P9-BHT-428

Contemporary
Literary Criticism

Guide to Gale Literary Criticism Series

For criticism on	Consult these Gale series
Authors now living or who died after December 31, 1959	*CONTEMPORARY LITERARY CRITICISM (CLC)*
Authors who died between 1900 and 1959	*TWENTIETH-CENTURY LITERARY CRITICISM (TCLC)*
Authors who died between 1800 and 1899	*NINETEENTH-CENTURY LITERATURE CRITICISM (NCLC)*
Authors who died between 1400 and 1799	*LITERATURE CRITICISM FROM 1400 TO 1800 (LC)* *SHAKESPEAREAN CRITICISM (SC)*
Authors who died before 1400	*CLASSICAL AND MEDIEVAL LITERATURE CRITICISM (CMLC)*
Black writers of the past two hundred years	*BLACK LITERATURE CRITICISM (BLC) AND BLACK LITERATURE CRITICISM SUPPLEMENT (BLCS)*
Authors of books for children and young adults	*CHILDREN'S LITERATURE REVIEW (CLR)*
Dramatists	*DRAMA CRITICISM (DC)*
Hispanic writers of the late nineteenth and twentieth centuries	*HISPANIC LITERATURE CRITICISM (HLC)*
Native North American writers and orators of the eighteenth, nineteenth, and twentieth centuries	*NATIVE NORTH AMERICAN LITERATURE (NNAL)*
Poets	*POETRY CRITICISM (PC)*
Short story writers	*SHORT STORY CRITICISM (SSC)*
Major authors from the Renaissance to the present	*WORLD LITERATURE CRITICISM, 1500 TO THE PRESENT (WLC)*
Major authors and works from the Bible to the present	*WORLD LITERATURE CRITICISM SUPPLEMENT (WLCS)*

ISSN 0091-3421

Volume 123

Contemporary Literary Criticism

Criticism of the Works
of Today's Novelists, Poets, Playwrights,
Short Story Writers, Scriptwriters, and
Other Creative Writers

Jeffrey W. Hunter
Polly Vedder
EDITORS

Justin Karr
Timothy J. White
ASSOCIATE EDITORS

GALE GROUP

Detroit
San Francisco
London
Boston
Woodbridge, CT

Library of Congress Catalog Card Number 76-46132
ISBN 0-7876-3198-1
ISSN 0091-3421

Printed in the United States of America
10 9 8 7 6 5 4 3 2 1

Contents

Preface vii

Acknowledgments xi

Preface

A Comprehensive Information Source
on Contemporary Literature

Named "one of the twenty-five most distinguished reference titles published during the past twenty-five years" by *Reference Quarterly,* the *Contemporary Literary Criticism (CLC)* series provides readers with critical commentary and general information on more than 2,000 authors now living or who died after December 31, 1959. Previous to the publication of the first volume of *CLC* in 1973, there was no ongoing digest monitoring scholarly and popular sources of critical opinion and explication of modern literature. *CLC,* therefore, has fulfilled an essential need, particularly since the complexity and variety of contemporary literature makes the function of criticism especially important to today's reader.

Scope of the Series

CLC presents significant passages from published criticism of works by creative writers. Since many of the authors covered by *CLC* inspire continual critical commentary, writers are often represented in more than one volume. There is, of course, no duplication of reprinted criticism.

Authors are selected for inclusion for a variety of reasons, among them the publication or dramatic production of a critically acclaimed new work, the reception of a major literary award, revival of interest in past writings, or the adaptation of a literary work to film or television.

Attention is also given to several other groups of writers—authors of considerable public interest—about whose work criticism is often difficult to locate. These include mystery and science fiction writers, literary and social critics, foreign writers, and authors who represent particular ethnic groups.

Format of the Book

Each *CLC* volume contains individual essays and reviews taken from hundreds of book review periodicals, general magazines, scholarly journals, monographs, and books. Entries include critical evaluations spanning from the beginning of an author's career to the most current commentary. Interviews, feature articles, and other published writings that offer insight into the author's works are also presented. Students, teachers, librarians, and researchers will find that the generous critical and biographical material in *CLC* provides them with vital information required to write a term paper, analyze a poem, or lead a book discussion group. In addition, complete bibliographical citations note the original source and all of the information necessary for a term paper footnote or bibliography.

Features

A *CLC* author entry consists of the following elements:

■ The **Author Heading** cites the author's name in the form under which the author has most commonly published, followed by birth date, and death date when applicable. Uncertainty as to a birth or death date is indicated by a question mark.

- A **Portrait** of the author is included when available.

- A brief **Biographical and Critical Introduction** to the author and his or her work precedes the criticism. The first line of the introduction provides the author's full name, pseudonyms (if applicable), nationality, and a listing of genres in which the author has written. To provide users with easier access to information, the biographical and critical essay included in each author entry is divided into four categories: "Introduction," "Biographical Information," "Major Works," and "Critical Reception." The introductions to single-work entries—entries that focus on well known and frequently studied books, short stories, and poems—are similarly organized to quickly provide readers with information on the plot and major characters of the work being discussed, its major themes, and its critical reception. Previous volumes of *CLC* in which the author has been featured are also listed in the introduction.

- A list of **Principal Works** notes the most important writings by the author. When foreign-language works have been translated into English, the English-language version of the title follows in brackets.

- The **Criticism** represents various kinds of critical writing, ranging in form from the brief review to the scholarly exegesis. Essays are selected by the editors to reflect the spectrum of opinion about a specific work or about an author's literary career in general. The critical and biographical materials are presented chronologically, adding a useful perspective to the entry. All titles by the author featured in the entry are printed in boldface type, which enables the reader to easily identify the works being discussed. Publication information (such as publisher names and book prices) and parenthetical numerical references (such as footnotes or page and line references to specific editions of a work) have been deleted at the editor's discretion to provide smoother reading of the text.

- Critical essays are prefaced by **Explanatory Notes** as an additional aid to readers. These notes may provide several types of valuable information, including: the reputation of the critic, the importance of the work of criticism, the commentator's approach to the author's work, the purpose of the criticism, and changes in critical trends regarding the author.

- A complete **Bibliographical Citation** designed to help the user find the original essay or book precedes each critical piece.

- Whenever possible, a recent **Author Interview** accompanies each entry.

- A concise **Further Reading** section appears at the end of entries on authors for whom a significant amount of criticism exists in addition to the pieces reprinted in *CLC*. Each citation in this section is accompanied by a descriptive annotation describing the content of that article. Materials included in this section are grouped under various headings (e.g., Biography, Bibliography, Criticism, and Interviews) to aid users in their search for additional information. Cross-references to other useful sources published by The Gale Group in which the author has appeared are also included: *Authors in the News, Black Writers, Children's Literature Review, Contemporary Authors, Dictionary of Literary Biography, DISCovering Authors, Drama Criticism, Hispanic Literature Criticism, Hispanic Writers, Native North American Literature, Poetry Criticism, Something about the Author, Short Story Criticism, Contemporary Authors Autobiography Series,* and *Something about the Author Autobiography Series.*

Other Features

CLC also includes the following features:

- An **Acknowledgments** section lists the copyright holders who have granted permission to reprint material in this volume of *CLC*. It does not, however, list every book or periodical reprinted or consulted during the preparation of the volume.

- Each new volume of *CLC* includes a **Cumulative Topic Index,** which lists all literary topics treated in *CLC, NCLC, TCLC,* and *LC 1400-1800.*

- A **Cumulative Author Index** lists all the authors who have appeared in the various literary criticism series published by The Gale Group, with cross-references to Gale's biographical and autobiographical series. A full listing of the series referenced there appears on the first page of the indexes of this volume. Readers will welcome this cumulated author index as a useful tool for locating an author within the various series. The index, which lists birth and death dates when available, will be particularly valuable for those authors who are identified with a certain period but whose death dates cause them to be placed in another, or for those authors whose careers span two periods. For example, Ernest Hemingway is found in *CLC,* yet F. Scott Fitzgerald, a writer often associated with him, is found in *Twentieth-Century Literary Criticism.*

- A **Cumulative Nationality Index** alphabetically lists all authors featured in *CLC* by nationality, followed by numbers corresponding to the volumes in which the authors appear.

- An alphabetical **Title Index** accompanies each volume of *CLC.* Listings are followed by the author's name and the corresponding page numbers where the titles are discussed. English translations of foreign titles and variations of titles are cross-referenced to the title under which a work was originally published. Titles of novels, novellas, dramas, films, record albums, and poetry, short story, and essay collections are printed in italics, while all individual poems, short stories, essays, and songs are printed in roman type within quotation marks; when published separately (e.g., T. S. Eliot's poem *The Waste Land),* the titles of long poems are printed in italics.

- In response to numerous suggestions from librarians, Gale has also produced a **Special Paperbound Edition** of the *CLC* title index. This annual cumulation, which alphabetically lists all titles reviewed in the series, is available to all customers. Additional copies of the index are available upon request. Librarians and patrons will welcome this separate index: it saves shelf space, is easy to use, and is recyclable upon receipt of the next edition.

Citing *Contemporary Literary Criticism*

When writing papers, students who quote directly from any volume in the Literary Criticism Series may use the following general forms to footnote reprinted criticism. The first example pertains to material drawn from periodicals, the second to material reprinted in books:

[1]Alfred Cismaru, "Making the Best of It," *The New Republic,* 207, No. 24, (December 7, 1992), 30, 32; excerpted and reprinted in *Contemporary Literary Criticism,* Vol. 85, ed. Christopher Giroux (Detroit: Gale, 1995), pp. 73-4.

[2]Yvor Winters, *The Post-Symbolist Methods* (Allen Swallow, 1967); excerpted and reprinted in *Contemporary Literary Criticism,* Vol. 85, ed. Christopher Giroux (Detroit: Gale, 1995), pp. 223-26.

Suggestions Are Welcome

The editors hope that readers will find *CLC* a useful reference tool and welcome comments about the work. Send comments and suggestions to: Editors, *Contemporary Literary Criticism,* The Gale Group, 27500 Drake Rd., Farmington Hills, MI 48333-3535.

Acknowledgments

The editors wish to thank the copyright holders of the excerpted criticism included in this volume and the permissions managers of many book and magazine publishing companies for assisting us in securing reproduction rights. We are also grateful to the staffs of the Detroit Public Library, the Library of Congress, the University of Detroit Mercy Library, Wayne State University Purdy/Kresge Library Complex, and the University of Michigan Libraries for making their resources available to us. Following is a list of the copyright holders who have granted us permission to reproduce material in this volume of CLC. Every effort has been made to trace copyright, but if omissions have been made, please let us know.

COPYRIGHTED MATERIALS IN *CLC*, VOLUME 123, WERE REPRODUCED FROM THE FOLLOWING PERIODICALS:

Artforum, v. XXVIII, May, 1990 for "Syncopated Thriller: Dennis Potter's 'Singing Detective'" by Therese Lichtenstein. © Artforum 1990. Reproduced by permission of the publisher and the author.—*Belles Lettres: A Review of Books by Women,* v. 9, Spring, 1994. Reproduced by permission.—*boundary 2,* v. 18, Summer, 1991. Copyright © boundary 2, 1991. Reproduced by permission.—*Chicago Tribune—Books,* September 15, 1991 for "Sustaining a Scream" by Madison Smartt Bell. © copyrighted 1991, Chicago Tribune Company. All rights reserved. Reproduced by permission of the author.—*Chicago Tribune-Books,* November 5, 1995 for "On 'The Concealed Side': Novelist Nadine Gordimer Explores the Interplay of Society and Self" by Philip Graham. © copyrighted 1995, Chicago Tribune Company. All rights reserved. Reproduced by permission of the author.—*Commonweal,* v. CXIX, March 27, 1992; August 15, 1997; v. 23, October 24, 1997. Copyright © 1992, 1997 Commonweal Publishing Co., Inc. All reproduced by permission of Commonweal Foundation.—*Contemporary Literature,* v. XXXII, Summer, 1991. © 1991 by the Board of Regents of the University of Wisconsin. Reproduced by permission of The University of Wisconsin Press.—*The Critical Quarterly,* v. 29, Winter, 1987. Reproduced by permission of Blackwell Publishers.—*Critique: Studies in Contemporary Fiction,* v. XXXII, Winter, 1990; v. XXXIII, Summer, 1992; v. XXXIV, Winter, 1993. Copyright © 1990, 1992, 1993 Helen Dwight Reid Educational Foundation. All reproduced with permission of the Helen Dwight Reid Educational Foundation, published by Heldref Publications, 1319 18th Street, NW, Washington, DC 20036-1802.—*Cross Currents,* v. 42, Summer, 1992; v. 47, Fall, 1997. Copyright 1992, 1997 by Cross Currents Inc. Both reproduced by permission.—*Essays in Theatre/Études Théâtrales,* v. 10, May, 1992 for "Delirious Subjectivity: Four Scenes from Havel" by Michael L. Quinn. Reproduced by permission of the author.—*Ethics,* v. 99, April, 1989 for a review of "Incercourse" by Deborah Harrold. Reproduced by permission.—*Feminist Review,* Summer, 1991 for "Review Article: Dworkin's Mercy" by Roz Kaveney. Reproduced by permission of the publisher and the author.—*Harper's Magazine,* v. 252, April, 1976. Copyright © 1976 by Harper's Magazine. All rights reserved. Reproduced by permission.—*The Hudson Review,* v. XVIII, Autumn, 1965; v. XXXVII, Winter, 1984-85. Copyright © 1965, 1984-85 by The Hudson Review, Inc. Both reproduced by permission./ v. 47, Winter, 1995 for "Auden's Local Culture" by Alan Jacobs. Copyright © 1995 by Alan Jacobs. Reproduced by permission.—*The Journal of Commonwealth Literature,* v. XX, 1985. Reproduced with the kind permission of Bowker-Saur, a part of Reed Business Information Ltd.—*Journal of Modern Literature,* v. XVIII, Winter, 1992. © Temple University 1992. Reproduced by permission.—*The Kenyon Review,* v. 15, Spring, 1993 for "Václav Havel: The Once and Future Playwright" by Robert Skloot. Copyright © 1993 by Kenyon College. Reproduced by permission of the author.—*Literature and Psychology,* v. 33, 1987; v. 39, Spring-Summer, 1992. © Editor 1987, 1992. Both reproduced by permission.—*Literature/Film Quarterly,* v. 21, 1993. © copyright 1993 Salisbury State College. Reproduced by permission.—*London Review of Books,* April 5-18, 1984 for "Saboteurs" by Sylvia Clayton. Appears here by permission of the London Review of Books and the Literary Estate of Sylvia Clayton./ v. 13, November 7, 1991 for "Off the Edge" by Frank Kermode; v. 13, December 5, 1991 for "Dry Eyes" by John Bayley; v. 16, September 8, 1994 for "What Nations Are For" by Tom Nairn; v. 17, January 12, 1995 for "Pale Ghosts" by Jeremy Harding. All Appear here by permission of the London Review of Books and the respective authors.—*Los Angeles Times Book Review,* October 6, 1991; September 18, 1994; March 16, 1997; May 3, 1987. Copyright, 1991, 1994, 1997, Los Angeles Times. All reproduced by permission.—*Michigan Quarterly Review,* v. 30, Spring, 1991 for "Pynchon's Groundward Art" by

W. H. Auden

1907-1973

(Full name Wystan Hugh Auden) English-born American poet, dramatist, librettist, critic, essayist, editor, and translator.

The following entry presents an overview of Auden's career through 1997. For further information on his life and works, see *CLC*, Volumes 1, 2, 3, 4, 6, 9, 11, 14, and 43.

INTRODUCTION

W. H. Auden is considered one of the preeminent English-language poets of the twentieth century. In many ways a contradictory personality, at once prudent, revolutionary, pious, and intemperate, Auden is distinguished for his enormous intelligence, technical virtuosity, complex philosophical and moral vision, and keen wit. His prodigious output, spanning nearly a half century, includes inventive experiments with lyric and prose poetry, verse drama, librettos, and notable contributions to literary criticism. His best known poetry, most of which appears in *The Orators* (1932), *Another Time* (1940), *Journey to a War* (1939), *New Year Letter* (1941), *For the Time Being* (1944), *The Age of Anxiety* (1947), and *Nones* (1951), reflects his life-long preoccupation with political, psychological, and spiritual conflicts. As an innovative dramatist and librettist working in operatic forms, Auden also displayed an intuitive musical ear and theatrical genius ahead of his time. A highly original poet and celebrated man of letters, Auden's large and varied oeuvre attests to the impressive range and profundity of his literary and intellectual endeavors.

Biographical Information

Born Wystan Hugh Auden in York, England, and named after a Saxon saint, Auden was raised in the industrial city of Birmingham by devout, well-educated Anglo-Catholic parents of clerical descent. His father was School Medical Officer and Professor of Public Health in Birmingham. The family library, reflecting his wide ranging interests in archaeology, psychology, the classics, and Norse saga, acquainted the young Auden with scientific subjects and literature. His mother, with whom Auden maintained a powerful attachment, held a degree in French and worked as a nurse. Auden attended preparatory school at Saint Edmund's between 1915 and 1920, where he befriended Christopher Isherwood. He then went to Gresham's School, Holt, where he wrote his first poems and began to come to terms with his homosexuality. His first published poem appeared in *Public School Verse* in 1924. A brilliant student whose

wealth of diverse knowledge dazzled his instructors and peers, in 1925 Auden began study at Christ Church College, Oxford, on a scholarship in natural science, though he later switched to English. At Oxford, Auden published poetry in *Oxford Poetry,* for which he served as an editor, and his first volume of poetry, *Poems* (1928), which was handprinted and privately distributed by classmate Stephen Spender. During this time, Auden was at the center of a group of emerging young writers including Spender, Isherwood, and Cecil Day-Lewis, alternately known as the "Oxford Group" or the "Auden Generation." While still at Oxford, Auden also wrote his first dramatic work, *Paid on Both Sides* (1930), which T. S. Eliot eventually published in the *Criterion.* After graduating in 1928, Auden spent a year in Berlin, then took up work as a schoolmaster in England and Scotland for several years while composing his first commercially distributed volumes, *Poems* (1930), *The Orators*, and a verse drama *The Dance of Death* (1933). Auden also collaborated with Isherwood on the verse dramas *The Dog Beneath the Skin* (1935), *The Ascent of F6* (1936), and *On the Frontier* (1938). Established as a major poet during the 1930s, Auden became increasingly interested in left-wing political movements and social causes. He travelled to Iceland with Louis MacNeice in 1936, documented in *Letters from Iceland* (1937); to Spain in 1937 to support anti-fascist Loyalists in the Spanish Revolution, inspiring the poem "Spain"; and to China with Isherwood in 1938, recounted in the travel book *Journey to a War*. He also worked with composer Benjamin Britten on several documentary films and librettos, including *On Hunting Fathers* (1936) and *Paul Bunyan* (1941). Auden married Erika Mann, daughter of Thomas Mann, in 1935 to provide her with British nationality enabling her to leave Nazi Germany, after which they divorced. In 1939, Auden moved to the United States with Isherwood, where he became an official citizen in 1946, remaining in New York City until 1972. Once in America, Auden underwent a religious conversion that restored him to the Christianity of his youth. His first American publication, *Another Time*, contains some of his most memorable poetry. During the next decade, Auden was the recipient of two Guggenheim fellowships, taught at several prestigious liberal arts colleges, and continued to produce important volumes of poetry, including *The Double Man* (1941), reprinted the same year under the title *New Year Letter; For the Time Being;* and *The Age of Anxiety,* for which he received the Pulitzer Prize in 1948. Auden also published the first of several collections of his work with *The Collected Poetry* (1945), for which he received the Award of Merit Medal from the American Academy of Arts and Letters. Auden suffered a fatal heart attack at his summer home in Kirchstetten, Austria, in 1973.

Major Works

Auden is best known as a poet of great erudition, wisdom, and remarkable lyrical gifts. His early verse in *Poems* (1930) is characterized by terse exposition, alluring abstraction, and inventive use of language, bearing the influence of Eliot and Thomas Hardy, Auden's initial master, as well as Laura Riding, Wilfred Owen, and Gerard Manley Hopkins. Auden's early poems also adumbrate his penchant for Anglo-Saxon phrasing, syncopated rhythms, traditional forms, the allegorical imagery of science and geology, and his deep-felt humanitarian concerns. Drawing on eclectic sources for the verse drama *Paid on Both Sides*, inspired by the lively dramatic action of the parlor charade and the plays of Bertolt Brecht and William Butler Yeats, Auden merges the archaic style and blood-feud theme of Anglo-Saxon poetry with structural elements of Greek tragedy and the fragmentary modernist presentation of Eliot's *The Waste Land*. Auden built upon these early experiments in the prose and verse of *The Orators*, drawing on Freudian psychoanalysis, Marxist doctrine, and the avant-garde techniques of Eliot, James Joyce, and Gertrude Stein to present a surreal vision of the revolutionary hero and a warning against the danger of fascism. Peppered with private jokes and allusions to his friends, *The Orators* laments and satirizes the

stagnation of English society and the dubious promise of untamed modernism. Similar political and psychological concerns are echoed in Auden's collaborative verse dramas with Isherwood from this period, including *The Dog Beneath the Skin, The Ascent of F6* and *On the Frontier. Look, Stranger!* (1936), reprinted as *On This Island* (1937), marks Auden's entrance into leftist politics and his shift toward an increasingly formal aesthetic. Turning away from the obtuseness of modernism and the subjective idealism of the Romantics, Auden invokes the directness and clarity of light verse to give serious expression to his strong ethical stance and to impose order upon the chaos preceding the Second World War. His poem "Spain," composed immediately after witnessing the brutal internecine combat in that country, reflects Auden's disillusionment with political causes and the indiscriminate violence of war. "In Time of War," a sequence of sonnets which appeared in *Journey to a War,* reveals the maturation of Auden's civic voice and liberal humanist creed. Published shortly thereafter, *Another Time* displays the full emergence of Auden's unique synthesis of technical mastery, moral probity, and spirited lyricism. This volume, his first American publication, contains many of his greatest poems, including "As I Walked Out One Evening," "Musée des Beaux Arts," "Lay Your Sleeping Head, My Love," "September 1, 1939," "The Unknown Citizen," "Letter to Lord Byron," and elegies to poets Matthew Arnold, A. E. Housman, and Yeats. The full impact of Auden's self-imposed exile and acute spiritual crisis, which led to his reversion to Christianity, is evident in *The Double Man.* This volume contains "New Year Letter," an extended epistolary poem on the evils of modern civilization rendered in Augustan form, and the sonnet sequence "The Quest." Influenced by the existentialist thought of Soren Kierkegaard and American theologian Rheinhold Neibuhr, Auden moved still further toward a cerebral style that sought universal harmony in a system of religious ideals. *For the Time Being* contains "For the Time Being: A Christmas Oratorio," an overt Christian allegory based on the Nativity in which he employs the terminology of science and psychology to rationalize religious faith, and "The Sea and the Mirror: A Commentary on Shakespeare's *The Tempest,*" an ambitious allegorical work that examines the complex relationship between life and art and the creative potential of literary interpretation. His next major work, *The Age of Anxiety,* subtitled "a baroque eclogue," relates the inner consciousness of four disparate characters as they converse among themselves in a New York City bar during the Second World War. Returning to the alliterative Anglo-Saxon versification of his early poetry, Auden explores the spiritual dimensions of their ordinary lives and individual failings within a religious context. The height of Auden's mature, intellectual style is evident in *Nones*, which contains "In Praise of Limestone," *The Shield of Achilles* (1955), featuring "Horae Canonicae" and "Bucolics," and *Homage to Clio* (1960), which includes "The Cave of Making" and "Tonight at Seven-Thirty." Devoid of the frivolity of his earlier poetry, the serene meditations of these late volumes, frequently in neo-classical or pastoral modes, displays Auden's unsurpassed technical control and deep insights into the nature of human existence and experience, particularly as informed by the philosophy of Martin Heidegger, medieval Christianity, history, and nature. Auden's highly perceptive critical essays, reviews, and lectures in *The Enchafèd Flood* (1950), *The Dyer's Hand* (1962), and *Forewords and Afterwords* (1973) document his intellectual concerns and artistic principles during his American period.

Critical Reception

Auden is widely regarded as one of the greatest poets of the twentieth century. Though a decidedly modern poet in terms of his radical politics and bold experimentation with accepted literary forms, Auden's idiosyncratic virtuosity and protean ethical perspective distinguishes him from his contemporaries. As many critics note, Auden's striking originality stems from his counterrevolutionary appropriation of traditional poetic forms, unabashed Christian faith, and mistrust of irrationalism, all seemingly at odds with the tenets of both modernism and romanticism from which his poetry derives. While most critics view Auden's poetry from the 1930s and early 1940s as his best, especially as found in *The Orators, Another Time,* and the poems "Spain," "In Time of War," and "New Year Letter," controversy surrounds evaluation of the middle and later periods of his career. "New Year Letter" continues to receive much critical attention, as does the relevance of Auden's self-imposed exile in America. Some critics believe that Auden's poetry lost much of its imaginative power and vitality after his emigration to the United States. However, others contend that the contemplative Christianity and Horatian intellectualism of Auden's American period represents the apogee of his disciplined style and sensibility, particularly as evident in *The Age of Anxiety,* "The Sea and the Mirror" from *For the Time Being,* and "In Praise of Limestone" from *Nones.* Many critics note a tendency toward obscurity in much of Auden's poetry throughout his career, variously attributed to his liberating genius, private satire, and cloaked references to his homosexuality. Despite Auden's significant contributions to contemporary musical theater, he remains largely unstudied as a dramatist and librettist, mainly due to the fact that the forms in which he worked have either fallen out of favor or never fully developed popular appreciation. A prolific poet of extraordinary technical dexterity, intellectual domain, engaging perspicacity, and epigrammatic wit, Auden forged a rare poetic voice that reconciled the opposing forces of tradition and modernism, for which he is hailed as a towering figure of twentieth-century literature.

PRINCIPAL WORKS

Poems (poetry) 1928

Poems (poetry) 1930

Paid on Both Sides (drama) 1931

The Orators: An English Study (poetry) 1932

The Dance of Death (drama) 1933

The Dog Beneath the Skin; or, Where Is Francis? [with Christopher Isherwood] (drama) 1935

The Ascent of F6: A Tragedy in Two Acts [with Christopher Isherwood] (drama) 1936

Look, Stranger! (poetry) [published in the United States as *On this Island,* 1937] 1936

On Hunting Fathers [with Benjamin Britten] (libretto) 1936

Letters from Iceland [with Louis MacNeice] (poetry) 1937

Spain (poetry) 1937

On the Frontier: A Melodrama in Three Acts [with Christopher Isherwood] (drama) 1938

Selected Poems (poetry) 1938

Ballad of Heroes [with Randall Swingler and Benjamin Britten] (libretto) 1939

Journey to a War [with Christopher Isherwood] (poetry) 1939

Another Time (poetry) 1940

The Double Man [republished as *New Year Letter*] (poetry) 1941

Paul Bunyan: An Operetta in Two Acts and a Prologue [with Benjamin Britten] (libretto) 1941

For the Time Being (poetry) 1944

The Collected Poetry (poetry) 1945

The Age of Anxiety: A Baroque Eclogue (poetry) 1947

Collected Shorter Poems, 1933-1944 (poetry) 1950

The Enchafèd Flood; or, The Romantic Iconography of the Sea (criticism) 1950

Nones (poetry) 1951

The Rake's Progress: Opera in Three Acts [with Chester Kallman and Igor Stravinsky] (libretto) 1951

The Shield of Achilles (poetry) 1955

Homage to Clio (poetry) 1960

Elegy for Young Lovers [with Chester Kallman and Hans Werner Henze] (libretto) 1961

The Dyer's Hand and Other Essays (essays) 1962

About the House (poetry) 1965

The Bassarids [with Chester Kallman and Hans Werner Henze] (libretto) 1966

Collected Shorter Poems, 1927-1957 (poetry) 1966

Collected Longer Poems (poetry) 1968

City Without Walls and Other Poems (poetry) 1969

Epistle to a Godson and Other Poems (poetry) 1972

Forewords and Afterwords (essays) 1973

Thank You, Fog: Last Poems (poetry) 1974

Collected Poems (poetry) 1976

The English Auden: Poems, Essays, and Dramatic Writings, 1927-39 (poetry, essays, and drama) 1977

CRITICISM

Samuel Hynes (essay date Winter 1982)

SOURCE: "The Voice of Exile: Auden in 1940," in *Sewanee Review,* Vol. 90, No. 1, Winter, 1982, pp. 31-52.

[*In the following essay, Hynes discusses Auden's emigration to the United States, his preoccupation with history and art, and "New Year Letter" as a reflection of Auden's historical sensibility.*]

What I am going to say here concerns the relations between poetry and history. I intend to deal with Auden as an historical poet—in the sense not of a poet reconstructing the past in the manner of Browning and Pound, but of one who saw human actions as conditioned by history, and history as the necessity that men must recognize if they are to be free; and who wrote his historical understanding into his poems. The focus of my attention will be on the years 1939 and 1940—a point in Auden's career at which his ideas (and his style) changed radically—and on what the poetic consequences of that change were. Underlying my remarks is the literary historian's assumption that all works of art exist in Time, and are therefore both historical and biographical, and that historical and biographical knowledge are therefore a necessary part of our understanding of a work of art.

My principal example will be **"New Year Letter,"** a long didactic poem that bears the date January 1, 1940. That date is obviously important, both in human history and in Auden's biography. On that day the thirties ended, and a new decade began: "Tonight a scrambling decade ends," Auden says in the poem. A few months earlier he had called it "a low dishonest decade," and we all know what he meant: we have learned the Myth of the Thirties—how Evil grew powerful and insolent then, while Good dithered and did nothing; how young writers tried to make writing a mode of action, and failed; and how a war that everyone foresaw and only the wicked wanted came at last. On January 1, 1940, England and France were at war with Germany; but it was the time of the "phoney war"—the fighting had not really begun. It was an odd, anxious time, between an ending and a beginning.

In Auden's life it was also an anxious, interim time. He had left England with his friend Christopher Isherwood in January 1939 and had emigrated to America, interrupting a promising career and alienating his English friends to go into exile among strangers. It was a move unlike those of any of the other famous modern literary exiles: if you compare the others—James, Conrad, Joyce, Mann, Pound, Eliot, Nabokov, Brecht—there is no other case of an *established*

writer who left his country *voluntarily.* If literary biogeography ever becomes a field of scholarship—and perhaps it should—Auden will provide a unique case for study.

To many of his countrymen Auden's motive for this extraordinary move seemed clear enough. It was clear, for example, to Major Sir Jocelyn Lucas, M.P., who asked in the House of Commons "whether British citizens of military age, such as Mr. W. H. Auden and Mr. Christopher Isherwood, who have gone to the United States and expressed their determination not to return to this country until the war is over, will be summoned back for registration and calling up, in view of the fact that they are seeking refuge abroad?" And when the parliamentary secretary of the ministry parried the question, Sir Jocelyn asked angrily: "Is my hon. Friend aware of the indignation caused by young men leaving the country and saying they will not fight?"

A careful historian will want to make two points about this incident. One is that though Sir Jocelyn was surely wrong in assuming that Auden's motive was simple cowardice, he cannot be dismissed as just another Blimp-in-office. He asked his question on June 13, 1940—ten days after Dunkirk and a week before the surrender of France. At that moment England was alone in the war, and had just been driven back onto her island. And Auden was an Englishman who had chosen not to be present. Historically speaking, one can understand Sir Jocelyn's anger. The other point is that Auden knew all this, that the anger and contempt of his countrymen—including many former friends—was a part of his consciousness, and we can therefore look to find it reflected in the work that he was doing. And in June 1940 that work was **"New Year Letter."**

Auden's actual motives for choosing exile are more difficult to determine. One *could* argue that his move was the expression of a fundamental change of belief: that he was sailing away from politics, and toward religion. And if you favor left-wing politics and deplore religion you will naturally take this change as a betrayal—not of country, but of ideology. Some critics—notably Randall Jarrell—did respond this way. And certainly Auden's beliefs *did* change at this time. Isherwood recalls a conversation that he had with Auden aboard their New York-bound ship:

> *Isherwood:* You know, it just doesn't mean anything to me any more—the Popular Front, the party line, the anti-Fascist struggle. I suppose they're okay but something's wrong with me. I simply cannot swallow another mouthful.
>
> *Auden:* Neither can I.

And we know that during 1940 Auden began to attend Episcopal church services in New York, and that before the end of the year he had returned to the church in which he had been raised.

But having taken note of these facts, we haven't explained a self-imposed exile. Many of Auden's friends had lost their left-wing faith by 1939, and had found it possible to go on living in England. And as for religion—it seems an odd, indeed a perverse move to leave England in order to return to Anglicanism.

Consider also the mysterious passage in his essay in *Modern Canterbury Pilgrims* (1956) that recounts Auden's state of mind at about this time:

> So, presently, I started to read some theological works, Kierkegaard in particular, and began going, in a tentative and experimental way, to church. And then, providentially—for the occupational disease of poets is frivolity—I was forced to know in person what it is like to feel oneself the prey of demonic powers, in both the Greek and the Christian sense, stripped of self-control and self-respect, behaving like a ham actor in a Strindberg play.

I quote this mysterious passage only to say that I don't know what Auden is referring to in his private life. The context suggests that it happened before he left England; and it may have been a part of his motivation for leaving.

"What I am trying to do, is to live deliberately *without* roots."
—*W.H. Auden*

I think Auden's emigration is better explained in more general terms, as a negative response to the historical situation as he saw it. By 1939 it seemed clear to him, as it did to many other Europeans, that the crisis they were facing was not simply another war but the failure of an ideology. *If* fascism existed, and dominated Europe, *if* another world war was coming, then the liberal western conception of man must be wrong in fundamental ways—more than wrong, *dead.* By leaving England when he did, Auden was freeing himself from that dead liberal ideology. Man's condition would have to be understood differently from now on: as existentially alone, cut off from the old roots, the old comforts and securities. And if that was true, then England was the wrong place for an English poet. When an old friend opposed Auden's move, on the grounds that it was dangerous for a writer to sever his native roots, Auden replied that the concept of roots was obsolete: "What I am trying to do," he explained to E. R. Dodds, "is to live deliberately *without* roots."

It was an extraordinary decision to make—to go in quest of a life that would be a parable of the condition of Modern Man, as though one could become a Kafka character, or the Wandering Jew, by an act of will. Even the word *quest* itself seems a bit literary and elevated for what was, after all, just another Atlantic crossing. I use it nonetheless, because it was a word—and a concept—that Auden was using a lot then, most notably in his other major poem of these years, the sonnet sequence called **"The Quest."** Questing was on his mind, because that's what he saw himself as doing: journeying to meet the future.

For a European writer who aspired to rootlessness, America was the obvious place to go. "The attractiveness of America to a writer," Auden told an interviewer for the *Saturday Review* in 1940, "is its openness and lack of tradition. In a way it's frightening. You are forced to live here as everyone will be forced to live. There is no past. No tradition. No roots—that is in the European sense." In this rootless society a European could escape the past, and become what Auden desired to be: the entirely Modern Man. And then, presumably, he could write Modern Poems.

What such poems would be like we may infer from the poems that Auden wrote during his first year in America—for example **"September 1, 1939,"** a poem that commemorates the day on which the Germans invaded Poland, and liberalism and the thirties died. In the poem a rootless man sits in a rootless place—what could be better for that than a New York bar?—and meditates on what has ended—and why. Around him are rootless, undifferentiated human beings—the faces at the bar, the dense commuters—none having any relation to the speaker, or to each other, none an agent in its own life. The forces that operate in the world of the poem are blank abstractions: Collective Man, Important Persons, Authority, the State. Even the skyscrapers are blind.

Nothing happens in the poem; nothing changes; nothing connects. Yet it ends with two stanzas of affirmation:

> All I have is a voice
> To undo the folded lie. . . .
>
> Yet, dotted everywhere,
> Ironic points of light
> Flash out wherever the Just
> Exchange their messages. . . .

The manuscript (in the Berg collection) shows that this floating affirmation was originally even stronger. Auden must have been thinking of two canceled stanzas when he said that the poem was "infected with an incurable dishonesty," and excluded it from later collections of his poems. For sentimentality is a form of dishonesty, and **"September 1,**

1939" is certainly sentimental: it sentimentalizes loneliness, it sentimentalizes the role of the artist (what good will his voice do in a world war?), and it sentimentalizes the idea of affirmation itself in that final image of the points of light that flash messages without content. (It is worth noting that Auden got that image from E. M. Forster, who had written, just the year before in *I Believe:* "It's a humiliating outlook—though the greater the darkness, the brighter shine the little lights, reassuring one another, signalling, 'Well, at all events I'm still here. I don't like it very much, but how are you?'" In the manuscript Auden first used Forster's word *little*, before he hit on *ironic*. Perhaps part of Auden's dissatisfaction with the poem was his recognition that he had not yet cast off Forsterian liberalism: he had brought some of his roots with him.)

"September 1, 1939" is an unsuccessful poem, but it is a useful one to begin with, because in it Auden made a first attempt to deal with the major problems that concerned him in these crucial years: how to think historically about present disaster; how to be an artist in a bad time; and how, and what, to affirm. The poem is therefore a sort of first draft of "New Year Letter." Thinking historically may be the most difficult task that a modern writer can assume, especially in a time of war. In the twentieth century it has been impossible to think about any war in historical terms while it was going on: war-writing, and war-thinking, is always apocalyptic. Auden tried in "September 1, 1939" to see the war, as it began, as an historical consequence: he mentions Protestantism and imperialism, and invokes Thucydides; but there is really no argument offered, only sketchy materials for one. One way to look at the work that followed is to regard it as a series of expansions and revisions of this first wartime view of Modern Man, in the mess of history that he had made.

The years 1939-1940 were productive ones for Auden. In those two years he published two books and wrote another, published more than fifty poems and many reviews, all this while lecturing and teaching, and even for a time running a Brooklyn boardinghouse. And he read: "I have never written nor read so much," he wrote to a friend in late 1939. What he was reading was not primarily literature but science, philosophy, and religion: the sorts of books that a man might turn to who was trying to construct for himself a new understanding of man-in-history. You can get some sense of what this reading was, if you look through Auden's notes to "New Year Letter": Hans Spemann's *Embryonic Development and Induction*, Margaret Meade's *Growing up in New Guinea*, the journals of Kierkegaard, Werner Jaeger's *Paideia*, Nietzsche's *Postscript to the Case of Wagner*, Charles Williams's *Descent of the Dove*, Collingwood's *Metaphysics*, Köhler's *The Place of Value in a World of Facts*.

If you read through the whole body of Auden's prose for these years, you will find that quotations from these writers keep turning up, often in quite unlikely places, sometimes more than once. And you will find other repetitions—certain definitions and analyses and formulations. You *could* argue from this evidence that he had simply overextended himself, and was meeting his journalistic deadlines by cannibalizing his own writings. But that doesn't seem an adequate explanation, given the extraordinary fertility of his mind; I think it would be more accurate to say that at this time Auden had certain preoccupations, and that his repetitions express the power of those preoccupations to force their way into everything he wrote. This is true of even his most casual book reviews, in which he would habitually swerve from his ostensible subject—a life of Voltaire or an anthology by de la Mare—to write about his real concerns.

You can group those concerns under three general headings: History, Art, and Necessity; *everything* that he wrote during these years had to do with one or more of these subjects. And you might go on to say that in fact these are all aspects of one master question. Auden put that question in a review he wrote of Harold Laski's *Where Do We Go from Here?* Laski's title, he said, posed an unreal question: "The only real question, and this itself becomes unreal unless it is asked all the time, is *where are we now?*" Everything that Auden wrote—every review, every lecture, every poem—was a draft of an answer to that question. Somewhere Auden quotes approvingly Forster's story of the old lady who exclaimed: "How can I tell what I think till I hear what I say?" And that's what he was doing during these years: listening to what he thought, working it out, until finally he put it all together in "New Year Letter."

Of the thirty or so prose pieces of these years there are five that I'll be referring to and that seem to me to be Auden's most substantial prose statements: "The Public v. the Late Mr. William Butler Yeats," published in the *Partisan Review* in the spring of 1939; "The Prolific and the Devourer," written during the spring and summer of 1939, but unpublished until Edward Mendelson included the first of its four parts in *The English Auden;* "Romantic or Free?", a commencement address given at Smith College on June 17, 1940; "Mimesis and Allegory," an English Institute lecture given on September 13, 1940; and "Criticism in a Mass Society," a lecture delivered at Princeton on November 7, 1940.

Beside this calendar of Auden's writings we might set a calendar of public history: while he was writing "The Public v. the Late Mr. William Butler Yeats," the Spanish Civil War ended; while he was finishing "The Prolific and the Devourer," the Russo-German pact was signed, and the war began; while he was giving his commencement address, the French were negotiating their surrender to Hitler; while he was reading **"Mimesis and Allegory"** to his New York audience of professors, the Battle of Britain was approaching its end. The point of this second calendar is not to lend a spurious drama to the literary record, but to remind you of Auden's exact location in history: that as he wrote, a peace ended and a war began, of which neither the scale nor the outcome could be predicted; that the Apocalypse that thirties writers had feared and expected was taking place. If we are to read Auden historically, we must imagine our way back to his state of mind, and his condition of ignorance, at that point in history now forty years in the past. This is the justification for reading a poet's forgotten lectures and reviews—that they contain the mind and the knowledge that made the poems, and reveal the poet's preoccupations more fully than the poems do, simply because they are not poems.

I have said that Auden's preoccupations during these critical years could be grouped under the headings of History, Necessity, and Art. Let me now try to give you, under these headings, a sense of where Auden thought the world was in 1939-1940.

History: Auden's recurrent theme is that man has come to the end of an epoch. The period that has ended he calls by various names: it is the end of the Renaissance, the end of the Protestant epoch, the end of liberal capitalist democracy. What these have in common is that they all acted to separate men from each other: the Renaissance "broke the subordination of all other intellectual fields to that of theology, and assumed the autonomy of each"; Protestantism made men's relations to God individual and autonomous; capitalism made men autonomous in their economic relations. The results were the atomization of society, the disintegration of tradition, the loss of community. The war, coming at the end of this process, is not therefore a struggle for the survival of western democracy, or of any other traditional system, but the final term in the disintegrating process, like the last scene of *Götterdämmerung*. The very fact that it was taking place seemed to confirm Auden's analysis: a war involving the whole world was the final disintegration of order. All through the thirties concerned men had said: "If a war comes, it will be the end of civilization." And here it was.

A subheading of History is Romanticism, Auden had called his address at Smith **"Romantic or Free?",** and early in the speech he explained what he meant:

> The term romantic I have chosen rather arbitrarily to describe all those who in one way or another reject the paradoxical, dialectic nature of freedom. Perhaps heretic would have been a more accurate term, but I chose romantic partly to avoid purely clerical associations, and partly because the particu-

lar forms in which these eternal heresies appear today took shape in the period that is historically called the Romantic Revival.

To be romantic, in Auden's view, was to simplify one's sense of man's dialectical existence: to believe that human beings are essentially good, or that they have absolutely free will, or that they are absolutely determined; or that they can live entirely by reason, or entirely by instinct; or that they will be happy and good if the structure of society is changed. Auden saw these "eternal heresies" manifested throughout history, but becoming political with the rise of industrialism, in Rousseau's theory of the General Will. As long as capitalism was expanding, Auden wrote in **"Jacob and the Angel,"** "the inadequacy of rationalist Liberalism to guarantee material happiness was unperceived by the majority, and it was not until after the Great War that political Romanticism became a great force and a great enemy." To Auden's mind the connection between romanticism and politics was crucial: when he taught a course on romanticism at Swarthmore he called it "Romanticism from Rousseau to Hitler." But romanticism was, to him, *more* than a political term: it was the generic term for all the errors in men's thought—political, philosophical, and religious—that converged at last in Nazism, and in the war. The war was therefore a climactic, terminal event: the ultimate expression of the eternal romantic heresies.

Necessity: Though by 1939 Auden had ceased to be a Marxist (if he can be said ever to have been one), he continued to quote Engels's definition of freedom: that freedom is the consciousness of necessity. The difference lay in what he meant by necessity. In essay after essay of these years he makes one central distinction: between *causal* necessity ("the external necessity of matter") and *logical* necessity, which he sometimes calls *moral* necessity (the internal necessity of moral decision).

> In earlier phases of social development [he said in his Princeton lecture, **"Criticism in a Mass Society"**] a man could be a member of a group (i.e. not, in our sense, an individual), and yet be a person; he could be accessory to his position because the latter was a real necessity, and by virtue of being a necessity, could make him free. Today a man has only two choices: he can be consciously passive or consciously active. He can accept deliberately or reject deliberately, but he must decide because his position in life is no longer a real necessity; he could be different if he chose. The necessity that can make him free is no longer his position as such, but the necessity of choosing to accept it or reject it. To be unconscious is to be neither an individual nor a person, but a mathematical integer in something called the Public which has no real existence.

You can see that this account of logical necessity is related to Auden's ideas of history: human society has evolved to a state of total separateness, in which every man has an absolute responsibility to make his own moral choices: *that's* the necessity. If he does not, if he creates or joins a society that *denies* that necessity, he ceases to be an individual, as in fascist states. (Again and again in the essays Auden defines fascism as a society in which everything that is not required is forbidden: that is, a society which denies the necessity of moral choice.)

Another name for human separateness is *loneliness,* a term which is recurrent and crucial in Auden's writings of this time. Loneliness was, for Auden, a kind of modern categorical imperative: an ethical term, primarily—to be lonely was to be conscious of the real human condition—but with political implications. "There can be no democracy," he told the women at Smith, "unless each of us accepts the fact that in the last analysis we live our lives alone." Auden's own political position was based on loneliness: "I welcome the atomization of society," he wrote in **"Tradition and Value,"** "and I look forward to a socialism based on it, to the day when the disintegration of tradition will be as final and universal for the masses as it is already for the artist, because it will be only when they fully realize their 'aloneness' and accept it, that men will be able to achieve a real unity through a common recognition of their diversity." This isn't everybody's idea of socialism, and it is certainly a long way from the cozy collectivism of the young English Left in the thirties, but it is a *possible* socialism, in which political equality acts to equalize men's opportunities for moral choice. (In unequal societies, Auden said, the *haves* usually believe in absolute free will, while the *haves-nots* are determinists. These are both, for him, romantic heresies, for which his kind of socialism would be a cure.)

Art: Auden made his most famous statement about aesthetics in the spring of 1939, in his elegy on Yeats: "Poetry makes nothing happen." He said the same thing, more elaborately, in his essay **"The Public v. the Late Mr. William Butler Yeats,"** written at about the same time:

> Art is a product of history, not a cause. Unlike some other products, technical inventions for example, it does not re-enter history as an effective agent, so that the question whether art should or should not be propaganda is unreal. The case for the prosecution rests on the fallacious belief that art ever makes anything happen, whereas the honest truth, gentlemen, is that, if not a poem had been written, not a picture painted, not a bar of music composed, the history of man would be materially unchanged.

This is, of course, a repudiation of conventional engagée thinking of the thirties. Its importance to Auden is suggested by the number of times that he repeated it: first in the poem, then in the essay, then twice in **"The Prolific and the Devourer":** "Artists and politicians would get along better in a time of crisis like the present, if the latter would only realise that the political history of the world would have been the same if not a poem had been written, not a picture painted nor a bar of music composed." And, a little further down the page: "art makes nothing happen."

Notice how far Auden goes here: he doesn't simply say that art doesn't affect politics: it makes *nothing* happen, it is not an agent in reality in any sense. Not only that. In **"Mimesis and Allegory"** he draws back from another conventional defense of art: "One of the romantic symptoms has been an enormous exaggeration of the importance of art as a guide to life."

Most of what Auden had to say about Art at this time is couched in negative terms: he was more certain of what it *didn't* do than of what it *did.* One can see why this should be so: a theory of Art would have to wait upon the answers to the larger philosophic questions. Still we can see the direction in which his thought about art was moving in two lectures that Auden gave in the autumn of 1940. First these sentences from the final page of **"Mimesis and Allegory":**

> I. A. Richards is right, I think, in his account of how art organizes attitudes, but the criterion by which we judge the value of such an organization lies outside art. . . . Art is not metaphysics any more than it is conduct, and the artist is usually unwise to insist too directly in his art upon his beliefs; but without an adequate and conscious metaphysics in the background, art's imitation of life inevitably becomes, either a photostatic copy of the accidental details of life without pattern or significance, or a personal allegory of the artist's individual dementia, of interest primarily to the psychologist and the historian.

So art has its value: it *orders.* But that order is not self-generated: art needs belief, needs absolutes, needs metaphysics. As Society does; in the same lecture, and in other writings of the time, Auden makes this point very strongly: societies come to grief when they have an inadequate metaphysics, or none.

Auden developed this idea further in **"Criticism in a Mass Society":** "We cannot live without believing certain values to be absolute. These values exist, though our knowledge of them is always imperfect, distorted by the limitations of our historical position and our personal character. However, if but only we realize this, our knowledge can improve." And he went on to ask himself what the consequences of this assumption would be for the judgment of art: "The critic who assumes that absolute values exist but that our knowledge of them is always imperfect will judge a work of art by the degree to which it transcends the artist's personal and historical limitations, but he will not expect such transcendence ever to be complete, either in the artist or himself."

The key word here is *imperfect:* it introduces a concept that becomes crucially important in Auden's aesthetic from this point on—what we might call the Aesthetics of Imperfection. Absolute values exist, but man can only know them imperfectly; and his art will mirror his imperfect knowledge. Indeed the very imperfection of a work of art may be a value, since it will enact and so remind us of our own imperfection. The idea of perfection is a romantic heresy.

One can see, in what Auden says about History, Necessity, and Art, a common factor: in every case he is repudiating the convictions and clichés of the thirties. History is *not* economically determined, man is *not* perfectible, freedom is *not* the knowledge of causal necessity, and art is *not* an agent. But he was also working toward his own alternative ideology, based on the need for absolutes. We sense the form that it will take in the vocabulary that he began to use at this time: words like *sin* and *damnation, heresy* and *orthodoxy.* But it is important to recognize that what we are observing in Auden's writings through 1939 and 1940 is not the record of a conversion experience and its consequences, but the evidences of a strenuous and open-minded effort to reconsider his ideas of man and history. His Christianity was not a *cause* of this effort but was a logical conclusion of it. "As to my return to the church," he wrote to Kenneth Lewars in September 1947, "it was a gradual business without any abrupt leaps. *The Double Man,* written Jan.-Oct. 1940 covers a period when I was beginning to think seriously about such things without committing myself. I started going to church again just about October." This is not the language of conversion (it's nothing like the tone of Eliot's announcement of *his* Anglicanism); Auden simply chose to renew an interrupted religious commitment.

What he found in Christianity was a system of beliefs that could contain his new conclusions: the ethic of loneliness; the aesthetic of imperfection; the paradox of necessary freedom. He found, you might say, that Modern Man and Christian Man were the same.

II

Auden's principal poem of this period, the poem in which he set down most fully his answers to that hard question Where are we now?, is **"New Year Letter."** It is the poem that stands most exactly at the point between the decades, between an ending and a beginning: in form and substance it repudiates the poetry that he had written during the thirties, and it points forward to all of the later work.

Readers coming to it in 1941 from the earlier work must have been shocked at how different, and how much less "modern," it was: neither elliptical, nor parabolical, not melodramatic, not imperative, but a long, relaxed, discursive poem in that most facile of meters, the tetrameter couplet. Furthermore it is written in the form of a familiar letter, with all that *that* implies: that though the poem may discuss public issues, the discourse will be private; and that the goal of the poem will be not action, but communion. Most striking of all, its tone is calm: at this dark time in human history Auden's verse is, for the first time, free of anxiety.

The occasion of the poem carries us a good way toward its meaning. In the dark hours after midnight, between the last day of the 30s and the first day of the 40s, the poet sits in his room in Brooklyn Heights, looking across the dark East River toward Manhattan. This is obviously an ironic version of a romantic convention that runs from Shelley to Yeats: the poet in his dark tower, elevated, isolated from the world, making the philosophic poem. But it is also an emblem of Auden's own situation—the self-exiled poet, alone in a foreign country. And, since Auden had come to see loneliness as man's real condition, it is also an emblem of universal human existence.

But if there is loneliness, there is also connection: he is writing a letter, and a letter, after all, implies an addressee. Auden's letter is addressed to Elizabeth Mayer—a German refugee who had made her Long Island home a haven for other exiles, and particularly for artists (including Auden and his friend Benjamin Britten). She and her home play an important symbolic role in the poem, as we shall see.

But though the addressee is important, the poem is less an actual letter than it is a series of meditations on those preoccupations that I've been talking about: History, Art, and Necessity; where we are now and how we got here. These themes interweave in the poem, as Auden saw that they interwove in life, one countering and qualifying another in the dialectic that was the model of Auden's reality. The whole discourse therefore moves disjunctively, from art to history and back, from art's value to its limitations, from necessity to choice, from personal recollection to historical example. The form is necessarily an open one: its very openness is *its* particular model of order—an inclusive shape that can be true to all of its terms, the poem of its time that is not closed to any aspect of its historical context.

A good place to begin looking at the poem is an early example of this kind of dialectic, in which Auden recalls the day the war began.

> . . . the same sun whose neutral eye
> All florid August from the sky

Had watched the earth behave and seen
Strange traffic on her brown and green,
Obedient to some hidden force
A ship abruptly change her course,
A train make an unwanted stop,
A little crowd smash up a shop,
Suspended hatreds crystallize
In visible hostilities,
Vague concentrations shrink to take
The sharp crude patterns generals make,
The very morning that the war
Took action on the Polish floor,
Lit up America and on
A cottage in Long Island shone
Where Buxtehude as we played
One of his *passacaglias* made
Our minds a *civitas* of sound
Where nothing but assent was found,
For art had set in order sense
And feeling and intelligence,
And from its ideal order grew
Our local understanding too.

In the immediate world of history a universal disorder
grows; in the world of art, a local understanding. Neither
term cancels the other; reality is the dialectic that contains
both. It remains true that art makes nothing happen; and in
a time of war that limitation seems very great. Yet it has its
value: it offers us models of order, and so sustains our efforts to give order to our lives.

> "New Year Letter" begins in darkness and
> aloneness—the universal disorders of the
> time, the disorders of history, the very
> principal of disorder itself.
> —*Samuel Hynes*

"New Year Letter" is a poem about history. But it is also
a poem that *contains* history. It has, for instance, a vast cast
of historical figures, from Aristotle to Hitler: some artists,
some philosophers, some scientists, some theologians, a few
simply English eccentrics. None gets more than a few lines'
attention, and all function illustratively (and so would seem to
be dispensable). What they are doing in the poem is simply
being historical: exemplifying man-in-time—acting, choosing,
being free and responsible and guilty. Their presence in the
poem is another departure from Auden's practice in the 30s;
then he had worked within a mythological world populated by
fictional characters like the Airman and the Uncle and the Spy,
and by Christopher and Stephen and Gerhart Meyer, the truly
strong man. But Auden had separated himself from that myth;
his emigration had cut him off from his generation, and now,
on January 1, 1940, he was making a new myth out of his-

torical persons. (There is a similar point in Yeats's career,
at which his poems begin to be invaded by persons from
his own and Ireland's history; and also in Eliot's: a point at
which art and history interpenetrate, because each poet has
found an ideology that can *contain* both.)

"New Year Letter" begins in darkness and aloneness—the two
fundamental realities—the universal disorders of the time, the disorders of history, the very principal of disorder itself. But it also
touches on points of order. I have quoted one—the day when war
was declared, and Auden, in the house of Elizabeth Mayer, shared
in the order of art. A second, occurring at the beginning of the third
part, is a recollection of a similar occasion, but only a week past
(so that would be Christmas Day).

Warm in your house, Elizabeth,
A week ago at the same hour
I felt the unexpected power
That drove our ragged egos in
From the dead-ends of greed and sin
To sit down at the wedding feast,
Put shining garments on the least,
Arranged us so that each and all,
The erotic and the logical,
Each felt the *placement* to be such
That he was honoured overmuch,
And SCHUBERT sang and MOZART played
And GLUCK and food and friendship made
Our privileged community
That real republic which must be
The State all politicians claim,
Even the worst, to be their aim.

This passage records an experience similar to the first, but
with a deeper significance; here art participates in the occasion, but the felt community is based on *love,* not on art
alone. The lines that follow make it clear that Auden ascribes a value to such moments much like that which Eliot
found in the rose garden in *Burnt Norton:* a moment out of
time, a glimpse of the Eden we cannot inhabit, an evidence
and a promise that the ideal exists. Such moments cannot
be sustained: they must be lost, Auden says, to be regained;
but because they occur, man can endure ordinary reality.

The common element in these two positive passages in
"New Year Letter" is the figure of Elizabeth Mayer, in
whose presence the two orders of love and art flourish. So
it is not surprising that in the final lines of the poem, as dawn
breaks on the first day of the 40s, another day of war and
suffering and necessary loneliness, Auden addresses her.

Dear friend Elizabeth, dear friend
These days have brought me, may the end
I bring to the grave's dead-line be
More worthy of your sympathy
Than the beginning; may the truth

That no one marries lead my youth
Where you already are and bless
Me with your learned peacefulness
Who on the lives about you throw
A calm *solificatio.*
A warmth throughout the universe
That each for better or for worse
Must carry round with him through life,
A judge, a landscape, and a wife.
We fall down in the dance, we make
The old ridiculous mistake,
But always there are such as you
Forgiving, helping what we do.
O every day in sleep and labour
Our life and death are with our neighbour,
And love illuminates again
The city and the lion's den,
The world's great rage, the travel of young men.

"We fall down in the dance . . ." This, of course, is from Mann's "Tonio Kröger," but Auden uses it to make a very different point. This is once more the aesthetic of imperfection, but here accepted, as a necessary imperfection of existence, unavoidable, but made forgivable by that love, that *agape,* of which Elizabeth Mayer is the human symbol, and art the ideal model. In the end the world goes on existing as it is: suffering continues, war continues, men continue in their imperfections. But love also exists, and art exists: order is possible, the world is redeemable—though not now, not here. This "moment" is the positive value that makes "living deliberately without roots" possible; it is another kind of community—momentary, imperfect, but *real*—that must replace the lost traditional community of place and class and nation.

"New Year Letter" is a very odd poem—at once historical and private, a war poem about not being in a war, a religious poem without a religion, a disordered meditation on the order of art. One way to describe it might be to call it a *witness,* as in Christian usage. A witness is not a confession, and Auden has not abandoned his customary reticence, but it is the revelation of a Self; and it is with this poem, I think, that Auden began to establish that self that so substantially and comfortably occupies the later poetry. The earlier poems, on the whole, don't have that kind of substantial presence: they are dramatic, mysterious, imperative; they create a world, but not a personal identity. But a letter implies a letter-writer, and in **"New Year Letter"** there is a knowable "I," who is doing the thinking and feeling, and whose expanding and coalescing understanding of the meaning of his personal situation is the content of the poem.

Contemporary reviewers were troubled by the poem's evident inconclusiveness. Edwin Muir, for instance, wrote in *Horizon* in August 1941 that "it seems to be making, with

a great deal of excellent argument, towards something which is never reached . . . ," and he concluded that Auden was "convincing when he expresses doubt, but unconvincing when he tries to find an answer to doubt, for the doubt comes from a deeper source than the answer." This is very acute; but I think Muir is wrong to take this quality as a flaw. Historically speaking, doubt and uncertainty seem inevitable in a poem written in 1940 to answer the question Where are we now? But doubt and uncertainty are more than historical conditions: they are, for Auden, inherent in the human condition (in his notes he quotes Pascal's *Pensées:* "Nier, croire, et douter bien, sont à l'homme ce que le courir est au cheval"—denying, believing, and doubting are to man what running is to a horse). The goal is not to resolve doubt, but to live in doubt without anxiety.

Like many modern poems **"New Year Letter"** is also a poem about poetry, and doubt and uncertainty have their poetic equivalent in the aesthetics of imperfection. Art is an ideal order that man strives for, but fails to achieve; imperfection is the human condition: all art is failure—including this poem, in which Auden writes:

> For I relapse into my crimes:
> Time and again have slubbered through
> With slip and slapdash what I do,
> Adopted what I would disown,
> The preacher's loose immodest tone;
> Though warned by a great sonneteer
> Not to sell cheap what is most dear,
> Though horrible old KIPLING cried
> 'One instant's toil to Thee denied
> Stands all eternity's offence,'
> I would not give them audience.
> Yet still the weak offender must
> Beg still for leniency and trust
> His power to avoid the sin
> Peculiar to his discipline.

But since the will to achieve order is a universal moral impulse, the artist is no different from any other man who falls down in the dance. There is no such thing as The Artist: the poet is everyman.

The later poetry of Auden, and the role that he assumed in his later years, begins here, in **"New Year Letter,"** with this perception. The poem is not exactly a crisis poem: the Hound of Heaven never barks, there is no wrestling with the Angel, and no Hopkins-ish agony. The process is more like what he wrote at the time about Melville: "Towards the end he sailed into an extraordinary mildness." This voyage into mildness has not been completed by the end of the poem, but the course has been set.

The price of this commitment for Auden as a poet has been

considerable. The later poetry has never gotten the attention and admiration that the earlier got; it has never been taken as the true expression of a generation or a decade, and many a reader has looked back nostalgically to the poetry of the 30s, when anxiety was really anxiety. But there is no point in regretting the change: For Auden it was simply an example of that necessary moral choice by which man affirms his freedom.

In one of the notes to **"New Year Letter"** Auden raises the question of Wagner, who was for him the greatest of the romantic artists, and the greatest romantic heretic. Why, Auden asks himself, do Wagner's characters behave so absurdly? Why do their actions deny their knowledge? And he answers: *"To allow Wagner to go on writing music and, moreover, the kind of music that he was good at writing."* This is no doubt one kind of genius: the genius of the romantic heretic who bends reality to his gifts. Auden's genius was of the opposite kind: he rejected the beliefs by which he had written his early brilliant poetry, because he found them to be untrue; and when he had thought his way to a new, true belief, he was content to write such poems as that belief would allow him to write.

"New Year Letter" stands at the crux of this transforming process, and it is therefore important to our understanding of Auden. But it is more than that: it is a poem about the meaning of history, and that too is important. When Auden spoke at Smith College, he justified his existence as a poet and an intellectual in these words: "To try to understand what has come upon us and why may not be the most heroic of the tasks required to save civilization, but it is indispensable." He spoke just four days after Sir Jocelyn Lucas had asked his question in the Commons. Auden couldn't possibly have known about that question, yet he was answering it. He would not fight, but he would perform a different and indispensable task: he would try to understand what had come upon the human race, and why—that is what this poem does. Writing as he did, not after the fact, but while the historical events were still in process, he wrote, not surprisingly, an imperfect and uncertain poem; but that would not have troubled Auden, and should not trouble us. For it is also a unique poem: a record of a great poet's effort to understand the meaning of history as it occurred, and to find the values by which he could live in history—as a poet and as a man. It is a part of *his* history; and it is a part of ours.

Ron McFarland (essay date Spring 1983)

SOURCE: "Auden's *Cena:* 'Tonight at Seven-Thirty,'" in *Southern Humanities Review,* Vol. 17, No. 2, Spring, 1983, pp. 139-47.

[*In the following essay, McFarland examines the significance of Roman satiric verse and the conventions of the* cena, *a Roman banquet, in "Tonight at Seven-Thirty."*]

Among W. H. Auden's many neo-classical poems, the dozen collected under the rubric, **"Thanksgiving for a Habitat"** (written between 1958 and July 1964), each poem dedicated to some personal friend or friends, constitutes perhaps the most outrageously (some might say self-indulgently) Augustan of his opus. "Every home should be a fortress," he writes in **"The Common Life,"** "equipped with all the very latest engines / for keeping Nature at bay." The recognizably Roman sentiments vary in conceptual significance from such comments on the relationship between man and nature to that which opens the title poem of the series: "Nobody I know would like to be buried / with a silver cocktail shaker." The poems range from the companionable yet serious colloquy on poetry in **"The Cave of Making"** (In Memoriam Louis MacNeice) to the Swiftian excrementalism of **"The Geography of the House"** (For Christopher Isherwood).

Readers who admire Auden's most anthologized poems, from **"Musée de Beaux Arts"** to **"In Praise of Limestone"** or **"In Memory of W. B. Yeats,"** must find most of the poems in **"Thanksgiving for a Habitat"** difficult of access for several reasons, not the least of which is Auden's voice, which, while sometimes intimate enough with regard to the person or persons named, is aloof with respect to the reader. **"Tonight at Seven-Thirty"** is a useful poem for analysis with respect to the relationship between poet and reader for several reasons. First, and most important, the poem has its basis in a sub-genre of Roman satiric poetry which has never been much pursued by English or American poets. Second, the poem is intriguing and rather difficult both in form and content. Third, it is representative in voice (including tone and diction) of other poems in the series and of Auden's later writing in general.

The conventions of the *cena* (banquet, dinner), as established in Roman satire—like Horace's 2.8, the dinner of Nasidienus, the rich man—include identification and behavior of the host; description of food served, along with its method of preparation and presentation; list of guests, invited or otherwise (i.e., "shadows"); account of events (e.g., arguments, insults, brawls, accidents) other than dining. Since the *cena* is satirical, there must always be some point of censure or reprimand: "satire feeds on the tension between what is ideal and what is real, and its purpose is to portray reality as a situation causing aversion or disgust." In the *Cena Nasidieni* the host is the object of satiric attack. "He stands for a type common enough in Horace's day," according to Niall Rudd, "a type which always appears when wealth is acquired without either education or social conscience."

For the modern reader, the boorish behavior of the guests, as recounted to Horace by Fundianus, far outweighs the *gaucherie* of the well-meaning host. As Rudd demonstrates, Nasidienus has bent over backwards to do everything right, but in the process he has overdone it; he has lost perspective, and as a result everything turns out wrong. There is not only fine Caecuban and "brine-free Chian" wine, but also the less worthy Alban and Falernian. In this regard, Rudd defends Nasidienus against any meanness of intent, but perhaps the error is not in offering the two lesser wines, but in offering them specifically to the wealthy connoisseur, Maecenas. At any rate, it is the "shadows" (uninvited guests, in this case cronies of Maecenas), Servilius Balatro and Vibidius, who cause most of the trouble. Nasidienus becomes overfastidious in explaining the origins and value of each item on the menu. As he loses sight of the proper role of the host, so Balatro and Vibidius, determining to get drunk and wreck the feast, lose sight of their place as guests. When the dusty wall hangings collapse on the lamprey, Nomentanus, the philosopher, hyperbolizes in defense of the distraught Nasidienus: "'Ah Fortune! What god more cruel than you?/ You always like to play around with mankind's hopes!'" Balatro, however, restores some perspective: "'Such is the nature of life, thus it happens / that our reputations don't correspond to hard work.'" Though presumably soothing the host, who has worked hard to stage a reputable banquet, the innuendo suggests that Nasidienus has not worked hard for his status in life. Balatro concludes that "'a party-giver's talent, like a general's, comes out / in case of trouble.'" Failing to find the perspective from which to deal with the disaster, however, Nasidienus thanks Balatro and proceeds to multiply the delicacies (a crane, "the liver of a fig-fed, albino gander," "boiled blackbird breasts served with de-assed doves") and then lectures "about their causes and essential natures." Given no other recourse, the guests flee. These somewhat riotous aspects of the *cena* tradition in Roman satire culminate in the *Cena Trimalchionis* episode of Petronius' *Satyricon.*

Juvenal's *cena* satires (the fifth and the eleventh) are more moderate than those of Horace or Petronius. He uses the comparative mode (essentially for contrast), which becomes something of a motif in the *cena* tradition, not only in satire, but also in epigrams, odes, and epistles, for the *cena* is not limited to the satire as a genre. In Satire V, which is double-edged, the guest, Trebius, is willing to endure Virro's outrageous insults for a free meal. The contrast here is between the fine food devoured by the host and the wretched fare offered to Trebius. The discrepancy in quality extends even to the water and to the servants who bring in the dishes. The serving of the lamprey, "the finest that the Straits of Sicily can purvey," to the master is countered by the following to grovelling Trebius:

For you is reserved an eel, first cousin to a water-

snake, or perchance a pike mottled with ice-spots; he too was bred on Tiber's banks and was wont to find his way into the inmost recesses of the Subura, battening himself amid its flowing sewers.

As Juvenal notes, should Trebius come into money, Virro's response would be altogether different. Nevertheless, the main thrust of Satire V is that if a man will put up with such shabby treatment, he deserves it. Martial uses a similar contrast as the subject of *Epigrams* III, lx.

In Juvenal's Satire XI, the contrast is between the sumptuous feasts of the present and the simple food (including a corresponding moderation in servants and types of entertainment) of earlier times. The modest repast also becomes a sort of motif within the *cena* tradition. Horace's *Epistles* 1.5, although really an invitation to a *symposium* (drinking and conversation, as opposed to dinner and, usually, entertainment), stresses the simplicity of the "unstylish couch," "plain vegetables," and "cheap plates." Martial's *Epigrams* V, lxxviii invites a friend to "fare modestly" on "cheap Cappadocian lettuces and strong-smelling leeks," among other things. Though the dinner may be small and poor, however, he can promise that "you will say no word insincere nor hear one, and, wearing your natural face, will recline at ease." In his *Odes* 3.29, inviting Maecenas to leave Rome for a visit to the country, Horace offers "a simple meal beneath the poor man's humble roof."

It is this particular development of the *cena* convention—the modest dinner combined with honest and straightforward conversation—that has most influenced English poetry. That small degree of interest in the *cena* that has surfaced in English poetry is limited, for the most part, to the work of Ben Johnson and his followers in the seventeenth century. Jonson's "Inviting a Friend to Supper" is probably the best known of the poems dealing with conventions of the *cena,* and it draws heavily on Martial's epigrams. Like Horace, Jonson catalogs the food to be served, then he suggests the evening's entertainment (readings not from his own work, but from Vergil, Tacitus, and Livy). Like Martial, Jonson concludes with a promise to part "innocently":

> . . . No simple word,
> That shall be utter'd at our mirthfull board,
> Shall make us sad next morning: or affright
> The libertie, that we'll enjoy to night.

Several of Robert Herrick's poems from *Hesperides* (1648) owe something to the *cena:* "A Country Life: To His Brother," "The Hock Cart, or Harvest Home," "A Panegerick to Sir Lewis Pemberton," "To His Peculiar Friend Master John Wicks," and especially "Oberons Feast" and "The Invitation." Part of a three-poem sequence, including "The Faerie Temple: or, Oberons Chappell" and

"Oberons Palace," "Oberons Feast" is a banquet cast in miniature and set on a mushroom table. Against the background
music provided by grasshoppers, crickets, flies, and gnats,
the fairy king, served by elves, dines on such miniscule fare
as "The hornes of paperie Butterflies," "Emits eggs," "a
Newt's stew'd thigh," and "The broke-heart of a Nightingale / Ore-come in musicke." "The Invitation" is a more
conventional poem in the *cena* tradition, in which the
guest, expecting "such lautitious meat, / The like not
Heliogabalus did eat" and "no less than Aromatick Wine
/ Of Maydens-blush, commixt with Jessimine," finds instead a cold hearth:

> At last, i'th'noone of winter, did appeare
> A ragd-soust-neats-foot with sick vineger:
> And in a burnisht Flagonet stood by
> Beere small as Comfort, dead as Charity.

Here, Herrick uses the comparative mode with good comic
effect, at the same time carrying the "poor home-plain food"
motif to an absurdity. Under these circumstances, the virtues of innocence and moderation are lost, and the guest
goes home with the ague.

Auden's **"Tonight at Seven-Thirty"** examines the nature
of the dinner party concentrating on a single aspect of the
cena: the guests. The point of view, unlike that of most poems in the tradition, is that of the host. The poem begins
incongruously: "The life of plants / is one continuous solitary meal." Ruminants scarcely stop eating, and predators
are "ravenous most of the time." None of these "play host /
to a stranger whom they help first," except man, that "supererogatory beast, / Dame Kind's thoroughbred lunatic."
"Supererogatory" is the first of several sesquipedalianisms
in the poem. Auden is reminiscent in his diction of Herrick,
with his "liquefaction" and "cunctation," "circumvolving"
and "excathedrated," but for Auden the polysyllables (usually Latinate) are a more prevalent characteristic of style.

It is hard to say exactly when one begins to realize that the
loose lines, variable in length from four to fourteen syllables
and frequently enjambed, constitute a stanzaic form. The
indentation makes the lines seem less regular than they are,
and the rhyme scheme is modulated through the use of near
rhyme and the rhyming of lines dissimilar in length.
Auden's sustaining of a fourteen-line scheme over six stanzas rivals the virtuosity of John Donne and perhaps of any
poet in the language. I will quote the second stanza for
closer examination. It begins with the conclusion of a sentence from the first stanza, "Only man . . . can do the honors of a feast . . ."

> and was doing so
> before the last Glaciation when he offered
> mammoth-marrow

> and, perhaps, Long Pig, will continue till Dooms
>   day
>   when at God's board
> the saints chew pickled Leviathan. In this age
>   farms
> are no longer crenellated, only cops port arms,
> but the Law of the Hearth is unchanged: a brawler
>   may not
>   be put to death on the spot,
> but he is asked to quit the sacral dining area
>   *instanter,* and a foul-mouth gets the cold
>   shoulder. The right of a guest
> to standing and foster is as old
>   as the ban on incest.

The rhyme scheme, with frequent off-stress rhyming, is
a, b, a, c, b, d, d, e, e, c, f, g, f, g. This configuration
defies division into quatrains and couplets, or into alternating and enclosed patterns, yet it is certainly not random, as examination of other stanzas will demonstrate.
The effect of this complex stanzaic form is that of the
baroque, properly considered: an impression of elaborate
ornamentation and activity beneath which (or within
which) operates a definite sense of form and order.

The formal tension in this poem between looseness and constraint reflects the interplay between the colloquial and the
erudite language, which one encounters frequently in
Auden's poems. Against phrases like "Long Pig" (a euphemism of Polynesian origin for human flesh as meat), "saints
chew pickled Leviathan," and "only cops port arms," we
have "dine *en famille*" and "the sacral dining area." This
sort of tension, in both form and language (and therefore,
in content), works best, I think, in the satiric poem where,
as I mentioned earlier, the poet is exploring the tension between the ideal and the real.

In modern times farms are not walled, and only the police are armed (Auden appears not to be thinking of the
United States in this context), but the rules of hospitality are unchanged: although a "brawler" is not "put to
death on the spot," he may be dismissed instantly ("in-
stanter" being the legal term) from the dining room. In
effect, then, the *cena* retains certain natural rules of decorum. It is an institution of civilized man who does not
need to wall himself in or arm himself against his neighbors. The guest has rights (the term "foster" derives from
the OE, *fóstor,* meaning "nourishment" or "food"). If man
is indeed a "supererogatory beast" and a "thoroughbred
lunatic," he is still superior to the plants, ruminants,
predators, and pack-hunters of the first stanza. It is
against the understood decorum of the hospitality code,
after all, that the Roman satires on the *cena* are offered.
Without such a code, there could be no tension between
ideal and actual behavior.

In the third stanza Auden advises, "for authentic comity," an assemblage both "small" and "unpublic," as opposed to "mass banquets where flosculent speeches are made / in some hired hall." Under such circumstances, he points out, we think either of ourselves or of nothing at all. Both "Christ's cenacle" and "King Arthur's rundle," he continues, "seated a baker's dozen," but today, when the host must be both chef, servant and dishwasher, even a dozen is too large a number. In fact, the "Perfect Social Number" these days is "six lenient semble sieges, / none of them perilous." The Latin (sometimes via French) of the latter phrase translates: "six soft assembled seats" ("siege" derives from OF for "seat," and ultimately from the Latin *sedere,* "to sit"). The play on "Siege Perilous," of course, refers to the vacant seat at the Round Table, which could be filled only by Sir Galahad, who was to find the Holy Grail, and which was fatal to anyone else.

In the fourth stanza Auden makes it clear that he is speaking of a "dinner party" and not just a casual supper or a covered-dish social. It is "a worldly rite that nicknames or endearments / or family / diminutives would profane." The language throughout the poem (e.g., "sacral dining area," "Christ's cenacle") has suggested that such a dinner retains some qualities of religious ritual. "Two doters," therefore, "who wish / to tiddle and curmurr between the soup and fish / belong in restaurants," and children, of course, belong in bed. The guests must be mutually agreeable; therefore, "married maltalents" and melancholy singles are to be avoided.

"Not that a god, / immune to grief, would be an ideal guest," the next stanza begins. A god would simply be "a bore." Here, Auden offers a portrait of the ideal guest, the "funniest" and "kindest" of mortals, "those who are most aware . . ."

> of the baffle of being, don't kid themselves our
> care
> is consolable, but believe a laugh is less
>   heartless than tears, that a hostess
> prefers it. Brains evolved after bowels, therefore,
>   great assets as fine raiment and good looks
>   can be on festive occasions,
>   they are not essential like artful cooks
>   and stalwart digestions.

Auden gives in these lines the perspective which any good satirist must have. It is not sufficient simply to indicate the sort of guests one should avoid (brawlers, foul-mouths, doters, *et al.*). The ideal guest knows the pain of the human condition, but he believes in laughter rather than tears as a response (plays Democritus rather than Heraclitus).

In the concluding stanza Auden gives a portrait of the ideal set of guests for a *cena:*

> I see a table
>   at which the youngest and oldest present
>   keep the eye grateful
>   for what Nature's bounty and grace of Spirit can
>   create:
>   for the ear's content
> one raconteur, one gnostic with amazing shop,
> both in a talkative mood but knowing when to
>   stop,
> and one wide-traveled worldling to interject now
>   and then
>   a sardonic comment, men
> and women who enjoy the cloop of corks,
>   appreciate
> dapatical fare, yet can see in swallowing
>   a sign act of reverence,
> in speech a work of re-presenting
>   the true olamic silence.

The acceptance of both men and women into the dinner party immediately sets Auden's banquet apart from the Roman and seventeenth-century English *cena,* but much of the same spirit of camaraderie remains. If Auden himself is not the "raconteur" and "gnostic with amazing shop," then he is certainly the "wide-traveled worldling" of that triumvirate.

The words "dapatical" and "olamic" are not to be found in standard lexicons, not even in *Webster's Third New International Dictionary,* but "dapatical" is listed in the *OED* as a synonym for "sumptuous," dating to the seventeenth century, and "olamic" is listed as a relatively recent coinage (1872 is its first appearance in English) from Hebrew meaning "vast" or even "perpetual." The erudite etymologies contrast interestingly with the echoic colloquial "cloop of corks." The allusions at the end of the poem are not merely eucharistic, but something more primitive. They refer to a cyclic concept of nature and time, in which man's relationship with other living things of the earth (as in the first stanza) is being asserted. Lévi-Strauss observes that the "gustatory code" occupies a "privileged position" in primitive mythology "since it is through myths explaining the origin of fire, and thus of cooking, that we gain access to myths about man's loss of immortality." Moreover, Lévi-Strauss continues, cooking marks "the transition from nature to culture."

"Tonight at Seven-Thirty" is not, of course, a true *cena* in the Roman satiric tradition. We have no recounting of boisterous, all-male feasts, no comparison of luxurious with simple fare, no scrumptious catalog of edibles indulged for its own sake. The Roman tradition forms the foundation for this poem, but the direct source for some references is neither Horace nor Johnson, but the woman to whom the poem is dedicated, the noted gastronomist M(ary) F(rances)

K(ennedy) Fisher. Her five most famous books, beginning with *Serve It Forth* (1937) and including the provocative title, *How to Cook a Wolf* (1942), had been reprinted in a single volume, *The Art of Eating,* in 1954 and again in 1963. Auden praised Fisher's prose and proclaimed that "*The Art of Eating* is a book which I think Colette would have loved and wished she had written." The last book of the volume, *An Alphabet for Gourmets* (1949), concludes with a brief essay entitled "The Perfect Dinner," from which Auden probably derived both the idea that six was "now a Perfect / Social Number" and the line-up of ideal guests in the concluding stanza quoted above:

> A good combination would be one married couple,
> for warm composure; one less firmly established,
> to add a note of investigation to the talk; and two
> strangers of either sex, upon whom the better-ac-
> quainted diners could sharpen their questioning
> wits.

Fisher adds that "it is ridiculous to threaten an evening's possible perfection in the name of democracy, gastronomical or otherwise."

But the *cena* offers a good perspective from which to examine **"Tonight at Seven-Thirty,"** especially because Auden makes explicit what has conventionally remained tacit about the banquet. In the *Cena Trimalchionis,* the *Cena Nasidieni,* the banquet poems of Juvenal and Martial, Jonson and Herrick, very little is said about what one needs in order to have an ideal dinner party. One does not, implicitly, want a host like Nasidienus or a guest like Trebius, but what are the desiderata? From the Roman poems one sometimes supposes that a properly cooked lamprey and a well-chosen wine are all. From the seventeenth-century English poets one might gather that simplicity and moderation are the essentials. Auden argues for a thoughtful selection of guests, for a proper guest-host relationship, and more: he insists that amidst the "sardonic comment" and the "cloop of corks" there be a mutual reverence for humankind, that "supererogatory beast" which remains the only one capable of doing "the honors of a feast." At the end of **"The Horatians,"** Auden speaks for Horace's odes:

> ". . . We can only
> do what it seems to us we were made for, look at
> this world with a happy eye
> but from a sober perspective."

Alan W. France (essay date Spring 1990)

SOURCE: "Gothic North and the Mezzogiorno in Auden's 'In Praise of Limestone,'" in *Renascence: Essays on Value in Literature,* Vol. 42, No. 3, Spring, 1990, pp. 141-8.

[*In the following essay, France examines Auden's historical perspective and juxtaposition of Latin and Gothic Christianity in his "In Praise of Limestone."*]

Critics of W. H. Auden's **"In Praise of Limestone"** have often been lulled by the poem's casual voice into overlooking its seriousness. It has been said, for example, to betray a "frivolity [that] has modulated into a quixotic, religious playfulness" ([Richard] Johnson) or the "indulgent . . . humor" of a "family portrait of Mother Nature" ([Edward] Callan).

A good reading of **"In Praise of Limestone,"** it seems to me, should account for the poem's centrality to the Auden corpus (it introduces, but one, both *Nones* and the concluding quarter of *Collected Shorter Poems*); such a reading should also incorporate our understanding of Auden's historical, cultural, and religious concerns of the post-war decade. The poem presents, I believe, a panorama of Western history, stretching from antiquity into the so-called post-Christian era, the poet's perspective being specifically, though only anecdotally, Christian.

"In Praise of Limestone" at once calls to mind several attributes of Eden from Auden's paradisical wish-list in the *The Dyer's Hand:*

> *Landscape*
>   Limestone uplands like the Pennines plus a small region of igneous rocks with at least one extinct volcano. A precipitous and indented sea-coast.

> *Religion*
>   Roman Catholic in an easygoing Mediterranean sort of way. Lots of local saints.

Auden remarks, as well, in a discussion of the sacred: "Many of us have sacred landscapes which probably all have much in common, but there will almost certainly be details which are peculiar to each." He makes it clear that his own sacred landscape is historical, "a world of unique events and unique persons," and that "tradition now means a consciousness of the whole of the past as present." Significantly, however, Auden blames Luther and Descartes for the destruction of "sacramental analogies" to the "phenomenal world." **"In Praise of Limestone,"** I am suggesting, is the poet's attempt to rediscover the sacramental quality in nature, a quality still animate in the "under-developed" regions of the Mediterranean South—in particular Italy below Rome, the Mezzogiorno—but thoroughly extirpated in the Germanic North by Protestant asceticism and modern science.

If this is so, **"In Praise of Limestone"** refutes the orthodox, "Whiggish," positivistic understanding of post-Reformation European history. The idea of the progressive enlightenment of the North is particularly evident in J. A. Symonds' massive *Renaissance in Italy,* a work Auden would most probably have known. Interestingly, Symonds used geological tropes to distinguish Latin, Mediterranean Europe as "backwaters and stagnant pools" of superstition from the scientific and rationalistic North, driven by the "tidal stress of cosmic forces." In the century-long religious struggles, Symonds imagined that northern Europe "heaved like a huge ocean in the grip of a tumultuous gyrating cyclone." **"In Praise of Limestone"** is a re-vision of this positivistic, Protestant understanding of modern history, a re-valuation of Europe's southern, cultural backwaters.

In **"Good-bye to the Mezzogiorno,"** Auden calls Germanic Europe the "gothic North" and the Latin, Mediterranean world the "sunburnt otherwhere." **"In Praise of Limestone"** extends the place-centered "psychic geography," *paysage moralise,* into the realm of spiritual history. The locus of the poem is the South—Ischia, presumably, but many other Mediterranean shores could serve as well. Limestone forms the geological substrate of the Latin South, and, more significantly to the poet, Latin culture is itself a substratum of the spirit: geological elements symbolize profound spiritual differences between North and South that have grown out of the particulars of European history.

The poet sees Mediterranean civilization as an expression of sibling rivalry
—Alan W. France

The cultural contrast between North and South is represented most clearly in the poem's insistent distinction between voice and vision. The poet speaks from within the spiritual tradition of the Gothic North, although he is a loving barbarian. The Latin South remains the observed "otherwhere," envisioned but voiceless.

"In Praise of Limestone" begins by attributing to the Mediterranean world the qualities of limestone; the poet, by contrast, is of other mettle: "If it form the one landscape that we, the inconstant ones, / Are consistently homesick for, this is chiefly / Because it dissolves in water. . . ." Limestone is, of course, a sedimentary rock, nicely connoting the sedentary, domestic qualities of Mediterranean civilizations: stratum accreted on strata like Minoa or Schliemann's Troy. It is a calcium compound rich in recycled organic material, shell and bones accumulated and compacted over eons. In its strata are traces of the individual organisms left as a fossil record of the past. The mineral is thus a geological metaphor for history. And the civilizations shaped by the Medi-

terranean are, with good reason, identified with limestone, since the calcium makes the stone water-soluble and, therefore, easily eroded by the action of tides and waves.

The result is life-sustaining: "caves and conduits . . . a private pool for its fish . . . / Its own little ravine whose cliffs entertain / The butterfly and the lizard." The poet then begins to invest this nurturing environment, the Mediterranean region in general and Latin civilization in particular, with a distinctly maternal personality:

> What could be more like Mother or a fitter
> background
>   For her son, the flirtatious male who lounges
> Against a rock in the sunlight, never doubting
>   That for all his faults he is loved; whose works
> are but
> Extensions of his power to charm?

The poet sees Mediterranean civilization as an expression of sibling rivalry, "a child's wish" domesticating the limestone substance of nature, "From weathered outcrop / To hill-top temple," formalizing "appearing waters" in "conspicuous fountains," transforming "a wild to a formal vineyard." Figuratively, the male in Latin cultures is the child who builds to please the eternal Mother, and the structures reflect the life-sustaining domestic concern of that Mother as the limestone itself is "built" into ecological niches, caverns, ravines, and basins by the Mediterranean mother-figure.

Lines 21-43 characterize the fundamental human qualities, spiritual as well as social, that limestone-based Mediterranean cultures nurture. The poet notes the innocent warmth and anarchic volubility of the

> band of rivals as they climb up and down
>   Their steep stone gennels in twos and threes, at
> times
> Arm in arm, but never, thank God, in step;
>   . . . knowing each other too well to think
> There are any important secrets. . . .

These indulged child-rivals play under the eye of the eternal feminine; they share an understanding that enforces rivalry at the same time it encourages unspoken intimacy. Most important, it precludes their conceiving of abstract causes and dicta that enlist both the best and the worst of human allegiances, and they are therefore "unable / To conceive of a god whose temper-tantrums are moral / And not to be pacified by a clever line / Or a good lay." The *double entendre* of the latter propitiation, suggesting both hymn and the readiness to coax with sexual favors, reinforces the female quality of Mediterranean religiosity.

According to the poet, then, Latin theodicy makes no provision for an angry God-the-Father, who, unmoved by in-gratiating gestures, drives the sons out of the house into the cold homelessness, "the granite waste" of an alien universe: "They have never had to veil their faces in awe / Of a cra-ter whose blazing fury could not be fixed." Here the poem suggests the rumblings of an angry God as well as the phal-lic symbolism of a volcanic cone erupting with the pent-up energy of irrepressible anger. In contrast to this primal, un-domesticated power of patriarchal aggression, the Mediter-ranean *Urmutter,* whose "rounded slopes" conceal a "silent system of caves and conduits," is comfortingly humane.

Pampered and protected, the sons of Mediterranean nurture occupy a locality "Adjusted to the local needs of valleys / Where everything can be touched or reached by walking" and have never had to look out "into infinite space." They have always stayed home, insulated from the world of up-rooted nomads, who must bump into evil, without and within: "born lucky, / Their legs have never encountered the fungi / And insects of the jungle, the monstrous forms and lives / With which we have nothing, we like to hope, in com-mon." The "we" of this last line again enforces the sense of otherness or "Northern-ness" of the poet's voice and iden-tity and, by extension, his identity with the God of moral temper-tantrums, blazing fury, and infinite (perhaps inhu-man) enormity.

Unacquainted with the possibility of profound evil, however, the adolescent "band of rivals" is itself incapable of enor-mities: "when one of them goes bad, the way his mind works / Remains comprehensible." Neither absolute evil nor ab-solute sanctity is a possible outcome of Mediterranean spiri-tuality: "to become a pimp / Or deal in fake jewelry or ruin a fine tenor voice / For effects that bring down the house, could happen to all / But the best and the worst of us. . . ." Again, "effects that bring down the house" suggests the do-mesticity of evil in its Latin manifestation and the local, fa-miliar, almost familial, psychological purpose it serves: "To receive more attention than his brothers."

In the first half of the poem, that preceding the ellipsis at line 43, the poet has spoken publically as a representative of his tradition, using the first person plural. He has spo-ken also in a sermonic imperative: "mark these rounded slopes"; "hear the springs"; "examine this region"; "Watch, then, the band of rivals." The rhetoric has been discursive and public; the perspective, historical; the audience, fellow communicants of Northern spirituality. In the latter half of the poem, another voice is heard, one that most often speaks privately, as "I." The audience has shrunk from a cultural community addressed sermonically to a single intimate ad-dressed as "Dear."

In the latter half of the poem, Auden gives the Northern ter-rain voices, but the limestone landscape of the Latin South remains the observed object of the ode. The poet speculates about the reasons that extremes of good and evil seem to prefer colder climates: ". . . I suppose, / The best and worst never stayed here long but sought / Immoderate soils where the beauty was not so external, / The light less public and the meaning of life / Something more than a mad camp." The spiritual attributes of the Gothic North are personified by means of geological metaphors in lines 47-59. The hard ascetic sanctities of Protestantism are "granite wastes" that cry to the indolent, indulged sons of Latindom: "Come! . . . How evasive is your humour, how accidental / Your kind-est kiss, how permanent is death." The Faustian temptations of science and technology and the monsters, the "Intendant Caesars" of political and ideological empires are "clays and gravels" purring "Come! . . . On our plains there is room for armies to drill; rivers / Wait to be tamed and slaves to construct you a tomb / In the grand manner: soft as the earth is mankind and both need to be altered."

The real animus of modernity is natural force, personified as "oceanic whisper"; it is "an older colder voice," this face-less power that erodes limestone and all the human jetties and levees against nihilism. This voice of benign indiffer-ence whispers and fetches "the really reckless": "I am the solitude that asks and promises nothing; / That is how I shall set you free. There is no love; / There is only the various envies, all of them sad."

Anthony Hecht has recently associated the triad of geologi-cal voices—the call of granite and of clays and gravels and of oceanic whispers—with the three temptations of Christ in Luke 4:1-13, respectively, spiritual pride, worldly pow-ers, and the existential freedom implicit in suicide. The con-text of the poem relates these temptations to modern, post-Christian equivalents, which the poet suggests have grown out of the ascetic Protestant tradition of the Gothic North.

The Dynamo, as Auden calls the faceless forces of moder-nity in his essay, **"The Virgin and the Dynamo,"** repre-sents the regimenting, arithmetical power of science, bureaucracy, and the state. The Mediterranean world of limestone—"the sweet home"—cannot maintain a separate identity against these corrosives of modernity. It cannot pos-sess "the historical calm of site / Where something was settled once and for all." The "settled" here again calls to mind the sedentary domesticity of Mediterranean cultures and the sedimentary stratification of their historicity.

But the Mezzogiorno is not merely a "dilapidated province" for German tourists (or English poets), an otherwhere "con-nected / To the big busy world by a tunnel." Its very exist-ence questions the legitimacy of all Gothic abstractions on which modernity is based; "it disturbs our rights," the poet insists, our aesthetic, ethical, and spiritual "Great Power" assumptions. Even poetry has become the exponent of those modernist orthodoxies, naturalism and subjectivism. The poet is now "Admired for his earnest habit of calling / The sun the sun, his mind Puzzle, is made uneasy / By these marble statues which so obviously doubt / His antimythological myth. . . ."

The Northern abstracting mind is distracted not only by marble beauty but also by hot carnal pleasure readily at hand: "these gamins, / Pursuing the scientist down the tiled colonnade / With lively offers, rebuke his concern for Nature's / Remotest aspects." Here, one is reminded of Mann's *Death in Venice:* the melting of Germanic will; the danger that the embrace of sordid pleasure poses to the Gothic sense of self; the contagion of disease corrupting that most abstract of entities, the soul. In this context, the reference to a young man "displaying his dildo" (line 12 of the poem as it appeared in *Nones* before Auden excised the phrase from the version in *Collected Shorter Poems*) fits much better.

The poet, assuming his private voice to the intimate, confesses his own Gothic vulnerability to forbidden pleasure: "I, too, am reproached, for what / And how much you know." He prays for protection against moral dissolution, which threatens to destroy the basis of his human freedom, to reduce him to the level of "beasts that repeat themselves" and elements "whose conduct can be predicted." Against this threat, the poet invokes "our Common Prayer, whose greatest comfort is music / Which can be made anywhere, is invisible, / And does not smell." "Common Prayer," of course, alludes to the Anglican liturgy, but beyond that, the "our" suggests a wider reference to Protestant spirituality of which the Prayer Book is an expression. The invisibility and incorruptibility of music calls to mind a line from Lincoln Kirstein's "Das Schloss": "Bach begs nothing but absolute all-mastering order." It is in this order, I think, that the poet finds at once the glory, the consolation, and the danger of Gothic spirituality. All-mastering order is superhuman, and the superhuman is in constant danger of hardening into the granite of the inhuman. Thus, the abstractions of science threaten to reduce humanity to something sub-human, a beast without freedom or a substance obedient to natural forces. The substantiality of limestone transformed into art is a spiritual declaration of independence from this naturalistic determinism.

In the concluding lines, the poet turns to the spiritual possibilities of human substance. Death, material dissolution, is a natural force, and one that is as certain and abstract as science. The "we" of the poem confirms this Gothic mortification of the flesh: "In so far as we have to look forward / To death as a fact, we are right." Death is a biological force, just as erosion is a geological force. The poet clings to "our Common Prayer" as the only hope for human freedom, and yet he is reproached by the worldly beauty of the Mezzogiorno.

"In Praise of Limestone" finally transcends these two partial views through the promise of resurrection. Resurrection raises humanity out of the geological metaphor, as the sculpting of stone into athletes and fountains raises stone out of the purview of natural forces.

> . . . if bodies rise from the dead
>   These modifications of matter into
> Innocent athletes and gesticulating fountains,
>   Made solely for pleasure, make a further point:
> The blessed will not care what angle they are
> regarded from,
>   Having nothing to hide.

Resurrection will reconstitute the individual corporeal elements, cleansed and transmuted by faith, into permanent form. Both elements of Auden's complex analogy are thus brought together. In nature, human material is formed into civilization as the forces of geology formed limestone: by sedimentation. The human art of sculpting marble—limestone transformed by fire—into human and aesthetically humane forms is like the resurrection of the human material into a purged and permanent form. As the vehicle of both metaphors, limestone is to be praised.

The poet concludes in his voice of private address to the intimate: "Dear, I know nothing of / Either, but when I try to imagine a faultless love / Or the life to come, what I hear is the murmur / Of underground streams, what I see is a limestone landscape." Resurrected nature, as distinguished from the resurrecting power, is imaginable in this world only in the beauty and pleasure of icons. Their provision is the Mezzogiorno's "worldly duty which in spite of itself it does not neglect." The poet associates this Latin spiritual vision with the eternal feminine; he perceives the *Urmutter*—sedentary, domestic, and fertile—in the civilization of the Mezzogiorno. It is a foreign, if beatific, vision and one he can only learn as second-sight.

The resurrecting power, the Word, is understandable to the strictly Gothic sensibility only in terms of abstractions of music and moral systems, notions of divine justice and majesty. The poet speaks from within this Gothic tradition of spirituality; but what he sees, finally, is the glory of the world and, thereby, the complementary nature of the two personalities of Western Christianity.

Patrick Deane (essay date Summer 1991)

SOURCE: "'Within a Field That Never Closes': The Reader

in W. H. Auden's 'New Year Letter,'" in *Contemporary Literature*, Vol. XXXII, No. 2, Summer, 1991, pp. 171-93.

[*In the following essay, Deane explores Auden's theoretical assumptions, linguistic techniques, and open-ended relationship with the reader in "New Year Letter."*]

In October 1941, the pages of Scrutiny registered the appearance of W. H. Auden's *New Year Letter* with characteristic acerbity. The long poem from which the volume as a whole took its title came in for particular excoriation, Auden's "wit" being described, somewhat condescendingly, as the sort of thing one might expect from "a theological student at a Scottish university." The conclusion of the reviewer, Raymond Winkler, was that "another edition of this book omitting the **'Letter'** and the notes [to it] would detract less from Mr. Auden's deserved reputation." But even that last concession to the poet's stature evaporates under the heat of what is actually being proposed: the excision of approximately 140 of the book's 188 pages.

The attack at times dissipates itself in silly innuendo—as in the comment on Auden's fondness for quoting from "suspiciously fashionable authors like Kafka, Kierkegaard and Rilke"—but it does eventually come to a point: namely, that **"New Year Letter"** inverts "the usual practice of good verse" by neglecting to "precipitat[e] . . . ideas" through "the concrete situation." I think this means that Auden abjures obliquity in favor of directness, that he does not "evoke" ideas and emotions through an Eliotic "objective correlative" or a Poundian "image" but instead expresses them in apparently abstract terms. Distrust of the abstract was of course at the base of *Scrutiny's* divergence from Eliot himself after 1939; and one sign of the journal's consistent animus against "unprecipitated" ideas is the fact that Auden's reviewer was later to write a general article lamenting what Francis Mulhern has called "the eclipse of the early 'empiricist' criticism by doctrinally induced generalization and abstraction." In 1941 Winkler's attack on **"New Year Letter"** focused repeatedly on the "simplicity" of Auden's ideas and the "bludgeoning" directness with which they are conveyed. "One is reminded," he writes, "that the Ministry of Information has lately found the same verse-form a convenient vehicle for National Savings propaganda."

What is quite obviously behind this attack is a hostile understanding of the "poetic," amounting almost to a repugnance for overtly "philosophical" poems, no matter by whom they are written or in whatever age. This aversion comes through especially in the disparaging comment that "it's only a matter of months before . . . [**"New Year Letter"** is] described in one university or another as a 'twentieth-century "Essay on Man"' or 'another "First Anniversarie."'" In fact, the Augustan character of the poem had already been remarked upon—six months before and

in the pages of the *Nation*—by Randall Jarrell. In that case the review was a cordial one. Jarrell saw the appearance of Auden's poem as an indication of the new life and direction of twentieth-century poetry, the norm of modernist poetic performance—"experimental, lyric, obscure, violent, irregular, determinedly antagonistic to didacticism, general statement, science, [and] the public"—having finally "lost for the young its once obsessive attraction." **"New Year Letter,"** he perceived as clearly as did *Scrutiny*, was a poetic performance of almost the opposite sort. It was, he wrote, "a happy compound of the Essay on Man and the Epistle to Dr. Arbuthnot, done in a version of Swift's most colloquial couplets. Pope might be bewildered at the ideas, and make fun of, or patronizingly commend, the couplets; but he would relish the Wit, Learning, and Sentiment—the last becoming, as it so often does, plural and Improving; and the Comprehending Generality, Love of Science, and Social Benevolence might warm him into the murmur, 'Well enough for such an age.'"

Jarrell praises Auden for leaving behind the obscurities of Pound and the high modernists and for making a "thoroughly readable" and accessible long poem "out of a reasonable, objective, and comprehensive discussion." In contrast, Winkler looks at the same thing—the discursive quality of the verse—and announces, somewhat puzzlingly, that "the effect is to hang a curtain between author and reader." One is tempted to probe more deeply the ground of this difference of opinion, but of greater interest for the moment is the single point on which these two appear to agree: namely, that the **"New Year Letter"** is a modern text in the Augustan tradition.

Auden's debt to the Restoration and eighteenth century in this and almost all of his poems has generally been regarded as one of the least problematic aspects of his art—*theoretically* the least problematic, I should say, since there have always been hairs split about precisely which Enlightenment figure is at any point the strongest influence. But unlike Eliot, whose acknowledgment of the importance of Dryden and Johnson is enigmatically impersonal, and whose imitations of Pope and the Augustans were largely edited out of his published poems, Auden's recognition of his debt has always been forthright, one of the few critical "facts" on which it appears possible to found an interpretation. For example, in **"Criticism in a Mass Society,"** an essay more or less contemporary with the **"New Year Letter,"** Auden includes the name of Pope among the three writers who have been the greatest influence on his own work. A similar acknowledgment is to be found, of course, in Part 1 of the **"New Year Letter,"** where the poet imagines Dryden in attendance at Auden's own literary trial: "There Dryden sits with modest smile, / The master of the middle style." Such acts of self-criticism have surely encouraged the formation of a kind of consensus on this issue. A. Alvarez wrote in

1958, "Of all twentieth-century poets Auden would feel most at home in the age of Dryden, the age of informed, satiric, and slightly gossipy occasional verse." This was the view adopted and expanded by Monroe K. Spears in his influential study of Auden in 1963, and it remains largely accepted, although "the age of Dryden" is usually extended to include the eighteenth century as well.

The Augustanism of **"New Year Letter"** is overt and seems on the surface to raise few problems. The poem is a Horatian verse epistle displaying many of the characteristics which typify eighteenth-century adaptations of the form. Its rhyming couplets, its wit, and its discursive style all seem to confirm Auden's temperamental and artistic affinities with the Age of Enlightenment. But they are also poetic characteristics which, as Paul Fussell has shown, are frequently linked to "social commentary or depictions of social or ethical action." That this is the case in Auden's poem is borne out by the responses of some of the early reviewers. Malcolm Cowley, for example, commented that the poem is marked by "a fanciful but fundamentally serious eloquence" and that its subject is moral. Charles Williams, whose *Descent of the Dove* was acknowledged by Auden as the source of "many ideas" in **"New Year Letter,"** wrote that the concern of the poem "is with the building of the Just City" and that "it is, after its own manner, a pattern of the Way; that it dialectically includes both sides of the Way only shows that it is dealing with a road and not a room."

If this proposition is true we have even firmer ground for linking the work with those of Dryden, Pope, and Johnson. What Williams is describing is a poem defined and conceived as rhetoric, a verbal contraption—to use Auden's own phrase from the essay **"Making, Knowing and Judging"**—which is intended to construct something beyond itself in the world of human and spiritual action. Or to develop Williams's other metaphor, the poem is a road intended to take the reader toward some perception or state of mind quite different from that in which he or she began reading. This concentration on the text as vehicle for the edification of the reader is an idea as peripheral to the poetics of modernism as it is central to the poetics of neoclassicism. It is what lies behind Dryden's commitment, in the preface to *Religio Laici,* to the "middle style"—the language of ordinary, worldly affairs—and it would seem to provide a compelling motive for Auden's preoccupation with the middle style in his poem. The essence of Auden's Augustanism in the **"New Year Letter,"** I would argue, is what Winkler identified when he compared the piece to government propaganda: namely, that the raison d'être of the poem is to accomplish some sort of mental reorientation in the reader that will have ramifications in the world beyond poetry.

At first glance this seems a relatively straightforward claim.

It would take a very obtuse reader not to notice that much of the poem is given over to sententious moralizing and that it is very conscious of its audience, and of its effects on that audience. At the end of Part I there is the wish expressed that the letter be sent as a "dispatch," in the midst of global turmoil, "to all / Who wish to read it anywhere" and that its message be "En Clair." That last wish of course accounts for the prominence in the poem of Dryden, "the master of the middle style." But as we consider this passage, we may well reflect that its overt gesture toward the poem's audience is still somehow less active and involving than the kind of thing suggested in Charles Williams's comments on the text, with their gerundial and present continuous forms and their preference for metaphors of process—"the Way," "a road and not a room."

Related to this discrepancy and not the smallest problem with the end of Part 1 is that it runs against the drift of the argument 243 lines earlier. Having been told that "To set in order—that's the task / Both Eros and Apollo ask" ("Art and life agree in this, / That each intends a synthesis"), we are cautioned that

> Art is not life, and cannot be
> A midwife to society,
> For art is a fait accompli:
> What they should do, or how and when
> Life-order comes to living men,
> It cannot say, for it presents
> Already lived experience
> Through a convention that creates
> Autonomous completed states.

If that is so, one might ask, what is the point of sending out a poetic dispatch to the world? And doesn't that phrase "autonomous completed states" contradict Williams's emphasis on Auden's art of process? Faced with this, one clings—with some justice, as we shall see—to the possibility that there is an equivocation in that word "states," a suggestion of some persisting connection between the "true gestalt" of art and the Just City. At the same time, however, one hears Auden's voice from twenty years later warning that "All political theories which, like Plato's, are based on analogies drawn from artistic fabrication are bound, if put into practice, to turn into tyrannies" (**"The Poet and the City"**).

We can find a useful gloss on this section of the **"Letter"** in **"The Public v. the Late Mr. William Butler Yeats,"** which Auden published in the *Partisan Review* in the spring of 1939, less than a year before he began work on the poem:

> art is the product of history, not a cause. Unlike some other products, technical inventions for example, it does not re-enter history as an effective

agent, so that the question whether art should or should not be propaganda is unreal . . . . the honest truth, gentlemen, is that, if not a poem had been written, not a picture painted, not a bar of music composed, the history of man would be materially unchanged.

A more familiar, potted version of this argument is to be found in the famous second section of **"In Memory of W. B. Yeats,"** which Auden added a month after the poem had first appeared in March 1939. "Ireland has her madness and her weather still," we are told, "For poetry makes nothing happen: it survives / In the valley of its saying where executives / Would never want to tamper." That valley is another version of the autonomous completed state referred to in the **"New Year Letter,"** and the poem appears to be making the same point as the essay: namely, that art, when completed, becomes in some sense detached from history and cannot "re-enter history as an effective agent."

Far from relieving the contradiction in **"New Year Letter,"** these two contemporary works appear to aggravate it. We have a Horatian verse epistle, the very form of which bespeaks at least some confidence in the ability of the text to act as an agent in history, which contains within itself both a denial of and a commitment to its own historical efficacy, and also from the same period we have Auden's obiter dicta on the subject, which are often taken to be an uncompromising rejection of the more "engaged" poetic which he had practiced during the thirties. The extent to which that rejection was compromised I will consider later, but it is unquestionably true that in the spring of 1939 Auden resolved "Never, *never* again . . . [to] speak at a political meeting" and almost simultaneously made the declaration of independence from politics that we have seen in his writings on Yeats. Given that, there is surely something perverse in his return soon afterward to the worldly and outwardly directed form of the verse epistle with which he had first experimented in 1937.

In that instance, paradoxically, the recipient had been someone already removed from history—Lord Byron—whereas in 1940 the **"New Year Letter"** was directed at Elizabeth Mayer, still very much alive and well at her home on Long Island. The choice of form appears particularly contrary when we consider that Auden's poetry of his self-confessedly political period was in the main not characterized as we might expect by the lucidities of the "middle style," nor by a compelling univocality. World events enter the realm of those poems obliquely, for the most part, and the perspective is marked by that intractable subjectivity which Lukács lamented is the distinguishing mark of literary modernism. Even **"A Bride in the 30's"** (November 1934) and **"Spain"** (April 1937)—in which the threat of war is felt relatively strongly—are the work of what Joseph Warren

Beach characterizes as "a typical 'modern' poet, who sedulously avoids the 'frontal attack' on his subject, whose thought is characteristically rendered by the 'oblique' or indirect method, the terms of his discourse being, not philosophical abstractions and plain statements of fact, but symbols, myths, and implications, and whose effects are complicated by the use of such rhetorical devices as irony, 'ambiguity,' and dramatic impersonation."

How odd it is to find that whereas Auden's poetic strategies as an avowedly socialist poet effect what Lukács would call an "attenuation of reality and dissolution of personality," **"New Year Letter,"** his first major work after his rejection of "engagement," appears by its direct methods and singular perspective to affirm that "unity of the world . . . as a living whole inseparable from himself" which in Marxist thinking provides an antidote to the bourgeois doctrine of alienation. And yet there we run aground—unsalvageably, it seems—on the content of the poem, on that idea, expressed very early on in the **"Letter,"** that works of art are "autonomous" and complete—"alienated," in some sense, from the processes of history.

Auden sees the origin of language in a sense of absence and alienation.
—*Patrick Deane*

All of these contradictions will continue to seem insurmountable so long as we assume that Auden's rejection of a "political" role for poetry necessarily involved the adoption of a formalist aesthetic. Winkler pointed, in his review of **"New Year Letter,"** to reaction as an important element in the content of the work; he argued that the author's "method implies reaction in Mr. Auden's system of ideas." And the point is not invalid, since the adoption of an eighteenth-century style is in some sense atavistic, evidence of a nostalgia for past values. In aesthetic terms, however, it does seem logical that reaction against the failure of political activism in art would be more likely to lead toward formalism than toward the didactic modes of the eighteenth century. But here it is necessary to look beyond the internal logic of criticism and toward certain facts about Auden's attitudes—facts which are often ignored as critics attempt to read the poet's life and career as a kind of "moral fable," illustrating either the reassertion of bourgeois values and the betrayal of the proletariat or the inevitable demise of socialist ideas and the triumph of liberal humanism.

The first of these facts is that Auden did not, in 1939, cease to hold the political views he had held before that date. Humphrey Carpenter tells us of the poet's answers to a questionnaire completed during that very summer, one of which declares "I believe Socialism to be right" but goes on to express the view that for himself ordinary political activity is no longer productive. Another, perhaps more important continuity in Auden's work and thought from before 1939 to the **"New Year Letter"** has to do with his attitude to language. One of his central documents on this subject is the essay **"Writing,"** originally published in 1932 as part of a curious primer for children of all ages, *An Outline for Boys and Girls and Their Parents*. Edward Mendelson was quite recently the first critic to point out the extraordinary extent to which that essay "offers a premature exposition of the central themes of structuralist literary theory and its successors." Auden sees the origin of language in a sense of absence and alienation; he argues that language, both written and spoken, is an attempt to fill the void, to bridge the gap between speaker and auditor, writer and reader; but then he also makes important distinctions between written and spoken language; and he insists on "the antagonism and difference between language and its objects." "All these," writes Mendelson, "are aspects of a late romantic theory of language, brought to a crisis by modernism, and agonized over by the young Auden a generation before Derrida and Lacan." Mendelson's point is convincing. The poet's views on language clearly have a great deal in common with those that are currently influential, and Stan Smith's recent "rereading" of the entire oeuvre is exciting testimony to Auden's amenability to poststructural approaches.

In his essay, Auden does not imagine a paradisal language in which sign and signified were ever identical. Language instead originates precisely as a result of a sort of internal dissociation of sensibility. We are told that "at some time or other in human history, when and how we don't know, man became self-conscious; he began to feel, I am I, and you are not I; we are shut inside ourselves and apart from each other" (**"Writing"**). Speech begins as an attempt to remedy the problem: "Words are a bridge between a speaker and a listener." This is extended in an interesting way under the rubric "Writing":

> The urge to write, like the urge to speak, came from man's growing sense of personal loneliness, of the need for group communication. But, while speech begins with the feeling of separateness in space, of I-here-in-this-chair and you-there-in-that-chair, writing begins from the sense of separateness in time, of "I'm here to-day, but I shall be dead to-morrow, and you will be active in my place, and how can I speak to you?"

To this idea of language as bridge across space and time, Auden adds another crucial element, which he deals with—rather curiously—under the rubric "Meaning," and which he calls "Intention": "Apart from what we say or feel we often want to make our listeners act or think in a particular way." The issue is elaborated under the heading "Why

People Read Books": "Reading and living are not two water-tight compartments. You must use your knowledge of people to guide you when reading books, and your knowledge of books to guide you when living with people. . . . Reading is valuable when it improves our technique of living." This stress on the nonliterary efficacy of writing and reading is an essential part of Auden's conception of language as a bridge between the limitations of a monadic psyche and the possibility of a fruitful society.

Auden's other essay called **"Writing,"** the more familiar one published in *The Dyer's Hand* exactly thirty years later, differs from the first in many ways, but there is still that original insistence on language as a social agent. Auden talks about the debasement of language in modern culture, and about the particular dangers which this presents to the poet, though not to the composer or the painter. "On the other hand," he continues, "he is more protected than they from another modern peril, that of solipsist subjectivity; however esoteric a poem may be, the fact that all its words have meanings which can be looked up in a dictionary makes it testify to the existence of other people. Even the language of *Finnegans Wake* was not created by Joyce *ex nihilo;* a purely private verbal world is not possible" (***Dyer's Hand***).

The fundamental point to be made about Auden's theories, then, is that in them language, which is in fact an index of the gap which separates subject and object, tends also to be thought of as the nemesis of that gap, the hope of escape from solipsistic subjectivity. One last gloss on this idea is to be found in **"The Sea and the Mirror,"** written between 1942 and 1944. In the third and last principal section, "Caliban to the Audience," we have a long disquisition on the conditions and aims of art. Toward the end, Caliban has this to say about the "aim and justification" of a "dedicated dramatist"—surely a type for all writers:

> what else exactly is the artistic gift which he is forbidden to hide, if not to make you unforgettably conscious of the ungarnished offended gap between what you so questionably are and what you are commanded without any question to become . . . ?—the more he must strengthen your delusion that an awareness of the gap is in itself a bridge, your interest in your imprisonment a release, so that, far from your being led by him to contrition and surrender, the regarding of your defects in his mirror, your dialogue, using his words, with yourself about yourself, becomes the one activity which never, like devouring or collecting or spending, lets you down.

Caliban's point is that even though art may be eternally isolated from life, and even though it may never be really possible to bridge the gap between writer and reader, it is imperative that we continue to work at bridge-building. In the most basic terms of Auden's belief, no bridge means no society at all, socialist or otherwise. And there we surely have one reason why Auden's retreat from active politics was not also a retreat into formalism. Some of his poetry in the thirties was written to "serve" socialist ideals, of course, but that was only part of a more fundamental intention to serve the construction of society in general. When socialism as an active political philosophy was discredited in Auden's eyes, the commitment to a "social" use of language remained unchanged. Indeed, a determination to reassert that commitment may lie behind his almost instantaneous decision—seemingly "perverse," as I said earlier—to adopt the sociable form of the Augustan verse epistle. The poem's own doubts about its historical efficacy may have something to do with what went wrong with European politics in the 1930s, but they are certainly connected with the more profound fear, expressed by Caliban in **"The Sea and the Mirror,"** that thinking that "awareness of the gap is in itself a bridge" may be simply a delusion. What remains, though, is the conviction that "your dialogue, using [an author's] words, with yourself about yourself, becomes the one activity which never . . . lets you down." This appears to me to point us directly into the rather troublesome realm of the psychology of reading, and so it is to the place of the reader in the poem, and that reflexive dialogue envisaged by Caliban, that I now wish to turn.

Here it is necessary to go back to both the **"New Year Letter"** and Auden's elegy for Yeats and to notice that in each case the denial of an effective historical role for literature carries with it a description of the way in which a text in its "autonomous completed state" will relate to the world around it. In the **"Letter"** this is relatively simple. We are told that once art is "realized" and separate from life, it can no longer function as a direct agent of the author's intention. It is, "though still particular,"

> An algebraic formula,
> An abstract model of events
> Derived from dead experience,
> *And each life must itself decide*
> *To what and how it be applied.*

(emphasis added)

The corresponding passage in the elegy for Yeats is somewhat more colorful but on the surface probably no more encouraging. Every reader of poetry is probably familiar with the lines, from Part 1, which tell us that "The words of a dead man / Are modified in the guts of the living," very much the point made in those lines from **"New Year Letter"** which I just quoted—except for the added suggestion that whatever dialogue occurs between reader and text is not purely a matter of the mind. But in the inserted second part

comes another relevant passage which, as Stan Smith has rightly commented, is much less frequently quoted. Poetry makes nothing happen, yes, but "it survives, / A way of happening, a mouth."

"This strange, dehumanizing metonymy," writes Smith, "insisting on the act of speech while simultaneously detaching it from any human hinterland in a speaking subject, catches the paradox of . . . [the text's] double historicity. A poem can be read at any time, and, in reading, it enters into a precise historical moment, the moment of the reader quite distinct from that of the originating author." This explication of the line seems to me entirely accurate, and it reveals the thread of hope that remains for Auden once the currents of history are resolved in the "true gestalt" of poetic art. It is precisely because "art is a fait accompli," which is treated on the surface as a matter for grief, that it is able to "survive." And surviving, it presents itself to all humanity not as a spoken thing, with a "meaning," but as a *means of speaking.* More than that, it provides a *way* of speaking, and *speaking* comes to define *being,* so the poem is "a way of *happening*" (emphasis added). This stress on the read text as the source of a subconscious experience rather than a specific "meaning" is supported by Auden's comment in *Secondary Worlds* (1968) that "in so far as one can speak of poetry as conveying knowledge, it is the kind of knowledge implied by the Biblical phrase—*Then Adam Knew Eve his wife*—knowing is inseparable from being known."

This line of argument effects a rather surprising refinement of the idea of language as a bridge. Entrenching that concern with the materiality of words which is already very evident in the **"Writing"** essay of 1932, Auden comes to think of language as something which is most powerful not when you have "decoded" it but when you are *on* it or *in* it. In the idea of poetry as "a way of happening" he is extending in a similar direction what in 1932 he had inappropriately called the fourth form of "Meaning": the intention "to make our listeners act or think in a particular way." Although the direct line of influence between writer and reader—his power to compel us through the expression of ideas—has become somewhat attenuated, an indirect one still persists. In the process of reading, the text becomes "the other" in a self-reflexive dialogue conducted by the reader, who for the duration will "be" as the poetry "happens."

This phenomenon in Auden is adequately but not perfectly rendered by Louis Althusser's term "interpellation," describing the process by which an ideologically fraught discourse constitutes, "recruits," or "transforms" its own subject. One important consequence of regarding **"New Year Letter"** primarily as an instance of interpellation is that the ambiguities and contradictions which ordinarily appear to surround the choice of its form, the Horatian verse epistle, no longer matter to quite the same extent. For if Auden wanted in his poem to construct a poetic "way of happening, a mouth," through which a subject position could be realized that was simultaneously ideologically well defined and yet also somewhat open, he could hardly have chosen better. That these two things—definition and openness—were important to him is testified to by a passage in **Secondary Worlds,** where he moves from a discussion of the sort of person who uses words as "Black Magic"—as "a way of securing domination over others and compelling them to do his will"—to make the point that "politics and religion are spheres where personal choice is essential." Propaganda he defines as an exercise of words without allowance for choice, and in that sense political and religious propaganda are unacceptable in his view. But writing *in the service of* those two human concerns, writing which does exercise some ideological power in the sphere of politics and religion—that is to him acceptable, and probably necessary, provided it makes an allowance for choice.

In a verse epistle, the "voice" which we become when we read is quite strictly defined. The reason must partly be the striking occasionality of the form. One is usually *prompted* to write a letter, even a very literary one, by some sort of external event—and what is more important, by a very specific response to that event, the kind which brings it all to the point of a pen. In Auden's poem the occasion is New Year's Eve 1939, the night when "a scrambling decade ends." His response is to revive and revolve upon the question of "who and where and how we are." And all of this adds up to a sense in the reader that the "mouth" with which we have begun to speak is not entirely detached—or detachable—from a historical "body."

More important than this, however, is the fact that the verse epistle is, conventionally if not theoretically, univocal. This particular example of the genre is emphatically so. The voice we hear when we set the "mouth" that is the poem in action is one very familiar from Auden's shorter poems: urbane, witty, outrageous—and for all that, remarkably consistent. The form of the octosyllabic couplet, persisting through over seventeen hundred lines, exerts a powerfully leavening influence on Auden's extravagant and colorful lexicon, and it asserts the continuity of his discourse. Indeed, even the eclecticism and eccentricity of the language seem to entrench our sense of the single voice; this is a powerfully individual speech, and every quirky linguistic gesture makes it less and less possible for us to efface the historically defined subject position of the poem, to make this "mouth" entirely our own. The total effect is a curious one: while the consistent univocality of the text facilitates the adduction of the reader to the position of speaking subject, the very way in which that univocality is realized (through the use of an intractably individual vocabulary and historical references) insists that adduction must also to some extent involve a translation, of the text by the reader

but also of the reader by the text. This is a point made explicitly by Auden in **Secondary Worlds,** where he writes that "every dialogue [which, as Stan Smith has noted, includes the act of reading] is a feat of translation." Smith explains the nature of the translation in reading as "an exchange of subject positions," but in this particular case it is perhaps more correct to talk of a mutual modification of subject positions. How profoundly appropriate, one reflects, was Auden's original title for the whole volume—***The Double Man.***

A further important way in which **"New Year Letter"** entrenches its apparent univocality is through self-reflexive commentary. I have already alluded to numerous instances of this: the discussion of the relation of poetry to history in Part 1, for example, and the closing lines of the same part, where the speaker expresses the hope that "This private minute for a friend" will be the "dispatch" that he intends "to all / Who wish to read it anywhere." But these are only two of a great many instances, occurring particularly in that first part. There is, for example, also the ninety-line section in which the speaker imagines himself appearing before "That summary [literary] tribunal which / In a perpetual session sits." This, as I said earlier, is a form of metapoetry, in which the discourse of the poem and discourse about the poem are consubstantial. And then there is commentary on the peculiar tone of the whole piece, that typically Audenesque mixture of flippancy and high seriousness:

> Though language may be useless, for
> No words men write can stop the war
> Or measure up to the relief
> Of its immeasurable grief,
> Yet truth, like love and sleep, resents
> Approaches that are too intense,
> And often when the searcher stood
> Before the Oracle it would
> Ignore his grown-up earnestness
> But not the child of his distress,
> For through the Janus of a joke
> The candid psychopompos spoke.

If Auden's position in the Yeats elegy is valid, and if in reading the poem we are, in some fundamental sense, merely reading ourselves, these moments of overt self-reflexivity both underline and exacerbate the solipsistic condition. **"In Memory of W. B. Yeats"** talks of individuals imprisoned—poetry notwithstanding—"each in the cell of himself," and in the **"New Year Letter"** the pervasive tenor of self-awareness does indeed make reading an act concentrated inordinately upon that "self" which the text constructs and which we assume. In all its complexity, that process is the essence of what I have been calling the poem's "univocality": its deliberately cultivated association with a purportedly coherent and exclusive "self." And yet, as the Yeats elegy again hints, the solipsistic experience of reading such a work is paradoxically at the root of whatever efficacy the text may eventually enjoy in history and in human affairs outside of literature. The reason is that although the poem appears on the surface so inseparable from one man's experience at one period in history—and thus of limited application to ourselves and our own time—the subject position defined by the text is so precise and so coherent that the "way of happening" which it provides future readers is quite exactly determined. The text may exist only as a "mouth," but the body which is implied whenever it is made to speak will always in some way be the same. Thus, rather surprisingly, what Caliban refers to as "an awareness of the gap" between the text and history, between one subject writing and another reading, turns out indeed to be "in itself a bridge" across space and history (**"The Sea and the Mirror"**), a way in which an author can—albeit obliquely—make something intentional "happen." This he does, in Auden's practice, by accepting that while lexical "meaning" will always be subject to alteration by time, significance inscribed in the processes of the text will enjoy greater power and endurance. Thus the work must be constructed in the awareness that once it is complete, it will be less important as a statement made than as "an infinite series of its own self-generating occasions."

Insofar as that is an accurate account of the status of the text of **"New Year Letter,"** a complementary account of the status of the reader is implied. For if the essence of the text is process, and if the process is subject to potentially infinite repetition, the constructed subject position which "is" the reader (for the duration of reading, at least) must be inseparable from that process, and also infinitely repeatable. And interestingly, this is precisely how **"New Year Letter"** defines the problematic notion of "self":

> each great I
> Is but a process in a process
> Within a field that never closes.

It would be difficult to summarize the reader's position in the text more effectively. This passage is doubly important for us, however, because it so happens that it is here that the content of the poem also comes to its sharpest point. While Part 1, as we have seen, takes art and its relation to history as its central concern, Part 2 explores our relation to time and space in a more abstract way. And it is here that Auden formulates the weltanschauung on which the more practical resolutions of the final, third part of the poem will be based. The passage I have quoted comes very early in Part 2, and its immediate context is a discussion of the difficulties involved in coping with life in a post-Einsteinian universe. The question of "who and where and how we are" is answered in part: we are "The children of a modest star, / Frail, backward, clinging to the granite / Skirts of a sen-

sible old planet, / Our placid and suburban nurse / In *Sitter's* swelling universe." Auden catches the challenge which that universe poses to us in a characteristic and wonderful paradox. We find it hard, he writes, "to stretch imagination / To live according to our station"; we find it difficult to think of ourselves as other than stable, to grasp that our reality is elastic and subject to constant change and that "we are changed by what we change."

A great deal of what comes before and after this point in the text finds its focus here. All of the intellectual temptations explored in Part 2—and they take up almost the whole section—involve false conceptions of stability, spurious arguments against the idea of a relativistic universe, self-limiting applications of logic, and crude empiricism. Such things, it is implied, are persuasive to a nerveless people, "The patriots of an old idea, / No longer sovereign this year." For the enlightened,

> all our intuitions mock
> The formal logic of the clock.
> All real perception, it would seem,
> Has shifting contours like a dream.

And furthermore,

> The intellect
> That parts the Cause from the Effect
> And thinks in terms of Space and Time
> Commits a legalistic crime,
> For such an unreal severance
> Must falsify experience.

At one point Auden has the devil argue in glozing and ingratiating fashion a position that is nevertheless taken by the poem to be fundamentally correct: namely, that Eden was lost when "the syllogistic sin took root." Adam and Eve became "Abstracted, bitter refugees," who "fought over their premises, / Shut out from Eden by the bar / And Chinese Wall of Barbara"—"Barbara" being "a mnemonic term for the first mood of the first syllogistic figure, in which both premises and the conclusion are universal affirmatives" (*Shorter Oxford*). Our longing for stability and certainty is thus the greatest impediment to our happiness.

Although we are told that to think "in terms of Space and Time" is to commit "a legalistic crime," the poem readily accepts that to think consistently in other, more comprehensive terms is perhaps beyond the present abilities of the human mind. In fact, a rather hard-nosed pragmatism in this regard reveals itself at various places in the text; for example, Auden denigrates the attitude of the zealot, his politics "perhaps unreal," who is tempted to martyr himself for a probably unrealizable dream. In physics, as in politics, nympholepsy is abjured. We are told that "we are conscripts to our age / Simply by being born, we wage / The war we are"; our task is to learn "how / To be the patriots of the Now." This statement has many meanings, but for the poem it represents an important acceptance of historic time as the apparent medium of our lives and actions:

> In Time we sin.
> But Time is sin and can forgive,
> Time is the life in which we live,
> At least three-quarters of our time
> The purgatorial hill we climb,
> Where any skyline we attain
> Reveals a higher ridge again.

Auden goes on at length to develop this analogy between temporal sequence and the hill of Purgatory. The basic position is very clear, however: acquiescence in "the formal logic of the clock" is, in the first place, our only choice, and in the second, it alone offers hope of an escape from this limited conception of time. Notice, though, the paradoxical suggestion that the possibilities for escape (forgiveness of "sin") seem to increase with the endlessness of time.

This is a most odd proposition, not at all unlike the kind of theological paradoxes which Auden was in fact shortly to re-embrace. But what it means in terms of theology, metaphysics, or indeed the new physics is not our immediate concern. The point is that at the root of this rather peculiar rapprochement between pre- and post-Einsteinian conceptions of time, there is a very simple pragmatism: "Time is the life in which we live," and though continuing to think in terms of the clock is "a legalistic crime," it is a necessary one. Throughout **"New Year Letter,"** pragmatism seems to triumph over theoretical purity in Auden's treatment of this complex relationship. He begins Part 2, as we have seen, establishing as our context "*Sitter's* swelling universe," and he not only explores with some relish the full and disconcerting implications of the general theory of relativity, but he also dwells with amusement on those "patriots of an old idea" who react against the new cosmos thus brought into view. Very soon, however, the dialectic between old and new ideas is translated into much more simple and comprehensible terms. Standing in the way of our advancement is "the Prince of Lies," "the Spirit-that-denies," and he encourages us to mourn the passage of time, "claiming it's wicked to grow older." This is not at all an argument against the world view of the new physics but simply a resistance to temporal process, traditionally conceived. In Part 3, all these ideas come to a focus in the passage which I have already cited, the one dealing with the necessity of our life in time. It will not do to simply argue that Auden's understanding of Einsteinian physics was naive and that he misread relativity through Heraclitean eyes; on the contrary, we can see in certain lines—such as the reference to the "le-

gal crime" which separates space and time—evidence of a quite confident knowledge of contemporary physics. Indeed, that reference alone tells us that he knew how the theory of relativity had discredited the notion of time as sequential process, replacing it with the more comprehensive, four-dimensional concept of space-time. I think the way to resolve this problem is to concentrate on his pragmatic acceptance of clock time as one of the grounds of our thought. He seems to latch on to the opposition between process and stasis as a more manageable analogue for the relationship between an Einsteinian and a Newtonian conception of reality. He uses temporal process as a rather traditional metaphor for a wider ranging and more radical press toward indeterminacy and instability.

Here I am talking about "use" at the level of content, but Auden also makes a similarly pragmatic "use" of temporal sequence at the formal level. If, as I have been arguing, the poem's commitment to an Einsteinian world view becomes concentrated (however illogically) on the idea of process, it seems natural enough that one of the non-rational ways in which the poet will seek to communicate that world view will be through constructing a text that seems in some sense essentially process—or, perhaps, essentially sequence. Whether or not it *is* pure process is not relevant; what matters is that when we read it we feel ourselves, to a very great degree, implicated in a linguistic and intellectual movement of potentially infinite extension: "a process in a process / Within a field that never closes."

Precisely how Auden sets out to accomplish this in linguistic, stylistic, and rhetorical terms is, of course, a complex question that I can only begin to answer in the space available. Among the formal techniques he employs to evoke in us a sense of inexorable process, perhaps the most important is the rhyming couplet—linked, invariably, to a grammar and syntax of proliferation. Let us look briefly at the passage which immediately follows the introduction of the purgatorial hill as a metaphor for that "Time [which] is the life in which we live":

> however much we grumble,
> However painfully we stumble,
> Such mountaineering all the same
> Is, it would seem, the only game
> At which we show a natural skill,
> The hardest exercises still
> Just those our muscles are the best
> Adapted to, its grimmest test
> Precisely what our fear suspected,
> We have no cause to look dejected
> When, wakened from a dream of glory
> We find ourselves in Purgatory,
> Back on the same old mountain side
> With only guessing for a guide.

In terms of **"New Year Letter"** as a whole, this is a very typical sentence, its length not at all unusual. There are, as I reckon, at least four places in this passage where we seem to have arrived at a syntactical terminus. Three of those coincide with a line-ending, so our expectation of closure is especially strong. But in each instance, the momentum flows over and beyond the point of possible arrest. That this happens three times after the first, and that in each case an apparently certain terminus is breached—all of this surely means that when we do finally reach a period, we can have no confidence in its integrity. This is where the rhyme scheme becomes especially important. It has, of course, participated in the subversion of stasis throughout the passage. For example, although the sense seems to reach a terminus at the word "skill," the rhyme scheme does not. "Grumble" has its "stumble," and "same" has its "game," but "skill"— if we stop there—lacks a partner. The idea of lexical partnership has been so powerfully entrenched in the previous 465 rhyming couplets that we are bound to look around for a companion to "skill," and by the time we find him at the end of the next line we are already drawn beyond that first periodic structure. What happens at the end of the passage I have quoted is very similar to this. Although we have a real syntactical terminus in the full stop, and although the end is strengthened by the completed rhyme—"side" and "guide"—the established pattern of rhyming couplets surely makes us expect that more will follow, as indeed they do to the number of 431.

From that example I think it is plain to see why this particular verse form suited Auden's purpose in the **"New Year Letter."** The effect is of a reading experience that is potentially open-ended, and this is true not only of Auden's appropriation of the form but of others' as well. In a very interesting passage on Johnson's "The Vanity of Human Wishes," Ezra Pound, for example, remarks on the sort of confusion induced by rhyming couplets. "The cadence comes to a dead end so frequently," he writes, "that one doesn't know the poem is going on." Perhaps more apposite in the context of Auden is this comment, again on Johnson's "Vanity," but by T. S. Eliot: "We do not ordinarily expect a very close structure of a poem in rhymed couplets, which often looks as if, but for what the author has to say, it might begin or end anywhere" (*On Poetry*). Paul Fussell is surely concerned with the same impression when he argues that "such couplets can be called stanzas only by courtesy. They could perhaps more accurately be called something like additive units, and perhaps a poem in heroic couplets is best thought of as essentially stichic, with a 'line' of twenty rather than ten syllables." Composition by "additive units," rather than strophes, makes simple succession appear to be the principal ground of coherence.

The couplets of **"New Year Letter"** are, of course, not heroic but Hudibrastic, and the pointedly crude rhymes and

octosyllabic line which typify the Hudibrastic form also contribute strongly to the sense of process as we read. The relative shortness of the line (compared with the decasyllabic heroic, that is) naturally increases the prominence of the end rhyme, something which is then further enhanced by self-conscious and unlikely choices in the end words themselves. To the reader, the principle of composition by "additive units" becomes in the case of this form even more apparent; the text reads like a potentially endless procession of discrete structures, which complete themselves quickly and disappear into oblivion. Stan Smith makes the further point that while "the stately heroic couplet of Pope and Dryden . . . is a spacious enough measure to allow for sense to be repeatedly contained within its formal antitheses," the Hudibrastic form "is constantly in its compactness overflowing its couplets, spawning a syntax that can find its resolution only after a proliferation of sub-clauses and amplifications, which seems to move in a permanent future tenseness. Such a style is flexible enough, but its pace is considerably more urgent and impulsive than the pentameter." In those words "urgent" and "impulsive" and in his description of that feeling of a "permanent future tenseness," Smith has caught the quality of affect engendered by the form of Auden's text, and it is very much in harmony with the reification of process which occurs in the poem at the level of content.

Smith has also pointed out the destabilizing effect of Auden's play with words. His tendency to make extensive use of foreign words and phrases serves "to break open the closed verbal universe of the poem," and his fondness for puns and other forms of wordplay frequently has the reader moving in two interpretive directions at once. The impulse behind the poem, as we saw earlier, was to approach truth "through the Janus of a joke," and linguistic two-sidedness is one of the text's most distinguishing characteristics. The act of reading is an almost constant negotiation of opposites. At the end of Part 2 the speaker sets himself apart from "The either-ors, the mongrel halves," whom he defines in the notes as "the impatient romantics," romanticism being defined in turn as "Unawareness of the dialectic." And a pervasive construction of dialectical relations is one of the most crucial ways in which the text nurtures our sense of process. At a rhetorical level this is particularly true. Edward Callan is correct to point out that Auden resembles Pope or Dryden in using the rhyming couplet as a vehicle for "reasoned argument," but his method of argument differs from theirs in being dialectical in the specifically Hegelian sense. In the poem we explore contradictions in order to approach a truth that in some way comprehends them all. Thus Auden says of the devil:

> he may never tell us lies
> But half-truths we can synthesize:
> So, hidden in his hocus-pocus,

There lies the gift of double focus,
That magic lamp which looks so dull
And utterly impractical,
Yet, if Aladdin use it right,
Can be a sesame to light.

Here we have another angle on the text as an ideologically powerful "contraption." Constructed as it is according to a consistent "double-focus," it may prove more "practical" than it at first appears. (Remember the Yeats elegy and its stand on the "impracticality" of art, the assertion that on the surface "poetry makes nothing happen"). Used "right" and by an Aladdin-type reader, it can open a way to new perceptions, "Can be a sesame to light." Aladdin, of course, did not unlock the secret power of his lamp by intellectual interrogation or by interpretation. He rubbed it, and in that way his experience foreshadows the one which Auden envisages for his reader: a continuous molding of the mind to the surfaces of the text; a horizontal and in the best sense superficial exploration of its inward and outward curves.

What is particularly interesting in the case of **"New Year Letter"** is that the verse epistle is appropriate to Auden's intention not only because of its expressive potential but also because its characteristic features—its rhyming couplets, its directedness and specificity, its dialectical substance—all seem to work affectively to produce in the reader a nonrational sympathy with the poem's world view. Thus the poem exercises an ideological power which can potentially be felt even beyond the specific historical occasion which produced it. When we shift our focus from Elizabeth Mayer, the historically specified recipient of the letter, onto that unspecifiable reader who will encounter the poem at some uncertain point in history, we see that the gospel of process, the vision of a new cosmos that the poem seeks to communicate, will to some extent still be available to a reader even after conventional interpretation has become problematized by the alteration of historic circumstances. For the ideational power of the text will continue to be exercised through its form, which as we have seen is peculiarly well suited to provoke in the reader a sense of the way, according to Auden, things ultimately are. It is less remarkable that Auden found the Augustan verse epistle a useful tool for *expressing* his post-Einsteinian vision of the universe than for affecting us with a sense of it.

James Held (essay date Winter 1992)

SOURCE: "Ironic Harmony: Blues Convention and Auden's 'Refugee Blues,'" in *Journal of Modern Literature,* Vol. XVIII, No. 1, Winter, 1992, pp. 139-42.

[*In the following essay, Held discusses the significance of* Auden's appropriation of blues music convention in "Refugee Blues."]

All art, Walter Pater declared, aspires to the condition of music. However, Pater's oft-quoted dictum hardly anticipates its ironic implementation in W. H. Auden's **"Refugee Blues."** **"Refugee Blues"** adapts the conventions of the blues to Auden's portrait of exiles in flight from Europe on the eve of the Second World War. Yet beneath the modifications which Auden grafts to it, the poem retains a core of integrity as a blues in form and theme.

"Refugee Blues" directly reflects Auden's experience of his new home after his emigration to New York in 1939. The city harbored thousands of refugees from Europe's upheavals, many of them persons of high attainments, as is the speaker of **"Refugee Blues."** Moreover, the city had become, with Europe's capitals effectively off-limits, the cultural nexus of the West, a fertile soil hospitable to artistic hybrids such as **"Refugee Blues."**

It is not possible to determine precisely what blues songs or performers Auden may have known; it is possible, however, to establish the ubiquity and popularity of the blues by 1939. Auden's familiarity with the blues forms and themes is manifest in the seamless mesh of his theme and lyric voice with the conventions of the blues.

> **"Refugee Blues" directly reflects Auden's experience of his new home after his emigration to New York in 1939.**
> —*James Held*

The blues is essentially a lyric form; its "message is delivered from a first person point of view." As lyric, the blues has an exceptional capacity for the expression of emotion. The scholar Paul Garon, paraphrasing a comment of André Breton's writes that "the blues represents a fusion of music and poetry accomplished at a very high emotional temperature." The primary characteristic of the blues, says Barry Lee Pearson, is the singer's involvement in "the subjects of his song through subjective presentation and emotional intensity."

The themes of the blues can be separated into two broad and necessarily simplified categories: suffering and celebration. David Evans notes that the primary themes which emerge from individual blues consistently reflect this basic dichotomy. Evans also identifies as hallmarks of the blues an overarching cynicism toward life, coupled with a secular outlook that places little hope in spiritual deliverance from suffering.

It is immediately clear that the tale of exile and persecution presented in **"Refugee Blues"** capitalizes on the emotional power of the blues, its theme resonant with the blues' great themes of suffering. The poem's debt to the blues extends, moreover, to the most fundamental levels of construction, a debt manifest in Auden's handling of blues conventions.

The basic stanza form of the blues is a three-line construction (AAB). The first line is repeated (with some variation), and the third line replies to the previous two, as in Robert Johnson's classic "Me and The Devil Blues":

> Early this morning when you knocked on my door
> Early this morning, wmh, when you knocked on
> my door
> I said, "Hello Satan, I believe it's time to go."

"Refugee Blues" is composed of three-line stanzas but does not exhibit the classic blues line sequence, although its rhyme scheme is AAB. Each third line of Auden's stanzas features a similar construction: a repeated statement of negation or exclusion bracketing the phrase "my dear." Auden appears to be inverting the classic blues stanza, with his first two lines now distinct and the third compressing the repetition of the AAB form into a single line. It is also possible that he is adapting a more obscure blues form, the AB-refrain stanza, in which a constant third line serves as a refrain throughout the song. In **"Refugee Blues,"** the phrase "my dear" employed in each third line performs an analogous function; however, the relative rarity of this form makes it a less likely model than the classic AAB form.

Whatever the changes that Auden rang upon the blues form, the stanzas of **"Refugee Blues"** retain what Evans calls "blues logic": the last line of each stanza answers the first two. Blues logic derives from the ancient African call-and-response pattern enshrined in the blues and exploits a sense of tension between the two parts:

> In the village churchyard there grows an old yew,
> Every spring it blossoms anew;
> Old passports can't do that, my dear, old passports
> can't do that.

The images of this stanza's first two lines suggest home and renewal; the tension of rising hope is released, and the hope dashed, by the third line's reply.

"Refugee Blues" also demonstrates attributes of the blues in matters of poetic diction and metre. The speaker of the poem in some lines omits the first-person pronoun or inverts the order of pronoun and verb:

> Went to a committee; they offered me a chair or:

> Dreamed I saw a building with a thousand floors.

Despite Auden's practice of excising the unnecessary word, in the syntax of these lines he deliberately echoes "the peculiarities of phrasing of the blues," as, for example, in Blind Blake's "Steel Mill Blues":

> Workin' in the steel mill, makin' pig iron all day.

The chief metric similarity of **"Refugee Blues"** lies—ironically enough for the poet who "'gave the caesura its freedom'"—in its placement of pauses. Many of the poem's lines are bisected by coordinating conjunctions or semicolons marking a natural caesura in mid-line, the standard point of placement for the caesura in the blues. The phrase "my dear" interjected in each third line also enforces a mid-line pause between the repeated halves.

"Refugee Blues," like its models, is iambic but only very roughly so; in the blues, considerable deviation results from individual style, or in this poem's case, from the demands of a conversational delivery.

There is a final technical parallel between Auden's poem and the blues that proves most intriguing of all: the relation of the interjection "my dear" to the blue note. The blue note is the insertion of a flattened or descending note, usually the third, but at times the seventh or fifth, into the diatonic scale. It is a practice derived from African music, and it is used to express powerful emotion. I believe that the "my dear" of **"Refugee Blues,"** while in one sense evoking blues apostrophes such as "lord," "baby," or "well, well," is more properly understood as a blue note. The first two lines of each stanza generate a tension that is released or exacerbated by the repeated statement in the third line. The interjection separating the initial statement from its repetition forces the reader to pause and consider the emotional consequences of this first reply to the preceding two lines; following the shock imparted by the first half of the third line, the interjection serves as a descending note on an emotional scale declining into despair, as the reiteration of that initial statement drives its import home with finality.

The kinship of **"Refugee Blues"** to the blues is thematic as well as formal. The poem's themes are manifestly those of the "suffering" blues: exile, self-pity, exclusion, and persecution. The lyric perspective of **"Refugee Blues"** conforms to the traditional stance of the singer of the blues; both express the personal impact of larger events. The speaker does not directly attack Nazism or racism (mention of Hitler notwithstanding), but focuses instead on the results of those evils in the lives of the speaker and of the woman whom he is addressing. It is also noteworthy that the speaker does not offer any prospect of redress; such hope in progress or ultimate justice is "alien to the spirit of the blues." The tone and impact of the poem's blues logic are unremittingly grim:

Saw a poodle in a jacket fastened with a pin,
Saw a door opened and cat let in:
But they weren't German Jews, my dear, they
weren't German Jews.

The message of the last stanza,

Stood on a great plain in the falling snow,
Ten thousand soldiers marched to and fro:
Looking for you and me, my dear, looking for you
and me,

seems hardly different in concept, tone, and imagery from
Robert Johnson's "Hellhound on my trail, hellhound on my
trail."

The imagery of **"Refugee Blues"** is not predicated on logic
or narrative clarity; rather, its emphasis is placed, as in true
blues imagery, upon a "wealth of unstated associated meanings permitting a maximum of content with a strict economy
of means." Auden chooses his images for their evocative
power: the churchyard yew conjures a mix of hope and nostalgia; the fish, freedom visible yet forever beyond reach;
the ten thousand soldiers, relentless pursuit by an implacable
enemy.

The poem's irony stems not from any disjunction between
the origin and nature of the blues with Pater's assumptions
about music, with Auden's classicism or political commitment. It evolves, rather, from the perfect harmony of the
blues with Auden's thematic concerns. The irony of **"Refugee Blues"** extracts its power from the moral bankruptcy
of the European culture from which Pater's aesthetic pronouncements derive. Europe's pretensions to cultural gran-
deur prove empty in the face of the persecution of the Jews;
the vehicle of Auden's indictment is the unschooled music
of another minority much despised and exploited by the
West.

Alan Jacobs (essay date Winter 1995)

SOURCE: "Auden's Local Culture," in *Hudson Review*,
Vol. 47, No. 4, Winter, 1995, pp. 543-68.

[*In the following essay, Jacobs examines Auden's
communitarian sympathies and moral vision. According to
Jacobs, "Auden understood both the costs and benefits of
choosing to cultivate local knowledge and local attachments
better than almost any political thinker writing about such
issues today."*]

I

One of the more interesting developments in American political and social thought in the last decade or so has been
the emergence of communitarianism—in large part because,
though no one knows exactly what communitarianism is,
people do tend to think good thoughts about the notion of
community. As Wendell Berry writes, "Community is a concept, like humanity or peace, that virtually no one has taken
the trouble to quarrel with; even its worst enemies praise
it." Perhaps some communitarians have chosen not to define their aims and goals too specifically because they know
that the cold light of specificity tends to dispel the warm
fuzzy aura that surrounds that word "community."

But some attempts at definition have been made. According to Christopher Lasch, who should know,
communitarianism "proposes a general strategy of devolution or decentralization, designed to end the dominance of
large organizations [this means multinational corporations
as well as the U.S. government] and to remodel our institutions on a human scale." Communitarians, then, inveigh
against the old habit of thinking of the *polis* largely in national terms, and advocate its replacement by more local-
ized forms of attention.

A curious trait of communitarians is that few of them seem
to have arrived at their position willingly. Rather, they have
become communitarians only because more grandiose and
universal systems (whether Marxism, old-fashioned liberalism, or state capitalism) have, in their view, failed us all.
In this regard the paradigmatic communitarian, it seems to
me, is St. Francis of Assissi. After he discovered the Biblical principles on which he and his followers would base
their brotherhood—by picking three verses at random from
the Gospels—he sought again and again to bring his message to other parts of the known world. But each time he
prepared to voyage forth to make his message universal,
some barrier (whether a Pope's edict or the collapse of his
health or God's unmediated will) would prevent him from
living Italy; thus he was forced, until quite late in his career, to cultivate the Franciscan spirit of community only
in his native Umbria. Like most communitarians, then,
Francis became one by default. No one, it seems, wants
cultiver son jardin as long as changing the world remains a
viable option.

This is especially the case for intellectuals, because, as Karl
Mannheim pointed out many years ago in his *Ideology and
Utopia,* intellectuals in Western societies form a distinct
class "whose special task is to provide an interpretation of
the world." An intellectual, then, by definition thinks glo-
bally rather than locally; so much so that to accept the validity of local concerns is to court excommunication from
the church of the clerisy. This danger may best be seen, I
think, in the example of Albert Camus. Think of some of
his most notorious statements about the Algerian conflict

in which his family was endangered: "I believe in justice, but I will defend my mother before justice." "Love is injustice, but justice is not enough." "If anyone . . . thinks heroically that one's brother must die rather than one's principles, I shall go no farther than to admire him from a distance. I am not of his stamp." If the virulence with which such statements were repudiated by the French intelligentsia seems shocking today, that is only because in the intervening thirty-five years we have lost confidence in the mental and moral detachment of the intellectual. Even if the detachment and objectivity of the intellectual is a fiction, it remains (if Mannheim is right, and I think he is) necessary to the very concepts of "intellectual" and "intelligentsia." To the adherents of that fiction, the celebration of local culture and local knowledge is anathema.

These reflections apply quite directly, I believe, to one of the more interesting, if largely unacknowledged, predecessors of the contemporary communitarian movement, the poet W. H. Auden. Though Auden settled on communitarian principles with great reluctance, after the defeat of his universalist hopes he articulated those principles with remarkable force and clarity in twenty-five years of beautiful, but to this day largely unappreciated, poetry. Moreover, I contend that Auden understood both the costs and benefits of choosing to cultivate local knowledge and local attachments better than almost any political thinker writing about such issues today. For that reason alone his work on this subject deserves our attention. But it also repays study because of certain conflicts into which Auden's particular brand of communitarianism drew him—conflicts that may have been inevitable.

2

What we need here is a vantage point from which to survey both the early and the later Auden, and that point is provided by **"New Year Letter,"** the first long poem Auden wrote after he moved to America at the outset of the Second World War. One of the most notable and surprising features of this poem is its celebration of local culture. Auden's conception of what local culture is and what it does develops throughout the **"New Year Letter,"** but finds condensed expression near the beginning, as Auden remembers a recent gathering of friends at the home of Elizabeth Mayer (to whom this "letter" is written). After describing the various objects and actions which with a "neutral eye" the sun observes on earth, he writes that this same sun

> Lit up America and on
> A cottage in Long Island shone
> Where BUXTEHUDE as we played
> One of his *passacaglias* made
> Our minds a *civitas* of sound
> Where nothing but assent was found,

> For art had set in order sense
> And feeling and intelligence,
> And from its ideal order grew
> Our local understanding too.

The phrase "ideal order" comes from T. S. Eliot's famous essay "Tradition and the Individual Talent": "The existing monuments [of European art] form an ideal order among themselves, which is modified by the introduction of the new (the really new) work of art among them." But while Eliot's concerns are merely intertextual, describing only how these "monuments" are organized and deployed in relation to one another, Auden's interests are markedly different: the question for him is, How does art help us (if indeed it does) to set our lives in order? For Eliot the ideal order is to be contemplated and celebrated; for Auden it is to be used. And it finds its use in the formation of "local understanding," of small groups of people united, if only temporarily, to become citizens of their own tiny republic.

Later in the poem, at the beginning of its third and last part, Auden returns to the same message:

> And SCHUBERT sang and MOZART played
> And GLUCK and food and friendship made
> Our privileged community
> That real republic which must be
> The State all politicians claim,
> Even the worst, to be their aim.

I quote this passage too because otherwise it might not be clear how such an apparently high view of art's utility could be reconciled with that famous opinion Auden had pronounced for the first (but certainly not the last) time almost exactly a year before, in his famous elegy on Yeats: "Poetry makes nothing happen." Does Auden now mean to say that if poetry can't make anything happen music can? There were certainly times in his later career when he came close to saying just that, but in the context of the **"New Year Letter"** I think the point is that art, while it cannot of its own power *enforce* any alteration of consciousness or morality, can *help* those who would be joined together to find their desired unity. Artists can never become the legislators of the world, either acknowledged or unacknowledged— Auden often expressed scorn and repulsion for Shelley's famous claim—but they can become after a fashion public servants. Yet even this they can only do successfully if the public they serve is small enough for real commonality of purpose to be possible: art can promote "local understanding" in a miniature *civitas,* but cannot change the world. And this is true not because art is weak, but because, in Auden's view in 1940, all dreams of universal or even national unity, dreams which he himself had tried for a decade to share in, are fundamentally absurd. Art can serve only local understanding because local understanding is the only understanding there is.

3

One of the more interesting points to be made about Auden's conclusion here is that he had been confronted with just such an example of perfect local understanding—an example even more perfect, and certainly far more dramatic, than he found in Elizabeth Mayer's Long Island home—less than seven years before, and had been unable to accept it. He did not provide a full account of the experience until 1964, thirty years after it had occurred, and even then he did not openly admit that the experience was his own. The account needs to be quoted at some length:

> One fine summer night in June 1933 I was sitting on a lawn after dinner with three colleagues, two women and one man. . . . We were talking casually about everyday matters when, quite suddenly and unexpectedly, something happened. I felt myself invaded by a power which, though I consented to it, was irresistible and certainly not mine. For the first time in my life I knew exactly—because, thanks to the power, I was doing it—what it means to love one's neighbor as oneself. I was also certain, though the conversation continued to be perfectly ordinary, that my three colleagues were having the same experience. (In the case of one of them, I was later able to confirm this.) My personal feelings towards them were unchanged—they were still colleagues, not intimate friends—but I felt their existence as themselves to be of infinite value and rejoiced in it.

> I recalled with shame the many occasions on which I had been spiteful, snobbish, selfish, but the immediate joy was greater than the shame, for I knew that, so long as I was possessed by this spirit, it would be literally impossible for me deliberately to injure another human being. I also knew that the power would, of course, be withdrawn sooner or later and that, when it did, my greed and self-regard would return. The experience lasted at its full intensity for about two hours when we said goodnight to each other and went to bed. When I awoke the next morning, it was still present, though weaker, and it did not vanish completely for two days or so. The memory of the experience has not prevented me from making use of others, grossly and often, but it has made it much more difficult for me to deceive myself about what I am up to when I do. And among the various factors which several years later brought me back to the Christian faith in which I had been brought up, the

memory of this experience and asking myself what it could mean was one of the most crucial, though, at the time it occurred, I thought I had done with Christianity for good.

This story fits nicely with the celebration of "local understanding" elaborated in **"New Year Letter":** here indeed is a tiny Athens, even a miniature New Jerusalem. But when Auden wrote a poem about the experience, soon after it happened, his chief concern was to articulate his sense that the acceptance of such an excessively local culture was morally and politically indefensible.

The early stanzas of the poem, which Auden would eventually give the title "A Summer Night," show no sign of uneasiness:

> Equal with colleagues in a ring
> I sit on each calm evening
>   Enchanted as the flowers
> The opening light draws out of hiding
> From leaves with all its dove-like pleading,
>   Its logic and its powers:

> That later we, though parted then,
> May still recall these evenings when
>   Fear gave his watch no look;
> The lion griefs loped from the shade
> And on our knees their muzzles laid,
>   And Death put down his book.

But as the poem moves on its center of interest shifts: what about those who are not so fortunate as to be enclosed within such an Edenic "ring"? How does an acknowledgement of their existence affect the comfortable insiders? Or is life in such an enchanted circle dependent on a studied ignorance of those outside? Perhaps the insiders, "whom hunger cannot move,"

>   do not care to know,
> Where Poland draws her eastern bow,
>   What violence is done,
> Nor ask what doubtful act allows
> Our freedom in this English house,
>   Our picnics in the sun.

> The creepered wall stands up to hide
> The gathering multitudes outside
>   Whose glances hunger worsens;
> Concealing from their wretchedness
> Our metaphysical distress,
>   Our kindness to ten persons.

This vision of love and community, then, may not be a free gift in which to rejoice, but a dangerous temptation to social quietism: it is at best a "doubtful act." What the Auden of 1964 celebrates as a blessed inability to harm others, the Auden of 1933 fears as an insidious tendency to be satisfied with one's "kindness to ten persons" while the "gathering multitudes" outside starve. The perfect local understanding which the Auden even of 1940 celebrates as an incalculable gift, the Auden of 1933 finds a scandal precisely because it is local and not universal.

How, then, did Auden get in less than seven years from the one position to the other? One might begin by describing his disillusionment with Marxism and his return to Christianity, a return which was not yet complete when **"New Year Letter"** was written but was nearly so. But we should be careful here. That Auden rejected Marxism and became a Christian is certainly true; but there is no necessary connection between Christianity and the embrace of local culture exemplified in **"New Year Letter."** In fact, it would be more accurate to say that Marxism and Christianity alike stand opposed to such localization of culture, which finds more sympathy in certain ancient Greek and Roman modes of political thought (Aristotle rather than Plato, Horace rather than Virgil). The cultivation of "local understanding," as is manifest in the passages quoted from both **"New Year Letter"** and **"A Summer Night,"** requires as an essential, perhaps *the* essential, component the cultivation of friendship—and friendship, while an Aristotelian virtue, tends to be suspect both to Marxism (which opposes to it the ideal of "comradeship") and to Christianity (which opposes to it the ideal of "brotherhood and sisterhood in Christ"). Jeremy Taylor, the seventeenth-century Anglican divine, wrote: "When friendships were the noblest things in the world, charity was little." In other words, when the ancient Greeks and Romans emphasized the great virtue of friendship, they neglected to care for those who stood outside *philia*'s charmed circle: the "gathering multitudes" outside the "creepered wall." Likewise Samuel Johnson: "All friendship is preferring the interest of a friend, to the neglect, or, perhaps, against the interest of others. . . . Now Christianity recommends universal benevolence, to consider all men as our brethren; which is contrary to the virtue of friendship, as described by the ancient philosophers." One might easily argue that Marxism inherits this Christian universalism, while proposing alternative explanations for its practical failure and alternative means for its eventual realization. Thus it is by no means obvious that Auden's embrace of Christianity would naturally lead to an embrace of local culture and local understanding.

> **A consistent theme in Auden's work of this period is that we lack the power to *undo* the evil that we have the power to *do*.**
> —*Alan Jacobs*

In fact, it seems to me that Auden's return to Christianity and his celebration of local culture form two rather distinct movements in his intellectual life that meet at only one point, a point which we will soon identify. First, it is vital to note that at no point in Auden's intellectual development does he deny that human beings are capable of creating universal *evil*. For instance, from **"New Year Letter":**

> And more and more we are aware,
> However miserable may be
> Our parish of immediacy,
> How small it is, how, far beyond,
> Ubiquitous within the bond
> Of an impoverishing sky,
> Vast spiritual disorders lie.

Then follows a catalogue of those "disorders," from China to Spain to Ethiopia to Poland. But a grave spiritual and moral danger, Auden argues, arises from the recognition of such universal evil. "Who," he asks,

> will not feel blind anger draw
> His thoughts toward the Minotaur,
> To take an early boat for Crete
> And rolling, silly, at its feet
> Add his small tidbit to the rest?
> It lures us all; even the best,
> *Les hommes de bonne volonté,* feel
> Their politics perhaps unreal
> And all they have believed untrue,
> Are tempted to surrender to
> The grand apocalyptic dream
> In which the persecutors scream
> As on the evil Aryan lives
> Descends the night of the long knives,
> The bleeding tyrant dragged through all
> The ashes of his capitol.

One might with cause assume that Auden here is arguing for pacifism, claiming that the attempt to defeat Hitler will reduce the Allies to Hitler's moral level. But Auden, though he felt the appeal of pacifism, never embraced it, and soon after writing **"New Year Letter"** explicitly rejected it. Instead, Auden is warning the Allies that they are not immune to the forces that (as he wrote about Germany in **"September 1, 1939"**) "have driven a culture mad"; the great if not inevitable danger of fighting the Nazis is that one may become contaminated by the very disorder one sets out to cure. Thus the little parable that, in the Notes which he originally appended to **"New Year Letter,"** Auden attaches to the lines about throwing oneself at the feet of the Minotaur:

> During the last war Frau M was in Tübingen. Walking home one cloudy night, she met two professors from the university, carrying rifles.

"What's the matter?" she asked.

"There's an enemy aeroplane overhead. Can't you see its pilot-light?"

"But that's not an aeroplane. That's Jupiter."

Having thrown themselves at the feet of what Auden calls in *The Sea and the Mirror* "the Minotaur of Authority," these men have lost their ability to make elementary moral and even perceptual discriminations. And let us not fail to note that these are professors, a fact that indicates that Auden's warning is chiefly directed against the intellectuals, who are in the greatest danger of all because of their conviction that their detachment and objectivity place them beyond danger. This is a lesson, I believe, Auden learned in Spain, where he saw how the Republicans (surely *hommes de bonne volonté*), consumed with hatred for anything associated with the old regime, had closed and in many cases wrecked or burned the churches of Barcelona—and without eliciting recognition of their act, much less disapproval, from their supporters among the intelligentsia.

Perhaps Auden's insistence upon the nearly infinite human capacity for evil would not have been so objectionable to the intellectuals of his time, were it not for his equally vivid insistence that it does *not* follow that humans are capable of equally great goodness. A consistent theme in Auden's work of this period is that we lack the power to *undo* the evil that we have the power to *do.* It is this belief that leads Auden to what would become one of the most persistent features of his poetry until his death: his praise of humility. *This* is the point at which his conversion to Christianity and his acceptance of the validity of local culture converge.

4

One of the first significant appearances of this *leitmotif* is in Auden's great sonnet sequence of 1938, **"In Time of War,"** which grew out of his and Christopher Isherwood's visit to China. In the last sonnet of the sequence, for instance, Auden describes the hopes for human perfection in a perfectly innocent past of what Eliot would call "unified sensibility" and in a perfectly ordered future—these being the dreams, as he would later write in the "Vespers" section of the **"Horae Canonicae,"** of the Arcadian and the Utopian respectively. But here he calmly rejects both visions of perfection as being incompatible with the fundamental human condition:

But we are articled to error; we
Were never nude and calm like a great door

And never will be perfect like the fountains.

A full understanding of this inevitable fallenness requires not only humility but a recognition of the historical value of humility: in the verse "Commentary" to the sequence Auden writes of the importance of giving "Our gratitude to the Invisible College of the Humble, / Who through the ages have accomplished everything essential." Auden's conviction on this point finds its most perfect poetic expression about a year after the completion of **"New Year Letter,"** in the penultimate (later, upon revision, to be the last) stanza of **"At the Grave of Henry James":**

All will be judged. Master of nuance and scruple,
Pray for me and for all writers living or dead;
   Because there are many whose works
Are in better taste than their lives; because there is
no end
To the vanity of our calling: make intercession
   For the treason of all clerks.

Auden's humble recognition of the profundity of human evildoing and the limited capacity for doing good has two major consequences for his thought: first, that the Christian belief in original sin and the concomitant need for salvation from God is, in all essentials, right; second, that one must do what one can, not what one wishes one could do, to make things better. In the famous phrase from **"Tintern Abbey,"** Auden determines to cultivate and to praise "that best portion of a good man's life: / His little, nameless, unremembered acts / Of kindness and of love"; and from Sydney Smith he learns (a phrase he would often repeat in prose and verse) to "take short views." This emphasis on limited aims, this desired reconciliation with inevitable incompetence, appears often in Auden's later poetry—to take but one example, in **"Memorial for the City"** (1949), in which a versified history of the failed Constantinian experiment of melding the City of Man with the City of God is followed by the voice of "our Weakness," a voice never acknowledged by the hubristic Constantinians whose best efforts culminated in the encompassing tyrannies of Hitler and Stalin.

Auden's replacement for these great dreams, his determination to cultivate his garden, may be chastised as a philosophy for the cosy, merely domestic ethics. But Auden is quite explicit in his belief that on these grounds and on these grounds only can meaningful culture—and moreover, the kind of culture which both safeguards us from as a culture being "driven mad" in the way the Germans were, and minimizes the danger of becoming like the Nazis in fighting them—be achieved. It is, of course, precisely this view that has caused so many critics to scorn the "new" Auden and long for the earlier, politically-committed Auden. Randall Jarrell, for instance, in a famous attack upon Auden in a 1945 issue of the *Partisan Review,* sneers at "that overweening humility which is the badge of all his saints" and condemns Auden for "moral imbecility" in seeking the salvation of his own soul while heedless of the world being destroyed around him. Jarrell feels that Auden should have somehow put his intellectual powers to work in the war against Hitler rather than criticizing, as Auden did in a 1944 review of a new edition of Grimm's *Märchen,* "the Society for Scientific Diet, the Association of Positivist Parents, the League for the Promotion of Worthwhile Leisure, the Coöperative Camp for Prudent Progressives and all other bores and scoundrels." To which Jarrell: "In the year 1944 these prudent, progressive, scientific, coöperative 'bores and scoundrels' were the enemies with whom Auden found it necessary to struggle. Were *these* your enemies, reader? They were not mine."

Auden did not respond to Jarrell's attack; he never responded to attacks. But someone should; therefore, the prosecution having made its case, I will now take the part of the counsel for the defense (on the model of Auden's own **"The Public vs. the Late Mr. William Butler Yeats"**).

5

Ladies and Gentlemen of the jury, it is customary at this point for the defense attorney to praise the eloquence of the prosecutor. That I cannot do, for it seems to me that despite the customary brilliance of his wit he has spoken neither well nor to the point. He has accused my client of a virtually treasonable disregard of his social and political duty as a writer, and this accusation, with all its unreliable inferences and misleading implications, it is my duty, and my pleasure, to refute. I think you will soon see, ladies and gentlemen, just how insubstantial these apparently weighty charges really are.

Where to begin? The distinguished prosecutor has made so many errors that I struggle to decide which to dispose of first. Perhaps we had best begin by clearing up a potential misunderstanding about the accusation itself. Members of the jury might be forgiven for assuming that the distinguished prosecutor meant at times to chastise my client for having failed to enlist as a soldier—whether of his native Great Britain or of our United States—and to fight in the most literal sense against Hitler's armies. But this cannot be what Mr. Jarrell intended: if such had been his charge, he would have complained that Mr. Auden was writing *at all,* rather than complaining about the specific content of his writing. (And Mr. Jarrell could not make a general attack on writing in wartime without, like King David, standing condemned by his own judgment.)

No, the essential charge the prosecutor levels against my client is the charge of *frivolity:* the allegation is that Mr. Auden fiddles while Europe burns. The cause of this frivolity, or rather its justification, according to the prosecutor, is Mr.

Auden's belief in the Christian doctrine (traditionally, if not accurately, identified with Calvinism) of human depravity: because Mr. Auden believes that *all* have sinned and fallen short of the glory of God, he has ceased to make moral discriminations, and this is inexcusably frivolous—especially in the midst of this war, when moral distinctions between the monstrous Hitler and his opponents are vital.

Were this an accurate representation of my client's views, he would indeed be guilty of, in Mr. Jarrell's memorable phrase, "moral imbecility." But it is a wildly and irresponsibly inaccurate account. Mr. Auden has time and again, in public and in private, expressed his opposition to Hitler and Hitler's cause. However, unlike Mr. Jarrell, he does not believe that in so doing he has exhausted his moral responsibilities, because, again unlike Mr. Jarrell, he does not assume that we have all honor and virtue thrust upon us merely through being attacked by an evil force. Mr. Auden never, even for an instant, questions whether the force that has attacked the Allies and Western civilization itself is evil; rather, he asks us to be watchful lest (possessed by a "grand apocalyptic dream" of revenge) we become infected with that same evil ourselves. What the doctrine of human depravity does for Mr. Auden is simply and constantly to remind him that no one can *assume* himself or herself to be invulnerable to the forces that led, first to the Nazis' supremacy in Germany itself, and later to the Nazis' determination to conquer all Europe. Mr. Jarrell, on the other hand, seems never to doubt his moral standing, and appears unaware that the war offers to him, or to any loyal citizen of the Allied nations, any moral temptations whatsoever. This is especially odd when one considers Mr. Jarrell's poems about the life of a common dogface soldier, which indicate his comprehension of the evil that can be done at least by the leaders of an army, even when that army fights in a just cause.

Moreover, the prosecutor has not just misrepresented Mr. Auden's understanding of evil and its manifestations in the current war; he has also simply missed the essential point of the writings by my client that most offend him. The key issue for Mr. Auden is not what the ordinary citizen can and should do in the war, but rather what responsibilities the artist, in particular the poet, must carry out. It is clear that Mr. Jarrell believes that the poet should in some way turn his or her talents to the fight against Hitler; but he does not, or cannot, explain just how this could be done. If he believes that Mr. Auden should be active in translation or propaganda, he should say so. Does he believe that Mr. Auden should write poems about the war? Well, Mr. Auden cannot, like Mr. Jarrell himself, write poems about the experience of being a soldier; what sort of poems, then, should he write? Whatever our prosecutor's answer might be, it appears that he has not thought seriously about Mr. Auden's striking claim that there is *nothing* a poet, *qua* poet, can do to fight against Hitler. "Poetry makes nothing happen," he has famously said; moreover,

> art is a product of history, not a cause. Unlike some other products, technical inventions for example, it does not re-enter history as an effective agent, so that the question whether art should or should not be propaganda is unreal. The case for the prosecution [of Yeats, my client's distinguished predecessor in the dock] rests on the fallacious belief that art ever makes anything happen, whereas the honest truth . . . is that, if not a poem had been written, not a picture painted, not a bar of music composed, the history of man would remain materially unchanged.

If Mr. Auden is wrong in this belief, then he is honestly wrong; and even the most cursory review of the history of Europe will suffice to show that the burden of proof rests on those who disagree. It is understandable that Mr. Jarrell would *want* to believe that art has the power to change the world, and thus that the writer *qua* writer can be a significant weapon against the evil incarnated in Hitler; but it is less understandable that he would exercise such virulence and scorn against a fellow poet who happens to disagree with that assessment of art's power.

Why does Mr. Auden write at all, then, given his skepticism about the power of art? Because while poets are not and can never be the unacknowledged legislators of the world—that job, Mr. Auden says, has been applied for by the Gestapo—they can serve their own community by calling certain important but easily neglected facts to remembrance, and by warning against some equally easily neglected dangers. Poets cannot fight against Hitler, but they can fight against the people and the tendencies in their own society which corrupt that society from within and on the foundational levels of family and locality. Moreover, it is not inconceivable that some of these corrupting forces are precisely those—"the Society for Scientific Diet, the Association of Positivist Parents, the League for the Promotion of Worthwhile Leisure, the Coöperative Camp for Prudent Progressives"—whom Mr. Jarrell explicitly claims *not* to oppose. It is evident, then, that while there is opposition between Mr. Jarrell and Mr. Auden it does not take the form that Mr. Jarrell claims it does: it is not Jarrell's concern for the world versus Auden's concern for his own personal salvation; rather, it is disagreement over *which* enemies may profitably be fought, *which* superindividual concerns the poet may effectively engage in.

Two conclusions, then, emerge from my exposition of the real ideas of the real Mr. Auden, as opposed to the prosecutor's imaginary versions. First, that if my client has sinned, it is only against Mr. Jarrell's high view of art, and

not against English or American society, or against the Allied war effort. And second, a man who goes out of his way, and against the current cultural grain, to warn us of the moral dangers that *we* face as we fight against Hitler, is guilty of anything but "moral imbecility," anything but frivolity. Mr. Auden's is a voice we need to hear, and not, as Mr. Jarrell would counsel, to suppress.

6

What we have done so far, then: first, to trace the history of Auden's conviction that significant culture is and must necessarily be local rather than universal; and second, to defend this conviction against certain misunderstandings, especially those which conceive it to involve a quietistic or even fatalistic withdrawal from all forms of superindividual concern. But what also emerges from reflection on this period of Auden's career is his equally important conviction that this local culture must be deliberately and personally *chosen*. Now, normally those who emphasize the inevitable chosenness of culture (for example, T. S. Eliot) tend also to emphasize its universality, while many communitarian devotees of local culture (for example, Wendell Berry) tend to avoid the question of choice. It is Auden's combination of these two positions that makes him particularly important today.

Let's look at Auden in contrast to the two representative figures I just mentioned. Eliot writes, in a famous passage from "Tradition and the Individual Talent," that tradition "cannot be inherited, and if you want it you must obtain it by great labour." Presumably, in light of other things he was writing at the time, Eliot means us to understand that this need to obtain tradition only through heroic effort and deliberate choice is the peculiar curse of the modern age; certainly it would not have afflicted John Donne, who (or so Eliot thought at the time) "could feel his thought as immediately as the odour of a rose," living as he did in an age of unified sensibility. It is incidentally important to understand Eliot's later career, his claim to classicism, traditionalism, and so on, to see these positions as choices rather than inherited givens. As Robert Langbaum wrote in *The Poetry of Experience* some thirty years ago: "Are not, after all, even our new classicisms and new Christian dogmatisms really romanticisms in an age which simply cannot supply the world-views such doctrines depend on, so that they become, for all their claims to objectivity, merely another opinion, the objectification of someone's personal view?" I am not sure that Eliot fully understood the implications of this point, but Auden did. The dialectic of choice and necessity is, as many critics have pointed out, an obsession of Auden throughout his career, but it is summed up with exemplary clarity in the prayer that concludes **"In Sickness and in Health,"** written just a few months after **"New Year Letter":** "O hold us to the voluntary way."

But in any case, what most clearly distinguishes Auden from Eliot is the fact that Eliot's chosen tradition is universal and objective: the "ideal order" of *all* great works of art, the forerunner of Northrop Frye's archetypically organized "imaginative universe." It by definition cannot be confined to a place; it repudiates the insular and parochial—opprobrious terms which in its dialect are synonymous with the local. But as we have already seen, for Auden it is precisely the locality and particularity of the gathering at Elizabeth Mayer's home that enables those people to come together as a genuine, if tiny, *civitas*.

Auden may equally well be contrasted with Berry, who relentlessly and eloquently has argued for the beauty of the local and its necessity as a foundation for significant culture. But Berry's consistent emphasis is on the need to conserve and protect existing communities, or to restore those that have fallen into neglect and disrepair; he always assumes a history of relations which, if they are not currently active, can be reestablished. In essays such as "The Work of Local Culture" and "Writer and Region"—many others could be cited here—Berry posits *memory* as a necessary component of healthy community. In Berry's scheme, it appears, Auden's first move toward community would have to be a return to England; yet England is the one place where, Auden believed, he could not find genuine community, in part because there was no place in England which he could think of as home, but also and more importantly because the English intelligentsia rejected and scorned the convictions he had come to find essential. (In 1940 Auden told Golo Mann, "The English intellectuals who now cry out to Heaven against the evil incarnated in Hitler have no Heaven to cry to; they have nothing to offer and their protests echo in empty space.") Berry cannot, or does not, explain how Auden might find significant local community in America, in New York City of all unlikely places. It is the creation of new community that Auden is concerned with—as he often tried to explain, in letters from this period, to his puzzled English friends—not the restoration of the old; and thus the question of choice, which Berry neglects but which is formulated so eloquently by Langbaum in the passage quoted above, is paramount for him.

From the preceding paragraph it becomes evident that, while I have identified Berry and Auden alike as proponents of local culture, "local" does not mean the same thing to both. There are common points: local culture as both men use the term is restricted in scope, humble in its aspirations, dedicated to preservation and conservation; moreover, it emphasizes and celebrates the social and communal formation of all personal identities. But for Berry—again see "Writer and Region," also "Poetry and Place"—healthy local culture must necessarily be rooted in a particular physical environment, a *place*. Auden does not seem to think so. For more than twenty-five years he lived in New York City, but for

only half the year; the other half being spent first on the tiny Italian island of Ischia, later in his beloved home in the village of Kirchstetten in Austria. Auden thought often and wrote beautifully about these localities, but clearly felt the need, as Berry perhaps does not, to maintain his community solely in his own mind and work. The nature of his profession—it is vital to remember that Berry is a farmer as well as a poet, and would necessarily have a very different understanding of community and local culture if he only wrote poetry—and of his apparently rootless way of life forced Auden to confront a difficult fact: if he were to experience the blessings of communal, local culture at all, he would have to find a means to cultivate such experience that would seem quite alien to more traditional local cultures.

Which is another way of saying that Berry's emphasis on memory does eventually come to be essential even to Auden's peculiar form of local culture: Auden does not have the luxury of beginning with a substantial history, but he soon develops one. From about 1940 on Auden very consciously builds a community of friends and colleagues that he sustains and memorializes through his poetry. No other major poet dedicates so many poems to his friends; the reader of Auden's correspondence, especially letters from the last twenty years of his life, finds that he spent an extraordinary amount of time typing up drafts of his poems for friends, and asking them if he could dedicate those poems to them. And often the themes of these poems involve Auden's reflections on the very issues of this essay: under what conditions communities can thrive, what dangers (internal or external) threaten those communities, and, especially, the importance of being continually thankful for the blessings of friendship and "local understanding." Thus a chief purpose of Auden's later poetry becomes the making of a permanent record of the nature and history of his friendships, that is to say, his community. Poetry—for Auden and, he hopes, for his friends—resumes an ancient (and by Auden much-lamented) function, as a mnemonic device. What must be remembered through poetry, however, is not the number of days in April, but rather the character of one's friendships and the virtues of one's community. Like the Jesuit missionary Matteo Ricci, Auden builds a memory palace, but this one does not remain a Prosperian "insubstantial pageant": it is inscribed on solid paper and bound between hard covers.

7

Earlier I mentioned, briefly, **"Memorial for the City"** as a poem in which Auden repudiates the Constantinian project. But the very title suggests that Auden retains as part of his conceptual framework the notion of a political entity larger than the tiny *civitas* made up of his friends and colleagues. Every local culture, Auden frequently implies, though it is a *polis* unto itself, also participates in that larger entity more usually called the *polis*. It does not often participate well and meaningfully, largely because it remains unconscious of its responsibilities to the greater City, but in the ideal commonwealth the smallest and largest polities will understand their relation: as he writes near the end of **"New Year Letter,"** "The largest *publicum*'s a *res, / And the least *res* a *publicum*."

One practical consequence of this view is that each local community must recognize the validity of other such communities and accept that each has a place in the fabric of the whole, Berkeley and Orange County alike. In **"Vespers,"** the fifth of Auden's **"Horae Canonicae"** (that great and potently condensed sequence of poems that he worked on for about seven years, from the late forties to the mid-fifties), Auden described a brief but significant crossing of paths. At dusk in "our city," the poem's speaker, an Arcadian devoted to contemplation of a charming and idealized past, meets his future-directed Utopian "anti-type"; however,

> Neither speaks. What experience could we possibly share?

> Glancing at a lampshade in a store window, I observe it is too hideous for anyone in their senses to buy: He observes it is too expensive for a peasant to buy.

> Passing a slum child with rickets, I look the other way: He looks the other way if he passes a chubby one.

The playful tone of the poem should not obscure the underlying seriousness of its theme: "You can see, then, why, between my Eden and his New Jerusalem, no treaty is negotiable." But this collision of opposites is not the poem's conclusion. It may be, muses the speaker as they move on in their different directions, that this twilit meeting, far from being an accident, is "a rendezvous between two accomplices," each of whom reminds the other "of that half of their secret which he would most like to forget." For "a fraction of a second" each remembers "our victim," a victim both human and innocent, whose blood enables the "secular wall" of the city "safely [to] stand." This victim—Auden says "call him Abel, Remus, what you will, it is one Sin Offering," but these are clearly shadowy types of Christ—in his innocence recalls the unspoiled perfection of Eden, the restoration of which is now the city's hope and goal; but this restoration is only made possible by the shedding of that very innocent's blood, for as St. Paul says, "without the shedding of blood there is no remission of sin"; and this is a fact only the Utopian, willing to make sacrifices for an imagined future, is able to face. Thus these two enemies are

in fact equally necessary members of their city, "our dear old bag of a democracy."

The challenge that Auden presents in this poem, then, is to maintain simultaneous allegiances to one's local culture and to the greater polity—assuming that that polity is a democracy, because only in democracy (thinks Auden) can such exceedingly varied and even contradictory local communities be formed and sustained. But it is extraordinarily difficult, even in times such as ours in which there is (supposedly) no higher virtue than toleration, to acknowledge and even celebrate the role one's political opponents play in the constitution of the society. And sad to say, as Auden got older the vision of this great twilit meeting receded and was replaced by withdrawal into the most local of all cultures, the garden cultivated *only* in the mind.

8

I have already said that Auden's lack of attachment to a place causes him to think of the formation of community in terms of thankfulness, remembrance, and inscription: to write poems to and for his friends is to remember and give thanks for their friendship, to build a community on the page that cannot, thanks to the international character of Auden's life and his connections, be built in a single location. But however necessary this form of community-building was for Auden, he pursued it with such vigor and determination that it gradually assumed a kind of perverse life of its own, so that the local culture that he conceived in his mind and memory became preferable to any more material kind. This tendency he was perfectly aware of, though it is not easy to tell if he regretted it. For instance, in **"Thanksgiving for a Habitat"** (written mostly from 1962-64), Auden writes that one of the greatest blessings of his Austrian home, a dwelling-place "I dared not hope or fight for," is that there "I needn't, ever, be at home to / those I am not at home *with*," which is pretty understandable; but he adds these curious lines in the third poem of the sequence, **"The Cave of Making,"** to his recently deceased friend Louis MacNeice:

> I wish you hadn't
> caught that cold, but the dead we miss are easier
>   to talk to: with those no longer
> tensed by problems one cannot feel shy and,
>   anyway,
>   when playing cards or drinking
> or pulling faces are out of the question, what else
>   is there
>   to do but talk to the voices
> of conscience they have become? From now on, as
>   a visitor
>   who needn't be met at the station,

your influence is welcome at any hour in my ubity

. . .

MacNeice's ghost might well be pleased at being named a "voice of conscience," but perhaps a little uneasy at being considered a more welcome friend now that Auden doesn't have to go to the trouble of meeting his train, and presumably feeding him and finding him a bed. It is true that the dead, as friends, are remarkably little trouble, but even to hint that this makes them *better* friends is to betray an unhealthy pleasure in keeping the garden of one's daily routine well-tended and undisturbed.

Such a tendency provokes a disturbing question: is something like this fate inevitable for forms of local culture that are not, as Berry would have them be, rooted in a particular place? Is the project of building local culture in poems of recognition and gratitude an impossible one? "The houses of our City," Auden writes in another poem from **"Habitat," "Grub First, Then Ethics,"**

> are real enough but they lie
> haphazardly scattered over the earth,
>   and her vagabond forum
> is any space where two of us happen to meet
>   who can spot a citizen
> without papers.

But is this good enough? Can a *polis* worthy of the name be sustained by occasional meetings of *cognoscenti* and equally occasional poems from one *cognoscente* to others? It seems that Auden feared just that, since the poem goes on,

>   So, too, can her foes. Where the
>   power lies remains to be seen,
> the force, though, is clearly with them: perhaps
> only
>   by falling can She become
> Her own vision, but we have sworn under four
> eyes
>   to keep Her up . . .

This is a curious passage, because it suggests that Auden's attitude toward the local culture he had striven to build closely resembles his attitude toward the poetic art to which he had dedicated his working life. To Louis MacNeice's ghost he writes,

>   . . . Speech can at best, a shadow echoing
>   the silent light, bear witness
>   to the truth it is not . . . ,

but this is an old idea with him. From **"New Year Letter":**

> Yet truth, like love and sleep, resents
> Approaches that are too intense,
> And often when the searcher stood
> Before the Oracle, it would
> Ignore his grown-up earnestness
> But not the child of his distress,
> For through the Janus of a joke
> The candid psychopompos spoke.

This idea finds its fullest development in ***The Sea and the Mirror,*** where Caliban, "beating about for some large loose image to define" the experience, recorded in *The Tempest,* of the disillusion of magic and the acceptance of bounds, finally settles on this: "the greatest grandest opera rendered by a very provincial touring company indeed." Paradoxically, it is the very poverty and ineptitude of the production that makes it valuable to its actors, for even though "there was not a single aspect of our whole performance, not even the huge stuffed bird of happiness, for which a kind word could, however patronisingly, be said," nevertheless it is "at this very moment [that] we do at last see ourselves as we are." At the moment when all pretense to aesthetic achievement helplessly falls away, and the actors are confronted with the authentic selves which they had used their performances to escape, they come to see God precisely in their distance from Him:

> . . . we are blessed with that Wholly Other Life from which we are separated by an essential emphatic gulf of which our contrived fissures of mirror and proscenium arch—we understand them at last—are feebly figurative signs. . . . it is just here, among the ruins and the bones, that we may rejoice in the perfected Work that is not ours.

It is just when the would-be proximity of mimetic art to truth fails that the distance of analogy, with its "feebly figurative signs," manages somehow to succeed.

In **"Thanksgiving for a Habitat,"** Auden seems to be saying something quite similar about the City of which he is a voluntary and self-selected citizen: "perhaps only / by falling can She become / Her own vision." A chief purpose, then, of all humanly built cultures is to produce recognition of the gaping chasm that separates all earthly cities from the City of God, all earthly communities from the Communion of the Saints. The failures of such cultures, then, are not only to be expected but to be welcomed—but only if the effort to perfect them (or at least "keep them up") has been genuine. As Simone Weil never tired of saying, you can confront your weakness only if you have reached the actual limit of your abilities; failures due to laziness have no educational value.

9

Is this a perverse and fatalistic conclusion? Or, to the contrary, an unrealistically hopeful one? For the reader who can share Auden's belief in an eternal City of God, his message is chastening but ultimately reassuring: "All will be judged," he says to Henry James, but in the (later excised) last stanza of that poem he also finds comfort in those words from the Prayer Book about "Him whose property is always to have mercy, the author / And giver of all good things." For the reader who cannot share that faith, Auden may seem to rest too comfortably in his own inevitable failure to sustain any ideal order, however restricted in its scope and aims. Members of either party, however, should, it seems to me, give thanks to Auden—as I have said, he was always one for giving thanks—for having shown us just how complex and difficult a project the formation of community is, and just how many and how serious are the virtues required to keep it alive and well.

Nicholas Jenkins (essay date 1 April 1996)

SOURCE: "Goodbye, 1939," in *New Yorker*, April 1, 1996, pp. 88, 90-4, 96-7.

[*In the following essay, Jenkins provides an overview of Auden's literary career and the significance of his expatriation in the United States.*]

No episode in the century's English-speaking literary world came as more of a surprise than the poet W. H. Auden's abrupt departure, in January of 1939, from Britain for the United States. Auden was the first major English-language poet to be born in the twentieth century (in 1907); now, as the century drains away, it seems likely that he will turn out to be the only poet of world stature born in England in the last hundred years. He is more widely read than he has been for many years, both here and in England, and Auden scholarship is flourishing. (A multivolume *Complete Works* is under way and, along with several memoirs, two major biographies have been written: the most recent, from Pantheon, is Richard Davenport-Hines's absorbing *Auden.*) Auden was perhaps the most important English poet since Tennyson, and yet he never aged into the role of National Fossil, like the author of "Idylls of the King." In 1892, Tennyson was laid to rest in Westminster Abbey, attended by the Foreign Secretary, the Lord Chancellor, Henry James, and Sir Arthur Conan Doyle. In 1973, Auden was buried in an Austrian village graveyard, watched over only by family members and close friends. "In relation to a writer, most readers believe in the Double Standard," he once commented tartly. "They may be unfaithful to him as often as they like, but he must never, never be unfaithful to them."

Although the state of exile became a virtually de-rigueur element of the modernist condition, none of the major literary expatriates before Auden had left their own countries voluntarily while they were at the height of their reputations. (Joyce, Pound, James, Eliot, Stein, and Conrad all emigrated before they hit their stride.) For Auden, who by the end of the thirties was distressed and exhausted by his public role as the poetic spokesman for a set of left-wing causes he believed in only half-heartedly, his move was a kind of dying and a kind of rebirth. The first poem he completed in America was an elegy for W. B. Yeats, who had just died. But in it he also mourned his former self, his British readership, his familiar cityscapes. Within the space of little more than a year in New York, he entirely recast the terms of his life and his career. He started the process of becoming a United States citizen; he lost his faith in the power of politics to alleviate unhappiness; he fell in love for the first time; he went back to the church he had been in flight from since childhood; and he gained literary access to an inner world that he had never before been able to write about directly.

This may sound like a triumph, but to Auden's enemies and venerators alike the consequences of his migration looked very different. Many British critics felt—and feel—that he was never as great a poet once he left England. (They conveniently forget that most of the poems they think of as his best work were written when he was abroad for long periods in the thirties.) Young readers felt abandoned by their spiritual leader, and members of the literary establishment raged—often for decades. When Auden died, the novelist Anthony Powell peered over the top of his newspaper at Kingsley Amis and announced, "No more Auden." Amis murmured something about the shock, and Powell fired back, "I'm *delighted* that *shit* has gone. . . . Scuttling off to America in 1939 with his boyfriend."

Throughout the thirties, Auden, though never a Communist Party member, had given expression to the emotions of a broad coalition of liberal and left-wing anti-Fascists and anti-imperialists. His emigration in 1939 came to be seen as the first in a sequence of notorious leftist betrayals: he belonged to the disaffiliated generation that included the spies Burgess, Blunt, Philby, and Maclean—the first important clutch of traitors in British political life for hundreds of years. Auden's offense was, of course, vastly different from that of the spies, but he felt his dissidence had similar causes. In the fifties, he told a friend, "I know exactly why Guy Burgess went to Moscow. It wasn't enough to be a queer and a drunk. He had to revolt still more to break away from it all. That's just what I've done by becoming an American citizen." At a single stroke, Auden generated an enduring parable of the edgy relationship between writer and audience. And, in doing so, he established his own rootless modernity.

Auden grew up on the outskirts of industrial Birmingham, Britain's "second city," the third son of a cultivated doctor father and a highly religious (and highly strung) mother. They were Anglo-Catholics, and Mrs. Auden loved to inveigh against the feebly progressive notions of the Birmingham church hierarchy; Auden wrote that on Sundays in that grime-caked city their life was suffused with "music, candles, and incense." In this intense, cloistered atmosphere, Auden picked up a fascination with "medicine and disease, and theology"—the sicknesses of the body and the spirit. "Health is the state about which Medicine has nothing to say," he later noted. "Orthodoxy is the state about which Theology has nothing to say." Happiness, he might have added, on the evidence of his own work, is the state about which Poetry has nothing to say.

Like most upper-middle-class English boys, he was sent away to prep school while still young, and it was there that he met the future novelist Christopher Isherwood, who was to become his closest friend. Auden wrote his first lyrics at the age of fifteen, and at sixteen he began reading Thomas Hardy fanatically, studying him under the bedcovers and writing Hardyesque poems during study periods. He also began getting up early and going to his desk unwashed, setting rigorous schedules for his literary projects—treating writing, he said later, not as an inspirational mystery but as "a real occupation like banking or fucking, with all its attendant egotism, boredom, excitement and terror."

Auden went up to Oxford in 1925 as a scientist, but he soon switched to English, and spent his free time in his rooms, reading and writing poetry, much of it bad. Nonetheless, he impressed his college acquaintances with his intellectual authority, and in 1930 he burst onto the British poetry scene, under the sponsorship of T. S. Eliot, who was an editor at Faber & Faber, with a volume of cryptic lyrics called simply *Poems.* Over the next few years, Auden's writing established him as the leader of a group of young, more or less left-wing poets including Stephen Spender, Louis MacNeice, and Cecil Day-Lewis. What united these poets was not their largely ineffectual political attitudes but their fascination with the look and feel of modern Britain. (Literature's first television set appeared in Auden's work, in 1932.) One critic called them "communists with an intense love for England." In Auden, that love was particularly sensuous and direct. He produced huge vistas of England's mines and millscapes, and the jagged, deserted upper reaches of the northern Lake District—and he invested these scenes with a reverent, filial longing.

The counterpoint to this tender side in Auden's early poetry was a tone of laconic, sometimes portentous toughness. Like Kipling, he loved to preach and playfully hector. "Something is going to fall like rain / and it won't be flowers"; "Go down with your world that has had its day";

Auden could reel off lines that reeked of threat and outrage. To a generation of young readers, dismayed by the economic conditions in their country and by the long slide of history toward the Second World War, Auden seemed to possess a communal voice, an imagination that was eerily in contact with their own hopes, fears, and resentments. The thirties was a time of weak political leadership in Britain, and an early phrase of Auden's about England—"this country of ours where nobody is well"—soon became a touchstone. As he became more famous, even his casual opinions were noted in gossip columns.

Auden was tall and thin, with a pale complexion and a cowlick of sandy hair that often fell over his brow ("the great big white barbarian" is how he imagined himself); his accent was plummy and Oxonian. He was often messily clothed: torn trousers, ragged tie, frayed or stained shirt cuffs and collar. (The economist John Maynard Keynes described him as "very dirty but a genius.") He smoked almost nonstop, and his nails were bitten down to the quick. Late in life, Auden would write, "The way he dresses / reveals an angry baby, / howling to be dressed."

He was relentlessly self-critical, partly, no doubt, as a result of the guilt programmed into homosexuals by British society. And yet his feelings of inferiority were tangled, overdetermined; sex was only a part of the configuration. On one occasion, he said that he felt embarrassed in the presence of anyone who was not in some respect his superior ("It may be a large cock, it may be sanctity"); indeed, for all his awareness of his own powers he thought of himself as clumsy, myopic, timid, sentimental, and overintellectual—a stranger to the world of physical sensations and strong feelings who, consequently, was obsessed by them.

From the summer of 1936, the year of Auden's second celebrated collection, *Look, Stranger!,* until the winter of 1939, when he left England permanently, Auden was never at home for more than six months at a time. In those two and a half years, he became a compulsive wanderer, circling the globe with Isherwood and spending substantial amounts of time in Iceland, Belgium, Spain, and China. And even while his reputation soared in Britain (George VI himself presented Auden with the King's Gold Medal for Poetry in 1937) Auden's work, and his comments to his friends, had begun to take on a pessimistic, sardonic flavor. When *New Verse,* the most influential poetry magazine of the decade, published an "Auden Double Number," which was entirely devoted to pieces about Auden and his work, Auden contributed **"Dover,"** a deliberately flat poem that offered an entropic picture of George VI's "Great" Britain. "All this show / Has, somewhere inland, a vague and dirty root," he declared. For all "the vows, the tears, the slight emotional signals" that have become routine here, England, he said

coolly, has become "of minor importance." It was a calculated diminishment of his own poetic cult and of the country that had exalted him.

> **Duty and responsibility kept drawing
> Auden back to England but, though he was
> writing prolifically, he felt that his sources
> of inspiration were drying up.**
> —*Nicholas Jenkins*

In reminiscences of Auden from these years, one often finds
him sitting alone by a window brooding, or keeping osten-
tatiously silent in company. In mid-1938, Isherwood saw the
poet who the year before had written a poem in praise of a
one-night stand "in tears, telling me that no one would ever
love him, that he would never have my sexual success."
Auden had had boyfriends, of course, but, partly because
he was usually attracted to teenagers, had so far had no enduring love. Loveless, faithless, and successful, he was in
the grip of a strange predicament. When he was abroad, he
wrote brilliant poetry, and was often personally happy.
When he was at home, he lectured and exhorted, his poetry
grew brittle, and he was filled with a gloom bordering on
despair. He spent most of his time in England living, like
an overgrown simpleton, at his parents' house in Birmingham. "I felt that I had to make some kind of radical change,
not knowing what it would be exactly," he told an interviewer late in life. "I would say that I felt the situation in
England for me was becoming impossible. I couldn't grow
up." Duty and responsibility kept drawing Auden back to
England but, though he was writing prolifically, he felt that
his sources of inspiration were drying up.

Around this time, Auden got a letter from a young poet who was
sending him some poems. When Auden replied, he gave the young
man some advice that he himself was having trouble following:

> Remember that another poet's work is not a pair of
> spectacles, but a key with which to unlock one's
> nature and find its unsuspected treasures. Ask your-
> self constantly and remorselessly "What am I really
> interested in?" "What do I know for myself?"
> "What, in fact, *are* my experiences?" And however
> boring or silly those experiences may seem at first
> sight, those and those only can be the subject mat-
> ter of your poems. Make the fullest use you can of
> your *own* visual and emotional experiences.

In January, 1939, Auden and Isherwood were on a French
liner, the Champlain, as she labored westward. (The same
ship, celebrated at the end of **"Speak, Memory,"** would
ferry Vladimir Nabokov and his family to the New World
the following year, before she was sunk by a mine near Bor-

deaux.) In the midst of featureless North Atlantic waters,
the two men found themselves shuffling off the coils of a decade's
worth of public aspirations. They had reached a state of emotional
exhaustion with the leftist rallies, the speeches, the petitions, the
worried dinner-table discussions. "'You know,'" Isherwood remembered telling his friend as they stood on deck, "'it just doesn't
mean anything to me anymore—the Popular Front, the party line,
the anti-Fascist struggle. I suppose they're okay but something's
wrong with me. I simply cannot swallow another mouthful.' To
which Wystan answered, 'Neither can I.'"

The ship ran into a blizzard off Newfoundland and,
Isherwood recalled, sailed into New York Harbor "looking
like a wedding cake." On the morning of January 26, 1939,
he and Auden stood on deck—tiny pristine bride and bride-
groom figures perched high on the tiers of snow—and
watched the skyline emerge, like a photographic print, out
of a fresh storm. To Isherwood the image was a terrifying
vision of "the Red Indian island with its appalling towers. . . . The Citadel—stark, vertical, gigantic, crammed with
the millions who had already managed to struggle ashore
and find a foothold." But for all its prestige as the center of
an advanced civilization, Manhattan was still recognizably
Whitman's "City of the sea! city of hurried and glittering
tides!" There were cannons and steamship offices at the end
of lower Broadway, and stores there where you could buy
a sou'wester; the port's channels brimmed with a slew of
vessels—ferries, barges, tugs, liners, and fishing boats.

Like most English people arriving in the city, Auden and
Isherwood fell among the English. They moved into the
George Washington Hotel, on Lexington Avenue, an unfashionable edifice with an ornate, toffee-colored facade (it
is still there, sagging among exercise studios and welfare
hotels). The manager, Donald Neville-Willing, was a queeny
English émigré who exulted in the news that he and Isherwood
had mutual acquaintances in Cheshire. The results soon began
to flow: special weekly rates, free late-night toddies, invitations
to parties in Neville-Willing's sitting room.

Auden liked the George Washington so much that he eventually wrote a valedictory poem about it, and he explained
to Benjamin Britten that New York itself was one "grand
hotel" in a world so destabilized that everyone had become
a traveller. A friend who went to see Auden one morning
found him busy in his "cell-like room, puffing cigarettes
amid suitcases, books, papers, old clothes and grounded
wall-decorations." In this clutter, Auden set about extricat-
ing himself from his roots. Besides his elegy for Yeats, he
composed memorial poems for the socialist playwright Ernst
Toller, who hanged himself in the Barbizon Plaza Hotel, and
for Sigmund Freud. Together, the subjects of these poems
formed a trinity representing the secular ideologies of cure
that he had toyed with throughout the thirties: visionary poetry, Marxist politics, and psychoanalysis. In prose, Auden

soon added an elegy for his first master and "poetical father," Thomas Hardy.

For a few years, Auden had barely kept up with his own father. But in February of 1939 Auden got a letter from Dr. Auden which was mildly critical. In a recently discovered reply, now in the Bodleian Library, at Oxford, Auden argued back at length. "Sorry you didn't like the little poem in the *New Statesman*," he began, and he went on to provide answers to the accusations that would later be levelled against him by his English audience. To his father's Why? Auden responded with a Because:

> You say you would like to see me the mouthpiece of an epoch: so, of course, would I, but I want to explain to you what being a writer looks like from the inside. . . . Basically the writer's problem is that of everyone, how to go on growing the whole of his life, because to stop growing is to die. . . . Because the actions which express his growth, ie his writings, are public, there are peculiar temptations for a writer.

> 1. If he does something which is successful, the public want him to go on doing it. Now he often Can. When you say, for instance "I liked your work before you turned away from the Romantic," I know that I could quite easily go on turning out the kind of Romantic poetry I was doing, but it would be destruction for me to do it, however popularly successful it was. I don't say that my work then was worse than now. Very likely it was better; but to go on doing it when I feel different would be to be false to myself and to art.

As Auden foresaw, he was to suffer a lifetime of such reproaches. He went on:

> If he wants to be the mouthpiece of his age, as every writer does, it must be the last thing he thinks about. Tennyson for example *was* the Victorian mouthpiece in "In Memoriam" when he was thinking about Hallam and his grief. When he decided to be the Victorian Bard and wrote "Idylls of the King," he ceased to be a poet. . . .

> What an age is like is never what it thinks it is, which is why the best art of any period, the art which the future realizes to be the product of its time, is usually rather disliked when it appears.

The letter from Dr. Auden must have hit a nerve; Auden soon composed a poem about Matthew Arnold's dutiful and self-mortifying relationship with his headmaster father, the Victorian patriarch Thomas Arnold, and he inserted a third

section into the elegy for Yeats, adding his famous and oracular definition of his art—"Poetry makes nothing happen." He wrote that poetry survives as "a way of happening, a mouth." It is a strange, almost erotic image: poetry was to be not a hard, impersonal artifact—the "mouthpiece" his father had spoken of—but the warm, vulnerable, yielding organ of song, speech, and love.

For a while, Auden continued to be tempted by his old English role, that of the political prophet. Then, in March, 1939, at a dinner at the Commodore Hotel to raise money for people who had fled from Franco's forces in Spain, he realized how terrifying and nihilistic the experience of prophetic power could be. He gave a talk on the significance of the Spanish conflict in which he castigated intellectuals for being "so damn conceited, selfish and lazy." What, he asked, is the real meaning of democracy? He answered himself with a burst of humanitarian boilerplate about decency and caring. And then he ended by envisaging the apocalyptic dissolution of his own class. He exhorted his listeners to behave more like democrats in their private lives. If we don't, he said, it will be "our own people who will say 'To hell with talk, to hell with truth, to hell with freedom,' will rise up and sweep us away, and by God, ladies and gentlemen, we shall deserve it." His listeners erupted.

Auden's initial reaction was a sense of exhilaration. The poet who a few years before had been guiltily aware of the gap between himself and his English admirers discovered an audience that he could feel transmitting a surge of ecstatic energy to him. He explained to a friend, "I suddenly found I could really do it, that I could make a fighting demagogic speech and have the audience roaring. And, my dear, it is so exciting but so absolutely degrading; I felt just covered with dirt afterwards." The contact high that Auden had intermittently sought from his audience throughout the thirties suddenly revealed itself to him as a demonic temptation.

When Auden asserted in his Yeats elegy that poetry makes nothing happen, part of what he wanted to convey was that, in a world so full of active evil, he *hoped* that poetry—especially his own—was not responsible for making anything happen. "Never, *never* again," he swore to a friend, "will I speak at a political meeting." In fact, Auden's comments at his next major public appearance in New York, a month later, were an almost explicit refutation of the Commodore Hotel speech. He and Isherwood were booked to participate in a reading on "Modern Trends in English Poetry and Prose" at a social club called the Keynote, in midtown, run by the Marxist-dominated League of American Writers. The writer Selden Rodman, who was a member of the audience that night, wrote in his journal that Auden's first words came as "a bombshell." The famous left-wing poet opened with his new aesthetic creed:

I don't want there to be any mistake about the responsibilities of the writer or the limitations of art. Two hundred years from now nobody will care much about our politics. But if we were truly moved by the things that happened to us, they may read our poems. In his time Dante was a reactionary. It is also deplorable that Yeats' last poem calls for war. But because Yeats was one of those most rare writers who continued to be moved by what happened to him right up to the day he died, his work will always have that authentic ring we recognize as poetry.

After Auden, Isherwood, and Louis MacNeice took turns reading, there was a beer-and-pretzels party, at which Auden and Isherwood met a fleshy blond undergraduate, Chester Kallman, and his boyfriend, Harold Norse. "Our first impressions of Auden, slovenly in rumpled tweed, were of disbelief," Norse remembered. "His shirt was unpressed, heavy woolen socks bunched limply around his thick ankles, and untied shoelaces flopped over his shoes." When he got a chance, however, Norse edged his way over and introduced himself to Isherwood, who gave him a card with the address of the apartment that he and Auden were renting.

When Kallman turned up at the flat two days later, Auden was disappointed. "It's the wrong blond!" he whispered to Isherwood. But Auden, who had been instructing his audiences in the necessity of "being interested in your fellow human beings not as 'subjects for reform' but as equal human beings," was ready for something to fill the hole left by the collapse of his political ideals. Kallman proved to be an adept (and funny) conversationalist, as well as a desirable sexual trophy. He stayed to tea and came back a couple of days later. By the beginning of June, Auden wrote to his brother, "It's really happened at last after all these years. Mr Right has come into my life. He is a Roumanian-Latvian-American Jew called Chester Kallman. . . . This time, my dear, I really believe it's marriage."

Auden told another friend that he was "mad with happiness"—and insecurity. A few years later, he explained, "I never really loved anyone before, and then when he got through the wall, he became so much part of my life that I keep forgetting that he is a separate person, and having discovered love, I have also discovered what I never knew before, the dread of being abandoned and left alone." Kallman's reactions were divided. He was exhilarated by the affair at first ("Auden is in *love* with me!" he crowed to Norse), but he was only eighteen, and almost straightaway his eyes started to wander. Even on their "honeymoon" trip ("honeymoon" was Auden's term; "*Such* a romantic girl" was Kallman's comment) to the Southwest in the summer of 1939, Kallman wrote to Norse that he "almost precipitated a domestic crisis by groping a boy sitting next to me between Jacksonville and Tallahassee. . . . Wystan was quite rightly exasperated."

While Kallman delighted in his emotional hold on Auden, he was intimidated by Auden's literary powers. Staying at a ranch outside Taos, Auden worked at his prose and Kallman, who had literary ambitions of his own, tried to write poetry. But he complained that his efforts were subjected to ruthless scrutiny: "Wystan reads them like a foreman and god I suffer under that clinical gaze. . . . He hardly approves at all, except for lines here and there—and almost never the ones *I* liked."

Kallman's sense of the distance between his own efforts and Auden's rapidly increased: Auden wanted to devote himself to Kallman; Kallman wanted to absorb Auden's talent. In a notebook of Kallman's dating from 1939 or 1940, there is a page covered by false starts—more writhing than writing. One quatrain has a callow, gloomy pathos:

> Upon the porch my inspiration ceases
> But upstairs Wystan paces
> Like a horse before it races
> Intoning one by one his quickie
>   masterpieces.

As Auden and Kallman headed back East from their honeymoon, the political realities of 1939 became inescapable. Sitting in a railway carriage in the middle of Kansas at the end of August, Auden wrote to a friend, "There is a radio in this coach so that every hour or so, one has a violent pain in one's stomach as the news comes on." He arrived in New York just in time for Europe's descent into the maelstrom. Hitler invaded Poland on September 1, 1939, and that night Auden went, apparently alone, to a place called the Dizzy Club, on West Fifty-Second Street. It was probably there, in the noisy bar—"packed to the rafters with college boys and working-class youths" is how Norse described it—that Auden began one of his most famous poems, **"September 1, 1939."** It was another elegy, this time a farewell to his generation's "clever hopes," aspirations that he had in part been responsible for molding. The thirties had been called "the Age of Auden"; now Auden himself wrote off the entire "low dishonest decade." Yet, oddly, given that this is one of Auden's most sombre poems, the opening cadence is borrowed from one of America's great comic poets, Ogden Nash. Auden, in his early months in the States, had self-consciously searched for American local styles, and had written to a friend about his discovery of Nash's idiom, misquoting from the poem "Spring Comes to Murray Hill": "As I sit in my office / On 23rd Street and Madison Avenue." Auden's new poem begins, "I sit in one of the dives / On Fifty-Second Street."

But Nash's equable comic accent is drowned out by a more strident rhetoric as the American bar scene gives way to the supercharged power of global indictment:

> Into this neutral air
> Where blind skyscrapers use
> Their full height to proclaim
> The strength of Collective Man,
> Each language pours its vain
> Competitive excuse:
> But who can live for long
> In an euphoric dream;
> Out of the mirror they stare,
> Imperialism's face
> And the international wrong.

Auden wrote the poem over a weekend, but he would spend a good part of the rest of his life regretting it. He soon came to loathe what he felt was its sanctimoniousness and (as he saw it) the frivolity of its famous assertion that "we must love one another or die." In a letter to a friend who had admitted that she found it memorable, he fumed, "The reason (artistic) I left England and went to the U.S. was precisely to *stop* me writing poems like **'Sept 1st, 1939'** the most dishonest poem I have ever written. A hang-over from the U.K. It takes time to cure oneself."

But poems, like children, defy their creators. Auden later made dogged attempts to extirpate **"September 1, 1939"** from his canon, but it has become one of his most quoted works. You can see why Auden was dissatisfied. After presenting a despairing picture of individual isolation, Auden asks portentously:

> Who can release them now,
> Who can reach the deaf,
> Who can speak for the dumb?

There is no explicit answer, but the implication is that it is the poet who can restore contact and community to the lonely and the self-immured. Yet, in spite of this remorseless self-elevation, **"September 1, 1939"** continues to be an important poem. Not since Andrew Marvell's "Horatian Ode" had a poet made equivocation and doubt in the face of a major political event seem so representative a condition. As a piece of emotional reportage, Auden's threnody is a perfect register of the strangely muted onset of the century's worst event, and as long as we read poems for what they describe as well as for what they diagnose, it will remain one of the century's key lyrics.

The final, harsh epiphany of Auden's first year in the States occurred in early December, in a movie theatre in Yorkville, a predominantly German neighborhood on the Upper East Side and a stronghold of both Nazi and anti-Nazi activism.

Throughout the year, Auden had been drawing parallels between the power of the poet and the power of the dictator ("The Dictator who says 'My People': the Writer who says 'My Public,'" he scribbled in a bitter comment), and in Yorkville he saw a dynamic illustration of the state of violence that a dictator could whip up in an audience.

Among the films showing that day was a newsreel accompaniment to a sappy German comedy, "Das Ekel." The headquarters of the local Nazi *Bund* was above the cinema and, as Auden later told his old tutor Nevill Coghill, who asked him why he became a Christian, "Every time a Pole appeared on the screen, the audience shouted, 'Kill him!' What was remarkable about the film was the lack of hypocrisy. Every value I had been brought up on, and assumed everybody held, was flatly denied. I was forced to ask myself: 'If I think their values are wrong, what basic reason can I give?'"

A reviewer for the *Post* (at that time a liberal paper) was struck by the same thing as Auden. He reported in his column that, after a melee of shots from the battlefield, "there was a picture of Hitler reviewing his troops." Then, "As the solid blocks of soldiers marched past, goose-stepping almost off the ground . . . the 86th Street Garden Theatre burst into sudden and violent applause."

In a review Auden wrote shortly afterward he excoriated the contemporary world for "an ecstatic and morbid abdication of the free-willing and individual before the collective and the daemonic." He went on, "We have become obscene night worshipers who, having discovered that we cannot live exactly as we will, deny the possibility of willing anything and are content masochistically *to be lived.*" Within a few months, though, Auden had "willed" a momentous decision: in downtown Brooklyn, he took out the first set of papers necessary to change nationalities. In a draft of a poem he was working on at the time, he wrote, "'England,' 'La France,' 'Das Reich,' their words, / Are like the names of extinct birds."

"Nineteen thirty-nine was a very decisive year for me," Auden told an acquaintance on the first day of 1940. He had begun the transition from subject to citizen, from liberal progressive to orthodox Episcopalian believer. (In the fall of 1940, he tentatively started to go to church again, in Brooklyn Heights.) Little more than a year before, Isherwood had heard Auden complaining that no one would ever love him. But now, in his new collection, he wrote of surveying the Manhattan harbor "with a lover's eyes." And yet his happiness was short-lived. Since the first summer of their relationship, Kallman had been unfaithful, and in July of 1941 there was a showdown during which Kallman told Auden that he had taken another lover, and that he would never sleep with Auden again. (That seems to have been the one vow in life which Kallman actually kept.)

For a while, Auden went to pieces—weeping, raging, even contemplating violence against Kallman and his new lover. After one savage row, Kallman woke up to find Auden's nicotine-stained fingers squeezing his throat. Auden quickly relented as Kallman pushed him away, and, though they were to live together on and off for the rest of their lives, their now sexless relationship was never free of emotional and practical tensions. Auden tried to persuade himself that he was grateful for the torments; as he explained to a friend in January of 1942, Kallman "makes me suffer and commit follies, without which I should soon become like the later Tennyson."

In fact, by 1942 Auden was very far from being treated like the Victorian Poet Laureate by anyone in his old country. In February of 1940, Cyril Connolly, for instance, had written silkily of two "far-sighted and ambitious young men with a strong instinct of self-preservation, and an eye on the main chance, who have abandoned what they consider to be the sinking ship of European democracy." And Auden was attacked by the right wing as ferociously as he was decried by his old left-wing friends. The week before his new book of poems, *Another Time,* was published, during the period of the Battle of Britain, a Tory M.P. asked questions about Auden and Isherwood in Parliament, demanding to know whether they would be recalled for armed service. (Both had offered to return to Britain, but the government had told them to stay where they were.)

The assaults continued throughout the war. And shortly afterward the august Sir Desmond MacCarthy described Auden and Isherwood as "leaders of the young, champions of the oppressed, beacons of the future, thinkers, who, when civilisation and their fellow-countrymen were in danger, promptly left for Hollywood!"

The resentment, for some, remained intense even after the war began to fade into history. In 1955, the poet John Wain wrote that for a young poet "the Auden line" was no use after the war: "It was worn out even before it got smashed, and what smashed it decisively was not the war, but Auden's renunciation of English nationality." And in 1960 Philip Larkin declared that Auden had "lost his key subject and emotion . . . and abandoned his audience together with their common dialect and concerns."

Larkin was right—Auden *had* abandoned his bond with his English audience. It was a decision that he never regretted. After moving around the States for several years in the wake of the crisis with Kallman, Auden made his home in Manhattan, until the very final years of his life. Like Yeats, he had "remade" himself; and he went on doing so throughout his life. "Who am I now?" he asked in a poem in 1967, called, defiantly, **"Prologue at Sixty."** His answer suggested that while he had given up his English nationality, he had

not become an American. He defined himself instead as a citizen of a polyglot world of transients; he wrote that he was "a New Yorker."

Even as Auden endured the jeremiads launched at him and his work, there is no evidence that he ever felt that he was anywhere but at the center of his era. It was almost as if he suffered while he was still alive the decline in interest that hits most writers only after they die. Now, though, his status is higher than it has been for more than fifty years. Since his death, his words have been "scattered among a hundred cities," sometimes in ways that would have dismayed him. At least four of the past seven Presidents (Johnson, Reagan, Bush, and Clinton) have quoted Auden publicly to drive home political points. And the recent resurgence of his reputation has carried him beyond the confines of the merely "literary" audience. A couple of years ago, a pamphlet of Auden poems, *Tell Me the Truth About Love,* sold over two hundred thousand copies in Britain.

At first glance, the rise in Auden's stock makes sense. The qualities once singled out by hostile critics—his un-English fondness for philosophical theory, his religiousness, his homosexuality, his fascination with the marginal and the neglected, his rootlessness—now look eerily contemporary. But some of Auden's coolly skeptical qualities are being forgotten or glossed over, and the old, approachable communal bard of the thirties is again in the ascendant. This adds up to a limited notion of his significance. Auden wrote some of his greatest verse after he emigrated—vivid poetry full of slang and archaism, which stands at a slight angle to the world of the "normal" and the "natural" so as to cut into our everyday pieties.

But these are literary issues on which one can agree or disagree. The lasting significance of Auden's decision to emigrate to the United States is not the insoluble calculus of whether he would have written better had he stayed at home. After all, many writers stay put and slump disastrously. The main point about Auden's departure is simply that he left. And, in leaving, he did perhaps more than anyone else ever has to extend the horizon for British writers. He made it possible—made it mandatory, in fact—to conceive of a literary map on which London was not at the center of the world; he defined cultural allegiances as something provisional and chosen; he gave a faint but indelible italic slant to the word "*home.*" It wasn't a particular place, Auden wrote riddlingly in 1942. Instead, home was

> A sort of honour, not a building site,
> Wherever we are, when, if we chose, we might
> Be somewhere else, yet trust that we have
>   chosen right.

Charles Berger (essay date Fall 1997)

SOURCE: "Auden in Time of War," in *Raritan,* Vol. 17, No. 2, Fall, 1997, pp. 79-89.

[*In the following essay, Berger examines the content, structure, and central themes of "In Time of War."*]

Auden's poetry of the thirties is suffused by a sense of diffuse crisis, or crises—economic, social, military—so there is no clear line of demarcation separating peace and war in his poetry. In fact, there is very little represented peace in the early poems; moments of refuge are always shadowed by the sense of what they defend against. Early on, Auden tries to imagine the role of poetry during revolution, or in a postrevolutionary society. This is the plot of **"A Summer Night,"** written in 1933. By the end of the decade, however, revolution has given way to war and the concept of a social avant-garde seems already to belong to an unrecognizable past. Auden's journeys to the various sites of wars in Spain and China are balanced by his journeys away from these hot spots—to Iceland and New York. In any event, the journey often seems more important than the destination. Although it inhabits so many named places of contention, his poetry nonetheless seldom seems topical, except perhaps for the masterful **"Letter to Lord Byron,"** whose satirical brio feeds on direct hits. The common reader in all of us latches onto those titles and poems where the reference to historical time and place is most recognizable— **"Spain 1937," "September 1, 1939"**—which might be one reason for Auden's disavowal of them. But it is more characteristic of Auden to blur spatial and temporal markers. He assigns and disperses blame and guilt, equates and differentiates nations. Stances, attitudes, are identified as inimical to "our" health, but who exactly the enemy is remains unclear, nor can we easily identify who "we" are. The aggressor may not be identified, but the burden of the victim is clear, as in **"Refugee Blues,"** where Auden brilliantly uses the literal "burden" of the ballad, its tailing refrain, to accentuate the lament of the refugee and his lack of a responsive audience: "But they weren't German Jews, my dear, but they weren't German Jews."

The sonnet sequence **"In Time of War,"** later titled **"Sonnets from China"**—though apparently only one of the poems was actually written in China—plays as many variations upon the dialectic of topicality and distancing as one might imagine. First published in the Isherwood/Auden volume *Journey to a War* (1939), an account of the collaborators' fifteen-week "tour" of China in 1938 during the Sino-Japanese war, the twenty-seven poem sequence displays an acute sense of the difference between journeying to, and standing in the time of, a war. Auden takes extraordinary care to distinguish between observers and participants, but he also complicates the category of the observer, not limiting it simply to the touring poet/journalist who seldom came close to the front. (Indeed, the threat of Japanese air attacks behind the lines extended the concept of the "front.") One of the poem's most durable discoveries involves locating ways in which strategizing generals and tactical technocrats are themselves observers—with the power to send others to their deaths. Auden displays a sharp sense, even in 1938, of how bureaucratized the coming war will prove to be, how strong a role in slaughter will be played by "the intelligent . . . with all their instruments for causing pain"; by "the conversation of the highly trained"; by "bombardiers remote like savants." The world of difference between Auden and Yeats can be compressed into their contrasting representations of modern aerial bombardment. In **"Lapis Lazuli,"** written in 1936, no expertise is required to "Pitch like King Billy bomb balls in / Until the town lie beaten flat." No comparison I know of has been made between **"In Time of War"** and **"Lapis Lazuli,"** though such a cross-reading would be a valuable one. Think of Yeats's Chinamen, with their "ancient glittering eyes," perched above it all. Auden's exemplary Chinese man, on the other hand, is the dead soldier of the sonnet, "Far from the heart of culture he was used," who "added meaning like a comma, when / He turned to dust in China."

Before turning to a sustained reading of the sequence I need to say a word about which text I am using, for this is, after all, Auden, which means that the textual situation is a complicated one. **"In Time of War"** is the title of the "full" twenty-seven poem sequence as it appears in *Journey to a War.* Readers of Auden's *Collected Poems* will find a revised, rearranged twenty-one poem sequence called **"Sonnets from China."** Those using the Edward Mendelson edition of the *Selected Poems* will find the "original" longer poem once again under the title **"In Time of War."** But there is still another choice, the text of the poem in Mendelson's *The English Auden,* where we find the full sequence *plus* the crucial dedicatory sonnet to E. M. Forster, which served as the dedicatory epigraph to the whole volume, *Journey to a War.* I characterize the Forster sonnet as crucial because Auden himself chose to end **"Sonnets from China"** with a revised version of the poem. Mendelson makes the sonnet to Forster something of an epigraph for the sequence, which strikes me as an inspired move. So, it is this fullest version of the poem, the one in *The English Auden,* that I regard as giving the reader more interpretive choices than any other. This is important, because I share Mendelson's opinion that **"In Time of War"** is "Auden's most profound and audacious poem of the 1930's." But it seems to me that readers are kept from realizing the full power of this poem when they cannot even be sure what to call it, nor how many sonnets it contains, nor where it really begins and ends. Tedious textual untangling of the sort that I have just had to perform can only get in a reader's way.

The opening dozen sonnets of **"In Time of War"** enact that *Journey to a War* of the volume's title, for they describe a genealogy and a chronology, if not a history, of civilization that, while inexorably forward marching, also demonstrates, at every turn, the inextricable involvements of culture with violence, progress with error. (*Error*, especially, is a crucial term in the sequence; its closing poem announces that we are "articled to error," as if this were an inherited fallibility.) The sonnets from this first movement of the sequence, though marked by archaic tokens and topoi, avoid any reference to specific place and time, thereby keeping a schematic open-endedness, an allegorical applicability to all times and places; they belie their prefatory stationing in the poem by their ever-present descriptive usefulness.

VI

He watched the stars and noted birds in flight;
The rivers flooded or the Empire fell:
He made predictions and was sometimes right;
His lucky guesses were rewarded well.

And fell in love with Truth before he knew her,
And rode into imaginary lands,
With solitude and fasting hoped to woo her,
And mocked at those who served her with their hands.

But her he never wanted to despise,
But listened always for her voice; and when
She beckoned to him, he obeyed in meekness,

And followed her and looked into her eyes;
Saw there reflected every human weakness,
And saw himself as one of many men.

VII

He was their servant—some say he was blind—
And moved among their faces and their things;
Their feeling gathered in him like a wind
And sang: they cried—"It is a God that sings"—

And worshipped him and set him up apart,
And made him vain, till he mistook for song
The little tremors of his mind and heart
At each domestic wrong.

Songs came no more: he had to make them.
With what precision was each strophe planned.
He hugged his sorrow like a plot of land,

And walked like an assassin through the town,
And looked at men and did not like them,
But trembled if one passed him with a frown.

These are not moments to be put behind us, for we have overcome nothing they emblematize. "We," now, are equally that "he" of poem after poem who begins by exerting his strong predilections, but ends, time and again, defeated, implicated, bewildered. As Stan Smith describes it: "Each of these crises of disappointment is a social and an epistemological one, and **'In Time of War'** links the two by situating each sonnet as a moment of knowledge in a particular knowing subject—a moment which carries with it, too, a complementary ignorance, that finally puts an end to that moment." The only concession Auden makes to the historicity of these vignettes comes by way of the speed of his narration, as the rise and fall of cultural actors and actions, the completion of cycles, are captured in portrayal, if not fully apprehended. They become, therefore, examples of poetic historiography, as opposed to history proper.

Within the sequence as a whole, the present, the in-time of war, arrives in sonnet 13, interestingly enough, with a song of praise: "Certainly praise: let the song mount again and again / For life as it blossoms out in a jar or a face . . . Some people have been happy; there have been great men." Though "history, always, opposes its grief to our buoyant song," though Auden has presented the genealogy of culture operating with a kind of machine-like precision, the story is not predetermined or fatalistic. Men and women, as sonnet 2 tells us, were not expelled from the garden: "They left." From sonnet 13 on, **"In Time of War"** is studded with references to the present, to the here and now; within this particular sonnet there is a strong homophonic pun on "hear" and "here": "But hear the morning's injured weeping." The fourteenth sonnet might be said to initiate full moral cognition of history's lesson to the autobiographer: the calamities that have happened to others can indeed happen to *me,* "who never quite believed they could exist, / Not where we were." This poem also marks an interesting counterpoint to a moment narrated by Isherwood in another passage from the book. Passing a Japanese gun emplacement, Auden and Isherwood were somewhat disappointed when the guns did not open fire. In a remark perfectly poised between a lament and a boast, Auden says: "You see, I told you so . . . I knew they wouldn't . . . nothing of that sort ever happens to *me.*"

Three poems later in the sequence there is a stunning rhyme of "now" with "Dachau," pointing to the unreadability of the still-to-be-revealed present. The sonnet in which this rhyme occurs, "Here war is simple like a monument," tells us much about Auden's attitude toward the poet's task and the poet's limits with respect to representing a violent or evil present. The sonnet points to the growing abstractness involved in the conduct of a modern war, with its emphasis on communication, with indeed the predominance of communication, so that "a telephone is talking to a man." Auden concentrates on the distant, removed strategist of war, the engineer or tactician with his penchant for maps, plans, ideas, he who most tellingly embodies the abstracting tendency of culture itself, as predicted in the earlier genealogical sonnets. Occasionally, the map points to a place whose name alone does indeed mean something: "Nanking, Dachau."

> But ideas can be true although men die,
> And we can watch a thousand faces
> Made active by one lie:
>
> And maps can really point to places
> Where life is evil now:
> Nanking, Dachau.

The close conjunction of *life* and *evil* points to the latent material or graphic pun spelled out by the word *evil* itself: *live* spelled backwards, the reversal of life, the turning of life against itself. *Evil* is a strong word for Auden; his customary terms of reproach more often involve words such as *error* or *mistake*. But the map simply points. The poet/observer follows the pointing, takes the point. It is worth nothing that Nanking and Dachau are the first named places to enter **"In Time of War."** They disturb the poem's level anonymity. These named places cannot yet be schematized, nor can they simply be equated with earlier places. They punctuate their present uniqueness with the simple punctuation of a period. They breed no commentary, as yet. They mark a point of silence.

"In Time of War" searches constantly for what the poet might indeed say—not so much in order to change history, as to avert, or interrupt some persons from their destructive course, and to cheer up others who are tempted to despair. Those familiar with the poem might recognize in my words allusions to the poem's overt gestures toward two modern writers never before or since conjoined, but here placed alongside each other as complementary figures who show, each in his different way, some strong use of his art to save, in a limited sense, himself and some others. These figures are Rilke and Forster. Rilke died in 1926, Forster, though living until 1970, published his final novel, *A Passage to India*, in 1924. When we note how many of Auden's poems from the mid-thirties through the early forties are addressed to writers, we should also observe that almost all of these figures were dead. This cannot simply be explained in terms of some elegiac imperative, for many of these poems were not addressed to the recently dead—witness the poems to Melville, Byron, Voltaire, Rimbaud, Edward Lear, Henry James, Rilke. The better question is: why was Auden so open to commemorating dead writers? What equation between the writer and death struck him so forcefully that he sought these subjects? And how might it have been related to his sense of imminent, or arrived, global catastrophe?

Rilke and Forster float to the surface in Auden's account as if they were the modern avatars of those anonymous, genealogical ancestors limned in the first part of **"In Time of War."** Of the present time, they are granted features, marks of identity, no longer recognizable in their precursors, though vestiges of schematic or anonymous portrayal still remain. But the question arises: do they change in any way the balance of power between poet and prince?

To E. M. Forster

> Here, though the bombs are real and dangerous,
> And Italy and King's are far away,
> And we're afraid that you will speak to us,
> You promise still the inner life shall pay.
>
> As we run down the slope of Hate with gladness
> You trip us up like an unnoticed stone,
> And just as we are closeted with Madness
> You interrupt us like the telephone.
>
> For we are Lucy, Turton, Philip, we
> Wish international evil, are excited
> To join the jolly ranks of the benighted
>
> Where Reason is denied and Love ignored:
> But, as we swear our lie, Miss Avery
> Comes out into the garden with the sword.

XXIII

> When all the apparatus of report
> Confirms the triumph of our enemies;
> Our bastion pierced, our army in retreat,
> Violence successful like a new disease,
>
> And Wrong a charmer everywhere invited;
> When we regret that we were ever born;
> Let us remember all who seemed deserted.
> To-night in China let me think of one,
>
> Who through ten years of silence worked and waited,
> Until in Muzot all his powers spoke,
> And everything was given once for all;
>
> And with the gratitude of the Completed
> He went out in the winter night to stroke
> That little tower like a great animal.

I have already discussed the different positioning of the sonnet to Forster in the different versions of the sequence. But it is important to mention that in the ordering of *The Collected Poems*, the Rilke sonnet is third from last, so the two poems are more openly connected. Auden changes some of the lines but the explicit dedication to Forster remains. Rilke, on the other hand, is never named directly, only kenningly referred to by way of Muzot, his Swiss minicastle. Rilke and Forster emerge, necessarily, as differing paradigms, but it is also important to think about the peculiar way each is invoked within the poem. Auden's quirky way of summoning each figure into the poem might put us on guard against glorifying mere aesthetic solutions to political and social problems.

The poem calls on Rilke without naming him openly, relying on the reference to Muzot, or perhaps to the tower, to spark recognition. This obscure, insider's reference asks the reader to acknowledge the myth of Rilke, or at the very least his celebrity, all of which is nicely supported by the heraldic tower, site of sublime poetry from Milton to Yeats. (Could one ever imagine Auden inhabiting a tower?) Yeats, a more pertinent example for Auden than Rilke, garners more critique than homage in the famous elegy. But Rilke, whose politics were fairly problematic in their own right, whose appeals to versions of organic selfhood could only have aroused skepticism and alarm in Auden, whose very pose as poet was so theoretically inimical to Auden—this same Rilke comes close to standing as a lonely figure of resistance, a rallying point for all who feel "deserted." He is said to have been "Completed" by his vision—quite a Yeatsian condition—which of course means that death was soon to follow. This sheds some light, perhaps, on Rilke's curious position in the sequence, for two sonnets earlier Auden writes: "The life of man is never quite completed." The kind of completion achieved by Rilke, and sought here by Auden as consolation in a moment of political despair, represents a profound renunciation of the poet's role in struggle as enunciated in **"Spain 1937,"** or the poet's role in the evolution of society, as seen in **"A Summer Night"** from 1933. But perhaps the most interesting way of contextualizing the example of Rilke is by reading him back into those earlier portraits of poet figures from what **"In Time of War"** leads us to believe is an earlier historical time. Sonnets 6 and 7, which I quoted earlier in the essay, excavate ancient models of sublime poets who are undone when they discover that they are "one of many men," or "tremble" if they are disapproved of. The independent, interpretive reader is led by Auden, I believe, to tie Rilke back into these examples, or to read those examples forward toward him, as a way of gaining perspective on the modern poet's supposed singularity. Rilke's greatness is cast in the image of the ancient. He is dangerous because alluring, and especially alluring in time of war, yet Auden nonetheless calls on him.

The example of Forster, whether placed at the head of the sequence in the form of a dedication, or used as the final, coda-like poem, is less generic than Rilke. Nothing about Forster, at first glance, appears to be in the high-heroic mold.

Here is Isherwood from his 1961 book, *Down There on a Visit,* explaining what Forster stood for in 1938—to him and, presumably, to Auden as well:

> Well, *my* England is EM: the antiheroic hero, with his straggly mustache, his light, gay, blue baby eyes and his elderly stoop. Instead of a folded umbrella or a brown uniform, his emblems are his tweed cap (which is too small for him) and the odd-shaped brown paper parcels in which he carries his belongings from country to town and back again. While the others tell their followers to be ready to die, he advises us to live as if we were immortal. And he really does this himself, although he is as anxious and afraid as any of us, and never for an instant pretends not to be. He and his books and what they stand for are all that is truly worth saving from Hitler; and the vast majority of people on this island aren't even aware that he exists.

Forster threatens to break the mold; nothing in the genealogical scheme of the opening sonnets prepares us for an artistic figure who interrupts us. The word bears thinking about: to interrupt is to break continuity, which is what a modern novelist like Forster might be said to do—far more so than Rilke. He checks us. One way he does so is by reminding us that the inner life shall pay, even as we lose ourselves in Hate, which Auden seems to equate with engagement in International Evil—either to resist that evil, or to promote it. Forster might seem an odd sponsor of the inner life but it is precisely because he avoids "the little tremors of the mind and heart" that he captures, according to Auden, the true measure of inwardness. Forster's distance from song, from *melos,* his channeling of his writing spirit into characters, leads Auden to make the reader dwell on the particulars of Forster's fictional world. Named fictional characters enter the poem—Lucy, Turton, Philip, Miss Avery—who serve as guarantors of the artist's engagement with the materiality of the world. Furthermore, this is a world seen not as international evil but as local complication. The enemy, as the example of Forster teaches, is abstraction—though Auden himself is much given to it, as the first part of **"In Time of War"** demonstrates. Forster cannot be read abstractly; his characters must be hasped onto.

The example of Miss Avery, outside her context, is unintelligible. She is the ghostly housekeeper of *Howard's End* who appears in the garden at the end of the climactic chapter 41, after Charles Wilcox has hit Leonard Bast with the *blade* end of the sword: "They laid Leonard, who was dead, on the gravel; Helen poured water over him. 'That's enough,' said Charles. 'Yes, murder's enough,' said Miss Avery, coming out of the house with the sword."

By citing so peculiar a moment, so idiosyncratic an event—

though one that ends with emphasis on the prototypical sword—Auden advocates a kind of pointed, nonabstract warfare. This sword-in-hand moment comes by means of a fictional character, a woman, who only uses the sword to rebuke the lie of a man who claims not to have really used it. Auden says that Miss Avery "comes out" as "we swear our lie," thus equating us with Charles Wilcox. The point here, I think, is that the sword gathers authority for Auden as long as it is *not* used for what it was intended. Auden—through Forster through Miss Avery—invokes the sword only to use it against the grain.

This is how writers resist, as writers, In Time of War, according to Auden in 1938.

Robert L. Caserio (essay date Fall 1997)

SOURCE: "Auden's New Citizenship," in *Raritan,* Vol. 17, No. 2, Fall, 1997, pp. 90-103.

[*In the following essay, Caserio discusses Auden's attitudes toward civic allegiance, the significance of his emigration to the United States, and the association of homosexuality with exile.*]

W. H. Auden underwent two conversions: one to Christianity, one to American citizenship. We treat the first conversion seriously. We have no serious account of the second. Is it a sign of our confused or divided attitudes towards citizenship that we gloss over the poet's manner of belonging to—or of appearing to own—one political state rather than another? Yes, we acknowledge Auden's civic voices. But as we work out the meanings of the poet's civic dimension, our understanding of the poet's feelings about civic attachments gets obscured by a typically Audenesque sleight-of-hand. We ask the post-1938 Auden to show us his proof of citizenship, his passport, so that we can examine the impact of concrete national allegiance on his civism; and what Auden extends in response are ambiguous identity papers from some timeless zion. Accordingly, we leap into spiritual dimensions, and read the poems, in spite of their relation to modern nationalism and the function of national citizens, not in terms of the realities of secular pledges of allegiance, but in terms of relatively unreal cities or city-states: with reference either to a sacred Kingdom, or to a secular civic model that is highly abstract and generalized. Criticism's preponderant attention to the spiritual city-state informs Anthony Hecht's recent study of Auden; and the abstract model, which turns citizenship into an exemplary habit of reading, not tied to historical national conditions, informs John R. Boly's *Reading*

Auden. I cannot hope to compete with Heeht's grace or Boly's analytic power. And there is certainly good reason for the critical tradition of connecting Auden to the city of God and utopia. But we have to think more about how Auden's abstract ideals are built upon the specifics of his shifting national ties.

As a start, I argue that Auden, even as he turns from one national citizenship to another, acts out, in his own terms, a conversion of citizenship itself, a new paradoxical—indeed perverse—characterization of it. Taking out American citizenship papers, Auden repudiates detached political neutrality; at the same time, by becoming a U.S. citizen during the wartime composition of *New Year Letter, For the Time Being,* and *The Age of Anxiety,* the poet uses the poems to redefine what it means to be a modern national. The redefinition limns the uncertainty of one's political passport. Auden's new citizenship strikes me as better figured by the displaced person, the real counterpart of the mythical Wandering Jew, than by the citizen who has a local habitation to which he can securely give a name. The subject and the origin of Auden's civic voice canonizes not a state of inclusion, but a state of allegiance-on-the-move, a refugeeism, whereby neutral citizenship is both canceled and reinstated. The refugee isn't *settled* by citizenship papers. Instead, Auden's new version of citizenship canonizes eccentric exile and involves a temporary act of allegiance at whose center a *pledge* of allegiance is absent. This is no merely abstract or spiritual condition. The poet's life as well as the poet's poems work to make his reader see that the dignity of citizenship inheres in a concretely enacted state of being *between* or *among* nations, and not *in* or *of* one. The state of wandering is one's refuge; and this state is what a new idea and practice of citizenship needs to admit, and be owned by. It's a pure inversion of the norm. The elevation of the refugee as the model, and not the antitype, of citizenship is influenced in Auden's case by his homosexuality. A refugee eros, no less than a refugee status and no less than a Christianity that is more renegade than orthodox, constitutes the passe partout that identifies citizen Auden.

Before moving to the verse, since I want Auden's life to bear on the readings to come, I need to rehearse the facts of Auden's conversion to the American State. In the fall of 1938, crossing the U.S. upon his return with Isherwood from China, Auden decided to emigrate from England. Once in New York at the start of 1939, and having fallen in love with Chester Kallman, Auden's intentions gained a motive: "I shall have to become an American citizen, as I'm not going to risk separation through international crises." But instead of international crises. Auden's taking on paying jobs in America violated his work visa, and risked the separation. To repair the violation, U.S. immigration advised Auden, in the fall of 1939, to go to Canada, and to return to the States as one of the quota of British immigrants from north of the border.

Thus by November of 1939, on returning from Canada, Auden had emigrated to America twice. He applied for citizenship, and registered for the draft in 1940, concurrent with the writing of *New Year Letter.* Auden's next long poem, *For the Time Being,* spans the end of 1941—not long after Auden discovered Kallman's secret infidelity (since late 1940) with an English merchant marine sailor—and September, 1942, when Auden was rejected by the draft board on account of his homosexuality. *For the Time Being,* as we shall see, uses the Nativity story in order to meditate on fidelity and infidelity in gay marriage, and on citizenship and exile; and the start of *The Sea and the Mirror* belongs to the moment of the draft board rejection. During the composition of these poems, Auden's citizenship application was in suspense. In 1943, still not a citizen, Auden began *The Age of Anxiety;* then, in the spring of 1945, with the war in the East continuing, Auden signed on to the Morale Division of the Pentagon's U.S. Strategic Bombing Survey in Germany. The rejected applicant to the draft board thus became a uniformed major, investigating, in a whirlwind five-month tour, the effects of American destruction on German civilians. It was not until May, 1946, six months before finishing *The Age of Anxiety,* that Auden became a citizen. One of the benefits of citizenship was eligibility for the Pulitzer Prize: *The Age of Anxiety* won in 1948-49. If we want to see the history of Auden's citizenship as the story of a successful reattachment of a civic voice from one nationality to another, it is notable that at this time the U.S. Navy reportedly purchased numerous copies of the poet's work.

These are the bare facts about Auden the citizen. But they are barely the facts. Apart from the erotically driven reason for citizenship, they give us no facts about Auden's motivations. And the facts show signs of factitiousness. Consider the story of the Navy's tasteful bent for Auden's poetry. Humphrey Carpenter's biography says the Navy bought eleven hundred copies of *The Collected Poetry* of 1945; Richard Davenport-Hines's biography says that the Navy ordered one thousand copies of *The Age of Anxiety,* the Pulitzer-prize winner. Are these two different purchase orders? The biographies don't answer, for the biographies don't document the orders—they say only that *Auden* is the source of the story; and they do not say where or when Auden tells this tale. Could the military purchases be an Auden fantasy, the result of his wishful thinking that *The Age of Anxiety* be a grammar for a new American citizenship? It would be a grammar ratified by the very armed forces which had treated queer Auden with the same anxiety with which, in Auden's poem, the U.S. Navy man, Emble, treats the sexual desire evinced for him by the poem's Canadian flier, Malin. For the Navy to be enamored

of *The Age of Anxiety,* given the homosexuality in the poem and what we will see to be the poem's version of citizenship, is a sort of joke Auden well might have invented.

Humphrey Carpenter complains that in 1940-41 Auden's thoughts about citizenship had "no apparent consistency." But Carpenter's complaint is unreliable, for he can not accept the consistent neutrality exhibited by Auden towards both citizenship status and enlistment, even as Auden pursued them. Auden "does not seem to have faced whether he had a moral duty to help . . . in the fight against Hitler," Carpenter asserts, thereby echoing Erika Mann's infuriation in 1940-41 at her husband Auden's "neutral manner" towards the conflict. (We must remember that Auden had married the refugee Mann in 1935 to make *her* an *English* citizen.) Auden's neutrality expresses itself in 1940 when he tells E. R. Dodds that America gives one the chance "to live deliberately without roots": a phrase in which Auden nicely fuses citizenship with permanent rootlessness, and a neutral manner with non-neutral opposition to virulent nationalism. And Auden also associated America with an embrace of loneliness, of a *common* loneliness, in a community whose essence is detachment. Again in 1940, in an essay on Rilke, Auden writes of the "courage" of political neutrality, and of a person's neutral dissociation from the state, which dissociation he says is "not to be confused with selfish or cowardly indifference." And while in 1941 Auden expresses to Spender an absolute impatience with pacificism, Auden's ties with Isherwood, who just then was about to become a conscientious objector, might have set up within him a check on his impatience. At the very time of the draft board rejection in 1942, Auden in Ann Arbor writes a poem, apparently lost, called "In War Time," expressing distrust of the combat. On patriotism's erotic front, meanwhile, we should probably include Auden's surprising love affair with Rhoda Jaffe in 1945-46 as entangled with the move towards citizenship: the affair not only avenges Kallman's infidelity, it shows the draft board, three years later, the stupid inflexibility of their erotic criteria for assessing a person's public value; and, understood as a masculinist experiment, it sets the stage, perhaps, for Auden's signing on with the Pentagon Survey team. Yet, no less than the Navy's book orders, this signing on resists explanatory documentation. Neither Carpenter nor Davenport-Hines can tell us *how* or *why* Auden undertook this Pentagon job. And Auden's report of his work has vanished. We only know (from a letter to Tania Stern) that he saw horrible effects of "wicked" American bombing, that on the verge of citizenship he documents his new country's depredations.

Perhaps the capstone irony of Auden's changing national allegiances is the fit between the moment of his Pulitzer, and his simultaneous struggle to award the Bollingen Prize not to the echt-American William Carlos Williams but to the traitor Ezra Pound. For this successful action Auden was widely abused in the press, so that we see in 1948-49 a repetition of attacks made on him in 1938-39 by the English press, and by some members of Parliament, for his alleged indecent desertion of the State and of a citizen's responsibilities. Thus within ten years of emigration, and within two years of the ratification of his new citizenship papers, Auden is already moving into the next expatriation. In 1951, in an essay on Auden and Rilke, D. J. Enright attacks Auden for using the imagination as a form of "dereliction of duty . . . even treason"; in the same year Auden finds himself involved, innocently, in the defection from England by the queer traitors Guy Burgess and Donald Maclean. Auden sympathizes with them, to the point of identifying his American citizenship with, of all things, a defection to Russia. "I know . . . why Guy Burgess went to Moscow," Auden explained in 1959, twenty years after leaving England. "It isn't enough to be a queer and a drunk. He had to revolt still more. . . . That's . . . what I've done by becoming an American citizen . . . crossed to the wrong side of the tracks." By 1959, however, Auden already had long crossed over from, or double-crossed, his American tracks. Isn't putting it this way justifiable, given that Auden's first trip to Ischia—his first voyage of disengagement from America—takes place in 1948? Carpenter quotes a poem from 1948, **"A Walk After Dark,"** and approvingly quotes a critic who calls the poem "a fitting farewell to [Auden's] American period." It's a sign of how little attention criticism has paid to Auden's acting out of the meanings for citizenship in the American period that Carpenter can notice this "fitting farewell" without blinking an eye. The poem is the farewell of a citizen whose American period lasted, legalistically speaking, for two years.

Motives are always what's lacking, or rather what's always cunningly hidden, in Auden's life and in his poetry.
—*Robert L. Caserio*

The Age of Anxiety, written along the way of Auden's path to citizenship, winner of a prize reserved for American citizens, is about the way in which, for Auden, real citizens—those worthy of the name because they redeem the name—have no national roots. The true citizen, the one we now need to value and to identify with authentic public virtue, is the one without a country. Of the poem's four characters, only Emble is American-born—and the narrative function of the poem's other characters is to exorcise Emble, to banish or exile the one man who is legally, by birthright, most American. The other characters are Malin, the queer Canadian airman; Quant, an Irish-born son of a refugee father who assassinated a landlord during the Troubles; and then, most importantly, Rosetta, the woman without a home

or a country. Since Rosetta describes herself as Time's stone or bedrock, presumably Auden wants us to think of her as Rosetta *née* Stein: although her home once was a tight little Island, she also has lived in Babylon and, at the poem's end, sits on her light luggage, waiting to leave if called to some new exile. The refugee who is a Wandering Jewess is the new muse—the new type and not the antithesis of citizenship. After all, the poem's part 2, which is about "The Seven Ages" of life, suggests that universal temporal patterns neither explain nor assuage "a sad unrest / which no life can lack." Explanation and assuagement seem promised, rather, by a seven-stage quest for "rare community" which Rosetta initiates in the poem's third part. But the quest is baffled. "The penultimate step is the State / Asylum"; but the ultimate state is always a stage yet to come, is transitional and transitory. The sad unrest is to be re-envisioned, and embraced. "To get on," to move on, "though passports expire," is a goal and a value for the poem's picture of community as well as for Rosetta. Only by emphasizing a passport-less goal for the poem, and the rootlessness of the Rosetta-Quant-Emble trio, can we approach the poem's motives.

Motives are always what's lacking, or rather what's always cunningly hidden, in Auden's life and in his poetry; above all, Auden's ventriloquial style—his ventriloquial *obsession*—loads his work with incitements for us to question his motives. What's his motive for becoming an American citizen? What's his motive for writing about it this way in *The Age of Anxiety,* for choosing these archaic metrics, this weird, anticolloquial, scarcely civic diction? As Boly points out, the difficulty of following the sense of the forward movement of Auden's verse tends to block, even to overrule, our usual questions about why it goes forward in the mode it does. We just want to keep hold of the sense, which is invitingly there, in spite of the complex voices in which the sense is distorted. But our grasp of Auden's sense can't go forward until we push back against the ventriloquism, until we hypothesize reasons for the disruptive voices or the discontinuity of tones that constitutes the headlong Auden intricacy.

In *The Age of Anxiety* a celebration of rootless refugees, of postnational wanderers, motivates the intricate vagaries of the poet's voices. But the style of the poem covers up, no less than it expresses, the motivation. It is as if the style plays for the verse the part that citizenship is supposed to play for the uprooted. The style *appears* to give the wanderers' voices and their wandering sense a permanent home. The style, as it were, repatriates the erring sense. But the repatriation is, as Auden works it out, itself the error. Repatriation is no stopping-place, repatriation takes no hold. No wonder one of the poem's mottos—at the start of "The Seven Stages"'s baffled search for a settled community—is, from Verdi's *Aida,* "O Patria, patria! Quanto mi costi!" Fatherland and motherland cost too much because their stability and security does not pay. In exiling Emble's presence from them, the others in *The Age of Anxiety* exorcise repatriation itself.

To put it this way gives one a key to Auden's motive for casting the exilic finale of *The Age of Anxiety* in a style that ventriloquizes *Finnegans Wake*. Edmund Wilson, excited into incoherence by his enthusiasm for Auden's poem and by his simultaneous disgust for Auden's assumption of Joyce's voice—an assumption that clogs the forward wandering transit of the poem's sense—in 1947 fired off a letter to Auden: "Your regurgitation of the last pages of [*The Wake*] in [Rosetta's final] speech over the sleeping [Emble] . . . is [your] only misstep." "Aside from the echo of Joyce," Wilson concludes his letter, "*The Age* really rivals *Finnegans Wake*." *Aside* from the echo of Joyce, Wilson thereby complains, Auden is *the same* as Joyce. Wilson's illogic shows him struggling with the hiddenness of Auden's compositional motives. Why *does* Auden's finale turn up the Joycespeak already mutedly present in the poem, so that Rosetta talks like Joyce's Anna Livia Plurabelle? One reason is that the Joyce style allows the verse to be composed in the key of exile. The Irish refugee's offspring Quant has a propensity to translate life into myth: in his figure, therefore, Joyce the mythmaker is encoded. Rosetta is something like a female emanation of Quant, for her vocation is to "make up mythical scenes" in which to enwrap ordinary citizens: the kind who like Emble think they're at home in any nationality-centered residence. She makes up "the Innocent Place where / . . . the leaves are so thick" that everyone can think patria is Eden.

But Auden's use of Joyce is double-edged. It suggests that insofar as Joyce makes myths, Joyce uses *his* A.L.P.-Rosetta, and *his Wake* to turn our world back into myth, and to relocate displaced Eden in a rediscovered hermetic-Edenic garden of historical and etymological "roots." In contrast Auden's uprooted Rosetta-A.L.P. reveals the illusion that is her own mythmaking. In fact her mythology aims to enclose the world's Embles in the delusion they pursue. What is the delusion? Emble is a male coquette, wanting men like Malin as well as women like Rosetta to desire him. He is not a willful tease—he just can't help it, any more than those smitten by him can help being smitten. He desires to be consumed, erotically, by both genders; but he is afraid of bisexual passion, for his desire cannot bear to be rootless and homeless. For Emble to be at home, he needs to repatriate desire, to bring it out of exile and to give it refuge within domestic limits, which typify a national home. The national home is a shabby delusion, however. Rosetta prays that Emble gets what his fear hopes for. "Make your home / with some glowing girl; forget with her what happens also." While Rosetta is thus praying for Emble, she also is cursing him, weaving the delusive scenes of a myth in which he seeks to be embowered. "What happens also" is

outside the bower. What happens also is unruly eros, and historical time, each the antithesis of myth and rootedness; what happens is a reality covered over by the Joycean (and the archaicizing) leafage, underneath whose camouflage Auden outruns leafy speaking.

To be sure, when Rosetta—for whom home is a "light elation," and, as she says, is a hope that has ended—takes up the burden of being an exile, she does so in a long monologue that ends with the most sacred name (in transliterated Hebrew) of a nation-centered He. He is not the Christ we expect from Auden, but Israel's God. But for Auden, Israel's God does not appear to be a Zionist. He is invoked as the divinity of ceaseless wanderings, not of a settled national homeland. For better or worse, He is a God of wanderings because He is the God of time—of time's dispersals and disseminations. Emble at home in a nation hides both from the Eros that creates homelessness, and from the temporal dimension that, just like Eros, makes one, in all anxiety, a refugee, perpetually on a frontier where "His ragged remnant," as Rosetta describes them, "seep through boundaries / Diffuse like firearms through frightened lands, / transpose our plight . . . / . . . time-tormented." And if we feel it is perverse not to say that Rosetta's long speech converts itself to orthodox theology rather than remains faithful to antimythological rootless temporality, we must look again. The sense of the monologue clings to an ironic or sarcastic repatriation. The He whom Rosetta finally invokes has been characterized by her as a lying shiftless nobodaddy: she recounts his infidelities, and wonders how he could have loved his new wife, Stepmother Stupid. "I shan't be at peace / Till I really take your restless hands / My poor fat father," Rosetta says. She does not lead him to a resting-place, however; although weary, she leads him on, blessed in restlessness.

This unsettling metamorphosis of He into "poor fat father," this counterconversion from theodicy to banality, is what I call ironic repatriation. It takes the supreme patria-figure and relocates him into banal secular self-division, alienation, displacement. Repatriation in Auden, like conversion, first allies itself to a god-term, a father-term (like fatherland), then counterconverts the god-term into distance from divinity and from the great good Innocent Place. The God who is prayed to at last is a god who is himself on the lam, an exile. Malin takes up the concluding meditations in *The Age of Anxiety*, and speaks as a new Rosetta. He speaks in her and Auden's "own / Contradictory dialect, the double talk / Of ambiguous bodies," who are "Temporals . . . finite in fact yet refusing" to recognize their inevitable double talk. Patrias and "patriations" refuse the double talk, the eternal dislocations that for Auden *should* invest all citizenship. When Malin's last words breathlessly fall forward into invocations of Rosetta's He, and sound the counterexilic note of infinite salvation—as if time were not the poor finite and displaced father that it is—Malin is fooling himself. He is not as anchored by assured salvations as his prayerful allegiances presume.

Here is the point at which Auden's civic voice, motivated by the impulse to value enduring expatriation, converges with Auden's religious voice. The religious voice complements the civic voice. The two voices both utter "double talk," because their author is conscious that, no less than nationalism, even theology might be an emblem of Emble— a woven defense against cosmic and ontological homelessness, a defense too against Eros's resistance to domesticity, and a defense against the temporal devolution of Our Father into the real old man. Yet precisely "double talk" in another sense, the incessant wavering between patria and expatriation, or between civism and refugeeism, is Auden's vital center of civic and religious belief. Consider the religious and patriotic virtue of doubleness implied in Auden's Kierkegaard-inspired version of "the existential." "I am free to make choices," Auden writes in **"Soren Kierkegaard"**; but "I cannot observe the act of choice objectively. If I try I shall not choose." Choice is a differentiation and commitment, and a leap in the dark. Translated into the realm of state allegiances, this means that one's civic and national ties and commitments always are partly blind choices. The blindness that inheres in these commitments produces edgy anxiety in us; but the anxiety perhaps is a disguised consciousness of the need to distrust commitments, in order to continue to be free. Harbored within both choice and anxiety is a need to maintain a mobile, vitally neutral perspective on even one's passionate attachments.

Like *The Age of Anxiety, For the Time Being: A Christmas Oratorio* (1941-42) is motivated by Auden's impulse to undermine the settling and stabilizing functions of nationality and religion. But *For the Time Being* is even more joined to a homosexual inspiration than the poem about Emble the flirty Navy man. We know about the inspiration thanks to Dorothy Farnam's publication of Auden's letter-poem to Kallman, dated Christmas Day, 1941, in which Auden elaborates point-for-point likenesses between the Nativity story characters and the Auden-Kallman marriage. The elaboration, at once impious—from a Christian convert of scarcely two years!—and earnest, identifies Kallman with Mary: "Because mothers have much to do with your queerness and mine, because we both have lost ours, and because Mary is a camp name; As this morning I think of Mary I think of you." With this Mary at the center, all Christmas becomes Christian High Camp. Because Auden recently had discovered Kallman's infidelity, Auden identifies with Joseph, who represents jealous male "vileness" and "conceit" at the discovery that his Mary has had intercourse elsewhere. He identifies with Herod, too, because Herod, jealous like Joseph, wants to kill whoever threatens devotion to him. (Significantly, Auden combines these identifications with a studied neutrality towards Joseph's and Herod's fixed, jealous attachments.) Auden also identifies his marriage to Kallman with "the Holy Family" ("because you are to me emotionally a mother, physically a father, and intellectually a son") and with the Paradox of the Incarnation ("because in the eyes of our . . . friends our relationship is absurd"). Since in the context of Auden's allegory, the Incarnation, whereby god becomes man, also sounds like a literalizing of gay awe at the advent of male beauty ("He's divine!"), perhaps it's not surprising that in Auden's fantasia even the shepherds at the crèche turn out to be gay sailors and rough trade.

But without knowledge of this letter, *For the Time Being* surely can't be read in this queer way. Hecht admires the letter's "very moving declaration" and its "brilliant ingenuity"; but he quotes it *outside* of his chapter on the poem. He doesn't know how to fit the letter into his interpretation. It is not easy. After all, the only gay man explicitly represented in *For the Time Being* is George, the soldier of fortune who reenlists in the Army "Just in tidy time," as the camp song about him says, "to massacre the Innocents." With homosexuality looking like an opportunistic, murderous arm of Herod, Auden has intruded homosexuality into the poem shockingly. He gives no explicit motive for assigning just this sexuality to the soldier. By identifying a homosexual figure with the villainous massacre, he seems to retract—homophobically—the Christmas letter's theologizing of queerdom. What *is* Auden up to? If the reprehensible George is gay, we aren't likely to read dear Mary as "Mary." In contrast to him, isn't she too good to be gay?

One answer emerges out of the shocking intrusion. Until this point in the poem, Auden's revisions of the Nativity stay within the story's conventional bounds. George breaks the bounds. But when a conscientious writer introduces material that seems purely disruptive, he might be inviting a reader to test the possible relevance, after all, of the irrelevance. This is just what Hecht does, unintentionally. By chance he calls George a refugee. Having called him this, however, Hecht does not note that George's public villainy reaches its apex when the refugee has stopped wandering, and enrolls himself as a solid citizen. George's wanderings are scarcely blameless; but the solid state of citizenship, the service to Herod, is the one in which the queer becomes vicious. George *was* without a country before he became a gay in the military and a good citizen. His intrusion in the poem suggests an equation between being a better queer and being a refugee. The better citizens, those more potentially the bearers of a redemptive public virtue, are migrating or in exile. This perverse suggestion lies behind Auden's burdening us with George. From this suggestion, the queer allegory of the letter to Kallman gets into the poem. Mary and her kind—that divine boy included—must migrate out of citizenship, become strangers in a strange land, because this is the nobler public-minded thing to do.

It is indeed an inversion, this idea that a citizen's virtue is best realized only before one has acquired one's national identity papers and one's passport, or only after one has left them behind. Still, in one of the poem's most moving passages, section 4 of "The Summons," *For the Time Being* insists on the idea. "We are not unlucky but evil, / . . . the dream of a Perfect State or No State at all, / To which we fly for refuge, is a part of our punishment," the poem says. I take this to mean that we are to recall how the imagination of man's heart is evil from its youth, and especially so when the imagination takes two political forms. One form is instanced by the refugee who insists on building and entering what he takes to be Utopia. The Utopia might be Brook Farm; it might be no more than complacent national allegiance. In either case, the refugee will find himself, inevitably, in Herod's house, enlisted in some slaughtering activity. Moreover, it is to be remarked that the Perfect State probably is also the Perfect Religious State, which Auden encapsulates in *For the Time Being* in **"The Meditation of Simeon."** Hecht takes much too earnestly this tour de force theodicy, which is undercut by its pedantic, assured assertiveness.

Simeon, I submit, is Herod doubled as a theologian. He is scarcely Kierkegaardian. In Simeon logical demonstration slaughters belief. But, alternatively, the refugee from Perfection will be wrong to dispense altogether with imagining civic values and ideals. To dream of No State at all is to be merely antisocial, or chaotic, and so to miss—for better or worse—incarnations and holy families like Auden-Kallman's. There is a middle (and paradoxical) ground between the evil alternatives of Utopia and the antisocial war of all against all. The Shepherds describe the paradox of the middle ground as "our lucky certainty / Of uncertainty." The Wise Men indicate the same middle when they say that love fraternizes with anarchy, but "vividly expresses obligation / With movement and in spontaneity." Exemplary citizenship would fuse obligations to the commonwealth with their spontaneous performance and vivid expression. (But this ideal model might indulge the evil of Perfection.) It is Mary and Joseph, in exilic movement, in between Perfect State and No State, who most vividly express obligation to the new citizenship. Once the pair has fled into Egypt, and are safe, their safety worries them. Safety is not responsive to the refugee's blessed, migratory intermediacy, to the queerness that feels most conscious of its responsibilities in a condition of political and national displacement. "For all societies and epochs are transient details." "Safe in Egypt," sing the gay Jewish couple Joseph and Mary, "we shall sigh / For lost insecurity; / Only when her terrors come / Does our flesh feel quite at home." To gestate and to enact the promise of public well-being one must resist the security of patriation.

Not just Auden's private letter to Kallman but an important literary influence bears on *For the Time Being*'s identification of Kallman with Mary, and helps shape Auden's new citizenship. In this influence the rebellious oddities of Auden's religious and national conversions converge. The Mary of *For the Time Being* derives, I submit, from Walter Pater's interpretation of Botticelli's Maries in *Studies in the Renaissance*. Pater tells us that Botticelli's virgins are inspired by Matteo Palmieri, the author of "La Città Divina," a poem which represents the human race as the incarnation of the angles who, during Lucifer's revolt, were neither for Jehovah nor for his enemies. In Botticelli's paintings, the Virgin too, Pater writes, "though she holds in her hands the 'Desire of all nations,' is one of those who are neither for Jehovah nor for his enemies; and her choice is on her face. . . . Her trouble is in the very caress of the mysterious child . . . who has already that sweet look of devotion which men have never been able altogether to love." A characteristic Paterian acid here, corroding theology, is too extreme to apply to Auden's Christianity. Still, as the source of a tradition of which Auden is a product, the acid bites deep. Not repatriation but re-Pateriation contributes to the neutral, in-between citizenship and the Ahasuerus-like burden of wandering in which Auden invests the desire of all nations.

FURTHER READING

Criticism

Boly, John R. "Auden and the Romantic Tradition in *The Age of Anxiety*." *Daedalus* 111, No. 2 (Spring 1982): 149-71.

Examines Auden's reaction against and assimilation of romanticism as reflected in the major themes, artistic concerns, and structure of *The Age of Anxiety*.

Bozorth, Richard R. "'But Who Would Get It?': Auden and the Codes of Poetry and Desire." *ELH: English Literary History* 62, No. 3 (Fall 1995): 709-27.

Explores the significance of private allusions, coded language, and ambiguity in Auden's poetry as an expression of his homosexuality.

Bryant, Marsha. "Auden and the 'Arctic Stare': Documentary as Public Collage in *Letters from Iceland*." *Journal of Modern Literature* XVII, No. 4 (Spring 1991): 537-65.

Examines Auden's interest in documentary filmmaking and the politics of representation as reflected in *Letters from Iceland*.

Christianson, Scott R. "The Poetics and Politics of Eliot's Influence on W. H. Auden." *Essays in Literature* 19, No. 1 (Spring 1992): 98-113.

Considers the genealogical and political influence of T.

S. Eliot's poetry and literary criticism on the development of Auden's own poetry and critical perspective.

Mendelson, Edward. "'We Are Changed By What We Change': The Power of Politics of Auden's Revisions." *The Romanic Review* 86, No. 3 (May 1995): 527-35.

Examines the ethical significance of Auden's frequent revisions of his poetry as indicative of his respect for the politics and shaping power of language.

Pascoe, David. "Auden and the Aesthetics of Detection." *Essays in Criticism* 43, No. 1 (January 1993): 33-58.

Explores Auden's interest in English detective fiction and elements of the genre in his poetry.

Riffaterre, Michael. "Textuality: W. H. Auden's 'Musée des Beaux Arts.'" In *Textual Analysis: Some Readers Reading,* edited by Mary Ann Caws, pp. 1-13. New York: Modern Language Association of America, 1986.

Examines the principles and function of literary intertextuality through analysis of Auden's "Musée des Beaux Arts."

Spears, Monroe K. "The Divine Comedy of W. H. Auden." *Sewanee Review* 90, No. 1 (Winter 1982): 53-72.

Examines the development of Auden's poetry and artistic concerns in relation to the three books of Dante's *Divine Comedy.*

Spiegelman, Willard. "The Rake, The Don, The Flute: W. H. Auden as Librettist." *Parnassus* 10, No. 2 (Fall-Winter 1982): 171-87.

Discusses Auden's interest in operatic forms and the artistic principles applied to his adaptations of *The Rake's Progress, Don Giovanni,* and *The Magic Flute.*

Additional coverage of Auden's life and career is contained in the following sources published by Gale: *Authors and Artists for Young Adults,* **Vol. 18;** *Concise Dictionary of British Literary Biography,* **1914-1945;** *Contemporary Authors,* **Vols. 9-12R, 45-48;** *Contemporary Authors New Revision Series,* **Vol. 5;** *Dictionary of Literary Biography,* **Vols. 10, 12;** *DISCovering Authors; DISCovering Authors: British; DISCovering Authors: Canadian; DISCovering Authors Modules: Dramatists, Most-Studied, and Poets; Major Twentieth Century Writers; Poetry Criticism,* **Vol. 1; and** *World Literature Criticism.*

Andrea Dworkin
1946-

American nonfiction writer, novelist, essayist, short story writer, and poet.

The following entry presents an overview of Dworkin's career through 1998. For further information on her life and work, see *CLC,* Volume 43.

INTRODUCTION

A highly controversial author and activist, Andrea Dworkin is a leading radical feminist and heterodox figure of the contemporary women's movement. Her provocative investigations into the cultural origins of misogyny and sexual violence have generated contentious debate among feminists, academics, politicians, and free speech advocates. A forceful spokesperson against pornography, Dworkin calls attention to the insidious sexual myths that perpetuate the role of women as degraded objects of male gratification and exploitation. Dworkin is best known for her nonfiction analyses *Pornography* (1981) and *Intercourse* (1987), as well as several collections of potent essays and speeches and two novels—*Ice and Fire* (1986) and *Mercy* (1990)—in which she illustrates the shocking brutality of female subjugation. Alternately revered and reviled for her firebrand polemics and castigation of mainstream feminists, Dworkin has exerted an important influence on public discourse surrounding the modes, extent, and human cost of male dominated sexuality and female oppression.

Biographical Information

Born in Camden, New Jersey, Dworkin was raised in a liberal Jewish home by her father, a guidance counselor, and mother, a secretary. While still in grade school, Dworkin expressed her desire to affect social change as a writer or lawyer. Her early literary interests were shaped by the writings of Arthur Rimbaud and Fyodor Dostoyevsky, and later Virginia Woolf, the Brontës, George Eliot, and revolutionary Che Guevara. Politically active by age eighteen, Dworkin was arrested at an antiwar rally in New York City in 1964. While jailed at the Women's House of Detention, she was sexually assaulted during an invasive body search, prompting her to lead a public demonstration upon her release. Dworkin attended Bennington College in Vermont, where she earned a bachelor's degree in 1968 after a one year leave of absence in Greece. Dworkin's writing first appeared in the privately printed volumes *Child* (1966), a book of poetry produced in Crete, and *Morning Hair* (1968), which consists of poetry and prose. Disillusioned

by American involvement in Vietnam, Dworkin moved to the Netherlands for a five year period after graduating from Bennington. During this time she endured a physically and emotionally abusive marriage to a Dutch man, whom she escaped in 1971 with the help of intervening feminists. Returning to the United States in 1972, Dworkin supported herself as a waitress, receptionist, secretary, salesperson, factory worker, and prostitute while periodically homeless. She was eventually hired as an assistant to poet Muriel Rukeyser while working on her first book, *Woman Hating* (1974), which she began in Amsterdam. Dworkin was also active in feminist demonstrations and established herself as a powerful speaker at the National Organization for Women's Conference on Sexuality in 1974. Two years later she published *Our Blood* (1976), a collection of essays and speeches, followed by *The New Woman's Broken Heart* (1981), a volume of short stories. During the 1980s, Dworkin joined forces with Catharine A. MacKinnon, a law professor at the University of Michigan, to campaign for antipornography legislation. Together they authored an important civil rights ordinance in Minneapolis that recognized pornography as a form of sexual discrimination. The ordinance was passed in 1983 and became a model for similar legislation in other American cities and Canada. Dworkin also appeared before the Attorney General's Commission on Pornography in 1986. Her research and lobbying resulted in *Pornography* and *Pornography and Civil Rights* (1988), a collaborative volume with MacKinnon. A frequent lecturer at feminist gatherings and contributor to numerous periodicals, Dworkin also published the book-length studies *Right-Wing Women* (1983) and *Intercourse,* the nonfiction collections *Letters from a War Zone* (1989) and *Life and Death* (1997), and the novels *Ice and Fire* and *Mercy.*

Major Works

The primary subjects of Dworkin's critical studies and fiction—sexual abuse, pornography, and female subordination—are introduced in her first book, *Woman Hating.* In this work, Dworkin examines the socialization of gender roles and misogyny through analysis of fairy tales and pornographic writings. Such cultural artifacts, according to Dworkin, represent a continuum through which hierarchical heterosexual relationships are prescribed from childhood through adulthood. Her examination of sources ranging from "Snow White" to Pauline Réage's *The Story of O* demonstrates that women are consistently portrayed as weak, submissive, and despised, reflected in cultural practices such as foot-binding and witch-burning. These themes are expanded upon in *Pornography* and *Intercourse.* In *Pornography,* Dworkin examines the content, social context, and effects of pornography as a tool of male domination over women. Dismissing claims that pornographic writings and images fall under the protected category of free expression, Dworkin asserts that pornography is an exploitative medium of mass propaganda by which the ideology of male supremacy is transmitted. Drawing attention to the victimization of real women who perform in pornographic films, Dworkin contends that the creation of pornography is inseparable from the degradation of women it falsely portrays as fantasy; thus the production of pornography embodies its harmful effect. In *Intercourse,* Dworkin discusses the physical act of heterosexual intercourse as the quintessential manifestation of male hegemony and female inequality. According to Dworkin, male penetration during copulation signifies possession of the woman, rendering impossible the notion of female liberation or selfhood, as she is compelled to submit to male desire as occupation. Incorporating analysis of religious and legal strictures governing female sexuality and texts by Leo Tolstoy, Kobo Abe, James Baldwin, Tennessee Williams, Isaac Bashevis Singer, and Gustave Flaubert, Dworkin maintains that—for women—the manipulative, demeaning experience of sexual intercourse precludes mutual respect or integrity. Dworkin's semiautobiographic novels, *Ice and Fire* and *Mercy,* give vivid expression to the conclusions in her nonfiction. *Ice and Fire* relates the experiences of an unnamed young feminist from Camden, New Jersey. She grows up in a work-class Jewish neighborhood, goes to college, marries an abusive husband, and eventually settles in New York City where she lives in squalor, prostitutes, and is brutalized by various men while attempting to write a book. After much difficulty locating a publisher, the protagonist finally gets her book into print, though it flounders due to its spiteful publisher and poor sales. Dworkin's alter ego in *Mercy,* also a young woman from Camden, is named Andrea. The first person narrative documents a long history of horrific sexual abuse inflicted upon its protagonist, beginning when she was molested in a movie theater at age nine. Andrea is sexually assaulted by sadistic prison doctors, raped and mutilated by her husband, and repeatedly violated while living a bohemian existence in New York City. Her rage finally gives way to retributive violence, leading her to firebomb sex shops and assault homeless men while envisioning an international guerilla war on men. The narrative action is framed by a prologue and epilogue, both entitled "Not Andrea," in which Dworkin parodies her liberal feminist and academic detractors. Dworkin's views on the political, cultural, and physical subjugation of women are further elaborated in the essays, columns, and speeches collected in *Our Blood, Letters from a War Zone,* and *Life and Death.* In the nonfiction work *Right-Wing Women,* written during the early years of the Reagan administration, Dworkin attempts to explain the appeal of the Republican party for women, despite its opposition to the Equal Rights Amendment and other legislation to enhance the well-being of women. According to Dworkin, fear of male violence compels many conservative women to relinquish their autonomy for the security of traditional sex roles which demand passivity and subservience. The book was in part an attempt by Dworkin to distance herself from the antipornography advocacy of anti-feminist, religious, and conservative groups such as the Moral Majority.

Critical Reception

Dworkin's compelling examination of sexual politics and pornography is the subject of divisive controversy in academic, political, and feminist circles. Though praised by some for her insightful, groundbreaking analysis of cultural misogyny and sexual exploitation, her detractors typically object to the abrasive presentation of her postulations. Critics frequently complain that Dworkin's bombastic rhetoric distorts and sensationalizes the substance of her findings while alienating much of her audience. Critics also condemn Dworkin's interchangeable use of literal and metaphorical statements and her tendency to construct sweeping generalizations based on overstated or anecdotal evidence. *Pornography* and *Intercourse,* her best known and most inflammatory works, are generally recognized as her most important contributions to feminist scholarship.

Negative critical response to *Intercourse* is directed primarily at elements of biological determinism in Dworkin's argument. According to many reviewers, Dworkin reduces the inequality of women to the inevitable anatomical facts of intromission. Though critics often dismiss her methodology and conclusions, many praise her highly perceptive critical analysis of literary sources in *Pornography, Intercourse,* and *Woman Hating.* Dworkin's vigilant condemnation of pornography has also caused fissures among feminist activists, especially those reluctant to challenge First Amendment rights. However, Dworkin's focus on pornography as a Fourteenth Amendment infringement instead of an obscenity issue, a strategy formulated with MacKinnon, is considered an important legal maneuver for antipornography advocacy. Dworkin is less appreciated as a novelist. While some reviewers commend her visceral evocation of sexual violence, most find fault in her simplistic prose, undeveloped characters, overt feminist agenda, and graphic sexuality which, as some reviewers note, resembles the pornography she decries. Eschewing theoretical abstractions and the insular ideological battles of academic feminists, Dworkin has won many supporters for her willingness to address distasteful and often overlooked aspects of sexual abuse. A formidable independent thinker and activist, Dworkin is recognized as one of the most articulate and influential voices of contemporary feminism.

PRINCIPAL WORKS

Child (poetry) 1966

Morning Hair (poetry and prose) 1968

Woman Hating (nonfiction) 1974

Our Blood: Prophecies and Discourses on Sexual Politics (essays and speeches) 1976

The New Woman's Broken Heart (short stories) 1980

Pornography: Men Possessing Women (nonfiction) 1981

Right-Wing Women: The Politics of Domesticated Females (nonfiction) 1983

Ice and Fire (novel) 1986

Intercourse (nonfiction) 1987

Pornography and Civil Rights: A New Day for Women's Equality [with Catharine A. MacKinnon] (nonfiction) 1988

Letters from a War Zone: Writings 1976-1987 [republished as *Letters from a War Zone: Writings 1976-1989,* 1989] (essays) 1988

Mercy (novel) 1990

Life and Death: Unapologetic Writings on the Continuing War Against Women (nonfiction) 1997

CRITICISM

Janice Mall (review date 3 May 1987)

SOURCE: A review of *Ice and Fire* and *Intercourse,* in *Los Angeles Times Book Review,* May 3, 1987, pp. 1, 7.

[*In the following review, Mall offers tempered criticism of* Ice and Fire *and* Intercourse.]

According to *Publishers Weekly,* Andrea Dworkin's first novel, ***Ice and Fire,*** was turned down by 20 American publishers before its appearance last year in England. One wonders why. True, Dworkin, known as a feminist particularly concerned with pornography, takes a flyer on surrealism in the novel, but the style works for her, at least at first.

Her protagonist is marvelous as a little girl on a working class Jewish block in Camden, N.J., in the 1950s, a girl who defies the unwritten law of her neighborhood by making friends with black and Catholic kids at elementary school and walking, in solitary curiosity and defiance, down the blocks where these proscribed people live. Childhood comes to glowing life on this single block with its alleys and, between the houses, spaces mysteriously large to children out playing "witch" on summer nights, the boys chasing the girls, putting the captured one in a homemade cage: "I would play witch, wanting to be chased and caught, terrified to be chased and caught, terrified not to be chased, racing heart. . . . Oh, it was incredible to run, racing heart. . . . If only that had been the game. But the game was to get caught. . . ."

When she grows up, this perceptive little girl is not going to buy into the games men and women play, right?

Wrong.

The never-named character finishes college, has an abortion, and passes the next few years in a squalor of drugs, poverty, prostitution and terror on the Lower East Side of New York. With her friend, like her a well-educated young woman and would-be artist/film maker, she makes her home in a filthy dangerous storefront, turning tricks with men or women for a cup of coffee. Why? Because, in the 1960s, "We couldn't be lacquered secretaries."

As Dworkin seems too smart to slip us the silliest cliche of that or any other decade, we begin to suspect that she has these women where they are to tell us about what men do to them. And tells us she does. What the men do is brutal, wanton, true to the worst newspaper headlines.

There are hardly any conventionally acceptable men in ***Ice and Fire.*** The narrator marries a man who is impotent, and patiently coaxes him to virility, whereupon he becomes a batterer. Her lover she calls "the sleeping boy," a passive ghost whose face reminds her of her brother as a baby. This brother, whom she loved when they were small, has died in Vietnam, but we learn this only in an oddly impersonal reference to the narrator's father having lost his son—as if this quintessentially male death should be tossed in male laps.

In short, once past that brief, magical childhood, Dworkin seems less concerned with her fiction than with its lesson, and there's not much artfulness in the lesson: Grown up men, potent men are dangerous for women.

Dworkin's new work of nonfiction, *Intercourse,* starting right off with Alma Mahler's and Sophie Tolstoy's touching diaries of lives with Gustav and Leo, is a far more entertaining work, full of drama, intellectual hops and skips and the surprisingly turned corners that her novel ought to have but doesn't.

Dworkin's question: Can women ever be equal or free if they engage in sexual intercourse? The act (Dworkin reminds anyone who needs reminding) involves male invasion of a private part of the female body—invasion sometimes by guile, often by force, and always within social, legal and religious structures created and run by men. Throughout history men have been extraordinarily prolific in demeaning words for both the invading act and the invaded body. But for Dworkin it isn't just the words that are demeaning. Germaine Greer has said, "Andrea Dworkin has confronted the question that no feminist hitherto has dared to ask, whether intromission is compatible with equal status."

Dworkin herself would hardly claim to be the first, since most of her first chapter is devoted to Leo Tolstoy's exposition about the same theory in his novel, *The Kreutzer Sonata.* Tolstoy was no feminist, but he did think that lust demeaned both sexes and that as swords were beaten into plowshares in some higher future of the race, intercourse too would disappear. Countess Tolstoy underwent 13 pregnancies as a result of the act her husband despised as much as he despised her person. After Tolstoy spoke of admiring a vegetarian diet he'd read about, Sophie wrote, "I expect the person who wrote the menu practices vegetarianism as much as the author of 'The Kreutzer Sonata' practices chastity."

Dworkin's book is fine for browsing. It could have been subtitled. "What Lots of Fascinating Authors Have to Say About Sex." Dozens of footnotes and 35 pages of bibliography are more inviting than the title, referring us to quotes from Tolstoy, Koko Abe, Tennessee Williams, James Baldwin, Isaac Bashevis Singer, Gustave Flaubert, Bram Stoker. These writers—and Joan of Arc in an engaging essay—are treated at length. But there are also many shorter takes, like the wife in Don DeLillo's *White Noise* who agrees to read pornography to her husband, but only if he does not choose anything that "has men inside women, quote-quote, or men entering women. We're not lobbies or elevators."

But Dworkin herself has much to say about the fact that the desire and ability to push a hard penis into a woman and to have one or more women available for this is the most profound definition of masculinity in this or any culture. That civilized people are appalled by violent abuses of the sexual act does not negate the fact that men, including the angry ones, must prove themselves upon women's bodies. Men who cannot or will not not do this are ridiculed, despised, persecuted and prosecuted.

But in the end, Dworkin too casually dismisses a social reality centuries old. Little matter whether it is the gods or Darwin who decree that it is our nature to perpetuate the race: Until recently, intercourse has been the only way to do it; and despite new technology, intercourse is going to be the only way to do it for most people for a long time to come.

And though Dworkin sprinkles the word *Amerika* about (always a banal shorthand), she in fact seriously neglects contemporary America with its appalling and unique level of sexual violence. She does offer a terrifying analysis of incest and child molestation, claiming that the frequency of it is "perhaps a sexual response to the political rebellion of adult women. . . . Women are supposed to be small and childlike, in looks, in rights. . . ." But while shuddering over this possibility, one wishes she'd had more to say about what can be done about violence among males. Considering what is wrong with intercourse doesn't take us far with that pressing question.

Maureen Mullarkey (review date 30 May 1987)

SOURCE: "Hard Cop, Soft Cop," in *The Nation,* May 30, 1987, pp. 720, 722-4, 726.

[*In the following excerpt, Mullarkey offers unfavorable assessment of* Intercourse, *which she describes as "a hate-mongering tantrum."*]

Is pornography a sex aid, like a dildo, hence undeserving of protection as speech? Is it a potent political message that should be denied protection before it leads to a Haymarket riot of rapists and pedophiles? By what criteria is an image determined "degrading"? Is the pet of the month a nastier purveyor of "bad attitudes" than Calvin Klein advertisements, rock videos, Harlequin romances or the *New York Post?* Is *Screw* an unusually dangerous product, like gunpowder, which places special liabilities on its maker? What effect will more laws have on the reasons isolated men masturbate in stalls at Mr. Peepers? Will they try it with chickens after they see *Leda and the Swan?* If Nazis can speak in Skokie and man-haters can speak anywhere, why can misogynists *not* speak in Indianapolis?

Andrea Dworkin and Catharine A. MacKinnon are not interested in clarifying issues. Co-authors of the 1984 Indianapolis civic ordinance that declared pornography a form of legally actionable sex discrimination, they prefer obfuscation and shock tactics. *Intercourse* and *Feminism Unmodified* should be read solely for clues to the crudity of the authors' assault on the First Amendment. This is lock-step, *völkisch* theorizing spun from the tribal myth of male depravity. With the dictatorial arrogance of traditional censors, the High Command disdains information and truthful discussion. (At an April 4 conference at New York University, titled Sexual Liberals and the Assault on Feminism, Dworkin trashed "the free market of ideas" because it does not guarantee that "good" ideas will win.) They rely on demagogic pronouncements and sensationalism, calculated to induce reflexive responses and hysterical acquiescence. Both books are ritual performances, hokey rallying points for the real agenda: the polarization of women along lines of sexual preference. Pure feminists (lesbians and nice asexuals) on one side of the sex code, collaborators on the other. The pornography issue is a stalking horse for power—within the feminist bureaucracy and its twin in academia.

Both books travesty debate with a pornography of their own: the reduction of men to their erections and the depiction of heterosexuality as vicious and degrading. Their styles are different—Dworkin's is Dzerzhinsky to MacKinnon's Lenin—but their substance is identical. Dworkin's lunatic *pensées* offer a glimpse at the hindside of MacKinnon's scholarly facade. These are the minds paving the way for censorship. The two take turns playing Hitler. The New "Jewish illness" is male sexuality. The world Jewish conspiracy is heterosexual intercourse (MacKinnon: "The institution of intercourse is a strategy for subordination"). The despised Jew-lover is any woman who prefers sex with a man. Implicit in their rhetoric is a condemnation of maleness itself, sub species *aeternitatis.*

Dworkin's strong-arm specialty is cuntspeak. *Intercourse* is a hate-mongering tantrum dolled up as a prolegomenon to the work of Tolstoy, Tennessee Williams, James Baldwin, Kobo Abe and Isaac Bashevis Singer. Nose-dive under the skunk spray, and forget the thirty-four-page bibliography. Dworkin's monomania has nothing to do with literature. Art and life are a ghastly jumble, the artist mistaken for the art and vice versa. Fantasy is equated with reality, metaphor taken for fact, in a global attempt to discredit all of West-

ern culture as pornographic. The muddle fulfills MacKinnon's belief that "existing standards of literature, art, science and politics, examined in a feminist light, are remarkably consonant with pornography's mode, meaning and message." Tolstoy's "goose-stepping hatred of cunt" is a synecdoche for men's universal "genocidal loathing" of women. In the Dworkin-MacKinnon pornotopia, there are only the fuckers and the fuckees. The sooner the fuckers' books are burned the better. Dworkin's readings are shackled like an S/M bondage slave to a primitive abhorrence of men, so blatant and compulsive that it obviates her pretense to critical analysis:

> But in the world of real life—and in the subtextual worlds of Brown [Norman O.] and Freud and nearly everyone else—men use the penis to deliver death to women who are, literally, in their genitals, dirt to men. The women are raped as adults or as children; prostituted; fucked, then murdered; murdered, then fucked.

Beware the party hacks who chirp encomiums to her "elegant" and "lyrical" prose. Dworkin lives in "Amerika," where "*violation* is a synonym for intercourse," and "incestuous rape is becoming a central paradigm for intercourse in our time." Her own description of intermission is as brutal and lewd as anything on Forty-second Street:

> The vagina itself is muscled and the muscles have to be pushed apart. The thrusting is persistent invasion. She is opened up, split down the center. She is occupied . . . This hole, her hole, is synonymous with entry.

Heterosexuality is on trial in a kangaroo court, and the judge talks dirty. Sex is a "humiliation ritual," and "penetration was never meant to be kind." (MacKinnon: "There is much violence in intercourse as a usual matter.") The "norms of disparagement and cruelty that constitute fucking male-to-female" are so horrific that even Nazi death camps do not compare:

> There is no analogue anywhere among subordinated groups of people to this experience of being made for intercourse; for penetration, entry, occupation. There is no analogue in occupied countries or in dominated races or in imprisoned dissidents or in colonized cultures or in the submission of children to adults or in the atrocities that have marked the twentieth century ranging from Auschwitz to the Gulag.

How did the submission of children slip in? What kind of submission? The rant is as slovenly as its innuendoes: "In the United States, incest is increasingly the sadism of choice." Dworkin suggests that incest is a male policy, not an aberrancy that occurs—initiated by both sexes against children of both sexes—in troubled emotional situations for a tangle of tragic reasons. She ignores the shared involvement, conscious or unconscious, of other family members. She does not distinguish between increased incidence of incest and increased reporting of it. (Patricia Foscato, a psychotherapist and coordinator of a sexual-abuse prevention program, testified before the Meese commission that she did not believe there was more incest now than thirty years ago, only "more exposure.")

Dworkin's regard for accuracy, like MacKinnon's, is matched only by her estimate of the reasoning abilities of her audience. Both women swing between biological determinism (the male is destined to exploit by his demonic arousal mechanism) and the wholesale denial of biology. Both grant canonical authority to the fashionable theory that gender is exclusively "a social construct," like the bourgeois-democratic state machine and credit buying. According to the new Ladies' Anthropology, sexual differences are not the sum of biologically determined morphological and physiological characteristics. "Opposites were created," says Dworkin, by such cunning conventions as "vagina-specific fucking," sodomy laws and the "martial aims of gender":

> The creation of gender (so-called nature) by law was systematic, sophisticated, supremely intelligent. . . . Fuck the woman in the vagina, not in the ass, because only she can be fucked in the vagina.

MacKinnon states the insight this way:

> Gender is . . . a social status based on who is permitted to do what to whom. . . . gender *is an ideology*. . . . Gender has no basis in anything other than the social reality its hegemony constructs. Gender is what gender means.

Neither scholar is concerned with the implications of this hash of sex and sex roles. With its tacit insistence on the absolute rule of social conditioning, for instance, it provides the heterosexual majority with a new rationale for imposing the tyranny of behavior modification on the homosexual minority. If all behavior is stored in culture, including our institutions of what it means to be human, the problem of incest, for example, can be solved merely by lifting the taboo. If everything is learned, any social system will do, because we can be trained to live in any kind of society. The word "inhuman" loses all meaning without a guide-pin to human needs by which to judge the world. . . .

The eye for smut is sharper than the eye for our own subterranean biases and fears. Behind the catch phrases of the porn squad ("subordination of women," "trafficking in

women's bodies") crouches the tattered old horror of masturbation. Lurking, too, is the ancient repugnance of the Better Sort for the desolate and down-and-out who inhabit porn districts. The sexuality of "that element" is a menacing nether world, condemned as obscene because it reminds us of the fragility of our well-being. Antiporn crusades are a symbolic barrier between us and them, illusory buffers against all wayward, darkling encroachments on our slender margins of safety. Such movements are cruel in that they fail to address the conditions that help create and sustain "offensive" populations of the economically or emotionally disenfranchised. They divert scarce resources from the enforcement of existing sanctions against actual harmful behavior. In addition, they contribute nothing to the material ability of women to leave abusive relationships or exploitative jobs.

MacKinnon and Dworkin are mountebanks strutting on a feminist stage. Women have much to lose by submitting to the regressive "protection" of these neobarbaric thought police and self-appointed arbiters of "correct" sexuality. Despite the reservations we might have about pornography, the only proven danger to date is the censorship mentality itself. There is no constitutional protection for women or men against uncertainty, ambivalence, dread or distaste. These are the hazards of living. By seeking legislation against speculative perils and whatever offends us, we invite suppression of any controversial speech. Such censorship is the cherished technique of every *Führer* who claims to know what is good for us.

Lorna Sage (review date 16 October 1987)

SOURCE: "Staying Outside the Skin," in *Times Literary Supplement*, October 16, 1987, p. 1129.

[*In the following review, Sage provides tempered criticism of* Intercourse.]

By the time Swift's Gulliver paddles away from Houyhnhnm-land in his Yahoo-skin canoe, he is so consumed with self-disgust and self-hatred (Yahoo-hatred) that it seems he has only two alternatives—to skin himself, to jump out of his skin, or (the one he chooses) to loathe everyone else, and particularly (when he gets home) his nearest and dearest, from whose foul closeness he escapes to the stable to inhale the horses. Andrea Dworkin's *Intercourse* is a book that belongs in a similar landscape of extremity. It's about skinlessness, about coming home to revulsion:

> In Amerika, there is the nearly universal conviction—or so it appears—that sex (fucking) is good and that

liking it is right: morally right; a sign of human health; nearly a standard of citizenship. Even those who believed in original sin and have a theology of hellfire and damnation express the Amerikan creed, an optimism that glows in the dark: sex is good, healthy, wholesome, pleasant, fun; we like it, we enjoy it, we want it, we are cheerful about it; it is as simple as we are, the citizens of this strange country with no memory and no mind.

This Amerika, though (think of Donne, "O my America! my new-found-land, / My kingdome, safeliest when with one man mann'd"), is somewhere we all live, or rather, that lives in us. You discover it—ironically enough—as a result of consciousness-raising, rather as Gulliver did.

Dworkin's position assumes an impasse in feminist thinking. The reformist strain is wearing itself out (this is almost a definition, in any case: it's about wearing itself out) in conflict with both consumerism (which makes use of "liberation" for its own purpose) and the various forms of fundamentalist backlash. At the same time, there is a retreat, a green retreat, into separatism, with the stress on feminine, nurturing qualities. All of these things keep women busy, patching and mending. Dworkin, however, is interested in picking off the cultural patina that persuades people of the naturalness of their "nature," and disputing over again the category of the human.

The literary examples from which she starts (Tolstoy on chastity, or Tennessee Williams on intimacy with strangers, or James Baldwin on "communion") aren't the kind that would make up a "women's studies" reading-list. Those work usually by cumulative comfort, the building of traditions, the argument of quantity, but this argument is opposite, and works (or wants to work) by way of quality, and stripping down, through the persuasiveness of images and metaphors. Here she is, improvising on the central metaphor of *The Face of Another* by Kobo Abe:

> The skin is a line of demarcation, a periphery, the fence, the form, the shape. . . . The skin is separation, individuality, the basis for corporeal privacy. . . . Especially, it is both identity and sex, what one is and what one feels in the realm of the sensual, being and passion, where the self meets the world—intercourse being, ultimately, the self in the act of meeting the world.

Woman's privacy (and hence her individuality, her integrity, her significance) is never real or complete—Dworkin cannot, any more than Milton, praise a cloistered virtue, virgin ignorance—because her meeting with the world is an invasion. She is not the owner or sole inhabitant (her privates we) of her own skin, "her insides are worn away over time, and she, possessed, becomes weak, depleted, usurped . . . ."

Dworkin has been accused of misunderstanding and/or being led astray by metaphors of penetration and possession. Certainly, the book develops and sustains its momentum on metaphor, and metaphor's powers of provoking recognition, of outwitting the rational desire to take things apart *only in such a way that they can be put together again*. Metaphors redraw the map, and put the boundaries in different places; *these* metaphors, in particular, make women into territory that has had a boundary drawn not round its edge, but on the inside, in the name of nature. It is an argument *ad feminam*, with all the unfairness that implies: if you can't recognize what I'm saying you're in thrall; if you can, you're in thrall too, but you've been rescued from banality, and can say, with all bitterness and bleakness, "we": "this elegant blood-letting of sex is a so-called freedom exercised in alienation, cruelty and despair. Trivial and decadent; proud; foolish; liars; we are free." This climax to Chapter Six ("Virginity," and Bram Stoker's *Dracula*) perhaps conveys something of the sublimity of the preacher's style that sells so bleak a sermon, and avoids (like the plague) any suggestion of patching and mending reasonableness. It's worth looking at what the book has to say about the production of meaning:

> It is human to experience these differences whether or not one cares to bring them into consciousness. Humans, including women, construct meaning. Humans find meaning in poverty and tyranny and the atrocities of history; those who have suffered most still construct meaning . . . we can understand some things if we try hard to learn empathy; we can seek freedom and honour and dignity; that we care about meaning gives us a human pride that has the fragility of a butterfly and the strength of tempered steel. The measure of women's oppression is that we do not take intercourse—entry, penetration, occupation—and ask or say what it means . . .

"Ask or say" are synonyms here: asking the questions, you supply the answers. The argument is weakened by this tactic, though not as much as might appear. It *is* cheap to ask, on page 128, "Is intercourse itself then a basis of or a key to women's continuing social and sexual inequality?" It is less so to ask, "To what extent does intercourse depend on the inferiority of women?" On this, the book suggests, for once, fewer answers than questions. The notion of the "real privacy of the body" ("There is never a real privacy of the body that can co-exist with intercourse") is for Dworkin inseparable from full selfhood, from freedom, from integrity, from the "discrete" individual. "Liberal" is for her a term of abuse ("A false sympathy of abstract self-indulgence"), but it's from that background that her sense of the human is derived. Or at least, it's on that sense of the self—as choosing, willing, meaning—that her map of women's possession is based. She is in this sense as much an "enlightenment" figure as Mary Wollstonecraft, who argued that she didn't want women to have power over men, but over themselves.

There remains the question, then, of human closeness under any circumstances—the Yahoo problem. And here the book is eloquent by its silence on lesbianism. By the logic of its own metaphors it should be saying that women's sense of their own sex is invaded by the "natural" and cultural climate, that they are no less "objectified" in relations with each other. But by the message of its silence it produces an unthought, unarticulated alternative, which does more than any of its rhetorical excesses to undermine it. Do women stay outside each other's skins? To ask the question is to flounder on a technicality. It's clear from the whole tenor of the argument that Dworkin will have no truck with tender, sentimental same-sex notions about peace and merging, but at the same time it's impossible not to suspect that this is also a question to which she feels she knows the answer. Either that, or there's the prospect of a kind of "existential" pathos, a celebration of the alienation caused by boundaries that's not so different from what Simone de Beauvoir grappled with in (with?) Sartre.

The voice, in fact, is very much that of the heroic polemics of the late 1960s. Dworkin describes (surely) herself when she bitterly praises those who refuse to submit to "the indignity of inferiority"—"the lone, crazy resisters, the organized resistance." *Intercourse* embarrasses not only by its visceral imagery, but by its refusal to speak any of the conciliatory public languages of feminism. The contrast with the tone of (say) Germaine Greer's preface to her collected essays and occasional pieces (*The Madwoman's Underclothes,* 1986) is instructive. Greer writes:

> The quality of daily life is what matters, the taste of the food on the table, the light in the room, the peace and wholeness of the moment. Perfect love casteth out fear. The only perfect love to be found on earth is not sexual love, but the wordless commitment of families, which takes as its model mother-love.

Dworkin's preoccupation is precisely the obscenity of the ordinary, a gross metaphysical joke played on women. None the less, there is a marked continuity with the tone of Greer's earliest pieces—"Morality is essentially connected with choice, with the exercise of will itself." And this same piece (1972, on abortion) provides a name for Dworkin's special quality: "spiritual muscle."

The days have (probably) gone when this metaphor could be put down to penis envy. Now it is merely unfashionably harsh and individualistic.

Leonore Tiefer (review date 1988)

SOURCE: A review of *Intercourse,* in *Sex Roles,* Vol. 19, Nos. 3-4, 1988, pp. 255-8.

[*In the following review, Tiefer offers qualified endorsement of* Intercourse. *"Dworkin's book," Tiefer concludes, "deserves appreciation and study for its challenging depiction of various aspects of heterosexual relations despite her overstatement of their importance."*]

As feminist historians are beginning to show, theories about sexual acts and values have played a central role in every feminist movement. Feminist sex reformers in the 19th and early 20th century argued intensely over women's and men's sexual "natures," and how best to construct sex to further women's interests. The recent wave of feminism beginning in the late 1960s and early 1970s found radical feminists such as Dana Densmore and Ann Koedt writing essays on sexual acts and attitudes that blew people's minds! Lacking awareness of earlier feminist positions, we naive readers excitedly read their claims, including that sexual intercourse was an act designed by men for male pleasure, and that the feminist revolution had to redefine and rechoreograph sexuality from women's point of view. These essays first appeared in pamphlets that circulated rapidly around consciousness-raising groups, generating hours-long discussions, the intensity and honesty of which are recalled to this day by the participants.

After the early clarion calls, however, matters for female sexuality rapidly became more complicated. The whole "discovery" of the extent of sexual assault/incest/abuse of women and girls replaced pleasure rechoreography as the central element on the feminist sexual agenda. The roles of pornography and of lesbianism in women's oppression and liberation became issues that bitterly divided feminists interested in sexual analysis. Battles over reproductive rights and the new reproductive technologies introduced unforeseen complexities and alliances. By the late 1980s, the once-unified and hope-filled feminist sexual analysis was as divided and factionalized as feminist sexual reform had been in earlier eras.

Andrea Dworkin's recent book, *Intercourse,* then, must be adequately contextualized—as a feminist statement about women's sexual interests, as a position paper supporting one particular faction in contemporary struggles with feminism, and as an echo of a purity movement from the *first* wave of feminism. Its central tenet, reiterated in many chapters with only slight variations, is that the act of heterosexual intercourse is an act of possession, of eroticized domination, an act that "distorts and destroys any potential human equality between men and women by turning women into objects and men into exploiters." "The political meaning of intercourse for women is the fundamental question of feminism and freedom; can an occupied people—physically occupied inside, internally invaded—be free?"

Intercourse is a series of separate essays on sexuality mostly focused on the deconstruction of the act of intercourse. The first chapter, "Repulsion," is stimulated by Tolstoy's novella *The Kreutzer Sonata,* the tale of a man so disgusted by his own passion and how it makes him treat women that he finally murders his wife! Dworkin's theme here is the physicalness of women as the basis for their exploitation, that women gain power through manipulating men's desire (because of their powerlessness in other arenas) leading to men's fear and hatred of women.

The second chapter, "Skinless," uses Kobo Abe's stories of sexual passion (best known: *The Woman in the Dunes*) to discuss the seriousness of sex, the intensity, the obsessiveness, the communion sought, and how men desperately seek human connection through sex to escape their self-absorption. The third chapter, "Stigma," uses selected works of Tennessee Williams to claim that sex has costs, and that the persons driven to sex know it. In the fourth chapter, "Communion," James Baldwin's work is used to demonstrate that sex can be a bridge from ignorance to truth, to really knowing a complex person, to developing the awareness that can eradicate racism. In Chapter Five, "Possession," an Isaac B. Singer story is used to show how women's capacity for sexual pleasure is developed within the narrow confines of male sexual domination. Women learn to experience "fucking" as being possessed and to feel possession as deeply erotic.

Joan of Arc and Flaubert's *Madame Bovary* are the centerpieces of Chapter Six, "Virginity." In this intellectual *tour de force,* Dworkin shows how Joan gained unprecedented freedom for herself by defying conventional femininity in the only effective way—rejecting all aspects of male desire. The so-called freedom of Emma Bovary, by contrast, consists in freedom to commit forbidden sexual acts. Dworkin claims that virginity here has been redefined—from freedom and self-determination to the status of pre-male intercourse. There is a lot of herstory in the chapter to chew over.

In Chapter Seven, "Occupation/Collaboration," Dworkin's voice is its most shrill, her language most concrete, and her vision of heterosexual intercourse most pessimistic:

> Male-dominant hierarchy seems immune to reform. . . . This may be because intercourse itself is immune to reform. In it, female is bottom, stigmatized. Intercourse remains a means or the means of physiologically making a woman inferior: communicating to her cell by cell her own inferior status, impressing it on her, pushing

and thrusting until she gives up and gives in—which is called *surrender* in the male lexicon. In the experience of intercourse, she loses the capacity for integrity because her body—the basis of privacy and freedom in the material world for all human beings—is entered and occupied. . . . What is taken from her in that act is not recoverable, and she spends her life . . . pretending that pleasure is in being reduced through intercourse to insignificance. . . . She learns to eroticize powerlessness and self-annihilation.

Intercourse, finally, is "the pure, sterile, formal expression of men's contempt for women," and here Dworkin's fury drives her language to extreme expressions of hatred and despair.

In Chapter Eight, "Low," Dworkin is persuasive in showing that intercourse is an act so controlled by statute and penal code that it can never be "private," but she surprisingly goes on to claim that sex laws are primarily a means for regulating men, for limiting male-male conflict to maintain male dominance. In the final chapter, "Dirt/Death," she concludes by showing how sexual language is "dirty" because women are dirty, inferior, "other," and women are sex.

I chose to present these capsule summaries of each chapter to give the reader the opportunity of experiencing both the monotony and the insight offered by this work. I, too, believe it is a mistake to see sex and intercourse as banal or as easily reformable. But, unlike Dworkin, I feel a universalistic description of the meaning and consequences of intercourse based on anatomical arrangements is not in women's best interests. Anatomy is never destiny in a world of socially constructed arrangements.

Stripped of its emphasis on genital layout and deployment as determinative, Dworkin can be read as reminding us that the very personal is very political, and that most heterosexual intercourse, by ignoring women's individuality and wish for self-determination, serves to trap women into compliance and collaboration that undermines their feminist integrity and commitment. As sex therapists have insisted on for two decades, intercourse-oriented sex is not woman oriented. The original insights of Koedt and Densmore are as valid today as in the early 1970s.

But Dworkin's message cannot be seen in the late 1980s as simply a reminder that our revolution must continue in the bedroom as it does in the courtroom and the boardroom. We cannot "strip" her argument of its focus of intercourse as "the fundamental question of feminism," because the anatomical focus is central to Dworkin's thinking. Further developing the arguments made in her earlier books on pornography, she continues to privilege sexuality as the central question for feminists. Nothing will happen in the boardroom or the courtroom, she insists, until and unless something happens to change male sexuality.

I do not think there is *a central question* for feminists. Gender arrangements are pervasive power differences, and influence all activities, feelings, and thoughts. Steadfast deconstruction and reconstruction of one thing after another is the formula for change. I personally also choose to write and work with a special emphasis on sexuality, but it is not because I think this or anything else is *the primal* issue. Dworkin's book deserves appreciation and study for its challenging depiction of various aspects of heterosexual relations despite her overstatement of their importance. I regret that her polemics will limit the audience reached by this book.

Hermoine Lee (review date 3 June 1988)

SOURCE: "Taking the Lid Off," in *Times Literary Supplement,* June 3, 1988, p. 611.

[*In the following review, Lee offers unfavorable assessment of* Letters from a War Zone, *which she dismisses as "an appalling book."*]

This is an appalling book, and it is hard not to be appalled by it for hasty reasons. Andrea Dworkin is a fanatic, a ranter and a bully. She represents, in her own sad words, "the morbid side of the woman's movement. I deal with the shit, the real shit." To read her is to go to prison: to become, like her, a monomaniac, confined inside the walls of her cruel theme, to the complete exclusion of other and kinder ways of thinking about being alive. She is profoundly offensive to "civilized" liberals because she denies all possibility of tolerant allowances or individual variations.

She is, also, particularly alien to most British readers, since, though she describes herself as a lone prophet in the wilderness of fascist "Amerika," she belongs to a very American tradition of inspirational platform speaking. *Letters from a War Zone* are mostly speeches, written in the 1970s and 80s as ways of circumventing the publishing and media industries which, Dworkin claims, have repeatedly censored and silenced her. But though she says she was forced into speech-making, public rhetoric clearly suits her: there is no great difference in style between the speeches, the essays and the books on the same themes (written at the same time as the speech-making) such as *Pornography* and *Intercourse.*

Dworkin's enraged abusing of abuses might seem a far cry from the charming, vague, utopian utterances of Henry

James's Verena Tarrant in 1886: "We require the lid to be taken off the box in which we have been kept for centuries. You say it's a very comfortable box with nice glass sides. . . . Good gentlemen, you have never been in the box, and you haven't the least idea how it feels!" There are no good gentlemen in Dworkin's war zone, and Verena's glass box has become a peep-show torture chamber, rigged with whips and belts. But James was using, however sceptically, Dworkin's own historical models, courageous platform feminists like Margaret Fuller, Susan Anthony and Elizabeth Cady Stanton. The occasions of Dworkin's writings—a peroration at the end of "a three-hour speak-out on sex" to over 1,000 women in New York City, speeches all over the country to "Take Back the Night" marchers in the late 1970s, an anti-determinist address to a roomful of angry women in "Lesbian Pride Week," testimony given to the Attorney General's Commission on Pornography in 1986—are the latest chapter in the 200-year history of American feminist oratory.

Dworkin is a little too fond of presenting herself as a martyr-hero ("If you can't stand the heat, / Step down from the stake," she says, quoting her friend Robin Morgan) whose life must be at once exceptional and exemplary. She is the lonely "free spirit," "set apart" by her dedication to her art and her cause: "I have learned to live alone, developed a rigorous emotional independence, a self-directed creative will, and a passionate commitment to my own sense of right and wrong." She is alternately ostracized and silenced by the establishment, and hailed ecstatically by the Movement: "Women were crying and shaking and shouting. The applause lasted nearly ten minutes." This may be irritating, but it is of interest to historians of the women's movement in America.

But an objective historical reading is not invited. Like all notable demagogues, Dworkin has one thing to say and says it relentlessly. No behaviour, under Dworkin's Law, is free from harm. Parents, children, lovers, spouses, friends, colleagues: all are trapped by the system, and all must play their parts as either terrorists or the terrorized. No one can claim to be civilized, since civilization itself is barbarous. The world we all live in is a constructed male-dominated system of social institutions, sexual practices and economic relations, in which women are silenced, exploited and damaged. There is ("thus") an essential connection between the foul end, the "real shit," of sexual relationships—pornography, rape, wife-battering, prostitution—and the sanctioned end, marriage, love, "so-called" normal intercourse. The conspiracy to believe that women like to be hurt extends throughout. Just as the law allows for unspeakable abuses of women in pornography, so it gives "protective legitimacy" for the ownership of women by men. *Ergo,* "Marriage is a legal license to rape," "fucking is the means by which the male colonizes the female":

Women are a degraded and terrorized people. Women are degraded and terrorized by men. Rape is terrorism. Wife-beating is terrorism. Medical butchering is terrorism. Sexual abuse in its hundred million forms is terrorism. . . . Women are an occupied people. . . . This fascist ideology of female inferiority is the preeminent ideology on this planet.

No remission is allowed: there is, for Dworkin, nothing else to say, no other way of saying, and nothing to do but say it.

The book is full of dreadful and convincing examples of the power and influence of the multi-million dollar pornography industry. Her stories of domestic brutality and abuse are appallingly authentic, and her evidence of the connections between pornography, rape and incest seems impossible to deny. Her most extreme instances—death by suffocation of victims of "deep throat" rapes, "snuff films" in which prostitutes in Central America are tortured, dismembered and killed for the camera, and the prints sold to private pornography collections in the States—should be considered by anyone wanting to argue for pornography as a benign aid to sexual pleasure.

But the sad truth is that, except for altogether like-minded readers, Dworkin's book is not persuasive. It is hard to be outraged all the time, and the writing suffers terribly from its inexorability: an essay on *Wuthering Heights* has to be on Heathcliff as a wife-batterer, a celebration of the eighteenth-century actress Susannah Cibber has to end with a statement on today's actresses "compelled to act out for us our most abject humiliations." She is a writer entirely without humour, and when she talks about recoiling from a telephone receiver because she knows it can be used as a sexual weapon against women, or describes an activist called Shell Wildwomoon pouring human blood over some didoes in a shop in Hartford Connecticut, or defines a friend as an anti-rape feminist (what is a *pro-rape* feminist?), derision is tempting.

There are more serious grounds for dismay. Though Dworkin hotly repudiates attacks on her as a biological determinist, she can still say "Men as a class are moral cretins," or "Men love death." Such diktats sit oddly with a polemic as full of utopian propositions ("We must use our bodies to say 'Enough'") as Verena Tarrant's speeches. Dworkin argues that her "facts" can only be done away with through a feminist revolution; till then they are universal and inevitable. But if statements such as "Women have to pretend to like men to survive," or "Relationships called love are based on exploitation," are simply not true to your own experience, you cannot be a follower of Dworkin's Law.

The totalitarian refusal to allow exceptions is part of some-

thing still more disturbing. In order to describe brutality and aggression, Dworkin uses a brutal and aggressive rhetoric. In order to attack the tedious dehumanizings of pornography, she tediously dehumanizes its agents. Since she has been censored she must demand a policy of censorship (hence her battles with the American Civil Liberties Union, and the attacks on her from the Left as a reactionary opponent of free speech). Dworkin is well aware of these traps, but she sees no alternative. What is most appalling about this significant and desolating book is that perhaps there can be no language of protest other than the language of what is opposed; that revolutionaries must always become tyrants, and thereby defeat themselves.

Deborah Harrold (review date April 1989)

SOURCE: A review of *Intercourse*, in *Ethics*, Vol. 99, No. 3, April, 1989, pp. 670-1.

[*In the following review, Harrold summarizes Dworkin's view of sexual inequality in* Intercourse.]

All right, strap on those crampons, and into the Abyss! How does intercourse relate to the status of women?

Intercourse is examined through a series of concepts—repulsion, skinlessness, stigma, communion and possession, and the opposing/complementary roles of virginity and occupation/collaboration. Dworkin uses a multiple approach to her subject and her subjection. She analyzes social practice and individual lives, and the use of language; she employs psychoanalytical concepts, legal interpretation, and literary criticism. The interpretation of literary texts is excellent—marked by generosity and effective, never strained, exegesis. The examination of legal definition and construction of gender and sexual practices (both legal and illegal) is especially fine.

Dworkin notes the constant challenge to the liberal notion of the individual that women present. Her property in herself is intrinsically compromised by that opening for men to penetrate. Woman is open, marked as penetrable and possessible in biology, personal relations, and law. Dworkin's positioning of intercourse in the foreground of the inquiry into woman's lesser worth has been burlesqued as an acceptance of biological determinism; as buying into a vulgar ideology of male supremacy. Yet the constructions of a hegemonic culture, whether true or false, define women's roles and lives. These constructions are no less powerful for being constructions.

Woman is defined in difference and in degradation as the opposite of man. Woman is socially constructed as a human being to be taken, entered, penetrated, to bear up, to bear children willingly or unwillingly. Rebels who choose to have none of this are not going their own way, they are going the other way, a form of rebellion defined in opposition to the dominant, dominating mode of being. Chastity, lesbianism, and alternate reproductive methods are commentaries, not challenges, to intercourse in a man-made world.

Is this penetrability of woman's body the principle reason, the first cause of her inferiority? Dworkin argues that there is more to penetration than social construction. But how much more? The strictly physical aspects of the female body, its openings and its fertility, indicate a natural sexual congress. But a proper use is charged with the abuse; the mock conquest of the first time with surprise, pain, and blood; or the risk and wearing away of health and mind by too many or too dangerous pregnancies; and woman's statistical infrequency of orgasm as reported anonymously to researchers. Dworkin suspects that our construction of intercourse is at the heart of the inferiority of women if physical construction is not enough. She notes that penetration could be interpreted differently. But a happy, self-willed, undominated sexuality that includes for women a positive and inclusive construction of mother, wife, lover is not the dominant set of meanings by which intercourse is interpreted. In fact, sometimes we cannot differentiate sexual activity from bloody murder: note the assumption that a glimpse of the primal scene by those of tender understanding will be devastating, and the confusion between violent murder and sexual congress in *Ruthless People*. It does not do to shrink from the unpalatable, and those who find the notion of the book preposterous should reflect on what it means to be fucked, fucked over, fucked up, or to do the fucking.

Lore Dickstein (review date 29 October 1989)

SOURCE: "Street Fighting Feminist," in *The New York Times Book Review,* October 29, 1989, pp. 11-2.

[*In the following review, Dickstein offers tempered criticism of* Letter from a War Zone. *According to Dickstein, "Much of what Andrea Dworkin has to say is important—whether you agree with it or not—but how she says it tends to undermine her argument."*]

Abbie Hoffman might have been pleased to see that someone still spells America with a "k," evoking in one small gesture the clenched fist, the pulsating energy and rebelliousness of the 1960's. Andrea Dworkin is still out there fighting, and hers is a very specific battle: against the way American culture treats women.

Ms. Dworkin, a novelist and the author of six books of nonfiction, is most famous for having initiated, with the feminist lawyer Catherine MacKinnon, legislation in Minneapolis in 1983 and 1984 that would have outlawed pornography as sex discrimination and a violation of women's civil rights. Passed by two City Councils, it was vetoed twice by the Mayor. Similar statutes in Indianapolis and in Bellingham, Wash., were struck down by the courts as a violation of the First Amendment right to free speech.

A political firebrand, Ms. Dworkin is a street fighter and an unswervingly radical feminist. Revolutions need people like her, women willing to draw fire on the front lines and the barricades. But when the heat of battle subsides, as it has in this country, such figures are inevitably left behind, railing at the departing troops. While some might be disappointed that other people did not share their fervor or staying power, Ms. Dworkin's reaction is a bristling fury: rage and self-righteous indignation suffuse this new collection of her work.

The pieces included in *Letters From a War Zone* are a mix of speeches delivered at protest marches and before college audiences, essays and an occasional book review or interview. They very in length from a few paragraphs to several pages, and each piece is prefaced by notes that succinctly place it temporally and politically. Ms. Dworkin uses these notes, as well as the introduction to the book, as an opportunity to vent her resentments and perceived slights; she considers any criticism of her ideas to be ridicule, any editing of her writing to be "police work for liberals."

In addition, Ms. Dworkin complains bitterly (and often) that she has been ostracized; "censored out of the Amerikan press" is the phrase she uses. The brunt of her anger is directed at the liberal press, including the Op-Ed page of this newspaper, which she once assumed, perhaps naïvely, would be her natural home. But, in fact, the lady protests too much: she has now had nine books published, almost all by mainstream houses.

Much of what Andrea Dworkin has to say is important—whether you agree with it or not—but how she says it tends to undermine her argument. The author writes in an incantatory, rhetorical style, probably effective when delivered from the soapbox but numbing to read. It rings in the ears, pummels the mind; one begs for release from this relentless harangue. But then, this is precisely Ms. Dworkin's point, her message as well as her method: to hound and harass, to respond to indifference or even civility with a shrill pitch of outrage.

She is not a subtle writer (she would probably consider it

an insult to be called that); the vulgarity and crassness of her language, much of it not fit to print here, are intentional—to shock, to be confrontational, to move to action. Her occasionally cogent insights are marred by a sweeping condemnation of any political stance but her own. She dismisses American feminism as an establishment that is "media-created and media-controlled . . . fairly corrupt." "Feminism is dying here," she says, "because so many women who say they are feminists are collaborators or cowards." The American Civil Liberties Union, which helped defeat some of her legislation, is characterized as "exceptionally corrupt, a handmaiden of the pornographers, the Nazis, and the Ku Klux Klan."

One piece, the transcript of Ms. Dworkin's 1986 testimony before the Attorney General's Commission on Pornography, stands out as free of the ranting polemics that marks so much in this collection. Here, with uncharacteristic grace, Ms. Dworkin gives an exceptionally reasoned, articulate and toned-down presentation of her case. Pornography, she tells the commission, "creates bigotry and hostility and aggression towards all women."

Using anecdotal evidence, she claims that pornographic materials are often used as instruction manuals in violent crimes. The women who pose for pornographic magazines and videotapes, she says, "are tortured as a form of public entertainment and for profit." She questions using the word "consent," because she feels that for women with few options (many of the models are poor, work as prostitutes and had been victims of childhood sexual abuse), freedom of choice is problematic at best. She would not use the obscenity laws to ban pornography, questioning what "community standards mean in a society when violence against women is pandemic." She would ban not just child pornography, a point on which she has lots of company, but all "sexually violent material," including mass-circulation magazines like *Playboy* and *Penthouse*. Here is where she gets into a legal tangle. Focusing solely on what she considers objectionable, she doesn't question what else might be banned if such a precedent were set. Finally, she calls for "federal civil rights legislation recognizing pornography as a virulent and vicious form of sex discrimination."

This same argument is repeated in many guises throughout the 11 year span of writing covered in this book. Only the language varies, with Ms. Dworkin pitching her most strident and graphic statements to the already converted. Some of these epigrammatic pronouncements have contributed to her notoriety and have pushed her to the far, lonely fringes of feminist thought. Here are a few emblematic examples:

"Romance . . . is rape embellished with meaningful looks."

"One of the differences between marriage and prostitution is that in marriage you only have to make a deal with one man."

"Marriage . . . is a legal license to rape."

"The hurting of women is . . . basic to the sexual pleasure of men."

"All men benefit from rape, because all men benefit from the fact that women are not free in this society."

Throughout *Letters From a War Zone,* Ms. Dworkin proclaims an unflinching, idealistic belief in the power of writing to effect change. "I am not afraid of confrontation or risk," she says, "also not of arrogance or error." This might well be her credo as a writer, a defiant finger thrust at the world. Yet Ms. Dworkin's pervasive senses of both persecution and superiority also lead her to say that she "never wanted to be less than a great writer," but that "great writing from women is genuinely—not romantically—despised." Her assessment of her own standing on the political scene is grim and defeated. "This essay, like others in this book," she says in the notes to one piece, "has no cultural presence: no one has to know about it or take it into account to appear less than ignorant; no one will be held accountable for ignoring it." In fact, Andrea Dworkin may not like the kind of attention her work receives, but she is hardly unnoticed.

Andrea Dworkin with Gail Dines and Rhea Becker (interview date June 1990)

SOURCE: "A Conversation With Andrea Dworkin," in *Sojourner,* Vol. 15, No. 10, June, 1990, pp. 17, 19-20.

[*In the following interview, Dworkin comments on pornography and contemporary feminist protest.*]

[*Gail Dines:*] *Why did you have to go to England to get* **Letters from a War Zone** *published originally?*

[Andrea Dworkin:] I can give you the reasons I know. In the United States the pornographers and the publishers see themselves as having identical interests—legal, social, and economic interests. In the United Kingdom that is not the case. Pornographers are still regarded as pimps and sleazeballs even though the consumers are your regular males, normal citizens. Publishers still see their responsibility as being to publish writers, and it has been in that kind of a social environment that I get published. People will say, "Whether we agree with you or not, you are a fine writer, therefore we will publish you."

It looks to me like pornography is getting worse, acts of violence are getting worse, and the younger the assailant, the more vicious and violent the act. But what I've found with a lot of women is, "Oh, pornography? We've dealt with the pornography question. Can't Dworkin give it a rest?". Do you agree that pornography is getting worse?

I think there's a certain detached objective way in which you can say it's not getting worse; it never gets worse in the sense that it has always been primarily about rape, sadism, and humiliation. I mean, what's worse than the Marquis de Sade? What is worse is that it is much easier to use real people in the production of the sadistic and humiliating pornography, and also that there are no limits on the kind of pornography that can be publicly displayed and sold. What we're seeing is a complete saturation of the society with pornography that grows more and more sadistic. What we know is that men become very quickly desensitized to whatever it is in pornography that arouses them to begin with. So that *Playboy*, alas, is losing subscriptions. I don't think it is because of our activism, in which case the pornography industry would be growing smaller in size, but because these men become desensitized and need more violent pornography.

Many of my students tell me they spend their Friday nights at gross-out parties. That is, you rent four or five of the worst slasher films, get drunk, and watch the movies throughout the night. Slasher films prime these kids at age fourteen or fifteen, then a bit later they become the real pornography consumers.

Statistics now indicate that boys are getting younger and younger when they first consume pornography. So very young adolescents see pornography and use it and have it as their primary source of sex instruction. And since there's really no limit on what's on the newsstands, it's not as if they're seeing what used to be called "soft-core" pornography. They're seeing the whole range of pornography, and because video pornography is so accessible, what they see is even more vivid and makes an even greater impression than the static pornography of the magazines. So it really is a very desperate situation, if you understand that pornography is—as I have come to think of it—the DNA of male supremacy. So if you want to do something about male supremacy, you had better understand that we have to do something about pornography. The average age of rapists, of course, is also going down, congruent with the consumption of pornography.

From what I read in news reports, it seems more and more men are filming rapes—and not just for making a fast buck by selling the film. But they keep it—the actual incriminating evidence that they committed a rape. I'm be- ginning to wonder if we've reached the point where there's no separation between media and reality, that the two are completely fused; that men need documentation of what they did because then it becomes real; that they're so trained to be voyeurs that it is now coded into their sexuality.

It's a vast question. I think that it's true, as you put it, that the form of pornography has become a part of male sexuality, but in a way you can say that the technology is taking over because the alienation is closer to complete. In fact, touching an actual human being is almost anticlimactic. The video is more real; the photographs are more real.

For me, the ethical basis of the issue has always been that if the person next to you in bed or in life is not real, it is impossible for the person down the street to be real to you. If you do not understand the humanity of the person you are with, you can't understand humanity, period. So what we have is a new generation of men who have been raised on these dead women, these pressed, flat cadavers of sexuality, and who are in fact behaviorally tied to two-dimensional, painted, leg-splayed, unreal, unhuman, dead women.

Also, as Jane Caputi points out in her book, The Age of Sex Crime, *serial killers often kill women before they are able to ejaculate. They want the woman to be like the one in the picture.*

I don't think that it's uncommon, but I know one serial killer that we were trying to deal with in Minneapolis who had killed—I can't remember the numbers, but it was in double digits—Native American women, and after he had killed them, he posed them like the pictures in pornography. Let all those academic women or men tell us that pornography has nothing to do with this; that's crazy. It has everything to do with it.

One of the most surprising developments in the feminist antipornography movement in recent years was the appearance of FACT [Feminist Anti-Censorship Task Force]. What do you think of this development?

For me, it wasn't FACT in particular, but the initial organizing of the s/m lesbians that did it for me, which preceded FACT by several years. FACT, for me, was a kind of inevitable aftershock of the s/m lesbians, because to me feminism is the antidote to sadomasochism. And to have sadomasochism proclaimed as a feminist practice of liberation is the ultimate mind-fuck.

Younger lesbians I've spoken to tell me that there is no place for them, particularly on campuses, if they are not practicing sadomasochism. Has this been your experience as well?

I travel widely, as you know. I travel throughout the country, through Canada and in many parts of Europe. And I have only found the s/m lesbians to be strong in New York, Boston, and San Francisco. I think it's actually a very narrow phenomenon. I think it's a media-supported phenomenon. You've got this one little reed instrument playing and suddenly we've got amplification and it makes it sound as though you've got a five-thousand-piece orchestra. But it's not. Part of what has happened in the feminist community is that the feminist media has come to distort real experience as much as the mainstream media does. It's a mirror, but it's more like a funhouse mirror than a real mirror.

In spite of the s/m movement, it seems to me that women are still organizing against pornography.

There's a huge women's movement in this country—there's a huge women's movement all over. There's all this grass-roots activism. The pornography issue has brought many women of different ideologies to a feminist perspective on male dominance. And it has also broadened the movement in that women who were excluded by virtue of race and class before now see pornography as one of their main issues. It's an issue of poverty. It's an issue of exclusion. It's an issue of sexual exploitation, the kind of sexual exploitation that the poorest women in this society experience. So what I see is this division among women where there's this reactionary old-guard feminism that has circled all of its wagons around so that everybody talks only to each other, and then there's this much broader feminism that the news media choose to ignore.

So the radical movement is outside the universities.

Absolutely. And one of the great disappointments is that women's studies movements have become so reactionary. The only regret that I feel in my life as a feminist is that in the first few years of being on the road I worked so hard for the establishment of women's studies departments. Now I think, "Why?" I thought it was so important then. So much had been lost, so much had been suppressed, and if we had women's studies departments, then we would have had that material. But what the women who have these positions of safety are choosing to do is to bury alive books like Kate Millett's *Sexual Politics* and Shulamith Firestone's *The Dialectic of Sex*. They don't teach them. They have allowed these fundamental feminist texts to go out of print.

It's interesting how the antipornography ordinance that you wrote with Catherine MacKinnon has been regarded. People say, "If it's not going to wipe out pornography, then we're not interested in the law." Yet I've not heard any of these same people argue that we should tear down the rape laws because we can't be sure they're not go-

ing to be used improperly. Battle lines have been drawn regarding pornography. Why?

This might sound really shallow, but I think that the reason is because pornographers fight back. Pornography is a locus of male power and the thing that has terrified feminists about fighting it is that it's real. It's real, it's specific, it's organized, it's institutional. In political terms that means it's good target, you can find it. But what is frightening about it is that you had better be serious. You had better be willing to put your life on the line if you are going to fight it, and that's very different from what liberal feminists had in mind.

Do you think other countries are going to have more success than us in fighting pornography? Right now, Clare Short, a member of Parliament in England, is trying to pass legislation similar to the ordinance you drafted. [In the United States, the civil rights ordinance has been passed by some city councils and public referendums, but it has been ruled unconstitutional by the courts.]

Clare Short is one of many women who are trying to do something. Women Against Violence Against Women has of course been active for a long time, and there's a new group, called "Campaign Against Pornography and Censorship," which is essentially trying to get the Minneapolis legislation passed in England. They have a very good, clear program, which is to enact legislation that recognizes pornography as sex discrimination.

But don't forget, also, that the other issue is that in England there are laws against racial hatred. They're very specific. Most Americans don't even know about them. They say you cannot say this, this, or this, because it incites racial hatred. And then it lists all the media in which you cannot say all these very specific things. Now the Liberals and Labour Party people have supported these laws in the United Kingdom so they have very little basis for refusing to support laws that do something about sexual hatred. And in fact, the Campaign Against Pornography and Censorship has gotten the National Committee on Civil Liberties in England to endorse what is essentially the Minneapolis ordinance because they convinced the membership that pornography acts as a force that subordinates women in society and therefore denies us our civil liberties. And every country in Europe that was occupied by the Nazis has laws against race hate and against speech that encourages genocide.

So the National Committee on Civil Liberties in England has actually endorsed the Minneapolis legislation.

Not by that name, but it is the same legislation. And in New Zealand, the Ministry for Justice has recommended passage of a similar law. In Germany, essentially the same bill has been endorsed by the Social Democrats and is being studied by the other parties. I think we'll see antipornography legislation passed in a lot of Western democracies.

Would you like to add anything?

Just that I am proud of the women I work with and how extraordinary they are. And I think that they are going to endure, and that we are going to win.

Ann Russo and Lourdes Torres (essay date June 1990)

SOURCE: "Why Feminists Should Read Andrea Dworkin," in *Sojourner,* Vol. 15, No. 10, June, 1990, pp. 16-7.

[*In the following essay, Russo and Torres provide a positive overview of Dworkin's feminist perspective and political activism through analysis of* Letters from a War Zone.]

The following retrospective essay provides an analysis of Andrea Dworkin's work from 1976 to 1989. It is based on Dworkin's newest book, a compilation of essays and speeches entitled **Letters from a War Zone: Writings 1976-1989,** *which covers subjects ranging from Hedda Nusbaum's experience of battery to the ACLU's stand on pornography.*

Dworkin has devoted her life to fighting violence against women in all its manifestations, particularly pornography. She co-authored, with attorney Catharine MacKinnon, an antipornography ordinance (known as the Minneapolis ordinance), which defines pornography as a violation of women's civil rights. The ordinance allows those who are hurt by pornography to sue for damages. . . .

Women, according to Andrea Dworkin, are socialized to be indifferent to our own situation and that of other women. She seeks through her essays and speeches, compiled in *Letters from a War Zone,* to compel women to fight for women's rights. Writing is her active response to the war being waged daily against women. She introduces her new volume of essays by stating:

> *I wrote [these essays and speeches] because I care about fairness and justice for women. I wrote them because I believe in bearing witness and I have seen a lot. I wrote them because I believe in writing, in its power to right wrongs, to change how people see and think, to change how and what people know, to change how and why people act. I*

wrote them out of the conviction, Quaker in its origin, that one must speak truth of power. . . . And I wrote these essays, gave these speeches, because I believe in people: that we can disallow cruelty and embrace the simple compassion of social equality.

Dworkin, an outspoken advocate for women's freedom, appeals throughout the volume for women to commit themselves to the struggle against sexual inequality and violence. She recognizes, in her powerful essay **"Feminism: An Agenda,"** that in doing this work "one of the things the women's movement does is to make you feel pain. You feel your own pain, the pain of other women, the pain of sisters whose lives you can barely imagine." Some women, feminists included, find her too depressing, negative, and angry, and refuse to believe the situation is really that bad for women. She has been much maligned in the mainstream and Left press, as well as in feminist and women's studies publications, for her forthright condemnation of male power, and particularly for her analysis of pornography.

Especially problematic for some feminists is the fact that Dworkin names the men we know—our fathers, husbands, lovers, brothers, uncles, friends, comrades, and co-workers—as potentially the most dangerous to us because they are the ones who have the most access to us. She challenges our most unquestioned and intimate relationships involving love, sexual desire, and sexual practices, including intercourse and sadomasochism, and analyzes them as social institutions centrally involved in women's oppression. To be critical of these particular men, and of these intimate and close relations, means challenging our relationships in fundamental ways, and so many would rather dismiss her analysis.

Dworkin is commonly accused of being a biological determinist. In feminist academic circles, this critique is enough to totally dismiss her work and any contribution she might have. Yet such a criticism shows that her critics either do not read her work or read into it whatever they want. Throughout, the volume *Letters from a War Zone,* Dworkin analyzes biological determinism as the underlying ideology of male supremacy—as the major rationale and justification for inequality, male violence, and female subordination throughout history. She emphasizes how biological determinism has been used historically to justify and orchestrate racial and ethnic bigotry, war, and genocide, as in the Nazi Holocaust and in U.S. slavery. Dworkin speaks out against such perspectives wherever she encounters them, even among feminists. For instance, in her essay **"Biological Superiority: The World's Most Dangerous and Most Deadly Idea,"** she describes a panel in 1977 on Lesbianism as a Personal Politic, in which she was hissed at and shouted down for criticizing the Super Woman ideology advocated by some lesbians. Dworkin firmly believes that acceptance of biological determination in any form is a fundamental mistake for any political movement.

Despite this analysis, many continue to call Dworkin a biological determinist because of her unflinching critique of male power as the power that men (as a group and as individuals) hold over women in this society. Dworkin does hold all men accountable for their violence and abuse no matter what their politics. At the same time, however, she has faith in men at some level and in the possibilities for social change. For instance, in **"I Want a Twenty-Four-Hour Truce During Which There is No Rape,"** she challenges the men at the 1983 Midwest Regional Conference of the National Organization for Changing Men: "I am here today because I don't believe that rape is inevitable or natural. If I did, I would have no reason to be here. If I did, my political practice would be different than it is. Have you ever wondered why we are not just in armed combat against you? It's not because there is a shortage of kitchen knives in this country. It is because we believe in your humanity, against all the evidence."

Central to Dworkin's feminist analysis and politics are the very women with whom the mainstream leaders of the women's movement have rarely identified: the poor, the homeless, prostitutes, women in pornography, women who have been battered, raped, and sexually abused as children. She does not distance herself from women who are victimized by men in this society nor does she make them into one-dimensional objects of discourse. In her writing, she identifies herself as a woman who has been hurt and battered, and as a survivor. She sees her work as part of the struggle of all women toward freedom. This is unusual in feminist theoretical and academic writing. Many feminists disassociate themselves from women who are victimized by male violence (even if they themselves have been victimized, and even when they are working on these issues). What perhaps is most frightening to academic and mainstream feminists about Dworkin's writing is recognizing themselves in these pages, realizing that the privilege they have acquired by distance or disassociation ultimately does not differentiate them: they are still girls, they are still raped, they are still battered, they still have pornography and hateful propaganda used against them.

Dworkin speaks on behalf of all women and children, of all races, because as she states, "By the year 2000, women and their children are expected to be one hundred percent of this nation's poor." She believes that women constitute a class by virtue of the fact that all women are oppressed through sexual subordination; but to say this is not to suggest that Dworkin fails to analyze women's condition in terms of race, class, and economic power.

Dworkin's writing, more than many white radical or liberal feminist analyses, illuminates how the histories of racial and ethnic hatred are integrally related to the history of sexism and male domination. The intersections of race, class, and sex, which are explicated throughout the book, are perhaps most directly articulated in this volume in **"Feminism: An Agenda,"** which outlines her vision for a women's movement, and in her analysis of *Wuthering Heights,* which documents how sexual sadism and racism are created and reproduced in personal relationships. Moreover, Dworkin consistently points out how rape has been used in this country to bolster racism. By focusing attention on stranger rape and by perpetuating the mythology of the black rapist, white men, both on the Right and the Left, prop up racism and simultaneously take attention away from themselves as potential (and actual) rapists.

In her analysis of men's control over women's reproduction, Dworkin focuses on the right of every woman to control her body and her sexuality. She reminds us that many poor women in the United States do not have access to abortions, and that feminists must demand the right of women of color and poor women not to be sterilized because of their race and class status. Similarly, in her analysis of pornography, Dworkin advocates for those who are most often left out of the debates: the women who work in the industry. She points out that 65 to 70 percent of the women in the industry are victims of sexual abuse. Most are poor women and/or runaways, women who entered the industry not because they weighed a series of viable options and found the pornography industry to be the most attractive, but because economic survival demanded it. Moreover, she consistently points out how race, color, and class also determine women's position within the pornography industry.

Dworkin is best known for her analysis of pornography as systemic and institutionalized sexual violence and abuse of women, both in and out of the pornography industry. She defines pornography as the graphic, sexually explicit subordination of women. Dworkin does not see pornography as simply ideas or images, but rather as a practice, which actively oppresses women through its production and consumption. For Dworkin, the question of whether pornography causes violence against women is not the issue, because "pornography *is* violence against women."

She demonstrates this claim in three ways. First, she emphasizes that the pornography is made with real women and so is not fantasy for the women who have to be and do whatever the pornographer asks, demands, or coerces them into doing. Secondly, she emphasizes the real effects of pornography on women not in the industry: women in personal and social relationships with men who consume pornography; women assaulted and abused by men who get their ideas, motive, and strategy from pornography; and all women living in a society in which women are consistently treated as sexual objects and less than human. Finally, in **"Why Pornography Matters to Feminists,"** she argues that "pornography is an essential issue because pornography says that women want to be hurt, forced, and abused; pornography says women want to be raped, battered, kidnapped, maimed; pornography says women want to be humiliated, shamed, defamed; pornography says that women say No but mean Yes—Yes to violence, Yes to pain." And these are the very beliefs and values that lead judges and juries to refuse restraining orders to battered women, acquit child abusers because the girl children seem "sexually provocative," award custody to fathers who sexually abuse their daughters, and acquit rapists because of the way the victim is dressed.

Integral to Dworkin's analysis of pornography is a discussion of how racism is sanctioned and encouraged concurrently with misogyny, both in the material itself and in the conditions surrounding its distribution. Dworkin points out that the most sadistic violence and hatred depicted in pornography is directed at women of color: video games encourage the rape of Native American women; Asian women are hung, dead, from trees; Jewish women are placed in death camp scenarios where they supposedly delight in torture by Nazi captors; snuff movies, where women are slaughtered and dismembered for male enjoyment, are advertised as being filmed in Latin America, "where life is cheap"; and black women are presented as slaves on plantations, begging for abuse. Dworkin, in her testimony before the attorney general's commission on pornography (**"Pornography Is a Civil Rights Issue"**), states, "In this country where I live, there is a trade in racism as a form of sexual pleasure. . . . Black skin is presented as if it is a female genital, and all the violence and abuse and the humiliation that is in general directed against female genitals is directed against the black skin of women in pornography." She thus develops how pornography sexualizes racial and ethnic bigotry and racializes sexual bigotry, and gives these processes significance in a society already permeated with such divisions and inequality.

In this collection, a number of essays are devoted to the civil rights approach to pornography that Dworkin and Catharine MacKinnon developed. The civil rights law is "based on the state's abdication of responsibility for assuring human rights for discrete groups of people, based on color or based on sex." It is absolutely distinct from obscenity laws. The civil rights approach has nothing to do with a criminal ban, police power, or prior restraint. Rather, it is a legal tool for women who have been hurt by pornography. In **"Against the Male Flood: Censorship, Pornography and Equality,"** Dworkin argues that a civil rights law "empowers women by allowing women to civilly sue those who hurt us through pornography by trafficking in it, coercing people into it, forcing it on people, and assaulting people directly because of a specific piece of it." Such a law stops the pornographers "from producing discrimination with the total impunity they now enjoy, and gives women a legal standing resembling equality from which to repudiate the subordination itself."

In debates on pornography, inevitably the question of free speech surfaces as an argument against doing just about anything to fight pornography. Dworkin's conception of freedom of speech recognizes that the most powerless people in society do not have free speech. In her essay **"For Men, Freedom of Speech; For Women, Silence Please,"** she writes:

> *The First Amendment, it should be noted, belongs to those who can buy it. Men have the economic clout. Pornographers have empires. Women are economically disadvantaged and barely have token access to the media. A defense of pornography is a defense of the brute use of money to encourage violence against a class of persons who do not have—and have never had—the civil rights vouchsafed to men as a class.*

Dworkin's concept of freedom of speech is not abstract, it is not about ideas; it is about the reality of who has power and who doesn't.

Dworkin's concept of freedom of speech is not abstract, it is not about ideas; it is about the reality of who has power and who doesn't.
—Ann Russo and Lourdes Torres

A major premise of Dworkin's is that silence does not mean consent. One of the purposes of her writing and activism has been to break the silence around sexual abuse. For example, she speaks as a formerly battered wife. Women who are beaten by their lovers or husbands, Dworkin argues, eventually lose language, stop trying to say anything, and become totally isolated, because their speech and their screams are ignored, denied, mistrusted and/or misunderstood. Until the speech of battered women, incest survivors, prostitutes, and the many other powerless groups in society has real social significance and power, the First Amendment and abstract ideals of "freedom of speech" are meaningless. They were never meant to protect the interests of women (or men for that matter) who have no money, property, or social and political power.

Dworkin describes the realities of incest, rape, and battery as they are enacted in and out of marriage and family, in public and private institutions, in prostitution and pornography, and demands that we take the lives of women seriously so that we may be motivated to action. She gives women's stories validity and importance, and she responds with outrage and grief to the suffering of women. She interprets acts of violence against women as atrocities, insists that they are serious human rights violations, and indicative of the cruelty arising from inequality, bigotry, and hatred. This interpretation is not typical, because in this society, women's lives don't carry that much weight, and mostly we are blamed for the violence against us. Because women are not accorded full human status, rape, incestuous assault, and other forms of sexual violence are accepted as part of "normal life."

Dworkin believes that foremost among the purposes of feminism must be the commitment to end human suffering. She challenges, "If you are a feminist, and if you have forgotten that our purpose is to *end* the suffering of countless unnamed and invisible women from the crimes committed against them—and yes, we may also end the suffering of the men who are committing the crimes, yes, we think we can—then your feminism is hollow, it doesn't count."

Many feel that the focus on violence presents a futile and pessimistic view of the world for women, and may even contribute to hurting women. While it may feel futile—because it is in so many ways the reality of many women's lives (just pick up the newspaper on any given day)—Dworkin offers hope to women in the form of anger, clarity, and indignation at the conditions of our lives. Contrary to much writing today about sexual violence, Dworkin never individualizes, psychologies, or neutralizes the violence (tendencies popular in much of the co-dependency, dysfunctional family, and similar literature) and she never blames women. Dworkin's feminism says to women: "It is not 'just life.' It is politics; it is history; it is power; it is economics; it is institutional modes of organization: it is not 'just life.'" Throughout her work, she emphasizes that while sexual inequality and pervasive violence is reality, it is not truth. Dworkin counters passive acceptance, resignation, pity, and sympathy. She offers hope for change in women's individual and collective lives, but it is *not* a hope that looks like storybook happiness. It is a hope that is dependent upon and embedded in personal, social, and political struggle.

Part of the struggle for social change, for Dworkin, is the commitment to individual integrity—a commitment to facing the truth, speaking truth to power, and basing our actions on a thorough understanding of our lives and the lives of all women, an understanding that is not filtered through male ideology. In her essay on theory and politics, **"Look, Dick, Look. See Jane Blow It,"** she writes:

> *The mind struggling for integrity will fight for the significance of her own life and will not give up that significance for any reason. Rooted in the reality of her own experience—which includes all that has happened to her faced squarely and all that she has seen, heard, learned and done—a woman who understands that integrity is the first necessity will find the courage not to defend herself from pain. The colonized mind will use ideology to defend itself from both pain and knowledge.*

Integrity, says Dworkin, is essential to political theory and practice. The danger in any political movement, she argues, is the compulsion to authority and to group ideology without reflection or thought. She suggests: "One may discover integrity in the companionship of others, but one does not ever discover integrity by bowing to the demands of peer pressure. The heavier the pressure is toward conformity—no matter how lofty the proposed final goal—the more one must be suspicious of it and antagonistic to it." Dworkin never trivializes or ridicules women's efforts for social change; she understands that everything women do in the fight against violence matters.

Throughout *Letters from a War Zone,* Dworkin speaks to the diversity and creativity of individual and collective actions women have taken in defense of ourselves and for freedom. Many of the speeches and essays were written as part of the grassroots feminist movement, for rallies and demonstrations, public hearings, and campus controversies. Throughout her essays, she pays tribute to women's courageous actions in fighting back, including killing their husbands, organizing demonstrations, committing civil disobedience, destroying pornography, creating legislation, writing letters, and petitioning governments.

One of the common misconceptions about Dworkin is that she is intolerant and narrow in her politics and vision. We disagree. What she asks is not that you follow her theory and agenda slavishly and unthinkingly, but that you do something to help stop the suffering of women that many of us take for granted:

> *I don't have an agenda. My agenda is everything I can think of, everything I think of doing, all the time: movement, movement, physical and intellectual and political confrontations with power. You have to write the picket signs, march, scream, yell, write the fucking letters. It's your responsibility to yourselves and to other women.*

Zoë Heller (review date 5 October 1990)

SOURCE: "Nasties," in *Times Literary Supplement,* October 5, 1990, p. 1072.

[In the following review, Heller offers unfavorable assessment of Mercy.*]*

In 1983, Andrea Dworkin gave a speech to students at Hamilton College in upstate New York. "I represent the morbid side of the women's movement", she began. "I deal with the shit, the real shit." Seven years on, Dworkin's commitment to the dirty work of feminism shows no signs of letting up. "The shit"—or more specifically, the physical abuse of women by men—is still her specialization.

Her second novel, *Mercy,* is the story of Dworkin's *alter-ego,* "Andrea", a young woman whose journey through the misogynist world ("this zoo of sickies and sadists") constitutes an almost encyclopaedic survey of male sexual violence. Andrea begins her first-person narrative with an account of being assaulted in a cinema at the age of nine. Adolescence is french-kissing dirty old men on buses, and sex at knife-point with the neighbourhood tough. Adulthood is heralded by being raped "properly" for the first time.

The young Andrea is a Walt Whitman fan. She wants to sing the body electric and contain multitudes. But wherever she goes and whatever she does, she confronts a relentless male hostility. She is sent to jail for being on a peace demo, and sadistic doctors rip her up inside with a speculum. She travels to Crete and is raped again. She returns to New York and is raped in her apartment by a local gang-leader. A man comes to rescue her but proceeds to rape her himself, biting her genitalia to shreds.

And on the brutalities go—not so much set down, as spewed out in an anguished, paragraphless emission. Her prose revels in its own paratactic disorder, rejecting all "bourgic" refinements. "Nightmares don't have a linear logic with narrative development," she explains, "Terror ain't aesthetic."

This is a tricky position for a novelist to adopt. "Andrea" insists on a raw, traumatized prose style because anything more "aesthetic" would, she says, let us off too easily—make the horror too palatable. This implies a curiously primitive notion of how art achieves its impact. By piling up the gore and punctuating each fresh grotesquerie with a yell of retrospective pain, Andrea isn't shocking us into truth. She is ranting. There is no suffering so profound that it cannot be rendered banal by bad prose, and *Mercy* confirms this uncomfortable fact.

Andrea also rejects theoretical subtleties. Evil things are evil, she says. Rape is evil. Men are evil. "You may find me one who ain't guilty but you can't find me two." One has a feeling that this rough and ready philosophizing is leading somewhere nasty, and sure enough, Andrea concludes her story by declaring war on the opposite sex. She has taken to roaming the streets at night, beating up male tramps. "I hurt them and I run; and I fucking don't care about fair; discuss fair at the U.N." She plans to expand her one-woman terrorism act into an international guerilla force. "I've always wanted to see a man beaten to a shit bloody pulp with a high-heeled shoe stuffed up his mouth, sort of the pig with the apple."

Ho hum. Anticipating the objections to this radical revenge strategy, Dworkin has framed Andrea's narrative with a prologue and epilogue entitled "Not Andrea." The woman who speaks in these sections is a parody of the fudging, liberal feminist. She insists that as a university academic, her interest is in theory, not "direct human experience." She says it is "tiresome" to dwell on sexual abuse. She suggests that rape has "transformative dimensions." She is, of course, offensive and ludicrous. And she is meant to make our weedy reservations stick in our throats.

It is immense intellectual dishonesty on Dworkin's part, though, to have characterized her critics in this way. One doesn't have to think rape is transformative to query whether all men are "Nazis without uniforms." One doesn't have to prize theory over experience to wonder about the efficacy of beating up tramps. Dworkin has written a mad, bad novel; and one doesn't have to be a man, a rapist, or a self-hating woman to admit as much.

Wendy Steiner (review date 15 September 1991)

SOURCE: "Declaring War on Men," in *The New York Times Book Review,* September 15, 1991, p. 11.

[In the following review, Steiner offers tempered criticism of Mercy. *According to Steiner, "Ms. Dworkin's argument, proceeding from pain, may be moving, but it is also intolerant, simplistic and often just as brutal as what it protests."]*

This past spring in London, with an hour to kill in a bookstore, I decided to read the first few pages of as many new novels as I could. Among the recent releases was *Mercy,* a second novel by the controversial feminist Andrea Dworkin, better known to me for her nonfiction tirades against pornography, against intercourse, against men. She was not a writer I would normally be drawn to, but in the spirit of experimentation I read through the first chapter. It was a representation of sexual trauma through a 9-year-old child's bewilderment, and I found myself utterly transfixed; I had to keep on reading. But although it seemed powerful to me as fiction then, I now see Ms. Dworkin's book in a larger context—as another salvo in the war between liberals and radicals. Once again the noddy head of tolerance is pummeled by the unbrookable demands of outraged pain.

Mercy is spoken in the voice of a woman named Andrea, who tells us the story of her life. It is a *Bildungsroman,* composed to explain why she now kills men. "I was born in 1946," she says, "after Auschwitz, after the bomb, I never wanted to kill, I had an abhorrence for killing but it was raped from me, raped from my brain, obliterated, like freedom. I'm a veteran of Birkenau and Massada and deep throat, uncounted rapes, thousands of men, I'm twenty-seven, I don't sleep." Brutally attacked and cruelly disillusioned in each of the novel's 11 chapters, Andrea goes from a child raised among liberal Jews in Camden, N.J., to an alcoholic bag lady who kills bums as they sleep in the streets of New York. *Mercy* is a monologue that almost makes her deviance seem normal; its voice speaks *in extremis* out of a pain so compelling that patience and reason appear to be obscenely insensitive responses. Andrea's experience is meant to stand as that of all women and to constitute an unassailable argument against the attempt to coexist peaceably with men.

Bracketing Andrea's monologue are a short prologue and epilogue, each called "Not Andrea," in which feminist voices express the very calm and temperance that Andrea's pain invalidates. "As a woman of letters, I fight for my kind, for women, for freedom," says the speaker in the prologue. "The brazen scream distracts. The wild harridans are not persuasive. . . . I will not shout. This is *not* the ovens." This point of view gets short shrift in *Mercy.*

Ms. Dworkin's book denies measure, denies the difference between the metaphorical and the literal. In *Mercy,* women's experience is the ovens; women *are* the mass suicides of Massada. Andrea is not a persona or a character but Ms. Dworkin herself; art *is* life. Pornography is evil because it condones and incites the rape of women. Representation is power. All men's behavior toward women is finally rape. "Your heartbeat and his heartbeat can be the same heartbeat and it's still" rape.

This degradation, for Ms. Dworkin, is inevitable, however women may strive against it: "My mother named me Andrea. It means manhood or courage. . . . This one's someone, she probably had in mind; a wish; a hope; let her, let her, something. . . . Don't, not with this one. Just let this one through. Just don't do it to this one. . . . My mama showed that fiction was delusion, hallucination, it was a long, deranged lie designed to last past your own lifetime." Men's fictions of bondage and rape are the truth; women's fictions of liberation and equality are lies. Representation is power only if you are a man.

But *Mercy* itself is meant to provide a new representational strategy. Andrea's language is lyrical and passionate—a cross between the repetition of the early Gertrude Stein and, ironically, the unfettered flights of Henry Miller. She describes sexual violence in graphic terms, risking the prurience of the pornography she deplores. But unlike any antipornography text that I know, *Mercy* defeats prurience. It is to pornography what aversion therapy is to rape. The titillating language of violation—"one hand's holding my neck from behind and the other's pulling off my T-shirt, pulling it half off, ripping it"—becomes noxious with Andrea's terror and pain and the inhuman viciousness and betrayal of the men she has trusted. Her stylistic breathlessness—repetition, rhythm, loss of control—conveys not rising passion but the desperate need to have the violence end.

Andrea writes to change reality: "I have to be the writer [my mother] tried to be—Andrea . . . —only I have to do it so it ain't a lie . . . [I'm] just going to bleed all over you and you are going to have to find the words to describe the stain, a stain as big as [my] real life, boy; a big, nasty stain, a stain all over you, all the blood you ever spilled, that's the esthetic dimension." In this way, Andrea says, she is giving men the choice to be human or not, and turning women's weakness and loss into gain: "The less, the more, you see, is the basic principle, it's like psychological jujitsu except applied to politics through a shocking esthetic."

The ambition, the verbal brilliance, in this "shocking esthetic" are profoundly affecting, and the repulsiveness of the Not Andrea voice in the epilogue is the great scandal of our times—reason's inability to offer an acceptable answer to the pain that everywhere surrounds us. This weakness is the undoing of liberalism: in the sordid mess of the political correctness debate, the Mapplethorpe debacle and Salman Rushdie's collision with Islam, in the failure of communication between feminists inside the system and those outside it.

Ms. Dworkin's argument, proceeding from pain, may be moving, but it is also intolerant, simplistic and often just as brutal as what it protests. Ms. Dworkin advocates nothing short of killing men. The last chapter ends: "I went out; at night; to smash a man's face in, I declared war. My *nom de guerre* is Andrea One; I am reliably told there are many more; girls named courage who are ready to kill." One cannot argue here, any more than Mr. Rushdie could, that statements in literature are not equivalent to statements in the real world. Ms. Dworkin's pain erases the boundary between the two spheres, declaring the distinction a male trick to justify pornography and rape. Either her book must be absolved of murderous intent through special pleading—

the invocation of that very magic circle around art that she has worked so hard to deny—or else we must accept that we are reading a political manifesto justifying and inciting illegal acts. Either way, we are caught in a bind. We must either deplore Ms. Dworkin's duplicity, which would be unfeeling, or have her arrested, which would mean we were assenting to the literalism that is our own undoing.

Perhaps the most glaring weakness in Ms. Dworkin's esthetic is her indifference to other people's pain. She keeps insisting on her debt to Walt Whitman, whose house was on her street in Camden, but she denounces him for his false promises of democracy, never considering the pain of his homosexuality. And she is completely ruthless with women who do not share her point of view.

The Not Andrea of the epilogue turns out to be a lesbian who gets along fine with exploitative men because she inflicts on her lover the same bondage and sadism that men practice. Not Andrea's arguments are undercut by this revelation and by the stiltedness of the language placed in her mouth, and this strategy on Ms. Dworkin's part is cheap. The issues are important enough to be raised by a character whose liberalism is not so obviously corrupt.

The question is how we can deal with pain, conviction, compulsions that we do not share. Or alternately, the question is whom Ms. Dworkin thinks she is speaking to. By reading *Mercy* we are meant to experience her pain, to know it as our own. Will we take the next step—as women, becoming Andrea Two or Three or Ten, or as men, bending to the task of describing the blood that has stained us? Or is the matter put in terms too crude, too intellectually violent, to offer us the possibility of action? If all women are either victims or collaborators and all men are rapists, can the cry for mercy fall on any but deaf ears?

Roz Kaveney (review date Summer 1991)

SOURCE: "Review Article: Dworkin's *Mercy*," in *Feminist Review*, No. 38, Summer, 1991, pp. 79-85.

[*In the following review, Kaveney offers tempered criticism of* Mercy, *which she describes as "an ambitious novel." Kaveney writes, "The real failure of this book is not in the cheating, or the calculated omissions, or the implicit elitism; it is in the deep solipsism that characterizes it from beginning to end."*]

Polemical novels are problematic, both ethically and aesthetically. When a novel is merely a novel, the aesthetic questions around it have to do with how well it achieves its artistic ends; a critic may prefer Alexandrian trickiness, or may prefer simple passionate utterance, but these preferences are matters of opinion. When we are considering a polemic, the questions that have to be asked deal with the position advocated, but also with the methods adopted; most would agree that a polemic in favour of an egalitarian project which manipulates by subliminal rhetorical cues is devalued thereby, because to influence rather than to argue is to adopt a position of superiority at odds with the ideology promoted.

When a novel is both art object and argument, the weighing of the two sets of judgements becomes complex. The duty to produce the best possible novel, and the duty to put a case as clearly as possible in a way that respects readers' understanding, might sometimes conflict and have to be balanced. In this as in so much else, Andrea Dworkin makes it clear that she would like things to be simple—'I wanted some words; of beauty; of power; of truth; simple words; ones you could write down; to say some things that happened, in a simple way.' The bitingly satirical approach she takes, in her prologue and her epilogue, to an imagined postmodernist, libertarian, feminist opponent, makes it clear that she will have nothing to do with irony, or trickiness or moral ambiguity. If we are to judge *Mercy* by Dworkin's own standards, we should expect it to be sensitive to both aesthetic and ethical approaches, not only in what it says, but in how it says it.

Much has been claimed for *Mercy,* not least by its author. It weighs in as a leading contender for the title of Great Feminist Novel of our time; we are told that its failure to find a publisher in the United States is, as indeed it may be, the result of the conspiracy to suppress the thought of a leading feminist. It has to be said, without putting too much stress on the issue, that, in general, conspiracies to suppress are rather more successful; having most of one's work in print, and freely on sale, in one's native language, and regularly appearing on talk shows and in newspaper interviews is a sort of suppression to which many famous writers of the twentieth century might aspire, many political and sexual dissidents vainly desire. It has further to be said that, within the novel, which generally portrays the author as lone and embattled, the single oppositional voice heard is obliged to validate the protagonist's viewpoint by acknowledging 'Sexual Jacobins . . . are sexualised in the common culture as if *they* are the potent women. Everyone pays attention to them . . .' Dworkin attributes this phrase to her opponent, but seems to accept the title with pride. (Does she not know what the historical Jacobins did to the French feminists of the Revolutionary period?)

We are told, often by mainstream literary critics like Lorna Sage, that Dworkin is an 'essential' feminist writer because she writes with such passion about intolerable transgression; we will note, in passing, the assumption that feminist literature, and feminism itself, should be about feeling rather than thought, the further assumption that there is a division between those two and a choice to be made. (The abusive caricature of her feminist opponents offered in Dworkin's prologue and epilogue makes these assumptions a clear part of her own discourse—her opponent is clearly, as they used to say in the Tory party, too clever by half.)

This prologue and epilogue aside, the novel offers us a series of monologues in chronological sequence, detailing the experiences of a protagonist who shares the author's name, but specific identity with whom the author has explicitly disavowed—'I am not the person in the book.' This woman is sexually assaulted, sexually brutalized during treatment by prison doctors, sexually harassed, raped, subjected to wife battering, involved in nonconsensual fellatio and sado-masochism, and outraged by pornography. She aligns these experiences to her intuition that she partakes, perhaps by reincarnation, in the experience of the concentration camps; there is a long sequence in which the mass suicide of the Jewish zealots at Masada is at once praised and blamed, and an earlier avatar of the narrator kills herself so as to be a dissident participant in it. Her early involvement in the peace movement leads her to identify in an abstract sort of way with men who burned themselves alive to promote peace. She argues for an aesthetic and a politics that will concentrate on convicting men, and punishing them; to this end, the protagonist fire-bombs pornographers and beats up random members of the dispossessed substance-abusing urban male proletariat, hoping that this will inspire emulation. To heighten our emotional involvement, the book is written in long spans of declaratory sentences hitched on to each other with semi-colons; its monologue is rarely broken by speech.

Mercy is an ambitious novel, and its author's ambitions are clearly not merely literary. It has always seemed like gratuitous abuse to accuse Andrea Dworkin of Messianic fantasies, and most, if not all, of her opponents in the women's movement have accordingly refrained; this will no longer be necessary. One of the two epigraphs to the book is a quotation from Isaiah, about the imminent return of God as the redeemer; the endless Job-like rebukes to a God who is not absent, but rather a sadistic father, possibly make this ironic, but at various points Dworkin makes it clear that what she is describing is a Stations of the Cross. Her narrator's side is pierced, literally by an appendectomy operation, and later in a receiving of the stigmata; when she fantasizes about the killing of her ex-husband by anonymous women guerrillas, she uses the language of the Mass—'for this; do this; for me'—to make it a sacramental participation in her redemptive acts. The protagonist's central insight—'It is important for women to kill men' comes to her from 'a woman I didn't know with the face of an angel,' and presumably an angel's origin and authority. This

is a book which claims privilege at various points and in various ways; principal among those privileges is the claim to be regarded as a Holy Book, and thus as, if not truth, gospel.

Even though the author has disavowed specific identification with the protagonist, this is a novel which claims the special privilege which confessional has traditionally held in the women's movement; its first epigraph is from one of Sylvia Plath's most famous confessional poems. Even a naive reader knows that, beyond this text, the author has written other texts which offer an analysis of women's lot, based in part on personal experience, and specific programmes to combat sexual oppression; that naive reader would accordingly be entitled to assume that what is on offer here is analysis, experience and programme.

By disavowing specifically autobiographical intent here, Dworkin does not so much remove the implied authenticity of the personal, but add to it a claim of even more generalized authenticity; this is the biography either or at once of a fictional character, of Dworkin herself, or of Everywoman remade, by literary technique, in Dworkin's own image. One could choose to regard this as a postmodernist deconstruction of a particular feminist literary technique, but, given the specific denunciation of postmodernism in the text, it seems more likely that this is an old-fashioned matter of having one's cake and eating it. It might also, by the not especially naive reader, be taken as an abuse of the reader's sisterly trust.

One of the ways in which this is done is by an at times highly sophisticated, and at other times surprisingly crude, literary manipulativeness masquerading as demotic simplicity. Generally, this is a book which claims its moral superiority from its appearance of simplicity, and that authenticity which the appearance of simplicity often claims, but which achieves that appearance by constructing webs of technique.

When Dworkin writes of childhood, she does so in a language of simple declaration, with much repetition, and many sentences that start with conjunctions and tag on to each other endlessly without punctuation.

> and you don't know the right words but you try so hard
> and you say exactly how the man sat down and put
> his arm around you and started talking to you and you
> told him to go away but he kept holding you . . .

This is not reportage of the actual language of an actual abused eight-year-old, but rather the use of a literary convention of representation of children's speech, itself based on assumptions about what a child is and what concepts a child is capable of forming. Innocence has a moral authority, which, according to magical thinking, can be appropriated by miming the surface of innocence.

There is a tradition in American literature, and demagoguery, of using contractions aggressively to demonstrate commitment to straightforward expression, ignoring effete correctness; this tradition has been adopted by much representation of street and black speech. When Andrea, the character, suddenly starts saying 'Ain't,' as in 'Terror ain't aesthetic' or 'You may find me one who ain't guilty, but you can't find me two,' it is this tradition, and the moral authority attached to it, which is being invoked. (When Andrea is mocking the idea that any SM porn could be a record of consensual acts, she invokes the struggle for black civil rights: 'If I saw pictures like that of a black man I would cry out for his freedom; I can't see how it's confusing if you ain't KKK.' Any dissent from the Dworkin line is straight complicity with fascism, it appears.)

Other examples of this appropriation have been referred to above in my synopsis, and it is worth citing at least one example in detail:

> Birch trees make me feel sad and lonely and afraid. There's astrologers who say that if you were born when Pluto and Saturn were travelling together in Leo, from 1946 to about the middle of 1949, you died in one of the concentration camps and you came right back because you had to come back and set it right. Justice pushed you into a new womb and outrage, a blind fury, pushed you out of it onto this earth, this place, this zoo of sickness and sadists . . . I consider Birkenau my birthplace.

At various points in the feminist debates around sado-masochism, some startling claims to moral authority were flung around, but for brazen cheek, and carelessness of offense to camp survivors, this appropriation of actual pain to literary effect takes the biscuit. It is also stunningly clumsy in its movement between the poetic, the pseudo-scientifically specific, the personified and the merely outrageous.

The book adopts magic-realist techniques freely; or, to put it another way, it complicates its realist description and analysis by incidents of doubtful likelihood. When one of Andrea's rapists kisses her body, his kisses open up as infected wounds; later in the book her unhealed wounds bleed the green of rot and corrosion. If these are to be taken as metaphors, which clearly they are, what are we to assume about the claim that fellatio has denatured the narrator's voice—'something hoarse and missing, an absence, a mere vibration'—is this a realist claim about physical injury, or a metaphysical claim about the loss of personal integrity and authenticity? In a text which is political and ethical as well as literary, we are entitled to know which; an author who is playing Prophet cannot also play Trickster.

On another occasion, Andrea protests against what has happened by setting herself on fire, by becoming flame; this is a metaphor for rage, and an appropriation of the moral authority of actual political suicides. What then of the narrator's fire-bombing of porn stores? Is this a political programme, or a prophesy, or another metaphor? Further, is this a complicated use of literary techniques in a way that brings out the ambivalences so loved by the postmodernism Dworkin ritually comminates, or is it a way of recommending illegal acts while avoiding charges of incitement?

The novel uses traditional Romantic sentimentality to an extent that is perhaps surprising, given the historic associations of that sentimentality with disempowering images of women. When Andrea consensually fellates a British taxi-driver, who proceeds to abuse the trust he has won by walking the dog she is too drunk to walk herself, by thrusting deep into her, she swoons; her pain and misery before and upon awakening from this swoon are heightened by the presence of the innocent and unknowing animal with 'its sweet melancholy look.' The streets of Andrea's passion are mean and neon-shiny and rain-swept; this is a book in which the pathetic fallacy is not only alive and well, but part of an implied claim that Andrea has, as Woman, the right to the overt sympathy of animals and the Weather.

The book sometimes makes eloquent, and intermittently effective, use of the graphically unpleasant, but more often places a screen of abstraction between what is shown and what is being described. The aforementioned swoon is not the only one of its kind in the book; Dworkin ritually denounces Sade, but has learned from him the teasing avoidance of the specific in descriptions of the sexual act that a heroine's momentary unconsciousness affords. Dworkin uses the word 'pain' a lot, but rarely, save through extravagant metaphors, is that pain described or made specific and concrete. The act of fellatio, for example, is described as disgusting on the ground that it is like the man trying to kill a small furry animal in your throat, or because DNA from his semen is colonizing your brain; we find oddly little here about the more obviously unpleasant aspects of oral-penile contact—the presence of smegma and the disinclination of many men to wash.

It is legitimate, indeed probably necessary, that a novel which takes rape as its subject makes no attempt to understand it in the sense of providing empathy with the rapist as well as with the victim; it is rather more doubtful whether it is a good idea for a study of rape, particularly one which makes extraliterary claim to experiential authority, to be so entirely without an analysis of what rape is, and the complexities of the ideology which serves it, an ideology which regularly sees potential victims as deserving of punishment.

It is interesting, however, how much that ideology permeates some of the novel's implied attitudes. Andrea talks of rape, particularly of the rape of children, as something which it is impossible that the victim can survive whole; she argues that most women with asthma are reliving paternal oral rape endlessly. To say that to be victimized once is thereafter to take your core identity from that victimization is perilously close to those patriarchal ideologies which kill rape victims as damaged goods. When Andrea talks of sex workers, it is in terms which animalize them; they are 'mules' and 'jackasses.' It is not always clear that it is their employers alone with whom she is angry; her language talks of the way they have been made, by pornographers, into objects, but does so in a way that fails to restore their humanity. The exception is Linda Marchiano, of course, whom she sees as a mystical sister, but then Linda Marchiano is the brand plucked from the burning.

Part of the purpose of this book must be, by describing rape in its various forms, to enhance the insight of Dworkin's previous book *Intercourse* that heterosexual, and, implicitly, penetrative, intercourse of all kinds is an untenable practice for women in a sexist society, that consent is impossible. The refusal to write in particularly evocative terms about bodily functions means that this argument is not made especially effectively; Dworkin does not appeal to common experience of the occasional awfulness of sex, which runs the risk of reminding how it can also occasionally be pleasurable, in specifics, but to a ritualized abstraction from experience. It is important not to eroticize rape, but, in a society where it is legitimized, it is also important to concretize its offensive assault on human decency.

This of course tallies with the aesthetic practice implicit in the Dworkin-MacKinnon ordnance; if Dworkin disapproves of most forms of sexually explicit representation, she cannot represent graphically sexual activity of which she disapproves even to make us recognize that we share her disapproval. Much of the ultimate weakness of this ambitious book derives from the fact that Dworkin's own positions on representation make it impossible for her to achieve her artistic and political ends by accurate simple representation rather than rhetoric and manipulation.

The real failure of this book though is not in the cheating, or the calculated omissions, or the implicit elitism; it is in the deep solipsism that characterizes it from beginning to end. Dworkin rightly mocks male writers like Norman Mailer for trying to conquer the universe by an act of egotistical will, but the list of male greats at whom she sneers indicates that she sees herself as in some sort of competi-

tion with them. This is a book in which, from the beginning to the end of the main text, there is not a single other developed character.

The male characters are plot functions, who appear, rape the protagonist and depart, while all of the women from mother to friends, with a couple of momentary exceptions—Marchiano and a friendly lesbian hooker in a gold lamé dress—are shadows who fail to protect Andrea. This is a book which preaches solidarity between women, but represents a lone individual's struggle against an unfriendly universe, a woman of sorrows and acquainted with grief. It is this self-regarding and self-constructed figure that calls women together in a crusade of pointless retributive violence; the worth of the crusade as an egalitarian project can best be demonstrated by the way that Dworkin describes other women in the text, and the contemptuous way she endeavours to manipulate her women readers with rhetorical trickery.

Madison Smartt Bell (review date 15 September 1991)

SOURCE: "Sustaining a Scream," in *Chicago Tribune Books*, September 15, 1991, p. 5.

[*In the following review, Bell offers favorable assessment of* Mercy. *Bell praises Dworkin as "a brilliant and passionate theoretician" whose "anger is a polished and dangerous instrument."*]

"Now I've come into my own as a woman of letters," goes the prologue of Andrea Dworkin's second novel, *Mercy*. "I admit to a cool, elegant intellect with a clear superiority over the apelike men who write...." Some apelike reviewers may find this sort of thing prejudicially annoying. Let the reader be warned.

But the main body of the novel is told in a different voice, by a first-person narrator named Andrea, presumably distinct from Dworkin herself and certainly different from the author of the prologue, who is somewhat confusingly identified as "Not Andrea." It's the narrating Andrea that controls most of the text, which is most interesting for its aggressive style. It's difficult to sustain a scream for over 300 pages, but Dworkin's narrator does quite a good job, using long tumbling run-on sentences to achieve a powerful effect.

Perhaps it would not have been too submissive for her to paragraph occasionally. But there's only one significant strategic error, the persistent misconjugation of verbs, which Dworkin deploys in hopes of sounding more proletarian or street-inured, maybe. This mistake is unlike her, for she is a very sophisticated and persuasive prose stylist whose craft and determination make her non-fiction manifesto *Intercourse* something to admire, whether the reader agrees with it or not.

For a writer who functions best at the highest levels of rhetoric, the dialect touches are a false note, but otherwise the fictional Andrea's voice is a potent mix, if not always a tasty one—something like a blend of Molly Bloom and Medea. At its best it can fuse a lyrical intensity with the sort of pointed abstract argument so strongly made in Dworkin's nonfiction work:

> I went to unlock the two locks on my door to my apartment and the first lock just crumbled, little metal pieces fell as if it was spiders giving birth, all the little ones falling out of it, it just seemed pulverized into grains and it just was crushed to sand, the whole cylinder of the lock just collapsed almost into molecules; and the second lock just kept turning around and around but absolutely nothing locked or unlocked and then there was this sound of something falling and it had fallen through the door to the other side, it just fell out of the door. It was night, and even putting the chain on didn't help. I sat with my knife and stared at it all night to keep anyone from breaking in. The crisis of getting new locks left me destitute and desperate and on such occasions I had to steal.

Structurally, the book seems more loose and amorphous than it really may be, patterned on the amoebic expansion and contractions of Walt Whitman's poetry. Andrea was born near Whitman's house in Camden, N.J., and the ambivalence of her relationship to the poet is reiterated in a looping pattern somewhere near the beginning of every of chapter. Andrea's voice generates a Whitmanesque interplay between world and self, without troubling too much about narrative specificity. The text is more concerned with the evolution of Andrea's sensibility than with the events of her life and although the events are related in chronological order they seem to float discontinuously within the sensibility.

Most of the significant events are rapes, beginning with a technically unconsummated molestation in a movie theater when Andrea is nine. This first chapter is one of the best, showing in swift sure strokes how not only the assault itself but also her parents' poor handling of it make Andrea feel completely isolated and abandoned by everyone, including God. But when she next appears she is five years older and involved in all sorts of rough, sordid but apparently consensual sex (though readers of *Intercourse* will know that in Dworkin's larger scheme of things any woman's desire for penetration by a man is merely the product and mechanism of her enslaved degradation).

It's unfortunate not to know how she got from the first stage to the second, for in the latter phase she often seems to be, like the character Tralala in Hubert Selby Jr.'s *Last Exit To Brooklyn,* as much a victim of her own carnality as of the lustful cruelty of others.

Between rapes, Andrea survives on the fringes of '60s political action, working for an anti-war organization. Estranged from her parents in her teens, she becomes a semi-street person, dependent for shelter on unreliable and often dangerous hippie hospitality. She takes some male lovers willingly and engages in some lesbian encounters that aren't much dwelt on. In Europe she marries a terrorist who, when romance wears thin, ties her up and beats and rapes her; these sadistic explosions become part of the routine of their domestic life.

Back in New York she returns to a bohemian twilight zone where she is vulnerable in many ways, not just sexually: often without money, food, or shelter, often helplessly drunk. Each chapter shows how these circumstances converge on another rape. The last, an especially brutal "deep throat" rape, so radicalizes Andrea that she begins car-bombing porno stores and murdering male winos on the street, telling herself, "none of them's innocent and who cares?"

There's hardly any plot in the conventional sense and not really any characters, except Andrea; the others are just more heads on the hydra that's out to crush and devour her. All the men are rapists and all the women let her down somehow: her mother (especially), her political acquaintances, the martial arts master she turns to when she begins to realize "it is very important for women to kill men."

Her only real friend is her dog; her eulogy to the dog is one the book's most affecting passages. Otherwise, the main virtues are prodigies of interpretation rather than imagination, an ingenious analysis of a Huey Newton newsphoto, an explosive attack on pornography. The book carries too heavy a polemical burden to work very well as a novel.

But very likely Dworkin is more interested in producing a politically effective text than an esthetic object. Indeed the prologue and epilogue, which turn out to be parody, are meant to preempt objections to her violent radicalism that more moderate feminists might raise. There are other objections, however, which she does not address.

If Andrea Dworkin is the Malcolm X of feminism, then this novel is her version of his *Autobiography.* Dworkin is such an astute political analyst that she certainly must know how her tactics resemble Malcolm's, especially the uncompromising demonization of all members of the enemy group. Black Island's "the whitey" has its analogue, too. For irony, compare the fictional Andrea's murders of winos with Eldridge Cleaver's rape of white girls. But the real catch is that while black separation is at least theoretically plausible, female separatism is not.

Dworkin does not supply any alternative myth; unlike some other feminists she has not gone Goddess-chasing. Never afraid to confront all the implications of her thinking, she concludes that only a male God could have devised a creation so inimical to women. But even with God declared non-existent, a biology that requires sexual intercourse for species survival remains, as she puts it in *Intercourse,* "immune to reform"—never mind the hope she holds for "new reproductive technologies."

What's next? An all-out war of women on men is no more likely to occur than the all-out war of blacks on whites that didn't happen in the '60s. Malcolm went to Mecca and came back changed, but it's hard to imagine where Andrea Dworkin can go from here. Still, she is a brilliant and passionate theoretician, her anger is a polished and dangerous instrument, and even some of the people she's marked as enemies can hope she finds her way.

Cindy Jenefsky (review date February 1992)

SOURCE: "To Remember the Pain," in *Women's Review of Books,* Vol. IX, No. 5, February, 1992, pp. 6-7.

[*In the following review, Jenefsky offers a favorable evaluation of* Mercy. *According to Jenefsky, "The result is a work of artistic integrity that, in the manner of Dworkin's body of writing generally, synthesizes form and content, art and politics."*]

In an interview with herself in *Yearning* (1990), bell hooks asks "Why remember the pain?" and responds:

> Because I am sometimes awed, as in finding something terrifying, when I see how many of the people who are writing about domination and oppression are distanced from the pain, the woundedness, the ugliness. That it's so much of the time just a subject—a "discourse." . . . I say remember the pain because I believe true resistance begins with people confronting pain, whether it's theirs or somebody else's, and wanting to do something to change it.

In contrast to the notion, popularly advocated by academic feminists, that focusing on women's pain accentuates our

victimization and powerlessness and thereby denies our agency, hooks claims that speaking from that place of pain is transformative—that it is the necessary location from which one learns about oppression and learns what is necessary to overthrow it.

Andrea Dworkin's most recent novel, *Mercy,* is written from that place of pain. Like all of Dworkin's works, this novel shows how male domination is maintained through "ordinary" sexual practices. In particular, *Mercy* picks up where *Intercourse* (1987), her last work of feminist theory, ends. Both books articulate the lack of clear distinction between sex and sexual abuse in contemporary sexual practices; both are written in a poetic style that fosters intellectual as well as visceral engagement with the ideas instead of a strictly academic apprehension of Dworkin's controversial analysis of sex. But where *Intercourse* centers on articulating the normative nature of abuse in sex, *Mercy* centers on illustrating the destructiveness of denying the abusive nature of sex.

Mercy is the story of one woman's survival of repeated sexual abuse and her struggle to overcome the denial of the pain it has caused her. Initially, the protagonist, Andrea, must contend with the denial of others: their denial of the fact that she has been sexually abused and of the extent of its injury. Then, in a pattern mimicking the lives of many survivors of sexual abuse, this external invalidation is joined by her own denial. In Andrea's case, this denial is manifested by self-doubt, loss of memory, the numbing use of drugs and alcohol, and her refusal to admit that she lacks self-determination in her sexual practices. While denial enables Andrea to survive the pain of poverty and multiple assaults, it also prevents her from making changes in her life; for denial—both her own and that of others—stops her from taking her abuse seriously and from actively rebelling against her perpetrators.

In the revolutionary spirit that hooks suggests, Dworkin attempts to get both Andrea and the reader to confront the pain that everyone in Andrea's life denies is real. *Mercy* is not a book to pick up if you're looking for light, weekend leisure reading; in the manner of Toni Morrison's *Beloved,* this book compels the reader to experience the pain the protagonist suffers. Even if you don't like Andrea—either her behaviour or her ways of thinking—you still cannot escape feeling her pain; the agony, confusion, terror, humiliation and anguish are built into the form of Dworkin's writing and, therefore, built into the experience of reading the work.

At the age of nine, Andrea is molested in a movie theater, and her parents fail to recognize her fear and sense of violation. Their denial exacerbates the child's confusion and makes her begin to doubt her memory. Dworkin conveys the child's breathless panic by intensifying the pace of her words: she elongates the structure of her sentences and gives the reader no space to pause for breath:

> You get asked if anything happened and you say well yes he put his hand here and he rubbed me and he put his arm around my shoulder and he scared me and he followed me and he whispered something to me and then someone says but did anything happen. And you say, well, yes, he sat down next to me, it was in this movie theater and I didn't mean to do anything wrong and there wasn't anyone else around and it was dark and he put his arm around me and he started talking to me and saying weird things in a weird voice and then he put his hand in my legs and he started rubbing and he kept saying just let me . . . . and someone says did anything happen and you say well yes he scared me and he followed me and he put his hand or hands there and you don't know how many hands he had, not really, and you don't want to tell them you don't know because then they will think you are crazy or stupid but maybe there are creatures from Mars and they have more than two hands but you know this is stupid to say and so you don't know how to say what happened and if you don't know how many hands he had you don't know anything and no one needs to believe you about anything because you are stupid or crazy and so you don't know how to say what happened and you say he kept saying just let me . . . . and I tried to get away and he followed me and he . . . . followed me and he . . . . and then they say, thank God nothing happened.

(author's ellipses)

As Andrea's parents continue to ask questions and make comments that minimize and trivialize her feelings, the young girl's story becomes progressively more convoluted. Each time her parents minimize the abuse, her confusion and panic intensify, culminating at the end of the chapter in a breathless sentence that spans three pages. The form of the text thus compels the reader to *feel* some of the panic the child experiences. Unlike everyone else in Andrea's life who hears her story, the reader is not encouraged to collaborate in denying the pain.

This first episode creates the foundation for the progressive annihilation of self caused by repeated assaults. All the ingredients are present: the invalidation, the shame, the disbelief, the trivialization, the self-doubt, the self-blame, the alienation. With each incident, Andrea continues to encounter barriers that prevent her from being able to comprehend and communicate the harm she experiences.

Most of these barriers are manifested as failures in lan-

guage, and much of this novel concerns Andrea's struggle with the inadequacy of words. First, she is unable to comprehend fully the violence she experiences because she has no words to describe it. Jailed for civil disobedience during the Vietnam War and repeatedly raped with a steel speculum, she is unable to comprehend the experience *as rape* because "no one said rape"; "it wasn't rape," explains Andrea, "because it wasn't a penis and it was doctors"; and since she "had never heard of any such thing happening before . . . it didn't seem possible to [her] that it had happened at all."

Even when she knows the words to describe her pain, language still fails her, for no one understands the meaning of her words: "When I feel something," she says, "no right words come or no one would know what they mean. It would be like throwing a ball that could never be caught." When she is beaten and raped by her husband, she wants to stand up in a public theatre and scream out his abuses, but she refrains because she knows she will not be taken seriously. While the inadequacy of Andrea's language keeps her isolated and hinders her from obtaining help from others, her poverty and progressive self-annihilation increasingly erode her capacity for meaningful speech: the success of one's words in **Mercy** corresponds to the degree of social, economic and political power one already possesses.

Ironically, this novel's most valuable contribution to feminist discussions of sexual abuse is precisely what makes the reader less sympathetic to Andrea's story: the lack of a clear distinction between Andrea's sexual pursuits and her sexual victimization. Andrea insistently seeks and relishes the raw intensity of sex and the fusion of self and other that is made possible by sexual intimacy; in fact, the intensity of her passion for sex reflects her passion of self-determination and for defiance of all the rules that are supposed to govern women in sexuality. Yet her sexual pursuits often end in sexual abuse, and it is very difficult to figure out where Andrea's sexual desire stops and the man's abuse begins.

This obfuscation in the boundary between sex and abuse sustains Andrea's own denial about the fact that she is sexually abused, for she believes that she is doing what *she* wants:

> I do what I want, I go where I want, in bed with anyone who catches my eye, a glimmer of light or a soupçon of romance. I'm not inside time or language or rules or society. . . . In my mind I am doing what I want and it is private . . . what I feel is the only society I have or know . . . I think I am alone living my life as I want. I think that when I am with someone I am with him.

What it takes her most of the novel to realize is that the

experience in her mind and body is circumscribed by the social reality of male domination. No matter how hard Andrea tries throughout her young adulthood to design sex to fit *her* desires, her repeated experiences with sexual assault force her—after a decade of resistance—to relinquish her illusion of self-determination:

> . . . I used to say I wanted to do it, what they wanted, whatever it was, I used to say it was me, I was deciding, I wanted, I was ready, it was my idea, I did the taking, I decided, I initiated, hey I was as tough as them; but it was fuck before they get mad—it was lower the risk of making them mad; you use your will to make less pain for yourself; you say *I am* as if there is an I and then you do what pleases them, girl, what they like, what you already learned they like, and there ain't no I, because if there was it wouldn't have accepted the destruction or annihilation . . . you say it's me. I chose it, I want it, it's fine—you say it for pride . . . .

Andrea's gradual recognition of the fact that she is denied self-determination in her sexual practices marks the shift in her life from self-annihilation to self-defense. But this recognition does not occur as a moment of epiphany that changes her life for the better from that point forward; rather, as in the life of most survivors of sexual abuse, the shift is painfully slow and intermittent. Even after finding the will to escape her abusive husband, she still lapses into moments of denial in which she refuses to believe that men want to hurt her. Each time she maintains this illusion, she is sexually victimized. Only when she allows herself to comprehend the magnitude of male violence against women—not just against her—does Andrea become resolutely defiant about defending herself and avenging the many lives that men have destroyed in the name of sex.

The fact that Andrea's gradual empowerment emerges from the recognition of her own sexual victimization is bound to generate hostility toward this book from those who have tired of a feminist emphasis on sexual victimization and who believe that empowerment is to be found in the discovery of female sexual *agency*. In fact, the structure of this novel anticipates just such criticism: Andrea's chronological autobiography (from "August 1956" to "April 30, 1974") is sandwiched between a prologue and an epilogue, both entitled "Not Andrea," which articulate hypothetical feminist objections to the novel.

The prologue warns Andrea and Dworkin not to indulge is hyperbole and "not to be simple-minded" about the nature of women's oppression; the epilogue uses hyperbole to explicate Andrea and Dworkin's simple-mindedness about sexual abuse. These parts that are "Not Andrea" circumscribe Andrea/Dworkin's story by invalidating or minimiz-

ing their words. This literal framing of the novel within its own critique represents both Andrea's and Dworkin's struggles to overcome others' denial of the destructive nature of sexual abuse in women's lives. Dworkin, then, accuses critics in advance of colluding in women's oppression; for, in the context of the narrative, those who minimize Andrea's words help to perpetuate abuse.

What is probably going to anger Dworkin's critics the most, however, is her implicit claim that the root of feminists' denial of Andrea/Dworkin's story is women's resistance to recognizing sexual victimization in their own lives. "Not Andrea" concludes the epilogue: "I have been hurt but it was a long time ago. I'm not the same girl." Dworkin implies that academic feminists in particular have adopted an intellectual analysis of sex at the expense of their (or other women's) concrete experiences with sex. Accordingly, both the prologue and epilogue are written in an analytic style, borrowing vocabulary from feminist theoretical debates on sexuality:

> There is no victim. There is perhaps an insufficiency of signs, an obdurate appearance of conformity that simply masks the deeper level on which choice occurs. . . . To their reductive minds prostitution is exploitation without more while those of us who thrive on adventure and complexity understand that prostitution is only an apparent oppression that permits some women to be sexually active without bourgeois restraints.

In contrast, Dworkin's poetic style in Andrea's autobiography is a formal effort to minimize the reader's intellectualization of sex and sexual abuse. The result is a work of artistic integrity that, in the manner of Dworkin's body of writing generally, synthesizes form and content, art and politics. The artistic form of *Mercy* fulfills its own political directives. It does what it says needs to be done to stop the cycle of violence against women: it confronts the pain of sexual abuse.

Lauren Glen Dunlap (review date Spring 1994)

SOURCE: A review of *Letters from a War Zone*, in *Belles Lettres*, Vol. 9, No. 3, Spring, 1994, pp. 74-5.

[*In the following review, Dunlap offers positive assessment of* Mercy.]

The urgency and rage that suffuse Andrea Dworkin's writing leave little room for savoring the distinctions between pre- and post-French Revolution pornography. In *Letters from a War Zone* (1993), Dworkin asserts that pornography remains essentially the same across eras and cultures precisely because women's oppression—"expressed in rape, battery, incest, and prostitution"—remains the same. "The change," writes Dworkin, "is only in what is publicly visible."

Dworkin never claims to be objective. "Objectivity, as I understand it, means that it doesn't happen to you." And "it" *does* happen to Dworkin, from the days when she was raped as a student and battered as a wife, to later, when her work made her the target of threats, including being made the subject of a sexually explicit cartoon in *Hustler.* ("A cartoon like that says, bang, you're dead, and one way or another you are, a little.") And "it" *does* happen to women every hour of every day (including one rape every three minutes), to women who have told their stories to Dworkin over the last two decades.

Dworkin is interested in drawing distinctions: between words and action, between political protest and literal physical torture, between the protected "free speech" of pornographers and the forceful silencing of women, between proclaiming equality and working to create it.

The pieces in this collection were written between 1976 and 1989. Many were written as speeches. Contexts range from Take Back the Night rallies to a debate with the noted civil liberties lawyer Alan Dershowitz who, at the time of the debate, had not yet gone on the payroll of *Penthouse.* Audiences range from separatist lesbians to a group of 500 Men's Movement men, from women law students and lawyers at Yale to a mostly right-wing audience. Also included in the transcript is the testimony Dworkin gave to the Meese Commission, during which she was heckled by ACLU lawyers and representatives from *Penthouse.*

Many of the pieces are published here for the first time. Virtually none of those previously published had wide circulation. Dworkin recounts a long history of publication difficulties. She underscores the irony in her being accused of having contempt for free speech. "Speech is what I do; it ain't free; it costs a lot."

Not all the pieces are on pornography. They include, for instance, the most lucid reading of *Wuthering Heights* I have come across. But pornography, in Dworkin's view, is a sort of missing link that ties together all the other phenomena of women's oppression.

. . . pornography, in Dworkin's view, is a sort of missing link that ties together all the other phenomena of women's oppression.
—*Lauren Glen Dunlap*

There are a number of reasons why people might find Dworkin's work unpalatable. There is, for instance, the subject matter. "I represent the morbid side of the women's movement," Dworkin begins one essay. "I deal with the shit, the real shit. Robin Morgan calls it 'atrocity work.' And that's pretty much what it is."

And there is the style. Dworkin's style is characterized by the severity of one who has survived much, by the passion of one who, against great odds, has not given up hope. That is not to say her logic suffers from her bias. As she quotes Wollstonecraft, "we reason deeply, when we forcibly feel."

Dworkin's arguments are, in fact, irrefutable. Dworkin cuts through the euphemisms, the subterfuge, the nonsense. She tells us that women are fighting not only for essential ideals such as social equality and justice. We are fighting for our very lives.

Andrea Dworkin with Michael Moorcock (interview date 21 April 1995)

SOURCE: "Fighting Talk," in *New Statesmen & Society,* April 21, 1995, pp. 16-8.

[*In the following interview, Dworkin discusses formative events in her life, her writings, and her views on pornography and free speech.*]

[*Michael Moorcock:*] *You were born in Camden, New Jersey, in 1946, had an admired father, went to a progressive school, led the familiar bohemian life of the 1960s, were active in protest politics, were arrested and received unexpectedly brutal treatment—but not as brutal as being a battered wife, stranded in Amsterdam with your monstrous husband, a political radical. Pretty traumatic stuff, yet you remain, I think, fundamentally an optimist.*

[Andrea Dworkin:] Optimism is what you do, how you live. I write, which is a quintessential act of optimism. It sometimes means the triumph of faith over experience, a belief in communication, in community, in change, and, for me, in beauty. The power and beauty of language. I act with other women to create social change: activism is optimism. I've always believed in art and politics as keys to transformation. Emotional authenticity and, if you will, social progress towards fairness and equality.

I was happy as a kid, although my mother was sick with heart disease, and my younger brother and I were often parcelled out to various family members, separated from each other and my parents. I grew up very fast and very early in all ways. That means I was independent, I did what I wanted. I learned to have a private life when I was very young, and also at different times I had to take care of my brother and mother. I lived a lot on the streets with my friends. It was a big part of my life. My family was poor and all these circumstances meant that I didn't have a stable or middle-class upbringing.

My father was—and is—very special, even back then noticeably different from other fathers: extremely gentle and caring, respecting women and children, listening to us, responding intellectually and emotionally. He worked in what was considered here a woman's job, as a teacher, and he worked at the post office; so I didn't get to see him much. But he was the great heart in our family. It would be hard to overstate how much he had to do with teaching me about human rights and human dignity, also how to talk and how to think.

The progressive school was Bennington, which I went to on a scholarship. I went to neighbourhood schools until college. I didn't think much of them because they were intellectually constricting, demanded conformity, especially for girls. My political life began long before I was arrested for protesting against the Vietnam war. I refused to sing Christmas carols in elementary school and was isolated and punished for it—as well as having "kike" written on my drawings on the bulletin board. In sixth grade, I couldn't decide whether to be a lawyer or a writer. I wanted to change the abortion laws . . .

Your first book was **Woman Hating** *in 1974. To make some sort of living from your work, you took to public speaking. This led to* **Our Blood,** *a collection of eloquent and finely written speeches, published in 1976. Where do you come from politically?*

Both my parents were horrified by US racism, certainly by *de jure* segregation, but also by all aspects of discrimination—black poverty, urban ghettoes, menial-labour, bad education, the lack of respect whites had for blacks. My father was pro-labour; he wanted teachers to be unionised. He refused a management job at the post office. My mother was committed to planned parenthood, to legal birth control (it was criminal then) and to legal abortion. We had immigrant family members who were survivors of the Holocaust, though most of my mother's and father's families had been killed. So I grew up taking hate and extermination seriously. I read all the time, as much as I could. My mother often had to write me notes so that I could have certain books from the library. After the high school board purged the library of all "socialist" and "indecent" books, I found this cute little book they'd missed called *Guerilla Warfare* by Che Guevara. I read it a million times. I'd plan attacks on the local shopping mall. I got a lot of practice in strategising real rebellion. It may be why I refuse to think

that rebellion against the oppressors of women should be less real, less material, less serious.

You've been described as a radical visionary rather than a practical politician. Do you enjoy politics?

I find compromise not impossible but incomprehensible. When Catharine MacKinnon and I were trying to pass the civil rights law recognising pornography as sex discrimination in Minneapolis in 1983, politicians kept talking to me about incinerators. I was bewildered. They'd vote for the civil rights bill if legislator X would vote to put some incinerator somewhere—not in their district, I think. My eyes would glaze over. Then I'd become enraged. The trade-offs, the pay-offs, sometimes actual blackmail and bribery. I was good at holding the politician's feet to the fire, in private and in public; to excoriate them, to move their constituents, but from a basis of principle. That I can do. I have good practical instincts on where dominant structures are vulnerable. This requires a high tolerance for risk and conflict.

I've always considered writing sacred. I've come to consider the rights of women, including a right to dignity, sacred. This is what I care about. I don't want to give up what I care about.

There's enormous substance and original insight in your work. Yet a book like **Right-Wing Women,** *a superb analysis of the kind of women presently very prominent in politics, is out of print in the US. Why?*

My novel *Ice and Fire* has never appeared in paperback here. For years, most of my work was officially out of print or simply unfindable. From when the civil-rights law was passed in Minneapolis until 1990, after I found a new publisher, *Pornography* could only be bought in northern California, via exceptionally resourceful distributors. There was a long period in the mid-1980s when it was easier to get virtually any book by me in English in Nigeria than in the US. Without belabouring any of this, I think these are the reasons: 1) In the US the pornography industry and the publishing industry see themselves as twin entities engaged in exercising and protecting the same rights in the same way. I stand against the pornography industry; the publishing industry see me as an enemy. 2) My work is radical. A lot of people, especially the already comfortable, don't like it. Men especially object. Women don't want to be associated with work that brings out unambiguous hostility in men. 3) The left refuse to change, and in order to organise for the equality of women, the left must change. Even to consider, for example, the analysis in *Right-Wing Women* means reconceptualising what it would take to organise women politically.

Having worked for porn publishers and knowing the

trade pretty well, I felt your 1981 **Pornography: Men Possessing Women** *offered clear insights into what made me uneasy about porn. Like you, I am an anti-censorship activist, but I didn't like what porn "said." Did you begin with the view that porn is effective propaganda against women?*

Like many women, I think, my life was different from my understanding. I didn't come to feminism until I was in my mid-20s. It's hard for younger women now to understand that women my age didn't have feminism as a movement or an analytical tool. I understood Vietnam right away. I understood apartheid. I knew prisons were bad and cruel, but I didn't understand why the male doctors in the Women's House of Detention essentially sexually assaulted me, or even that they did. I knew they ripped up my vagina with a steel instrument and told dirty jokes about women while they did it. I knew they enjoyed causing me purposeful pain. But there was no public, political conception of rape or sexual assault. Rape rose to being a political issue only when it involved false accusations made by white women against black men.

I prostituted on the streets for several years. I had no political understanding of that, nor even of my own homelessness or poverty. I was battered—genuinely tortured—when I was married, but I thought I was the only woman in the world this had ever happened to. I had no political understanding that I was being beaten because I was a woman, or that this man thought I belonged to him, inside out. I came to pornography, which I had both read and used, just as I came to fairy-tales: to try to understand what each said about being woman. There was the princess, the wicked queen or witch; there was O, there was the Dominatrix. I had somehow learned all that, become all of them; and figured I'd better unlearn some of this shit fast or I was going to be dead soon but not soon enough.

I once heard a pimp say he could turn any woman out but no one could make her stay on the streets. But what happens when you find the inside worse than the outside? What happens when the marital bed with your revolutionary lover/ husband is worse than any two-second fuck in any alley? I was a believer in sexual liberation, but more important I had believed in the unqualified goodness of sex, its sensuousness, its intensity, its generosity. I've always loved being alive. I've no interest in suicide, never have had. The battering destroyed me. I had to decide whether I wanted to live or die. I was broken and shamed and empty. I looked at pornography to try to understand what had happened to me. And I found a lot of *information,* about power and the mechanisms by which the subordination of women is sexualised. I want you to understand that I didn't learn an ideology. For me, it's been a living journey. I began to examine the use of force in sex, as well as the kind of sa-

dism I'd experienced in prison. I had so many questions, why do men think they own women? Oh, well, they do; here are the laws that say so; here's how the pornography says so. Why do men think women are dirty? Why is overt violence against women simply ignored, or disbelieved, or blamed on the woman?

I read all I could and still found the richest source of information on women's lives was women, like me, who wanted freedom and were willing to fight for it. But a big part of the fight was facing facts; and facts had a lot to do with what men had done to us, how men used us with or without our own complicity. In pornography I found a map, a geography of male dominance in the sexual realm, with sex clearly defined as dominance and submission, not as equality or reciprocity.

After **Right-Wing Women** *and* **Ice and Fire** *you wrote* **Intercourse.** *Another book which helped me clarify confusions about my own sexual relationships. You argue that attitudes to conventional sexual intercourse enshrine and perpetuate sexual inequality. Several reviewers accused you of saying that all intercourse was rape. I haven't found a hint of that anywhere in the book. Is that what you are saying?*

No, I wasn't saying that and I didn't say that, then or ever. There's a long section in **Right-Wing Women** on intercourse in marriage. My point was that as long as the law allows a statutory exemption for a husband from rape charges, no married woman has legal protection from rape. I also argued, based on a reading of our laws, that marriage mandated intercourse—it was compulsory, part of the marriage contract. Under the circumstances, I said, it was impossible to view sexual intercourse in marriage as the free act of a free woman. I said that when we look at sexual liberation and the law, we need to look not only at which sexual acts are forbidden, but which are compelled.

The whole issue of intercourse as this culture's penultimate expression of male dominance became more and more interesting to me. In **Intercourse** I decided to approach the subject as a social practice, material reality. This may be my history, but I think the social explanation of the "all sex is rape" slander is different and probably simple. Most men and a good number of women experience sexual pleasure in inequality. Since the paradigm for sex has been one of conquest, possession, and violation, I think many men believe they need an unfair advantage, which at its extreme would be called rape. I don't think they need it. I think both intercourse and sexual pleasure can and will survive equality.

It's important to say, too, that the pornographers, especially *Playboy,* have published the "all sex is rape" slander repeatedly over the years, and it's been taken up by others like *Time* who, when challenged, cannot cite a source in my work.

What do you say to committed feminists who disagree with your approach to pornography and say porn is merely one manifestation among many of a problem with deeper roots?

I say solve the problem you think is more urgent or goes deeper. Pornography is so important, I think, because of how it touches on every aspect of women's lower status: economic degradation, dehumanisation, woman hating, sexual domination, systematic sexual abuse. If someone thinks she can get women economic equality, for instance, without dealing in some way with the sexual devaluation of women as such, I say she's wrong; but I also say work on it, try, organise; I will be there for her, as a resource, carrying picket signs, making speeches, signing petitions, supporting law suits for economic equality. But if she thinks the way to advance women is to organise against those of us who are organising against sexual exploitation and abuse, than I say I don't respect that, it's horizontal hostility, not feminism. Women willing to let other women do the so-called sex work, be the prostitutes, while they lead respectable professional lives in law or in the academy, frankly make me sick. I concentrate my energy, however, on uniting with women who want to fight sexual exploitation, not on arguing with women who defend it.

You have been wildly and destructively misquoted. I've been told that you hate all men, believe in biological determinism, write pornography while condemning it, have been censored under the very "laws" you introduced in Canada and so on. I know these allegations have no foundation, but they're commonly repeated. Do you know their source?

Playboy, Penthouse, Hustler and lobbying groups for pornographers. Some of the lobbying groups call themselves anti-censorship, but they spend so much time maligning MacKinnon and myself that it is hard to take them seriously. And it seems to be only defending pornography that brings them out. I would define illiteracy as the basic speech problem in the US, but I don't see any effort to deal with it as a political emergency with constitutionally based remedies, such as law suits against cities and states on behalf of illiterate populations characterised by race and class, purposefully excluded by public policy from learning how to read and write. Fighting MacKinnon and me is equivalent to going to Club Med rather than doing real work.

What's your position on free speech?

I don't think the British understand US law. Here, burning a cross on a black person's lawn was recently protected as free speech by the Supreme Court. It's obviously a big subject, but the First Amendment, which keeps Congress from making laws that punish speech, doesn't say, for instance, that I have a right to say what I want, let alone that I have right to say it. *After* I have expressed myself, the government isn't supposed to punish me. But women and people of colour, especially African-Americans, have been excluded from any rights of speech for most of our history. In the US it costs money to have access to the means of speech. If you're a woman, sexual assault can stop you from speaking; so can almost constant intimidation and threat. The First Amendment was designed to protect white, landowning men from the power of the state. This was followed by the Second Amendment, which says, ". . . and we have guns." Women and most blacks were chattels, without any speech rights of any kind. So the First Amendment protects the speech of Thomas Jefferson, but has Sally Hemmings ever said a word anyone knows about? My own experience is that speech is not free; it costs a lot.

What do you think about the current shift to the right in US politics?

Here, in blaming and shaming the oppressed, the powerless, the left colludes with the right. There's no reason to look to the left for justice, so people look to the right for order. It's pretty simple. The victory of the right also expresses the rage of white men against women and people of colour who are seen to be eroding the white man's authority. Of course, we need to keep eroding that authority. The pain of destroying male rule won't be worse than the pain of living with it.

David Futrelle (review date 16 March 1997)

SOURCE: "Battle-Ax," in *Los Angeles Times Book Review,* March 16, 1997, p. 9.

[*In the following review, Futrelle offers an unfavorable assessment of* Life and Death.]

To read Andrea Dworkin is to enter into an alternate universe.

In her Amerika—yes, she still spells the word with a K— we live in the midst of an obscene, unending war: the war of the sexes. Women live, she says, "under martial law . . . in a situation of emergency . . . under a reign of terror . . . brutalized by 'pimps' and pornographers and just plain ordinary men."

These dramatic phrases are not, to Dworkin, simply examples of poetic license, the sort of boilerplate bellicosity that can give spice to an otherwise tepid political speech—Dworkin believes "the war against women is a real war. There's nothing abstract about it. This is a war in which his fist is in your face."

Readers familiar with Dworkin's work will find very little in *Life and Death,* her newest collection of essays, that is new or surprising. In the writings contained within it—some originally given as speeches at feminist gatherings, others reprinted from magazines and journals and even the pages of this newspaper—Dworkin plays variations on the themes she's explored in her previous books: pornography, prostitution, rape and violence against women.

These are all serious subjects—indeed, in some cases, deadly serious—but Dworkin's reflexive rhetorical overkill, her unrelenting outrage, serves to cloud rather than clarify the issues. And by collapsing the distinctions between real life-and-death issues (rape, brutality) and what are at worst trivial annoyances (*Playboy* centerfolds), she manages to trivialize all she touches.

Intercourse and *Pornography: Men Possessing Women* may indeed have been, as her publicist rather perversely puts it, "seminal works," but *Life and Death* is, for the most part, Dworkin by-the-numbers.

At the heart of "the continuing war against women" that Dworkin refers to in her subtitle is, of course, pornography. Far from being a "superficial target," as some might claim, pornography is "the DNA of male dominance" or (to change the metaphor) the "Pentagon" of male violence. "Pornographers train the soldiers; then the soldiers go out and do the actions on us," she writes. "We're the population that the war is against."

It's often said that pornography leads to rape—an assertion that seems to most free-speechers a little simplistic. To Dworkin, though, the issue is even simpler than that. Pornography, in effect, is rape, no different from "any other historically real torture or punishment. . . ." Pornography isn't fantasy—"pornography happens." Dworkin may be the only person alive who believes that the letters in *Penthouse Forum* are real.

This conflation of pornographic pictures and real-world rape is typical of Dworkin's style. She carefully elides the distinctions between all that she opposes: Pornography is prostitution, prostitution is rape and rape, finally, is not altogether distinct from normal sex. "You cannot separate the so-called abuses of women from the so-called normal uses of women," she writes. "Men use sex to hurt us. An argument can be made that men have to hurt us, diminish us, in order to be able to have sex with us. . . ."

In Dworkin's view, women live in a charnel house of torture and degradation—most just don't realize it yet. "When one thinks about women's ordinary lives and the lives of children, especially female children, it is very hard not to think that one is looking at atrocity—if one's eyes are open," Dworkin tells her readers. "We have to accept that we are looking at ordinary life; the hurt is not exceptional; rather, it is systematic and it is real."

Given such high stakes, it's hardly surprising that, to Dworkin, "free speech fetishists" seem as bad as street pimps and snuff pornographers. Indeed, she is enthusiastic in abusing her foes, describing them as "gutless wonders," "male supremacists" and worse—the sort of people who can work up hypocritical sympathy for a murdered girl even though they "would not really mind her being beaten to death once she was an adult."

In one extraordinary essay, she suggests that male writers who challenge her views are no better than serial killer Marc Lepine, the brutal misogynist who gunned down 14 women in Montreal a little over seven years ago. "It is true that not every man picks up a semiautomatic gun," Dworkin writes, "but a lot of them don't have to, because they have pens." The pen, it seems, is indeed mightier than the sword.

Dworkin's reflexive name calling serves as a kind of substitute for reasoned argument. She asserts; she does not prove. She proclaims; she does not support her proclamations with anything beyond anecdotal evidence. (Her most compelling "evidence" comes from statements given at a public hearing she helped to organize.)

Though she's quick to attack critics of her arguments (and her "evidence") as arrogant misogynists, she manages to avoid mentioning more than a handful of her critics by name, and she does not attempt to respond to their arguments in detail—perhaps because it is easier to deal with caricatures of critics than it is with real people and real arguments. Dworkin rails at a vague, malevolent "they."

In most cases, of course, the gender of Dworkin's accused is male. But it would be unfair to label her, as some have done, as a man-hater—in part because her most contemptuous treatment is reserved for those women who disagree with her.

Dworkin is loath, however, to even admit that any woman might differ with her, much less intelligent and eloquent anti-censorship feminists, such as Susie Bright or Sallie Tisdale—it spoils her picture of a world overwhelmed by "male supremacists." Showing certain women a contempt even greater than she shows for the typical man, she refuses even to name her female opponents—referring to one, for example, only as "*Playboy*'s hired girl."

She dismisses serious feminist criticism with an impatient wave of her hand: Those women who don't see the world as she does are "liars and deniers," cowards and fools.

So much for dialogue, so much for real debate; those who disagree with her might not even deserve to live.

There are to be sure, a few chapters of *Life and Death* not utterly disfigured by hysteria—the first chapter, an often eloquent account of Dworkin's life as a writer, and a tender closing chapter detailing her visit to the Holocaust Memorial Museum in Washington. In both of these essays, Dworkin seems to be honestly interested in exploring the issues at hand, willing to suspend for a moment the dogmatic certainty of most of her writing, to challenge herself to learn something new from the world.

But there is little in *Life and Death* that will challenge anyone, much less Dworkin herself. The book is designed to reinforce the dogmatic outrage of committed Dworkinites and to offend and anger those "free speech fetishists" unlucky enough to find themselves reading it.

As something of a "free speech fetishist" myself, I found it merely depressing yet another sign that our national "debate" about pornography is anything but a real debate. The Dworkinites will continue to make their speeches; we free-speechers will make our replies. But we won't really be talking to each other at all. We live, after all, in very different worlds.

Kristen Golden (review date March-April 1997)

SOURCE: A review of *Life and Death*, in *Ms.*, Vol. 7, No. 5, March-April, 1997, p. 82.

[*In the following review, Golden offers praise for* Life and Death.]

Twenty-five years ago, after a feminist helped her escape from her brutally violent husband in Europe, Andrea Dworkin made a vow: "I would use everything I know in behalf of women's liberation," she recalls in *Life and Death,* an impressive collection of speeches and articles she wrote between 1987 and 1995.

And Dworkin knows a lot. In *Life and Death,* her eleventh book, it is clear that she knows—firsthand—about rape, prostitution, battery, pornography, child sexual abuse, and poverty. She knows, deeply, how patriarchy works and how it sustains itself. And she knows how to tell the truth about women's lives, especially those women in prostitution and pornography.

Dworkin's critiques are original and compelling. In stark, powerful prose, she bears heartbreaking and relentless witness to the violence and degradation that women suffer, leaving the reader awash in indelible, haunting images. "My only chance to be believed is to find a way of writing bolder and stronger than woman hating itself—smarter, deeper, colder," she writes in **"My Life as a Writer."** In other pieces, she takes on the State of Israel, the creators of the Holocaust museum, the rulers of the Serbian death camps, and, as always, the pornographers. Part of what makes Dworkin's analyses so affecting is that she sees no middle ground—you are literally either on top or on bottom. She argues persuasively that pornography and prostitution must be eradicated before women can be free, equal, or even just safe.

While her uncompromising views have long inspired the wrath of male supremacists, journalists, pornographers, and some feminists, Dworkin remains undaunted. "When I look at my own life, I think about the difference between being beaten because I didn't clean the refrigerator and having my life threatened because I am fighting the pornographers," she writes. "There is a better and a worse, and it is better to encounter anything when you have made a choice that puts you where you want to be, fighting for your own freedom and fighting for the freedom of the women around you."

In these essays, Dworkin makes a passionate case that women's equality is a matter of life and death.

Martha C. Nussbaum (review date 11 August 1997)

SOURCE: "Rage and Reason," in *The New Republic*, August 11, 1997, pp. 36-42.

[*In the following review, Nussbaum comments on* Life and Death *and provides sustained analysis of the philosophical, legal, and moral dimensions of Dworkin's case against pornography.*]

I.

Prophets don't write like philosophers. Why not, since they seem to have a common goal? Since Socrates, philosophers, like prophets, have been dedicated foes of ethical complacency, and of the many forms of moral disease complacency conceals. Socrates's call to the examined life was inspired by a concern for the health of souls. He once described the insides of his interlocutor as filled with tumorous growths, and his arguments as purgative drugs that would carry away the diseased material. This vivid sense of the ugliness of evil and the urgency of ethical change makes itself felt in the arguments of many of the greatest moral philosophers. Even when philosophers write calmly, as they usually do, an intense engagement with corruption can frequently be detected beneath the serene surface. (It would not be wrong to see the arguments of John Rawls, a deliberately abstract, cool philosopher, as motivated by the ugliness of human dignity violated, and a longing for the world that would be constructed by "purity of heart, if one could attain it.")

And yet, as I have said, philosophers do not write like prophets. If they excoriate evil, or call the heart to an acknowledgment of its transgressions, this is not their immediate business. That lies in the construction and the dissection of theories and arguments, often intricate and rather removed from the practical matters that were their starting point. They address the reader not with a cascade of resonant denunciation, but with delicacy and logic; not with "Woe unto you!" but with "Many different kinds of things are said to be just and unjust. . . ." (That is Rawls, in an Aristotelian mode.)

Why do philosophers proceed in this way, when real evil is at hand? Sometimes it is because they are profoundly unworldly people who just don't know how to confront bad things. (Edmund Husserl, completely bewildered by the evil of Nazism, wrote shortly before his death in 1938 that he hoped soon to be in a "realm of truth," where such things do not exist.) Sometimes, too, it is because they are gentle, polite people who don't feel comfortable denouncing others, even if they know there is evil at hand. Often, though, there is a better reason for their restraint. It is that they share with Socrates a commitment to reason as an indispensable instrument in the struggle for good.

What do philosophers have to believe about people, in order to believe that a logical argument can produce a result in calling the soul to an acknowledgment of its own deficiencies? They have to believe, I think, that at least a part of evil is not innate or necessary, that at least a good part of evil is based on error, whether social or personal. (These errors may be very deep-rooted, shaping emotions as well as thoughts.) They also have to believe that people have many good beliefs and good intentions, so that there is at least a chance that, confronted with an argument that reveals hidden contradictions in their view, they will select the better and reject the worse. They probably need to believe, too, that reason is a morally good way to approach adversaries, one that shows respect for their humanity. Finally, they need to believe that the patient work of theory-construction can deliver a practical benefit in the long run, systematizing the best of our beliefs and intuitions in a way that reveals new possibilities for politics or morality.

All these beliefs, of course, are questionable. No philosopher's work can prove that the conditions for the worth of philosophizing are satisfied in the world, and to that extent all the work of philosophy is built upon what Kant would call a "practical postulate," a faith in a kind of goodness that is not empirically verifiable.

Prophets, by contrast, believe that the urgency and the magnitude of the evils that they see admit of no delay, no calm and patient dialogue. They believe that only by violently shaking the heart can they make progress against the complacency that is evil's great ally. Argument looks too unengaged, theory-construction too remote from the practical task. Jeremiah did not write a theory of justice, nor did Isaiah address the Israelites with dialectic. Even the philosopher's interest in the nuances of individual cases seems to prophets a dangerous detour, when by and large things are so hideously bad. Suppose Jeremiah had said, "The heart of Israel is corrupt utterly, but on the other hand there are some very nice people there." Or suppose Frederick Douglass had excoriated the evils of slavery but pointed to the moral goodness of certain individual slaveowners. Such philosophical delicacy would have undermined their purpose, which was to terrify and thereby to prompt tears and repentance and change.

In any movement for social justice, then, philosophers and prophets are likely to be somewhat at odds. To prophets, philosophical patience looks like collaboration with evil. (This impression is magnified when, as frequently happens, philosophical calm brings academic security, while the prophet is a despised outcast.) Philosophers, on the other hand, are likely to conclude that prophets do not get to the root of the problem, because they aren't patient enough to do the necessary work. They will be suspicious of the prophet's lack of attention to variety and nuance. They may sense that the prophet's way of speaking shows insufficient respect for the adversary's dignity. It just is not true that people are utterly corrupt; and we get the best out of our dealings with them by proceeding on the assumption that they want to think well and to be good.

Still, it is possible for philosophers and prophets to be (uneasy) allies. Philosophers may judge that their own methods are not the only ones that we need to approach human beings in a time of moral unrest, and they may grant that change sometimes requires a more confrontational style of discourse. (Mill's *The Subjection of Women* didn't have much influence with its calm, rational arguments, and its failure cannot be ascribed to Mill's philosophical insufficiency.) They may also feel some doubts about their practical postulate itself, wondering whether it is merely a convenient way of justifying a personal preference for detachment from politics, or even for personal comfort.

The whole idea of a feminist philosopher can thus be seen,

by these philosophers themselves, as a problematic one, and the feminist prophet can prove as compelling as she is disturbing. Is it really right to proceed as if one can make progress by calmly arguing with men? Should one really assume that they are basically good, so that argument can change them? Should one say, "Yes, some are corrupt, but others are very nice"? Or isn't that the very cop-out that Jeremiah rejected?

II.

Andrea Dworkin knows that good men exist. Indeed, among the most moving passages in the autobiographical essay that opens her book (alongside portraits of strong women who inspired or helped her) is the portrait of her father, a gentle man who adored her and treated her with respect, challenging her Socratically to debate and to argument. Once in high school, asked to give an example of a great man in history, she named her father and was ridiculed. "But I meant it—that he had the qualities of true greatness, which I defined as strength, generosity, fairness, and a willingness to sacrifice self for principle." Dworkin also warmly praises her brother, a Jewish scientist who married an Austrian Catholic, also a scientist. They transcended "cultural differences and historical sorrow," she writes, "through personal love, the recognition of each other as individuals, and the exercise of reason, which they both, as scientists, valued." At his funeral, the chief rabbi of Vienna officiated and her father sat with the women, in protest against the Orthodox separation of the sexes. And finally there is the man with whom Dworkin has lived for twenty years: "I love John with my heart and soul. . . . We share a love of writing and of equality; and we share each ·and every day. He is a deeply kind person, and it is through the actual dailiness of living with him that I understand the spiritual poverty and the sensual stupidity of eroticizing brutality over kindness."

So: Dworkin, whose history includes child molestation by a stranger, sexual abuse by prison guards, domestic violence and prostitution, also knows that the world is complicated and contains some very good male people. She knows, too, that reason may do some good in this complex world. (Both her father and brother are portrayed sympathetically as reason-loving types, and her Jewish education is praised for teaching her the argumentative skills.) But Dworkin aims to deliver shocks to the heart. Her political hero is not Socrates or Kant, it is Frederick Douglass, "someone whose passion for human rights was both visionary and rooted in action," whose political speech "was suffused with emotion: indignation at human pain, grief at degradation, anguish over suffering, fury at apathy and collusion."

Dworkin's prose is a powerful instrument. (Less so in her fiction, with its frequently turgid stream-of-consciousness.) She is inspired to indignation and grief by the evils of vio-

lence against the female body, in rape, in domestic violence, in prostitution: and by the sheer fact that women throughout so much of the world's history have been understood to be mere objects for the use of men. To make a difference (she reports her own earlier reasoning), she will need to write in a way that strikes readers as "nightmarish and impolite," denying them the option of seeing themselves as "innocent bystander[s]." And she will have to give up "sentimentality" toward men in favor of a "militarist's" stance. What this means, among other things, is a focus on the evils perpetrated by "the collective him" and a refusal of sympathy, and of mercy, to many individual hims, each of whom a philosopher might hold to be basically good at heart, and capable of being persuaded.

Life and Death returns to some of the topics of **Woman Hating, Pornography** and *Intercourse,* and adds some new topics—the status of women in Israel, the Holocaust Memorial Museum in Washington. But its primary focus is physical violence against women—stalking, misogynistic homicide, rape and, above all, domestic violence. (There is a fine piece on Nicole Brown Simpson.) Dworkin's essays have provoked much hostility, inside feminism and outside it. She is frequently called a man-hater, a foe of free speech, and many other things that are more expressive than precise. So any critical response should begin by trying to get clear about what she has actually claimed.

At the heart of Dworkin's position are two theses, one normative and one diagnostic. The normative thesis is that women deserve to be treated with a dignity equal to that of men, and given rights fully equal to those of men. (This idea is unmistakably Kantian.) The words "dignity," "human rights," "equality," "fairness" suffuse this text, making Dworkin's affiliations with a certain type of radical Enlightenment vision clear. For Dworkin, the central moral sin is treating a human being as an object.

Objectification, as Dworkin defines it, has a number of different aspects, which are not always clearly distinguished. Sometimes to objectify someone is to deny the person's autonomy; sometimes, to show indifference to the person's feelings and experiences; sometimes, to proceed as if the person's boundaries are not deserving of the same respect that one's own deserve; sometimes, to treat the person as fungible, easily replaceable by other similar objects. (Of course, these different ideas are closely linked, and one can well see how one might lead to the others.) But the central concept, I think, is that of instrumental use: what is always morally problematic, for Dworkin, is to treat other human beings as mere tools, rather than as ends in themselves. "The issue here," she concludes, "is the rights of human beings. And if you understand that women are human beings you must ask: What is the right and honorable and proper way for this person to be treated by that person?"

Why would a person treat another person as a mere thing? There may be many reasons in different contexts: but Kant held that this happens inevitably between men and women in the context of a sexual relationship. Sexual desire, he believed, makes people lose their grip on the moral point of view: "as soon as a person becomes an Object of appetite for another, all motives of moral relationship cease to function." Its intense sensations drive out, for a time, all thought of respect for humanity as an end, leading partners to treat one another as mere tools of their own urgent desires for pleasure. At the same time, their keen interest in pleasure leads them to permit themselves to be used as things by one another, indeed, to volunteer eagerly to be dehumanized so that they can dehumanize in turn.

Kant apparently thought that this tendency was intrinsic to sexual desire itself. This led him to conclude that desire should only be expressed within a relationship—marriage, as he saw it—that constructs moral regard institutionally by making the parties promise to care for one another. This proposal completely ignored the asymmetrical character of marriage and the extent to which its conception of women as property reinforces the thing-like treatment of women, giving men limitless sexual rights over women's bodies and making it very unlikely that the law will intervene to protect the women's boundaries from violence.

Without explicitly discussing Kant, Dworkin departs from the Kantian view in two important respects. First, she denies that the baneful tendencies that Kant imputes to sexual desire belong to it inevitably or as such. Indeed, Dworkin thinks that it is always a mistake to read existing social behavior as reflecting desire's underlying "nature," given the depth at which social and political structures contribute to shaping what we find desirable in a partner. And, apart from the social deformations caused by asymmetrical structures of power, Dworkin holds that sexual relationships can express regard for humanity.

Second, she focuses (as Kant did not) on the role of male-female asymmetry in constructing a pernicious form of sexual exchange in which men come to be aroused by the idea of turning a woman into a thing, and women come to find excitement in the thought of volunteering to be used as things. Here Dworkin's analysis lies close to that of Mill, Who argued in *The Subjection of Women* that men, wishing to make willing rather than unwilling slaves of women, have "put everything in practice to enslave their minds," teaching women that "meekness, submissiveness, and resignation of all individual will" is "an essential part of sexual attractiveness." The idea that women's current behavior reveals their "nature" is scoffed at as much by Mill as by

Dworkin, when he says that this is just like putting a tree half in a vapor bath and half in the snow, and then, seeing that one part is luxuriant and the other part withered, saying that it is "the nature of the tree" to be that way.

Dworkin does not speculate about how the sexual objectification of women began, though she suggests (again with Mill) that it is greatly helped along by the legal construction of marriage as involving limitless rights of sexual access. (Mill already argued in 1869 that the absence of laws against marital rape made women's status lower than that of slaves. Today most states in the United States still have some form of spousal exemption for rape.) What she does emphasize—this is her diagnostic thesis—is that men have been pervasively socialized to think that aggression, violence and the treatment of women as objects are just normal male attitudes, "boys being boys," and that women just have to put up with that. Given our society's tendency to glorify and to eroticize male violence, men frequently learn to find sexual satisfaction only in situations of dominance. The cultural portrayal of intercourse as conquest has deformed sexual relations, making it difficult for men to accept women both as sexual partners and as equals. "In order to get a response from men, one has to be the right kind of thing." And "[w]hen you enter the sexual agreement to be a thing, you then narrow your own possibilities for freedom."

Dworkin has frequently been portrayed as holding that all sexual intercourse is rape. Some of her more sweeping statements have supported such a reading. She should have been more circumspect here, demarcating her claims more precisely. Still, examining her rhetoric with care, one may discern a far more plausible and interesting thesis: that the sexualization of dominance and submission, and the perpetuation of these structures through unequal laws (such as the failure to criminalize marital rape or to prosecute domestic violence effectively), have so pervasively infected the development of desire in our society that "you cannot separate the so-called abuses of women from the so-called normal uses of women." This sentence certainly does not say that all acts of intercourse are abuses. It does say that the dominant paradigms of the normal are themselves culpable, so we can't simply write off the acts of rapists and batterers by saying that they are "abnormal." Gendered violence is too deep in our entire culture.

Dworkin observes that, no matter how often males use violence against other males, nobody concludes that men like being beaten up, or that it is in the nature of men to provoke violence by their bodily appearance. But women who do not leave abusive marriages, on account of economic dependence or terror or a conviction that they will die sooner or later anyway, are often portrayed as wanting abuse, and the abuse is often portrayed as a natural reflex of the jealous male nature. Again, until very recently it was standard courtroom policy to portray a rape victim as someone who "asked for it"; but such judgments are rarely made about men who get mugged. "There's a different standard of dignity," Dworkin concludes. What we should say, in both cases equally, is that human rights have been violated. But we don't say that frequently enough about women.

Up to this point, Dworkin says what few feminists today would find controversial. The legal proposals that her arguments have promoted or supported now enjoy widespread support in our society. Most feminists welcome the changes that have made it possible to complain of sexual harassment in the workplace and to demonstrate that an asymmetry of power is frequently at the root of what creates a "hostile work environment." These concepts, developed by Andrea Dworkin and Catharine MacKinnon, are now commonplace in our legal culture, and have been validated recently in workplace opinions by such non-radical judges as William Rehnquist and Richard Posner.

Most feminists would hardly wish to return to the situation of thirty years ago, where a raped woman would have to show that she resisted "to the utmost" or was physically harmed in a struggle, and where a woman's prior sexual history would be used against her as evidence in a rape trial, to show that she "asked for it." Most feminists also would gladly concur with Dworkin's central conclusion in her new book: that laws against domestic violence should be far more effectively enforced, and that our society should intervene in many more ways to provide women with alternatives to staying in abusive relationships. Dworkin's suggestion that women who retaliate violently against their batterers should in some cases be allowed to plead self-defense also enjoys widespread support.

It is a curious feature of contemporary feminism that one repeatedly encounters women who denounce MacKinnon and Dworkin as man-haters, but who gladly enjoy, and even take credit for, the legal reforms that were made possible only through concepts they introduced. Dworkin and MacKinnon are radicals; but their radicalism has proven broadly acceptable, in large part because they call a culture based on rights and equal dignity to full consistency with itself.

III.

Pornography is a different matter. *Life and Death* describes the episode in Dworkin's career that has, more than any other, led to widespread vilification: her association with MacKinnon working for legal changes in this area. It is extremely common to hear the two assailed as apostles of censorship; but often the ideas themselves are not described with any precision.

Dworkin's persuasive argument about cultural patterns of objectification prompts an obvious question. How are these bad attitudes about women reproduced, in a culture that in some respects accords women equal dignity as persons? Dworkin answers that a key part of the causal story is violent and humiliating pornography. Pornographic images repeatedly portray women as dirty and debased, as asking to be raped, as deserving violent or abusive treatment. Pornography commonly portrays the will of women from a fictive male viewpoint, expressing the thought that they want to be used as things for male pleasure. Describing a photograph in which a pregnant woman gleefully sticks a hose up herself, Dworkin comments: "This is not a human being. One cannot look at such a photograph and say, This is a human being, she has rights, she has freedom. She has dignity, she is someone. One cannot. That is what pornography *does* to women."

In Dworkin's view, of course, our whole culture is suffused with such attitudes, and pornography is far from being their only source. Yet she argues, drawing both on experimental evidence and on testimony from women whose batterers made them re-enact pornographic scenarios, that it is a very prominent cause of the "boys-will-be-boys" indifference to violence. (It is hard not to think this way, when Larry Flynt, who portrayed the dismemberment of a woman in a meat grinder as arousing, is canonized as a saint of free speech, while the Nazis who marched in Skokie are regarded as despicable scum whose rights just might be protected by the First Amendment. What does this difference show us about ourselves?) Regarding pornography as rather like a dangerous drug that causes harm, she and MacKinnon have attempted to create a legal remedy for women who are victims of these harms.

Neither MacKinnon nor Dworkin recommends using the criminal law to punish the makers or the distributors of pornography. Nor have they called for censorship of pornographic materials. What they have proposed (with brief success in Indianapolis, before a federal appellate court ruled against them) is a civil ordinance, under which women who have been harmed by pornography can sue its makers and distributors for damages, and ask an administrative agency to issue an injunction against the offenders. The potential plaintiffs were envisaged as of two types: actresses who are harmed while making pornographic films, and battered women who can show a sufficient causal connection between the abuse and the man's use of pornographic materials. The category of material that would be potentially actionable is both narrower and broader than the materials that are potentially illegal under current obscenity law: narrower because sexual explicitness by itself is not found problematic, if there is no humiliation or violence; broader because there is no escape clause for redeeming social value, and no permissible appeal to the sense of the work as a whole to establish such redeeming value.

People who attack this proposal simply on the grounds that they are in favor of the First Amendment are not saying anything intellectually respectable. The First Amendment has never covered all speech; bribery, threats, extortionate offers, misleading advertising, perjury and unlicensed medical advice are all unprotected. Indeed, in 1918, when Eugene Debs went to jail for sedition on account of speeches urging people to resist military service, the First Amendment wasn't even held to cover the type of political speech that is currently recognized as lying at its very core. So the argument cannot be that pornography is speech, so it must be protected. Instead, the argument must be made that it is the type of speech that ought to be protected by the First Amendment.

Such an argument against Dworkin must be based on extensive legal analysis, something that many of her opponents (but not all of them) fail to offer. They need to grapple also with the fact that we currently have a legal obscenity standard that renders illegal (on other grounds) most of the materials that concern Dworkin; and that we also have a variety of other laws—against cigarette and alcohol advertising, for example—that reflect our society's view that some speech is harmful and needs regulation. Moreover, we now permit people harmed by tobacco products and the advertising surrounding them to sue the makers of those products for damages. Under certain circumstances, sellers of alcohol are also liable for damages their products have caused. (But we do not currently allow damage suits against those who speak or write in praise of alcohol or tobacco.) Most Western democracies, moreover, allow more regulation of hate speech than we do: Germany's restrictions on anti-Semitic speech and Britain's Race Relations Act, for example, need to be considered as we ponder what we really want to say.

How, then, should one object to the MacKinnon-Dworkin proposal? Certainly one should begin by acknowledging that it addresses the proper moral target, in the sense that material depicting the abuse of women as sexy is morally problematic in a way that the traditional category of the "obscene" does not seem to be. (Defined in terms of the vague notion of appeal to "prurient interest," that category has frequently led to a focus on depictions of reciprocal sex that are just a little too frank for some judge's taste—as with *Lady Chatterley's Lover.*) One should also grant that such representations of women as made for abuse are likely to contribute in some way to the general climate of violence against women that is among our pressing social problems. And then the objections should begin.

One reasonable objection might be that MacKinnon and Dworkin have never satisfactorily articulated a theory of the distinction between law and morals, and that we need a general account of this notoriously problematic line in order to carry the argument further. Many bad things aren't, and shouldn't be, illegal. Even under Mill's "harm" principle, a case can surely be argued for some regulation of pornography. But Dworkin never argues such a case, though she seems to agree with Mill's objection to laws against the merely offensive. More argument might have clarified her position.

Next, given the ubiquity of violence in our society, the causal links between pornography and any particular case of harm are probably too difficult to establish. With cigarette smoking, we have a control group cigarette smoking, we have control group of non-smokers to examine. Men in America have been exposed to a wide range of images of women, in the media, in advertising and, in many cases, in pornography. Perhaps we cannot adequately distinguish the contributions of these different sources, showing that in a given a case of abuse pornography, and not the man's earlier socialization, was the primary cause.

It is unclear, moreover, under what circumstances we should hold the producer of a work liable for the harms that it inflicts. *Crime and Punishment* gave rise to copycat murders. Nietzsche's writings influenced the Nazis. In both cases, the murderers were to some extent misreading the work, whereas the batterer who imitates a violent porn book or video is not misreading (except in the sense that the maker of the work plainly aimed at masturbation, not real-life enactment). But MacKinnon and Dworkin probably cannot use this distinction, given their rejection of the appeal to the sense of the work as a whole. It seems plausible, then, that making authors liable for what copycat criminals do will exert a stifling effect on some valuable speech.

Fourth, we might object that such an ordinance is very likely to be abused in practice. Judges are likely to prove bad analysts of sexual stereotypes and their effect. The history of obscenity law shows us that work of high human value is likely to be targeted, while much harmful trash escapes unscathed. Indeed, insofar as they refuse appeal to the sense of the work as a whole, MacKinnon and Dworkin make it possible to indict some feminist work—say, Dworkin's fiction—that graphically portrays the sexual abuse of women, with the overall purpose of sensitizing us to its terrible character. James Lindgren has shown that 63 percent of students who were shown an extract from Dworkin's novel **Mercy** ranked it as pornographic under MacKinnon's and Dworkin's own definition of pornography (almost as high a proportion as *The Story of O*, one of Dworkin's central examples of pornography)—though they did not rank it as obscene under a modified version of the current Supreme Court obscenity test.

This points to another and more fundamental issue. There is value in Dworkin's prophetic examination of the pornographic; the ability to study troubling cultural representations without fear of legal penalty is an important part of affecting social change, and so even someone convinced of the moral case against pornography might plausibly be disturbed by the legal pressures such an ordinance might create. But should we accept Dworkin's moral thesis? Many objectors have defended the value of a type of pornography that she does not attack (works involving consensual, nonhumiliating activity that would be far more likely to be targeted by the current obscenity test than by her test). Others have simply refused to acknowledge that there is any moral problem in the representation of women as meant for abuse and humiliation. (This, I think, is an implausible position.) But there is another position, one that appeals to the all-important issue of context and sense in the work as a whole.

Sexual objectification of various types occurs within many relationships that are, in their larger structure, relationships of equality and respect. Within such an established context, forms of treatment that might otherwise undermine dignity (for example, treating a person, for a time, as identical with his or her bodily parts) do not undermine dignity. One might reformulate Kant's position as the claim that one moral goal of an intimate relationship is to establish a context within which respect can be taken on trust, so that acts that would elsewhere mean domination and subordination do not, therefore, mean this. Dworkin allows that in individual lives penetration and receptivity may have other meanings; but the ordinance that she proposes makes no distinctions of context, and thus it might be used to target representations that even a sympathizer with Dworkin's argument might judge morally good.

For a combination of these reasons, I am inclined to oppose the MacKinnon-Dworkin ordinance as a legal remedy for the harms of violent pornography. Still, Dworkin has identified an urgent problem that needs to be treated with moral seriousness. Feminists who deny this should ask whether women can really make progress in areas such as rape law and the prosecution of domestic abuse, when a jury of their peers has been raised on images that depict such abuses as exactly what women are about.

IV.

Prophets may also be false prophets. That is how many feminists view Dworkin's attacks on sexual corruption. A calm examination of Dworkin's views can help to articulate more precisely the sense of her claims, and to show what is plausible and valuable in them; but that is not the end of the matter, even philosophically. There are some general worries about the nature of Dworkin's undertaking that must be faced.

The first worry concerns Dworkin's obsessive focus on the sexual as the locus of women's subordination, and her apparent indifference to economic issues. Dworkin holds that it is because men view women as sex objects that women do not enjoy equal dignity. She therefore sees a change in socially constructed forms of sexual desire as the key to women's equality. Yet men have traditionally viewed women in other ways as well: as bearers of, and carers for, children; as homemakers; as performers of domestic labor. It is plausible to think that these powerful interests reinforce and perpetuate the more narrowly sexual forms of subordination, and may even collude in their creation.

If one sees things this way, one will think that the key to women's equality is to promote their economic advantage, focusing on employment, credit, land rights and other issues of daily self-sufficiency. In developing countries today, feminists are split over these issues: some reject projects as non-feminist if they do not focus, Dworkin-style, on the criticism of sex roles, while others insist that such criticism can never bear fruit unless women first enjoy greater economic self-sufficiency. There is no necessary incompatibility between the two approaches; but Dworkin's failure to acknowledge the economic aspect of inequality means that she offers very uncertain guidance for practical change, especially in the developing world.

> **In her new book [*Life and Death*], one finds less hostility to argument than in her other writings, but Dworkin's contemptuous attitude to her opponents, and her failure to engage in calm exchanges of ideas, has not disappeared, and it is troubling.**
> —*Martha C. Nussbaum*

Another worry concerns Dworkin's attitude to reasoned persuasion. In her new book, one finds less hostility to argument than in her other writings, but Dworkin's contemptuous attitude to her opponents, and her failure to engage in calm exchanges of ideas, has not disappeared, and it is troubling. Maybe Dworkin is right. Maybe most people are so distracted, or obtuse, or jaded, that only highly colored rhetoric can shake them, and a calm argument will leave their prejudices untouched. But it seems more productive to believe that people are innocent of the refusal of reason until proven guilty over a long period of time, and that we should always make the first move toward them on the assumption that they would like to search along with us for an adequate account. Doesn't prophetic rhetoric of Dworkin's sort objectify people in its own way, reducing them to their sins rather than regarding them with respect, as ends in themselves?

I have referred to Dworkin's "fire-and-brimstone" rhetoric. My deepest concern about her project lies here. Dworkin's attitude to men exemplifies the unattractive traits that are commonly, and falsely, attributed to the Jewish god: a focus on retributive justice, a total absence of compassion and mercy. Her novel *Mercy* is all about why it is correct to refuse mercy to men, and best to regard them in the light of strict retributive justice, paying them back in kind for the wrongs that they have done to women. Like most old-time retributivists, Dworkin doesn't even think it terribly important which individual gets the punishment, since the sins are understood to belong to the whole "house" or race, and individuals are guilty in virtue of this membership.

Life and Death, too, contains the denunciation of evil without the vision of reconciliation, fury without mercy, hatred without love. Indeed, Dworkin repeatedly expresses sympathy with violent extralegal resistance against male violence: "If we have to fight back with arms, then we have to fight back with arms. One way or another we have to disarm men." Dworkin is right to claim that feminists have used "extraordinary patience and self-restraint" by responding with words and not with violence, as have most other oppressed groups; but this does not mean that a commitment to nonviolence is not a good feminist choice. Surely it must not be a source of shame. ("I have a long history of violence against me, and I say, to my increasing shame, that everyone who has hurt me is still walking around.")

One might favor legal and nonviolent means while still being a strict retributivist, opposed to sympathy and mercy. Kant, who denied a right to revolution, also held that only the retributive attitude expresses respect for the criminal's personhood. Pleas for sympathy (attributing the wrong, for example, to bad cultural forces rather than personal evil) are seen as diminishing personhood by negating responsibility. (Justice Thomas has recently followed Kant's lead in his remarks about criminal sentencing of minority defendants.) But sympathy and mercy need not diminish personhood. They may simply express the thought that all human beings are weak and fallible, in part the creation of their social milieu and not fully culpable for evils that are bred into them by the unjust conditions they inhabit.

Such an idea is a valuable one for a prophet of social change, for it can forge a link between the corrupt world that the prophet decries and a new world of equality and respect. Martin Luther King Jr. understood this well. He saw that a prophet must lead people out of something bad *and* into something good. His use of prophetic language created a space within which love might come to exist, and a world made ugly by hierarchy might be redeemed by the beauty of equality. Dworkin's rhetoric, by contrast, contains no space for reconciliation, no positive vision. Her non-forgiveness toward men, like her refusal of reason, is itself an act of violent aggression, expressing the thought that men will be punished forever for their bad acts by being refused entry into any world that is good.

This is a message that is ultimately at odds with Dworkin's own view of the possibilities of human life, though it is perhaps entailed by her decision to talk about a "collective him" rather than to make more fine-grained distinctions. Certainly it is a vision that cripples social progress by identifying the call for justice with a state of permanent hostility. Mercy may be given from a position of weakness, because one has been taught that women are sympathetic creatures who shouldn't demand their rights. Yet it may also be given from a position of strength, because one is confident that one has dignity, and one has some confidence in the possibilities of reason and reconciliation. Nietzsche once said that mercy toward the aggressor is "the self-overcoming of justice." Dworkin gives us the call for justice without any space for its self-overcoming.

Cindy Jenefsky and Ann Russo (essay date 1998)

SOURCE: "The Art of Confrontation," in *Without Apology: Andrea Dworkin's Art and Politics,* Westview Press, 1998, pp. 78-93.

[*In the following essay, Jenefsky and Russo examine Dworkin's political methods and rhetorical discourse as an antipornography activist. According to the critics, Dworkin's approach centers upon strategies of "concretization" and "de/centering," by which she draws attention to the real-life implications of pornography while undermining familiar constitutional arguments in its favor.*]

Dworkin's advocacy against pornography is shaped by her commitment to confrontational politics as "the essence of social change." "The way that you destabilize male power," she says, "is basically not by seduction, and not by begging, and not by any of the female stratagems that [women] are essentially taught should be the basis of our politics. . . . The places where society has moved, it has been because of confrontation." Accordingly, Dworkin rejects all "female stratagems" as ineffective political methods and expressly devotes herself to confrontational politics: "My activism is centered on my notion that what's important is to confront male power; that's the standard by which I decide what I will and won't do." This standard abides in her artistic practice and demands that the form and content of her writing be as direct and concrete as possible:

The form, the voice, the diction of the writing itself confronts male power directly. My writing is concrete as opposed to abstract. It goes right to the political heart of things. It doesn't go through a veil of ideas nor does it interpret the world through others' ideas, weighing and balancing them. It's very direct, and that's something about both form and content that's extremely important and substantive.

Both substantively and stylistically, Dworkin's antipornography discourse enacts this political commitment to confrontation through two prominent rhetorical strategies: concretization and de/centering. Concretization—making something concrete by focusing on its tangible properties—strips pornography of its ideological garb of sexual libertarianism and directly zooms in on its real-life harm. De/centering places women's destructive experiences with pornography at the *center* of her texts and *de*-centers all other experiences and competing perspectives on pornography. Combined, these two strategies enable Dworkin to confront pornography in a direct manner by "go[ing] right to the political heart of things" (concretization of harm) and refusing to "interpret the world through others' ideas" (de/centering). With these strategies, Dworkin produces a set of ironic reversals that switch the premises upon which pornography has been widely debated, radically substituting *her* concerns about pornography in place of those of pornography's defenders. These reversals constitute an act of political disruption boldly displacing the premises of the status quo. This chapter examines this confrontative form of Dworkin's antipornography advocacy, focusing on the political utility of her artistic practices.

Privileging the Concrete

Throughout all of Dworkin's work, she expresses contempt for abstraction and stresses the necessity to understand social phenomena in concrete material terms. She writes in **"The ACLU: Bait and Switch"**: "There is nothing as dangerous as an unembodied principle: no matter what blood flows, the principle comes first." Dworkin says she refuses "to sit around and argue ideas with people." Ideas are important only insofar as they are relevant to real people's lives and the material conditions underlying them: "I care about some idea where somebody's life is at stake; and if there isn't that interrelationship between idea and somebody's life, you know, I don't care about the argument." She often characterizes abstract discussion as a frivolous practice of the privileged—that is, as an activity performed by those who do not recognize or experience the harmful consequences of the "ideas" they discuss. For example, she says of the abstract conception of censorship in the United States:

It gets to be, in silly countries like this one, whatever people say it is, separate from any material definition, separate from police power, separate from state repression (jail, banning, exile, death), separate from devastating consequences to real people (jail, banning, exile, death). It is something that people who eat fine food and wear fine clothes worry about frenetically, trying to find it, anticipating it with great anxiety, arguing it down as if—if it were real—an argument would make it go away; not knowing that it has a clear, simple, unavoidable momentum and meaning in a cruel world of police power that their privilege cannot comprehend.

In contrast to such abstraction, Dworkin describes her own approach to political issues as a process of drawing conclusions inductively from lived experiences (her own or other people's). For example, she says of her process of writing **Woman Hating** after escaping the brutality of her marriage: "The battering destroyed me. I had to decide whether I wanted to live or die. I was broken and shamed and empty. I looked at pornography to try to understand what had happened to me. And I found a lot of *information,* about power and the mechanisms by which the subordination of women is sexualized. I want you to understand that I didn't learn an ideology. For me, it's been a living journey." Similarly, she says of her antipornography work generally: "I know about the lives of women in pornography because I lived the life"; and again:

I knew how women were hurt by pornography. My knowledge was concrete, not abstract: I knew the ways it was used; I knew how it was made; I knew the scenes of exploitation and abuse in real life—the lives of prostitutes, daughters, girlfriends, wives; I knew the words the women said when they dared to whisper what had happened to them; I could hear their voices in my mind, in my heart.

Dworkin thus characterizes her concrete approach to political analysis in explicit contrast to ideological approaches that begin with a theoretical framework which is then applied to life. "What I try to do in my work," she states, "is to look at what the concrete scenario is and then understand the meaning of it from that, rather than go backwards. . . . I just think it's pointless to have one's ideas about society and then try to lay them on the pornography—that you find out more if you look at the pornography and try to figure out what it is that it's doing in relationship to everything you know about the ways in which various groups are being hurt in society." She claims that she must be able to see a phenomenon "in action" before she can understand it and write about it. "In other words, I don't accept it from an ideological point of view or a dogmatic or programmatic point of view . . . My books don't come from dogma." As she says, they come from lived experience: "mine or other people's, all experience that I know of that is available to me in any way: through books, through what happens to people."

Dworkin's rejection of abstraction is manifested stylistically in her own rhetorical practice: her analyses of social phenomena are directed toward that which is concrete—behaviors, life experiences, material conditions—rather than ideas and principles. Her ideas are always embodied in her discourse; she presents them in terms of their concrete implications for real people's lives. Her analysis of pornography is no exception. In contrast to usual public debates about pornography, she does not address pornography in terms of what it symbolically presents (its ideas about women or sex or perversion) or symbolically presents (such as being a metaphor for women's oppression or a symbol of free speech, sexual freedom, or moral depravity); nor does she frame her discussion in terms of constitutional principles (such as the First or Fourteenth Amendment). Her analysis of pornography centers on what pornography *does:* its tangible function in sustaining male sexual domination and the tangible ways it harms women. Her "ideas about" pornography are made concrete by embodying the lived experiences of those women—including herself—exploited, used, humiliated, and abused through the production and consumption of pornography. "Autobiography is the unseen foundation of my nonfiction work," writes Dworkin; "when I wrote *Intercourse* and *Pornography: Men Possessing Women,* I used my life in every decision I made. It was my compass. Only by using it could I find north and stay on course. If a reader could lift up the words on the page, she would see—far, far under the surface—my life. If the print on the page turned into blood, it would be my blood from many different places and times." She is intolerant of pornography "being treated as if it's some kind of university debating issue. That's never been what it's been. Women's lives have always been at stake." She summarizes this point in **"Pornography Happens to Women."** She states that the sexualization and dehumanization of women in pornography are "always concrete and specific"; they are "never abstract and conceptual."

> That is why all of these debates on the subject of pornography have such a bizarre quality to them. Those of us who know that pornography hurts women and care, talk about women's real lives. Insults, and assaults that really happen to real women in real life—the women in the pornography and the women on whom the pornography is used. Those who argue for pornography, especially on the ground of freedom of speech, insist that pornography is a species of idea, thought, fantasy, situated inside the physical brain, the mind, of the consumer no less.

> In fact we are told all the time that pornography is really about ideas. Well, a rectum doesn't have an idea,

and a vagina doesn't have an idea, and the mouths of women in pornography do not express ideas.

Accordingly, Dworkin describes pornography exclusively in terms of its tangible qualities. The above passage, for instance, contrasts defenses of pornography based on concepts of free speech, ideas, thoughts, and fantasies with her concretized notion of pornography's use of women's rectums, vaginas, and mouths. A short three sentence excerpt from **"Against the Male Flood"** also captures this strategy of concretizing social phenomena. She writes: "The pornographers actually use our bodies as their language. We are their speech. Our bodies are the building blocks of their sentences." Note how she focuses not on what pornographers say but on how their speech entails doing something concrete to women: literally using women's bodies, not merely spreading false ideas about women. Pornographers' speech is not just words or pictures here but is *comprised* of women's bodies: "our bodies *as* their language," "We *are* their speech," "Our bodies *are* the building blocks." Without women's bodies, pornography as such would not exist.

The pornographers actually use our bodies as their language. We are their speech. Our bodies are the building blocks of their sentences.
        —Andrea Dworkin

In a similar example from her 1986 testimony to the Attorney General's Commission on Pornography, Dworkin states: "Our bodies are their language. Their speech is made out of our exploitation, our subservience, our injury, and our pain, and they can't say anything without hurting us, and when you protect them, you protect only their right to exploit and hurt us." By presenting pornography solely from the perspective of women harmed by it, Dworkin frames pornographic *speech* in terms of *physical* properties: "our bodies," "our injury," "our pain," "exploit and hurt us." Pornographic speech is thereby transformed from a cultural artifact to a concrete practice within her prose by infusing it with material harms done to women. In **"Silence Means Dissent"** (1984), Dworkin concretizes the usually abstract concepts of "sexual subordination" and "hierarchy"—two *practices* central to her conception of pornography—by describing how these practices are manifested behaviorally in women's lives:

> Pornography is the sexualized subordination of women. It means being put down through sex, by sex, in sex, and around sex, so that somebody can use you as sex and have sex and have a good time. And subordination consists of a hierarchy that means one person is on the top and one person is on the bottom. And while

hierarchy has been described in beautiful ideological terms over thousands and thousands of years, for us it is not an abstract idea because we know who is on top. We usually know his name and address.

Whereas many perceive pornography as the sexual expression of pornographers, Dworkin sees it from the perspective of women used in pornography and the tangible acts done to them: "Society . . . says that pornographers must not be stopped because the freedom of everyone depends on the freedom of pornographers to exercise speech. The woman gagged and hanging remains the speech they exercise." And again: "pornographers use our bodies as their language. Anything they say, they have to use us to say . . . we . . . are their ciphers, their semantic symbols, the pieces they arrange in order to communicate." In every instance, Dworkin linguistically concretizes pornography by embedding within it the experiences of women exploited.

No matter which dimension of pornography Dworkin addresses—sexual subordination, sexual objectification, racism, economic exploitation, discrimination—her descriptions always revolve around actual harms done to women. In each of her works on pornography she focuses on a range of harmful behaviors: from dehumanization and humiliation to various forms of violence and even death—essentially, all of the ways she claims pornography sexually subordinates women though its production and consumption. And as all of the examples in the previous two paragraphs illustrate, Dworkin never simply claims pornography is a concrete practice that harms women; rather, she always linguistically *constructs pornography as an active agent responsible for material consequences to women's lives.* Her texts function iconically, as pornography's performance in her texts mirrors its performance in society.

Dworkin's lengthy description of pornography in **"Against the Male Flood"** summarily represents this stylistic strategy of concretization. In each sentence, "what pornography is" (its ontology) consists of "what it does" to women. In this way, pornography is textually comprised of its tangible acts of sexual subordination. She writes:

In the United States, it is an $8-billion trade in sexual exploitation.

It is women turned into subhumans, beaver, pussy, body parts, genitals exposed, buttocks, breasts, mouths opened and throats penetrated, covered in semen, pissed on, shitted on, hung from light fixtures, tortured, maimed, bleeding, disemboweled, killed.

It is some creature called female, used.

It is scissors poised at the vagina and objects stuck in it, a smile on the woman's face, her tongue hanging out.

It is a woman being fucked by dogs, horses, snakes.

It is torture in every prison cell in the world, done to women and sold as sexual entertainment.

It is rape and gang rape and anal rape and throat rape: and it is the woman raped, asking for more.

It is the woman in the picture to whom it is really happening and the women against whom the picture is used, to make them do what the woman in the picture is doing.

It is the power men have over women turned into sexual acts men do to women, because pornography is the power and the act.

It is the conditioning of erection and orgasm in men to the powerlessness of women: our inferiority, humiliation, pain, torment; to us as objects, things, or commodities for use in sex as servants.

It sexualizes inequality and in doing so creates discrimination as a sex-based practice.

It permeates the political condition of women in society by being the substance of our inequality however located—in jobs, in education, in marriage, *in life.*

It is women, kept as a sexual underclass, kept available for rape and battery and incest and prostitution.

It is what we are under male domination; it is what we are for under male domination.

It is the heretofore hidden (from us) system of subordination that women have been told is just life.

Under male supremacy, it is the synonym for what being a woman is.

It is access to our bodies as a birthright to men: the grant, the gift, the permission, the license, the proof, the promise, the method, how to; it is us accessible, no matter what the law pretends to say, no matter what we pretend to say.

It is physical injury and physical humiliation and physical pain: to the women against whom it is used after it is made; to the women used to make it.

As words alone, or words and pictures, moving or still, it creates systematic harm to women in the form of discrimination and physical hurt. It creates harm inevitably by its nature because of what it is and what it does.

Pornography—its production, products, dissemination, and use—is the subject of each sentence; "what happens to women" is the predicate of each sentence. Pornography is concretized within the texture of her discourse by being constructed as an agent acting upon women's bodies. The audience is thus invited to experience "Pornography" within her texts exclusively in terms of the concrete experiences of those it harms.

Pornographers do not do something as benign as "speak" in Dworkin's discourse: "they traffic in women . . . they sexualize inequality in a way that materially promotes rape, battery, maiming, and bondage; they make a product that they know dehumanizes, degrades, and exploits women; they hurt women to make the pornography and then consumers use the pornography in assaults both verbal and physical." Looking at pornography narrowly as a form of speech elides all of the ways it also functions as an *act;* it eliminates from view all of the women whose lives are diminished by pornography. Just as pornographic speech never exists in isolation from its production and consumption, so "pornography" in Dworkin's work always textually embodies actual harmful experiences of women used to make pornography and women on whom pornography is used. "Pornography happens," states Dworkin in a 1993 speech delivered at the University of Chicago Law School: "It happens. Lawyers, call it what you want—call it speech, call it act, call it conduct . . . but the point is that it happens. It happens to women, in real life." Through this strategy of concretization, she asserts women's lived experiences as the basis of her "theory" about pornography's function in our male supremacist society. Dworkin writes a "theory in the flesh"—one that uses "the physical realities of [women's] lives": "flesh and blood experiences to concretize a vision" of pornography as she knows it.

Centering the Margins

Noticeably omitted from Dworkin's textual representations is mention of benign or valued properties of pornography. For Dworkin, discussing pornography's social, educational, political, or entertainment value is akin to discussing Nazi anti-Semitic propaganda in terms of its merits as intellectual, artistic, entertainment, or educational media: in both cases, it requires one to close one's eyes to systematic cruelty and atomistically sever the product from all the ways it harms real people. Dworkin never denies that pornography gives people pleasure; rather, she problematizes the pleasure as a source of pornography's propagandic success and renders it insignificant in comparison to pornography's harm. "The pleasure." She states,

> is at a cost to women, including when it comes from dehumanization and not from violence. . . . The fact

that somebody gets an orgasm from anti-Semitic material makes the anti-Semitic material, what, good? Legitimate? What? With women, we're talking about a fundamental political condition where people's pleasure is coming from the subordination of women. It's whole range of pleasure. So if what you're going to say is, "pleasure is our ultimate value," then essentially you're going to be defending the subordination of women all across a long continuum of acts.

For Dworkin, pornography's harm outweighs all other possible values attached to it. Any positive value accorded pornography—whether it be pleasure, edification, or political import—exacerbates and veils its real human destructiveness. Consequently, all positive associations with pornography are rendered invisible in her discourse; only the negative dimensions are given presence in her work.

The absence of competing perspectives within Dworkin's works is a brazen artistic and political choice. She places the harm to women at the center of her discourse and marginalizes all contrasting ideas about pornography. As a result, she gives undivided attention to the experiences of those whom pornography harms, particularly poor women, prostitutes, and survivors of incest, rape, and other forms of sexual violence.
—*Cindy Jenefsky and Ann Russo*

The absence of competing perspectives within Dworkin's works is a brazen artistic and political choice. She places the harm to women at the center of her discourse and marginalizes all contrasting ideas about pornography. As a result, she gives undivided attention to the experiences of those whom pornography harms, particularly poor women, prostitutes, and survivors of incest, rape, and other forms of sexual violence. This shift in perspective—from prevailing interpretations of pornography to her radical reconception of it—enables previously invisible qualities of pornography to be seen. As Deirdre Lashgari writes in her introduction to *Violence, Silence, and Anger: Women's Writing as Transgression:* "When those who are marginal to the dominant power re-place the center, making the margin the new center of their own subjectivity, different perspectives on violence become possible. . . . Shifting the vantage point of the subject allows one to see forms of violence that had been invisible, or to see in unfamiliar ways." In describing pornography exclusively from the perspectives of those it most exploits, Dworkin places pornography's harm at the center of her audience's vision. "What I'm concerned about," says Dworkin. "is the way that the hierarchies are arranged in each situation . . . . and then the meaning that comes from that for the people who are the ones exploited."

In the introduction to *Returning the Gaze: Essays on Racism, Feminism, and Politics*, Himani Bannerji describes this rhetorical de/centering as a revolutionary strategy for disrupting and reconfiguring hegemonic representations. She writes: "By understanding 'representation' to mean representation of our realities, from a foundationally critical/revolutionary perspective, there can emerge the possibility of making our very marginality itself the epicentre for change. This has always been the principle of any fundamentally revolutionary or critical perspective." Similarly, bell hooks finds revolutionary potential in utilizing the margins as "a space of resistance": "a central location for the production of a counter-hegemonic discourse." According to her, moving the margins to the center of one's vision is a radical act of intervention. While hooks insists on not "only speak[ing] your pain" when speaking from the margins, Dworkin's rhetorical intervention articulates only the "pain." Her texts are spaces where the harm of pornography is made central and prominent, with all other perspectives absented from the discussion.

Moving the margins to the center and excluding competing perspectives within her texts is a form of rhetorical distillation that enhances the direct, confrontative quality of Dworkin's work. By articulating only the experiences of those harmed by pornography, she presents her messages in a concentrated form, neither diluted nor distracted by opposing perspectives. Such rhetorical distillation is a bold artistic move that reflects her expressed determination to engage her audience in the most direct manner possible. As she says, she will not "go through a veil of ideas nor . . . interpret the world through others' ideas." She resists all pressures to frame her knowledge in relationship to other, existing bodies of knowledge on a topic and insists, instead, that her texts be inhabited by her insights alone. In doing so, she violates what she calls "a whole bunch of unwritten rules for women": "Some of the rules are academic, some of the rules are clearly gender-related. All of them have to do with hedging your bets—you know, with expressing ambivalence, with never really asserting that you know what it is you see or what you're about." She says female writers in particular are expected to couch their ideas in relationship to a host of other perspectives in order to demonstrate knowledgeability. "You're supposed to say," says Dworkin:

> "now there's that, now there's that, there's that, there's that and there's that, and this one's wrong, this one's wrong, this one's wrong, this one's really stupid and dedadedadeda, and I hate oppression, I hate racism, I hate classism, and I hate this," and then you come to

your conclusion. And what you've demonstrated is that, yes, you know how to dance. I mean, that's it; that's all you've done.

Dworkin also rejects these unwritten rules as middle-class conventions inapplicable to her life as a writer. She says,

> I'm not a middle-class writer. I can't be. It's not the kind of life I've had . . . the forms of courtesy [others] expect in writing are essentially middle-class conventions that mean nothing to me . . . manners, and a sense of respect and, especially, a belief that there is a tomorrow so you can hoard your resources, and there's time—that if you don't do it now, you'll do it later. First you'll say this, and then you'll wait five years, and then you'll say that. Whereas for me, every day is the last day, and that's not going to change. If I don't do it now, if I don't say it now, I don't get it done now, I don't have tomorrow. . . . I don't write with the sense that I have anything to lose.

Rhetorical theorist Kenneth Burke provides a useful framework for explicating the difference between Dworkin's direct writing style and the style Dworkin describes as "academic" or "middle-class." The latter is labeled a "proportional" mode of interpretation, whereas the former is termed an "essentializing" mode. The proportional mode seeks to interpret something by explicating its meaning explicitly in relation to all of the parts that make up the whole. For example, in a proportional interpretation of a proposed law, "the court would note that the legislation in question would be wholly irrelevant to certain of the wishes, would wholly gratify one or some, would partially gratify others, and would antagonize the rest. And its judgment would be rationalized with reference to this total recipe." An essentializing interpretation, in contrast, would pick one representative clause in the Constitution and evaluate the legislation in reference to it alone. Similarly, a proportional interpretation of pornography might present it in terms of the broad expanse of pornographic media and images, the wide variety of people's responses to it, people's many uses of it, the sexual pleasure and sexual freedom it provides to some, the detriment it causes to others, etc. Or it might present one perspective on pornography and contrast it in relation to a spectrum of differing viewpoints. But in Dworkin's essentializing interpretation, she defines pornography strictly from the perspective of those harmed by it. All other perspectives are excluded from her texts. She thereby requires her audience to step into her world as she sees it, rather than presenting her world *in relation to* the perspectives of others. When her perspectives stands alone, she states her message directly without interference or distraction.

This refusal to entertain competing perspectives within her

discourse has resulted in characterizations of her work as myopic, distortive, hyperbolic. Alice Echols criticizes Dworkin for leaving "no room for ambiguity, contradiction, or nuance in her writing." In a review of *Pornography: Men Possessing Women,* Ellen Willis writes: "The misogyny Andrea Dworkin decries is real enough—it is just not all of reality." In David Pannick's review of the same book, he maintains, "A lack of perspective and proportion considerably weakens the worth of this book." Alan Wolfe claims that Dworkin's thought (and that of others who fight against pornography) has "none of the contingencies and ambiguities of language, representation, and meaning that one finds in thinkers like Derrida or Rorty." Based on his belief that all representations are open to multiple interpretations, he insists that "pornography is not, as Dworkin claims, *only* about men brutalizing women." Janice Winship's review of *Pornography* also criticizes Dworkin's exclusive focus on male domination in pornography as reductive and unreflective of people's capacity "to make different readings." And similarly, Nancy Wechsler impugns the book for its "blanket assertions" about pornography that dismiss the experiences of "the women who use porn, who enjoy it, who are turned on by it. Women who enjoy porn are silenced by these books." Each of these critics judges Dworkin for failing to present a proportional portrait of pornography, yet each also omits any consideration of the possible artistic or political functions of her rhetorical form. Their judgments are confined to the referential content of her political analysis and fail to recognize the meaning imparted by the artistic form she has chosen.

Dworkin interprets "that expectation about giving the whole picture as a serious part of the double standard around gender." She says:

> Women academics are presenting it as if it's academic, but it's not. It's a lie. Foucault does not give the whole picture. Derrida does not give the whole picture. They don't spend any single part of their time essentially describing the world from other people's point of view unless their point is to undermine or destroy that point of view. And to me all that it means is that it's an expectation of gentility and politeness and courtesy and a notion that I have to prove that I'm a good girl, in this case meaning a good student, before I'm allowed to say what it is I think. Whereas my view is that my relationship with the world is a direct one.

Woman Hating and, especially, *Right-Wing Women,* contain elements of a proportional writing style. So does the book she coauthored with MacKinnon, *Pornography and Civil Rights,* as well as a few of her speeches and essays. But most of her work on pornography and her two most artistically sophisticated nonfiction writings, *Pornography: Men Possessing Women* and *Intercourse,* contain exclu-

sively her own vision in its most intense, distilled, and direct form. "By the time I wrote *Pornography,*" says Dworkin, "I was determined that I was going to write a book that did not have a word of apology in it. . . . And that became to me a fundamental principle of the politics of writing."

Ironic Reversals: Switching the Grounds of Debate

The two prominent rhetorical strategies in Dworkin's advocacy—concretization and de/centering—produce a set of ironic reversals; that is, they switch the foci and premises that underlie the public debate on pornography from a concern with the individual rights of pornographers and consumers to the civil rights of those exploited through pornography's production, distribution, and consumption. Dworkin rejects a narrow view of pornography as a cultural artifact (desirable to some, undesirable or immoral to others) and constructs a contextualized portrait of an exploitive social practice with concrete, damaging consequences to women. In the process of centering and concretizing these harmful experiences, Dworkin implicitly switches the guiding constitutional framework circumscribing pornography. Even though she does not argue in constitutional terms, she nonetheless implicitly displaces pornographers' and consumers' First Amendment speech rights to the inaudible/invisible margins of her discourse and implicitly places women's Fourteenth Amendment rights to equal protection at the center of her vision. "I am not interested in hearing arguments by people who claim to be protecting their precious little rights as intellectuals," states Dworkin, "their precious little status quo in the face of what is massive sexual abuse of women presented as entertainment." Instead of couching her critique of pornography in terms of constitutional arguments (whether First or Fourteenth), she marginalizes constitutional arguments and simply speaks within a separate paradigm wherein the harm to women is palpable and visible.

Placing women at the center of her discourse displaces a host of other premises undergirding current defenses of pornography. Similar to *Woman Hating,* Dworkin is still challenging sexual libertarian notions about "sexual freedom." "There are those who say [pornography] is a form of freedom," she states. "Certainly it is freedom for those who do it. Certainly it is freedom for those who use it as entertainment, but we are also asked to believe that it is freedom for those to whom it is done." This statement evidences the shifting vantage point from the pornographers and consumers of pornographic products to the women on whose bodies the pornography is produced and used. "Freedom looks very different when you are the one it is being done on," she states. Dworkin displaces the notion of pornography as an expression of sexual *freedom* and couches it, instead, in terms of its role in sexual *subordination.*

Whereas civil and sexual libertarians express concern about sexual repression and state intervention in sexual expression, Dworkin expresses concern about sexual oppression and violence. She switches the terms of the debate by exposing how pornography's so-called sexual freedom is, in fact, a practice of sexual oppression. From this perspective, ridding society of pornography is not a repressive measure but an urgent, necessary tactic for liberating women from one of the key mechanisms of sexual subordination.

Another significant ironic reversal emerges in Dworkin's work when she talks about free speech rights. She refers to the speech rights of women harmed by pornography and not, as is usually implied, that of pornographers and consumers. In **"Pornography Is a Civil Rights Issue,"** she writes:

> Now, we have been told that we have an argument here about speech, not about women being hurt. And yet the emblem of that argument is a woman bound and gagged and we are supposed to believe that that is speech. Who is that speech for? We have women being tortured and we are told that that is somebody's speech? Whose speech is it? It's the speech of a pimp, it is not the speech of a woman. . . .

The reality for women in this society is that pornography creates silence for women. The pornographers silence women.

The first women silenced are those in the pictures. The construction of the pictures and the discourse that accompanies them are from the perspective of the pornographers, not the women themselves. The pornographer's voice is made to seem as if it is the woman's voice and perspective, but in actuality the women have no control over the words attributed to them. The women's own voices are absent from the text. Dworkin writes in **"Against the Male Flood"**: "The women flattened out on the page are deathly still, except for *hurt me. Hurt me* is not women's speech. It is the speech imposed on women by pimps to cover the awful, condemning silence." And then there is, as well, "the silence of the women not in the picture, outside the pages, hurt but silent, used but silent." Dworkin presents pornographic artifacts as material evidence of women's silence rather than material expressions of men's speech: "Splayed legs are silence. Being beaver, pussy, cunt, bunnies, pets—that is silence. 'Hurt me, hurt me more' is silence. And those who think that it is speech have never heard a woman's voice, not ever." Again, this shift in perspective is accomplished by writing from the perspective of women used in pornography and women against whom pornography is used.

In Dworkin's writing, the relationship between pornography and women's silence is not confined to descriptions of what pornography "represents." She sketches a dynamic relationship as multidimensional as her conception of pornography itself. Based on all the complex ways pornography is invested with social power to harm women, it serves as a powerful mechanism to enforce women's silence. Pornography as hegemonic speech, for instance, functions generally to silence dissenting interpretations of experience—by drowning out, rendering incomprehensible, or trivializing speech that counters prevailing interpretations of reality. As legal scholar Richard Delgado explains, "the dominant paradigm renders certain ideas unsayable or incomprehensible; and our system of ideas and images constructs certain people so that they have little credibility." Dworkin considers pornography "a weapon of power—used to destroy the expressive abilities of the powerless by destroying their sense of reality . . ." and their credibility. Pornography also actively suppresses women's speech in its function as an instrument of sexual abuse against those women used to produce pornography and those on whom the pornography is subsequently used. This dimension of women's silence includes the literal loss of speech incurred by victims of sexual abuse, especially victims of incest and wife battery. Every causal claim about pornography silencing women is based on these organically interrelated aspects. In direct response to these forms of silencing, Dworkin presents the civil rights antipornography ordinance as a means for silenced women to reclaim their voices. In speaking of the women who testified at the 1983 Minneapolis public hearings on pornography, she writes: "What the survivors said was speech; the pornography had been, throughout their lives, a means of actively suppressing their speech. They had been turned into pornography in life and made mute; terrorized by it and made mute. Now, the mute spoke."

Pornography's function as hegemonic propaganda and its role in sexual abuse and in other forms of sexual subordination operate dialectically with one another to silence women. As is evidenced in the following abridged excerpt from **"Against the Male Flood,"** this dialectic is the foundation of Dworkin's conception of pornography's capacity to silence women:

> Subordination can be so deep that those who are hurt by it are utterly silent. Subordination can create a silence quieter than death. . . . The women say pimp's words: which is worse than silence. The silence of the women not in the picture, outside the pages, hurt but silent, used but silent, is staggering in how deep and wide it goes. It is a silence over centuries: an exile into speechlessness. One is shut up by the inferiority and the abuse. One is shut up by the threat and the injury.

Note how subordination is the context in which women are silenced to produce pornography, which is itself a representation of women's silence and further creates the conditions and the incentive to intimidate, humiliate, and terrorize women into remaining silent about the ways pornography has exploited and subordinated them. These elements do not function in a linear manner, nor even in a neat circular manner—in this passage or in society; they build upon one another in an ever-expanding dialectical pattern. As is usual for Dworkin, she makes no explicit claims about the dynamic nature of the relationship between pornography and women's silence. Instead, she iconically reproduces it within the texts themselves.

Whereas defenders of pornography seek to *preserve* the speech rights currently exercised by pornographers, Dworkin seeks *access* to speech for those who are socially silenced by male domination. "I am talking about a deep silence," writes Dworkin:

> a silence that goes to the heart of tyranny, its nature. There is a tyranny that preordains not only who can say what but what women especially can say. There is a tyranny that determines who cannot say anything, a tyranny in which people are kept from being able to say the most important things about what life is like for them.

Within Dworkin's texts, the social context of male domination and its attendant suppression of women's speech is central to her conception of freedom of speech. Her textual displacement of pornographers' and consumers' First Amendment rights is based upon both her contextualized portrait of pornography—detailed in the previous chapter—and this contextualized understanding of speech as consonant with power relations in society. It is within this larger social context that it is possible to see pornography's active participation in the institutionalized suppression of women's speech. Dworkin argues that, in fact, pornography's continued existence is *dependent upon* the coerced silence of those it exploits.

Contrary to those who claim that protecting the speech of pornographers is essential to protecting the speech of all, Dworkin claims that fighting against the pornographers "is as much a fight for my life as a writer as it could possibly be." She says she has "learned what it is that keeps women from being able to say anything at all; and the fact that I'm constantly engaged as somebody who is a professional writer, still trying to be able to get speech to exist socially, is something that keeps me from being able to be glib about it." Twice in her life Dworkin literally lost her ability to speak: once after she was raped in the Women's House of Detention in New York City and again after years of abuse from her husband. "I am talking about speech," writes Dworkin. "It isn't easy for me. I come to speech from under a man, tortured and tormented. What he did to me took

away everything; . . . He hurt all the words out of me, and no one would listen anyway. I come to speech from under the brutalities of thousands of men. . . . And so for twenty years now I have been looking for the words to say what I know."

Based on the silencing effects of pornography, Dworkin's discourse accomplishes another ironic reversal: she casts pornographers as censors. "Writers do not do what pornographers do," states Dworkin. "Secret police do. Torturers do. What pornographers do to women is more like what police do to political prisoners than it is like anything else." Only if one isolates pornographic speech from its larger social context—including its production, dissemination, and use—is it possible to consider pornography merely a form of speech. Within Dworkin's framework, pornography is a "system of terror that stops speech and creates abuse and despair. The pornographers are the secret police of male supremacy: keeping women subordinate through intimidation and assault." From this perspective, intervention in pornographers' and consumers' so-called "speech" is not censorship; it is an act of justice designed to protect women from the harm pornography proliferates, including its role in intimidating women into silence. The issue of free speech rights is not whether pornographers get to *retain* their right to speak, but whether they are going to be stopped from creating hostile conditions that make it impossible or unlikely for women's contrary speech to be heard and believed. This ironic inversion of the issue of free speech is no more apparent than when Dworkin describes the civil rights antipornography ordinance as "women's speech." She writes: "It defines an injury to us from our point of view. . . . It breaks the silence. It is a sentence that can hold its own against the male flood. It is a sentence on which we can build a paragraph, then a page."

Dworkin never explicitly argues against the premises underlying contemporary defenses of pornography. But her analysis subverts these defenses without allotting any textual space to articulating competing voices. As she says of this strategy, "I know what the givens are of the world that I live in, and I'm trying to undermine them. I want to knock them loose. I want them to fall." These "givens" include the necessity to uphold First Amendment protection for all speech, especially that which we dislike (despite specified legal exceptions); trust in the neutrality of the law to protect the speech rights of all people equally; belief that state intervention poses the greatest threat to sexual freedom and freedom of expression; faith in the "marketplace of ideas" as the best means for sifting falsity from truth; the notion that pornography is a private matter in which the government has no right to intervene; belief that all attempts to legislate pornography are acts of repression that curtail sexual freedom and freedom of expression; belief that women pose in pornographic representations because they "freely choose" to do so; a conceptual distinction between pornographic artifacts and the labor used to produce them; and denial of the harm of pornographic artifacts.

In contrast, the premises underlying Dworkin's position include the necessity to uphold Fourteenth Amendment protection for all people, even when such protection demands abrogating First Amendment rights of others; a belief that the First Amendment is a tool for preserving the speech of only the most privileged in our society and that, thereby, it preserves existing power hierarchies; the belief that hegemonic speech is differentially more powerful than that of socially, politically, and economically dispossessed groups; a rejection of the public/private distinction in law as a false dichotomy preserving systems of domination that thrive in private domains; and a belief that pornography is a practice of discrimination that impedes women's equality and freedom, including sexual freedom, and therefore must be subjected to civil litigation by those who can prove its harm. In short, defenses of pornography are premised on the right of individuals to be free from government interference in their private lives, whereas Dworkin seeks freedom from sexual exploitation and a right to equal protection from discriminatory practices. Her strategic reversals in the grounds of the pornography debate culminate in a direct conflict of rights that demands resolution: pornography precludes women's civil equality; so either pornographers and consumers get rights or those women harmed by pornography do. There is no compromise possible here.

As Dworkin and MacKinnon point out in their coauthored book, ***Pornography and Civil Rights,*** this clash of rights echoes earlier conflicts, most notably the battles against slavery and segregation. In both of these cases, a dispossessed group sought the aid of the federal government in an attempt to gain rights to equal treatment. In doing so, each clashed with the existing constitutional rights of white supremacists to be free from federal intervention in their lives: defenders of slavery sought to keep the federal government from interfering with states' right to conduct their own affairs, and defenders of segregation sought to keep the federal government from interfering with whites' rights to free association. Dworkin's antipornography argument is analogous to both of these civil rights struggles: current constitutional interpretation protects the rights of pornographers to engage in practices which actively subordinate a class of people. "Those who have power over others," explain Dworkin and MacKinnon, "tend to call their power 'rights.' When those they dominate want equality, those in power say that important rights will be violated if society changes. . . . Change has come from sustained, often bitter rebellion against power disguised as 'rights.'"

Subverting Pornography

More than anything else, the strategies of concretization and de/centering enable Dworkin to confront audience denial of pornography's harm. Her use of concretization strips pornography of its abstract, theoretical defenses and reconstitutes it in terms of its material properties: its real-life tangible harms to women's bodies and lives. At the same time, she excludes all notions of pornography's so-called socially redeeming or benign attributes and centers her texts exclusively around its massive destructiveness to women. She simultaneously makes the harm visible and provides no relief from it in her texts. This enables her to confront her audiences with the problem in the most direct manner possible. And the resulting intensity matches the urgency of the crisis she addresses.

Her reconstitution of pornography in terms of its harm is a rhetorical intervention that subverts the premises upon which pornography is currently defended—primarily as an emblem of free speech and as a crucible of sexual privacy and freedom. As Dworkin explains, "virtually all power, in cultural terms, in 'winning an argument' comes from how you define the problem. I mean, . . . a person who sets up the premises is the person who sets up the conclusion. And so I am setting up my own premises, and I think they're premises that help to undermine the general premises and, therefore, the status quo conclusion."

The civil rights antipornography ordinance is constructed from the premises of Dworkin's analysis. It is designed as a material remedy to the material problem she addresses: it attempts to provide individual women with a legal mechanism for redressing class-based subordination perpetuated through the production, distribution, and consumption of pornography. It provides a legal definition and description of pornography's concrete discriminating practices from the perspective of those it subordinates. It draws upon the Fourteenth Amendment guarantee of equal protection rather than the First Amendment right to free expression. It repudiates the public/private dichotomy that protects sexual exploitation in individuals' private lives. It recognizes the injury pornography does to women (and sometimes men) and empowers those harmed by pornography to hold accountable those involved in the subordinating practices.

As Dworkin explains, the ordinance is designed to change "the power relationship between the pornographers and women." Like her antipornography discourse generally, the ordinance undermines the premises of pornography by infusing the law with "the flesh-and-blood experiences of women . . . whose lives have been savaged by pornography." She writes:

> Using the Ordinance, women get to say to the pimps and the johns: we are not your colony; you do not own us as if we were territory; my will as expressed through

my use of this Ordinance is, I don't want it, I don't like it, pain hurts, coercion isn't sexy, I resist being someone else's speech, I reject subordination, I speak, I speak for myself now, I am going into court to speak—to you; and you will listen.

In a manner duplicating Dworkin's rhetorical confrontation with the pornography industry, the civil rights antipornography ordinance authorizes those harmed by pornography to use their concrete life experience as the basis for confronting pornography's subordination of women. The ordinance embodies the political imperative at the heart of Dworkin's feminist resistance: "to use every single thing you can remember about what was done to you—how it was done, where, by whom, when, and, if you know, why—to begin to tear male dominance to pieces, to pull it apart, to vandalize it, to destabilize it, to mess it up, to get in its way, to fuck it up." The civil rights antipornography ordinance communicates faith that women can transform pain into political knowledge useful for destroying the system of male supremacy.

FURTHER READING

Criticism

Eberly, Rosa A. "Andrea Dworkin's *Mercy*: Pain, Ad Personam, and Silence in the 'War Zone.'" *Pre/Text* 14, Nos. 3-4 (Fall-Winter 1993): 273-304.
    Examines Dworkin's literary reputation and critical response to *Mercy*.

Jenefsky, Cindy, and Ann Russo. *Without Apology: Andrea Dworkin's Art and Politics*. Boulder, CO: Westview Press, 1998, 163 p.
    Book-length critical study of Dworkin's nonfiction writings and feminist discourse.

Wolfe, Alan. "Dirt and Democracy." *The New Republic* (19 February 1990): 27-31.
    Discusses Dworkin's objections to pornography as delineated in *Pornography*.

Additional coverage of Dworkin's life and career is contained in the following sources published by Gale: *Contemporary Authors*, **Vols. 77-80;** *Contemporary Authors Autobiography Series*, **Vol. 21;** *ContemporaryAuthors New Revision Series*, **Vols. 16, 39; and** *Major Twentieth Century Writers*.

Nadine Gordimer
1923-

South African novelist, short story writer, and essayist.

The following entry provides an overview of Gordimer's career through 1996. For further information on her life and works, see *CLC*, Volumes 3, 5, 7, 10, 18, 33, 51, and 70.

INTRODUCTION

Gordimer is a well-known and acclaimed writer who explores the social effects of South Africa's apartheid system and the consequences of its demise. Although political themes are central to her work, Gordimer focuses on the personal aspect of political turmoil. As a white in South Africa, Gordimer occupies a difficult position in relation to the country's racist institutions. Although opposed to racism, Gordimer benefitted from racist institutions with a privileged place in South African society. Many believe that this explains why Gordimer's storytelling talent was not acknowledged by the Nobel Committee until the dismantling of the apartheid system began.

Biographical Information

Gordimer was born on November 20, 1923, in a mining town called Springs, South Africa. Her father was a Latvian Jew who emigrated to South Africa and had a jewelry shop in Springs. Her mother was born in London, but emigrated to South Africa with Gordimer's grandfather, who was a diamond miner. Gordimer's family was not well off, but they had a black servant from the time she was 2 until she was 30. Gordimer was warned to stay away from natives as a child, and she knew nothing about native life or culture. Her childhood was filled with solitude and extensive reading, and it was this exposure to literature that caused her to adjust her view of native people. Gordimer began writing at an early age. She published her first short story at the age of 15, and her stories appeared in such American publications as the *New Yorker* and *Harper's*. In 1946 Gordimer began studying at Witwatersrand University and, for the first time, had contact with blacks who were not servants. It was a turning point in her acceptance of blacks as human beings. Gordimer's political consciousness developed slowly, but she eventually became ardently and vocally opposed to apartheid. She left the University and returned home after a year to concentrate on her fiction. In 1949, Gordimer married Gerald Gavronsky. The two had a daughter and then were divorced in 1952. After the divorce Gordimer struggled to make ends meet. A friend sent her

stories to a publisher in New York. Not only were her stories accepted for publication, but she signed a contract to write a novel, too. Gordimer was married again in 1954 to Reinhold Cassirer, with whom she had a son. Gordimer has continued to publish both short stories and novels, as well as lectures and essays. She has remained active in the fight against racist practices in South Africa, and in 1990 she joined the African National Congress. Gordimer thought about leaving her country; she even lived for a time in Zambia. However, she decided that she belonged in South Africa and would rather fight to change what she did not like. She received the Nobel Prize for Literature in 1991.

Major Works

Gordimer's fiction chronicles the struggles and turmoil in South Africa surrounding apartheid and the aftermath of its dissolution. Gordimer's early work centers on the intrusion of external reality into the comfortable existence of middle-class white South Africans. Her first novel, *The Lying Days* (1953), is about an Afrikaner woman who gains political consciousness through her affair with a social worker. The stories in *Not for Publication* (1965) and *Livingstone's Companions* (1971) depict ordinary people defying apartheid in their daily lives. *The Conservationist* (1974) focuses on a wealthy white industrialist who struggles with his guilt and sense of displacement as his estate is overcome with poor black squatters. *Burger's Daughter* (1979) follows the struggle of the daughter of a slain leader of the South African Communist Party to find an apolitical existence. *July's People* (1981) is one of Gordimer's few novels that is not set in the present. It is set in the aftermath of a future revolution. The story revolves around a liberal white family who is forced to depend on a black man who was their former servant. The reversal of roles allows Gordimer to explore different aspects of racism and how it affects relationships. The stories in *Something out There* (1984) examine the temperament of individuals who unwittingly support the mechanisms of racism. Like *July's People, A Sport of Nature* (1987) focuses on the creation of a new black nation out of what once was South Africa. The protagonist Hillela is a white South African who inherits the cause of her slain black husband. At the end of the novel she becomes the First Lady of the newly created nation.

Critical Reception

Gordimer is lauded for her authentic portrayals of black African culture. Dick Roraback comments on her ability to assume a universal voice, remarking "Gordimer is multilingual. She can speak male and female, young and old, black and white." Many reviewers praise her use of precise detail to evoke both the physical landscape of South Africa and the human predicaments of a racially polarized society. Sylvia Clayton notes that Gordimer "places her figures exactly in the landscape, and the contrast between their precarious lives and her own controlled poise yields a high imaginative tension." Many commentators feel that her best talent is in her chronicling of contemporary South Africa. Some argue that because Gordimer is part of the privileged white class of South Africa, she is automatically complicit with a racist society. Other reviewers point to her liberal views and her balanced portrayal of all aspects of South African society to disprove her association with racist institutions. Roraback calls her "the conscience of the white South African." Others claim that Gordimer's detached narrative voice lacks emotional immediacy, but many regard her fiction as compelling and powerful. Various critics have argued that Gordimer's talent is better suited to either the short story or the novel. Barbara J. Eckstein states, however, that "Evidence of success in both genres disproves any assertion that Gordimer's talent is better suited to one fictional form than to another." Critics also note thematic repetition in Gordimer's fiction, some accusing her of rehashing and others praising how she breathes life into persistent themes and situations.

PRINCIPAL WORKS

Face to Face (short stories) 1949
The Soft Voice of the Serpent, and Other Stories (short stories) 1952
The Lying Days (novel) 1953
Six Feet of the Country (short stories) 1956
A World of Strangers (novel) 1958
Friday's Footprint, and Other Stories (short stories) 1960
Occasion for Loving (novel) 1963
Not for Publication, and Other Stories (short stories) 1965
The Late Bourgeois World (novel) 1966
A Guest of Honour (novel) 1970
Livingstone's Companions (short stories) 1971
African Literature: The Lectures Given on This Theme at the University of Cape Town's Public Summer School (lectures) 1972
The Black Interpreters: Notes on African Writing (criticism) 1973
The Conservationist (novel) 1974
Selected Stories (short stories) 1975
Some Monday for Sure (short stories) 1976
Burger's Daughter (novel) 1979
A Soldier's Embrace (short stories) 1980
What Happened to Burger's Daughter; or, How South African Censorship Works [with others] (nonfiction) 1980
Town and Country Lovers (short stories) 1982
July's People (novel) 1981
Something out There (short stories) 1984
Lifetimes under Apartheid (nonfiction) 1986
A Sport of Nature (novel) 1987
The Essential Gesture: Writing, Politics, and Places (essays) 1988
My Son's Story (novel) 1990
Jump, and Other Stories (short stories) 1991
Writing and Being (lectures) 1995

*This work contains stories from previously published collections.

CRITICISM

Charles Poore (review date 8 May 1965)

SOURCE: "Her Field Is People: People Are the World," in *The New York Times,* Vol. CXIV, No. 39,186, May 8, 1965, p. 29.

[*In the following review, Poore praises the stories in* Not for Publication.]

The coolly controlled fury of Nadine Gordimer's storytelling stands out in this new collection [***Not for Publication***]. It is Miss Gordimer's best book.

Not many authors in her field accomplish what she sets out to do with so much force and grace. Her aim is nothing less than to advance the amenities of civilization. A tall order. But she goes about it with a kind of brilliantly deceptive casualness. You are caught up, first of all, in a story—the loves of men and women, the confrontations of growing up—the elemental business, in short, of life, liberty and the strenuous, faltering pursuit of happiness. Along the way, though, Miss Gordimer never fails to dramatize the dreams of glory, the petty subterfuges born of elemental insecurity, the odious side of power.

A number of these stories appeared first in *The New Yorker*, a magazine that, for all the recent tohubohu about it, can stand securely on the fact that it has never had a successful rival. Others were published in *Harper's, The Saturday Evening Post, The Atlantic, Mademoiselle, The Kenyon Review,* all stalwarts in the vital business of keeping the art of the short story alive. A bookkeeping doctrine in publishing is that short story collections don't sell lavishly. They should when they are written by the likes of Miss Gordimer.

There's no use trying to kraal her as a South African regional writer. True, she lives there. But her field is people and people are the world. Superficial proof lies in noticing that she sometimes sets her scene in England, on shipboard, or elsewhere. A deeper confirmation may be observed when you see her turning a Johannesburg suburb into an annex of Westchester or Grosse Pointe. She is quick to examine persons called troublemakers—and quicker to expose the mean disquiet of authoritarians who try by foul means to get rid of "troublemakers." The slave-driving instinct, she shows us, has an amazing variety of manifestations in our world.

> **. . . her field is people and people are the world. Superficial proof lies in noticing that she sometimes sets her scene in England, on shipboard, or elsewhere. A deeper confirmation may be observed when you see her turning a Johannesburg suburb into an annex of Westchester or Grosse Pointe.**
> **—*Charles Poore***

One of her best stories is **"The Worst Thing of All."** In structural essentials, the tale may well rank high among the ten most shopworn themes in literature. It's about the reappearance of a man's troubling early love. The generic title should be: "The Old Flame Burns Again."

The old flame, here, is a wildly magnetic woman, Sarah, who was long ago the mistress of Denys, a reformed Johannesburg playboy happily married to Simone and a tobacco fortune. Once upon a time Denys helped Sarah put on daring plays in a disheveled little theater; once upon a time they fought with deeds, not hypocritically safe words, to lower the racist color bar.

Now, fresh from heady theatrical triumphs, Sarah is a talk-of-the-town visitor from Europe, where she went after ditching Denys. Will he be drawn back into her beguiling orbit? Simone, and the town, wonder.

The ending will surprise you. The mis-en-scène is acutely sketched. The local worldlings see how gauche they really are: "They were the ones who used the language of the avant-garde, learned from the appropriate reviews" . . . while Sarah spoke "in everyday words that, among them, would have been taken as signs of naïveté and ignorance. . . ."

Time and again Miss Gordimer decides in these stories at the last moment, as it were, that T. S. Eliot was right in favoring music with a dying fall. The burst-of-fireworks-at-the-end school holds for her little appeal.

In **"Not For Publication,"** the promising African boy who will one day help lead his territory to freedom from colonial rule disappears from the mission school that is determined to prepare him for Cambridge. The desperately lost stateless man in **"Son-in-Law"** achieves, through human attrition, a bleak security. **"The Pet"** presents a parallel between the fate of a servant and the fate of a household dog that is rather in the Katherine Mansfield tradition.

Have you ever noticed that when grown-ups offer children ice cream they seldom fail to take a good helping of it for themselves? Some such manifestation of the mutual benefit drive animates Miss Gordimer's observation of the ways of the old with the young.

In **"A Company of Laughing Faces,"** a terribly devoted mother decides to take her 17-year-old daughter, Kathy, to an African affluent-society beach so that Kathy can have fun with people of her own age. Incidentally, of course, the mother loves life there. A shocking experience or two makes Kathy want to go home before the holiday is due to end. Her mother objects—briskly.

Adrian Mitchell (review date 23 May 1965)

SOURCE: "Pervaded by the Strangeness of Africa," in *The New York Times Book Review,* May 23, 1965, pp. 5, 47.

[*In the following excerpt, Mitchell focuses on Gordimer's narrative technique in* Not for Publication.]

It would be futile to look for a flowering of experimental writing among the fiction published about Africa today. The continent is dominated by race war and the state of the Republic of South Africa is such that it dictates a mood—and even a style—to those who try to write of it. Almost every public action in that country, and many private actions, too, add impetus to a revolution which seems as inevitable as anything in history.

Everyone who writes about Africa is affected by this shadow. In such a situation a novel is hard to make. A novel takes too much time to write, a novel takes too much time in which to unfold. Perhaps this is the reason why so much of the best writing about Africa, much of it conceived in exile, is poured into the short-story mold. With foreknowledge of the holocaust, these writers are like photographers whose city is doomed, urgently recording their last pictures of people and scenes which will be gone or transformed tomorrow.

There are masterly performers among them, with wildly dissimilar styles. Among the best is Nadine Gordimer, a writer with an enviable range of techniques. One of her most arresting methods is this: to concentrate the reader's attention on one particular moment, one gesture.

In her new and exhilarating collection of 16 stories [*Not for Publication*] this method can be seen at its best in **"The African Magician."** An apparently incompetent conjurer has been trying to entertain the white passengers on a liner. They demand that he demonstrate his hypnotic powers. Suddenly a girl, who is on her honeymoon, rises from her place and walks calmly to him:

> She stood directly before him, quite still, her tall rounded shoulders drooping naturally and thrusting forward a little her head, that was raised to him, almost on a level with his own. He did not move; he did not gaze; his eyes blinked quietly. She put up her long arms and, standing just their length from him, brought her hands to rest on his shoulders. Her cropped head dropped before him to her chest.

This quarter-paragraph is far from typical of Miss Gordimer's style. But, placed at the pivot-point of the story, it is completely effective. There is an alien, translated quality about the sentences and a near-biblical, magi-

cal rhythm to the words. From this stylized description the author moves immediately to a description of the gesture in social, sexual, esthetic, religious and political terms. It is this passion to explore the hidden significance of a particular moment and this discovery of historical meaning in the movements of one girl which make Miss Gordimer's work so exciting.

In **"Something for the Time Being"** the central gesture—the decision by a newly-released political prisoner to wear his African National Congress badge—is more obvious, but the author's examination is just as subtle. In **"The Pet"** she ends her story of a man who feels kinship with no human being with the only action left to him—he throws a piece of bread to an unpleasant and hated dog. But although these stories have in common a welcome care for language, a controlled wit, a sense of the strangeness of Africa and a driving concern for its future, there is a healthy variety of tales. **"Message in a Bottle,"** for instance, has no conventional plot. The outline of a thoroughly bad day, it works less like a story than like an Alexander Calder mobile, a pattern of isolated events revolving. But it works. . . .

The Times Literary Supplement (review date 22 July 1965)

SOURCE: "Alone, Obsessed, Outsmarted," in *The Times Literary Supplement,* No. 3308, July 22, 1965, p. 609.

[*In the following excerpt, the critic highlights the theme of lonliness in* Not for Publication.]

Although Miss Nadine Gordimer's scene in her short stories is often South Africa, and her themes therefore often have to do with the colour bar, she is not an explicitly "liberal" writer: she nearly always writes of the best, the most humane side of her characters—even the thick-headed policemen who arrest the gallant Mrs. Bamjee for her anti-racialist activities in **"A Chip of Glass Ruby"** are decently abashed and sorry (as far as their natures will allow them) for what they have to do. Miss Gordimer's real theme is loneliness—the loneliness of all kinds of exile (of, for example, "free" South African Nationalists who are being trained in sabotage in a free republic, or of a German *au pair* girl in a sympathetic London family), including the kind of exile that comes simply from possessing one's own identity in a world composed of others similarly endowed. This latter theme is finely explored in **"Good Climate, Friendly Inhabitants",** which describes the impact of a shady, faintly sinister young man on the life of an aging female garage worker. In this story the woman overtly shares the vulgar and humanly degrading prejudices of most of her white compatriots about "colour", yet Miss Gordimer demonstrates, with an irony that is restrained to exactly the right degree, and which totally avoids any propagandist overtones, just how strongly her essential self remains unprejudiced: it is a Negro fellow-worker who saves her from the consequences of her own helplessness in the hands of the heartless young white man.

And Miss Gordimer is versatile: at the end of **"A Company of Laughing Faces"** she achieves a moment of genuine horror when she describes, in a memorable image, the consequences of a seemingly innocent gregariousness on the part of a foolish mother, who is determined that her shy daughter should enjoy a holiday, and of a not particularly vicious sexual advance on the part of a brash boy who crudely misinterprets the girl's willingness to be with him alone. *Not for Publication* is unsentimental and scrupulously observant. . . .

Patrick Cruttwell (review date Autumn 1965)

SOURCE: A review of *Not for Publication*, in *The Hudson Review*, Vol. XVIII, No. 3, Autumn, 1965, pp. 444-45.

[*In the following excerpt, Cruttwell contrasts the mood of Gordimer's fiction with Flannery O'Connor's.*]

. . . It is mainly in male authors that the posturing seems obligatory (though I'm not so sure of that, now I've written it; I can think of some female ones, but I'd better not name them); and so it may not be coincidence that a quite unfair proportion of the interesting, the distinguished, the *literate* writing among the fiction I have received is the work of women. Three in particular: two volumes of short stories by Flannery O'Connor and Nadine Gordimer [*Everything that Rises Must Converge* and *Not for Publication*], and one novel so short as to be almost a short story, by Elizabeth Spencer. These are what I call literature. They are, that is, works of art, in which very distinctive personalities and clear, strongly held viewpoints on life are presented in such a way that they are absorbed into the imagined world of the fiction: there is no need, no temptation, to look outside that world for explanation or completion. Both the volumes of short stories are set in societies tortured and obsessed by the problems of race and colour: Nadine Gordimer's in South Africa, Flannery O'Connor's in the American South. But they make a remarkable contrast in this with the work of some other writers on race, more heavily publicized: James Baldwin, for instance. In him, the agony is being exploited—used as a screen on which to project a vast magnification of some personal disorder; in these stories, it has its place, neither played down nor softened, but viewed and felt as it has to be by real and ordinary people who must go on living in such a society.

Flannery O'Connor's stories are fiercer, more fanatical than Nadine Gordimer's, and in some of them hysteria is not far away; she is capable of greater intensity, but pays for it by a lack of pure serenity at the centre of tragedy, such as Gordimer achieves superbly in a story called **"A Company of Laughing Faces,"** which describes a young girl on a seaside holiday in which nothing "real" seems to happen to her in spite of her desperate efforts to persuade herself she is enjoying it all—until, right at the end, she has a glimpsed vision of a boy drowned in a pool. That is a moment of pure lyrical poetry; O'Connor's poetry is grotesque and neurotic, but it might be said to hit harder: and if it does, this is because her writing is clearly the work of an authentically religious writer, Catholic but not obtrusively or aggressively so (in which respect I found the introduction by Robert Fitzgerald, which is obtrusively Catholic, unfortunate and misleading). Now and then, the fierce contempt for liberal humanist do-gooders on the one hand and hellfire Biblical sectarians on the other seemed to me to twist and bias her vision—as it does in "The Lame Shall Enter First," a story of enormous power, but power warped and cruel; pity, for once, is lost in anger and scorn. It is certainly a strange world her stories live in: I never cease to wonder (speaking as an alien) at the American South as its writers portray it. Is it "really like that"? I wonder naïvely—or is it as much the invention of untypical geniuses as the wind-tortured moorlands, peopled by demons in human shape, of *Wuthering Heights*? Something that O'Connor herself said (quoted in Fitzgerald's introduction) seems to suggest that this is the case. "I doubt," she said, "if the texture of Southern life is any more grotesque than that of the rest of the nation, but it does seem evident that the Southern writer is particularly adept at recognizing the grotesque; and to recognize the grotesque you have to have some notion of what is not grotesque, and why."

Gordimer's stories keep much closer to what one had thought the real world was like: she is capable, therefore, of an accurate, undistorted social satire which is not in O'Connor's range—see, for instance, **"The Worst Thing of All,"** the story of the return to South Africa of a woman theatrical genius become world-famous and her impact on the associates of her early obscurity. Gordimer is cooler, less fevered; one might almost have guessed, if one didn't know, that Flannery O'Connor died young of a terrible disease, for there is something in her prose which seemed to me very close to the poetry of Anne Sexton and Sylvia Plath—the poetry of exposed and tortured nerve-ends. . . .

Gail Godwin (review date April 1976)

SOURCE: "Out of Africa and India," in *Harper's Magazine*, Vol. 252, No. 1511, April, 1976, pp. 101-02.

[*In the following excerpt, Godwin discusses the changing African dimension of the characters in* Selected Stories.]

Reading a collection of stories by a good writer affords a pleasure quite distinct from reading a novel by the same writer. The pleasure comes from the activeness demanded from the reader, from the quick leaps of synthesis he must make as he skips around in the book, pouncing on the stories that promise to attract him most, surprising the author in a variety of themes, moods, and stances as the author moves through his own time: the writing-time of the stories. Reading a collection of stories written out of a high-quality perceptiveness is like stalking the master stalker: you can sneak up on him at any angle and watch him pursue the prey. There are no long securities staked out for you at the beginning, as in a novel. Each story is a brand-new beginning, a new hunt. But as you read on, you form a composite picture of his territory. You get to know his allurements, his hunting habits, the terrain of his mind as well.

When I finished Nadine Gordimer's collection [*Selected Stories*] (composed of stories she chose from the many she wrote between the ages of twenty and fifty), I felt I knew her territory ("My time and place," she states, "have been twentieth-century Africa") in a way history and geography could not purvey it. (How purvey mutability when it happens inside the minds of people who live decade after decade in the same landscape *except* through cumulative fictions?) And I had become related to the writer through following her consciousness through its own mutability and growth, as well. Her "territory," of course, exists nowhere in its entirety except in this marvelous collection, which she has had the good sense to arrange chronologically; the Africa of her first page, on which the white girl's relationship with a black man is that of victim and attacker, is no longer the Africa of the girl in **"The Smell of Death and Flowers,"** with her passionate involvement in the black cause; and she, in turn, inhabits another world from the rather cynical and weary liberal in the last story, **"Africa Emergent,"** whose long, intense work with the blacks has led him into a self-righteous bind, making him suspicious of any black who hasn't proved himself by going to jail for the cause.

Though many of the stories reflect the author's political conscience, and her awareness of the complex tangles in which single-minded devotees of good causes can trap themselves, her subject at large, her Big Game, is Africa in the sense that the great fiction writers have always stalked it: a beautiful and dangerous land of opposites, both a test and a mirror of the psyche, where Kurtz went mad and Isak Dinesen fell in love with everything, and Jung, while dancing with natives, came perilously close to being swallowed by his id. Africa, some particular aspect of African life, is often used to reveal a character's inner life. For the romantic young city woman in **"The Gentle Art"** (my favorite story), a crocodile hunt starts out as a deliberate form of symbolic adultery in the presence of her husband. The crocodile hunter, who has invited them to come along in his boat, is everything she fantasizes a real man should be, while her husband, whom she calls "Poor Ricks," is "shut up in a blue suit in town." But when she finds herself gazing into the eyes of a live baby crocodile, which the hunter has pulled out of the river just for her amusement, she has something much closer to a religious experience.

In **"Livingstone's Companions,"** a foreign correspondent from London, who has been robbed, by his own "wry, understated" way with words, of his capacity for living and his sensual wonder, is revived through getting lost in a strange, out-of-the-way resort during an assignment which would have required him to retrace Livingstone's last journey. The most compelling stories in the volume are the ones of this nature, in which the sheer terror or beauty of being somewhere bigger than one's petty concerns imposes itself on a character.

But there are unforgettable moments in the "provincial" stories as well. I don't mean Nadine Gordimer is provincial, I mean her characters in these stories never realize that *they* are not seeing beyond the tips of their noses—or their suburban *kopjes*. Their plights are no less poignant, however, because of Gordimer's true artistic self-effacement. The epiphany of every character, however small, is realized with absolute fidelity, from the stale fantasy summoned by a guilty suburban housewife (in **"The Life of the Imagination"**) whose lover has left and forgotten to lock the door (she imagines a native coming in to kill her) to the old aristocratic lady in **"Enemies"** who meets her aging, complaining self—the self she has never acknowledged—on a train from Cape Town to Johannesburg, and *snubs her*. (Her alter ego dies during the night; the survivor sends a triumphant telegram to her chauffeur the next morning: "It was not me.")

Of interest to writers as well as readers is Miss Gordimer's introduction to her story collection. It contains more wisdom about the writing process in a few pages than many entire semesters of creative-writing classes. She has answers for the feminists ("My femininity has never constituted any special kind of solitude for me. . . . All writers are androgynous beings"); she has answers for the accusation that a writer "uses" people ("A writer sees in your life what you do not. . . . Fiction is a way of exploring possibilities present but undreamt of in the living of a single life"); and she knows what a short story is, and why she writes one rather than a novel ("A short story is a concept that the writer can 'hold,' fully realized, in his imagination, at one time. A novel is, by comparison, staked out, and must be taken possession of stage by stage. . . . A short story *occurs,* in the imaginative sense. To write one is to express from a situation in the exterior or interior world the life-giving drop—sweat, tear, semen, saliva—that will spread an intensity on the page; burn a hole in it"). . . .

George Kearns (review date Winter 1984-85)

SOURCE: A review of *Something Out There,* in *The Hudson Review,* Vol. XXXVII, No. 4, Winter, 1984-85, pp. 619-21.

[*In the following excerpt, Kearns discusses the politics of Gordimer's fiction in* Something Out There.]

. . . Nadine Gordimer's **Something Out There** is a collection of nine short stories and the title piece, a long novella that might have had greater impact if published separately. Gordimer is a writer of political fiction whose assurance has become finer with time. Her South Africa is a country torn apart not by "racial problems" or "terrorism," but by what she wants us to know is nothing less than civil war. Lush patches of safety in this battlefield are supported by a "grand illusion," and are under attack from enemies within and without. It is a country from which so many have "skipped"—a word with reverberations: "This one or that has skipped; the laconic phrase contains, for all this generation of South Africans in the know, dumped by their elders with the deadly task of defending a life they haven't chosen for themselves, the singular heritage of their whiteness." This writer is unconcerned with distancing her views by ascribing them, even nominally, to some stand-in or narrator. Nor do drama and conflict have to be devised: they are inherent in a place where everything is visibly dramatic and political, at least to Gordimer's fine eye for detail—every nuance of speech, every choice of dress is necessarily charged with irony. In the title story, for example, Joy, a white revolutionary, is caught in a delicate crisis when she must deal with a black visitor who is capable of blowing the cover she's providing for two black terrorists:

> Joy slept in an outsize T-shirt; she put her Indian skirt over it and went out into the yard with the right amount of white madam manner, not enough to be too repugnant to her, not too little to seem normal to the former Kleynhans laborer.
>
> —Yes? Do you want something?—
>
> Mild as her presence was, it clamped him by the leg; caught there, he took of his hat and greeted her in Afrikaans.—*More missus, more missus.*—

She changed to Afrikaans, too.—What is it you want here? . . . They knew exactly how to lie to each other.

Gordimer supplies some views of the lives and thoughts of her conservative/reactionary fellow citizens, and of the merely bewildered, but the characters she's most interested in, clearly, are those whites who fall within a range closer to her own politics, and the blacks and coloreds whose lives provide not even an illusion of refuge from politics. She is writing for her countrymen today, and for the world today; she is also preserving, in a society where truth is more than ordinarily manufactured and suppressed, a record for the future of what it felt like to be a South African now, of what people said, of how they behaved. It's that part of the record only art can preserve. Gordimer is aware of every problem writing political fiction poses, as she showed in her supportive, but tortured and tortuous recent review of the South African J. M. Coetzee's *The Life and Times of Michael K.* Her own decisions as a writer are clear and, in what she writes, brave. She's willing to sacrifice transcendence. . . .

Sylvia Clayton (review date 15-18 April 1984)

SOURCE: "Saboteurs," in *London Review of Books,* April 15-18, 1984, p. 23.

[*In the following excerpt, Clayton comments on Gordimer's writing style in* Something out There.]

Nadine Gordimer continues to send sane, humane reports from the edge of darkness. In her finest stories she fixes authoritatively the experience of her South African characters, who exist in the shadow of a gun. They are menaced by repressive laws, unpredictable violence and a cruel historical process; their small domestic treacheries can carry a fatal undertow of danger. In this latest collection [*Something Out There*] her tone remains cool, diagnostic, her brilliant camera eye unfazed. Even in a few pages she produces not a tentative sketch but a finished drawing. She places her figures exactly in the landscape, and the contrast between their precarious lives and her own controlled poise yields a high imaginative tension.

> **Even in a few pages [Gordimer] produces not a tentative sketch but a finished drawing. She places her figures exactly in the landscape, and the contrast between their precarious lives and her own controlled poise yields a high imaginative tension.**
> **—*Sylvia Clayton***

The education of a middle-aged, liberal-minded divorcee, Pat Haberman, becomes, in her beautifully constructed story, **'A Correspondence Course'**, a taut, ironic drama. Pat has rejected her husband's money-grubbing, country-club life' for independence with her daughter Harriet, now a graduate student. 'Harriet has been brought up to realise that her life of choices and decent comfort is not shared by the people in whose blackness it is embedded . . . And since she has been adult she has had her place—even if silent—in the ritualistic discussion of what can be done about this by people who have no aptitude for politics but who won't live like Haberman.' An English journalist serving nine years in a maximum-security jail in Pretoria for political offences responds to an article by Harriet in an academic magazine. A regular, censored, monthly correspondence begins. Pat supports her daughter. She is proud of their shared compassionate attitude; she talks about the letters at parties; she is gleefully excited when he makes his escape with five years left to serve. But when she finds a bundle of clothes that Harriet has left out for the escaped prisoner, and when the man actually appears on the doorstep, she is overcome by terror.

The pressures of living in South Africa are revealed within this close mother-daughter relationship; the rhythm of the story unfolds them with increasing clarity. A mother's protective regard for her child is central to another brief, intense story of conflicting loyalties, **'A City of the Dead, a City of the Living'.** Here everything happens inside the overcrowded little house of Moreke, a jobbing gardener. A stranger, a man with a gun, comes to lodge with Moreke, his wife and baby. Moreke feels in duty bound to give him shelter. For a week the wife watches him as she does her crochet. 'The tiny flash of her steel hook and the hair-thin gold in her ear signaled in candlelight.' Eventually, acting entirely on her own, the wife betrays him, one of her own people, to the police. The woman who keeps the shebeen spits in her face. The story leaves behind a faint doubt about the author's timing, especially about the moment she chooses to stop. Since the scene has been set and the tensions have been built up with such skill, it comes as a letdown to find no explanation of the mother's decision to turn informer and no hint as to her husband's reaction.

The stories seldom convey the sense of biting pain that charges Athol Fugard's plays about South Africa. Some vital information or necessary energy is missing. A novella, **'Something Out There'**, offers a panoramic view of Johannesburg, where an ape-like animal is at large in the suburbs. Young Stanley snaps it with his camera, a bar mitzvah present. The picture is printed in a newspaper; an elderly estate agent's wife welcomes the headlines as a distraction from worse horrors. Doctors at the golf club are convinced it is a baboon. It startles a couple who are having an illicit affair; it steals food from a policeman's kitchen. Meanwhile, in a run-down rented house four people, a white couple and two blacks, are planning to blow up a power station. The interlocking lives of the saboteurs as they wait, disguised as an unremarkable suburban household—two young married whites and two black servants—are watched by the author so intently that the peripheral business of an ape at large seems unnecessary packaging. She describes magisterially their movements, their irritations with each other within a conspiratorial intimacy, yet she contrives to keep a distance from their inner struggles. The young woman has decided that she will stay with her partner, even though their six-year relationship is over, because the mission has long been planned and is important. How she arrives at this decision and what cause she is supporting are not explained. All four are in deadly danger; their purpose is destruction: urbanity seems the wrong mode in which to write of their crisis.

This is a book in which Nadine Gordimer steps outside the South African territory she has made her own; her most adventurous excursion is into the past. **'Letter from his Father'** is supposed to be written in self-defence by Hermann Kafka to his son, Franz. It is easy to feel that the relatives of a genius sometimes get a raw deal. There were friends of D. H. Lawrence's family who objected strongly to the portrait of his father in *Sons and Lovers*: they denied that he was a coarse, unfeeling husband, unworthy of his wife's long-suffering refinement. Friends of Kafka *père* agreed that he had much to put up with from his difficult son. It is one thing to question a character study from direct personal knowledge, quite another to impersonate the subject and pretend to be answering false accusations. Kafka wrote a letter to his father, which he never sent, perhaps never intended to, and which was published only in 1954 in a volume consisting mainly of posthumous fragments. Ms Gordimer's letter purports to be written from heaven, where Hermann, though not Franz, Kafka is to be found. Its style is stage-Jewish and the effect of its bluff reproaches is embarrassing. She is a wonderfully clear-sighted writer, innately courteous, like Ruth Prawer Jhabvala or E. M. Forster, to the creatures of her imagination. It is foolhardy of her, though, to take on Kafka, whose work remains a set text for any examination on the 20th century. . . .

Judie Newman (essay date 1985)

SOURCE: "Prospero's Complex: Race and Sex in Nadine Gordimer's *Burger's Daughter*," in *The Journal of Commonwealth Literature*, Vol. XX, No. 1, 1985, pp. 81-99.

[*In the following essay, Newman analyzes the psychological connections that Rosa makes between race and sexu-*

ality in Burger's Daughter *in relation to prevailing cultural attitudes toward each.*]

Nadine Gordimer has remarked that all South African novels, whatever their political intentions, involve the question of racism:

> There is no country in the Western world where the creative imagination, whatever it seizes upon, finds the focus of even the most private event set in the social determination of racial laws.

There are those who have argued that the white South African novelist is automatically corrupted by a privileged position, that Gordimer's audience can only be other privileged whites, and that the products of her creative imagination are therefore intrinsically a part of a racist society. In ***The Conservationist*** Gordimer focused upon the disjunction between the internal, subjective reality of her white protagonist and the external reality of political consensus, employing as her principal strategy the translation of political problems into other languages, particularly into sexual terms. In the novel sexual fantasy functions as a surrogate for colonial lusts. The sexual body of woman, the body of a murdered black, combine to form one massive image of colonial guilt. As her use of the language of Zulu culture, and Zulu dreams, indicates here, Gordimer is clearly aware of the dangers of solipsistic art, an art which may articulate only the dominating power of the white imagination.

Rosa Burger begins her tale with the recognition that:

> one is never talking to oneself, always one is addressed to someone . . . even dreams are performed before an audience.

In ***Burger's Daughter*** Gordimer focuses upon the fantasies of the white subconscious, in order to undermine their power. Once again, a body lies below the level of conscious articulation, here the body of a white woman. In the opening scene of the novel Rosa is presented as she appears to other observers, as seen by casual passers-by, as reported on by her headmistress, and as transformed by the rhetoric of the Left, which converts her into "Little Rosa Burger" "an example to us all." The later Rosa reflects on her invisibility as a person:

> When they saw me outside the prison what did they see? I shall never know . . . I saw-see-that profile in a hand-held mirror directed towards another mirror.

As the daughter of a Communist hero, it is assumed by others that Rosa's views reflect her father's. Rosa is thus trapped in a hall of mirrors, an object in the eyes of others whose internal reality remains unknown. A figure in an ideological landscape, she is placed by observers only in relation to their own political position: an image of the struggle in the "bland heroics of badly written memoirs by the faithful," a suspicious object to State surveillance. This public rhetoric of South Africa contrasts with a bleeding body, invisible to all shades of South African opinion. For Rosa these external views are eclipsed by her awareness of the pains of puberty:

> real awareness is all focused in the lower part of my pelvis . . . outside the prison the internal landscape of my mysterious body turns me inside out.

In the novel Rosa's sexuality forms the point of entry to an exploration of the topography of the racist psyche. The disjunction between external and internal realities is rendered in the form of the novel in the alternation of first and third person narratives, narratives which interact in order to explore the roots of racism.

Burger's Daughter poses the question of racism as primary or secondary phenomenon. Is racism the product of a political system (capitalism) as Lionel Burger would argue? Or is racism a screen for more primary sexual insecurities? The central images of the novel are drawn from an informed awareness of the principal arguments involved here. Racism has been generally understood by various commentators as a product of sexual repression. In his early, classic study of prejudice Gordon Allport notes that to the white the Negro appears dark, mysterious and distant, yet at the same time warm, human and potentially accessible. These elements of mystery and forbiddenness are present in sex appeal in a Puritanical society. Sex is forbidden, blacks are forbidden; the ideas begin to fuse. White racism expresses itself in response to ambivalence towards the body, conceived of as both attractive and repugnant. In *White Racism: A Psychohistory* Joel Kovel developed the argument, describing aversive racism as the product of anal repressions. In his view the Negro is not the actual basis of racism but a surrogate or substitute. In white culture bodily products are seen as dirt. The subject therefore splits the universe into good (clean, white, spiritual) and bad (dirty, black, material). Things associated with the sensual body are dirty; those things which may be seen as non-sensuous are clean. Racism therefore depends upon the displacement of "dirty" activities onto an alter ego. Fantasies of dirt underlie racism, which is a product of sexual repressions.

Octave Mannoni offers a rather similar analysis, though with greater emphasis on sexual fantasy. Nadine Gordimer entitled her Neil Gunn Fellowship Lecture **'Apprentices of Freedom'** quoting Mannoni. In *Prospero and Caliban* Mannoni argues that colonial racism simply brings to the surface traits buried in the European psyche, repressed in Europe but manifest in the colonial experience. Colonial countries are the nearest approach possible to the archetype of the desert island. Colonial life is a substitute life available to those who are obscurely drawn to a world of fantasy projection, a childish world without real people. For Mannoni, European man is always in inner conflict between the need for attachments which offer emotional security, and the need for complete individualisation. Revolt against parents is an important factor here. When a child suffers because he feels that the ties between him and his parents are threatened, the child also feels guilt, because he would also like to break those ties. He therefore dreams of a world without bonds, a world which is entirely his, and into which he can project the untrammelled images of his unconscious. This desire to break every attachment is impossible, of course, in fact. But it is realised by the colonial when he goes into a "primitive" society, a society which seems less "real" than his own. In the modern world this urge may be realised by the substitution of depersonalised links for original attachments. Mannoni cites the film star and pin-up girl as examples. These people are still persons, but only just enough for the subject to form unreal relations with them. The more remote people are, the easier they appear to attract our projections. Prospero's relation with Caliban and Ariel, Crusoe's with Friday, are cases in point. In Gordimer's **July's People** a similar relationship obtains between white woman and black servant. Maureen Smales comes to realise in the course of the action that the traits she admired in July were not his real character but only assumed characteristics, assumed in order to conform to Maureen's mental image of him. In the literature of colonialism the native woman is more commonly a focus for this type of projection. The white colonial marries the native girl because her personality is so little externalised that it acts as a mirror to his projections. He may then live happily among these projections without granting that the Other has autonomous existence. In Mannoni's words:

> It is himself a man is looking for when he goes far away; near at hand he is liable to come up against others. Far-away princesses are psychologically important in this respect.

As will become evident, Rosa Burger almost becomes identified with the image of the far-away princess, inhabiting a world of erotic fantasy, though in her case Europe becomes the magic island, and her guilty revolt against her father is only temporary.

In this connection Mannoni's analysis of the roots of racism in a patriarchal system is particularly important. For Mannoni the antagonism between Caliban and Prospero in *The Tempest* hinges upon Miranda's presence as the only

woman on the island. Having first treated the black (Caliban) as his son, Prospero later accuses him of having attempted to rape Miranda, and then enslaves him. In short Prospero justifies his hatred of Caliban on grounds of sexual guilt. Analysing the "Prospero complex" Mannoni draws a picture of the paternalist colonial whose racism is a pseudo-rational construct to rationalise guilty sexual feelings. In his view the sexual basis of racism is revealed in the old cliché of the racist: But would you let your daughter marry one? Uneasy incestuous feelings in the father are disturbed by this argument. For Mannoni it is easy to see why it is always a daughter, sister or neighbour's wife, never his own, whom a man imagines in this situation. When a white man imagines a white woman as violated by a black man he is seeking to rid himself of guilt by projecting his thoughts onto another (Caliban), putting the blame for his "dirty" sexuality upon someone else. In *The Tempest* Prospero's departure from the colonial island is accompanied by his renunciation of his art, in this case magical arts which enable him to dominate a world created in his own image. Caliban remains behind, however, as disowned son and slave. There are clearly extremely interesting connections here with the character of Baasie (adopted as a son by Lionel Burger but later abandoned) with Rosa's relationship with her father, in whose shadow she lives, and with the nature of Gordimer's art.

Mannoni's is, of course, a highly ambivalent analysis of the colonial enterprise. His central thesis, that the dependence and inferiority complexes are present in rudimentary form in everyone, too easily elides into the untenable hypothesis that people are colonised because they want to be colonised, at least subconsciously. Communists, in particular, have denounced the search for psychological solutions, as too easily providing an alibi for those who refuse to confront political problems. In *Black Skin, White Masks* Fanon contested Mannoni in detail. While Fanon allows that the "civilised" white may retain an irrational longing for areas of unrepressed sexuality which he then projects onto the Negro, he argues that this image of the sexual-sensual-genital Negro can be corrected:

> The eye is not merely a mirror, but a correcting mirror. The eye should make it possible for us to correct cultural errors.

For Fanon, sexuality need not remain at the level of frustration, in authenticity or projection. True authentic love is "wishing for others what one postulates for oneself." Confrontation of one's psychic drives is only a necessary part of a process of cultural evolution:

> The tragedy of the man is that he was once a child. It is through the effort to recapture the self and to scrutinize the self, it is through the lasting tension of their free-

dom that man will be able to create the ideal conditions for a human world . . . Was my freedom not given to me in order to build the world of the *You*?"

Burger's Daughter charts just such a process of self-scrutiny. Rosa remembers and observes her past self, in an extensive attempt to recapture and reconstitute it, and to engage with the world of the "You". Rosa's first person narrative is directed to three people, each addressed as "You": Conrad, a surrogate brother with whom she enjoys childish erotic freedom, Katya, a sexually permissive replacement mother, and finally Lionel Burger, the father to whom she eventually returns. "You" is obviously also the reader, who is initiated into these three identities. The reader participates in the fantasy while also measuring the distance between these surrogate people and himself. At key points Gordimer adopts Fanon's phraseology. For Conrad, the significant dynamic is "the tension between creation and destruction in yourself". Rosa describes Lionel, however, in antithetical terms: "the tension that makes it possible to live lay, for him, between self and others." In the novel Gordimer's narrative technique draws the reader into a tension of freedom, progressing from Conrad's inner psychological existence to a fresh orientation towards the world of the autonomous other. The alternation between first and third person narrative creates a tension between external image and internal voice, between "She" and "I". As "You" the reader continually mediates the two, correcting the errors of the eye, emerging from the spell of the internal voice. The reader is therefore offered a choice. He may place the voice addressing him as initiating him into a secret intimacy. Or he may refuse to identify with a surrogate "You" and thus register the possibility of a world in which communication is not limited to depersonalised stereotypes.

In the first movement of the novel, Rosa Burger disowns her original attachments in order to enter a world in which surrogate brothers and mothers replace them in a fantasy landscape. She does so largely as a result of ambivalence towards the body, as one example will indicate. When Rosa meets Marisa Kgosana (gorgeously regal while buying face cream) their embrace is described as a step through the looking glass.

> To enter for a moment the invisible magnetic field of the body of a beautiful creature and receive on one-self its imprint—breath misting and quickly fading on a glass pane—this was to immerse in another mode of perception.

To the salesgirl Marisa appears in the image of the sensuous black woman, distant and unreal. She asks, "Where's she from? One of those French islands!" Marisa, however, has returned, not from the exotic Seychelles or Mauritius, but from Robben Island, the island to which white racist attitudes have banished her husband. From Marisa, Rosa's mind moves at once to Baasie, who is remembered quite differently as a creature of darkness and dirt. Rosa remembers Baasie wetting the bed which they shared as children:

> In the morning the sheets were cold and smelly. I told tales to my mother—Look what Baasie's done in his bed!—but in the night I didn't know whether this warmth . . . came from him or me.

Quite obviously the two images suggest the twin racist strategies delineated by Kovel and Mannoni—the attempt to use blackness as a way to sensual liberation (Marisa), the attempt to blame "dirty" actions on the black (Baasie). Rosa exists in tension between these two forms of racism, but it is a tension Gordimer's complex art transforms into a political challenge. Key terms and images—island paradise, incestuous desires, projection onto mirrors, far-away princesses—recur in the novel from Mannoni's thesis, as do images of dirt, guilt, bodily products and repugnance, taken from Kovel. The language of racism is exploited, however, in order to confront the reader with a series of questions. Which vision of Rosa do we accept?—that of a white woman who is part of a racist society and who can address a "You" who exists only in her own projections? Or that of a woman confronting and correcting a stereotyped image and painfully learning to address herself to a world of other autonomous beings? It is my contention that the complex narrative art of ***Burger's Daughter*** refuses to maintain the text at the level of private fantasy or dream, and also avoids the danger of the depersonalised image. Gordimer employs the terms of the white racist subconscious in an attempt to free her art from Prospero's complex, and to direct it towards a world where "You" is not a fantasy projection, but real.

> **Gordimer employs the terms of the white racist subconscious in an attempt to free her art from Prospero's complex, and to direct it towards a world where "You" is not a fantasy projection, but real.**
> —*Judie Newman*

Gordimer's daring strategy, here, is to select as the focus of the novel a white woman attempting to achieve autonomy by emerging from her father's dominance. As the daughter of a white Afrikaner Communist, Rosa is an extremely complex figure. She may be defined in terms of sex, race, and position in the class struggle, and thus encapsulates the warring explanations of South African racism. In order to assert her autonomy Rosa can rebel only against another rebel. Her father is fighting political repression, so to fight his psychological influence is to join with the forces of political repression. This paradoxical situation is made evident from the beginning. In the eyes of the faithful, Rosa is desexualised and infantilised, maintained in the image of the faithful daughter. In the opening scene Rosa is described as having already "taken on her mother's role in the household" "giving loving support" to her father. That father cheerfully permits Rosa to have boyfriends while laughing at them for "not knowing she was not for them". In the Burger household the children have few exclusive rights with their parents for whom intimate personal relationships are subordinate to the struggle. As a young woman Rosa gains her parents' approval by posing as the fiancée of Noel de Witt, a device to enable him to receive visits in prison. Decked out, scented, "a flower standing for what lies in her lap" Rosa presents herself as a sexual object in prison, conveying a political subtext beneath innocuous lovey-dovey phrases. She returns to her mother's welcoming expression, the expression reserved for her "as a little girl" returning from school, and to her father's "caress". Rosa's parents are blind to the fact that she *is* actually in love with Noel. They are happy to cast her in a surrogate sexual role, a role which denies the reality of her emotions, confining her sexuality within prison walls. In the overall action of the novel, Rosa moves from prison to prison. Infantilised as "Little Rosa Burger" at the start, she becomes in the final pages, once more a child. Flora describes her at the end: "She looked like a little girl . . . About fourteen." In the eyes of the faithful Rosa has not changed at all. She is still her father's daughter, and is living out the historical destiny prepared for her by him. Imagistically, the prison is connected to the dichotomy of "inside" and "outside" in the novel. The reader, with access to Rosa's internal voice, knows that Rosa defected from her father in a belated revolt against the ideology of the parental generation. Does Rosa return from France to continue the political struggle, making a free choice on the basis of internal understanding? Or has Rosa simply fled from the erotic life of Europe in order to return to a desexualised security, a prison of women where she is once more her father's daughter? Rosa is finally imprisoned on suspicion of abetting the schoolchildren's revolt—a revolt informed by consciousness of black brotherhood, and directed against paternalism, whether white or black. Rosa's return follows her encounter with Baasie who denies her "brotherhood". In external political terms the white is rejected by blacks and retreats into paternalism. In internal psychological terms, however, the position is more complex.

That Rosa's rejection of her father is connected to sexual assertion is made clear in the scene with Clare Terblanche, daughter of Dick and Ivy who have been as surrogate parents to Rosa. Rosa is tempted by the parental warmth of their welcome and recognises their attraction:

> In the enveloping acceptance of Ivy's motherly arms—

she feels as if I were her own child—there is expectance, even authority. To her warm breast one could come home again and do as you said I would, go to prison.

Clare Terblanche lives with her parents and her life is devoted to their cause. As a result she is desexualised, in contrast to Rosa who is beginning to emerge. Clare appears at Rosa's door as a shadow which "had no identity" glimpsed through a glass panel. In Rosa's eyes, Clare is still her childish playmate, sturdy as a teddy-bear, suffering from eczema and knock knees which went uncorrected by parents for whom the body is unimportant. Where Rosa's is a body with "assurance of embraces" Clare, faithful to her father's ideals, has "a body that had no signals" and is "a woman without sexual pride". Clare has two purposes here—to recruit Rosa as a political intermediary, and to rent a flat for her lover. The first is clearly the dominant motive. Rosa refuses on the grounds that she will not conform to her parents image of her:

> Other people break away. They live completely different lives. Parents and children don't understand each other . . . Not us. We live as they lived.

One event specifically links Clare to the earlier Rosa. When Rosa shows Clare the vacant apartment, Clare discovers a used sanitary towel in a cupboard. As they leave she removes this unmentionable object to the waste-bin, "and buried her burden . . . as if she had successfully disposed of a body." Disposing of her body is, of course, what Clare has done. Supposedly involved with the people's struggle, her background isolates her from the realities of the body. Irony cuts both ways here, however. In the background a radio announcer is:

> reciting with the promiscuous intimacy of his medium
> a list of birthday, anniversary and lover's greetings for
> military trainees on border duty.

Rosa's refusal to help Clare aligns her with this promiscuous intimacy. In South Africa there appears to be no possible mediation between the desexualised image and an erotic intimacy which is the voice of the repressive state.

This erotic intimacy is developed in the person of Brandt Vermeulen. Breaking her attachments to the original family, Rosa sets out to obtain a passport, aligning herself with an alternative family. In order to defect, she makes a series of visits to Afrikaners "whose history, blood and language made (Lionel) their brother." Of them all, she selects as her ally Brandt Vermeulen, member of the Broederbonde, the Afrikaner political "brotherhood" which runs South Africa from within Parliament. Brandt's house expresses the psychological reality of colonialism. The facade is that of a Boer farmhouse of seventy or eighty years ago. Within, however, all the internal walls have been demolished to create one large space of comfortable intimacy, with glass walls giving access to a secret garden. Behind the facade of historical legitimacy there exists a vast personal space, inhabited by the erotic male. Brandt runs an art publishing house, and is about to publish a book of erotic poems and woodcuts. By participating in a racist political system Brandt has found sexual liberation. Rosa's attempt to escape from her father has brought her to a "brother" whose facade of reverence for the traditions of his fathers conceals a sophistic eroticism. Rosa is placed here against a highly representative background of *objets d'art*. Brandt's walls are hung with Pierneef landscapes, modernist abstractions, a print of the royal Zulu line, and images of tortured bodies. The room is dominated, however, by a sculpture, a perspex torso of a woman's body, set upon a colonial chest. Described as suggesting both the ice of frigidity and the hardness of tumescence the sculpture presents an image of erotic woman as a reified object of display, possessed by the male and existing only in his internal space. It is on this erotic object that Brandt's more "sophisticated" art depends, as Prospero's art draws upon a complex of sexual motives. In the garden a small black boy plays, amidst chairs spattered with messy bird-droppings, indicating *his* place in Brandt's internal landscape. To escape desexualisation by a father Rosa has entered a landscape organised by a surrogate brother to reflect his own fantasy.

Conrad is another such "brother". (The watchman for whom he places bets describes him to Rosa at one point as "Your brother".) Rosa's relation with Conrad is foreshadowed in the visit she pays to the Nels' farm when first separated from her jailed parents. At the farm "More and more, she based herself in the two rooms marked Strictly Private—Streng Privaat." On the door hangs a wooden clock-face on which visitors mark the time of their call. To Rosa it is:

> immediately recognizable to any child as something from childhood's own system of signification. Beyond any talisman is a private world unrelated to and therefore untouched by what is lost or gained . . .

The dummy clock marks the entrance to the timeless world of the child's psyche, a place to which Rosa returns when separated from her parents. The visit to the Nels also marks the disappearance from Rosa's life of Baasie. Rosa recalls that she and Baasie had both been given watches, but that Baasie ruined his in the bath. To Rosa, Baasie has become timeless, existing only in her memory. When Rosa is permanently separated from her parents, she sets up house with Conrad in a world which is also outside time and place. Their cottage, soon to be demolished in favour of a new freeway, is let without official tenure at "an address that no

longer existed". Set in a jungle of palms, beneath a bauhinia tree, the house is "safe and cosy as a child's playhouse and sexually arousing as a lovers' hideout. It was nowhere." In the dark of their secret cottage, Conrad and Rosa act out their dreams of a private erotic world in which parents are no longer controlling. For Conrad, a man with no political affiliations, only psychological events matter: Sharpeville passes unnoticed, obscured by the realisation that his mother had a lover. Freed from his Oedipal conflicts by the awareness that his mother was no longer the sole possession of his father, Conrad became obsessed with her.

> I was mad about her; now I could be with someone other than my father there already.

Rosa admits a kinship with Conrad:

> We had in common such terrible secrets in the tin house: you can fuck your mother and wish your father dead.

Conrad's reaction to Lionel's death is "Now you are free." Freedom from the father liberates Rosa sexually, but is attended by guilt. She wished for this freedom. She obtained it on her father's death. She concludes, "I know I must have wished him to die." In the psyche there is no distinction between what she has actually done and what she has imagined. This criminality of the white imagination is seen as liberating by Conrad. For him Rosa can only begin to live once she blasphemes her father's ideology. He quotes Jung in his support:

> One day when he was a kid Jung imagined God sitting up in the clouds and shitting on the world below. His father was a pastor . . . You commit the great blasphemy against all doctrine and you begin to live.

As Conrad's choice of example suggests, he and Rosa are still inhabiting a world structured around the opposed terms of racist language. When Rosa ends her relationship with Conrad she does so in terms which suggest important connections with Lionel and Baasie:

> I left the children's tree-house we were living in, in an intimacy of self-engrossment without the reserve of adult accountability, accepting each other's encroachments as the law of the litter, treating each other's dirt as our own, as little Baasie and I had long ago performed the child's black mass, tasting on a finger the gall of our own shit and the saline of our own pee . . . And you know we had stopped making love together months before I left, aware that it had become incest.

Rosa recoils from Conrad's erotic activities—activities which depend upon the replacement of the father—because these activities are perceived as dirty and incestuous. The closer Conrad becomes to Rosa, the more he blasphemes against her family's beliefs, the more he approaches Baasie, the black "brother" with whom her first "dirty" acts were performed. For Rosa sexual freedom is forever connected to images of the black, and to imperfectly suppressed incestuous desires. Significantly Conrad later sails off upon a yacht to islands in the Indian Ocean. Rosa departs for Paris—an unreal place, "Paris—a place far away in England" as she describes it to the Nels' maids—and thence to the South of France, to the arms of a surrogate mother, Lionel's first wife, who placed erotic freedom before the needs of the Party.

Rosa's arrival in the South of France is described in terms which establish it as the enchanted land of fantasy. "The silk tent of morning sea" tilts below her plane, glimpsed through the distorting glass of the window. Below, tables outside a bar become "tiny islands" in "a day without landmarks". On the verge "roadside tapestry flowers grow" and in the background "a child's pop-up picture book castle" stands against a landscape of sea and flowers, where

> People were dreamily letting the car pass across their eyes an image like that in the convex mirror set up at the blind intersection.

Rosa's perceptions are dazed here, as if entering a dream world, a world drowning in sensuality. Katya's dining room appears as "swimming colours, fronds blobbing out of focus and a sea horizon undulating in uneven panes of glass." Katya's reminiscences of the Party—vodka, parties, sexual affairs—accompany Rosa's meal while she is "dissolving" in the pleasures of wine, and French sights, sounds and tastes. A room has been prepared for Rosa at the top of the house, full of feminine bric-à-brac, flowers, mirrors, and peaches:

> a room made ready for someone imagined. A girl, a creature whose sense of existence would be in her nose buried in flowers, peach juice running down her chin, face tended at mirrors, mind dreamily averted, body seeking pleasure. Rosa Burger entered, going forward into possession by that image.

Rosa is thus presented with an image of herself as sensual woman, created by Katya, an image which she delightedly assumes, enjoying the sensual pleasures of an unreal country, where her projections are reflected back to her, where she ceases to be her father's daughter and becomes instead the mistress of Bernard Chabalier. The particular features of the landscape—islands, tapestry, flowers, mirrors, silk tent—are focused in the tapestry series, "*La Dame à la Licorne*" which is presented to the reader after Rosa's return to Africa.

Rosa's lover plans to show her these tapestries. He also takes her to see an exhibition of painting by Bonnard. As he says, "In Africa, one goes to see the people. In Europe, it's paintings." The white in Africa sees people as objects to be contemplated, objects which mirror their own projections. In Europe art offers a timeless substitute reality. To Rosa the paintings of Bonnard are just as real as the French people she lives among. These people are "coexistent with the life fixed by the painter's vision". Bernard points out that Bonnard's style and subjects never changed. The woman painted in 1894, the mimosa painted in 1945 during the war are treated in the same way. In the fifty years between the paintings there was the growth of fascism, two wars, the Occupation, but for Bonnard it is as if nothing has happened. The two paintings could have been executed on the same day. In Bernard's analysis, the woman's flesh and the leaves around her are equal manifestations:

> Because she hasn't any existence any more than the leaves have, outside this lovely forest where they are . . . Your forest girl and the vase of mimosa—C'est un paradis inventé.

With Bernard, Rosa lives in a similar invented paradise, a world of sensual pleasures, divorced from the world of historical events, cut off from both future and past, a world in which she is only a timeless image. Rosa meets Bernard for the first time in the bar owned by Josette Arnys, a Creole singer. The bar is mirrored and suggests the solipsism of France for Rosa. "In the bar where she had sat seeing others living in the mirror, there was no threshold between her reflection and herself." In the background runs a recording of Arnys' unchanging voice, singing about "the island where she and Napoleon's Josephine was born." Arnys is quite unaware of the naive political content of the song. For her, art is timeless in its eroticism. She argues at one point that "the whole feminist thing" will mean the death of art, as women will no longer be able to sing of love. In her view, "the birds sing only when they call for a mate". Katya is associated with the same vision, when she takes Rosa to hear the nightingales singing. Rosa's final rejection of this world is linked to a different voice—that of Baasie—and to the image presented in the tapestry series.

The tapestries of the Musée de Cluny have been very variously interpreted both by artists and scholars. Discovered by George Sand, who featured them in her novel *Jeanne*, they were also the inspiration for a ballet created by Jean Cocteau in Munich in 1953. Rilke was also attracted to them, and celebrates them in one of his Sonnets to Orpheus, which begins "O dieses ist das Tier, das es nicht gibt" (This is the creature that has never been.). Rilke also described the tapestries in detail in The *Notebooks of Malte Laurids Brigge*. The hero, Malte, has found that growing up is a process of reducing and distorting experience to make it fit conventional categories, thus acquiring a false identity or mask. To his horror that mask becomes more real than his inner self; the self he sees in the mirror is more real than the person it reflects. When he observes the tapestries, however, Malte feels a restored sense of totality. From the tapestries he gains a sense of total or simultaneous time, with no sense of an absent future.

> Expectation plays no part in it. Everything is here. Everything forever.

Forced as she grows up into a similar assumption of a fixed role, Rosa is also attracted at first to the tapestries, as part and parcel of her assumption of the role of Bernard's mistress.

> Bernard Chabalier's mistress isn't Lionel Burger's daughter; she's certainly not accountable to the Future; she can go off and do good works in Cameroun or contemplate the unicorn in the tapestry forest. "This is the creature that has never been"—he told me a line of poetry about that unicorn, translated from German. A mythical creature. Un paradis inventé.

Scholars have suggested various interpretations for the tapestries, seeing them as representing a Turkish prince and his lady, as celebrating a marriage between two noble houses, as an act of homage to the Blessed Virgin Mary, and most importantly, as a celebration of the five senses, to name only a few of the available explications. A particular focus of difficulty is the sixth tapestry, in which the lady, on a blue island, against a rose background strewn with tapestry flowers, stands in front of a silk tent over which hangs the banner motto "A mon seul désir". The Lady appears to be taking a necklace from a box and the tapestry has thus been understood as celebrating a gift of love. Nadine Gordimer draws upon both Rilke's vision of the tapestries and the most recent scholarly explanation. In the text, she describes the first tapestry, in which the lady holds a mirror in which the unicorn is reflected, and then simply lists the four following tapestries as "the representation of the other four senses", hearing, smell, taste and touch. The text then moves to the sixth tapestry which is described in more detail. In 1978, Alain Erlande-Brandenburg agreed that the tapestries represent the five senses, but suggested that the meaning of the sixth tapestry lay not in the acceptance of a gift, but rather in its renunciation: the lady is not receiving the necklace but replacing it in the box. The sixth tapestry may therefore be understood as signifying the need not to submit to the power of the senses, but to exercise free will in their control. The necklace is therefore a symbol of the renunciation of the passions, which may inter-

fere with our ability to act morally. "A mon seul désir" translates as "by my own free will" and is linked to the *Liberum arbitrium* of Socrates and Plato. Where formerly the tapestries were seen as celebrating the senses, as embodied in a beautiful woman, the understanding of the sixth panel has now corrected the eye of the observer.

On the simplest level, therefore, the tapestries indicate that Rosa's decision to abandon the luxuriant sensual joys of life with her lover is an act of free will, and a renunciation of the fantasy eroticism of projection, mirror images and magic islands. Life with Bernard would remove her from her historical destiny to a "place" outside time. Gordimer's description of the tapestries is entirely in the present tense, a timeless participial present which creates an impression of enchanted stillness. "The Lion and the Unicorn listening to music. . . . The Lady weaving . . . The Lady taking sweets from a dish . . . " In France Rosa has been possessed by an image of herself as sensual, floating like the lady on "an azure island of a thousand flowers", hearing nightingales sing, delighting in the taste of French foods and the sights of France, enjoying the touch of a lover. For all their beauty, however, the tapestries were executed in "the age of the thumbscrew and dungeon". Bernard would take Rosa away from a similar world of pain and imprisonment in order to sequester her in a private world of sensual joy and art, a world in which he could show her the tapestry he loves—"to love you by letting you come to discover what I love". What Bernard loves is an image of Rosa to which she does not entirely correspond. In the extremely complex presentation of the tapestries, Gordimer describes a woman gazing at them, a woman who has all the time in the world to do so.

> There she sits gazing, gazing. And if it is time for the museum to close, she can come back tomorrow and another day, any day, days.

> Sits gazing, this creature that has never been.

In the "Sight" tapestry the lady is also gazing, into a hand-held mirror, but she sees only the reflection of the unicorn, the mythical creature which has never existed outside the human mind. In the tapestry the oval face of the lady with her hair twisted on top is echoed in the oval frame of the mirror and the unicorn's twisted horn. Rosa Burger may become, like the lady, a gazer into a hand-held mirror which reflects back to her only an unreal and mythical creature, a woman who has only existed in the projections of others. In returning to South Africa, however, Rosa chooses not to be such an image, an object to be displayed and desired, a figure in an erotic or political iconography. In South Africa, Rosa, like Rilke's Malte, acquired a false identity imposed upon her by others. Pursuing a personal erotic course, however, simply creates an alternative mask. Rosa's progress towards autonomy involves coming to terms with the mythic masks which men have fastened over the female face—whether desexualised or erotically reified—and correcting the errors of her own internal eye.

Where the tapestry series articulates the necessity of correcting the errors of the eye, Baasie's voice establishes the autonomous existence of "You". Rosa wakes in the night to "the telephone ringing buried in the flesh" and in the darkness at first assumes it is her lover, Bernard. When she realises it is Baasie she tries to put him off. When Baasie keeps telling Rosa to put on the light, Rosa refuses on the grounds that it is late; she will see him "tomorrow—today, I suppose it is, it's still so dark." Rosa would very much like to keep this conversation in a timeless darkness. To her, Baasie is not a person with an autonomous existence, but a creature of her own mind.

> The way you look in my mind is the way my brother
> does—never gets any older.

She addresses him as Baasie. The childish nickname, insulting in the world of *baasskap,* infantilises and desexualises an adult male, converting him into a "boy". For Rosa his real name—Zwelinzima Vulindlela—is unknown and unpronounceable. Infantilised and desexualised by Rosa's impersonal greeting at the party, Baasie angrily insists that he is not her "black brother" and doesn't have "to live in your head." He will not enter into a relationship with her in which he functions as a psychological surrogate. His insults force Rosa to put on the light, transforming his voice:

> the voice was no longer inside her but relayed small,
> as from a faint harsh public address system.

Baasie's insults externalise his voice, no longer a part of Rosa, but a person in his own right, challenging her. By taunting her,

> he had disposed of her whining to go back to bed and
> bury them both.

Burying the body is a part of Rosa's strategy, as much as it is Clare Terblanche's. She, too, would like to live in a world which corresponds to childish projections, a world in which the childish magical landscape is more real than a "Suffering Land" (Zwelinzima). In the conversation, Baasie can only be "You", a voice without pronounceable identity. Up to this point in the novel Rosa may be said to have addressed a "You" of fantasy. Now, however, "You" answers back. At the end of the conversation, vomiting in front of the bathroom mirror, Rosa sees herself as "Ugly, soiled", "filthy" and "debauched". She comments, "how I disfigured myself." Disfiguration is an essential step in Rosa's progress to autonomy, an autonomy which depends upon

confrontation with her real body, repugnant as well as beautiful, a body which cannot be split into good, clean, white or bad, dirty, black.

The realisation is also a product of the subject of Rosa's conversation with Baasie—their respective fathers. In the conversation Rosa tries to assume responsibility for Baasie's father. She says that she was responsible for getting a pass to him, a pass with which he was caught, and as a result died. Baasie, however, refuses to allow whites to assume responsibility for blacks: "it's nothing to do with you . . . who cares whose 'fault'". Baasie rejects Lionel as spokesman for the black cause, as he rejects white paternalism. Rosa's desire to assume responsibility for her "brother's" father's death is finally checked here, as she emerges from the world of the psyche into the light of conscious action. What Baasie says to her ends her fantasy guilt over a white father, but does not absolve her from political responsibilities. She leaves behind an incestuous psychological world, in the recognition that blacks are autonomous beings, who are not bound to her by imagined ties of dependence.

Rosa returns to South Africa to take up her father's work again, in two senses: firstly in terms of a renewed political commitment, and secondly in the tending of black bodies. As a physiotherapist, Rosa (like her doctor father) restores feeling to the nerves of injured black people. Rosa's return is to a world of repugnant bodies—horribly mutilated in the Soweto riots—but she is now able to face these bodies and act in their world. When Rosa is charged with "aiding and abetting of the students' and schoolchildren's revolt" the reader knows of no external evidence for the truth of the accusation. Internally, however, Rosa had participated in a schoolgirl's revolt against paternalism, a revolt which has brought her to political consciousness. The novel ends with a revolt against parents which is not the product of white fantasy, but a political and historical reality. The schoolchildren's revolt in Soweto is directed at the white paternalist state, but also at the political compromises of black fathers. Fats Mxenge is such a father, a man who appears at the end of the novel like "someone brought abroad out of a tempest."

The extent to which she has left Prospero's complex behind is indicated in the art of Gordimer's novel. Two points are important here. In the final pages of the novel the third person view is emphasised and Rosa appears flatter and more distant than before. Gordimer also introduces into these final pages a statement from the Soweto Students Representative Council, ungrammatical, misprinted and rhetorically crude. Rosa comments:

> They can't spell and they can't formulate their elation
> and anguish. But they know why they're dying.

In the prison Rosa obtains drawing materials and produces paintings which are also crude in their expression. Failures in aesthetic terms, they are however politically valuable. One drawing is a Christmas card. Ostensibly an innocuous group of carol singers, the card represents the clumsily drawn figures of Marisa, Rosa and Clare, signalling to its recipients that the women are in touch with each other. In the prison Marisa sings—not of love—but in order to announce her presence to the other prisoners. Rosa has also found her political voice and as a result her inner voice has become silent. The other picture is a

> naive imaginary landscape that could raise no suspicions that she might be incorporating plans of the layout of the prison.

In this crude drawing tiny boats appear "through some failure of perspective" to be sailing straight for a tower. Rosa's drawing is an analogy to the art of Gordimer's novel, which takes the landscape of the racist psyche and inverts it to political ends. At the end of the novel Rosa is distanced as a result of a creative change in the reader's perspective. The "You" of fantasy has disappeared, replaced by the political voice of autonomous blacks (the S.S.R.C. statement). The internal voice has been silenced in favour of communication directed towards the world of the Other. *Burger's Daughter* opens with the epigraph

> I am the place in which something has occurred.

Gordimer's aesthetics are directed against the constructs of a racist imagination, constructs which depend upon psychological displacement in order to relocate the individual in a real political perspective.

Dick Roraback (review date 6 October 1991)

SOURCE: "Gordimer Is in the Details," in *Los Angeles Times Book Review,* October 6, 1991, pp. 2, 10.

[*In the following review, Roraback notes the freshness of the themes in* Jump, *despite their familiarity.*]

Nadine Gordimer takes you by the hand. Sometimes she leads you gently. Sometimes, impatient, she yanks. Come, she says, there are things I want you to see.

We've been over Gordimer turf before. We know the field is not level. As always, there are salients of insensitivity, injustice, inhumanity—apartheid. After so many tours, can there be something we missed?

There can. There is [in *Jump*]. Our cicerone knows where

the real stuff is—new insights, apercus, epiphanies, buried under layers of complacency. She knows where to dig.

As the conscience of the white South African, Gordimer could be expected to pause here and there to pontificate. Instead, in the best African tradition, she favors the role of a *griot,* a storyteller, who encourages her auditors to draw their own conclusions from the behavior of the characters she conjures up out of an endless imagination.

> **As the conscience of the white South African, Gordimer could be expected to pause here and there to pontificate. Instead, in the best African tradition, she favors the role of a *griot,* a storyteller, who encourages her auditors to draw their own conclusions from the behavior of the characters she conjures up out of an endless imagination.**
> —*Dick Roraback*

Here, in **"My Father Leaves Home,"** we are introduced to an impoverished and persecuted Eastern European youth who migrates to Africa, where he discovers that no matter how humble one's origins, white makes right. There, in **"Keeping Fit,"** we meet his foil, a well-to-do white jogger who strays into the teeming shantytown across the highway. Abruptly, he finds himself a cipher, generic, "only another white man, no other identity, no other way to be known." They all look the same.

In **"The Ultimate Safari,"** the very young and very old of a village are forced by strife to leave and traverse a vast game reserve to gain safe haven with another branch of their tribe. Creation of the park—"the place where white people come to look at the animals"—has arbitrarily split the tribal homeland, and as a small girl, ravenous, trudges through the reserve, she cannot help but note that "the animals ate, ate all the time . . . and there was nothing for us."

In another game park, this one private, weekend guests, leaving a cozy campfire, are driven by an African servant to watch, in something approaching awe, as lions feast on a fresh-killed zebra. The balance of nature is served when the driver hacks off a cut of loin, a small one: "The lions know I must take a piece for me because I find where their meat is. But if I take too much they know it also. Then they will take one of my children."

As in any well-planned tour, there are side trips—to London, where an intensely quiet Arab radical lures a commonplace Cockney girl to the ultimate betrayal; and, in blessed comic relief, to an English seaside resort where "a man who had had bad luck with women" finds a valuable ring, advertises in Lost and Found, and is braced by a beautiful claimant who couldn't possibly have lost it.

There are O. Henry endings that would make the master curl his toes in glee (the last four words of **"The Moment Before the Gun Went Off"** hit like a sledge). And there is even a parable.

The island of **"Teraloyna,"** whose original shipwrecked inhabitants have dispersed generations ago—some now white, some black, some "colored"—is now overrun by descendants of two imported cats. A planeload of young soldiers, one of distant Teraloynan heritage, is dispatched to get rid of the pests. "He is going home to the island. He is looking forward to the [fun] he and his mates will have, the beer they will drink, and the prey they will pursue—this time grey, striped, ginger, piebald, tabby, black, white—all colours, abundant targets, didn't matter which, kill, kill them all."

In this tour de force don't be afraid that you may misunderstand the guide. Gordimer is multilingual. She can speak male and female, young and old, black and white, and ginger, piebald, tabby.

Her voice is that of a Siren, simple words arranged like flowers, or embers:

—"The hyenas with their backs that sloped as if they were ashamed."

—"He went to the compounds where black miners had proudly acquired watches as the manacles of their new slavery."

—"Schoolgirls tramped onto the bus with their adolescent female odours and the pop of gum blown between their lips like the text balloons in comics."

—"We wanted to go away from where our mother wasn't and where we were hungry. We wanted to go where there were no bandits and there was food. We were glad to think there must be such a place; away."

These are Gordimer's tales. Go with her; there are things to see.

John Bayley (review date 5 December 1991)

SOURCE: "Dry Eyes," in *London Review of Books,* Vol. 13, No. 23, December 5, 1991, p. 20.

[*In the following excerpt, Bayley discusses the stories of Jump in the context of classic stories by literary masters of narrative art.*]

A Jane Austen of today is barely imaginable: but if one nonetheless imagines her, and locates her in South Africa, how would she be exercising her art? Could she find any subject other than the one Nadine Gordimer writes about? A great, even a good writer does not find his subject, it takes him over: he becomes it, and the world it has brought with it. But there exist situations in which this is necessarily not the case. Not only the subject but the way to treat it is handed to the talented South African writer in the most unambiguous terms. His success must be measured, not in terms of the world he has made by his art, but by what his art reveals of a particular world.

Jane Austen's sense of the society she lived in is subject to a variety of interpretations. D. W. Harding detected her 'controlled hatred' for it, while most of her fans regard her as supremely at home in it, using it as a vehicle for amusement and perception and something like comfortable fantasy. She repels and attracts; she can be attacked and defended. Nadine Gordimer, on the other hand, can only earn a chorus of dutiful praise. It must exasperate her sometimes to read that her novel or story is 'not to be missed' by anyone who cares what has been happening in South Africa; or that by revealing what has happened she has 'earned herself a place among the few novelists who really matter'. An honourable place, of course, and earned by the demonstrational sympathy and intelligence of **Burger's Daughter** and **My Son's Story** and **The Conservationist.** But her real talents are compromised by this style of celebrity in a way that does not reflect on them, yet imprisons them; and that seems not to happen to a novelist like Amos Oz, whose subject is not so much Israel and its future as some vision of his own about human beings and their spiritual insides. This is not the same as 'intertwining the personal with the political', and delineating 'each shift' in the African situation as a literary keeper of records'. With fans writing that on the dust-jackets of Nadine Gordimer's books, who needs depreciatory critics?

The success of the story or nouvelle stands in particular need of an equivocation the art of the form brings into being. A real masterpiece like *The Aspern Papers* reveals James's own fascination with the phenomenon of greed and power: the greed of the narrator for possession of the papers, whose ownership is poor Miss Tita's only weapon in her struggle for power and for possession of him. Every touch in James's evocation of Venice, like the statue of Colleoni, the indomitable warrior and ruthless mercenary, makes its ambiguous undercover point: and yet the touchingness of the tale itself seems not to be aware of what is going on, just as the governess-narrator in *The Turn of the Screw* is not aware of what is going on in the children's private world. This is the freedom of the story form, and it is a freedom sadly withheld from Nadine Gordimer's searching talent and narrative skill. **'Safe Houses',** one of the best stories in this collection [*Jump*], suffers from the parameters it cannot avoid. A white political subversive, in hiding from the Police in Johannesburg, meets a rich woman whose business husband is away on frequent trips to Germany or Japan. Their meeting on a bus—her car has broken down and she has never been on a bus before—and their subsequent affair is immaculately described; and the end is not betrayal, for she never finds out who he really is, but a succession of less glamorous safe houses and eventual arrest. The donnée of the story is of course the contrast between his own secret dedicated life and her idle and privileged one, but it is not a theme which allows room for manoeuvre, or freedom for the story to surprise us and itself.

And yet it is possible to feel the author willing it to have such a freedom, and putting her skill into two kinds of understanding of the pair. They are representative, emblems of their time and place, but they are also physically realised. Their relation is observed with the tough business-like sympathy Nadine Gordimer has developed over the several volumes of her stories. She is more at home with physical notation than with what goes on in people's minds. Her episodes are to inform rather than to move us, and this means that a story which explores its own possibilities is more likely to reach our emotional responses than one which indicates a proper way to think and to feel. These stories are trapped inside the nature of their event. In one, a white farmer accidentally shoots his unrecognised son, a black boy whom he favours and who goes everywhere with him. In another, **'Some are born to sweet delight',** a London family (locations outside Africa are left deliberately vague) acquires a Middle Eastern lodger. The daughter of the family falls in love with him and gets pregnant. She goes abroad to have the child with relatives, and he gives her a plastic toy to take to them. She thinks fondly of the way he watched without taking his eyes off her as she went through the barrier into the passport and security area. The plane blows up in mid-air.

The trouble is that a story can have nothing to add to such an event. Like Mérimée or Maupassant or Somerset Maugham, Nadine Gordimer seems most at home when no commentary is necessary: most of all when even an implicit ideology can be sidetracked. **'A Find'** is about a man powerful and prosperous enough to have got through two designing wives, and who then goes to take a bachelor holiday on a Riviera beach. Among the sea stones he finds a valuable ring, and decides to make use of it through an advertisement. The dénouement is admirably done, and the author seems rather disconcertingly at home in it, as if easing herself with a holiday from normal duties and commitments.

Connoisseurs of the short story will remember the use that Maupassant, Maugham and James all make of the same theme: the jewellery whose value or lack of it gives a quick print-out of individual human reactions. James is of course the one who in his tale 'Paste' ponders the notion most effectively, starting from the inheritance of some trumpery jewellery which turns out to be the real thing. The psychology of acquisition then breeds a whole new generation of victims and predators.

Nadine Gordimer wisely leaves her participants without any inner life. In her title story **'Jump'** this pays off with a Science Fiction setting in which a new black world houses in conditions of privileged nightmare a white renegade, a former 'supporter'. The awful futility of the isolation is treated inconspicuously and dryly, and the ambiguity of anti-climax has spread even into the concepts of revolt and repression. The image of a jump, a leap in the dark, borrowed from Conrad's *Lord Jim,* is neatly turned round, so that it never seems quite time to make the final gesture, the right moment for what was once the dangerous challenge of an assignment, and would now be simply the one to bow out on, to confront extinction. Freedom-fighting necessarily takes place in a slot like the one now occupied for life by the nameless hero, a slot isolated from the other realities of Africa—hyenas on the prowl, a lioness stalking a zebra—which are the subject of the laconic **'Spoils'.** Lamb chops flavoured with rosemary for camp dinner fit together, in the indefinable degradation of a 'safari park', with the excitement of watching from the safety of a jeep a carnivore devouring a herbivore. . . .

Barbara J. Eckstein (essay date Winter 1992)

SOURCE: "Nadine Gordimer: Nobel Laureate in Literature, 1991," in *World Literature Today,* Vol. 66, No. 1, Winter, 1992, pp. 7-10.

[*In the following essay, Eckstein discusses the political atmosphere of South Africa and how it affected Gordimer's career and fiction.*]

The world literary community has noted each year the prevailing tastes and proclivities of the Nobel jury. So rare was the choice of the Nigerian Whole Soyinka in 1986, for example, that it evoked comment from many quarters. John Kwan-Terry has speculated on the reasons for the exclusion of Chinese names from the list of winners. The paucity of women recipients is no less cause for speculation. In addition, commentary on the Nobel Prize traditionally includes the observation voiced here by John Banville: "The committee has always appeared distinctly chary of anything that smacks of art for art's sake, preferring its literature well salted with political or social concerns." Alfred Nobel's stipulation that his money reward literature of benefit to mankind [sic] and many of the jury's choices through the years do contribute to this perennial observation that artists' artists (e.g., Borges and Nabokov) do not win the Nobel Prize. Writers' and critics' common assumption that esthetic experiment and political commitment are incompatible is, however, equally responsible for this Nobel lore. The jury's awarding of the Nobel Prize to Nadine Gordimer in 1991 provides an opportunity not only to congratulate her for a reward earned through a lifetime's work but also to challenge the assumption separating esthetic complexity and political engagement.

Gordimer's receipt of the award in 1991, rather than earlier, speaks to the recent negotiations of the South African apartheid regime and leaders of the black majority population. The overt white supremacy practiced by the South African government has long been, at the very least, an embarrassment to Europeans and other people of primarily European descent, regardless of our own sins. Until that embarrassment had reason to abate, or seemed to, no white South African living in material comfort in South Africa, whatever the individual's stated resistance to apartheid, could receive a Nobel Prize, the major European prize. As a black African, the moderate but nonetheless worthy Bishop Desmond Tutu could receive the Peace Prize in 1984 for his resistance to the recalcitrant apartheid government. Still, separation of black rights and white rights being what they are in South Africa, the awarding of a Nobel Prize to a white South African would, until this year, have been untenable for the jury—or so I am guessing. This is, of course, not to say that Gordimer's prize also belongs to the South African government or that it deserves it. It is to speculate that, from the jury's point of view, the time is right to reward Nadine Gordimer and the political commitment her work has expressed for over four decades.

In her career, to date, Gordimer has published eight collections of short stories, ten novels, and two nonfiction works, has contributed excerpts from her fiction to two fine collections of photographs by David Goldblatt, and has given numerous interviews, now collected in one volume. This large body of work has prompted some reviewers and critics to assert that Gordimer is at her best in the short story and others to insist that the novel is her milieu. Having succumbed to this comparative thinking in the past, I now suspect my judgment—all these judgments—were based on the wrong question. Evidence of success in both genres disproves any assertion that Gordimer's talent is better suited to one fictional form than to another. She has also published less-polished pieces in both genres. Her work is not more accomplished in the one than in the other. Reflecting on her body of work, I realize instead that she repeats certain social situations in a number of works and

that this repetition sometimes results in powerful work and sometimes not. The question to ask, then, is how repetition of these certain social situations has served Gordimer's fiction.

In a recent essay Irene Gorak points to a situation repeated in much of Gordimer's work. "Interpenetrating white and black bodies . . . forms the hidden center of all her books," Gorak asserts. Gorak criticizes what she calls the political quiescence of this repeated situation, dubbing it "libertine pastoral." I agree that much, though not all, of Gordimer's work describes bodies, explores the role of sex in life, and imagines the possibilities and difficulties of interracial sex. But Gorak is wrong to see this crucial repetition as a separation of private appetite from social choice. Examining the role of repetition in linking Gordimer's esthetics to her politics and ethics, I find that private life and public life, desire and choice, are also inextricably linked.

I use the term *repetition* thinking of Edward Said's essay "On Repetition" and Henry Louis Gates's use of the concept of repetition and reversal to explain signifying as it is practiced primarily by African Americans. Both critics focus on what Said describes as "Marx's method [which] is to repeat in order to produce difference." Said concludes:

> Probably repetition is bound to move from *immediate* regrouping of experience to a more and more *mediated* reshaping and redisposition of it, in which the disparity between one version and its repetition increases, since repetition cannot long escape the ironies it bears within it. For even as it takes place repetition raises the question, does repetition enhance or degrade a fact?

Does Gordimer's repetition of black-white sexual relations "enhance or degrade" the fact? Is the hegemonic fear of rape by the black man that dictates the behavior of the white woman in **"Is There Nowhere Else Where We Can Meet?"** enhanced by the cruel law and white self-interest imposed upon the young black women with white sexual partners in **"Town and Country Lovers"**? Is the Utopian interracial union that represents a new nonracial political state in *A Sport of Nature* enhanced by the interracial extramarital affair that finds itself at the margin rather than the center of *My Son's Story*? To both questions I answer yes, in short, and see clear value in the mediated repetition. In other stories of interracial sexual union the repetition is less successfully reshaped. Even in these stories, however, one can understand the need for and the use in repeating the problem and the question in response to the apartheid government's reiteration of unchanging racialist answers and solutions.

But why this particular repetition, this "interpenetrating of black and white bodies"? An answer lies in these repetitions' struggle to elucidate what are the political powers of intimate relations. By this I mean not only how state political powers define the limits of personal desire by such acts as a law against miscegenation; but I mean also how all private spheres, all families of whatever ethnicity, perpetrate sets of gender and racial ideologies. This Gordimer shows masterfully in a number of pieces, among them the early story **"Something for the Time Being"** and the recent novel *My Son's Story.* Thus when sexual partners of different races meet, Gordimer postulates, a possible interpenetration of these different privately held ideologies occurs. In its best fictional forms this interracial intimacy asserts itself as more than an allegory for a nonracial state.

Racial supremacists' fear of miscegenation—promoted as fear of black man's rape and enforced by laws, lynchings, and torture—occupies considerable space in South African and United States history (to name two). That fear, obscured by violence, derives in part from the possibility that the interpenetration of ethnically different private spheres and their ideologies would result in ideological accommodations threatening to absolute separation and one group's assumption of supremacy. Individuals' attempts to wrest personal appetite or desire from ideological determination are social choices. Interracial sexual relations are one means Gordimer used to explore the possibility of a social choice free from ideological determination. Her fiction repeatedly demonstrates, however, that such choice is rarely, if ever, achievable in any situation. Nevertheless, in repetition is "mediated reshaping," the possibility of change.

South African writers of every ethnic origin face the question, "Am I politically radical enough?" Whether or not they ask it of themselves, it is asked of them by reviewers and critics both inside the country and out. Behind the question is the model of the martyrs, those South Africans, like Steve Biko, who believe that only overcoming fear of death will free them to oppose the apartheid regime as one must. Theirs is a standard of sacrifice difficult to match or to doubt. Reviews and essays about Gordimer's work frequently raise the question of political commitment through a comparison of her to another South African writer (often John Coetzee), and often these essayists formulate the comparison by means of the dichotomy between so-called modernist esthetic experiment and so-called historically determined revolutionary commitment. The usual strategy assumes that the modernist esthetic is ahistorical and therefore incompatible with political commitment. In 1983 Rowland Smith compared the work of Gordimer and Coetzee, arguing that her writing is historically grounded and, thus, preferable. Richard Martin begins his 1986 comparison with the promising idea that both Gordimer's and Coetzee's uses of history are borderline cases in their

treatment of realist and nonrealist form and content, but Martin returns in the end to the favored assumption. Paraphrasing Gordimer's review of Coetzee's 1983 novel *The Life and Times of Michael K,* Martin asserts that the novel demonstrates a revulsion of history. On the other hand, Martin concludes that Gordimer's 1979 novel **Burger's Daughter** is "at home in history and in language, [and so] the text can take its place in the struggle for . . . a solution." Irene Gorak turns the tables of the dichotomy in her 1991 essay, declaring Gordimer the modernist whose "radical aesthetic tradition [is] yoked to a quiescent political one" and quoting Coetzee's review of **The Conservationist,** in which he asserts that Gordimer's novel has not laid the Afrikaner pastoral to rest. Although my cursory treatment does not do justice to these arguments, it is, I believe an accurate characterization of the tendency to polarize narrative experiment and political engagement, the same tendency which influences Nobel lore. This polarization, together with the tendency also to compare Gordimer to other writers in order to measure relative political merit, elicits in me not the question "What should the relation of 'modernist' literature and political change be?" but "What *can* the relation between any literature and political change be?"

It is possible that no direct relation exists between literature and political change, regardless of how prescriptive or how paradoxical the literary form; but I reject the certainty of this idea, just as I do the certainty that literature does produce political change. Instead it is probable that no easily determinable relation exists between literature and political change. Gordimer clarifies in part why this is true in numerous stories about the difficulty of beginning and maintaining direct political action and the dubious relationship between that action and greater justice. *A Sport of Nature* aside, the skepticism with which Gordimer depicts political change in most of her fictions prevails; it is obvious, for example, in *A Guest of Honor,* **"A Soldier's Embrace,"** and **"A City of the Dead, a City of the Living."**

As a teacher of Gordimer's fiction, I have witnessed what the relation between her fiction and political change might be. All her best work undoes easy outrage and assumption about blame. It demonstrates the complicity with racist injustice of those who seem innocent, uninvolved, or even possessed of the correct sympathies. It teaches the careful student how to read politics as systems of power reaching into private life, lying with lovers. Those who learn what her fiction shows from affiliative bonds, links to consciously learned ideas challenging the intimate ideologies of unexplored assumptions. Whether or not these affiliative ideas provoke action and action produces change are another matter.

The strength of Gordimer's fiction lies less in what her

characters say than in her careful descriptions of how they move through different private, public, physical, and political landscapes. Her characters' essential gestures speak. They tell of the characters' cruelty and grace, vulnerability and will, desires and choices.

> The old man from Rhodesia had let go of the coffin entirely, and the three others, unable to support it on their own, had laid it on the ground, in the pathway. Already there was a film of dust lightly wavering up its shiny sides. I did not understand what the old man was saying; I hesitated to interfere. But now the whole seething group turned on my silence.

Characters within a story often repeat a gesture, turning habits of living into statements of belief, and sometimes Gordimer repeats a gesture of a character from one piece in another character of another work, but repeats it with a critical difference. These modest changes are both credible and moving. One such example occurs in two works separated by decades: **"Is There Nowhere Else Where We Can Meet?"** and *My Son's Story.* The first, the story Gordimer chose to begin her *Selected Stories,* describes a meeting in an isolated field between two strangers, a young white woman and a poor black man.

> . . . any move seemed towards her and she tried to scream and the awfulness of dreams came true and nothing would come out. She wanted to throw the handbag and the parcel at him, and as she fumbled crazily for them she heard him draw a deep, hoarse breath and he grabbed out at her and—ah! It came. His hand clutched her shoulder.

The ambiguity of this isolated encounter in which the woman interprets the man's gestures through the fear she has learned becomes in this second scene a passing encounter in a crowd. Hannah, a white woman, attends memorial services for slain young men in a black township.

> . . . moving over forgotten graves with the party from the combis she stumbled on a broken plastic dome of paper flowers and was quickly caught and put on her feet by a black man in torn and dirty clothes: *sorry sorry.* They were all around, those who had followed the convoy, and those who were streaming down from all parts of the township to the graveyards.

With the absence of isolation, separation, and unmediated fear in this second scene, the hand that seemed to clutch now quickly put her on her feet. This is repetition with a difference—not necessarily in the black man's hand but in the white woman's head.

While congratulating Gordimer on her achievement, it is important to concede what she herself would concede: her opportunities as an artist in South Africa between the 1940s and 1990s have, because of her "color," surpassed any available to artists of other "colors" whom political conditions have often forced into exile. Ezekiel Mphahlele, one of those exiles, gracefully illustrates this point at the end of his 1959 autobiography *Down Second Avenue.* Having escaped the confines of South Africa and gone to Lagos, he sits in a garden listening to Vivaldi and remembers an afternoon in Gordimer's garden where they also listened to Vivaldi. The memory serves as a reminder that Gordimer's garden could only be a temporary oasis; in Lagos Mphahlele felt the full refreshment of Vivaldi in his own garden. Perhaps the Swedish Academy has contributed to the dismantling of the apartheid government's separate systems of opportunity by honoring Nadine Gordimer's art and its resistance to injustice.

Nadine Gordimer with Claudia Dreifus (interview date January 1992)

SOURCE: "Nadine Gordimer: 'I've never left Africa,'" in *Progressive,* Vol. 56, January, 1992, pp. 30-2.

[*In the following interview, Gordimer discusses her work and political change in South Africa.*]

It was a frosty New York autumn afternoon, and Nadine Gordimer, South Africa's pre-eminent novelist, was sitting in the Union Square offices of her American publisher, Farrar, Straus & Giroux. Just a week later she would become the first woman in a quarter century to win the Nobel Prize for Literature and the second member of the African National Congress to win any Nobel. (Chief Albert Luthuli won the Peace Prize in 1960.)

Gordimer, sixty-seven, had come to New York to see her grown son, to do some public readings, and to promote her newest book of short stories, *Jump.* Like most of her fiction, *Jump* is full of realistic political tales of how apartheid destroys the souls of all who live in South Africa—though this collection also includes stories set in Mozambique, England, and the South of France.

During our two hours together, I mentioned that Gordimer had made the Nobel short list several times but had never received the award. "I *really* don't think about it," she said. "It's really unlikely to happen if I think about it."

A week later, the Swedish Academy made its announcement: "Nadine Gordimer, who through her magnificent epic writing has—in the words of Alfred Nobel—been of very great benefit to humanity. . . . Her continual involvement on behalf of literature and free speech in a police state where censorship and persecution of books and people exist have made her 'the doyenne of South African letters.'"

I spoke with Gordimer again, briefly, on the day of the Nobel announcement. The interview that follows is an amalgam of the two conversations.

[*Dreifus:*] **Jump** *seems like a set of transitional stories for you. Are you living now in a transitional country in a transitional time?*

[Gordimer:] Well, I always think of a line from Gramsci, "living in the interregnum." But you know, there have been few times in the last ten years that haven't been a kind of interregnum—in Europe, too, though that one will be more quickly resolved than the one in South Africa.

Few writers have been able to influence the politics of their place as much as you have.

I wonder if I have. A handful of South African writers, including myself, if we helped at all to bring about change there, we helped through our influence on the outside world. In what countries have writers been influential? It seems to be happening again now that you have Václav Havel in Eastern Europe.

In Latin America, the writers have been influential.

Yes, in Latin America. But it's pretty rare. Can you imagine writers influencing things in this country? Can you imagine a writer in England influencing? Absolutely not. And in France? It used to be, but no more—absolutely not. France used to, at least, have writers as diplomats, but not any more.

In a country like South Africa, we have nuisance value, because those of us who have become known overseas have certainly helped to inform people about what life is like there.

Is the Nobel Prize an endorsement of your anti-apartheid work over the years?

I really can't say. I can only say that if you look at the recent Nobel Prize winners, one couldn't say that the work didn't matter and the political commitment did. Who had ever heard of the Egyptian writer Naguib Mahfouz? He is not politically involved. Octavio Paz is a great poet, also not politically involved. The Nobel Prize is for literature, for the quality of work over the years.

Some of your recent writings have been set in places far from South Africa. Do you consider yourself primarily a South African or a citizen of the world?

I don't think I am a citizen of the world; I am very much a citizen of my own country. But my own country is closely related to other parts of the world and influenced by what happens there. I think this has happened more and more in my lifetime. When I was a child, we seemed to be living in a world remote from the rest of the world. But television has made a great difference to all of us. If something happens where I live, you see it tomorrow or perhaps even at the same time it is happening there.

It's not "one world" in the sense that conflicts are resolved in the world. But we are more one world in that we know what is going on and are psychologically influenced by what goes on around us.

The Afrikaner government long resisted putting television in. South Africa was the one place in the world where Dallas *wasn't to be seen on a Friday night. What was their problem with it?*

Well, I think they made quite a wrong calculation; they thought television would spread ideas that were inimical to the kind of society they were trying to preserve. But when television was brought in—now about twelve years ago—it was entirely state-owned, and they discovered they had been neglecting the most effective tool for the propagation of their ideas. From their point of view, they had made a mistake to keep it out so long.

I myself have not appeared on South African television.

Are you semi-banned from South African television?

I banned myself! I decided that I wanted nothing to do with South African government television while any of my fellow writers were banned and couldn't speak publicly. Once you have some sort of reputation in the outside world, they will try to woo you. They will say, "Won't you come and be on a talk program about books? That's not political." Then they can say to the outside world, "See how free it is, she appears on television. See how free it is." So I refused to have anything of mine read or dramatized on South African television.

In 1990, when the African National Congress and the other movements were unbanned and Nelson Mandela and our other leaders came out of prison, they had to make an agonizing decision, which was then passed on to the rest of us: whether to continue to boycott South African television. Nelson and our other leaders decided that the time had come to use television. Once he'd done that, we writers met and discussed our position again.

In the meantime, the cultural section of the South African Broadcasting Company was beginning to woo us. They wanted to do an in-depth program about my work. So I went to the African National Congress, of which I was a member, to discuss what I should do. We asked how this was to be done, if I would have final cut. I also made a condition that I wouldn't be told afterwards that it was a half minute too long and had to be cut. So everything that I said went out exactly, intact. It was quite a breakthrough.

When did you join the African National Congress?

A year ago last March. I had been a long-time supporter. I had identified with the ideas of the ANC, and now one could come out and make one's allegiance public. I still hope that many other white people will follow suit. There are many people who are sympathetic toward the Congress but haven't actually gotten to the point of joining. In Johannesburg, there's quite a large membership of white people.

Who are they?

Well, it's quite interesting. In the area where I live, they get a mixture of elderly people who've been in the left-wing movement—some were in the Communist Party—and you get fighters for justice and liberation.

People like "Lionel Burger," the fictional anti-apartheid leader of your **Burger's Daughter***?*

Well, people of that generation. And then, a lot of young people. Where I live is near the university, and a lot of the young people are joining.

And then, of course, you get an amazing mixture, because quite near where I live there's a crowded apartment-house area where lots of black people have moved in, whether it's legal or not. So this chapter of the ANC now has quite a lot of blacks, even though it is not near a black township or a black ghetto.

How did it happen that a neighborhood in central Johannesburg came to be integrated?

Well, it was a triumph of people power. Two things have brought about change in South Africa. One was the incredible endurance and determination of black people who really hung in there. One can't measure how a mood of confidence comes about. Somehow, in the last ten years, blacks have simply begun to move in where they've always been kept out. It's partly the fact that you could no longer run a country of something like thirty-six million people with four-and-a-half million whites. So areas where blacks have never been able to get jobs before have had to be opened to them.

Banks, for instance. Banks have had to train black tellers. And by blacks, I mean all kinds of people—people of mixed blood, people who are completely black, Indians, and so on.

Then people began to use facilities that had not been open to them, and with that came the confidence that when an apartment building had some apartments to let, when the building had been empty for some time, the owner would decide she would risk prosecution and black people would move in. And so this whole area is now full of people of all colors.

What have the last two years—as you've watched such intense social change in South Africa—been like for you personally?

Very exciting, certainly. It was something you would hardly believe would happen because it had gone on so long. It had been deadlocked for so long.

If the heroine of **Burger's Daughter,** *a young white woman whose father dies in prison for his anti-apartheid work, were living in the South Africa of today, what would she be doing?*

It's interesting that you asked. What was she doing at the end of the book? She wasn't active in politics. I think, as she put it, she was teaching victims of apartheid, children, "to put one foot before the other." Now that the ANC is unbanned, I think she would probably be running one of its branches. She would be living a much freer and open sort of life.

John Edgar Wideman, in a review of a recent book of yours, wrote, "Her withering insights deflate us; they show a fine contempt for the human species." Do you think that's accurate?

Totally inaccurate. I don't know what is meant by "contempt for the human species." It's the last thing in the world I have. I couldn't be sufficiently interested in human beings to be a writer if I had contempt for human beings.

Are the people you know personally happier now that apartheid has eased up?

Certainly the people who are close to me are happier. They feel freer. I'm thinking, for example, of a black friend, a regional organizer for the Congress. He's twenty-nine. At the age of seventeen, when he was in the youth group of the ANC, he went to prison, to Robbin Island, for five years. After prison, he went into trade-union work. He's spent his whole life in black ghettos in great poverty with great dignity. And now he and his young wife, who is an actress, have just moved into an apartment where only whites have lived before. They have no furniture there, just a bed for themselves, a bed for the baby, and a big TV, of course. But I think the very space around them is something extraordinary.

It's still a struggle, but they are living more fully than they did. But they are city people; for country people, things are as they were. They are very remote, very poor, very dependent on the white farmers they work for. It's very difficult to organize them.

There are still huge, huge problems to be tackled.

Doris Lessing, in the preface of her African Stories, *says Africa provides no end of source material, no end to the horrors and dramas and joys and the courage you can witness. Do you agree?*

About the joys and the courage, I really don't know what other people think. I just know that I've never left Africa. I've lived there all my life. And one of the wonderful things, in spite of all the terrible things that happen in South Africa, is the way people continue to keep their dignity. They continue to love, to laugh, to get pleasure out of life.

People come out of jail and pick up their lives and go on. I've met people in exile who have gone through terrible prison experiences—I'm talking about blacks now—and who've gone through all the terrible experiences that exile can mean, and suddenly they discover they've fallen in love. They marry and produce a baby—even though they know that they may be shot where they are, that they may have to move on to somewhere else, without any of the bourgeois calculation of, "How can I bring up children if I can't give them a settled life?" They just have the idea that you simply live your life to the full and accept whatever comes.

This idea that revolutionaries are martyrs who go around looking gloomy and noble, this is a romantic idea for people who've never met anybody who's gone through the experiences.

In your newest collection of short stories, **Jump,** *you have one about a Middle Eastern terrorist who moves in with a working-class English family, impregnates the daughter, and then sends her on a plane with a bomb. This sounds suspiciously like a true-life story that I read some years ago.*

Yes, it's one of the few stories in my whole life that has ever come out of three lines in a newspaper.

Could you say something about the process?

I read the newspaper account. Journalism picks up the dra-

matic point, but what led up to it? What happened after? How did these people meet? One simply doesn't know, so this intrigues the writer's imagination, and you invent the life.

I think Graham Greene once said, "We invent alternative lives for people." We catch a glimpse that intrigues us of somebody's life, and we invent an alternative life for them. And that's what happened with that story.

Did the events strike you as particularly horrible, so that you felt a need to write about them?

No. I mean, what he did was inconceivably awful. But if you've known people who believe that the cause they work for justifies everything, and that everybody else is to blame for this, and he belongs, as he must have, to some cell, and he's disciplined to do what he's told. . . . The mystery remains for me, when he started sleeping with that girl, or further on, when she was pregnant, at what point did he actually decide to give her that bomb to carry on? But to me this is what fiction is about; it asks questions, and it doesn't answer.

Another story in **Jump** *tells about the current nightmare of civil war in Mozambique through the eyes of one child-victim.*

People should know more about that situation. Two years ago, I made a documentary film with the BBC on Mozambique, on the South African side, where these camps are. And I realized, though I live just over the border from where these camps are, that I didn't know what a terrible, terrible thing this war in Mozambique is. And it is something being done in our name.

The changes in South Africa seemed to occur almost in response to the changes in the Soviet Union.

I think it was coincidental. The real influence of the events in the Soviet Union was to spread a lot of unease and anxiety in the African National Congress, because the Soviet Union had been the only country, really, that had stood by us all those years.

The West never lifted a finger or gave a cent to the African National Congress. America, England, Germany—everyone supported the South African government against the attempts of the African National Congress to bring about change. So actually, there was worry about losing that support—somewhat offset by the fact that now the ANC began to receive support from the West.

Of course, the strange thing is that the South African government is now madly wooing the new Soviet Union, or what is left of the Soviet Union. So we have Russian journalists there, and a Russian trade commission is coming, having lunch one day with the government and the next day with the ANC.

When Nelson Mandela emerged from prison two years ago, he seemed to be almost the last person on Earth who still spoke about "socialism."

I know. But the Communist Party is very popular in South Africa, especially among the young people. Never having had a chance to travel, and having suffered so much under capitalism, they still can't believe that the Russian people themselves have rejected it.

What are your impressions when you come to the New World Order, U.S.A.?

I come to this country a lot, and have for over twenty years. I've seen New York City, where my son lives, go up and down, and it seems to be in a down phase at the moment. People have had this idea of how wonderful it would be to live in America—the dream of so many Europeans, so many Africans—but it doesn't seem to be a desirable dream to have at all.

I find it odd how now, with the breakup of the Soviet Union, America has become so powerful internationally. You call the tune wherever you are, whereas at home, things just seem to be getting worse and worse. I would have thought this would have caused President Bush to lose a lot of popularity, because by and large people only care about domestic policy.

I wonder what's going to happen here, because it seems to me the material life in this country has decayed.

How do you feel about President Bush recently having lifted sanctions against South Africa?

I am pro-sanctions, and I was very sorry to hear that President Bush had made the decision to lift sanctions. I know, as someone living there, that sanctions have been tremendously important in forcing the South African government to finish the job.

If the sanctions are removed prematurely, what will happen?

I share the fear of Mandela and others that there will be a sliding back, that we will stay only halfway to freedom.

Thomas Knipp (essay date Spring 1993)

SOURCE: "Going All the Way: Eros and Polis in the Novels of Nadine Gordimer," in *Research in African Literatures*, Vol. 24, Spring, 1993, pp. 37-50.

[*In the following essay, Knipp traces the thematic development of traditional expressions of Western liberalism in Gordimer's fiction.*]

Nadine Gordimer's ten novels and seven collections of short stories constitute an impressive fictional achievement that is remarkable for its unity of vision and singleness of purpose. Gordimer has been preoccupied with a single great theme: the fate of ideological and methodological liberalism in South Africa since World War II. In interviews, essays, and speeches, she has clearly stated that she dislikes being called a liberal. Writing as a liberal and writing *about* liberalism are not the same, but Gordimer does both. Her commitment to the African National Congress and to the United Democratic Front are "radical" in the sense that they reflect her commitment to fundamental change—a *root* change—in the political and economic structure of South Africa. Nevertheless, values of the future South Africa that she envisions in her fiction, speeches, interviews, and essays (the values that form the moral basis of the struggle in which her protagonists are engaged) remain deeply rooted in a Western tradition of liberal individualism.

> Nadine Gordimer's ten novels and seven collections of short stories constitute an impressive fictional achievement that is remarkable for its unity of vision and singleness of purpose. Gordimer has been preoccupied with a single great theme: the fate of ideological and methodological liberalism in South Africa since World War II.
>
> —*Thomas Knipp*

In two of her most important essays, **"Living in the Interregnum"** and **"The Essential Gesture,"** she advocates non-racialism, constitutional freedom, and the writer's need to respect "the will to liberty" wherever it might appear. She is an outspoken defender of "basic rights" and "guaranteed" individual rights. In a 1987 conversation with Margaret Walters, for example, she says, "I am concerned with the liberation of the individual no matter what sex or color." The ends and premises of the liberal individualism that she defines in such statements are the same ends and premises that concern the protagonists of her fiction through whom she most fully delineates her moral vision. She herself recognizes this, admitting in **"The Essential Gesture"** that "nothing I say here will be as true as my fiction."

When she declared that learning to write "set [her] falling, falling, through the surface of 'the South Africa way of life,'" she was intimating that writing was, for her, the process of discovering the nature of state and society in South Africa. What she finds is a tangle of race and sex and politics. "In a fumbling way that sometimes slid home in an unexpected strike, I was looking for what people meant, but didn't say, not only about sex, but also about politics and their relationship with the people among whom we lived." She found what she was looking for, examined her findings from the perspective of liberal individualism, and reported them in her novels and stories. In the novels, this reporting follows two different narrative patterns. The minor pattern involves the presentation of South African life through the lens of a foreign liberal sensibility such as that of Toby in *A World of Strangers*. Variations upon this narrative pattern can be found in *A Guest of Honor* and *Occasion for Loving;* in the latter, it is interwoven with Gordimer's dominant narrative mode—a maturation plot in the form of a quest in which a South African girl (woman) searches for a liberal moral center in an illiberal land. This quest is Gordimer's great story, a theme upon which she orchestrates variations in *The Lying Days, Occasion for Loving, The Late Bourgeois World, Burger's Daughter,* and *A Sport of Nature.*

In these novels, similarity of plot and singleness of theme lead to the creation and variation of a single type of protagonist. Helen in *The Lying Days,* Jessie in *Occasion for Loving,* Liz in *Late Bourgeois World,* and Rosa in *Burger's Daughter* are all thoughtful, self-absorbed, self-reflexive, intelligent women who seek to make their way through the moral wilderness of apartheid. The fact that Hillela in *A Sport of Nature* is an antithetical character who does not engage in introspection merely serves to underscore Gordimer's awareness of the "unity in variety" of her protagonists. Hillela's life is also a sad commentary upon the failure of intellectual liberalism to transform South Africa. She does what others don't and can't do. She intuits the distinction between liberal ends and radical means, and she acts on the implications of that distinction.

Gordimer presents this search as a sexual guest. Eros is her primary symbol. Each heroine's success in harmonizing the psychological with the political—in moving toward a liberal moral position in an illiberal political context—can be measured in terms of the political attitudes of her lovers. In a sense, each of Gordimer's female protagonists makes love to her own principles. For example, Liz in *The Late Bourgeois World* moves from her origins in the white South African petite bourgeoisie through a marriage to Max, the failed radical, and a love affair with Graham, the liberal lawyer, to a flirtation and collaboration with Luke Fokase of the PAC. In all these relationships, including those that are not overtly sexual, Gordimer (or her protago-

nist-narrator) emphasizes the erotic. Luke and Liz have not made love by the novel's end, but their relationship is charged with eroticism:

> He put his hands at once on the top of my arms and let them slide down towards the elbow, squeezing me gently. We stood there a moment grinning, flirting . . . he gave me a little appraising lift, with the heel of the hand on the outer sides of my breasts, as one says, "There!"

Gordimer's ten novels were written during a thirty-seven-year period when South Africa was undergoing momentous changes. Through 1985 the nationalist government became increasingly fascistic, and the implementation of apartheid grew more ruthless and arbitrary. The options available to liberals changed during this period because many liberal attitudes and activities were declared criminal. Gordimer's fiction reflects these changes and marks the tragedies that occurred at Sophiatown, Sharpeville, Soweto, and elsewhere, but she herself always writes *about* liberalism and *as* a liberal. She writes about personal relationships and personal moral choices—about what Emerson called "the infinitude of the private man." For her, the individual moral choice is not just the focus of art but the pivot of history.

Liberalism can be said to function at four levels: as an ideology, as a mythology, as a collection of attitudes, and as a predisposition toward particular sorts of behavior. Ideological liberalism is rooted historically in Christian moral teaching and, as a secular political philosophy, has a long and complex history; but its fundamental principles are that individuals have rights, responsibilities, and the capacity for individual moral action. Over time these principles have been expressed through a variety of political and economic systems, sometimes giving rise, ironically, to structures and systems that contradict and subvert the principles upon which they themselves are based. International capitalism in its exploitative neo-colonial phase is an example of this tendency. The application of liberal principles across racial and cultural barriers has always been difficult and marked by failure. Numerous racial or cultural mythologies have emerged to justify these failures: manifest destinies, racial stereotypes, etc. Thus liberal principles have often become the bases of illiberal political and economic cultures.

An example of this process has clearly arisen in South Africa, where liberal political ideals are espoused by a minority of enfranchised citizens at a time when liberal attitudes and behaviors have been criminalized. Under such circumstances, liberals soon discover that traditional liberal institutions such as jury trials, legal codes, and proportional electoral representation have been coopted by an illiberal power structure. The challenge to the liberal is to find alternate forms of action that express liberal principles. The individual search for such principles and such actions constitutes Nadine Gordimer's major theme, a theme that she has projected as a woman's erotic quest. Politics and sexuality, *polis* and *eros*, public and private, move in tandem as the erotic becomes the vehicle for the political. If *The Lying Days* provides a paradigmatic example of this theme, her later works contain deeper, richer variations of it. *A Sport of Nature* might well be the summative formulation of the theme. (Note that the questing liberal heroine is absent from her most recent novel, *My Son's Story,* the protagonists of which are a black [coloured] father and son.)

The Lying Days is the first-person narrative of Helen Shaw's quest-journey from childhood to womanhood, from a South African mining town through the university and the city to Europe. This journey outward is also a journey inward, because, for her, the discovery of the other (i.e., the male, the black) is also the discovery of the self. Moving from a closed world to an open one, Helen's journey begins in the limited world of her mother, of whom she says: "Wives and husbands and children and the comfortable small plan of duties they owed to one another—for her, this was what living was."

The novel's opening incident compresses within itself the moral force and narrative design of the whole novel. Committed to an afternoon of tennis (a trivial pleasure in the closed world of white privilege), Mrs. Shaw hesitates to leave her daughter Helen alone. Her reluctance has its origins in the unarticulated fear of the suppressed black man:

> "You know I can't leave you on your own, the girl's out." Yes, I knew that, an unwritten law so sternly upheld and generally accepted that it would occur to no child to ask why: a little girl must not be left alone because there were native boys about.

But Mrs. Shaw does leave and Helen does go out, away from the closed world of the mine: "I went straight down the garden path and out of the gate into the world," she said, "somewhere I had never been," and "there were dozens of natives along the path." But if she goes out, she also returns, a pattern that is repeated several times in the novel.

The Lying Days is divided into three sections: "The Mine," "The Sea," and "The City." These are way stations on Helen's journey away from the closed world of the mine and toward an open, liberal world. Her quest is not unsuccessful, but it is incomplete. The progress that she makes is marked by her erotic encounters with Ludi and with Paul, and it is placed into perspective by Joel, the lover with whom she never makes love.

Alienated from bourgeois South African life and from its values, Ludi is absent without leave from the army. From a perspective based on his instinctive harmony with nature, he shows Helen the limits of mine location life, which, under "a surface of polite triviality," is "the narrowest, most mechanical, unrewarding existence you could think of in any nightmare." He makes her feel "lonely . . . for something [she] had not yet had," and his kiss awakens "the beginning of desire," but it is a desire he does not fulfill because of his own limitations: his lack of intellectuality and ideology. Ludi is a drop-out, but he succeeds in convincing Helen that she needs to escape from her own small world, and he launches her on a search for a world where sexual fulfillment and social commitment are the same.

Paul, a social worker struggling with the housing problems of the blacks in the townships, seems to offer the possibility of such a world. He works within the system to ameliorate the lives of blacks and, in his free time, he works outside the system to help them organize politically. Reflecting Gordimer's belief that love is a process by means of which sex and society come together as value and meaning in the person of a lover, Helen says:

> So I, who had inherited no God, made my mystery and my reassurance out of human love; as if the worship of love in some aspect is something without which the human condition is intolerable and terrifying, and humans will fashion it for their protection out of whatever is in their lives.

In fashioning her love, Helen focuses on the "aspects of Paul" that are traditional expressions of liberalism. "The job that Paul did first interested *then excited me*" (emphasis added), she says. In fact, she loves him because of his job, "the only kind of job . . . that could bring a white man deep into the life . . . of the Africans who surround us." Summarizing her love, Helen exclaims, "not only was Paul the source of joy, he was also at grips with the huge central problem of my country," the problem of recognizing and responding to the human individuality of black Africans. In other words, she loves Paul because he *embodies* the liberal ideology and *lives* the liberal agenda.

Or so she believes at the time: "I was at that stage in idealism when the gesture was satisfying in itself." What she learns is that the gesture (Paul's life) is futile. He himself becomes fragmented and sneers self-deprecatingly at his job: "It matters so little whether it goes on or not." He is, in reality, outside the historical process, doomed to irrelevance, not because his liberal ideology is invalid but because his traditional liberal methods are ineffective against the oppressive control of the apartheid state. A growing realization of this futility pulls the two lovers apart. Helen's love no longer has a viable context. As a result, she admits that, "intense love-making was all we had now." Her complaint, "nothing fits," suggests a dysfunction that is both sexual and social. "I loved Paul and part of my loving him was my belief and pride in the work he had chosen." The failure of the work is the death of their love. Thus, Paul proves to be only one encounter in Helen's ongoing search for herself in the selfhood of others.

Joel, the son of a poor Jewish shopkeeper in the mining town where he and Helen had grown up, embodies the traditions of a Jewish liberalism that endow him with the sense of self for which Helen is searching: "His nature had for mine the peculiar charm of the courage to be itself without defiance." Their friendship almost but never quite takes on an erotic dimension, but whether they are conversing alone in a house, picnicking in the country, or dancing in Durban before their respective departures for Israel and London, the erotic is always just beneath the surface of a relationship that is studded with symbolic action. With Joel she drives beyond the reef, with him she climbs the kloof.

Joel is Helen's guide through the moral swamp of South African life. She clearly accepts him as a mentor, and as she prepares to sail for London at the end of the novel, he offers her a final insight when he tells her that, in searching for herself in others, in attempting to fuse eros and agape (of which liberalism is the secularized ideological expression), she is both snobbish and lazy:

> "You always set yourself such a terribly high standard, Helen. That's the trouble. You're such a snob when it comes to emotion. Only the loftiest, the purest, will do for you. Sometimes I've thought it's a kind of laziness, really. If you embrace something that seems to embody all this idealism, you feel you yourself have achieved the loftiest, the purest, the *most* real."

The novel ends in the middle of Helen's journey. Armed with a heightened self-awareness and a tinge of disillusionment, she anticipates her London adventure calmly, knowing, "I'm coming back here." When she returns, she will have become Rosa Burger.

A World of Strangers is almost the structural obverse of *The Lying Days*. The protagonist is male, not female; he is outside the South African ethos looking in, not inside struggling to get out; he is selfishly liberal, not an avid seeker after a liberal basis for selfhood. Toby is a young English publisher recently arrived in Johannesburg in whom liberal principles have deteriorated into a thoughtless and self-indulgent individualism. He insists upon maintaining a "private life" and a personal perspective unencumbered by causes and commitments. Drawn into a friendship with Steven Sitole (a self-absorbed black) and into a love affair with Cecil (a thoughtless white suburban beauty), he keeps Sam (the committed black) and Anna Louw (the white activist lawyer) at an emotional distance.

> About South African life, Toby observes: I felt the attraction of this capacity for joy as one might look upon someone performing a beautiful physical skill which one has lost or perhaps never had. Lopped off, gone, generations ago, drained off with the pigment fading out of our skin. I understood, for the first time, the fear, the sense of loss there can be under a white skin. . . .
> I was drawn to the light of fire at which I have never warmed, a feast to which I had not been invited.

This effusiveness is sentimental, but Sitole's meaningless death awakens Toby to the real human cost of this *joie de vivre*, and the pain-filled lives of Sam and the other township blacks sensitize him to the exploitative racial basis of Johannesburg's vitality. His heightened awareness of South African reality and his growing commitment to black aspirations are symbolized by his willingness to act as godfather to Sam's newborn child. Nevertheless, *A World of Strangers* ends in uncertainty as Toby leaves Johannesburg, promising to return to his newly acquired commitments and relationships.

A World of Strangers is the first novel in Gordimer's secondary mode—that in which an outsider comes to terms with Africa by experiencing it and by placing his or her experience into a matrix of liberal values. *Occasion for Loving* brings this mode together with the dominant one in her fiction. The protagonist of this novel is Jessie Stillwell, a South African liberal in her late thirties who is contentedly married to a university lecturer in history. Like Helen Shaw, Jessie moved from childhood in a mining town through several erotic encounters, including two marriages, to her present situation in the liberal bourgeoisie. During the course of the novel, she discovers the ironies of this situation as she is drawn into the experiences of Ann Davis, a self-willed young woman who had been raised in England and who has a love affair with Gideon Shibalo, a black South African painter. As a witness to this affair and its consequences, Jessie comes to understand the untenable nature of her and her husband's liberal attitudes and behavior. Once again, *polis* is revealed in terms of *eros*.

Jessie's "journey" is a flight as much it is as a guest. It is a flight from her home on the mine location and from her mother, a symbol of white South Africa's emotional and intellectual aridity. Her first husband who had been killed in the war was a man whose limitations mirrored her own at the time of their marriage. He was father of Morgan, the son whom she does not and cannot love. When the novel opens, Jessie "still belonged to the height of life, the competitive sexual world." And "for the best part of eight years she had lived honestly, wholly, even passionately. But for some time now she had been aware that though this was the way she had chosen to live . . . it was not the sum total of her being." Such an existence did not satisfy all her inner needs because it did not respond adequately to the external realities of her world. That is, Jessie's life is inadequate because its characteristic liberal responses are ineffective in the face of the increasing repressions of the apartheid state. This inadequacy is epitomized by the career of her husband Tom, who is working on a history of Africans as invaded peoples rather than as "fauna dealt with by the white man in his exploration of the world." Tom's inadequacy and, by extension, that of Jessie, are symptomatic of the liberal failure, as an African colleague makes clear when he talks to Tom about the tightened restrictions on the education of Africans: "Fight them over this business if you want to, man, but don't think anything you do really matters." This sense of irrelevance marks the limitations of Jessie's inner life (*eros*) as well as the failure of her liberalism (*polis*).

In contrast to Jessie, Ann, like Toby in **A World of Strangers,** has an outsider's perspective and cultivates the selfish individualism of an unreflective Westerner. She "has no work of her own" and "is easily amused." She indulges "her impatience with . . . limitations" in small matters such as pushing her way to the head of queues and in the large issue of the love affair. However, she is interested neither in the limitations placed upon Gideon's life, nor in the politics that are contingent upon them. She is in love with his body and his talent, not with his principles and his struggles. The result is "a reckless love affair" marked by "emotional anarchy." She derives pleasure from scandalizing strangers in public places, and she has no compunctions about inconveniencing black people when she and Gideon are traveling together. Ann brings only ego and passion to the love affair, not awareness and commitment. But Gordimer (and Jessie) insist, "There are certain human alliances that belong more to the world than to the people who are amusing themselves by making them." Because Ann refuses to engage this world, to integrate *eros* and *polis,* all her attempts to flee from it with Gideon are futile. Their affair becomes a journey without a destination, an idyllic but ephemeral interlude.

Ann's blindness allows Jessie to see clearly. "Like a kid playing hide and seek," Ann flees with Gideon, willfully ignoring South Africa's political realities. "She did not love him across the colour bar; for her the colour bar did not exist." By denying the political realities of the larger world, Ann reduces their lovers' world to the dimension of the automobile in which they are riding; when the car breaks down, they are drawn back into the real world where they are obliged to dissimulate. In their final bid to live outside the real world, they seek seclusion in the seaside summer home where Jessie is spending several weeks with her chil-

dren. Initially resentful of their intrusion into *her* temporary escape from the real world, Jessie gradually accepts not only their presence but her own reluctant awareness of what they *mean* for her and in her world. As Ann becomes restive within the constraints of her limited world and anxious to have her affair resolved "by something drastic, arbitrary, out of her own power," Jessie comes to *know* Gideon in his blackness and in his particularity:

> A black man sitting in the car with the small ears they have, and the tiny whorls of felted black hair. . . . A black man like thousands, the Kaffir and picanin and native nig of her childhood, the "African" of her adult life and friendships; the man, the lover. He was these. And none of them. Shibalo.

Thus individualized, Gideon is drawn into Jessie's personal world. He becomes the temporary patriarch of her family, playing with the children, carrying them from the beach, holding them while they fall asleep. But unlike Ann, Jessie also sees *his* world "where people were born and lived and died before they could come to life."

Occasion for Loving is a subtle, complex novel. The core of it is the taxonomy of a love affair. The point of it is the response to the affair by a number of people who are differently situated in relation to the political realities of South Africa: Gideon, who knows "the only thing possible—the struggle"; Ann's husband, who "cannot kick a black man in the backside"; Ann herself, for whom "everything was taken for granted, everything that had ever been struggled for and won with broken bodies and bursting brains"; even Tom with his self-appointed task of writing history from a black perspective. But it is Jessie who learns from Ann's erotic failure to comprehend the limits of her own moral world:

> [She and Tom] believed in the integrity of personal relationships against the distortion of law and society. What stronger and more personal bond was there than love? Yet even between lovers they had seen blackness count . . . nothing could bring integrity to personal relationships.

> The Stillwells' code of behavior toward people was definitive, like their marriage; they could not change it. But they saw that it was a failure.

The implication of this discovery is not that the Stillwells should abandon their liberal principles, but that they should embrace a radical means of achieving them. And Jessie, who had come to see Gideon as a lover, albeit somebody else's, would be the one to act upon this insight. "Tom began to think there would be more sense in blowing up a power station; but it would be Jessie who would help some-one do it."

The Late Bourgeois World is the shortest of Gordimer's novels. A first-person narrative, it depicts the events that take place on a particular Saturday in the life of the pro-tagonist, Liz van den Sandt, who also recalls the past events that help explain the meaning of that day's agenda. At the beginning of the novel, Liz receives notice that her ex-hus-band has committed suicide; by the end of the novel, she has all but agreed to smuggle money into the country for Luke Fokase and the PAC. In the meantime, she visits her son and her grandmother and receives a visit from her lover. Liz's life reveals a pattern of personal experience similar to that of Helen Shaw in **The Lying Days**—a movement away from her origins and a simultaneous inward journey toward a moral center that would enable her to embrace radical means to achieve liberal ends.

Confronted by Max's death, Liz recalls his futile life. As an undergraduate Marxist, Max had rebelled against his family's "moral sclerosis" and its exploitative bourgeois gentility. At the time of his death, he was a failed radical. "Max, three years ago, tried to blow up a post office," but he was arrested, convicted, and imprisoned. During the trial, he turned state's witness. As Liz observes, "He wasn't the sort of person he thought he was." More importantly, he was not equal to the expectations she had for him:

> I wanted to make love to Max, and I wanted to give him the approval he wanted. I wanted to please him. But it wasn't a matter of watching your husband rising a notch in the salary scale. *What I wanted was for him to do the right thing so I could love him.* (em-phasis added)

Max is Liz's unsuccessful attempt to achieve the moral high ground of liberal individualism through the actions of a sexual partner—to define her own liberated self on the ba-sis of her lover's deeds.

Liz is presently involved in a comfortable, non-demanding love affair with Graham, a liberal lawyer who "defends many people on political charges." Graham works with and within the law; he "has defined the safe limits of what one can get away with." Liz asks herself: "If I wanted a man here at this time, in this country, could I find a better one? He doesn't act, that's true; but he doesn't give away, and that's not bad, in a deadlock." But for all his virtues, Graham demonstrates the futility of liberal methods. Due process, trial by jury, and other procedures are useless once they have been co-opted by fascists. He and, through him, Liz are among "the liberal minded whites whose protests, petitions, and out-spokenness have achieved nothing." All they really have is an inward daintiness and a code that does not address the real problems of "the people who . . . crowded in on us with hurts and hungers kindliness couldn't appease."

During the course of her long Saturday, Liz visits both her son and her grandmother, the white future and the white past in South Africa, but when the day ends, she is still contrast-ing the moral tension between means and ends in her own life as she dines tête-à-tête with Luke Fokase. A member of the PAC, Luke has requested that she smuggle money into the country by taking advantage of her grandmother's bank account. That is, he has asked her to go beyond the discredited liberal means that have achieved nothing—to go beyond the "safe limits."

During their encounter, the political and the erotic are united. Gordimer presents Luke's political request as a se-duction. Liz recognized Luke as "an expert in what might be called sexual regret: the compliment of suggesting that he would like to make love to you if time and place and the demands of two lives were different." His action and his words are a kind of foreplay. "He trailed the tips of his fingers along my ear and down my neck," Liz says. And he calls her Lizzy. "The play on my name, using incongruously, intentionally clumsily and quaintly the form in which it is a kitchen girl's generic, made a love-name of it." As the novel ends, Liz looks back on a day in which she has moved reflectively from Max to Gordon to Luke. She hasn't made love to Luke or promised to smuggle funds, but the reader is left with the impression that she will. In her mind, the two represent complementary aspects of the same experi-ence, part of the movement away from the mine and toward a racially egalitarian world. Lovemaking is a political act:

> A sympathetic white woman hasn't anything to offer him—except the footing she keeps in the good old white Reserve of banks and privileges. And in return he comes with the smell of the smoke of the brazier in his clothes. Oh yes, it is quite possible he will make love to me, next time or sometime. That's part of the bargain. It's honest, too, like his vanity, his lies, the loans he doesn't pay back; it's all he's got to offer me.

Burger's Daughter is a variation upon Gordimer's domi-nant theme and mode. Like its predecessors, it is the story of an outward journey which is also an inward journey—a quest during which the personal parallels the political. The erotic motif is more muted in **Burger's Daughter** than in the earlier novels and occasionally transformed into a se-ries of non-erotic personal and familial images of the in-terpenetration of the public and the private. This version of the motif is illustrated by Rosa's recollections of the on-set of puberty and of a later menstrual period when her mother and father were being arrested:

> The bleeding began just after my father had made me

go back to bed after my mother had been taken away.... But outside the prison the internal landscape of my mysterious body turns me inside out, so that in that public place on the public occasion ... I am within that monthly crisis of destruction, the purging, tearing, draining of my own structure.

The juxtaposition of "outside" and "internal," the fusion in the memory of the two "landscapes," the repetitive emphasis on the word "public" all bridge the gap between *eros* and *polis*.

The erotic motif is muted in ***Burger's Daughter*** because the main point of the story is Rosa's discovery that the love of her *father* and the love of her country are the same in the sense that they combine to impose a sense of commitment upon her. But, as with Helen and Liz, Rosa's erotic encounters are part of the process of discovery. As she withdraws from anti-apartheid politics after her father's death in prison, she becomes involved with the moody, self-absorbed Conrad, who has adopted an egocentric form of individualism. He says, "I don't give a fuck about what is 'useful.' The will is my own. The right to be inconsolable. When I feel, there's no 'we,' only 'I.'" Later, she recalls Conrad as part of the process by means of which she has come to understand her father's house, its *liberal* foundation, and her commitment to it. "The creed of that house discounted Conrad's kind of individualism, but in practice *discovered and worked out another*" (emphasis added). In the South African context, Lionel Burger's Communist Party membership is an expression of liberal individualism.

Indulging in her own version of Conrad's *selfish* individualism, Rosa leaves South Africa for the Mediterranean coast of France, where "you forget all about degrees of social usefulness." There she learns, or learns to articulate, the crucial distinction between liberal ends and liberal means, as this exchange illustrates:

> "Oh well, ordinary civil rights. That's hardly utopia. You don't need a revolution for that."

> "In some countries you do."

On the French Riviera, she enters into a love affair with Bernard, a member of the French leftist bourgeoisie. Ironically, his relaxed but committed liberalism helps Rosa to comprehend her own destiny as a South African. The thought process that culminates in her decision to return to South Africa is complex, but Bernard's assurance that "you can't enter someone's cause of salvation" and her awareness that she is gradually drifting into an acceptance of permanent exile catalyze the realization that her own salvation is at stake as well as that of black South Africans such as Bassie, her now exiled childhood playmate. Rosa learns that the only success is a life "that makes it all the way." Reflecting on her own attempt to flee South Africa and to build a life with Bernard, she concludes that "Nothing can be avoided ... no one can defect."

She returns to South Africa not to indulge in overtly radical behavior but to practice her profession as a physical therapist and to accept the fate of those who bear witness to the truth. She is imprisoned without charge together with her black friend Marisa Kgosana. There are homoerotic undertones in Rosa's attitude toward Marisa, who is first presented in terms of sexual splendor "jerking her beautiful breasts." There is also an erotic energy in the language she adopts to express her feelings for Marisa: "I felt a dangerous surge of feeling, a precipitation toward Marisa ... [a] longing to attach myself to an acolyte destiny; to let someone else use me, lend me passionate purpose, propelled by meaning other than my own." When she flees South Africa, Rosa "abandons" Marisa "without saying goodbye," and when she returns, she comes back to Marisa, who "got permission to be escorted to Rosa's cell twice weekly for therapeutic exercises for a spinal ailment she said was aggravated by sedentary life in prison. Laughter escaped through the thick diamond mesh and bars of Rosa's cell during these sessions."

Hillela, the protagonist in *A Sport of Nature,* begins her erotic and political quest more or less where Helen Shaw, Jessie, and Liz end theirs. She matures in a household where the adults are increasingly confronted by the failure of liberal modes of behavior to stem the advance of apartheid. She spends most of her adolescent years in the home of her liberal Aunt Pauline and Uncle Joe, a lawyer who defends blacks and activists indicted for violating apartheid statutes and regulations. However, unlike Rosa and other Gordimer heroines, Hillela is not introspective or self-reflexive. Early in the novel, we see Hillela as Pauline does: "One of the problems with Hillela was that she never seemed able to explain what made her do what she did." She responds to every situation in and through her body. Ben, the psychiatrist for whom she works briefly, reflects on "the unselfconscious ease with which she was at home with her body." Arnold, her radical friend on the beach in Tanzania, asks, "What are you saying? You don't trust anything but your own body?" She answers in the affirmative. The insight of her second husband, Reuel, is summative: "Everyone has some catch of trust, while everything else—family love, love of fellow man—takes on suspect interpretations. In her it seemed to be sexuality."

This seems unmistakably clear. For Hillela, eros and agape are the same, love and justice two aspects of the same experience. More unequivocally than in the case of Gordimer's more thoughtful and self-aware heroines, her erotic adventures are an integral part of a political quest.

This quest is anticipated by the friendship she forms, while at school, with a coloured boy and by the scandal that results in her expulsion from school. It begins in earnest when, having violated in spirit the taboo against miscegenation, she violates that against incest by seducing her cousin Sasha, a rebellious heir to the bankrupt tradition of decorous liberal behavior. She proceeds from Sasha to Andrew Key, the double-dealing radical journalist who made her aware "of the orchestration of her body conducted by him," to Udi, the aging German labor organizer who teaches her about commitment by not making love to her, to the French diplomat who becomes her lover. This social-sexual quest ends when she meets Whaila Kgomani, the militant Azanian revolutionary who becomes her lover and then her husband.

Whaila is the fulfillment of her instinctive erotic search to discover herself in the other. His blackness and maleness make her complete. She says, "When we are together, when you're inside me, nothing is missing." In her authorial voice, Gordimer says, "If Pauline and Joe had known it, the daughter of feckless Ruthie had what they couldn't find, a sign in her marriage, a sense and certain instruction to which one could attach oneself and feel the tug of history." In fact Hillela senses that this attachment will *produce* the political future—a new "rainbow coloured" people who will be free and in possession of their individual selves. With Whaila she had "animated confidence that she was escorting the first generation that would go home in freedom." However, he is assassinated by the fascists, and she miscarries her second child. One beautiful black daughter is all she has; Whaila and the unborn "rainbow" children are the price she pays for having found herself in the answering self of a black man. It is the price demanded by the political struggle against the apartheid state.

The last hundred pages of the novel are curiously futuristic and redundant. They constitute a reprise with variations upon the erotic journey/political quest that constitutes the first two-thirds of the narrative. At home in the cause of Azania, Hillela wanders the world on its behalf, encountering a series of lovers who parallel those in the first part of the novel—Karel and Pavel in eastern Europe, Bradley in the United States, and finally Reuel, her second black husband, the successful liberator-president of his unnamed country. At the end of the novel, a new flag is raised over a free Azania. Hillela attends the ceremony with Reuel, who is serving as the president of the OAU. Standing next to her black lover-husband, "Hillela is watching a flag slowly climb. . . . It writhes one last time and flares wide in the wind, is smoothed taut by the fist of the wind, the flag of Whaila's country."

In this image of the miscegenous lovers united under the flag of a free Azania, the liberal goal of the two-fold quest of Gordimer's heroines has finally been achieved because, in Hillela, the white sensibility has finally accepted radical means without abandoning liberal ends. This goal has also been achieved incrementally from one novel to the next. Helen leaves South Africa to test her liberalism, intending to return. Partly because she is witness to a miscegenous love affair, Jessie learns the futility of liberal means in an illiberal land. Liz hovers on the brink of commitment to radical means. Rosa completes the journey Helen had begun, accepting imprisonment as the inevitable consequence of her commitment to Marisa. For each protagonist, the erotic parallels and defines the political. For each protagonist, the act and process of love develop the soul and reveal the world and establish a connection between the two.

Hillela recapitulates and completes Gordimer's characteristic paradigm. She completes it by living the truth that William Plomer's protagonist had discovered and turned away from in the explosive 1926 novel *Turbott Wolfe*, the truth with which the liberal South African novel might be said to have begun. Wolfe loved the African woman Nhliziyomi and knew that his salvation—and South Africa's—resided in that love, yet he failed to act. From novel to novel, Gordimer's heroines move toward this truth until the moment when Hillela and Reuel stand together before the Azanian flag. The truth that inheres so tightly in the novels as to be part of their structure is really a plexus of truths: the journey outward is also a journey inward; *eros* and *polis* are the same—facets of the same existential experience; in an illiberal land, liberal ends require radical means; and finally, the most radical act in every sense of the word is the act of love.

Graham Huggan (essay date Winter 1994)

SOURCE: "Echoes From Elsewhere: Gordimer's Short Fiction as Social Critique," in *Research in African Literatures*, Vol. 25, No. 4, Winter, 1994, pp. 61-73.

[*In the following essay, Huggan applies Gordimer's short story theory to her practice, analyzing "Six Feet of Country" in comparison to three later stories.*]

Nadine Gordimer's novels have done much toward "articulating the consciousness" of contemporary South Africa. What is not often realized, or not realized often enough, is that her short stories also contribute to this articulation, and that the short story is just as well-equipped as the novel to attempt it. Gordimer has proved herself over time to be one of the foremost exponents in the world of the modern short story. Yet her critics have tended, almost exclusively, to focus on her novels. Why should this be so? The main reason for the critical imbalance in favor of Gordimer's novels might be brought down, perhaps, to a lowest common denominator: that critics have had and continue to have difficulty with the short story. The lack of theoretical groundwork does not help; for while theories of the novel abound, it has not been until relatively recently that short story theory has awakened academic interest, most noticeably in the United States. Recent theoretically informed studies such as Susan Lohafer's *Coming to Terms with the Short Story* and Bill New's *Dreams of Speech and Violence* act as valuable correctives to those who persist in seeing the short story as a "minor" genre or, still worse, as an incipient or microcosmic form of the novel. Two collections of nineteenth- and twentieth-century views of the short story, Charles E. May's *Short Story Theories,* and its "sequel," Susan Lohafer and Jo Ellyn Clarey's *Short Story Theories at a Crossroads,* are also particularly useful, although it seems significant that most of the views provided in either collection are by short story *writers* rather than by short story critics. It is in May's collection that Gordimer's most succinct statement on the short story can be found: her essay **"The Flash of Fireflies,"** which first appeared in *The Kenyon Review* in 1968. In this paper, I shall look first at some of the propositions put forward by Gordimer in this earlier essay, and compare them to later statements made in her introduction to the 1975 *Selected Stories.* I shall then go on to suggest how her short story theory may be applied to her fiction, beginning with a detailed analysis of the early story **"Six Feet of the Country,"** and continuing with brief, comparative comments on three later stories: **"A Company of Laughing Faces," "Livingstone's Companions,"** and **"Keeping Fit."**

The essay **"The Flash of Fireflies"** opens with the question: "Why is it that while the death of the novel is good for post-mortem at least once a year, the short story lives on unmolested?" Gordimer's contention is that "[i]f the short story is alive while the novel is dead, the reason must lie in approach and method." Yet how do the approach and method of the short story differ from that of the novel? Gordimer argues that the strongest convention of the novel, its "prolonged coherence of tone," is also potentially its weakest aspect, since it is "false to the nature of whatever can be grasped of human reality." The short story, which relates to "an area-event, mental state, mood, appearance which is heightenedly manifest in a single situation," is, according to Gordimer, "better equipped to attempt the capture of ultimate reality." Shelving for a moment the problem of what Gordimer might mean by "ultimate reality," I shall focus on her concept of "heightened manifestation." Reminiscent of Joyce's epiphanies or Woolf's moments of being, the "heightened manifestations" of the short story are posited by Gordimer as being particularly appropriate to modern consciousness, which "seems best expressed as

flashes of fearful insight alternating with near-hypnotic states of indifference."

> **Reminiscent of Joyce's epiphanies or Woolf's moments of being, the "heightened manifestations" of the short story are posited by Gordimer as being particularly appropriate to modern consciousness, which "seems best expressed as flashes of fearful insight alternating with near-hypnotic states of indifference."**
> —*Graham Huggan*

So far in her essay, Gordimer would seem to be doing little more than restating Frank O'Connor's influential thesis that the short story is somehow a more "authentic" form of self-expression than the novel, and that the self it expresses is more often than not lonely, alienated, idiosyncratic. Gordimer goes on, however, to ask what I believe to be the most challenging question posed in the essay: "What about the socio-political implications of the short story's survival?" For Gordimer, the novel "marks the apogee of an exclusive, individualist culture. . . [I]t implies the living room, the armchair, the table lamp." The short story, like the novel, presupposes leisure and privacy, but it does not have "the consistency of relationship" of the novel; because of its limited duration, fragmented form and immediate impact, it "depends less than the novel upon the classic conditions of middle-class life, and perhaps corresponds to the breakup of middle-class life which is taking place." It is not clear what Gordimer means here by the "classic" conditions of middle-class life. Presumably she is referring to the security and tendency toward a reassuringly integrated outlook that are reflected in the literary conventions of, say, the nineteenth-century realist novel. It is debatable, of course, whether the novel is as consistent and integrated, or the society it supposedly reflects as secure, as Gordimer implies; her own novels, in any case, expose the flaws and contradictions inherent in middle-class ideology. Her second point, however, is more illuminating: for if the short story corresponds to a breakup of contemporary life, its implicit expression of the disintegration of the existing social order makes it an ideal vehicle for radical social critique. The anti-authoritarian potential of the short story has not been lost on other commentators: O'Connor, for example, suggests that "we can see in it an attitude of mind that is attracted by submerged population groups, whatever these may be at any given time." It is precisely this attitude of mind which emerges from Gordimer's short fiction, corresponding to the short story writer's attempt to articulate what I shall refer to here as a "submerged consciousness." This hypothesis suggests that the reader should treat the primary narratives of Gordimer's short stories with suspicion, and should look instead for what emerges from beneath the surface or between the cracks of these narratives. Terry Eagleton's comments are useful here:

> It is in the significant silences of a text, in its gaps and absences, that the presence of ideology can be most positively felt. It is these silences which the critic must make 'speak'. The text is, as it were, ideologically forbidden to say certain things.

Eagleton is describing Pierre Macherey's theory of literary production, but he could equally well be describing the politically repressive conditions under which Gordimer's work has been—and continues to be—produced. In Macherey's model, however, ideology is unconsciously produced by the literary text; in Gordimer's, it emerges from a *deliberate* strategy of textual interruption. Repressed narratives rise to the surface and make their presence felt: a technique Gordimer uses most obviously in the novel *The Conservationist,* but which is used in intensified form in several of her short stories. The literary devices of inference and ellipsis—not restricted to the short story, of course, but at their most telling in the short story—are particularly well-suited to Gordimer's exposure of the politics of repression. By using inferential techniques to articulate a submerged consciousness, Gordimer identifies the short story as a powerful agent of social critique in a country where freedom is strictly limited.

Gordimer outlines her approach toward the short story more clearly in her introduction to the 1975 edition of her selected short stories. The problematic "ultimate reality" to which she refers in her earlier essay, implying that her primary interest is in portraying "universal" aspects of the human condition, is this time more closely identified with her immediate social environment. "A writer is selected by his subject [*sic*]," claims Gordimer, "his subject being the consciousness of his own era." The short story, in this context, is not political by design but by necessity: "ultimate reality" is indissociable from social reality. This does not mean that Gordimer's short stories need subscribe to the "dreary" social realism she disparages in **"The Flash of Fireflies"** but rather that, irrespective of their artistic handling, they are the products of a specific set of social and historical conditions. Gordimer suggests further that, since the writer is "selected by his subject," he or she is highly likely to inquire into the mode of production of his/her work, to explore both the social conditions which have given rise to it and the ideological presuppositions on which it is based. It is true of course that in her explicitly political novels (such as *Burger's Daughter*) and her implicitly political ones (such as *The Conservationist*) Gordimer does just that, but the most succinct and, in my view, most pertinent expression of the limits of the ideol-

ogy within and against which she writes is in short stories where an elided sub-text, submerged beneath the body of the presented text, implicitly challenges and undercuts the dominant narrative voice. I would like to demonstrate what I mean by taking a closer look now at some of the narrative tactics employed in Gordimer's short stories, beginning with the early story **"Six Feet of the Country."**

> **The literary devices of inference and ellipsis—not restricted to the short story, of course, but at their most telling in the short story—are particularly well-suited to Gordimer's exposure of the politics of repression. By using inferential techniques to articulate a submerged consciousness, Gordimer identifies the short story as a powerful agent of social critique in a country where freedom is strictly limited.**
> **—*Graham Huggan***

For a reader accustomed to the complex narrative displacements of Gordimer's novels, the apparently univocal and syntactically uncomplicated story **"Six Feet of the Country"** might seem disarmingly simple. The disarmed reader is the deceived reader, however, for the apparent simplicity of the story is part of a greater narrative strategy which consists in presenting the reader with an illusion of completeness while allowing him/her (if he/she reads carefully enough) to see through that illusion. The reader recognizes, in the process, that the content of the story is not so much contained in the form as *omitted* from it. The central technique, then, is that of irony; the most telling literary device, that of ellipsis.

The plot of **"Six Feet of the Country"** can be quickly summarized as follows: The anonymous narrator, a travel agent in the city, has bought a nearby farm for himself and his ex-actress wife in the hope that it will improve the quality of their lives and give some stability to their unhappy marriage. Neither happens, and matters are complicated further when Petrus, one of the black farmhands, informs the narrator that his brother has died. Petrus's brother is taken away by the authorities for post-mortem and duly disappears; but Petrus and his family insist on (and pay for) the right to bury their own. After some delay, the coffin is returned, and the funeral takes place; it transpires, however, that the body in the coffin is not Petrus's brother. The mistake cannot be rectified, and Petrus loses both his brother and his money.

The story seems well rounded: beginning with background, it proceeds with action and moves on to dénouement in conventional realist fashion. Yet, from the outset, the reader is led to suspect that the narrative is unreliable and incomplete. "My wife and I are not real farmers," says the narrator at the beginning of the story, giving the reader immediate grounds for suspicion: for if he is not a "real" farmer, who is he "really"? Significantly, we never learn his name; and although his is certainly the dominant narrative voice, the "real" voice is suggested as being *elsewhere*. This initial suspicion increases when we learn that his wife would like to be an actress (i.e., to play another role), and increases still further when he compares his wife unfavorably with his female visitors: his wife, "her hair uncombed, in her hand a stick dripping with cattle dip," is contrasted with "some pretty girl and her husband shambling down to the riverbank, the girl catching her stockings on the mealie stooks." The impression given to the reader in the first few pages is of an unstable marriage in uncertain surroundings; for the narrator lives neither in the city nor, properly speaking, on the land: instead of "having it both ways," he finds himself with "not even one way or the other but a third, one he had not provided for at all." The implication is that the narrator's control over his subject is at best limited, and that he is offering us a falsification—or at least an abridged version—of the story.

Out of this uncertainty, the possibility emerges of a sub-text (or texts) which tacitly inform(s) the reader of the "real" conditions that drive the narrative. This sub-text can be located in two areas: first in (his wife) Lerice's, second in (his farmhand) Petrus's version of events. That there is a large degree of coalition between these two versions is suggested by the narrator's discovery of a strange similarity between his wife and Petrus:

> She and Petrus both kept their eyes turned on me as I spoke, and oddly, for in those moments they looked exactly alike, though it sounds impossible: my wife, with her high, white forehead and her attenuated Englishwoman's body, and the poultry boy, with his horny bare feet below khaki trousers tied at the knee with string and the peculiar rankness of his nervous sweat coming from his skin.

Although their social status is obviously very different, Lerice and Petrus both occupy a *subordinate* subject position; as Martin Trump puts it: "Gordimer has perceived a common element in the degrading way in which black people and women are treated in her society." Indeed, the major source of irony in the story can be traced back to the narrator's failure to recognize that the third possibility, the one he has not provided for at all, is that his own patriarchal values are complicitous with the more obviously divisive and inhumane practices of the apartheid state. His failure to acknowledge his wife's right to her own voice is thus consistent with the authorities' failure to acknowledge the blacks' right to bury one of their own people.

Let me return for a moment to the notion of "submerged consciousness." Gordimer's belief in the heightened manifestations which suddenly illuminate the narratives of short stories to produce "flashes of fearful insight" can be interpreted in this context as an attempt not merely to capture momentarily an "ultimate reality," but to identify this reality with the emergent consciousness of a beleaguered social group (or groups). The two groups I have in mind, of course, are the blacks of South Africa and the women of South Africa and elsewhere. The narrator of **"Six Feet of the Country,"** rather like Mehring in Gordimer's novel ***The Conservationist,*** only provides the "principal" voice of the narrative; he does not provide the "real" voice, which belongs to a "submerged consciousness" functioning as sub-text to the presented text. In ***The Conservationist,*** the sub-text, Henry Callaway's *The Religious System of the Amazulu,* gradually comes to the forefront of the narrative to dispossess Mehring of his "inauthentic" version of events and relocate them within an "authentic" Zulu context. The sub-text not only destabilizes Mehring's narrative; it also provides an *alternative* narrative (even if, as Brian Macaskill points out, that narrative continues to function within a counter-hegemonic interruptive framework that eschews interruption as mere replacement). In **"Six Feet of the Country,"** however, the sub-texts of Lerice and Petrus are precisely that: sub-texts, drowned out by the patriarchal rhetoric of the dominant narrative voice. Neither Lerice nor Petrus is given an opportunity to give their side of the story, and when the opportunity would seem to arise, they are immediately cut off, or accounted for, by the narrator. Noticing that in Petrus's presence, his wife seems "almost offended with him, almost hurt," the narrator refuses to elucidate: "In any case, I really haven't the time or inclination any more to go into everything in our life that I know Lerice, from those alarmed and pressing eyes of hers, would like us to go into." Like Lerice, Petrus is condescendingly accounted for by the narrator; when he hands over the money for his brother's exhumation, for example, we are duly informed that "[t]hey're so seldom on the giving rather than the receiving side, poor devils, that they really don't know how to hand money to a white man." The narrator thus covers up his earlier, mistaken assertion that the possibility of Petrus ever obtaining the money was something "so unattainable that it did not bear thinking about." This persistent strategy of self-exoneration complements the central image of the story, that of Petrus's brother "somewhere in a graveyard as uniform as a housing scheme, somewhere under a number that didn't belong to him or in the medical school, perhaps, laboriously reduced to layers of muscle and strings of nerve." Buried and forgotten in some unknown place, Petrus's brother becomes a metaphor for an apartheid régime which withholds the identity of its subjects by denying them a sense of place. He also represents the disenfranchised voice which can neither speak nor be spoken about, being submerged instead beneath a strident rhetoric of authority that at best restricts, at worst annuls its own freedom of expression. The health authorities' mistake in digging up the wrong man, and their apparent unconcern in looking for the right one, thus mirror a mistake-ridden but self-exonerating narrative: a narrative that seeks spurious legitimacy by dismissing the whole affair as "a complete waste" and by glossing over potentially incriminating alternatives.

There are occasional moments, however, when these alternatives provide, against the grain of the narrative, their "flashes of fearful insight." Such moments, for example, are those when, in Johannesburg, "a black man won't stand aside for a white man" or when, during the funeral procession, "the old man's voice was muttering something. . . . [T]hey could not ignore the voice; it was much the way that the mumblings of a prophet, though not clear at first, arrest the mind." It is precisely when the mind is arrested, when the flow of the narrative is interrupted, that the flash of insight occurs. The reader is informed, at these moments, that the primary narrative has been false all along; that the narrator has either been consciously diverting us from truths he does not wish us to understand, or unconsciously diverting us from truths he does not fully understand himself.

Quite clearly, the narrator of **"Six Feet of the Country"** is not in full control of his narrative. His lack of control is made manifest in two ways: first, in his attempt to hide or cover up his mistakes; and second, in his ignorance of his mistakes, as when, for example, he ironically upbraids the health authorities for their lack of principle, unaware that their principles coincide largely with his own. It is significant that at his moments of greatest stress, the narrator experiences, or claims to experience, a sense of unfamiliarity. Thus, when he first sees the dead man, Petrus's brother, he admits to feeling "extraneous, useless"; similarly, his wife, in her moments of greatest emotional intensity, is described as looking "searchingly about her at the most familiar objects as if she had never seen them before." These admissions of unfamiliarity seem suspiciously disingenuous, however, for the narrator proves adept, throughout the story, at *laying claim* to the unfamiliar: a self-protective ruse that includes, for example, his perception of blacks refusing to stand aside for whites as "strange," or his description of Petrus's wish to give up a large part of his earnings to rebury his brother as "incomprehensible." In these cases, it is not that the narrator does not understand, but rather that he does not *wish* to understand: calling an action "strange" or "incomprehensible" becomes a convenient means of repressing its deeper implications.

Let me dwell for a moment on the further implications of the unfamiliar. Defamiliarization has been seen by many critics and theoreticians as a characteristic effect of the short story. For the Russian Formalists, defamiliarization was primarily a question of *stylistics* (the "making new" of form within the structure of the literary text through the "laying bare" of its technical devices); but for contemporary critics of the short story such as Charles May, it becomes a question of *epistemology* (the unsettling effect of the text on the reader's knowledge of the world). According to May:

> The reality the short story presents us with is the reality of those sub-universes of the supernatural and the fable which exist within the so called 'real' world of sense perception and conceptual abstraction. It presents moments when we become aware of anxiety, loneliness, dread, concern, and thus find the safe, secure and systematic life we usually lead disrupted and momentarily destroyed.

May concludes from this that "the short story is closer to the nature of reality as we experience it in those moments when we are made aware of the inauthenticity of everyday life . . . those moments when we sense the inadequacy of our categories of conceptual reality." As Gordimer shows, however, these categories of conceptual reality are based on existing social conditions and prevailing ideologies: the "familiar" and the "unfamiliar" are finally questions neither of stylistics nor of epistemology, but rather of social and cultural *context*. Defamiliarization therefore becomes a means of "laying bare" both the form of the text and the form of the society in which the text has been produced; by internalizing the defamiliarizing effect of the short story, making it operative on its narrator, Gordimer effects the critique of a society in which it is possible for the narrator's "ordinary" world to be the world of apartheid. By jolting the narrator's "categories of conceptual reality," Gordimer exposes the false consciousness of the narrative and validates the "submerged consciousness" beneath it.

"Six Feet of the Country" provides an early example, then, of the ways in which Gordimer uses the formal devices and generic conventions of the short story to social ends. Similar techniques are applied in a story Gordimer wrote nearly ten years later, in her fourth, ironically entitled collection **Not For Publication**. In the story, **"A Company of Laughing Faces"** (itself ironically entitled), the seventeen-year-old ingénue Kathy Hack is escorted by her mother to the beach resort of Ingaza for the Christmas holidays. In a company of dutifully laughing faces, amid the empty rituals of a holiday entertainment carefully orchestrated for Kathy and her adolescent companions by their overprotective parents, Kathy meets, and is seduced by, an arrogant young man. Shaking off his crude advances, shocked by the apparent indifference with which he makes them, Kathy turns her attention instead to a small boy of nine: a loner, like herself, who prefers his own company to the comforting anonymity of the crowd. But no sooner has Kathy befriended the boy than disaster strikes: the boy goes missing and Kathy finds him, drowned. Kathy cannot bring herself to break the news to the boy's big sister, however; and long after the boy is discovered, lamented, and—presumably—forgotten, Kathy still guards her complicitous secret.

In **"A Company of Laughing Faces,"** Gordimer uses inferential strategies—litotes, prolepsis, innuendo—to convey the ironic discrepancy between a world of glittering surfaces and a darker world within. The flash of fearful insight that occurs when Kathy finds the boy is a moment not of shock, but of recognition. For the lagoon in which the boy lies drowned, "not a foot below the water . . . held up by the just submerged rock that had struck the back of his head as he had fallen into [it]" harbors another secret: Kathy's realization that her "sight [of the boy], there, was the one real happening of the holiday, the one truth and the one beauty." As in **"Six Feet of the Country,"** a previously hidden sub-text reveals itself through layers of geographical metaphor. In the earlier story, Petrus goes missing and is never found; in the later one, the boy is eventually retraced. But both figures, in a sense, form the absent center around which their respective stories revolve. The boy's death and his subsequent unreported discovery by the protagonist allow for the articulation of a submerged consciousness that underlies, but also undercuts, the superficially "correct" but unprincipled conventionality of the primary narrative.

In **"Six Feet of the Country,"** Gordimer had used short story techniques to uncover a repressive politics of race and gender; in **"A Company of Laughing Faces,"** she uses similar techniques to expose the hollow value-system of a white middle class which seeks to disguise its privilege by "giving some semblance of productivity to [its] leisure." The adolescent holidaymakers in Gordimer's story seek solace in the crowd; initiated into this willfully homogeneous world, Kathy experiences the momentary "thrill of belonging." But she senses, even as she makes polite conversation with her newly acquired boyfriend, that

> the only part of her consciousness that was acute was some small marginal awareness that along this stretch of gleaming, sloppy sand he was walking without making any attempt to avoid treading on the dozens of small spiral-shell creatures who sucked themselves down into the shore at the shadow of an approach.

Through proleptic moments such as this one, Kathy foreshadows her own subjection; she also anticipates her alliance with the young boy whose drowning is itself foreshadowed when, in the "pause that comes in the breath-

ing of the sea," and muffled music from the beach tearoom wafts up to her hotel bedroom, Kathy imagines herself "under the sea, with the waters sending swaying sound-waves of sunken bells and the cries of drowned men ringing out from depth to depth long after they themselves have touched bottom in silence." Sights and sounds from below rise to the surface of Gordimer's fractured narratives, imposing themselves upon the consciousness of their narrators, their protagonists and, not least, their readers. The novel, says Bakhtin, resonates with a multitude of voices. So too does the short story, but many of its voices, and some of the most insistent among them, do not emanate from "within" the text; instead, they reverberate from "outside" or "beyond" it: from behind walls or beneath floors, from underwater or underground. Through their troubled visions and unsettling "absent presences," Gordimer's stories resurrect a series of unquiet ghosts; through their conspicuous silences, embarrassing interruptions, and vaguely threatening undertones, they orchestrate a sequence of echoes from elsewhere.

In the title story of Gordimer's 1972 collection *Livingstone's Companions,* echoes well up from the graves of Livingstone's eponymous companions: unsung heroes of his last expeditionary party. Sent by the newspaper he works for to retrace the steps of Livingstone's last journey, Carl Church finds himself drawn not to Livingstone himself, but to the pages of Livingstone's journals, where the celebrated explorer pays rich, if patronizing, tribute to those who died on his behalf. Searching for the graves of these "companions," Church loses his way and ends up at an isolated hotel: itself something of a ruin, a product of former colonial times, now a weekend retreat and haven for those, like Church, who seek temporary refuge from their worldly responsibilities. Church spends a few untroubled days at the hotel: "This sort of hiatus had opened up in the middle of a tour many times [before]," he consoles himself, "lost days in a blizzard on Gander airport, a week in quarantine at Aden." The difference? "This time he had the Journals instead of a Gideon Bible." But the journals, as Church discovers, open up a different kind of hiatus: a submerged counter-narrative that throws ironic relief on his own explorations in Africa; on his allegedly compassionate liberal politics; and on his frustrated desire for personal companionship.

In **"Livingstone's Companions,"** Gordimer employs similar interruptive techniques to those used in her novel *The Conservationist.* But the random clippings from Livingstone's journals, unlike the accumulated excerpts from Callaway's *Religious System of the Amazulu,* fall short of establishing an alternative narrative. Instead, they alert the reader to a submerged consciousness within the primary narrative: a consciousness which speaks the silences of the colonial past, but which also gives voice to the contradictions of a neo-colonial present. (Set in Central Africa, in an unnamed country which sets itself apart from the white-supremacy states south of its borders, Gordimer's story explores the ironies of an emergent nation which claims to have thrown off the shackles of its former oppressors—to have disabused itself of the legacy of the colonial past—but which continues to be driven by social, political, and economic differences: differences that are submerged beneath a rhetoric of national unity, but are clearly unassimilable to that rhetoric.)

By adopting a technique of multiple ventriloquism—Church speaking Livingstone speaking Livingstone's companions—Gordimer draws attention, once again, to the palimpsestic structure of her short story narratives. As in **"Six Feet of the Country,"** the sociology of narrative voice—who speaks, and for whom; who does not speak—is closely related to the politics of territorial claim. The owner of Gough's Bay Hotel, like the narrator in **"Six Feet of the Country,"** appears to have few doubts about her territorial rights. The graves of Livingstone's companions, she tells Church, are only two minutes' walk from the hotel: "My graves. On my property." But as Church discovers, the graves, and the submerged narratives they contain, cannot be so easily accounted for. Another grave lies alongside them: that of Richard Macnab, the original owner of Gough's Bay Hotel and its current owner's former husband. This grave, too, contains its own hidden story: a story, like the stories of Livingstone's companions, which effectively challenges the entitlement of the primary narrative. Who "owns" Gough's Bay Hotel and the land that surrounds it? Who is the story of Gough's Bay Hotel "about"? And why is the hotel still there: a survivor, like the graves of Livingstone's companions, from another era? These questions remain unresolved in Gordimer's story; by presenting a surface narrative which then cracks and ruptures to reveal other narratives sedimented beneath it, Gordimer articulates rival claims to a "new" but residually colonial country that remains, like the story itself, unfinished, unstable, and subject to dispute.

In a story from a more recent collection, *Jump,* Gordimer provides a further variant on the intrusive sub-text. A bird, trapped in a drain-pipe outside the protagonist's bedroom window, cheeps plaintively from somewhere behind the wall, disturbing his sleep, "penetrating the closed space of his head from some other closed space." As in **"Livingstone's Companions,"** a voice from elsewhere impinges upon the protagonist's consciousness, defamiliarizing the world of his everyday experience. The bird's accident reminds the protagonist of his own misadventure earlier that morning when, jogging in the indeterminate area between his protected white suburb and a neighboring black township, he had witnessed a brutal murder and had been forced to run: not for his health, this time,

but for his life. Unlike the bird, or the latest casualty of South Africa's intertribal violence (if that is the reason for the murdered man's death, for we never find out), the protagonist eventually gets away; but not before he is trapped into complicity with the events of the morning. For in a sense, like both bird and man, the protagonist has no place to go: he can only escape into further captivity.

As in so many of Gordimer's short fictions, the absent presences of the text—the suffocating bird, the murdered man—become the invisible nodes around which the story coheres. Both creatures are robbed of their most fundamental of rights: "the first imperative [of life] . . . to breathe." But breathing depends on space as well as air; and space depends, in turn, on social status. After witnessing the murder, the panic-stricken protagonist crosses over into the "forbidden territory" of the township, where he is rescued by a family who offer him temporary, if understandably grudging, shelter. The protagonist is well aware of his intrusion: the intimacy of his new—and wholly unfamiliar—surroundings "pressed around him, a mould in which his own dimensions were redefined. He took up space where the space allowed each resident must be scrupulously confined and observed." The inferences are easy enough to draw: the protagonist is reminded that the air is not his alone to breathe; that privacy elides privilege; that physical freedom masks psychological entrapment; that the accidental intruder can also be an inadvertent accomplice.

"Keeping Fit"—the title, once again, is heavily ironic—provides the latest instance of a preoccupation in Gordimer's fiction with the politics of space: a politics in which text and sub-text, surface narrative and submerged narratives, interact with one another in a complex imbroglio of territorial disputes. These disputes, needless to say, are conducted on unequal terms; but paradoxically, it is within the more concentrated form of the short story, rather than the more elaborate structure of the novel, that the enormity of this discrepancy makes itself most readily felt. It is hazardous, of course, to make categorical distinctions between the novel and the short story; Gordimer's fictions are no exception. But by using the inferential techniques of the short story to articulate the submerged consciousness of marginalized and/or oppressed groups, and by using the defamiliarizing effect of the short story to expose the moral bankruptcy of a white bourgeoisie intent on "naturalizing" its unearned privilege, Gordimer illustrates that the seemingly innocuous short story may well cut deeper than the ostensibly political novel into the fabric of society.

Rosemary Dinnage (review date 9 September 1994)

SOURCE: "In a Far-off Country," in *Times Literary Supplement*, September 9, 1994, p. 20.

[*In the following review, Dinnage outlines the narrative of* None to Accompany Me.]

For forty years Nadine Gordimer has been revealing to us the splendours and miseries of life in her extraordinary country; now in this latest novel [***None to Accompany Me***] she takes us through the dramatic and confused transitional period just before the establishment of South African majority rule.

The narrative (there is no "story" in the usual sense) centres on two couples, one white and one black, and parallel with the political events that carry them along, is an account of the vicissitudes of long marriages. Vera Stark (the name must indicate special endorsement for the character) has been married since the 1940s to Bennet. She has two secrets: their elder son may actually have been fathered by the husband she had lived with in a brief first marriage; and along the way, she has had an intense adulterous affair. As a lawyer she has been consistently involved over the years in the struggle for black freedom, while Bennet's role has been to run the business that supports the family. The other couple, Sibongile and Didymus Maqoma, have been even more deeply a part of the movement and have spent time in exile and in jail. Now, though, it is the wife, Sibongile, who has been chosen to help set up the new regime, and Didymus has to accept that he is an ex-hero. So in both couples there is a strong woman and relegated man.

As always, Gordimer impeccably exposes how the times they are living through affect every aspect of their lives. Vera can hardly bear the weight of Bennet's love, that it never changes: "It hasn't been taken up into other things. Children born, friends disappearing in exile, in prison, killings around us, the death of his father in the house, the whole country changing. It hasn't moved", she says in her exasperation to her son. Sibongile, on her side, has had to go through long periods of separation: "Parted so often; what happens in these partings, his, now hers, in the one who goes away? Is the one who left ever the one who comes back?" The comradeship of having to face violence and disruption together makes Vera closer to her black colleagues than to Bennet: she survives a physical assault with only a leg wound, while her friend Oupa dies slowly and excruciatingly from the complications of his own wound. The cruelty and injustice and punitiveness that are the background of their day-to-day lives are indicated at every point, simply taken for granted. Sibongile gets a letter telling her she is on a hit list. Bullets could come from a passing car, or through an open window; she has to go out of the house at unpredictable times, put out notes in case she never comes back, always leave things in place.

The politics of the time make new ethical dilemmas; Didymus's is that he once had to work in a camp for traitors to the movement. Terrible things were done there, and he had eventually managed to disengage himself. But the problem of keeping clean hands while opposing a soiled regime is one of the preoccupations of the group.

Vera gradually separates herself from her husband, who goes away on a visit from which, it becomes clear, he is not going to come back. The theme of woman alone, facing up to truth, finding herself (and so on) has become something of a current fictional cliché, and one feels a touch of disappointment here. But again it is the South African context that matters. It seems to be not so much Vera's past sexual secrets that dissolve the marriage, but the fact that she has been the active campaigner, going ahead alone. The marriage of Sibongile and Didymus remains close because, though they have been physically separated, as blacks they have to be together in their commitment. The question of whether South African whites can really belong on the continent is always implicit. But there are the splendours as well as the miseries of the country: dedication, sacrifice, heroism. In raddled, cynical Britain these come from a very long way off.

Richard Eder (review date 18 September 1994)

SOURCE: "Faces of Revolution," in *Los Angeles Times Book Review*, September 18, 1994, pp. 3, 10.

[*In the following review, Eder emphasizes the theme of change, both social and personal, in the South Africa of* None to Accompany Me.]

There are revolutions—the French, the Chinese, the Russian—that devour the children who made them. More often, perhaps, it is a matter not of being devoured but of being digested. A little ahead of the curve of history, as always, Nadine Gordimer writes of two anti-apartheid fighters from whom victory, like a river rising and jumping its bed, has begun to withdraw and leave stranded.

None to Accompany Me takes place in the blurred and confusing excitement of South Africa in the early 1990s. Nelson Mandela was out of jail and negotiating with the government, the black exiles were returning and change was happening too quickly to be legalized or stopped—or safe. What with so many straws, leaves and twigs in the wind, it was like Birnam Wood advancing.

Two of the characters, for example, meet at an elegant gallery. It was showing a black painter "whose work had become fashionable since city corporations and white collectors had seen such acquisitions as the painless way to prove the absence of racial prejudice." Gordimer is a master ironist; here she plays in light tones.

She can play in darker ones. Odendaal, an Afrikaner farmer, refuses to negotiate with several thousand squatters. At the same time—if you can't lick the devil perhaps you can make a profit off him—he quietly but unsuccessfully tries to get the government to proclaim the land a black township and buy it up.

In a patriarchal fury, but not really losing his head as it turns out, he enlists a band of white commandos. Nine squatters are killed and many wounded, including their leader, Zeph Rapulana, one of the book's pivotal figures and one of its richest. Zeph is not happy about it—Gordimer is rarely simplistic—but he recognizes the advantage. Both sides will profit. With nine dead, at a time when De Klerk and Mandela are subtly maneuvering toward change, the government will have to give the squatters the land. And Odendaal will be handsomely paid.

> **As other authors use sexual passion, Gordimer is able to use politics as the fine psychological matrix of her characters.**
> *—Richard Eder*

Two families are the center of the novel. Their fortunes, their nerves and their deepest sense of themselves all refract the change between the old struggle and the new times. As other authors use sexual passion, Gordimer is able to use politics as the fine psychological matrix of her characters. (In this novel Gordimer uses sex too, and in some detail, but she uses it awkwardly; it lacks pheromones.)

Vera and Ben Stark are privileged and conscientious whites. She has worked for 20 years as the indomitable moving force in a foundation that fought apartheid in one of its cruelest aspects: its forced displacement and resettlement of rural black communities. Her husband, a sculptor once, became a businessman to provide security for her dangerous life.

In their youth two of their closest friends had been Didymus Maqoma, a budding Soweto lawyer, and his wife, Sally. Their families would spend weekends together at the Starks' pleasant house, despite the apartheid restrictions. Then the Maqomas disappeared, ostensibly abroad. In fact, while Sally lived in London, Didymus went underground as one of the top leaders of the African National Congress resistance inside the country.

Now they are back. Among the hundreds of returned exiles

he has pride of place—a chauffeured car met him at the airport—as one of the movement's authentic heroes. But he had made enemies; and in any case his courage and fighting qualities are not what are wanted. Flexibility and the ability to negotiate with the white powers are what counts. Shockingly, he is excluded from the newly elected executive committee.

Sally, on the other hand, who had lived quietly during the fighting years and held their family together, is elected in his place. She had been put in charge of finding jobs for the returning exiles. To do so she had to deal with the business community; and she showed such tact, energy and talent for it that she has become a rising star. The night of her election, and his defeat, she rages and mourns in their bedroom; at the same time she feels a dizzying exhilaration.

Vera's passage is less marked and less dramatic. She remains active in her mission to fight for displaced black claimants. She works with Zeph against Odendaal. And, reluctantly, she will let herself be elevated to the mixed commission in charge of drafting the crucial document of the future: a constitution. Her decline has to do with a gradual loss of function: White heroes will no longer be relevant to the fight for black empowerment. The word itself is a displacement for her. "What is this new thing?" she asks Zeph. "What happened to what we used to call justice?"

There is a hint of "Animal Farm" foreboding here and in a few other places, but it is only a hint. Gordimer can at the same time be ironic about the changes, committed to them and capable of seeing the dangers. There are shadows on the new forces; there is also the infinitely promising figure—though with his own dangerousness—of Zeph. By the end of the book he has achieved stature, deepened mystery, and perhaps large promise.

None to Accompany Me is a political novel of intelligence and subtlety and it brings us news that we need. It is more than that, as well; though its more is somewhat less successful. The characters have an expository function, and for the most part what they have to expound is worked into their vital condition. Several are memorable; particularly Vera's endearing assistant, Oupa, who becomes a tragicomic victim of the changing times, and Didymus and Sally. Their reciprocal rise and fall makes a political point, but it is also a moving and beautifully imagined account of the intimate shifts within a marriage.

Gordimer works them all hard, though, and sometimes their duties wear their essences pretty thin. The writing grows rough when it tries to do too much, knotting into an odd mix of the baroque and the elliptical. This is particularly true with Vera, the novel's main voice. Her personal history, her emotions and her character get the fullest treatment of anyone. She has a gnawing will to power, as well as genuine nobility, and Gordimer works it into her two marriages and her two adulterous affairs. The more deeply she is opened up to us, though, the more effortful and less real she becomes. She and the author seem to need a certain distance from each other.

Measured distance lights up the book's most haunting link between the political and the personal. Vera's function as white mentor dissipates gradually; gradually too, she is growing old. Her last love—her husband has faded away—can exist only as a relinquishing. *No One to Accompany Me,* alludes both to the waning of all white hegemonies, even that of heroic idealism, and the waning of old age. Gordimer's novel is prophetic, and it has the very still quality of what is already passing. Your truest revolution is your clock's: recurring each 24 hours, always predictable and always a dismay.

Richard Bausch (review date 25 September 1994)

SOURCE: "After the Euphoria," in *New York Times Book Review,* September 25, 1994, p. 7.

[*In the following review, Bausch praises Gordimer's personal approach to social and political issues in her* None to Accompany Me.]

I read somewhere long ago that a good novelist is also a social historian; the operative word there is also. And while literary criticism, at least in the United States, has lately become more and more a kind of ersatz social science, where worth is judged according to social impact or a political agenda, one is always grateful for writers like Nadine Gordimer whose fiction is so often categorized as work of social significance, and who, when one actually reads her novels and stories, shows herself again and again, in the face of enormous pressures, to be insistently personal in her approach.

> We may turn to the historians, we may even turn to primary sources like newspapers and letters, yet it would be hard to find a more direct experience of the times through which South Africa has passed over the last 40 years than in the intimate portrayals Ms. Gordimer has given us.
> —*Richard Bausch*

Ms. Gordimer is concerned, as all good writers are and al-

ways have been, with the individual cost of the events she depicts. Because she has had a long career and has been prolific, producing to date 11 novels and 9 collections of stories, her writing life creates a kind of record of her troubled country. We may turn to the historians, we may even turn to primary sources like newspapers and letters, yet it would be hard to find a more direct experience of the times through which South Africa has passed over the last 40 years than in the intimate portrayals Ms. Gordimer has given us. Now, as the country tries to re-create itself, to make the shift from repressive white rule to a democratic government with full participation by blacks, Ms. Gordimer has, once again, provided a clear window through which to witness the ramifications of these momentous changes on particular lives.

None to Accompany Me concerns two couples, one white and one black, and the people around them—their children, the men and women they work with and have lived with and loved. While we are given glimpses of events through the eyes of each of them at various points in the novel, its central figure is Vera Stark, a progressive white woman, and experienced lawyer who has abandoned a prosperous firm to become a mainstay of the Legal Foundation, which "is not a legal aid organisation in the usual sense," but "came into existence in response to the plight of black communities who had become so much baggage, to be taken up and put down according to a logic of separation of black people from the proximity of white people." As Ms. Gordimer wryly notes, "a logic can be made out of anything; it lies not in the truth or falsity of an idea, but in the means of its practical application."

Apartheid has been defeated, and efforts to forge a progressive government are under way. The black couple, once exiles are in hiding, are struggling with the many changes wrought by the new reality. Didymus and Sibongile (Didy and Sally) Maqoma have a history with Vera Stark and her husband, Bennet, an English professor. But each of the four has a private history as well, a store of memories that lies beneath the euphoria of political liberation, that cannot entirely be put aside, even when they and their friends seem "giddy with discovery."

As time passes, new tensions emerge. Didy, his wife observes, "seems to be living in the past," unable to jettison his carefully acquired habits of deference and caution. Matters are not helped by the fact that Sally is a rising star in the new political movement—or that their 16-year-old daughter, Mpho, raised in England, is out of touch with the culture her parents have sacrificed so much for. There are conflicts for Vera, too—most immediately obvious in her work, where she and her colleagues struggle over policies for the redistribution of land, seeking to return some of it to blacks who were evicted during the long repression.

But all of these conflicts, while providing an outer shell of plot, serve mainly as a kind of shifting backdrop to the central drama of the novel, which takes place in Vera Stark's soul. Here is a journey to what, at least on the surface, looks like a remote kind of personal independence, a distancing in which Vera becomes, rather oddly only her public self. Her husband is "worried about her way of life, apparently so completely involved, in public, always part of group thinking, group decision, and so withdrawn outside that." But "wherever she was now, it was not a form of escape."

Paradoxically enough, as Vera seeks to disentangle herself we become ensnared in the process—because we have been allowed to know her in the way that we know any artfully created fictional character. We have shared Vera's memories and her own assessments of her actions. We have witnessed her nightmares and her hopes for some sort of authenticity, and we have eavesdropped on her failures of understanding. We know that she left her first husband to marry Ben, and that because she allowed that first husband to make love to her one last time after the divorce, her older child, Ivan, may not be Ben's son. She has been unfaithful to Ben, and she fears that it was because her daughter, Annick, divined this in early childhood that she has grown up to become a lesbian. Vera also broods over the broken marriage that her son describes in his letters to her from London. And she feels some sense of sorrow over Ben's very constancy; she is achingly aware of what he has given up to love her, as though it were a form of imprisonment to be that important in another human being's life.

This portrait of Vera's internal turmoil is delivered with a fierce clarity in the light of the social moment, so that external events give it resonance without ever taking over. There are no puppets in Ms. Gordimer's work, no mouthpieces; her people are all afforded the dignity of human vanity and complexity. Black and white, they are neither very noble nor very bad. They are people whose failures almost always stem from lack of courage—or from their stubborn attempts to journey toward self-knowledge.

As I followed Vera's journey, I kept thinking of the old existentialist idea that we are doomed to fail in our search for authenticity because authenticity requires solitude and we exist in society. Vera manages to divest herself of so much—her family, her whole personal life, really—that we feel her hard-won freedom as being ironic and sad. Her journey ends in a solitude that finally seems rather pathetic. This passionate presence becomes a quiet lady living in an annex, a sort of docent in the museum of her own private history, a committee woman. One middle-of-the-night encounter with a young naked woman in the corridor of her landlord's house makes us feel her separation, not only from her family, but from all the sources of joy.

About midway through this capacious novel, there is a passage that reports an attack on two people who are on a fact-finding mission; one of them, we soon learn, is Vera. Here the novelist addresses us directly: "What were they doing on a road far from the site of any state land on their itinerary? To know that would be to have to enter their lives, both where they touched and widely diverged, to be aware of what they knew about each other and what they did not know; where they had expectations, obligations operating covertly one upon the other. To know at least that much."

Even as she reminds us of how little we can really know, Ms. Gordimer's every fictional gesture aims at knowing everything; the result is what is, at times, an almost blinding particularity. In the midst of her affair, we are told of Vera's fears "that when she began to grow old she would become one of those women who have a fancy for young men, that she would dye her hair and undress in the dark to hide drooping buttocks and sad belly from a lover paid with—what? Gold weights and silk shirts are only the beginning. Thank God, no sign of any taste for young men was occurring, but the passing mistrust of self projecting upon the commanding outer reality of a community only just breathing under its own rubble . . . what meaning could the mistrust of self have, what reality, standing against that!"

The answer to this unanswered rhetorical question provides a kind of ironic reverse image of the way Ms. Gordimer's fiction really works: what meaning could these events, for all their enormity, have without the intensely personal mirrors of personality through which they shine forth?

Michael Wood (review date 1 December 1994)

SOURCE: "Free of the Bad Old World," in *New York Review of Books*, Vol. XLI, No. 20, December 1, 1994, pp. 12-3.

[*In the following review, Wood concentrates on characterization in* None to Accompany Me, *detecting autobiographical impulses in the narrative.*]

Prisons have opened, exiles have returned, the notion of apartheid is in ruins. Blacks have moved into white suburbs, a new constitution is being drafted, the old opposition is practicing for new habits of rule. But there are hit lists, muggings, murders; violent rearguard actions; there is a housing shortage, there are land disputes, squatters risking their lives to reverse old patterns of settlement. There are unheeded warnings that corruption doesn't vanish easily, and isn't a respecter of race or class or political and tribal boundaries. This is the last year of the old South Africa, or as Nadine Gordimer puts it in her new novel [***None to***

Accompany Me], "this is the year when the old life comes to an end." The year, as she says later in the same book, "of the last white parliament that would ever sit," but also of the rise of the swastika "from bunker to blazon."

History has moved on since then, and many things have changed (utterly) in a very short time. Other things, reports suggest, have changed less than we might have thought, former structures and familiar faces looking to linger well into the foreseeable future; and of course the moment just before change, that last old year, would in any case be a gift to any novelist who cared about times and places, and was ready for the formidable challenge the moment presents. But what sort of gift would it be?

Nadine Gordimer is interested in what history does to particular people, both those who embrace it and those who seek to ignore it, and also in what history forgets, or cannot afford to remember. The end of the old life, as a setting and a story, allows her to weave personal and political destinies into an inconclusive but disturbing question about solitude. "Perhaps the passing away of the old regime makes the abandonment of an old personal life also possible." Perhaps. But wouldn't you then just be exploiting the public moment, making a false equation between your needs and the country's? Or would you be saying that history really has written itself into your most intimate assumptions, that the end of public lying may be a start of private truth?

Vera Stark, the person around whom these questions circle in the novel, abandons everything *except* a certain kind of public life, her work on the new constitution and at the Legal Foundation, but what does she find? She gives up her property, the house that came to her with her divorce long ago, and becomes the tenant of a black landlord, ironically miming in white, so to speak, the insecurity of the black lives she has been trying to protect. She is fond of her children and her second husband, but has slipped away from them into a kind of anonymity, because her children don't need her and her husband does. The final straw, after an incident in which she has been wounded by casual assailants, is her husband's saying, after forty-five years of marriage, that he couldn't live without her. "What am I to do with this love?" she thinks; and to her daughter she formulates a riddling answer: "I cannot live with someone who can't live without me."

So what she has found is a form of privacy, an edgy kind of independence, something she used to seek, perhaps, in sex and infidelity, and has probably always sought in her work. She is free, let us say, but she has locked herself out of most of the things other people want freedom for. Her closest associate at the end of the novel is the man whose tenant she is, a former schoolmaster and representative of squatters' rights who is now "a director on the boards of several finance companies, a development foundation, two banks." There is no sexual activity between them—"sex had no part in their perception of each other except that it recognized that each came from a base of sexual and familial relations to a meeting that had nothing to do with any of these"—but Vera is disturbed and attracted by the echoes of sex in their friendship, an old "chemistry of human contact" turned to new uses.

Vera has gone too far, as one of the epigraphs to the novel suggests ("We must never be afraid to go too far, for truth lies beyond"—Proust) but her truth, if that is what it is, is pretty icy. The other epigraph, a haiku by the Japanese poet Basho—

None to accompany me on this path:
Nightfall in Autumn

—acquires, in the context of the novel, an oddly positive ring. It's only at the end of stories (days and seasons and lives), maybe, that you get to shake off all that company, and find the solitude you wanted all along. The difficulty of this novel, which makes it, in spite of the smoothness of its writing and a certain ready-made quality in a number of its characters, one of Gordimer's most ambitious, arises from this mixture of ice and fulfilled desire. You can't tell whether Vera is wonderful or repellent; you certainly can't feel sorry for her. "Everyone ends up moving alone towards the self." That is what Vera thinks, and she enacts the thought. But is it an uncomfortable truth or a simple withdrawal into egotism? If it were true, would it be so even in times of great change? Especially in times of great change?

Here is our last glimpse of Vera. She has just bumped, during the night, into the girl her friend and landlord is sleeping with; a sign that sex really is over for her, that she is outside all that too. She steps into the garden.

> Cold seared her lips and eyelids; frosted the arrangement of two chairs and table; everything stripped. Not a leaf on the scoured smooth limbs of the trees, and the bushes like tangled wire; dried palm fronds stiff as her fingers. A thick trail of smashed ice crackling light, stars blinded her as she let her head dip back; under the swing of the sky she stood, feet planted, on the axis of the night world. Vera walked there, for a while. And then took up her way, breath scrolling out; a signature before her.

This is courageous writing, because it gives so much away. It ends on an upbeat, and perhaps even wants to celebrate the cold as a kind of clarity. Vera has her wish, she has no regrets, she is free of the bad old world, part of the new one. She has done a lot of good in her life, she has rarely deceived herself, and she doesn't condescend to anyone.

She makes a pause in the night and she takes up her way; she still has a signature. But she is also blinded and freezing; the necessary fate, perhaps, of those who can't live with those who can't live without them.

The plot of the novel is quite slight, although it's not all about Vera. Her black friends Didymus and Sibongile Maqoma have returned from secrecy and exile to open politics at home, except that Sibongile, the former waiting wife, is the figure of tomorrow, while Didymus, once the man of action, is the sidelined hero. This situation causes them difficulties, but they handle them with grace. Their daughter, Mpho, half Zulu, half Xhosa, but mostly a teen-age Londoner, brings out the mild gush that black beauties tend to provoke in Gordimer:

> This schoolgirl combined the style of *Vogue* with the assertion of Africa. She was a mutation achieving happy appropriation of the aesthetics of opposing species.

Mpho gets pregnant and is forced to have an abortion. Later she takes off to study drama at NYU. Just the child of important people; not the future for South Africa. One of Vera's employees at the Legal Foundation is shot and appears to survive, but later dies of internal leakage from his wounds. Vera's son Ivan, who lives in London, gets divorced and sends his faintly delinquent son to live for a while with his grandparents in Johannesburg. Vera's daughter Annick turns out to be a lesbian who lives with a loving friend and adopts a baby. This is all very decent, but a bit perfunctory, as if Gordimer's mind were not entirely on it, as if the charm of Vera's austerity and the fine offhand intelligence of the prose had taken up all her interest. "No doubt every divorce is a soap opera," Ivan writes to his mother. No doubt if you can't concentrate on the details, and if you are surprised to find you are like everyone else.

What is striking in this book is its array of apparently casual insights: the sense of how much an old photograph reveals and conceals ("There's always someone nobody remembers"); the effect of old faces returning from clandestinity or dispersion ("the weight their lives had was the weight of the past, out of storage and delivered to those who stayed behind"); of a shantytown with an eager, unmanageable ambition to be a suburb ("The assertion of this half-built house is so undeniable . . . the sudden illusion of suburbia, dropped here and there, standing up stranded on the veld between the vast undergrowth of tin and sacking and plastic and cardboard that was the natural terrain, was something still to be placed").

There are sensitive discussions of violence, of moments when outrage gives way to a murky understanding ("If they killed that good man, why not deal back death to them—she understood with all her impatient angry flesh the violence that, like others, she called mindless"); and hauntingly, through this book dedicated to a moment on the edge of an extraordinary future, runs the refrain of a complicated loyalty to the past: not nostalgia, not guilt, but an acknowledgment of what Gordimer calls "uninterpreted life"; a belated and continuing attempt to see who we were. And who they were; and what "we" and "they" have meant. "Does the past return because one can rid oneself of it only slowly, or is the freedom actually the slow process of loss?"

Kathrin Wagner's book [*Rereading Nadine Gordimer* (1994)]is an intelligent and informed account of her "deep-seated discomfort with the claim that [Gordimer] should be seen as *the* spokesperson for white South Africa." Given this angle, Wagner can hardly be generous, but she doesn't explore her discomfort as she might. It's not enough to say that domestic audiences "may find merely banal what the outsider finds illuminating" or may think Gordimer's depictions of South African conditions "tired or clichéd." Wagner and the domestic audiences could be right, but we need to know what's banal or tired in the writing; we need to know that the natives are not just blasé or envious. We do know that fans are often as silly as they seem ("If one were never to read any other literature about South Africa, Gordimer's work would be enough"—Penny Perrick, quoted by Wagner); but that doesn't mean what they are seeing is silly. Wagner says South Africans share "an unease with the quality of Gordimer's vision, a sense . . . that there is something fundamentally unsatisfying and even misleading about her interpretation of the South African experience," but this is a strangely foggy claim. Interpretation scarcely ever sets out to satisfy, and Gordimer's fiction can be "misleading" only if we forget the partiality of all fiction, and also assume she is our only source of news. Similarly, it seems perverse on Wagner's part to assume that only liberals feel queasy about violence, and to attribute Gordimer's complex and courageous views on this subject to a "pre-feminist" construction of femininity ("such as the expectation that women function as the civilising, nurturing, all-giving and all-sacrificing power which would redeem the crude excesses of the male world").

It's true, though, that there is a certain "thematic predictability" in Gordimer's work, and that, like Vera escaping her family, we could long to be freed from the sheer political decency of what she is doing. Wagner finds at the end of **A Sport of Nature,** in the young woman who is allowed "to disappear into the political irrelevance of a private life," a "small but potent symbol of hope for a New World whose hall-marks will be not only a non-racial community of men, but also, perhaps more significantly, a society in which the individual will be liberated from the stranglehold of the imperative to radical political action." The trouble is that this sounds like a travesty of the liberal dream of ease ("Everyone ends up moving alone towards the self"), and I was only halfway through typing it out when I wanted to go back to politics.

None to Accompany Me is a novel about the deep politics of the unpolitical person, as well as about the intricate politics of political people. The solitude it projects is not a refuge but a zone of peace in an intensely contested place. Vera says she distrusts power because she has "belonged to a people who used it horribly." Her black friend Zeph says her work on the new constitution will mean "real empowerment for our people," and this delicate linguistic reflection follows:

> It was accepted tacitly that when he spoke of "our" people it was a black speaking for blacks, subtly different from when he used "we" or "us" and this meant an empathy between him and her. They continued to accept one another for exactly what they were, no sense of one intruding upon the private territory behind the other. It had come to her that this was the basis that ought to have existed between a man and a woman in general, where it was a question not of a difference of ancestry but of sex.

Ought to have. There is a poignancy in the tense, as if only a historical nightmare could bring us, and even then bring us too late, anywhere near this understanding.

Gordimer is quoted by Wagner as saying she has been interested "all my life" in the "oblique picture of the narrator himself, emerging from the story he tells and the way he tells it; an unconscious revelation." The narrator of *None to Accompany Me* is sprightly and personal, full of reflections, but doesn't give much away. Yet I can't help thinking that the figure of Vera, distinguished, lonely, admirable, a little forbidding, must have something of an autobiographical edge. When Vera steps out into the garden, Gordimer is not picturing the coldness she is often accused of, and she is not claiming for herself the warmth Vera lacks. She is saying: Don't think I haven't thought about this, don't think I'm not still thinking.

Jeremy Harding (review date 12 January 1995)

SOURCE: "Pale Ghosts," in *London Review of Books,* Vol. 17, No. 1, January 12, 1995, pp. 20-3.

[*In the following excerpt, Harding assesses the narrative strengths of* None to Accompany Me.]

. . . Nadine Gordimer's novel [*None to Accompany Me*] is set in the period after Mandela's release. It is about homecoming and transition. The heroine, Vera Stark, who works

for a progressive legal foundation, is not an exile as such, but she has lived at a distance from herself, which is slowly closed by her encounter with a black land rights spokesman, courageous, ambitious but unpretentious—virtues that are not confined to Mandela, but which try a novelist's skills, and occasionally a reader's patience. Didymus and Sibongile, old friends of Vera, have returned from Europe and Africa. Didymus, an ANC worthy, fails to land a senior post at home—his wife gets one—and it transpires that he has been involved in the persecution of ANC members (during the Eighties, both the ANC and Swapo detained and tortured their dissidents) up in some front-line state 'where the methods of extracting information by inflicting pain and humiliation learnt from white Security Police were adopted by those who had been its victims'.

This thread is spun pretty much in passing. It is taken up again at a party in Johannesburg, but here Gordimer forecloses any discussion by making the speaker a ludicrous cameo character—a young English journalist 'in a catfish-patterned dashiki', whose motives for bringing up the subject of ANC detention camps are suspect. Gordimer's books often unstitch their own politics in this way and, as derision of one thing becomes extenuation of another—or vice-versa—it does no harm, even at the risk of appearing a fool, to slip into a dashiki by about page nine and start mumbling one's objections; tricky, however, for readers who are close to Gordimer's world—everyday 'Movement' folk, of whom, and in many ways for whom, *None to Accompany Me* is an ordinary tale.

The rhythm of the novel is good. It glides easily from the inside of Vera's head, with its round-the-clock screenings—first husband, second husband, erstwhile European lover, thoughts on middle age, the struggle, children—to the outside, where events are moving almost as hectically. But the interior is always vivid while the world is sketchy, forever in draft. Being with Vera, whose sensibilities are the main thing, is like being on a ship at night in rough weather, where there is little by way of a view beyond the rise and fall of cabin furnishings. But this has its purpose. The rewards of personal freedom after years of general misery would not be grasped in a novel that divided its attention more evenly. 'Everyone ends up moving alone towards the self,' Vera reflects, in the calm at the end of the book, when she has left white suburbia. She has thrown over the old life, just as the old politics has been overthrown, and in her connection with the land rights activist, who embodies her own hopes as well as those of the people who queue outside her office at the legal foundation, she seems at last to become her own woman—'*herself* a final form of company discovered'. . . .

Philip Graham (review date 5 November 1995)

SOURCE: "On 'The Concealed Side,'" in *Chicago Tribune Books,* November 5, 1995, pp. 6-7.

[*In the following review, Graham describes Gordimer's artistic ethos as outlined in* Writing and Being.]

This collection of Nadine Gordimer's recent Charles Eliot Norton Lectures at Harvard University [**Writing and Being**] offers six lucid and interconnected essays on fiction that should be read by every serious reader and writer. Throughout this slim yet intellectually hefty volume Gordimer—the distinguished South African novelist and Nobel Prize winner—succeeds in elegantly explicating her hard-won artistic ethos, a moving and fluid blend of personal discovery and commitment to the wider world.

Gordimer's first essay, **"Adam's Rib: Fictions and Realities,"** explores with a wry eye the persistent desire of some critics and readers to play the game of "I Spy": trying to discover who a fictional character "really" might be. Such an endeavor is, of course, quixotic, for even if a writer "wanted to replicate, there is no seeing, knowing, the depth and whole of anyone, and therefore no possibility of so-and-so being you-know-who. . . ." Yet Gordimer is unwilling to embrace the counter argument that an author's characters are wholly imagined; instead, she writes, they are an artful blend. "Imagined: yes. Taken from life: yes."

Gordimer then offers a personal account of how she imagined the lives of people she only peripherally knew for the novel that is perhaps her masterwork, **Burger's Daughter.** She remembers seeing outside a prison courtyard a young girl she knew, the daughter of a political prisoner. As this child—white, privileged—waited for a brief visit with her father, Gordimer wondered "What was she thinking?" The result was a novel that, in attempting to imaginatively capture a moment in the life of a single person, grew to embrace the complex moral dilemmas of her divided nation.

Not until the second essay, **"Hanging on a Sunrise,"** does Gordimer explicitly offer her definition of literature: the "exploration of the possibilities of language, the power of insight to human behavior beneath its outward manifestation, the unending expedition into the mysteries of existence, the creation of a world of words." Fiction's crucial aim, she argues, is to uncover what she calls The Concealed Side, that elusive knowledge of the inner life that each writer must struggle to discover for him- or herself, for it has no "final containing design." Yet once achieved, each writer's truth becomes a secret home, "the final destination of the human spirit beyond national boundaries, natal traditions."

Gordimer claims that this always uneasy, always provisional understanding is a powerful source of strength, a place from which a willing writer can "counter the lie in one's society." For Gordimer, the highest form of literature is an unflinching acknowledgment of the inescapable mirroring of inner history and metahistory, "the pull between the personal and the historico-political."

> **For Gordimer, the highest form of literature is an unflinching acknowledgment of the inescapable mirroring of inner history and metahistory, "the pull between the personal and the historico-political."**
> —*Philip Graham*

To illustrate her point, she examines in her following three essays writers who have been molded by a particularly dramatic historical time and place: Chinua Achebe, Amos Oz and fellow Nobel Prize winner Naguib Mahfouz. In her lovingly detailed mappings of Mahfouz's *The Cairo Trilogy,* Achebe's *The Anthills of the Savanna* and Oz's *Fima,* Gordimer demonstrates that "where society is perceived as devious, all angles of approach to possible truth may have to be tried."

In her final essay, **"That Other World That Was the World,"** Gordimer returns to autobiography, a moment of personal revelation which, it becomes clear, she has been leading up to all along. She describes her early years as an isolated young woman in a South African rural community and writes poignantly of the physical and intellectual confinement of South African apartheid, which, she makes clear, extended to the white world as well as the black. Only many years after Gordimer left her parents' home did she realize that Archbishop Desmond Tutu had once lived a portion of his own childhood in the black ghetto across from her white enclave. "There was as much chance of our meeting then," she writes ruefully, "as there was of a moon landing."

Because Gordimer understood intuitively that she needed to create and discover herself in order to avoid becoming "the dangling participle of colonialism," she turned to the world of books, that other world that was the world: "I ate and slept at home, but I had my essential being in books."

Literary revelations led, inevitably, to personal and political revelations. At the age of 20, Gordimer, as a member of an amateur theater company, performed *The Importance of Being Earnest* in a black township. At first, the audience's easy laughter seemed to bless the production with success, but then Gordimer "came to the full appreciation that the audience, those people with drama, tragedy and comedy in their own lives about which we knew nothing, were laughing at us."

When Gordimer began her first attempts at creating her own fiction, her early stories were a looking outward as well as a turning inward. "In my desire to write, in the writing that I was already doing out of my pathetically limited knowledge of the people and the country where I lived, was the means to find what my truth was." So it was imperative that her personal and artistic revolution include the political revolution of her troubled nation. "I had to be part of the transformation of my place in order for it to know me."

Because Gordimer is as rigorous a thinker as a prose stylist, following the eloquent argument that she weaves through these six essays is a pleasurable task. Some readers, however, may find Gordimer's belief that fiction should be wedded to political commitment to be unnecessarily narrow. Yet if, as Henry James once elegantly asserted, the house of fiction has many windows, then Gordimer's passionately described view is bracingly clear and inspiring particularly when she declares, "The expression in art of what really exists beneath the surface is part of the transformation of a society. What is written, painted, sung, cannot remain ignored."

Nancy Topping Bazin (essay date 1995)

SOURCE: "Southern Africa and the Theme of Madness: Novels by Doris Lessing, Bessie Head, and Nadine Gordimer," in *International Women's Writing: New Landscapes of Identity,* edited by Anne E. Brown and Marjanne E. Goozé, Greenwood Press, 1995, pp. 137-49.

[*In the following excerpt, Topping Bazin discusses how utopian and dystopian visions of Gordimer's novels reflect past and present racism in South Africa.*]

However different their lives, Doris Lessing, Bessie Head, and Nadine Gordimer share the common heritage of having grown up in southern Africa. All three were profoundly affected by that experience. Their responses to the colonialist, racist, and sexist attitudes that permeated their lives have determined, to a major extent, the nature of their fiction. Their novels reflect the grotesque situations and bizarre human relationships created by prejudice, injustice, and the desire to dominate. These three authors focus on the mad nature of this social and political situation in southern Africa. In their works, dystopian and utopian visions of the future provide perspectives from which to view the nightmarish quality of the past and present. These writers seek to communicate the horror of what they have known and their longings for something else—other ways of being and acting than those that characterize not only most whites of southern Africa but also most people of all colors. . . .

The sight of a violent black man in Nadine Gordimer's novel *Burger's Daughter* functions . . . as a recurring spur for the protagonist, Rosa Burger, to persist in her political activities. Such moments make her intensely aware of the necessity for an alternative. Born and raised by white activist parents in South Africa, Rosa Burger is driving along when she sees a donkey-drawn cart with a woman and child huddled in terror among the sacks. The black driver, frustrated by his own victimization, in turn, abuses his animal and his family. Rosa sees him standing on the moving cart:

> Suddenly his body arched back with one upflung arm against the sky and lurched over as if he had been shot and at that instant the donkey was bowed by a paroxysm that seemed to draw its four legs and head down towards the centre of its body in a noose, then fling head and extremities wide again; and again the man violently salaamed, and again the beast curved together and flew apart.

For Rosa, the donkey, cart, driver, and mother and child behind him "made a single object that contracted against itself in the desperation of a hideous final energy." What that scene represents for her is:

> the entire ingenuity from thumbscrew and rack to electric shock, the infinite variety and gradation of suffering, by lash, by fear, by hunger, by solitary confinement—the camps, concentration, labour, resettlement, the Siberias of snow or sun, the lives of Mandela, Sisulu, Mbeki, Kathrada, Kgosana, gullpicked on the Island, Lionel [her imprisoned father] propped wasting to his skull between two warders, the deaths by questioning, bodies fallen from the height of John Vorster Square, deaths by dehydration, babies degutted by enteritis in "places" of banishment, the lights beating all night on the faces of those in cells.

Faced with so much suffering that she cannot determine when or how to intervene, Rosa's first reaction is to leave her native South Africa: "After the donkey I couldn't stop myself. I don't know how to live in Lionel's country." But later in the novel, Rosa Burger realizes that she cannot stay away and ignore this suffering; her place is in South Africa. She must rejoin the struggle. This is symbolized by the epigraph for section two of the novel: "To know and not to act is not to know."

Through writing her next novel, *July's People,* Nadine Gordimer seeks an end to the psychological and social madness created by apartheid or any master-servant relationship. She reveals how even the white South African liberals are collaborators benefiting from racist policies. In this book Gordimer presents a dystopian vision of the future. Through it she can perhaps move white readers to take action to abolish apartheid and the many injustices suffered by blacks, thereby preventing the situation described in the novel from becoming a reality. In *July's People,* violence has erupted. With the help of Cuban and Soviet missiles, the black Africans are taking over the cities, and the white Smales family is saved, presumably from death, only by the ingenuity of their servant July, who allows them to escape with him to his village. However, in the village the power shifts from the whites to the blacks, just as it had in the city. Roles are reversed; July, the servant, becomes the master. Once again there is dominance rather than equality.

Through depicting in *July's People* what it would be like to be a white person abruptly thrown into a basically hostile black African village, Gordimer conveys a little of what the black person experiences when thrown into an alien white environment. To survive in the white world, July had to learn English; Bam and Maureen Smales need to know, but do not know, July's African language. Unable to speak and comprehend the dominant tongue, they are rendered powerless. Unable to understand local customs or methods of getting food and necessities, the Smales family becomes almost entirely dependent upon July for its survival. Because Bam cannot be seen driving his own small truck, called a *bakkie,* July keeps the keys. A little later, Daniel, one of the villagers, steals Bam's gun and goes off to fight against the whites for possession of the country. The Smales no longer have any police protection, and both the chief of the village and July have the power at any time to deny them the safety the village provides. On one hand, they are—like the urban blacks—invisible, nonparticipants in the social system; on the other hand, they are totally visible because they are watched closely by every villager.

Both Bam and Maureen Smales lose their status and traditional roles when they enter the African village. Their marital relationship is destroyed by this breakdown of their social order. Powerless, Bam can no longer support or protect his family. He does not know anymore how to speak to his wife, Maureen, because, without their roles, they seem to have no self or identity. He is unable to see this woman he lives with now either as Maureen or as someone functioning in any of her past roles—wife, mother, partner, dance teacher, daughter; therefore, he views this female as "her." He views her as a presence whose "sense of self he could not follow because here there were no familiar areas in which it could be visualized moving, no familiar entities that could be shaping it." Likewise, Maureen can no longer identify Bam as the man she had known back home in the "master bedroom." No longer able to function as her financial and physical protector, he seems useless; "she looked down on this man who had nothing, now." When the village chief asks Bam to explain what is currently happening in South Africa between the blacks and whites, Maureen is quick to perceive that what he was really ask-

ing about was "an explosion of roles, that's what the blowing up of the Union Buildings and the burning of the master bedrooms is." Similarly, July had lost his macho role and status when he had gone to the Smales to work, for Maureen had been his daily master and he her "boy." July tells her bitterly, "Fifteen years / your boy / you satisfy." Just as Maureen lost her respect for her husband in the black African village where he had no power, the black African wife's respect for July had been permanently diminished by his lack of power in the white-dominated city. To become powerless and hence to lose control over one's own life mean a loss of social status but also a loss of self-esteem and a clear sense of one's own identity. This loss of identity and well-defined roles is central to the terror evoked by this South African dystopia.

In desperation, Maureen seeks to play a subservient and semi-intimate role with July. She discovers, however, that she, who had had control over his daily life, rather than Bam, the real white power, has earned all of July's hostility. Furthermore, she has absolutely no power over him anymore, for "his measure as a man was taken elsewhere and by others. She was not his mother, his wife, his sister, his friend, his people." His lack of response to her plea for a new kind of relationship makes her understand for the first time the true nature of their prior employer/employee interactions. She suddenly "understood everything: what he had had to be, how she had covered up to herself for him, in order for him to be her idea of him."

More quickly than Bam, Maureen sees the total impossibility of their situation. July will obey black soldiers when they show up in the village just as he had obeyed whites, and for the same reason: he is powerless. By hiding his white family instead of staying in town to fight with his own people, July was already a traitor, a nonhero. So, too, in the village Bam is a nonhero. He will not fight with the village chief, who wants to defend himself against the revolutionary blacks. Politically, Bam is on the side of the revolutionaries; ironically, these same rebels may kill him.

It is not surprising then that, deserted by Bam and July, Maureen runs toward the helicopter that one day lands near the village. From the noise of the helicopter, "her body in its rib-cage is thudded with deafening vibration, invaded by a force pumping, jigging in its monstrous orgasm." This masculine symbol comes down with "its landing gear like spread legs, battling the air with whirling scythes." Concerned only for her own survival, Maureen is instinctively drawn toward this representation of male power. Her fantasy is of "a kitchen, a house just the other side of the next tree." The book ends with the two words "She runs," and critics have speculated about what it is she is running toward. Will the helicopter contain saviors or murderers? If black men will be inhabiting the new master bedrooms of Africa, will Maureen be accepted inside?

In Gordimer's next novel, *A Sport of Nature,* she develops further this desire of a white woman to share the future of black Africans as an insider. Being in the master bedroom with the new men in power makes that possible. The white South African protagonist, Hillela, crosses over the racial barrier effectively, marrying first a black revolutionary and then a black ruler. Under their aegis, she works continually and efficiently for the new black Africa. The latter part of *A Sport of Nature* is a fantasy in which we witness "the proclamation of the new African state that used to be South Africa." Hillela can be part of the new world, but only because, as Nadine Gordimer says, "'Hillela is a kind of freak. She represents a break with all the ways that have been tried.'" Hillela is a "sport of nature" (defined in the epigraph as an "abnormal variation") in South African society, because she is free of racial prejudice. Distrustful of words, her decision making is determined by instinct and sexual passion. Meanwhile, her cousin Sasha, who makes decisions based upon political commitment, spends time in jail and then leaves the country. Despite his revolutionary commitment, he is unable to achieve the degree of integration into the black revolutionary societies of southern Africa that Hillela does through marriages.

Nevertheless, Hillela has to face the fact that the time was not yet right to realize her utopian dream of having an "African family of rainbow-coloured children." Loving the skin and hair of the Other cuts at the root of racism; yet love between a few interracial couples cannot by itself alter an oppressive social structure. Moreover, this white female/black male attraction often hurts the black female—which a close reading of *A Sport of Nature* and Gordimer's next novel, *My Son's Story,* makes all too evident. Physical and spiritual love between whites and blacks is one way to undermine the madness of racism, but that love will be fragile in a struggle for dominance or in a racist or patriarchal context—white or black. Will the new African government itself be free of racism, and will black women be empowered? At the end of this futuristic novel, the answers to those questions are not clear. Still, the image of an interracial couple at the founding of the new African nation suggests that racial harmony may eventually prevail.

For Nadine Gordimer, as for Doris Lessing and Bessie Head, the future could be a dystopia or a utopia, depending upon the decisions we make in the present. Growing up in southern Africa made all three writers especially sensitive to the barriers between people. Barriers that separate, based on race or gender or class, breed madness in individuals as in social policies. Their novels suggest that experiencing mystical moments and/or witnessing moments of grotesque human violence convinced them that

alternatives had to be found. Their dystopian fantasies and hallucinations help readers better understand the nature and the consequences of injustice and evil. Their utopian fantasies enable readers to imagine positive alternatives. In the words of Sasha, Hillela's cousin in *A Sport of Nature,* a utopia may be unattainable but "without aiming for it—taking a chance!—you can never hope even to fall far short of it." He concludes that "without utopia—the idea of utopia—there's a failure of the imagination—and that's a failure to know how to go on living." The novels of Doris Lessing, Bessie Head, and Nadine Gordimer make clear that to alter attitudes and behavior to support what is just, rationality and sanity are necessary. Until individuals not only know this but also act accordingly, the madness will continue.

Edith Milton (review date June 1996)

SOURCE: A review of *Writing and Being,* in *Women's Review of Books,* Vol. 13, No. 4, June, 1996, p. 8.

[*In the following review, Milton comments on the themes of* Writing and Being.]

Nadine Gordimer is a writer whose moral vision predicates her literary one. The same could be said, to some degree, about any writer one would willingly read. But I see Gordimer's perspective on good and evil as being quite different from that of many, or even most, of the thinking writers of our day: Gabriel Garcia Marquéz, say, or Günther Grass or Doris Lessing, who are so burdened by the madness of contemporary society that they often need to break out of the confines of realism to give sufficient voice to their sense of absurdity.

By contrast, there is something almost old-fashioned about Nadine Gordimer: not only because she stays within the limits of exactness and reason—even when she writes prophetically as she does in *July's People*—but because she seems to have been able to balance a sober, often somber, outlook with innate respect for her neighbors and the hope that the human race may deserve a future.

Perhaps this balance stems from a well-focused vision and a sure sense of where she belongs. There are remarkably few serious writers nowadays who describe the world securely from the viewpoint of their native place in it, or even of their accustomed place. Many live in exile, either voluntary or involuntary; and if they speak for a particular landscape or for a particular country—as Tolstoy did, and Hardy did, as Hawthorne and Balzac and Austen did—it is usually from the perspective of an outsider.

Nadine Gordimer, to the contrary, was born in South Africa, and has stayed there. She lives in Johannesburg; in her writing, certainly, as well as in some more personal ways that she insists were merely modest, she took part in the struggle against apartheid, until justice, finally, seems to have prevailed—though one should be cautious about all political prophecies. Far from being alienated from her world, she is deeply involved in recovering its good health and in its survival; her moral outlook is a matter of daily life, not a literary abstraction. One could call it, simply, her conscience.

Writing and Being, which encompasses the six Charles Eliot Norton lectures Gordimer gave at Harvard in 1994, bears witness to that conscience both in Gordimer's perception of herself as having done, if anything, too little and in the generosity and admiring insight with which she reads the writers she reflects on here. It is interesting that all of them share her secure sense of place—that, like her, they have documented, passed judgment on and suffered from the political and social conditions of their native countries—which are also where they still live. Gordimer is emphatic about the fact that none of the work she is discussing "belong[s] to the main stream of Euro-American literature. . . . These writers," she says,

> know *who* they are; their work is no part of the Euro-American search for identity; what it expresses is . . . not that the individual does not know himself, it is that as Amos Oz's character Fima says, *"his place does not know him."*

In her opening essay she speaks rather generally about the transactions between life and art, reader and writer, introspection and morality. The second essay becomes specific. It describes the work of several South African revolutionaries: the autobiographies of the quiet Carl Niehaus and the charismatic Ronnie Kasrils; the poetry of Jeremy Cronin, who is white, and of Mongane Wally Serote, who is black. With her third essay Gordimer arrives at the heart of her subject as she begins to draw evidence about the moral uses of fiction from the work of three writers. Her discussion centers on *The Cairo Trilogy* by the Egyptian Nobel laureate Naguib Mahfouz, *Anthills of the Savannah* by the Nigerian writer and activist Chinua Achebe, and *Fima* by the Israeli novelist Amos Oz.

The authors she has chosen are immersed, have always been immersed, like Gordimer herself, in the cultural milieu which they document. But though these are, I suppose, political novels in a larger sense, their political bias transcends the specifics of the world in which they are so firmly placed and looks towards the common struggles and insistent failures of human history.

"These . . . are works that go too far, they're after

Zaabalawi, looking for Home on The Concealed Side," notes Gordimer—who, it should be said, is neither at her most simple nor her most eloquent as a critic, particularly when she adapts this idiosyncratic series of borrowed metaphors and phrases to serve as her critical tools. Let me offer a translation.

Gordimer takes the concept of "going too far" from a passage in Proust, "Do not be afraid to go too far, for the truth lies beyond." The phrase becomes her touchstone for everything that is virtuous in literature. "Home" she defines as "truth . . . the final destination of the human spirit beyond national boundaries, natal traditions."

"The Concealed Side" translates two Aramaic words quoted by Amos Oz, and incorporates a concept I am at a loss to interpret—though one can pretty much intuit its meaning. As for Zaabalawi, he is adopted from a parable—something of a shaggy dog story, in fact—which Gordimer finds in *The Cairo Trilogy.* The holy man Zaabalawi, it seems, the object of a sick man's passionate pilgrimage, is so elusive that the poor invalid has fallen hopelessly asleep by the time the seer appears, sprinkles him with water and disappears again before he has woken up.

There may be a certain defensiveness in the eccentric wording Gordimer uses for her analysis: a sort of linguistic self-protection against the snobbery of more conventional criticism. But it is not without other uses. Once you become accustomed to her borrowed vocabulary, which is simultaneously homespun and global, what she says proves powerful. And you begin to feel a sort of intimacy with her, a sense of privilege both in getting to know the particular person she is and in being introduced to the vast subject she is addressing.

What she sees everywhere is incompleteness. In *The Cairo Trilogy* sons and grandsons struggle for political, moral and spiritual enlightenment but fail to overcome the damage caused by the primordial narcissism of the patriarchal system. In *Anthills of the Savannah* the battle for economic and military control—in an imaginary country much like Nigeria—stems from British colonial domination: but liberation merely contorts the already established injustice and sends violence into new and larger channels.

Gordimer describes Fima, Oz's verbally blocked and morally paralyzed poet, as suffering from "an existential heartburn the antacid tablets he's always munching after indigestible snacks are powerless to appease." Israel's suppression of the Palestinians appalls him. He is particularly disgusted by the sleights of language in which this suppression is habitually disguised. Something of an anguished clown, Fima "has *chosen to fail* in the terms of success his society recognizes because he believes it has lost its way. . ."

In *Fima*, Gordimer discovers emphatically two characteristics she admires: self-doubt and contradiction. She quotes a passage in which Fima meets a cockroach and, about to smash it with his shoe, recognizes himself: "He is himself the cockroach, and so are the blacks, and . . . the Palestinians. And he himself . . . is the hater, the persecutor, the one with the . . . raised shoe."

Her sympathies are clear. For Gordimer, one of the highest moral achievements may be an ability to disagree with oneself, an uneasy, self-contradictory humanity. Ambivalence is the attribute for which she commends Achebe when she cites his "deep distrust of Right and Left" and which she admires in Carl Niehaus, who can identify equally with the oppressed black majority for whom he is fighting, and with the white Afrikaaner oppressors who are his family and have become his enemies.

The strongest thread which runs through ***Writing and Being*** is a disdain for simplistic alliances and self-righteousness; with each essay, this thread—and the writing itself—becomes stronger. The last essay addresses colonialism—less in its conventional political and cultural dimension than as a potent state of mind. Diffidently and sketchily, Gordimer outlines her South African growing-up. She is wary of autobiography, but she paints a formidable portrait of colonialism as a species of exile. Since law and custom permit her no association with Africans, she can have no understanding of Africa. Though she is brought up on the model of the proper English schoolgirl, she has never been near England. She grows up, in effect, marooned between two societies, a dismal condition which she notes was shared by Marguerite Duras, who spent her early years in Indochina, and by Albert Camus, raised in Algeria. "Colonial: that's the story of who I am," she writes of her childhood. "The one who belongs nowhere. The one who has no national mould."

Yet it strikes me that this state of isolation she describes has given her place and purpose. In the end, her condition as outcast in her own country has served her well: she has stayed in place and her place has come to know her. When her personal triumph in the wake of South Africa's newly-found democracy leads her to declare "I am no longer a colonial. I may now speak of 'my people,'" most of us can only envy her. And remark how few writers there are, these days, with an equal sense of hope or of belonging.

FURTHER READING

Criticism

Beauman, Sally. Review of *Livingstone's Companions*, by Nadine Gordimer. *New York Times Book Review* (31 October 1971): 6, 22.
    Lauds the stories in Gordimer's *Livingstone's Companions*.

Broyard, Anatole. "The New African Landscape." *New York Times* CXXI, No. 41,554 (1 November 1971): 39.
    Presents a stylistic and thematic overview of Gordimer's *Livingstone's Companions*.

Digilio, Alice. "South Africa and the Storyteller." *Washington Post Book World* XIV, No. 29 (15 July 1984): 4-5.
    Asserts that there are some weak links in Gordimer's *Something Out There*.

Enright, D. J. "Which New Era?" *Times Literary Supplement*, No. 4,226 (30 March 1984): 328.
    Discusses Gordimer's *Something Out There* and asserts that "Nadine Gordimer survives as a writer of distinction by virtue less of her themes than of her distinction as a writer."

Hayes, Richard. "The Moment of Illumination." *Commonweal* LVI, No. 8 (30 May 1952): 204.
    Lauds the stories in Gordimer's *The Soft Voice of the Serpent*.

Jones, D. A. N. "Limited by the Law." *Times Literary Supplement*, No. 3,852 (9 January 1976): 25.
    Discusses Gordimer's *Selected Stories* and asserts that "Besides being a good sort of propaganda, these stories are gracefully and, sometimes, beautifully written, and may be read as poems."

Kanga, Firdaus. "A question of black and white." *Times Literary Supplement*, No. 4,619 (11 October 1991): 14.
    Lauds Gordimer's brilliance in *Jump and Other Stories*, but points out some extravagances in her style.

King, Bruce. *The Later Fiction of Nadine Gordimer.* New York: St. Martin's Press, 1993, 249 p.
    Provides critical analysis of Gordimer's later fiction.

Mathabone, Mark. "Tales of the White Tribe." *Washington Post Book World* XXI, No. 36 (8 September 1991): 9.
    Discusses Gordimer's *Jump and Other Stories*.

Mazurek, Raymond A. "Gordimer's 'Something Out There' and Ndebele's 'Fools' and Other Stories: The Politics of Literary Form." *Studies in Short Fiction* 26, No. 1 (Winter 1989): 71-9.

Compares the role of politics in the work of Nadine Gordimer and Njabulo Ndebele.

Nordell, Rod. "Miss Gordimer and Africa." *Christian Science Monitor* 48, No. 270 (11 October 1956): 10.
Discusses the stories in Gordimer's *Six Feet of the Country* and asserts "All of them go beyond provincial applications to make a statement, however bleak, however limited, on the ways of mankind."

Peden, William. "Eternal Foreigners." *Saturday Review* XXXIX, No. 43 (27 October 1956): 16-7, 25.
States that "With *Six Feet in the Country* Nadine Gordimer emerges from the category of gifted beginner and assumes the stature of one of the most distinguished younger contemporary writers."

Phelps, Lyon. "Humane Comedy." *Christian Science Monitor* (22 June 1965): 9.
Praises Gordimer's *Not for Publication and Other Stories.*

Schwartz, Lynne Sharon. "Figures in a Landscape of Sun and Shadow." *Washington Post Book World* X, No. 36 (7 September 1980): 1, 4.
Lauds Gordimer's *A Soldier's Embrace.*

Theroux, Paul. "The Presence of Africa." *Chicago Tribune Book World* V, No. 48 (28 November 1971): 19.
Provides a thematic overview of the stories in Gordimer's *Livingstone's Companions.*

Tuohy, Frank. "Breaths of Change." *Times Literary Supplement,* No. 4022 (25 April 1980): 462.
Presents that merits and faults of the stories in Gordimer's *A Soldier's Embrace.*

Interviews

Topping Bazin, Nancy and Marilyn Dallman Seymour. *Conversations with Nadine Gordimer.* Jackson: University Press of Mississippi, 1990, 321 p.
Contains interviews with Nadine Gordimer from throughout her career.

Additional coverage of Gordimer's life and career is contained in the following sources published by Gale: *Contemporary Authors,* **Vol. 5-8R;** *Contemporary Authors New Revision Series,* **Vols. 3, 28, 56;** *DISCovering Authors; DISCovering Authors: British; DISCovering Authors: Canadian; DISCovering Authors Modules: Most-Studied* **and** *Novelists; Major Twentieth-Century Writers; Short Story Criticism,* **Vol. 17; and** *World Literature Criticism Supplement.*

Václav Havel

1936-

Czechoslovakian dramatist, essayist, and poet.

The following entry presents an overview of Havel's career through 1997. For further information on his life and works, see *CLC*, Volumes 25, 58, and 65.

INTRODUCTION

An internationally renowned Czechoslovakian statesman and champion of human rights, Václav Havel is among the most important East European dissident writers of the Cold War period. His relentless political activism and avant-garde plays established him as a leading voice of protest against the repressive communist government of Czechoslovakia during the 1960s, 1970s, and 1980s. A frequent political prisoner whose writings were banned in his native country, Havel resisted totalitarianism in influential essays, speeches, and popular underground plays. As a dramatist, he is best known for *Zahradní slavnost* (1963; *The Garden Party*) and the trilogy of "Vanek" plays performed during the 1970s. Associated with the Theatre of the Absurd, his satiric dramas caricature the dehumanizing conditions of political tyranny and technocratic society. Havel was elected president of Czechoslovakia in 1989 after sweeping democratic reforms dissolved the nation's communist regime. A charismatic folk hero and public intellectual, Havel is recognized worldwide as a leading humanitarian and political visionary.

Biographical Information

Born in Prague, Czechoslovakia, Havel spent his formative years under Nazi Occupation and Stalinist hegemony. The son of a wealthy industrialist and property owner, he was denied access to a higher education in keeping with the communists's program to disenfranchise members of the bourgeoisie. Havel worked as an apprentice in a chemical laboratory while in school and, beginning in 1951, as a laboratory technician. Over the next several years he attended evening classes to earn a secondary degree in 1954. Havel studied economics at the Czech University of Technology from 1955 to 1957, during which time he published his first essays on literary topics. In 1959, after completing two years of compulsory military service, Havel found work as a stagehand for Divadlo ABC (the ABC Theatre of Prague). The next year he moved to Divadlo na zábradli (Theatre on the Balustrade), where he initially worked as a stagehand, then as a secretary, manuscript reader, and literary manager from 1963 to 1968. In 1961, Havel collaborated with Ivan

Vyskocil, artistic director of Theatre on the Balustrade, to produce his first play, *Autostop* (1961; *Hitchhike*). Havel's first full-length independent play, *The Garden Party*, premiered in 1963, followed by *Vyrozumení* (1965; *The Memorandum*), winner of an Obie (Off-Broadway) Award, and *Ztizená moznost soustredení* (1968; *The Increased Difficulty of Concentration*)—all produced at Theatre on the Balustrade. He also published *Protokoly* (1966; *Protocols*), a collection of his early drama, essays, and poetry. While working and writing for the theater, Havel studied drama at the Academy of Art in Prague from 1962 to 1967. He married Olga Splichalova in 1964. During the "Prague Spring" of 1968, Havel was a leading activist for artistic freedom and democratic reforms. With the Soviet invasion of Czechoslovakia in August 1968, Havel's works were banned and he was subjected to repeated arrests, periods of imprisonment, and more than a decade of virtual house arrest. During the 1970s he remained an outspoken advocate for human and civil rights. He was a contributor to Charter 77, a human rights manifesto made public in 1977, for which he was incarcerated for four months. In 1978, Havel founded the Committee for the Defense of the Un-

164

justly Persecuted (VONS), leading to another six-month imprisonment. Havel also wrote several plays for underground circulation, including *Spiklenci* (1970; *The Conspirators*), *Zebrácká opera* (1975), an adaptation of *The Beggar's Opera, Audience* (1975), *Vernisáz* (1975; *Private View*), *Horsky hotel* (1976; *The Mountain Hotel*), and *Protest* (1978). For continued acts of political protest, Havel was sentenced to four and a half years imprisonment in 1979. Upon his early release in 1983, he produced *Dopisy Olze* (1983; *Letters to Olga*), a collection of letters written to his wife while imprisoned; *Dálkovy vyslech* (1986; *Disturbing the Peace*), an interview with Czech journalist Karel Hvizdala in which Havel discusses his childhood, literary career, and political experiences; *Václav Havel, or Living in Truth* (1987), which contains six essays by Havel—notably "The Power of the Powerless" and "Politics and Conscience"—along with texts in honor of Havel by Samuel Beckett, Heinrich Böll, Tom Stoppard, Milan Kundera, and Arthur Miller; and the plays *Pokouseni* (1985; *Temptation*) and *Largo Desolato* (1986), both of which won Obie awards. After two years of intensified protest and labor strikes, in 1989 Czechoslovakia renounced its communist government for new democratic elections. Havel was unanimously appointed interim president by the Czechoslovakia Parliament in December 1989 and officially elected president in 1990. Havel resigned the presidency in 1992 to protest the imminent division of Czechoslovakia into Slovakia and the Czech Republic. He was elected president of the new Czech Republic the same year. His political views and experiences are recorded in *Open Letters* (1991), which contains essays dating from 1965 to January 1990, *Summer Meditations* (1992), and *The Art of the Impossible* (1997).

Major Works

Havel's dramatic works are dominated by themes of alienation, malcommunication, betrayal, and the search for identity and truth. According to Havel in *Disturbing the Peace*, his plays are intended to portray "modern humanity in a 'state of crisis.'" Influenced by the writings of Albert Camus and Samuel Beckett, Havel's early absurdist comedies expose the ineptitude and depersonalization of bureaucratic institutions. In *The Garden Party* protagonist Hugo Pludek pursues a position at the Office of Liquidation through Orwellian doublespeak and linguistic contrivance. A shrewd careerist who easily assimilates party platitudes and clichés, Pludek eventually becomes the director of two agencies—the Office of Liquidation and the Office of Inauguration. However, an attempt to eliminate the Office of Liquidation raises an intractable dilemma, since only the Office of Liquidation can dissolve itself and once terminated would no longer exist to complete the process. Alluding to the structure of a chess game, Pludek's paradoxical checkmate signifies his compromised self-identity as a pawn of the nonsensical system. *The Memo-*

randum further examines the alienating effect of bureaucratic discourse. The plot involves Josef Gross, an office manager who attempts to decode an official document written in "Ptydepe," a new scientific language designed to banish ambiguity and emotion from human communication. Gross's efforts to decipher the incomprehensible memorandum are harried by irrational bureaucratic policies and a manipulative underling who has him demoted. Gross eventually convinces Maria, a secretary, to translate the memo which, ironically, is revealed to be itself a directive for the elimination of "Ptydepe" as an ineffective language. *The Increased Difficulty of Concentration* involves Dr. Eduard Huml, a social scientist who attempts to balance conflicting obligations to his wife and mistresses. While participating in a farcical computer experiment and composing a lecture on the complexity of modern life, Huml's personal life is increasingly complicated by multiple sexual infidelities that reveal his flawed personality. Havel's "Vanek" trilogy consists of the one-act plays *Audience, Private View*, and *Protest*. Each of the three plays is connected by the semiautobiographic protagonist Ferdinand Vanek, a dissident writer who witnesses the degrading forces of corruption, false ideology, and socioeconomic coercion. In *Audience* Vanek works in a brewery where the drunken head malter pressures him to write weekly reports on himself for the secret police in exchange for lighter work. Vanek refuses to assist the government that he openly opposes by betraying himself, demonstrating the inviolable principles of the artist in contrast to the malter's demoralization. In *Private View*, Vanek visits Michael and Vera, a superficial couple who have sacrificed moral consciousness for material advantage and social respectability. While proudly displaying their newly redecorated apartment, they espouse the conditioned values of Western consumerism and chastise Vanek for his stubborn idealism and alleged cowardice. In *Protest*, Vanek is approached by Stanek, a noncommittal fellow writer, to draft a protest letter on behalf of an imprisoned rock star who is involved with his daughter. When Vanek presents the document for Stanek's approval, Stanek loses his nerve and launches into a convoluted debate through which he affirms the status quo and dismisses his obligation to act. In the end, Stanek learns that the rock star is released and protest is unnecessary. In all of the "Vanek" plays, Vanek's self-effacement and humble integrity offer a foil for the sophistry and duplicity of those he encounters. *Temptation* is Havel's interpretation of the Faust myth in which Dr. Foustka's occult meddlings reveal the evil of instrumental truth and postmodern relativism. *Largo Desolato* centers upon the existential crisis of Professor Leopold Nettles, a persecuted intellectual who must renounce a controversial passage that he has written by denying its authorship. Confined to his apartment—a symbolic prison cell—to contemplate authority and subjectivity, Nettles's becomes consumed with self-doubt regarding his identity and the possibility of truth.

Critical Reception

Havel is widely praised as an uncompromising artist, human rights activist, and leader of democratic reforms in Czechoslovakia. Though best known for his political activities and message of hope, Havel's dramatic works are highly regarded as provocative commentaries on life in a totalitarian state. The majority of critical attention is directed at *The Garden Party, The Memorandum,* the "Vanek" trilogy, and *Largo Desolato,* generally considered his most effective plays. *The Garden Party* remains Havel's most popular and acclaimed literary work. Critics frequently comment on the significance of distorted language, moral abdication, and lost self-identity in Havel's parodies of oppressive sociopolitical structures. In addition to the absurdist influence of Camus, Beckett, and Eugene Ionesco, many critics compare Havel's bureaucratic nightmares to those depicted in the writings of fellow Czech-born author Franz Kafka. Critics also note Havel's philosophical debt to Martin Heidegger and existentialist Jean-Paul Sartre. Though recognized as one of Eastern Europe's most important playwrights, some critics question Havel's literary accomplishment when measured against his contemporary Western counterparts. The reluctance of some Western critics to judge Havel's writing is attributed to fear that unfavorable evaluation of his literature may jeopardize his political stature. Havel's affinity for existentialism and outmoded theatrical devices of the 1960s, cited by some as a weakness in his work, is indicative of the cultural stagnation under the East Bloc regime Havel strove to overcome. Despite such qualifications, most critics view Havel's plays and essays as forceful philosophical statements on the degrading conditions of authoritarianism and the moral responsibilities of dissenters.

PRINCIPAL WORKS

Autostop [with Ivan Vyskocil; *Hitchhike*] (drama) 1961
Zahradní slavnost [*The Garden Party*] (drama) 1963
Vyrozumení [*The Memorandum*] (drama) 1965
Protokoly [*Protocols*] (drama, essays, and poetry) 1966
Ztizená moznost soustredení [*The Increased Difficulty of Concentration*] (drama) 1968
Spiklenci [*The Conspirators*] (drama) 1970
Audience (drama) 1975
Vernisáz [*Private View;* also translated as *Unveiling*] (drama) 1975
Zebrácká opera [adaptor; from the drama *The Beggar's Opera* by John Gay] (drama) 1975
Horsky hotel [*The Mountain Hotel*; also translated as *A Hotel in the Hills*] (drama) 1976
Protest (drama) 1978

Dopisy Olze [*Letters to Olga: June 1979 to September 1982*] (correspondence) 1983
A Private View [contains *Audience, Private View,* and *Protest*] (drama) 1983
Pokouseni [*Temptation*] (drama) 1985
Dálkovy vyslech [*Disturbing the Peace: A Conversation with Karel Hvizdala*] (interviews) 1986
Largo Desolato (drama) 1986
Václav Havel, or Living in Truth [with others] (essays) 1987
The Vanek Plays: Four Authors, One Character [contains *Audience, Private View,* and *Protest*] (drama) 1987
Open Letters: Selected Writings (essays) 1991
Summer Meditations (essays) 1992
The Art of the Impossible: Politics as Morality in Practice: Speeches and Writings, 1990-1996 (speeches and essays) 1997

CRITICISM

Irving Howe (review date 26 May 1991)

SOURCE: "One Can Stand Up to Lies," in *New York Times Book Review,* May 26, 1991, p. 5.

[*In the following review, Howe offers positive assessment of* Open Letters. *"We turn to Havel," Howe writes, "not for theoretical innovation but for the consolidation of truth."*]

There is a pleasing anecdote about Vaclav Havel, perhaps true, perhaps not. During the years he was being hounded by the Stalinist dictatorship in Czechoslovakia, he would spend part of his time in the country, watched day and night by the secret police. Once, a policeman is supposed to have said to him: "Why go back to Prague? Why don't you remain in the country, where we have such a nice, quiet life together?" Intuitively, this policeman had come to grasp the moral power of the writer he was watching.

For there is a mystery to Mr. Havel. Now the President of his country and, before that, a leading dissident spokesman and playwright, he has come to occupy a special place in our imaginations. We think of him as . . . well, an unheroic hero. **Open Letters,** his new collection of writings, which range from the time of his first hesitant statements in 1965 to the soberly triumphant inaugural address of January 1990, can be read as a political history in miniature. Yet I found myself more deeply interested in Mr. Havel as a phenomenon—the writer as popular leader—than in the events he charts. Others have written quite as well about the struggle for freedom in Central and Eastern Europe, but what is remarkable about Mr. Havel is his emergence as public man. Why and how did he win the affection of people throughout the world? And still more, the confidence of Czechoslovaks long immured in skepticism about all varieties of politics?

Mr. Havel's essays are lucid, sometimes even luminous, but their content is either topical (this protest, that arrest) or derivative. It would not be hard to name a dozen Central and East European intellectuals who write with more flair and provide more original analysis—I think, for instance, of George Konrad and Leszek Kolakowski. Yet there is something peculiarly gripping about Mr. Havel, something that makes him central to this historical moment. A touch of charisma? A chastity of voice?

Once in a rare while he succumbs to the vanity of verbal display, as in writing that people must "assume the existential responsibility for their own truth." What, after all, would be lost if he had scrapped that pulpy word "existential"?

In the main, however, Mr. Havel writes in a transparent style (competently rendered into English by a variety of translators) and out of an ethic of community. He talks to people, to factory workers, common readers, learned colleagues, sometimes even party apparatchiks. He seems still to believe that in this age of debased "communications" it is possible to have an exchange of thought. And thereby he achieves the eloquence of simplicity, so that, as we keep reading, this simplicity comes to seem charming, a smile of friendship.

The longest essay in *Open Letters* is a 1978 piece entitled **"The Power of the Powerless,"** an anatomy of totalitarianism about which the Polish Solidarity leader Zbigniew Bujak said: "It gave us the theoretical underpinnings for our activity." Now, anyone familiar with the literature on totalitarianism will recognize echoes in Mr. Havel's essay from, say, Hannah Arendt and Andrei Sakharov, as well as several others. But it doesn't really matter, since we turn to Mr. Havel not for theoretical innovation but for the consolidation of truth. **"The Power of the Powerless"** gave sustenance to the opponents of Stalinism—though I suspect that many of them shrugged their way past Mr. Havel's concluding slide into Heideggerian reflections about the dangers of technology.

Mr. Havel can be amusing about himself. He remarks that after he composed his stern 1975 letter, **"Dear Dr. Husak"** (to the then Stalinist boss of Czechoslovakia), "one friend told me he secretly suspects that I wrote [it] mainly to avoid having to write my play." He can be modest about the perils of dissidence in a dictatorship: "I've put together something I call my 'emergency packet' containing cigarettes, a toothbrush, toothpaste, soap, some books, a T-shirt,

paper, a laxative." But there are moments when he lets himself go, rising to strong ethical statement:

> People [should] realize that it is always possible to preserve one's ideals and one's backbone; that one can stand up to lies; that there are values worth struggling for . . . and that no political defeat justifies complete historical skepticism as long as the victims manage to bear their defeat with dignity.

Mr. Havel is at his best when writing brief pieces that somehow survive their moment. There is a **"Letter to Alexander Dubcek,"** sent after the defeat of the 1968 Prague Spring, in which he begs Mr. Dubcek to speak out for the values of "socialism with a human face." Later Mr. Havel would add, "I know that [Mr. Dubcek] got the letter; I don't know what he thought of it. He disappeared rather quietly and inconspicuously from political life; he didn't betray his own cause by renouncing it, but he didn't bring his political career to a very vivid end either." There is something very fine about the mixture of generous feeling and severe judgment in that last sentence.

Especially moving is an essay Mr. Havel wrote in 1988 about Frantisek Kriegel, a medical doctor and reform-minded Communist, the only one in the Dubcek leadership who refused to sign the Moscow agreement sanctioning the Soviet invasion of Czechoslovakia in 1968. Kriegel then became an outcast, joining with the dissidents in the 1970's while still continuing to call himself a Communist. Tenderly but with a touch of asperity, Mr. Havel studies the paradox—still more, the complexities—of "a man who believed heart and soul in the equality of all people, but who was also a member of a party that claimed for its members a higher status than anyone else."

Throughout the years of opposition to Stalinism and then after the "velvet revolution" of 1989, Mr. Havel embodied what I'd call a mood of ethical fraternity. People of varying opinions joined together, first in spreading Charter 77, the manifesto of freedom, and then in the Civic Forum, the dissident political movement, to oppose the sclerotic version of Stalinism that had been imposed on their country since 1969. In that mood—it often flourishes during the initial phases of revolution—there is a tacit agreement to brush aside ideology, political platforms, plans for the future. All that matters is linking hands in behalf of simple freedoms—a phase Mr. Havel nicely calls "a period of youth." In that time, "a new and quite unusual etiquette appeared: no one bothered with introductions, getting acquainted, or feeling one another out. The usual conventions were dropped and the usual reticence disappeared."

An exalted moment, and of course, it could not last. In Czechoslovakia today the movement that raised Mr. Havel to the presidency is gradually, inevitably coming apart. At one pole there is a social democratic tendency, and at the other a free market tendency. Politics will return, good politics and bad politics, as the "period of youth" gives way to anxieties of maturity. And then, if he's lucky, Mr. Havel may go back to writing his plays.

Veronika Ambros (essay date Summer 1991)

SOURCE: "Fictional World and Dramatic Text: Václav Havel's Descent and Ascent," in *Style,* Vol. 25, No. 2, Summer, 1991, pp. 310-9.

[*In the following essay, Ambros examines the interplay of fictional constructs, representations of reality, and dialogue in* The Garden Party.]

Because the theory of fictional worlds concentrates primarily on narratology, work on drama is rare. The reason for this lack of interest lies in the very nature of the theater, which involves the audience's entering an "as if" world. This characteristic of a theater performance is attributed almost automatically to the text of drama. So, for instance, the construction of the dramatic world in the rendition of Keir Elam presupposes a spectator; it is more the world of theater than that of written drama which he has in mind. Moreover his elements of a fictional dramatic world, such as "a set of physical properties, a set of agents and a course of time-bound events," are not distinctive features of drama as a literary text. Elam's elements suggest that the fictional world of drama is similar to that of narrative. Yet, as I will point out, the dramatic text enjoys a unique position among literary genres. Its two layers, the dialogical and the extradialogical discourse, mark its special structures and provide distinctive devices for creating a dramatic fictional world. And it is theater that combines both textual and extratextual features (stage movements, props, nonverbal sounds, and so forth) and that assumes a spectator. In contrast, a drama is the entirety of the text that, though designed for the theater, hopes as much as any other text for a reader.

A distinction between the two types of discourse was first elaborated by representatives of the Prague Linguistic Circle, who initiated a new approach to the problems of drama and theater. At best, drama had been treated as a marginal literary genre and at worst as mere material for the theater performance. The Czech aesthetician Otakar Zich is an example of this approach. In his *Estetika dramatického umení (Aesthetics of Dramatic Art)*, he separates drama from literature and refuses to regard the dramatic text as a work in its own right. The dramatic text is only part of the work of art. Hence for Zich, dramatic

art means not so much the text as the performance based on a text. His only exception is texts that as literary works are what Miroslav Procházka calls "self-sufficient."

In contrast to Zich, Jirí Veltruský, a member of the Prague Linguistic Circle, maintains that "drama is a work of literature in its own right" and that "it is a text that can, and mostly is intended to, be used as the verbal component of theatrical performance." The provocative title of Veltruský's important article "Drama jako básnické dílo" ("Drama as a Poetic Work") reflects its author's understanding of drama as literature focuses on the literary characteristics of dramatic texts.

As Veltruský emphasizes, "the semantic construction of a play relies on the plurality of contexts that unfold simultaneously, relay, interpenetrate, and vainly strive to subjugate and absorb one another." He indicates that all the different semantic contexts create semantic unity: the plot "provides all those semantic changes with a single motivation." Veltruský speaks in this context about "a central operative subject" controlling the different semantic contexts. Such an opinion strips the dramatis personae of their determination as representatives of actual persons and emphasizes their identities as literary constructs. The "central operative subject" is implicitly inherent in the special organization of the dramatic text. Its peculiarity lies in the distribution of the text: that is, in the distinction between the discourse of the characters and the extradialogic text.

In drama's capacity as a literary genre Veltruský regards dialogue as its most distinctive feature. In this he follows the ideas of Jan Mukarovský whose articles on dialogue and monologue hold their place among the fundamental works of Czech structuralism. Mukarovský lists three essential aspects of dialogue: 1) "The communication between the participants designated as the relationship between 'I' and 'you'"; 2) The relationship between the participants of a discourse and the real, material situation which surrounds them at the moment of the discourse; 3) "Dialogue is impossible without the unity of theme" (*The Word and Verbal Art*).

The importance of the last point is underscored by an ironic Czech folk saying: "Já o voze, on o koze" ("I talk about a cart, he talks about a goat"). Such a splitting of theme is also described by Peter Szondi, who takes his example from Chekhov's play *Three Sisters,* where a deaf person speaks to one of the characters. Szondi calls such a dialogue of participants lacking a common theme "aneinder-vorbei-Reden" ("talking past one another") and concludes that by this device the dramatic form itself is questioned.

Veltruský complements Mukarovský's theory with a special feature of dramatic dialogue: "Unlike the ordinary dialogue of everyday life, dramatic dialogue is both the sequence of alternating utterances made by several speakers and an utterance made by a single speaker, the author. The speeches attributed to each character are constructed in such a way as to be intelligible not only to the other character, but also, to the reader" ("Basic Features"). The unifying force of the author lies in the coordination of all constituents of the dramatic text.

Concentrating on the fact that the extradialogic text is transposed into another semiotic system, namely that of performance, Veltruský offers an explanation for why its role has been underestimated. It has generally been considered a mere instruction ("stage directions") for transforming the text into a theatrical performance and therefore subordinate to the main text: that is, the discourse of the characters. Veltruský observes that the less extradialogic text is employed, the shorter the gaps between each reply; the longer the extradialogic text, the greater the distance between the discourses of the characters. As a result, more physical action will be inserted in the latter case. Hence, both text layers are complementary. For this reason, the extradialogic text cannot be reduced to a framework of the discourse of the characters nor to directions for performance.

Depending on the epoch, literary trend, theater tradition, and so on, the extradialogic text might also perform the function of narrator. In spite of its rudimentary nature the extradialogic text approximates even the different narrative modes. And it is this part of the dramatic text that can primarily be endowed with authentication force. The "authentication function" is, according to Lubomír Dolezel, "absolutely essential for the construction of fictional worlds. It determines, first of all, what exists and what does not exist in the world and, no less importantly, assigns specific modes of existence to the fictional entities."

In opposition to narrative textures with a strong authentication force, Dolezel places the skaz: "The skaz-narrator constructs a non-authentic fictional world whose mode of existence is uncertain, ambiguous, where everything is open to doubts." In drama, a similar effect is achieved by a contradiction between the two layers of the dramatic text. One of the most notorious examples is the ending of Beckett's *Waiting for Godot:*

> Estragon: Yes, let's go.
> (*They do not move.*)

The action announced in the dialogue contradicts the nonaction indicated in the extradialogic text. The extradialogic text of *Waiting for Godot,* like the skaz-narrator's, does not fully authenticate the fictional world.

On the contrary, the reader as much as the spectator of this play (for the nonaction indicated in the extradialogic text can easily be transformed into performance) faces doubts about the nature of Beckett's world. As this example shows, the authentication of the dramatic fictional world is negotiated in two kinds of textual contrast: the semantic confrontation between the discourses of the different characters and that between the characters' discourse and the extradialogic text. These diverse sources of authentication support each other, conflict with each other, or do anything in between. Obviously, authenticating the fictional world of drama is a rather complex undertaking, which offers a spectacular range of different solutions.

Václav Havel's *Zahradní slavnost* (*The Garden Party*) will be used to illustrate the authentication of the dramatic fictional world. In Martin Esslin's view, the play belongs within the Theater of the Absurd. *The Garden Party,* however, is a special, Czech variety of this category. In the 1960s, critics often labeled contemporary Czech drama "model-drama," a tag based on certain features that these plays have in common: presenting a possible world and modeling rather than depicting or representing the actual world. In contrast to the existential core of such plays as Beckett's *Waiting for Godot,* the Czech authors construed a model of a hypothetical world, one where political and moral issues of power distribution are raised.

Esslin states that *The Garden Party* "displays a mixture of hard-hitting political satire, Sweikian humour and Kafkaesque depths." He applies the worn-out clichés used as a rule by Western critics introducing a new work of modern Czech literature. But Havel follows different traditions: on the one hand, logically constructed models of a world (represented by Sartre or Camus) and, on the other, the Dadaist and surrealist tradition of "free," playful, hyperbolized language. The events in *The Garden Party* follow the pattern of a weird chess game played by Hugo Pludek, the protagonist: "Instead of a total victory one time or a total defeat another, he prefers to win a little and lose a little each time." Havel's play opens with Hugo playing simultaneously the black and the white figures and ends with the protagonist's announcing a checkmate. The four acts present a game within a play. Hugo's other game—a play on words—is a means to ascent in his career. He pursues it in different places (at home, at the gate of the garden where the party takes place, at the office of Ministry for Inauguration) and eventually returns to the starting point without actually coming back. Although he succeeds at this game, he is defeated as a human being: his identity vanishes. So the closing checkmate is, in fact, a defeat of Hugo by Hugo. The world of *The Garden Party* resembles a tightly meshed mechanism where the ascent of a character also means his concurrent descent.

Hugo's character depends on the construction of as well as the destruction by his basic deictic definitions:

> Me? You mean who am I? Now look here, I don't like this one-sided way of putting questions, I really don't! You think one can ask in this simplifying way? . . . Truth is just as complicated and multiform as everything else in the world . . . and we all are a little bit what we were yesterday and a little bit what we are today; and also a little bit we are not these things. Anyway, we are all a little bit all the time and all the time we are not a little bit . . . some only are, some are only, and some are only not, so that none of us entirely is and at the same time each one of us is not entirely. . . .

> (*The Garden Party*)

Hugo suffers not only the loss of his identity index by undergoing a transformation from "I" into "we." When his own parents fail to recognize him, his pronominal status is questioned. The pronominal chaos reaches its peak when Hugo, in a dialogue with his mother, refers to himself as "he," imitating the impersonal speech of politicians:

> Hugo: He [i.e., Hugo] has a friendly word for everyone, even for the simplest folk. As a matter of fact, I'm counting on it myself. I've come here to have a little chat with him and see if perhaps I might not give him a hand with this or the other. What about that nice cup of coffee?

> Mrs. Pludek: Yes, of course, as soon as our darling little Hugo arrives.

> Hugo: He's not home yet?

The deictic transformations entail the destruction of the protagonist's persona. According to Jindrich Honzl, "verbal deixis serves as a semantic filter that enables the dramatist to create and image of the world and of people. . . . Such a semantic filter, which does not admit images undesired by the dramatist, alters the profile of those real elements out of which the representation of a human being and his behavior is created in a play." Though Honzl relates his notion to ancient drama, the deictic transformations in *The Garden Party* can also be considered a "semantic filter" generating ambiguity in the fictional world.

Hugo's career is the final evidence of his identity loss. The promising son turns out to be a lost son. In the dramatic fictional world, however, he still retains his function of agent. The extradialogical text guards the status of the figure by providing its authentication.

The world in which Hugo rises consists of words. Like Hansel who, in Grimms' fairy tale, gathers stones to find his way back, Hugo collects words that guide him. In the second act, he memorizes such combinations of words as "lyrical-epic verses." This phrase then becomes a weapon to defeat a man from whose utterance it was originally taken. Hugo equips these overheard words with a new logic, so that their original meaning is twisted. As his discourse becomes more and more "sophisticated," the words lose their meaning more and more until a semantics of nonsense is brought about. In contrast to the nonsense of *Alice in Wonderland,* the nonsense of Hugo's utterances expresses the mechanistic character of the world of *The Garden Party.*

The plot of *The Garden Party* is modeled on the *Bildungsroman,* in which the hero sets off to explore the world. On his way, he faces various difficulties, finds himself in the thick of adventure, and finally settles down as a better man. Hugo, too, is a sort of pilgrim. But his journey is different: he progresses and regresses at one and the same time. His voyage starts at home, which is not a homely place at all since there is no difference between private and public life in the world Hugo tries to conquer. And unlike the *Bildungsroman* hero, he is not in the end a better man but ceases to exist altogether as a person. He lives on only as a legend in telegrams sent to his father's friend. Kalabis, and in the dialogues with his parents, where he speaks of himself as of someone else:

> Hugo: So your Hugo is liquidating not only the Liquidation Office, but the Inauguration service as well?

The positive hero of socialist realism is kin to the protagonist of the *Bildungsroman.* *The Garden Party* rebels against this poetics. The positive hero is a spokesman for the socialist ideology, capable of reforming his surroundings for the better. Hugo, however, is anything but a conqueror of the "old and rotten world of the bourgeoisie" or a spokesman for the "right philosophy of the working class." Quite the contrary: Hugo makes his career "because he clearly has in his veins the healthy philosophy of the middle class!" His character demonstrates the fusion of two ideological layers—middle-class beliefs and vulgar Marxism—which make up the base of Havel's absurd fictional world. Hugo's father's reflection is worth quoting:

> You can't fry chickenweed without straw. And why? Whereas all other classes in history kept exchanging their historical positions, the middle classes have come down through history untouched, because no other class has never tried to take their position, and so the middle classes never had anything to exchange with anybody and have thus remained the only permanent force in history.

A monologue of this type displays empty words, a desemantization of the dialogical text. A similar effect correlating the dialogical and extradialogical texts indicates that the utterance is comprehended literally and as a result entails action not at all intended. So, for instance, an exclamation "mami" is meant as a confirmation that Hugo accepts the offer to fraternize with the director and to see the latter as if he were a mother. The extradialogical text, though, announces "Hugo's mother." A short exchange between Hugo and his mother clarifies that the clamor was meant figuratively.

In his introduction to the Czech edition of the play, Jan Grossman, the former producer of the Theater on the Balustrade where *The Garden Party* was first staged, points out that the generating mechanism of Havel's first two plays is the cliché. Grossman even claims that the cliché is the real protagonist of *The Garden Party.* It is this special use of language that assumes a pivotal role. Marxist vocabulary merges with parodied proverbs into new phrases. Havel's concept of "gag" here jumps to the fore. In the essay **"Anatomie gagu"** (**"Anatomy of the Gag"**), published at the same time as his first play, Havel writes that a gag consists of a combination of automatisms.

Language consisting of elements of the new ideology combined with the distorted folk tradition signals what Herta Schmid calls "Verlust der Geschichtlichkeit" ("loss of historicity"). *The Garden Party* presents a distortion of the language and hence the dissolution of both the collective and the individual memory. So at the end of the first act, for instance, both parents use quotations from Czech literature. These fragments manifest how limited individual memory is. The parents' dialogue develops what is already indicated by their first names, Oldrich and Bozena, names that refer to a couple who represent the Czech national myth. The world of *The Garden Party* is that of determined national entity. The proverbs and their parody create an atmosphere of the Czech folk tradition artificially exhumed and peddled by the official ideology.

The Garden Party exhibits a contrast between both text layers as the contrast between a speech and action, akin to that mentioned in *Waiting for Godot.* In the first act the family expects the father's friend, Kalabis:

> *Pludek: (To Mrs. Pludek)* If he doesn't come, somebody else will! *(Just then the door-bell rings.)*
>
> *Mrs. Pludek:* Nobody will come! Nobody will write! Nobody will call! We're alone. Alone in the whole world!
>
> *Hugo:* And there are more and more Japs every day. Did somebody ring?

> *(Peter enters.)*
>
> *Mrs. Pludek:* Peter! Go and hide in the pantry! Kalabis is here!

Kalabis has not arrived, contradicting the announcement in the dialogical text. As a result the cause-and-effect order of the actual world is reversed. The succession of ringing a bell and the expected announcement of a guest customary in the actual world is here violated. Moreover, the text underlines the contradiction between the action expressed by the extradialogical text and the utterance of the person. Breaking the law of the actual world raises the "as if" character of the dramatic world.

Yet another relation between the two discourses appears in the course of Hugo's apprenticeship in the world he is about to conquer. Accumulating combinations like that of the "lyricoepical verses," Hugo mumbles them "for himself." An aside is a typical device that as a rule provides the audience a surplus of information and in consequence produces so-called dramatic irony. But Hugo's murmur breaks this norm: it does not shed any light on the action or on any of the characters. On the contrary, when Hugo eventually repeats these mumbled words, his utterance proves that he only had been practicing the nonsense. Hence it is not only the expressions themselves that underscore that empty words with no enigma are involved. The very way the two text layers are juxtaposed results in an ambiguity similar to that of skaz.

Hugo's ascent is signaled by a nose made out of papier-maché that originally was a sign for Plzák's superiority. In the fourth act this prop also indicates Hugo's descent, his loss of identity. Hence the nose epitomizes the fictional world as a unit, where the opportunism destroys both the collective and the individual memory.

Investigating Beckett's *Quad,* the German semiotician Schmid comes to the conclusion that "the absence of all traditional means of drama, reveals the constant inner form of dramatic theater, that means a theater, which is governed by the verbal element." One can add that it is the very organization of the dramatic text that keeps this inner form together. *The Garden Party* shows the consistency of a dramatic fictional world in spite of the ambiguity displayed on different levels. Moreover, it is the ambiguity that emphasizes the fictional status of the presented world. This is how the text points to itself, becomes self-reflexive.

Most of the dialogue of *The Garden Party* is constructed according to the principle of "aneinander-vorbei-Reden." Instead of verbal exchange, the dialogue resembles a chain of fragmentary soliloquies. Even though the utterances are attributed to different persons, they often do not have distinct characteristics.

As a consequence, *The Garden Party* exposes the limits of human communication. The figures do not address each other in order to communicate; words serve another purpose: ritual. The very core of it is the "metaphysical dialectic," a term Havel coined in an essay published shortly after the opening night of *The Garden Party.* There Havel specifies metaphysical dialectic as the attitude that follows very much the logic expressed by Hugo: "In fact, they were both sort of right and sort of wrong, or rather, on the contrary, both were wrong and both right, weren't they? I mean, they were, were they not?"

Havel's target in the essay is the dominating vulgar and dogmatic understanding of dialectic and the neglect of its virtual philosophical qualities. He objects to the fact that the dialectic became a fetish: "Instead of the dialectic helping reality, it is the reality that serves the dialectic." Both the play and the essay about it try to disclose the mechanism of this absurd reversal.

The steps Hugo takes are akin to the pattern of the Dutch painter M. C. Escher's impossible configurations in, for example, *Ascending and Descending,* where the staircase leads simultaneously up and down. Concurrent ascent and descent is the overall pattern of the course of events in *The Garden Party.* At one point, the offices for Inauguration and for Liquidation fuse, a synthesis of thesis and antithesis. In accord with this dialectic principle, the play exhibits both the construction and deconstruction of its fictional world. At the end, when the bureaucrat Plzák crawls out of Hugo's cupboard and addresses the audience with "And now, without any sort of ado—go home!" Havel pays tribute to Brecht's "V-effect" (defamiliarization). He erases the opposition between the fictional world and the actual world. This breaking of the fictional into the actual is the final authentication of the dramatic world.

Phyllis Carey (essay date September 1991)

SOURCE: "Contemporary World Drama 101: Václav Havel," in *Thought,* Vol. 66, No. 262, September, 1991, pp. 317-28.

[*In the following essay, Carey provides an overview of Havel's literary career, major works, and critical reception.*]

The performance of Vaclav Havel as Czech President since December 1989 has thus far met with mixed reviews from Western observers. But Western fascination with the popu-

lar and colorful Havel himself remains high as he continues to play a key role on the center stage of Czechoslovakia. English translations of Havel's political writing, his letters from prison, and his drama have rapidly appeared in book stores. So far a representative sampling is readily available; it is more than enough to whet the appetite. Most provocatively from a Western perspective, Havel's writings suggest that the drama that continues to unfold in Eastern bloc countries has the power to reveal to the West "its own latent tendencies" (*Living in Truth*). As the Iron Curtain continues to rise, the spectators of the West may glimpse, if Havel the philosophic playwright-president is to be believed, a reflection of themselves on the other side.

BIOGRAPHY

Havel insists that in all of his writings his starting point is his own experience. The events of his life have provided recurring themes for both his plays and his essays. Born in 1936 into a bourgeois family, he was isolated as a child because of the privileges of his class, but after World War II under the Communists, the family's property was confiscated, and Havel was repeatedly rejected for a higher education because of his class. After serving two years in the army, he began working as a theater technician, learning drama from the ground up, finally staging his first independent full-length play. *The Garden Party,* when he was 27—although he had begun writing and publishing before he was twenty years old and had authored or co-authored five other plays between 1959 and 1962.

Havel wrote three major plays in the 60s: *The Garden Party* (1963), *The Memorandum* (1965), and *The Increased Difficulty of Concentration* (1968), the latter two each receiving American Obie awards. During this time he also wrote a radio and a television play. In the 70s he wrote *The Conspirators* (1970), his own version of John Gay's *The Beggar's Opera* (1972), several one-act plays, including a trilogy on a "dissident" writer, Ferdinand Vanek, and a play about writing plays, *A Hotel in the Hills* (1976). His major plays of the 80s include *Largo Desolato* (1984)— named a Best Play of 1986 for Broadway and off-Broadway—and *Temptation* (1985). The early plays are absurdist theater, but as Milan Kundera describes it, Havel's drama portrays the absurdity of the rational, when bureaucracy reigns, and means and methods become ends in themselves. Havel himself has described his plays as depicting "modern humanity in a 'state of crisis'" (*Disturbing the Peace*). Besides rational extremes, Havel's drama satirizes careerism, irresponsibility, and abuses of language. The plays richly dramatize the themes that preoccupy him in his essays: betrayal, manipulation, exile, and isolation as well as truth, responsibility, and the search for identity.

Although Havel's public political views date back at least

to 1956, it was not until 1969—after the Prague Spring followed by the Soviet invasion of 1968—that he was charged with subversion for his protests of the "normalization" process, and his plays, along with the works of several other Czech writers, banned.

The 70s and 80s in Czechoslovakia saw two literary circles at work: the official public writers and an unofficial "underground" group which circulated typewritten manuscripts, termed *samizdat* editions, some of which found their way to the West.

Havel's work in helping to initiate Charter 77, a manifesto for human rights made public in 1977, led to his first detention for four months. In 1978 he helped form the Committee for the Defense of the Unjustly Prosecuted (VONS in its Czech acronym), was detained for six more weeks, and was virtually under "house arrest" when he was not in prison. Finally in May 1979, Havel and five other members of VONS were arrested. At their October trial, Havel received a four-and-one-half-year sentence. While in prison he wrote 144 letters to his wife, whom he had married in 1964, the letters becoming the substance of *Letters to Olga.* Because of pneumonia and other serious health problems, Havel was released early, in March 1983.

In 1985, Havel was detained twice for forty-eight hour periods. He remained active in the late 80s, writing both essays and plays in *samizdat* versions, and spending brief periods of time in detention. He served four months in prison in early 1989 for taking part in a memorial for Jan Palach, the young Czech who immolated himself in protest for the 1968 Soviet invasion. Havel also took part in the dramatic events in late 1989, finally leading a delegation of the Civic Forum to negotiate with the Communist government after the general strike in November. He was elected president of Czechoslovakia in December 1989.

LIVING IN TRUTH

Of the three most available volumes in English that explore in vastly different ways Havel's political ideas, *Living in Truth* provides the best introduction. The volume originated with the Erasmus Prize Foundation in Amsterdam, which awarded Havel the Erasmus Prize in 1986. The book is a collection of six essays by Havel and sixteen miscellaneous texts by several writers, mostly Czech, written specifically for Havel. Among the contributions by other writers are a response to Havel's *Letters to Olga* by Heinrich Böll, a prose poem by Arthur Miller, an introduction to Havel's play *The Memorandum* by Tom Stoppard, and *Catastrophe,* a one-act play written by Samuel Beckett for Havel when he was in prison in 1982.

Havel's own six essays come from the ten-year period 1975-85, two written before and four written after his three-year imprisonment. The first text, which contributed to Havel's initial detention in 1977, analyzes what he terms the "crisis of human identity" (*Living in Truth*) and presents an argument against censorship. In his published **"Letter to Dr. Gustáv Husák, General Secretary of the Czechoslovak Communist Party"** (1975)—whom he replaced as Czech leader in 1989—Havel points out that beneath the superficial adaptation and rising standard of living of the mid-seventies, the Czech people are undergoing spiritual, political, and moral degradation: "What social conscience only yesterday regarded as improper is today casually excused; tomorrow it will eventually be thought natural, and the day after be held up as a model of behavior." Callousness, moreover, not only breeds greater insensitivity but also blinds the society to its own degradation. The human is the "obedient member of a consumer herd."

Havel's letter is primarily an appeal for the free exercise of culture as "the main instrument of *society's self-knowledge.*" The "official" writers practice the "aesthetics of banality . . . culture in the consumer philosophy: not to excite people with the truth, but to reassure them with lies." The suppression of other writers and artists becomes a suppression of history, for which (here echoing Ghandi and Martin Luther King, Jr.) the suppressors will suffer as much as the suppressed. The government in immobilizing culture also immobilizes itself and creates its own political entropy. But beneath the "heavy lid of inertia," a "secret streamlet trickles on" and—in one of many statements that now seem prophetic—Havel warns that the conflicts, demands, and issues growing beneath the surface will "burst forth when the moment arrives when the lid can no longer hold them down. That is the moment when the dead weight of inertia crumbles and history steps out again into the arena." Havel's letter, in summary, appeals morally to Husák and the other Communist leaders to exercise their authority responsibly and at the same time encourages the Czechs themselves in their resistance of the seventies for the sake of their own history.

The Power Within

Havel's **"The Power of the Powerless"** (1978) is perhaps his best-known and most influential political essay. As the title suggests, Havel argues that humans acting morally have the power to overthrow dictatorships. Havel asserts in the essay's introductory paragraphs that the Communism of the Eastern Bloc is not a classical dictatorship but rather another form of a consumer and industrial society, what Havel terms a "*post-totalitarian* system" (*Living in Truth*). As "an inflated caricature of modern life in general," the Eastern bloc stands "as a kind of warning to the West, revealing its own latent tendencies."

And what are those latent tendencies? According to Havel, they are not accidents of history or decrees of fate, but rather they are tendencies within humans themselves to create systems, adapt to those systems, and then maintain the systems in order to avoid acting responsibly as individuals:

> A person who has been seduced by the consumer value system, whose identity is dissolved in an amalgam of the accoutrements of mass civilization, and who has no roots in the order of being, no sense of responsibility for anything higher than his or her own personal survival, is a *demoralized* person. The system depends on this demoralization, deepens it, is in fact a projection of it into society.

But if humans become the system by surrendering to automatism, they also have the power to destroy the system because they are capable of living responsibly and in integrity. Morality comes from humans, not from systems nor from legality, Havel avers. Only by creating a better life can a better system—and better laws—be developed. The power of the powerless is, therefore, the potential to spread the "virus of truth" by living in integrity and, thereby, helping to reform society. Havel argues that moral acts have a power of illumination that can make an apparent wall of stone as transparent as a tissue.

Havel devotes a large portion of the essay to showing by specific examples the many ways that the powerless have provided illumination in Czechoslovakia. He also analyzes the nature of "opposition" and the term "dissidents." Havel finds the latter term especially misleading; he himself prefers to speak of a "parallel" or "second" culture.

Havel concludes the essay by underlining the universality of its theme. The "power of the powerless" does not refer only—nor perhaps even primarily—to people living under Communist regimes. Rather, the moral crisis Havel sees in his own country is just one expression of a global crisis of technological automatism, a theme he pursues in greater detail in another essay discussed below, **"Politics and Conscience."** Moreover, because manipulation is more subtle in Western democracies, Havel thinks that those who are ostensibly "free" may be the most unaware of their actual subjugation to a utilitarian automatism.

Havel suggests that the only true solution to the crisis of the world may lie in what he terms a "post-democratic" existential revolution, a moral reconstitution of society:

> . . . a radical renewal of the relationship of human beings to what I have called the "human order," which no political order can replace. A new experience of being, a renewed rootedness in the universe, a newly

grasped sense of "higher responsibility," a new-found inner relationship to other people and to the human community. . . . In other words, the issue is the rehabilitation of values like trust, openness, responsibility, solidarity, love.

Havel is not proposing a future organized movement, but, rather, an ongoing resurrection of the individual human spirit. He queries at the end of the essay whether such a renovation is not already taking place, whether "only our own blindness and weakness has [sic] prevented us from seeing it around us and within us, and kept us from developing it?"

Post-Imprisonment Essays

The four essays from the mid-eighties echo the themes established earlier but add new dimensions and implications. "Six asides about culture" examines in six parts the plight of the unofficial writer in Czechoslovakia and attempts to define the unique Czech spirit expressed by the "parallel" writers. **"Thriller"** (1984), using the name of Michael Jackson's best-selling video, playfully explores the strange remnants of the primitive mixed with the technologically sophisticated in modern man. **"An Anatomy of Reticence"** (1985) contrasts the Western European peace movement with the efforts of the East European "dissidents" to reveal the complex ambiguities that prevented a totally united peace movement.

To Save the Earth

Of the four "post-prison" essays, **"Politics and Conscience"** (1984)—a speech that Havel would have given if allowed to attend the ceremony awarding him an honorary doctorate at the University of Toulouse—provides perhaps the greatest challenge to Western Europe and the United States. Drawing from his own experience and echoing Martin Heidegger's "Essay Concerning Technology," Havel laments the devastation of nature and the denaturing of the human that result from a wholesale adaptation to a scientific-technological world view. He sees in the pollution and degradation of the planet—and in the inability to conceive of any remedies outside of technological ones—the paradoxical triumph of an objectivizing that has subjugated the natural world:

> The fault is not one of science as such but of the arrogance of man in the age of science. Man simply is not God, and playing God has cruel consequences. Man has abolished the absolute horizon of his relations, denied his personal "pre-objective" experience of the lived world, while relegating personal conscience and consciousness to the bathroom, as something so private that it is no one's business. Man rejected his re-

sponsibility as a "subjective illusion"—and in place of it installed what is now proving to be the most dangerous illusion of all: the fiction of objectivity stripped of all that is concretely human. . . . (*Living in Truth*)

Havel, of course, is not advocating a return to the Middle Ages. But neither does he believe that the evil humans have done to the environment—and to themselves—can be remedied without addressing its cause. Hence, his attempts to make explicit the hidden scientific-technological ideology underlying both capitalism and Communism.

In the realm of politics, he uses the Czech philosopher Václav Belohradský to point out the "rational technology of power" that can be traced back to Machiavelli "when human reason begins to 'free' itself from the human being as such, from his personal experience, personal conscience and personal responsibility." Havel acknowledges that the depersonalization of power is naturally linked with Eastern totalitarian systems but that these systems were in fact forced on the world by the Western European intellectual imperialism of natural science, rationalism, scientism, the industrial revolution, continuing down to the cult of consumption, the atomic bomb and Marxism:

> I think that, with respect to the relation of western Europe to the totalitarian systems, no error could be greater than the one looming largest: that of a failure to understand the totalitarian systems for what they ultimately are—a convex mirror of all modern civilization and a harsh, perhaps final call for a global recasting of that civilization's self-understanding.

For Havel, the question is clearly not whether capitalism or socialism will prevail. Nor is he convinced that people in the West understand what is actually at stake: "I cannot overcome the impression that Western culture is threatened far more by itself than by SS-20 rockets." The global answer for the planet as Havel sees it is a return to our humanity in its fullness: a reaffirmed human responsibility, a trusting in the voice of conscience, an honoring of the mystery of the natural world, a resistance to the anonymous, inhuman power of ideologies, systems, bureaucracies, artificial languages, political slogans, advertising, and consumption. For Havel, a single person who "dares to cry out the word of truth and to stand behind it with all his person and all his life, ready to pay a high price, has, surprisingly greater power, though formally disfranchised, than do thousands of anonymous voters." Havel ends the essay with a call for the "solidarity of the shaken," an international community of human conscience—a call he realizes will be ridiculed "by the technicians of power."

LETTERS TO OLGA

As the direct experience of Havel the prisoner, *Letters* belongs not so much to the epistolary genre but to that indefinable category of writings that springs from the direct experience of prison life, including in our century such writers as Dietrich Bonhoeffer, Viktor Frankl, Etty Hillesum, Martin Luther King, Jr., and Alexander Solzhenitsyn, to name only a few. Havel began serving his nearly four years knowing his letters would be circulated among friends but not realizing how vital those letters would become to his own survival. They were written under strict regulations and censored. No more than four standard pages per week, no humor, no rough drafts, no copies were allowed.

Letters to Olga contains 123 letters written between June 4, 1979 and September 4, 1982. Havel himself calls the volume a "very strange book" that "helped to save my life" (*Disturbing the Peace*). The letters contain very little about prison life itself as the prisoners were allowed to write only about family affairs, and Havel soon discovered that the more complex and intellectual the letters were, the easier it was to get them through the censors. The result is a form of "encoding"—occasional indirect expressions and convoluted sentences that point to a sub-text; for example, "some predetermined framework" (*Letters to Olga*) clearly includes the censors of the letter. Of the prison experience itself Havel has said, "The most important thing about it is incommunicable" (*Disturbing the Peace*).

Havel has also indicated that the "main hero, though admittedly hidden," is Olga (*Letters to Olga*), and—like the "dark lady" of Shakespeare's sonnets—the mysterious recipient of the letters intrigues the reader. The carping in Havel's early letters, however, is irritating despite the excuses in the introduction that Havel was deeply anxious and that Olga was the only person he could write to or receive letters from (others could communicate only through her). Havel instructs Olga on how she is to live her life while he is in prison and criticizes the frequency, length, content, and style of her letters. He evaluates her appearance after each visit—as well as the visits themselves—and at times what she said and brought. As the letters progress, however, Havel does seem to become more accepting of Olga as she is, and as Jan Lopatka, the Czech editor of the letters suggests, the volume can be seen on one level as a novel of "maturing love." In addition, however, "Olga," besides being Havel's wife, seems to become both the "outside world" and—in the late letters—the part of the self that listens.

In reading the letters, one becomes gradually aware of the human degradation from which they are emerging—the crowded cells, the filth, the restrictions on space and pencils and on what can be said, the disappointment over letters not delivered or refused. Havel's own physical ills, which he mentions almost in passing, contribute to the bleakness: flu, fevers, infected gums—which he lances himself—hemorrhoids (requiring surgery), a hernia. One of Havel's defenses for this misery is the "rage for order" underlying many of the requests he makes of Olga. He practices his own rigid routines within the narrow restrictions of space and time. He mentally composes and recomposes the letters themselves before the time appointed for letter-writing. The symmetry and schemes for organizing that are a prominent feature of Havel's drama seem to derive from his basic need to rescue experience from impending chaos through arranging and ordering.

But if ordering becomes a means of imposing meaning on experience, the language itself of the volume provides a measure of the weight of that meaning. Havel, commenting on Saul Bellow's *Herzog,* notes that in a society that permits total intellectual freedom, language has no weight. In Havel's own society, however, "words have so much weight that you must pay quite dearly for them" (***Letters to Olga***). Correspondingly, as ***Letters to Olga*** progresses, the language becomes denser.

The final letters of the volume express "existence at the edge"—a tenuous holding on to sanity that gives these "meditations" a dramatic intensity. They language grows more and more abstract but at the same time paradoxically more intensely concrete and particular:

> We live in an age in which there is a general turning away from Being: our civilization, founded on a grand upsurge of science and technology, those great intellectual guides on how to conquer the world at the cost of losing touch with Being, transforms man its proud creator into a slave of his consumer needs, breaks him up into isolated functions, dissolves him in his existence-in-the-world and thus deprives him not only of his human integrity and his autonomy but ultimately any influence he may have had over his own "automatic responses." (***Letters to Olga***)

The volume ends with the admission that in all his letters from prison, nothing has been said that "hasn't already been discovered long before and expressed a hundred times better" but that these meditations have been a source of personal growth. Like Camus's Sisyphus, who ironically finds contentment in confronting absurdity, Havel asserts, "I may well be happier now than at any time in recent years."

One of the last letters (number 138) contains a "confession" that some have seen as the "climax" of the collection. Havel describes his misjudgment in requesting release from his 1977 imprisonment—which officials subsequently used to disgrace him—and admits that he has spent years excusing himself through a "psychological process" that he sees as "that typically modern way of excluding the self from the 'category of blame.'" He concludes, on the

contrary, that "only by assuming full responsibility today for one's own yesterday, only by this unqualified assumption of responsibility by the 'I' for itself and for everything it ever was and did, does the 'I' achieve continuity and thus identity with the self." Havel's deep shame and anguish dramatize an implicit corollary to his explicit comments on responsibility: If the price for living responsibly is high—and all of the evidence suggests that Havel and the other "dissidents" paid dearly—the price for failing to take responsibility is for Havel clearly much higher.

The "catharsis" of the confession comes in the final group of letters; what initiates it is a trivial but Kafkaesque event that crystallizes many of the themes of the letters. Havel is watching the news one evening when the sound system of the television studio apparently fails. An anonymous television weather-woman realizes with great embarrassment that the sound system is not functioning and that her words are not being heard. Watching her predicament, Havel is moved almost to tears. The woman's vulnerability bespeaks naked human existence, which evokes compassion from those who are no less vulnerable. The picture of the mute human trying futilely to make contact from the machine-prison becomes a remarkable image for a great deal that Havel is trying to convey about human responsibility in a desensitized world; in addition, it becomes a convex image of Havel himself trying to communicate from his own prison cell in his letters to Olga what he has described as essentially incommunicable.

DISTURBING THE PEACE

Disturbing the Peace originated as an interview with Karel Hvízdala, Czech journalist and playwright living in West Germany. In 1985, Havel, nearing 50, reflected on his experiences via tape recorder in response to Hvízdala's questions. Havel's answers were transcribed, edited, and the volume was published in *samizdat* in Czechoslovakia and translated into English in 1989 by Paul Wilson.

> **"My plays are consciously, deliberately, and obviously constructed, schematic, almost machinelike"**
> —*Václav Havel*

The volume provides a behind-the-scenes view of Havel discussing his childhood, his political experiences, his career in the theater, and his ideas on both politics and drama. Basic themes of the essays and the letters from prison—responsibility, identity, hope—are reiterated. The volume will be most useful for those who are already familiar with Havel and interested in the personal details, e.g., Havel's own experience of the Soviet occupation, his involvement in the various resistance movements, the memories and details of prison life. Unique to this volume, nevertheless, are reflections on his own poetics and extended meditations on the nature of human hope.

Havel's Poetics

As a literary critic of his own drama, Havel confirms the most striking features of his plays as intentional: "My plays are consciously, deliberately, and obviously constructed, schematic, almost machinelike" (***Disturbing the Peace***). Readily apparent are the symmetry and patterns in the plays, manifested in repetition and almost mathematical variations in actions and dialogues. Nevertheless, although Havel himself does not mention it, one may see a difference between the pre-prison and the post-prison plays. The plays of the sixties and seventies seem both more "absurd" and playful; the plays of the eighties, on the other hand, are much more serious. The protagonists, moreover, become increasingly more human as one progresses through Havel's oeuvre.

As to Hvízdala's charge that Havel's plays are pessimistic—a charge that may not coincide with the experience of Western readers who are used to far bleaker fare—Havel responds that his plays are intended "to warn, to predict horrors, to see clearly what is evil. Face to face with a distillation of evil, man might well recognize what is good."

Havel also discusses his fascination with language and his attempts to show how language shapes life, hence the need to be sensitive to the many shades of abuse that language both reveals and perpetrates. In ***The Garden Party,*** Havel concedes, the main hero is the cliché, which mechanically subdues human identity. In ***The Memorandum*** Havel invents the language of *Ptydepe*, an artificial scientific language designed to banish the imprecision and ambiguity of "natural" languages. *Ptydepe* becomes a wonderful satire on the many technical languages—including those in contemporary literary criticism—that manifest specialized knowledge today and that in turn create the illusion of sophistication and superiority.

The Paradoxes of Hope

The final section of ***Disturbing the Peace*** provides a glimpse into the many paradoxes that comprise Havel: He is a political activist who has never been a politician, a philosophical writer who is not a philosopher, a playwright who dislikes reading plays as well as most theater. The public Havel is "an eternal rebel and protestor" while the private Havel is a lover of harmony and peace; the public Havel is a pillar of strength while the private Havel is inwardly shy and diffident; the public Havel loves crowds while the private Havel thrives on solitude; the public Havel preaches hope and responsibility while the private Havel is wracked with fears and doubts.

But if Havel sees many contradictions in his own life and temperament, it is partially because of the fundamental discrepancy he sees between the seeming randomness and chaos of human existence and its call to the fullness of identity, displayed in the nature of human hope itself. Havel describes hope as "an orientation of the spirit" that is "anchored somewhere beyond [the world's] horizons" (***Disturbing the Peace***). He differentiates hope from joy in that joy is related to successful outcomes, whereas hope pertains to "the certainty that something makes sense, regardless of how it turns out."

In working for something "because it is good" rather than because it may be successful, Havel demonstrates the link between responsibility and human hope. What humans are willing to risk their beings for defines not only their hopes but also two they are—their own identity. And in this regard, Havel again provides a mirror for the West in its condoning of Libyan leader Moammar Khadafy while he supplied oil: "Westerners are risking their security and their basic moral principles for the sake of a few barrels of crude oil." For Havel the hope for nations—similar to the hope for individuals—derives from a sense of responsibility to something beyond, that which gives risking one's being a meaning.

HAVEL ON STAGE: THE INITIAL REVIEWS

Patocka once told me: the real test of a man is not how well he plays the role he has invented for himself, but how well he plays the role that destiny assigned to him. (***Disturbing the Peace***)

Havel seems eminently unqualified to be president of a country, but then, as the above quote implies, that may not be the issue. Nevertheless, he has been criticized for indecisiveness, choosing amateurs for positions demanding specialized skills, and visiting Austrian leader Kurt Waldheim despite the protests of many Jewish leaders. His country is undergoing a difficult economic transition, is suffering from deep internal divisions, and must come to terms with environmental pollution that may well be the worst in Eastern Europe.

What the world will ultimately make of Havel's performance as president is much too early to predict, but Havel himself has anticipated the conflict of image and identity in his most recent plays, ***Largo Desolato*** (1984) and ***Temptation*** (1985). As ***Largo Desolato*** suggests, a leader can become the embodiment of the hopes and expectations of the people he represents, to his own detriment; he may lose his own identity entirely in trying to measure up to the expectations—and consequent demands—of others. *Temptation,* based on the Faust theme, which runs through Havel's political writings, explores the subtle prostituting of one's ideas and integrity when they become calculated or useful, qualities that are considered simply good politics by many Westerners. Both plays dramatize the pressures, the temptations, and the ambiguities of leadership.

Havel's leadership also embodies the problem of "role reversal." Historically, Havel has thrived as a "dissident" who—despite pressure—refused to leave his own country in a century where political exiles have won the vast majority of literary and political kudos. His forte is pre-eminently the role of internal antagonist. Nevertheless, as the feisty president of a newly-reborn democracy with a tradition of philosopher presidents, Havel may yet find his most challenging role in confronting the smug "superiority" of the West. Havel, the Czech "dissident," has prepared the stage for the role of Havel, international protester.

And the critics are ready. Western intellectuals who hear echoes of Heidegger, Sartre, Camus, and Kafka in Havel's writings may label him a "preposterous idealist" (Havel's own term for what critics call him), an anachronistic Existentialist in a postmodern world, an obvious example of the intellectual backwardness of Eastern Europe—or worse. The task of protesting the deadening of the human in a Communist bureaucracy may turn out to be Havel's dress rehearsal for the challenge of confronting the self-propagating and seemingly impregnable automatism of a global technocracy.

In his writings, nonetheless, the folk-hero Havel has already pricked the sleeping Giant of the West. But if Havel's thought is taken seriously, it is not the response of the superpowers—or the intellectuals—that matters. Rather, it is the response of each seemingly powerless individual, assuming the roles assigned by destiny, that will make the difference in contemporary—and future—world drama. And no better example of this philosophy in action can be found than Václav Havel himself.

Michael L. Quinn (essay date May 1992)

SOURCE: "Delirious Subjectivity: Four Scenes from Havel," in *Essays in Theatre,* Vol. 10, No. 2, May, 1992, pp. 117-32.

[*In the following essay, Quinn explores delirium, namely in the form of misunderstanding and confusion, in Havel's dramatic works. According to Quinn, Havel typically incorporates elements of delirium to evoke irony and satire.*]

Setting the Stage: The Negative Concept of Delirium

One of the most interesting products of the contemporary critical focus on semiotics in the formation of subjectivity is the "negative theory" of delirium. Unlike an ordinary analytic theory, which tries to construct coherent references, delirium involves a theory of mistaken references, of incoherence; as a supplement to theories of communication, which are designed to explain how we keep messages straight, this theory explains how sense gets lost, and the interesting things that happen when people lose it.

As a theory of confusion, delirium has several uses, especially philosophical, psychoanalytic and aesthetic ones. As it has emerged in deconstructive philosophical writing, it provides an occasional tropology for the slippage of signs in relation to their conventional functions. For some psychoanalytic theorists delirium is a political solution, a valorized term that opens the utopian prospect of free play to the searching eyes of the anxious subject. In this case delirium serves as an utterly skeptical qualification to the logic of reference, as the shadow-side of a coherent, perhaps oppressive order of determinate things and events that produces symptomatic non-sense. My focus in this essay is on delirium's aesthetic interest, since it provides for both the vivid expression of character and the playful use of signs as they are imaginatively received by an interpreting community.

In *The Logic of Sense* Gilles Deleuze compares the tree of "ordo" with the roots, the "rhizome" of delirium. A logical analysis of representations typically ends in paradox; in delirious analysis the paradoxical "lekta" of representation—its gesture or, in Peirce's terms, interpretant—produces a series of semiotic associations. When these associations fall within the logical status of fictions, they have nothing to do with truth claims; their relations are with other signs, and they cease to function as propositions ([John R.] Searle). Even though such a situation causes the subject to lose contact with the phenomenal "manifold of perception," delirious association does seem to involve the mysterious perception of semiotic resemblances, whether of the homonymic type that exists between similar sign materials, or of the synonymic type that relates similar meanings ([Sergei] Karcevski).

Delirious analysis, as a semiotics of mental association like Freud's master tropes of condensation and displacement, may be brought to bear on any subjective context involved in the production and reception of drama. In the authorial context, delirious association provides the source for surrealist playwriting's not-so-random techniques of automatic writing and the journal of dreams; in this form, which communicates without coded associations, the entire appearance of the drama becomes a play of resemblant signs. Yet as a technique of dramatic writing, delirium appears most often as a crucial tool for the representation of character. When the confusion of a central character spins into an aesthetically fascinating dementia, an aesthetics of delirium can be used as a way to express or comprehend the progress of the unravelling mind. The idea of delirium exists as a safe categorical standpoint from which an audience or another character can explain what is being shown after the delirious subject becomes—however poetically—inarticulate.

Václav Havel has, since his first works, written characters whose mental states verge on the delirious. To describe all such moments would require much more than a short essay, so for the present I will describe four representative "moments" of delirium in his plays, together with the subjective situations, both cultural and dramaturgical, that helped to produce them. From this standpoint I am not following the thesis of Deleuze and Guattari, that the whole structure of thought in western culture is paranoid; I merely intend to use historical circumstance as the subjective, often culturally conditioned scene in which delirium erupts as an important part of dramatic texts or performances. In principle the notion of delirium does not imply any particular politics, but delirious expression does bear with it the conditioning limits of experience and culture, of what can be combined in unverifiable or unlikely scenarios according to the ruling lekta of association that constructs the series.

Only rarely does Havel employ the authorial context in his writing of delirium; the most obvious example is *The Mountain Hotel*, in which the delirium of the authorial persona overpowers the characters by making them all subject to the same repeating semiotic series. More often Havel uses a central moment of delirium—almost a borrowed technical "turn" from the rhetoric of expressionism—as a way of dramatizing the crisis of conscience (of consciousness) in the life of his central character. Fortunately, from the audience standpoint, he has produced these images of delirium in the context of an "inferential dramaturgy," which interprets the significance of delirium through an ordinary semantic and aesthetic context, encouraging delirious moments to be perceived as a means for the expression of irony and satire. The audience is supposed to be able to understand delirium, and even embrace it in dramatic form, but it is not supposed really to endorse it, and certainly not to imitate it.

Scene I: Motomorphosis

Havel's first use of playful delirium feeds on the formalist tradition of comic theory. I'd like to rehearse this tradition in relation to one of its master tropes, to give an example of the way that even delirious signification establishes a tradition within which its aesthetic uses can become clear.

One of Victor Shklovsky's favorite metaphors for the art work was a motor car. Writing in 1928, on the cusp of Formalism's official disappearance, he explained:

> If you wish to become a writer you must examine a book as attentively as a watchmaker a clock or a chauffeur a car.

> Cars are examined in the following ways: The most idiotic people come to the automobile and press the balloon of its horn. This is the first degree of stupidity. People who know a little more about cars but overestimate their knowledge come to the car and fiddle with its stick-shift. This is also stupid and even bad, because one should not touch a thing for which another worker is responsible.

> The understanding man scrutinizes the car serenely and comprehends "what is for what": why it has so many cylinders and why it has big wheels, where its transmission is situated, and why its rear is cut in an acute angle and its radiator unpolished.

> This is the way one should read.

Yet from the point of view of delirious analysis, what is most interesting is the way in which the first contacts with the car establish a relation, from which other relations begin to emerge. Shklovsky would have people know how the machine works as such, yet delirious resemblance accommodates the ridiculous efforts of the "stupid" to comprehend the car's significance much more coherently than does their out-of-hand practical dismissal. Only a mad theory of confused association can explain the sorts of uses that automobiles have acquired, for example, in contemporary advertisements for trucks or sports cars, in which the relations of cars to cultural signs of power, pleasure and identity far outweigh their importance as machines for transportation.

The potentially delirious aesthetic play in the metaphor of the motor car was noticed by Shklovsky's friend Roman Jakobson when it occurred as a joke in one of the plays of Prague's Liberated Theater. Jakobson's "Letter to Voskovec and Werich on the Noetics and Semantics of Fun," written for the Czech theater's outstanding pair of clowns, gives this example of how a delirious view of the sign for motorcar was staged in one of their revues, as a phenomenal "negative object":

> Bun: Well, you know that big Sentinel sports car? The hood with all that chrome, six meters long?

Hand: Well, yeah, that's my dream!

Bun: Well, that hood, you see, I don't have that at all. But then again those six exhaust pipes, so nice one under the other . . .

Hand: Well, yeah, I know them!

Bun: Well, I don't have those, either.

To mistake the sign for the thing it represents becomes, in Jakobson's view, a convenient vehicle for the disruption of the "automatism of habit," which in the formalist tradition after Bergson usually implies a laugh. There are many darker shades of delirium in Czech literature and theory, like the fervent imaginings of Ladislav Klima or the "negative objects" in Kafka's works, (such as *The Castle* or the "The Oklahoma Nature Theater,") but delirium knows no genres, either—even though Havel's early perspective as a protegé of Jan Werich was doubtless conditioned by comedy. Havel seems to have inherited both the motorcar and a delirious, comical way of looking at it.

Havel's first three experiments in the professional theater were formally complex revues, commissioned for the Theater on the Balustrade by Ivan Vyskocil, a charismatic cabaret performer who specialized in what he called the theater of "text-appeal" (Horinek). These were collaborative projects: one was co-written with Vyskocil, one with Milos Macourek (an imaginative author of children's literature), and another, called *The Demented Dove*, dramatized the delirious transformations of language through the use of verse texts from writers working in the modernist Czech tradition of Poetism. The first of these was published as **Auto-Stop** (or **Hitchhike**); it consists of three one-act plays introduced by a "demonstrator," played by Vyskocil. All three one-acts are about the impact of the motorcar, but in the central one the demonstrator takes on the part of a university docent (an assistant professor without tenure) who is presenting research "On Motomorfosis," i.e. on an "essentially complex disease process of psychoneurotical origins, consisting in the graduated and general transformations of persons into an automobile or other kind of motorized vehicle."

After presenting his dissertation work, docent Macek (which means "tomcat") introduces a friendly case-study named Felinka ("feline"?) who drives himself on stage, parks, turns his motor off so that he can talk to the doctor, and then starts himself back up again so that the audience can ask amusing technical questions about things like the vibration in his carburetor and the mixture of oil and gasoline in fuel cylinders (since, like most Eastern bloc cars, he has a two-cycle engine). Finally Felinka drives back to his "ambulanci," which is the Czech word for both an ambulance and an outpatient clinic. In the next, crucial scene, the enthusiastic docent argues that Felinka's motomorphosis is not merely a delusion, but a real physiological disease, a "pathological process consisting in a complex stalling out of natural physiological functions . . . evidently declinating from all normal forms of everyday biology in humans," which is even verifiable "empirically and statistically."

When the audience objects to this bizarre physiological theory, the docent becomes extremely angry, proclaiming that they had better examine their relationship to his contemporary discovery, for they will be unmasked if they are revealed to be "among the members of the union hostile to motorism." In the final scene, the "transformation and conclusion," the audience for the presentation and the docent begin to "sound like klaxon horns," then assemble in formation behind a Mr. Bursik ("Exchange"), and "toodle" offstage together. They have been changed perhaps too literally into the "desiring machines" of Deleuze and Guattari, but in the context of a critical artistic tradition that was clearly moving the metaphor of the motorcar in just that nonsensical direction.

Scene II: Logical Disappearance

This sort of strange episode relates to Havel's study of absurdists like Ionesco—even though it predates *Rhinoceros,* which tells the same story through the more ominously Fascist myth of the savage beast that man can become. The influence of Ionesco asserts itself in Havel's work more obviously in the way Havel's dialogue imitates the theories of the linguistics professor in *The Lesson.* Signs which seem to be the same acquire different meanings in different moments, or their meanings are simply determined subjectively by the force of their speaker's assertions. In Ionesco's work the play's dialogue often suspends its ordinary relation to reality, despite its pretentions to logic. Such a profound loss of connection between signs and their coded references can strike at the very foundations of understanding, including supposedly self-evident notions like Descartes's cogito.

In Havel's case the metamorphic "mechanization" of man, seen as a goal in earlier theories like Italian Futurism, is also a metaphor for the forced reorientation of subjectivity that Czechoslovaks experienced after the Nazi occupation in 1938 and the subsequent Communist coup in 1948. As Czeslaw Milosz describes them in *The Captive Mind* (still the classic study of artistic subjectivity in the context of ideological drift), the rigid dialectical and historical requirements of the Soviet ideology established absolute connections between signs and reality that were not subject to judgement; the official ideology became a mechanism which threatened to overpower the traditional critical powers of thought. Consequently the concept of "mechanization" in Havel's work provoked a great deal of explanation in the first phase of his critical reception. The effort to think through the subjective effects of ideological transformation did not yield easily to logical analysis, but rather led Havel to the sorts of paradoxes of being that also provide the springboard for Deleuze's leap into the theory of delirious subjectivity.

The clearest example of this paradoxical problem with identity comes through the self-analysis carried out by Hugo Pludek in *The Garden Party*. This central character has a talent for logical games, and an uncanny ability to manipulate discourse into unexpected pseudo-logical formulations and strategies. Leaving the house where he compulsively plays chess with himself (and loses!), Hugo goes to a Party social gathering where his imitations of official language eventually lead the head of the Inauguration Dept. to deduce that the Liquidation Dept. has decided to dissolve his organization. Hugo, when he visits Inauguration the next day, is quick to understand that the liquidation can never begin if there is no Inauguration department to start it; Hugo ends up in charge of a newly-designed central commission that will administer both departments.

This pseudological semiotic game might seem to be a simple indictment of the bizarre Communist practice of strictly categorizing business responsibilities under government bureaus, but Hugo also extends his analysis into an examination of human identity. When the new, powerful Hugo returns home his parents can no longer recognize him, nor does Hugo really know himself; he is caught up in a delirious frenzy of dialectical language, which leads to the kind of semio-poetic analysis in which the connections between signs take on a life of their own apart from their referential uses. In this case the shorthand of representational logic slips into infinite regression:

> Hugo: I? Who am I? Now look, I don't like such one-sidedly formulated questions, I really don't! How can you even ask in such a simplified manner? No matter how one answers questions like these—one can never encompass the whole truth, only its limited part: a Person—that is something so richly complex, changeable, and diversified, that there is no sentence, book, nothing at all that could define one in its totality. There is nothing permanent, eternal, absolute in persons, they are perpetual change, proudly ringing change, of course! Nowadays the time of static, unchangeable categories is over; nowadays, A is not just A, and B just B; today we know that A can often also be B, and B at the same time be A; that B can be B, as well as A and C; by the same token, C can be not only C, but also A, B, and D, and under certain circumstances, F can be Q or even Y or R!

Hugo's talent for analysis eventually helps him to theorize the delirious erasure of the possibility of his own being. Echoing Hamlet, he concludes: "I don't know whether you want to be or want not to be, and when you want to be and not to be; but me, I want to be always—that's why I must always a little bit not be." This satisfies Hugo's parents, and as the play ends the audience in the theater is subsequently told to "split."

Yet the audience's perception does not split; their identification with the delirious hero does not logically imply their imitation of Hugo's fragmentation into an aspect of political discourse. The coherence of the play's delirious elements depends upon their maintaining an understanding that the signifier for Hugo in the world of the play, the actor playing Hugo, remains recognizable. Hugo may seem to be logical, but he is also so badly mistaken about his place in the world that he is utterly ridiculous, and consequently completely fascinating.

Hugo represents the delirious potential of logic, just as the well-known effects of artificial language in *The Memorandum* represent a linguistic equivalent, in which the principles for the construction of the proposed "official" languages conform precisely to the poles of linguistic confusion and differentiation identified by Karcevski. Because logical arguments can maintain their logical form without maintaining the material correspondences that judgement must establish between signs and their referents, the logical connections between signs do not by themselves provide a secure context for stable judgements of identity. In *The Garden Party* one character goes adrift in an ocean of signs; in *The Memorandum* the whole world of the play risks being similarly overwhelmed by delirious signification.

Scene III: Time/Space Discontinuum

In *The Increased Difficulty of Concentration* Havel dramatizes the consciousness of a system of order even more vertiginous than language: social philosophy. Eduard Huml, overcome by anxiety, has retreated to his apartment, and Havel's play is cross-cut through time to show his confused interactions with the four women who meet with him there. In this play Havel uses time-sequence displacements to demonstrate confusion—disruptions of regular narrative chronology that also create spatial disturbances as characters move in and out of different doors in different costumes during time-spans that seem impossible. Havel wrote a thesis on this play in which he illustrates the disruptions in a chart. The left hand column is a list of the sequence of chronological events, beginning when Huml has breakfast with his wife, continuing through a series of episodes with a stenographer, mistress and visiting research team, and concluding with his wife's return from work. The right hand column shows the order of events in the plot, beginning and ending with the breakfast scene, and intercutting the action in what looks like a random sequence. In Deleuzian terms, the chart is the rhizome, the root system for an elegant, formally circular play in which the clarity of the dramatic structure is entirely at odds with the confused experience of the hero that it conveys. This elegant form is unmistakable for the audience, since the structure is bracketed by the first scene after Huml wakes and its twin, the last scene before he goes to sleep. With time, and consequently the spatial coordinates for time, in such formally imposed confusion, the hero literally cannot tell when and where people are; he lapses into repetitive behavior, confuses the identities of the women in the play, and loses any concept of the relative values of behavior.

At the climax of this formal structure is a crucial scene with the research group. In addition to the leading researcher, Jitká Balcarkova—who begins an unlikely affair with the confused Huml at the end of the play—the team includes a computer named PUZUK, the nickname of Havel's younger brother. This early computer brain is supposed to have enormous powers of calculation and scientific prediction, yet the hermeneutic burden placed upon its sensitive mechanical subjectivity is so great that when it is ordered to perform, it complains that it is tired, and asks for some rest. Later on, forced like Huml to cooperate with the research program despite having made its excuses, the computer becomes delirious, and begins to generate impertinent, surreal and embarrassing questions. Triggered by the machine, Huml's consciousness, too, spins out of control. In a bizarre sequence out of time and space, characters from earlier in the play re-appear in rapid sequence, repeating non-sensical questions that fruitfully combine their lines with others: "Fishing for fresh green apples, are you? Tomorrow I'm going carroting, so there! Give me your mountain dog-plums! Wherein lies the nucleus? Do you piss in public, or just now and then?" The burden of a theory of knowledge which makes the unit of data an absolute fact, but offers only an infinite context for judgement, is too great for either Huml or the little computer to bear, resulting in their parallel episodes of delirious imagination.

Huml, who dictates a lecture throughout the play, had theorized values in the broadest of relativist terms. After this delirious episode Huml can only restore his perspective through a new discovery that he works out in a long speech near the end of the play: the re-discovery of a personal hermeneutic perspective. Centered in the horizon of interactive experience, the human valuation of humans is a matter of shared judgment, and not necessarily an invitation for infinite "factual" ratiocination:

> Huml: I'm afraid the key to a real knowledge of the human individual does not lie in some greater or lesser understanding of the complexity of man as an object of scientific knowledge. The only key lies in man's complexity as a subject of human togetherness, because the limitlessness of our own human nature is so far the only thing capable of approaching—however imperfectly—the limitlessness of others. In other words, the personal, human, unique relationship which arises between two individuals is so far the only thing that can—at least to some extent—mutually unveil the secret of those two individuals. Such values as love, friendship, compassion, sympathy and a unique, irreplaceable mutual understanding—or even mutual conflict—are the only tools which this human approach has at its disposal. By any other means we may perhaps be able more or less to explain man, but we shall never understand him—not even a little—and therefore we shall never arrive at a basic knowledge of him.

Though such a perspective is still vulnerable to problems of interpretation, and especially to any loss of the context for shared communication (either of which could be a pretext for new delirious "miscognitions"), Huml's discovery does solve the problems of spatial, temporal and self perception that can result when the subject exists in semiotic singularity.

Scene IV: Delirium and Political Paralysis

Havel's regular theoretical solution to the problem of delirious subjectivity has been a consistent faith in the intuitive hermeneutic power of the audience to infer appropriate judgements of the play's events. In technical articles on playwriting from the 1960s he consistently described conventions themselves as tending to construct "vicious circles"; without the semiotic discretion of the historical audience, any innovation, meaning, and even Deleuzian "sense," would be impossible to communicate. In this regard Havel's conclusions are very much like those of Gadamer, which suggest that interpretation occurs as a negotiation of perspectives on signs. The loss of this audience resource for Havel after the Prague Spring eventually led him to adopt a communicative ethics of dissent that closely resembles a phenomenological version of the late Habermas, in which the crucial concerns are access to communication, the sincerity of communication, and shared rules of legitimate argument. The ability to communicate becomes the foundation for democratic politics.

The political pitfall of delirious subjectivity, then, becomes apparent in Havel's work in the case of isolated characters like Leopold Koprivá, the dissident phenomenologist in *Largo Desolato.* The play begins with three identical scenes:

> As the music dies away the curtain rises slowly.

Leopold is alone on stage. He is sitting on the sofa and staring at the front door. After a long pause he gets up and looks through the peep-hole. Then he puts his ear to the door and listens intently. After another long pause the curtain drops suddenly and at the same time the music returns.

The same scene closes the play, modified only to include a curtain call. Leopold, isolated and deprived, exists in a situation in which the only important signs are outside, sensible only through the lens of a peep-hole and the muffled sounds that penetrate the door. Such a situation, the metaphoric equivalent of Havel's imprisonment, provides no reliable or coherent hermeneutic perspective, and requires change.

Left as it is, Leopold's life continues under conditions in which the delirious imaginings of the persecuted subject can only be allayed by the gestures that he gradually adds to his routine in the course of the play: pacing, taking medication, washing, and gasping for air. Even Leopold's monotonous, uneventful life becomes too complex to be tolerated in the context of his delirious situation; his lack of confidence about the truth of signs finds its analogous expression in his lack of personal confidence. Like Huml, late in the play Kopriva's consciousness yields to a delirious, imagined scene of veiled threats. The characters appear outside of the plot sequence, speaking lines from earlier in the play that focus on Leopold Kopriva's self-doubts:

Leopold: I don't exactly know what I was saying—

First Sidney: But we know—
(At that moment the bathroom door opens. Bertram is standing in the doorway talking to Leopold.)

Bertram: I don't want to be hard on you or hurt you in any way.
(At that moment the kitchen door opens. Edward is standing there speaking to Leopold.)

Edward: Were you worried?
(At that moment the door of Suzana's room opens. Suzana is standing there speaking to Leopold.)

Suzana: Are you sure you didn't get yourself into trouble again somehow?

Bertram: I'm not just speaking for myself.

Edward: Perhaps you should take some pills—
(At that moment the balcony door opens. Lucy is standing there in her bedspread and speaking to Leopold.)

Lucy: You sang a different tune the first time you got me to stay here with you.

Edward: You ought to go and see Lucy.

First Sidney: This could be what people are waiting for—

Second Sidney: You'll find a way

Suzana: What is there to consider, for heaven's sake.

Bertram: And how are things between you and Suzana?

Lucy: You've had enough of me and now you want to get shot of me—

Edward: Did you sign anything?

First Sidney: We've only taken the liberty of giving you our opinion—

Second Sidney: The opinion of ordinary people—

First Sidney: Lots of ordinary people—

Edward: Some hero.

Suzana: Some hero.

Bertram: Some hero.

Lucy: Some hero.

First Sidney: You've had enough of me and now you want to get shot of me.

Second Sidney: Some hero.

First Sidney: Did you sign anything?

Leopold: (Shouting) GET OUT!

Leopold, paralyzed by dread, fluctuates between a delirium that sometimes becomes a sustained, defensive indifference, but at other times emerges as an indiscriminate desire that has collapsed upon itself, so that he cannot resume his marriage, cannot commit to political action, and cannot conceive of meaningful alternatives to confinement. Even formerly convincing political arguments seem questionable, as Leopold admits to an admiring female student:

Leopold: On the other hand there is the fact—as I've already tried to show in Ontology of the Human Self—

that there's a certain non-verbal, existential space in which—and only through which—one can get hold of something through experiencing the presence of another person—

Marketa: Forgive me, it's exactly that part—it's from chapter four—which made me decide to come and see you—

Leopold: There you are! But I wouldn't like to raise your hopes unduly, because the fact that I'm meditating on this topic doesn't automatically mean that I am myself capable of creating such a space—

Marketa: But you've been creating it for ages—by talking to me at all—by understanding me . . .

Leopold, unlike Huml, does not recapture a hermeneutic perspective, yet it has been taken up by an attentive reader. In this regard Marketa's understanding imitates the receptive understanding of the play's audience, which anchors every instance of delirium in Havel's imaginative work.

Havel uses delirious episodes throughout his later career; even in so apparently documentary a play as the Vanek "Audience," the Brewer's progressive drunkenness conjures a fluidly discontinuous whirlpool of subjectivity, against which the stoic dissident strives to communicate. In *The Mountain Hotel* the entire play is like Huml's nightmare, a delirious permutation combining characters, scenes, actions and dialogue into new sequences and effects. In *The Beggar's Opera* the delirious moment comes late in the play, when MacHeath finally realizes that his basic assumptions about the world were mistaken; deception is the rule, not the exception that makes truthfulness an issue, and at the end of the play he embraces the delirious implications of moral chaos. In ensemble pieces, like *Temptation* and *Redevelopment,* the delirious moment is a drunken party— a black mass and a celebration. Many of these moments have proven extremely difficult to stage, especially for the plays written during the time when Havel was without a theater. Earlier plays, carefully revised in rehearsal to respond to the dynamics of audience reception, augmented the coherent context of audience understanding with a strong aesthetic effect.

Curtain Call: Havel's Semiotic Self

I have argued elsewhere, in a piece called "Vanek for President," that the reception of Havel's authorial persona has been similarly susceptible to delirious permutations, many of which contributed to the man's unlikely yet all the same inexorable rise to power during the revolution. In **"Stories and Totalitarianism"** Havel had begun to discover a distinct cultural community, in Czechoslovakia's prisons, that

still regarded proceedings beyond the prison walls with something like the theater audience's human perspective of hermeneutic engagement:

> While I was in prison I realized again and again how much more present, compared with life outside, the story was. Almost every prisoner had a life story that was unique and shocking, or moving. As I listened to those different stories, I suddenly found myself in something like a pre-totalitarian world, or in the world of literature. Whatever else I may have thought of my fellow prisoners' colorful narratives, they were not documents of totalitarian nihilization. On the contrary, they testified to the rebelliousness with which human uniqueness resists its own nihilization, and the stubbornness with which it holds to its own and is willing to ignore this negating pressure. Regardless of whether crime and misfortune was dominant in any given story, the faces in that world were specific and personal.

Dialogic narrative, and the affirmation of understanding that occurs during its plural, inter-subjective coherence, provides a context for identity and experience that extreme commitments to logic and dogma cannot easily contradict. Havel, known as a historical hero with singular talents, nevertheless theorizes a dialogic construction of the self.

For many contemporary philosophers responding to the delirious post-deconstructive discourses of identity, the "logically simple" factor of the person—as Strawson puts it—in semiotic dialogue with others offers new hope for an answer to Christopher Norris's uneasy question, "What's Wrong with Post-modernism?" If the phenomenon of the person is a semiotic creation of communication, then delirium, as a crisis of semiotic coherence that disrupts interaction and isolates people, is a serious political problem.

Havel may very well emerge as a kind of proto-type of the generative self: creator of signs, pseudonyms, self-interpretations and public meditations.
—*Michael L. Quinn*

The perspective on the semiotic self that Havel seems to encourage in his "living in truth," a new phenomenological politics of communication, is much like the one described by Hugh Silverman in *Inscriptions:*

> In a hermeneutic semiology of the self, meaning cannot be relegated on the one hand to pure consciousness nor on the other hand to a simple chain of signifiers. Pure consciousness is only another substitute for a beginning and a pure chain of signifiers re-

places goal-like objectives. The system of signs must arise out of the self's interpretive activity. It must be realized through the grasp of consciousness (prise de conscience), not through consciousness itself—through the meaning of sign systems, not through their external manifestations. Interpretive experience is an ongoing activity that creates meaning, leaves signs and tends toward the production of new signs. If I AM my system of signs, the interpretive mode will have turned into a concatenation of objectivized identifications. The non-objective characters of these identities cannot be over-stressed. The signs of the self are produced through the interpretation and maintained through the ongoing activity of interpretive experience. Self-knowledge therefore will depend upon a careful understanding of signs in relation to one another. These signs, however, are not separable from the understanding that reveals them. This ambiguity is the perplexity of western philosophy . . .

This ambiguity is also the place in which the delirious self slips under the horizon, unable to translate signs into representations of experience and hence unable to experience more than the querulous self-expression of an excessively meaningless transcendental intentionality—otherwise known as desire. These coherent expressions of experience admit others to the pleasures of an effective code, unfolding in the historical perspective of the interpretive community; for the delirious subject, expression is merely more nothing.

Havel may very well emerge as a kind of proto-type of the generative self: creator of signs, pseudonyms, self-interpretations and public meditations. Certainly his dramaturgy suggests that he manages a careful balance between the expression of delirious characters and the coherent audience interpretation of their playful mental associations. This paradox of aesthetic technique seems sensible in the case of a public figure who asserts a conspicuous lack of desire for power, yet conversely gains power through altruism. The successful subject in post-modern culture is not only reflective, but expressive and receptive, able to balance self-assessment with the ongoing social project of personal interpretation. Canadian philosopher Charles Taylor sums up the contemporary notion of a "dialogic" self in terms that seem to imply just this conclusion about Havel, so I will allow his summary to conclude my argument:

> Much of our understanding of self, society, and world is carried in practices that consist in dialogical action. I would like to argue, in fact, that language itself serves to set up spaces of common action, on a number of levels, intimate and public. This means that our identity is never simply defined in terms of our individual properties. It also places us in some social space. We define ourselves partly in terms of what we come to accept as our appropriate place within dialogical actions. In the case that I really identify myself with my deferential attitude toward wiser people like you, then this conversational stance becomes a constituent of my identity. This social reference figures even more clearly in the identity of the dedicated revolutionary.

Phyllis Carey **(essay date Summer 1992)**

SOURCE: "Living Lies: Václav Havel's Drama," in *Cross Currents*, Vol. 42, No. 2, Summer, 1992, pp. 200-11.

[*In the following essay, Carey provides an overview of Havel's creative periods and major dramatic works.*]

Americans were captivated by the 1989 election of Vaclav Havel, a human rights activist who spent almost four years in prison, as the first president of post-communist Czechoslovakia. Many who had heard that his ideas had played a vital role in the country's "Velvet Revolution" were introduced to his thinking through interviews, particularly the extended dialogue in *Disturbing the Peace,* as well as occasional pieces in the *New York Review of Books.* They learned even more from the philosophical-political essays of *Living in Truth,* and from *Letters to Olga,* the collection of fascinating, philosophical letters Havel wrote to his wife while he was in prison. Havel's political writings emphasize, among a great many other things, the "power of the powerless," the ability of seemingly impotent individuals to transform their societies through assuming responsibility for their humanity and living in truth.

Fewer Americans have been introduced to Havel's dramatic oeuvre, which provides a fascinating counterpoint to his philosophical and political thought. His plays, which have earned an international reputation and have won several awards in the U.S., were banned in Czechoslovakia between 1969 and 1989. In contrast to the moral clarity of the political essays, the plays explore the ethical ambiguity that plagues modern life regardless of its political context.

Havel, who served for a number of years as literary manager of the Balustrade Theater in Prague, has defined his dramatic goal as forcing the viewer/reader "to stick his nose into his own misery, into my misery, into our common misery, by way of reminding him that the time has come to do something about it. . . . Face to face with a distillation of evil, man might well recognize what is good" (*Disturbing the Peace*). Three major phases characterize Havel's drama:

the early absurdist comedies; the Vanek morality plays; and the psychological-prison plays.

Absurdist Plays of the 1960s

Havel's first full-length play, **The Garden Party** (1963), demonstrates his enduring interest in the many roles language plays in modern society. As Havel himself notes, the action of **The Garden Party** is controlled by cliché, which not only inundates the dialogue but becomes the objective correlative of the humans who have surrendered themselves to the bureaucratic system.

The play derives its name from a garden party at an anonymous Liquidation Office. Hugo Pludek, the would-be protagonist, seeks a career in the system, but because each bureaucrat has become merely an interchangeable functionary, Hugo ends up compromising himself out of existence, unaware that the "Hugo Pludek" he is waiting to see at the end of the play is himself. As in the game of chess that forms a recurring motif in the play, the characters move in grid-like fashion within the rigid confines of prescribed, lifeless systems—social, political and linguistic—only to checkmate their own meaningless existences. Like a political address that avoids offending any group or individual, Hugo's final speech, echoing both *Hamlet* and Beckett's *Watt,* reduces the question of being to verbal gymnastics:

> . . . we are all a little bit all the time and all the time we are not a little bit; some of us are more and some of us are more not; some only are, some are only, and some only are not; so that none of us entirely is and at the same time each one of us is not entirely; . . . I don't know whether you want more to be or not to be, and when you want to be or not to be; but I know I want to be all the time and that's why all the time I must a little bit not-be. . . .

If the language games of **The Garden Party** relativize the human out of the equation, the use of a synthetic language—*Ptydepe*—enables Havel in **The Memorandum** (1965), winner of the Obie Award (1967-68) for best foreign play, to focus on the process by which humans abdicate their humanity to linguistic and/or political systems.

Josef Gross, the Managing Director of an anonymous bureaucracy, receives a memorandum in *Ptydepe,* an artificial language designed to make human communication scientifically precise by making words as dissimilar as possible. In his attempts to get the memo translated, Gross experiences the paradoxes of bureaucracy: he can obtain the documents he needs to authorize the translation only by having the memorandum already translated. While he struggles with the irrationality of the system, he falls victim to a subordinate's power play, is demoted, but eventually convinces Maria, a secretary, to translate his memo; the message, ironically, confirms in *Ptydepe* the inadequacy of the new language, urging its liquidation. The play ends with Gross back in charge and with the prospect of a new synthetic language—*Chorukor*—which will operate on linguistic principles of similarity.

In **The Memorandum** Havel explores the scientific effort to transform language into a technological tool. Here, the drive for scientific precision contends with the apparently human need for unpredictability. The language instructor's lesson on saying "boo" in *Ptydepe* illustrates how analysis increasingly deadens spontaneity: The decision as to which *Ptydepe* expression to use for "boo" depends on the rank of the person speaking and whether the "boo" is anticipated, a surprise, a joke, or a test, as in "Yxap tseror najx." Another hilarious example of a simple expression made as complex as possible is the word "Hurrah!," which in *Ptydepe* becomes "frnygko jefr dabux altep dy savarub goz texeres."

The precision exercised on analyzing the trivial contrasts with the imprecision in expressing what may be humanly significant. The ambiguous term "whatever," deemed the most used human expression, is rendered by the shortest *Ptydepe* word, "gh." Ironically, beneath all of the scientific pretensions, body language communicates and carries much of the action.

The preoccupation with using an artificial language in **The Memorandum** draws attention to the technological propensity to focus on means instead of ends. Enormous efforts to communicate precisely are undercut by the banality of what is expressed. Knowing the system, however, enables one to participate in the illusion of power and control. Like the specialized jargon of most professionals, *Ptydepe* represents an elitist code that paradoxically limits human communication both to a small group of *cognoscenti* and to those issues that can be analyzed and labeled.

Gross is caught between the need to fit into the system and his own humanistic platitudes. When Maria, fired because she translated the message without authorization, asks for his help, Gross excuses himself on the grounds that he cannot compromise his position as the "last remains of Man's humanity" within the system. He moves Hamlet's dilemma into Camus' theory of the absurd, and as so often in a scientific age, the descriptive becomes the normative:

> Like Sisyphus, we roll the boulder of our life up the hill of its illusory meaning, only for it to roll down again into the valley of its own absurdity. . . . Manipulated, absurdity . . . automatized, made into a fetish, Man loses the experience of his own totality; horrified, he stares

as a stranger at himself, unable not to be what he is not, nor to be what he is.

Gross, the would-be existentialist who is always wishing he could start his life over, cannot translate his own language into responsible action. If Pudnik is entangled in language games devoid of human integrity, Gross demonstrates that when language becomes an end in itself, even the most accurate or the most eloquent expressions become impotent.

In the tradition of Kafka, Camus, and Beckett, probably his most significant mentors, Havel explores in **The Garden Party** and **The Memorandum** the paradox of human rationality pushed to its absurd logical extreme. As in Kafka, anonymous authority figures loom behind the absurd context; as in Beckett, the habits and rituals of daily existence frequently deaden people from the horror of their predicament; as in Camus, there is occasional recognition of the absurdity. But Havel's characters, unlike those of Camus, do not rebel; rather they adapt and use the absurdity as an excuse for their own inhumanity.

The Vanek Plays

Havel wrote three one-act plays in the mid-to-late 1970s that are based on one character, a Czech writer named Ferdinand Vanek: *Audience* (1975); *Private View* (1975); and *Protest* (1978). (In a fascinating twist to dramatic history, three other playwrights adopted Vanek for their own plays—Jiri Dienstbier, Pavel Kohout, and Pavel Landovský.) Havel's Vanek plays focus on the role of the writer in a society whose corruption extends from the workplace to the privacy of home, and even to the professional life of writers.

Audience (also published with **Private View** under the title **Sorry . . .**), is probably Havel's best known work in the United States: it is often paired with *Catastrophe*, a one-act play Samuel Beckett wrote and dedicated to Havel while the latter was in prison in 1982. Although superficially simple, *Audience* raises complex ethical questions. Essentially a dialogue between Vanek and the increasingly drunken head-malster of the brewery where Vanek works, *Audience* focuses on the brewmaster's attempts to persuade Vanek to compose the brewmaster's weekly reports in exchange for an easier job. To do so, however, Vanek would, ironically, be supporting the system he is against by informing on himself.

Vanek's reluctance to accept the offer precipitates the brewmaster's assault on intellectuals, which some critics see as the heart of the play:

It's all right if I get filthy—so long as the gentleman stays

clean! The gentleman cares about a principle! But what about the rest of us, eh? He couldn't care less! . . . Principles! Principles! Sure you hang on to your flipping principles! Why not? You know damned well how to cash in on them, you know there's always a market for them, you know bloody well how to sell them at a profit! Thing is, you live on your flipping principles! But what about me? . . . Nobody's ever going to look after me, nobody's afraid of me, nobody's going to write about me, nobody's going to help me, nobody takes an interest in me! I'm only good enough to be the manure on which your flaming principles can grow!

The play ends with Vanek making a mock exit and re-entrance, starting the dialogue anew with the malster, this time readily accepting the proffered beer and joining immediately in camaraderie. The "underlying message" of the play, as Damien Jaques (drama critic of *The Milwaukee Journal*) notes, would seem to be that "artists can have principles that they refuse to violate [but] the common man doesn't have that luxury."

But truth, as Havel dramatizes it, is almost never so obvious. Among the inescapable ironies of *Audience* is that the brewmaster—rather than not having principles of his own—has merely exchanged them for the mechanics of the bureaucracy and, as a result, has become a slave to the system. Although ostensibly the one in power—he is in charge of Vanek and several other workers—he confesses himself powerless because he is a mere dispensable cog. Vanek, on the other hand, is a threat by virtue of being an authentic human being. The drunken brewmaster, a blustery administrator of the powers-that-be, ends up begging the timid Vanek to bring an actress to see him so that he can believe "I didn't live for nothing—." To "live for nothing," however, as Vanek's reticence implies, is as much a choice as to live on principle, to live for something. The ending of the play, suggesting an alternative scenario, leaves the larger "audience" with the question of which alternative is preferable.

"Living for nothing" comes in many different packages, however, as *Private View*—perhaps the most accessible and humorous of Havel's Vanek plays—amply illustrates. Michael and Vera are Westernized Yuppies who have invited Vanek for a "private view" of their newly redecorated apartment. That their lifestyle has become their only absolute is clear early on as Michael proudly shows Ferdinand the Madonna he has long sought in order to fit his "niche." Rather than adjusting the niche, he has traveled widely to find a Madonna the right size. Correspondingly, he and Vera fit all of life's experiences into the niches of their consumer clichés, which they try to convince Vanek are the "solution" to all of his presumed problems: he should redecorate; he should have a child; his wife should take cooking lessons, etc.

As the play progresses, Michael and Vera increasingly sound like commercials. When they reach the topic of their sex lives, they are quite willing to perform a demonstration for Vanek. As Michael notes,

> "Vera has remained as smashing as ever. . . . The body she's got now! It's a knockout! So fresh and young! Well, you can judge for yourself. Darling, do you mind just opening your dress a little bit? . . . After we've finished our little chat, we're going to show you some more, so you'd see what sophisticated things we do to one another."

When Vanek demurs and starts to leave amidst a barrage of advice, Michael and Vera suddenly fall apart. Their facade is their existence, and with no one to impress, they lose their only reason for being. They browbeat Vanek into staying, and the play ends where it began.

Private View provides a glimpse of private life withdrawn and alienated from public and political concerns. Michael and Vera accuse Vanek of being a coward and a romantic because he will not compromise enough to get a socially respectable job. They, on the other hand, in substituting consumer comforts and "self-fulfillment" for social responsibility, have become dehumanized, merely part of the decoration in their apartment. The satisfaction Michael finds in the almond peeler he has brought back from the States suggests the way in which their being and purpose have been trivialized, their identity subsumed in the objects that they serve.

Havel, describing elsewhere the interdependence of the social and the private, the historical and the personal, alludes to the problem at the core of *Private View:*

> . . . even the most private life is oddly distorted, sometimes to the point where it becomes implausibly bizarre, the paradoxical outcome of a paralyzing desire for verisimilitude. It is obvious what has made this desire so intense: the subconscious need to compensate for the absence of the opposite pole—truth. It is as though life in this case were stripped of its inner tension, its true tragedy and greatness, its questions. (**"Stories and Totalitarianism,"** *Open Letters*)

If the "crisis of human identity" that Havel sees as the central question of all of his plays (*Living in Truth*) afflicts the bureaucrat, the blue-collar worker, and even the purely private relationships of spouses, it also afflicts writers themselves as the Vanek play *Protest* illustrates. Like all of his plays, *Protest* contains vague allusions to actual events or experiences in Havel's life.

As in the other two Vanek plays—and most of Havel's

oeuvre—the action takes place in the language, in this case the dialogue between Vanek and Stanek, a fellow writer whose daughter is pregnant by a pop star who has just been arrested on a pretext. Stanek, who enjoys political immunity presumably because he can straddle issues, asks Vanek about protesting the pop star's arrest. When Vanek, who has already written a protest, presents Stanek with the document for his signature, Stanek's inner conflicts come to the fore. In a lengthy monologue Stanek analyzes the "subjective" and "objective" arguments for signing the protest, demonstrating through convoluted logic both how "they"— the authorities—think and how he excuses himself from taking responsibility. His speech embodies "double think," becoming a brilliant exercise in reducing morality to rationality. Stanek does not sign the document and the play ends when Stanek learns that the pop star has been released, making the protest superfluous.

Part of Stanek's rationalizing anticipates what Havel explores in greater detail in *Largo Desolato:* the widespread abdication of personal responsibility to the professionals in morality. Stanek points out that "the rest of us—when we want to do something for the sake of ordinary human decency—automatically turn to you [Vanek], as though you were a sort of service establishment in moral matters." The question of Stanek's signature, therefore, involves his claiming identity as a responsible human being, a claim he is unable to make.

Havel's Vanek, however, around whom moral issues arise, does not play the role of a moral authority; rather, he comes off as a self-ironic, timid soul whose occasional embarrassment becomes the only comment on the "bad faith" of the brewmaster, Michael and Vera, and Stanek. In all three plays Vanek, who speaks very little, becomes a sounding board for the characters' reflections on their own identities and concerns. His simplicity contrasts with their sophistication and sophistry. He occasionally questions, often offers understanding, never condemns. Rather, he allows his own integrity and motives to be questioned and attacked as the other characters attempt to implicate or discredit him. If he is an alter-ego of Havel, he is also an anti-hero, his humility and self-effacement pointing beyond the human to a standard of truth that enables the other characters to glimpse their own duplicity and that gives his own character both its quiet dignity and its self-parody.

Psychological-Prison Plays

When Havel returned from his stay in prison as a result of dissident activities, he wrote a short play (1983) in response to Beckett's *Catastrophe.* The play, entitled *Mistake,* foregrounds the human tendency—regardless of political system—toward totalitarianism, not only politically but privately as well. The plot is simple: four inmates in a prison—who have formed their own subsystem with their own kingpin—indoctrinate a new prisoner, who has inadvertently smoked a cigarette before breakfast, on his rights and responsibilities within the system. The new inmate, XIBOY, says nothing throughout the play, merely shrugging and looking embarrassed, to the increasing anger and frustration of the "King" and his cohorts, who finally realize that XIBOY is a "bloody foreigner." The play ends with King's "death sentence" for XIBOY.

The prison setting as a totalitarian system—although no doubt inspired by Havel's own recent experiences—underscores the human propensity not only to adapt to repressive systems but to duplicate them in subsystems, and to subjugate others, attempting to force them into uniformity. The seemingly trivial offense against "non-smokers' rights" becomes a major crime in the context of the repressive systems operating without and within and suggests a subtle challenge to the West's preoccupation with minor "rights" when larger questions of human survival and identity are at stake. The foreigner's death sentence comes about because, speaking another language literally and perhaps metaphysically, he cannot be indoctrinated and subsumed into the system. His silence and lack of complicity become a threat to the status quo.

Havel's two full-length post-imprisonment plays, *Largo Desolato* (1984) and *Temptation* (1985), further explore the themes of *Mistake.* Unlike the relatively flat characters of Pudnik and Gross in the earlier plays, the post-imprisonment drama excavates much deeper psychological terrain. In addition, the archetype of Faust joins Hamlet as the subtle distortions of truth become both increasingly ambiguous and perverse.

Largo Desolato, which won a Best Play Off Broadway award for 1985-86, probes the relationship between human identity and the roles one plays. Professor Leopold Nettles, an existentialist philosopher who has been under police surveillance and harassment for writing a paragraph "disturbing the intellectual peace," can escape from his dilemma by declaring that he is "not the same person who is the author of that thing." Nettles is so tortured by the expectations of his friends and by his own self-doubts, however, that he has virtually imprisoned himself within his own apartment and his own mind.

Like Vanek in *Protest,* Nettles has been the vicarious moral voice upon whom all his friends, who have surrendered their own voices, depend. He is their excuse not to be. Their vague expectations and dependence contribute to his identity crisis: is there a split between who he is and the roles others expect him to play? The dichotomy between Nettles's current internal torment and the image he has projected in the past is revealed through the other characters.

His friend Bertram notes, "I can't escape the awful feeling that lately something inside you has begun to collapse . . . that you are tending more and more to act the part of yourself instead of being yourself."

In fact, Nettles in his desperation increasingly acts the roles that others project on him, using the same phrases they have addressed to him. Urged to put his philosophical ideas to some practical use, he ironically does just that: he uses his reputation and writings to seduce Marguerite, a young student whom he sees as "in mid-crisis about the meaning of life." Before the seduction is complete, however, the agents of the authorities appear. Nettles takes a stand, swearing that he will not disclaim his paragraphs, that he will not give up his "own human identity." The agents inform him that his protest comes too late: he has already given up his identity, and his signature, therefore, "would be superfluous." Like Stanek, Nettles has spent so much time analyzing and worrying about his image that he has lost his own identity in the process. The play ends where it began, but with Nettles taking a bow as the actor playing a role in a play about playing roles.

Largo Desolato anticipates *Temptation* in its depiction of the external and internal demons that make Nettles's existence a living hell. The prospect of going to prison seems trivial in comparison with the the torment and restrictions that Nettles experiences as a result of trying to serve all of his self-imposed masters, of playing all of the roles others expect of him. As in a dysfunctional family, most of the other characters have already abdicated their identities, becoming mere stage props or interchangeable characters, as evidenced by their very names—"First Sidney" and "Second Sidney," "First Chap" and "Second Chap," "First Man" and "Second Man." *Largo Desolato* depicts the loss of human identity both by those who depend on others to save them and by those who would save others from their own burden of humanity. For Havel, there are no specialists in being human; every human is challenged to be—or not to be.

Havel's long-term interest in writing a play based on the *Faust* legend found its fruition in *Temptation,* his latest full-length play. *Temptation* is by far Havel's wordiest play as he explores in depth the question of truth and the ways truth can be perverted. Havel's Faust, Dr. Foustka, who is a scientist, has been secretly studying black magic. Fistula, who plays the Mephistopheles role, becomes his mentor and points out that "the truth isn't merely what we believe, after all, but also why and to whom and under what circumstances we say it!" Here, ironically the Devil is paraphrasing Havel, who expressed this definition of truth in a 1982 letter to his wife (*Letters to Olga* [No. 138]). Later, the Deputy of the Institute in the play convolutes the definition:

The truth must prevail, come what may. But for that very reason we must remind ourselves that looking for the truth means looking for the whole, unadulterated truth. That is to say that the truth isn't only something that can be demonstrated in one way or another, it is also the purpose for which the demonstrated thing is used or for which it may be misused, and who boasts about it and why, and in what context it finds itself.

Foustka begins his struggle with truth where Nettles left off in *Largo Desolato;* Foustka's philosophic description of modern humanity leads Marketa, a secretary at the Institute, to fall in love with him. When, his ego inflated by the "conquest," Foustka is confronted by the Director and accused of pursuing unscientific knowledge, Foustka appeals to scientific truth and morality to exonerate him. He claims that he has studied the occult in order to expose its unscientific basis. Marketa, who has believed Foustka's appeal to a higher authority as a basis for truth, ends up as Foustka's Ophelia, dismissed from the Institute and singing in madness. Foustka later learns that Fistula is a secret agent of the Institute, sent to test his fidelity to scientific truth. Foustka is finally entrapped by the complex web of lies he has woven; like Nettles, he has created his own hellish prison.

Finally aware that his attempts to manipulate the system have failed, Foustka acknowledges the devil—"here among us"—not Fistula, but "the pride of that intolerant, all-powerful, and self-serving power that uses sciences merely as a handy weapon for shooting down anything that threatens it, that is, anything that doesn't derive its authority from this power or that is related to an authority deriving its powers elsewhere." The play ends with a witches' sabbath, chaos, Foustka being set afire, and a fireman coming to put out the flames.

Temptation constantly challenges common definitions of truth while affirming its fundamental significance. Havel masterfully demonstrates how the most "truthful" expressions can be demonic when truth is instrumentalized, made a tool for some human purpose. At the same time, he creates seemingly demonic characters who see clearly the logical inconsistencies of selective duplicity. Ironically, it is a devil figure quoting Scripture who points out that living in lies carries its own rules: "You cannot serve two masters at once and deceive them both at the same time! . . . You simply must take a side!" The play suggests, moreover, that to reduce truth to the limits of rationality in turn distorts the "truths" of that rationality. *Temptation* becomes a comic-bitter indictment of the postmodern mind.

The setting of Havel's plays alternates from modern apartment interiors to anonymous bureaucracies. Although the characters all seem to be aware of "higher authorities,"

those in charge might as easily be representatives of free-market countries as of communist or socialist regimes. As in Beckett, Havel's perennial setting is metaphysical: the contemporary human mind, imprisoned in its rationality, substituting scientific, political, and consumer systems to fill the need for an absolute.

The question of human identity that Havel explores in all of his works is not the issue of individual self-fulfillment that seems to preoccupy Americans. Rather, it is the universal question of the human on the brink of the twenty-first century, in which technical specialization has, paradoxically, produced greater standardization, and more and more people are living in an artificial environment, seduced by the comforts of effortless existence. The question for Havel from Pudnik to Foustka is whether humans choose to be or not to be human beings, to live in truth rather than to support the lies that make them mere adjuncts of one or another system: "Human identity, simply put, is not a 'place of existence' where one sits things out, but a constant encounter with the question of how to be, and how to exist in the world" (*Letters to Olga* [No. 139]).

> **Truth for Havel seems inextricably linked with assuming responsibility for one's humanity.**
> —*Phyllis Carey*

And what is truth? Havel never tells us directly in his plays. He assumes that we will recognize the many forms of its opposite—the excuses, subterfuges, rationalizations, illusions, pretexts, sophistries—even if many of his characters do not. Truth for Havel seems inextricably linked with assuming responsibility for one's humanity. To the extent we fail, his drama implies, we live in misery; hope lies in recognizing and taking responsibility for "our common misery."

Alfred Thomas (review date Summer 1992)

SOURCE: A review of *The Vanek Plays* and *Living in Truth,* in *Slavic Review,* Vol. 51, No. 2, Summer, 1992, pp. 348-51.

[*In the following review, Thomas offers positive assessment of* Living in Truth *and* The Vanek Plays. *According to Thomas, Havel's dramatic works "are more complex, darker studies of the human spirit than the Czech tradition of 'humanist' criticism would suppose."*]

Predating the tumultuous political events of 1989, both volumes here under review—one a collection of political essays by the playwright Václav Havel, the other an anthology of plays by Czech dissident writers including Havel—can and should be assessed in the light of subsequent events. It would be facile to claim that these books have become outdated by the political changes in central Europe; rather, Havel's essays, contained in *Living in Truth,* form a continuity with President Havel's more recent pronouncements on the fortunes of his country as it evolves into a democratic, pluralist state.

Living in Truth consists of six seminal essays by Havel himself (including **"Letter to Dr. Gustáv Husák," "The Power of the Powerless"** and **"Politics and Conscience"**) and sixteen additional works of homage to Havel by writers as diverse as Samuel Beckett, Heinrich Böll, Jiří Grusa, Pavel Kohout, Milan Kundera, Ludvík Vaculík, Arthur Miller and Timothy Garton Ash. The need for this type of *hommage* is understandable: artists, critics and journalists from Czechoslovakia and the west were at pains to demonstrate their moral support to a persecuted fellow artist in the years of so-called "normalization" when Havel spent many years in prison. With historical hindsight, one cannot help but regard these expressions of support as the nascent development of what I choose to term the western-inspired "phenomenon" of Václav Havel. In the present Czech and Slovak Federal Republic Havel is frequently the object of criticism yet here in the west he remains the object of unqualified praise and admiration. The "phenomenon" of Havel is inviolate in the west perhaps because of his status as the embodiment of the spirit of central European democracy. During and following the revolution of 1989 Havel was synonymous with freedom and reform. Criticism of Havel in the west would probably be construed, therefore, as automatically harmful to renewed Czech democracy itself. (It is perhaps a sign of the healthy resilience of democracy in the Czech and Slovak Federal Republic that the figure of the President is not untouchable.)

While it is understandable, maybe even desirable, for western commentators and critics to desist from criticism of a brave individual who is struggling to keep his internally beleaguered country together, this kind of unqualified admiration can interfere with a truly objective critique of Havel as an *artist.* All too often Czech literary criticism fails to distinguish between politics and critical evaluation. Markéta Goetz-Stankiewicz's introduction to *The Vanek Plays* exemplifies the unfortunate tendency of certain modes of scholarship to subordinate disinterested criticism to the imperatives of the partisan politics. Let us illustrate what is meant: Professor Goetz-Stankiewicz informs us that Havel is the recipient of many western awards and accolades. What does this have to do with being a good playwright? When we read criticism on Harold Pinter or Sam

Shepard we do not expect to be told how many trophies they display on their mantel. (Incidentally, the Czech *fin de siècle* critic Arnost Procházka regarded the Czech need for praise from foreigners as a peculiar failing of the "small nation" mentality.) Professor Goetz-Stankiewicz sees a "common idea of human value" running through the Vanek plays. We might ask what "human value" means here—human goodness perhaps? Such an emphasis is reminiscent of T. G. Masaryk's concept of *humanita,* the ethical system which perceives the quality of "humanity" as immanent in the Czech intellectual tradition from the Hussites to the present.

It is my belief that Havel's plays—both those of the "Vanek" cycle contained in the present anthology (*Audience, Protest* and *Unveiling*) and the later drama *Temptation* and *Largo Desolato*—are more complex, darker studies of the human spirit than the Czech tradition of "humanist" criticism would suppose. As Havel points out in his collection of essays *Dálkový výslech,* the figure of Vanek in his plays serves as a "dramatic principle," a foil which highlights the moral predicament of the principal protagonists. In *Audience,* for example, Vanek is a dissident prisoner harangued by the drunken Brewmaster who is demoralized not by Vanek's impassive responses but by his own personal sense of inadequacy. In *Unveiling,* Vanek is a visitor at the apartment of a couple, Michal and Vera, who have sold out to the regime. Their materialistic lifestyle includes free access to western travel and luxury goods. The couple attributes to Vanek's marriage the misery which underlies their own personal life. In a fine example of the circular structure of theatre of the absurd, the play ends with the all-suffering Vanek coerced by his neurotic hosts to stay on—a conclusion reminiscent of Josef Topol's play *Slavik k veceri* (*Nightingale for Dinner*) in which the eponymous Mr. Nightingale is emotionally bullied and finally murdered by a grotesque bourgeois family. In the third Havel one-act play, *Protest,* Vanek pays a visit to Stanek, another of Havel's self-hating conformists who is trapped between the poles of political expediency and private conscience. By the end of the play, Stanek has managed to persuade himself by means of a dialectical process of reasoning that the political status quo is acceptable.

For Goetz-Stankiewicz, Vanek is a positive, steadfast character, the "quiet eye of a hurricane" whose eloquent silence proves the falseness of the language by which the other characters live. In claiming that language has been emptied of metaphysical meaning, Goetz-Stankiewicz is subscribing to a "modernist" reading of the "Vanek" plays which, to my mind, overlooks their more radical pessimism. Goetz-Stankiewicz perceives a seamless unity between Havel's essays and his fiction, each mutually illuminating the other. I am rather of the opinion that Havel's drama undermines some of his most cherished ethical ideas as expounded in essays like **"The Power of the Powerless."** Goetz-Stankiewicz states that in Vanek Havel has created a "new hero," a representative of that strong, if silent majority which will prevail against the forces of reaction and oppression. This is a prescriptive, programmatic criticism which is belied by the internal evidence of the plays themselves. In *Unveiling* Vanek (a latter day variation on the Czech ideal of the virtuous little man typified by Masaryk's *Kleiner Mensch* and Karel Capek's *obycejny clovek*) emerges as a weak, pathetic individual who is unable to resist or oppose the predatory instincts of his interlocutors. One might even notice a latent contempt for this Czech ideal of compliance and obedience.

On a philosophical note, Havel's plays reveal a radical critique of a solipsistic ontology. In *Protest,* for example, Stanek is trapped in a dilemma *of his own making,* whether to subscribe to the "objective" world of political pragmatism or the "subjective" world of private conscience. As the character puts it: "Should I be guided by ruthless objective considerations, or by subjective inner feelings?" On one level Havel's plays are programmatic in their desire to illustrate the ethical need for personal responsibility (a key word in Havel's essays). For him the individual *is* society. Yet the playwright's ethical agenda is complicated, even contradicted, by his more original insight that personal responsibility is all but impossible to achieve in the modern world where the exercise of power is no longer objective and externalized but, as Foucault put it, "internalized." It is impossible in the modern world, Havel seems to be saying, to draw a clear dividing line between the public and private self. The objective-subjective dichotomy, maintained by Stanek, breaks down; political exigency is as subjectively determined as the dictates of social conscience; that is to say, "inner feelings" can be both political and personal. According to Foucault, the post-Enlightenment world involved a gradual movement from power conceived as a crude, unilateral coercion imposed on the individual from outside (such as imprisonment and torture) to a more subtle, "internalized" mode of control in which the individual checks his own behavior. Stanek, Michal, Vera and the Brewmaster are subjects *and* objects of power in that they regulate and are regulated by power. There seems to be no way out of this dialectic. Goetz-Stankiewicz proposes a humanistic "happy-ending" by attributing to the disenfranchised Vanek the role of a positive hero. But Havel's drama is of a distinctly darker hue: there simply is no hero or self uncontaminated by corruption, greed and the lust for power. To make of Vanek the redemptive hero is to play down the tragic-comic absurdity that identifies Havel as a direct spiritual descendant of Franz Kafka and Jaroslav Hasek.

Havel treats the problem of power and subjectivity with consummate skill in *Largo Desolato.* In this play (to my mind his best) the philosopher's living room has become a metaphor for the prison of the mind. The tragi-comic absurdity of the action is generated not by the scenario of surveillance but the hero's inability to distinguish between external and subjective reality. In this solipsistic hell it is impossible to tell whether the other characters (Kopriva's contemptuous wife, his bullying fellow-dissident Bertram and those Kafkaesque doubles who drop in at regular intervals) are intended as real people or fragmented projections of the hero's psyche. Havel's "Vanek" plays can be read in an analogous fashion as subjective monologues masquerading as dialogues wherein the individual struggles in vain to demarcate the boundary between objective and subjective experience.

In conclusion, we can claim that Havel's plays are more ambiguous and pessimistic than many commentators have suggested. In highlighting the plays' ethical-humanistic message, critics risk oversimplifying their dramatic power. Far from being positive affirmations of "human value," Havel's plays are tragi-comic allegories about the insidious configuration of power in the modern world—insidious precisely because its starting point is the private domain of the self.

George F. Kennan   (review date 24 September 1992)

SOURCE: "Keeping the Faith," in *New York Review of Books,* September 24, 1992, pp. 3-4.

[*In the following review, Kennan offers favorable assessment of* Summer Meditations, *praising Havel's courage to "offer to the public so unsparingly an exposure of what one can only call his political and personal philosophy."*]

Václav Havel, the courageous leading dissident in the years of Communist control of Czechoslovakia, and more recently president of that country, needs no introduction to the readers of *The New York Review.* His name has appeared on the pages of the *Review* in a number of capacities. Known originally primarily as a playwright, Havel has always been a prolific and engaging writer. His literary output in later years has taken exclusively the form of essays, letters, and unpublished interviews; and after his release from prison in 1983, several volumes of English translations of such materials saw publication, prior to the appearances of the volume here under review.

With very minor exceptions, the materials contained in those volumes were written during the Communist period of Czechoslovak history and reflected Havel's preoccupation with the tremendous strains that rested upon his life and those of so many others in those tragic years. The volume to which this present discussion is devoted was written in the summer of 1991 and reviewed by the author in early 1992—that is, during his second presidency of that country, now terminated by his recent withdrawal.

It is the first such volume, therefore, to reflect the author's reactions to the tremendous events, including prominently his own experiences, of the period of liberation. It speaks, however, for the depth and solidity of his thinking that this fundamental change in political environment occasioned, and required, no significant revision of the convictions and principles that had inspired his earlier writings. These last were simply applied to the new situation; and they seem to have lost none of their relevance or their force in the process.

Leaving aside the first section of the book entitled "Politics, Morality, and Civility" (which was placed last in the original Czech edition and will be given similar place here), the first material to meet the reader's eye is the long section (the longest in the book) that deals, under the title "In a Time of Transition," with the internal political problems of the Czechoslovak state as they presented themselves to Havel during his second presidency, when the book was written. Much of this section is devoted to constitutional problems. The present constitution, inherited from the Communist period, being plainly unsuitable for the present era, Havel, a strong opponent of proportional representation and advocate of the strengthening of the presidency, pressed hard, while president, for the early preparation of a new one. But this question soon became enmeshed with the problem (among others) of Slovak separatism; and pending a resolution of that problem, no serious progress in the constitutional question was possible.

This being the case, it was not surprising that a large portion of this first section of Havel's book was addressed to the future of the Czech-Slovak relationship. And an agonizing matter this was for a man of Havel's generous impulses, torn between a broad-minded sympathy and understanding for Slovak national feeling, on the one hand, and exasperation with the erratic and irresponsible behavior of Slovak politicians (and some of the Czech ones as well) in the official discussions of this bitter problem. It remained throughout his conviction, and one for which he offered a number of serious arguments, that a complete separation of the two peoples would be nothing but "a grave misfortune" for all concerned. And his reluctance to preside over a break-up of the country was apparently one of the principal reasons for his withdrawal from the presidential office.

There is a particularly tragic aspect to Havel's helplessness in the face of this problem, for it is hard to believe that the Slovaks, whether independent or otherwise, will ever have a fairer, more tolerant, or more understanding chief of state than Václav Havel would have been at the head of a continuing Czechoslovakia. And indeed, this writer knows of no evidence that the majority of the Slovaks, if challenged by the sort of referendum Havel has urged, would favor a complete separation. But here is where the professional politicians come in. The drift toward separation appears to have been largely the product of their narrowness of concept and their tendency to play with words and slogans that would shore up their own positions. Things will no doubt continue to be this way.

Among Havel's comments on this subject there were a few observations about politicians and politics that were clearly part of his general political philosophy and had a much wider relevance than to Czechoslovak problems alone. He did not challenge the usefulness or the necessity of the political party as such. He saw it as "an integral part of modern democracy and an expression of its plurality of opinion." But he minced no words in expressing his impatience with what he calls "the dictatorship of partisanship," which he defines as "the excessive influence of parties in the system of political power." Political parties, he writes, can become "a shadow state within a state." The loyalties they demand "can count for more than the will of the electorate." Their pre-electoral maneuverings have a tendency to supersede society's interests. Electors come to be governed by people they never elected. Political decisions come to be determined by the tactics and strategies of partisan competition. "A few months before the election," he noted,

> electoral politics are already dominating political life. . . . There are articles about partisan bickering, bragging and intrigue, predications about who will join with whom and against whom, who will help (or harm) whose chances in the election, who might eventually shift support to whom, who is beholden to whom or falling out with whom. Politicians seem to be devoting more time to party politics than to their jobs. Not a single law is passed without a debate about how a particular stand might serve a party's popularity. Ideas, no matter how absurd, are touted to gain favour with the electorate. . . . All this displaces a responsible interest in the prosperity and success of the broader community.

These views were written, of course, about conditions in Czechoslovakia; and this being a country in which, according to Havel's translator, Paul Wilson, "forty parties, coalitions, and movements" were competing in the most recent election. They are not surprising. But no one who has been following pre-election developments in the United States will fail to note the wider connotations of Havel's remarks. It is not hard to detect in them not only echoes of early

Federalist anxieties about "factionalism" in the emerging American political system, but also something of the impatience with rampant partisanship that caused so many Americans to greet with sympathy and satisfaction Mr. Ross Perot's strictures on the American political establishment of this day.

It is in fact a question whether Havel, in these observations, did not strike a chord that resonated with the public of a number of modern democracies. It would be hard, of course, to deny the vulnerability of modern democracy generally to domination by party machines and personalities in whose motivation for political involvement a devotion to the public interest is diluted to put it mildly, by considerations of another and less admirable nature. It has been customary in the past for most Western peoples to accept this situation with a resigned shrug of the shoulders as one of the prices for political freedom. But the years immediately ahead mark the passage not only of a century but of an age in Western civilization, and the advent of an age that is bound to place many new and unprecedented strains on the resources of modern democracy. What Havel has done, intentionally or otherwise, is to raise the question whether these developments do not call for adaptive changes in democratic systems, and whether, in particular, the democracies can continue to afford the luxury of leaving the great affairs of state so extensively dependent upon the outcome of struggles among political factions more immediately concerned with their own competitive fortunes than with the major problems of national interest. This comes out particularly clearly in his opposition to proportional representation and in his feeling that the choices the common citizen should be asked and permitted to make in the election booth should be ones among individuals, not among parties.

The next section of Havel's book, entitled "What I Believe," is devoted primarily to questions of ideology, doctrine, dogma—whatever one wishes to call it. It places principal emphasis on his skepticism and aversion with relation to all schematic thinking of this nature. He firmly rejects what he describes as the Communist effort "to unite all economic entities under the authority of a single monstrous owner . . . one central voice of reason that deems itself more clever than life itself"; and he accepts without stint the basic necessity of a market economy. But he warns against making a dogma out of the attachment to the free market. The state, too, has its part to play; but this is limited to the establishment by legislation of the rules of the game, to making the usual "macroeconomic decisions," and to formulating clear policies for all those situations in which government finds itself compelled to accept involvement. All this admittedly requires some sort of a master plan, or strategy, the aim of which should be the maximum gradual reduction of precisely this involvement, recogniz-

ing, of course, that its total elimination will never be possible.

The chapter "The Task of Independence," which follows, is devoted to the foreign policy of the Czechoslovak state as it existed at the time of Havel's writing (although there is no reason why most of it should not be applicable to the rump "Czech" state by which that older one will presumably be replaced). Not surprisingly, it is a moderate and thoroughly peaceable policy that Havel envisages. It is marked by an eagerness for association with the remainder of Europe through whatever international bodies, whether the European Community or the Council of Europe, or the CSCE, or even NATO, lend themselves to this relationship and this, then, in whatever ways seem possible and promising. Of all this it can only be said, with assurance, that a Europe concerned for its own peace and prosperity will encounter no obstacles in any Czechoslovak or rump Czech state dominated, as either of these would be likely to be, whether or not Havel is in the presidential office, by his ideas and personality.

In his observations on this subject, Havel could not avoid the effort to come to terms with one of the great overarching problems of the international life in the emerging age, which is the tension, everywhere, between the forces of integration and disintegration—this is a problem that embraces not only the restlessness of national minorities within the framework of a larger state but also the struggles of new and small states to find a middle ground between their overpowering longing for the trappings of sovereignty, on the one hand, and the obvious fact, on the other hand, of a degree of real dependence on outside forces that make a mockery of all strivings for total independence. Underlying this entire problem is of course the lack of a suitable intermediary status between that of complete formal subservience of a minority within a larger state, and, on the other hand, its total (but unreal) independence and equality with all other states as a member of the universal UN community. What Havel has to say about Czechoslovakia's relationship to these problems is thoughtful and sensible; but no more than anyone else is he in a position to come up with sweeping and universally applicable and acceptable answers to this most baffling and recalcitrant of contemporary world problems.

The chapter entitled "Beyond the Shock of Freedom" sets forth Havel's vision—a dream he calls it—of Czechoslovakia as he would hope to see it one or two decades hence. The text of this chapter having appeared in somewhat different form in *The New York Review* of June 25, 1992, under the title **"My Dream for Czechoslovakia,"** there is no need for a recounting of its many features at this point. Suffice it to note that Havel would be the first to deny that what he is presenting is a plausible utopia. He is well aware that his dream could never be realized in its totality:

> A heaven on earth in which people all love each other and everyone is hard-working, well-mannered, and virtuous, in which the land flourishes and everything is sweetness and light, working harmoniously to the satisfaction of God: this will never be. On the contrary, the world has had the worst experiences with utopian thinkers who promised all that. Evil will remain with us, no one will ever eliminate human suffering, the political arena will always attract irresponsible and ambitious adventurers and charlatans. And man will not stop destroying the world. In this regard, I have no illusions.

But all great statesmanship, as Martin Luther King suggested, must begin with some sort of a dream; and the one Havel describes—the dream of a small people with limited resources that has nevertheless come to terms with its international entourage, its natural environment, and itself—is so far ahead of most of the dreams that have inspired statesmanship in this brutal century that the reader can only acknowledge his respect for the dreamer, even if this means sharing the wistfulness that inspired the dream.

Havel denies being a philosopher. He describes himself, instead, as "only an occasional essayist or a philosophically inclined literary man."
—*George F. Kennan*

In the first chapter of this book (which I, like the original Czech publisher, have reserved for the end of this discussion) Havel sets forth and defends his effort to move his country, despite the many obstacles that lie across the path, in the direction of his dream. Of the difficulty of the task he has no illusions. He is aware, as few others could be, of the damage done to the moral fabric of Czechoslovak society by decades of Communist abuse. He had made this clear in his earlier writings. But the reality, as observable in the years since the liberation, exceeded his worst fears. What followed upon the removal of the heavy Communist hand was "an enormous and dazzling explosion of every imaginable human vice." Society had indeed freed itself; but in some ways it was behaving "worse than when it was in chains"; and it would take years to develop and cultivate a new moral order.

This, however, in Havel's view, was no cause for despair. "The only lost cause is one we give up on before we enter the struggle." And he had no doubt that the people at large would be responsive to his effort to create that new order. There was among them a dormant good will that needed only to be touched—that longed in fact to be recognized and cultivated. Nor was there any need for cynicism or deception in the approach to them. Politics was *not* essentially a disreputable business. There *was* no ultimate conflict between morality and successful political leadership. Politics as the practice of morality was not easy; but it was possible.

In this moving affirmation of confidence in the decency, the good will, and the latent responsiveness of the common man to responsible leadership there was bound to be, one might suppose, even in a man as little given to outward piety as Havel, a touch of something very close to a religious faith, guarded and undemonstrative, if you will, but none the less since. "Our death," he wrote,

> ends nothing, because everything is forever being recorded and evaluated somewhere else, somewhere "above us," in what I have called "the memory of Being"—an integral aspect of the secret order of the cosmos, of nature, and of life, which believers call God and to whose judgment everything is subject. Genuine conscience and genuine responsibility are always, in the end, explicable only as an expression of the silent assumption that we are observed "from above," that everything is visible, nothing is forgotten, and so earthly time has no power to wipe away the sharp disappointments of earthly failure: our spirit knows that it is not the only entity aware of these failures.

Havel denies being a philosopher. He describes himself, instead, as "only an occasional essayist or a philosophically inclined literary man." But what emerges from these pages is a remarkably integral view, and a strongly held one, of many things. And it is surely rare for the president of a modern country, while still in office, to offer the public so unsparing an exposure what one can only call his politically personal philosophy. And what is even more striking still is the elevated quality, morally and intellectually, of philosophy that emerges from this effort. If we look for its origins, we find that they were forged and tempered in the grueling experience of his long personal conflict with a Communist regime (an experience that included some four years in prison), and in persistent effort to understand both that regime and his own people's reaction to it.

Is there not, one wonders, a lesson in this? How much more comfortable and easy it was, by comparison, for leaders of Western societies never touched by the Communist hand to concentrate their heavy-lidded gaze exclusively on the material aspects modern life—such things as economic growth, unemployment, budgetary problems—and to leave the moral condition of society to the public schools, the churches, the commercially dominated mass media. But can this, one asks, go on? Will there not have to be a more determined and structured effort to confront young people with the seriousness of life and its problems, and with the full measure of their responsibility for responding to it, if they are to meet the coming age head-on? These, in any case, are the questions with which at least one reader puts down Havel's book; they suggest that in the writing of it he was serving purposes wider than those of which he was aware.

One cannot leave this subject without a word of recognition for the quality of Paul Wilson's translation. Wilson has been translating Havel's books for several years, and the intimate acquaintance with Havel's thought that this engendered has no doubt been uniquely helpful to him in finding the proper terms for its rendition in another language. The reader, in any case, is grateful for a text of such fluency and naturalness that he is allowed to forget that it is a translation.

Robert Skloot (essay date Spring 1993)

SOURCE: "Václav Havel: The Once and Future Playwright," in *Kenyon Review,* Vol. 15, No. 2, pp. 223-31.

[*In the following essay, Skloot considers the literary accomplishment of Havel's drama in relation to the works of Harold Pinter, Tom Stoppard, Eugene Ionesco, and Samuel Beckett.*]

In the short space of a few years, we have been witness to a Havel industry. Images of the Czech playwright-politician appear frequently in the West, and his words are quoted often whenever democrats of all kinds convene. His life is held up as an example of resistance to the tyrant's authority and the terrors of the state, and he is celebrated by those who have suffered brutal indignities as well as by those who have suffered not at all.

In 1992, with the fragmentation of his bipartite nation and the loss of his presidency, the simple fact of his unwavering commitment to human rights and to policies of tolerance and trust has introduced into the politics of the 1990s new spirit of both personal courage and political resolve. The mention of Havel's name is, for most observers, an occasion to chart the possibilities of changing old, repressive, tribal ways for new, humane ones, an exercise all the more needed as neighboring countries hemorrhage in an agony of self-destruction. In this essay, I want to explore the nature of political Havelism by temporarily disengaging it from the newspaper headlines and looking at a number of his plays. In doing so, I want to point out their distinctiveness as well as their problematic aspects and to ask whether, were it not for Havel's political importance, we

should attend to (or attend at all) the theater of this astonishingly undramatic actor on the stage of modern history.

One result of Václav Havel's recent celebrity has been references throughout the media to his plays which, it is quite likely, have never been seen or read by most American commentators or journalists. Since 1963, when *The Garden Party* was first produced, Havel has written four short and five full-length plays which are available in English translation, the language in which I have come to know them, and several others. The remainder of Havel's artistic energy has been expended in political essays and correspondence, the latter including *Letters to Olga* (published in English in 1988), *Disturbing the Peace* (in English, 1990) and *Summer Meditations* (in English, 1992). Havel's plays have been generally neglected by most American theaters. Because the predominant concern of most American theater has been, and continues to be, to provide entertainment for the dwindling numbers of middle-class audiences, Havel is not good "box office." For a while, smaller and "engaged" theaters and a few in universities, will produce Havel's plays as a statement of political solidarity with the momentous changes in European politics. At the same time, they will confirm the feebleness of America's theatrical art to rouse anyone to thought or action.

Aside from its political context, what is the artistic relationship between Havel's plays and those of his contemporaries? Discerning the thread that binds the plays of Czechoslovakia's ex-president to other modern playwrights is important in understanding his theater. One dramatist who comes to mind is Harold Pinter who, not surprisingly, acted in two of Havel's short plays (*Audience* and *A Private View*) in 1977 on the British Broadcasting Company. Pinter shares with Havel an interest in how people respond to the space in which they live, particularly the enclosed kind of space which makes Havel's *Audience* and *Largo Desolato* reminiscent of Pinter's *The Dumbwaiter* and, especially, *The Birthday Party.* In the latter, first produced in 1958, Pinter creates the figure of Stanley, the inarticulate recluse who is, depending on the interpretation of the text in production, destroyed by a thuggish, malevolent society or "birthed" into a culture which may not be as corrupt as it is pragmatically brutal. In fact, such opportunities for interpretation separate Pinter's plays from Havel's. Pinter's plays suffer markedly when they are "located"; Havel's, on the other hand, are conceived within a specific political context which is very difficult to separate out from the texts and their implications. Pinter, who writes in a democracy, is interested in existential freedom and is nonideological in his plays; confinement is a condition of life, not of politics. Trying to make his plays overtly political (as in the presentation of McCann's Irishness in *The Birthday Party*) restricts and diminishes them.

Havel, who wrote his plays under tyranny, is deeply ideological in both attitude and experience. His plays embody a knowledge of history and are always attached to a context; Pinter's float free and are open to multiple inferences. For Pinter, the threatening "Other" is whoever happens to be the annihilating force of the moment; for Havel, the Other is always the state which may be, depending on the depth of our compromise with its invidious demands, surprisingly benign. Pinter's people talk elliptically, trying to conceal motive and expressing a wide range of psychological subtexts; Havel's people talk ambiguously, seeking to avoid blame or shame, but expressing a very narrow choice of psychological motive. Both writers do create a very powerful sense of the sinister, and Havel's plays may be called, as Pinter's have been, "comedies of menace." Pinter frequently creates a feeling of threat through the use of an enclosed space; Havel often achieves the same effect by including in his plays a character or two, perhaps silent, who represent the omnipresent repressive state, for example Pillar in *The Memorandum,* the Two Chaps in *Largo Desolato,* and the Secret Messenger in *Temptation.*

An even closer theatrical affinity exists between Havel and the English playwright Tom Stoppard, who was born a few months after Havel, also in Czechoslovakia. Kenneth Tynan has written a splendid comparison of the lives, plays and temperaments of the two writers. Suffice to say that the two playwrights share a deep mistrust of all orthodoxy and authority, and an identical delight in the liberating power of satirical language. The beginning of Stoppard's *Travesties* with its multilingual, arch use of language made both artistic and incomprehensible (to the audience) in the hands (or at the scissors) of Tristan Tzara, James Joyce and Vladimir Lenin reminds us of Havel's invention of Ptydepe, the unlearnable bureaucratic babble of *The Memorandum,* written in 1965. And, equally important, the "time slips" in *Travesties* have been an identifying feature of Havel's plays since *The Garden Party,* a theatrical device where one scene or piece of dialogue is repeatedly replayed, perhaps modified by changing who says a certain speech or who performs the repeated action.

In Stoppard's play, the "slips" are "under the erratic control" of Henry Carr, his irascible curmudgeon of a protagonist, and Carr's frequent narrative recapitulations in the performance of *Travesties* are intended by Stoppard to be metatheatrical intrusions. Havel uses the technique more as a metaphorical device, apart from character, in order to signal either a world careening out of control (when the words and actions are accelerated), or one denuded of objective meaning, leaving its inhabitants to their meaningless lives. Stoppard has adapted Havel's *Largo Desolato,* written the introduction to *The Memorandum* in its English translation, and has dedicated his own brilliant political comedy about life under tyranny in Czechoslovakia,

Professional Foul, to Havel. Geographically speaking, Stoppard is the cultural and national bridge between Havel and Pinter since he was born in Czechoslovakia but relocated to England at an early age. Artistically, he has been more prolific and inventive.

The third and even greater influence on Havel, of an entirely continental source, is Eugene Ionesco. With *The Bald Soprano,* first produced in 1950 and called an "anti-play" by its Romanian-born author, Ionesco began a series of theater pieces extraordinary for their antic humor and complete disregard of what can be called the logical necessities of stage realism. Well into the 1960s, his work endured as one of the dominant influences on European playwriting, and his shadow looms large as a presence in Havel's work. In a brief tribute to Havel, Milan Kundera asserts that

> . . . no foreign writer had for us at that time [the 1960s] such a liberating sense as Ionesco. We were suffocating under art conceived as educational, moral or political . . .

> One cannot conceive of Havel without the example of Ionesco yet he is not an epigone. His plays are an original and irreplaceable development within what is called 'The Theater of the Absurd'. Moreover, they were understood as such by everyone at the time . . .

Looking at *The Garden Party* with its loopy dialogue, nonsensical action and its fragmentation of character (by the end of the play, the protagonist Hugo Pludek has assumed a second identity of the same name), or noting the pretentious social chatter and bourgeois accumulations in *A Private View,* it is impossible not to perceive the Ionesco of *The Bald Soprano, The Lesson* or *Jack, or the Submission,* the first two of which were produced by Havel's Theatre of the Balustrade in the early 1960s. And Havel's use of doors in *The Increased Difficulty of Concentration* and *Largo Desolato,* in particular as an expression of the intrusions of an erratic, malignant external universe, has Ionesco's type of comic paranoia as its model. Havel, however, adds the political context missing in Ionesco, and Kundera is but one of many observers who see this Absurdism with a political face as a true moment of cultural liberation in the dark history of postwar Czechoslovakian politics.

One additional name must be mentioned in relation to Havel, though not for his structural, scenographic or linguistic similarities. It is a thematic thread that ties Pinter, Stoppard, Ionesco and Havel together with Samuel Beckett who wrote this small *Catastrophe* in 1983 to commemorate and excoriate (though subtly, minimally) Havel's lengthy and near-fatal imprisonment. This thematic line can be expressed as the well-worn theme of "respect for individual worth and the individual's need for dignity," though it is the unique genius of each of these five artists that keeps this concern meaningful and frequently moving. The painful and occasionally fanciful existence of Pinter's Stanley, of Stoppard's Henry Carr, of Ionesco's Berenger and of Beckett's Gogo and Didi are all images of their creators' devotion to the irreducible minimum of human freedom, and it is no coincidence that all of them in their personal lives (though some more than others and Beckett least of all) have committed themselves to fighting on several fronts for a humane existence for all the world's abused inhabitants.

With his election to the presidency, Havel's career in the theater was suspended, and his political commitments needed to be worked out in the "real world." In this connection, I think of the Chilean poet and politician Pablo Neruda (who took his name from a lesser-known Czech writer of the nineteenth century), for just as Neruda's Nobel Prize was earned for literature, Havel may receive his for peace.

Currently, the great attraction to Havel's writing in the West is extratheatrical, based on its antitotalitarian ideology of tolerance and responsibility, as well as by Havel's personal drama of exemplary courage in the face of oppression. One curious result of recent events in Czechoslovakia is that Havel's political failure now aligns him better with the failure of his plays' protagonists (who share occasional details of a common biography with their author). But if we examine Havel's artistic endeavor apart from his political life, how can we measure his achievement?

Looking at Havel's plays leads even a sympathetic reader to conclude that the stylistic and structural repetitions, for example, the time warps, the repeated gestures and bits of business, the identical dreary "journeys" of the protagonists (Gross in *The Memorandum,* Huml in *The Increased Difficulty of Concentration,* Nettles in *Largo Desolato* and Foustka in *Temptation*) show Havel repeating himself too much. Thus, *Largo Desolato* and *Temptation,* Havel's last two plays, reveal a continuing preoccupation with outdated theater forms and an inability to drive his thinking or technique into a more moving creative expression than it possessed before the time of his imprisonment in 1979. In his brief tribute to Havel, Timothy Garton Ash assesses the situation thus:

> . . . I still cannot avoid a deeper disappointment. The play [*Temptation,* produced in 1986 in Vienna], even as Havel has written it, is weak. And it is weak, it seems to me, for reasons directly related to his situation. For a start, the dramaturgy and stage effects envisioned in his very detailed stage directions are stilted, and if not stilted, then dated—all stroboscopes and

smoke, *circa* 1966. Not surprising if you consider that he has been unable to work in the theater for eighteen years.

In 1986, in a culinary metaphor Brecht would have loved and perhaps agreed with, Ash concludes about *Temptation* "The thing is overcooked."

The comparison to Ionesco now becomes useful, for it has long been noted that the best efforts of Ionesco are the early, short plays like those mentioned above. Absurdist drama, already a historical detail in the postmodern theater and unknown firsthand to anyone under thirty, was most successful when it remained playfully brief. When lengthy, as is Ionesco's work since *Exit the King* (1962), Absurdism turned turgid and not a little pompous because the fun (often touched with horror) and the spirit of invention was unsustainable. Consider the conclusions of *The Garden Party* and *Temptation,* two Havel plays separated by almost a quarter of a century. The former ends with a character hidden inside a large cupboard (eavesdroppers appear in several Havel plays), making a surprising entrance, walking down to the footlights and directly addressing the audience: "And now, without sort of much ado—go home!" For this play, essentially a cartoon, the ending is abrupt, silly and appropriate. But the ending of *Temptation,* a play that attempts to deal with some of the same themes as *The Garden Party* (the language of bureaucracy, the description of life without commitment), seems to result from an exhausted imagination that has reached a point of no return, and no advance. The concluding dance which Havel describes as "a crazy, orgiastic masked ball or witches' sabbath" is accompanied by excruciatingly loud music and an auditorium full of smoke. The stage direction reads:

> The music suddenly stops, the house lights go on, the smoke fades and it becomes evident that at some point during all this the curtain has fallen. After a very brief silence, music comes on again, now at a bearable level of loudness—the most banal commercial music possible. If the smoke—or the play itself—hasn't caused the audience to flee, and if there are still a few left in the audience who might even want to applaud, let the first to take a bow and thank the audience be a fireman in full uniform with a helmet on his head and a fire extinguisher [a major prop in *The Memorandum*] in his hand.

Temptation explores in greater measure Havel's major theme of betrayal (by society, of self), but its satirical attack on a world destined to disappear in flames is too discursive and distended, lacking precision or sting. *Temptation* features the usual Havel touches: repetitive and replayed dialogue or action, long speeches of apology for or exculpation from corruption (Havel's protagonists are frequently compromised intellectuals and/or academics), an environment of bureaucratic timeserving and political cowardice, and ample though insufficient flashes of antic wit. But, unlike Beckett whose work traced an endangered and dying universe with ever greater austerity and concision (including *Catastrophe*), Havel's proliferating scenic and linguistic excesses provide a smaller payoff.

In Tynan's essay referred to earlier, he discusses Stoppard's difficulty in expressing genuine emotion and in creating convincing female characters. These are Havel's problems too, although in his defense it could be argued that in the kind of comic universe he creates, having either would be unusual. Nonetheless Havel's comic plays, essentially cerebral and objective, exclude the opportunity for the expression of deep, genuine feeling. His world is usually one of evasion and avoidance, like the world of classical farce which it frequently resembles in its dependence on rapid entrances and exits through a multiple number of doors. At his weakest, Havel replaces feeling with activity, providing gestures instead of activated concern. When this occurs, as in the recurrent business with PUZUK the computer in *The Increased Difficulty of Concentration,* the face washing/door slamming of *Largo Desolato* or second dance sequence of *Temptation,* the plays lack, in Tynan's phrase, "the magic ingredient of pressure toward desperation."

The most common Havel story (and clearly a political one) involves the increasing pressure of a (male) protagonist to decide whether or not to betray himself or his friends. Mostly, Havel's characters fail the test miserably. But on the way to failure, the plays suggest a way to a true if limited salvation: the involvement in a genuine experience of love with a woman. Thus, in *The Memorandum,* Gross is attracted to the pure adoration of the office clerk, Maria, but he abandons her at the moment of her greatest need and marches off to lunch with his office staff. That Maria remains "happy" because "nobody ever talked to me so nicely before" does not excuse Gross's avoidance of moral action nor his failure to reciprocate Maria's genuine expression of love toward him. Similarly, at the conclusion of *The Increased Difficulty of Concentration,* Huml almost reaches an expressive emotional reciprocity with Miss Balcar who, at one moment in the final scene, is reduced to tears by her need for Huml despite the gassy academic discourse he puts between them. Though he embraces her and kisses her "gently on her tearful eyes," and she exits "smiling happily," it is clear that Miss Balcar will be the fourth of Huml's failures with women in this play and additional proof of his intellectual and political cowardice.

At the end of *Largo Desolato,* Marguerite arrives to give Leopold Nettles one final chance for rejuvenation through love. "You have given me back the meaning to my life," she tells him, "which is to give you the meaning back to yours."

But their intense embrace is interrupted by the doorbell, and a terrorized Nettles leaves her immediately to chase after and to be humiliated by the two sinister chaps who inform him his gesture of "heroism" will no longer be required. Lastly, in *Temptation,* it is Marketa who serves as the abused image of innocence when her moment of courage in defending Foustka in front of their hostile bosses ends only in her summary dismissal after Foustka's betrayal of her. She returns later in the play dressed and behaving like a lunatic Ophelia, the one serious moment in the "witches' sabbath," but one deprived of tragic resonance because Havel has her return under peculiar circumstances for a last appearance as one of Foustka's tormentors.

In all of these scenes, I sense that Havel is flirting with a way to express a potentially liberating emotional occasion, liberating to his protagonists and to himself as a playwright of satirical political comedies. But in all of them, he deflects the serious tendencies of the characters and himself, preferring to avoid the entanglements of emotion with a disengaged, objective posture. It would be possible to argue that this lack of emotional commitment is the *result* of the political environment of his country, but I do not believe this is the case. Instead, I see this pattern as a refusal to extend these wonderful comedies into a more profound and troubling territory which would have serious and I think very positive results on Havel's playwriting. Havel turns back to his satire of bureaucratic and academic language in the arias of his cowardly protagonists, preferring the Ionesco "anti-play" to, say, Beckett's "tragicomedy." In this critical context, I would choose the two short pieces *Audience* and *Protest* as Havel's most successful plays, although I have a great liking for the stylish, sustained confidence of the comic ironies of *The Memorandum.* These plays are relatively brief, with all male characters, and emphasize the anguish of moral action and the fallibility of the human character, and are very funny.

> **For a brief political moment, Havel's was the triumph of life over art, though the future may demand otherwise.**
> —*Robert Skloot*

In the third of his "Six asides about culture" (1984), Havel compares the Czechs with their northeastern neighbors: "We live in a land of notorious realism, far removed from, say, the Polish courage for sacrifice." I understand Havel to refer to the Polish inclination toward the deathly side of human existence rather than his own Czech appreciation of the dark side of human organizations, and to the Polish strain of fatalism which is outside of and resistant to Havel's satirical assault on the notorious political realism of Czechoslovakia. Havel has yet to write a play as powerful, as, say, Mrozek's *Tango,* that terrifying exposure of malignant brutality which, it should be mentioned, was adapted for the English stage by Tom Stoppard.

In John Webster's early seventeenth-century tragedy, *The Duchess of Malfi,* the title character confronts her state supported executioners and replies to their murderous threats with an ingenious and unlikely metaphor:

> I know that death hath ten thousand several doors
> For men to take their exits, and 'tis found
> They go on such strange geometrical hinges,
> You may open them both ways.

Havel's stage world until now has had the doors but not the death. His new, resumed life as an ex-president may include an appointment with the theater where, contemplating the murderous world around him, he will be hard pressed to avoid writing pointedly about how countries and peoples die. In his part of Europe the dire situation isn't, or isn't only, a joke.

". . . if you must have a revolution," wrote Timothy Garton Ash, "it would be difficult to imagine a better revolution than the one Czechoslovakia had: swift, nonviolent, joyful, and funny. A laughing revolution." This revolution culminated in Havel on the balcony overlooking a huge public square, in Prague's open air, unconfined, and recorded by accredited journalists rather than hidden informers. As president, Havel's voice was aspiring and consoling, simple and moral, a deliberate rejection of the anxious volubility and fussy cowardice of his absurd protagonists. Now it appears that he has been given a new, unwanted freedom so that he may, in the words of the Israeli novelist David Grossman, "hallucinate another kind of future," or perhaps, another kind of play. For a brief political moment, Havel's was the triumph of life over art, though the future may demand otherwise.

Erwin Knoll   (review date April 1993)

SOURCE: "The Poet as President," in *Progressive,* Vol. 57, No. 4, April, 1993, pp. 40-3.

[*In the following review, Knoll offers favorable assessment of* Open Letters, Summer Meditations, *and* Living in Truth. *Knoll praises Havel's "literate, profound, and humane essays."*]

When I talked with Czechs about Václav Havel during a brief visit to Prague last fall, I was surprised to find that many did not share the esteem and enthusiasm with which their illustrious compatriot is so widely regarded in the West.

Havel had just resigned as president of Czechoslovakia so that he would not have to preside over the dissolution of his country. He would return in a few months to head the new, truncated Czech Republic. His symbol-rich exit from the Prague Castle—wearing a T-shirt, carrying a backpack—had made more of an impression elsewhere in Europe (and in the United States) than at home.

Czechs criticized Havel for not fighting hard enough against the breakup, after seventy-four years, of Czechoslovakia. (I heard this, curiously, even from some who claimed not to care about Slovak independence and who said, dismissively. "Let them go!") Other Czechs—or, sometimes, the same ones—complained that Havel had deepened the nation's economic crisis by dismantling much of its arms industry and curtailing overseas weapons sales. And the most virulent attacks focused on Havel's opposition to the "lustration" law that stripped former communist office-holders of their civil rights regardless of whether they had, themselves, engaged in human-rights violations. Czechs who had suffered under the communist regime—though few had suffered more than Havel—simply could not understand his concern for the rights of those associated with their and his former tormentors.

All of this suggested to me that Havel was a decent, thoughtful, generous, and compassionate human being—qualities rarely encountered in those who hold high political office. And I concluded that the Czechs were in the extraordinary, almost unique position of having a leader better than they wanted or deserved.

These impressions were emphatically confirmed by the literate, profound, and humane essays compiled in Havel's ***Open Letters*** and ***Summer Meditations,*** and in ***Václav Havel: Living in Truth,*** which includes six pieces by Havel as well as sixteen appreciative essays by, among others. Samuel Beckett, Heinrich Böll, Milan Kundera, Arthur Miller, and Tom Stoppard.

The first essay in ***Open Letters,*** and the only one out of chronological sequence (it was originally published in 1977), is autobiographical and presents an excellent introduction to the man and his work.

"I do not belong to that fortunate class of authors who write constantly, quickly, easily, and always well, whose imaginations never tire and who—unhampered by doubts or inhibitions—are by nature open to the world." Havel writes. "Whatever they touch, it is always exactly right. That I do not belong in such company, of course, bothers me and sometimes even upsets me: I am ambitious and I'm angry with myself for having so few ideas, for finding it so difficult to write, for having so little faith in myself, and for thinking so much about everything that I often feel crippled by it."

That modest disclaimer notwithstanding, Havel has been remarkably prolific in the last thirty years—though less so while preoccupied by his presidential duties. His plays, with which I am, for the most part, unfamiliar, have been produced to critical acclaim in Europe and the United States. His letters and essays, of which these three collections constitute only a small part, are a formidable body of work.

Though he abandoned early efforts at writing poetry, he still writes as a poet, bringing pellucid insights even to political analysis, and achieving lyricism even while engaging in polemics. Here is Havel in a 1984 essay called **"Thriller"**: "I am unwilling to believe that this whole civilization is no more than a blind alley of history and a fatal error of the human spirit. More probably it represents a necessary phase that man and humanity must go through, one that man—if he survives—will ultimately, and on some higher level (unthinkable, of course, without the present phase), transcend."

And here is his compelling argument against censorship, understandably a recurrent theme throughout Havel's work: "A great many people can peck at a typewriter and, fortunately, no one can stop them. But for that reason, even in *samizdat* [work unofficially circulated underground], there will always be countless bad books or poems for every important book. . . . But even if, objectively, there were some possibility of selection, who could claim the right to exercise it? Who among us would dare to say that he can unerringly distinguish something of value—even though it may still be nascent, unfamiliar, as yet only potential—from its counterfeit? Who among us can know whether what may seem today to be marginal graphomania might not one day appear to our descendants as the most substantial thing written in our time? Who among us has the right to deprive them of that pleasure, no matter how incomprehensible it may seem to us?"

Havel was born in Prague in 1936 and established himself as a dissident and irritant to the Czech state even before Alexander Dubcek's Prague Spring of 1968. The earliest essays in **Open Letters, "On Evasive Thinking,"** delivered as a speech to the Union of Czechoslovakian Writers in 1965, ranks with the best of George Orwell's work as an analysis of the use and abuse of political language.

"We never seem to notice," Havel writes, "how suspiciously often what happens—in fact—does not conform to what—according to our prognoses—was to have happened. We know with utter certainty what should happen and how it should happen, and when it turns out differently, we also know why it had to be different. The only thing that causes

us trouble is knowing what will really happen. To know that assumes knowing how things really are now. But that is precisely where the catch lies: between a detailed prediction of the future and a broad impression of the past, there is somehow no room for what is most important of all—a down-to-earth analysis of the present."

That isn't just communist Czechoslovakia Havel is describing. As with the work of his compatriot, Franz Kafka, we are stunned by the generalizations we can draw from Havel's particulars.

In 1976, Havel attended the trial in Prague of four musicians from the Czech underground music scene—a travesty he recounts in a furious essay whose title must resonate in Prague: **"The Trial."** From that point on, Havel's dissidence was irreconcilable. He was a founder of Charter 77, the Czech human-rights movement, and in 1979 he was sentenced to four-and-a-half years in prison, during which time he produced letters and commentaries of lasting value. In 1989, he helped found the Civil Forum, the first legal opposition movement in postwar Czechoslovakia, and late that year his Forum colleagues unanimously elected him president.

"It would have been irresponsible of me," Havel writes, "to criticize the communist regime all my life and then, when it finally collapsed (with some help from me), refuse to take part in the creation of something better."

In **Summer Meditations,** a set of essays written while he was president of Czechoslovakia, Havel grapples with some of the troublesome questions that preoccupied him in this difficult period of transition—the split with Slovakia, the role of the "free market" in his country's emerging economy, the structures of constitutional government, the perpetual tension between politics and morality.

With admirable candor—especially for a chief of state— he agonizes aloud: He is constantly told, Havel says, that he "should be tougher, more decisive, more authoritative. For a good cause I shouldn't be afraid to pound the table occasionally, to shout at people, to try to rouse a little fear and trembling. Yet, if I wish to remain faithful to myself and my notion of politics, I mustn't listen to advice like this—not just in the interests of my personal mental health (which could be seen as a private, selfish desire), but chiefly in the interests of what most concerns me: the simple fact that directness can never be established by indirection, or truth through lies, or the democratic spirit through authoritarian directives. Of course, I don't known whether directness, truth, and the democratic spirit will succeed. But I do know how *not* to succeed, which is by means that contradict the ends. As we know from history, that is the best way to eliminate the very ends we set out to achieve."

There is only one way, Havel adds, "to strive for decency, reason, responsibility, sincerity, civility, and tolerance, and that is decently, reasonably, responsibly, sincerely, civilly, and tolerantly. I'm aware that, in everyday politics, this is not seen as the most practical way of going about it. But I have one advantage: among my many bad qualities there is one that happens to be missing—a longing or love for power. Not being bound by that, I am essentially freer than those who cling to their power or position, and this allows me to indulge in the luxury of behaving untactically. I see the only way forward in that old, familiar injunction: 'live in truth.' But how is this to be done when one is President?"

This eminently decent citizen—I absolutely believe him when he says he has no longing or love of power—is, of course, capable of error. His grasp of economics is, at best, tenuous. In understandable reaction to the abuses of the communist regime under which he lived and suffered, he has exaggerated expectations of the benefits to be derived from the market—and acknowledges as much. His determination to see the best in his fellow Czechs blinds him, perhaps, to the full ramifications of the worst: the pervasive greed, corruption, chauvinism, and pinched conservatism now on flagrant display in his country.

But Havel's most serious mistake may be the decision he reached, after much private and public self-questioning, to return to the Castle as president of the Czech Republic. "I have been thinking about this decision for a long time," he says in an afterward to *Summer Meditations,* "and it presents me with a genuine dilemma. There are so many arguments for and against." In the end, the arguments for prevailed—especially the arguments that being president affords him an opportunity to work for his "civil program."

But the news from Prague indicates that right now—and for the foreseeable future—the Czechs need Havel the critic, Havel the pamphleteer, Havel the playwright, Havel the poet, more than they need Havel the president.

"Modern man, that methodical civil servant in the great bureaucracy of the world, mildly frustrated by the collapse of his 'scientific' world view, finally switches on his video recorder to watch Michael Jackson playing a vampire in 'Thriller,' the best-selling videocassette in the history of the world, then goes into the kitchen to remove from a thermos flask—behind the backs of all animal-welfare societies—the still warm heart of a hoopoe. And he swallows it, hoping to have the gift of prophecy conferred on him."

Someone who can write like that has no business wasting

his time as president of anything. He needs to devote every available moment to helping all of us understand the human condition.

Peter Majer (essay date 1994)

SOURCE: "Time, Identity and Being: The World of Václav Havel," in *Twentieth-Century European Drama,* edited by Brian Docherty, St. Martin's Press, 1994, pp. 172-82.

[*In the following essay, Majer examines the influence of totalitarian oppression and imprisonment on Havel's existentialist concept of time, individual identity, and the possibility of meaning in his dramatic works.*]

In his first speech to the Federal Assembly in Prague (25 January 1990), playwright Václav Havel, in his new role as President of the Republic of Czechoslovakia, focused on the phenomenon of time:

> In my offices in the Prague Castle, I did not find one single clock. To me, that has a symbolic meaning: for long years, there was no reason to look at clocks, because time had stood still. History had come to a halt, not only in the Prague Castle but in the whole country. So much faster does it roll forward now that we have at long last freed ourselves from the paralysing straitjacket of the totalitarian system. Time has speeded up.

As Guillaume Apollinaire notes, in his poem, 'La Zone', 'les aiguilles de l'horloge du quartier juif vont à rebours'. The clock in the Prague Jewish quarter, at the Jewish Town Hall tower, moves backward, as if symbolising—poetically as well as historically—the absurd movement of time: no longer forward, no longer even static, but really moving back. Czech history has moved back a number of times. The dormant and petrified beauty of Prague, a city described by Franz Kafka as the mother with claws, with its backward-moving clock, with its legends of slumbering knights who would return 'when the time is right', made the theme of Time a central feature of Czech philosophical thinking, traceable in the writings of Comenius, Bernard Bolzano, T. G. Masaryk and, more recently, Jan Patocka.

The dramas of president-philosopher Václav Havel contain many elements which relate directly or indirectly to Time, which in Havel's interpretation is primarily an existential category, in the same sense as viewed by Albert Camus, Jean-Paul Sartre, or Martin Heidegger. But to Havel, Time is quite a specific entity. It is more tangible and man-related than Heidegger's Time, which has always a metaphysical, abstract dimension, and relates to existence itself, as expressed in the very title of Heidegger's major philosophical work *Sein und Zeit* (Being and Time), published in 1927.

Heidegger's concept of Time, as interpreted by Jan Patocka (in whose clandestine seminars Havel took part when he wasn't serving a prison term), helped Havel survive some depressing times of isolation. In isolation, be it physical or psychological, time slows down. The very private and inward-looking existence forced upon people by a totalitarian regime which inspires fear of meaningful action and interaction, lest the meaning they produce turns out to be subversive, are the stuff from which Havel weaves his slow-moving but inwardly intense drama. He represents a conflict of the individual struggling with events and human relationships stuck in a time warp. His characters struggle to escape from a cobweb of meaningless events which move predictably and tediously in a closed circle. Their struggle seems equally meaningless to those for whom suspended time has become the only tangible reality, in which they know only how to function, and survive. In Havel's plays, individuals struggle with a world which is grinding to a halt, and that threatens to blur any difference between people and to bring human existence to a fossilised end.

This bleak picture is most poignantly illustrated in Havel's play **The Mountain Hotel** (1976), whose characters meander in circles, repeating phrases which betray nothing of their individuality or any personal thoughts, and which gradually become interchangeable to a point where personal identity no longer matters and communication becomes impossible. No one listens to anyone and no one expects to be listened to. As if they were all a single character, a hydra-like monster speaking through several mouths, they say the same things, becoming a symbol of uniform repetitive thinking. Any yet, at one point, out of the blue and almost out of character, one of the mouths (Drasar) says:

> Isn't it time to break the barriers between us? To take off our conventional masks and open up to one another just a little? We may not realise it but time flies, life is short and your sojourn here flows like water—and before you notice, some of you begin to leave, and those who stay behind feel remorse—unfortunately too late—how little they were able to say to those who are now irretrievably gone, how little they were able to let them know that—in spite of everything—they cared and felt something deeper for them—

Milan Uhde, the playwright and now the Czech Minister of Culture, describes the characters in this play. They are

> not people with a past, a present, or an identity, with attributes and relationships. They are sloughing all of these off and one wonders if they ever wore them. The only thing that covers them now are their names. Their actions, their status, careers, destinies, feelings, dreams, dialogues, amours, flirtations, peel off their personalities like a label off a bottle. The labels are interchangeable, the content evaporates. Void is all that remains.

This is a reflection of a deformed social reality as Havel perceives it, a society which extols empty slogans and makes them into yardsticks with which to measure non-existence, often masquerading under the banner of bizarre ideological facades.

In this kind of world, one might as well be in prison. Havel was offered a choice between prison and exile. As if to discover for himself the meaning of life separated from time, to clarify, as he calls it, the 'naked values', timeless and eternal, which would give human existence a meaning in any circumstances, any conditions, Havel chose prison. In his letters from prison to his wife, Havel writes:

> I think a great deal about the meaning I should give to the prison years which I am facing. Last time, I wrote about the possibility that it might lead—if I manage it well—to an overall psychological and mental reconstruction of myself. Why do I believe that? In recent years, I have lived rather an odd, unnatural, exclusive existence, as if in a glasshouse. That is going to change now. I shall be one of many small and powerless ants. I shall in a sense be returning to the old times, thrown into the world in a similar way I was when I worked as a lab assistant, as a stage-hand, or when I was a soldier or a student. I shall be a mere number, I shall be one of many and no one will expect anything of me or take any special notice of me. For some people outside, I shall probably be an 'institution,' but I shall know nothing about it, I shall live in a different world with different problems. This return to the earlier existential situation—a situation in which I thrived best and in which I also created most—might help me with this inner reconstitution which I spoke about last time (losing my stiffness and lack of self-confidence, stop seeing myself through the eyes of others who expect something from me, give up my nervousness, self-doubt, etc.) One of the specific things I might do is to start writing more for the theatre again—as an observer of 'the theatre of the world' . . .

Serving time in prison and attempting to reconstruct Time internally helped Havel focus on the deformations of time existing in the world outside. For Havel as a playwright, the static cobweb of Czech totalitarian tedium was the framework within which drama was created by the two clashing concepts of time, with a predictable end: whatever happens, whatever action an individual might take, round in circles he goes. For Havel as a philosopher and politician, the unpredictable and exciting events of November 1989 provided the explosion through which compressed time burst out with speed and confusion, and which required a playwright to take charge. Too many suppressed dramas were now writing themselves out and needed to be harnessed. And an observer cannot escape the impression that, just as Havel the playwright once struggled to speed time up, Havel the statesman may now be struggling, if not to slow time down, then at least to channel the millions of accelerated personal dramas into a coherent dramatic shape.

Focus and purpose, which Havel has been trying to give his confused nation, are to him not merely a philosophical concept, but a specific entity linked to a restoration of individual identity lost in years of meaningless, mechanised, uniform patter and prescribed action. Years in which people could lose their sense of identity to a point when they could end up visiting themselves, like Pludek in *The Garden Party* (1963).

The threat to identity is real in any political system, so much more so in a totalitarian one. Havel's *The Garden Party* has two absurd organisations, whose job is to ensure loss of identity: the liquidation department and the commencing service. Between them, they make people blend into each other and gradually liquidate them by making them indistinguishable. Uniformity is the ideal, exceptions are out. When the play's protagonist, Pludek, becomes director of both institutions, even the institutions themselves blend into each other and become indistinguishable. Their activities are an Orwellian pretence, a cover-up of some mysterious activity which is the opposite of what the institutions claim to stand for.

Similarly, *The Memorandum* (1965) takes us to an unspecified office where scientists are mere officials and administrators pretending to be engaged in scientific experiments, exchanging repetitive meaningless banalities. Havel further foregrounds this pseudo-reality of pretence and camouflage by their concern with an artificial language—'Ptydepe', which destroys universal human values by depriving people of the ability of communicate anything sensible, and by stripping words of their meaning.

In most of his plays, Havel deals with the issue of 'The Inner Lie' and the possibility of dismantling it, be it a self-deception or deception about the world. However, many of his characters simply refuse to find out anything about themselves, to identify who they are. In *The Garden Party,* Hugo Pludek's father, when asked who exactly he is, replies with dismay: 'I? Who am I? Look. I don't like such one-sided questions. I really don't!'

In their search for identity Havel's heroes get entangled in situations of existential conflict with established social structures. They need to defend their identity, if for no other reason, then at least to come to terms with, and to be able to survive in, a totalitarian society. Those who do not defend their identity often end up like the protagonists of *The Increased Difficulty of Concentration* (1968), where a conflict occurs when two sets of 'scientists' meet and make each other's work impossible. They are mainly clerks or bureaucrats or scientists from a variety of ephemeral institutes and establishments, who carry out their activity with enthusiasm but without any results. Everything degenerates into personal and sexual relationships between secretaries and bosses, superiors and their staff.

Havel returns to the atmosphere of pseudo-science of his earlier plays in his more recent work, *Temptation* (1985). *Temptation* presents a renowned scientist, Dr Foustka, tempted by the devil. Foustka is one of those scientists engaged in unspecified work for an institution with unspecified purpose. His job is to protect and supervise the 'scientificality of science' and guard it against any infiltration by unscientific irrationality. But Foustka dabbles in the esoteric, the occult and the magical, so his encounter with the devil is only a matter of time, and to fall into the devil's, claws means never to be able to get out again. The devil, here, functions as a system from which there is no escape. Foustka's identity has to be defended in conflicts with his boss and colleagues, in an atmosphere of fears and anxiety, seeping through from outside.

The Faustian theme, which Havel knew as early as 1977 (at the inception of Charter 77), had by then acquired a specific Czech significance. In the Czech predicament of that time, the inept and comic devils were personified by interrogators and supervisors. In order not to lose himself, not to betray those he represented or ideals he believed to be true, Havel, like his protagonist, Foustka, had to strive for personal integrity or, in Heidegger's terms, authenticity, truthfulness, and loyalty to one's true self. He had to struggle to preserve his identity in the face of the devil, in the face of temptation by evil. Evil was seen as loss of identity, through collaboration with, or connivance at, the dehumanising machinery of totalitarianism, and was to be fought. Pressure to conform in return for relative comfort had to be resisted. All these became issues of everyday existence, not only for characters in dramas, but also for individuals in Czech society.

In this situation, drama becomes a way of expressing and defining models of existential conflicts resembling simulated situations in experimental psychology. An illustration of a psychological premise in specific human situations is often carried ad absurdum.

The absurdity of totalitarian politics is parodied in Havel's play *Conspirators* (1970), where general prosecutor Dykl describes the new candidate for the dictator's job, Colonel Moher, with these words: 'Let me be frank. His awful self-confidence scares me. He considers all his decisions automatically correct, however many proofs one may present of his errors. Or take his dreadful implacability. I am an old veteran but I must say that when he described how severely he was going to deal with the students, he scared the daylights out of me. Imagine a situation when practically all power is concentrated in his hands.' Major Ofir replies: 'His measures are, admittedly, often somewhat harsh. But what matters is that his goals are beneficial.' Dykl: 'Forgive me, Major, but history will not judge our intentions but only and solely our deeds. We may repeat a hundred times that we are building a new and more humane world. But what will all this mean when the imprints of our blood-stained hands cry out from every single stone of our glorious edifice.'

Havel makes a direct attempt to decode and identify the absurd features of totalitarian pseudo-government in *The Beggars' Opera* (1975), linking it with criminality which does not stop short of murder. The city chief in the play is, at the same time, chief of all gangsters. Whoever leads a gang must also report to the police, and the chief of police runs the entire criminal network. He does, to be sure, solve some crimes and prosecute some criminals, but does not forget to use this to enrich himself and strengthen his personal power.

Such a deformed society induces a crisis of awareness of the meaning and purpose of life and the world, and leads to a dissipation of human identity. Man goes on living merely as a robot. Havel's dramas, in his own view, carry the dissipation of identity into 'a dismemberment of the dramatic character, suspension of time and absence of a coherent story on which an identity of a character could assert itself. Time loses its human dimension, comes to a halt or runs around in a circle.' Events do not connect or relate to each other any more, and are not heading towards a solution or conclusion. Man, instead of being their creator, becomes their powerless victim. In the dismemberment of the storyline into disconnected elements which do not match, traditional drama, as a sequence of time, disappears. It becomes, as it has in Havel's plays, a psychodrama—a conflict of psychological states rather than real characters.

Havel's early plays, such as *The Garden Party, The Memorandum,* and *The Increased Difficulty of Concentration,* can be seen as an updated illustration of Existentialist philosophy, a philosophy of a man on the run. Havel's Existentialism, however, is returning to humanism steeped in a passionate desire to make sense out of absurdity. The running man will soon have nowhere left to run, he has to seek

certainty within himself by reclaiming and accepting responsibility for his actions, and even for events which he might have thought were not of his own doing. Hence the often repeated claim, in his addresses to his fellow citizens: 'We all have our share of responsibility. All of us carry totalitarianism within ourselves.'

With the Soviet invasion, in 1968, and Jan Palach's death a few months later, the political climate changed drastically. For Havel, it meant that he could no longer maintain his ironic distance. He wanted to scream rather than laugh. If, in his earlier plays, he had been ironically modelling the totalitarian machine, he was now becoming vitally interested in the destiny of the human individual crushed under its wheels.

> **Havel's meticulously constructed plays are not always easy to decode, and the level of abstraction often makes identification and empathy with individual characters impossible.**
>
> —*Peter Majer*

The philosophy of integrity and responsibility is what informs his later plays and what gives them the shape of Socratean dialogues. In the '*Vanek Plays*', Havel introduces the protagonist, who serves as a catalyst, bringing to the surface and exposing the existential dilemmas of his environment. Often silent and self-doubting, Vanek is a kind of a modern Socratic character leading his co-players, but also readers and viewers, to clarify the nature of their 'presence in the world'. By his very presence, Vanek challenges basic ethical categories of human responsibility and integrity.

Havel's meticulously constructed plays are not always easy to decode, and the level of abstraction often makes identification and empathy with individual characters impossible. The Vanek plays—*The Audience* in particular—enjoyed international success, perhaps mainly because they clearly drew on Havel's personal experience, presenting real and tangible situations and characters.

Prison may have damaged Havel's health, but it did, as he acknowledges, wake him up from understandable lethargy and laziness to systematic and serious philosophical work. Having experienced, in prison, the Sartrean 'Hell is being with others', he could no longer satisfy himself with Sartre's intellectual 'roads to freedom', but had to reach for concrete tangible freedom, for himself and his nation, for which he felt responsible.

Havel used his prison time to search for his inner self, identity, individuality. In a letter to Olga, no. 13, he writes:

You may find it odd that prison of all places should serve me for a self-reconstitution, but I truly believe that cut off for a longer period of time from all ties which I myself turned into limitations, I could gain inner freedom and a new sovereignty. This is not, of course, merely a revision of my view of the world, my aim is a better fulfillment of the tasks imposed on me by the world—as I see it. I do not want to change myself but be myself in a better way. This may resemble somewhat the hopes with which Dostoyevsky's heroes go to prison—but in my case, it is not so pathetic, so absurd, or so religious . . .

Largo Desolato (1984) bears the mark of Havel's experience of life in prison and of interrogations leading to it. Its main character is a man who falls victim to fabricated accusations, an intellectual whose identity is destroyed by the whims of officialdom, by a power system which wears him down and makes him not just its victim but also its co-creator. However steadfastly the hero, philosopher Kopriva, may hold to his intellectual integrity, he remains unable to maintain human relationships.

Havel is not just a playwright dealing with philosophical questions, but a philosopher in his own right. His plays, which started as jolly and absurd comedies, Ionesco style, gradually turned into modern Socratean philosophical dialogues. In them, however, wisdom is not imparted by a teacher to a student, but discovered in the course of a lonely character's conflict with a world whose reality does not match its established description.

To Havel, the appearance of absurd drama—which has also been referred to as 'anti-drama'—is a result of living under stress, with no obvious way out. Remove the stress and drama is set in motion anew, returning to its classic story shape. With no way out, Havel searches for a way in—a rediscovery of his identity which would no longer depend for its creation on external circumstances but could start creating itself from its own resources. From the discovery of a higher, timeless and self-generating dimension of Being, which Havel believes is present in man's inner self in any circumstances, comes that which removes the stress of absurdity. The rediscovery of a man's intrinsic higher identity is, to Havel's philosophical thinking, absolutely essential for any serious and systematic creative work. It is that which brings about the integration of the dissipated elements of man—and thus generates meaningful action.

One of the principal philosophical problems for Havel is probably the very concept of Being, which was the pivotal issue with all existentialists, Heidegger in particular. But Heidegger, or other existentialists, never presented a precise definition of the concept of Being. Havel felt a need to define it. While Heidegger's approach is focusing on the awareness of death, on 'Sein zum Tode' (Being towards Death), Havel affirms life as the absolute horizon and parameter of Being, including the human individual. Being as a philosophical issue is very much present in his later letters from prison. Havel writes:

> The orientation of Being as a state of the spirit can also be interpreted as faith: a man oriented towards Being has profound faith in life, the world, morality, a purpose of things and of himself: his attitude to life is accompanied by hope, awe, humility and spontaneous respect for its mystery.

Havel is not only trying to define this concept in the context of awareness, consciousness, thinking, but also as a reflection of the spirit. He writes, 'What exactly is spirit, a reflection of consciousness? I would say that this dimension of "self" can be seen as a certain "duplication" of Being.'

The awareness of Being, which, for Havel, may be given any name including God, is a gradual integrative process, completing man inwardly and enabling him to reach self-realisation. It is an essential need of any man to aspire to his inner integrity, an ability to find within himself the very essence of Being, and identify with it.

Havel's entire work, dramatic, philosophical and political, is permeated with a desire to set things right, to rectify the absurdity of the world he lives in. To free the individual from lies, from meaningless phrases, from enforced pretence. He struggles against all that is shallow, vague and false in human relations. His quest is to help create a society in which individuals will again desire to understand each other, tolerate each other's shortcomings and forgive each other's mistakes and lapses. He refuses to be the judge of his persecutors because he knows that they, as tiny screws in a dehumanised machine, did not know any better.

His life as a writer, philosopher and statesman is an attempt to realise the utopian vision of a world where, in the words of a 1989 revolution poster, 'truth and love shall triumph over lie and hate'.

Jude R. Meche (essay date Winter 1997)

SOURCE: "Female Victims and the Male Protagonist in Václav Havel's Drama," in *Modern Drama,* Vol. 40, No. 4, Winter, 1997, pp. 468-76.

[*In the following essay, Meche discusses the role of subordinate or victimized women in Havel's drama as a symbolic foil for deficient male protagonists.*]

Václav Havel's recent rise to political power in the now-dissolved Czechoslovak Republic has only confirmed some critics' contentions that Havel's dramatic works are all basically political in origin and theme. These critics' beliefs are supported by some striking similarities in many of Havel's plays; the bureaucracies that are often seen as thinly veiled representations of totalitarian regimes, for example, are present in or alluded to in all of Havel's major works beginning with *The Garden Party* (1963) and ending with *Temptation* (1985). But while the existence of these bureaucratic systems and the protagonists' struggle to retain their personal identity in their dealings with such systems may suggest a political theme, they by no means limit Havel's plays to political matters. The appeal of Havel's plays in the West—especially in the United States, where threats of totalitarianism are distant—seems to suggest that these works hold within themselves something beyond their political content, something capable of capturing the attention of a large portion of the Western hemisphere.

Martin Esslin offers perhaps a better perspective to Havel's plays (or at least one that is better able to explain the playwright's international popularity) when he identifies Havel as an absurdist. Esslin's absurdist playwrights strive to express "the senselessness of the human condition and the inadequacy of the rational approach by the open abandonment of rational devices and discursive thought"; and indeed, Havel injects a multitude of contradictions and paradoxes into his plays, seemingly to express this very idea. And alongside these paradoxes and contradictions, Havel's works also mercilessly employ repetitions of words and actions. The end result of these techniques is a world—often centered around scientific or business affairs—where the human is remote or even alien; and it is in such a world that Havel's protagonists confront the absurd in the guise of bureaucracy and inner-office power struggles. For Hugo Pludek, Josef Gross, Leopold Nettles, or any of Havel's other heroes, the seemingly-arbitrary rise and fall of fortune is akin to Sisyphus's meaningless but interminable struggles to roll a boulder uphill only to have it roll back down. Unfortunately, the protagonists in these dramatic works fail to face the absurd with the heroic acceptance that Camus attributes to Sisyphus. In *The Garden Party,* for instance, Hugo's "swift career is . . . realized at the expense of his personality," and Marketa Goetz-Stankiewicz describes this loss of individuality as a fall from humanity: "Hugo has become a talking machine, a robot, repeating language which has become independent of its user. He has become a well-functioning particle in a system."

Havel's other protagonists, like Ionesco's rhinoceroses, also abandon their humanity or compromise themselves to become more easily assimilated into the inhuman bureaucracy that surrounds them. However, if Havel's heroes are not representative of the human in these plays, questions concerning whether such a representative exists and who such a figure would be follow logically. In searching for answers to these questions, Havel's viewer quickly finds that the only figures who consistently stand in contrast to the absurdity of the dramatist's bureaucracies are his female characters, particularly his secretaries.

In his own life, Havel seems to find an element of innate humanity in women. Certainly, his wife serves almost as an anchor, in *Letters to Olga,* to keep him connected to the normal, human world outside of his prison routine of work and interrogation. And Phyllis Carey identifies as the climactic catharsis of *Letters to Olga* one moment when, while Havel is watching television in prison, the television studio's sound equipment fails and "[a]n anonymous television weather-woman realizes with great embarrassment . . . that her words are not being heard." Carey notes that

> The woman's vulnerability bespeaks naked human existence, which evokes compassion from those who are no less vulnerable. The picture of the mute human trying futilely to make contact from the machine-prison becomes a remarkable image for a great deal that Havel is trying to convey about human responsibility in a desensitized world.

Of course, Havel's female characters do not, like Olga, have fully fleshed-out identities. Havel's females are much closer to the two dimensional image that Havel views in prison (though a number of his female characters precede his experience with the mute weather-woman). As is often typical in absurdist plays, these human shells are not meant to be actual human beings; instead, they are part of "concrete stage images," to use Esslin's words, meant only to represent an abstract mood, situation, or idea. Havel's women are such characters. They respond to kind acts and kind words with love; they become willing to help or protect those they love, even if such assistance violates the laws of the synthetic world in which they are placed. Inevitably, these female characters are punished (literally or figuratively) for violating bureaucratic procedures; and/or worse, their love for the male protagonist is unrequited since he has by now assimilated himself into the bureaucracy he has initially struggled against. These actions or slight variations of these actions occur again and again throughout Havel's earliest works as well as in *Largo Desolato* (1984) and *Temptation.*

The first of Havel's female characters to follow or approximate this scheme is the Secretary in *The Garden Party.* This Secretary, who lacks a name and is only identifiable by her title, is tending to her duties at the Liquidation Office's garden party until Falk brings up the subject of love. Prior to this, as Paul I. Trensky observes, each character (with the exception of Hugo) has a "particular lingo": "The language of the [Clerk and Secretary] is characterized by excessive literariness. Both speak as if they were citing a prepared text; their language is dry, precise and complex." However, when love arises as a topic of conversation and when the Clerk and Secretary interpret Falk's praises of love ("a bloody useful thing—so long as one knows how to latch on to it" [*Garden Party*]) as a suggestion that they should try love, their language begins to fall apart:

> CLERK I say, sparrows are flying—the boss mlossoms—the meadows are a-humming—
>
> SECRETARY Oh, I see—nature!
>
> CLERK Yes. Well now. You have hair! It's pretty—gold—like buttercrumbs—I mean buttercups—and your nose is like a rose—I'm sorry—I mean like a forget-me-not—white—
>
> SECRETARY Look—a sparrow!
>
> CLERK What?
>
> SECRETARY It's flying!
>
> CLERK And you have breasts.
>
> SECRETARY I know.
>
> CLERK Two—like two—like two—two little founts—(*Pause.*) I'm sorry—I mean footballs—like two footballs, that's what I meant to say—sorry—
>
> SECRETARY That's all right—go on—

Trensky calls this dialogue "a grotesque demonstration of their emotional bankruptcy," but as "grotesque" and utterly pathetic as the Clerk's advances are, the Secretary welcomes them. This "love affair" progresses to further levels of intimacy, which the Clerk sums up for Falk:

> we exchanged various facts from our private lives—we threw pine cones at each other—we tickled each other—nudged each other—tried to throw each other off balance—I pulled my colleague the Liquidation Secretary by the hair—my colleague the Liquidation Secretary bit me—but all just in fun, you know! Then we showed each other various peculiarities of our persons—we both found it very interesting—and we also touched each other—and, finally, we even called each other by our first names a few times!

Unfortunately for the Secretary, the Clerk quickly loses interest in love when he learns that the Inauguration Service is to be "liquidated." And when he turns their conversation to speculations about how the liquidation is to be carried out, she becomes distraught. Further, when the Clerk encourages her with "Be glad it's all over," she *begins to sob*" and runs toward the exit. This disappointed sobbing is to occur again in later plays.

In contrast to this Secretary, who develops genuine human feelings, the Clerk and Hugo show badly. The Clerk clearly has no interest in anything remotely human; he prefers the sterile procedures of the Inauguration Office's bureaucracy. Hugo's transformation, though, is inversely proportional to the Secretary's. As she becomes more human, as she begins to experience love, Hugo loses any humanity that he had at the play's opening. When Hugo returns home, for example, he does not realize that he has entered his own home nor does he realize that he is in search of himself. He is seemingly so transformed that not even his parents recognize him upon his return. In contrast to Hugo's loss of humanity, the Secretary's failed love affair—though bringing the Secretary grief—reveals her as a character conscious of her emotions and, in this most basic way, human.

While the Secretary in **The Garden Party** reveals Hugo's inhumanity by way of a juxtaposition with her ability to love, Maria in **The Memorandum** shows Josef Gross to be another failure as a human being. This time, though, Havel's protagonist is directly involved with the secretary and, this time, it is Gross who disappoints the female character and ruins her professional prospects. Havel's change in tactics from simple juxtaposition of characters to direct involvement between Gross and Maria serves to better reveal Gross's loss of interest in non-professional human affairs and relationships after he again acquires the Director's chair. Ironically, her translation of Gross's typed memo makes his second rise to power possible, and Maria voluntarily performs this act despite the distinct possibility that she will be punished for it.

Of course, Maria's willingness to risk termination in translating the memorandum does nothing to condemn Gross; her willingness only testifies to her courage and sympathy for a fellow human being in need. Gross condemns himself by not only "abandon[ing] her at the moment of her greatest need" but by excusing himself from this debt with a wave of self-important rhetoric. He explains:

> Dear Maria! We're living in a strange, complex epoch. As Hamlet says, our "time is out of joint." Just think, we're reaching for the moon and yet it's increasingly hard for us to reach ourselves; we're able to split the atom, but unable to prevent the splitting of our personality; we build superb communications between the continents, and yet communication between man and

man is increasingly difficult. . . . Dear Maria! You can't begin to guess how happy I would be if I could do for you what you've just asked me to do. The more am I frightened therefore that in reality I can do next to nothing for you, because I am in fact totally alienated from myself. . . .

The twentieth-century alienation of man from his fellow man is no more a reason to refuse Maria's plea than is Hamlet's lamentation directed at the twentieth century. Of course, Gross is correct in blaming his alienation from himself as the reason for his refusal, but the Director's awareness of the problem may just as easily make his behavior toward Maria more hateful as it is capable of excusing his actions. And finally, Robert Skloot adds: "[t]hat Maria remains 'happy' because 'nobody ever talked to me so nicely before' does not excuse Gross's avoidance of moral action nor his failure to reciprocate Maria's genuine expression of love toward him."

Havel's next major work, *The Increased Difficulty of Concentration,* provides yet another variation on the same male/female situation. While Hugo Pludek and Josef Gross lose themselves in the machinations of their respective bureaucracies, Dr. Eduard Huml drowns in the growing complexity of his private life; but oddly, this complexity is caused by Huml's own womanizing. Huml is married, but he also has a mistress. Meanwhile, he makes repeated, violent sexual advances to his secretary Blanka. Finally, toward the play's end, he embarks upon a fourth romantic entanglement with Miss Balcar. Huml's wife, to complicate matters, is aware of Renata, her husband's mistress, and continually prods him to break off his relationship with her. At the same time, Renata urges Huml to take action and leave his wife. Through the course of the play, Huml quickly goes from woman to woman while events speed up and Huml becomes increasingly confused, using the same pet names and the same lines of dialogue for all four women.

Eventually, Huml begins to alienate these women. Renata complains that her lover never says anything tender to her, and when Huml protests that he only lacks the "imagination" to say "big words," Renata exclaims "I'm a fool, I really am!" running from the stage in tears. Later Mrs. Huml makes a similar complaint about Huml's lack of "one kind word" and then laments that Huml never kisses her neck. She then uses the exact words to her husband that Renata uses in frustration with him: "I'm a fool, I really am!"

Huml's advances to his secretary are less emotional and more primitive than his dealings with either his wife or his mistress. Repeatedly, Huml stops his dictation, staring strangely at her turned back. And after a pause,

HUML leaps towards BLANKA, falls on his knees, grabs her shoulders and tries to kiss her. [. . .]

A short struggle ensues. . . . BLANKA resists, finally she gives him a push," HUML *loses his balance and falls down.* (intervening stage direction and outcry from Blanka omitted)

This scenario occurs repeatedly throughout the course of the work. And like his dealings with Renata and his wife, Huml's dealings with Blanka reveal the protagonist's inability to function normally on either an emotional or sexual level. His advances are almost attempts at rape, primal in nature and lacking any civilized human finesse. Further emphasizing the primal nature of Huml's attacks is their spontaneity. Like rapes, they occur without any clear reason or provocation.

Finally, Huml's dealings with women return to a more civilized though no less inept level with Miss, actually Dr., Balcar. Huml devastates her with a long and rhetorical speech against her career as a social scientist in which he argues the impossibility of ever understanding man "even a little." Miss Balcar responds to this attack with tears, and Huml responds in turn with a recantation and gentle sexual advances. "HUML *watches her for a moment in some embarrassment, then he quickly approaches her, takes her gently in his arms and begins to stroke her hair."* This embrace leads to several kisses and then to *"passionate kissing."* As he does with Blanka, Huml reveals, through his actions, a seeming inability to deal with women in any way other than as sexual objects. He is embarrassed and seemingly puzzled about what he should do since he has hurt Miss/Dr. Balcar. The only solution he can devise is to treat her the same way as he treats the other women in his life; he sets out to seduce her.

> **Like Havel's other protagonists, Leopold suffers from a loss of identity.**
> —*Jude R. Meche*

Indeed, Edward Huml reveals his limited ability to behave in a genuinely human manner by his consistently uncivilized treatment of the four female characters in the play and by contrast with them. On the other hand, Leopold Nettles in *Largo Desolato* shows his withdrawal from humanity and his ensuing lack of social skills through the difficulty he experiences in maintaining a successful emotional relationship. As Huml's four female companions suffer from his lack of humanity, so Lucy suffers in *Largo Desolato* because of Nettles's similar deficiency. Lucy sacrifices herself to rebuild Leopold, and she admits, "Everything I've done for us I've done freely and willingly, I'm not complaining and I don't want anything in return." However, Lucy does complain; she is clearly not happy with the state of their relationship; and immediately after protesting that she wants nothing, Lucy adds "I only want you to admit what is true," that she and Leopold are lovers. Leopold recoils from this request, though. In fact, he recoils from anything having to do with human emotions, failing to start work on his highly academic treatise which argues the thesis "that love is actually a dimension of being—it gives fulfillment and meaning to existence." Indeed, Leopold appears to be an even worse case than Huml, for Huml at least seeks out physical love. Leopold is repulsed by public acts of love. And in contrast, Lucy's openness and her aggressive efforts to strengthen Leopold through love testify to her acceptance of this emotion and all of its consequences. The contrast between Lucy and Leopold, for instance, is especially evident as Lucy promises to "unblock" Leopold, "*embrac[ing]*" him and "*kiss[ing] his face.*" During Lucy's embraces and promises, "LEOPOLD *sits perplexed and remains quite passive.*"

Lucy's efforts, though, lead to the same fate as befalls many of Havel's other female characters: tears. She realizes that Leopold is worse off than she believed. Saying, "All this talk—it's nothing but excuses!" She confronts him with the fact that he is a hopeless case. Leopold again shows his unwillingness to help her when she is detained by both the First Man and the Second Man. He fails to act on her behalf or even to visit her after her release, claiming: "I can't possibly leave here!" And finally, Leopold reaffirms his failed character by abandoning his second love when, "terrorized," he "chase[s] after and [is] humiliated by the two sinister chaps who inform him his gesture of 'heroism' will no longer be required."

Most likely, he would, like Josef Gross, excuse these failures because

> In reality I've had the feeling for some time now that something is collapsing inside me—as if an axis holding me together has started to break—the ground crumbling under my feet—I lack a fixed point from which everything inside me could grow and develop—I get the feeling sometimes that I'm not really doing anything except listening helplessly to the time going by.

Like Havel's other protagonists, Leopold suffers from a loss of identity. Not only has he lost the drive to continue his work, he has also lost, seemingly, a part of his humanity, as is obvious first in contrast to Lucy and later in contrast to Marguerite's hope and optimism that she might save him.

Havel incorporates this male/female relationship into *Temptation,* his version of the Faust myth. In fact, Goetz-Stankiewicz observes that the secretary Marketa fits perfectly "in the tradition of Goethe's Gretchen," and that Havel appears to take advantage of the character's appearance in Goethe's Faust play as an opportunity to again juxtapose the male protagonist who compromises his soul to the innocent woman who retains a basic element of humanity. Indeed, Dr. Henry Foustka's seemingly sincere discussion of "moral action" strikes a chord in Marketa. She exclaims: "Yes, yes, that's exactly how I've felt about it all my life!," and believing that Foustka is as moral as she is and as he appears to be, she falls in love with him, declaring to him that she would "rather be ruined with you and live the truth than be without you and live a lie!" Havel's protagonists, though, never choose to live in truth, and Foustka is no exception. Like his predecessors, he offers no help to the woman who has, ironically, sacrificed herself in defense of him. He simply lets her lose her position. The only difference is that, on this occasion, the audience witnesses the consequences of Foustka's actions, for Marketa later reappears as a lunatic Ophelia.

However, the greater tragedy in this work comes as Foustka loses his moral compass, manipulating truth for his own benefit. Such actions are despicable enough, but when Foustka's morally-barren efforts to retain his position are contrasted to Marketa's honest words prior to her termination, Havel again succeeds in further disgracing his male protagonist while retaining a model of truth for his audience to celebrate and (possibly) emulate.

Throughout these works, Havel exhibits an amazing consistency in his presentation and use of secretaries and victimized female characters as foils to his male protagonists. As far as the reason Havel uses female characters as representative examples of fully-functioning human beings (in contrast to his deficient protagonists), one might only speculate. Certainly, if Havel is working on a somewhat symbolic level as he appears to be, a female character might be an appropriate choice because—archetypically—women are viewed as more nurturing and more likely to show their emotions. Whether such archetypal perceptions are true seems to be of little concern to Havel, for he deals not in fully developed female characters but—like many absurdists—in concrete representations of abstract concepts. Similarly, Havel's frequent use of females in secretarial roles might be explained (in addition to matters of setting and the status of women when these plays were written) by the low status of the secretary in bureaucracies and in relation to the male protagonist. The secretary is a person who can be taken advantage of by the protagonist. Treatment of his underlings becomes yet another facet of the comprehensive test of his humanity that Havel sets before him. Indeed, Havel appears to make much use of the contrasts that he repeatedly establishes between male protagonists and their female foils.

Walter H. Capps (essay date Fall 1997)

SOURCE: "Interpreting Václav Havel," in *Cross Currents*, Vol. 47, No. 3, Fall, 1997, pp. 301-16.

[*In the following essay, Capps examines Havel's artistic and philosophical development in the context of Czechoslovakian intellectual tradition and contemporary politics.*]

Though the intellectual and academic worlds haven't caught full sight of it yet, we are standing on the threshold of a new era in thought, idea, and cultural construction. This new era has been made possible by the ending of a prolonged Cold War, and the sudden, unexpected opportunity to learn how the people of Eastern bloc nations sustained themselves culturally and spiritually during the time of their subjection to totalitarian forces. For most of the Cold War period, philosophical and artistic expression in Marxist countries was neither widely known nor acknowledged in the western world. Since the appropriate evidence was not readily available, it was too easy to assume that not much of significance was happening.

Yet, one can quickly appreciate how untrue such an assumption is. Human nature being human nature, there is never a time or circumstance that does not produce ideas or cultural expressions. Indeed, many of the most profound ideas and the most stirring expressions have been created during times of greatest social, political, and economic unrest, and by those who were the most seriously affected. We learn about the character of the struggles of the time, for example, through Dietrich Bonhoeffer's *Letters and Papers from Prison,* Martin Luther King's "Letter from the Birmingham Jail," Nelson Mandela's autobiography, the *Diary of Anne Frank,* the testimony of dissidents, and the literature of marginality. And when the portion of the world that is now being referenced deserves to be called the "new Europe," one recognizes that the social, cultural, religious, and intellectual fallout is of significant proportions and dimensions.

Of course, a single essay cannot attempt a comprehensive sketch of pertinent developments in Eastern Germany, Bulgaria, Romania, Hungary, the Czech Republic, Slovakia, Poland, Latvia, Lithuania, Estonia, not to mention Bosnia, and the provinces of the former Soviet Union. But we can focus attention on one of these places, namely, the Czech Republic, knowing that the other regions can also boast of important and exciting occurrences and developments. In this essay we wish to focus specifically on the intellectual and political life in the city of Prague, prior to the successful "velvet revolution" of 1989—a subject that is magnetized by another remarkable piece of prison literature, namely, Václav Havel's *Letters to Olga*—and then to give consideration to Havel's thought and vision for politics.

Prague's Intellectual Life during the Cold War

It is difficult to imagine what was transpiring in the city of Prague during Soviet occupation. But we do know something about how intellectual freedom survived, and how it was advanced. For clues I am indebted to the insight and analysis of the late Ernest Gellner, Prague-born Cambridge University philosopher, who, at the time of his death, was the director of the Center for the Study of Nationalism at the new Central European University in Prague, and whose most recent book is *Conditions of Liberty: Civil Society and Its Rivals* (1994). My thinking on these matters has also been influenced by Dinko Tomasic and Stjepan G. Mestrovic, whose work is referenced in Mestrovic's highly provocative *Habits of the Balkan Heart: Social Character and the Fall of Communism* (1993), which builds its case in brilliant conversation with Alexis de Tocqueville, Thorstein Veblen, Erich Fromm, David Riesman, Robert N. Bellah, and Seymour Martin Lipset. Also supporting Mestrovic's analysis are the writings of Friedrich Tonnies, and, in particular, Tonnies's distinction between *gemeinschaft* and *gesellschaft,* as this is the central focus of Tonnies's *Community and Society.* But I am following Gellner's analysis because it is compatible with that offered by Václav Havel (b. 1936), the famous playwright and essayist, who currently serves as president of the Czech Republic.

The sequential development can be traced and sketched. Prague is invaded in 1968 when the Soviet tanks come rumbling into the city and make their indomitable presence felt in Wenceslaus Square. The citizens of the city try to make some accommodation to the Soviet presence. Promises are offered but promises are broken. The people suffer increased disappointment and disillusionment. Suddenly, with the frustration level high, a certain Jan Palach, hardly a well-known or prominent citizen, in protest against the repressions of occupying Soviet forces; burns himself to death in front of the statue of St. Václav in Wenceslaus Square on January 19, 1969.

A few months after Palach's suicide, Václav Havel, already known as a superb essayist and dramatist, appealed to President Alexander Dubcek to institute democratic reforms, proposing that such an act of defiance against the Soviets "would place before us an ethical mirror as powerful as that of Jan Palach's recent deed." Dubcek listened to Havel's plea, but, under pressure from the reigning Communists, took no action. But the tide of revolution was already in process. Havel commented that Palach's self-immolation marked the beginning of a period in which nothing short of "human existence itself is at stake."

None of this happened, of course, in isolation, but rather was part of an intricate set of interconnecting influences. A prominent background presence is Tomas Garrigue Masaryk (1850-1937), a brilliant philosopher who served for fifteen years as a member of the Austrian Parliament. Opposed to Germany's nationalism in Austria and Austria's adventurous policies in the Balkans, Masaryk became convinced that Austro-Hungary could no longer serve as the common homeland for the small nations of Central Europe. Thus, dramatically, following the outbreak of World War I, Masaryk became the champion of an independent Czechoslovakia, leading troops who fought successfully alongside Allied forces. At the end of the war, Masaryk became president of the first Czechoslovakian Republic, from 1919 to 1938.

Primarily a philosopher, Masaryk had come under the influence of Franz von Brentano (1838-1917) during his studies in Vienna. Subsequently, when he was twenty-seven years old, in Leipzig, Masaryk developed a friendship with Edmund Husserl, and was instrumental in convincing Husserl to switch from the study of mathematics to philosophy. Through Masaryk, Husserl was directed toward the work of Brentano. And from Masaryk, Husserl acquired a heightened sense of the spiritual crisis of the modern world. Masaryk was concerned about the loss of religious faith. Alarmed that increased scientific sophistication did not bring moral progress, he feared that modern reason had become detached from the world of good and evil, which for him was the foundation of lived reality.

Husserl extended Masaryk's analysis to include the judgment that theoretical knowledge had lost contact with living human experience. Eventually Husserl wrote a powerful treatise on the subject, *The Crisis of European Sciences* (1936), in which he affirmed that the morally ordered world of our prereflective lived experience is indeed the common life-world. Masaryk would have said the same, though with greater emphasis on matters of religious belief. For our purposes, it is significant to note that these Masarykian and Husserlian themes are perceptible in Václav Havel's thinking and writing.

In addition, Masaryk affirmed that Czech national consciousness had been grounded and shaped by the Hussite movement. Through Masaryk's testimony, the national martyr, Jan Hus (1370-1415), gained fresh place in contemporary Czech thinking. So when Jan Palach burned himself after the Soviets invaded Czechoslovakia, it was appropri-

ate for Czech patriots to assign Hussite martyr symbolism to the event.

We must also cite the strong influence of the philosopher Jan Patocka (1907-77), who studied under Husserl, taught Václav Havel, and subsequently was instrumental in publishing Charter 77, the statement of resistance to Soviet occupation and communist ideology, Patocka, whose philosophical work at last is becoming better known outside the Czech Republic, drew upon the thought of his significant predecessors. First, he studied under Husserl, and devoted a good portion of his graduate work to a systematic study of Masaryk's thought. (When Husserl was expelled from Freiburg University by the Nazi rulers of Germany, Patocka was instrumental in bringing him to Prague to deliver guest lectures.) Then too, like Masaryk, Patocka exhibited respect for religion, and spent considerable time studying theology. In one of his earlier essays he wrote, "without God the world is unthinkable." He admitted, however, that God was not accessible to him through lived experience.

Patocka's final set of writings, grouped under the title *Heretical Essays in the Philosophy of History,* provides evidence that the subject that most captivated him is the requirement of the human struggle. The final essay in this collection, "Wars of the Twentieth Century and the Twentieth Century as War," offers a commentary on Heraclitus's understanding of *polemos,* which Patocka translates as "struggle, fight, and war." The reference is to Heraclitus's Fragment 26: "It should be understood that war is the common condition, that strife is justice, and that all things come to pass through the compulsion of strife." Here Patocka affirms that this struggle possesses the kind of ontological fundamentality that others accord to love, justice, compassion, happiness. Indeed, there is evidence that Patocka would vote for other thematic possibilities himself, were it possible to do so. But the always necessary struggle against the world—which is nothing less than an adversarial conflict with reality—forces him to give priority to *polemos.*

Patocka employed Heraclitus to correct and amend Husserl's Phenomenological assumptions about reality's underlying harmony. The conclusions of *Heretical Essays* are thoroughly compatible with Patocka's understanding of his cultural task. In fact, the publication of the *Essays,* in informal typescript copies, received widespread attention, and served to rally the Czech citizenry against the oppressions being inflicted by the occupying forces. Patocka's readers understood that hope is paradoxical: when its ontological supports fail, hope must be re-established on grounds intrinsic to the person. Paradoxically, the collapse of confidence in external supports evokes personal responsibility; there emerge twin needs to save one's soul in the midst of war's apocalypse and to establish a community of solidarity among those who have been shaken. This "solidarity of the shaken" provides them with that refuge and strength which is "the power of the powerless."

He even took on the alien, adversarial powers, with the promulgation of the Charter 77 texts, prompted by the 1977 Helsinki Agreement on human rights which affirm that human beings are obliged to discover and protect a valid moral foundation since there can be no rightful expectation that salvation will be provided by the state, or that it can be effected by any combination of social powers and forces. In a message to the Czech people, Patocka explained the creed of Charter 77 as follows:

> Something fundamentally non-technical and non-instrumental must exist. There must be a self-evident, non-circumstantial ethic and unconditional morality. A moral system does not exist in order to help society function but simply so that man can be human. It is not man who defines a moral order according to the arbitrary nature of his needs, wishes, tendencies, and desires, but, on the contrary, it is morality which defines man.

Patocka and the other signers of Charter 77 urged their Czechoslovakian compatriots to resist injustice by assuming the responsibility of free citizens, in accordance with the Helsinki principles. For Patocka, *polemos* both separates and unites people. The solidarity it enjoins is the basis for establishing the *polis,* and for seeing oneself and other citizens as members of the *polis.*

Predictably, the promulgation of Charter 77 incensed the authorities. Patocka, whose publications were already censured, was brought in for long hours of intensive interrogation. It was too much for him emotionally and physically, and he was transferred to the hospital after suffering heart trouble. Still, he kept up his resistance, promulgating an explanatory statement: "conformity has not yet led to any improvement; what is needed is to speak the truth." Under continuing pressure from the authorities, on March 13, 1977, just a few days prior to his seventieth birthday, he died of a severe brain hemorrhage. More than a thousand mourners came to his funeral, all under the watchful eyes of police agents and cameramen. Several of his friends were taken into custody. Havel, calling Patocka Czechoslovakia's "most important philosopher," named it a martyr's death. On March 19, Paul Ricoeur, in a commemorative essay in *Le Monde,* attested that it was because he "knew no fear that he has literally been put to death by the authorities." Havel was also arrested and jailed for four months for his part in Charter 77 activities. In 1979 he was convicted again, this time sentenced to four-and-a-half years in prison, but received a suspended sentence because of poor health and an international protest campaign.

It was during his second stay in prison that he wrote the letters to his wife that were subsequently published as *Letters to Olga.*

Masaryk, Patocka, and Havel

Before analyzing the career and thought of Václav Havel in more detail, we must call attention to similarities in the principal ideas and sense of vocation of Masaryk, Patocka, and Havel. Note, first, that all three mixed keen interest in theory and unfailing commitment to scholarship with dedicated involvement in direct political activity. As noted, Masaryk was a member of the Austrian parliament, the leader of a Czech movement for independence, and the first president of independent Czechoslovakia. Patocka dedicated much of his philosophical career to identifying reality's most distinctive principle; after according centrality to strife, he then rallied his fellow citizens to support freedom and responsibility, before succumbing to a martyr's death. Havel was a playwright and essayist, who, following the "velvet revolution" of 1989, became the first president of the newly (re-)established Czech Republic.

Note, second, that the lives and careers of all three exhibit narratives that support the collective identification of the Czech people with the martyrdom of Hus. Masaryk invoked the memory of Hus to facilitate independent Czech national identity. Patocka, following Jan Palach's self-immolation, was interrogated so severely that his death was perceived as suffering on behalf of the Czech people. When Patocka died, Havel wrote his testimonial, **"The Power of the Powerless,"** and dedicated it to Patocka's memory. Havel's own qualifications for martyr's status are to be found in his imprisonments.

Third, the intellectual intentions of all three were remarkably similar. All three took their intellectual cues from the shared recognition that, as a result of disjuncture, disharmony, or pervasive conflict, European life and thought were in profound crisis. In *The Crisis of European Sciences,* Husserl's extensive commentary on the principles according to which Descartes established modern philosophy, this disjuncture was portrayed as a crisis of self-alienation. Such profound alienation could not possibly be resolved, Husserl argued, except through attribution of normative status to the *Lebenswelt* (life-world), which is the basis for ethical autonomy. Masaryk perceived a crisis too. For him, the traditional habits and patterns of religious faith conflicted with a technological world increasingly devoid of moral and ethical meaning. As Masaryk saw it, nineteenth-century science had usurped the authority previously accorded to faith and reason, and the moral and ethical repercussions were catastrophic. In *Suicide as a Mass Phenomenon of Modern Civilization,* Masaryk traced the reversal of moral progress which had accompanied the loss of religious faith. For him, science was both mechanistic and materialistic, and, in these senses, substituted dysfunctionally for an awareness that human life belongs to an ordered moral universe. Following Brentano, Masaryk believed it crucial that human beings return to the world of primary experience, there to be reconnected with a vital sense of good and evil.

Václav Havel's Philosophical and Political Program

Václav Havel, then, did not emerge out of nowhere, he is part of an ongoing Czech intellectual tradition. When he needed ideas by which to counter oppressive Marxist thinking, he found the key in Husserl's concept of *Lebenswelt.* For Havel, the resort to *Lebenswelt* fostered the conditions of "living in truth." The alternative to top-down, mechanistic, manipulative theoretical deduction (which, in Havel's view, is the tendency of Marxism) is acute attention to what Havel's calls "the flow of life." And "flow of life" (a phrase Heraclitus might well have incorporated in his "everything flows" [Fragment 20] and "time is a river into which one cannot step twice in the same place" [Fragment 21]), evidences deep contracts between the superficiality and artificiality of ideology and the dependability of fundamental ideas.

It is also important to recognize that Havel understood that he too was responding to the problematic identified in Husserl's *Crisis.* In **"Politics and Conscience"** (1984), Havel calls Husserl's understanding of "the natural world" and "the world of lived experience" reliable vectors through which to approach "the spiritual Framework of modern civilization and the source of the present crisis." In the same passage, reflecting Masaryk's fundamental trust in what Erazim Kohak describes as "the prereflective certainty of Moravian peasants," Havel identifies children, working people, and peasants as "far more rooted in what some philosophers call the natural world, or *Lebenswelt,* than most modern adults." Then, in direct response to the self-alienation Husserl addressed in the *Crisis,* Havel explains:

> They have not grown alienated from the world of their actual personal experience, the world which has its morning and its evening, its *down* (the earth) and its *up* (the heavens), where the sun rises daily in the east, traverses the sky and sets in the west, and where concepts like "at home" and "in foreign parts," good and evil, beauty and ugliness, near and far, duty and rights, still mean something living and definite.

It is significant that Havel employed his predecessors' commentaries on "the crisis" to criticize the totalitarian system under which the people of (then) Czechoslovakia were subjected. Indeed, the untrustworthy mechanistic world of impersonal agents and forces is vividly illustrated in Soviet Marxist rule. In **"What I Believe,"** Havel becomes quite specific. He criticizes "systematically pure market economics," while seeking to cast suspicions on Marxist ideology. He chastises both for presuming that "operating from theory is essentially smarter than operating from a knowledge of life." The alternative—again following the guidance of Masaryk and Patocka—is a true "understanding of individual human beings, and the moral and social sensitivity that comes from such understanding." In other words, "social life is not a machine built to any set of plans known to us." Rather, in true Heraclitean fashion, "new theories are constantly being fashioned." And in this essay, Havel invokes *Lebenswelt* as "the flow of life which is always taking us by surprise."

Through all of this it becomes apparent that Havel and his colleagues interpreted the Czech situation under Soviet rule to be a vivid exemplification of the fundamental challenge that both Masaryk and Patocka had identified, and Husserl had conceptualized. In *Disturbing the Peace,* Havel thanks Patocka for teaching him that "the real test of a man is not how well he plays the role he has invented for himself, but how well he plays the role that destiny assigned to him."

Put the ideas together, and they come out like this: there is a fundamental contrast between the world that can be constructed out of some presumed ideological viewpoint and the world that is rooted in trustworthy lived-experience; impersonal, mechanistic, manipulative force can be effectively resisted only by the one true power that all persons have at their disposal, their own humanity. Ivan Klima, a brilliant contemporary Czech writer, in *The Spirit of Prague* finds the same lesson in the teachings of Prague's Franz Kafka:

> [Kafka's] hero is, above all, a hero for our time, a godless age in which power endowed with a higher meaning has been replaced with a vacuous power of tradition and legal and bureaucratic norms, that is, by human institutions. Man, deprived of all means and all weapons in his effort to achieve freedom and order, has no hope other than the one provided by his inner space.

Havel and the Language of Being

The pattern was established by Masaryk. After the basic human conflict has been identified and described and effective ways of responding are proposed, the question becomes what portions and degrees of the religious or spiritual world can be invoked. Masaryk found satisfaction in traditional Christianity. Patocka flirted with religious resolutions, but adopted the position that strife is the source of all things. Havel moved in a distinctive direction, keeping faith with the intellectual tradition in which he had been raised and trained, while continuing to combine insights from Husserl and Heidegger, both of whom employed the language of being and felt constrained to come to terms with the transcendent.

> **Humans, he says, have lost respect—self-respect, respect for others, and respect for what Havel calls "the order of nature, the order of humanity, and for secular authority as well."**
> —*Walter H. Capps*

It is hardly surprising that Havel writes (in *Letters to Olga*, Letter 76):

> Behind all phenomena and discrete entities in the world, we may observe, intimate, or experience existentially in various ways something like a general "order of Being." The essence and meaning of this order are veiled in mystery; it is as much an enigma as the Sphinx, it always speaks to us differently and always, I suppose, in ways that we ourselves are open to, in ways, to put it simply, that we can hear.

Consequently, when addressing an audience at the Stanford University Law School, September 29, 1994, Havel referred to "unconscious experience" as well as to "archetypes and archetypal visions." His point was that cultures formed thousands of years ago, quite independently of one another, nevertheless employ the same basic archetypes. This suggests that "there exist deep and fundamental experiences shared by the entire human race." Further, "traces of such experiences can be found in all cultures, regardless of how distant or how different they are from one another:"

> . . . the whole history of the cosmos, and especially of life, is mysteriously recorded in the inner workings of all human beings. This history is projected into man's creations and is, again, something that joins us together far more than we think.

The idea is extended even further: "after thousands of years, people of different epochs and cultures feel that they are somehow parts and partakers of *the same integral Being,* carrying within themselves a piece of *the infinity of that Being* [italics mine]." In the final take, Havel asserts that "all cultures assume the existence of something that might be called the *Memory of Being,* in which everything is constantly recorded." The guarantees of human freedom and personal responsibility lie neither in programs of action nor systems of thought, but, rather, in "man's relationship to that which transcends him, without which he would not be and of which he is an integral part."

Havel's Stanford University discourse carried the title **"The Spiritual Roots of Democracy"** and was designed to delineate his understanding of the fundamental crisis in the modern world. Humans, he says, have lost respect—self-respect, respect for others, and respect for what Havel calls "the order of nature, the order of humanity, and for secular authority as well." When respect is lost, laws, moral norms, and established authority are also undermined. Gone is the sense of responsibility that inhabitants of one and the same planet have toward one another:

> The relativization of all moral norms, the crisis of authority, reduction of life to the pursuit of immediate material gain without regard for its general consequences [originates] in that which modern man has lost: his *transcendental anchor,* [italics mine], and along with it the only genuine source of his responsibility and self-respect.

When explaining how human dignity, freedom, and responsibility can be secured, Havel makes the same point again: "The source of these basic human potentials lies in man's relationship to that which transcends him." And what is this? Havel answers not by talking about God, or even about Being (though both may be implied), but by referring to the universal experience of the human race. He pleads that humankind today must become connected (or is it reconnected?) to "the mythologies and religions of all cultures" so that all humans, together, may "engage in a common quest for the general good." And what is the general good? Havel's somewhat apocalyptic answer is that "global civilization" is already preparing a place for "planetary democracy." And what is this? It is "the very Earth we inhabit, linked with Heaven above us":

> Only in this setting can the mutuality and the commonality of the human race be newly created, with reverence and gratitude for that which transcends each of us, and all of us together. The authority of a world democratic order simply cannot be built on anything else but the revitalized authority of the universe.

In an essay entitled **"Politics and the World Itself"** (*Kettering Review,* Summer 1992), Havel criticized the Marxist presumption that reality is governed by a finite number of universal laws whose interrelationships can be grasped by the human mind and anticipated in systematic formulae. According to Havel, there are no such laws or theories, just as there is no comprehensive ideology that can either explain or direct human life. The demonstrable weakness of Marxist philosophy carries profound implications for the future of the world. Indeed, it calls for an abandonment of "the arrogant belief that the world is merely a puzzle to be solved, a machine with instructions for use waiting to be discovered, a body of information to be put into a computer with the hope that, sooner or later, it will spit out a universal solution." Havel understands that there is no "universal key to salvation." The alternative is to recognize the pluralism of the world, which does not reduce to "common denominators" or to a "single common equation." Havel's alternative to proposed keys to salvation begins with "an elementary sense of transcendental responsibility," to which he appends "archetypal wisdom, good taste, courage, compassion, and, not least, faith in the importance of particular measures."

The Global Agenda

Several extraordinary addresses he has given in the United States provide a clear sense of Havel's aspirations. One of the most compelling was his February 1990 address to the U.S. Congress on the subject of democratic ideals and the rebirth of the human spirit. The previous bipolarity of the Cold War has yielded to "an era of multipolarity in which all of us, large and small, former slaves and former masters, will be able to create what your great President Lincoln called 'the family of men.'" His experience with antagonists, Havel said, had taught him that "consciousness precedes being, and not [as Marxist philosophy erroneously teaches] the other way around." This means that "the salvation of this human world lies nowhere else than in the human heart, in the human power to reflect, in human meekness and in human responsibility."

To be more specific:

> Without a global revolution in the sphere of human consciousness, nothing will change for the better in the sphere of our being as humans, and the catastrophe toward which this world is headed—be it ecological, social, demographic, or a general breakdown of civilization—will be unavoidable.

So, what is to be done? Havel's answer is not a specific program, or a prescribed philosophical or ideological point of view. Rather, the only way to progress is through dedication to responsibility:

> Responsibility to something higher than my family, my country, my company, my success—responsibility to the *order of being* [italics mine] where all our actions are indelibly recorded and where and only where they will be properly judged.

On June 8, 1995, in a commencement address at Harvard, Havel sounded similar themes in recognizing that the world has already entered a single technological civilization. He commended the scientific achievement that made such a civilization possible but—in the spirit of Masaryk, Husserl, and Patocka—sounded the alarm. In fact, to counteract this single technological civilization, a contrary movement is occurring which finds expression in dramatic revivals of ancient traditions, religions and cultures. Havel explained the phenomenon as the recovery of an "archetypal spirituality" that is "the foundation of most religions and cultures"—"respect for what transcends us, whether we mean the mystery of Being or a moral order that stands above us."

> We must divest ourselves of our egoistically anthropocentrism, our habit of seeing ourselves as masters of the universe who can do whatever occurs to us. We must discover a new respect for what transcends us: for the universe, for the earth, for nature, for life, and for reality. Our respect for other people, for other nations, and for other cultures, can only grow from a humble respect for the cosmic order and from an awareness that we are a part of it, that we share in it and that nothing of what we do is lost, but rather becomes part of the eternal memory of Being, where it is judged.

His intention was to invite the Harvard graduates to accept responsibility for creating "a new order for the world."

Havel's May 15, 1996, address in Aachen, called **"The Hope for Europe"** (*The New York Review,* June 20, 1996), stands as a provocative survey of Europe's influences, both destructive and constructive, on human civilization, and envisions the role that the countries of the region might exercise today. The contrast on which he draws derives from an application of key distinctions in Husserl's *Crisis.* (Indeed, the Aachen address can be read as an updated, contemporary response to prior Czech analyses of the principal challenges of European culture.) Havel identifies "the starting point" with "a discussion about Europe as a place of shared values" (recall what he said the previous year at Harvard on this topic). And this is to talk about "European spiritual and intellectual identity or—if you like—European soul." Havel hopes that post-Cold War Europe "might establish itself on democratic principles as a whole entity for the first time in its history." But this will happen only if the "values that underlie the European tradition" are supported by "a metaphysically anchored sense of responsibility." In short:

> The only meaningful task for the Europe of the next century is to be the best it can possibly be—that is, to revivify its best spiritual and intellectual traditions and thus help to create a new global pattern of coexistence.

The word "global" is central.

A Personal Word

I have been reading and contemplating Václav Havel's essays for the past several years because I know of no one writing about politics today whose work is more inspirational. A brilliant intellectual, playwright and essayist, he believes with passion that essayists, poets, dramatists, artists, musicians, and philosophers carry responsibility for the well-being of the societies in which they live. In describing the role of politics in the world today, he exhibits a keen grasp of prevailing global dynamics. He knows from conviction and experience why a politics that is not attached to an anchored spirituality carries no lasting promise. When addressing religion, he affirms what believers wish to avow without falling into debilitating dogmatic or parochial traps. In assessing the present conditions of the world, he warns against utilitarian, pragmatic techno-culture. He respects the innate human aspiration to become rooted in that which most profoundly binds us to the core of being. In evaluating the Cold War, he is confident he knows why Marxist philosophy failed. It was not that it was beaten by a rival system but "by life, by the human spirit, by conscience, by the resistance of Being and man to manipulation." Havel expands on this thesis with a Heraclitean corollary: "it was defeated by a revolt of color, authenticity, history in all its variety, and human individuality against imprisonment within a uniform ideology."

I am not sure I know how to translate such ideas into contemporary American political thinking, or even if it is appropriate to try. After all, Washington is not Prague, and the history of the United States is not interchangeable with the history of communist and post-Cold War Europe. Moreover, I sometimes fear that politics in the United States no longer has a philosophical context, and this is why what content there is derives so directly from ideology or is so swiftly transposed into public relations. I am often suspicious of American calls for more vital moral and spiritual foundations, because we all know how quickly they can dissolve into rancorous requests for audible prayer in the schools. Do our citizens understand that ours is a culture in crisis, not because we are following the misguided counsel of an incorrect politics, but because whatever remains of the flow of life has been overwhelmed by unjustifiable confidence in code, formula, policy, and divisive special interests?

When I consider the fullness of spirit with which Havel believes reality deserves to be engaged, I fear that the weakest of alternatives is to try to live life as an analyst, critic, or spectator. When he strives vigorously to resist depersonalization, I question our depth of commitment to keeping intuitive faculties alive. With profound respect for the priority he accords moral guidance, I ask how we can expect to get by on substitutes for a primary trust that our own subjectivity is linked to the subjectivity of the world. When I hear Havel extol the needs of the global community, I worry that post-Cold War America has become too isolationist, too shockingly and embarrassingly greedy.

I do not know whether a political philosophy like Havel's can function effectively in a world like ours. But I know that we are deriving less substance and direction from it than we ought. I hear him plead that politics and politicians must cultivate new attitudes if they are to meet the challenges and opportunities of our world. He is surely correct when he observes that it is not enough for us to try to reform political methods and procedures. We must revise not our procedures but our view of reality. We must subject ourselves to an authority now ignored—of real persons in their life-world.

I do not know how this transformation can be effected, but I believe I do know where and how it starts. Václav Havel writes frequently of soul and spirit, and points to where "living in truth" takes place. Whenever he invokes these terms he links them to "the humility that is appropriate in the face of the mysterious order of Being." In **"The Politics of Hope"** we read: "in my own life I am reaching for something that goes far beyond me and the horizon of the world that I know; in everything I do I touch eternity in a strange way." With this grounding, politics becomes "the universal consultation on the reform of the affairs which render man human."

Translating this vision into American terms is difficult. Yet Havel is admired and loved within the United States. His 1990 address to Congress continues to evoke approval and excitement. He lectures often at American institutions. Increasing numbers are becoming acquainted with his writings. Does the fact that more Americans than one might expect attend to his views and support his vision stand as evidence that citizens of this country are searching for alternatives to our prevailing fare of divisive, uninspiring politics? Is it confirmation that people would welcome an intellectually substantive, culturally satisfying, and spiritually nurturing politics?

I do not know, but I am confident that this strong voice of the post-Cold War "new Europe," with its insistence that politics be accorded a transcendental source and foundation, is a resounding testimony to hope.

Jean Bethke Elshtain (review date 24 October 1997)

SOURCE: "Philosopher President," in *Commonweal*, October 24, 1997, pp. 23-4.

[*In the following review, Elshtain offers a positive evaluation of* The Art of the Impossible.]

President Václav Havel of the Czech Republic is one of the great spokesmen for the "return to Europe" of countries formerly compelled to inhabit that political nowhereland called "Eastern Europe." He is an urbane intellectual, a playwright, and a moralist. That he is also the president of a nation-state is for him one of life's great ironies, even miracles, and he claims that he can scarcely believe it most of the time: one day an infamous dissident slated for harassment and incarceration; the next a famous dissident addressing hundreds of thousands gathered in Wenceslaus Square in defiance of a corrupt, authoritarian regime; and then a bit further on, the president of (then) Czechoslovakia proclaiming, on January 1, 1990: "People, your government has returned to you!"

It has not been an easy return. Havel knew it would not be. In October 1992, in a conversation with a small group gathered in Prague, Havel was sober to the point of being somber. The two republics were breaking up. The process of crafting a new constitution was then frustrated—so much so that Havel declared that he felt rather like locking up a group of clever constitutional lawyers and not permitting them to leave the building until they had forged a draft constitution. And, as well, Europe, his part of Europe, had "entered the long tunnel at the end of the light." This was a brilliant reversal of a standard metaphor. Havel has never been a utopian; indeed, much of his life has been dedicated to defeating all utopian politics, all ends-of-histories and overarching world views that promote ugly social engineering and destroy human freedom, mutual self-help, and even minimal decency.

And yet the title of this book is *The Art of the Impossible.* What, then, does Havel mean? He means hopefulness, a kind of canny insightfulness, energy for the tasks ahead. So much has happened so fast. How can one not believe in "miracles" [his word]? But such miracles are not wholly within our grasp. At best, we can see the possibilities immanent in a situation and screw up our courage in order to act, knowing that human events are not wholly under our own control. Much of this collection of speeches and essays written between 1990 and 1996 traverses the in-between—in-between quiescence and arrogant overreach. That is Havel's terrain. How well does he traverse it? Passing well, I would say, although he does seem to falter from time to time and he thinks aloud about the reasons why. He struggles with Oxford fellow Timothy Garton Ash's critique of intellectuals in politics, for example. Ash had worried in print about the confusion of independent intellectual and practicing politician that he believed plagued post-1989 Europe: become one or the other, Ash more or less urged. Either stay outside and maintain your intellectual independence or take up a post and start to act, well, Weberian. (Weber, remember, distinguished between an ethic of "ultimate ends," too good for this world, and an "ethic of responsibility," one that is forced to choose between imperfect alternatives.)

Many of the most interesting reflections in this volume show Havel grappling with Ash's criticism. He understands "how difficult it is for an independent intellectual to adjust overnight to the world of practical politics when he has spent his whole life critically analyzing the world and defending certain chemically pure tenets." And there is a tendency for the intellectual to "resort to philosophical meditation, which in most cases makes things worse" than they would have been if he had just opted for an alternative, even a bad one. Another temptation is to launch into "complex reflections that voters find difficult to follow"— a charge lodged frequently against Havel—when what he ought to be about is saying "in clear and unambiguous terms that he is running for office because he is the best person for the job. . . ." He shouldn't spend a lot of time hesitating, doubting, refusing to fight, questioning his own motives—again the sort of thing Havel is taxed with. He should shoulder the burden that is his and just get down to it.

Practical politics, yes, but never a politics shorn of morality. Havel's great fear is that relinquishing a politics of high morality often leads to a politics of brute instrumentality; thus, he rejects politics that is simply "the art of the possible." No, one should lift up politics. It is a nobler craft and a more demanding art than the technicians and power mongers allow. Politics has to do with hope and with purpose, with the articulation of a "spiritual dimension." It has to do with accepting responsibility, not of a total and unlimited sort, but of a carefully defined sort, and going on to approach that responsibility neither from a "will to power nor an ideological vision of the world but, rather, a moral stance."

What does Havel have in mind here? The verities and virtues he embraces are basic decencies, Christian in origin, but honed and shaped through the struggles with human dignity, rights, and power in modernity. Havel is clear that the source of the sense of responsibility he embraces is "metaphysical." This probably doesn't win many votes, and it frustrates some of his admirers and friends, especially when he starts to talk about "the order of Being" and the like. These Heideggerian turns of phrase turn lots of folks off. And I must say that the references to "Being" at times seem rather off-hand in these writings. Perhaps Havel needs to flesh out a bit more the conceptual and moral work his frequent references to Being play in his overall moral and political thinking.

That having been said, it is refreshing to read the words—

most of them spoken aloud—of an erudite thinker and writer and political leader who unabashedly celebrates certain universal truths and rebukes "moral relativism" and "the denial of any kind of spirituality, a proud disdain for everything suprapersonal," and other features characteristic of the late modern West. For Havel, human beings need a "transcendental anchor, . . . the only genuine source of [their] responsibility and self-respect." Without these we forfeit much of the credibility of our own political affirmations and we blight our spirits. Havel manages to say all this in a way that avoids tub-thumping and breast-beating. But he is insistent. If we pit politics and morality against one another, we give politics over to the devil. We lose "the moral integrity of society" and relinquish "responsibility for human lives."

There are those who believe Havel's moment has come and gone. I don't think we've arrived at that moment yet.

FURTHER READING

Criticism

Bradbrook, M. C. "Václav Havel's Second Wind." *Modern Drama* 27, No. 1 (March 1984): 124-32.

> Provides an overview of Havel's dramatic works and literary influences.

Procházka, Martin. "Prisoner's Predicament: Public Privacy in Havel's *Letters to Olga*." *Representations* 43 (Summer 1993): 126-54.

> Examines Havel's philosophical meditations and elements of public discourse in *Letters to Olga*.

Trensky, Paul I. "Havel's *The Garden Party* Revisited." In *Czech Literature Since 1956: A Symposium,* edited by William E. Harkins and Paul I. Trensky, pp. 103-18. New York: Bohemica, 1980.

> Offers critical analysis of *The Garden Party.*

Interviews

Emingerová, Dana, and Lubos Beniak. "'Uncertain Strength': An Interview With Václav Havel." *New York Review of Books* (15 August 1991): 6, 8.

> Havel discusses his presidential experiences, literary interests, and Czechoslovakian politics.

Additional coverage of Havel's life and career is contained in the following sources published by Gale: *Contemporary Authors,* **Vol. 104;** *Contemporary Authors New Revision Series,* **Vol. 36, 63;** *DISCovering Authors Module: Dramatists; Drama Criticism,* **Vol. 6; and** *Major Twentieth Century Writers.*

Dennis Potter

1935-1994

(Full name Dennis Christopher George Potter) English playwright, novelist, essayist.

The following entry presents an overview of Potter's career through 1996. For further information on his life and works, see *CLC*, Volumes 58 and 86.

INTRODUCTION

Dennis Potter's main contribution as a writer is to television drama and film. He began his career, however, with non-fiction commentary on post-war English society, notably the politics of class and the personal costs for those crossing traditional class demarcations. Potter's sensitivity to English class tensions expressed itself in early work such as his prose piece *The Glittering Coffin* (1960), in which he explores the issue of upward mobility, drawing on autobiographical details, and in *The Nigel Barton Plays* (1965) which Potter adapted from television to the stage and whose multi-layered scenes and interlocking flashbacks foreshadow the techniques of his later work. In his early years he was also a journalist, most notably a television critic. After some time spent writing for the theater he developed a long-standing relationship with the BBC and produced works of exceptional quality for television, among them *Pennies from Heaven* (1978), *Blue Remembered Hills* (1979), and *The Singing Detective* (1986). His thematic concerns, whether in his non-fiction, his novels (most of them adapted for television) or his plays, include betrayal in love and of family (by sexual infidelity and by passing class lines), the persistence of the past in one's present, the blending of reality and imagination, and sexuality. In terms of style and subject matter, Potter brought the television drama to new heights, exploring a personal vision while exploiting the medium's features like no one before him.

Biographical Information

Potter was born in the Forest of Dean, an English mining district by the Welsh border in Gloucestershire in 1935. Although his father was a miner, after a grammar school education in the area Potter went to Oxford on a scholarship where he obtained a B.A. in 1959 with Honors in Philosophy, Politics and Economics. Oxford proved to be a turning point, as it gave him the opportunity to move beyond his class. However, it was also a source of guilt because Potter felt he had somehow betrayed his roots. Several of his works reflect the tensions between Potter's

background and education; among them are: *The Changing Forest* (1962), *The Glittering Coffin*, a denouncement of class snobbery and critique of post-war socialism and the Labour Party, and *Stand Up, Nigel Barton* (1965), his first play. Potter's sense of guilt about betraying his working-class past was to become a running theme in his work and led to his involvement in politics (he was a Labour candidate for parliament, East Herefordshire, in 1964), and has been seen as a factor in his being drawn to the popular medium of television, to which he was to devote most of his creative energy. In television he found a way to enter homes of all types and to work out his ideas about class, his ambivalence about popular culture and his own personal ghosts. At the age of 25 he became afflicted with psoriatic arthropy, a severely disabling hereditary disease that enforced his resolve to be a writer; it also served as a convenient metaphor for an internal, psychological affliction that pervades his work. He worked at BBC television and as a feature writer, television critic, and book reviewer at several English newspapers during the 1960s and 1970s. In this period he developed his notions about television and the cultural and political issues of his time. Potter is the recipient of numerous prizes and high critical acclaim, but controversy surrounds many of his works, which have been accused of being provocatively pugnacious (*The Glittering Coffin*), smutty (*Brimstone and Treacle*, 1978) or blasphemous (*The Son of Man*, 1969, in which Christ is depicted as a hippie). Potter died in 1994 of pancreatic cancer.

Major Works

Potter's masterpiece is *The Singing Detective*. Broadcast as a television mini-series in 1986, it is the story of a pulp mystery writer named Marlow who is hospitalized for a severe skin and arthritic condition similar to Potter's own. While at hospital he mentally works through the plot details of his fiction, the central character of which is Marlow the private detective, a figure borrowed from Raymond Chandler. At the same time, someone in another bed is reading one of the protagonist's novels. The divisions between fiction, imagination, memory and the "reality" of the play are blurred, as scenes from the author Marlow's imagination are represented alongside scenes in the hospital, and alongside scenes from Marlow's childhood. Potter used this multilayered, self-referential quality in his later work, notably in the posthumous *Cold Lazarus* (1995) about a writer named Feeld whose head is frozen in cryogenic suspension until revived 400 years in the future by Professor Emma Porlock, a scientist who insists that he revisit his childhood traumas for scientific investigation. In Potter's earlier posthumous play *Karaoke* (19) the frozen writer, Feeld, was writing a play about cryogenic suspension called *Cold Lazarus*. *Blackeyes* (1989), which appeared as a novel, a television serial and a film, uses similar devices. It is a story about a retired fashion model who appears as a vapid sexual object in a pulp novel written by her uncle. She attempts to change her fictional identity, but runs into the problem of mixed real and fictional lives. Clearly, Potter favored non-naturalistic devices, which he used in almost all his work, except for *Christabel* (1989), a drama set in Third Reich Germany which Potter wrote, in his words, to satisfy a need "to do a piece of naturalistic, chronological narrative as an act of writerly hygiene, just as you might wash your brain under the tap." Songs, which Potter called "chariots of ideas" pervade much of his work, notably *The Singing Detective* and *Pennies from Heaven*. The latter is a story involving a '40s-era sheet music salesman who ends up on death row for a murder he didn't commit and is saved by a non-naturalistic trick of the writer's pen which transports him beside his loved one on Hammersmith Bridge in the closing scene. (Potter later reworked the script for a film version by MGM with actor Steve Martin, set in Chicago.) As one critic noted, the "overall proposition is that, however false, rose-hued and saccharine the songs may be, the dreams they peddle are necessary to human survival as the premise of religion used to be." Other works of note are *Brimstone and Treacle*, which was banned by the BBC

on the premise that its objectionable features (the play involves the rehabilitation of a crippled, vegetative young woman by having her raped by a demonic young man) were not redeemed by its artistic merit, and *Blue Remembered Hills*, a play that explores memory and the loss of childhood innocence. In the first, the psychological themes of moral ambiguity and cathartic violence are explored, as are the ideas of intrusion and privacy. The second has the unusual feature of adult actors playing children.

Critical Reception

Potter's work has consistently met with controversy. Much of the controversy surrounds his anger and irritation at the liberal left in the political climate of his youth, notably his disenchantment with and chastisement of the Labour party in *The Glittering Coffin*, which reviewers responded to with an appreciation of his intelligent critical spirit, but with some irritation at his iconoclastic scattershooting. His subsequent work has delighted most critics for its daring with dramatic conventions and dramatic innovations, especially of the popular television drama which critics believe Potter has brought to an unprecedented level of achievement. His choice of themes, particularly his depiction of repressed sexuality; Oedipal guilt; the latent misogyny of his male characters; the occasional voyeuristic features; and his depiction of woman as adulteress, earned him at one time the tabloid label of "Dirty Drama King" and "Television's Mr. Filth." Other critics have detected a fear of strong women, since the male characters can only be aroused by the stereotypical mindless siren, or the good, nurturing woman. But some reviewers maintain Potter is depicting a prevalent attitude, especially among members of his own generation. His self-referential, multi-layered style has had many championing critics, notably Rosalind Coward, who sees in his work, particularly *The Singing Detective*, a shining example of cutting edge notions of textual creation and exploration of the authorial presence in fiction. Some commentators have complained that after *The Singing Detective* Potter resorted to recycling his ideas and looking down at his audience, and that his work became marked by mannerism. Potter has been compared to stage writers such as Tom Stoppard and Harold Pinter, and many acknowledge that he has had a profound influence on television writing. Several critics assert that he has been responsible for the awakening of a realization of the possibilities of the television medium. As critic Jenny Diski pointed out, Potter is "one of television's very few intellectually respectable gifts."

PRINCIPAL WORKS

The Glittering Coffin (non-fiction) 1960

CRITICISM

Anthony Crosland (review date 12 February 1960)

SOURCE: "Smashing Things," in *The Spectator,* February 12, 1960, p. 223.

[*In the following review of* The Glittering Coffin, *Crosland examines Potter's critique of the Labour Party and the politics of social class in 1950s England.*]

Mr. Potter is a twenty-three-year-old exchairman of the Oxford University Labour Club, who was also a prominent figure in the old *Universities and Left Review.* His book [*The Glittering Coffin*] is part autobiography, part polemic—against present-day British society, and against the Labour Party for allegedly not wishing to change it. It is disarmingly candid, and indeed courageous, since he wishes to go into Labour politics and fears that his outspokenness may be held against him. It is also muddled, inconsistent, and almost wholly negative; Mr. Gaitskell, if he read it, would certainly not obtain a clear idea of what, in detail, he was supposed to do. Nevertheless, it expresses an attitude of mind which deserves to be seriously considered.

Its most conspicuous, and probably significant, feature is the extreme contrast between the intellectual argument on the one hand, and the tone, the language and the emotional atmosphere on the other. The former (in so far as it can be separately distilled) is moderate and intelligent, the latter crude and intemperate.

On the plane of argument, Mr. Potter (whom I shall henceforth use to stand for many of the younger Left) concedes that the traditional Labour Left, still 'shrieking incoherently about good red-blooded Socialism,' no longer makes a relevant appeal; it has failed to recognize the fact of Keynes, the managerial revolution, and the more complex character of present-day capitalism. This capitalism, however, although more prosperous and stable, is still rotten with social evils; and a new, radical Left is needed to challenge these effectively.

The evils are as follows: the rigid and snobbish character of our class relations, our élite system of education, the maldistribution of wealth, the serious gaps in the Welfare State, Conservative policies on Suez and Africa, the H-bomb, racial intolerance, the smugness of our middle-class-dominated culture, the ugliness of our towns, the materialistic standards cultivated by commercial advertising, and the present national mood of smug, self-satisfied conformity. Scattered hints are dropped as to how some of these evils might be remedied. But virtually nothing is said about further nationalisation or detailed planning; indeed the traditionalist Left is treated throughout with considerable disdain.

Here the puzzle begins. This all sounds like an orthodox revisionist manifesto. I personally would accept 80 per cent. of the statement of aims; indeed, through the chance of being older, I have been writing and speaking on many of them for much longer than Mr. Potter. And the ideological debate between revisionists and traditionalists has been precisely about the relevance of the 'red-blooded Socialism' which Mr. Potter dismisses so disdainfully. Why, then, does he harbour so venomous a hatred for Mr. Gaitskell, the 'new thinkers,' and indeed the whole Labour Party (dismissed contemptuously as a 'part of the Establishment,' against which the young intellectual instinctively reacts)?

Why, again, the almost hysterical language, which seems grossly disproportionate to many of the evils under discussion? Labour leaders may be bad; but they hardly deserve to be described, as they are here, as hypocritical, stinking, pin-striped, slovenly, stupid, tatty, and (Mr. Gaitskell, this) a 'fun-fair barker with a false nose.' Conceivably I am prejudiced, being personally the object of abuse. But others, not themselves victims, have agreed with me that the tone of malice and contempt is, to put it mildly, rather striking.

A similar disproportion is apparent in Mr. Potter's description of present-day British society. He admits, briefly and grudgingly, that a welcome rise has occurred in the standard of living. Nevertheless he thinks the whole society rotten, ugly and evil, a 'synthetic Madison-Avenue-constructed way of life,' utterly dominated by the filthy, debased standards of commercial advertising, the women's magazines and the juke box. The picture is ludicrously one-sided; one gets no hint of the wider vistas and opportunities open to the average family as compared with thirty years ago. Of course there are immense vulgarities to be attacked. But this kind of indiscriminate abuse is not only inaccurate; it is positively inhumane. It could be made only by one wholly outside, and hostile to the society in which he lives.

How is this resentful alienation to be explained? By personal temperament? Clearly not, since it is by no means unique to Mr. Potter. True, the typical young worker would not know what on earth he was talking about; and even in University Labour Clubs his attitude is probably a minority one. Nevertheless, enough young intellectuals feel this way to make it a group and not an individual phenomenon. Is it, then, simply the fact of youth, of which Mr. Potter himself makes so much? Again I think not. The young intellectual Left in the 1930s, although possessing an élan and a set of fighting issues which the present young Left nostalgically envies, did not in fact adopt this tone. It was hot-blooded, violent, passionate. But the note of frustrated personal resentment was much less evident.

Is it, perhaps, that the present Labour leadership, through being exceptionally somnolent or reactionary, gives rise to exceptional feelings of discontent? I personally believe that the leadership is too acquiescent and complacent on some of the social and cultural issues which Mr. Potter discusses. Nevertheless, it shares his views on many other issues, from Africa to the distribution of wealth; and it is not notably Right-wing by past Labour Party standards. Nor is it obviously worse than the leadership of most Socialist parties abroad; and we have to explain the fact—commented on by every visiting Socialist—that this particular form of Left-wing bitterness has no close parallel in any similarly placed European country.

We must ask, then, what factors most obviously differentiate Britain today from other countries at a comparable state of political and economic development. One such factor, which Mr. Potter castigates with my total support and sympathy, is the enveloping blanket of smug, lethargic conservatism which descended on Britain during the 1950s. This can be seen almost everywhere one looks: in our lagging rate of economic growth, the sluggish pace of technical innovation, the complacency about our institutions, the absence of civic initiative, the lack of revolt against the public schools, the number of taboo subjects from the Monarchy to the Trade Unions, our laws on homosexuality and hanging, the level of public patronage to the Arts, our insular nationalism, our attitude to Europe, and so on indefinitely. It is not only that these things persist longer than in other countries; but they persist with the full support of most of the population. No wonder that young, radical intellectuals feel discouraged and frustrated.

The other unique British phenomenon, now at last being openly discussed, is our exceptionally rigid class structure, with its deep social and cultural divisions. Upon this rigid structure we have now imposed a (limited) degree of upward social mobility through the educational system. The result is a direct confrontation of social classes, notably at Oxford and Cambridge, on a scale not previously known: and out of this confrontation sometimes comes an understandable explosion of class resentment, sharper than in other countries precisely to the degree that the social contrasts were initially more marked.

As Mr. Potter correctly observes, 'talking about class in highly personal terms is a shocking and embarrassing thing for an Englishman to do; there is a kind of pornography about the subject, an atmosphere of whispered asides and lowered eyes.' His honest and courageous account of his own 'confrontation' at Oxford is therefore particularly welcome. He describes, feelingly, the dilemma of working-class students who are unsure of the class to which they belong, culturally divorced from the one in which they grew up, resentful of and still outside the one into which their ability has thrown them. Some are quickly assimilated; others remain alienated and (as it were) detribalised.

One can easily exaggerate the size of this group. Outside Oxford and Cambridge, and still more outside the Universities, the confrontation is not so dramatic or direct; and there is no clear sign that social mobility is leading to greater class tension. One can also exaggerate its likely permanence. No one can tell what process of cultural assimilation may or may not occur, or whether class rigidities will gradually give way under the pressure of rising consumption or technological change. But today, and in the group for which he speaks, Mr. Potter's insistence on the factor of class resentment cannot be denied; and it is this factor which accounts, in part at least, for the feeling of being outside the society and hostile to it.

That is why it is futile to be angry at his anger, or to return the insults which he hurls. I personally regret the anger and dislike the insults. Besides, they make him incoherent, and will infuriate many of his readers, thus neutralising the effect he seeks. But at least they have a cause. Mr. Potter remarks that he has written his book now, lest age and assimilation gradually mollify his feelings. Personally, I hope they do. The Labour Party badly needs a dose of iconoclasm at the present moment; and the young University Left has picked on many of the icons which most need smashing. But if they wish to be effective, Mr. Potter and his friends must abate some of their resentful, almost hysterical anger and curb their tendency to wild and inaccurate overstatement. Then they will direct fewer and better-chosen arrows which actually hit the target.

Richard Wollheim (review date 1960)

SOURCE: "How it Strikes a Compatriot," in *Partisan Review,* Vol. 27, 1960, pp. 353-62.

[*In the following review, Wollheim discusses the ideas on politics and class in* The Glittering Coffin, *providing a brief historical backdrop and examining the personal and social issues implied in the English class structure.*]

In *The Glittering Coffin* Mr. Dennis Potter, a young working-class undergraduate just down from Oxford, raises a voice of genuine social protest. Unfortunately he accompanies it with so much rant and rhetoric that he virtually drowns his own words. It seems to me dubious whether the few scraps of coherent sense that are likely to drift across to the reader will mean much to him, particularly if he is at all unfamiliar with their place of origin. May I say how it strikes a compatriot?

But to do so one must go back in time. In 1853, Gladstone, then Chancellor of the Exchequer, asked Sir Stafford Northcote and Sir Charles Trevelyan to prepare for his use a report on the general condition of the Civil Service. In November of that year the report appeared, a highly conscientious piece of work, complete with criticisms from eminent administrators and educationalists and with replies to these criticisms from the two authors. Amongst other things the report recommended that the old system of patronage—whereby, as Bright said, the Service was the outdoor relief department for the aristocracy—be abandoned, and instead recruitment be effected by open examination. This dry, practical document was one of the great formative factors in the creation of modern English culture: for it secured the establishment of the class out of which this culture sprang.

Nor was this result so alien or so tangential to the motives of the reformers as one might suppose. Undoubtedly part of their inspiration was the desire to have an efficient bureaucracy and to remove excrescences of which Dickens' Circumlocution Office was no great parody. But another aim, of which they showed themselves to be not totally unconscious, and between which and the original purpose of the operation they saw no real conflict, was in some way to "provide" for the younger generations of the new middle class: not of course in *any* way, but in a recent and suitable way. For there were around, in increasing numbers, young, intelligent, conscientious men who were not particularly interested either in money-making or in money-spending, who wanted to do something for others, provided that doing so would also do something for them. They wanted a worthy, respectable yet comparatively lucrative occupation. It was quite evident that a reformed Civil Service, if such a thing could be brought into being, would be the answer to their problem.

By 1870 the recommendations of the report had been implemented in full. Meanwhile the older universities, shaking themselves out of their eighteenth-century slumbers, had come to see that increasingly their role would be to prepare young men to take up their place in the reformed

bureaucracy: or if not exactly in the bureaucracy then in some other profession that by virtue of resemblance or of propinquity to the bureaucracy had acquired a parallel status and respectability. The result of these various operations was that something like a funnel or chute was set up in the very middle of English life: graduated in degrees marked "Public School, Oxford or Cambridge, Profession": and into this chute and up it were drawn, in their generations, the sons of the middle classes, instructed, as they progressed through it, in the classics, in the value of character, and in distrust of the emotions. English culture, as it exists today and as it has existed for nearly a hundred years, is to be understood in terms of, even if it is not wholly produced by, what comes out of the top of this chute. Both the good features and the bad features of the culture are very intimately connected with this fact: on the one hand, for instance, the closeness of the intelligentsia to practical concerns, and on the other hand, a large number of less desirable features, which it is not my duty here to rehearse.

In recent years something has happened. The bottom of the chute has been unmistakably splayed out so as to bring into its field not just the children of the middle classes but also the cleverer children of the working-classes. An important qualification is that the public schools remain the preserve of the middle classes, but, setting aside this anomaly and the extent to which it weighs educational opportunity in favor of one class, one may say that today access to the professions via Oxford or Cambridge is, both in theory and practice, open to all. It is merit that counts: not class or money.

But all this has been achieved without there being any corresponding change in the old nineteenth century pattern of life, society and culture. In England there is a far greater social mobility than there was: but what is on the move, moves along old established channels. Under the new dispensation the role of Oxford or Cambridge is to absorb the abler and more ambitious sons of the working class into the bourgeoisie—or, in the case of the less successful, to equip them for some comparatively classless role in one of the interstices of the hierarchy. I remember seeing this process at work in Oxford in my own day. And if one suspected that it was done at a price, at the cost of considerable pain and emotional confusion, one also thought that the pain and confusion were justified, that they were necessary evils in what couldn't be anything but a long and tedious process: the "liberalization" of English life. And around the whole process there grew up, need I say, the conspiracy of silence, which is the inevitable embarrassed response of English gentility to anything that relates to class conflict or class difference.

Two years ago Mr. Potter broke the silence. I don't mean that no one had ever broken it before, but he broke it very effectively. At a time when people were deceiving themselves into thinking that Britain was a totally fluid society, Potter wrote an article in the *New Statesman* describing in detail the anguish of a working-class boy in a good Oxford college. He described the awkwardness of his relations with undergraduates coming from very different backgrounds, and who, in their rooms, their girls, their clothes, their conversation, showed the difference, *wore* it one might say. But the anguish of the story is not here. It lies rather in the change that a scholarship effects in the relations between a working-class boy and his working-class parents. In some cases, the result may be that the boy is ashamed of his parents. Those in a sense are the easy cases, and certainly not the ones Potter is thinking of. His cases are where the boy feels gratitude to his parents for what they have done for him: and yet realizes that what they have in effect done for him is to push him into a world that is different and apart from theirs: and no sooner realizes this than wishes he didn't, for how can one remain for long conscious of "the two worlds" without making a qualitative judgment between them? And not only is the boy aware of the two worlds, but three times a year he has to perform the physical journey between them.

Potter describes these things excellently: with a little exaggeration perhaps, but with no more than is pardonable. For the courage it must have taken to set it all down is considerable. And now that we have the descriptions between the covers of a book, I hope that they will secure a wide audience. Much of what he says is bound to cause considerable surprise even to those who feel that they know English life well. The class system in England is not what it was. It is now more like an "open" prison than the old-fashioned penitentiary it used to be: indeed at any given moment a large number of its members are out on parole. But the appearance of freedom, of continuity in social life that this gives is in part illusory, and this book for all its rhetoric is calculated to call one to a better sense of reality.

It is, however, quite another matter when Potter passes from description to diagnosis and cure. For what he stated in the *New Statesman* article and what survives as the center-piece of **The Glittering Coffin** is essentially a *personal* problem, a problem about feelings and emotions, to which one could think of a variety of possible solutions. One might, for instance, think that toleration, or a measure of stoicism, or the working through to a more realistic conception of what is and what isn't important in life would be the best means of transcending the problem.

But Potter denies this. According to him the problem is a cultural one. By which is implied that it arises from the conflict of two cultures, and that a solution to it must consist in the elimination of this conflict. Personally I am skeptical about this diagnosis. I suppose that there is a sense in

which we can talk of a working-class culture and a middle-class culture in England, but it must be emphasized that this is a very loose sense indeed, and not one in which the confrontation of two such cultures is tantamount to a cultural conflict. For confrontation means conflict only when a culture contains as part of its constitution jealous things like values and exclusive attitudes. But is this true of either of the so-called class cultures of England? I cannot see anywhere, either in this book or outside it, any reason to be sure that such is the case.

Of course what there is a great deal of in England is snobbery. But snobbery is no part of either of the two class cultures. It is an attitude *about* class and its *differentia;* it is not itself one of the *differentia.* Snobbery is in effect the attachment of value to differences of habit and behavior that have in reality no significance. And therefore the fact that we think it is snobbish to make so much of class differences is some evidence that we are not here dealing with rival ways of life that cannot peacefully co-exist in a plural society.

But suppose that Potter is right in his diagnosis of the evils in our transitional society as arising out of the clash of cultures, there are at least two solutions other than the one that he gives, and these he passes over. The first solution would be the gradual diffusion of existing middle class culture so that it became the culture of the society. Potter gives no reasons for rejecting this solution—which after all has been inspiration of many educational reformers—but what his reasons would be can, I think, be inferred from his treatment of the second alternative solution, to which I shall immediately pass. This is the transcendence of the existing class-cultures into an all-embracing "classless" culture: a process which is certainly well on its way in this country, and which is generally referred to as "Americanization." Now, significantly, it is for this, for what he calls "the synthetic, Madison Avenue-concocted way of life" that Potter reserves his deepest contempt. He cannot deny that Americanization is likely to produce and diffuse a higher standard of living than anything known in the past, but this he dismisses not just as an advantage that is outweighed by other disadvantages but something that is not really an advantage at all. It ministers, he asserts, only to conditioned wants and imposed choices—though he nowhere subjects these concepts to the scrutiny they deserve. But for him the real trouble with classless culture is not its content, but just its classlessness: its lack of roots, its non-organic character. And from this we can reconstruct why Potter would reject the universal diffusion of middle-class culture: his argument would be that if this culture were universalized, it would inevitably lose its class character, and losing its class character it too would become synthetic and lifeless.

So we arrive by elimination at the true solution: the reconstitution of working-class culture. The idea is one that is much in the air, but it must be said that in *The Glittering Coffin* it is argued for even more perfunctorily than is usually the case. For what is there—we have the right to ask—what is there in working-class culture to be reconstituted?

It is tempting to assimilate the problem with which Potter deals to another to which it bears a strong resemblance: that of the children of immigrant groups in a new society. For we might think that it is highly desirable that these children should benefit from the kind of "race-less" education that a plural society has to offer, and yet at the same time retain some of the distinctive cultural features of their racial group. And the experiment of the New World has shown how difficult this is for the non-privileged, i.e., non-Anglo-Saxon, groups to achieve. It is the justifiable boast of the Jew and the Negro that he can come up from the bottom and yet retain his cultural peculiarities. Can the same be said for the Pole, for the Greek, for the Chinese?

But the analogy is deceptive: for of course in the case of those groups who cannot preserve their distinctive culture, we know at the same time that there is a distinctive culture that they might have been able to preserve. But do we have the same assurance about the working-class boy? What on this score do we find asserted if we comb our way through *The Glittering Coffin?* I cannot see that Potter in his celebration of working-class culture manages to claim as its manifestations more than the following: football matches; chapel twice a Sunday; street carnivals; and the ability to turn one's back on the television. And if someone urges that it would be fairer to judge working-class culture by its distinctive attitudes rather than by its distinctive products, it seems to me that these relate almost exclusively to courage under adversity: and, it should be said, under adversity that an advanced industrial society need no longer tolerate.

What sort of basis do we have here for the culture of the future? That Potter cannot see the obvious answer to this question can be given a dual explanation. In the first place, he confuses dream and reality. On to the grim enough accounts of life in the mining villages of the Forest of Dean, he projects a kind of William Morris utopia, in which every job done is a job worth doing, where a man fulfills himself in his daily work, where everyone is bound to his fellow workers by ties of community and brotherhood, and in which the higher interests of man rest upon the more lowly interests, so that the genius at the top speaks in the vernacular and out of the experience of all. Some find such a utopia a dream of overwhelming appeal. I happen not to. But whatever our predilections on this subject, it cannot be denied that this would in no way count as a true picture of working-class Britain twenty, fifty, a hundred years ago. The second reason why Potter is so absurdly over-optimistic

about the future of working-class culture is that for all his talk of culture he really is not interested in or concerned by the subject on any level higher than that of a hobby. To the arts, to the free occupations of man, to the expressive function of culture, he shows himself indifferent, if not cold. At one or two points in his book he detects the first marks or intimations of a sunrise on the damp, murky, English horizon. Where does he see these marks? In Free Cinema, in the Royal Court Theatre, in the Theatre Workshop Stratford. Now I have no wish to decry these efforts. There is much here that is intelligent, much that is amusing, much that is disturbing, a great deal that is lively and provocative: but little that is substantial, and even less that is vigorously creative. I cannot believe that the main stream of the art of our future will stem from this thin trickle of social realism.

> **Potter criticizes the Labour leadership for its "cautious and feeble pragmatism," but he nowhere suggests a single step, not one, that he would take beyond it.**
> **—*Richard Wollheim***

The Glittering Coffin was conceived as an act of political dedication: an effort by a young man who would "very much like to make a career in politics" to remind himself as he grows older and stuffier of "what I once believed and hoped": a kind of *memento vivere*. But, it may be said, what has all this about class and culture to do with politics? And Potter's answer would be, roughly, Everything. For him and those who think like him the future of progressive politics in England, and of the Labour Party in particular, is to be found in the "oblique" approach to politics. And by this what is meant is that political programs should be created out of our awareness of what we wish society to be like, that practical policies should be composed under the influence of some vision of men living and working and creating together.

To this approach I am not unsympathetic. But surely it is unjustified to call our speculations about society and culture "political" until we have worked our way back from the more imaginative vision to some suggestion, however fragmentary, of how the vision can be realized. Furthermore, to attack the suggestions of others not because they disagree with what ours are or would be, but just because they *are* practical suggestions and not visionary speculations, is absurd. Potter criticizes the Labour leadership for its "cautious and feeble pragmatism," but he nowhere suggests a single step, not one, that he would take beyond it. His criticisms are directed not against the play, but against the production: and a bit, it must be said, against the accents of the actors. If Potter were not such a young man, one might well think that oblique politics was going to be another word for misguided thinking.

Benedict Nightingale (review date 6 December 1968)

SOURCE: "Backwoodsman," in *New Statesman,* Vol. 76, No. 1969, December 6, 1968, pp. 812-13.

[*In the following brief review of* Vote, Vote, Vote for Nigel Barton, *Nightingale points out Potter's lack of "critical astringency" while appreciating his daring.*]

Dennis Potter has adapted his Barton plays from television to the stage under the title of the second and better of them, **Vote, Vote, Vote for Nigel Barton**—or, rather, he has shuffled them together like two decks of cards. There are scenes within scenes, flashbacks from flashbacks from flashbacks, and great must be the bustle among the shifters and carriers in the wings of the Theatre Royal, Bristol, where the piece opened last week. Back we go from a rural by-election, to Oxford, to the pit village where Nigel was born and bred, to and fro, back and forth, and all through the eyes and under the guidance of a Labour agent, played by Martin Friend rather like the spoof Beaverbrook newshound in *Beyond the Fringe.* This seedy, cynical creature gives the play a superficial unity and brings out its unifying theme, which has to do with compromise. Pity poor Nigel, marooned in the no-man's-land of class warfare, alienated from the miners by virtue of his education and yet unable to commit, or even attach, himself elsewhere; reviled as teacher's pet by his classmates, wrongly dressed at the slick Oxford parties, restless on the hustings. As Labour candidate he can't bring himself to be nice to the proletarian racist, or cadge a vote from the mumbling old snow who, in a dialectically lurid but theatrically effective moment, asks him to sew back an amputated leg. In Potter's view, this is a grubby world in which it's impossible to reconcile moral chastity with political effectiveness. Frank Barrie's riven Nigel—plebeian voice, patrician looks, a sort of social struggle in microcosm—won't compromise and doesn't win.

> **In Potter's view, this is a grubby world in which it's impossible to reconcile moral chastity with political effectiveness.**
> —*Benedict Nightengale*

Much of the case is passionately and intelligently argued; yet I couldn't avoid feeling that somehow, somewhere, Potter is cheating. His deck is overstacked with court cards—not kings and queens, perhaps, but well-bred knaves in abundance. We begin with a comic hunting scene, replete with upper-class whinnies—'He's broken his neck: oh, I say, what a damned shame'—and we end with a snob banquet, at which Nigel commits harakiri, homing in with a V-sign on an outrageously blimpish Tory candidate. No wonder Potter calls the place Barsetshire: it's scarcely less fanciful than a Loamshire or a Whimshire. I can't think that even the country gentry presents quite so glaring a target these days. Surely the social enemy, rural and urban, is more devious than this. How easy it would be if one had only to do battle with stuffed shirts, empty leftovers from Trollope.

This isn't to accuse Potter or his Nigel of unjustified prejudice. No feeling person could contemplate our history of human waste and unmerited privilege and *not* have what it pleases some to call a 'chip'. Indeed, this is the very point Nigel himself makes, apropos his deprived and deserving father. But isn't it rather self-indulgent to respond to admitted injustice by prosecuting the most noisy, stupid and irrelevant reactionaries you can ferret out of the backwoods? That might relieve the feelings, but it has no place in a useful political debate—and **Vote, Vote, Vote** aspires, I think, to be taken seriously as such. By all means let Potter go on to conclude, with Bevan, that Tories are vermin, but let him choose the right Tories, those with influence and power. Let him visit the commuter dormitories, the suburbs, the Billericays and the Wolverhamptons, the City, Whitehall, the swinging metropolitan funhouse, all or any of these; let him leave this obsessive Barsetshire of his and perhaps tackle the Wilson party with more critical astringency than he displays here. The result could be—could have been—a genuinely challenging play in a genre that the Americans have had entirely to themselves recently.

Paul Allen (Review date December 1977)

SOURCE: "Stirrings in Sheffield," in *Plays and Players,* Vol. 25, No. 3, Issue # 290, December, 1977, pp. 36-7.

[*In the follwoing excerpt, Allen reviews a stage production of* Brimstone and Treacle, *examining the play's premise, its characters and the production itself.*]

Brimstone and treacle is apparently what the Victorians, stern administrators of all kinds of purgative, dosed themselves with in cases of constipation: the brimstone to do the job, the treacle to make the medicine go down. What if, so far as the swallower is concerned, they become as one? The medicine in Dennis Potter's **Brimstone and Treacle** (much publicised on account of its having been commissioned then rejected by BBC TV) comes in the form of a young man smelling faintly of sulphur, rather given to 'tempting' talk, quite capable of delivering the goodies of the kingdoms of the earth, and with the unctuous air of a curate who has caught his bishop fiddling the tax returns. Treacly.

Is he the devil? The stage direction says: Martin is, or imagines himself to be, a demon. It is more helpful than it seems: Potter's concern is with good and evil—larger concepts than a generation which limits itself to talk of lifestyle, situational ethics and social progress is comfortable with—and in particular with the ambiguities in the relationship between good and evil.

Thus Martin, having got himself into a house where Mr and Mrs Bates are slowly being driven mad by the strain of looking after a daughter turned into a vegetable by a car accident, takes the pressure off them at once; but when he has got them out of the house he rapes the paralysed and gibbering victim: surely an act of extreme evil? Yes, but. When he does it again her brain is restored: it was shock, not physical injury, which kept her prisoner. So, a happy ending? Again, yes but. As she comes round she sees her father and remembers his part in her accident—she dashed out into the street after seeing him with her girlfriend, a girl we have just heard him describe as a slut. The moral complexity goes further. The father is, apparently, a puritan of sorts, suspicious of Martin at once (and in a sense rightly so). He flirts with the National Front, but it is Martin's relish for the destructive and hate-filled logic of NF policies that pulls him back from it. Mumsie is an apparently silly suburban housewife at the end of her tether. But she has faith and trust and a kind of simple goodness that are in fact repaid. Who is the stronger?

David Leland's production of this deep and complicated (though sometimes sloppily written) play gives the Crucible Studio's New Play Festival an impressive start. Where Potter's effects are betrayed they are by his own obsession with forging a sense of complicity between Martin and the audience, and by the furore which was attached to the play's history: we needed to be shocked, badly, by the central rape scene and we knew too much about it. But there are four very good performances from Sean Scanlan (Martin), Christopher Hancock and Ann Windsor (the parents) and Adrienne Byrne as the girl. Adrienne Byrne is required to spend the play writhing and moaning, but both moves and sounds are very specifically scripted and for good reasons and the performance is a very strange kind of tour de force.

Philip Purser (essay date 1981)

SOURCE: "Dennis Potter," in *British Television Drama,* ed. George W. Brandt, Cambridge University Press, 1981, pp. 168-93.

[*In the essay below, Purser examines Potter's work in chronological order, exploring connections to biography, Potter's developing aesthetic and thematic interests and ideas about the medium of television.*]

Dennis Potter's titles are meticulously chosen even when they're filched from popular songs, but none gives such a clue to the ruling passion of his work as the one he picked for a now forgotten—indeed, lost—little play of 1966, *Emergency Ward 9.* It was, obviously, set in hospital, which was a recent experience of Potter's, and one unfortunately to be repeated many times, but the theme is not noticeably derived from personal suffering, nor in fact much concerned with suffering at all. It's a slight comedy of attitudes between patients in the ward, one unruly and working class, one prim and middle class, one black. The point is that Potter seemed deliberately to be adapting the formula of the popular hospital soap operas of the day, and was quite certainly echoing—down to the way it was universally misread—the name of the most popular of all. *Emergency—Ward 10* was the first twice-weekly serial on British television, running from 1957 to 1967. Though it was supposed to roam over all the departments of a big general hospital, with Ward 10 a purely representative location for the drama and urgency invoiced in the title, its devotees steadfastly ignored the dash whenever they talked about their favourite programme, thereby transforming it into the annals of a mythical 'emergency ward' where all the hopes, disasters, sunshine and tears of hospital life could be handily concentrated. In this respect they displayed a better understanding of the nature of soap opera than the programme-makers, and Potter followed suit. The play affirmed his allegiance to television as the true national theatre and common culture of the people. That was the audience *he* wanted to reach, though it was to be many years before he achieved anything like mass popularity in terms of ratings. He is, or at least was until 1979, extraordinarily indifferent to the stage adaptations he occasionally made from his television originals, or to the two or three screen plays he has written to commission; while frequently and publicly despairing of the use made of television both at the sending and the receiving ends, he remains its ardent champion.

Dennis Christopher George Potter was born in 1935 in the village of Berry Hill in the Forest of Dean, the son of a coalminer. Every writer is the product of his upbringing, but here time and place and community conspired together with unusual attention to detail. A working-class background (or working-class passport, as Alan Brien has termed it) was almost a literary requisite in the early sixties, in the wake of Alan Sillitoe and Shelagh Delaney and *Billy Liar,* and the best qualification of all was a dad out of the pits. So many gnarled specimens were depicted in films and plays, failing to understand their soft, déclassé sons, that by the end of the decade the funny television show *Monty Python's Flying Circus* could mount an inversion of the formula in which the father, now a scarred old author, berated the son for opting for the security of a well-paid job at the coalface. 'Civic luncheons, lad? Ah've eaten more civic luncheons than tha've had hot dinners.' It is a small but impressive indication of the vigour of Potter's dialogue and characterisation that *Lay Down Your Arms* (1970) went out only a few weeks later containing the straight-forward version (coalminer father, scholarship boy) and still managed to give the scene freshness and love. Potter's relationship with his father, whom he had also 'put' into *Stand Up, Nigel Barton,* as finely played by Jack Woolgar, was exceptionally close, and the strains of finding himself drawn into a world far removed from his home and family were very real.

The Forest of Dean is, or was in Dennis Potter's formative years, a peculiarly remote, inward-turned corner of England. 'Enclosed, tight, backward' were his own adjectives I quoted in a magazine profile. Until he left home he had never seen a flush toilet or a washbasin with running water. The slops were thrown on to the vegetable patch as fertiliser. There were neighbours who had never been out of the Forest in their lives. And although the working population was an industrial one, the scenery was as rural as that of Hardy's Wessex. Directly or indirectly it is the setting for a great deal of his invention. When Potter was fourteen the family moved to London, staying with relatives in Hammersmith. After two and a half years Potter's father tired of odd jobs in the building trade and went back to the Forest and the mines; but Dennis, doing well at St Clement Dane's Grammar School, stayed on. Hammersmith, especially Hammersmith Bridge, is another favourite location.

He won a place at New College, Oxford and after two years' national service which we will consider when they surface in dramatic form went up to read Philosophy, Politics and Economics. Brought up in a solidly Labour, chapel-going community he threw himself into left-wing politics but also acted, debated and edited *Isis.* In his third year he wrote his first book, *The Glittering Coffin,* a swipe at Oxford, the class system and metropolitan culture in the mood of the 'angry young men' of the day. Like many an undergraduate shocker, it was written with one eye on Fleet Street and the hope of attracting an offer, as a notorious young writer, from one of the papers. This came to pass for Potter but not immediately, for *The Glittering Coffin* was not published until 1962 and in the meantime he had been accepted as a BBC general trainee, the one lucky spermatozoon from the hundreds of arts graduates who used to apply every year at this time. Potter worked on *Panorama* and according to popular legend wrote his first-ever lines of dialogue when for an early book programme he furnished

the little dramatised excerpts from novels which were then thought to be the only way of making literature visual.

His most important assignment, though, was to work with the film-maker Denis Mitchell, under whose supervision Potter wrote and directed a documentary called *Between Two Rivers* (1960) about his beloved Forest of Dean and the threat to its particularity posed by television and the Light Programme and advertising and all the other manifestations of a popular, generalised culture. The angry tone of the commentary caused most comment, anger still being a quality eagerly sought in young men. I quote from my review in the old *News Chronicle,* not with any great satisfaction but because it is to hand and because I spotted the fact that Potter was to some extent putting it on.

> He hates the idea of this once-proud, distinctive mining area becoming submerged in a colourless, supermarket England. He hates status-seeking, hidden persuasion, the acquisitive urge, publicists, pop music and pop TV. He likes brass bands, pubs, working men's clubs, Methodist chapels, independence and that most comforting of concepts, 'community'.

> Most young men of sensibility could produce a similar reaction, and in his vehemence Mr. Potter came close to over-stating his case. People and places that on his own admission had oppressed and confined him only three or four years earlier were now bathed in golden approval. Though it was a shame the old pub was to be modernised, I must say it was pretty bleak as it stood.

Potter's relationship to at least two of the bogeys on that list (television and popular music) must have been ambivalent even then. Certainly he went over the same ground in a much less strident and more tolerant—indeed, often gentle—voice in a monograph called *The Changing Forest* (1962) for a Secker & Warburg series to the brief of 'Britain Alive'. Meanwhile *Between Two Rivers* had failed to please his superiors at the BBC. Denis Mitchell took no more pupils. Dennis Potter, disillusioned with broadcasting and impatient of the political neutrality expected of broadcasting, went off to the *Daily Herald* as a leader-writer. The episode was an early demonstration of the Potter knack of generating controversy, but it may have left scars of a different—and graver—sort. He already felt guilty about the elitist education (as he called it) which separated him from his working-class compeers. The reactions of family and friends and neighbours to his film made him secretly afraid that he had patronised them, made use of them and, worst of all, pronounced upon them. In later years he would sometimes date his illness from this moment.

In November 1962 the BBC launched its satirical Saturday night *That Was The Week That Was,* which became first a national sensation, then a national institution. Potter and a *Herald* colleague, David Nathan, formed one of the writing partnerships that flocked to exercise their wits on the lovely new audience that was suddenly available, a bourgeoisie waiting to be affronted. By definition most of the material was pretty ephemeral, but a reminder of four or five Nathan-Potter contributions is preserved in print in a *TWTWTW* compilation. Two of them are openly political: the Conservative Party had just issued a pamphlet tearing some Labour proposals out of context, so Nathan and Potter applied the same technique and same rhetoric to the Tory record; neater and more enduring, really, because it draws on a recurring human foible, is a sequence of remarks made about Clement Attlee by his political adversaries over the years, gradually warming from hostility to benign approval as Attlee passes out of power and into history. The item likeliest to be remembered, however, was called 'Mother's Day'.

What is a Mum?

A Mum lives with a Dad and 2.4 children in a rented house where the neighbours notice her washing on the line. A Mum relies upon secret ingredients and instant cake-mixes. She has kids with dirty teeth who regularly shout 'Don't forget the Fruit Gums, Mum.' A Mum is full of faith. She thinks every wash-day is a miracle. And since she adds the extra egg to everything except the bacon, she is probably constipated as well.

And so on. If wit was shit, as they say in Suffolk, tha'd be constipated, too, Dennis and David. But it was a neat enough concatenation of all the most grating assumptions aired in the TV commercials of the day, and with Mum impersonated by Rose Hill it seemed at the time to be a funny and scathing *aperçu,* as well as an early example of the obsession with the ruses of advertising which was to colour several of Dennis Potter's plays.

While covering a political progress by Hugh Gaitskell for the *Daily Herald,* Potter suddenly felt his knee lock as he was trailing along the street in the wake of the party. It was the first serious intimation of the mysterious illness, eventually diagnosed as psoriatic arthropathy, which was to beset him on and off—but increasingly on—for the next fifteen years. He would suffer intense skin irritation coupled with painful stiffening of the joints; his hands in particular were affected, in the end permanently. Treatment by various drugs brought some relief but distressing side-effects. Only the intervention of doctors who read of his plight and suggested, in 1977, a trial with a new drug,

Razoxin, finally brought about a substantial and sustained improvement in his health.

One immediate consequence of his illness was that Potter had to be taken off his existing duties at the *Daily Herald.* The paper gave him the job which he wryly defined as the refuge of the sick and the crippled, that of television critic. Actually, morning-paper reviewing was quite a nervy task when a good deal of television was still live and there were few previews for the press. Some hundreds of words of judgement might have to be telephoned in by a deadline only five minutes after the show finished. Potter evidently enjoyed both the subject and the spontaneity demanded of him. Television could be 'dreary, repetitive, sordid, commercial and second-rate', he had written in *The Changing Forest,* and it was regrettable that this was so often what the folks chose to watch; but television was also the only unstuffy medium capable of reaching everyone and independent of the snobberies and superiorities of an educationally privileged minority. To yell for the best in television and deride the worst was an honourable calling; and what truer, less stuffy way of doing it than by spilling out the hot reaction, without the opportunity to sit down and compose mandarin second thoughts? Though after two years Potter took advantage of a period of remission in his illness to pursue an old ambition to enter politics, and never returned to a staff job on a newspaper, the instant satisfactions of journalism would always attract him. He wrote a personal column for his old paper—by now the *Sun*—in the mid-sixties; he contributed book reviews to *The Times,* and throughout most of the seventies acted as television critic first for the *New Statesman,* then *The Sunday Times.* Whether he applied to these last tasks the whoopee-doo of extemporisation I don't know, but he told me once that his measured book pieces for *The Times* were sketched out only in note form and then ad-libbed over the telephone to a patient Printing House Square copytaker. By this time, it has to be added, his hands were irretrievably injured by the illness; typing was out of the question, and dictation to a typist, judging by the fury it induced in the temporarily crippled writer-hero of *Only Make Believe* (1973), did not suit him. He had to master a new longhand with pen wedged in his fist, and while it is unlikely that this necessity will have much affected his dramatic works, his only published novel *Hide and Seek* is written in such an obsessive prose that you can almost see, through the print, the lined paper and crabbed racing hand.

Potter stood as a Labour candidate in the 1964 General Election that brought Labour back into power after thirteen years, but against Derek Walker-Smith in the safe Tory seat of Hertfordshire East a young and emotional tyro stood little chance. Potter found the campaign exhausting and the baby-kissing and glad-handing sickening. Politics were not for him. He now knew for certain that what he wanted was to be a writer. Like most young journalists, he had started a novel in his spare time. A friend, Roger Smith, had become a story editor in BBC television drama. Why didn't Dennis turn his plot into a television play instead? If accepted, it would bring a much quicker return than slogging on to complete the statutory seventy thousand words and then waiting the best part of a year for publication. And, of course, it was in accord with all his cultural ideals. Potter accepted the suggestion and with it a challenge that might have been framed for him.

In his first fifteen years as a television dramatist Potter completed twenty-five single plays, of which all but *Cinderella* were produced ....
—Philip Purser

The Confidence Course went out as a *Wednesday Play* in February 1965. The plot concerns a trio of smooth operators endeavouring to enroll a group of potential pupils into a personality class supposed to make the recipient happier, more successful and, obviously, more confident. They are defeated by a kind of Holy Fool among the aspirants who keeps breaking in with dissertations on such Potterish preoccupations as the advertisements in the London Underground and finally, by casting doubts on the list of attributes the Confidence Course claims to bring out, converts everyone back to the comfort of being unconfident. It seemed to me at the time to be a consummation rather too easily obtained, but, alas, nothing of the production survives. In the expressive and understandably aggrieved jargon of the National Film Archive, the recording has long since been 'junked'. Nor is it the only one. The tapes of *Message for Posterity* (1967) and *Angels Are So Few* have also been wiped. *Emergency Ward 9* belonged to a fad for half-hour studio plays on both BBC-2 and ITV (Rediffusion) around 1966-7 prompted partly by stinginess, partly by a kind of Pre-Raphaelite urge to get back to the roots of television drama as a live, compact, enclosed performance, and by definition has vanished into the great blue yonder. *Cinderella* was rejected at the script stage, though not without earning the author some of his customary publicity in the process. *Shaggy Dog* (1968) I saw but have quite forgotten. Scripts, of course, exist, and in one or two cases I have consulted them to check points of detail; but Potter has written somewhere of the 'soup' of television, the non-stop swirl of sport and news and second-hand movies and idiot panel games from which every programme has to sing out or go under. In braver moments he has intimated that he likes his own work to be experienced in this context rather than in the isolation of the Steenbeck Room, so I propose to pay him the compliment of relying chiefly on what the good critic Maurice

Richardson used to call the cauliflower-shaped tape-recorder.

In his first fifteen years as a television dramatist Potter completed twenty-five single plays, of which all but *Cinderella* were produced, though another was famously never transmitted; two original six-part serials; and two serials and one single episode adapted from literature. Though many of them reveal recurring obsessions, and some of them even share a circumstance in the plot, to try and classify the single plays alone would require one of those complicated patterns of eccentric and partially overlapping circles—however recognisable the tone of voice may be. The nearest thing to a common factor is that most of the time Potter is dealing in what he has himself defined as 'interior drama'.

> I'm much more concerned with interior drama than with external realities. Television is equipped to have an interior language. Certainly one of the strands in TV drama is that of the interiorising process, the concern with people's fantasies and feelings about the shape of their lives, and about themselves. It seems very important to me that television should be concerned with that, because the people watching it are watching it in a very peculiar way, with all their barriers down. You've got a huge audience on the one hand, and yet it's also a series of very informal, very tiny audiences, multiplied X times, and the interior drama, if you like to call it such, can work in those conditions almost better than anything.

This pronouncement comes from Paul Madden's useful interview with Dennis Potter in the duplicated programme to the season of British Television Drama held at the National Film Theatre in October 1976. Potter was represented by his two Nigel Barton plays from late 1965 and, pausing only to forgive him for 'interiorising', we might as well deal with them at this point. Both are autobiographical, though Potter was at pains in the same Madden interview to stress that he likes using only the external circumstances of his own life. The hero's hopes, fears, fantasies and revulsions are not necessarily his own. The autobiographical element is a framework for the play rather than the play itself. *Vote, Vote, Vote for Nigel Barton* was written first, as an angry lampoon on politics inspired by his Hertfordshire candidature but owing something to *TWTWTW* and his two years as a critic. Having been on the receiving end of so much television drama, he told Madden, he was anxious not to furnish merely more of the same when he changed roles. He wanted to use a brisker narrative style and, in particular, experiment with direct address to the audience. A political subject with everyone making speeches was obviously suitable. It is interesting to note how in *Pennies from Heaven* thirteen years later Potter—or his director then, Piers Haggard—used the same, if by now familiar, device of opening on the politician as if he is making a speech direct to camera and only pulling back after a moment to relocate him within the geography of the play.

Stand Up, Nigel Barton, which fortuitously went out first, is the better play in Potter's own opinion. Certainly his command of what is soon to become the identifiable Potter style is surer, though there is also an early warning, in an Oxford party scene populated by vapid upper-class undergraduates, of the rather silly and curiously anachronistic caricatures Potter sometimes draws instead of characters. The action flicks to and fro between present and remembered time to follow Nigel through the same convulsive process that heaved his creator from miner's cottage to dreaming spires, only instead of making a television film Nigel takes part in one. He watches it with his family at home. His father sweeps out in disgust. Nigel catches him up and they head for the pub together, but the last scene direction in the published script has father and son walking away from the camera 'separated by a mutual anxiety'.

The most original device in **Stand Up** is to have all the children in the remembered classroom scenes, including Nigel himself, played by adult actors 'imitating childish manners and movements in a horribly precise style'. It is possible that Potter had seen an item in the current-affairs programme *Tonight* in which a number of adult contributors to a collection of memoirs called *John Bull's Schooldays* were sat at little school desks to discuss the book. It was still a brilliant extension of the conceit to apply it to drama; Nigel is one minute able to address the viewers directly with the hindsight of the man and lapse the next into the boy taking the first steps along the road to the scholarship that is to distance him from his fellows. And a sharp, unexpected reminder of the nature of childhood comes from seeing actors slipping into the giggles, snivels, innocences, treacheries and capricious alliances of infancy. Fourteen years later Potter expanded the novelty into the whole device of his little masterpiece **Blue Remembered Hills.**

The remaining play written to the autobiographical convention is **Lay Down Your Arms** (1970), which drew on Potter's two years' national service between school and Oxford. In company with Michael Frayn and other misfits he was sent on one of the army's celebrated crash language courses which had been instituted to provide an ample supply of interpreters should the Cold War produce some warmer skirmishes, and ended up as a Russian-language clerk in the War Office. What the play makes of this employment is a good illustration of the liberties Potter feels free to take with his own—or anyone else's—history. He deferred the action a year or two in order to have it taking place during the Suez crisis, a time of righteous indigna-

tion for all left-wing writers, added a visit by the Moscow Dynamo football team for good measure and converted the bunch of officers with whom his hero had to work into a collection of upper-class numskulls as caricatured as anyone in **Nigel Barton.**

One tiny bit of business remains sharply in my mind after more than ten years: the ritual of the morning coffee or afternoon tea, with the clerk carrying a tray of mugs to each officer in turn for the drill of being offered first the sugar and then the use of the communal stirrer. Obviously it was an even more vivid memory to Potter, perhaps because it encapsulated a distinction between officers and other ranks which seemed especially fatuous and especially humiliating when everyone was in civilian clothes. Potter uses it in drawn-out detail, twice if not three times, as a piece of the apparatus of life he reproduces very carefully while whizzing off in all directions for the imaginative content of his plays. Here, he never quite settles whether to go for a serious diatribe (Suez), a farcical climax (his hero trapped by his fantasies into impersonating the Dynamo goalkeeper) or a happy ending (anxious quest for a girl friend succeeding at last). The production was nevertheless an entertaining instance of what might be called the virtues of transience in television drama, which is something I want to expand on later but brutally simplify just now to mean that at the particular season it went out, the play's evocation of another particular season seemed very apt. Though it wasn't the first time Potter had taken his title from a popular song and used the same song on the sound-track, it was, until **Pennies from Heaven** the only occasion on which the song was at all contemporaneous with the events of the play, and belted out by Anne Shelton in the authentic mid-fifties version it carried all sorts of resonances— not quite nostalgia, more than simple remembrance—besides furnishing an ironic chorus to the martial and amatory strands of the story. Potter and the director, Christopher Morahan, also demonstrated a casual mastery of the narrative devices which Potter now commanded: newsreel clips, overlapping voices, flashbacks, a little play within the play and that familiar scene between coalminer father and grammar-school son which even Monty Python hadn't been able to blight.

A natural companion piece to **Lay Down Your Arms,** if more sombre in tone, is **Traitor** (1971). Potter's renegade British agent self-exiled in Moscow has some antecedents in common with Kim Philby, including a responsibility for the betrayal and death of former allies, but biography is no more Potter's concern here than self-revelation is in his autobiographical pieces or Christology in **Son of Man.** It is an attempt to bring alive as 'Adrian Harris' one kind of person who might have behaved as Philby did and offer an explanation of why he did so. The proposition of the play is beautifully explicit, with a party of English correspondents climbing flight after flight of stairs to their quarry's bleak Moscow flat, speculating the while as to why he has invited them and what they will hear. And notice again this curious whiff of impermanence about the production (director, Alan Bridges), as if it were deliberately geared to transmission at this very conjunction of the planets on 14 October 1971. Instead of one of the heavyweight actors who might have been expected, Bridges cast as Harris John le Mesurier, an actor identified not merely with comedy but with the immensely popular *Dad's Army,* then in the third year of a run which lasted from 1969 to 1978. By being such a familiar of the screen, I noted at the time, he lent proceedings 'a curious and rather valuable quality of being about someone whose picture really was on the front pages day after day, a while ago now'.

Potter's explanation of Harris's behaviour is revealed by the characteristic injection of flashbacks and lightning interior images as he answered his visitors: childhood under the shadow of an eminent archaeologist father, the one direct borrowing from Philby's background; schooldays transposed from the village primary of Potter's experience to a posh prep school but with Authority stamping down even more harshly on childish individuality and infirmity, e.g. the young Adrian viciously persecuted for stuttering over a line from Blake; the upper-class mill grinding on through public school and Oxbridge to the Foreign Office, while in newsreel clips the poor languished in slums and the unemployed marched.

'Traitor?' muses the exile in his Moscow flat,'—to my class, yes. Not to my country, not to England.' For his England is the England of Constable landscapes and, ironically, the romantic socialist visions of the very poet for whom he had been made to suffer in the classroom. His hatred is of his upbringing, not his fellow countrymen, but by a further irony it is his upbringing which had prevented him from ever knowing his fellow countrymen. Only to an ex-public schoolboy in the party of journalists, significantly, can he really make himself understood. If less glib and more sophisticated an explanation than I have perhaps made it sound, in retrospect it is still not strong enough to support the disconcerting durability of a Philby's or an Adrian Harris's convictions. Not for the first time, the play itself seemed less persuasive than the glittering extemporisation on patriotism and treason which Potter delivered on *Late Night Line-Up* afterwards. Who was it that, in praising Shaw's prefaces, wondered why he bothered to append those silly little plays?

Potter's own patriotism is intense and localised. He did not go abroad for the first time until well past forty. Even to venture out of England for the 1977 Edinburgh TV Festival was an ordeal, he told the delegates. His England is the Forest of Dean, Hammersmith Bridge and a fervent old-fashioned socialism rooted in chapel and pit. His scorn for the superficial, flag-waving, who-won-the-war-then patriotism is correspondingly fierce. But so is a distrust of foreigners and foreign influence which can only be described as xenophobic. When these two impulses coincide, as they did in the thoroughly bad and best forgotten *The Bonegrinder* (1968), it is difficult not to suspect that it is Dennis Potter himself, like one of his Puritans who protest too vehemently at filth and unchastity, who is secretly and ashamedly the Little Englander.

Traitor slides us towards the plots which Potter has acquired from legend or observation rather than from his own depths, and which therefore tend to take place a little less inside the head. In this early-to-middle period, *Alice* (1965) is a sympathetic study of Lewis Carroll, *Where the Buffalo Roam* (1966) a lurid parable about a youth with a Wild West fixation, *Message for Posterity* (1967) the clash of an indubitably Churchillian elder statesman with the doughty old painter who has come to do his portrait. The most interesting, on several counts, is *A Beast with Two Backs* (1968), which Potter took from a Forest of Dean story he had perhaps heard as a boy, of how the locals once attacked and killed a dancing bear which came wandering into the area. Potter gives the episode an authentic folktale atmosphere while rooting it firmly in period (the 1890s) and place. It is the only play of his set solely and specifically in the Forest and the first to be shot (by the veteran director Lionel Harris) wholly on film. But I suppose the piece which still dominates this particular batch is *Son of Man* (1969). Potter wrote it at a bad time in his illness and a time of change in his political convictions. He was still a socialist, as he is today, but during the revolutionary fever of 1968 he happened to come into contact with some of the leading zealots and was suddenly disenchanted with the materialism of their aspirations. From childhood he had been susceptible to the intimidating face of religion—in an oft-quoted reminiscence, the Valley of the Shadow of Death was, for little Dennis, a sunken lane near his home down which he scuttled with his heart in his mouth. Now in his pain and his disillusionment, he saw the reverse side. He was overcome by—and wished to communicate—the enormity, as he put it, of Jesus's simple message of love.

It is difficult now to evaluate either that 1969 production or the script underlying it. The common reaction was respect rather than enthusiasm among those disposed to accept the play, resentment rather than indignation among those who disliked Potter's indifference to the divinity of Christ and concentration on the humanity of Jesus. The scene everyone remembers is Colin Blakeley, as a muscular, earthy, journeyman carpenter of a Messiah slapping the cross (in an early confrontation with the machinery of crucifixion) and lamenting the abuse of good timber which might have been turned into tables or chairs. Otherwise it seems to be one of the few Potter plays which somehow missed the tide when they were first done, and it will be seen clearly to be a HIT or a MISS only if it is one day reproduced, with different actors, a different attack and a different set of expectations.

Seven plays written between 1970 and 1976 are linked by filaments sometimes so fine that they seem only to be coincidences, the author nodding over his typewriter and inadvertently punching up the exact sentiment he gave another character in another world, sometimes so specific—in the production and casting if not in the text—that the connection is proclaimed. In **Only Make Believe** (1973), a play about the writing of a television play, and more particularly the use an author makes of his own experiences, the play in question is **Angels Are So Few** (1970), and clips from it are sewn into the action. As an extra nudge in the BBC production, the actor playing the author was Keith Barron, previously Nigel Barton in the Nigel Barton plays. The relationship between an author and his character is also the device of the novel **Hide and Seek,** which, published in 1976, is clearly an honorary member of this group. The relationship between an author and the actor—or in this case, actress—inspiring his play is one of the concerns of **Double Dare** (1976). The relationship between an actor and the parts he plays is the sour joke of **Follow the Yellow Brick Road** (1972).

Another regular obsession is voiced by Jack Black, the paranoid hero of that play and star of the dreadful TV commercials which punctuate its narrative. Despite the ignominy of being pushed into a pond by a Great Dane avid for Waggytail Din-Din or creeping downstairs in the dead of night to catch his wife at the Krispy Krunch biscuits, he professes to prefer the sunny world of the commercials, where families are happy and husbands and wives love each other, to the sordid home truths of the television drama of the day.

> JACK. Filth—that's what *oozes* out of these plays. Filth of all kinds to mock virtue and to encourage doubts. They turn gold into hay, these people. Angels into whores. Love into a s-s-sticky slime—and Jesus Christ into an imbecile bleeding and screaming on a cross. God! I hate them. I bloody hate them, and their rotten, festering, suppurating scabs of ideas!

Potter is, of course, settling a few old scores. The language is the language of the most ignorant and least temperate among those who sought to 'clean up' television at this time. 'Filth' was almost an obligatory word. In just such terms had Potter's own plays been described: the angels turned into whores may be a sly reference to **Angels Are So Few;** the line about Jesus Christ is certainly an allusion

to **Son of Man.** But Black is no yahoo. He is the hero of this play, the character with whom the audience is invited to identify. In common with other Potter characters, and for that matter with a substantial section of humanity, he is both attracted and repelled by sex; the panting excitement of the moment is instantly followed by a Swiftean disgust with the bodily plumbing involved; ideals of love and ethereal sensation wither before the readiness of others to feign, sell or otherwise betray their intimacies. In Jack Black's case the revulsion dates from the discovery, glimpsed in flashback, of his wife not at the Krispy Krunches but satisfying a rather different appetite, with a naked man. In **Double Dare,** by a complete reversal, the playwright's disgust is focussed on a commercial made by the actress he wants, in both senses, in which she was evidently willing to fake the most intimate caress available to a woman in order to sell a chocolate bar.

Illusion and reality, performance as against genuine behaviour, the transmutation of life into fiction, the consolations of fantasy, the eternal struggle between the id and the ego—the permutations are always ingenious, often funny and made absolutely plain by Potter's technique, now fully developed, of cutting instantaneously between present and past, between objective and subjective versions of events. But it has to be said that the interplay of author and character or actor and role cannot help seeming too easy, too private a metaphysical concern. It's one that any writer is going to have his nose rubbed in; it is not one that necessarily fascinates everyone else. Certainly the most exciting—if ultimately disappointing—of the seven plays, **Double Dare,** toys with an altogether more heady set of speculations. The actress playing the actress who is helping the dramatist overcome a nasty case of Writer's Block also plays a call-girl visiting a boorish, red-faced client in the same hotel. Cross-cutting between the room dominated by the typewriter and the room dominated by a bed makes a familiar Potter connection between sex and creativity. But what is this trick of the dramatist's of anticipating what the girl is going to say? Why does he keep quoting from Dante Gabriel Rossetti's *Sudden Light*?

> I have been here before,
> But when or how I cannot tell:
> I know the grass beyond the door,
> The sweet keen smell,
> The sighing sound, the lights around the shore.

It looks as if Potter is going to explore something he hasn't explored before, the possibility much loved by J. B. Priestley and of appeal to anyone who has experienced one of those sensations of *déjà vu,* that time unfolds in loops and there may be a Second Chance or at least some precognition of things to come. But he settles for a variant on the solipsist dénouement he has already used in

Schmoedipus (1974): actress and whore are the same person and the red-faced client is the writer's *alter ego;* it's all in the mind.

Schmoedipus is one of three or four plays in the group sharing the same little circumstance of a young man who turns up on the doorstep of a private house and claims acquaintance with someone within. In *Schmoedipus* it is the housewife, and he says he is her long-lost son, which she is delighted to accept; but in the end—if much more skillfully and compassionately than this bald summary can indicate—he is revealed to be a figment of her guilt and yearnings. In *Joe's Ark* (also 1974) the visitor is real and legitimate and means well, a friend from student days of the young girl in the house who is dying of cancer. In *Brimstone and Treacle,* recorded in 1976 but never transmitted, he is still real, if hardly human and certainly not legitimate. He is a genuine devil complete with cloven feet; his pretence of having known the now brain-damaged, inanimate daughter of the house is a whopping lie; and he means very badly indeed. His sexual possession of her body—twice—is truly shocking. But it achieves what all her parents' wan efforts have failed to bring about: it jolts her back into sapient life. Potter is deliberately inverting the proposition of *Angels Are So Few* (which had a real angel) and the pieties of *Joe's Ark* to see if the other side has anything to offer. 'Why don't people accept evil when they are offered it?' the little demon wonders, genuinely puzzled.

> **Denied transmission by Alasdair Milne, then BBC Director of Programmes, *Brimstone and Treacle* became the focus of much agitation about censorship.**
> —*Philip Purser*

Denied transmission by Alasdair Milne, then BBC Director of Programmes, *Brimstone and Treacle* became the focus of much agitation about censorship. The text was published first in the *New Review,* then as a paperback. The tape was shown on closed circuit at the 1977 Edinburgh Television Festival at which Potter was due to speak, and delegates were moved to send a telegram of protest to Milne. A stage version was produced shortly afterwards (October 1977) at the Studio Theatre, Sheffield; a further production was mounted at the Open Space, London, in February 1979. Alasdair Milne's grounds for his decision were that the rape scenes would provoke such outrage that Potter's 'point of serious importance' would be prevented from getting across, and certainly it is not easy to watch an inanimate girl being unbuttoned—or in the Sheffield stage version, even more explicitly, having her plastic pants lowered—preparatory to being violated. But rationally it is the

outcome of the assault which demands the bigger swallow of acceptance. Is Pattie's (the girl's) reclamation any less fortuitous a turn-up than one I still remember from a boy's magazine story and rejected as unlikely even at the age of ten, whereby the hero took his crippled friend for a ride on his motor-bike, they crashed, the friend's leg was injured, but at the hospital, gosh, they found that the new injury had corrected the old infirmity? After all, brain damage is usually held to be irreversible. I believe that Potter does make the miracle work, if only because a miracle is obviously admissible in any play that contains a paid-up supernatural being. Where, on reflection, he forfeits the more extravagant claims made for *Brimstone* after its banning is in what look suspiciously like stand-by elements in the plot. One is a set of National Front attitudes on the part of the girl's father, which he is made to re-examine by the visitor's acting, appropriately, as Devil's Advocate as he leads the conversation to the logical conclusion of concentration camp and gas chamber. The other is a tatty little injection of secret guilt into the father's concern for Pattie. The accident which turned her into a cabbage, it transpires, happened as she ran headlong from discovering Daddy in the arms of her best friend.

The poor bastard has enough sadness to bear, you might think, without this added burden. An interpretation, I suppose, is that the demon doesn't really exist—he is the phantom representation of Daddy's secret self just as the client is the playwright's secret evil self in *Double Dare* or the visitor in *Schmoedipus* is the heroine's phantom son—but to support this logically the paternal lusts should have been directed at Pattie herself, not at her friend. Potter has written of the fierce religious beliefs he absorbed in the revivalist chapels of his boyhood, the certainty that there was an eagle-eyed God noting every sin and programming due retribution. It looks here, as it looks in many of his works, as if he is still reluctant to accept that ill fortune can descend at random and needs at all costs to trace it back to one fatal lapse. In this respect he follows the author he presumably much admires and has twice adapted for television, Thomas Hardy. The trouble is that the visual shorthand he employs is always in danger of seeming too glib, too mechanical. These recurring scenes, flashes of memory, fleeting visions, are removed only in style from the ponderous flashbacks, invoiced by a rippling screen or echoing music, at which we smile in old Hollywood epics.

All television drama is collaborative, and Dennis Potter's connection with a comparatively small number of producers and directors has been vital to his developing confidence as a writer. No fewer than nine of his early plays were directed by Gareth Davies. Barry Davis, Alan Bridges and, more recently, Brian Gibson have each directed at least two plays. But the relationship with the producer, who in television acts as impresario, moving spirit and buffer between the author and everyone else, has evidently been even more important to Potter. Kenith Trodd, a friend from early political days, is a former story editor at the BBC (he worked on **Emergency Ward 9**). In 1968 with Tony Garnett, David Mercer and the late James MacTaggart he set up an independent production company, Kestrel Productions, for whom Potter wrote **Moonlight on the Highway** (1969). When Kestrel folded after a few years in the face of the programme companies' reluctance to share whatever credit was available with a subcontractor, Trodd became a straightforward freelance producer and the man who has nursed most of Potter's later works on to the air. Their maiden collaboration, **Moonlight on the Highway,** is not only an adroit and intriguing comedy but also Potter's first real raid on the mythology of popular music. His hero runs a society dedicated to the memory of Al Bowlly, the crooner killed in the London Blitz; Bowlly's songs swirl in and out of the action, his photographs are everywhere; and when the hero tries to charm a girl he's met, they are Bowlly's words he reaches for.

It was when, years later, he was brooding over an idea for a further play about Bowlly and found he was really more interested in the songs than in the singer, Potter has said in an interview, that he began to hatch the work which has brought him a wider audience than anything else. **Pennies from Heaven** (1978), described as a play in 'Six Parts with Music', is in fact a serial *to* music, in a particular and quite novel sense of the words. Some sixty original recordings from the Bowlly era, including some by Bowlly himself, are woven into the story. Since Potter's hero, Arthur, is a sheet-music salesman of the period, this may seem perfectly natural, but the use to which Potter applies the songs is far from naturalistic. Without any hesitation or change of expression, characters step out of the play and into a rendition—I choose the word with care—of the number, miming to the original voice or voices and frequently adding a snappy little dance routine for good measure. Sometimes it is in enhancement of the mood of the scene, as in a Hollywood musical of the era, more often in ironic contrast to it. When, at the outset, Arthur's amorous advances are rebuffed by his pretty but cold and socially ambitious wife, he slips into 'The Clouds Will Soon Roll By'. Driving to Gloucester next morning, 'Prairie Moon' sets the optimistic mood of the journey and is also the song which he is carrying in his attaché case to push in the music shops along the way. Tracking down the pretty schoolteacher from the Forest of Dean (of course) who has taken his fancy, he croons 'Love Is the Sweetest Thing'. Sometimes a song is used more than once or used in opposite contexts by different parties. In one really surrealist instance the mysterious 'Accordian Man' whom Arthur also meets on the road leads a workhouse ensemble of sleeping tramps through 'Serenade in the Night'. The overall proposition is that, however false, rose-hued and saccharine the songs may be,

the dreams they peddle are as necessary to human survival as the promises of religion used to be; indeed, they represent what heaven once represented to the devout, a truer and more enduring reality than the mundane ups and downs of the day. 'Songs', someone says, 'are the same as pictures. They drop into your head and 'elp you to understand things.'

This gives Potter his ending, widely but gratuitously thought to be Brechtian, whereby Arthur—sentenced to death for a murder he did not commit—is dematerialised from the execution shed to turn up 'like a bad penny' by his loved one's side on Hammersmith Bridge. 'The song is ended but the melody lingers on,' he says as the title song plays and the credits roll. It is, of course, an old-established dramatic get-out, used by John Gay in the original *Beggar's Opera* long before Brecht's version, by Jean Anouilh in *L'Alouette* and by Elliot Silverstein in the movie *Cat Ballou*. The author shifts into the Great Key and the players step away from the scaffold. Why not? My difficulties with the 1978 production, blurred at the time, sharper in retrospect, in fact had little to do with any of the conventions, though I must say the injection of the songs did lose its novelty over six weeks and an increasing proportion of them seemed to be there because it was time for another break or they were favourites of Potter's which he hadn't otherwise been able to place, and in either case were cued in a rather literal and certainly non-contrapuntal way—'Radio Times' for instance, by the happy accident of a railway traveller immersed in the *Radio Times*. But the real stumbling-block is that Potter's objective England of 1935 is not really any more substantial than the dream world of the songs. It is drawn not from life but from superficial associations with which the thirties are lumbered. It was a good decade for murder, so there are a couple of murders. Prostitution flourished. Tory M.P.s were corrupt hypocrites clinging to their military rank. Head waiters put jumped-up diners in their place. Buskers entertained the cinema queues. You get the feeling of time and place assembled from Great Western Railway posters, old Sunday papers and the novels of Patrick Hamilton.

The detective on Arthur's trail speaks in the accents of a floor-walker and coughs genteelly, *ahem*, behind his hand. His idea of justice is summed up in an exchange with Arthur's wife Joan, characteristic of Potter's humour but indicative, again, of this rather tuppence-coloured, derivative picture of a harsh bourgeois society. Arthur's best chance, the detective tells Joan, is to give himself up. 'What? And hang?'—'He'll have a fair trial first.' As for Arthur himself, he is—or was in Bob Hoskins's performance on television—an extraordinary mixture of a few period cockney features with the truculent whine and interrogative interjections ('Innit?', 'Aren't I?') of the Greater Londoners heard complaining on the radio any morning today.

The most prominent consequence of the original production was a revival of interest in the songs it pressed into service, with Dennis Potter's name written large in the advertisements for two **Pennies from Heaven** albums of 'Original recordings of 40 years ago by the most famous Bands and Vocalists of those Dizzy Dancing Years!' Though the show was subsequently bought for the cinema, with a screenplay by Potter transposing the action to Chicago, it seemed to me to belong absolutely to the whizzing traffic of television which Potter half enjoys and half regrets: something to hop on to and enjoy at the time, without too much brooding.

An apparent anomaly of the close Potter-Trodd partnership is that while Potter has, as recently as 1976, gone on record as preferring electronic drama to film, Kenith Trodd is a leading advocate of putting it all on to film and the compiler of the famous 'Trodd List' of the first three hundred British television dramas so to be made. His third production of a Potter script, the wry newspaper comedy **Paper Roses** (1971) for Granada, was filmed; so were **Double Dare**, at Ealing Studios, and the piece which followed it on the air a week or two later in 1976, **Where Adam Stood.** Potter took this from an episode in Edmund Gosse's *Father and Son* in which Gosse recalls the impact of Darwin's theory of evolution on his stern Victorian papa, a leading natural scientist but also—as a member of the Plymouth Brethren—a fundamentalist Christian committed to the literal truth of the Bible. His struggle to reconcile his beliefs with what he recognises to be irresistible scientific argument is played out against a small clash of wills with the boy Edmund as the two of them (the mother is dead) spend a holiday together in the West Country. It is on any estimation one of the half dozen best things Potter has done, and I would rate it as one of the two indisputable masterpieces: intellectually faultless, warm, tender and sly, with the boy unwittingly turning a prayer session intended to disabuse him of his desire for a model boat into a demonstration of the Darwinian principle of learning to adapt.

The director was Brian Gibson, who had moved across to drama from making scientific documentary films. In the summer of 1978, with Nat Crosby as cameraman, he shot the other outright masterpiece, **Blue Remembered Hills** (televised 1979), in which seven adult actors recreate the activities of seven seven-or-eight-year-olds on a summer's day in the middle of the Second World War; and for the first time it is quite impossible to consider the author's contribution apart from the director's. There is a scene, for instance, in which the craven Willie, having been subdued in a fight by the bully Pete, is getting his own back by means of a resourcefully improvised scare-story on the dangers of eating dirty apples ('They drop them on Germany, the R.A.F. do, so the Germans will eat them and die. . .'). As Pete, who has been eating a dirty apple, begins to half-believe him and lose his top-dog assurance, Gibson has Willie idly scuffing along a fallen tree-trunk so as to put himself first on a level with the other boy, then above him. Or when the two girls in the gang are pushing their battered old pram through the grass and it gets stuck, Gibson lets them struggle with it instead of going to a retake, and instinctively the plain, devoted one does all the work while the pretty one looks on.

The convention of the play works perfectly to throw into sharp relief the differentness of childhood—the lightning shifts of mood and loyalty, the fantasies, the schemes, the cruelty, the remorse. Childhood innocence, Potter is saying, is really unspoiled original sin. It is also the only convention he uses here: none of the other devices from the armoury—no cross-cutting, no time-jumps, no flashbacks, no inner visions, no pop tunes (instead, a jaunty little march by Marc Wilkinson). The unities are observed. You are reminded of a painter who has discarded the stylistic tricks which brought him fame in favour of simplicity of line.

Perhaps the permanence of film makes a television dramatist aim a little more consciously for immortality. On celluloid his handiwork is more accessible, more easily consulted, more readily distributed, more of a property. It is going to be seen again and again in years to come. Certainly Potter has bemoaned the destruction of his lost plays, and it is not unreasonable to find in **Where Adam Stood** and **Blue Remembered Hills** signs of someone who, after years of revelling in the hit-and-miss, hurrying traffic of television, is now ready to leave a few monuments. But to infer too much would be to misunderstand what makes Dennis run. His impulse is not to store up, it is to splash out. All that output, all that journalism on top—he is the last of the big spenders. After the débâcle of **The Bonegrinder,** Potter devoted his column in the *Sun* to his compulsion to be a writer. He knew he was destined either to be a laughable failure or a good writer—perhaps he dare not say 'a great writer'. He was interested in nothing between. All he knew was that he could only write by using himself, indeed using *up* himself. 'So when I die I want to be completely emptied and completely exhausted. Which means of course, that I am still rejoicing. Only a happy human being can write a sentence like that.'

Rosalind Coward (essay date Winter 1987)

SOURCE: "Dennis Potter and the Question of the Television Author," in *Critical Quarterly,* Vol. 29, No. 4, Winter, 1987, pp. 79-87.

[*In the following essay, Coward uses Potter's* The Singing Detective *to consider the role of the author in the medium of television and as a case study in recent theories of meaning and authorship in a text.*]

The question of the author poses particularly difficult problems for any attempt to understand the mass media by reference to critical models drawn from literary studies. While 'authorship' may not be the only or indeed the most crucial factor in the academic study of literature, it would be hard to deny its significance as a way of organising the disparate elements that constitute the study of literature. As Stephen Heath said in the *Nouveau Roman:* 'the institutionalisation of "literary criticism" (in faculties, journals, newspaper reviews, etc.) . . . depends on and sustains the author (enshrined in syllabi and examinations, interviews and television portraits). The task of criticism has been precisely the construction of the author. It must read the author in texts grouped under his name. Style in this perspective is the result of the extraction of marks of individuality, and creation of the author and the area of his value.'

Conceived thus, the study of the author seems a peculiarly limiting way of approaching the mass media, encompassing as it does the popular, commercial and above all *collective* productions of film, radio and television. Such forms of production, requiring division of labour, disparate skills and shared responsibilities have more immediately in common with industrial production than with the literary image of the individual author or artist. However, although these forms of production seem to suggest that almost any criteria other than the study of the individual author might be more appropriate, it would be misleading to suggest that the question of the author has been irrelevant to the study of mass media. It is an interesting reflection on the interdependency on the idea of art and the idea of the individual artist, that the higher the valuation of the medium *as an art,* the more likely you are to find the quest to establish an author for a work. Indeed with the recent 'season' of Dennis Potter plays and films on television we can witness the simultaneous 'literary' commitment to the idea of an individual author, and the desire to elevate the status of television through the existence of 'great' television writers.

The author in film studies

This quest for the idea of the individual author has particularly marked the critical study of film. Apart from one or two isolated attempts to treat film as an art, such as Gilbert Seldes's 1937 book *Movies for the Millions,* film (and particularly Hollywood film) was regarded as not worthy of serious study before the 1950s. Much of this attitude derived, as in the case of television today, from an unwillingness to treat an industrial, collective and popular medium as likely to be worthy of serious critical attention,

and again it is worth noting here the way in which criticism inscribes the creative individual as the crucial factor, differentiating art from mass entertainment. In the late 1950s and early 1960s the film journal, *Cahiers du Cinéma,* produced a manifesto arguing for what it called a *politique des auteurs,* which was regrettably mistranslated into English as 'auteur theory'. The motive behind the position of *Cahiers du Cinéma* was twofold. On the one hand there was a desire to challenge some of the snobbish hostility to American cinema, and on the other there was a move against studying film only for its sociological contents and themes without any regard to *how* a film might produce its effects.

The journal argued on behalf of the existence of distinctive *auteurs* in cinema who could be seen to stamp their work with marks of their own personality. The cinematic author was taken to be the director (or *cinéaste*) who, through the translation of the script and the overall arrangement of the disparate elements which make up film, could be seen to be determining the overall shape and meaning of the film. Clear examples could be found in the popular genre works of John Ford, Howard Hawks and Nicholas Ray. What this approach offered was a serious study of film technique, with attention to the codes of shooting, lighting, editing and how these were combined by individual directors to produce their distinctive styles. In paying attention to these factors, the writers for *Cahiers* drew attention to the particularities of cinematic language, and especially to the concept of *mise-en-scène. Mise en scène* was seen as the most usual method the director used to imprint his distinctive style on the film. *Mise en scène* was understood as the various elements that went into the staging of a shot, including the scene arrangement, the camera movement, details of dialogue and the style of its delivery and the transitions from shot to shot.

The limitations of the *auteurist* approach were considerable. Most serious was the fact that it introduced a whole new hierarchy in the critical study of film. Only those films, or groups of films, which could be demonstrated to bear the distinctive marks of an 'individual' author became worthy of serious study (even if the canon did now include some Hollywood directors). And as a concomitant it followed that the quest to establish the author also became a method of evaluation. Individual personality, or distinctive traits of personal style, became methods of establishing value.

The criticism which Roland Barthes levelled at the obsession with the idea of the individual author of the written text is just as relevant to cinema. Barthes challenged the obsession with the idea of the individual creative genius as the explanation for the meanings revealed in a text. For him, the idea of individual creativity blinded critics to the process of production and the characteristics of the material in which that production was accomplished, be it film or writing. In *auteurist* approaches to film, this elevation of the individual at the expense of understanding the processes by which meaning is arrived at took a particularly romantic turn. Given the collective and industrial nature of film production, it was regarded as all the more remarkable that individuality could be achieved against such odds. Just as in the study of literature, the pre-eminence given to the individual as the explanation for meaning acted as a closure on what could be said about a film in terms of the social forces in which it was produced.

The same tides which brought Barthes's criticisms to bear on the literary text and the enshrinement of the individual also turned against the *auteur*ist approach to cinema. But it is generally recognised that the *politique des auteurs* did something for film studies which is rarely accomplished in literary studies when it focuses on the individual author as a means of understanding that text. What *auteur*ism accomplished in film was in fact the beginnings of an elaboration of film language. In attending to *how* the individual *auteur* transformed the elements of the raw material into a meaning and a style which was distinctive, this approach to film did in fact bring critics into a close *textual* analysis of the visual image. Perhaps for the first time, the idea of the transparency of the photographic image was effectively challenged. (By this I refer to the prevailing 'common-sense' belief that the camera simply records what is there and is therefore the medium most likely to accurately record reality.) In studying the elements which are arranged in a shot to produce its particular meaning, in studying the codes of lighting, of how shot follows shot, of the positioning of figures and objects within a shot, and the general composition of the image, what began to emerge were the tools of material analysis of film which deals with codes, ideologies, orders of discourse (the social factors in determining meaning rather than the life or personality of an individual). To some extent *auteur*ist approaches to film laid the groundwork for the approaches which superceded it, approaches influenced by semiology which insisted on studying *how* meaning comes about in a filmic text, in the combination of all its signifying elements or codes—including as a minor, but rather privileged code, the '*auteur*ist' interpretation, relating one film to others 'by' a particular director.

Television authorship

The situation with television is peculiarly pointed. The history of broadcast television certainly shows an institutional sympathy to the idea of the author, perhaps even greater than that of film. Probably deriving its direct descent from radio, television carries with it a firm belief in the value of the written word, and with that come the inevitable ideologies about the significance of the individual author. The history of BBC radio is marked not only by an extreme reverence to the great authors of the literary establishment, but also by 'episodes' where significant literary figures were courted by the new mass medium. What is more, much of radio's history is marked by a denial of the essential characteristics of the medium of radio and an insistence that radio was simply a spoken 'version' of the written text, involving very little technical interference between the written word and its delivery to the audience. Even if it may not have appeared so to the average listener, the author, both in the form of literary figures and in the form of the individual scriptwriter, was enormously important in radio's self-perception.

Television at its inception acquired wholesale a series of values from radio in which the 'writer' is privileged above any of the 'technical' tasks such as direction and production. Yet in spite of this willingness to found its more 'serious' productions on the idea of authorship, this has proved a relatively intractable task. For the average consumers such as ourselves, television is virtually an anonymous medium. The bulk of its output—news, documentaries, soap-operas, serials, adverts, come to us without any obvious 'organising consciousness'. Indeed, very often quite other criteria apply in what we consider to be the most important factor in an individual programme. Even in programmes such as sitcoms where the *cognoscenti* might recognise authorship in the form of scriptwriters, the significance of character actors is often thought to at least equal, if not outweigh, the significance of the scriptwriter in determining the meaning of a production. Here television shares some of the same problems as film in terms of ascribing authorship. For film critics often felt that the 'star' of a film was perhaps finally the crucial factor in the film's meaning. For example, we are far more likely to think of a Garbo film than know the name of Clarence Brown, who in fact directed seven of Garbo's films.

In fact, many of the constraints on an easy recognition of television authorship are similar to those of film. Radio can inspire the illusion of very little technical intervention between the written words of the author and the audience's reception of these words. But film and television both present us with a complexity of production, and division of labour within that, which makes the image of the transparent communication between one author and his or her audience, hard to credit. But in spite of this, television itself and television critics do struggle hard to retain a regime of individuality. Indeed it is a fundamental value of television. At moments this regime of individuality is quite different from that of literature, as in the inscription of the idea of the television personality attaching to frivolous and serious alike, encompassing presenters like Wogan at one end, and a 'personality' reporter like John Pilger at the other. At other moments, however, the idea of the individual author derived directly from literary models reigns supreme. First, much of television's quality output is based on 'dramatisations' of authors—Dickens and Shakespeare are favourites but there are many others, like the Brontes, Jane Austen or more modern writers like Malcolm Bradbury. These productions reinforce the idea of the text (and create the idea of the programme) as the emanation of one individual mind. *The History Man* is far more likely to be remembered as a dramatisation of Malcolm Bradbury's novel than by any specifically televisual attribute it might have acquired in the process of dramatisation. These productions are much more common than a second relation which television has to the literary author, which is the commissioning of original works by 'quality' writers. There is surprisingly little traffic between, say, the Booker Prize shortlist writers and television. Fay Weldon's successful incursion on to TV with *The Heart of the Country* and Alan Bennett's TV plays are the exception rather than the rule.

It is rare for something originating from within television itself to be regarded as 'quality' entertainment in the same way. In fact that notion of quality seems curiously parasitic on the literary establishment. The only hope which television offers itself for claiming an intrinsic cultural quality is through the notion of the playwright. And this notion of the playwright owes nothing to specific skills within the medium of television, and everything to the institution of literature. The playwright is the lure held up to television. If the playwright is good enough, television too might become an art.

Critics are claiming that with the success of his last production, *The Singing Detective,* he has established himself as the first 'great' television writer.
—*Rosalind Coward*

Dennis Potter and **The Singing Detective**

The example of Dennis Potter is both timely and relevant. Critics are claiming that with the success of his last production, *The Singing Detective,* he has established himself as the first 'great' television writer. Television itself was fast to respond to the critical success which *The Singing Detective* accomplished in the press. Firstly, Dennis Potter became the subject of an Arena programme, which has previously expressed a clear commitment to a highly traditional notion of the Arts. Secondly, and more recently, there has been a Dennis Potter retrospective, showing work, of rather variable quality, dating from the 1960s. Both of these are indeed high accolades for a writer who has worked almost exclusively within the medium of television. In so far as television does reflect on itself, it has been (es-

pecially recently) the presentation of television as social history, and with little claim for 'cultural achievement'.

The elevation of Dennis Potter to television *auteur* is not without a hidden agenda. The retrospective of his plays has allowed inclusion of **Brimstone and Treacle,** a play banned under the previous BBC regime of Alisdair Milne (in 1972). By constructing Potter as the first great television playwright, the new regime at the BBC can mark its distance from the previous one, but without having to defend the play itself. It simply becomes an important example of the *oeuvre* of Dennis Potter. But long before the retrospective, the Arena programme made it quite clear that Potter had already been claimed by the ideologies surrounding the individual author in literary criticism. Potter was interviewed by Alan Yentob, Head of Arts Programmes for the BBC, whose questions emphasised the importance of Dennis Potter's life as the way of understanding his work. The questions sought to establish recurrent themes in Potter's output and, in particular, they revealed the desire to relate those themes to the individual's autobiography. Much of the programme was geared to understanding Dennis Potter's previous output, in the light of **The Singing Detective,** as if **The Singing Detective** was the laying bare of the themes and obsessions which previous works began to explore.

In criticising this approach to **The Singing Detective,** I am in no way trying to lessen its significance. Far from it. Watched by eight million people, (and source of offence to a sizeable minority) it was certainly an important cultural event, putting forward extremely complex, perhaps even radical, ideas about male sexuality, fantasy and history in a highly entertaining way. Indeed, it could be argued that the series was far more important and searching than anything which has appeared on these subjects in the literary text over the last decade. However, far from 'authorship' being necessary to guarantee this significance, the concept, if anything, seems to get in the way, and block recognition of some of the truly radical aspects of the series.

The Singing Detective

The reception of **The Singing Detective** shows up the inadequacies which the search for authorship imposes on a medium like television. The Arena programme attempted to construct the television *auteur,* with snippets of previous productions, with questions designed to tell the story of his own life, and then an attempt to find the points of contact between these two. The retrospective series has offered a number of disparate programmes, linked by the author, in which we are invited to find recurrent themes, and distinctive stylistic traits. Both these approaches limit what can be said about texts. They attempt to impose one meaning on Dennis Potter's work, either a meaning which can be explained by his life (themes) or by his character and distinctiveness (style). By this operation, his most important series, *The Singing Detective,* can be understood as the apotheosis of these themes. But just like the attempts to establish the author in early *auteur* writing about the cinema, even these questions open up onto another, more important approach to television. For in attempting even to talk about the author's style in relation to *The Singing Detective,* we are forced into questions about the nature of the medium of television itself. The questions which present themselves here are about how the meaning is produced in a text which is using visual, verbal and musical language, which moves complexly between fantasy and 'reality', and which self-consciously refers to the conventions and styles of television and film.

What is striking about *The Singing Detective,* is the mixing of televisual or film genres. Scenes of intense, almost documentary realism set in the hospital are quickly replaced by perfect parodies of *film noir,* or give way to musical numbers.
—*Rosalind Coward*

What is striking about **The Singing Detective,** is the mixing of televisual or film genres. Scenes of intense, almost documentary realism set in the hospital are quickly replaced by perfect parodies of *film noir,* or give way to musical numbers. A perfect example of this occurs in the first episode. During the consultant's ward round, the stark, alienating reality of the hospital is suddenly transformed into *a smoky* where the entire hospital staff perform the musical number 'Dem bones, dem bones, dem dry bones'. The sequence returns with surprising ease to the painful 'reality' of Marlow embarrassing the doctors by weeping bitterly about his condition. Although Marlow's head is the point which we gradually learn unifies the disparate fragments of memory, fantasy and experience, there is no hierarchy of discourses, where for example the scenes of hospital realism are given greater significance than other scenes. The first episode starts firmly located in the fantasy thriller genre, and it is only some time into the episode that we are given a 'realistic' location, the hospital ward where Philip Marlowe, writer of second-rate detective fiction is incapacitated with a horrific skin complaint. The juxtaposition marks a series of significant oppositions (between fantasy and reality, between 'art' and life) which dominate the series in the very process of their breaking down.

In attempting to analyse the style and effect of these passages, the links to be made with 'previous Dennis Potter productions' and with 'the life of Dennis Potter' are rather limiting. Much more important is an attention to the text which reveals very precisely the culminative impression of

meaning formed by the juxtaposition of known film and television genres with each other. There is no clear unilinear narrative development; scenes are juxtaposed rather than being connected in any linear 'cause' and 'effect' sequence. Throughout the series, the genres shift as the scenes shift; often 'scenes' are played out in a mixture of genres. In conventional TV production, a programme either stays within one genre for its duration or makes clear how we can evaluate a hierarchy of genres, that is, it observes the conventions of television realism, unless it clearly marks its departure into dream or day-dream (even then, the fantasy insert often remains in the same style as the so-called reality sequences). In *The Singing Detective* the switch between genres is crucial to exploring the themes of reality and fantasy; often the distinction between the two is only marked by quite subtle changes in television style.

Episode five provided a particularly good example of the intercutting between genres, both marking and blurring the distinction between fantasy and reality, and used for cumulative effect. The sequence starts as a ward scene with a strong connotation of hospital realism, signalled by the loud soundtrack of hospital noises. The scene continues with a move into close-up and focus on the dialogue of Philip Marlowe and his girlfriend Nicola. The predominating style is that of TV drama, with an emphasis on acting and witty repartee between the protagonists. Very quickly the scene moves to fantasy; at first this is clearly marked, but gradually the distinctions become harder and harder to maintain. The distinction between Philip and Nicola's 'real' exchange in the hospital, and Philip's fantasy of her involvement with Mark Finney, is at first easy to maintain. However, the distinction becomes increasingly untenable. Nicola does indeed seem to be trying to 'cheat' on Marlowe just as his fantasy suggests, and the Mark Finney figure starts appearing in the hospital setting. At one point, two figures who had previously clearly inhabited Marlowe's fantasy world as writer, signified by their heavy (heavy-handed) connotations of *film noir,* merge into the hospital realism, culminating in a strange and inexplicable chase from the hospital (again whose unreality is only signified by knowledge of the American TV thriller drama). At moments the rapid shift from genre to genre, from fantasy to reality, is foregrounded, as in one moment where Nicola and Mark Finney are interrupted by the sound of Nicola's voice in the hospital and turn towards the interruption as disgruntled actors.

There is no guiding or explanatory voice through sequences like this. Meaning arrives only through the culmination of juxtaposed scenes. Over the six episodes there are repetitions. Certain scenes begin to appear in shorthand, such as the scene of the woman's body being brought out of the river, or the scene of his mother making love to an unknown soldier in the woods. These scenes, or parts of these scenes, are repeated, set first against one scene then against another, beginning to transfer meaning from the first scene to the third. At first the woman's body appears closely in relation to Marlowe's fantasies, in particular his thriller and detective fantasies. Gradually the scene begins to reappear more and more in relation to other more personal memories, of his childhood and of his mother's 'betrayal'. Only at certain moments in the entire six episodes is there any definitive linking and locating of the various memories and fantasies. This occurs in a scene where Marlowe is dragged into an unwilling word game with a psychotherapist which leads at increasing pace to 'shit', 'women', 'sex', 'death'. And as those words arrive, so too do the various recurrent visual themes. This scene foregrounds one of the important aspects of *The Singing Detective*—precisely this use of repetition and rhythm. The only overall comprehension which is possible for the series derives from recognising the pattern of repetition and recognising the build-up of rhythm to the significant moments where memories and fantasies are linked together.

What is important about this approach to the series is that it emphatically reveals the importance of the viewer as the place where the meaning of the text ultimately (if anywhere) resides. What we need to recognise is that viewers of this series are being called on to recognise (and use) television genres and codes in order to recognise the differences between fantasies, and between fantasy and reality. No text could more vividly illustrate Barthes's description of what makes up all texts, 'the text is a tissue of quotations drawn from innumerable centres of culture' (*S/Z*). Each element is a trace of what has previously gone before, a reworking of previous cultural usages; the programme is 'an intertextual space' (Kristeva). But unlike most television and popular entertainment, which simply repeats previous cultural usages in worn stereotypes, *The Singing Detective* takes up these 'quotations', and by juxtaposition and repetition, uses them to explore themes of memory, repression, the past and the present. And what is revealed by Dennis Potter's particular exploration of these themes through the medium of television is how complex and sophisticated is the ability of the average television audience to 'read' the codes of television. Nothing could more dramatically reveal the continued disregard of the television audience's intelligence than the fact that such a 'complex' programme (in the aesthetic terms of television management) could be so popular. None of these things can be said from a form of criticism which is determined to explain *The Singing Detective* by reference only to the author Dennis Potter.

In a sense *The Singing Detective* is 'about authorship'—about a writer, Philip Marlowe, his need to fantasise to assuage his personal pain, and his desire to impose (or at least present) his fantasies on others. But if we see the series

as simply governed by the central character's consciousness (a central character, as the press kept telling us, who is very like Potter), then we miss the point—the final episode where the petty gangsters come in search of their author, and Nicola has apparently murdered Finney. These cannot be seen as simply emanations of the author, Philip Marlowe. The characters have gained a life of their own—and only the inadequacies of that life are the author's responsibility. Perhaps then, Potter himself, doyen of TV 'authors' is telling us that authorship is a relatively unimportant, if ego-inflating, critical question. Or, as he put it in the Arena programme: 'Nowhere but nowhere in the script did I mention the Forest of Dean' (Potter's own birthplace). So who set the series there? It must have been the producer Kenith Trodd—a great promoter of Potter as author. Such are the tangles that the hunt for the television will snare us in. . . . The 'author' is an external and uncomfortable import in television criticism. Nevertheless the existence of the author is being made a condition of television being taken seriously as a cultural product. I hope to have shown that neither film nor television can usefully be forced into that particular obsession, which only serves to hide knowledge of the media from us and therefore make us complicit in the belief that film and television are not in fact constructs but are instruments of personal expression.

Therese Lichtenstein (essay date May 1990)

SOURCE: "Syncopated Thriller," in *Artforum*, Vol. XXVIII, No. 9, May, 1990, p. 168, 170-172.

[*In the following essay, Lichtenstein studies the complexities of* The Singing Detective*'s plot and its devices of merging and superimposing different levels of fiction.*]

Oedipalized scenarios, traumatic psycho-sexual dynamics, and violence are the stuff that Dennis Potter's television plays and films are made of, moving across the taboo terrain of sexuality within the seemingly orderly nuclear family. The vehicle for these "perverse" scenarios is a dazzling montage of familiar dramatic genres, including the detective story, the musical, the psychological autobiography, and the bildungsroman, all intersecting in a series of interpenetrating narratives that deny any linear structure. Much of the language of "post-Modern" Western culture involves just this kind of self-conscious hybridization, a lifting and appropriating of different languages. Often such work reifies and estheticizes history, making it static, but Potter's complex reconfigurations of the past show it vitally present. They explore how stereotypes function culturally, how our own fantasies and realities are mediated by cultural myths that inhabit us as "natural" identities. Such recent movies as Spike Lee's *Do the Right Thing* and Steven Soderberg's *Sex, Lies and Videotape,* both of 1989, also reveal the spasms of difference between shared stereotypes and individual selves, and expose the stereotype as a dangerous, threatening construction. Potter's vision is no less dark, but also far more ambivalent.

How do the public and the press react to Potter's psychosexual dramas? During the first broadcast of *The Singing Detective,* on the British Broadcasting Company's Lionheart Television in December 1986, the London *Times* reported a rash of callers outraged by "scenes of a boy watching a couple engaged in explicit lovemaking in a wood." (The boy is not just any young boy watching just any couple, but a son, in his private perch in a tree, watching his adulterous mother with her lover.) Though *The Singing Detective* also received rave reviews, both in England and on its PBS broadcast in the U.S., in 1988 (it was also given limited release here as a movie), it is important to remember that TV shows literally enter the home, the sacred, private space of the family, and in doing so they reach, at least potentially, a larger, more heterogenous public than the cinema does. Within the framework of current television, and in the broader conservative cultural and political contexts of Britain and America, *The Singing Detective* is stylistically and conceptually radical.

> . . . it is important to remember that TV shows literally enter the home, the sacred, private space of the family, and in doing so they reach, at least potentially, a larger, more heterogenous public than the cinema does. Within the framework of current television, and in the broader conservative cultural and political contexts of Britain and America, *The Singing Detective* is stylistically and conceptually radical.
> —*Therese Lichtenstein*

Potter was born and raised in Gloucestershire's Forest of Dean, in southwest England, in a working-class coal mining town that he feels was "more democratic and powerful in its emotions than English country villages." In 1961, when he was 26, he began to suffer from a chronic inherited disease, psoriatic arthropathy, a devastating illness that continues to plague him for around three months each year. Its symptoms are burning, blistering skin, high fevers, and swollen joints, which cause general physical immobility. Potter has referred to his psoriasis as the "shadowy ally" of his writing, because, he says, "it makes me introspective." In fact his career as author began not long after the disease's onset, and so far comprises numerous television dramas and miniseries, three novels, and the screenplays

for the movies **Pennies from Heaven,** 1981, a version of his own miniseries; **Brimstone and Treacle,** 1982; and the less successful **Track 29,** 1988. His most recent venture was to adapt his novel **Blackeyes** for television. For the first time, Potter directed.

Picture this. The night air is filled with moist memories of a recent rain. The camera apprehensively pans the slippery, secret-ridden streets to take in a lone busker playing the plaintive notes of "Peg o' My Heart" on the harmonica. A man drops a coin wrapped in paper inscribed with the word "Skinskapes" into the busker's hat.

Cut to a nearby club. Above the entrance, a blue-and-pink neon sign flashes the word "Skinskapes" and the outline of a cocktail glass. The man hurries inside down the steep stairs. The song "I've Got You under My Skin" permeates the tense air. A voice-over says, "And so the man went down the hole, like Alice. But there were no bunny rabbits down there. It wasn't that sort of hole. It was a rat hole." We have just entered the 7 1/2-hour miniseries *The Singing Detective.*

The scene switches to a hospital where a patient is wheeled into a ward full of sick and bedridden men. His face (and body, we soon discover) is covered with red and white patches of blistering, flaking skin. He can barely move without pain, yet his cantankerous personality is glaringly alive as he directs bitter and ironic comments, with piercing precision, toward almost everyone around him. When a hospital staffer asks "What do you believe in?" he replies with a long list: "cholesterol, cigarettes, alcohol, masturbation, carbon monoxide, the Arts Council, nuclear weapons, the *Daily Telegraph,* and not properly labeling fatal poisons. But most of all, above all else, I believe in the one thing which can come out of people's mouths. Vomit." What an endearing fellow! Who is this man? He calls himself the singing detective, though at the moment it is doubtful that this pathetic-looking creature could either sing or sleuth.

One moment we see a ward full of invalids and a moment later a scene of seduction and intrigue at the Skinskapes club. Next we are back in the hospital, with a close-up of the singing detective's face, but this soon dissolves into a shot of a naked woman being fished out of a river on a murky, misty night. A healthy-looking version of the singing detective observes her from a nearby bridge. What is happening? Multiple clues flash in front of us, but information is constantly withheld.

Who is the singing detective? He is the protagonist of the story, Philip Marlow, or I should say he is two Philip Marlows—the man in the hospital, a middle-aged writer of detective fiction, and that writer's alter ego, the hero of his eponymous book *The Singing Detective.* Both Marlows are played by the same actor, Michael Gambon. In this fantasized masquerade of identity, Marlow the detective is everything that Philip the writer is not. The detective is cool and suavely macho. Like Philip's father, he sings in his own band. (The name "Philip Marlow," of course, deprived of its final *e*, is lifted from Raymond Chandler's detective hero of the 1930s and '40s.) The writer, on the other hand, is full of self-pity, caught in a psychic crisis that both produces and is produced by a profound loss of belief and commitment. To his neighbor in the next bed, Philip laments, "One thing about this place, Ali—it strips away all the unimportant stuff—like skin—like work—love—loyalty—like passion and belief."

A brief, conventional synopsis of Potter's unconventional narrative might run like this: Philip is confined to a London hospital by a chronic illness, psoriatic arthropathy (the same condition that afflicts Potter). He is emotionally as well as physically beset: preoccupied with his wife, Nicola (Janet Suzman), who visits him only twice during his three-month stay in the ward, he imagines her having an affair with the hack writer Mark Finney (Patrick Malahide), and suspects they are plotting to steal Philip's old screenplay, an earlier version of *The Singing Detective.* Still, he slowly recovers, gradually becoming able to light a cigarette, turn his head, and, eventually, walk. His body is greased periodically by the beautiful Nurse Mills (Joanne Whalley), and he attends psychotherapy sessions with Dr. Gibbon (Bill Paterson), with whom he eventually develops a positive transference.

The narrative complexifies as we follow Philip through his fantasies, his hallucinatory visions, and his mental revisions of his *Singing Detective* novel (which another of the patients is reading throughout). All of these scenes appear on screen, undifferentiated from the "real" action in the ward. In a second, intertwining level of fiction, for example, we see Philip's childhood memories. He is a lonely and unhappy boy. We watch him at school in Gloucestershire in the '40s, playing a scatological prank on his authoritarian schoolmistress. We see him escaping into the branches of his special tree in the Forest of Dean; the tree gives him a refuge from impinging familial and social strictures, a place where he thinks, dreams—and witnesses his mother's adultery. He is over-whelmed by feelings of guilt and responsibility for his parents' difficulties. "It's all my doing" is a constant refrain. The young Philip often soliloquizes about how he will become a detective when he grows up and everything will be all right—he will find out "who done it."

Philip's mental reenactment of his novel about Marlow the detective is another interlacing narrative strand. Taking place in 1945, it recreates the film noir tradition, replete with spies, betrayals, murder, prostitution, moody music,

chiaroscuro light and shadow, and period dialogue right out of Chandler. Marlow is hired by Mark Binney to protect him from a murder rap. Later, Marlow discovers that Binney is a Russian spy who trades with the Nazis. Actually, Binney has multiple roles in the different layers of the work. A classmate of the young Philip's is named Mark Binney, and the actor who plays the Binney in the detective story also appears as the writer Mark Finney. This actor also plays Raymond, the lover of Philip's mother. Thus all the different narratives mesh, making it difficult to distinguish between fiction, reality, and fantasy.

The viewer probably identifies less with Philip's difficult character than with the kinds of emotional and intellectual processes he goes through. The way Philip combines memories, fictions, fantasies, and actual perceptions is closer to our own thought patterns than is the conventional linear narrative. The viewer is placed in the role of detective, the quintessential voyeur, putting together shards of evidence, clues that slowly start making sense. It is as though Freud had met Columbo in a psychological thriller, their purpose to reveal the monad of Philip's identity. Potter carefully manipulates us into this position of detective and keeps us guessing. And like good detectives, or like psychotherapists, we maintain a certain distance. Every clue emanates from within Philip's mind; the detective story, then, becomes an allegory for the therapeutic experience, and the film work becomes equivalent to the dream work—a working through, a rite of passage, a journey toward an integrated self. Potter explains that *The Singing Detective* "is a detective story about how you find out about yourself, how an event has lodged inside you and affects how you see things. . . . Out of this morass of evidence and clues we can start to put up this structure of self."

The images and stories in the kaleidoscope of Philip's memory reveal a dialectic of censorship or repression and recognition or insight. Simultaneously imprisoning and liberating, memory is experienced as an interplay of remembering and forgetting, all set in motion by the impossible search for one's origins. Erupting into Philip's consciousness like the fragmentary aftereffects of dreams, psychic formations left from his childhood trauma are censored, edited, and embellished as dreams are, becoming staccato, briefly glimpsed gasps of images—the return of the repressed. These images are repeated like musical variations, always slightly different, added to, altered. But Potter also uses Marlow's interior state to attack external conditions—establishment values, organized religion, and the indecencies of the social relationships called into being by such bureaucratic institutions as the hospital. From the outset, the hospital is targeted as a callous, inhumane place that reinforces a power hierarchy of patronizing, condescending doctors and nurses. The patients are the bottom of the pyramid. During the first episode, "Skin," a vulnerable

Philip is humiliated by the diagnostic "experts" gathered around his bed. The camera views the scene from overhead, pinning the nearly naked "speciman" to his sheets. When Marlow cries out, in utter despair, "I'm a prisoner of my own skin and bones," the doctors shout for Librium, tranquilizers, barbiturates, and antidepressants, in a devastating parodic chorus of clinical insensitivity.

Philip momentarily escapes from this abuse by hallucinating some comic relief: suddenly the light takes on a vaude-villian cast, and the ward is transformed into a musical stage where the staff performs a song-and-dance routine to Fred Waring's Pennsylvanians' song "Dry Bones," of 1949. The women nurses become a seductive, short-skirted, high-heeled chorus line, and another staffer plays a xylophone of human skulls. "Sometimes—sometimes these—hallucinations," Philip claims, "they're better than the real thing." Feverish musical numbers like this one have an uncanny quality, not only because they rupture an already fragmentary narrative (and one much darker in tone than the conventional musical, in which such interruptions are expected) but because of their peculiar combination of the familiar and the strange. The characters do not sing in these scenes; they lip-synch to songs from the '30s and '40s, making themselves into dummies, mechanical but lifelike. They lose their own voices. This device of Potter's, which he also used in *Pennies from Heaven,* reveals his characters' internal division, their masquerading doubleness, their lack of a stable and coherent identity. Or, rather, since these scenes are all phantasms of Philip's thoughts, they reveal his own divided self. But the songs, sung by Bing Crosby, the Andrews Sisters, the Mills Brothers, Vera Lynn, and others, also make a broader social point. (Their ironic, ambiguous presence here is not nostalgic; Potter describes nostalgia as a "second-rate emotion.") These artifacts of popular culture reveal the fantasies of their collective audience, or the building blocks with which the public constructs its desires. Relieving its listeners' pain and expressing their feelings, the music also suggests how the past lives and assumes meaning in the present, how it speaks through individuals, provides the vocabulary for even the most intimate of their emotions. It is as though their culture were speaking through them at the expense of their identities, as though they were empty shells or vehicles for their culture, as though they had no autonomy.

The loss of control, both physical and in terms of one's ability to direct one's own life, is a major concern for Potter. Philip hallucinates and fantasizes not only to block out the harsh reality of the ward but to gain imaginary control over his body. During periods of physical illness one sometimes feels inhabited by a hostile, foreign other, producing a state of alienation—a division between body and mind. In one of the more comically grotesque scenes in *The Singing Detective,* the beautiful Nurse Mills greases Philip's hot,

feeble, blistered flesh. As she slips on her tight plastic gloves and dips into the jar of grease, she says politely, "All right. I'll start down below first." To keep himself from sexual arousal, Philip tries to "think of something boring— For Christ's sake think of something very very boring— Speech a speech by Ted Heath. . . Australian barmen ecologists semiologists. . . ." But the nurse soon says, "Sorry. But I shall have to lift your penis now to grease around it." We are immediately transported to Skinskapes, where Mills becomes a glamorous singer performing (in lip sync) "The Blues in the Night." The song is followed by loud applause from the mostly male audience and by the humiliated Philip apologizing, "I'm very sorry. It—that's the one part of me that still sort of functions." His orgasm here is a symbol not so much of male potency as of potency made passive, out of control. Like the other patients in the ward, Philip speaks out of a marginalized position— out of an unhealthy, even grotesque male body, a site of oppression. Presenting male subjectivity as divided and crisis-stricken—the way women are so often portrayed on television—Potter disrupts the familiar, idealized images of masculinity that populate the mass media.

Women, however, do not escape any more lightly. The young Philip's disillusionment with his mother, her transformation, for him, from pure and "virginal" to adulterous "whore," develops into a tendency to class women into these two-dimensional categories. Philip's mother, in fact, has doubly disappointed him: he experiences her adultery as betrayal and her eventual suicide as an abandonment. But he also feels responsible for her acts, and internalizes them, besieging himself with self-loathing and guilt so that he can exonerate her and restore her as the good mother. This psychic displacement, of course, is no substitute for her love, protection, and nurturing. As a result, his attitudes toward women combine adoration and hate, alienated identification and misidentification, and an uncomfortable symbiotic dependency.

Philip's mistrust of women becomes clear in the connection his imagination makes between sex and death. At one point, Dr. Gibbon plays a word-association game with Philip, who matches "woman" with "fuck," "fuck" with "dirt," "dirt" with "death." Later Philip sees George, an older patient, suffer a heart attack as he tells a story about a sexual encounter he had with a blonde during the war. The sounds of the machine with which the doctors try to revive George combine in Philip's mind with the sounds and images of his mother's adultery. Her lover's orgasm and George's death occur simultaneously. Such associations between sex and death are familiar in Western cultural history: in France, orgasm is called "*la petite mort*," and the verb "to die" appears often in English Jacobean drama as a synonym for coitus. For Philip, sexual climax represents a deathlike loss of power, and an intolerable melting of the boundaries between men and the frightening figures of women. He tries to resurrect these boundaries by his compulsive voyeurism—by participating in sex vicariously, through others, without risk to himself. Voyeuristic scenes often occur in his fantasies, compulsively repeating the primal scene on which he has actually, and accidentally, spied. His physical illness becomes a metaphor for his psychic paralysis and his repression, an outward sign of his inner loss of power. Yet the "impotent" position of voyeur also provides a desperate sense of power and control.

Small wonder that in *The Singing Detective,* sex is never represented as mutually pleasurable for men and women. It is passionless, guilty, often paid for in one way or another, and often related to death and violence. This, at least, is Philip's view, and his viewpoint structures the values of the entire drama. But the work probes his attitudes toward women, and reflects the pain they cause, rather than simply passing them on. Dr. Gibbon asks Philip, "You don't like women, do you?" Philip defensively retorts, "Which sort do you mean? Young ones. Old ones. Fat ones. Thin ones. Faithful ones? Slags? Sluts? Try to be more specific." And Dr. Gibbon replies: "All right. Let me rephrase that. I'm reasonably sure that you think you *do* like them. That you even think they are—well—capable of being idolized, or—You don't like *sex.* You probably think you do. I mean, we spend a great deal of time thinking about it, don't we?" Philip's attitudes toward women, both tender and cruel, are emblematic of attitudes in society at large. And Potter doesn't so much justify them as suggest their causes, and the way they victimize those who possess them as well as those who suffer them. Finally, by the end of the series, Philip's identity is better integrated, and he is better able to trust his wife, Nicola—able to overcome his feelings that since she is not a virgin she must be a whore.

This ending, however, sounds a curious and paradoxical note: Marlow the detective enters Philip the writer's hospital room and shoots him, saying in a voice-over, "I suppose you could say we'd been partners, him and me. . . . But, hell, this was one sick fellow, from way back when. And I reckon I'm man enough to tie my own shoelaces now." Fiction has burst into the filmic "reality." Now we see the ward again, transformed into an orderly place after the shooting, and Philip, completely recovered from his illness, dressed in a suit instead of hospital cloth, and looking exactly like Marlow the detective. He is leaning on Nicola's arm—they have been reconciled. From "a starting point of extreme crisis and an utter lack of belief," the protagonist has rebuilt and regained his autonomy. On the soundtrack, however, Vera Lynn sings "We'll Meet Again." The song is ironic, referring not only to Philip's reunion with Nicola but to the inevitable return of his illness. And since the work has dealt so consistently with interpenetrating, inseparable layers of "fiction" and "reality," we may also see here an allusion to Potter himself, and an allegory for the writer's return to a theme. (Potter has said, "I think any writer has a small field to keep plowing . . . and eventually you turn up the coins you want. I know I always return to the same motifs.") There is also another ambivalence in this ending: if *The Singing Detective* moves toward Philip's moral and physical regeneration, the temporary return of his sovereignty, it does so by resurrecting the conventional terms of masculinity that have been subverted throughout. The killing of sick Philip by strong Marlow—a type, the stereotypical gumshoe, an artifice from a book—is a contradictory return to health: as if we could not sustain ourselves on our own without standing on the forms of the past, which both limits our future and makes it possible.

Mary Gordon (essay date Fall/Winter 1990/91)

SOURCE: "Who's not Singing in *The Singing Detective*," in "Some Things I Saw," in *Salmagundi,* No. 88/89, Fall/Winter, 1990/91, pp. 118-122.

[*In the following excerpt, Gordon opposes the "pervasive and seductive elements of adolescent male fantasy" that she suggests permeate the hard-boiled detective fiction that* The Singing Detective *is modeled after.*]

The dreaming boy alone in the lush tree. The crooner by himself before the microphone. The walking detective (hard boiled dick), solitary, gun in hand, his heels clicking along the rainy pavement. Is he by himself because he wants to be? Is the role of the isolate, in proximate relation to things longer than they are wide, the role he chose first for himself or is it the austere and wise second choice of the man who knows too much?

Dennis Potter's *The Singing Detective* is all about the stuff male dreams are made of: obviously, deliberately, self-consciously this is the case of the work. The brilliant technique is there to interweave dream and wakefulness, real (nineteenth century) reality and primitive fantasy, the numbing, nullifying pressures of present life and the simple voluptuousness of the old songs and the older stories. I watched, at first, transfixed by the verbal and visual facility but as the hours drew on I found myself more and more alienated from what I was seeing, more uneasy, until finally I had to force myself to watch. The techniques of the singing detective are new, but the message is certainly not. Dennis Potter is merely saying something we have heard for a very long time: at the center of the boy's dream is the treacherous, transgressing cunt.

The point of *The Singing Detective* is that it functions simultaneously on many levels. There is the level of the present: Philip Marlow, a washed up writer of third-rate detective fictions, lies in his bed in a hospital ward. He is the victim of arthritic psoriasis, which renders him loathsome to look at (his skin has turned to horrifying scales) and makes most movements of his limbs and head excruciatingly painful. Around him, the flotsam and jetsam of English society suffer, decay and die. (Men make far less attractive patients than women. Perhaps it's all those catheters, all those grizzled faces, degenerate looking because unshaved.) They reveal themselves to be, like the rest of Marlow's humankind, small-minded, mischief-making, lewd, self-deceiving, foolish, devoted to others' harm. The occasional ray of decency pierces the pervading fog: an Indian man, who has the good sense to understand that Marlow's racial slurs are ONLY A JOKE, offers Marlow a sweet and then dies. But sweetness and light come to the ward in the presence of a pretty nurse, who is not only cheerful and understanding, but covers every inch (*every inch*) of Marlow's damaged body with cold cream. This is an important part of his therapy, and Marlow tries to be good, but what would you do, male viewer, if a pretty girl were greasing your penis with cold cream? You might try, like the noble Marlow, thinking of the most boring possible things (the Arts Council, the Guardian Woman's page, your own work even) but against your will you would succumb. Against your will. The only other time we see Marlow as a sexual performer he is calling his partner (a whore) filthy names at the climactic moment. But at Nurse Mill's hands, there is no need for nasty language. Marlow's orgasm is entirely unvolitional. It occurs through the ministrations of a woman who asks nothing of him, not even money. She doesn't require so much as a touch. Contact is limited to his penis and her greasy plastic gloves. How could he possibly fail her? Wiping the semen with the Kleenex, she only half blames. She is the perfect woman. "You're the girl in all the songs," Marlow says, and he's right, not just because she's pretty and nice but because she offers sexual satisfaction while eliminating entirely the risk of sexual failure. Marlow loathes himself; of course he would expect that women would loathe him. How could sex with anything like mutuality be anything but terrifying for him? What reason would he have to *feel good about it,* that mandate that we have been given from the sixties on? Why would he trust women, when his early experience of them shows them to be betrayers and tormentors? How could he be other than he is?

Of course the *self* that Marlow is is enormously complicated; that is the point of *The Singing Detective* and particularly its technique. He is his present and his past, his psychoanalysis and his characters, his mordant, nasty, witty language and the soothing words of the songs, "Banality with a beat," he calls them. In the experience of the past which the suffering Marlow remembers, popular songs are an important backdrop. In fact, they solidify the tone of

childhood wishes: simplicity and harmony, delicious temporary yearning with no sense that finally it cannot be fulfilled. In Marlow's memory of his childhood, his mother is hysterical, and frustrated, but she *moves*. She is imprisoned in her husband's family house with her appalling father-in-law who projects missiles of phlegm onto the fire in the middle of dinner, and her mother-in-law, who keeps reminding her that it is not her house. It is not surprising that she takes a lover. We are not surprised at this turn of events, but we are mournful. For who is she betraying? The kind, stoical, anxious to please father, his eyes always close to tears, his ears vulnerable below his too short haircut. And the father sings. The loving joyous words of the song come from his mouth, as he leads a sing-song in the pub. Impotent in life, he is potent in his singing. He owns the important language: the language of the songs. In *being the singer*, he is able to be self-expressive, to express the deepest desires of the community and therefore to be its point of cohesion. And what is mummy doing all the while? Accompanying him on the piano. She is the silent handmaiden. Only when she is deprived of language and it becomes the property of the father in a way that excludes her are there moments of family happiness. It is interesting to note who sings in *The Singing Detective.* The only solo female voice which is accompanied by a specific female face is that of Dietrich singing Lili Marlene. This is the voice of the foreigner, the one who could not be mother. "A tart," Phil's maternal grandfather calls her, tart being synonymous for him with non-English. The foreign spy, who is killed by the enemy, is a special locus of desire for Philip as he takes on the skin of his third self, the character of the Singing Detective he has created in his novel. The spy who sings Lili Marlene is given the face of Philip's real life mother. In Philip's detective-novel life, she is shot dead. She is the only female solo singer in the film. The important female characters—Philip's tormenting teacher and his complicated wife—are not allowed into the dream world of the songs.

> When *The Singing Detective* works, it works because it embodies and indeed canonizes extremely pervasive and seductive elements of adolescent male fantasy. The Philip Marlow-Sam Spade character makes sacred, honorable, and noble the male fear of intimacy with the female.
> —*Mary Gordon*

There are important reasons for this, and they are connected with the ultimate failure of *The Singing Detective* to achieve cohesion or a satisfying end. When *The Singing Detective* works, it works because it embodies and indeed canonizes extremely pervasive and seductive elements of adolescent male fantasy. The Philip Marlow-Sam Spade character makes sacred, honorable, and noble the male fear of intimacy with the female. The detective is always the moral center of the fiction. He is poor and unsuccessful because his standards are incorruptible. For the same reason he is alone: he is purer than the rocks on which he sits. Occasionally, he is tempted, either by a need for love or for sex, to join himself with a female, but it is always to his peril. The beautiful face is always the face of the betrayer and the murderer. Only his secretary understands him, and she is willing to love him in agonizing silence, making him coffee, bailing him out, helping him with his hangover, and being told that she's a great girl and he's sorry he's too ruined to be the man she really deserves. The fiction embodied by the '30's and '40's songs embodies as well a world of female un-dangerousness. One yearns and is yearned for; one loves and is loved, but the high point of erotic imagination is the kiss, not the fuck. Obviously we (contemporary men and women) are supposed to know better than all this, we are supposed to want the loving partnership of equals. But in fact, the loving partnership of equals has very little mythological furniture to make habitable its bare rooms. The stories and the songs that all of us grew up on are based on relationships of unequal and skewed power. There is simply nothing that has been imbedded in popular culture long enough to render luscious the model of two adults struggling in the modern world. Tracy and Hepburn, Russell and Grant, exist in the realm of comedy, whose touch by its very nature is light, too light to make the deep impress of melodrama on the molten wax of yearning. Too light and too far from death. We see Ingrid Bergman leaving Humphrey Bogart at the Airport and there is music in the background; there is no equivalent to "As Time Goes By" running through our brains as we see Russell and Grant in the newsroom or Tracy and Hepburn on the golf course or in court. There is no theme song for mutuality, just as there is no embodied romance for the female isolate. Humphrey Bogart can walk off alone or with Claude Rains, but Hepburn and Russell have to have a man. It is impossible to say that we can't believe in the female isolate because of our conviction of female bodily weakness. Even Amelia Earhardt went up in flames. Shane rides off into the sunset alone; the female on the frontier must be accompanied.

The romances of popular culture make no place for the solitary female. She can't look death in the face; she has to be saved from it. A stronger presence (male) has to intervene between her and death. She is the conduit of death but she can do nothing to keep it back. If she can never be alone, how can we ever know who she is? And if she is only death or betrayal, how can there be a truthful end that includes her in any of the traditional, delicious genres?

At the end of *The Singing Detective,* Marlow walks out of the hospital with his wife. Why isn't this woman singing? There is a perfect opportunity for her to do it. Near the end, in the process of Marlow's cure, the Ink Spots are singing "You Always Hurt The One You Love." The voice we hear next is Ella Fitzgerald's. But do we see Marlow's wife's face? No, the voice is disembodied.

In life real change does not amputate the child's life, or the dreamer's, it moves it along. In the context of the film's shaping myth, the force bringing about change would not be the psychiatrist or the sexy soubrette wife, but the pretty nurse, who cures by her unselfish love. In the last encounter with her, Marlow tells the nurse she is the nicest and most beautiful person he's met in a long time. He mentions how wonderfully her head sits on her neck. Then he quits, dropped; he becomes a grownup. We are meant to believe that the boy in the tree will stay there, he will come back, but he will not be powerful enough to defeat the good (adult) man and the good woman, walking down the hospital corridor into the modern world. In the context of everything that went before, this is unbelievable, the stuff of post-therapeutic thought against the heady concoction of non-linguistic, culturally enshrined desire.

Potter's techniques—this ability to harness television's fragmentariness and quick shifts—are new, but the story is a very old one. You can't put old wine in new bottles, and the final product lacks bouquet; the sediment settles at the bottom: the stuff of undigested dream.

Richard Alleva (review date 27 March 1992)

SOURCE: "Silly Secrets," in *Commonweal,* Vol. CXIX, No. 6, March 27, 1992, pp. 24-25.

[*In the following review, Alleva comments on Potter's directorial debut with his film* Secret Friends.]

Dennis Potter's *Secret Friends* is a jigsaw puzzle that doesn't give you much to look at once you've assembled it. Of course, the fun of jigsaw puzzles is in the assembly, not the final result. But *Secret Friends* fails as mind teaser, too, because too many of its narrative twists can be easily anticipated. This movie testifies more strongly to Potter's work ethic than to his art. For his first directorial effort, he's written a script that's very busy yet quite cold, extremely intricate, and utterly hollow.

The premise is interesting. A man on a train (Alan Bates) is quite obviously having an emotional breakdown. He weeps hysterically as he stares down at his luncheon fish but can't communicate to conductor and passengers the turmoil in his brain. As the film enters his mind we begin to understand that he fears he has murdered his wife (Gina Bellman) in a fit of insanity. Or has he merely imagined the deed? Until the last few minutes resolve the mystery, Potter devotes his story not to the immediate circumstances of the real or imagined crime, but to the reasons why such a murder *might* have been committed by this particular man.

Potter's narrative method is one used in certain films of the 1960s and early 70s, all of which were inspired by *Last Year at Marienbad*: short, nonconsecutive scenes (sometimes no more than single-shot glimpses of an action) that don't unfold a linear story but challenge us to assemble the story ourselves. This method made sense in *Last Year* because that film was about doubt: how can we know if a love affair took place if the male affirms that it did while the female denies it? The method makes even more sense for **Secret Friends** because that subject is not only doubt (did Bates murder his wife or not?) but the sort of extreme anguish that can scramble chronology in the mind of the sufferer.

But making sense and giving pleasure are different things. By the end of **Secret Friends,** the puzzle pieces all fall into place but we couldn't care less. There seem to me two reasons why this is so.

First, the motives for the putative crime are all grounded in the neurosis of Bates's character. This is a man who cannot function sexually except in the arms of whores, yet who also harbors an extreme detestation of whorishness. Emotionally in love with his wife, he forces her to disguise herself as a call girl so that they can have sex, but then his feelings curdle murderously at the effectiveness of the disguise. But this is absolutely all there is to Bates's character. The psychosis isn't just an important component of the role, it *is* the role. Every scene, every flashback, every exchange of dialogue, relates to this sexual aberration, yet there is no exploration of it, only reiteration that the neurosis exists. This not only exhausts the viewer's patience but limits Alan Bates as an actor. With only one note to hit, he does his best to hit it with varying degrees of force, from different points of attack. Bates's virtuosity is impressive, but watching him here is like watching a great juggler discover how many ways he can juggle one ball. If Gina Bellman seems more lively, it's only because the script lets her contrast the behaviors of mousey wife and sexy prostitute, both of which she enacts admirably.

Second, Potter seems to underrate our ability at jigsaw-puzzle solving. He wastes so much time teasing us that he doesn't give himself enough time to open the characters up and make them truly complex and interesting. Long after we have guessed that the modestly dressed woman in Bates's home and the slit-skirted temptress in the London hotel are one and the same person, Potter is still trying to

titillate us with identification games. And long after we have guessed that the phantom who looks exactly like Bates and who promises to do his murder for him is, in fact, Bates's imaginary doppelgänger (the "secret friend" of the title), Potter feels the need to explain the childhood origins of this double in a long, not very interesting monologue with which Bates embarrasses a dinner party.

There's so much fancy cinematic and narrative cakewalking in this movie that both the roots and the results of the hero's problem are scanted. That old British standby, the puritanism of middle-class parents, is pressed into duty yet again as an explanation of what's wrong with the hero, and a nice heart-to-heart with the wife in bed seems to clear everything up at the end. All very tidy. And inadequate.

Did Potter, an enormously gifted writer (**Pennies from Heaven, Dreamchild, Gorky Park, The Singing Detective**) give himself this schematic script as an exercise so that he could worry less about characterization than about where to place actors and camera? If so, he certainly has come through creditably as a technician. The choice of camera angles, the duration of each shot, the alternation of fixed shots with long smooth pans, are all excellent. Now, if only Potter the talented writer would give his artistic doppelgänger, Potter the accomplished director, something interesting to work on! That would be a not-so-secret act of friendship from which we could all benefit. . . .

Mick Imlah (review date 26 March 1993)

SOURCE: "Surreptitious Overturnings," in *Times Literary Supplement*, No. 4695, March 26, 1993, p. 17.

[*In this short review of* Potter on Potter *and* Lipstick on Your Collar, *Imlah briefly examines the elements of Potter's dramatic devices.*]

Dennis Potter is exceptional: a television dramatist worth the weight of a whole book of interviews. What justifies **Potter on Potter,** though, is less the special quality of the work it analyses—some of which was screened once and can never be seen again—than the hard intelligence with which Potter surveys the personal history that informs his plays to such an unusual extent: the working-class upbringing in the Forest of Dean, National Service, the scholarship to Oxford that severed him from his roots, and above all, the crippling and disfiguring illness, psoriatic arthropathy, which struck at twenty-six to deny him a life in politics but about which, even at its first outbreak, he claims to have had positive feelings in terms of his writing.

Potter chose what he calls "the Palace of Varieties in the

corner of the room", and a career whose highlights, the acclaimed serials *Pennies from Heaven* and *The Singing Detective,* made innovative use of popular songs (respectively of the 1930s and 40s), mimed by his characters as part of a consciously de-naturalized drama.

In his introduction to *Potter on Potter,* Graham Fuller calls *Lipstick on Your Collar* the "third part" of Potter's "song-cycle"; but set in the 1950s and powered by the longings of the young, this has a much lighter, more careless and more positively sexy atmosphere than its predecessors. The narrative unfolds in a relatively uncomplicated present tense, and despite its ration of rough scenes—the appeasement of a sobbing beaten wife by firm inward pressure on a nipple; a bully plunging his victim's head down an unflushed WC ("Take a closer look—shit to shit")—the story is essentially comic. It contrives a crossover of desires between slick Mick Hopper, a clerk in the War Office during the Suez crisis, and his naive scholarly colleague from Wales, Francis Francis. The latter makes the mistake of falling for the gorgeous, mercenary wife of the brutal career soldier, Corporal Berry, while Hopper wastes his coffee-bar charm on Lisa, the Ibsen-loving niece of a visiting American general. After Berry has been run over and killed by a drunken Light-Programme organist (Roy Hudd) in the penultimate fifth episode, Hopper moves in on the lightly bereaved Sylvia, while Francis finds a marriage of minds with the booklorn Lisa. The exchange is confirmed in a dazzling celebratory finale, full of winks of forgiveness and resurrection, set in the cinema where Sylvia works as an usherette.

With the lyrics randomly distributed among the actors, the songs here are less meditations on the narrative than riotous disruptions of it—a reflection no doubt of Potter's low estimate of the emotional resonance of early white rock 'n' roll. Most of them are fantasies by which Hopper—an aspiring drummer—escapes the boredom of his clerical subordination. He has routinely to ask "Permission to speak, sah!" of a quartet of senior officers; but his imagination makes these middleclass soldiers prance about with a spangled, naked Eve to some of the worst records ever made: proof of his observation that "People can sing even when they've got their mouths shut". These surreptitious overturnings have their political counterpart in Britain's failure to go into Egypt; an abdication which reduces Hopper's boss, Lt Col Bernwood, to a breakdown which is rivetingly rendered by Peter Jeffrey.

Jeffrey's is only one of a dozen absorbing cameos by some of Britain's best-known television actors. But Potter's rich script, and Renny Rye's ebullient, expansive direction, are equally well served by the unknowns imaginatively cast in the three leading roles. Of these Louise Germaine, a twenty-one-year-old model from Margate, has never even

acted before: yet her innocence of what she is doing, except with her figure, makes her the perfect vehicle for Sylvia's guileless manipulations.

Martin Wiggins (essay date 1993)

SOURCE: "'Disgusted, Shepherd's Bush': *Brimstone and Treacle* at the BBC," in *Essays and Studies, 1993: Literature and Censorship,* Vol. 46, 1993, pp. 131-43.

[*In the following essay, Wiggins discusses* Brimstone and Treacle *and the issue of censorship in relation to the themes and dramatic features of Potter's teleplay.*]

Any discussion of censorship at the BBC will necessarily contain an element of speculation. All successful censorship makes its object invisible, but at the BBC the censorship itself is also invisible. The decision not to broadcast an item is entirely an internal matter, closed to public scrutiny and accountable to no outside body: there is no right of appeal, and there can be no informed public debate, since the BBC has no statutory obligation to explain its actions. This is one reason why the suppression in 1976 of Dennis Potter's television play *Brimstone and Treacle* did not become the *cause célèbre* that Potter evidently hoped. Other post-war censorship cases, such as the prosecutions of *Lady Chatterley's Lover* in 1960, *Oz* 28 in 1971, and *Gay News* in 1977, became notorious because the proceedings were conducted in open court, and people were therefore able to develop sophisticated opinions and write letters to *The Times* about them. In the case of Potter's play, however, there was only the impersonal and uninformative press announcement that, 'in the opinion of the BBC television service, *Brimstone and Treacle* ought not to be shown since it is likely to outrage viewers to a degree that its importance as a play does not support'.

The case has also lacked the feeling of deprivation which successful censorship tends to incite, for Potter went to great lengths to circumvent the BBC ban and bring his play before a public audience. The script was published in the May 1976 issue of *The New Review,* and a stage adaptation was produced at the Crucible Theatre, Sheffield in the autumn of the following year; it was also performed in London early in 1979. Potter then collaborated with Kenith Trodd, who had been the BBC's in-house producer of the play, to make a film version, which was released in 1982. Finally even the BBC relented, and broadcast the original television production for the first time as part of a Potter retrospective in August 1987. In different forms, then, the play has been more widely available than many BBC drama productions which were not banned.

Brimstone and Treacle is a black parody of a popular genre best represented by the film *It's a Wonderful Life* (1946). It begins with suburban despair, and it ends with a miracle: in a climate of incipient marital break-up, Mr and Mrs Bates care for their daughter Pattie, reduced to a gibbering vegetable after a hit-and-run accident; and in the course of the action a charming and mysterious stranger, Martin, enters their lives, cures Pattie, and then disappears into the night. Familiar, perhaps, but with a twist: this time the household has not entertained an angel unawares. Where *It's a Wonderful Life* and its kind spooned out treacly sentimentality, Potter's play offers a touch of brimstone: the devil has all the best miracles.

Where *It's a Wonderful Life* and its kind spooned out treacly sentimentality, Potter's play [*Brimstone and Treacle*] offers a touch of brimstone: the devil has all the best miracles.
— *Martin Wiggins*

The two unscripted epigraphs which punctuate the first scene are the best guide to this aspect of the play. First: 'There resides infinitely more good in the demonic man than in the trivial—Kierkegaard.' Then, with no variation of the voice-over speaker's tone: 'A spoonful of sugar helps the medicine go down—Andrews.' Angel in the house is a syrupy role which Martin plays to win the Bates's confidence and with it an invitation to stay and help with Pattie. Once installed, he rapes her, and the shock restores her to mental normality; like medicine, it is nasty, but curative. The demonic man has done good in spite of himself.

Broadly speaking, it is understandable that the BBC should believe that offence might be caused if the play were transmitted. Rape, religion, and mental illness are all sensitive topics, but Potter does not treat them sensitively: they are the incidentals of the plot rather than the objects of reverent analysis; it is not a play 'about' those subjects. It does not follow from this, however, that the ban was justified. It is notable that Potter's efforts to get his play seen brought it, with more or less the same manifest content, into an arena where it was subject to the Obscene Publications Acts 1959 and 1964, the Theaters Act 1968, the judgement of the local licensing authorities for cinemas, and, informally, that of the British Board of Film Censors. It was neither banned nor prosecuted, and this safe passage past the instruments of public censorship inevitably calls into question the BBC's private, institutional act of censorship in 1976.

Brimstone and Treacle was made at a time of reaction and retrenchment at the BBC: Kenith Trodd later characterized

the 1970s as 'the censorship decade' for television, after the liberties of the 1960s. Underlying the very different policies followed by the BBC in each of these decades was the Obscene Publications Act 1959, which expressly excludes BBC broadcasts from its scope. Under Hugh Greene, the liberal intellectual Director-General appointed in 1960, this was interpreted as a license to dare, and the result was the emergence of organized opposition in the form of the Clean-Up TV Campaign (later the 'National Viewers' and Listeners' Association'), a rightwing and extremist Christian pressure-group led by Mary Whitehouse. One of the central objectives of this group was a change in the law to make the BBC accountable to a Broadcasting Council.

Greene's confrontational approach, then, entailed the risk of a political backlash that might cost the BBC its autonomy. The Corporation's interests were better served by seeking an accommodation with the protesters, and Greene's successor, Charles Curran (appointed in 1969) accordingly made a point of paying greater attention to Whitehouse, without necessarily acceding to her demands outright. The crucial *volte-face* was the issue in 1973 of new guidelines on taste and standards in BBC programmes. The document recognized that, in the past, the BBC had made and broadcast outstanding programmes (*The Wednesday Play, Culloden,* and *Till Death Us Do Part* were named) which had 'come about through apparent defiance of accepted practice', and it did not repudiate their artistic success; but it was clear that, in future, the forestalling of public criticism was to have a higher priority. In other words, the BBC entered the mid-1970s determined to impose a narrower standard of acceptability, in the hope that it would be understood to be putting its own house in order without the need for legal or constitutional coercion.

Brimstone and Treacle was the first play that Dennis Potter submitted to the BBC after the issue of these guidelines. The script was delivered in December, 1974, and was approved for production by the Head of Plays, James Cellan-Jones. The finished version was seen and approved by Bryan Cowgill, the Controller of BBC-1, and it was scheduled for transmission as part of the *Play for Today* strand on 6 April 1976. At the last moment, less than three weeks before the play was due to go out, and after the *Radio Times* for that week had gone to press, it was announced that *Brimstone and Treacle* would not, after all, be broadcast. Alasdair Milne, BBC Television's Director of Programmes, had seen the play, and, repelled, decided to withdraw it from the schedules. He later wrote to Potter to explain his decision: 'I found the play brilliantly written and made, but nauseating. I believe that it is right in certain instances to outrage the viewers in order to get over a point of serious importance, but I am afraid that in this case real outrage would be widely felt and that no such point would get across.'

This was, to say the least, an extraordinary way for the BBC to conduct its affairs, even allowing for its increased proneness to impose censorship at this time. Potter himself said as much in a grumpy article published soon afterwards in the *New Statesman:* for the Director of Programmes to ban a play which had been discussed and scrutinized for fifteen months at every level from tea boy to channel controller, and finally pronounced acceptable for transmission, looked alarmingly like a personal whim—and, when that play had cost around £70,000 to make, quite a costly whim at that. The price tag signifies more, however: it may have been managerially inept to leave the decision so late, but even an inept executive does not knowingly waste so much money without a compelling reason. Milne was frustratingly vague and reticent about what this reason might be—the quotation in the last paragraph was the entirety of his argument—but with hindsight, his objection to the play becomes clearer.

Brimstone and Treacle deals with intrusion. The essence of the plot is that Martin, pretending to be someone he is not (Pattie's friend and would-be fiancé), and something he is not (the ideal house-trained man, 'mumsy's little helper'), enters the Bates household and, left alone, abuses his position. As such, the play addresses a very ancient human demarcation of space into inside and outside: 'outside' is the jungle, 'inside' a place of safety which is today called 'home'. At one level, then, the conflict is between the civilized values of 'home' and the feral savagery of the outside. Martin is a creature of the latter. Early on, he sneers at the traffic in the street: 'Sick, sick people in metal boxes. They do not know the taste of blood in their mouths. They do not know the glory of the hunt as I know it, as *demons* know it.' (p. 33) Later, he uses Pattie to satisfy humanity's most animal drive, sexual lust. He is dangerous because, unlike the beasts of the jungle, he is intelligent and articulate. 'I can smell the domesticity on your clothes, you sick grey blobs, you timid *mortals*' (p. 32), he says in a scripted line cut from the finished version. His rejection of domesticity, of the 'inside' he seeks to penetrate and disrupt, is conscious and considered: it is something he recognizes well enough to imitate.

Martin brilliantly mimics the petty gentility, the religiosity, the sentimentality, of the environment he enters. 'The plain truth is,' he lies, 'that I once dared to ask Patricia to be my bride' (p. 38), the last word playing up to the romantic fantasies of his suburban middle-class hostess with chilling precision. Accordingly, Mrs Bates—whose greatest pride seems to lie in not using tea-bags or instant coffee—is entirely taken in by this 'nice young man . . . who says his prayers and knows long poems *off by heart*' (p.

46). Her husband is harder to convince. His most revealing domestic trait is that he 'can't stand stains' (p. 37)—a finicky distaste for chaos in the home which reflects a larger fear of intrusion. On the widest scale, his political views are underpinned by the same concern: he has recently left the Conservative Party to join the National Front. Among his worries he lists 'Drugs. Violence. Indiscipline. . . . Strikes. Subversion. Pornography' (p. 49), but his *bête noir* is immigration: 'There'll always be an England. Ha! Not with half the cities full of coloured men, there won't!' (p. 49) He is the archetypal Englishman whose home, even in suburban Archenfield Avenue, is his castle. No wonder he is instinctively suspicious of Martin, even without recognizing him as a kind of immigrant from another metaphysical plane.

The different levels of Mr Bates's concern reflect the concentricity with which the play treats Martin's intrusiveness. The action is structured like a camera zoom as he enters the different degrees of private space. First he bumps into Bates in the street, then (having obtained his address by stealing his wallet) crosses the threshold of his home. The focus on an objective sharpens with the next stage: he is invited to spend the night in Pattie's old bedroom, preserved as she had left it, and he amuses himself by rifling through her underwear and squeezing blood out of a bra. Finally he invades the most private space of all when he rapes Pattie.

Martin is, then, a character who violates boundaries: he resists containment. This is true even of the containment which delimits every character in every play. He has an unnerving habit of looking at the camera—one of the cardinal sins for an actor in realist film and television. It is as if he is the only one who knows he is taking part in a television play, knows that there is an audience watching—us. The impression is confirmed when, just before the first of the two rape scenes, he turns to address the audience directly in sing-song 'Patience Strong' couplets:

> If-you-are-a-nervous-type-out-there,
> Switch-over-or-off-for-cleaner-air.
> But-you-have-to-be-very-smug-or-very-frail
> To-believe-that no *man* has-a-horn-or-tail. (p. 42)

The perpetrator of the outrage usurps the role of the neutral continuity announcer, warning us that what we are about to see is unsuitable for children or persons of a nervous disposition.

Now we are better placed to understand Alasdair Milne's objection to ***Brimstone and Treacle***. Broadcasting has been called 'of its nature both a private and a public practice', and it is this dichotomy which is central to the debate on television censorship. One prevalent BBC philosophy holds that television offers its viewers a 'window on the world' (the phrase comes from the Richard Dimbleby era of *Panorama*), making available aspects of life which lie beyond their everyday experience. But since the days of Lord Reith, the Corporation has also been conscious that its broadcasts, though transmitted through the public airwaves, are received in a private place, the home, and that this imposes certain standards and conventions: the notorious dinner jackets that Reith's announcers wore behind the microphone were simply the appropriate dress for visiting. Shaun Sutton, who headed the BBC's Television Drama Group in 1976, is quotably succinct in his account of the reasoning as it applied in his field:

> If a play offends it is an assault within the home and
> its outrage is the greater. Television invades man's pri-
> vacy to an extent he would not tolerate from friend or
> neighbour. Drama, traditionally the host of the evening's
> entertainment, is now the guest in the house. As such,
> it should assume the graces and responsibilities of a
> guest.

The feeling that the home was being violated by the intrusion of undesirable broadcast material was the driving force of Mary Whitehouse's campaign, and, drawing in its horns in 1973, the BBC accepted that radio and television drama could not be judged by the same standards as the other media: 'drama to be seen or heard at home must accept restraints which do not necessarily apply to the theatre or the cinema'.

This is one reason why *Brimstone and Treacle* could be printed, staged in a public theatre, and projected onto a cinema screen, but also be considered unsuitable for broadcast television. The other is that much of its impact derives from its being a television play: to have it performed in a public place was an unsatisfactory compromise. To transmit the play, with its sensitive content, into the home could be seen as an enactment of the intrusion it represents in its action. To make matters worse, this intrusion is committed knowingly: when Martin acknowledges the audience, he becomes a presence in the room, looking through at us from the other side of the screen. If television is a window on the world, then *Brimstone and Treacle* seems to deny its viewers the benefit of net curtains.

It follows, that, in one respect, Milne's judgement was valid: the play would be likely to outrage some of its viewers if broadcast. The next stage of his deliberation, as his letter to Dennis Potter indicates, was to balance that outrage against an assessment of the importance or triviality of the play itself. In this respect he was following the procedure which has been used in obscenity trials since 1959, when the Obscene Publications Act provided for a defence of literary or artistic merit—though he, of course, consid-

ered the play in camera and without benefit of expert testimony.

The key issue is the play's objective—in Milne's terms, whether it seeks to make 'a point of serious importance'—and to some extent this is bound up with Martin's objective. Martin is the character through whom we see: we share in his knowledge and ignorance of key information, such as (respectively) the fact that he is not human and the full circumstances of Pattie's accident (known, until the end, only to Pattie and her father). This creates a disturbing impression of complicity, which is enhanced when he glances to camera: by drawing us in like this, he makes us voyeuristic intruders in the household too. Crucially, Martin is given no adequate motive for what he does. The play opens with him searching for bourgeois prey: 'Which one? Which one will it be?' (p. 31) Selection is difficult because it doesn't really matter whom he picks: disruption is an end in itself (he acts for the hell of it, so to speak), and the choice of victim will make only a minor difference in the quality of the aesthetic experience. Martin doesn't need a motive (after all, he's a demon), but *Brimstone and Treacle* does. If we identify his mischief (or anarchism) with the values of the play itself, we must conclude that it is brilliantly and gratuitously offensive (and therefore, in Milne's terms, should be banned).

That is the misjudgment on which, presumably, the decision to withdraw the play was based. It disturbs by showing the invasion of a home, and suggesting the invasion of our own. At a more sophisticated level it disturbs, too, by making us, in our homes, identify more with the feral Martin than with the domesticated Bates—with violator rather than victim. But these disturbances are the vehicle for the point of the play, not the point itself. That point is to question the mythology of 'home': crossing boundaries is the first step towards challenging their illusory absoluteness.

Before Martin arrives at Archenfield Avenue, during perhaps the first fifteen minutes of the action, there is a lot of verbal imagery of human beings inside enclosed spaces; this helps to establish the play's concern with inside and outside, home and foreign territory. Some of these spaces are protective, like the 'metal boxes' (p. 33) which the rush-hour commuters drive home. What is significant is that more are claustrophobic and threatening. The idea that Pattie might still be sentient somewhere inside her body is one that upsets Bates: 'to be cooped up, inside your own head and be unable to-to-' (p. 34) As for Mrs Bates, housebound for two years since Pattie cannot be left, she tells her husband, 'I feel as though I'm scraping my nails on the lid. . . . The lid of my coffin.' (p. 35) 'Home' has become confining as well as secure: the absolute dichotomy between the safety of inside and the danger of outside is already starting to break down.

That dichotomy is the basis of the opposition between Bates and Martin which is the axis of the drama. As a denizen of that dangerous outer world, Martin has bestial tendencies which he does his best to keep hidden in company. Besides his unpleasant sexual propensities, he is also a sadist, and becomes injudiciously excited during a discussion with Bates of the consequences of National Front policy, consequences which lead from deportation to concentration camps to genocide: 'Think of all the *hate* they'll feel! Think of all the violence! Think of the pain and the degradation and in the end the riots and the shooting and the-' (p. 50) All this makes Bates first uncomfortable, then repelled, and finally he decides to cancel his National Front subscription—another case of the demonic man doing good in spite of himself. But, again, an absolute dichotomy is impossible to sustain. In an isolated but very striking moment early on, Bates pronounces against the driver who hit Pattie and caused her condition: 'He should be hung up. On a steel rope. . . . All I hope is that whoever did it dies full of cancer, screaming his head off.' (p. 38) Even allowing for the understandable vindictiveness of the bereaved, the steel rope is the product of a sick imagination. It shows that Bates contains the same nasty streak of sadism that we later see in Martin: it is not so wide, nor so powerful, but the point is that it is there.

Bates is more overtly concerned with matters of sexual decency. In the past he has disapproved of Pattie's friends, his wife tells Martin, and in particular of Susan, whom he calls 'a slut . . . one of those girls who'll—'. (pp. 47—8) Now, he refuses to go out with his wife for fear that Pattie will expose herself to the babysitter, and he is concerned that Martin's help should not extend to washing or changing her: 'Her brain may be damaged. But her body is that of an attractive young woman.' (p. 46) Martin puts his finger on it brilliantly when he summarizes, as if offended: 'He means that it would be *indecent* for me to see her poor, helpless body, *obscene* for me to help make her more comfortable, and *lewd* and disgusting to-to-'. (p. 46) Mrs Bates is not far from the truth when, responding to this prompt, she rounds on her husband and accuses him of filthy thoughts—even though she is wrong to go on to say that such thoughts would never enter Martin's head. For if in Martin sexuality is rampant, in Bates it is not absent but merely repressed.

Bates is exposed as a corollary of Pattie's recovery, and this gives us the hindsight to see that his despair of that recovery, expressed throughout the play in marked contrast with his wife's optimism, was in part a form of repressed hope. Martin is the unwitting agent of this exposure in raping Pattie into articulate consciousness. This is not just a somewhat unorthodox form of shock therapy: it is a brutal reminder of the circumstances which led up to the accident in the first place—which is why both rape scenes induce flashbacks to that event. It becomes clear in the final moments of the play that Pattie ran out into the road after finding her father in bed with her friend Susan. Her mental incapacity has been the invisible keystone of the Bates household, ensuring her silence about the home-wrecking adultery she has witnessed.

In short, the difference between Martin and Bates is one of degree, not antithesis, and this has implications for Bates's isolationist philosophy as a whole. Not only is it politically undesirable at its widest dilation, it is also based on a fallacy: the things that he tries to keep outside, the wild, savage traits that give Martin his true identity, are already inside, at the centre of the home he wishes to protect. At the deepest level of enclosed space, within his own psyche, the binary distinctions of inside and outside, civilization and savagery, man and beast, collapse into one another.

The development of the play, then, is away from the disconcerting surprise which, at first, we are induced to feel as we are made to see things through Martin rather than through Bates. That initial discomfort arises partly from our preconceptions about the moral nature of Martin's actions, but also from our awareness that Bates belongs to the same home environment in which we sit watching the play: he is the one we feel we should identify with, and are not allowed to. But by the end of the play, such feelings have become irrelevant.

So far I have argued that this irrelevance follows from the play's skepticism about the privileged status of home space compared with outside, and its resistance of binary oppositions between the two. But not all viewers are so responsive, or so sympathetic: some may find the entire play irrelevant, either through lack of interest or (more importantly here) through hostility. In revealing the similarity that underlies the seeming antithesis between Martin and Bates, ***Brimstone and Treacle*** asks a disturbing question about our own pretensions to civilization. This is the crucial point in the censorship process. Viewers who cannot face that question will operate a personal censor mechanism which enables them to discard the play: to them it becomes trivial, or nauseating, or outrageous, a programme unfit for broadcasting. It only takes a position of power for an individual to turn his personal, psychological act of censorship into an institutional ban.

That there is such a connection between censorship and repression is evinced by the difficulty of establishing in specific terms what it is in a work's content that will cause it to be banned, or prosecuted. Advocates and practitioners of censorship tend to prefer imprecise pejorative terms like 'filth', which save them from having to engage with the nature of the material they seek to suppress. Even the keystone of English legal censorship, the concept of 'obscenity', has been defined since 1868 as a 'tendency . . . to deprave and corrupt', without any apparent need to establish what depravity and corruption might be. Subjective terms 'define' one another in a meaningless hall of mirrors: juries who convict in censorship cases may not know much about obscenity, but they know what they don't like. Or rather, they know it when they see it, for censorship, whether personal, institutional, or public, is very much an *ad hoc* practice. Because there are no precise rules, only a body of case law, it is not always possible to foresee trouble with the censor, as the BBC Drama Group found out in 1976.

This is, of course, a very one-sided account: one might put it differently by saying that censorship is a reactive rather than a proactive phenomenon, incited by a work's transgression of boundaries, albeit sometimes ill-defined ones. The process is itself part of the effort of definition: material is suppressed when (with whatever degree of intelligence or articulacy) it reminds us of the relativity of principles which we should prefer to think of as absolute. Usually this serves to afford a degree of legal or institutional protection to culturally sensitive ideas; in modern Britain, the censor is called upon to defend from question and challenge beliefs about such things as sex, religion, and the innocence of childhood. The paradox is that, to its supporters, censorship may itself be an absolute to be protected by these means, and in a sense this was the root of *Brimstone and Treacle*'s troubles at the BBC.

This is not to say that the play deals directly with censorship—patently it does not, and in practice to ban such a play would anyway have been too embarrassing to contemplate—but in Bates it presents a prime example of the censorship mentality. His concern to keep his household undefiled, to make it a privileged space by means which the play identifies as psychological repression, is a physical correlative for the censorship process in general, and an exact analogy with the ideas used to defend television censorship in particular. As Potter had recognized, the suburban setting of Archenfield Avenue is typical 'National Viewers' and Listeners' Association' territory. 'Potter . . . loves the idea of Mrs Whitehouse,' wrote a *Guardian* interviewer in 1973. 'He sees her as standing up for all the people with ducks on their walls who have been laughed at and treated like rubbish by the sophisticated metropolitan minority.' The ducks on the wall are an especially telling detail. No doubt it would be in such households, so like that of Mr and Mrs Bates, that the transmission of *Brimstone and Treacle* would have provoked the greatest outrage: in challenging the sanctity of the home, the play calls into question the fundamental principles of the advocates of television censorship; to them, more than anyone else,

Brimstone and Treacle would have seemed eminently censorable.

The play glances briefly at its own exclusion from the airwaves when Bates remarks that he has bought his wife a colour television. Martin promptly starts a conversation about *Songs of Praise*—the epitome of 'wholesome' television to the advocates of programming suitable for viewing at home (meaning a suburban, middle-class, ducks-on-wall home). What concerned Potter about the BBC's mid-1970s trend towards a tighter control of broadcast content was that its output might become restricted to such programmes. Not long after *Brimstone and Treacle* was accepted for production, he wrote in *The Observer*:

> The [late nineteenth-century] theatre was waiting for something like moving pictures to go down into the nightmares of dislocation and unease which both scar and ennoble modern man. The television play has this freedom, and it is seriously threatened at the moment precisely because its stumbling innovations and infant awkwardness are seen by the programme planners as disturbances, which mix ill with the treacle of TV entertainment or the 'balanced' editing of TV journalism.

In the play, the irony is that Bates has bought the television set to enable his housebound wife to get out vicariously. In practice, however, all the 'window on the world' lets into their home is more of its own stuffy atmosphere, in the form of *Songs of Praise* and its ilk: the sort of 'treacle' which, Potter argued, gums up a medium which could be used for serious, challenging plays. In acting to protect Britain's ducks-on-wall homes from such a play, Alasdair Milne simply proved the thesis.

Robert H. Bell (essay date 1993)

SOURCE: "Implication Without Choice: The Double Vision of *The Singing Detective*," in *Literature/Film Quarterly*, Vol. 21, No. 3, 1993, pp. 200-08.

[*In the following essay, Bell elaborates a reading of* The Singing Detective *as the story of "a sick man's soul," "a pilgrim's progress from despair to redemption," and looks at the significance of Potter's contribution to the television mini-series.*]

The Singing Detective, the six-episode film broadcast on BBC in 1986 and on PBS in 1988, is an extraordinary achievement for which its author, Dennis Potter, has been justly celebrated. Vincent Canby hails Potter for setting "a new standard for all films. He has also, single-handedly, restored the reputation of the screenwriter, at least in television." Uncommonly sensitive to what one character calls "langwidge," *The Singing Detective* is an equally impressive cinematic vision which exploits fully the potential of a television series to focus and refocus upon a complex subject. After the six hours and forty-two minutes of *The Singing Detective,* all those faces contorted by complicated extremes of feeling seem both weird and deeply familiar, while the tableaus of the forsaken father, the drowned woman, and the observer on the bridge remain as haunting as our own dreams. Directed by Jon Amiel, *The Singing Detective* is evocatively visual, compelling us long before it begins to come clear, but—notwithstanding many disorienting narrative strategies—it ultimately makes richly satisfying sense as the hero's psychological odyssey, the discovery of what it means to be a guilty viewer and auditor.

The protagonist of *The Singing Detective* must be one of film's most objectionable, least sentimentalized figures, and he is flamboyantly unreliable. He is depicted in relentless close-ups, and (as his Detective would say) it's not a pretty sight: his skin is so hideously scorched from psoriatic arthropathy that it shocks even the hospital orderly. Though fully aware of the psychosomatic component in his affliction, Marlow seems to revel in his heart of darkness, doing everything possible to repudiate sympathy and forestall assistance. He is a geyser of smut, hostility, profanity, and abuse. In one horrible scene, perhaps his nadir, he listens to his fellow-patient George recall the glory days of '45, when British soldiers occupying Hamburg could barter cigarettes for sex: "couple of fags it was for a shag." Just then, George is arrested by heart seizure, but Marlow reacts to George's obviously critical plight by taunting and mimicking him. As George expires, Marlow, figuratively arrested by his own version of heart seizure, pronounces sentence: "You can't say you haven't asked for it, George old son" (109).

The scene is characteristic of *The Singing Detective* in several ways. We view both George and Marlow in extreme close-up, not a place where anybody would choose to be: George is grotesquely lascivious and Marlow's feverish, blistered face appears demonic. George's account is punctuated by visual interpolations, connecting his Hamburg *frauleins* with the mysterious blonde Lili from Marlow's detective story. And the hero's reaction seems inexplicably cruel. The scene is characteristically off-putting and baffling, yet comprehensible once we have re-viewed the film. A hint is implicit in Marlow's curse, "You can't say you haven't asked for it . . . old son" (109). Here Marlow has a partial self-revelation, recognizing himself, an old son, in George. Moreover, Marlow is in this scene an audience, sensing his culpability in the story of another.

As the scene transpires, Marlow and we cannot fully com-

prehend the causes or implications of such connections, so this moment remains one piece of a puzzle, and of a character, not yet made whole. Marlow lives helter-skelter in four distinct but related worlds: the hospital or "real ward," the detective fiction he has written and is reworking in his mind, recollections (especially of his tenth year), and nightmare visions. Reality, imagination, memory, and hallucination merge and cross-pollinate. Though each world is rendered with remarkable detail, clarity and power, all are ultimately subordinate to a highly-determined psychic drama.

Marlow takes refuge in his novel *The Singing Detective,* visualized as *film noir,* a dimly-lit, smoky chiaroscuro world, and narrated by the tough, side-of-the-mouth Marlow, the singing detective. Here everything is B-movie ominous: people cast suspicious glances, play both ends against the middle, and attract murderous secret agents. Camera angles are titled, as in *The Third Man,* to suggest a world off-balance. Stock characters, "strays from a bad film" (80), or allusions to great ones like *Shoot the Piano Player,* abound. This overly portentous and enigmatic thriller is wonderfully cooked up and parodically exaggerated, so that its tone is persistently "jocoserious," to borrow a Joycean portmanteau word. Odd occurrences are taken for granted: a taxi materializes at 3 a.m. or pistols fire a ridiculous number of shots.

One of the great tricks of *The Singing Detective* is to sustain our interest in this hackneyed detective story, though (unlike *The Third Man*) it doesn't really lead anywhere. The whole thriller plot is a MacGuffin, a Hitchcockian pretense, to grab and compel our attention while the real story, the psychodrama, is developing. We soon realize that action often takes place in the thriller because something is happening in the "real ward" to the author, such as when the feverish patient imagines his protagonist Binney "hot . . . burning up" (23), or when he metamorphoses pretty Nurse Mills into a torch singer at the Skinskapes Club. Though he sometimes seems to slip into his story of *The Singing Detective,* this world is usually one that Marlow, needing evasion and refuge, chooses to enter and controls. But Marlow is hardly in control: memory and hallucination are of course uncontainable, memory being at least partially shaped by what happened, and hallucination being by definition uncontrollable apparition.

Marlow (and, as we shall see, his surrogates) are far more disoriented yet much more culpable than the traditional innocent protagonist of a thriller, unknowingly enmeshed in a sinister plot, like the Joseph Cotton character in *The Third Man* or the Cary Grant character in *North By Northwest.* As in *Psycho* and other Hitchcock films, the viewer is drawn willy-nilly into the heart of darkness. *The Singing Detective,* for all its obfuscation, has a central and sustained strategy of implicating all of us without choice. Part of Marlow's plight is that he suffers from paranoid delusions and is haunted by ghosts, which the film forces the viewer to share, to piece together Marlow's condition.

Confusion is thus both a result and a primary theme of *The Singing Detective.* Potter's characters are very often puzzled, baffled, clueless—interlocutors are constantly asking, "What do you think you're doing? Where do you think you are" (84)? Though much of the film is set in such everyday places as a schoolroom or a hospital, reality is made strange, calling for a double take, including the primary and persistent question, is this "real?" The ordinary appears ludicrous or bizarre, and not just in the savagely hilarious musical number. The doctors inspecting Marlow's wretched body or the evangelical medics presenting Sunday morning hymns seem grotesque even before they are suddenly transformed into antic performers, bursting into songs by The Inkspots or Dick Haymes.

Though my analysis focuses upon Marlow's grim business, *The Singing Detective* is often mordantly uproarious, especially depicting the daily humiliations of being in a hospital, such as needing a bedpan or avoiding arousal during the greasing of private parts. Then Marlow desperately thinks of boring things, like *Finnegans Wake,* Yoko Ono, everything in *Punch,* and Ethiopian relief. Such distractions failing, Marlow tries to enter the story, where Binney is handing money to the detective as though to a prostitute, and draws a pistol from the drawer. The pistol is the wrong thing for the patient to think about, and, just when the detective is pausing to inspect Binney's picture of a Nicola-like model, the poor patient apparently climaxes. Potter's humor is always multiply linked to his themes. It's no accident that this occurs shortly after Marlow has recalled in detail the primal scene of his mother in the forest, or that the flustered nurse reproaches him like a mother toilet training a child: "I would have thought you had better control of yourself" (124)!

The joke resonates self-reflexively because the film makes a primary subject of its narrative control; much of it at first appears to be sporadic or random. The principal source of the viewer's confusion is the disjunction and multi-layering of narrative. Sounds are separated from their images; sequence is abandoned; characters lip-synch famous forties songs. While some intersections between reality and fantasy are immediately apprehensible, many other quick cuts initially appear arbitrary and cryptic. Throughout this long film, barely visible threads connect worlds and comprise thematic motifs, even when the action seems inexplicable, such as when the Russian whore Sonia startles Binney by eating his five-pound notes. "Is shit," she says. "Mon-ey is" (47). Much later, playing word associations with the therapist Gibbon, the patient links "Shit" to

"Money" (175). This excremental imagery is pervasive and coherent: the boy who deposits a turd on the teacher's table is both bestowing a gift to a mother figure and fouling both of them, for reasons that come clear.

Many implicit associations emerge out of ordinary language and gather metaphoric momentum. George, the doddering patient who cannot remember his wife's name, insists she's called "Mum," a word which has talismanic potency to shape what Marlow now experiences and imagines. The pretty nurse hears George, then brings water to the dangerously feverish Marlow: "You *must* drink. Come on. There's a good boy," and she addresses him this once as Philip, as though she were his mother. Typically, they misunderstand one another. He says "Spring," and she replies, "No. Tap water" (73). He is remembering his mother's piano piece "Rustle of Spring," which flows into his more sinister sense of water, the river into which she flung herself. Such connotations are left implicit, rather than abruptly enacted or, worse, explicated.

Incomprehensible bits fit into an elaborate puzzle, which inexorably takes shape as we perceive that everything emerges from the consciousness of the patient Marlow: "In my head. Yes. In my head" (139). Marlow's detective story vision of the woman's body being hauled from the river yields to a forest scene: a woman, later identified as his wife Nicola, seen by the boy making love on the ground with an unidentified man, casually looks up to chastise him: "Don't be a spoilsport. Why don't you join us?" In retrospect we realize Marlow's psyche, his inexorable double vision, has simply substituted Nicola for his Mum, whom he actually observed in the same situation.

With the sly algebra of a dream and the uncanny logic of the unconscious, characters are regularly displaced, standing for other figures: if Mother can't be trusted, then no woman can be. Doubles crop up everywhere, appearing as pairs or opposites (two mysterious men, two Skinskapes hostesses, patient and therapist, client and detective). Actors play multiple roles: Michael Gambon is both the ailing writer and the suave hero, Patrick Malahide is the lover of both Philip's Mum and Marlow's wife Nicola, as well as the protagonist of the mystery story. Images are constantly superimposed, frequently reiterated, or repeated with variations, so that identity is fluid and ambiguous. Doubling is of course a convention of the thriller, with its double-crosses and split lives: Binney is a double agent, the hero both a singer and a detective, and girls (the Detective remarks) are never what they seem. Binney negotiates an evening with the "hostess" Amanda but inexplicably ends up with Sonia, which is an early hint of the way a character may play a role cast for someone else. Even the aggravating hospital idiom ("How are we today?") suggests doubling.

More subtle and provocative kinds of doubling pervade *The*

Singing Detective and require continuous sorting out. At first the relationship between P.E. Marlow and his imagined story seems to be a simple case of compensation, the helpless patient casting himself as the adroit hero, which is how the sick author appears to understand it: "Don't you know who I am?" he gasps to himself. "I'm the Singing Detective—" (6-7). But a more revealing sort of bonding emerges between the real Philip Marlow and Binney. In the classroom sequence, the boy Philip eludes retribution at the hand of the schoolteacher by pointing the finger at Mark Binney, son of the man whom Philip spied copulating with his mother. Later the delirious and paranoid writer imagines Nicola plotting with a made-up lover Mark Finney to purloin Marlow's screenplay of *The Singing Detective.* In witnessing his mother making love, the boy simultaneously identifies with and is repulsed by the lover Binney, who, raising Mrs. Marlow's skirt, sighs, "I could look at that all the live-long day" (111). Fused in his disturbed imagination with this demonic double, both the boy and the actual lover deserve to be wiped out like the ladybug Philip squashes and smears on himself.

This connection between the boy's trauma and the adult's guilt helps explain some loose ends in the detective story, such as why the Two Mysterious Men are gunning for both Binney and Marlow. Eventually and comically. those trenchcoated characters in search of an author glean their own fictivity and resent the fact that they have never even been fleshed out enough to merit names: then they step out of the thriller world to pursue the patient Marlow in the hospital. And the link between the real Marlow and Binney accounts for some of the mystery character's strange behavior. Under his civilized demeanor is a rat's heart, exposed (though he won't undress) in his urge to abuse prostitutes. In a suggestive narrative dislocation we view one scene twice, with a difference: first Binney rolls off Sonia, insults her and contemplates the filth in the river; later the scene is re-enacted with Marlow standing in for Binney, apologizing for the names he's called Sonia, asking if her actions don't disgust her, and observing that the river is "full of filth" (182).

What is full of filth is the sick man's soul. Fortunately Marlow is aided in his struggle by Dr. Gibbon, the Scots psychiatrist, who is another disguised double: playing Gibbon's word game Marlow associates "You" and "Me" (175). In the elaborate mirroring of this film, the relationship between therapist and patient echoes and is echoed by the dialogue between the singing detective and Binney. Gibbon, having read *The Singing Detective,* quotes and even imitates Detective Marlow. Like a generic private·eye, the therapist seeks clues and distrusts his client, with whom he is intimately connected and desperately struggling: "You don't have to like me, and I don't have to like you," remarks the suspicious detective. Binney, terrified that the murder of Sonia will be pinned on him, swears "on my mother's grave" that he isn't guilty. Marlow snarls, like a tough psychiatrist, "Dogshit by any other name smells just as foul, my friend. And it still sticks to the bottom of your shoe no matter what you call it. Be as mealy-mouthed as you like, but not around *me,* OK? You've stepped in something nasty, and you want me to clean it up" (61).

A clue which strikes Gibbon forcefully is a disgusting depiction of intercourse found in Marlow's novel and read aloud to the patient, who furiously comments, "Oink! Oink! Oink!" (58)! The passage Gibbon reads is another variation on doubling ("skin rubbing at skin") and a process, says the novel's narrator, in which "We are implicated without choice." The author acidly comments, "The Milk of Paradise," which cues the scene between Binney and Sonia. The connection between Milk and Mother, Paradise and Forest, is crucial, for it helps us perceive the terrible implications of what Philip saw and heard. This nine-year-old, on whom nothing is lost, knows more than is good for him: having witnessed his mother's fall, Marlow spends the rest of his life punishing Binney and himself. "After such knowledge, what forgiveness?" The question haunts not only the hero but the viewer, for we are all confused, transfixed voyeurs.

The main object of her son's intense, disconcerting gaze is Mrs. Marlow, another vividly rendered figure, seen from several points on the moral compass. Banished to the hinterlands of West Gloucestershire, near the Welsh border, far from her native London, she is cramped in a tiny cabin with her husband's parents. Her father-in-law, afflicted with miner's lungs, throws up gobs of spit during tea time, and her mother-in-law openly resents her dainty airs. Her husband, a miner and featured singer at the local pub, is a weak figure, whose farewell gesture is aptly juxtaposed with that of a scarecrow, for he is a straw man, rarely opening his mouth except to sing. Miserably estranged, Mrs. Marlow plays piano, applies lipstick, and indulges a romantic impulse with the local Romeo who sings with her husband. Her regrets are poignantly conveyed by her objections to Binney's "crude talk" (115) afterwards—"I ain't a sow," she complains, providing another connotation to Marlow's oinks. The tight shots of characters' suffering are affecting. She weeps desperate tears both on the ground and later on the train by which she leaves her husband and returns with Philip to her home in London. The one detail of Philip's story which doesn't come clear is what happened between his parents: whether the affair was discovered, or she left of her own volition, we can only guess, like the boy, who would not have access to this information.

In London Philip is miserable, missing "our Dad" and his beloved trees, bothering people with his strange dialect and that penetrating stare. He keeps asking when his father will join them, and when his mother finally admits he won't,

Philip wants to know if it's because of what that bloke did to her in the woods. Stunned, she slaps him; he retaliates with the reproach, "Shagging!" (186), and runs through the underground tunnels. While the soundtrack mixes the echo of the boy's footfall and The Ink Spots' "You Always Hurt The One You Love," in a brilliant evocation of the past invading the present, the boy runs from the 1945 underground into the "real ward" of the 1986 hospital. (It is also in the underground confrontation with his mother that she and we see the first signs of Philip's affliction, a hideous lesion on his arm.)

The soundtrack also ties things together by making echoes of what we might call "binary" or double sounds: the clackety-clack of the train, the wheelchair, the boy's shoes, or Gibbon's footsteps. Voices float free of speakers, with ironic and pointed implication. Marlow's reverie of running from his Mum is interrupted by some disembodied voice, asking "Oo killed'er, then?"—the very question haunting and plaguing the patient, who keeps seeing a naked woman's body fished from the black Thames. It's Reginald from the ward, who has just learned that the author of the book he's painstakingly reading is also there, more or less—for he is a double man, both absent and present. Author and reader have a comical and pathetic conversation, which jocoseriously mirrors the relationship between film/text and viewer/reader. When Reg again asks (very simply) whodunit, Marlow replies (very truly, unhelpfully) "A swine" (188). Brooding upon his story, contemplating who might be the killer, Marlow mutters, "Well—it can't be *me,* that's for sure. . . *I* didn't do it" (143).

This stubborn protestation of innocence links the author Marlow to Binney and recalls another extraordinary sequence in the classroom. Implicated in something so fundamentally dirty, the model student and good boy behaves, as the outraged teacher says, like a pig by fouling her table, and spends the day, as it were, studying his own shit. Finally blaming his hapless classmate, he insists, "I saw him. I saw Mark, Miss. With my own eyes" (190). When he tells his distraught Mum that he saw them with his own eyes, he condemns her to an unendurable shame and ultimately suicide in the vile river. You always hurt the one you love, which of course includes oneself most of all, because, in the title of another tune Marlow croons, "I've got you under my skin." Thus P.E. Marlow's condition is a hysterical phenomenon, at least partly psychosomatic. "Chronic illness," says the doctor, "is an extremely good shelter" (97); psoriasis is the body's effort to replicate epidermis, and Binney's club is called "Skinskapes" (altered from the more emphatic "Skinscapes" in the text). Tortured by guilt, Marlow lacerates himself and lashes at women, who are always filthy sluts, lying on the ground with their legs spread. Trying, in Potter's phrase, "to be sovereign human beings,"

these characters are battlegrounds, sites of contending discourses, fields of unruly strife.

The Singing Detective derives some of its power from its clash of vituperative cynicism and profound optimism: one way to describe its narrative structure would be as a pilgrim's progress from despair to redemption. Though no television production has more vigorously rubbed our noses in offal—Marlow's leprous disfigurement and disablement, scatological imagery and an actual turd, the filthy Thames, profane language, and the primal scene of a man and woman humping on the ground—the film is aptly characterized by the Bishop of York as "classically Christian drama." Speculating sardonically on the name his mother bestowed upon him, the patient says he should have been christened Christopher, then recalls lines about Judgment Day from *Dr. Faustus:* ". . .where we are is Hell,/And where Hell is, there must we ever be—." Appropriately the patient's fever rises until he feels he's burning up, and the common salve for psoriasis is a sulphuric compound.

The patient is subjected to mortifying indignities, displayed to the callous scrutiny of the doctors with only a loincloth like some medieval saint. Exposure is his ultimate humiliation, a Dantesque retribution for the little boy whose unblinking stare unfixed everybody and unhinged his mother. His favorite oath is "Christ" or "Christ Almighty," by which he echoes his mother's "language," and indirectly implies that he cannot mend himself unaided. In panic he blurts out to the doctors, "And if I don't tell someone, if I don't admit it—I'll never never get out of it" (28). His condition seems unalterable, so long as he despairingly clings to it. He tells his fellow patient Ali that there's no place else to go and he likes it here, where Hell is: "I'm never going to leave" (30). What he believes in most of all, he proclaims, is "the one thing that can come out of people's mouths. Vomit" (40).

But other forces are at work in and on Marlow, though they come in disguise or are dimly perceived through a glass darkly. In this double vision apparently random events may be viewed as providential. Typically, Potter's spiritual theme is both parodied and enabled by rollicking slapstick; many moments are ominous and ridiculous, so that we are always unsure how to situate ourselves, never knowing how seriously to take it. Those gazing doctors burst into a raucous vaudeville version of "Dry Bones," which dramatizes Marlow's estrangement and their outrageous clinical detachment. Yet the hallucination also plants, antically but emphatically, the seed of regeneration. Shall these bones live? Or will Marlow stay imprisoned in his own hell? Ironically, Marlow castigates the evangelicals, but he will, as they urge, "Be In Time." Similarly, he contemptuously compares Dr. Gibbon, who indeed becomes the patient's savior, to Billy Graham. Like his namesake the historian, the psychiatrist has no illusions about human nature but sustains a tenacious faith in the light of reason to illuminate and perhaps dispel the powers of darkness. In this conviction the psychiatrist and the film are surprisingly optimistic. Dennis Potter has said that he depicts "characters that, *until* they work things out, are going to have the whole sting and stretch of human feelings" (my emphasis).

Though *The Singing Detective* explores the origins and elaborates the nature of the hero's plight comprehensively, some viewers may feel that Marlow's recovery is too abrupt and thoroughly affirmative for such a complex story. In some ways the final episode, "Who Done It," resolves almost like an old-fashioned thriller. Yet we might remember that Marlow the author proclaims a preference for stories with "Plenty of clues. No solutions" (140): *The Singing Detective* remains less emphatically closed and more engagingly problematic—more stubbornly double—than it first appears. Clearly, Marlow now confronts more directly his demons: in a terrifying sequence he is stalked by the scarecrow, singing à la Al Jolson "After You've Gone" ("you miss the bestest pal you ever had"), its blank-eyed, distorted, snarling face blending into that of the teacher. Next day, though, the patient can analyze his nightmare with Gibbon, who asks if the face is Philip's mother and how she died. Directly Marlow makes the connection between the scarecrow specter and the old teacher; he insists, "I didn't kill my Mum. It wasn't my doing" (211) and confesses how he beshat the teacher's table and "implicated" poor Mark Binney. His angry outburst at the teacher suggests that she represents his mother. Then fury yields to shame that he himself was not punished severely for being "a filthy, wicked, horrible" boy. Marlow breaks down and stammers, "S-orry," embarrassed by his tears and finally acknowledging his grief and guilt, something he could never do for his teacher or his Mum.

It is here that the therapy revolves perhaps too simply around a single trauma, a kind of cankered "Rosebud," and Gibbon's powers appear rather too miraculous, for he successfully urges the patient to rise and walk. In some respects—but not quite—this resembles the conventional solution one expects from a miniseries, which is perfectly willing to show all hell breaking loose, as long as it solves it in six. What saves the scene from superficiality is that Marlow's recovery is not the end-all but only a step in the process. Marlow still has demons to exorcise, and he calls upon them with characteristically malicious relish. He imagines Nicola's humiliation at the hands of Mark, and her anguished exclamation, "You're a killer. My God, you're a killer!" which Marlow now understands to be apposite to himself. The link between Marlow and Mark is reinforced when Nicola proclaims, "you use your illness as a weapon against other people and as an excuse for not being properly human. . ." (218). In Marlow's fantasy, he creeps into

Mark's flat to eavesdrop (just as he was surreptitiously present for his Mum's tryst), and as Nicola delivers these lines, her gaze shifts from Mark to Marlow, who acknowledges their pertinence by shifting his eyes. Yet even as *The Singing Detective* tends toward a tonic resolution, it continues to dramatize turmoil, for Marlow's purgation also involves violence, the imagined murder of the traitor Mark Binney, aka P.E. Marlow, by the hysterical Nicola. That her knife strikes his throat is a suitable execution for a con man and thief of words, as well as for his double, the speaker of hasty words he can't recall.

It is appropriate that Nicola (played by Janet Suzman) articulates Marlow's condition so lucidly, for she has borne the brunt of his raging paranoia and will be a primary agent of his regeneration. Like everybody in *The Singing Detective,* she is by turns baffled and inscrutable, by profession double, an actress capable of magisterial poise yet unnerved by Marlow's attacks. So skillful is the indeterminacy with which the narrative unfolds that it is possible to watch much of *The Singing Detective* under the illusion that Nicola is actually conspiring with a lover to defraud her husband. Marlow's febrile fantasies of Nicola elide with and are almost indistinguishable from her real appearances; her image blurs and blends into the erotic portrait on Binney's staircase, or becomes the face of the drowned woman. In one visit, Nicola exhorts the evasive Marlow, "It's up to you now. Look at me" (136). Speaking of his story, he insists, "it has nothing whatsoever to do with you" (136), which, like his other denials, reinforces the opposite possibility.

After such cathartic releases and piercing recognitions, the healing patient can remember more soothing memories, like his return to "Our Dad." Mr. Marlow picks up Philip at the station after his wife's suicide and, too poor to pay for a bus, walks his boy home. Holding his son's hand, he asks, tentatively and heart-rendingly, "Lovely, was her?" "Yes." "Peaceful, like?" "Yes." But all is not reconciliation and redemption, even in these apparently consoling memories. Already the boy has discovered the need for the saving lie, for his mother's end was neither lovely nor peaceful. Soon young Philip is hiding from everyone and expressing to the trees what he has really learned: "Don't trust anybody again! Don't give your love. Hide in yourself. Or else they'll die. They'll die. And they'll hurt you! Hide! Hide" (232)! The film's signals are mixed, its rapprochement only partial, its ultimate indicators consistently ambiguous. We see the boy descending the tree, a "slow and difficult climb down" (232), to witness his father's desperate wail. Running to grasp hands, the boy still resists his father's urgent expression of love, by saying that somebody might hear: that scarecrow will stalk him for a long time.

Another hallucination enables Marlow to confront his terror of love, loss, and pain. He envisions a policeman informing him that Nicola eluded the arresting officers and, of course, threw herself into the river. But daylight, which brings an actual policeman, releases him from this scenario, for the bobby is only visiting his mother. The climactic hallucination is the arrival of the Two Mysterious Men, projections of his guilt, gunning for Mark Binney and his alter ego (the chubby man might be a grown-up version of the slandered boy Mark). Like Stoppard's Rosencrantz and Guildenstern, the Two Mysterious Men resent their vague status and demand to know "Who we are. What we are" (246); denied any satisfaction, they torture and assail Marlow.

Detective Marlow to the rescue! Here it is tempting to see the detective as a boy's-eye reincarnation of his Dad: both are singers, and in one moment, Phil Marlow on the dais gestures like Mr. Marlow waving goodbye. He drills the two men, and pronounces, side-of-the-mouth, words that Dr. Gibbon might say of his patient: "I'd suppose you could say we'd been partners, him and me. . . . But, hell, this was one sick fellow, from way back when." With the bad guys dispatched, the real Marlow and Detective Marlow can reunite: "And I reckon," says the Detective, "I'm man enough to tie my own shoelaces now" (248).

The patient, able to stand "on my own two feet," rises and dresses himself, and announces to the arriving Nicola that he's "cracked this case" (248). Sporting a hat, the patient winks, as debonaire as his Singing Detective. Just then Reginald finishes his novel, which, true to formula, concludes with an embrace, to which the reader comments both aptly and naively, "Lucky devil" (249)! The exit of husband and wife is celebrated by Vera Lynn's rendition of "We'll Meet Again." The final shot depicts Philip in his tree, repeating that when he grows up he'll be a detective—and flashing his first grin. Philip's final grin implies an equanimity which of course the boy is far, far from attaining; we know he is doomed to a long, hellish struggle. And only hours before he and Nicola emerge together, the patient Marlow is caught in a desperate fantasy of violence and retribution. If his visions are cathartic, his consciousness still seems febrile, disoriented, and afflicted. For all the cascading recognitions and resounding affirmations, there are lacunae, or deliberate points of stress in the affirmative denouement. The vision of the film remains aptly double.

The Singing Detective requires such elaborate reconsideration because of its linkages, reversals, and revelations, and because of the complexity with which it shows itself regarding so many details. The obnoxious patient Mr. Hall might be seen as merely colorful, until we perceive him as a foil, a two-bit Gloucester to Marlow's Lear, in complaining that daily injustice "eats the insides out of you" (8) and makes life "Living hell" (9), and in veering from abject need to excoriating vituperation for the Nurses. So

much discourse applies doubly that almost everything begins to seem multiply-pertinent, as when the old teacher, celebrating the impending collapse of Nazi Germany, exults, "But it won't be long now, the way things are going. . . . The big day is coming" (92)! Because the patient, like the Allied forces, has been probing "Deeper into the black heart of the Evil Land" (91), his soul, the big day of his triumphant exit *is* coming. Even minor characters we might be tempted to dismiss for their apparent double talk, like the hospital Registrar, offer meaningful insights: "You ask those questions as though someone else was responsible for your condition. But no one is or, at least, in the unlikely event that someone, anyone, is—then that someone cannot be anyone other than yourself" (39). Marlow doesn't yet want to hear this, but the film persuades us that we should be hearing and seeing everything.

I have made, and I hope justified, some vast claims for *The Singing Detective.* Part of my argument has been for the literary fecundity of Potter's screenplay, which has Harold Pinter's pungent idiom of confoundment and comedy of menace, and Tom Stoppard's ironic self-reflexivity and antic delight. *The Singing Detective* also resembles the "Circe" episode in Joyce's *Ulysses:* its mixture of dreamlike fluidity and transformation, burlesque or music hall extravagance, raunchy humor, uncanny possibilities, and unsparing psychodrama. The other part of my argument, fueling my enthusiasm for the film, is that it marks a coming of age for the television miniseries, realizing its potential for process, texture, felt life; the solution of the mystery, the whodunit rationale of the story, is in this sense subordinate, the meat thrown to distract the watchdog while the burglar goes about his business. This spirit runs counter to the fundamental tactic of thrillers, to sort through and differentiate the separate elements, and to achieve a sweeping closure. *The Singing Detective* heralds something new for television, the possibility of artworks themselves full of double takes which amply reward second looks, because they dramatize the vexed process of discovery for both the protagonist and the viewer, rather than delivering an illusory sense of scope and completion. Within the expansive format of *The Singing Detective,* character can be explored, not simply defined, situations elaborated, not merely reiterated. Narrative has an organic rhythm, emerging out of the material to complete a story, yet flaunts the artifice of story telling and insists on the problematics of viewing and knowing. Perspective may be panoramic, scanning a whole community, or deep-focused, rendering inner space. The camera has time for visions and revisions, inviting us—requiring us—to view events doubly, hear things polyphonically, and comprehend implications many-mindedly.

Joost Hunningher (essay date 1993)

SOURCE: "*The Singing Detective* (Dennis Potter): Who Done It," in *British Television Drama in the 1980s*, Cambridge University Press, 1993, pp. 234-55.

[*In the following essay, Hunninger, Principal Lecturer in Film and Television Production at the University of Westminster, examines every aspect of the production of* The Singing Detective *to determine how it is able to represent "objective and subjective realities" in the extraordinary manner that he suggests it does.*]

Dennis Potter dislikes academic critics. In the preface to **Waiting for the Boat: On Television,** he wrote: 'It is no news that there is a contemptuous, hard-eyed hatred of humanistic culture all around us . . . the long, grey, ebb tide of so-named Post-Modernism, pseudo-totalitarian, illiberal and dehumanizing theories and practices lie on top of the cold waters like a huge and especially filthy oil slick. . . The Academic critic reigns, intimidatingly.

Understandably, I tread cautiously over this bridge shrouded in fog except for an overall hunch, no, conviction, that I should declare now. **The Singing Detective,** expressly conceived for a television mini-series in 1986, is a vision of life, family, love, illness, art and sex that in its form provocatively challenges and uses television and film conventions, and realises in production terms a dazzling and sensitive creative collaboration. This is not to suggest that this process, which lasted well over a year, did not have its share of tensions, insecurity, arguments and, in thriller terms, back-stabbing. Nonetheless, the series reveals a rich process started by the skill and vision of Potter which interacted with the creativity of a production team and an ensemble of actors to produce a unique series which must be the most original British television drama of the decade. My aim is to investigate aspects of this process and find clues as to why **The Singing Detective** is such an inspiring work.

The body

At 9.00 p.m. on 16 November 1986, 8.12 million people turned to BBC1 to watch 'Skin', the first 75-minute episode of **The Singing Detective.** Philip Marlow's 7-hour odyssey had begun and continued its powerful emotional unravelling for six weeks, ending on 21 December with an audience of 6 million. The initial reactions from television critics varied from enthusiastically cautious to the totally engaged. 'You didn't know where you were with Dennis Potter's **The Singing Detective:** and it made it all the more exciting'. 'Still, this is not the week to linger over the down side of television, for it was the week that launched Dennis Potter's first new work for the BBC for eight years, **The Singing Detective**—an effort as remarkable as most telly presenters are unremarkable. It has been worth the wait'. ' . . .

reserve the following five Sundays as well. That way you will be sure to see every moment of **The Singing Detective,** probably the most compelling piece of original television fiction that I have seen in 16 years as a critic'.

What did the audience and these critics react to? Piecing together the construction of the opening episode which starts the manipulation of the multi-layered odyssey of the main character—Philip Marlow—we see how Potter introduces the themes, images and motifs that are to reveal Marlow to us and to himself.

The ingredients seem familiar enough: 'a misty, moody, atmospheric, "thrillerish" winter's evening in London, 1945'; we see a labyrinth of dissolving wet alleyways and pavements, 'a pathetic old busker is playing an achingly melancholy "Peg O' My Heart" on his mouth organ', the well-dressed Binney wearing a trilby and wrapped in an overcoat appears down the 'misty paving stones'; the busker inserts a bar of 'Deutschland über Alles', a coin and a message are exchanged: what is this—treachery? So far the cluster of film noir images seems as familiar as Harry Lime, 'but anyone beguiled into settling down to enjoy a piece of pleasantly stylish pastiche was to be sharply shaken up'. [Lucy Hughes-Hallet, *London Standard,* 17 Nov. 1986.] Binney descends into the Skinscape Club, a side-of-the-mouth voice-over, 'it was a rat-hole. . . Into the rat-hole. Down, down, down. And the one thing you don't do when you find yourself in one of those is to underestimate the rats in residence—' Suddenly we are in a daytime hospital in a skin-and-cardiac ward—the music changes to 'I have you under my skin'. Mr Hall moans to Reginald about the tea trolley. Reginald pays little attention—he is reading what we later discover to be a copy of **The Singing Detective.** The central character Philip Marlow is being wheeled back to his bed. 'Marlow is glowering morosely, crumpled into himself, and his face badly disfigured with a ragingly acute psoriasis, which looks as though boiling oil has been thrown over him'. The pain is underlined by the black porter who takes Marlow's smock off, 'hoo, man, razz', he stares at Marlow's 'cracked, scabbed, scaled, swollen scarlet and snowy skin'. Marlow is a writer, we have guessed this with his voice-over: 'No, sir. The way those creatures gnaw and nibble can do a lot of damage to your nerves full stop new paragraph. . .' Cut. Disorienting tilted film-noir shots as 'Binney, now appearing to be a nervous and hesitant businessman not certain that he is going to have a good time, or even that he should' descends into the Skinscape bar. Back to reality, and the hospital, as Marlow in his wheelchair composes the story.

BARMAN (*voice over*): G'evening, sir. What is your poison? What'll it be, sir? Ouch-h-!

Marlow, jolted by a bump on the chair as it trundles along the corridor, winces with pain.

MARLOW (*to himself, hiss*): Concentrate. Concentrate. . .

The bar at Skinscrape's reasserts its occupation of the screen. . . Binney looks from side to side, along the empty stools, and empty spaces which fade off into arches of near darkness.

BINNEY: Well. Company for a start.

A big close-up of a bell being pressed and suddenly Amanda, a young hostess in sailor's suit, is sitting next to him.

AMANDA: Hello, sugar.

BINNEY: Hello yourself. Sugar. Would you like a—

AMANDA: Champagne, toots.

BINNEY: Yes. Ah. Of course. Toots.

And so we get clues that Potter is exploring, as in **Double Dare,** the relation between the writer and his creation. Marlow imagines and creates and 'imitates exactly what he mostly cannot possibly have heard'.[Here as above and continuing though the essay, the author is quoting from Potter's **The Singing Detective.**] He is an unlovable, churlish detective writer who, helpless and paralysed by psoriasis, can only escape into the interior landscape of his imagination. As Potter says, 'That's the way you have to deal with physical pain, you know. You have to sort of stand outside it and say, "OK destroy me if you must, but I am going somewhere else."' Marlow, left alone, hums, 'I've got you under my skin', we dissolve to Hammersmith Bridge, a medium close-up of a naked drowned woman as she is pulled from the Thames, Amanda's voice-over says, 'A girl's got to live hasn't she?' On the bridge 'there is but one person, there now, in a trilby, his coat collar turned up, distantly lonely like the man in the old cigarette advertisement. ("You're never alone with a. . .") It is Marlow, 1945-style, without psoriasis or seized joints. He is watching the recovery of the body with a burning intensity of expression.' Throughout the series, again and again, dead, naked female bodies are pulled from the river. Are they new bodies or repeated memories? The labyrinthine story continues with parallel threads of images that smartly and wryly keep us guessing. Is this a Chandleresque thriller, a psychological drama, a hospital soap? Whatever it is, we are hooked as Potter 'swings with seeming effortlessness through time and space, carrying us repeatedly . . . into the condition of a drama, where action and reaction, normal chronology and

the shared assumptions of existence, dissolve. Visually everything remains sharp and clear, but a new internal logic dictates the way that the obsessive images come and go'. [Nicholas Shakespeare, *The Times*, 22 December 1986.] Back in the hospital, Marlow's relationship with Ali, the cardiac patient in the next bed, is affectionately offensive, Alf-Garnett style.

MARLOW: That's you cardiacs. You heart patients, nig-nog. I'm *skin,* Ali. Skin!

Ali lights Marlow's electronic lighter, the flame shoots out.

MARLOW: I could see the headlines. 'Another Asian Burnt to Death.'

The sexual tension first established in Skinscape is now transferred to the angelic nurse Mills who comes to relieve Marlow's pain by greasing him. The curtains are drawn and erotic polythene gloves massage Marlow's thighs in big close-ups.

Marlow's face fills the screen with intense concentration. . .

MARLOW (*voice over*): Think of something boring— For Christ's sake think of something very very boring—Speech a speech by Ted Heath a sentence long sentence from Bernard Levin a quiz by Christopher Booker a—oh think think think!—Really boring! A Welsh male-voice choir-Everything in *Punch*—Oh! Oh!

Nurse Mills is suddenly in the Skinscape Club as a singer crooning 'Blues in the Night'. Her singing and the massaging build and when she finally says in her role as the club singer, 'Sorry. But I shall have to lift your penis now to grease around it', all the paunchy middle-age men in Skinscape cheer and bang their palms on the tables as Marlow ejaculates into nurse Mills' plastic glove.

MARLOW (*off*): I'm—ah—nurse. I'm very sorry. It—that's the one part of me that still sort of functions. I do beg your pardon.

Cut to the Skinscape Club, Binney discovers the busker from the opening sequence murdered and hanging in a cupboard. Lights of a train approach through a tunnel—a woman's voice yells, 'Philip, Philip.' Suddenly with a dynamic fast-moving camera track, the hospital consultants arrive—they hardly hear Marlow's agony, 'God! Talk about the Book of—the Book of Job—I'm a prisoner inside my oooh own skin and bones'—and just as suddenly the consultants burst into Fred Waring's Pennsylvanians' musical number 'Dry Bones'. The number 'transforms the oppressive hospital ward into a hallucinating night club with high-kicking nurses and bossy doctors made into chorus boys'. Big tilted close-ups of Marlow convey his disorientation. Again the train approaches through a tunnel and the consultants' entourage sweeps away. Big close-up of Marlow. On soundtrack we hear Marlow's father, Mr Marlow.

> MR MARLOW (*voice over*): Philip! Phil! Philip! Where bist? Philip—Why doesn't thee answer?'

> The Forest forms itself out of Marlow's dead eyes. The small boy is in the treetop, high above the rolling lesser trees.

Unblinking close-ups of Marlow, back at the Skinscape Club Binney speaks Russian, another naked female body is pulled from the river (she seems slightly different from the first one), now all the patients from the hospital ward are standing on Hammersmith Bridge looking down. Back at the ward, the senile Noddy climbs into bed with the paralysed Marlow and starts humping him. Marlow, helpless to push off this sexual attack, yells for help. The amused night nurse brings the situation to order. During the day a registrar probes,

> REGISTRAR: It must be hellishly ticklish to work out a plot in a detective story, I should think. I suppose you have to scatter clues all over the place.

And the episode draws to a close with Ali insisting on giving Marlow a sweet. As Ali leans forward, he has a massive heart attack. The bag of sweets, in a big slow-motion close-up, falls from his hand. Emergency! Intercut with big close-ups of Marlow, the medical team assault Ali's body, a fist blow to the chest, electric shocks, mouth-to-mouth resuscitation, an adrenalin injection. The cardioscope shows no pulse. Ali is dead. Marlow reveals no emotion; not until later when he is given one of Ali's sweets. Then suddenly he cries like a child. Back to Philip in the treetop.

> PHILIP: I'll find out, I'll find out who done it.

End of episode 1.

'If all this sounds complicated, so it is—but in a wonderfully entertaining way. Here we have not some old novel adapted for television, but an original work created specifically for the electronic medium by a master craftsman who has served a long and productive apprenticeship. Today, Potter uses television with the familiarity and assurance that Dickens brought to the writing of novels'.[Christopher Dunkley, *Financial Times*, 12 November 1986, 23]

The form in all its complexity is stunning, but the Regis-

trar is right. Potter does scatter clues all over the place. There are clues about sex, family, treachery, guilt, illness, creativity, death, and they point to motifs throughout the work. These motifs are not just a fragmented patchwork, but relate to Marlow the patient, to Marlow the imagined detective, to Marlow the boy in the treetop, and reveal the fundamental psychological significance of Marlow as a whole character. These motifs also give a unity to six episodes which becomes increasingly evident to the viewer, and this growing awareness runs parallel with Marlow gaining understanding and self-insight. '*The Singing Detective* is an outstanding case in favour of the unique qualities of the TV serial . . . The spacing out over time of the serial . . . allows the plots and motifs to stay with the viewer and grow in his/her mind'. [George Brandt, from unpublished lecture at Leeds Polytechnic, 4 June 1991]. It also allows for a scale in dramatic complexity which is comparable to the novel, while the structural tightness of a television play or feature film is comparable, in scale, to a short story. As the director Jon Amiel explained to me, *The Singing Detective* 'involves you in a central mystery. Why is this man Marlow the way he is? The series had the faith in its audience to say, this human mystery is of such consummate complexity that you'll want to stay involved and continue to watch. And they did. The lesson I learnt, with great humility, was never ever underestimate your audience'.

The vision and plot

In the *Radio Times*, Dennis Potter said, 'The whole thing began to take shape several years ago when I was feeling rather sad about the death of the studio TV play. It seemed to have gone for ever, but I wrote down some ideas I had, a series of scenes in a hospital ward which I thought were quite promising. I just wanted to make use of some of the comedy that takes place in a hospital'. Potter's first ten plays between 1965 and 1968 were substantially created in the television studio; he knew what was possible there and felt the hermetic artificiality suited his dramatic focus. 'What I liked about the studio was that you could actually get inside people's heads more—if you weren't writing naturalism, that is. And because the temptation for the director was so severely limited, he couldn't embroider and run away with it'. Potter also knew a lot about hospitals. Although he strenuously denies that the events are autobiographical, it is well known that Potter has suffered from severe psoriasis since 1962. The hospital experience and the comic ideas were the starting-points. 'I had no idea what story [the hospital ideas] fitted into, but the ideas stayed with me and much later they fell into place'.

A great deal is revealed about Potter's dramatic construction and use of juxtaposition by the fact that he should decide to develop his 'comic ideas' through a tragic middle-aged detective writer—a character physically paralysed with pain and as mentally shipwrecked as Hamlet. It would be 'a journey in which a man in extreme pain and anguish tries to assemble the bits of his life'. As in much of his previous work, Potter is concerned with 'interior drama' and explores the man's life by juxtaposing complex strands of internal emotion about the present, the past, fantasies, artistic creation, and neurotic insecurity. Rapidly displacing scenes represent his objective and subjective realities. Marlow's development is structured as a psycho-analytical investigation, 'the unearthing of buried memories is consistently linked with the idea of detection in which information blockages have to be overcome. The author's carefully planted narrative blockages (retardations and digressions) are useful not only in sustaining dramatic interest: they mirror Marlow's resistance to analysis and self-insight'.[Brandt]

Potter deliberately avoids the narrative clarity of a chain of events in a cause-and-effect relationship set in chronological order. Yet if we step back from dazzling dramatic and technical innovations in *The Singing Detective,* there is a clear journey. We start with a man who is paralysed, whose body is out of control, who believes in nothing and who, after probing all the elements of his life in seven hours of television time, walks from the hospital having overcome his physical adversities and having found a way through his emotional labyrinth. The illness incites the crisis and starts the complex causal conflicts within Marlow. As Potter said on *Arena,* 'It is the illness which is the crisis. It is the illness which has stripped him . . . in dramatic terms it needed exactly that—that starting point of extreme crisis and no belief'.

Throughout the exploration of Marlow's complicated realities and fantasies, 'we alway[s] return to one point of contact,' Potter says, 'the man in a hospital bed. . . That's what it is really all about'.

The syndicate

In early 1979 Potter and producer Kenith Trodd had a two-year contract with London Weekend Television to produce six television plays. When the director of programmes, Michael Grade, announced in July 1980 that, after having produced three plays, LWT would not proceed with the arrangement because of 'insurmountable difficulties' and 'generous budgets being heavily overspent', Potter hit back in an article in the *Daily Mail* entitled, 'Why British TV is going to the dogs: and I'm going to California'. Potter did go to California to work on rewrites of his script *Pennies from Heaven* for Herbert Ross's film version, released by MGM in 1982. There, other sorts of barriers were up. 'When I was working at MGM in Hollywood I realised that the studio based all narrative forms entirely upon category. At the beginning of a project they would ask what particu-

lar bag it was in. Was it a detective story? Was it a musical? Was it a romance? They saw it as a marketing problem, even before the first shot,' says Potter. 'That sort of thinking throws a terrible carapace over the writer and one of the things I want to do in *The Singing Detective* is break up the narrative tyranny'.

Potter has long argued for plays that challenge the viewer's passive consumption of naturalistic television drama.
—*Joost Hunningher*

Potter has long argued for plays that challenge the viewer's passive consumption of naturalistic television drama. In 1984 he wrote, 'Most television ends up offering its viewers a means of orientating themselves towards the generally received notions of "reality"—that is, the way things are, which is more or less the way things have to be. There is not much space left for what it is that "Art" can do'. Insisting on the artificiality of the television play—'that a play is a play is a play'—his declared aim is to stimulate and thus 'to disorientate the viewer', to break out of 'the prevailing, unexamined "naturalism" of the medium as a whole . . . [which] continually works against the alert attention which any writer wants to evoke in . . . his audience'. As early as 1965 he assaulted the naturalistic mode with schoolchildren played by grown-ups in *Stand Up Nigel Barton,* a device which he repeated in *Blue Remembered Hills* (1979). In *Pennies from Heaven* (1978), as in *The Singing Detective* (1986), he threw characters, without warning, into miming songs of original thirties and forties recordings which comment, ironically or ambiguously, even sympathetically, on the dramatic moment.

In *The Singing Detective* Potter uses a growing arsenal of non-naturalistic devices—a range of provocatively integrated stylistic conventions, a range of acting styles and even some actors playing multiple roles, cross-cutting and flash-backs to moments of memory, actuality and fantasy, dancing and singing, etc. 'The advantage of this dramaturgic technique is to energise the viewer—he/she has to put in some effort in order to follow the story'. It is 'creative participation by the audience—they cease to be just spectators "consuming" but are asked to question that very process of consuming by the entertainment of the spectacle itself'.

Jon Amiel says,

> The script is written with dazzling confidence and certainty and an extraordinary feel for the power of the cut. Dennis understands how to juxtapose scenes in a way that gives a tremendous sinewy energy to the story.

Many writers put in a lot of camera directions, extreme c.u. or cut to w.s. . . . Dennis never does that, there are never any camera directions at all. However . . . when a close-up is necessary he will describe an event in such detail that the only conceivable way to match the intensity of that description is with a close-up.

Referring to the tea scene with the mother and the Gran in the second episode, Amiel gives an example from the shooting script:

> 'Swot! a gobbet of spit hits the grate and sizzles'. It both graphically describes the smell and event and sound and you have to find a visual way of matching it. . . . So what Dennis's writing does, rather than insist on or direct you to do something, is to inspire you to do something with the same passion and same specificity. That's what's so remarkable about his script.

The contract

Kenith Trodd is the prolific producer whose first Potter production was *Moonlight on the Highway* (1968) and who then produced most of his television plays up to *The Singing Detective.* He told me that *Pennies from Heaven* was a clever mixture of video tape and film, while *The Singing Detective* is all film and that was one of the big differences in creative taste between 1976 and 1986.

> By 1986, I would not have been able to get a director who was willing to work on a hybrid, even on a play by Dennis Potter. In 1976, it was the norm. Dennis by 1986 had not caught up to changing norms, because he had expected, and indeed wrote, all the hospital scenes, expecting them to be made in the television studio. He wanted to go on the prototypes of the sitcom for those scenes and expected the rest in film.

Trodd had always wanted to shoot on film and he remembers saying to Potter that it was necessary because he couldn't find a good enough director. Trodd feels that directors like Piers Haggard, who in 1976 directed *Pennies from Heaven* and could successfully integrate studio video and location film work, had become in the 1980s almost an 'extinct breed'. He told me that *The Singing Detective* was turned down by

> the cream of the British film industry, such as it was, Stephen Frears, Richard Eyre, Malcolm Mowbray, Pat O'Connor—nearly all on the basis that they couldn't interrupt their movie careers to do a Dennis Potter sitcom. So I got turned down by all these names and I then had to start looking, as I've often done, for less

tried talents. . . Amiel had brought me one or two projects . . . but not very much. He'd been a script editor: and unlike some directors, he had an attitude towards the script as well as to the visual realisation. . . I thought . . . it's probably Jon, and I took a chance . . . not knowing if he was going to live up to the job or not . . . it was a gamble.

Jon Amiel told me he was surprised to get the job.

> I know that the script was offered to five or six people who were more eligible or more distinguished than I was at the time. So Ken Trodd first came in and asked me to read the scripts and said, 'It's not an offer, there are other people, but have a look and see what you think'. I remember clearly reading these scripts, and by the time I was half-way through the first script my hands were shaking as I was turning the pages. I knew for an absolute certainty, because all of my training had been basically in script development [he had been a literary manager in the theatre and a story editor in television], that I was reading a masterpiece. The thought of directing this thing filled me with complete terror and the thought of not being asked to direct it filled me with as much terror. After having read the six episodes, I went to Ken Trodd, and in a surprisingly calm voice I said, 'Look, I think they are wonderful. I think it is a masterpiece, but I think A,B,C,D—all of this work needs doing on the scripts. The sixth episode is not the sum of the five previous ones, the singing detective story needs some detailed work on it, the relationship with Nicola needs looking at—and so on' . . .I couldn't believe that I was really saying these things. But the five more distinguished directors had all turned it down and the project evolved to me. And this is often the way things happen. Most people get their breaks that particular way.

After Amiel was appointed to direct in September, he had a series of meetings with Potter. The first two were exceedingly difficult. Amiel felt insecure but 'floundered on'. Then at their third meeting both men seemed to put aside any misgivings and launched into a 'truly joyful' collaboration. They had six further meetings before Amiel received a telephone call from Potter saying he was going to rewrite all the scripts right from the beginning. The pre-production schedule was very tight (two and half months) and Amiel remembers saying, 'Dennis hold on, not the whole script!' Potter insisted and then,

> while under attack from this awful disease psoriasis, he launched into one of the most extraordinary processes I've ever witnessed, he rewrote one episode a week for six weeks. He wrote with the most astonishing and unerring editing instinct I have ever come

across in a writer—he rejigged, rebalanced the whole thing and after that even went back to rewrite the sixth episode again.

Amiel found that the more he worked on rewritten scripts the more confident he felt about the production. As he told me, 'my conviction that I was working on a masterpiece only grew'.

Further enquiries

Designs

In *The Singing Detective* the expressive resources of film—decor, costume, make-up, visualisation, lighting, camera and editing rhythms, sound, music, acting—were used very creatively to realise the script and to enhance characters, emotions and the significance of each scene. Considerable creative contributions and collaborations are necessary to achieve such a unity. Besides interviewing the producer and director, I discussed this process with the designer, Jim Clay, and the make-up designer, Frances Hannon.

Jim Clay told me that 'making *The Singing Detective* was a wonderfully uninhibited process'; there was total creative freedom with very little interference from management. After long discussions with Jon Amiel about characters, plots and sub-plots, set designs evolved and models were built. 'Jon's precision is a treasure. He is hard work, but you don't mind it, because he's always pushing you a bit further'. Each set developed a great deal: Amiel never just accepted the first one offered—but this always led to better solutions, Clay says. 'For example, it took a long time to evolve the "Dry Bones" sequence. Dennis had written it in a black void with skeleton costumes . . . which we thought was terribly old-fashioned—so we wanted to use some hospital elements and struggled for a long time to find a solution for transforming the hospital into a dance sequence'. He remembers that finally they hit upon the solution as Jon Amiel, Quinny Sacks, the choreographer, and he sat having a cup of tea one afternoon in a hotel room in the Forest of Dean. 'One of us said, "Let's make the hospital into the club", and the three of us yelled, "That's it!"'. Suddenly it appeared obvious, and so in episode 1

> we were leaping backwards and forwards to the Skinscape Club, we should transform the hospital ward into the Skinscape Club and use neons for bars on the windows; it would become partly a prison, partly a club. The club was his escape, the hospital his prison. So the whole idea then developed into this huge dance routine with nurses dressed as waitresses and so on. We had done a million storyboards and a million

sketches on variations, but nothing felt right until we hit on this.

Although people tell Clay that they recognise his design style, he doesn't think of himself as 'having a recognisable style from one film to the next'. However, his back ground in architecture encourages him to design spaces in terms of how light would affect it—that is 'where I place doors, windows and openings. . . I try to make these as realistic as possible—even in a stylised set'. He also is realistic in terms of surfaces and how they are painted and what goes into a set. In his designs he thinks about how the set will help reveal the characters. 'I learnt a lot from working with the director Mike Leigh on how to dress a set for character. For example, he'd come on the set of *Four Days in July* and ask, "Who framed that picture on the wall?" and I'd say, "My assistant, Martin," and he'd say, "No, no, which member of the family?" So I learnt to work closely with actors and to dress a set with characters in mind'.

A set Clay particularly liked in *The Singing Detective* was the scene in the working-men's club. Amiel's brief had been that it should have an overriding sadness about it. They had found a church hall which was a perfect location, but how to make it look sad?

> It is easily done when Marlow is sitting there in the derelict club on his own with cobwebs and dust sheets over the piano. But when the whole community is there, it's another matter. I can't tell you how we did it. In the end, I used boring things like texture and colour, shape, placing windows in certain places, one pane of the window broken. They seemed fairly mundane things, but I guess as a whole they come together to make a dramatic space.

Given the effective lighting and camerawork and the strong smoky atmosphere of the scenes in the working-men's club, I was surprised to learn that Jim Clay did not have constant planning meetings with the lighting cameraman, Ken Westbury. Clay felt it was really a matter of Ken Westbury making the most of 'the lighting opportunities' built into the set.

In terms of camera style, Jon Amiel said that he wanted to use a very mobile camera technique, which thematically works effectively to suggest the detection that runs throughout the work. 'For the genre thriller I evolved with Ken Westbury a distinctively old-fashioned style of lighting . . . using hard source lights, key lights, pin spots, charley bars to get angles of light, a very distinctive noir lighting style'. To begin with, Amiel had wanted to shoot the detective story in black and white, but Potter persuaded him not to, saying, 'Don't do it in black and white, it gives everybody a very easy signal, when you're in the past and when you're in the present, it breaks the thing into two halves like a walnut'. Amiel also realised that working in short fragmented scenes meant that each scene had to be direct and powerful and graphically almost 'cartoon shots'. 'I knew that each scene had to hit hard, had to say, what's the essence of this scene, what is the emotional centre of it, what does it want to deliver? Then focus everything in delivering that moment as vividly, powerfully and truthfully as I could'.

On the whole, Potter did not get very involved in the production process. He came to the set only a few times and after seeing the rushes on tape would talk to Amiel every four or five days. Amiel took this as a remarkable sign of Potter's confidence in his direction of the script.

Cover-up

In **The Singing Detective,** getting under a character's skin starts with what was put on it. The outer casing of the characters provides clues about the different time periods, the stylistic leaps and the various multiple echoing roles that some actors play. The artistic contribution and skill of a department like Make-Up is of considerable importance. For example, Marlow's physical surface in the hospital appears as painful as the turmoil we discover underneath it. As John Wyver reported in *The Listener,* 'The dominant, almost overwhelming image of the film is of Marlow in a hospital bed, his outer layers scraped away, with raw, exposed tissue fighting across his face and body and the peeling areas of parched, translucent, dead skin'.

Frances Hannon, the make-up designer, told me, 'If you didn't have make-up in **The Singing Detective** it couldn't have worked . . . there would be no progression. . . Make-up is a very good indicator of things happening that people may not lock into but read subconsciously'. Before **The Singing Detective,** Hannon hadn't done 'anything of great standing', but Ken Trodd started sending her scripts as early as six months before the start of production. The greatest challenge for Hannon was the make-up for Marlow in hospital. Believing that make-up should be 'as real as possible', she began by researching the characteristics of psoriasis. She saw the top medical consultants in England and Wales plus a variety of drug companies who were all very helpful, showing her patients, slides and records. She told me that there are hundreds of forms of psoriasis and that, after looking at different forms, she and Jon Amiel agreed that Marlow's form should be arthritic psoriasis—physically the type of psoriatic symptoms that Dennis Potter had suffered from in the sixties until medical advances improved the control of the disease. 'Once I knew what it had to look like, it took me a long time to find out how to make it work. I had to find something which anyone's skin could take every day and not with an allergic reaction. . . It was a cre-

ative process of elimination'. In the end Hannon designed a complicated 'recipe' for Michael Gambon. She started with a water-based spray to seal the skin and then used six different colours to shade it; that was covered with petroleum jelly, talced, then painted again, sealed, plastics were added to give a three-dimensional look, and she used further sealers and then finished the surface with hot gelatin to give it a crusty finish. The process would take four hours to complete, and Hannon and the make-up team would start on Michael Gambon's make-up at 6.0 a.m. to be ready by 10.0 a.m.

> The make-up had to be filmed in the first four hours of the day . . . because after some time, due to the heat of the lights and Michael's varying body temperature, the gelatin would not stay hard and crusty, and [would] go soft. We used air-conditioning units around the bed to try to keep the temperature down and took them away just before each take.

Michael Gambon's acting technique added to the heat problem.

> Michael has a very expressive and mobile mouth, and with all that shouting and screaming he did, the scabs would be hanging off his mouth at the end of each take. We'd all rush in to repair the make-up. The make-up had its time limit. . . Michael Gambon was frequently uncomfortable, but took it all in his stride.

Hannon had plotted the cure element, so that Marlow's skin condition improved over the six episodes. Despite shooting out of sequence, it was scheduled to minimise intermixing Marlow with severe psoriasis and mild psoriasis and as the singing detective. She said that artistic collaboration went on continuously 'and we needed only one meeting in the beginning to know if we were all on the same wavelength'. With Amiel encouraging and co-ordinating decisions, the various departments evolved close working relationships 'to achieve the same mood and look'. For example, Hannon's collaboration with Ken Westbury, the cameraman, was important. Every night Westbury would describe the lighting for the following day and leave a set of the same lighting gels that were being used on the scene. Hannon then lit the make-up room with these gels, so that she could see how the filtered lights would affect her make-up design. 'If I hadn't had this information, Ken could completely destroy my work if he used, let's say, a red light instead of a blue one'. Having agreed on the severity of the make-up on Marlow after some film tests on Gambon, Hannon told me that Amiel had second thoughts. 'The night before we started shooting, we were in the hospital in Tottenham [where the ward sequences were shot] and Jon came up to me and said did I think we should take Marlow's psoriasis down slightly. I think he suddenly had the fear that the audience would be so revolted by the make-up that they wouldn't even look in'. Hannon agreed that slightly less would be enough.

Musical stings

A headline in *The Sun* wittily stressed the musical elements of *The Singing Detective* with 'Marlow's Singing in the Pain'. As in *Pennies from Heaven,* the songs 'distract, tickle, upset', but now they do more than provide an ironic counterpoint to the dramatic action: all relate to the young Marlow's 'troubled childhood' when he heard them 'drifting up the stairs from the crackling wireless' and thus 'connect and underline' different narrative strands in the work.

When, for example, Mr Hall and Noddy mime the words to the Mills Brothers' 'You Always Hurt the One You Love', the associations in Marlow's head lead from memories of a shallow experience with a prostitute, to the working-men's club where his father and Binney (with Mrs Marlow on the piano) are singing the same song, then to the woods where Mrs Marlow is in tears after her adultery with Binney, to Mrs Marlow on Hammersmith Bridge and finally to her naked body pulled from the Thames. The Mills Brothers' song is ironic in its jazzy harmonies, deadly accurate in its 'trite sentiments', and it also effectively binds the narratives.

Even the songs that are not mimed have thematic significance and reveal dramatic contrast. After climbing to the top of his tree in the Forest of Dean, the young Marlow says the Lord's Prayer and on the sound-track Bing Crosby croons 'Don't Fence Me In'. As the camera sweeps back from the forest, we cut to a radio in Gran's house where Bing's song continues and, in contrast to the boy's vision of freedom, we see Mrs Marlow imprisoned by the domestic and social conventions of matrimony. 'Putt thik racket, off!' instructs Gran.

In the final episode, Potter uses the lines from 'The Teddy Bears' Picnic'—'If you go out in the woods today, you'd better not go alone, It's lovely out in the woods today, but better to stay at home'—as a moment of Marlow's self-recognition. The song binds his memories and fantasies—the fictional detective singing, the mother and Binney on the ground, the young Marlow running away, the loneliness of the father, the hospital experience—and it finally releases 'all of Marlow's fatal traumas. . . The lyric's power is therapeutic enough to lift the arthritic Marlow to his feet'. Amazed, he stumbles forward and calls out, 'Look, I did it! I walked! I can walk!'

Since the nineteen songs dominate stylistically, Amiel was at first unsure about what music to use for the title theme and dramatic transitions. Eventually he decided that since Potter was playing with derivative styles, he should echo it and turn to an effects disc library. He 'got in over fifty albums of these weird generic titles with short pieces called something like "shock blood corridor" or "stirring chilly crescendo ending in a tympani climax" . . .[he] came up with about forty different bits of totally generic music, which was cut together'. The stings and transitions were assembled into a compelling soundtrack which, as in the title sequence, draws the viewer in and underlines the suspense of the investigation.

Casting accomplices

In their themes and explorations, other Potter films, such as *Secret Friends* and *Blackeyes,* explore some of the same territory as *The Singing Detective,* but in emotional terms none achieves the depth of character sustained by Amiel's cast. I was intrigued to find out how Amiel chose and prepared actors. He gave me some clues.

'I didn't find the casting difficult. I found I was like a kid in a sweet-shop, because suddenly I had these absolutely wonderful roles that I could take to actors whom I had admired for many years and finally say, here is a role worthy of you, Bill Paterson, Alison Steadman, Ron Cooke, Michael Gambon'. Amiel relied on instinct, often casting an actor for a very large role 'simply on the basis of a 20-minute conversation'. Sometimes he had a specific idea, 'but many times casting would actually surprise me'. He gave me an example: 'I had no idea what the father should look like, but at the time I was casting for the second of the mysterious men, I had already cast little Ron Cook for the first one, I knew I wanted someone either very tall or fat to play the other one—I wanted them to be a complete odd couple. Michele Guish, a casting director, had said there is this marvellously funny guy who is 6 ft 4 inches tall and was in *Guys and Dolls* playing Big Julie, and in came Jim Carter for the role of the second mysterious man'. Amiel talked to Jim for about 15 minutes: 'I listened to his lovely sad brown voice . . . his big earlobes made him look tremendously vulnerable and gentle'. He remembers watching him walk away down the corridor 'with this slightly stooping walk that rather tall men have and feeling an odd mixture of sadness and tenderness and knowing that this was the feeling that I wanted the father to evoke. I had not been able to visualise the father until Jim walked in'.

Amiel believes in the importance of rehearsals with actors before shooting. Many producers balance slipping schedules and financial problems by cutting rehearsal periods. Amiel pushed hard for extra rehearsal time and Kenith Trodd gave it to him. The series was in production for five and half months. Amiel had two weeks of rehearsal at the beginning and a further two in the middle.

In rehearsal period, I used to allow the characters [the actors] to explore the relationship with each other so that a feeling of familiarity that you get within families evolved . . . a sense of the things that people express, but don't need to say. We also worked very hard on the text, a great number of alterations were made to the text during the rehearsal period.

Jon told me, 'The great value of rehearsal is that it allows you to make that kind of vulcanised weld between the actors and the text where you can no longer see where the character begins and the actor ends'.

Characters, motives and further evidence

The Marlow family's disintegration sits like a knot in the stomach. The young unblinking Philip, played with an air of inquisitive innocence by Lyndon Davies, takes in the beauty of the forest, but also the human cruelty and treachery around him. His indirect revenge on the son of his mother's lover is chillingly determined. Again, his confused cruelty in abandoning his mother in the underground only surfaces slowly as the guilt for his mother's suicide becomes clear to the older Marlow. We've heard the sound 'motif' of his mother's voice yelling after him, 'Philip, Philip', from the first episode. Associated with that cry are the lights of the train in the underground that, like a hearse, probe Marlow's subconscious again and again. The young Philip's unblinking stare haunts the series. The same stare that watched his mother's infidelity with Binney in the forest in episode 2 also watches his father in the last episode throw back his head and let out 'one long and strange and almost animal-like cry of absolute grief and despair. Philip, in cover, watches this terrible release of anguish with wide eyes, and yet no obvious expression'. It is a riveting mixture of bereavement, guilt, innocence and emotional withdrawal. Earlier, the father, played by Jim Carter, had taken young Philip's hand in the forest,

MR MARLOW (*suddenly*): I love you, Philip. I love you, o'but. With all my heart.

PHILIP: Shhh!

MR MARLOW: What—?

PHILIP: Somebody might hear us!

The young Philip holds back and cannot trust himself to feel love ever again. Later we hear the vow that he took then, 'Don't trust anybody again! Don't give your love. Hide in yourself. Or else they'll die. . . And they'll hurt you! Hide! Hide!'

As viewers, we long for him to reach out to his vulnerable

father. He cannot do it. In the hospital, Michael Gambon as the older Marlow says 'Dad—?' and we remember the echo in the crowded working-men's club in episode 2, where a grown Marlow in his hospital pyjamas appears (at the end of a slow pan) watching his father singing and imitating bird-calls. He says, years later, what he should have said then in the forest as a boy.

MARLOW: That was *my Dad* doing the birds! That's my Dad on the platform—(*shouts*) Dad! Dad! Over here, o'butty! Come over here! Dad! Thee's know how much I'd care about tha—.

But the past and present are not merged and the scene switches quickly to Marlow alone in the empty, poorly lit working-men's club. 'The upright piano on the platform is draped with long, dusty cobwebs'.

Michael Gambon, as Philip Marlow, balances the complexities of the drama of the family's disintegration, the unravelling of his psychological turmoil, the cruelty of his revenges, the sharpness of his wit, the softness of his own human vulnerability with the fictitious wry cynicism of the singing detective. As the detective in episode 3,

MARLOW (*thinks*): There are songs to sing. There are feelings to feel. There are thoughts to think. That makes three things. And you can't do *three* things at the same time. The singing is easy. Syrup in my mouth. The thinking comes with the tune—so that leaves only the feelings. Am I right? Or am I right? I can sing the singing. I can think the thinking. (*Suddenly savage*) But you're not going to catch me feeling the feeling. No, sir.

His cruelty is sudden and deadly. He turns on the oppressive, revolting George (Charles Simon) for disgusting him with stories of 'shagging Frow Lines' for a few fags. The stories set off Marlow's own memories of his mother's infidelity in the woods, and when George suddenly has a heart attack, the sequence intercuts George's final life struggle with Mrs Marlow and her lover violently 'shagging' in the woods and with Marlow in his hospital bed. And equally cruelly, Marlow claws at Nicola (Janet Suzman), who in his suspicious mind is as unfaithful as his mother and uses sex for money and advancing her career. Gambon gives us much more than just the character's turmoil and revenge and the cool elegance of the detective, he also has us laughing, as is clear in the scene with Ali and the lighter, and sobbing, when suddenly Ali is no longer there. Gambon deserved much critical praise for his performance and he got it. Even the *News of the World* wrote, 'Michael Gambon had me reeling from laughter to tears. That speech of despair, Got under my skin'.

Janet Suzman, the ex-wife Nicola, matches the emotional

onslaught with a sad humanity and understandable self-defence. There are obsessive echoes among the ex-wife, the mother and the whores. Women and sex draw Marlow in and, at the same time, push him away. Philip's mother, played by Alison Steadman, is the main cause of the complexity and the play's turmoil, but she is no villain. Her love and concern for Philip are clear. She is a metropolitan character miscast in the Forest of Dean community. In ironic contrast to Philip's father's cuckoo and birdsong imitations, she plays the 'Rite of Spring' on the piano. The powerful tea scene where the dour Gran (Maggie Holland) goes on about a 'lovely bit o' plum' while Grancher (Richard Butler) emphatically spits into the grate has us on the verge of retching with Mrs Marlow. She explodes about 'being squashed up in this poky hole' and accuses her husband of not being 'any sort of a man'. (Philip's vulnerable Dad is not the man to stand up to his mother and wife.) Mrs Marlow's escape from this misery is into the woods with Binney. Alison Steadman's portrait merges with the Lili Marlene character in the fictional story and transfers to the sexual film noir motif of the women's naked bodies being pulled from the river (the mother, Russian Sonia and Nicola are all echoed in that recurring image).

A key role in freeing Marlow's helpless but fertile mind is that of Dr Gibbon, the psychiatrist, cunningly played by Bill Paterson. Dr Gibbon sees that Marlow has a psychosomatic illness caused by repression of painful childhood memories—that his psychological development is reflected in his illness, his writing and his relationship with Nicola and other people. Eventually through the probing and goading of Dr Gibbon, Marlow is able to overcome his paralysis and, in the last episode, he stands for the first time and dances with Dr Gibbon. Potter undercuts the dramatic impact of the moment with an ironic musical number as the two men mime to Ella Fitzgerald and the Inkspots singing, 'Into Each Life Some Rain Must Fall'. It is Dr Gibbon who gets Philip, as Nicola says, to 'come down from his tree'. But walking is not enough, psychologically; Marlow still has one score to settle—that is to resolve the struggle between Marlow the writer and Marlow his creation—the Singing Detective. With typical Potterian irony, the creation—the Singing Detective—tops the creator—Marlow the writer—with a bullet drilled into the forehead.

But these are the heavyweight parts, and in contrast there is much light and amusing comedy acting. The mysterious men, played by Ron Cook and George Rossi, are dressed up to suggest suspense and evil, but in fact add buffoonery to the detective narrative. They are Stoppardian characters looking for roles. As they say in the last episode, 'We're padding. Like a couple of bleed'n sofas', 'Our roles are unclear. . . No *names*, even. No bloody handles'. From the beginning we have known that this team was playing at being gangsters and are as innocently dangerous as Wilmer

in *The Maltese Falcon*. Mr Hall (David Ryall) and Reginald (Gerald Horan) also continue their endless humorous bickering about tea, bedpans and hospital company. And Reginald, of course, embodies Potter's playful device of reading the book of *The Singing Detective,* which allows him the opportunity of recapping the events for us at the beginning of 'Pitter Patter', episode 5. The relationship Marlow has with nurse Mills is in contrast to the tormented one he has with Nicola. Nurse Mills is never fished from the Thames. Marlow says to her, 'You are the girl in all those songs'—and so she is. Nurse Mills, played by Joanne Whalley, is an uncomplicated, sensuous 'angel of mercy' who delivers mental, physical and sexual comfort. Joanne Whalley's eyes stare down sympathetically at Marlow. She injects a strong life-force into the play. While most of Fleet Street debated the graphic details of the adultery scenes, *The Times* at least recognised the alluring danger of nurse Mills to male middle-aged viewers. 'Joanne Whalley's eyes ought to carry a Government health warning'.

Patrick Malahide plays three characters: Binney the spy in the detective story, Mark Binney who seduces Philip's mother and the modern film producer Finney who steals Marlow's book and wife. We think of him as the slightly pinched evil-hearted catalyst who pushes forward Marlow's real and imagined events. In all three parts, Malahide gives the character the air of predatory treachery suitable for generating injury and neuroses in the young and old Marlow. We never do find out if he smuggled Nazis out of Britain. But does it matter?

There is another kind of treachery in the frightening authoritarian country-school teacher played by Janet Henfrey. As in **Blue Remembered Hills** and **Stand Up Nigel Barton,** Potter shows us 'childhood innocence [as] unspoiled original sin' filled with snivelling, hypocrisy, betrayal and guilt. Janet Henfrey echoes a strong performance in **Stand Up Nigel Barton** and creates an almost religiously fanatical character who will have created traumatic psychic damage in Philip and in generations of her pupils.

The cast of **The Singing Detective** made their own powerful contribution to the play, achieving that invisible seam where the character begins and the actor ends.

Who done it?

The more I investigate clues as to why **The Singing Detective** is such an inspiring work, the more I discover 'further surprising revelations' in the creative journey of making it. The journey certainly seems elliptical, but that undoubtedly is normal in making any television drama involving sixty or more people. Talent does not drop out of the sky, it is fostered and encouraged. Although the series was a relatively low-budget production (about £400,000 per programme), it is not surprising that it was made at the BBC in the mid-eighties when the organisation encouraged confidence in its programme-makers and was comparatively generous in germinating and realising new work.

Potter's script mapped the terrain, but the achievement was the locking together of many artistic instincts. So Who Done It? Well, like Poirot in *Murder on the Orient Express,* I conclude, 'They were all in it . . . it was a perfect mosaic, each person playing his or her allocated part'. The process was a creative collaboration which made us sit up and watch television drama, not as an apology for a mini-movie, but as a creative and powerful dramatic medium. ***The Singing Detective*** was inspiring because it showed us the dynamic possibilities of television drama. Nancy Banks-Smith in *The Guardian* summed it up with, 'If the BBC and its Empire lasts another 50 years, men will still say, "This was one of their finest plays."'

As Poirot would say, 'Having placed my solution before you, I have the honour to retire from the case'.

Boyd Tonkin (review date 17 June 1994)

SOURCE: "The Last Blast," in *New Statesman and Society,* June 17, 1994, p. 40.

[*In the following brief obituary Tonkin comments on Potter's life and influence.*]

The green remembered glades from Dennis Potter's Forest of Dean childhood nestle on the edge of the Cotswold Euro-constituency, which Labour came within 4,000 votes of capturing this week. Among his many roles, the late playwright gave new voice to the survival of a historic rural radicalism. He helped explode the lie that only the metropolitan "chattering classes" really bother about social change. Potter was many things; but he was never trendy.

In spite of these roots, though, his journey up what he called "the tick-tick-tick examination ladder" pulled him up fast into the core of national culture. His early plays went out at prime-time, on BBC1 and even on the long-forgotten Rediffusion. Can you imagine a Potter premiere on Carlton?

That centrality, with all its opportunities for preaching or prodding, has vanished for ever from TV drama. Potter knew very well what his niche as a licensed irritant permitted. This recognition—even, sometimes, his amazement at what he got away with—shines through the two books Faber has just published. "Potter on Potter" (edited by Graham

Fuller) blends commentary and interviews on all his major work, with a complete filmography. "Seeing the Blossom" reprints last year's MacTaggart Lecture blast at Birt and Murdoch, along with the already legendary encounter with Melvyn Bragg in March and an earlier conversation with Alan Yentob.

Pluralism and profit have made the cliché come true. We really shall never see his like again: a TV "auteur" with access to the hottest slots for audacious work that rattled middle England and yet spoke from it as well. In the zap-happy future of few owners but multiple channels, market forces won't mind a bit if some tiny pay-per-view or cable outfit can finance the odd daring Potter-ish film for a minute audience.

Should we care, since radicals now assume the idea of a unitary culture was just another ruling-class fraud? As Potter said, "the BBC of my childhood was . . . paternalistic and often stuffily pompous". But it didn't slice up its publis into labelled consumer strata. "Those plummy voices spoke as from another land, and yet they did not seem to be trying to make one a stranger in it, let alone a shopper."

Of course, market-driven fragmentation does open some doors. They may lead, say, to the Asian-interest magazine, the feminist chat show, the gay shopping street. The trouble is that the handful of operators with real clout go on growing as their target groups shrink and scatter. Hence Potter's scarily intense hostility to Murdoch ("I would shoot the bugger if I could"). Fans of media diversity often overlook the wood in their passion for the trees. That is not an error the prophet from the forest ever made.

Christopher Hitchens (essay date August 1994)

SOURCE: "Potter's Field," in *Vanity Fair,* Vol. 57, No. 8, August 1994, pp. 36, 38, 40.

[*In the following essay Hitchens assesses Potter's life work, his achievements as a writer and his contributions to television and to English society in general.*]

You might care to picture this. A man—you may tell by the deference paid him that he is a celebrity of some sort—is being escorted into a television studio. The technical staff is tense and expectant, and the interviewer is grinning with nerves. All this the audience sees, because in a concession to *vérité* the preliminaries are being broadcast. A certain latitude is permitted to the interview subject, as is obvious from the drink (plainly alcoholic) that is placed before him. And the ashtray. And the flask, which isn't obvious until the subject calls attention to it by asking, "Is that too conspicuous there? I'll only need it if there's any spasms."

The flask contains a cocktail of liquid morphine. And the ashtray is because the patient is past caring about the sagacity of any surgeon general. This is a deathbed interview transferred to a modern setting and a modern set. Dennis Potter knows that he may be gone—really gone—before most people see the show. He also knows that he'll need pain-management techniques to get through the hour. We are watching a dead man on furlough.

Dennis Potter wrote **Pennies from Heaven** and **The Singing Detective.** He did the screenplays for **Tender Is the Night** and **Gorky Park.** He was once called, by a friend of mine, the Arthur Miller of his generation. When I told Arthur Miller himself that Potter was dying, he was instantly and terribly shocked.

"Dennis Potter was the first writer and perhaps the only one to take television as a new form and to use it as a form of handwriting," he said. "His work is tremendously important for the future, because people can see that the medium need not dictate the mere formula that it so often does now. Potter could convey a true *interior,* as the films sometimes do and as literature does. He gave television drama its own real personality."

Miller, of course, went from triumph on the stage to a later distinction as someone adapted for movies and for television. With Dennis Potter, the evolution was in the other direction. It was only in 1988 that critic Vincent Canby decided to place all his chips on one square and say (under the heading "Is the Year's Best Film on TV?") that **The Singing Detective**—which put Chandler's Philip Marlowe through his paces as a child, a fantasist, and an analysand—was "better than anything I've seen this year in the theater (live or dead)." He went on to compare it to *Citizen Kane, Napoléon* and *The Invisible Man.* Joseph Papp's Public Theater made a special effort to put the series before the public. Despite having been chosen by only a few PBS stations on its initial run, **The Singing Detective** made people Potter-conscious. So will the deathbed interview when it is broadcast in this country later this year.

Britain's leading arts broadcaster, Melvyn Bragg, best known to Americans as the host of the *South Bank Show,* made the interview as a self-contained special and sold it to Britain's Channel Four this past spring. The difficulties of recording it were daunting. Potter's body temperature was fluctuating so much that extra filters were needed to cool the lights, which also had to be kept at the farthest possible distance from him. They could not schedule "breaks," because Potter might (and in fact did) need to resort to the morphine bottle at any time.

"As we settled down," Bragg recalls, "we talked and both of us made that silent pact that can happen before an interview—the decision that we were going to go flat out for it." For days after the show aired, letters and telephone calls came streaming in, and Potter's gritty defiance of extinction became a surefire topic not just at dinner tables but in pubs—partially vindicating his dream that television, properly used, could become the "true national theater."

If you yourself have ever indulged the fantasy of being given, say, six weeks to live, you might like to check your dreams and needs against Potter's flinty stoicism. Emancipated by his intimacy with awaiting death, he elected to keep the appointment by demonstrating an unusual combination of bile and sweetness. Old antagonists such as Rupert Murdoch (with whom Potter has been competing for years for the soul of mass culture) received their blasts of grapeshot. "My cancer, the main one, the pancreas one, I call it Rupert, so I can get close to it, because the man Murdoch is the one who if I had the time—in fact, I've got too much writing to do and I haven't got the energy, but I would shoot the bugger if I could."

On nostalgia, the trope at which he always excelled in his writing and which he once memorably termed "a second-order emotion," he had this to say about his first published book (a study of the British "affluent society" called **The Glittering Coffin**): "Typical young man's title, you see, typical piece of that sort of humbugging, canting rhetoric which young men—bless their hearts—specialize in. I think we should always look back on our own past with a sort of tender contempt."

The arresting feature of Potter's appearance was his unfeigned ability to speak of himself essentially in the past tense, but without self-pity or sentiment. He had been apprenticed to tough-mindedness in a very hard school. Born to a coal-mining family in the Forest of Dean, which is a sort of English Appalachia in its geographical remoteness as well as its bald-faced lack of amenity, Potter escaped to Oxford as a clever scholarship boy and wrote his first successful play—**Stand Up, Nigel Barton**—about the hidden injuries of class as they inflicted themselves on the upwardly mobile.

Moving to Fleet Street and on his way to making a success of journalism, he was attacked—"savaged" might not be too strong a word—by the vile and incurable affliction of psoriatic arthropathy. Viewers of his terminal interview gradually noticed that his hands were like gnarled bludgeons and his skin flaky, but that was because he was in relatively good shape. At the worst moments of his illness, he could only move his lips. His own description of the disease:

It was like one of the plagues of Egypt. With 100 percent psoriasis you lose control of your body temperature. You semi-hallucinate. You're in danger of septicaemia, and therefore you're in danger of dying. People say they've got psoriasis, and they mean they've got some really uncomfortable itches, which don't hurt and don't make the skin flake off. With the extreme psoriatic arthropathy that I have you can't find a point of normal skin. Your pores, your whole face, your eyelids, everything is caked and cracked and bleeding, to such a degree that without drugs you could not possibly survive. It was physically like a visitation, and it was a crisis point, an either-or situation: either you give in, or you survive and create something out of this bombsite which you've become—you put up a new building.

He was 26 when he was first flayed by what he later came to call his "shadowy ally." The poet James Fenton recalls visiting him in the hospital two decades ago and seeing piles of human-skin scales lying on and under the bed. But there were medications available that could keep Potter going. Powerful medications, which were later discovered to have carcinogenic side effects, and which eroded his liver and pancreas and slew him at the height of his powers, at the age of 59. A tough sentence. That's about 33 years on the cross—the very place where Potter hung Colin Blakely in his irreligious play *Son of Man.* But, trite though it surely is to say so, the Potter oeuvre is by no means exclusively bleak. This is partly because Potter understands that illness forced him to discover and develop his real talent.

As he once told Graham Fuller of *Interview,* "The need to recreate myself coincided with finding the way to do it, which was through drama. I could have gone the 'theater' way or the 'novel' way, but something—maybe the guilt and anxiety about the gap between my origins and what I had become—steered me towards television. The palace of varieties in the corner of the room."

To that palace of varieties, which, as he said, was unlike the theater in that it brought "dons and coalminers" together to watch the same output, Potter devoted his life. He hoped to redeem the mass medium from the lowest common denominator, and did succeed in building a large audience for serious plays.

At one level, it's not hard to see why Arthur Miller esteems Potter so greatly. *Pennies from Heaven* concerns a traveling salesman of no great polish (played by Bob Hoskins) who hawks sheet music and suffers from the sexual inhibitions of his wife. The corny, uplifting messages of the ballads he peddles nag the salesman, who is called Arthur Parker, to contrast wife with life and life with lyric. Songs such as "The Clouds Will Soon Roll By" come to sound positively dire. Thus, by evoking the music of the people

and the easily accessible idioms of mass entertainment. Potter was able to hold attention for something more than a soap opera. Miller told me he'd seen the play on a cassette in London and wondered aloud why such fare was impossible or unthinkable for a mass market in the U.S.A. But actually it was *Pennies from Heaven* that, with the help of director Herbert Ross, allowed Potter to jump the Atlantic gap and catch Hollywood's attention.

An obliquely related theme, of father-son embarrassment and love, is one which obsessed Potter all his days. Bookish and studious where his father was not, and uneasy about deserting his "roots" in the chronically unfashionable mining community, Potter confessed to Melvyn Bragg in the dying interview that, having so often told his father to leave him alone, he now wished he could say, "'Come on in, Dad, for Christ's sake. Sit down and let. . . It doesn't matter about that now.'" This was a rare moment of relative clumsiness in Potter's speech, which generally came out in proper sentences, delivered in a fine Gloucestershire accent. In *The Singing Detective,* the same claim on the dead is made but with much more subtlety, and in words that no one who has lost a parent, or who can imagine such a loss, and who has seen the show is likely to forget:

> Are you saying my dad is dead? But no—but you see—there's so much that I want to say—I need to talk to him, very badly. . . . But he was there—he was!—My lovely dear old dad was there—that was him whistling. I heard him—I heard him! All the birds in the trees—all the love in the world—I heard him. I *saw* him.

You need an exquisite handling of words to avoid the mawkish, and to get the best out of the semi-articulate. (It was almost impossible to digest the news that, two months after the interview, Potter had to face the death from cancer of his wife, Margaret, who had been his nurse, ally, and comrade for 35 years. Potter himself died a week later, on June 7.)

Potter was a worker, in every sense of that word. Like many English radicals, he possessed a stubborn residual Puritanism that despised and distrusted those who took, or who found, things easy. Also in that tradition, he was conservative about matters such as family, countryside, money, and probity—hence his fierce hatred of things such as Murdoch's instant tabloid commercialism. With his mitts like suppurating claws from disease, he insisted on writing everything in longhand and at night. Whether composing or adapting for the screen, he never objected to putting his labor through another draft unless he thought the pressure was to soften or to blur (or to spare genteel viewers: he had several titanic rows with the BBC on this front).

Restless in his search for new and nongimmicky means of

catching and holding attention, Potter had great success with simple but daring ideas. For his television play *Blue Remembered Hills* (which is almost the perfect title for the evocation of nostalgia) he wondered how to get over the traditional problem of the child actor. Children, he realized, don't make long speeches, and you can't use flashbacks for people with no real memories. But you do need, and children can deliver, "continual, twitchy action."

His solution was to have his group of seven-year-olds played by seven adults. It was a nerve-racking moment in the history of television drama, as he recalled, because of "the panic of the first five minutes, when I think, My God, is this—Colin Welland's great fat ass and great shorts waddling, sploshing through mud, making airplane noises, and chewing on an apple—I thought . . . it's going to be one of those dire, dread embarrassments, because it ain't gonna work." But the audience saw at once that they were watching children at play, and *Blue Remembered Hills* is one of the reasons Potter is actually known by name at street level in England. (Another reason was the hatred shown him by the tabloid press, which cordially returned his dislike' and used to attack him for obscenity, blasphemy, and elitism. "Television's Mr. Filth" was the title he earned from one Murdoch organ for his play *Blackeyes,* in which he tried to explore feminism for the first time by depicting the exploitation of fashion models.)

> **In spite of endless reverses in his personal life, and constant battles over censorship and the limits of good taste, Potter never gave up on the medium of TV and displayed toward it a fidelity which one critic likened to that of a Labrador retriever.**
> **—*Christopher Hitchens***

In spite of endless reverses in his personal life, and constant battles over censorship and the limits of good taste, Potter never gave up on the medium of TV and displayed toward it a fidelity which one critic likened to that of a Labrador retriever. This was because, in his culture-starved childhood, he had always had the little window provided by the public-service radio broadcasts of the BBC.

He never forgot the chance encounters with a wider world that this box afforded him. The bigger box, he reasoned, must be even more important and even more worth fighting for. In his last extremity, he battled to finish a play called *Karaoke,* which took on the idea of virtual virtuosity. "There's the music, and you have your little line, you can sing it, and everything is written for you, and that is the way life appears to a lot of people and feels to a lot of

people. . . . You haven't got much space, and even the space you've got, although you use your own voice, the words are also written for you."

The dumbing-down attempt to script everybody and everything, and to identify the process as popular culture, had what I was going to call an undying foe in Dennis Potter, who was secure enough in his plebeian roots to contest the idea that "the people" wanted what they got, and therefore got what they wanted. I can remember once having him to dinner, along with some very clever television and literary types, all of them used to getting their way on talk shows and at supper tables. Potter didn't *say* all that much that evening, but his presence in the circle had the amazing effect of making people less glib. They would cast an anxious glance his way before launching and then abandoning some tried and tested piece of hilarious chicanery. I don't mean to make him sound forbidding; it was just that integrity can be as infectious as bullshit. How apt that he should have wasted no material, and enacted his own passing on the small screen, to which he gave his life.

Richard Eyre (essay date 3 May, 1996)

SOURCE: "The Man in Short Trousers," in *New Statesman and Society,* May 3, 1996, pp. 18-19.

[*In the following essay, Eyre offers personal impressions of Potter, places him in television history, considers his work among his contemporaries writing for the stage, and discusses the aptness of Potter's work for the medium of television.*]

I first met Dennis in 1978, just before I joined the BBC as producer of *Play for Today.* We were in Edinburgh for the annual television conference and somebody introduced us. I remember advancing my hand and Dennis glaring at me. "I don't shake hands." No explanation, no "sorry", just this childlike, abrasive, bullying quality that's absolutely characteristic of the man and his work.

Of course, I already knew Dennis's work. One of the first TV plays that really made a mark on me was *Stand Up Nigel Barton* (1965). I didn't go to the theatre as a child because we lived in Dorset, which was more or less a theatre-free zone, and my family weren't particularly interested. So this play struck me with great force. Although my social background was very different from Potter's, when I went to Cambridge I found I was as remote from the world of my parents as Potter was from his. He caught this dislocation between generations with extraordinary vividness.

Then when I arrived at the BBC, I shared an office with Ken

Trodd (producer of many of Potter's plays) who was curator of conscience in the BBC drama department. He had this constantly fluctuating relationship with Dennis and had just produced *Pennies from Heaven* (1978). When I saw *Pennies,* it seemed to me that Dennis had matured into a writer with an unmistakable voice. He had created a television form which was completely singular and he had done it within the confines of what the BBC offered in those days.

The limits were to do with length, budget and scheduling, and they were limits that don't exist in the same way in the theatre. Before Potter's big works, the only TV drama series were versions of classics or quasi-soaps. So to take a popular form and a popular medium and use it as a means of expressing sophisticated emotional, social and political ideas was extraordinarily adventurous.

Later, I was asked to direct several of Dennis's scripts, including *The Singing Detective* (1987). Unfortunately, when this came up, Alan Bennett had already offered me his play about Kafka, *The Insurance Man.* But Dennis was a hard man to say no to. We met at our mutual agent's and I explained that I had this other script that I was committed to doing. Dennis said: "You're making a terrible mistake. I'm offering you the chance to make television history." No irony. Wonderful. He was absolutely certain that *The Singing Detective* was a remarkable piece of work. And it was.

In the end, I never worked with Dennis, though I was well aware that his relationship with directors was fairly vexed. He always claimed that he wasn't a difficult writer for a director to deal with. That's true, as long as the director regarded himself as the medium through which Dennis expressed himself.

It wasn't a question of whether my ego would succumb to the considerably mightier force of Dennis. But it is true that in a medium where the director, by definition, has to have a point of view—by determining, literally, where the camera goes, what the audience look at, how they look at it—it is an anomaly that Dennis sought to retain that control.

If you look at his scripts, they not only have an emotional point of view and an authorial voice, they have a literal point of view. He tells you where to put the camera, where to cut. For a lot of directors, this is extraordinarily inhibiting.

But if you're working with a man like Dennis, you have to get over that and ask yourself: do I have anything more interesting to say than Dennis? In effect, he directed his own work in the spirit that typified all he did: curmudgeonly, emotional, generous, mean-spirited, splenetic.

So I was surprised to be asked to look at the script of *Karaoke.* In the end, it became clear that Dennis's deathbed wish had been for the play to be directed by Rennie Rye. Anyway, given the day job, I wasn't available. But I did read the script—it was a sort of painting-by-numbers approach. The means of telling the story, the form of telling the story, couldn't be separated from the story itself. So, in that sense, you would simply have to take Dennis's script and translate it into three-dimensional terms. His presence from beyond the grave is still that powerful.

But there are parts of *Karaoke* that are really extraordinary. Within a scene you can go from the sublime, if not to the ridiculous, then to the banal.

This is entirely characteristic of Dennis's work, which has a sort of childlike quality. It is a world of innocence, a sort of Arcadia which exists in all his writing. A sense that there was once a time when the world was uncorrupted, but that even in this mythical time, the world carried the seeds of its own corruption. That's the seam he explores throughout his work.

In a way, it's all part of Dennis's messianic, evangelical side. In the early 19th century, he would have been a Wesleyan preacher. You can hear this in his language, it's directly descended from the King James Bible. All his work comes across as both a personal story and a fable of the postwar years because the narrative of Dennis's life coincided with the hope of the 1945 government, the subsequent loss of the promise of New Jerusalem and all that went with it. It's a very, very potent British myth.

What makes Potter's work simultaneously attractive and disturbing, even repellent to some people, is the way he connects the personal and public in that rasping, insistent voice. Like all the most successful art, it's personal, but it reaches out and helps us make sense of the world.

I was born in the year in which *Blue Remembered Hills* (a 1979 Potter play currently playing at the National Theatre) is set. And I, too, feel a terrific pull to the allegory of the golden world, the New Jerusalem of the postwar years, and the tragedy of the loss of that Arcadia.

It is, in one sense, a distinctively Christian vision. But from another angle, Potter is clearly a writer of the left. He believes in social justice, has a vehement contempt for privilege, and is fuelled by a kind of class resentment.

He resisted any kind of classification. He'd say his concern was the ambiguity and fallibility of human beings. And his work is full of paradox: alongside the spleen, ill-temper and boorishness is the radiant optimism of so many of his main characters. Perhaps most memorable is the Bob Hoskins character in **Pennies from Heaven.**

Karaoke and **Cold Lazarus** are absolutely distinctive Potter, but they're not late plays with that brooding, elegiacal quality you get in, say, *The Tempest.* This is not the work of a man going gently into the good night. Artistically, I think these plays don't rank with **Blue Remembered Hills, The Singing Detective** or even **Brimstone & Treacle. Karaoke** is not brilliant by Potter's own standards, but it's extremely entertaining stuff.

We also cannot deny the importance of Potter's defiant stand against corporatism. Here, at his death, he demands a bargain that BBC 2 and Channel 4 work together, as if he's saying that it takes someone to die before the people who run television will be fully open to a writer's cantankerous and subversive view of our world. Dennis defined the limits and powers of expression of a new medium. Television drama hadn't really existed before, and he made it something that was wayward and idiosyncratic, unlike the movies or theatre.

I find it difficult to say where you put a Dennis Potter piece alongside the great plays of the contemporary stage, but I'd rank him alongside Tom Stoppard or Harold Pinter: a singular voice who chose to write for this weird medium. Some people might say it isn't a medium, just a hybrid, but he made a virtue of the fact that it is a hybrid.

A few of his plays will certainly live on in stage versions, like **Blue Remembered Hills** and possibly **Brimstone & Treacle.** But some of his finest work, such as **The Singing Detective,** could not work on the stage. I'm sure, though, that we'll be watching television re-runs of Dennis's work for a long time to come.

Blue Remembered Hills is right for the stage because, formally, it is very, very simple. It just has one quirkish device, which is that of adults playing children—a quintessential Potter idiom. In a sense, Potter was always an adult who kept his short trousers on. That was what made him so perceptive about the child in all of us and so regretful about the way in which the child within us is corrupted. It's like a fairy story in that it gives you the impression that you know it before it happens. It is full of truisms about childhood that are also true.

Quite where the genre of the TV play goes beyond Potter is less clear. Today, the culture is strongly quasi-filmic; that's where the liveliest voices are. Irvine Welsh's *Trainspotting* is an example, as is Jimmy McGovern's work. But when you're aiming at a first run in the cinema, the costs are that much greater.

Still, you can never predict genius. I'd say the most startling new voice in the English-speaking theatre is Tony Kushner. His *Angels in America* has Potteresque ambition. It's about the millennium and Mormonism and un-American activities and Aids. It's hard to see that kind of range and ambition emerging in television, because the culture that is seeking to encourage those wayward individual voices—writers with a strong point of view—doesn't exist. But then, if you'd said six years ago that the greatest new work for the English-speaking stage would come out of America, where theatre was moribund, everyone would have said you were crazy. Talent like that emerges unexpectedly, like the eruption of a sunspot.

In the end, Potter's most important legacy is his voice. That's where the argument about his talent still polarises. When someone like A. A. Gill (the *Sunday Times'* TV critic), who's just a journalistic yahoo who deplores the strength of Potter's voice, begins accusing British television of being sycophantic towards him, he's missing the point. Dennis, along with writers like Jack Rosenthal, Alan Bleasdale, Peter McDougall, Charles Wood, Alan Bennett, Jimmy McGovern and Trevor Griffiths, came through as authorial, strong voices. This extraordinary organisation, the BBC, somehow enfranchised these voices, allowed them to express themselves.

Today, there's a mounting anxiety about impartiality in broadcasting. But impartiality is the enemy of art. We must beware of any temptation to confine individuality of voice and authorial power to the theatre: it demands to be there on television, the most popular medium. Dennis was the most conspicuous champion of that tradition of writing for television, and he conquered territory that will be lost if British television follows an American course.

We must hope that, in these days of opportunistic culture, there are still enough people out there with the will to recognise and enfranchise another Potter, if a Potter were to come along.

Fay Weldon (review date 3 May 1996)

SOURCE: "Sex-lies on Videotape," in *New Statesman and Society,* Vol. 9, No. 401, May 3, 1996, p. 20.

[*In the following review, Weldon looks at the gender issues raised in* Karaoke *and* Cold Lazarus, *and evaluates the merit of these plays.*]

I watched four Potter **Karaokes** and **Cold Lazaruses,** at one sitting, and was, let me declare myself at once, absorbed, moved and exhilarated by the experience. Glued, as they say (or used to say when such things were more common), to the set. Writers' television once again.

What a relief. The technology serving the words on the page; actors obedient and trusting; producer and director as the writer's servants, not masters, not uppity, claiming moral authorship. A return to the old days, the opening years of the television age, when the box in the corner was seen as the key to social reform, personal enlightenment, and, believe it or not, the refreshment of the soul.

Took Potter's death to do it: as in his stage play **Son of Man** (1969), Jesus, that bolshie shop steward, has to die nastily and publicly to get a fairer deal for mankind. And how both stage-managed their own deaths. . .

Potter's narcissism was outrageous, his vanity noticeable, the contents of his head not overly likable, his distaste for the flesh quite horrible, his attitude to women neurotic to a degree, but what the hell—he was funny, bitter and alive— and the bitter liveliness has merely been exacerbated by the ironies of his death.

Now there's immortality for you. Potter offers us his head—wittily and literally in **Cold Lazarus,** frozen and detached in cryogenic suspension, 400 years in the future, still open for inspection—and it does not behove us to be ungrateful. But nor does it behove us to mince words.

Potter's attitude to women can only strike the contemporary viewer as antiquated, or at any rate—so long, long ago that decade seems in gender terms—stuck in the 1960s. Potter remained hopelessly unreconstructed, the most unnew of men; forever prey to that dreadful sexual anxiety, common in so many men over 50, who were determined to see women not as fully human, but existing as the object of desire. It opened such men up to dreadful humiliations.

Bluntly, to be a man at the mercy of a penis not fully under his control, which would rise, not where he admired, liked or trusted, but where he lusted, is no happy thing for a man. It rose when presented with a young female without brain, but fell if presented with a female of equal or greater intelligence, and that was the honest truth of it, and why should Potter, or we, tell it differently? And are we so sure this has changed?

The women in **Karaoke,** being the products of Potter's particular gender imagination, are enough to make a feminist writhe. Sandra Sollars is the 22-year-old bar-girl with whom the ageing writer, Feeld, in the TV play within the TV play, falls in love. Sandra is six foot two, uneducated, naive, badly spoken, working-class, kind and petulant by turns, and can't understand the long words our hero uses.

At which he just laughs and finds her the more endearing. She is the taught, he—when he is sober enough—the teacher: she the victim, he the saviour and comforter. She blesses him just by existing.

But careful! Sandra has an alter ego, Linda, another girl with no brain and long legs, with whom the director of the play within the play is obsessed. But this time the child-girl is not in danger but the source of danger: Linda takes advantage of her lover's married vulnerability; she does her best to blackmail him, destroy him. Detumescence is instant.

Anna, the producer of the play within the play, middle-class, educated, described by all the men around as a pain in the arse, is unable to cope, hopelessly neurotic, laughed at by everyone and fancied by no one. This, in Potterland, is the penalty paid by Women Who Aspire. Out of the running, in a race only men can win.

The middle-aged wife of the faithless director is made to suffer the humiliation—often enough experienced by the womenfolk of the over-fifties in real life—of being told by her husband that for a time he fancied someone younger and fresher than she—but it's over now. In Potterland, man has his fling but keeps his wife. It is his due.

In **Cold Lazarus,** 400 years hence, the world is run by nasty, sexually voracious, face-lifted matrons with obedient toyboys, who speak the cost-cutting language of BBC management, spattered by foul language. And though we are given as an antidote Professor Emma Porlock, an effective, dedicated and intelligent scientist, albeit renowned as a fearful bully, she turns out to be cruel beyond belief to our writer, in her insistence that he relive his childhood traumas for the benefit of science. (Potter chose to do it in his plays: here he is without choice—unless, unless he has invented her and the whole caboodle simply to do it again.)

But at least the professor is beyond the menopause, and so not going to make anyone sexually anxious. Emma utters the plangent line, when proposing to go out alone to lunch with a powerful man: "Don't worry. He's not going to rape me. Alas."

Ah, Potter's Emma knows where her bread is buttered, or was, until age put a stop to it. Rape is better than no sex at all, which leaves MEN ON TOP.

I am merely observing, not complaining. I enjoy this glimpse of gender's past. Balance and maturity is what you hope to find in a BBC documentary, not in drama.

If we go on as we are, with our politically and emotionally correct, well-behaved, committee-built, unvisionary dramas, with their tedious theme of strong women, noble ethnics and designated victims, we will all switch off yawning, and TV drama will die with a whimper of fading police sirens and gurgling saline drips.

The posthumous Potter plays, brilliant, imperfect, tricksy, unreformed and neurotic, give TV drama a shot in the arm which might even enable it to get up off its deathbed and walk.

John J. O'Connor (review date 20 June 1996)

SOURCE: "A Posthumous Send-Off for a British Original," in *New York Times*, June 20, 1996, p. 133.

[*In the following review, O'Connor comments on* Karaoke *and* Cold Lazarus *in which the author recognizes Potter's distinctive devices and themes.*]

Dennis Potter, the most important voice in television drama (***Pennies From Heaven, The Singing Detective***), died of pancreatic cancer two years ago this month. Appropriately, the notoriously cantankerous British writer has been given an extraordinary send-off.

While he was dying, and sipping morphine to ease the pain, he told Melvyn Bragg in a Channel Four interview that since he had spent his life in television, and since that life had "not been insignificant in television," he would like to see his last two plays produced posthumously: ***Karaoke,*** on the BBC and then repeated on Channel Four, and ***Cold Lazarus,*** on Channel Four with a BBC repeat.

Astonishingly, Alan Yentob of the BBC and Michael Grade of Channel Four agreed to the joint undertaking, rustling up a budget of more than $15 million.

Broadcast in England a few weeks ago, the productions, each consisting of four 55-minute episodes, elicited extreme reactions, the negatives in part stemming from something of a backlash in what sometimes seemed a cultural canonization of Mr. Potter.

No matter. After the keen disappointments of some of his later works, including the mini-series ***Lipstick on Your Collar*** and the film ***Midnight Movie,*** the two last plays are quintessential Potter, not reaching the near-perfect pinnacle of ***The Singing Detective*** but certainly qualifying in the same league.

Beginning today and continuing through Oct. 6, the Museum of Television and Radio (25 West 52d Street, Manhattan) will offer alternate-week screenings of the mini-series,

starting this week with ***Karaoke.*** Parts 1 and 2 will begin on Thursdays at 6 P.M., Parts 3 and 4 on Fridays at 6 P.M.

Screenings will also occur on the same days at the Museum of Television and Radio in Los Angeles. (There are currently no plans to broadcast the programs on television in the United States.)

In New York this week for the occasion, Kenith Trodd, Mr. Potter's longtime producer, speaks candidly of their stormy relationship. After a couple of years of professional estrangement, Mr. Trodd was personally summoned back for these productions by the writer who, ever the control freak, also specified who should be the director (Renny Rye) and which actors he would prefer.

Mr. Potter did not get his way in the casting of the central character of the writer Daniel Feeld, clearly based on the writer himself. The producers thought a star was needed and signed Albert Finney.

Mr. Trodd sees in the last works a renewal of Mr. Potter's powers as he compiles in white heat, racing the deadline of death, a summation and even a resolution of all his themes and obsessions. To the end, Mr. Trodd says wryly, Mr. Potter remained as abrasive and spiky as ever.

Karaoke (and was there ever a more perfect Potter toy for the mouthing of words to old songs?) opens in a seedy club where the gangster-proprietor, Arthur (Pig) Mailion (Hywel Bennett), is miming to a recording of "Why Must I Be a Teen-Ager in Love?," the lyrics projected on a screen for his customers in English and Japanese. Meanwhile, Daniel is in a hospital having a barium enema, muttering, "It's all undignified, isn't it?"

As usual, a Potter work plays out on several levels: in a cutting room, where Daniel's new film is being edited; in the film itself, where the characters mirror Daniel's reality; and in Pig Mailion's shady club, a monument to entertainment hustles.

Apart from his smoking, drinking and near-constant pain, Daniel must cope with the sudden conviction that the real people around him are speaking the lines from his script. His doctor says, "We're all in a kind of drama, perhaps, in which each one of us is center stage."

Matters reach a crisis point when middle-aged Daniel meets 22-year-old Sandra (Saffron Burrows), who reminds him of the young woman who is murdered in his film. He feels he now must write a happy ending that saves this aspiring hairdresser. She humors him even though, as she puts it, "I'm not saying that you still don't give me the willies." Virginal love sprouts in a world where there are, says Daniel, "no longer citizens or creatures of God but mere consumers."

Cold Lazarus jumps 374 years into the future where an antiseptic world of nonconnecting relationships seems to be ruled by muck merchants of entertainment, primarily the elderly and brassy California mogul named Martina Masdon (Diane Ladd), who goes through youth-pursuing contortions to keep up with her stable of muscular boy-toys, and David Siltz (Henry Goodman), an entertainment czar whose network offers "interactive sex with whoever you like."

Meanwhile, back in not-so-merrie olde England, at the Masdon Science Center in London, formidable Emma Porlock (Frances de la Tour) and her staff are digging into the memory of a man whose disembodied head has been frozen for centuries.

Kept under glass, the head belongs, of course, to Daniel Feeld, who in *Karaoke* was completing a play, *Cold Lazarus,* about cybernetics.

When David finds out about the experiment he moves quickly to secure the rights to Daniel's memory. "Who would want made-up stories from a hack when you can mainline into the real thing?" he asks. "At last, privacy has a true market value."

In short, here is the ultimate in reality programming, television style. But as Mr. Rye, the director, has remarked: "For Dennis, anything less than actual reality was unacceptable. To him, virtual reality was potentially a palliative for the masses much as 'soma' was for Aldous Huxley in *Brave New World.*"

These mini-series, independent though interlocked, are riddled with familiar Potter devices, not least the use of a double (Daniel has a twin brother) and doppelgängers (Pig can be seen as the dark side of Daniel).

There is also the sexual ambiguity that finds unsettling expression in traumatic incidents (young Daniel, played by Mr. Finney in short pants, is raped by a wanderer in the Forest

of Dean) and a tendency to label women as either virgins or whores. In addition, while Mr. Finney is generally superb, his Daniel is far more theatrical than the performance perfected by the always wily Mr. Potter. What is to be said of a writer egomaniacal enough to envision a future preoccupied largely with the thoughts within his own head?

But to enter Mr. Potter's fiendishly clever world means going along with him, no matter the occasional qualms. Political correctness was always a challenge to his instinct for provocation.

In the end, the trip proves enormously invigorating. It is surprising to be moved by the sight of Daniel winding up in Pig's club and mouthing the lyrics to a Bing Crosby recording of "Pennies From Heaven." Daniel does eventually regain control of his own story and, making his exit, specifies: The End. Full stop. Underlined.

Not quite yet. With these miniseries, Mr. Potter remains in remarkable control.

FURTHER READING

Criticism

Diski, Jenny. "Made for TV." *London Review of Books* 17, No. 24 (14 December 1995): 16-17.
    A review of two books on Potter that presents its own evaluation of the development of the themes and devices of Potter's work.

Fuller, Graham. "Dennis Potter." *American Film* XIV, No. 5 (March 1989): 31-3, 54-5.
    An essay presenting an overview of Potter's work in relation to his life which provides an analysis of the development of his thematic concerns and style.

Stead, Peter. *Dennis Potter.* Bridgend: Seren Books 1993, 147 pages.
    A book-length study of Potter's life and work—published just before his death—from his early days, through his developing years as a writer, until his last few years as a prominent and influential figure.

Thomas Pynchon

1937-

(Born Thomas Ruggles Pynchon, Jr.) American novelist, short story writer, and essayist.

The following entry presents an overview of Pynchon's career. For further information on his life and works, see *CLC*, Volumes 2, 3, 6, 9, 11, 18, 33, 62, and 72.

INTRODUCTION

Thomas Pynchon is considered among the most brilliant and controversial American novelists of the twentieth century. Drawing upon disparate elements of science fiction, fantasy, satire, myth, and advanced mathematics, Pynchon's complex novels feature enormous casts of unusual characters whose interrelated misadventures and burlesques signify the chaos and indeterminacy of modern civilization. The famously reclusive author of *V.* (1963), *The Crying of Lot 49* (1966), *Vineland* (1990), and *Mason and Dixon* (1997), Pynchon is best known for his acclaimed third novel, *Gravity's Rainbow* (1973), which established his reputation as one of the most formidable American writers of the postwar period. Often studied as a postmodern exemplar, Pynchon's far-flung novels are distinguished by allegorical characters, emblematic black humor, and encyclopedic appropriation of Western history and popular culture to illustrate the perilous tension between modern technology, political causes, and individual autonomy.

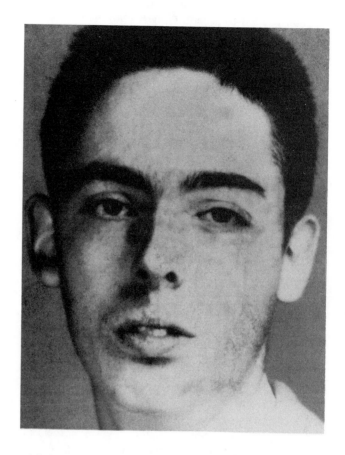

Biographical Information

Born Thomas Ruggles Pynchon, Jr., in Long Island, New York, Pynchon descends from a distinguished line of early Americans with ancestral origins in eleventh century England. William Pynchon, the first American to bear the family surname, emigrated from England to the Massachusetts Bay Colony in 1630, where he wrote a controversial theological tract deemed heretical and publicly burned. Pynchon's great-grand-uncle and namesake, Reverend Thomas Ruggles Pynchon, was a noted nineteenth-century novelist and president of Trinity College. An exceptional student who authored a column in his high school newspaper, Pynchon received a scholarship to attend Cornell University beginning in 1954, where he studied engineering physics and English. While at Cornell, Pynchon took a class with Vladimir Nabokov, befriended folksinger-novelist Richard Fariña, and worked on the undergraduate literary magazine *Cornell Writer*, to which he contributed poetry and short stories, including "The Small Rain," which appeared in 1959. During this time he also wrote and later published the following short stories: "Mortality and Mercy in Vienna" in *Epoch*, 1959; "Lowlands" in *New World Writing*, 1960; "Entropy" in *Kenyon Review*, 1960; and "Under the Rose" in *Noble Savage*, 1961, which later became material for his first novel, *V.* Pynchon graduated from Cornell with honors in 1958 following a two year interruption during which he served in the United States Navy. After spending a year in Greenwich Village, where he set to work on *V.*, Pynchon took a position as a technical writer with Boeing Aircraft in Seattle. Upon leaving Boeing in 1962, Pynchon traveled to Mexico and California to finish *V.*, published the next year. His debut novel won enthusiastic reviews and the William Faulkner Award in 1963. An extremely private, enigmatic literary figure, little is known of Pynchon's personal life from this point forward. His second novel, *The Crying of Lot 49*, also won acclaim and a Rosenthal Foundation Award from the National Institute of Arts and Letters in 1967. Portions of the novel appeared earlier in *Cavalier* magazine and as the story "The World (This One), The Flesh (Mrs. Oedipa Maas), and the Testament of Pierce Inverarity" in *Esquire* in 1965. While working on *The Crying of Lot 49*, Pynchon also published

"The Secret Integration" in *Saturday Evening Post*, 1964, and "Journey Into the Mind of Watts" in the *New York Times*, 1966. His next novel, *Gravity's Rainbow*, won a National Book Award and the Howells Medal of the American Academy and Institute of Arts and Letters, which Pynchon refused to accept. *Gravity's Rainbow* was also unanimously selected by the judges of the Pulitzer Prize committee as the best novel of 1973, though their decision was overruled by the Pulitzer advisory board who rejected the novel for its alleged obscenity and unintelligibility. Pynchon's long awaited fourth novel, *Vineland*, appeared after a seventeen year interim, during which he published *Slow Learner* (1984), a collection of his previous short stories, and the essay "Is It O.K. to Be a Luddite?" in the *New York Times Book Review* in 1984. Pynchon produced a fifth novel, *Mason and Dixon*, in 1997.

Major Works

Pynchon's challenging fiction is characterized by intricate nonlinear plots rife with conspiratorial paranoia, abrupt spatio-temporal dislocations, epistemic conundrums, incessant punning, frequent allusions to history, science, technology, and mass culture, and flat characters with overtly symbolic names whose inability to find meaning bespeaks a quest theme in all of his work. Pynchon's first novel, *V.*, embodies many of his trademark thematic concerns and narrative devices, particularly his preoccupation with historical design, the opposing forces of chance and determinism, and the ambiguity of truth. A long, sprawling work nominally set in the 1950s, the story revolves around the picaresque adventures of Benny Profane, an itinerant odd jobsman, and the historiographic sleuthing of his alter ego Herbert Stencil, the son of a British spy. While Profane hunts alligators in the sewers of New York City and fraternizes with "The Whole Sick Crew," an assemblage of libertine bohemians who represent the decadence and moral decay of modern society, Stencil engages in an obsessive hunt for the identity of V., a mysterious female persona whom he believes is involved in the 1919 murder of his father. V.'s chimeral appearances throughout Europe and Africa lead Stencil to the scene of various geopolitical crises between 1898 and 1956, but ultimately he fails to fix her identity with any certainty. *The Crying of Lot 49* similarly involves a detective story motif and an elusive entity that harries the protagonist's search for truth. Set in California during the 1960s, the novel centers upon Oedipa Maas, a suburban housewife who uncovers a renegade postal system called Tristero while investigating the bequest of real estate mogul Pierce Inverarity, a former lover who has named her executor of his will. In her efforts to penetrate the mysterious workings of Tristero—represented by a post horn insignia and the acronym W.A.S.T.E. ("We Await Silent Tristero's Empire")—Oedipa eventually becomes en-

gaged in an existential search for meaning, alluding to her Greek namesake, Oedipus, who solved the riddle of the Sphinx. While offering a parody of mainstream America and counterculture activity during the 1960s, Pynchon invokes the Second Law of Thermodynamics as a metaphor for the inevitable movement toward stasis and conformity in contemporary society. *Gravity's Rainbow* represents Pynchon's most ambitious effort to reorder and contextualize the major social, political, and philosophical developments of the twentieth century. A massive accumulation of historical, cultural, and scientific information, particularly related to rocketry and physics, the complicated meta-narrative involves hundreds of characters, divergent plotlines, flashback sequences, and hallucinations that present multiple levels of reality. Set in England, France, and occupied Germany in 1945, much of the novel relates the covert operations of German rocket scientists and Allied counterintelligence near the end of the Second World War. The principal character is Tyrone Slothrop, an American lieutenant unwittingly programmed by a behavioral scientist to predict Nazi V-2 rocket strikes with his erections. The dominant metaphor of the novel is the rocket, an undisguised phallic icon that signifies both the culmination of man's technological achievement and morbid obsession with self-annihilation. While presenting a grim portrait of a modern techno-industrial death culture, as in previous novels Pynchon also explores vying aspects of personal freedom and organizational coercion; manipulating entities are referred to as "Them" by exponents of resistance in the novel. Returning to the subject of the United States in *Vineland*, whose title alludes to Lief Ericson's 1000 AD discovery of America, Pynchon satirizes the failure of 1960s idealism and the conservative political climate of the Reagan administration. Set in California in 1984, the central plot involves Zoyd Wheeler, an aging hippie, and his teenage daughter Prairie, who leaves the fictitious redwood community of Vineland to pursue her long lost mother, Frenesi Gates. A former radical filmmaker and activist during the 1960s, Frenesi is seduced by Brock Vond, a sadistic federal prosecutor for whom she betrays her revolutionary cohorts and enters into government service as an undercover agent, though she later disappears in the Witness Protection Agency. Here Pynchon portrays a media-saturated consumer culture addicted to television and an unreal state of technological and bureaucratic complicity enforced by the omnipresence of commercial and government subversion. *Mason and Dixon* also focuses on the history and national identity of the United States. Set in colonial America during the 1760s and narrated by the Reverend Wicks Cherrycoke in a pastiche of eighteenth century language and punctuation, the novel relates the serio-comic adventures of astronomer Charles Mason and surveyor Jeremiah Dixon, famed navigators of the eponymous geographic demarcation separating Pennsylvania and Maryland. As the future boundary between free and slave states during the Civil War, the Mason-Dixon line represents a metaphorical division between liberty and tyranny, suggesting both the aspirations and failures of the American people. The presence of a wide array of fantastic characters and historical personages, such as a talking dog and a pot-smoking George Washington, further underscores the nebulous intersection between fact and fiction, particularly in a society where imaginary boundaries determine the destiny of real people.

Critical Reception

Pynchon is considered one of the most gifted and challenging American novelists of recent decades. The subject of rigorous scholarly interpretation, Pynchon's heteroclite fiction is acclaimed for its vast range, idiosyncratic comic voice, experimental synthesis of narrative voices, and profound philosophical insights into the nature of truth and historical reality. Associated with contemporaries Kurt Vonnegut, John Barth, Norman Mailer, and William S. Burroughs, Pynchon's satirical novels of ideas derive from the literary models of Francois Rabelais's *Gargantua and Pantagruel,* Candide's *Voltaire,* and Jonathan Swift's *Gulliver's Travels.* While *V., The Crying of Lot 49* and *Vineland* are highly regarded examples of Pynchon's prodigious talent, *Gravity's Rainbow* remains his seminal work, a landmark of postmodern literature compared to James Joyce's *Ulysses* for its extraordinary scope and originality. Most critics praise Pynchon's work for its erudition, dark humor, and provocative narrative constructs, though others find fault in its fragmented plots, flippant word play, and proliferation of empty allusions and undeveloped characters. Many critics also comment on Pynchon's affinity for binary oppositions, viewed by some as an effective strategy for exposing multivalent realities and the hypocrisy of extremes. However, his detractors dismiss such Manichean divisions and equivocal outcomes as simplistic and evasive. The comprehensive vision and exuberance of Pynchon's metafiction is often viewed as both a strength and liability. As many critics note, the result is a simultaneously bewildering and bemusing accretion of witticism, linguistic hieroglyph, and multidisciplinary referent that functions on the verge of incoherence and obscurity. A highly imaginative fabulist and innovative postmodern stylist, Pynchon is recognized as among the most inventive and important American authors of contemporary fiction.

PRINCIPAL WORKS

V. (novel) 1963
The Crying of Lot 49 (novel) 1966
Gravity's Rainbow (novel) 1973
Slow Learner: Early Stories (short stories) 1984
Vineland (novel) 1990
Mason and Dixon (novel) 1997

CRITICISM

Lance Olsen (essay date Spring 1986)

SOURCE: "Deconstructing the Enemy of Color: The Fantastic in *Gravity's Rainbow,*" in *Studies in the Novel,* Vol. 18, No. 1, Spring, 1986, pp. 74-86.

[*In the following essay, Olsen examines elements of postmodern fantasy in* Gravity's Rainbow.]

Oh, THE WORLD OVER THERE, it's
So hard explain!
Just-like, a dream's got, lost in yer brain!

—Thomas Pynchon (*Gravity's Rainbow*)

I.

Gravity's Rainbow—what one reviewer frustrated by its length, structure, and seeming lack of control tagged "a magnificent necropolis that will take its place amidst the grand detritus of our culture"—was probably the most unread best seller in America during 1973, and perhaps ever. It teetered at the bottom of the *New York Times Book Review* list for two weeks late in April and another two early in May before it toppled off altogether to make way for the likes of Susann's *Once is Not Enough,* Forsyth's *The Odessa File* and, of course, Bach's *Jonathan Livingston Seagull,* the last of which was soaring toward its sixtieth week as Pynchon's text tumbled. When later that year a team of distinguished judges met for the fifty-eighth annual Pulitzer Prize decision and recommended it, the journalists on the advisory board overturned their verdict because for them it was "unreadable," "turgid," "over-written," and "obscene." Nonetheless, almost immediately critics like Richard Poirier and Edward Mendelson placed it in the company of other encyclopedic works such as Dante's *Divine Comedy,* Rabelais' books of *Gargantua and Pantagruel,* Cervantes' *Don Quixote,* Sterne's *Tristram Shandy,* Goethe's *Faust,* Melville's *Moby-Dick,* and Joyce's *Ulysses.* And since then *Gravity's Rainbow* has generated a critical industry of its own, an academic cult, and more exegetic "apoplexy than any novel since *Ulysses,*" as one reader has commented, examined as it has been in a host of essays and dissertations, and no fewer than fifteen books, for its handling of history, war, mythology, literary echoes, cinematic qualities and influences, pop culture, religion, philosophy, psychology, politics, sex, death, music, feminism, engineering, ballistics, mysticism, Menippean satire, science fiction, the quest, parody, the lyrical impulse, irony, allegory, gothicism, comedy, and on and on and on.

But with the exception of Rosemary Jackson's brief mention of *Gravity's Rainbow,* insufficient attention has been given to Pynchon's third novel as a work of fantasy, a mode of discourse that has engaged the imagination since *Gilgamesh,* and a mode that has become a particularly prevalent trait of what has come to be known as postmodernism. One finds the fantastic impulse employed by contemporary writers as diverse as Borges, Beckett, Fuentes, Garcia Márquez, Barthelme, Irving, Kundera, O'Brien, Vonnegut, Heller, and Calvino. And there is little wonder for its omnipresence. Since postmodernism arose in response to a universe it saw under both physical and metaphysical erasure, and hence since it tries to face a situation it believes fantastic, there is little surprise that the mode of discourse chosen as a vehicle for the postmodern consciousness is the fantastic. In this essay I should like to devote my attention to the relationship of this mode of discourse to *Gravity's Rainbow*—first by delineating a working definition of the term; second by exploring what the idea of the fantastic yields concerning character, time, space, and language in Pynchon's "magnificent necropolis"; and third by examining reader-response to Pynchon's use of those constructs, and the cultural suppositions behind them.

II.

In the preface to *Slow Learner* (1984), his one and only literary-autobiographical essay, Pynchon with characteristic irony and ambiguity both talks disparagingly of fantasy literature and admits to being profoundly influenced by it. Early in the piece he equates "seriousness" in fiction with "an attitude toward death"; the one goes hand in hand with the other. He continues: "I suspect one of the reasons that fantasy and science fiction appeal so much to younger readers is that, when space and time have been altered to allow characters to travel easily anywhere through the continuum and thus escape physical dangers and timepiece inevitabilities, mortality is so seldom an issue." So the fantastic is for the younger, less sophisticated reader because it allows for an escape from the concerns of mortality. In other words, it is "escapist." But toward the end of his essay, Pynchon recounts taking a course in modern art while at Cornell. There he first encountered Surrealism, one of the major fantasy movements in the twentieth century. The Surrealists, he writes, "really caught my attention." What fascinated him was "the simple idea that one could combine inside the same frame, elements not normally found together to produce illogical and startling effects." The fantastic, then, contains an element of disruption (in

space or time, for instance) which results in unreason and surprise.

Tzvetan Todorov, in his cornerstone study of the fantastic in literature, carries this idea further. Fantasy, he argues, "lasts only as long as a certain hesitation" in the text and the reader between the uncanny (where "the laws of reality remain intact and permit an explanation of the phenomena described"—the land, in other words, of mimetic discourse) and the marvelous (where "new laws of nature must be entertained to account for the phenomena"—the land of gothic fiction, fairy tales, surrealist fiction, et cetera). Inexplicably, though, Todorov maintains that fantasy finds its purest form in the nineteenth century; and often he slips into the ethnocentric position of believing that terms like "laws of reality" and "laws of nature" are stable and sure. This is where Rosemary Jackson comes in. She takes Todorov's primary ideas and reshapes them, moving them from a quasi-epistemological to a narrative concern and defining fantasy as a mode of discourse that exists on a continuum between two other modes: at one end the marvelous and at the other the mimetic. Fantasy, she argues, can and has existed in all cultures at all times, but becomes particularly widespread in a culture experiencing excessive unease (as with the flourishing of gothic fiction at the turn of the eighteenth century, or the dominance of fantasy in our own culture since, roughly, the second world war).

The fantastic, then, plays one universe of discourse off another thereby creating a dialectic that refuses synthesis; the result is textual instability. As Caillois points out, "the fantastic is always a break in the acknowledged order, an irruption of the inadmissible within the changeless everyday legality." One may think of fantasy as a mode of narrative "illegality" whose intent is to dislocate and remain hostile to anything static. As a result, it rejects any definitive version of "truth" or "reality." Its mission is to disrupt cultural unities of character, time, space, and even language; to reveal that which must be concealed in order that one's internal and external experience may be comfortably known. Jackson suggests that "fantastic literature points to . . . the basis upon which cultural order rests, for it opens up, for a brief moment, on to disorder, on to illegality, on to that which lies outside the law, that which is outside the dominant value systems. The fantastic traces the unsaid and unseen in the culture."

In this way fantasy becomes the literary equivalent of deconstructionism, since both the narrative and critico-philosophical modes are designed to surprise, to question, to put into doubt, to create anxiety, to make active, to make uncomfortable, to rebel, to subvert, to render ambiguous, to make discontinuous. They may be seen, as Jacques Derrida intimates, either as "sad, *negative* . . ., guilty" modes or as "the joyous affirmation of the freeplay . . .

without truth, without origin." Both interrogate all we take for granted about language and experience, giving these no more than a shifting and provisional status. Within themselves they hold a radical skepticism that believes only in the impossibility of total intelligibility, the endless displacement of "meaning," the blocking of conceptual closure, the bottomless relativity of "significance"—all of which also may serve as a description of Pynchon's universe in *Gravity's* (a word associated with the static weight of the mimetic) *Rainbow* (a word signaling the weightless iridescence of the marvelous): a universe primarily of disorder, heat-death, white noise, communication collapse and existential blur, to which I should now like to turn my attention.

III.

The notion of *character* gives rise to larger questions about identity, wholeness of personality, three-dimensionality, stability of the self over time, what it means to be human. And, to begin with a commonplace, Pynchon's third novel is crammed with a cast of somewhere between three and four hundred (which roughly averages one new face every two pages), making it virtually impossible to pluck out a protagonist and—given how little the reader sees of each character—making it even more difficult to say anything serious and helpful about any of the characters' psychological makeup. As one early reviewer pointed out about *Gravity's Rainbow:* "Pynchon doesn't create characters so much as mechanical men to whom a manic comic impulse or a vague free floating anguish can attach itself" (see [Richard] Locke's review). They are, as so many critics have pointed out, cartoon characters—and in this context one should keep in mind Pynchon's pronouncement in *Slow Learner*'s preface: "May the Road Runner cartoons never vanish from the video waves, is my attitude"—with outlandish names that refuse to be taken as earnestly as one might someone named Dorthea Brooke, Marlow, Daniel Martin: Teddy Bloat, Corydon Throsp, DeCoverly Pox, Lord Batherard Osmo, Oliver Mucker-Maffick, Blodgett Waxwing, and so forth. What Pynchon has done in his international novel is to generate a geographical breadth of character by employing Americans, Britishers, Dutchmen, Germans, Japanese, Africans, Argentines, and on and on, without generating emotional depth.

In fact a register of the characterlessness of the text appears in several characters' breaking up, losing a discrete wholeness of personality. Tyrone Slothrop, as much a protagonist as *Gravity's Rainbow* can conceive of, by the end fractures into a number of identities. "Some believe that fragments of Slothrop have grown into consistent personae of their own," the reader finds. "If so, there's no telling which of the Zone's present-day population are offshoots of his original scattering." In a way Dr. Lazlo

Jamf, the man who conditioned Slothrop when the chubby American was a baby, is everyone, or so the reader gathers from Slothrop's recurrent dream in which he "had found a very old dictionary of technical German. It fell open to a certain page prickling with black-face type. Reading down the page, he would come to JAMF. The definition would read: I. He work begging It *no.*" A more minor example shows up in Gavin Trefoil, one of the "new varieties of freak" that have been turning up at "The White Visitation," the one-time madhouse become Pavlovian lab. Trefoil suffers from what Rollo Groast wants to name *autochromatism;* "he can change his color from most ghastly albino up through a smooth spectrum to very deep, purplish, black." He has metamorphosed into a human (?) chameleon.

The text thereby comes to interrogate what Robbe-Grillet has referred to as "the old myths of 'depth.'" In *For a New Novel* he continues: "The creators of characters, in the traditional sense, no longer manage to offer us anything more than puppets in which they themselves have ceased to believe. The novel of characters belongs entirely to the past, it describes a period: that which marked the apogee of the individual." In Pynchon's fantastic high-tech nuclear world what was called the individual has—like Slothrop, Jamf, and Trefoil, among others—scattered and vanished. Significantly, behaviorism and not Freudianism surfaces as the dominant psychological mode in the text. A mode of surfaces comes to replace a mode of depths. While for a time along with Oberst Enzian, commander of the Schwarzkommando, Slothrop may hope against hope that "somewhere . . . is the key that will bring us back, restore us to our Earth and to our freedom," the fact remains that by the time he enters the Zone he believes he is the essence of Conditioned Man, programmed and monitored since infancy, the exquisite Skinnerian Black Box. This is Lazlo Jamf's universe, Edward Pointsman's universe, the universe of faultless behavioral determinism.

In addition to disintegrating what Robbe-Grillet calls the Balzacian mode of character, Pynchon's fantastic text disrupts the mimetic belief in the stability of time and space. By doing so, it raises questions about chronology, logic, reason, order, and constancy. Often it has been pointed out that *Gravity's Rainbow* has affinities with the Nordic and the Russian sagas with their huge casts and multiple plotlines, but if this is so it is also so that in Pynchon's text the saga is told from the point of view of Faulkner's Benjy Compson. The text disjoints and conflates past, present, and future as well as here and there. Although the major action takes place between September 8 and November 30, 1944 (during the V-2 bombardment of London), and April or just before May 8, 1945 (either Eliot's cruelest month or just before V-E day, during the firing of the 00000 and 00001), in England and Germany, abrupt dislocations in time and space throw us back to biblical events, the middle ages, the seventeenth and nineteenth centuries, the 1920's and 1930's, and ahead to Jack Kennedy's and Malcom X's assassinations, mentions of Nixon, and even apparently to the beginning of World War III as the rocket screams down on the thereafter in Los Angeles, as well as across to New England, Southwest Africa, Argentina, the Russian Steppes, France, Switzerland, and Holland. Moreover, any attempt to reconstruct a clear and unambiguous chronology and series of settings may in the end clarify the text, but its result would be the manufacturing of a text that Pynchon did not write. To add to the confusion, what in traditional mimetic discourse should take a relatively long time (the conclusion of World War II, for instance) is passed over so quickly many readers miss it, and what "normally" should warrant a relatively brief mention (the extermination, for example, of the dodo birds by one of Katje's ancestors) lingers for pages. Consequently, as many have indicated, the reader senses that he is viewing some sort of crazy documentary on the second world war and its aftermath, but that the reels have gotten mixed up. And so have the projectors, apparently, since time in the text can even run backwards: "agents run around with guns which are like vacuum cleaners operating in the direction of life—pull the trigger and bullets are sucked back out of the recently dead into the barrel, and the Great Irreversible is actually reversed."

These disruptions of mimetic discourse's space-time conventions do not only exist at the stratum of plot; they manifest themselves in the very way the language is constructed. Notice, for instance, the way the text opens:

> A screaming comes across the sky. It has happened before, but there is nothing to compare it to now.
>
> It is too late. The Evacuation still proceeds, but it's all theatre, There are no lights inside the cars. No light anywhere. Above him life girders old as an iron queen, and glass somewhere far above that would let the light of day through. But it's night. He's afraid of the way the glass will fall—soon—it will be a spectacle: the fall of a crystal palace. But coming down in total blackout, without one glint of light, only great invisible crashing.

Just as the collapse of the "crystal palace"—the nineteenth-century monument to reason, optimism, progress, stability—of iron and glass is imminent, so too is the collapse of nineteenth-century "realistic" narrative. Without having some knowledge of at least the next few pages of the text, the reader cannot interpret the situation that confronts him on the first page. The reader comes upon something, but what that something is is impossible to say. The text opens with the present tense, one still slightly unsettling to a reader comfortable in the Balzacian mode of discourse; at the same time it withholds key orienting words, refuses to interpret fully the data in presents: "A screaming comes across the sky" (a human screaming? something else? where are we?). Next it withholds specific time references: "It" (again, *what?*) "has happened before but there is nothing to compare it to now" (how long before? when is now? where is the traditional hint of time-locus?). In the next few sentences the text provides just enough information to perplex. Why, for instance, is it too late? What kind of evacuation, and why the capital letter? How is an evacuation "all theatre"? What kind of cars have no light in them? Who is the "him" in the seventh line? The reader hears all the words of anxiety—*too late, no lights, total blackout,* and so on—and he realizes that either none of its is real, or all of it is reminiscent of something in some horror film, or both. The reader becomes a witness to actions he cannot understand, and an accomplice to them since he must to some degree originate his own version of them, hence entering into participation with the text. Over the course of the next few pages he slowly comes to realize the action involves a train during a bombardment, perhaps in London. Not until two full pages after the text has commenced does Pirate Prentice, the British commando who plays a very small role in the novel, sit up in bed and look around him, thinking "How awful. How bloody awful," and the reader can piece together enough to surmise he has probably been in Prentice's (?) dream.

Whether that dream beginning the text ever ends is another question. One way to read *Gravity's Rainbow* is to see it as either Prentice's or—more likely—a paranoid narrator's unending nightmare, drugged hallucination, autistic fantasy, or protracted hypnogogic state—that semi-conscious state of drowsiness and reverie one experiences just as one is falling into dreams, the state where one drifts away from an awareness of external reality and the body and in which the closed eye sees a continuous procession of vivid and constantly changing forms. Whatever the case, the text certainly concludes with another altered state as the A4 rocket 00000 fired by Weissman/Blicero, the German lieutenant, from the Luneburg Heath in the last days of the war merges with the A4 rocket 00001 carrying Enzian. Perhaps, then, the whole text is the story of one rocket shrieking down on an LA movie theater and what one imagination contemplates between the perception of it and its reaching the last delta-t just above the roof.

Following this line of reasoning, everything in the text occurs at roughly the same time. All the past, present, and future is contained in a brief narrative *now*. This notion would jibe with Kurt Mondaugen's, the radio electronics specialist's, Law of Temporal Bandwidth he propounds in his Peenemünde office. According to him, one's personal density is proportional to one's Temporal Bandwidth which is "the width of your present, your *now*. . . . The more you dwell in the past and in the future, the thicker your band-width, the more solid your persona. But the narrower your sense of Now, the more tenuous you are." Slothrop, Mondaugen argues, is an extreme case of someone who has an infinitesimally thin Bandwidth since he cannot remember what he did even five minutes ago, and has no idea what he will do the next second; in fact, by the end it is so thin his personality dissipates completely. If one looks around, one finds that just about everyone in the novel has a thin (though not as thin as Slothrop's) Bandwidth. Only the narrator in his paranoid schizophrenia seems to have enough density to live in a wide Bandwidth. For him, the past, present, and future all happen *now*. They are almost interchangeable. Consequently, the idea of Newtonian time, where there exists a clear demarcation between one moment and the next, becomes meaningless. Instead, the text abandons the Newtonian belief in cause-and-effect and drifts into a world of statistical probability that de-emphasizes temporal sequence. "The blurring of causal relationships and the flux produced by rapid shifts in setting and unforeseen turns of events in Pynchon's fiction," John Stark notes in his study of the writer, "indicate that theory of time developed here is [an] ongoing one rather than the traditional theory that postulates a series of frozen moments that can be distinctly separated and remembered." Again to quote Robbe-Grillet, whose discussions of narrative often seem like descriptions of Pynchon's project: "Time seems to be cut off from its temporality. . . . Here space destroys time, and time sabotages space. Description makes no headway, contradicts itself, turns in circles." In the fantastic mode of discourse, time ceases to be linear and space ceases to be discrete. The universe tends toward indeterminacy like the infinitely extended library in Borges' fiction—and Pynchon makes multiple mention of him in his novel.

As I intimated in my reading of the opening pages of Pynchon's text, inherent instability displays itself even in the way the language functions. While earlier twentieth-century writers like Proust, Stevens, and Mann possessed an almost religious faith in the power of words to encompass and order reality, Pynchon rebels against the constraint of symmetry and harmony by trying to subvert "the insanely, endlessly diddling play of a chemist whose molecules are words," to overthrow the mystical power that accomplishes no more than "setting namer more hopelessly apart from named." For him language becomes a meaningless and joyous affirmative freeplay in a world without truth. As opposed to the uniform language employed by texts like *Clarissa, Pride and Prejudice, Portrait of a Lady,* or *The Sun Also Rises*—texts that fashion through their uniformity of language a uniform view of reality while insuring the reader that no adjustment to style and viewpoint will be demanded in the course of reading—***Gravity's Rainbow*** employs a mixed language that revels in variety and potentiality. Such a language is an ideal vehicle, as Leonard Lutwack notes in his discussion of the novel form. "for the writer who is motivated by the spirit of irony and parody and who finds it impossible to remain committed to a single vision of reality." Further, he argues, the mixed style "has the effect of making the reader pass through a succession of contradictory and ambiguous attitudes; it offers no sure stylistic norm by which the reader may orient himself permanently to the fiction and to the point of view of the author." Thus, the use of mixed language refuses narrative closure.

Another way to discuss the disruptive capabilities of the language in Pynchon's text is to borrow Stephen Ullmann's concept of the lexical field, which he defines as "a closely organized sector of vocabulary, whose elements fit together and delimit each other like pieces of a mosaic. In each field some sphere of experience is analyzed, divided up and classified in a unique way." Pynchon continually frustrates reader-expectation by jamming one lexical field against another. He suspends traditional laws of lexical and tonal consistency and the verbal anarchy triggers the downfall of the narrator's attempt at self-confident syntax (hence, perhaps, his frequent breathless stutter). While such linguistic ruptures occur often at the level of page-long passages such as the narrator's long discussion of polymers (the lexical field of the chemist) or the derivation of a phrase like "Shit 'n' Shinola" (the lexical field of the etymologist), they also occur at the level of paragraph, and even sentence:

> Most people's lives have ups and downs that are relatively gradual, a sinuous curve with first derivatives at every point. They're the ones who never get struck by lightening. No real idea of cataclysm at all. But the ones who do get hit experience a singular point, a discontinuity in the curve of life—do you know what the time rate of change is at a cusp? *Infinity,* that's what! A-and right across the point, it's *minus infinity!* How's *that* for a sudden change, eh? Infinite miles per hour changing to the same speed *in reverse,* all in a gnat's ass or red cunt hair of the t across the point. That's getting hit by lightening, folks.

Within these nine sentences play the lexical fields of the mathematician ("sinuous curve," "first derivatives"), physicist (" t across the point"), pop philosopher ("Most people's lives have ups and downs that are relatively gradual"), wit ("They're the ones who never get struck by lightening. No real idea of cataclysm at all."), breezy American ("*Infinity,* that's what!"), perhaps even pervert ("in a gnat's ass or red cunt hair"), and the colloquial speaker ("That's getting hit by lightening, folks."). The outcome is the linguistic equivalent of the pratfall, language slipping on a wordy banana peel and stumbling over its own feet. The value of one language register—and, finally language itself—is questioned by the existence of a multitude of others.

Such prose, reminiscent of chameleonic Gavin Trefoil, manifests as well an extremely high information density resulting from a chaotic epic cataloging of a grotesquely decedent universe. It is, as Jackson points out, a prose that "gathers together a massive amount of Cultural material as if it were so much waste matter, the waste of 'culture,' culture as waste, or garbage or excrement, on the page." It is manufactured by an unreliable narrator of indeterminate gender in an indeterminate place and time in, at very best, an indeterminate, mental state—less a narrator, actually, than a Beckettian Unnamable, a protean field of consciousness that can metamorphose into separate personae and—like the pod people in Don Siegel's 1956 version of Jack Finney's *Invasion of the Body-Snatchers*—incorporate their thought and language patterns. His (?) existential problem appears to be that in a universe of statistical probability rather than cause-and-effect he seems to know absolutely everything and everyone except what will happen in the next sentence. His is a consciousness that indicates radical alienation from Cartesian reason, and hence from society and history as others share it; a drive toward disruptions in human systems; an extreme dislocation from nature and deity; a subversion of the belief in form, balance, and order; a disintegration of public discourse and the production of an autodestructive mode of noncommunication.

IV.

No wonder, then, that those journalists on the fifty-eighth annual Pulitzer Prize committee found Pynchon's third novel "over-written," "turgid," and "unreadable" (their "obscene" raises somewhat different questions concerning fantasy's ability and tendency to treat the underside of a culture). *Gravity's Rainbow* generates uncertainty and instability on both narrative and epistemological strata, casting the reader either in the role of "seeker" or "sought." The text force him to become either its We (the victim manipulated by the narrative equivalent of the Firm; an actor in a movie where the pages of the script have been shuffled like a deck of playing cards) or its They (the omnipresent "Pernicious Pop"; the unknowable manipulator who demands control over a text). Or perhaps, even more disconcerting, by some paranoid magic he must become *both* We and They at the same moment in this book of "nonanswers" ([David] Leverenz in *Mindful Pleasures*), this "metaphysical opposite of God's grace" ([Richard] Siegel), where he finds that those "like Slothrop, with the greatest interest in discovering the truth, were thrown back on dreams, psychic flashes, omens, cryptographies, drug-epistemologies, all dancing on a ground of terror, contradiction, absurdity." Enzian and the reader discover that:

We have to look for power sources here, and distribution networks we were never taught, routes of power our teachers never imagined, or were encouraged to avoid . . . we have to find meters whose scales are unknown to the world, draw our schematics, getting feedback, making connections, reducing the error, trying to learn the real function . . . zeroing in on what incalculable plot?

In other words, both Enzian and the reader realize that the fantastic text and universe require creative cooperation while at the same time interrogating all Enzian's and the reader's primary assumptions about the text and the universe. The reading process—both of the book and the universe—becomes one, then, of "decoding the Text, thus coding, recoding, redecoding the holy Text," but in the back of the Reader's mind always hovers the question: "If it is in working order, what is it meant to do?" Like the V-2 that both screams at the heart of the text and encloses it, the text offers itself to the Reader as "both organizer and destroyer." If he chooses to enter the text, the Reader must become the ultimate protagonist—and prevaricator—in a book that seeks to undermine the modernist paradigm of narrative and epistemological constructions; at one and the same time, he must live in a state of paranoia, where everything is connected, and what Pynchon calls *anti-paranoia*, "where nothing is connected to anything, a condition not many of us can bear for long."

Gravity's Rainbow, then, does not only question what it is to structure a traditional story, as in the section recounting Prentice's nightmare (?) of the giant adenoid attack or the passage about the woman who drowns and—like the text itself—teams with life and potential; it also questions what it is to structure a traditional culture, our Western culture gone consumer-oriented corporate American (*"dawn is nearly here, I need my night's blood, my funding, funding, ahh more, more . . ."*) a culture based—like the language of the text itself—on an excess of matter and signs, destructive ambition, power struggles. By presenting their opposites (Pudding and the Domina Nocturna sequence), it examines what it is to structure a conventional grid of aesthetic and moral tastes. In this way, it lends itself as a subtle offer to transgress, to cross over into that which the dominant culture has silenced. A register of this is Pig Bodine's and Roger Mexico's verbal disruption of officialdom at the dinner party; through a careful escalation of deliberate misreadings of the menu, they move from "surprise roast" to "snot soup," "pus pudding," "menstrual marmalade" and "discharge dumplings." Theirs is the impulse of fantasy and deconstructionism—a bizarre freeplay among texts, a delight in possibility, a joyous affirmation of kinesis, an invitation to narrative and cultural illegality, a thrust outside dogma and law, an interrogation of ethnocentric constructs such as "reality," "reason," "order," "identity," "decorum," "truth," and "meaning," an over-whelming sense of frustration before a culture that jams desire. *Gravity's Rainbow,* then, may be read as a deconstructive fantasy that battles the prevalence of white-ness within itself—that omnipresent colorlessness associ-ated with the behavioristic investigations at The White Visitation, that "dead" blankness, that "enemy of color," the image of closed systems, stasis, certainty—while delight-ing in the possibility of the rainbow, multiplicity, uncer-tainty, mindless pleasures, the metaphysical equivalent of the Zone, where "all fences are down, one road as good as another . . . without elect, without preterite, without even nationality to fuck it up."

Kathryn Hume (essay date 1987)

SOURCE: "*Gravity's Rainbow:* Science Fiction, Fantasy, and Mythology," in *Intersections: Fantasy and Science Fiction,* edited by George E. Slusser and Eric S. Rabkin, Southern Illinois University Press, 1987, pp. 190-200.

[*In the following essay, Hume explores the intersection of science fiction, fantasy, and mythology in* Gravity's Rainbow.]

Gravity's Rainbow has been hailed by John Brunner as an "incontestably science-fictional retrospective parallel world," (that is, an alternate wartime London); also, by Geoffrey Cocks as the Miltonic epic of science fiction that "has taken science/speculative fiction beyond the genre's limits into metaphysics, metapsychology, and cosmology." It has also been identified as gothic, as encyclopedic, and as various kinds of satire or anatomy. I am particularly sym-pathetic to the desire of some critics to claim *Gravity's Rainbow* for science fiction, because so little mainstream fiction engages with science in any significant way, and be-cause the identification would perhaps attract more atten-tion from the academy for that uncanonical literature. However, the problems of defining science fiction com-plicate the ascription, and any single label blinds us to the generic interactions within this maverick work. I would prefer to work with a broader palette of terms when trying to describe the experience that is *Gravity's Rainbow,* and would like to focus on the interrelationships between three: science fiction, fantasy, and mythology. (In no way do these three exhaust the generic possibilities.)

I am going to argue that Pynchon draws on science and con-tributes to science fiction by creating a fictive analogue to the post-Newtonian universe, and he forces us to consider probabilistic and uncertain realities in a way that we nor-mally avoid, even if we are aware of the implications of contemporary science. However, it is not science, but rather

his arsenal of fantasy techniques that allows him to create this fictive analogue to scientific reality—each one of those techniques flagrantly nonrational and nonrealistic. Counterpointing the fantasy and science fiction is a tradi-tional yet technological mythology, through whose repeti-tions, oppositions, and mediations we can find some of Pynchon's values, including a modified hero monomyth. Let me fill in this picture—the three generic forces interact-ing—and then consider briefly the implications to ques-tions of definition and canon.

Since our society is fundamentally technological rather than scientific, contemporary non-Newtonian science has had remarkably little effect on our everyday thinking about life. The ten or eleven dimensions now favored by cosmolo-gists rarely impinge on our consciousness. Reality, for us, is the stone that hurts our foot when we kick it; our as-sumptions do not reach to empty space, interrupted here and there by atoms, let alone to the energies which make up those atoms. All our normal assumptions about what is real are, as Rosemary Jackson puts it, bourgeois catego-ries of the real. They assert the nature of reality in terms of practical material concerns, quite regardless of any in-sight or contradictory evidence available through science or philosophy.

Science fiction has done relatively little with the implica-tions of non-Newtonian science in everyday life. When black holes turn up as grist for the story mill, they are of-ten hunted down and captured for commercial purposes; the unimaginable is thus domesticated and made normal. Un-certainty in most science fiction is usually confined to our not knowing in detail how the story will come out. Unknowability does appear in Lem's *Solaris,* for instance, but most science fiction is predicated on the mysteries of the physical universe proving knowable. As Gary K. Wolfe puts it, these stories celebrate our turning chaos into cos-mos by means of scientific method. Uncertainty, unknowability, and other aspects of nonmechanical phys-ics are usually ornamental, if present at all, in much sci-ence fiction.

Pynchon creates a world in which some subatomic char-acteristics of reality are dealt with at the level of everyday life. Pseudo-Heisenbergian uncertainty bedevils the main characters, but even more important, it constrains the read-ers. We cannot know some things. Contradictory evidence is given, and at best we can work out some sort of proba-bilistic and nonvalidatable answer. Slothrop is convinced that he was conditioned to the smell of Imipolex G, though he and we know that it was not invented, or at least not pat-ented, until 1939. Gottfried, too, impossibly knows that smell from his childhood. Slothrop's sexual adventures at sites soon to be blasted by V-2s cannot be explained by normal science, and we are left wondering just what, if any, is the relationship between these parallel series displayed on identical maps. The existence of "Them" is undeterminable. The novel's many paranoids detect multitudinous plots, but readers cannot verify the reality of those conspiracies.

What Pynchon creates is a fictional analogue to the post-Newtonian universe. We and his characters have to operate in his world as if such subatomic constraints as uncertainty and complementarity could operate at the quotidian level. If we really worried about the implications of the new science or philosophy, we might not make many casual assumptions about reality, such as the existence of cause and effect, or the communicability of anything. Pynchon helps us experience a world in which it is a survival factor to be aware of such unsettling possibilities and shape one's actions to this new, nonbourgeois reality.

Contrary to the assumptions of some literary critics, however, his is not scientifically a non-Newtonian world. There is no way that even his characters worry about determining the momentum and location of an electron at the same time for everyday living. One might call Pynchon's a parallel universe in which subatomic irrationalities become quotidian, rather than a direct translation of science into life; more accurately, however, I think one can say that his is a philosophical universe, and that he is using science as a structural metaphor to embody and reinforce the philosophical principles. I would argue that Pynchon's cosmos is not intended as an alternative to wartime London (in a Moorcock sense—as Brunner claims), nor as an alternate reality based directly on scientific theory. Rather *Gravity's Rainbow* is science fiction in the metaphorical manner of "Heat Death of the Universe," and as a celebration of technology, however ambivalent that celebration may be.

In order to create this fictive analogue to the universe that science gives us, Pynchon relies on fantasy techniques. To create a world scientifically and philosophically more real than our bourgeois reality, he resorts to what we would usually call the nonreal and nonrational, elements we would normally label fantastic.

To begin with, Pynchon establishes that his is a pluriverse, a realm of multiple realities which cannot be put in a hierarchy from the more to the less believable or real. Until physicists arrive at a satisfactory Grand Unification Theory, we are in approximately that position of being unable to unify multiple realities, but we don't worry because it doesn't affect our getting three square meals a day. Pynchon presents us with multiple realities that one does have to deal with, and leaves us to cope with the influx of data rendered nonclassifiable by such plurality.

One of his realities is that generated by dream: the book starts with an imagistic but apparently realistic sequence during the Blitz in London, only to be relabeled as Pirate Prentice's dream after we have oriented ourselves in this carefully-visualized reality, which includes such loving detail as the old-fashioned style of pulley wheel with S-shaped spokes.

Drugs also blur the lines we normally maintain between reality and fantasy. Parts of Slothrop's sodium amytal vision are documentable (indeed, the details come from Malcolm X's autobiography). But Slothrop's malaise with blacks becomes a fantasy of sodomy, and he struggles to elude this fate by diving down the toilet bowl. His subsequent trip down the sewer never explicitly ends. Both Pirate's dream and Slothrop's drug-vision are open-ended, thus erasing our guidelines to reality and making a statement about what comes afterward. The rest of the novel is in a sense an extension of the V-2 bombings, and Slothrop's excremental vision is symbolically the future his Harvard classmates will have to face, in which their WASP reality is shattered and they will be known not by family names or money, but by the kind of shit they produce.

Pynchon also destabilizes our novelistic ontology through a technique that Brian McHale calls attention to. Many characters map onto each other, and most map onto Slothrop at some point. A vivid example of such peculiar cross-overs occurs between Slothrop and Gottfried. Gottfried ends up riding in the V-2, which we might have expected to be Slothrop's fate, given his "precognitive" attraction to these rockets and his quest for their secrets. As Gottfried snuggles down in his Imipolex G insulation, the narrative voice remarks: "The soft smell of Imipolex, wrapping him absolutely, is a smell he knows. It doesn't frighten him. It was in the room when he fell asleep so long ago, so deep in sweet paralyzed childhood." But it is Slothrop who was apparently exposed in infancy to Imipolex G by its creator, Laszlo Jamf. As if this exchange of childhoods weren't enough, Slothrop experiences Gottfried's take-off in the rocket. When making love to Bianca, he starts to experience his own orgasm as if he were within his own cock, about to be launched: "his sperm roaring louder and louder, getting ready to erupt, somewhere below his feet [. . . .] an extraordinary sense of *waiting to rise* [. . . .] their own flood taking him up then out of his expectancy, out the eye at the tower's summit and into her with a singular detonation of touch. Announcing the void, what could it be but the kingly voice of the Aggregat [that is, the V-2] itself." Thus, in fantasy, the two men exchange places, and destroy our readerly assumptions about individuals as entities with well-defined limits.

Pynchon also creates fantastic vantage points to disorient us. We see a Pavlovian lab, and suddenly find ourselves in among the rats, who are grown to human size and who sing a beguine. At another point, we overhear skin cells in our own bodies parodying World War I heroics as they talk of "going epidermal," and facing the deadly ultraviolet radiation. Or we find ourselves in a future where men with machines can monitor stray thoughts of members of a crowd.

All of these manifestations of the fantastic reinforce messages Pynchon gives us at other levels. The world he describes is the world of modern science, philosophy, and language theory—the world of Heisenberg, Nietzsche, and Saussure. This fashionable negativity is what has most attracted the attention of critics. Indeed, they focus so exclusively on this void containing both nothingness and infinite possibility that they have almost entirely overlooked Pynchon's stabilizing mythology, so let me turn to it next.

"A mythological universe," remarks Northrop Frye, "is a vision of reality in terms of human concerns and anxieties." He points out the tendency of myths to aggregate into mythological universes, and offers the Bible as the prime Western example. Pynchon's mythological universe certainly takes some of its form from the biblical prototype. The paradise is America as virgin continent; the fall is the inability of the settlers to live within the cycles of nature, their choice of what became technology and capitalism; Gottfried's ascent in the rocket corresponds to the crucifixion as central symbol of violence; and there are allusions to several possible futures, all apocalyptic in the sense of being both destructive and revelatory. With appropriate modifications, Pynchon tells this linear tale of origins-to-apocalypse at four levels: for Western technological civilization; for Tyrone Slothrop; for the V-2; and for the history of technology.

I believe this can be called mythographic writing: first, because it works to fill the ontological gap between event and meaning, between our absent origin and the meaning of our place in the world; second, because it explains the world in human terms, measures it in human values (Northrop Frye); third, because of the archetypal nature of the major units of this symbolic history; and fourth, because it both shows us the shortcomings of the myths of our culture and manages to suggest the values that will have to supervene if we are to survive in a post-Newtonian, post-Darwinian world. Pynchon's four strands of story add up to a complex account of Western civilization and the danger it is approaching, namely *immachination,* or marriage between man and the machine. (Let me remind you that Pynchon explores a related theme in his first novel, *V.,* namely, the process by which animate flesh and spirit become inanimate, a process he represents symbolically by having V replace more and more parts of her body with mechanical prostheses.)

The mythology is not just a symbolic story line; it embraces Pynchon's entire cosmos. His world is mythic: directions like south and north have meanings. Illuminations and breakthroughs, partial though they usually are, take place in high places, or in the depths, or in wastelands. The Other Side, a pastiche of otherworlds from several traditions—insists not so much on the reality of its own details as on the existence of something beyond material reality. Pynchon's world is inhabited by more entities than is ours—the omnipresent Them; angels (Moslem, Rilkean, Kabbalistic, and the Angel of Death); the Titans; Pan. It lacks a benevolent deity and exhibits a bias toward the demonic, but is quite as much a mythological world as that in the Bible.

Let me sketch briefly the contents of Pynchon's mythology, and then sum up what Edmund Leach's structuralist approach to myth can tell us about this literary mythology. Then we will be in a position to see how this stabilizing pattern interacts with all of Pynchon's aggressively destabilizing strategies linked to science and fantasy mentioned above.

The early stages involve America as a potential paradise for the death-oriented European cultures. The settlers fail to realize this potential, and Slothrop's ancestors, the patriarchs of this new world, decline from God-smitten Puritans to Yankee materialists dealing in paper—the medium for shit, money, and the Word. Parallels to this Europeanization of the American continent are alluded to in stories about Katje's ancestor on Mauretius, in tales of Tchitcherine's literacy campaign in the Russian steppes, and in references to Weissmann's colonialist exploits in Southwest Africa. As these cultures stamped from the European matrix develop, we also watch the development of various technologies—dyes and plastics and rocketry in particular. Franz Pökler sees the early firings of the *Verein für Raumschiffahrt,* and takes part in the failures and advances of the A-2 and A-3 rockets. That the plastics and the V-2 take on mythic values is obvious in the way that the rocket draws first blood, lives on the lives of those dedicated to it. Similarly, the plastic Imipolex G is semialive, erectile.

World War II coincides with the New Testament of this mythology. In a heavily mythological passage reeking of ritual sacrifice, we see Gottfried's wedding to the rocket, his immachination, which is made literally a wedding, with "bridal costume," "white satin slippers," "white stockings" a "bridal" room, careful physical mating, a pressure switch that is the clitoris of the V-2. When Pynchon used the term immachination earlier, he shows us another form of the hybridization of man and machine, a futuristic space helmet: "The eye-sockets are fitted with quartz lenses. Filters may be slipped in. Nasal bone and upper teeth have been replaced by a metal breathing apparatus, full of slots and grating. Corresponding to the jaw is a built-up section, almost a facial codpiece, of iron and ebonite, perhaps housing a radio unit, thrusting forward in black fatality." Such Darth Vader suits will be worn in the high tech future in a society governed by the "Articles of Immachination." The rocket limericks that follow this future fantasy celebrate man's mating with machines in yet another mode. The theme surfaces in another strand of the plot, for Enzian supposedly had "a wet dream where he coupled with a slender white rocket." Plasticman, the hero of the comic Slothrop enjoys, and Rocketman, the persona he adopts, also embody variants of man united with technology. Whereas the central death in Christianity supposedly promises an end to death, immachination ultimately promises an end to life as we know it. Human life will depend on the machine for continuance, as happens in space, for instance, where one must abide by the rules and limitations of the machine or die. Or man and machine will perish together in the Liebestod of rocket falls.

The apocalyptic ends are only alluded to, but Pynchon does sketch four, all sharing the feature that man lives and dies by his technology; he is no longer separate or separable. Immachination in space is one. Rocket-borne war is another. The future (almost our present) of multinational corporations and of Them might be called the *1984*-version of our future, with its elite and its helpless preterite. The web of control exercised by I. G. Farben and its present-day counterparts, is real enough. A minor figure suggests that "Once the technological means of control have reached a certain size, a certain degree of *being connected* one to another, the chances for freedom are over for good." Pynchon also alludes in passing to what might be called a *Brave New World*-form of the future. The City, as it is called, is a living complex based on verticality, with elevators whose interiors are more like courtyards, with their flowersellers and fountains. There, uniformed, good-looking young women, "well-tutored in all kinds of elevator lore," refuse to answer questions about such taboo subjects as the Rocket, and the narrative voice alludes to social repression. This vision of the future is followed by a description of a Hitler Youth Glee Club, reminding us of the polished orderliness that was one of the Hitlerian ideals, and which is a powerful force in this City of the future, and in *Brave New World*. Other writers to explore this kind of dystopian future include Zamiatin, *We;* Vonnegut, *Player Piano;* and Levin, *This Perfect Day.* All show worlds in which poverty and material suffering have been reduced to negligible levels, only to leave other, more hopeless suffering, the more complete damnation of the preterite because they are inferior to machines. Such worlds find humanity acceptable only to the degree that it can become machine-like.

Turning from general history to an individual, we see the origins-to-apocalypse of Tyrone Slothrop. His ancestors, the patriarchs of the new era, fill us in on the development of Yankee know-how, capitalism, and the exploitation of the new continent. Slothrop himself is conditioned as a baby to respond sexually to a mystery stimulus (that he later concludes must have been Imipolex G). Sexual conditioning to a product of technology puts in symbolic terms Western man's fascination and obsession with his own technological creations. Slothrop is later crammed with rocket information, and goes in quest of V-2s. In the course of his search, he does indeed find the Mittelwerke where they were assembled, and Peenemünde, the "Holy Center" of rocket technology, but like Parsifal, he fails to ask the right questions, and does not reach true insight at the birthplace of the rocket. As Technological Man, or even The American, Slothrop's end is particularly interesting, for Pynchon imagines him as becoming briefly a vatic harmonica-Orpheus in the Zone, who ultimately disintegrates. His sparagmos is appropriately orphic, but this loss of identity and then of substance for Technological Man seems to suggest either that man as individual will similarly disintegrate when wedded to the machine, or that the only escape from immachination will be such total dismantling of the ego, or both. Whether you cooperate with the machine and power structure or oppose it, the end is the same. Life as we know it will disappear.

When we look at this mythological history, using Edmund Leach's basic characteristics of myth—redundancy, binary organization, and mediation—we find that they effectively point to the values the myth inculcates, and they show us how the myth works as a stabilizing structure amidst the uncertainty and unknowability set up by the fantasy and science. The process of applying Leach is long, so I can only summarize here a few of the results relating to redundancy.

Redundancies are seen most clearly when characters map onto each other, for they undergo the same experiences, share the same insights, and—usually—fail the same tests. Slothrop is the most heavily redundant character, in this sense; his actions help alert us to what to look for in the others. Among those shared experiences or characteristics most frequently found in the redundancies are:

(a) the shock of discovering a They-reality superimposed on our quotidian, material reality;

(b) the tantalizing awareness that higher illumination is possible, coupled with the failure to achieve the breakthrough;

(c) the desirability of becoming open to the Other Side;

(d) the development of a kind of flexibility to meet whatever improbability next appears;

(e) acceptance both of one's own preterition and one's death;

(f) the importance of kindness to ameliorate our preterite lot, and indeed a general shift from eros toward kindness;

(g) the need to avoid exerting control over others;

(h) the necessity of imposing some limits on one's own freedom in order to survive and be part of a social complex, but the desirability of not letting these limits multiply and become tyrannic bonds; and

(i) the need to recognize that we have fallen into time and cannot go back to living within a totally renewable cycle of nature, and must therefore make intelligent choices when we reach the cusps that history offers us.

What emerges from looking at the myth in modified structuralist ways is, in part, a new hero monomyth, or new concept of the individual and that individual's pattern of development. Given Western assumptions—including our rather inflamed egos and romantic concepts of the individual—we are likely to find Pynchon's alternative pattern spineless and shiftless. Within the new pattern, there is none of the respect which we shower on certain obsessions (for knowledge, money, material possessions, power, persuasiveness, competitiveness, and the like). They belong to the elect, not the preterite. In essence, Pynchon seems to be arguing that even survival values are changing, that flexibility and openness are more valuable than aggressive self-interest if the species (as opposed to the individual) is to survive; that whatever nature may be, man had better not be red in tooth and claw, or the result will be the stockpiling of means of death, the ICBMs of today, made possible by the V-2s.

Without wishing to belittle Pynchon in the least, I think him more traditional and less deconstructive than do most other critics. All the fantastic effects that destabilize novelistic ontology are there to create the fictive embodiment of the new cosmos we must face, the cosmos of modern science, philosophy, and language theory; of uncertainty, unknowability, of arbitrary relationships, and ultimate incommunicability.

Generically, we have the interplay of one kind of science fiction (science as metaphor) with fantasy. The technologically oriented mythology is another kind of science fiction, however, that functions to give warning, and to suggest possible ways of changing so that we could survive in the new cosmos. Particularly in its apocalyptic arguments, it reflects the dystopian strain in science fiction. We also have the science-fictional theme of man's relationship to the machine. The celebration of technology reflects yet another branch of science fiction. And some of the values that emerge from the mythology are the values Pynchon seems to feel we need to live in a post-Newtonian, post-Darwin-

ian world, which amounts to a kind of moral-scientific speculation.

In conclusion, I'm not sure that in most literary analyses we should even think of reducing any complex work to a single generic label. Yes, *Gravity's Rainbow* is science fiction—by several definitions if not by all—but to have called it science fiction, or fantasy, or mythological literature, and to have limited oneself to the insights available through one of those perspectives, would have distorted our understanding of what it achieves. Even limiting the discussion to these three genres is unwarrantable. In addition to casting doubt on the wisdom of such labels (except to use them as a temporary tool or starting point), this experience with *Gravity's Rainbow* suggests the usefulness of our defining science fiction as a family of related but competing literary strains, (as Michael McClintock argues elsewhere in this volume) rather than our trying to create a single exclusive definition. We can define science fiction in an exclusive and limiting fashion—be it as cognitive novum, or as informed extrapolation based on firm knowledge of science, or celebration of ritual transformation of chaos into cosmos via scientific ritual, or as investigation of human interaction with technology. But any such unitary definition is likely to distort our reading of any one work—if we try to apply the definition with any seriousness.

David Cowart (essay date Winter 1990)

SOURCE: "Attenuated Postmodernism: Pynchon's *Vineland*," in *Critique: Studies in Contemporary Fiction*, Vol. XXXII, No. 2, Winter, 1990, pp. 67-76.

[*In the following essay, Cowart examines Pynchon's mytho-historical perspective in* Vineland, *drawing comparison between the literary aesthetics of Pynchon and James Joyce.*

Thomas Pynchon, creator of the most significant body of fiction in contemporary America, may have spent some of the last 17 years discovering the limits of the postmodernist aesthetic. *Vineland,* his long-awaited fourth novel, appears 17 years after the publication in 1973 of the monumental *Gravity's Rainbow,* widely recognized now as the most important American novel published since World War II. One naturally asks whether this author's art has developed or stagnated over those 17 years. The bad news: Pynchon has made no effort to surpass *Gravity's Rainbow.* The good news: he has not stood still as a maker of fiction. In *Vineland,* which may represent a turning point for Pynchon, the author keeps his hand in, modifying some of his old tricks and trying out new ones. In a consideration of this novel's traditional and contemporary features, one encounters an evolutionary text, an experiment in literary hybridization. Conceding that the postures of literary exhaustion may themselves be exhausted, the author combines modernist concerns and postmodernist techniques with some of the features of two kinds of realism: social and magic. The following essay, while scrutinizing the vestiges of a style of aesthetic that Pynchon seems to be outgrowing, will glance at the Abish-like question, *how postmodern is it?*, in the course of gauging the traditional elements and fresh invention that compose this hybrid. The argument here, introduced in a brief comparison of Pynchon's career with that of Joyce, will focus on technique and the treatment given history and culture (including myth). The author of **Vineland** views these topics through a postmodern lens: they appear foreshortened, flattened, all surface. Yet the novel's title and its mythic extension of contemporary history hint at a broader view. Though Pynchon tends to deconstruct the myths he invokes, they complicate the rendering of an otherwise comprehensively ahistorical contemporaneity. Through a combination of this eccentric mythography with a moral earnestness expressed as a penchant for political didacticism, Pynchon produces, in **Vineland,** a fiction devoted less to indeterminate postmodernist "play" than to totalizing modernist "purpose."

On the face of it, Pynchon's is the definitive postmodern career. In book after book, he has seemed to be Bloom's "strong poet," creatively misreading his modernist forebears. Indeed, a comparison of his work with that of Joyce, a literary father to generate considerable anxiety, reveals some interesting parallels. With the exception of the late sport **Slow Learner,** Pynchon's 1984 collection of early stories, the fiction-publishing careers of these two writers match up, volume for volume. Joyce's first book-length fiction appeared in 1914, his fourth and last 25 years later, in 1939. Pynchon's first novel and his fourth span a nearly identical period: the 26 years from 1963 to 1989. In the space of exactly a quarter of a century, each of these writers has given his age its gold standard in fiction, the one defining modernism in the novel, the other postmodernism. Yet the two careers move toward an instructive divergence.

The early volumes of Joyce appeared within two years of each other; those of Pynchon, within three. Joyce's first book, *Dubliners* (1914), is a meticulously structured set of linked fictions that anatomize a culture. Pynchon's *V.* (1963), a highly episodic and fragmented novel that at least one early reviewer (Meixner) took to be a congeries of cobbled together pieces of collegiate creative writing courses, is also meticulously structured, also a cultural anatomy. *Dubliners* moves toward a final vision of snowy paralysis, *V.* toward the triumph of the inanimate. *V.* was followed in 1966 by **The Crying of Lot 49,** in which the failure of American promise gradually manifests itself to

a protagonist, Oedipa Maas, whose age (28 in 1964, the novel's present), education (Cornell), and places of travel and residence (Mexico and California) seem to make her a female Thomas Pynchon. A kind of oblique spiritual autobiography or conversion narrative, **Lot 49** is Pynchon's portrait of the artist in youth and, as such, corresponds to Joyce's autobiographical novel, *A Portrait of the Artist as a Young Man* (1916).

The seven-year period between **Lot 49** (1966) and **Gravity's Rainbow** (1973) corresponds to the six-year period between *Portrait* (1916) and *Ulysses* (1922). **Gravity's Rainbow** and *Ulysses* are quests, "encyclopedic" fictions that, epic in scope, catalogue whole cultures with broad attention to the literary and historical past. Each is, in its own way, a strange amalgam of family romance and Telemachiad: Stephen Dedalus discovers a father in Leopold Bloom, Tyrone Slothrop in the evil scientist Dr. Lazslo Jamf. Stephen, of course, is Joyce's autobiographical character, and perhaps one recognizes a further element of autobiography in the Pynchon novel too, inasmuch as it concerns a person who, like the author, simply fades from sight after embarking on a quest that makes him the "Zone's newest celebrity" and brings him face to face with the possibility that Western culture "might be in love, in sexual love," with its own death.

As the years went by after **Gravity's Rainbow,** one wondered whether its successor would, unimaginably, sustain the Joycean parallel. What complex, Viconian meditation, its hour come round at last, slouched toward Little, Brown to be born? In what idiom would it be written—would it be dense with Herero and Maltese portmanteau words? Pynchon's fourth novel was announced for early in 1990, but it was actually in the bookstores in late December of 1989. In terms of the paradigm, both dates are significant. The earlier is the 50th anniversary of the publication, in 1939, of *Finnegans Wake,* which appeared 17 years after Joyce's previous novel, *Ulysses.* The year 1990, of course, marks the same 17-year period since the publication of Pynchon's last novel, **Gravity's Rainbow.**

But the parallel falters: **Vineland** is not the postmodern *Finnegans Wake.* At most one can say that Vineland County, California, is as mythic a landscape as "Howth Castle and Environs" and the River Liffey. One can note, too, that Leif Ericson, who gave America its first name and Pynchon his title, is among the innumerable strands in the weave of the *Wake:* "lief eurekason and his undishcovery of americle." But these are frail and exiguous crossties for continuing the parallel rails laid thus far. The breakdown in the parallels suggests that the fate reserved for Pynchon's aesthetic differs radically from that reserved for Joyce's. Modernism, it seems, was fated to end with a bang, postmodernism with a whimper.

Though *Finnegans Wake* announced a new aesthetic in its structure—that of a giant Mobius strip—and in its parodic features (it burlesques the medieval dream vision), it is, first and last, the supreme modernist text. Like its modernist predecessors, it exploits myth, probes consciousness and its mysterious subsurface, and outrages aesthetic sensibility in a prose and structure of consummate "difficulty" (to use Eliot's unpretentious word). The parody, like that of *Ulysses,* is reconstructive rather than deconstructive. If like other modernist works it holds a mirror up to cultural fragmentation (it was published on the eve of the century's climacteric, World War II), it composes the fragments artistically, for the program of modernism, however iconoclastic, was always some kind of cultural reclamation.

But postmodernism has no such pretensions. It was always a holding action, a "literature of exhaustion," self-canceling in its most basic premises. Parody and replication in postmodern literature exist to underscore the death of the author and to allow an extra season or two to exhausted forms. In Jean-Francois Lyotard's formulation, postmodern literature "puts forward the unpresentable in presentation itself." A literature largely about itself and its own strategies of re-presentation, it perennially enacts the universal Semitic law: there is no "transcendental signified" behind the arbitrary signifiers—presence is infinitely deferred. The postmodern aesthetic, like signification itself, is a house of cards, and it seems naturally to exhaust itself at a faster rate than other literary movements. Thus the literary apotheosis toward which modernism moves (in a number of texts) is not available to postmodernism, and thus **Vineland** corresponds not to *Finnegans Wake* but to the new literary start Joyce did not live to undertake.

Vineland does not seem to be "self-reflexive" in the approved contemporary manner—a manner that, in all three of his previous novels, Pynchon has shown he can execute brilliantly. But it features at least a few of the quarterings of a postmodern pedigree. It relies heavily on parody, for example, and it favors historical surface to historical depth. It also resists the hierarchization of culture. This refusal to differentiate high culture from low, like the attention to surfaces, is a prominent feature of postmodernist aesthetics. The denial of authority, in all its senses, means the deconstructing of high culture's pretensions to that authority. Thus Pynchon can imagine Pee Wee Herman starring in *The Robert Musil Story.* Thus, too, in the multiple parody in **Vineland**—of Ninja fictions, television soap operas, espionage novels, and detective thrillers—Pynchon tends to minimize the "critical distance" that, according to parody theorist Linda Hutcheon, commonly accompanies the specific type of "repetition" that is parodic.

Where he does not parody popular culture, he catalogues it. What is remarkable is that, in contrast to his previous practice, he catalogues little else. He systematically denies himself the usual resources of allusion in its full range. In fact, he limits himself to one compound literary allusion and a couple of musical allusions. Only the literary reference—to an Emerson quotation in William James—is presented seriously. Both musical allusions, on the other hand, are comically undercut. When Prairie starts to learn about her mother from Darryl Louise Chastain, she appropriately hears music from *Tosca,* for the tale she will hear concerns the suffering of her Tosca-like mother and the Scarpia-like Brock Vond. But the music is played by a pseudo-Italian band at a Mafia wedding. Similarly, in the novel's elegiac conclusion, an entire Thanatoid village awakens to the strains of Bach's *"Wachet Auf,"* evidently with the chorale's powerfully suggestive opening line intended to come to mind: *"Wachet auf, ruft uns die Stimme."* The music materializes as a "piping, chiming music, synchronized, coming out of wristwatches, timers, and personal computers, engraved long ago, as if for this moment, on sound chips dumped once in an obscure skirmish of the silicon market wars . . . as part of a settlement with the ever-questionable trading company of Tokkata & Fuji."

Normally this author peppers his fictions with references that establish historical depth as well as cultural breadth, and readers have marveled at his ability to evoke, in *V.,* turn-of-the-century Alexandria, Florence, or South-West Africa, not to mention, in **Gravity's Rainbow,** the places and feel of much of Europe in 1944 and 1945. These evocations of place and time have generally involved a considerable body of cultural allusion, both high and low. Even in **Lot 49,** where the California setting is not particularly congenial to evocations of high art, one finds painting, literature, music, and film to be important features of the fictional landscape. But through a kind of *askesis* (to "misread" a term of Harold Bloom's), Pynchon here dispenses with the high-culture allusion almost entirely.

Meanwhile the density of reference to the ephemera of popular culture is almost numbing. Pynchon refers often to movies, as in **Gravity's Rainbow,** but here he neglects historic films and art cinema in favor of *Gidget, Dumbo, 20,000 Years in Sing Sing, The Hunchback of Notre Dame, Godzilla, King of the Monsters, Friday the 13th, Return of the Jedi, and Ghostbusters. Psycho* and *2001: A Space Odyssey* are the most substantial films mentioned. The author helpfully supplies dates for these films, parodying scholarly practice, and he invents a number of droll film biographies, including *The Frank Gorshin Story,* with Pat Sajak, and *Young Kissinger,* with Woody Allen. Even more insistently jejune are the allusions to the titles, characters, stars, and music of such television programs as *Star Trek, The Brady Bunch, Gilligan's Island, Jeopardy, Wheel of Fortune, I Love Lucy, Green Acres, Smurfs, CHiPs, Superman,* and *Bionic Woman.* This depressing litany—the intellectual horizon of the American mass mind—subsumes less obvious manifestations of popular taste as well: mall culture, "roasts," video and computer games, new wave hairstyles, breakfast cereals, even "'sensitivity' greeting cards." Pynchon's intent here is not entirely satiric, for no doubt he is genuinely fond of much popular culture. In the introduction to **Slow Learner,** he declares that "rock 'n' roll will never die," and the sentiment is shared by the founders of the People's Republic of Rock and Roll, who name their new state "after the one constant they knew they could count on never to die." Perhaps, too, Pynchon wishes to eschew cultural elitism and demonstrate solidity with the masses. But the virtual absence of historical depth in this body of allusion makes a devastating statement about the shortness of the American cultural memory. This, ultimately, is the point of his constant allusion to the signs and texts of popular culture. Pynchon denies himself much of the cultural and historical dimension of the previous novels and commits himself to imagining the relentlessly a historical consciousness of contemporary American society. The implicit judgment of this shallowness, finally, reveals a moral dimension—always in fact an element in Pynchon's work—that distances this author from the moral neutrality or nihilism sometimes alleged to be the postmodern norm.

Unlike the world he describes, Pynchon himself has an acute sense of history that also leavens his brand of postmodernism. His historical consciousness reveals itself in the guise of that universal history called myth. If the myths invoked in **Vineland** coexist uneasily at the edge of a mutually deconstructive exclusivity, they nevertheless provide the story's action with a temporal depth: they render it "historical" in spite of itself. Thus Terrence Rafferty does not err when he observes that "American history plays itself out" in the bed of Brock Vond and Frenesi Gates. The play of myth, then, circumvents the nominally a historical vision in **Vineland.**

One can sometimes differentiate modernists from postmodernists in their treatment of myth—where modernists exploit myth as universal, instinctual truth, their successors either deconstruct myth as an unreliable "metanarrative" (the breakdown of metanarratives, says Lyotard, is the ground for "the postmodern condition") or examine it as a language that, like all language, speaks its speakers rather than the other way around. Pynchon, as Kathryn Hume demonstrates in *Pynchon's Mythography,* has never divorced himself entirely from the modernist position on myth; and in **Vineland** he has it both ways—privileging at least one myth, deconstructing at least two others. The Faust myth, for example, seems to function in a fairly conventional manner: the federal prosecutor is Mephistopheles; filmmaking Frenesi is Faust. Yet the myth and the mythical identities prove unstable. The Faust here

is also an Eve in the American Eden who betrays her Adam, the hapless Weed Atman. The Mephisto figure, Brock Vond, is also the serpent who tempts them to a fall and a primal murder. These two myths, however, are not at odds, for Faust's passion merely updates that of Adam and Eve. The stories contain the same elements: a diabolical tempter and human souls reaching for forbidden knowledge. But Pynchon complicates matters by introducing, through Sister Rochelle, a *mise en abyme:* a subversive, feminist version of the Eden myth with Frenesi and DL as the primal Eve and Lilith in an Eden in which "the first man . . . was the serpent." This revision of the story seems a minor detail in the novel, and perhaps one at first disregards or discounts it in the desire for a totalizing version of a cherished American literary myth. But its seeming insignificance reveals the deconstructive point: it is one of the aporias around which at least one weave of meaning begins to unravel.

Feminism, by its very nature, is deconstructive—it locates the aporias in the "phallogocentric" discourse of patriarchy. In **Vineland,** the familiar myth undergoes a twofold feminist deconstruction: the patriarchal version of the myth is undercut once by Sister Rochelle's version—and again by the mythic action as Pynchon shapes it. For the mythic individual who makes the moral choice (traditionally an Adam in American fictions: Hawkeye, Huckleberry Finn, Isaac McCaslin) is the American Eve, Frenesi Gates. **Vineland,** then, is a surprisingly "writerly" text: it invites its reader to grapple with closure-resistant, open, multivalent myths that self-de(con)struct under the instruments of analysis.

Yet **Vineland** retains a myth that its author celebrates rather than deconstructs. Pynchon's setting is a representation of the American land; and he refuses to surrender the myth of American promise, which he seems to construe in terms of some continuing, provisional validity of a leftist political alternative to contemporaneous conservatism. The novel's title announces the mythic ground. It evokes more than the California setting and reputation for viniculture. The author situates the imaginary town that gives the novel its name up near the California border with Oregon, and he expects the reader to make the nominal connection with a town on the other side of the continent. The latitude of the real Vineland—Vineland, New Jersey—pretty much coincides with that of the imagined California "Vineland the Good," haven for immigrants like Zoyd Williams and others like him. This implied spanning of the continent at the latitude of its greatest breadth jibes with the novel's symbolic detail to suggest that Pynchon's setting is really the whole vast tract that the Vikings discovered and named Vineland at the end of the first millennium. Thus the title of Pynchon's new novel, published at the end of the second millennium, reminds his American readers that their land has been known to history now for exactly a thousand years.

The novel contains other miniaturized symbols of America. A central example is the People's Republic of Rock and Roll, symbolically the counterculture America of the sixties, delirious with freedom, under surveillance, doomed, the Richard Nixon monolith at oceanside casting its shadow, an obvious symbol of repression to come. Perhaps, too, Zoyd Williams's house, of which he has been forcibly dispossessed by unconscionable federal power, is another such symbol. At the end, he is flirting with the idea of putting it to the torch—which America's dispossessed may yet do to the house they are unable fully to enter. As in *Lot 49*, Pynchon contemplates the paradoxes of dispossession and preterition in the land of promise. "How had it ever happened here," wonder Oedipa Maas in that earlier novel, "with the chances once so good for diversity?"

Vineland, then, is a meditation on the American social reality, a return to the ground Pynchon seems to think he did not cover adequately in *Lot 49* (he remarks in the introduction to *Slow Learner* that he thinks his second novel merely a long story, not technically accomplished). Though *Vineland* is not *Lot 49* redivivus, one notes points of contact—most obviously the California setting—between the two. In the earlier novel the heroine, Oedipa Maas, meets a member of the Paranoids, an aspiring rock group, and offers to give her DJ husband, Mucho, a tape to plug. Now the reader learns that Mucho "after a divorce remarkable even in that more innocent time for its geniality," has become a successful recording industry executive (like *V*.'s Rooney Winsome)—and that he has shepherded Miles, Dean, Serge, and Leonard to success.

But where is Oedipa in the new novel? Oedipa realizes at the end of *Lot 49* that the only way she can go on being relevant to her country is "as an alien, unfurrowed, assumed full circle into some paranoia." The heroine of the new novel, Frenesi Gates, is a version of that new, desperate Oedipa—estranged from a man with a Dutch surname and living a furtive, underground existence. Oedipa seems a less flawed person than Frenesi, but both characters are symbols of the American conscience—radicalized in the sixties, coopted in the eighties. The two novels also explore the significance of drug use. In *Lot 49,* Oedipa does not perceive Mucho's involvement with LSD as positive, but it does link him to the marginalized Americans she will come to embrace. In the later novel, the reader learns that Mucho proceeded to addict himself to cocaine before giving up drugs altogether. Mucho's addiction and the horrors, however comic, of the 'Room of the Bottled Specimens' are among the book's few concessions that there might be a down side to drug use. But Mucho becomes an entrepreneur as he goes straight—and his entrepreneurism makes

him suspect in Pynchon's economy. Here one glimpses the equation that partially accounts for Pynchon's somewhat disturbing refusal to depict drugs in a negative light: taking drugs (as opposed, perhaps, to dealing them) remains a powerful metaphor for the idea of an alternative to the rapacious capitalism and consumerism that afflict American society.

One sees a more meaningful contrast between these books in their handling of history. Oddly, it is the book with ostensibly the more shallow historical draft—*Vineland*, with its one-generation memory—that reveals its author as truly concerned about the way the present evolves out of the past. In *Lot 49,* several hundred years of history are the means to make Oedipa's quest interesting and complicated, but this past is only superficially imagined as accounting for her American present (Oedipa's historical research serves the epistemological theme—the infinite reticulation of "paranoid" interconnectedness—rather than the sociological one that links her story to Frenesi's). In *Vineland,* by contrast, Pynchon again examines the American present, but with specific reference to a recent—and radically different—past. This equipoise between sixties and eighties keeps *Vineland* from being the simple-minded exercise in nostalgia some have taken it for. Far from the sour grapes of some bitter ex-hippie, it is a treatise on the direction history has taken, without our having given it much thought. Moreover, his own implicit political orientation notwithstanding, Pynchon exposes the millenarian canker in the flower children as rigorously as he diagnoses the reactionary carcinoma of the next generation. *Lot 49,* set in 1964, is a story of consciousness being raised—an allegory of sixties America repudiating conformity, racism, and militarism. It looks backward to the Eisenhower fifties and forward to the Summer of Love. *Vineland,* set a generation later in the portentous year of 1984, looks backward to that summer—and forward to some Republican version of the thousand-year Reich. It reveals how the nation has allowed an earlier passion for justice to go dead, to be coopted by a conservative backlash and an attendant dissipation of liberal energy.

In a single generation—from the mid-sixties to the mid-eighties, America veered from a liberal to a conservative bias, from the New Frontier and the Great Society to "Reaganomics," from hordes of student demonstrators to whole undergraduate populations majoring in business, from Yippies to Yuppies. In *Vineland* Pynchon examines these societal extremes and the historical currents they ride or embody. Interestingly contemporaneous with David Lodge's *Nice Work,* a refitting of the nineteenth-century "condition-of-England" novel, *Vineland* would seem in its hybridization also to undertake such an old-fashioned assessment. It is a condition-of-America novel. That condition, as a result of the Reagan revolution and, before that, the "Nixonian Repression" or "Nixonian Reaction," is imagined as darkening, a "prefascist twilight," if not the actual night. "Nixon had machinery for mass detention all in place and set to go," says a Pynchon character. "Regan's got it for when he invades Nicaragua." The "Reagan program" is to "dismantle the New Deal, reverse the effects of World War II, restore fascism at home and around the world."

Pynchon makes his political sympathies plain enough. But the polemics have little do to with the novel's art, which one sees in the indirection and economy that deliver this and other Pynchon works from the realm of propaganda and didacticism. This author's art—an art far superior, it seems to me, to that of such novelists on the left as Dos Passos or Steinbeck or Vonnegut—commands the aesthetic interest of readers who may find the politics somewhat overwrought. Pynchon contrives, by diving into the wreck of mythic metanarrative, to imbue with extraordinary historical resonance a story that ostensibly depicts the vitiation of the historical sense. He remains the only contemporary writer whose grasp of history's mythic dimensions merits comparison with that of Joyce—and he may yet present us with a fiction on the scale of that writer's last book. One doubts that he spent the seventeen years after *Gravity's Rainbow* on *Vineland* alone. Who knows what post-postmodern extravaganza may follow in its wake?

Richard Powers (review date Summer 1990)

SOURCE: "State and Vine," in *Yale Review*, Vol. 79, No. 4, Summer, 1990, pp. 690-8.

[*In the following review, Powers offers a positive evaluation of* Vineland.]

A Corporate State, as the quickest study among slow learners long ago pointed out, knows how to turn even innocence to its many uses. Childhood, vulnerability, every fairy tale that ever soothed us to sleep will, along with the rest of individual experience, be exploited, interrogated, made to turn a profit, put to efficacious and pacifying work by the controlling powers. Such a nightmarish historical motion pervades *Gravity's Rainbow,* one of the most astonishing and urgent American novels ever written. Politics, that exhaustive, eschatological proverb for paranoids sez, advances inexorably on the moment when the State will achieve its program, when government will at last seal off and package innocence, gaining a legislative stranglehold on pleasure. Pynchon's first novel in the seventeen years since *Gravity's Rainbow* suggests that this moment has already arrived, is here, in the United States of the eighties, a sad, hilarious, self-parodic, sprawling, terminally straightjacketed, desperate,

co-opted, but somehow still kicking and innocent place: *Vineland,* Vineland the Good.

It says something about how very different this new book is for Pynchon that a plot synopsis is at least possible, if only just. And especially for a book that revels in invention and event, plot is the only map into the heart of the matter. At the center of the story, yet disturbingly elusive, is this world's Chief Innocent, Frenesi Gates. She is, by turns and depending upon the observer, "a little kid alone at a dangerous time of day, not yet aware of her mom's absence," and a "third-generation lefty who'd likely've bombed the Statue of Liberty if she could." Born into California labor-movement lineage just after World War II, named for an Artie Shaw tune, and brought up during the 1950s in Hollywood, where her parents suffered political persecution, Frenesi comes of age at Berkeley and joins the radical, high-sixties film cooperative, 24fps. Celluloid is this group's Semtex:

> They particularly believed in the ability of close-ups to reveal and devastate. When power corrupts, it keeps a log of its progress, written into that most sensitive memory device, the human face. Who could withstand the light? What viewer could believe in the war, the system, the countless lies about American freedom, looking into these mug shots of the bought and sold?

Frenesi's foil and physical intimate in the film collective is Darryl Louise (DL) Chastain, an Eastern mystic and martial-arts adept, aggressive and pragmatic where Frenesi is idealistic and ethereal. The group travels to the tiny Southern Californian College of the Surf, which has just declared itself the People's Republic of Rock and Roll, "the one constant they knew they could count on never to die." Filming the formation of this fledgling, few-acre sovereign state, Frenesi becomes the lover of the activist leader Weed Atman and, at the same time, of the federal prosecutor villain, Brock Vond, who has been sent in to subvert the ingenuous uprising.

Prosecutor Vond, a thoroughly sadistic control freak, exercises hypnotic sexual power over Frenesi, who has inherited her mother's obsession with uniforms:

> [Frenesi's mother] on her own had arrived at, and been obliged to face, the dismal possibility that all her oppositions, however just and good, to forms of power were really acts of denying that dangerous swoon that came creeping at the edges of her optic lobes every time the troops came marching by, that wetness of attention and perhaps ancestral curse.

Frenesi's swoon, her involvement with Vond, deepens until she is supplying him with film, then information, then assistance. As her ultimate act of servility, she discredits the activist Weed and then facilitates his murder. Weed's death precipitates the collapse of the People's Republic, and Vond's forces ice the demise with a massacre midway between Kent State and Tiananmen Square. Frenesi is rounded up, along with others from the collapsed revolution, and taken to a detention camp, part of Vond's pet Political Re-Education Program (PREP) to turn civil detainees into government snitches. Her friend DL, loyal despite the evidence, springs the at-best-ambivalent Frenesi from the camp. But when Frenesi confesses everything, the two women split in mutual recrimination, the film cooperative dissolves, and the sixties come to an inglorious end, much as they did in the wider world.

The seventies, too, play out true to the big picture: a more or less lost decade for this lot. DL is conscripted into a Mob effort to eighty-six Vond, now her sworn enemy. She attempts to hit him with the Vibrating Palm, or Ninja Death Touch, a delayed-action lethal technique picked up from her years at that "Esalen Institute for lady ass-kickers," the Sisterhood of Kunoichi Attentives. By mistake, she instead zaps a Japanese speed-chomping investigator named Takeshi Fumimota. As an antidote and act of contrition, she becomes Takeshi's assistant, and the two of them set up business in Karmic Adjustments. Their principal clients are the Thanatoids, a community of damaged souls who have given up all worldly interests except watching the Tube and concentrating on "emotions helpful in setting right whatever was keeping them from advancing further into the condition of death."

Meanwhile, Frenesi wanders directly from her break with DL and 24fps into marriage with Zoyd Wheeler, a druggie piano player with the Corvairs (also known, in an attempt to catch a meager wave, as the Surfadelics). The match is more for cover than for love. Equally rapidly, she has a baby girl, Prairie. But redemption and family are not enough. When Vond suddenly reenters her life—pulling her over on the highway, spreading her legs, and frisking her—Frenesi abandons husband and infant to pursue the old obsession with uniforms and power.

Vond uses a DEA narc named Hector Zuniga, whose calling it is to torment eternally Frenesi's ex-husband, to set Zoyd up. Then Vond cuts a deal with Zoyd: take the infant Prairie, and regular government checks, and never let Frenesi near her daughter again. Zoyd chooses these terms over life in prison, and he brings Prairie up the California coast to Vineland, a last redwooded stand of American wilderness. There, in order to continue receiving the checks, officially for mental disability, Zoyd must perform some suitably insane act annually. He specializes in transfenestration—plunging through windows.

Frenesi, too, must accept terms from Vond. When the decisive year 1984 arrives, she is living a dismal, transient existence as a member of that very species her whole upbringing and conscience have taught her to detest: a government snitch, sting specialist, independent operator. She is remarried, to another low-level government snitch—again not for love—with whom she's had a son. They are being sheltered by the government in a witness-protection program. But "independent operator" is a euphemism for "instantly deniable," and it is this denial—Frenesi's removal from the files and abandonment to Reaganomic cutbacks—that launches the last chapter of these interlocked lives.

Narc Hector returns to plague Zoyd, telling him that Frenesi, long underground, has been flushed from the government computers and forced back to the surface. Hector seeks Zoyd's help in finding Frenesi, whom Hector wants to star in his government-backed feature film on the horrors of drug ingestion. But the DEA man now has a substance-abuse problem of his own: he has escaped from a Tubaldetox clinic, where treatment strategies for Tube addiction range from the homeopathic ("a retinal diet of scientifically calculated short video clips of what in full dosage would, according to theory, have destroyed his sanity") to the New Age cure of Transcendence Through Saturation. Hector, a real cop, has delusions that he is a TV one.

At the same time, Zoyd's house is seized by a military strike force under civil RICO. Zoyd goes into hiding, and his daughter Prairie, now a very mature fourteen, takes off with her punk-rocker boyfriend Isaiah Two Four, whose band, Billy Barfand and the Vomitones, metamorphoses into Gino Baglione and the Paisans in order to play a Mafia wedding. ("Mr. Wayvone says he was hoping he wouldn't have to go into too many details with you, but that he was thinking more along the lines of 'C'e la Luna,' 'Way Marie'—you know, sing-along stuff.") At the wedding, a transmitter business card that Zoyd once received from Takeshi for saving his life and that Zoyd has passed on to his daughter brings Prairie to the attention of her mother's old friend DL, who is there as the guest of the man who once hired her to kill Brock Vond. (As in other Pynchoniana, everyone connects to everyone else, and nobody knows anyone.) DL takes Prairie under her wing and, through computer files and old 24fps footage, introduces Prairie to the mother she never knew.

All paths converge, in the end, up in Vineland. Frenesi and her new family, on the run, are lured there by Hector and his insane movie scheme. Vond and his army pursue hotly in Huey gunships. DL and Takeshi are summoned north by the Thanatoids, who have been awakened to life and memory ("What was a Thanatoid, at the end of the long dread day, but memory?") by countless Tokkata & Fuji microchips programmed to erupt simultaneously in Bach's "Wachet Auf!"

Frenesi, her parents, Prairie, and Zoyd all descend on their extended family's annual reunion. Denouement comes at night, when Vond, too, descends on a helicopter umbilical cable to try to kidnap Prairie, sleeping alone under the stars. He tells the girl he is her father, a claim Prairie rejects. At that moment, as if in a fairy-tale snap, Vond's authorization for rampage (a Reagan evacuation exercise called REX 84) is withdrawn and he is winched back to heaven. He tries to return alone but winds up delivered to the Yurok land of death, where Indian spirits remove his bones. Yet the story ends darkly, with Prairie in the night forest whispering her own ancestral cop fantasies to the empty sky, telling Vond that he can come back, take her anywhere he wants. She wakes to a morning evocation of nature, Vineland, as if there were still a tiny sliver of land indifferent to politics, psychology, the pathology of civilization.

Not, perhaps, your average story. At the same time, *Vineland* clearly represents a return, for Pynchon, to a more traditional novel. As the synopsis reveals, there is still a great deal of tragical-comical-historical-pastoral mode-mixing here, but what's new this time around is that these stances are by and large subordinated to the central thrust of the story, however much that story is a setup for the old Manichaean struggle. Once again, he do the police in many voices, and he do a dozen of the police-victim dialects as well. Only now, rather than letting those voices and moods and genres proliferate polyphonically into an immense symphony of possible worlds (ultimate tonality always withheld), the grand master of the postmodern returns to an older trade, that of writing a character-driven commentary, without sardonic deflation, about what we can know of *this* world, however fragmented and fantastically extended. If Frenesi herself remains a deliberate center-stage cipher, other people in Vineland are more multidimensionally flesh and blood than anyone I can remember from Pynchon's previous books.

This is not to say that he's spun a conventional tale here—not by any stretch of the imagination. Stretched imagination itself sends this book into a place all its own. The outrageous plot—impossible but meticulously justified, close enough to surreal to be our own, mundane daytime soap—the page-after-page mordents and flourishes of syntax, the manic wordplay (Check's in the mayo, Midol America, Marquis de Sod lawn care), the endless invention (reified worms playing pinochle up a man's snout, suicide fantasy packages, Sister Vince and the Harleyite order, a male biker gang posing as a convent for tax purposes), the raw specificity of detail, all trademarks of Pynchon's unique version of Brechtian epic theater, are here put to another working purpose (the same, as Vineland folks are constantly saying, only different): not *Verfremdung*, but a police dossier of the bizarrely, banally familiar. The book is a riot of

genres and genre parodies—California gumshoe, comic book, Japanese sci-fi, kung fu, prime-time sitcom. Half its sentences perch somewhere between high and low burlesque. But his characters are too engaging, the landscape—the "thousand bloody arroyos in the hinterlands of time that stretched somberly inland from the honky-tonk coast of Now"—too close to the calcium and limestone for us to deny or fail to recognize vast tracts of it.

It would be a mistake, I think, to find in *Vineland* only a diminished *Gravity's Rainbow* or *V*, although the book does ask, of late-in-the-year America, what to do with a diminished thing. Nor is it simply a more mature *Crying of Lot 49*, which it superficially most resembles (it even features a walk-on by Mucho Maas, disk jockey now turned music industry biggie). It cannot be called realist; nor does it belong to any antithetical category. Rather, it is a deliberate departure, deploying existing motifs in a new variation, a strange hybrid of what would until now have seemed inimical ways of narrating. Dementedly *and* dryly funny, one of those entertaining, accessible novels that grows harder, richer, more problematic on second reading, it will nevertheless surely send ripples of shock and surprise through the raging pseudo-debate between the Pre- and Post- folks. If scope and scale are somewhat reduced, by Pynchon's standards, the concerns are not.

There is a large dose of Pynchonesque grassy-knollism in this book. References abound to resettlement camps for ensuring the domestic tranquillity come the impending confrontation (and there is some precedent for these, after all). But by and large, Pynchon's previous conspiracies of megamachine death are replaced here by more overt, visible enemies. At the rolling family reunion that ends the book, voices are "heard arguing the perennial question of whether the United States still lingered in a prefascist twilight, or whether that darkness had fallen long stupefied years ago, and the light they thought they saw was coming only from millions of Tubes all showing the same bright-colored shadows."

Here is the core argument of the book itself: the Vineland it hurts to read about is our own heartbreaking, magnificent mess of a nation-state, a self-proscribing society fervently proclaiming its freedom, plunged in a great constitutional debate over whether to jail cloth-burners, celebrating the blow for order, the flex of enforcement that allows it to nab at least certain Capital offenders without armed invasion. In Vineland, Brock Vond's forces do in fact storm "up and down the dirt lanes in formation chanting 'War-on-Drugs! War-on-Drugs!' strip-searching folks in public . . . as if they had invaded some helpless land far away." Drug-taking (which Pynchon admits in a few deft characterizations is not exactly yer best long-term liberator of individual potential) must be read as just one of a comprehensive range of individual pleasures under siege, the front-line target of a broader, more sadistic social regimentation: "Perfume Police. Tube Police. Music Police. Good Healthy Shit Police. Best to renounce everything now, get a head start."

The book would be far less interesting if it went no further than dopers and narcs, hedonism versus the Boys in Blue. But alongside Hector's hapless hippie-hounding and Vond's strike force thrashing about in the name of national security, there is a more insidious threat to freedom afoot, an abuse of private innocence even more fascistically comprehensive than law enforcement: the *corporate* in Corporate State. Everyone must be kept on the treadmill of diversion—brand names, tunes, shows—amusing themselves to death (in Postman's phrase). The deadly satellite-computer combo, the Information Age tools that make Vond and his sort invincible head-on, are supplemented by a far more deadly weapons combination: Cap'n Crunch. Film Noir Shopping Malls piping "a sprightly oboe-and-string rendition of Chuck Berry's 'Maybellene.'" Pee-wee Herman in *The Robert Musil Story*. A docudrama of the NBA '83-'84 championship, aired a few months after the "event." In order to keep the pump sumping, we are to accept lifestyle in place of life, to sit still and wait until the portal of retail and broadcast anesthesia pulls tight over our last lucid thoughts. Vineland, as Robert Hughes might say, has become not so much a place as a Ride. Thinking, moving, living are overwhelmed by "the ever-dwindling attention span of an ever more infantilized population."

Ultimately, from the dedication ... to the closing image of a girl invoking a father of impossible blood type to come back and ravish her, *Vineland* comes down to a story about parents and children—the stories one tells to placate, appease, mislead, control, co-opt, escape, and earn the love of the other.

—*Richard Powers*

"God," Zoyd laments, nostalgically recalling days of Vine and roses, old acid-dropping insights, "I knew then, I knew...." "Uh-huh, me too," Mucho Maas echoes:

"That you were never going to die. Ha! No wonder the State panicked. How are they supposed to control a population that knows it'll never die? When that was always their last big chip.... Give us too much to process, fill up every minute, keep us distracted, it's what the Tube is for ... just another way to claim our attention, so that beautiful certainty we had starts to fade, and after a while they have us convinced all over

again that we really are going to die...." It was the way people used to talk.

Mediated lives and deaths, in all senses of the word: if there is something squirmingly uncomfortable about this encyclopedic, inexhaustibly inventive talent repeatedly invoking the Smurfs, well, that's where we *live*, Foax.

There is a third leg to this grand unified isosceles of corporation, state, and abused innocence. Data, assault helicopters, all the brutal machinery of law and its execution, even the saturation of broadcast jingles would all be helpless, Pynchon suggests, without some degree of willing assistance on the part of the victim. The assertion, over three generations of heroines, that every woman might secretly love a fascist (somewhat problematic in real life) is just for starters; we must also own up to the recognition that we secretly hope, all of us, to entrust our innocence to the State. Everyone in this book is co-opted, turned, bought off to some degree or another. "Everyone's a squealer," Frenesi's squealer husband whines. Or a collaborator, in this country under occupation. This 1984 is even more *Animal Farm*. Even the Harleyites are turned from their program of mayhem by a stint on "Donahue." There seems to be, in the heart's deep core, some tacit complicity pact between Light and Dark, between Hayley and Satanic Mills.

The pact results from the fact that the struggle between social order and private anarchy is not just cops versus criminals, but Id versus superego, Eros versus Thanatos:

Brock Vond's genius was to have seen in the activities of the sixties left not threats to order but unacknowledged desires for it. While the Tube was proclaiming youth revolutions against parents of all kinds and most viewers were accepting this story, Brock saw the deep—if he'd allowed himself to feel it, the sometimes touching—need only to stay children forever, safe inside some extended national Family.

A theory of history is tucked away in here, plotting the progress of revolutions from the People's Republic of Rock and Roll ("this geist that could've been polter along with zeit") to the Reagan Bargain-Counter Reformation ("restore fascism at home and around the world.") The imminent expectation of revolutionaries is born in the child's hope for a "world newly formatted, even innocent," while the death wish of "the fascist monster, Central Power itself" against its own children has its source in a parental fear, like Brock Vond's, that "each child he thus produced, each birth, would only be another death for him." Vond and Frenesi's victim, Weed Atman, come back from the dead to walk the earth awhile among the Thanatoids, relates a dream where his two corpse-bodyguards debate Vond's motive for murder. "'It was all for love,' says one, and 'Bullshit,' the other replies, 'it was political.'" Yes, *Vineland* concludes, these two may come to the same thing.

This is a profoundly American book, oddly but squarely in the frontier tradition, where the bank jobs are pulled off by gangs of roller-skating mall rats in black T-shirts, where corrupt civilization is written out in endless digitized ones and zeros circumscribing all life and death, where the Redskins are called in to fillet the lawman alive, and where the West one might still escape into is reduced to a tiny but still unsurveyed enclave along the coast. *Vineland* is a pained comic cry for "the scabland garrison state the green free America of their childhoods even then was turning into," for "another planet . . . they used to call . . . America, long time ago, before the gutting of the Fourth Amendment."

A burlesque but deeply engaged fairy tale with real people setting the allegories in motion, the novel perilously straddles a dialogic rift: the stubbornly miraculous opposing the brutely real; inevitable annihilating power countered by a gust of antinomianism in a compliant time. Such a hybrid book runs the risk of disappointing the champions of experimentalism while still not behaving cleanly enough to satisfy the traditionalists. But as with all intensely imagined and closely observed worlds, this one is best lived in for the pleasure of engagement, without categories or preconceptions.

Ultimately, from the dedication ("to my mother and father") to the closing image of a girl invoking a father of impossible blood type to come back and ravish her, *Vineland* comes down to a story about parents and children—the stories one tells to placate, appease, mislead, control, co-opt, escape, and earn the love of the other. Its most engaging scenes, most convincing dialogue, most hilarious punch lines all involve mothers and fathers searching, seizing, and loving sons and daughters, and these sons and daughters refusing to submit while loving bewilderingly back.

All fallen and even abused children, like Frenesi, with her "shadows of her shoulder blades, like healed stumps of wings ritually amputated once long ago," will, for better or worse, never escape the need for parenting, for a bedtime story. Yes, narrative may be a form of paranoia, a frightened systems-building to counter or create conspiracies, real and imagined. But narrative can be more: in *Vineland* it is an interrogation of power, a flexing of imagination and observation, an urgent verbal gag straining to redeem what innocence is left us by the State. In this, its only weapon, as always, is continuous telling and retelling. Whatever other astonishments and innovations have landed him securely in American readers' imaginations, Pynchon remains above all a story-spinner, winning an-

other few moments for the mind's eye. So tell us another one, Pop, before it gets too dark.

Joseph Tabbi (review date Spring 1991)

SOURCE: "Pynchon's Groundward Art," in *Michigan Quarterly Review*, Vol. 30, No. 2, Spring, 1991, pp. 375-82.
[*In the following review, Tabbi criticizes Pynchon's artistic complacency in* Vineland.]

As long as the novel remains a popular medium, it is probably inevitable that readers should regard the artist before the work of art, and tend to celebrate the performing, rather than the creative, personality. An abdication as extreme as Thomas Pynchon's only proves the rule. He has given no interviews and made no public appearances, personal friends keep quiet, and there are only a scattering of photographs from the 1953 Oyster Bay High School yearbook that editors, in an act of pure revenge, have kept reprinting in feature articles and national reviews. For someone of Pynchon's stature, the sheer effort of maintaining anonymity has to be an occupation in itself, and reason enough to avoid publication for seventeen years.

Now that *Vineland* has appeared, however, it is clear that the most strenuous public relations campaign could not have stimulated as much interest. Nearly everything leading up to the appearance—the long wait, the award to the author some years previously of a MacArthur grant, and the secrecy in which Little, Brown cloaked the manuscript—worked to ensure its being read and reviewed, like any novel of note today in America, as news. Clinching the American reception was Salman Rushdie's front-page review in the *New York Times Book Review* (January 14, 1990), a message direct from the underground pronouncing the voluntary exile's literary return a "triumph." Dissenting reviews by Frank Kermode and Brad Leithauser registered a cooler international reception, but this has not kept academic critics here from taking up the novel's explication and getting started on the inevitable revisions of the Pynchon canon. Within a year of publication, there are already the beginnings of a *Vineland* industry, and it is against this large and continuing response that the novel itself will have to be understood.

Now more than ever Pynchon, by avoiding publicity, has created it, and, whatever his intentions, by his own elusiveness he has helped to serve the celebrity function of literature. The difference this time, though, is that the work would appear to rest comfortably in its publicity, offering very little in the way of critical resistance to the cultural climate in which it appears. We are used to hearing about media depredations on literary talent; about Norman

Mailer's having been ruined, for example, by his wasted efforts either to change or live up to his public image. But I wonder if reticence might not have its own price. At its worst, self-promotion in Mailer has been a way at least of making contact with an audience, and of testing its reality. Yet it is hard to know for whom, precisely, **Vineland** was intended, unless it be for the very audience that, through demographic studies and proven interest, the media and the marketplace have themselves created and sustained. With its laid-back style, American matter, and deliberately conventional sixties nostalgia, the novel is all too easily *placeable* in the field of current writing. And this is neither a sell-out nor an especially welcome bid for "accessibility" so much as an imaginative short-cut on Pynchon's part, an acceptance of a ready-made audience that frees him from the responsibility of creating the sensibility by which he will be understood.

My dissatisfaction with **Vineland** is not that the book is a falling off—"what wouldn't be," was a friend's fair response. After *Gravity's Rainbow,* a direct treatment and "return home" to America does make a kind of sense. But for the reader who has been moved by complexities of form and language beyond the alienation depicted in *Gravity's Rainbow,* the return can seem imperfectly achieved, the new optimism arbitrary, settled in advance, and sustainable only by an almost willed holding back from darker forces and paranoia that still come obscurely through. A relaxation of tension is apparent in the way that Pynchon allows the language and mannerisms of the time and place—mostly Northern California in the sixties and the eighties—to shape his own style; and, where he had often been accused in the earlier novels of creating cold, abstract characters (they are not), now there is an evident and mostly unironic fondness for all but the cops (and even for some of them) that has led many to believe that this, at last, is Pynchon's true face: an Old Lefty nostalgic for the lost radical history of Pacific Northwestern logger unions and Wobblie politics, and who is willing to assert, against all the co-opted radicalism, fallen ideals, and unfulfilled "acid adventures" of the sixties, a positive sense of community with his contemporaries.

His loyalties are political and generational rather than literary, as they always have been. But the left wing politics don't quite sit with a new, right-leaning aesthetic. In two recent semi-autobiographical essays introducing his own and his college friend Richard Farina's apprentice work, he showed signs of dissatisfaction with the flashy technique and experimental difficulty of his writing. After taking pains to criticize the short story, **"Entropy,"** an early show-off piece that remains nonetheless a good introduction to Pynchon's abstract imagination, he spoke of preferring fiction that has some "grounding in human reality" and an authenticity "found and taken up, always at a cost, from

deeper, more shared levels of the life we all really live." This change in attitude may account for the new attention to scenes of family life and general suburban ordinariness of the people of Vineland (even when they happen to be undercover agents, ex-anarchist bombers, or a bad-ass woman warrior like DL Chastain). Gone are the abstract epistemological quests that, for many, made the earlier novels such attractive allegories of contemporary reading, whose main characters are acutely aware of themselves as makers and interpreters of signs, and who because not conventionally "full" or "real" have been thought to be only elements in a game. Like Stencil in his first novel, *V.,* Pynchon must surely have seen the likelihood of his work being turned into "merely a scholarly quest after all, an adventure of the mind." The demands made by the earlier work may have selected a more cerebral audience than he ever wanted, and the anti-intellectual rhetoric of the prefaces, like the populist language and mock scholarly references in **Vineland,** seem designed to reach a wider audience, and to defend the work against the allegorizing critics.

In keeping with the new realism, the quest this time is less formally self-conscious, more personal and direct: a young girl, Prairie Gates, after years of separation comes to learn about her mother, Frenesi, and in the process is given a pretty good American political education. Frenesi lost the upbringing of her daughter in the early seventies when, having betrayed her radical friends to the Drug Enforcement Agency, she leaves her family home in Vineland for the security and protective anonymity of a bureaucratic career in the government. To Pynchon's credit, the betrayal is sought not in any simple rejection by Frenesi of her youthful ideals (which are shown to have been vague and naive at best), but in the larger spirit of sixties radicalism—most obviously in the cult of youth, but more subtly in a generation's unthinking embrace of media and technologies that set life at a distance. Even during her most idealistic years at Berkeley, Frenesi had sought a kind of immunity in film work, imagining that "as long as she had life inside her Tube-shaped frame, . . . nothing out there could harm her." The government offers merely another kind of immunity, one that seems neverending until her budget is cut and she not only loses her job, but—in ironic confirmation of her already lost identity—she has her entire file erased from the Agency's computer.

We could welcome the story as a domestic gloss on the earlier novels, a gloss that reduces, to be sure, but that does serve to correct our overly literary and de-politicized readings of Pynchon. The injunction to "be experimental" can be as much of a trap as any other creative prescription, and he can hardly be blamed for choosing not to push the limits of his art. Yet, for all the reputed ease and accessibility, he can't resist giving his own, indeterminate twist to his popular and realistic material, and the hybrid fiction that results has neither the emotional charge of realism nor the rich fabulism and science-based clarities of the earlier, more overtly experimental work. For long stretches the novel resembles nothing so much as recent cyberpunk fiction in which the deepest, most "shared levels of the life we all really live" are often hard to separate from the collective reality of brand names, corporations, and network television. If *Gravity's Rainbow* engendered a taste for technological complexities and multiple otherworldly bureaucracies in a younger science fiction writer such as William Gibson, there is now, in *Vineland,* a hint of Gibson in the ninjette training of the young DL Chastain, and in the subtle alterations, made in bed and on the operating table, to Takeshi Fumimota's nervous system. Here is the same mixture, as in Gibson, of a mock oriental mysticism (Chastain has touched the Japanese businessman with the Fatal Palm, which will cause instant death exactly one year later) and an equivalent, simulated mysticism in the West (Fumimota can be cured only by the most advanced procedures, involving endless use of the most costly medical equipment). A society of half-alive "Thanatoids" living on junk food and television re-runs are also reminiscent of Gibson's "flatliners" and of other technological "constructs" of once living personalities. Yet the Thanatoids, too, were anticipated in the final scattering of Tyrone Slothrop in a passage from *Gravity's Rainbow* that gestures, as Christopher Walker has remarked, toward Pynchon's "own disillusionment with the whole novelistic project":

> There is also the story about Tyrone Slothrop . . . and there ought to be a punchline to it, but there isn't. The plan went wrong. He is being broken down instead, and scattered. His cards have been laid down, Celtic style, in the order suggested by Mr. A. E. Waite, laid out and read, but they are the cards of a tanker and feeb; they point only to a long and scuffling future, to mediocrity (not only in his life but also, heh, heh, in his chroniclers too, yes yes nothing like getting the 3 of Pentacles upside down covering the significator on the second try to send you to the tube to watch a seventh rerun of the Takeshi and Ichizo Show, light a cigarette and try to forget the whole thing)—to no clear happiness or redeeming cataclysm.

It may be, as Walker suggests, that "*Vineland* is the fruit of this tubal immersion," and that the form of the TV re-run has to an extent replaced "the logic of quest, knowledge and apocalyptic revelation" in the first three novels. Yet this passage also reveals Pynchon in the earlier work as a writer who is capable of questioning his own plots, metaphors, and quests, so as to constantly resist the apocalypse he imagines. The endless replication in *Vineland* of already known forms, like the cyberpunk's retro-future in which the end seems to have already come, can only make

any further resistance seem pointless. Pynchon has been criticized for indulging an easy cold war rhetoric, but the apocalyptic threat could at least make us feel the present urgencies that impel us to act. Slothrop's scattering, described elsewhere in *Gravity's Rainbow* as a mindless collapse into a wholly discontinuous present, was in part a way of showing what can happen when we stop worrying and learn to love the bomb. The Thanatoids, existing "safe in some time free zone" of their own choosing, take this a historical mindlessness a step further—into the age of Star Wars and the postmodern eighties.

Whatever the differences between this novel and the last, Pynchon shows no sign of diminishing inventiveness, although the Thanatoid and Chastain/Fumimota subplots, evolving to the complexity of a suburban sprawl, only incidentally touch on the central story of Prairie and Frenesi. In the absence of the deferred apocalyptic moment, that story is even less compelling. A number of readers have expressed disappointment with the anticlimax of the last chapter when, for the first time after some 350 pages of preparation, the mother and daughter finally meet. From the little we are told about it, Prairie seems to have felt more emotion in long sessions of watching Frenesi on film. And if comments on clothes and hairstyle had recently given the exact right emotional coloring to the parting, probably for good, of Prairie and a teenage friend, they don't quite play in this much more important encounter. Despite the betrayals and adult experience she has been through, there is little about Frenesi that has changed since the sixties, even if the imagery that describes her refers not only to film now, but to the "falsely deathless perimeter" of a video screen. Her loss of immunity and corporate identity, and a suspect promise of a role in a movie, are all, really, that bring her home to Vineland.

Of course, there is also the presence of DEA agent Brock Vond to bring her back. Vond is the cartoon bad-guy who got Frenesi to come over to his side in the first place, which he accomplished mainly through the force of his sex. Now it is true that sex and power have always been connected in Pynchon's work, but never so bluntly, and without entering into a Vond-like fantasy of macho attractiveness, what reader, male or female, would accept Frenesi's plea of helplessness whenever her "pussy's running the show"? Even less satisfying is the bad joking arbitrariness with which Prairie is rescued from Vond at the novel's end, when, after his magical disappearance, even she is not sure she wanted to *be* rescued. Brock, descending on a helicopter cable to grab the girl out of her sleeping bag, is yanked back at the last second when the Reagan administration suddenly defunds *his* program; then he is carried off to hell. And this is how, in the post-ideological eighties, even the prototypal agent of oppression is made subject to the same economic contingencies as the rest of us.

Maybe it is to be expected that Pynchon, working closer than ever to conventional novelistic forms and evoking conventional expectations, would subvert them. But with our expectations Pynchon also raises significant political concerns that are later dropped with the same nonchalance. The novel purports to be about a generation's missed chances, about its addictions and betrayals, and about its replacement, among the educated classes, of an uptight morality and blatant racial prejudice with more subtle forms of mental and economic oppression (there is a running satirical commentary on television, yuppies, and New Age music). Pynchon's refusal to push the narrative to some plausible formal conclusion drains these issues, again, of any felt urgency; and the slapdash, indeterminate ending left me doubting the seriousness of his project in the book.

But then it is not at all clear that he *wants* to be taken seriously, at least not with the kind of seriousness that scholars and admiring critics have brought to the study of his work. Ever since the appearance of *Gravity's Rainbow*, many people have worked very hard to get at Pynchon's accomplishment, and to make its importance more widely felt. It is this critical group, myself included, that *Vineland* is most likely to have disappointed, even if, academic industry being what it is, there will continue to be those among us who will go on tracking *Vineland* arcana and the minutest allusive droppings without asking whether the work this time will bear the scrutiny. The famous assertion in *Gravity's Rainbow* that "*everything is connected*, everything in the Creation," offers a certain justification for the mass of critical explication devoted to *that* novel, if only in nervous and prolific denial of the less frequently cited counter-assertion that "nothing is connected to anything." But is *Vineland* better for our knowing, say, that a minor character named Van Meter might refer to Bob Feller, the great Cleveland Indians pitcher known throughout the nation at the age of 17 as "the farmboy from Van Meter," Iowa? Or that Frenesi's relative, Eula, may have been named after Eula Varner in Faulkner's Snopes novels? Might the appearance on page 97 of an *Italian Wedding Fake Book*, by Deleuze & Guattari, open up a whole psychic subtext? (More relevant may be the surname of one Weed Atman, the influence of Hindu Religion on *Vineland* having been noted in at least one review.)

Pynchon's attitude toward his interpreters might be gathered from his introduction, at the start of the book, of the character Zoyd Wheeler, who must do something certifiably crazy at least once a year if he is to continue to receive his "mental disability" checks from the Government. Zoyd's dangerous leaps through the front windows of various establishments in Vineland County are filmed every year by local television crews and subjected to endless scrutiny by panels of experts, the most recent "including a physics professor, a psychiatrist, and a track-and-field

coach . . . discussing the evolution over the years of Zoyd's technique." Pynchon is nothing if not self-conscious, and, in the passage describing Zoyd's reluctant leap, through a window whose glass turns out to have been replaced by a pane of "clear sheet candy," he could be summing up the effect that intense critical exposure in a culture sustained by media simulations has had on his own style in the book:

> [Zoyd] knew the instant he hit that something was funny. There was hardly any impact, and it all felt and sounded different, no spring or resonance, no volume, only a sort of fine, dulled splintering.

At the start of *Gravity's Rainbow*, Pynchon taunted us with one of the most brilliant author figures in recent fiction—Pirate Prentice, a kind of fantasist surrogate whose novelistic powers of dreaming other peoples' dreams are all too readily put into service by the "Firm" and the State. Prentice knows that his talents, his body, and even his own private fantasies are subtly implicated in sources of power within the culture; and his eventual initiation into a political "Counterforce" and social "We-system" (as against a decentered and relational "They-system") is a study in power and compromised resistance that rivals and anticipates Foucault's. Now, early in *Vineland,* we have Zoyd, the aging doper who remains uncorrupted in his refusal to collaborate or inform, but who made his peace with the Feds by agreeing to the ineffectual role of clownish eccentricity. These contrasting projections (of the artist, not the person), might mark an increasing marginalization of the creative subject; his feeling of ease proving to be little more than the freedom that comes when one has ceased to resist any more.

This is why *Vineland* should disappoint more than the scholars: for all Pynchon's evident warmth and generational identity, and for all the new realism, the America he returns to in the book remains a land of simulation—better observed and more fully experienced, surely, than in Jean Baudrillard's *America,* but no more engaging for that. Maybe that is not Pynchon's fault, but what we need, and what has been oddly lacking in recent fiction and theory, is a *style of resistance* to the forms of unreality in America that *Vineland* documents. For the moment, the best we can do is to continue to work through the refractoriness and literary complexity of *Gravity's Rainbow,* and hope that *Vineland* turns out to be only an outrider for a harder, more resilient fiction.

Alan Wilde (essay date Summer 1991)

SOURCE: "Love and Death in and Around Vineland,

U.S.A.," in *Boundary 2*, Vol. 18, No. 2, Summer, 1991, pp. 166-80.

[*In the following essay, Wilde examines the major themes, narrative presentation, and parody in* Vineland. *Citing the problem of indeterminacy and equivocation in the novel, Wilde contends that "*Vineland *seems from time to time to become what it beholds; a busy, pop version of America more attentive to momentary surfaces than to depth."*]

Presided over by "the hacker we call God," populated by characters who are "beneath [His] notice," who are in fact only so many "digits in God's computer," *Vineland* returns Pynchon's readers to threatening but familiar ground. We are back, it seems, in the world of Oedipa Maas, with its "zeroes and ones twinned above, hanging like balanced mobiles right and left, ahead, thick, maybe endless." Actually, all of Pynchon's novels stipulate opposition as their basic formal principle, but in *V.* and *Gravity's Rainbow,* one term (Street, Zone) is effectively privileged over the other (Hothouse, System). What sets *The Crying of Lot 49* apart is the absoluteness of the balance, and the fact that its contrasting terms are linked, as Oedipa despairingly thinks, in "a symmetry of choices." Predicated on the same sort of opposition, *Vineland* descends (in this respect at least) from *Lot 49,* as its California does from the earlier book's "legacy America." There, in and around Vineland, Brock Vond, agent of the Justice Department in both the Nixon and Reagan administrations, and Frenesi Gates, the novel's tarnished, unholy grail, who is variously his lover, informer, prisoner, and prey, act out the roles of zero and one—complementary images, as it turns out, of what is wrong with the country whose destiny their lives chart from the 1960s to 1984.

Brock is, among other things, the emblem of *Gravity's Rainbow*'s "masculine technologies," as well as of the treacherous System "They" represent in *Vineland:* "the State law-enforcement apparatus, which was calling itself 'America.'" Even more insidiously, he suggests the murderous embrace of sameness and stasis that is summed up most succinctly in his devotion to "the Lombrosian concept of 'misoneism' . . . this deep organic human principle, which Lombroso had named after the Greek for 'hatred of anything new.'" With his own grandly proportioned and ubiquitous hatred, Brock becomes the most vivid marker of the death or deathliness that leaks into every corner of *Vineland*'s volatile, hectic landscape. It is hardly accidental that he reminds Frenesi's ex-husband, Zoyd Wheeler, "of self-destructive maniacs he'd ridden with back in his clubcar days . . . dreaming away with these romantic death fantasies, which usually gave them hardons they then joked about all night."

The conjunction of death and sex provides the necessary

clue to the deeper and more contested levels of Vond's personality, where the stability he cherishes proves to be a necessary, but barely tenable, lie, so that while "everywhere Brock looked he saw some defects of control . . . others, in their turn, were not so sure about Brock." And with good reason, since under his carefully composed exterior there lurks "his uneasy anima," the "watchful, never quite trustworthy companion personality, feminine, under-developed," who visits him "in a number of guises, notably as the Madwoman in the Attic." That the Madwoman speaks to something in Brock at once feared and desired is obvious. The suggestion, echoed and amplified by an inner voice "whispering *Kick loose*," is of subterranean, inchoate impulses that lie below or above the level at which he deliberately chooses (or, alternatively, is compelled, self-protectively) to live. But to say that what most obsesses Vond—himself, women, sexuality—is also what he is most afraid of; or to note that his radically insecure ego marks the precise, vulnerable source of his overly valued sense of control is only to ripple the psychological and ontological surface of his being. Closer to the mark is the recognition that if his deepest desire is to be more (or less) than human, his greatest and attendant fear is of the human body—that uncertain, destructible vessel of human incarnation, messy, uncontrollable, and unavoidably committed to death. This may well explain why, at the point that Brock learns about Frenesi's daughter, Prairie, "something else, something from his nightmares of forced procreation, must have taken over." "Each birth . . . would be only another death for him," we're told later on, and so he begins the demented pursuit of the girl that leads in time to the prophetic fulfillment of his terror, which links the body's sexual activity (could Prairie be *his* daughter?) with its destruction.

In terms of these various equations, the connection between Frenesi and Vond becomes clear when, after the angry, defeated rejection of her baby, Frenesi imagines (at least she appears to be imagining) that Brock is with her: "With his own private horrors further unfolded into an ideology of the mortal and uncontinued self, Brock came to visit, and strangely to comfort. . . . Whispering, 'This is just how they want you, an animal, a bitch with swollen udders lying in the dirt, blank-faced, surrendered, reduced to this meat, these smells.'" As the passage ends, with Frenesi picturing herself as "only an animal with a full set of pain receptors after all," the last piece of the puzzle falls into place, and the ultimate horror of Pynchon's world reveals itself. No reader of *Gravity's Rainbow* needs to be reminded of that novel's obsessive concern with bodily functions, its dialectic of fascination and repulsion, its establishing of the body as the site of both mortality and its transcendence. What *Vineland* adds (can add, perhaps, because Pynchon seems less personally implicated now in the disgust he attributes to his characters) is not only the perception that the human, reduced to mere body, becomes animal but the awareness that Frenesi, "surrendered" in this phantasm of degradation, is less Brock's victim than his mirror—control and surrender being, as Eliot and other modernists recognized in their time, intimate and indivisible in their dynamics.

Frenesi's preferred mode of coping with the terrors of time and mortality appears nonetheless to be very different from what is imaged here. More characteristic is her dream "of a mysterious people's *oneness,* drawing together toward the best chances of *light,* achieved once or twice that she'd seen in the street, in short, *timeless bursts,* all paths, human and projectile, *true,* the people in a *single presence,* the police likewise *simple* as a moving blade—and individuals who in meetings might only bore or be pains in the ass here suddenly being seen to *transcend,* almost *beyond will*" (my emphasis). Sounding like something out of an Auden-Isherwood play, the passage recalls more generally modernism's wistful, obsessive longing for transcendent unity; and it is no accident that Frenesi, whose thoughts are haunted by the specter of time, dwells repeatedly on the transhuman, transhistorical, ultimately spatial moments that define the modernist imagination. Nothing I've just said, however, is meant to set Frenesi psychologically or ideologically apart from Brock. Nor is the issue simply that her sexual enthrallment allows her to live not according to "the time the world observed but [in] game time, underground time, time that could take her nowhere outside its own tight and falsely deathless perimeter." If Frenesi's desire is "to ignore history and the dead, to imagine no future," if she grieves over having been "brought back to the world like silver recalled grain by grain from the Invisible to form images of what then went on to grow old, go away, get broken or contaminated," Brock, man of the world though he is, longs no less for "a world of simplicity and certainty." And he participates no more than she in the ragged contingency of history and time. Embodying the ahistorical and the narrowly historical, hungering for timeless moments or for logical causality, figuring, as I've already noted, surrender and control, Frenesi and Brock, devotees respectively of camera and gun, are the obverse and reverse of the same coin. It hardly needs saying that if, in Frenesi's "world based on the one and zero of life and death. Minimal, beautiful. The patterns of lives and deaths," Brock is patently the Zero of death, her own minimal One has little more to do with life and living. Certainly, much in *Vineland* suggests that men are the villains of all psychic and political wars, but in the novel's moral economy, Frenesi comes across as no better than Brock—only, unfortunately for her, as less calculating and powerful.

. . . .

If I have dwelt at such length on Frenesi and Brock, it is because they, more than any of the other characters, inti-

mate the novel's moral position: roughly, an existential imperative to accept the undeniability of time and the imperfection of "the spilled, the broken world." *Vineland,* in short, prods the self to move toward exactly what Frenesi dreads—"another stage . . . further into adulthood perilous and real, into the secret that life is soldiering, that soldiering includes death." Although some critics find an unbridgeable gap between Pynchon's postmodernism and his ethical concerns, he is, in fact, not only a moralist but an insistent, urgent, and sometimes (most notably in *V.*) a heavy-handed one. That being the case, it seems plausible to ask whether *Vineland*'s moral dimension defines itself only in opposition to Brock's and Frenesi's evasions of life's dense complexities—that is, negatively and obliquely—or whether, as in the other novels, there is an exploration of some middle ground between the postulated extremes.

At this point, which is to say, in most of the book, matters quickly become more problematical. In their different ways, all three of Pynchon's earlier novels engage the question of middles, though in *V.* and *Gravity's Rainbow* (where they are specified most directly in McClintic Sphere's "keep cool, but care" and as Roger Mexico's "probabilities") they remain largely notional, subverted as they are by the novels' subtextual fascination with extremity. Only in *Lot 49* is there, in the notion of diversity and in Oedipa's intent, active pursuit of it, a genuine formal and ideological realization, or at least intimation, of the desired middle ground. The question is whether in this respect, too, *Vineland,* in its own thematic explorations and structural enactments, harkens back to the earlier book. Ironically, but significantly, the closest approach to a middle in *Vineland* comes by way of parody. Commenting, presumably, on Frenesi's polarized "one and zero of life and death" and on Brock's veneer of linearity and logic, Pynchon introduces into his novel the bizarre, ontologically ambiguous Thanatoids, who, like Barthelme's Dead Father, are "*dead but still with us, still with us, but dead.*" Reminiscent in some ways of *Gravity's Rainbow*'s "moderate little men," who are held, always, "at the edges of revelations," the Thanatoids are kept back, not from illumination but from death, and not by fear but by feelings of resentment and desires for revenge. Beyond that, one can only speculate on what exact role these mysterious characters are meant to play in the novel, though it seems safe enough to see in their "karmic imbalances" a clue to the nature of the larger American population, traumatized by television and possibly by memories of the sixties—"not living but persisting, on the skimpiest of hopes."

Is there any larger hope in *Vineland* as a whole? Between the deathliness of Brock Vond and the death-in-life of the Thanatoids, between Frenesi's surrender and Brock's control (or in opposition to them all), does there emerge some time or place that embodies Pynchon's repeated pursuit of what is at best an always elusive goal? Not unexpectedly, given the genealogy of Pynchon's fiction, it is the sixties that offer themselves as the most plausible candidate, and the novel does indeed present from time to time an idea or ideal form of the decade that readers of a certain age will find familiar. So we hear about "the Mellow Sixties, a slower-moving time, predigital, not yet so cut into pieces, not even by television" and about "a world sprung new, not even defined yet, worth the loss of nearly everything in this one." Most of all, we come upon this typically plangent, resonant contrast: "Outside spread the lampless wastes, the unseen paybacks, the heartless power of the scabland garrison state the green free America of their childhoods even then was turning into." Echoing Oedipa's plaintive "how had it ever happened here, with the chances once so good for diversity?," the description differs in subtle but important ways. Whereas Oedipa's alternative America is placed firmly in the past (or in the parallel world of the Tristero), *Vineland*'s other, greener, freer America is alive enough around 1969 to be under siege and dying. The effect of the shift is telling. By locating the ideal in the lifetime of his characters, Pynchon betrays again his nostalgia for the regretted time before the eclipse of "the analog arts ... by digital technology."

Still, however impassioned these occasional tributes are, there is another, darker side to Pynchon's portrait of the age, with its betrayals, shallowness, irresponsibility, and fears, its obsessive avoidance of death, and the desire, shrewdly recognized by Brock, for order, "the deep ... need only to stay children forever. . . . Children longing for discipline." Summed up in his comments about the debasement of the decade's talismanic word love—"its trivializing in those days already well begun, its magic fading, the subject of all that rock and roll, the simple resource we once thought would save us"—Pynchon's indictments go even further. As we learn, for example, about Frenesi's collusion with Brock in the murder of the now-Thanatoid Weed Atman, it becomes increasingly difficult to overlook the fact that Pynchon's attitude is not only critical but acerbic: a reflex, quite possibly, of a more intimate, local, personal sense of betrayal—the betrayal of the variously rendered ideal of simplicity and wholeness his fiction constantly returns to and that *Vineland* intermittently locates in the decade of light and love. More is at stake, however, than complex reactions to a complex period. In problematizing all of the decade's longings, Pynchon simultaneously problematizes his own. The results are most apparent in a curious, tonally enigmatic scene between Zoyd and Mucho Maas (a record producer now, divorced from Oedipa) as they reminisce about the good old drug days and the knowledge those days brought that "you were never going to die." For the reader at least, the conclusion is unavoidable: Mucho's "beautiful certainty," the acid-induced dream of

immortality, is only a replay of Frenesi's desire for timeless moments. The narrator's perspective, sympathetic and distanced by turn, is harder to pin down: "It was the way people used to talk," he says about Mucho's and Zoyd's wistful memories and then goes on shortly to invoke his own romantically "green free America." Less evenhanded than discordant, these sinuous twists and turns hint at just how indeterminate Pynchon's rendering of the sixties is throughout the novel.

. . . .

Pynchon's treatment of the decade implies, in turn, a more fundamental, at any rate a more widespread, equivocation emblematic of *Vineland* as a whole. Most notably, the novel vacillates between what I earlier called its existential morality and the Romantic primitivism that it inherits from *Gravity's Rainbow*. Rather more spotty and attenuated than in that book, *Vineland*'s primitivist leanings are nevertheless unmistakable. They announce themselves, as usual, in Pynchon's familiar vocabulary of the mysterious and the invisible, with its references to "another deep nudge from forces unseen," "hidden structures," "signs and symptoms," "the realm behind the immediate," "another order of things," "a world behind the world she had known all along," "some invisible boundary," and so forth. As so often in Pynchon's fiction, the common thread is loss: the sense of some innocence, wholeness, and unity overcome, as in the story of the *woge,* not by this or that human action but simply by the fact of human presence. That the *woge,* having withdrawn "before the influx" of humanity, might "if we started fucking up too bad ... come back, teach us how to live the right way, save us," highlights primitivism's usual contrast of now and then, here and elsewhere, which is the burden too of Sister Rochelle's pivotal, quietist parable of being:

> "It takes place [she begins] in the Garden of Eden. Back then, long ago, there were no men at all. Paradise was female. Eve and her sister, Lilith, were alone in the Garden. A character named Adam was put into the story later, to help make men look more legitimate, but in fact the first man was not Adam—it was the Serpent. . . . It was sleazy, slippery man," Rochelle continued, "who invented 'good' and 'evil,' where before women had been content to just be. . . . [M]en also convinced us that we were the natural administrators of this thing 'morality' they'd just invented. They dragged us all down into this wreck they'd made of the Creation, all subdivided and labeled."

"'Don't commit original sin,'" she ends, "'Try and let her just be.'" Who "her" is needn't concern us now. What is striking about the parable's feminist message is its echo of the description, already quoted, of "the Mellow Sixties ...

not yet so cut into pieces" and, still more, of *Gravity's Rainbow*'s indictment of "human consciousness, that poor cripple, that deformed and doomed thing . . . [whose] *mission* [it is] to *promote death.*"

Vineland's accusation, if less vehement and fervent, is no less to the point, and as in the earlier book, it reveals Pynchon's habit of locating his ideal time or place, the realm of being, somewhere before or outside the world that consciousness perversely segments and destroys. But for all its manic energy, *Vineland* is more hectic than persuasive—which may be why one is prompted to ask of it, more than of his other fiction, what exactly the referent of its Edenic vision is. The novel's title points toward "Vineland the Good": both Leif Ericson's pre-Columbian discovery and, almost a millennium later, "'A Harbor of Refuge,' as the 1851 survey map called it." But Ericson's eastward-lying America is only an unearned suggestion hovering weightlessly above the novel's action, and Pynchon's renamed Eureka, though buttressed by stories of the woge and the Yuroks and by intimations of preternatural light, a "call to attend to territories of the spirit," is hardly more substantial. Brad Leithauser's remark that "there is little 'behind' all the clatter in *Vineland,* nothing transcendentally spiritual or beautiful or numinous—or even overarchingly malignant" seems to me exactly right. It may well be the absence of some glamorously threatening force—something on the order of V., Blicero, or the inscrutable Tristero—that accounts for the absence of a persuasive, compelling Counterforce. Brock Vond, the most likely candidate, hardly measures up to this standard; and it is, in any event, arguably the case that the major villain of *Vineland* is not even intended to be the death-dealing Brock but "television, which . . . had trivialized the big D itself."

Certainly, much of the novel's satire centers on America's response to what is generally called the Tube. Not surprisingly, the Thanatoids "watch a lot of Tube," but so do most of the book's characters, their fate ironically inscribed in the story of Zoyd's longtime pursuer, Hector Zuniga, the DEA agent who has become a "tubal freak" and who throughout the novel is in flight from the Tubaldetox Squad. Furthermore, according to Prairie's young friend, Isaiah Two Four, Zoyd and his hippie generation are no better: "You believed in your Revolution . . . but you sure didn't understand much about the Tube. Minute the Tube got hold of you folks that was it, that whole alternative America, el deado meato." That Pynchon's analysis is neither new nor probing matters less than the fact that it is itself to no small degree trivialized by the novel's immersion in the culture it holds responsible for the failure of the sixties ideal. Filled not only with actual television trivia but with easy, one-liner references to imaginary TV shows—"John Ritter in *The Bryant Gumbel Story,*" "Woody Allen in *Young Kissinger,*" "Pat Sajak in *The Frank Gorshin Story,*" and so on—

Vineland seems from time to time to become what it beholds: a busy, pop version of America more attentive to momentary surfaces than to depth. It follows that Pynchon's insistent suggestions of mysterious and possibly redemptive dimensions beyond the two-dimensional tubal world lack sufficient contextual support. Whatever their local and occasional energy, these references appear unintegrated; and the possibility of "that whole alternative America" sinks under the insubstantial weight of TV culture. As it does so, the novel's balance shifts still further away from whatever its primitivist references are meant to express—away, among other things, from Sister Rochelle's way of being and toward the more arduous path of becoming. The failure of the mythic in *Vineland* requires a pursuit of Pynchon's moral intentions not in some hypothetical "elsewhere" but in the concrete, death-tormented world his characters inhabit.

. . . .

What remains, with the compromised sixties and the epiphenomenal Vineland out of the way, is the novel's final chapter, where against the abundant manifestations of Thanatos (presided over, as usual, by the omnipresent arch-individualist, Brock Vond) are massed the congregated forces of Eros: home, family, union, reunion, and love—including Zoyd's love for Prairie, which, as a more concrete revelation of Vineland's "goodness," bestows on him "his belated moment of welcome to the planet Earth." But since endings are structural as well as thematic, I want to pause first over Pynchon's narrative strategies. What they reveal again, now in a more formal way, are the underlying tensions that have by now become characteristic and familiar. No reader of *Vineland* has to be told just how dense, difficult, sinuous, and excessive the novel's plot is or how attentive one needs to be to its abrupt swerves and backtrackings, its embedded stories and endless, erratic flashbacks, its modal mimicry of any and all cultural forms, high and low, from comic strip to parable. Nevertheless, as the fluid, associative, non-linear interfaces of some computers mask the tight, digital logic of what transpires beneath their user-friendly graphics, so Pynchon's narratives, calculated though they are to undermine the symmetries of Frenesi's or Oedipa's ones and zeros, conceal their own structural economies. That *Vineland,* unlike the other novels, then proceeds to undo these economies is another matter, one I will come to shortly. For the moment, what is significant is that, beginning with the latest of the annual Traverse-Becker reunions (the gathering in Vineland of Frenesi's and Prairie's many and varied relatives), everything in the book *seems,* in apparent defiance of its narrative movement up to this point, to move toward resolution and reconciliation.

This movement explains, I suspect, why several reviewers

have discovered various signals of counterentropic hope: "some faint possibility of redemption, some fleeting hints of happiness and grace"; "faint signs of optimism"; or "some small possibility of faith-keeping and love inside a family." The invariable qualifications and hesitations are telling, but they don't, I think, go far enough. As Pynchon assembles or reassembles all of his major characters and not a few of the minor ones in this chapter, it is hard to resist the feeling that we are reading, incongruously, some odd, revisionist text modeled on, say, *Howards End* or *To the Lighthouse*—or even that we are watching some peculiar, postmodern variation on the finale of a Hollywood musical comedy. On the other hand, something unifying does emanate from the occasionally grotesque vitality of the gargantuan Becker-Traverse get-together. Conceivably, one might even argue that a ritual as sacramental as *Howards End*'s hay-cutting inheres in the Rabelaisian scene of community eating: "It was the heart of this gathering meant to honor the bond between Eula Becker and Jess Traverse, that lay beneath, defined, and made sense of them all."

But the most plausible token of small, faint possibilities (though it is not the one the reviewers I've quoted from have in mind), actualizes itself in the story of two characters so far unmentioned: DL Chastain, Frenesi's one-time friend, and Takeshi Fumimota. For reasons too complicated to spell out here, the two come together under the sign of death when DL mistakenly inflicts on Takeshi the Vibrating Palm (also known as the Ninja Death Touch), which is intended for Brock Vond. When, thereafter, both come to the Kunoichi Retreat (DL in flight from what she has done, Fumimota in pursuit of her), Sister Rochelle, just before she recounts her parable of being to Takeshi, scathingly orders DL "to become this fool's devoted little, or in your case big, sidekick and to try and balance your karmic account by working off the great wrong you have done him." Partners now, the two go appropriately into the "karmic adjustment business," with the Thanatoids as their anxious clients; and what signifies is that, for all their limitations, which Sister Rochelle is always more than ready to point out, they are in their own way involved, responsible, and concerned for others. This, and the fact that the trajectory of their lives moves them from death inflicted and received to life restored, even transformed into something like love. So, DL, who has, for better or worse, inherited her teacher's "entanglement in the world" and is clearly intended as Frenesi's foil, becomes the conduit through whom Prairie learns about her mother; Takeshi initiates their dealings with the Thanatoids, one of whom, ironically, but more wisely than he knows, compares his attempt to recover from the Vibrating Palm to TV shows "where, you got love, is always winnin' out, over death"; and in the chapter that was my starting point, the two, still fallible and uncertain but among the novel's most attractive characters, renego-

tiate the "no-sex clause" of their agreement and get on, in Sister Rochelle's words, with "the usual journey from point A to point B"—an accomplishment, in the context of *Vineland,* of no small magnitude.

But if, for now, Eros, in the form of both family unity and DL's and Takeshi's commitment to each other, appears to have overcome Thanatos and its individual discontents, still, as Jess recites to his assembled relatives a passage from Emerson that promises "secret retributions [which] are always restoring the level, when disturbed, of the divine justice," it is all but impossible to resist the feeling that, for whatever reason, Pynchon is overplaying his hand. Against Jess Traverse's comforting Emersonian gospel one needs to set Zoyd's lawyer's pithier, more contemporary estimate of the universe's workings, summed up in the phrase "life is Vegas" or the narrator's own description of "a sunset that was the closest we get to seeing God's own jaundiced and bloodshot eyeball, looking back at us without much enthusiasm." Besides, there are particular incidents and attitudes that contravene the possibilities of unity: Zoyd's failure to recover his house, "his own small piece of Vineland" from Brock's men; the fact that Frenesi, her daughter, and her mother, all three brought together now, are at best *"perilously* reconnecting" (my emphasis); or that Weed Atman, who has "lately . . . just been letting [Frenesi] be," still remains "a cell of memory, of refusal to forgive." In short, like the "long, desolate howling" of the Thanatoids that follows hard upon a morning when, "often for the first time, [they] sought contact with the eyes of other Thanatoids," hope, as often as not, peters out, the victim of its own longing imagination. Kin to the novel's thematic openendedness and its wild, associative discursiveness, these scattered loose ends are obviously subordinate to, or in a tensive relationship with, its gesture of formal closure. Nevertheless, despite my invocation of Forster and Woolf, *Vineland* is no modernist novel (as the contrast of the formal and the thematic might suggest), and I've deliberately used the word "gesture" to suggest, additionally, how unresolved, even on a structural level, the novel's ending proves to be.

Consider the bizarre events that bring the book to its close. They begin with the attempted, perhaps incestuous kidnapping of Prairie by Brock, an airborne Hades come for his Persephone, and then move on, in a reversal of the usual deus ex machina, to the foiling of the attempt, as he is hoisted back into his helicopter (thus his colleagues' name for him: "Death From Slightly Above") thanks to the suspension of REX 84, "Reagan's so-called readiness exercise"). Next comes the convenient elimination of Vond by "the legally ambiguous tow-truck team of Eusebio ('Vato') Gomez and Cleveland ('Blood') Bonnifoy," turned for the occasion into antic psychopomps who lead a puzzled Brock to "the land of death." And, finally, there is the scene that ends *Vineland,* in which Prairie, after a hectic night in which she disconcertingly calls upon the absent Brock to return,

> settl[es] down into sleep, sleeping then unvisited till around dawn, with fog still in the hollows, deer and cows grazing together in the meadow, sun blinding in the cobwebs on the wet grass, a redtail hawk in an updraft soaring above the ridgeline, Sunday morning about to unfold, when Prairie woke to a warm and persistent tongue all over her face. It was Desmond [her lost dog], none other, the spit and image of his grandmother Chloe, roughened by the miles, face full of blue-jay feathers, smiling out of his eyes, wagging his tail, thinking he must be home.

The recall of the novel's opening, where Zoyd awakes to "a squadron of blue jays stomping around on the roof," suggests symmetry, as the passage itself, read (if that is possible) with a deliberate absence of irony, suggests unity. But such a reading is, of course, out of the question. Whether structurally climactic or anticlimactic, whether tonally sentimental, melodramatic, or cartoonish, this incident and the others that lead up to it have about them the feel of myth transmogrified into parody. And nowhere more than in this description. Moving from the all too romantically picturesque to the deliberately whimsical and arch, it evokes such intertextual sources as *Lassie Come Home* and *The Wizard of Oz* and, in the process, dissolves the chapter's dissembled closure, along with the novel's intimations of Eros ascendant, in a farrago of pastoral farce.

I want to make clear that, in talking about the novel's ending, my intention is in no way to fault Pynchon for a failure to achieve New Critical aesthetic harmonies. Nor is it, alternatively, to praise him, by way of the newer poststructuralist aestheticism, for his refusal of totalizing visions, since the effect of this particular vision is not to defer or disseminate meaning but to rob it of its temporality. The issue, in other words, is not the lack of resolution, but its inversion in parody. Some could argue, I suppose, that Pynchon's picture-postcard conclusion is intended as a send-up of happy endings, whether transcendental or mundane, and that it therefore means to establish, precisely by way of parody, a more imperfect, precarious terrain for the meeting of self and world in the contingency of time. The reappearance of DL and Takeshi just a few pages before the novel's close would seem to support this reading, as does the report that is given of their most recent visit to the Kunoichi Retreat. Balancing her earlier story of Eden, Sister Rochelle now tells Takeshi a particularly opaque parable about hell, the point of which seems to be "that its original promise was never punishment but reunion, with the true long-forgotten metropolis of Earth Unredeemed." Certainly, Earth Unredeemed is very much

the locus of Pynchon's concern in *Vineland;* and hints of moderated, earthly reunion follow as he describes the couple's departure in "the year the no-sex clause didn't get rolled over": "You could tell that the Head Ninjette was interested at least in a scientific way in whether the Baby Eros, that tricky little pud-puller, would give or take away an edge regarding the unrelenting forces that leaned ever after the partners into Time's wind."

To the degree that DL and Takeshi conjure up thoughts of Eros and, more importantly, to the degree that whatever hope Sister Rochelle imagines for them is at best hesitant, tentative, subject to the whims of "the faceless predators . . . who despite every Karmic Adjustment resource brought to bear so far had simply persisted," a case can be made for the novel's willing acceptance of time and uncertainty—and thus too for parody as a limited, world-salvaging, recuperative maneuver: *Vineland*'s answer to Frenesi's timeless moments and Brock Vond's relentless logic of linear control. All of this is possible, even plausible, but problems persist nevertheless. Less easy to rationalize than this or that incident and far more difficult to convey is the actual experience of reading the novel: the immediacy of response that, even the second or third time around, precedes the sorting out. There are exceptions to what I'm about to say, and I've noted some of them, but on the whole, it appears to me that *Vineland* is a less poetic and impassioned book than *Gravity's Rainbow.* Evil is more commonplace, banal; good, even weaker and more ambiguous than it usually is in Pynchon's fictional world. That may be the reason why the novel's narrative and textural excesses register as more self-indulgent than heuristic. In other words, Pynchon's characteristic extremism focuses differently here. In place of the recurring rhetoric of salvation and possibility and, more particularly, in place of *Lot 49*'s inconclusive, but intensely generative, "waiting"—its hedged promise of an alternative world hanging within or behind constellated ones and zeros—we are presented with a gallimaufry of conflicting, equivocal messages; an evasion, perhaps, of the unresolved tensions I've been discussing.

If, as indicated, the parodic scene of Prairie's awaking can be bent to the shape of the novel's morality, it is considerably harder to account for the equally parodic episode in which Brock Vond is so effortlessly rendered hors de combat. Despite the presence of Baby Eros, DL and Takeshi manage, after all, only to steal "a couple of innocent hours away from the harsh demands of their Act, with its imitations of defiance . . . of gravity and death." What sense, then, are we to make of the novel's urgent ethical message(s) in light of this too convenient disposal of the figure who throughout the book is death's chief emissary and its major embodiment of Thanatos? Only this, I think: that, possibly in unacknowledged response to all of *Vineland*'s tensions and irresolutions, Pynchon at the last overreaches himself. Parody, less a recuperative maneuver than a personal dodge, comes across (in aesthetic terms) as self-indulgent play, and the effect is to vacate the book of the moral content that presumably underlies and validates its judgments both of characters and of America as garrison state. The most heteroclite of authors, Pynchon uncovers his own parodic emblem in "the Harleyite Order, a male motorcycle club who for tax purposes had been reconstituted as a group of nuns . . . [and who] pursued lives of exceptional, though antinomian, purity." It is to the Sisters that Zoyd looks for help in recovering his home, his friend, Van Meter, having "run across them in the course of his quest after the transcendent." Unfortunately, after their appearance on the Donahue show, the Sisters lose interest, both in transcendence and in Zoyd; but here too they are emblematic—this time, of *Vineland*'s very different dereliction: its refusal of the existential commitment it ponders only to evade.

Kathryn Hume (essay date Summer 1992)

SOURCE: "Repetition and the Construction of Character in *Gravity's Rainbow*," in *Critique: Studies in Contemporary Fiction*, Vol. XXXIII, No. 4, Summer, 1992, pp. 243-54.

[*In the following essay, Hume considers mythographic, modernist, and postmodern aspects of Pynchon's characters in* Gravity's Rainbow. *According to Hume, the novel's major characters are subjected to a common set of situations and relationships that reveal Pynchon's underlying humanism.*]

Thinness of character in *Gravity's Rainbow* disquiets even the book's partisans. Pynchon confounds us with an opulent Ulyssean world but denies us the filigrain complexity of Joyce's psychological portraits. Weissmann's squalid attempts to transcend, for instance, glisten darkly in the ashes of the Zone, but Pynchon does not ground that quest in the psyche of the individual—a puzzling failure by the standards of realistic literature.

Pynchon's admirers have tried to explain away this "fault" in two fashions. One consists of redefining the genre: if *Gravity's Rainbow* is a satire rather than a novel, argues Alfred MacAdam, we can expect flat figures. Much the same goes for calling it an encyclopedic narrative, a menippea, a jeremiad, or a gothic novel. The other consists of invoking postmodernism by any of several definitions. The intermapping between characters destroys conventional individuality (Brian McHale) or creates prismatic figures, without "core or identifiable inner self"—the absent center beloved of deconstructors (Carol Richer). Richer fo-

cuses on the dispatterned elements and ignores some obvious formal schemata. McHale notes the existence of repetitions that support his definition of postmodernism but pays no attention to those that build meaning in a conventional fashion. Without intending to attack critics who follow a postmodernist line, because I certainly accept their readings up to a point, I would like to focus on material that their assumptions necessarily obscure for them and their readers.

Through frequent repetition of certain situations and relationships, Pynchon subjects almost all of his characters to a fixed array of pressures. Major characters experience most of the possibilities; minor characters deal with fewer. Such repetition signals Pynchon's lack of interest in individuality. Within his aesthetics of character, individual variations are trivial when compared to the overwhelming problems facing everybody in his fictive universe.

Putting characters to the same tests makes sense if he wants to define some general features of human nature and renegotiate the terms of what it is to be human—normally the concerns of a mythographic writer. His situations and relationships introduce values and shed light on the question, "What is right action?"—again, a question basic to mythographically oriented works, an orientation that I have argued elsewhere to be relevant to *Gravity's Rainbow*. Generalizations about postmodernism have led critics to believe that Pynchon's vision is dehumanizing. His prominent use of repetition, however, has the potential to reinstate some values and to set boundaries to his particular form of postmodernism.

The repeated situations to be discussed represent a simplification of Pynchon's complexities. Having at one time traced and compared as many as thirty forms of repetition, I sought common denominators and reduced the variables to six, a manageable but admittedly arbitrary number. Each one exposes a character to an overlooked facet of reality or to our means of organizing such reality. The first two, (1) symbol systems and (2) the void, form an opposition. Symbol systems represent fundamental methods of ordering experience, whereas the void is that which cannot be ordered by such systems. The next two, (3) technology and science and (4) multiple realities, augment humanist, Western reality at both ends of the spectrum, the rational and the non-rational. The last two, (5) activity as game and (6) kindness, ask what human beings may be and what obligations we may have to them, given the nature of reality as defined in the other repeated situations. Establishing nondestructive relationships with other people is a major part of Pynchon's solution to the problems he poses, a significant component in the message of his mythology. After seeing the coherent power of these repetitions, we can return to the problem of how they and their implications relate to character construction and the postmodernism of *Gravity's Rainbow*.

Symbol systems. The presence of symbol systems in the novel has been frequently noted but not in relation to the formation of character. Pynchon reveals the power inherent in letters or numbers to his major figures. Tchitcherine is chagrined to discover that his life and happiness have been subordinated to letters by the powers-that-be: "all the Weird Letter Assignments have been reserved for ne'er-do-wells like himself." He notes the power of these letters in concatenations as religious texts and as anti-establishment graffiti. He realizes that the form taken by the letters used to transliterate the language of the Kirghiz tribes—Cyrillic, Arabic, or Roman—will channel their relationship to the world. For Enzian and Weissmann, the word is the basic unit, whether words of Rilke or of the African mythologies. Together they approach Absolute Presence, when "words are only an eye-twitch away from the things they stand for." Leni Pökler resists words as tools of political oppression: "'Mother,' that's a civil-service category, Mothers work for *Them!*" Roger Mexico learns to wield words with comic potency when he disrupts the banquet with his revolting alliterative menu, offerings such as booger biscuits spread with mucus mayonnaise and abortion aspic in dandruff dressing. Geli Tripping works magic with words of power.

Franz Pökler's symbols are mathematical; with numbers he can tame the terror of exponential curves and reduce the universe to our feeble human capacity to assimilate it. The bombs falling in London manifest the power of his calculations. Roger Mexico displays the power (and the impotence) of the Poisson distribution, in that he can predict rocket falls statistically but not individually. Pointsman revels in zeroes and ones, the elegant binary opposites that he expects to yield a perfectly mechanical explanation of life.

Slothrop's experience with verbal and numeric symbol systems is more diffuse than those just described but includes letters, words, and numbers. He tangles with single letters in Imipolex G, D wing, and stimulus x. Like his ancestors, he is "word-smitten." The numbers and letters of rocket equations give him erections. He chases the 00000. In addition, he is also exposed to secondary symbol systems: mandalas, chess as metaphor for life in the Zone, and the coercive force of heroic narrative. This last system of symbols causes him to plunge into personal danger because his Rocketman costume engenders powerful generic expectations in himself and others.

By confronting his characters with symbol systems, Pynchon makes them at least marginally aware of forces that control their lives. For most, however, awareness of primary symbol systems does not lead to decisive action, for few members of an advanced society would jettison the alphabet or numbers. However, if they recognize that they have been controlling others through these means, they try to repudiate such power. Roger admittedly uses alliterative words to manipulate the Elect, but Pynchon appears to condone this because his prank is explosive, dionysian, and self-consuming; the power could not readily be exercised over others not could Roger use it to overcome his present victims a second time. Enzian's mission of building a new mythic consciousness for his people forces him to use such verbal powers. His status as racial underdog wins reader sympathy, but he is likened to a lion, emblematic animal of the Elect, a suggestion that we should be wary of taking him as model for actions or values. The characters who use such power without scruple, Weissmann and Pointsman, provoke revulsion.

The void. The void and our symbol systems are naturally opposed. Whether the absence is the existentialist *néant* or the radiant void of mysticism, it is generally acknowledged to be ineffable, beyond the powers of mere words or numbers. Pynchon repeatedly exposes his characters to a nexus consisting of the void, silence, and illumination. This repetition functions in two fashions: it opens characters' minds to something beyond material reality and it demonstrates that symbols, for all their hidden coercive powers, are helpless to describe or tame or control this aspect of existence.

The void manifests itself in many forms. As vacuum, it threatens Pökler and encroaches upon Katje with Enzian. As silence, it is the Brennschluss of the sun, the stillness sensed at the Fair for double agents, the stillnesses of the Asian steppes, the stillness of a leaking toilet valve that signals a police raid. Stillnesses choke the narrative after Slothrop sees the Hiroshima headline. His harmonica blues fall silent. Pauses dominate melody in the quartet. Orpheus puts down harp.

As mystic void, we find it in Nora Dodson-Truck's experiences, in the spots on Tchitcherine's horse's hide, and in the Aqyn's song about the indescribable Kirghiz Light. Mystic vision is available to the major figures: Mondaugen in the Kalahari; Enzian near zero; Weissmann while firing the rockets; Slothrop at the Mittelwerke and Peenemünde. As Molly Hite has shown, Pynchon characters typically hover at the edges of illumination but fail to connect. Slothrop does manage to achieve one form of mystic consciousness as Zonal Orpheus, but can only express his feelings in wordless music.

When exposed to various voids, characters become aware that quotidian reality is bounded, as are our symbol systems. At the limits, something else commences. By repeating exposure to the void as a means of unfolding characters, Pynchon explores the gap between our ordinary reality and what our imagination yearns for. All the unobtainable, missing centers shed light on the limitations of our symbol systems and the reality they tame. As Charles Russell has remarked, the Fall from a paradise now lost is a fall into consciousness and into language.

Science and technology. When we come to science and technology and to multiple realities, we find Pynchon systematically augmenting the reality recognized by Western civilization. The Judeo-Christian-Hellenic tradition pays little attention to science or its implications. To that tradition, reality is something outside of human control. Hence, Pynchon's repeatedly linking characters to science or technology invites us to consider the often unacknowledged power of such forces within our lives. The relationship is sometimes metaphorical. For Tchitcherine, molecular chemistry is both an avocational interest (psychoactive drugs) and a figure expressing his way of life. He is "a giant supermolecule with so many open bonds available at any given time." As one of Tchitcherine's linguistic colleagues muses, molecules and alphabets are alike; letters can be modified and polymerized into texts.

For several characters, engagement with the sciences comes through mathematics. Katje, as intelligence agent, casually juggles the conversion factors between information and lives. She thinks of sex in terms of rocket trajectory equations. She is technically informed enough to test Slothrop on boundary layer temperatures, Nusselt heat-transfer coefficients, methods of computing Brennschluss, and jet expansion angles. Calculus lets Franz and Leni characterize experience. In Leni's case, calculus is her metaphor for trying to explain to Franz a world with multiple levels of reality. Roger Mexico operates as a statistician.

Enzian's metaphor is the atomic particle: "Well, I think we're here, but only in a statistical way." "Enzian would like [. . .] to be able to see where it's going, to know, in real time, at each splitting of the pathway of decision, which would have been right and which wrong. But it is *their* time, *their* space [. . .] each particle with its own array of forces and directions.'" This subatomic terminology also attaches to Squalidozzi, the Argentine Anarchist; although he has stayed invisible to the law, his trail is discernible, like "the vapor trail a high-speed particle leaves" in a cloud chamber.

In addition to such ornamental links to science, most characters maintain a professional bond with the Rocket. Mexico plots rocket-falls and becomes (in Jessica's eyes) a creepy creature of the rocket. Pointsman studies the fall in terms of Slothrop's amours. Pirate Prentice receives a "morning packet" in the rocket that landed in Greenwich.

Katje spies on the crew that launches them, and Weissmann fires them personally, a perk he enjoys after having administered the rocket program throughout its troubled development. Franz Pökler and Kurt Mondaugen help make the Rocket possible; Leni protests against it; Ilsa dreams of going to the moon in it; and Gottfried ascends in it. Enzian, Tchitcherine, and Slothrop quest for the elusive missile.

The rocket's ubiquity marks Pynchon's concept of reality, for his is not just the humanist's world of character, education in past cultures, and moral choice. Reality is not something separate from human invention, but is itself created through our science and our other professional activities. The Rocket may have peaceful applications in space exploration, but its powers as a weapon hold the foreground, and the various futuristic Rocket-cities are not utopias.

By repeatedly showing his characters engaged in rocket-related work, Pynchon insists that we take our relationship with technology into account when defining humanity. Through the complicity of all these characters, Pynchon suggests that people are responsible on the individual as well as the national level for the developments of human and social reality. We create the world; we do not just live in it.

Multiple realities. Pynchon's presentation of humanity insists on science and technology as an inescapable factor, as something that cannot merely be ignored or deplored, as usually happens in humanist visions. In addition to technology, he insists upon another ignored feature of reality, namely, its multiplicity. He repeatedly exposes his characters to at least two dimensions of reality that transcend the quotidian. The first, which he generally calls the Other Side, features Angels, Titans, the sentient dead, and other supernatural presences. The second is the world of Them-with-a-capital-T. Many readers have commented on the role of Them in *Gravity's Rainbow* but have fastidiously passed over The Other Side despite its raucous demands for our attention.

The denizens of the Other Side are capable of penetrating our own. Angels enter the lives of Slothrop, Tchitcherine, Weissmann, and the fliers bombing Lübeck; furthermore they haunt the text in the name of a nightclub for Katje and Pirate and in the name of a snow game for Roger and Jessica. Titans and Pan are real for Katje and Geli. Moreover, the dead are curiously lively in this novel. By means of séances in Berlin and London, we see Weissmann, Enzian, Roger, Jessica, and Leni exposed at least tangentially to revenants. Slothrop generates his own in Nice. Pirate and Katje are haunted by Katje's long-dead ancestor Frans van der Groov. Enzian as a Herero may consider such contact with one's tribal dead ordinary, but Tchitcherine does not suffer gladly the twisted vision of his dead father.

Besides these loosely classifiable forms of Other-Side power, there are the many invoked only once—Lyle Bland's astral intelligences, the "claws and scales" Slothrop hears as he absorbs data on Imipolex G, the miniature dwarves who attend one's transference to a new world after being hit by a bolt of lightning. Weissmann indeed may become an Other-Side power while still alive. Other dimensions of reality take on life when skin cells, rats, and trees talk.

Strangely, almost all the characters accept the remaking of their cosmic picture without hesitation once they have been exposed to some other plane of reality. Pirate is slightly slow to credit his dreaming the dreams of others, but his marginal hesitation is the most resistance mounted. Those who see the Lübeck angel accept it but do not report it, knowing that their bosses (Them) would call the seers insane. Jessica may or may not accept the séances, but she does not doubt that a woman at the White Visitation can read her thoughts. This uniformity of response is, in its fashion, amazing and clearly must be worked into one's understanding of Pynchon's endeavor. As a preliminary observation, I would simply point to the parallelism between Pynchon's tactic here and his approach to science: he is insisting through all the repetitions that non-rational and non-rationalizable forces of some sort are unavoidably part of life, and that we cannot begin to make sense of experience without taking this augmentation of material reality into account. Our assumptions about what makes a person or character must include responses to multiple realities.

In addition to traditional supernatural forces, we also see Them. Many characters realize that another reality is superimposed upon their own lives when they stumble onto the activities of Them. For the major characters, this revelation radically alters their sense of the world. For Roger Mexico, the insight comes when he learns that I. G. Farben had been spying on Slothrop even before the war. He realizes in a flash how he has been manipulated, how Jessica has been used to control him. Enzian concludes that the bombed-out Jamf Ölfabriken Werke AG is not a ruin. "It means this War was never political at all, the politics was all theatre, all just to keep the people distracted . . . secretly, it was being dictated instead by the needs of technology [his version of Them]."

Tchitcherine meets the Marxist Them governing history in an Oneirine haunting. Leni identifies Them right from the start and rebels against Their uses of "Mother." Franz Pökler recognizes the existence of another level of reality when talking with Weissmann: questions and answers about combustion and funding "were not exactly code for something else, but in the way of an evaluation of Pökler personally."

He intuits that behind the professional chitchat lies the fate of his wife and child.

Slothrop, as usual, enjoys the most elaborately orchestrated version of this revelation. Throughout his sojourn at the Casino Hermann Goering, and especially in the Himmler Spielsaal, he senses "an order whose presence among the ordinary debris of waking he has only lately begun to suspect . . . everything in this room is really being used for something different. Meaning things to Them it has never meant to us. Never. Two orders of being, looking identical." "What Slothrop has been playing against [is] the invisible House, perhaps after all for his soul." Slothrop accepts this restructuring of his world picture so totally that he throws away his chance for normal life by deserting the army.

The repeated appearances of supernatural beings and of Them mark Pynchon's cosmos as mythological. Although the presences do not conform to any neat taxonomy, the fabric of this fictive reality has enough structure to challenge the notion that it merely reflects random fragmentation. Granted: it resists closure. The various elements do not fit the same puzzle, and in that sense remain fragments. But within the pieces there are local orders if not Order-with-a-capital-O (the distinction is Hite's), and characters need to reach some sort of accommodation with this divided nature of existence.

Activity as game. With this fifth repetition, we come to attitudes toward humanity. Particularly central are those moments of recognition that afflict characters with a sense that professional activities are a game. Goals and rules suddenly appear arbitrary, not sanctified by any humane value. Moreover, those goals and rules do not necessarily nurture the best interests of the characters themselves. This discovery is closely linked to identifying a Them reality. The game is Theirs, and characters discover themselves to be lowly pawns. When they achieve this insight, they must choose how to respond.

Pynchon mostly portrays recoil and a gesture of withdrawal. Katje grows tired of the games as agent and as Weissmann's Gretel, and "quits the game for good." She goes on to serve the White Visitation as Domina Nocturna, but she leaves even that in her search for Enzian and ends by accepting a sense of guilt and responsibility at the fair for double agents, and by refusing to accept easy answers or "some shallow win." Like Katje, both Pirate Prentice and Roger Mexico recognize how they have been pawns in the games of Them, and quit—both to seek Slothrop. Pökler offers his supposed daughter her freedom: "Pökler committed then his act of courage. He quit the game." He continues working on the rocket but starts trying to investigate Camp Dora. He no longer pretends that the camp is irrelevant to rockets and has nothing to do with him. Like Katje, he admits complicity; he leaves his ring with an anonymous victim of Dora. Slothrop spots Their game while on the Riviera, and he quits by going AWOL and seeking rocket information on his own. Tchitcherine rebels against Soviet games playing (exposed by Wimpe) and escapes partly through drugs and partly by hunting both rocket information and Enzian.

The game They play revolves about death and control, as is learned variously by Tchitcherine, Enzian, and Roger. Father Rapier expresses a fear that They are becoming immortal, and their control, eternal. In his idealistic view, our only hope of escaping from Their game is to "choose instead to turn, to fight: to demand, from those for whom we die, our own immortality. They may not be dying in bed anymore, but maybe They can still die from violence. If not, at least we can learn to withhold from Them our fear of Death." This answer to the discovery that we are pawns in obviously two-edged. Learning not to fear death can also help resign us to serving Their ends as cannon fodder.

When life is a game, people are things—this is one of Pynchon's important insights. As an agent, Katje learns that Jews are as negotiable as candy bars or sex, and that their lives have a departmental value equal to set quantities of information. Tchitcherine muses on the convertability between human pain and goal and is rendered uneasy by the Marxist vision of history when Wimpe explains how it makes him and everyone expendable. Slothrop sees how people are being used as counters in a game when small honesties or kindnesses from Tantivy and Sir Stephen get them silently removed from his purview. Pirate and Roger revolt at the way Slothrop is being used as a thing. Leni and Franz both rebel against being used as if their human feelings and concerns were of no account. In contrast, Pointsman and Weissmann both use their subordinates as pawns.

Basically, Pynchon seems to favor withdrawal to the extent possible, upon recognizing the existence of Them and Their game. He gives us no hope of effective counter action: individual and improvised gestures, such as the alliterative menu, are possible; but concerted effort is not because that would involve hierarchy and control. We can only abjure control and extend ourselves to do small kindnesses.

To sum up the argument thus far: by means of this series of repetitions, Pynchon exposes his characters and his readers to a cosmos that is far from value-free. They come to understand some of the ways in which cultures and people are controlled by symbol systems. They are also pressured to realize that symbol systems do not provide any ultimate meaning because such systems are helpless when faced with the void, whether that void is radiant or merely empty.

Nor do symbol systems appear adequate to encompass the multiple realities offered us in this text. Pynchon insists that we live in a pluriverse and may discover that Titans or Angels are observing our actions—for what purpose we will never know. Words can acknowledge the presence of such forces but cannot delve into their motives or assign a logic to their actions.

Nor can words protect us from the powers called "Them." At any moment, we may became aware of a Them-pattern making us do things toward ends quite different from those we had in mind. We may find ourselves cheap counters in some unimaginable game that is being played at a higher level.

Kindness. Given the nature of Pynchon's universe, what advice does he offer? What *is* the nature of right action? The sixth repeated situation comes about when characters quit the game and feel impelled to some act of kindness rather than treating someone as a thing. In the worlds of hardship experienced at the end of the war, any kindness is a candle lit against the darkness. Leni, Franz, Pirate, Roger, Slothrop, Katje, Geli, Pig, and Bianca all offer kindness, gestures meant to help someone. The other person may be oblivious, as is the unconscious woman to whom Franz gives his ring, but the gesture helps him reverse the attitude that had once let him consider Dora inmates faceless, insignificant things. Pynchon associates love with mental bondage and control; but when it disintegrates, it leaves a capacity for kindness. The willingness to give something without expectation of a return is a move meaningless within a game and hence it puts one outside game-board relations with others.

These, then, are the six repeated recognitions of some aspect of reality or some value to which Pynchon systematically subjects his characters. What do these repetitions tell us about Pynchon's construction of character and how do such value-building structures relate to the value-fragmenting postmodernism of the novel?

Any work of art embodies a struggle between tradition and novelty and criticism will always branch, to some extent, as it pursues one or the other of these inherent orientations. The postmodernist readings help us see what is new; they help habituate us to the jagged, unstable vision of our time, to the denial of closure or perfect system. Such critics rightly make the point that traditional, rounded characters would contradict the world-vision of postmodernism. Characters with well-established selves are incompatible with deconstructive absent centers. But this in only half of the picture. Character is indeed irrelevant and the individual is diminished in this book—in part by the magnitude of Them and the supernatural power who are presented in repeated situations. The paranoid and multiple nature of reality affects Pynchon's construction of fictional people. Instead of focusing on character—the darling of realist and modernist fiction—Pynchon focuses on humanity, a very different concept. If we grant Pynchon the mythological, supernatural and fragmented nature of his cosmos, then we must ask how humanity is to operate within such a threatening world, how humanity is to survive in it. Thought his repetitions, he both warns us of what we must take into account—symbols, science, other realities and the like—and gives us his low-keyed suggestions for attitudes and behavior.

Pynchon's aesthetics of character emerges as a necessity of postmodernism and as a feature of several generic influences, for mythology as well as satire, gothic novel, menippea, and jeremiad, depends more on generalized figures than on individuals. It also emerges as the product of his concepts of a supernatural and Them-dominated reality, his passionate concern with humanity's possible future and our poor means of ensuring that we have any future at all. If we simply follow the highroad of postmodern orthodoxy, we will fail to grasp the humane orientation of his concerns.

The mechanisms by which postmodernism integrates with conventionality are little studied, but we have here an example of such a mingling. Jürgen Habermas has delineated two strains of postmodernism, one radical and one so conservative that it is reactionary, a Reaganite denial of modernism. He is excluding the middle, and excluded middles, as Oedipa Maas points out, are "bad shit." Pynchon seems to represent a middle position, one in which the old-fashioned material universe of science is undone by the unexpected presence of gods and angels; but those powers give us no new assurance because their ontological status, in turn, shimmers uncertainly. He fragments the self, and we discover that our systems for ordering experience all lack a firm center. Such a postmodern cosmos may drive us to agree that conventional logic lacks any foundations "reality," but people—however decentered Lacan may declare them to be—must blunder on in such a postmodern world, their emotions active even though thinking has been rendered problematic. Pynchon's mode of constructing characters is addressed to the problems of such people. Now as much as any time in the past, we need generalized thinking about what it means to be human and about the ordinary concern of how to survive, because we, too, live in the postmodern world. To overlook this conservative moral and prophetic strain in Pynchon's endeavor because we are intellectually drawn to the radical and postmodern is to impoverish our experience with the complexity of his text.

William Gleason (essay date Winter 1993)

SOURCE: "The Postmodern Labyrinths of *Lot 49*," in *Critique: Studies in Contemporary Fiction,* Vol. XXXIV, No. 2, Winter, 1993, pp. 83-99.

[*In the following essay, Gleason examines the postmodern attributes and "labyrinthine" structure of* The Crying of Lot 49, *particularly as found in the novel's indeterminate language, puns, "symbolic landscape, narrative design, and sexual dynamics."*]

> [M]an now lives in a circle without a center, or in a maze without a way out.
>
> —Edward Said, "*Abecedarium Culturae:* Structuralism, Absence, Writing"

Said's twinned metaphors concisely, if somewhat sexistly, limn recognizable features of contemporary society and employ terms that appear more and more frequently in our literary, critical, and social discourses. Wendy Faris's recently published *Labyrinths of Language,* for example, focuses on Said's latter possibility; the book attempts to illustrate "the central place of the labyrinth in the modern western [literary] tradition." Faris traces the labyrinth as both textual symbol and narrative structure through several European and Latin American texts but notes at the end of her introduction that the image seems less central to North American writers, owing perhaps to the "continuing force of the myth of the 'virgin land'" on this continent. This comment seems rather odd; one wonders how familiar she is with the work of Thomas Pynchon, for example—or that of a number of other notable North American authors—for the labyrinth seems as prominent in Pynchon's work as it does in her chosen texts. I will reconsider Faris's thesis, then, by taking issue with her regional corollary: I offer here a "labyrinthine" reading of Pynchon's second novel, **The Crying of Lot 49,** that focuses on its symbolic landscape, narrative design, and sexual dynamics and that means to throw some light into one corner of that maze-like concept known as postmodernism.

Faris attributes several key tensions and ambiguities to the labyrinth. First, it can be spatially modeled as uni- or multicursal, that is, having one or many possible paths. The multicursal labyrinth adds human choice to the ancient configuration and thus increases the opportunity for confusion, for error, for dead ends, for retracing one's steps. (Faris also considers a third variation offered by Umberto Eco in *Semiotics and the Philosophy of Language*—the labyrinth as net, or rhizome—which I'll argue later is a more suitable postmodern model.) Second, the labyrinth can be imagined either with or without a center, the center itself representing potential sanctuary, revelation, or confrontation. A third ambiguity concerns the ways in which the labyrinth may be perceived. One may enter the labyrinth as an explorer (a Theseus figure) and experience it through time (diachronically—or, as a reader) or view it from above as a designer (a Daedalus figure) and see it all at once (synchronically—or, as a writer). Thus the labyrinth may appear ordered, even delightful, to the designer and at the same time chaotic, even terrifying, to the explorer. Finally, although the labyrinth's formal structure, its conscious articulation, places it within the traditionally masculine realms of order, language, and intellect, its earliest associations are with traditionally feminine spaces. For according to Fairs the labyrinth's original contours were "designed to duplicate symbolically the form of sacred labyrinthine caves," thereby associating the labyrinth with "the traditionally feminine domain of the earth mother." Faris thus suggests that the labyrinth can be seen as a mediating form between matriarchal and patriarchal systems of power. This notion of meditation or integration will become important in *Lot 49.*

Literal and symbolic labyrinths lace the novel as Oedipa Maas (whose very name invokes ancient myth and also encodes a labyrinth—*maas* is Afrikaans for *mesh*) follows the twisting paths opened for her by Pierce Inverarity's will. Oedipa first encounters San Narciso as a labyrinthine printed circuit: "The ordered swirl of houses and streets, from this high angle, sprang at her now with the same unexpected, astonishing clarity as the circuit card had." She views the city from above (as a designer) and sees it—for the moment—synchronically. But Oedipa will not remain a Daedalian observer; she will enter San Narciso's curving streets as a Thesean explorer, intent to discover meaning: "Though she knew even less about radios than about Southern California, there were to both outward patterns a hieroglyphic sense of concealed meaning, of an intent to communicate. There'd seemed no limit to what the printed circuit could have told her." Oedipa senses potential "revelation" and feels herself "at the centre of an odd, religious instant."

Her pursuit of this central space takes her through a number of other labyrinths, in San Narciso and in Northern California, as she tries to trace the "languid, sinister blooming of The Tristero." But even before stumbling onto W.A.S.T.E. and the post horn, she responds to patterned stimuli. The map of Fangoso Lagoons that flashes on the TV at Echo Courts, for example, immediately recalls for Oedipa San Narciso's printed circuit. This new development, "laced by canals," promises equally mysterious elucidation: "printed circuit, gently curving streets, private access to the water, Book of the Dead. . . ." This last reference connects the Lagoons, with their sunken dead men's bones, to Mr. Thoth, the close-to-death senior citizen Oedipa meets in Vesperhaven House, who is named for the Egyptian god of learning and magic, the inventor of letters and numbers. The Book of the Dead is also known as the Book of Thoth, a

written guide for the dead to secure eternal life, typically inscribed on or inside sarcophagi. Faris points out that passage through death to another life is one journey symbolized by passage through the labyrinth; and we can, perhaps, read part of Oedipa's journey in the novel as one from her comfortable, suburban, Young Republican life in Kinneret to a new life that includes an awareness of and sensitivity to the vast and convoluted underground of the disinherited that lies beneath the mantle of America.

Pynchon's 1996 essay, **"A Journey Into The Mind of Watts,"** suggests that very few of Oedipa's suburban neighbors would consider following her through such a maze. A year after its explosive summer riots, Watts remained for Pynchon "country which lies, psychologically, uncounted miles further than most whites seem at present willing to travel." Yet white culture "surrounds Watts—and, in a curious way, besieges it"; the impoverished black community "lies impacted in the heart of [a] white fantasy." Faris notes that labyrinths have in the past served as protective city barriers: convoluted walls at a town's periphery (think of Hissarlik, Homer's Troy, for example) discourage invasion. But these very protections, she points out, can also imprison, for labyrinths trap within just as easily as they keep without. The mid-1960s Watts landscape that Pynchon describes is similarly confining. Alameda Street, the "gray and murderous arterial" at Watts's eastern boundary, for example, is as impassable as "the edge of the world." Inside Watts, little changes; blacks are "stuck pretty much with basic realities like disease, like failure, violence and death, which the whites have mostly chosen—and can afford—to ignore." When the trapped blacks turn to violence (which Pynchon feels "may be an attempt to communicate"), they metamorphose into modern urban minotaurs.

Images of blacks—and blackness—recur throughout *Lot 49.* Oedipa's husband, Mucho, could not ignore the endless parade of "Negro, Mexican, cracker . . . bringing the most godawful of trade-ins" to his used car lot on another "pallid, roaring arterial." Here blacks are one part of a multicultural "salad of despair"; at the Yoyodyne Cafeteria they become tray-toting kitchen servants "preparing to feed a noontide invasion of [presumably white] Yoyodyne workers." In **"Journey Into The Mind of Watts,"** Pynchon describes the frustrations of black job-seekers denied meaningful employment, or counseled to "look as much as possible like a white applicant." The blacks with steady jobs Oedipa encounters in *Lot 49,* other than the Yoyodyne waiters, include Winthrop Tremaine's San Diego "niggers" turning out swastika armbands and "an exhausted busful of Negroes going on to graveyard shifts all over the city," working the jobs no one else wants. The rejected positions blacks are forced to take recall the detrital landscape of Watts itself: "busted glass, busted crockery, nails, tin cans, all kinds of scrap and waste." This junk can be transformed into the Watts Towers, Simon Rodia's fantasy of fountains, boats, tall open-work spires, encrusted with a dazzling mosaic of Watts debris"; or reborn as the apocalyptic post-riot sculpture Pynchon sees at an Easter week arts festival: "In one corner was this old, busted, hollow TV set with a rabbit-ears antenna on top; inside, where its picture tube should have been gazing out with scorched wiring threaded like electronic ivy among its crevices and sockets, was a human skull. The name of the piece was 'The Late, Late, Late Show.'"

How can junk communicate so powerfully? Jonathan Culler, drawing on the work of Mary Douglas and Michael Thompson, points out that "[w]hat is marginal or taboo turns out to be essential to the study of the system that excludes it." The marginal category of rubbish turns out to be the "point of communication between categories of value." Waste, he claims, is thus found at the heart of value—and language—systems. Oedipa herself finds "God knew how many citizens" who deliberately communicate through the WASTE system rather than the U.S. Mail, or who, "even, daring, spent the night up some pole in the lineman's tent like caterpillars, swung among a web of telephone wires, living in the very copper rigging and secular miracle of communication." Unsuspecting, Oedipa searches the margins, searches WASTE, searches language itself, in order to understand the labyrinthine "legacy [of] America" left her by Inverarity.

Oedipa's penetration of his alternate system takes her through many more mazes. To get backstage at the Tank after watching *The Courier's Tragedy,* for example, she wanders in an "annular corridor," circling twice before settling on a shadowy door, finally walking in on "soft, elegant chaos." After attending the Yoyodyne stockholders meeting, she gets lost on a tour of the plant and experiences the acute anxiety of a solitary labyrinthine journey—although she is not entirely alone:

> Somehow Oedipa got lost. One minute she was gazing at a mockup of a space capsule, safely surrounded by old, somnolent men; the next, alone in a great, fluorescent murmur of office activity. . . . She began to wander aisles among light blue desks, turning a corner now and then. Heads came up at the sound of her heels, engineers stared until she'd passed, but nobody spoke to her. Five or ten minutes went by this way, panic growing inside her head: there seemed no way out of the area.

She finally reaches a potential center—Stanley Koteks doodling the muted post horn on an envelope—but he turns out to be an unwelcome sort of minotaur. His description of the Nefastis Machine makes Oedipa suddenly afraid that, "with a thousand other people to choose from," she walked "uncoerced into the presence of madness." Koteks is not a center—indeed, revelation in the novel is persistently deferred—but another clue, another piece of information.

Oedipa eventually heads north, following clues, entering and enacting more labyrinths. In her Berkeley hotel she is guided by a clerk "through corridors gently curving as the streets of San Narciso." She spends the next night wandering through San Francisco, finding the image of the post horn over and over; the following morning she encounters the tattooed sailor. After embracing him, physically touching one of the alienated, the withdrawn, the unloved, she takes him upstairs and enters a "warren of rooms and corridors," finally reaching his room, and his mattress—which she reads as yet another printed circuit, containing coded information about "all [the] men who had slept on it." While staring at the mattress and thinking of the sailor's DTs, Oedipa figures metaphor itself in distinctly labyrinthine terms: "The act of metaphor then was a thrust at truth and a lie, depending where you were: inside, safe, or outside, lost. Oedipa did not know where she was."

This is not the first time that Oedipa has lost herself (at Echo Courts, after the aerosol can woven its "complex web" about the bathroom, reticulating the mirror in the process, she looks for but cannot find her image), nor her first encounter with a metaphorical labyrinth (we recall, for example, Inverarity's "tangled" assets, the convoluted plot of "Cashiered" [and the submarine net within it], plus the "labyrinth of assumed motives" that leads Tony Jaguar to believe "he could surely unload his harvest of bones on some American someplace"). Nor is it the reader's first encounter with Pynchon's somewhat labyrinthine prose. Pynchon frequently duplicates at the level of narrative the indeterminacy, the confusion, the ambiguity that Oedipa experiences in her search. While terse detective-fiction patter drives much of the prose, Pynchon backtracks, interrupts (frequently using parentheses—or dashes), or layers his descriptions. Colons, semi-colons, and commas gently, rhythmically tug the reader through convoluted paragraphs:

> Through the rest of the afternoon, through her trip to the market in downtown Kinneret-Among-The-Pines to buy ricotta and listen to the Muzak (today she came through the bead-curtained entrance around bar 4 of the Fort Wayne Settecento Ensemble's variorum recording of the Vivaldi Kazoo Concerto, Boyd Beaver, soloist); then through the sunned gathering of her marjoram and sweet basil from the herb garden, reading of books reviews in the latest *Scientific American,* into the layering of a lasagna, garlicking of a bread, tearing up of romaine leaves, eventually, oven on, into the mixing of the twilight's whiskey sours against the arrival of her husband, Wendell ("Mucho") Maas from work, she wondered, wondered, shuffling back through a fat

deckful of days which seemed (wouldn't she be the first to admit it?) more or less identical, or all pointing the same way subtly like a conjurer's deck, any odd one readily clear to a trained eye.

This sentence meanders toward its main verb and then momentarily pools there ("wondered, wondered"), pausing before the final, not-quite-illuminating comparison. Only the next sentence reveals the goal of Oedipa's mental wandering: her recollection of Inverarity's late-night phone call a year earlier.

A few pages later, Pynchon amasses details until they blur:

> Maybe to excess: how could he not, seeing people poorer than him come in, Negro, Mexican, cracker, a parade seven days a week, bringing the most godawful of trade-ins: motorized, metal extension of themselves, of their families and what their whole lives must be like, out there so naked for anybody, a stranger like himself, to look at, frame cockeyed, rusty underneath, fender repainted in a shade just off enough to depress the value, if not Mucho himself, inside smelling hopelessly of children, supermarket booze, two, sometimes three generations of cigarette smokers, or only of dust—and when the cars were swept out you had to look at the actual residue of these lives, and there was no way of telling what things had been truly refused (when so little he supposed came by that out of fear most of it had to be taken and kept) and what had simply (perhaps tragically) been lost: clipped coupons promising savings of 5 or 10¢, trading stamps, pink flyers advertising specials at the markets, butts, tooth-shy combs, help-wanted ads, Yellow Pages torn from the phone book, rags of old underwear or dresses that already were period costumes, for wiping your own breath off the inside of a windshield with so you could see whatever it was, a movie, a woman or car you coveted, a cop who might pull you over just for drill, all the bits and pieces coated uniformly, like a salad of despair, in a gray dressing of ash, condensed exhaust, dust, body wastes—it made him sick to look, but he had to look.

This single sentence (possibly *Lot 49*'s longest) curls always from its initial observation ("Maybe to excess:") into coils of connected, yet sometimes confusing prose (the midpoint parentheses needs at least one rereading to align the "he supposed" and the "that" properly). While elsewhere in the novel repeated "or's" suggest bifurcating possibility—alternate paths in the maze—here they heighten indistinctness; for all the bits and pieces, whatever they might be, are "coated uniformly . . . in a gray dressing of ash."

Pynchon's mazy prose is not confined to the beginning of the book. The plot of *The Courier's Tragedy*, for example, is also endlessly convoluted—the narrated version no less confusing than the unloosing description provided Oedipa by the Paranoids and their girl friends, "as strange to map as their rising coils and clouds of pot smoke." And mazy, for Pynchon, is not always hazy: he also frequently constellates related, yet distinct details to suggest a network of interlacing observations. Faris, quoting Michael Butor, claims that we can call an author's prose labyrinthine if in it "narration is no longer a line, but a surface in which we isolate a certain number of lines, points, or noteworthy groupings." Furthermore, labyrinthine writing branches; it expands. As Oedipas crisscrosses the San Francisco night, for example, she tries to group her own observations into clusters that signify. In the following sentence, semicolons connect one individual to the next, while each succeeding description—until the last, when Oedipa sees an image of herself—unfolds a title further into the narrative space:

> Among her other encounters were a facially-deformed welder who cherished his ugliness, a child roaming the night who missed the death before birth as certain outcasts do the dear lulling blankness of the community; a Negro woman with an intricately-marbled scar along the baby-fat of one cheek who kept going through rituals of miscarriage each for a different reason, deliberately as others might the ritual of birth, dedicated not to continuity but to some kind of interregnum; an aging night-watchman, nibbling at a bar of Ivory Soap, who had trained his virtuoso stomach to accept also lotions, air-fresheners, fabrics, tobaccoes and waxes in a hopeless attempt to assimilate it all, all the promise, productivity, betrayal, ulcers before it was too late; and even another voyeur, who hung outside one of the city's still lighted windows, searching for who know what specific image.

And yet can we, with confidence, call these Oedipa's own observation? So intimate a knowledge of the Negro woman's "rituals of miscarriage," or the night-watchman's "virtuoso stomach" seems beyond even a searching, hypothesizing Oedipa. Although the narrative has never been truly first person, these insights must belong to the narrator, speaking over, or more precisely, through Oedipa. As a result of this narrative ventriloquy, Oedipa's own sensitivity is sharpened; she retains an awareness, however subconscious (even subvocal?), of these details. The self-awareness, and indeterminacy of the last encounter—with "another voyeur . . . searching for who know what specific image"—returns us more firmly to Oedipa's point of view.

Such narrator/character distinctions blur elsewhere in the novel as well. In the used car lot section, for example, point of view shifts among Oedipa, Mucho, and narrator, "You're too sensitive," Oedipa tells Mucho a paragraph earlier. And then, in her mind: Yeah, there was so much else she ought to be saying also, but this was what came out. It was true, anyway." The remainder of this paragraph can also be read as Oedipa's, even up to "Yet at least he had believed in the cars" at the beginning of the next. But soon in this paragraph (quoted above) the details become too fine, the layering too thick, to be Oedipa's—we must be hearing "hyperaware" Mucho. That is, until the narrator's voice gradually takes over, suggesting probabilities and propositions of which Mucho would have been less and less aware:

> If it had been an outright junkyard, probably he could have struck things out, made a career: the violence that had caused each wreck being infrequent enough, far enough away from him, to be miraculous . . . But the endless rituals of trade-in, week after week . . . were too plausible for the impressionable Mucho to take for long.

We can read the first conditional clause a one Mucho himself might have considered; but at "far enough away from him" we edge further away from Mucho himself, and by "impressionable" we've left him. Are we back to Oedipa, because "impressionable" recalls "but there was your Mucho: thin-skinned" at the end of the previous paragraph? Possibly. But the next sentence's proposition—and tricky tense sequence—seem beyond either character; we're hearing the narrator's voice: "Even if enough exposure to the unvarying gray sickness had somehow managed to immunize him, he could still never accept the way each owner, each shadow, filed in only to exchange a dented, malfunctioning version of himself for another. . . ."

This voice returns in *Lot 49* to comment on Oedipa's quest ("If she'd thought to check a couple lines back in the Wharfinger play, Oedipa might have made the next connection by herself") or express her thoughts in decidedly un-Oedipan fashion ("Cammed each night out of that safe furrow the bulk of this city's waking each sunrise again set virtuously to plowing, what rich soils had he turned, what concentric planets uncovered? What voices overheard, finders of luminescent gods glimpsed among the wallpaper's stained foliage. . . ?"). Oedipa may not be incapable of such reflections, but the diction is a stretch ("cammed," "flinders") for an exhausted, immobilized, "beat up on" detective. The labyrinthine sentence structure (particularly in the first clause) also suggests the controlling hand of the narrator—or of Pynchon. Oedipa makes connections, while this voice plays incessantly with language. She holds the sailor and feels his DTs, then remembers time differential dts from calculus—but the etymological gloss on delirium tremens ("a trembling unfurrowing of the mind's plowshare," for instance, isn't convincingly Oedipa's. The narrative voice, moreover, is here as mazy as Oedipa's own adventures.

Perhaps critics who argue that Oedipa is too insubstantial a character have moments like this in mind. They mistakenly assume that she has to—or even intended to—carry the "weight" of the narrative. But the constant disruption of boundaries in *Lot 49* calls into question our ability to define Oedipa precisely. Just as narrator and Oedipa merge, so too reader and Oedipa—we co-experience her anxieties, her confusion, the ambiguities forced upon her by the narrative. We follow Oedipa, Theseus-like, as she reads clues, gets lost, explores the mazy underpinnings of The Tristero. At the level of narrative, we work our way through Pynchon's convoluted prose. But we also attempt to interpret the labyrinthine design in the text itself; we thus try to read both diachronically and synchronically. Near the end of the novel Oedipa tries to read this way, too:

> Meaning what? That Bortz, along with Metzger, Cohen, Driblette, Koteks, the tattooed sailor in San Francisco, the W.A.S.T.E. carriers she'd seen—that all of them were Pierce Inverarity's men? *Bought?* Or loyal, for free, for fun, to some grandiose practical joke he'd cooked up, all for her embarrassment, or terrorizing, or moral improvement?

When Oedipa finally confronts her alternatives—that The Tristero is real or a complicated joke/plot or that she's nuts—she sinks almost irretrievably into solitary despair: "For this, oh God, was the void. There was nobody who could help her. Nobody in the world." Unable to resolve ambiguity, she attempts suicide.

But after her frustrating phone call to the Inamorato Anonymous at The Greek Way, feeling entirely alone in a "desolate, unfamiliar, unlit district of San Narciso," Oedipa paradoxically reconnects with the surrounding landscape by becoming lost within it:

> She stood between the public [phone] booth and the rented car, in the night, her isolation complete, and tried to face toward the sea. But she's lost her bearings. She turned, pivoting on one stacked heel, could find no mountains either. As if there could be no barriers between herself and the rest of the land.

Pynchon lets "desolate," "isolation," and "lost" resonate together here, emphasizing the dissolution of boundaries taking place for Oedipa. *Lost* is etymologically related to Old English *los*—a loosening, or breaking up—and though Oedipa has just nearly dissolved herself (blind with bourbon, driving a sightless car down a midnight L.A. freeway), what really begin to loosen are the barriers that have isolated her from her surroundings. *Isolated*'s Latin root is *insula* ("island"), and Oedipa has felt strangely isolated, buffered since the beginning of the novel. Just as a labyrinth may both protect and imprison, so too does insulation work doubly: one may feel protected (as insulating Tupperware protects food), or detached, cut off (as an island from the shore). For Oedipa, San Narciso, too, has seemed separated from the rest of the land. But San Narciso's boundaries dissolve simultaneously with her own; redeeming, even magical: "San Narciso at that moment lost (the loss pure, instant, spherical, the sound of a stainless orchestral chime held among the stars and struck lightly), gave up its residue of uniqueness for her; became a name again, was assumed back into the American continuity of crust and mantle." This accomplished, Oedipa can look beyond San Narciso to what the narrator calls "The higher, more continental solemnities—storm-systems of group suffering and need, prevailing winds of affluence." No longer buffered, she recognizes "the true continuity."

In several ways, particularly in these last few pages, *Lot 49* makes us aware of its own continuity with another American novel, namely *The Great Gatsby*. That text, too, is arguably "about" America (Fitzgerald himself considered changing the title to *Under the Red, White and Blue*), and one is tempted to read Pierce Inverarity as the embodiment of American capitalism that Jay Gatsby's father hoped his son would be. But Gatsby's illegitimate "gonnegtions" make him less like James J. Hill and more like Jay Gould—the unscrupulous financier whose bust Inverarity kept over the bed, and who, like Gatsby, died virtually friendless. Other odd details connect the two narratives. These include swastikas (compare Meyer Wolfsheim's "Swastika Holding Company" and Winthrop Tremaine's "swastika armbands"), bouncing (juxtapose the "gold-hatted, high-bouncing lover" in Fitzgerald's epigraph with Inverarity's exhortation to "Keep it bouncing"—which Oedipa recalls in a passage concerned with her love for that wealthy man), and also ash (match *Gatsby*'s "valley of ashes" to the "gray dressing of ash" inside Mucho's used cars). The connections are more than superficial. Waste and entropy, for example, are example, are key tropes in both novels. And Pynchon's "stainless orchestral chime held among the stars and struck lightly" carefully echoes Fitzgerald's "tuning-fork . . . struck upon a star." In the earlier novel these words mark Gatsby's magical starting point—the first time he kissed Daisy—and also designate his initial entry into a world previously closed to him. Pynchon's chime, too, invokes boundaries; but at the same time marks a loss—and an ending.

Wordplay in the novel—particularly the pun—helps activate this notion of boundary, of inclusion and exclusion. Puns, writes Culler, "present the disquieting spectacle of a functioning of language where boundaries—between sounds, between sound and letter, between meanings—count for less than one might imagine." Puns have, argues

R. A. Shoaf, "no 'inside' or 'outside.'" *Lot 49* is riddled with puns. A quick sampler might feature the blunt, anagrammatical "KCUF," the covert, translingual "K. da Chingado and Company" (Chicano slang, roughly, for the "What a Fuckup" Company); the satiric, suburban "[w]e still need a hundred-and-fourth for the bridge," and the cryptic, Jacobean plays on "encre," "anchor," and "tryst or odious awry." Many early reviewers derided the novel, it seems, for this very activity, denouncing *Lot 49* as "formless gush," "glossolaliac gibberish," and an "intellectual parlor trick." One critic, unable to resist a pun of his own, claimed the book revealed "a waste of considerable talent." Puns themselves have traditionally been thought an "excrescence of literature," consigned to language's wastebasket. Yet Mary Douglas reminds us that "there is energy in the margins" of any system; and what seems marginal, Culler argues, may actually be at the heart of the system itself.

This would appear to be the case in *Lot 49*. Oedipa herself is aware of "that high magic to low puns," which allows her to know "that the sailor had seen worlds no other man had seen." Puns, we are told in a passage linking saints, clairvoyants, paranoids, and dreamers, "probe ancient fetid shafts and tunnels of truth." Pynchon, I suspect, would agree with Culler's formulation: "puns are not a marginal form of wit but an exemplary product of language or mind. . . . The pun is the foundation of letters, in that the exploitation of formal resemblance to establish connections of meaning seems the basic activity of literature." Oedipa's quest to make connections, to see what she "might find out," propels the novel, and certainly her own synecdochic nickname—Oed, suggesting the *OED*—highlights the book's reliance on words and wordplay. Maureen Quilligan even argues that *Lot 49* is an allegorical novel generated by wordplay; for her the narrative unfolds from an initial pun on "will" (Inverarity's, Oedipa's, even God's).

Quilligan may overstate the case somewhat, but she is right to observe that punning for Pynchon "ground[s] the book's structure in polysemy." On its surface, *Lot 49* offers a series of either/or possibilities: either *Cashiered* will end happily, for example, or it won't; either Oedipa is sensitive and can work the Nefastis Machine, or she isn't and can't; either The Tristero exists, or it doesn't. But this matrix of twinned "zeroes and ones . . . hanging like balanced mobiles right and left," scarcely conceals what Thomas Schaub calls the novel's "essential ambiguity." The irresolvability of *Lot 49*'s polar oppositions enforces uncertainty; multiple possibility displaces binary order. Molly Hite's study of "ideas of order" in Pynchon reformulates Schaub slightly: "[Pynchon's] own fictional worlds . . . are pluralistic—governed not by a rigid, absolute, and universal Idea of Order but by multiple, partial, overlapping, and often *conflicting* ideas of order." Both critics thus rightly emphasize a both/and multiplicity operating in *Lot 49,* noting that the work, in the words of its narrator, opens up "excluded middles" and implicitly allows "the symmetry of choices to break down, to go skew." This even works on the narrative level; Pynchon's frequent use of the conditional mode, Schaub argues, causes the text to oscillate "like a standing wave between nodes of meaning."

Pynchon's puns impact the text this way as well, undermining binary oppositions by multiplying meanings. According to Frederick Ahl, puns "confuse binary though because they add the complexities of 'both/and' to 'either/or', thereby blurring the lines we like to draw between truth and falsehood, fact and non fact." Like metaphor, which "incites us to think and hear on more than one level concurrently," the act of punning, too, is "a thrust at truth and a lie." *Lot 49,* despite Oedipa's efforts (and those of some subsequent critics), refuses to rest at any pole of meaning, preferring to dance, ever-changing, like the neon Lissajous figures outside The Scope. The role of puns in reinforcing such ambiguity is further clarified by Derek Attridge, in terms strikingly applicable to the experience of reading Pynchon's novel: "In place of a context designed to suppress latent ambiguity, the pun is the product of a context deliberately constructed to *enforce* an ambiguity, to render impossible the choice between meanings, to leave the reader or hearer endlessly oscillating in semantic space."

Oedipa also wonders whether she is meant to discover signs of The Tristero at all—that is, is the evidence "encrypted" by Inverarity into the will? Or does Oedipa merely come upon it by "accident"? Perhaps, instead, both accident and design contribute to Oedipa's acquisition of knowledge—and given that *Lot 49* is often seen as a novel of "education," these comments of Culler's on the pun seem especially appropriate:

> What, then, does the pun teach? I have suggested that it foregrounds an opposition that we find difficult to evade or overcome: between accident or meaningless convergence and substance or meaningful relation. We treat this opposition as a given, presuming that any instance must be the one or the other. But puns, or punning, may help us to displace the opposition by experiencing something like "meaningful coincidence" or "convergence that affects meaning" convergence that adumbrates an order *to be* comprehended or explored.

The novel's suspended ending certainly suggests that whatever order inheres in The Tristero remains, for Oedipa, to be comprehended. And Oedipa seems more willing at the end to accept a theory like "convergence that affects meaning" regarding her discoveries. For within her own either/or dialectic rests both/and possibility; even if there is no Tristero, she can only live on as though there were, and she were a part of it; "For there either was some Tristero be-

yond the appearance of the legacy America, or there was just America and if there was just America then it seemed the only way she could continue, and manage to be at all relevant to it, was as alien, unfurrowed, assumed full circle into some paranoia."

Mary Allen sees Oedipa fighting madness throughout *Lot 49.* Besides any Tristero-induced paranoia, beneath Oedipa's "frustrating life"—particularly the incapacity of the men around her for "real human love"—lurks an "underlying hysteria." Indeed, an exploration of the novel's sexual dynamics may bring together certain elements of the labyrinth and language play already limned. Oedipa is decidedly a woman among men in this text. Only two other women are specifically named, and Oedipa's own identity blurs at times. She is alternately "Margo" (Inverarity's Lamont Cranston sidekick), "Oed" (a de-, or perhaps resexed Oedipus), "Rapunzel" (a captive maiden), a "heroin(e)" (at one point imagining herself as "some single melted crystal of urban horse"), a "nymph" (at Echo Courts), "Arnold Snarb" (at The Greek Way), "Mrs. Edna Mosh" (Mucho's pre-rendering of her name for the airwaves), and "Grace Bortz" (when she feels pregnant). Men provide the clues during her investigation of an alternate mail (male?) system, and the first man's name in the book (Pierce) points toward potential male sexual domination. Yet several other men—Fallopian, Koteks, Emory Bortz—bear named that link them to distinctly female systems.

Lot 49 thus compels us to ask whether the alternate mail system is in fact a female one (an "other" system) or just another (male) system. Faris points out that the labyrinth, built by Minos to conceal the product of the illicit love between his wife Pasiphae and the sea-bull sent to Crete by Poseidon, is on one level a male design that represses female desire. Oedipa uncovers a Tristero darkly mysterious, itself described as the magical "Other," representing a system of the marginalized, the repressed. The Tristero is first figured as a "malign and pitiless" striptease dancer, and in Driblette's staging of *The Courier's Tragedy,* the dark assassins appear in "lithe and terrible silence, with dancers' grace, . . . long-limbed, effeminate." These figurations thus connect The Tristero to the earliest—and most explicitly feminine—labyrinths, the "ritual floor designs upon which the priestess danced the myths of the mother Goddess." Driblette's own face is a furrowed labyrinth: Oedipa "couldn't stop watching his eyes. They were bright black, surrounded by an incredible network of lines, like a laboratory maze." He chastises Oedipa for her logocentric concerns ("The words, who cares?") and inspires her to consider being a world-projector, a refiguration of herself as maiden, trapped in the tower, weaving the tapestry of the world—but also a recognition of herself as heroine, outside the tower. Oedipa later tries to reconnect with Driblette, only to discover that he has walked into the Pacific and drowned. Sitting on his grave the night of his funeral, Oedipa reaches out to whatever "transient, winged shape" of his spirit might remain, trying "some last scramble" through the imprisoning maze of the earth. She feels "briefly penetrated, as if the bright winged thing had actually made it to the sanctuary of her heart," but the "winged brightness" never escapes the earth's labyrinthine space.

Winged escape from a labyrinth suggests Daedalus, the cunning designer imprisoned in his own design (as Driblette drowns, dressed/trapped in his own Gennaro costume), and also Icarus—particularly his failed escape and subsequent watery death (too close to the sum—too much "winged brightness"?). Oedipa too is frequently bothered by excessive sunlight. Oedipa believes in the sea as a principle of redemption, inviolate, representing "some more general truth." For her the "lonely sea" of the Paranoids' "Serenade" is "the hole left by the moon's tearing-free" and "that vast sink of the primal blood the Pacific," and thus distinctly connects redemption—and truth?—with the feminine. Unpatterned, unordered, the sea also opposes the labyrinth. Faris suggests that where labyrinths require the postponed desire of a journey, nonlabyrinthine spaces like the sea may offer the satisfaction of place of rest. Yet the sea, too, can host a quest, even claim a life. Ariadne herself was trapped at sea, abandoned by Theseus on the island of Dia. Oedipa's men have been stripped away as well, although, Ariadne-like, she was counting on them to lead her, the Thesean explorer, out of the maze.

Thus, Oedipa drifts, "reluctant about following up anything," in a space that has become more like Eco's third labyrinth, the net. Eco borrows the organic model of the rhizome suggested by Gilles Deleuza and Felix Guattari to describe this net, nothing that unlike the classical, linear design and the Mannerist multicursal mazes, the rhizomatic labyrinth has no center, no periphery, and no exit. Oedipa wonders if the Tristero's communication network is an alternative to the "exitlessness . . . that harrows the head of everybody American," and comes to believe that this system has "no boundaries." The novel certainly makes the question of "center" problematic. The six-chapter structure denies any one chapter such status, although several individual episodes offer themselves as central to the text. Oedipa's encounter with Mr. Thoth at Vesperhaven, which occurs practically at the novel's center, is a leading candidate. Here several narrative images converge: the play of bright day and dark night, the post horn symbol on the signet ring, the yarn, needles, and patterns in the knitting bag, the invocation of God. Oedipa herself feels "as if she had been trapped at the centre of some intricate crystal." And yet she quickly admits how tenuous, "like a long white hair, over a century long," the correlations may be. All that Mr. Thoth's recollections provide her, or, for that matter, her

brief meeting with Driblette, her talk with Koteks, her attempt at rousing Maxwell's Demon, her voyeuristic San Francisco night, her embrace of the tattooed sailor—all potentially central episodes—are clues. Oedipa, at the literal center of the Bantam paperback (the middle of page 69) even suspects that revelation will always, in this novel, be deferred:

> Oedipa wondered whether, at the end of this (if it were supposed to end), she too might not be left with only compiled memories of clues, announcements, intimations, but never the central truth itself, which must somehow each time be too bright for her memory to hold: which must always blaze out, . . . leaving an overexposed blank when the ordinary world came back.

The decentered quality of the rhizome connects it, according to Faris, with feminist critiques of patriarchy. She sees a link, for example, between the rhizomatic labyrinth and Julia Kristeva's "semiotic," or *chora.* Both are connected to the maternal (the rhizome is an earth-root, the *chora* is "anterior to naming, to the One, to the father, and consequently, maternally connoted"); both also disrupt traditional symbolic boundaries. In the decentered rhizomatic maze, every point connects with every other point, and every path with every other path; to its unlimited territory, therefore, there is no real "outside." The rhizome, then, like feminist discourse, can be said to replace either/or poles with a both/and continuum, with non-hierarchical plurality, with unlimited, heterogeneous connectivity. We have already seen that puns work largely this way; Gregory Ulmer notes that for Derrida, punning also "challenges the logocentric structure of concept formation." Oedipa, although she continues with varying degrees of effort to locate the "central truth," seems to recognize that this, too, "the direct, epileptic Word"—the logocentric, patriarchal, symbolic order—may ultimately be lost, leaving only clues. We could assemble certain "clues" in the novel to support Faris's tentative suggestion that the presence of labyrinths (particularly rhizomatic ones) in postmodern texts indicates the return of the repressed: the discovery of and emphasis on a marginalized, somehow feminine system representing the disinherited; the opening up of a both/and continuum (corresponding to the "both/and vision" Rachel Blau DuPlessis sees as a defining feature of a feminist aesthetic); the de- or multi-centered narrative itself; even the miraculous, feminine multiplicity of the deaf-mutes dancing to "some unthinkable order of music, many rhythms, all keys at once." For DuPlessis, artwork produced by a feminist poetics will further "incorporate contradiction and nonlinear movement into the heart of the text." *Lot 49* seems motivated by similar concerns.

Multiple though these concerns are, and multiple the very subjects I've been considering in this easy—labyrinths, prose mazes, puns, feminist discourse—I will argue that they may together converge in a more particular concept: the postmodern. The term itself, of course, has supported several definitions. An eclectic, "grab bag" multiplicity may in fact be one of the postmodern's determining markers. I invoke the term, moreover, not to attempt my own restrictive definition, nor to champion one already offered—I'm more interested in noting in this conclusion how the various convolutions in *Lot 49* help make the text a postmodern one. By using the word "text," for instance, I deliberately call up the writing of Roland Barthes; many of his propositions regarding the "Text" seem to me not only reasonable descriptions of *Lot 49,* but also fair enunciations of the postmodern. The Text, for example, "practices the infinite deferral of the signified" (as in *Lot 49*) revelation is continually postponed); it is "structured but decentered" (as the novel follows several parallel structures—including a structure by constant deferral—but resists a definite central space); and it is governed by a logic of "associations, contiguities, and cross-references" (as Pynchon's mazy prose constellates detail into interlacing networks). Indeed, Barthes's metaphor for the postmodern text is the network. This metaphor recalls Eco's rhizomatic net—and I think both mode adequately describe the postmodern labyrinths of *Lot 49,* particularly its labyrinths of language.

Language seems to be at the root of my several topics here (symbolic landscape, narrative design, and sexual dynamics). We might suggest, then, that language serves to negotiate between particular text (*Lot 49*) and the world. But it is primarily the play of (and in) language, I believe, that gives the novel's networks their special charge—as well as makes them postmodern. Pierce Inverarity, in fact, gives us a perfect (and playful) dictum for postmodernism: "Keep it bouncing." The imperative exhorts us to keep things in play—and precisely captures the ludic quality of the postmodern. Some critics, including Frederic Jameson, dismiss this play element as an endless superficially that self-consciously exalts pastiche while effacing both affect and history. These critics themselves, unfortunately, efface the pleasures of this play—and overgeneralize. *Lot 49*'s playful pastiche does not entirely obliterate economic and social concerns, (consider the interaction with Pynchon's **"Watts"** essay described above, plus Oedipa's late-found "new compassion"), nor does the novel become mere disclosure or textual play. *Lot 49* is certainly more trenchant than the detractors of the postmodern seem ready to admit. I maintain that its carefully crafted labyrinths help make this the case.

James Wood (review date 4 August 1997)

SOURCE: A review of *Mason and Dixon,* in *The New Republic,* August 4, 1997, pp. 32-8.

[*In the following review, Wood offers unfavorable assessment of* Mason and Dixon, *finding fault in Pynchon's equivocal allegories and indeterminate multiple meanings.*]

It is a problem for allegory that, while going about its allegorical business, it draws attention to itself. It is like someone who undresses in front of his window so that he can be seen by his neighbors. Allegory wants us to know that it is being allegorical. It is always saying: watch me, I mean something, I mean something. In this, it is very different from most great fiction. (It resembles bad fiction.) Why does anyone tolerate it? In literature, we rarely do. It is forgiven its hieroglyphics when it overcomes itself and behaves like great fiction (Kafka, some Dickens); when it elaborates complicated and deep truths (Dante, Kafka again); or when it explodes itself in the hunt for deep truth (Melville). It is tolerated when it is not only a map, but a landscape, too.

Thomas Pynchon is the most allegorical American writer since Melville and, for better or worse, the clear inheritor of Melville's broken estate. But his novels behave like allegories that refuse to allegorize. They pile up meanings and disown them at the same time; it is no accident that Pynchon so loves the shaggy dog story, which does the same. (His new novel is built on the shaggy dog story.) Thus he has created readers who think that he is a great occultist and readers who think that he is a visited hoaxer. His novels are huge manic factories that seem alive but are deeply static. They do not move. Yes, they twirl meanings around, they displace meanings; but they do not finally produce meaning. The factory has no products.

Pynchon's readers often mistake bright lights for evidence of habitation. One saw this in the reception of **Mason & Dixon.** It drew gasps: here is a novel set in the eighteenth century, wrote the reviewers, in which we see the first English pizza being made, and a dog that talks, and two clocks in conversation, and a vast octagonal Gloucestershire cheese, and George Washington smoking a joint, and a mechanical duck; and a crazed Chinese man who lectures everybody in sight on the magic of feng shui, and a giant Golem, and a severed ear that moves. They listed these things as if they were scenes and not objects, as if they constitute the movement, the workings, of the novel. But on the whole these occurrences do not move, are not scenes. They are fixed in a lively grid. Yet it was taken as brilliant that the book merely contains these things, like a cabinet of wonders; they were listed as simple natural marvels, whose presence was in itself evidence of significance. There was no need to ask what these marvels were for. They were read as signs; they were taken allegorically. Signs were taken for wonders.

There are delights in Pynchon's book, and some wonders. Chief among them is his language, which is notionally a pastiche of mid-eighteenth-century prose, but is in fact a beautifully flexible alloy, capable of bending calendrically, to take in early eighteenth-century styles as well as late-twentieth-century incursions. The novel's story is told by one Reverend Cherrycoke, who accompanied the surveyors Mason and Dixon on their trip to divide Pennsylvania and Maryland in the mid-1760s. Verbally, the reverend is metaphorical, sententious, rounded, periodical, lawless. All this is to the prose's good. It is the novel's achievement to create a prose, when it is working well, that seems not so much antiquarian as pristine—an American language before it knew itself as "an American language." Indeed, the capitalized nouns that are flaked all over the book begin to seem like the capitals of line-breaks: the prose is sometimes like a poetry that was written out in prose by mistake.

> Below them the lamps were coming on in the Taverns . . . the wind was shaking the Plantations of bare trees, the River ceasing to reflect, as it began to absorb, the last light of the Day. They were out in Greenwich Park, walking near Lord Chesterfield's House,—the Autumn was well advanc'd, the trees gone to Pen-Strokes and Shadows in crippl'd Plexity, bath'd in the declining light. A keen wind flow'd about them.

Yet this language, despite its beauty, is only a refined game. On its own, it is not enough to make a novel great. And the limitations of **Mason & Dixon** are the limitations of allegory. Truly, **Mason & Dixon** is not a novel. It functions as an allegorical picaresque, rolling the brougham of itself from implication to implication, taking on extra implications at one town and throwing off a few at the next. It tamps its characters down into little plots of meaning, then uproots them. Its characters exist to dispense lessons, ideological or philosophical. They do not exist as people. As usual in Pynchon, there are scenes that mean too much and there are scenes that mean too little.

Thus the Mason-Dixon line, which the eponymous heroes are drawing, is made to stand for several things: the good rule of law and the tyrannical rule of law, freedom and imperialism. George Washington smoking cannabis is no doubt supposed to instruct us in the importance of liberality at the highest levels. But the octagonal Gloucestershire cheese and the mobile ear are just diversions, scattered throughout the book—they act like the money that politicians used to throw to voters from the cart: they distract us from the truth.

How we respond to such comedy will depend on our tolerance for these sorts of japes and frolics. Pynchon is famous for his fantastic comedy. But too much, even in this benign book, seems willed, unfree, a hysteria that he forces onto his scenes because without it they would not really exist. It is the difference between the comedy of character and the comedy of culture. Pynchon does not, or cannot, do the former; what he can do, sometimes powerfully, is to make the culture vibrate at high speed, and to whip comedy from the rotations.

To be fair, in this book, and for the first time in his writing, his two protagonists have some concreteness. Both are English. Charles Mason is from Gloucestershire, a melancholic deist in long mourning for his dead wife Rebekah, and essentially conservative in temperament. Jeremiah Dixon is from the north of England, near Durham. He is a Quaker, an instinctive radical and populist, who finds himself appalled by the cruelties of American life (Indian-killing and slavery) even while enamored of its rebellious volume.

> Truly, *Mason & Dixon* is not a novel. It functions as an allegorical picaresque, rolling the brougham of itself from implication to implication, taking on extra implications at one town and throwing off a few at the next. It tamps its characters down into little plots of meaning, then uproots them. Its characters exist to dispense lessons, ideological or philosophical. They do not exist as people. As usual in Pynchon, there are scenes that mean too much and there are scenes that mean too little.
>
> —*James Wood*

Mason and Dixon are a double act; most of their reality is complementary. They are most full as characters when they are acting as halves to each other. Mason is gloomy, Dixon is cheery; Mason is sophisticated, Dixon a bumpkin; Mason is an astronomer (he looks up), Dixon a surveyor (he looks down); and so on. The comedy that Pynchon extracts from this is familiar, and occasionally touching. The novel opens with the pair voyaging to South Africa, to the Cape of Good Hope, to chart the Transit of Venus. (Since everything is always connected in Pynchon, the two also conduct some transits of Venus on land, in the shape of the highly sexed Vroom sisters, who tease them, Fielding-style.) At this time, Mason and Dixon are hardly on speaking terms, and cannot look each other in the eye. But they are not long in Capetown. By the end of the book, having spent more than four years in America and badged with all kinds of adventure, they have developed a deep fondness for each other.

This pattern has the guiltless banality of celluloid. It seems likely that Pynchon is burlesquing the buddy movie—the novel ends with the two men, now retired from their surveying labors, fishing together on an English river, grumpy old men, but learning to talk about their wives and children. This is a reduced comedy, comedy in prison. It relies entirely on fixed forms and the fixed escape from those forms. For example, the picaresque. The two heroes are invited to come to America to survey the state boundaries, and there they move from adventure to adventure—and this has the ridged, repetitive quality of the picaresque: however dissimilar each new adventure is from its predecessor, it resembles it in its mere adventurousness. Pynchon throws at us a giant Golem, the threat of Indian scalping, the lost tribe of Israel (apparently living in the Delaware forest), a mechanical duck, the long story of a French chef who moved from his native country to Pennsylvania, a story about rapacious Jesuits in Montreal, the late appearance of Johnson and Boswell, and on and on. The variety becomes homogeneous. One would like these fattened incidents to shrink into life; the road to become a current. The bloating is familiar from other Pynchon books, a weakness about knowing when to stop accumulating.

The comedy is fixed in other ways, too. Pynchon's most usual trick is anachronism: to confront the apparently antiquarian eighteenth-century form with unexpected modernities such as pizza, or the Malayan ketjap, or ketchup, with which Dixon lathers his food, or a woman asking: "Hallo, d'you think he'll get much of a hard-on, then?" There are puns ("Suture Self, as the Medical Students like to say"), and some charming sillinesses (some twins "nam'd Pitt and Pliny, so that each might be term'd 'the Elder' or 'the Younger', as might day-to-day please one, or annoy his Brother"). The comedy is most funny when least knowing. But too much of it works simply at the level of reader-recognition, a ticket-punch whereby we acknowledge the prompt presence of a Pynchon joke: the writer of sea yarns called Pat O'Brian, or the moment when Dixon goes into a Philadelphia coffee-house and asks for "Half and Half please," the punch coming a second later, when he clarifies: "Mount Kenya Double-A, with Java Highland. . . ." Or when a character called Mrs. Eggslap quotes Tammy Wynette: "Sometimes, 'tis hard, to be a Woman." (Again, this is rarely comedy about people; it is comedy between cultures, the old and the new, and between the writer and his text.)

One of the least funny and least likable scenes involves Mason's and Dixon's meeting with Colonel Washington at Mount Vernon. It is emblematic of Pynchon's comic vision elsewhere—its desperation, its desire to squeeze meanings, its inability to resist a kind of comedic harlotry. Washington is first seen "talking real estate." He offers the English visitors some dope, while dispensing realpolitik about why Americans will always kill Indians. Washington likes to say

"Proclamation-Shmocklamation" and "It's makin' me just mee-shugginah," a habit traceable to his African servant, Gershom, who is Jewish. At first we see Gershom serving coffee, and Pynchon notes only that he has "an ambiguous expression."

A moment later, though, Gershom breaks in fondly: "Don't bother about that Israelite talk, anyhow . . . it's his way of joking, he does it all the time." The scene ends with Gershom singing "Havah Nagilah, a merry Jewish Air, whilst clicking together a pair of Spoons in Syncopation."

This moment feels characteristic of many others in Pynchon's work: the expected is disrupted by the zany, and a purchaseless benignity falls over the whole scene. At such a moment, one realizes why so many of Pynchon's characters, here and elsewhere, have an irritating habit of breaking into song: the principle of Pynchon's comedy is the principle of the stage-musical. Everyone gets to sing their song, however senseless. Pynchon's farce floats in the watery democracy of the musical, the idea that everyone sings as well as the next person and deserves a moment under the lights, that many tunes are better than one tune. Gershom turns and reveals that he is not really a slave, but a mild Jew. Good for him!

Of course, the novel-form is a warmly democratic form, in the sense that the smallest people are noticed—Nabokov, writing about Dickens, claimed this for it. But there is a difference between descriptive charity and comic subsidy, which is the difference between real comic sympathy and the lend-lease of allegory. For Pynchon wants something back from Gershom, for Gershom's twirl on stage. He wants Gershom to signify politically.

It is a moment of utopian wish-fulfillment: oh, if the whole world were like this! Gershom must pay us back by fulfilling our wish. And thus it is, in part, that this scene is not funny, and has no stringency. Since it is not human comedy, it is not freely given—characters are not allowed to exist in "the irresponsible plastic way" in James's lovely phrase. Indeed, the comedy is not given at all: it is extracted from the characters, at their expense. Pynchon does not seem to care for a Washington or a Gershom who might move us or truly interest us. And this is the burrowed agenda of Pynchon's writing: scenes like this one can be strictly meaningless on the surface, because they are supposed to represent something underneath their surface. The comedy is not about the people involved. It is about a cultural moment, about an idea or an ideal—not a moment of free fiction but of unfree allegory.

This is the principle of Pynchon's fiction, and it drives this book, particularly its politics. The America in which Mason and Dixon travel resembles the America of *The Cry-*

ing of Lot 49; there is not such a great distance between 1766 and 1966. Both are ruled by what Pynchon once called "an emerging techno-political order that might or might not know what it was doing." America is both pure possibility and deep degradation, in Pynchon's vision. His diagnosis veers between the wildly dystopian and the wildly utopian.

The degraded America is the country about which Pynchon wrote in a short essay on **"Sloth,"** in 1993, in *The New York Times Book Review.* In the eighteenth century, he observed, America was "consolidating itself as a Christian capitalist state." In *Mason & Dixon,* the Christian capitalist state has been seeding itself, it seems, by laying waste the land. Both Mason and Dixon are shocked by the subjection of the Indians, and by slavery. In South Africa, they saw a similar tyranny. "Whites in both places," thinks Mason, "are become the very Savages of their own worst Dreams. . . ." Dixon recalls "the iron Criminality of the Cape" and "the beefy contented faces of those whites," but decides that "far worse happen'd here," in America. The Reverend Wicks, narrating the novel, plunges this truth home: "the word Liberty . . . was taken in those Times to encompass even the darkest of Men's rights,—to injure whomever we might wish,—unto extermination, were it possible. . . ."

As Mason and Dixon make their way along what they call "the Visto," the wide trench they cut from the Chesapeake Bay to the Ohio River, they meet various Indians and slaves. They are tutored in corruption. Near the end of the book, Dixon decides that he is no better than these white Americans, "having drawn them a Line between their SlaveKeepers, and their Wage-Payers. . . ." For in cutting a line between a slave state and a free state, he has simply shared in the general illusion that slavery is "ever somewhere else"—in South Africa, or in Maryland—"but oh, never in Holland, nor in England, that Garden of Fools." "Where does it end?" he laments. "No matter where in it we go, shall we find all the World Tyrants and Slaves? America was the one place we should not have found them." This is the busted dream that Pynchon writes about in *The Crying of Lot 49,* a land "with the chances once so good for diversity."

What troubles is not the relative ordinariness of these ideas, but their lumpy deployment in fiction. Mason's and Dixon's blotter-like receptivity to every bloodstain of American capitalism seems a little convenient, artistically. His characters might be freer as characters if Pynchon allowed them to put up some resistance to Pynchon's view of things. But that would be fiction, not allegory. Of course, they do respond to the freedoms, the unscored music of early American life. Pynchon especially enjoys the democratic anarchy of American religious life. There are insane German sects

and dour Puritans and strict Quakers and busy Catholics, all of them at stormy war with one another. Politically, there are British patriots and American rebels and mild indifferents. The Indians are fighting the Americans who are fighting the British; and beneath it all, the dried powder of slavery, ready to fire.

In the usual Pynchon way, this world is furrowed with paranoia. Each American suspects the next of being an agent or a spy. The Jesuit network is especially feared, and Mason's and Dixon's cutting party is joined by a mad Chinese, Captain Zhang, who is on the run from the Jesuits. Indeed, it emerges that most of the surveying group are agents of one power or another, including Mason and Dixon, as Dixon observes. To a skeptical Mason, he declares that both of them are paid employees, and therefore agents, of the British crown. They are servants of the oppressor of both black and white Americans.

So this is America in the 1760s. But really, it is the thickly sown lot of Pynchon's mind. For the wartime London of *Gravity's Rainbow* is a similar place, less a city of one noble British defense than the site of internecine paranoias, a city of shadowy groupings and official acronyms: "Everyone watching over his shoulder, Free French plotting revenge on Vichy traitors, Lublin Communists drawing beads on Varsovian shadowministers, elas Greeks stalking royalists, unrepatriable dreamers of all languages hoping through will, fists, prayer to bring back kings, republics, pretenders, summer anarchisms that perished before the first crops were in. . . ." (Pynchon's inability to stop accumulating meanings finds its verbal embodiment in his fondness for lists and catalogs.) And this is the California of *The Crying of Lot 49,* where Oedipa Maas voyages among secret groups and inflamed syndicates, trying to read the signs and the clues that Pynchon throws to her.

Paradoxically, it is in this sea of paranoia that the drowning may be saved. Pynchon seems to cherish the contradictory energy of diverse paranoias because of their lust for confusion. Their busyness confounds the single ruling order, that "techno-political order." In *Mason & Dixon,* a young radical praises the jumbled street music of America, especially "the Negroe Musick . . . 'tis there sings your Revolution." In *The Crying of Lot 49,* Oedipa realizes that "the only alternative was some unthinkable order of music, many rhythms, all keys at once. . . ."

What is the vehicle of this plotlessness, this new music? It is the novel—more, the sliding chromaticism of Pynchon's novels. Against the plot of government stands the musical novel, with its many plots or tunes. In case we miss this, Pynchon uses his characters to remind us. In *Mason & Dixon,* a character informs us that

Who claims Truth, Truth abandons. History is hir'd, or coerc'd, only in interests that most ever prove base. . . . She needs rather to be tended lovingly and honorably by fabulists and counterfeiters, BalladMongers and Cranks of ev'ry Radius, Masters of Disguise to provide her the Costume, Toilette, and Bearing, and Speech nimble enough to keep her beyond the Desires, or even the Curiosity, of Government. . . .

Then he stops, and the Reverend Cherrycoke warns us of "the danger of reading these storybooks,—in particular those known as 'Novel.'" It is the beautiful paranoids ("Cranks of ev'ry Radius") against the government; and fiction is a local branch of this beautiful paranoia. Pynchon is hippie-ish, a moist anarchist. Pynchon's fiction elaborates an allegorical politics. Partial truths are forced into a bent absolutism. It is a system whose vents and flaws seem only to make it stronger, more wrongly consistent, like medieval astronomy. Pynchon's world is a planetarium devised by a myope. The forces of evil, in Pynchon's vision, are the straight, the linear, the rule of governance. Mason and Dixon, though likable men, are agents of fixity. They are surveyors, and knowledge is power. Dixon recalls that, back in England, he laid out the boundaries that enforced the hated and unfair system of land-enclosures: "He had drawn Lines of Ink that became Fences of Stone."

Yet underneath the soil the anarchy of non-linear freedom lives. "Down Below, where no property Lines existed, lay a World as yet untravers'd." Captain Zhang, with his love of feng shui, reminds the surveyors that their line "acts as a Conduit for what we call Sha, or, as they say in Spanish California, Bad Energy. . . ." The Mason-Dixon line is like a dragon's tooth across the free flesh of the land, he warns. The Reverend Cherrycoke explains that Pennsylvania and Maryland are white man's abstractions. They do not exist, but are merely "a chronicle of Frauds committed serially against the Indians dwelling there."

The forces of good—who may be as crazy as the forces of evil—are all those who drift out of the reach of governance and rule. Dream is the utopian space of resistance. *The Crying of Lot 49* ends by praising "drifters" who live as if "in exile" from America. In *Gravity's Rainbow,* Tyrone Slothrop battles unseen enemy forces and is thrown back, as resistance, onto "dreams, psychic flashes, omens, cryptographies, drug-epistemologies, all dancing on a ground of terror, contradiction, absurdity. . . ." In the paranoia of dreams, there you feel free. In *Mason & Dixon,* all the uncharted America west of the Mason-Dixon line is the land of dream, "serving as a very Rubbish-Tip for subjunctive Hopes, for all that may yet be true. . . ." And these dreams are "safe till the next Territory to the West be seen and recorded, measur'd and tied in. . . ." Dreams are safe until they are ruled.

It is a sign of how greatly Pynchon's indexical intelligence intimidates his readers, a measure of his powers of evasion and self-subsidence, that few question the triteness, or the truth, of these notions. (And their ungainliness as fictional ideas.) But one of the advantages of the utopian is that it is impossible to fulfill. Pynchon's utopian good is good exactly because it is the uncharted. It is futurity or dream. It dwarves one's known littleness. Similarly, Pynchon's evil works in his fiction as an inverted utopia, a nightmare that has no streets or fixtures, that cannot be named. In *Gravity's Rainbow,* Slothrop, an American intelligence officer based in wartime London, is obsessed with the idea that "they" are out to get him. He wonders if "they" will explode a rocket over London with his name on it. But "they" are not the Nazis, who are actually sending rockets to London. No, "they" embrace "possibilities far beyond Nazi Germany." But we never find out who "they" are.

Only very occasionally does Pynchon become specific; only rarely does he come out of hiding. Perhaps it is just as well. For Pynchon's *Times* essay, in which he attempts to give body to the forces of evil and the forces of resistance, is dismayingly incoherent. In it, he suggests that, in mid-eighteenth-century capitalist America, time—clocktime—became a tyrannical linearity that ruled all citizens. Only the "ungovernable warp of dreams," or a secularized form of the old sin of sloth, could counter time. The modern equivalent of enforced linearity, he argues, is television. And how might we fight this televisual governance? With the VCR! "We may for now at least have found the illusion, the effect, of controlling, reversing, slowing, speeding and repeating time—even imagining that we can escape it." And then, in a characteristic move, almost as if Pynchon has seen that he has revealed too much, that he has been spotted, that without his novelistic clothes he looks only like a survival of Evergreen or a member or the editorial board of *Social Text,* he retreats. He seems to mock the very idea that he has proposed, to disown his own allegory. When he writes, for instance, that "sins against video time will have to be radically redefined," it is difficult not to hear Pynchon's snicker. He is having us on. Perhaps he is making fun of Andrew Ross; perhaps not. But he has certainly disappeared.

In this way, Pynchon covers his allegorical hide. At first sight, he seems to avoid a too-schematic war of good and evil by confiscating the identity papers of both sides. Maybe, Pynchon asks, good and evil are one side, not two. How would we ever know? The real forces of government are as invisible as the unreal forces of dream, and it is the fate of Pynchon's characters to search a landscape of toppled signs. This, Pynchon suggests, is the real terror of modern society, this cloud of unknowing. Pynchon appears to free his allegory into fiction. In *Mason & Dixon,* the English surveyors are good men serving a bad King. The line they draw is a gesture of imperial rule, yet it also rules between good and bad, between free men and slaveholders. Captain Zhang, who complains so bitterly that the Mason-Dixon line is a bad force, is himself a bad force, a mono-maniac in a world that should be plural and drifting. All this would, on the face of it, seem to be properly contradictory, negatively capable, and so on. Pynchon believes in the importance of plurality. He resents lines and therefore struggles to diversify his own sometimes schematic fictions. He fends off any single allegorical direction or reading. He wants his people to have many choices, including his readers, and he thinks that this is pluralism. Oedipa Maas is waiting for the end of normative America, "waiting for a symmetry of choices to break down, to go skew. . . "

The problem is that Pynchon's allegories are themselves tyrannical. This is his great failure. His belief in plurality is itself an inflexible bolus. His characters do not move us, because they are not free. They are serfs to allegory. They exist to generate meanings or to dissipate meanings. Even in **Mason & Dixon,** where character is given much greater play, one sees Pynchon forced to award his characters an extraneous flamboyance—as with zany Captain Zhang—because they cannot generate interiority. They must be theatrical, because all they are for is to enforce meanings. They are not human, they are agents; they not only think of themselves as agents of various forces, but they act as agents for their author. This is a vision that bullies not only its characters but also its readers into paranoid hunting. (Tony Tanner, the critic whose generous reading of Pynchon is now influential, argues that it is one of Pynchon's achievements to force his readers to read him paranoically.)

Pynchon may long for the polyphonic music of the fabulist, but his novels enforce a strict binarism even as they congratulate themselves on deconstructing this binarism. Oedipa may want "a symmetry of choices to break down," but Pynchon's very fiction is built on a symmetry of choices. Either utopia or dystopia; either governance or dream; either too much meaning or not enough meaning. At the end of **The Crying of Lot 49,** Pynchon offers Oedipa a choice: if the shadowy organization ("The Tristero") that she has been tracking exists, she will join it and escape, because she cannot wait any longer for America to mend its ways. And if the organization does not exist, then she must live in America. And if she must live in America, then she will have to be paranoid.

At first, Pynchon seems to be suggesting that this ordeal of choice is what is wrong with America: it is America that forces us to choose between exile or madness. But since we cannot verify that such a choice need exist (the novel leaves open the possibility that The Tristero is merely Oedipa's hallucination), since Pynchon's vision is itself so

ungrounded, all we can say is that this ordeal is Pynchon's problem, not America's. It is Pynchon, not America, that offers secrecy or dissolution as the only choice.

Pynchon's novels have a certain power—the agitated density of a prison, a closed system. But can one construct and disown allegory without producing incoherence, and an incoherence that seems evasive rather than suggestive? In *Moby-Dick,* Melville came close to destroying his book, by loading its circuitries of significance with so much energy that the novel was in danger of meaning too much and therefore too little. In *Moby-Dick,* the whale is good and evil, it is truth and it is blankness. It is a thousand things. But what is at stake in the novel is supremely human; it is the fate of one's soul. Melville used allegory to hunt down truth, and in so doing he exploded allegory into a thousand pieces. Pynchon uses allegory to hide truth, and in so doing he expands allegory into a fetish of itself. Melville raced with the danger of nothingness while running after truth. Nothingness was a wound in truth's side. But what is left when allegory does not believe in the possibility of truth is merely the allegorical; or a dogmatic faith in it. What is left are novels that draw attention only to their own significations, which hang without reference, inflamedly pointing like a severed arm to nowhere in particular.

Frank McConnell (review date 15 August 1997)

SOURCE: A review of *Mason and Dixon,* in *Commonweal,* August 15, 1997, pp. 20-2.

[*In the following review, McConnell offers high praise for* Mason and Dixon, *which he describes as "one of the most stunning novels I've ever read."*]

I've never been any good at keeping secrets. So: Thomas Pynchon's **Mason & Dixon** is not only the most stunning novel I've read in the last twenty years, but one of the most stunning novels I've read, comma, period. At this point I think we can safely argue that the radiant center of American fiction is inhabited by only three characters, Melville, Faulkner, and Pynchon, and I'm not too sure about Melville, and I left out the unapproachable Henry James only because he didn't really want to be American. So am I telling you that if you don't read **Mason & Dixon** your life will be, by that measure, impoverished? You bet. But of course most of you won't—or at least you won't finish it. It's long, by which I mean long; it's involuted, convoluted, self-referential—it's Thomas Pynchon—and it has, as all of Pynchon's novels, virtually no plot. It is, simply, magnificent.

I've been haunted by Pynchon for thirty-four years. In 1963, my Notre Dame classmate Mike McClintock—now a distinguished professor of literature at the University of Montana—loaned me a copy of *V*—Pynchon's first novel—suggesting that I might enjoy it.

Well, "enjoy" was not precisely the word. I was at first amused, then fascinated, and then I fell into the book, and, to tell you the truth, I'm not sure I ever got back. This man, I thought then and am sure now, possessed or was possessed by the right and real voice of his, which also happened to be my, moment—and yours, too, like it or not. The voice is irreverent—Pynchon loves jokes, the dumber the better, erudite, ranging from physics to Kabbalah and back again—and breathtakingly eloquent, nearly every sentence, as in Faulkner, a tiny masterpiece.

It is also profoundly, maybe despairingly, religious; we'll get to that.

Mason & Dixon is Pynchon's fifth novel, after *V, The Crying of Lot 49, Gravity's Rainbow,* and *Vineland.* And it continues a pattern in his work first noticed, I think, by my brilliant student Parker Douglas: one large, sprawling novel embracing as much Euro-American history as possible, then one shorter and jokier novel set in California, jokiest state of them all, then another large, sprawling novel und so weiter.

Well, *Mason & Dixon,* right on schedule after *Vineland,* is large and sprawling—or better (Pynchon imposes these paradoxes upon you), focused and sprawling.

This much is fact. Between 1763 and 1767, Charles Mason, a British astronomer, and Jeremiah Dixon, a British surveyor, were commissioned by the Crown to determine the exact boundary between Pennsylvania and Maryland. A more tediously quotidian task could probably not be invented—except that the Mason-Dixon Line became the demarcation of America's very own Gulag Archipelago, the line between our free and our slave states, still the symbol of our national failure to live up to our promise to ourselves.

But Pynchon can't deal with one theme without dealing with all the related themes, and all themes, are, finally, related. This was also Faulkner's curse and blessing.

What I mean is, this isn't a novel about slavery—though it is a novel about slavery—and it isn't a novel about America—though it is a novel about America—and it isn't even a novel about the limits of reason, thought it's surely that, too.

At last—and this is why I believe Pynchon is the only living and maybe the only American novelist who deserves to be called "great"—it is a novel full of nostalgia for the departure of God.

> "I was back in America once more, finding, despite all, that I could not stay away from it, this object of hope that Miracles might yet occur, that God might yet return to human affairs, that all the wistful Fictions necessary to the childhood of a species might yet come true,. . . a third Testament. . . ."

That is said by the Reverend Wicks Cherrycoke (yeah, yeah—Pynchon likes making up dopey names). Cherrycoke is the main storyteller of *Mason & Dixon,* reminiscing years later about accompanying them on their survey, after they're both dead. But other narrators, some identified and some not, weave intricately in and out of his tale, in this, the greatest eighteenth-century novel of the twentieth century.

Everett Zimmerman, in his recent book, *The Boundaries of Fiction,* argues persuasively that the novel as a form exists, ab origine, in the creative tension between history and myth, the urge to describe the world as it is and the urge to imagine the world as we desire it. We need novels, that is, because they articulate our condition as cosmic amphibians, living in the ineluctable pressure of the real and in the hope of a final, human meaning—forever speaking, as Karl Rahner writes, into the endless desert of God's silence.

Now all Pynchon's books are set on this boundary: His Central Plot is that an investigator finds him/herself embroiled in a wide-ranging conspiracy—a plot which has no name—which may be directed either toward the final dehumanization of the human race or toward a moment of dark/radiant transcendence.

But never before have the terms been stated as uncompromisingly as here. Bear of little brain that I am, I was halfway through the book before I got the sublime point of Pynchon's choice of subject. Mason and Dixon—a melancholy, vaguely spiritualist astronomer and a jovially carnal surveyor; a disciple of the stars and a disciple of the earth—what are they doing? They are using the stars and the earth to draw an imaginary line that will determine the course of American history, and therefore—at least for Pynchon—the fate of hope, in our world, altogether.

Their journey into America, which occupies the great bulk of the novel, is a journey into hallucination—nothing new for our lad Tom—but hallucination whose point is simply that all our national agonies and glories lie implicit in the conditions of our founding, a Republic of Reason administered by Born-Again Christians. If this is a great eighteenth-century novel, it's an even greater twentieth-century one, a perfect distillation the of the ironies of faith and despair that define the America of the soul.

I don't have space to tell you about Mason and Dixon smoking dope with George Washington and his black-Jewish-slave-stand-up-comic Gershom; or about Ben Franklin, or Samuel Johnson, or the cameo performance by an unnamed Thomas Jefferson; or the performing electric eel Felipe; or Fang the talking dog or the robot Duck who wants to learn about sex; or the squint-eyed, large-forearmed, pipe-smoking sailor who translates God's eyeh asher eyeh into "I am that which I am." You'll have to find them yourselves. Pynchon is as metaphysically serious as Rahner, and also—I think—as funny as George Carlin. If a new character is introduced on every other page of this book, a new joke—and a good one—is told on every page. His laughter, like Lord Byron's, is the laughter of a kind of cosmic sanity, humanizing us even as we guffaw.

This is the book of a lifetime, and God bless him for it.

Edward Gray (review date October 1997)

SOURCE: A review of *Mason and Dixon,* in *William and Mary Quarterly,* Vol. 54, No. 4, October, 1997, pp. 877-9.

[*In the following review, Gray offers favorable assessment of* Mason and Dixon. *According to Gray, Pynchon "transforms what might have been a merely amusing historical novel into a moving and profound meditation on the search for truth."*]

Historians should not read Thomas Pynchon's 733-page novel, *Mason and Dixon,* for information about the book's main characters, Charles Mason and Jeremiah Dixon, the two English astronomers who spent five years (1763-1768) establishing the boundary between Maryland and Pennsylvania. For that, they will find most of what is known in the brief entries in the *Dictionary of Scientific Biography.* There are, however, other reasons to read Pynchon's bestseller. First, historians will find that, although Pynchon has a penchant for caricature—which yields a Jewish George Washington and a Benjamin Franklin who in ordinary conversation utters epigrams such a "strangers heed my wise advice,—never pay retail price"—the range and depth of the author's historical knowledge is astonishing. He has mastered both the particulars of eighteenth-century astronomy and the cultural history of colonial Pennsylvania. Scholars will also find that Pynchon's faux-Augustan prose, invented doggerel, and numerous madcap characters—including a talking dog and an exiled French master chef—lend *Mason and Dixon* the appealing feel of an eighteenth-century

novel. Above all, historians should read *Mason and Dixon* because Pynchon approaches his characters and their world with rare compassion and seriousness. He transforms what might have been a merely amusing historical novel into a moving and profound meditation on the search for truth.

Pynchon has long been interested in the problem of certainty in a modern world whose boundaries in time and space are everywhere giving way to a vast and nebulous media-created reality. His protagonists, in their quest for certainty, often come upon alternate realities, shaped by dreams or hallucinations and freed from the disintegrative forces that make modern life alienating and dull. Before reaching the utopian realm, his protagonists must first recognize that their own reality is the result of dissimulation, duplicity, fakery, double-dealing, conspiracy, lying, cheating, cunning, and the paranormal—forces that, in *Mason and Dixon,* surface as conspiring Jesuits, Freemasons, illuminati, Kaballists, and Jacobites (of whom the older Mason tells the younger Dixon, "anyone who was seventeen that summer [of the '45] . . . was a Jacobite." In the America Pynchon writes about, things are not what they appear to be. If for characters in Pynchon's earlier novels this realization was something discovered, for the two protagonists of *Mason and Dixon,* it is taken fully for granted and also something that science somehow promises to overcome.

In addition to establishing the boundary line that bears their name, Mason and Dixon took part in the largest scientific undertaking of the eighteenth century: the tracking of the transit of Venus. The purpose of that project was to determine the distance between the sun and the earth—a result, participants hoped, that would permit the complete charting of the universe. Mason and his assistant Dixon, in their capacity as observers of the project, found themselves in Dutch South Africa, where Pynchon begins as account of their partnership. Born of an eighteenth-century belief that the universe is finest and fundamentally rational, their partnership rests on the assumption that the face of the earth can be comprehended through the careful application of universal, rational principles. None of this characterization is to suggest that Pynchon depicts Mason, Dixon, and their world as purveyors of mindless optimism. Instead, he implies a pervasive and melancholy sense that rational means may not yield rational ends. Hence the Reverend Wicks Cherrycoke, an alleged associate of Mason and Dixon and the narrator of Pynchon's story, says of the two astronomers' best known achievement.

> Here at the northeast corner of Maryland, the Geometrickal Pilgrim may well wish to stand . . . at this purest of intersections mark'd so far upon America. Yet, Geomancer, beware,—if thy gaze but turn Eastward by an Eye-lash's Diameter, thou must view the notorious Wedge,—resulting from the failure of the Tan-

gent Point to be exactly at this corner of Maryland, but rather some five miles south, creating a semi-cusp or Thorn of that Length, and a doubtful ownership,—not so much claim'd by any one Province, as prize'd for its Ambiguity,—occupied by all whose Wish, hardly uncommon in this Era of fluid Identity, is not to reside anywhere.

Wrongly plotted, the Mason-Dixon line could produce some sort of mysterious nether world. Whatever one may think of such an assertion, it has the effect of elevating the work of two minor astronomers to the sublime.

In present times, one does not need an astronomer to establish a boundary line. We live on land covered with benchmarks, often indicated by small concrete or stone monuments. These marks correspond to points on an imaginary grid composed of an infinite number of lines of longitude and latitude. Mason and Dixon were among those who first transformed that grid from the imaginary to the material by looking to the only fully accurate benchmarks available to them: the stars. To be a surveyor in colonial America was thus to be in a place where locations and boundaries between property and people had as much to do with the movement of the heavens as with distances and divisions between points on the land. It was also, Pynchon believes, to be the forger of a nation. For Pynchon, America before Mason and Dixon, was a giant, grinding, and licentious place—a place of oceans, continents, peoples, and races; a place vast in its wealth, vast in its misery, vast in its desires, and vast in its distances; a place of mixing and mingling; a place of crooks and cretins; a place of little quaintness or quietude. It was, in short, a place whose bounds were few.

Pynchon knows that Mason and Dixon's Ahab-like struggle to impose just one boundary on America was ultimately in vain. He knows that the boundary, which was meant to end confusion and conflict in the eighteenth century, became the center of conflict—bloody, damning conflict—in the nineteenth. He does not, however, fall prey to crude portent. Instead, he relishes his protagonists' determination to struggle against forces that are everywhere and always making the universe chaotic and incomprehensible—a determination driven by certainty about the existence of ultimate truth and the idea that, if people could only grasp that truth, they would all be much, much happier.

FURTHER READING

Criticism

Ames, Christopher. "Power and the Obscene Word: Discourses of Extremity in Thomas Pynchon's *Gravity's Rain-*

bow." *Contemporary Literature* XXXI, No. 2 (Summer 1990): 191-207.

> Discusses the function of obscenity in *Gravity's Rainbow* as a counteractive force against scientific jargon, the language of authority and oppression in the novel.

Caesar, Terry. "'Take Me Anyplace You Want': Pynchon's Literary Career as a Maternal Construct in *Vineland.*" *Novel: A Forum on Fiction* 25, No. 2 (Winter 1992): 181-99.

> Explores suggestive issues of origin and maternity in *Vineland* in terms of Pynchon's virtually unknown personal life.

Cowart, David. "Continuity and Growth." *The Kenyon Review* 12, No. 4 (Fall 1990): 176-90.

> Provides extended critical analysis of *Vineland.*

Gibb, Robert. "Ideas of Order: The Shapes of Art in *The Crying of Lot 49.*" *Journal of Modern Literature* XVII, No. 1 (Summer 1990): 97-116.

> Examines the paradoxical significance of closed systems in the narrative structure of *The Crying of Lot 49.*

Hans, James S. "*Gravity's Rainbow* and the Literature of Renewal." *Essays in Literature* 15, No. 2 (Fall 1988): 267-84.

> Explores positive aspects of multiplicity in *Gravity's Rainbow,* presented as an antidote to oppressive binary logic.

Hume, Kathryn. "Views from Above, Views from Below: The Perspectival Subtext in *Gravity's Rainbow.*" *American Literature* 60, No. 4 (December 1988): 625-42.

> Examines the significance of shifting vertical and horizontal perspectives in *Gravity's Rainbow* as a component of the novel's multidimensional subtext.

Putz, Manfried. "The Art of the Acronym in Thomas Pynchon." *Studies in the Novel* 23, No. 3 (Fall 1991): 371-82.

> Discusses the function of acronyms in Pynchon's fiction as a source of parody and satire.

Robberds, Mark. "The New Historicist Creepers of *Vineland.*" *Critique: Studies in Contemporary Fiction* XXXVI, No. 4 (Summer 1995): 237-48.

> Examines elements of poststructuralist theory and allegory in the historical underpinnings of *Vineland.*

Schachterle, Lance. "Bandwidth as Metaphor for Consciousness in Pynchon's *Gravity's Rainbow.*" *Studies in the Literary Imagination* 22, No. 1 (Spring 1989): 101-17.

Discusses the metaphorical significance of bandwidth in *Gravity's Rainbow* in the technical context of communication theory.

Weisenburger, Steven. "Hysteron Proteron in *Gravity's Rainbow*." *Texas Studies in Literature and Language* 34, No. 1 (Spring 1992): 87-105.

Examines the significance of "hysteron proteron" in *Gravity's Rainbow* as an element of satire and narrative disruption.

Additional coverage of Pynchon's life and career is contained in the following sources published by Gale: *Bestsellers*, 90:2; *Contemporary Authors*, Vols. 17-20R; *Contemporary Authors New Revision Series*, Vols. 22, 46, 73; *Dictionary of Literary Biography*, Vols. 2, 173; *DISCovering Authors*; *DISCovering Authors: British*; *DISCovering Authors: Canadian*; *DISCovering Authors Modules: Most-Studied, Novelists, and Popular Fiction and Genre*; *Major Twentieth Century Writers*; *Short Story Criticism*, Vol. 14; and *World Literature Criticism*.

Edward W. Said

1935-

The following entry presents an overview of Said's career through 1996.

Palestinian-born American critic and essayist.

INTRODUCTION

A Palestinian refugee in his youth and a respected though controversial professor of English and comparative literature at Columbia University, Said (pronounced sah-EED) is an influential and often polemical cultural critic. Said is a public intellectual who frequently writes about the Arab-Israeli conflict in the Middle East and actively supports the cause for Palestinian national rights. His most celebrated and contentious work, *Orientalism* (1978), which examines Western representations of Middle Eastern societies and cultures, established his reputation for innovative and provocative explorations of the interrelationships between texts—literary and otherwise—and the political, economic, and social contexts from which they emerged. In his writings Said adopts a Continental, interdisciplinary approach to literary criticism and uses the principles of phenomenology, existentialism, and French structuralism to make connections between literature and politics. Although his theories and methods have exerted a profound influence on the American academy, especially on literary theory and cultural studies, Said often is the target of phone threats and hate letters, principally for his unwavering advocacy of Palestinian political and cultural rights in the Middle East. "Said occupies a unique place in contemporary literary criticism," wrote John Kucich. "He is a much-needed link among humanistic values and traditions, theories of textuality, and cultural politics. His work is . . . a careful integration from these various positions and an original prescription for the renovation of literary and cultural study."

Biographical Information

Said was born November 1, 1935, in Jerusalem in what was then Palestine. The only son of Wadie and Hilda Musa Said, prominent members of the Christian Palestinian community, he was baptized as an Anglican and attended St. George's, his father's alma mater. In December, 1947, his family fled to Cairo, Egypt, to avoid the turmoil surrounding the establishment of Israel as a nation. In Cairo, Said studied at the American School and Victoria College, the so-called "Eton of the Middle East," before he completed his secondary education at a preparatory school in Massa-

chusetts. Said became a naturalized citizen of the United States in 1953. After graduating from Princeton University in 1957, he undertook graduate studies in comparative literature at Harvard University, where he earned his M.A. in 1960 and his Ph.D. in 1964. His dissertation on the psychological relationship between Joseph Conrad's short fiction and his correspondence became his first published book, *Joseph Conrad and the Fiction of Autobiography* (1966). Hired as an instructor in English at Columbia University in 1963, Said became a full professor by 1970; his distinguished teaching career at Columbia included two endowed chairmanships in the 1980s and 1990s. Said enhanced his growing reputation for literary scholarship with *Beginnings* (1975), which won Columbia's Lionel Trilling Award in 1976. During the 1970s Said actively involved himself in the Palestinian cause by writing numerous essays for scholarly journals and independent publications. From 1977 to 1991 he belonged to the Palestinian National Council, the Palestinians' parliament in exile, meeting Yasir Arafat many times and helping to draft the Palestinian declaration of statehood in 1988. Said pursued his work following the groundbreaking *Orientalism,* which was nominated for a National Book Critics Circle Award, with the publication of two "sequels," *The Question of Palestine* (1979) and *Covering Islam* (1981); the essay collection, *The World, the Text, and the Critic* (1983); and a meditative essay on Palestinian identity featuring the photographs of Jean Mohr, *After the Last Sky* (1986). During the 1980s and 1990s, Said was named to several visiting professorships and lectured extensively on both literary and political themes. In 1991 he published *Musical Elaborations,* a volume of original music criticism that grew out his lifelong fondness for playing the piano. Said was diagnosed with leukemia in 1993. His subsequent works—*Culture and Imperialism* (1993), *The Politics of Disspossession* (1994), *Representations of the Intellectual* (1994), and *Peace and Its Discontents* (1995)—continue to provoke controversy.

Major Works

Said's writings cover diverse topics, but at their center lies a concern for the multiple relationships between the act of writing and cultural politics, language and power. *Beginnings* theorizes about the reasons several writers begin their works the way they do, demonstrating that prevailing cultural ideas of the beginning act change and limit a writer's choice to begin. *Orientalism* reveals how Western journalists, fiction writers, and scholars helped to create a prevalent and hostile image of Eastern cultures as inferior, stagnant, and degenerate, showing the extent to which these representations permeate Western culture and have been exploited to justify imperialist policies in the Middle East. *Orientalism* provides much of the theoretical and thematic groundwork for many of Said's subsequent works, and it contains the dictum of orientalism: "They cannot represent themselves; they must be represented." *The Question of Palestine* outlines the history of the Palestinians and the Arab-Israeli conflict, describing the opposition between an Israeli world informed by Western ideas and the "oriental" realities of a Palestinian culture. *Covering Islam,* elucidating the themes of Said's previous books in more practical terms, investigates the influence of orientalist discourse on the Western media's representation of Islamic culture. Written between 1968 and 1983 on wide-ranging literary and political topics, the twelve essays comprising *The World, the Text, and the Critic* offer an assessment of contemporary criticism and scholarship in the humanities, highlighting Said's notions of "antithetical knowledge" and the synthesis of literary and political writing. *Culture and Imperialism* examines how imperialism, the "culture of resistance," and postcolonialism helped to shape the French and English novel, exemplified by close, provocative readings of Conrad, Rudyard Kipling, Albert Camus, W. B. Yeats, and Jane Austen. The essays in *The Politics of Dispossession* critique the Islamic revival, Arab culture, Palestinian nationalism, and American policy

in the Middle East, revealing a moderating stance toward Israel and a distancing from the Palestinian Liberation Organization (P.L.O.). *Representations of the Intellectual* is a case study of the intellectual persona.

Critical Reception

Owing partly to the nature of his thought and partly to his allegiance to the Palestinian cause, Said has generated controversy upon publication of nearly every book. Despite his persistent denials, he has been questioned about terrorism throughout the course of his career. Robert Hughes has reported that "none of Said's political foes have been able to cite a single utterance by him that could be construed as anti-Semitic or as condoning either tyranny or terrorism." Most scholars, however, have recognized the extent to which his oppositional criticism has influenced debate beyond literary issues and cultural politics, especially *Orientalism,* which has been cited as often as criticized by literary theorists, historians, anthropologists, and political scientists—the book even has spawned a new subdiscipline, the cultural study of colonialism. "The Orient was a product of the imagination," opined Albert Hourani of that book, "and Mr. Said's delicate and subtle methods of analysis are good tools for laying bare the structure of the literary imagination." Dinitia Smith remarked that *Orientalism* "has changed the face of scholarship on the Arab world and the Third World in general." Although many critics have praised the study, some have focused on imperfections in the argument of *Orientalism,* accusing Said of perpetuating the same Eastern stereotypes for which he had faulted the Western imperialist. Some critics have noted that although many of Said's writings have been translated into many different languages, his books on Palestinian affairs had not been published in Arabic by 1994. Robert Hughes has described Said as "a scholar and humanist, . . . the controversial voice of Palestine in America and an eloquent mediator between the Middle East and the West."

PRINCIPAL WORKS

Joseph Conrad and the Fiction of Autobiography (criticism) 1966
Beginnings: Intention and Method (criticism) 1975
Orientalism (criticism) 1978
The Question of Palestine (criticism) 1979
Covering Islam: How the Media and the Experts Determine How We See the Rest of the World (criticism) 1981
The World, the Text, and the Critic (criticism) 1983
After the Last Sky: Palestinian Lives (essay) 1986
Blaming the Victims (criticism) 1988
Musical Elaborations (criticism) 1991

CRITICISM

Albert Hourani (review date 8 March 1979)

SOURCE: "The Road to Morocco," in *The New York Review of Books,* Vol. 26, March 8, 1979, pp. 27-30.

[In the following review, Hourani details the principal arguments of Orientalism, *discussing their strengths and weaknesses.]*

The theme of this powerful and disturbing book [*Orientalism*] is the way in which intellectual traditions are created and transmitted. They do not simply arise, Edward Said argues, in the solitude of a thinker's or a scholar's mind. The scholar may "attempt to reach a level of relative freedom from . . . brute, everyday reality," but he can never quite escape or ignore his "involvement as a human subject in his own circumstances."

> . . . the possibilities for work present in the culture to a great and original mind are never unlimited. . . . The work of predecessors, the institutional life of a scholarly field, the collective nature of any learned enterprise: these, to say nothing of economic and social circumstances, tend to diminish the effects of the individual scholar's production. A field like Orientalism has a cumulative and corporative identity . . . the result has been a certain consensus: certain things, certain types of statement, certain types of work have seemed for the Orientalist correct.

"Orientalism" is the example Mr. Said uses to illustrate his theme, and by it he means something precise. The scholar who studies the Orient (and specifically the Muslim Orient), the imaginative writer who takes it as his subject, and the institutions which have been concerned with "teaching it, settling it, ruling it," all have something in common: a certain representation or idea of "the Orient," defined as being other than the "Occident," mysterious, unchanging, and ultimately inferior.

This representation has been created by the Western mind in more or less complete freedom, for "the Orient as a genuinely felt and experienced force" has been almost to-

tally absent from Western culture. It has been developed and maintained by a kind of implicit partnership between scholars, writers, and those who have won and governed empires. Scholars and writers have been conscious of the sheer fact of Western strength in a passive and powerless Orient waiting to be ruled or manipulated, and the men who ruled have drawn a moral justification, and therefore a kind of strength, from the Western idea of the Orient. The partnership has been mediated through institutions—certain formalized ways of teaching and writing—which have limited what can be thought and said about the Orient.

It is this cumulative way of thinking about the Orient and acting toward it that Edward Said calls "Orientalism." Of course, any kind of thought involves making distinctions, and distinctions establish limits, but it is his contention that this kind of definition has been particularly harmful. It may have acted as a spur to the European imagination and helped to shape the Western sense of identity, but since it is a distinction based ultimately on religious and cultural difference it has led to a misunderstanding of historical processes. It has made it impossible to see "orientals" as individual human beings, since their identity has been absorbed into the idea of "the Muslim," "the Arab," or "the Oriental"; and, like all very simple binary oppositions of "us" and "them," it has given rise to judgments of moral worth. The Orient is seen as strange and distant, malignant and dead unless we bring it to life, the haunt of "monsters, evils, heroes; terrors, pleasures, desires."

The germ of this vision of the Orient Mr. Said finds in the first encounters of Western Europe with the world of Islam: the struggle for control of the Mediterranean basin caused a recurrent trauma in the Western mind, and it could only be controlled by trying to explain Islam in familiar terms, as a false revelation or a Christian heresy. Then, in the second half of the eighteenth century, structures of thought inherited from the past were "secularized, redisposed and reformed"; under the influence of a new kind of intellectual curiosity and the expansion of European power, the image of the Muslim enemy turned into the modern image of the "Oriental." There appeared the first modern "Orientalists," the Frenchman Anquetil-Duperron, who discovered and translated Avestan texts, and the Englishman Sir William Jones, who translated Sanskrit poetry and studied Hindu laws, and who "before he left England for India in 1783 . . . was already a master of Arabic, Hebrew, and Persian." Jones was particularly important because his career was bound up with the first effective and permanent rule of Europeans over an Oriental society, that of the East India Company in Bengal; in his life and work, the link between political domination and the urge to understand becomes explicit.

A generation later there came a European incursion into the

heart of the Muslim Orient. The French occupation of Egypt in 1798 was not only an incident in the revolutionary wars, it was a movement of the imagination. Bonaparte had read the Comte de Volney's *Voyage en Egypte et en Syrle* and other writings about Egypt, and they helped to shape his actions there: he was conscious of forty centuries looking down on him and his soldiers: he thought of himself as coming to bring back life to a lifeless world, and the scholars and scientists who went with him carried out the first systematic appropriation of an Oriental society and culture.

The French expedition perhaps did more for the "imaginative geography" of the Orient than for the real Egypt. To represent the Orient intellectually and imaginatively, to dominate it and bring it back to life: these endeavors were to create the Orientalist "field" during the next seventy years or so. Scholars discovered, edited, extracted, translated, and interpreted texts; at first an individual effort, their work was later codified and embodied in institutions and traditions. Mr. Said is mainly concerned with two of the traditions, the French which begins with Silvestre de Sacy, author of works on grammar and an Arabic anthology, and the English which goes back to Edward William Lane, lexicographer, translator of the *Arabian Nights,* and author of a work still widely read, *An Account of the Manners and Customs of the Modern Egyptians.*

These traditions were enriched by ideas drawn from the general culture of the age, and Edward Said is right to lay emphasis on the science of philology, and in particular on Ernest Renan, who applied its methods to the study of the Semitic languages. Philology was one of the seminal studies of the nineteenth century, almost a secularized religion. Renan called it "the exact science of mental objects," and it seemed to offer a way of understanding not only languages but the nature and history of mankind. By reducing languages to their roots, it was able to group them into families, and it suggested that the families of languages could also be families of all those entities which expressed themselves through language: religions and mythologies, cultures and races.

Within a family, languages could be arranged in order of generations, and the classification of languages and cultures could therefore give rise to a history of them, and to a purely human history in which God had played no part. But Mr. Said contends that, in so far as it was used in the Orientalist field, philology itself was confined within the "Orientalist" frame and was used to give a "scientific" basis to the binary opposition which was already there. For Renan, the Semitic languages were essentially inferior to the Aryan, and incapable of developing beyond a certain point: "we refuse to allow that the Semitic languages have the capacity to regenerate themselves." In a particularly

brilliant passage, Mr. Said suggests that this idea comes from an application to philology of certain ideas current in the anatomical science of the age: Semitic for Renan is what an anatomical monster was for Etienne Saint-Hilaire, not an exception but an anomaly, a phenomenon of degraded or arrested development.

Parallel to the process of scholarly investigation went that of exploration. Some travelers to the Orient, like Lane, went as scholars to gather materials; some, like Chateaubriand, to discover or assert their identities; others, like Burton, from a mixture of motives. In a subtle analysis not only of what they said but of the ways in which they said it—arrangement, style, and "tone"—Mr. Said uncovers the "latent Orientalism" beneath their differences of approach. For all of them, the fact of empire, the assertion and domination of Europe, was a present reality; the Orient appeared as a fallen being, attractive but full of danger, in particular sexual danger.

The modern Orient that they found was not the real Orient but a dead shell into which only Europe could breathe life again; travel in the Orient was a kind of pilgrimage, which bore fruit only when the traveler had encountered dangers and overcome them, seen strange places and turned his back on them, and returned to his own self enriched. In spite of the similarities, Mr. Said is aware of differences between British and French attitudes, and perhaps he overstates them. For the British, securely established in India, he says, the Muslim Orient is a region of potential domination; for the French it is haunted by a "sense of acute loss." But in this period the French had not irretrievably lost the Middle East, and they had won for themselves a new province of the imagination in Algeria.

In the last quarter of the nineteenth century a new phase begins. The imperial governments take on new responsibilities, the British in Egypt and the French in Tunisia; then the division of the Ottoman Empire, foreshadowed before the First World War, is accomplished at its end, and the Arabic-speaking provinces fall under British and French control. The relationship between scholarly work and political action becomes closer and more complex. The institutions through which the Orientalist tradition is transmitted are larger, more formally organized, and more closely linked with governments. Within this tradition, new human types of the "Orientalist" emerge. In the generation before 1914, the age of light-hearted, combative, and self-assured expansion, there appears the "imperial agent," the man who puts his knowledge and ideas, his feelings and impulses, at the service of empire.

As a student of Joseph Conrad, Mr. Said is at his ease with this kind of ambiguous personality, mysterious, in the end unknowable, seeking some personal redemption by way of some difficult and secret mission. The archetypal agent is T. E. Lawrence, and Said has new and penetrating things to say about the complex interweaving of motives in Lawrence's active life, and of narrative and personal vision in *Seven Pillars of Wisdom.* For Lawrence as for Bonaparte, it was by way of an imaginative vision of an epic, to be first lived and then written, that he "drew these tides of men into my hands"; his actions were then re-molded into the vision we find in his flawed masterpiece, but it is impossible to tell where narrative ends and where vision begins, whether Lawrence's aim has been "to make a new nation, to restore a lost influence," or to make and discover himself. He himself becomes the Orient; one man becomes an entire history.

[Said's] writing is forceful and brilliant . . . and he has the skill to penetrate human wills and to delineate the structure of human visions. But can it be that he himself has fallen into the trap which he has exposed, and has sunk human differences in an abstract concept called "Orientalism"?
                                        —*Albert Hourani*

In the years after 1918 the Orientalist vision changes. Europe is in control of the Orient; its ultimate power cannot be shaken, its right to rule is scarcely questioned, but the resurgence of the peoples of Asia is now seen as a challenge, and the typical Orientalist of the age is the adviser who, while accepting the ultimate reality of Western domination, tries to show the way to a peaceful resolution of differences, a kind of mutual acceptance. The English and French traditions culminate in two figures who seem to sum them up: the first is the Frenchman Louis Massignon, whose evocation of the mystical writer and martyr Mansur al-Hallaj has been formed not only by the European tradition of Islamic studies but by an aesthetic sensibility and a Catholic consciousness typically French and of that time; the second is the Scotsman Hamilton Gibb, whose lineage goes back through Thomas Arnold and Robertson Smith to the same origins, and whose vision of the continuity and development of the Muslim community through history would come most easily to a mind conscious of imperial responsibilities and holding a certain Protestant view of the Church.

Mr. Said writes of both of them with respect for their culture, the quality of their thought, and their courage, but regards them both as being caught within the "Orientalist" cast of mind: "Oriental studies" had not turned critically upon their own tradition, as other human sciences were doing at the time, and for both Massignon and Gibb the ultimate re-

ality was something called "Islam," eternally present, always different from the West, in which the individuality of human beings, the differences of times and places, were dissolved.

Massignon died in 1962, and Gibb in 1971; for those of us who knew them and can compare our memories with what Mr. Said writes of them, doubts and questions may arise. His writing is forceful and brilliant (sometimes too forceful for comfort, sometimes too brilliant to be clear); and he has the skill to penetrate human wills and to delineate the structure of human visions. But can it be that he himself has fallen into the trap which he has exposed, and has sunk human differences in an abstract concept called "Orientalism"? What is the status of this concept? What kind of validity can he claim for the general statements he makes—such statements as these: "Orientalists are neither interested in nor capable of discussing individuals"; the Orientalist is marked by "absence of sympathy covered by professional knowledge"?

In a sense, the answer is simple. What Mr. Said has done is to construct an ideal type of "the Orientalist," made up of a number of elements logically connected with each other, and free from extraneous and accidental elements. But as every social scientist knows, such ideal types must be used with care and caution in order to explain particular events or human beings. No person fully exemplifies one type: each must be seen in the light of several types. One of them may explain him more than others, but in the end some irreducible individual flavor will remain. Having admired the elegance of Mr. Said's construction, we must still ask how far it will serve as a principle of explanation of the human beings about whom he writes. The politicians and colonial servants? On the whole, yes. His quotations from Lord Cromer (the British administrator of Egypt after 1883) and others are apt, and he could have found many more to prove his point: the conscious opposition of "East and West," ideas such as those of "oriental despotism" and "oriental stagnation," and the view that "Orientals" only understand force, did give Englishmen and Frenchmen the assurance that their rule over Eastern peoples was natural and right. Imaginative writers can also be understood as working within such assumptions, especially writers of the romantic age, Chateaubriand, Lamartine, Flaubert, de Nerval; their Orient was a product of the imagination, and Mr. Said's delicate and subtle methods of analysis are good tools for laying bare the structure of the literary imagination.

It may be, however, that he is not treading on such sure ground when he writes about scholars. Here too he has found some telling quotations: Theodor Noldeke saying that his life's work had only confirmed his "low opinion" of the Eastern peoples, or Gibb claiming that "the Arab mind" is incapable of rational thought. Some element of "latent

Orientalism" was indeed present in the minds of most of the Oriental scholars of the period he deals with; if it was not a certain contempt for those about whom they wrote, it was at least a conviction that they understood these people, knew their languages and beliefs, better than they did themselves. We must still ask, however, to what extent this conviction entered into their work and determined its direction and limits. To answer this, we must go beyond their *obiter dicta* to their serious professional work, and ask whether it was shaped and distorted by the crude opposition of "Orient" and "Occident," rather than by concepts more suited to its subject matter, and how far its products served to confirm and strengthen that opposition.

It is not necessary to be intelligent to become a scholar, and there have been many scholars who, even in their most substantial work, have shown no skills except those of language, and made use of no ideas except those drawn from the commonplaces of the age. Even great Orientalists found themselves obliged by circumstances to speak and write far beyond the limits of their real competence, and when doing so made use of ideas picked from the surrounding air. When most of them wrote about politics, or sociology, or "national character," or history, or literature, they wrote on the whole as amateurs.

There is, however, running through the work of the great Islamic scholars, one central strand of concern—for the origin and development of all those systems of thought which attempted to articulate what Muslims believed to be the revelation given to mankind through the Prophet Muhammad: tradition, law, theology, mystical thought. A hundred years of study of these matters have produced a body of work which cannot be regarded as badly done. There is in this work a cautious and careful use of original sources, an avoidance of unfounded generalization, a sense of the interrelations between intellectual movements and social and political events, and a feeling also for the quality of individual thinkers in so far as their works reveal them. The individual is not absorbed into a general concept in such detailed explorations of personal "thought-worlds" as Louis Massignon's work on al-Hallaj, Laoust's on Ibn Taimiya, and Ritter's on Farid al-Din ᶜAttar. It is true that a general concept has shaped such work; it is that of "Islam" as a system of thought, seen in its relations to earlier systems, Greek, Christian, and Jewish. But this concept is not another form of the idea of the "Orient" as Mr. Said has described it; it is Islam not seen as the reverse side of something else but in its specific nature, and this surely is a concept appropriate to the subject matter. Within the limits of this work, those whom the world calls "Orientalists" were not guilty of what Mr. Said calls "Orientalism."

In principle, Mr. Said knows about this, and he acknowledges "the work of innumerable devoted scholars." But he

has not in this book really come to terms with it. There may be two reasons for this. One of them is that he has omitted from his survey the scholars who wrote in German. He has done so because, in Germany, "at no time . . . could a close partnership have developed between Orientalists and a protracted, sustained *national* interest in the Orient." This is a valid reason, given his own terms of reference, but it has led him to neglect something important. Secondly, the work on religious and intellectual history, painstaking and solid as it is, has for the most part been rather dull, and has lacked that spark which would excite Mr. Said's mind.

But there was one exciting man of genius among them, the Frenchman Louis Massignon, and he has called out all the powers of Mr. Said's mind. His pages on Massignon are among the best in the book, but in a sense they show how little the ideal type of the "Orientalist" helps us to understand him. Mr. Said maintains that "in one direction his ideas about the Orient remained thoroughly traditional and Oriental," but what he says of him may leave us with the contrary impression. He writes of "the overwhelming intelligence . . . the sheer genius and novelty of Massignon's mind"; "the refinements, the personal style, the individual genius, may finally supersede the political restraints operating impersonally through tradition and through the national ambience."

For Massignon, indeed, the Muslim world was not, in the deepest sense, a region where his country pursued political interests, it was a place filled with individual men and women, loved, understood, grasped in their individual nature; the relationship of Christianity and Islam was not one of being and non-being, but of exchange and substitution. As the French scholar Jacques Berque has said, for those who knew him there are places—a certain church in Cairo, a certain street—where he will always be present.

Questions like these are raised also by the last section of the book, "The Latest Phase." Mr. Said's thesis is that the tradition of European "Orientalism" has now been transplanted to the United States, expressed in the language of the social sciences, embodied in institutions closely linked with American interests and policies in the Middle East, and used as a weapon in the conflict of Israel and the Palestinians. Once more, he is probably right in so far as he is dealing with popular images: for the movies, the politicians, and much of the press, the Arab is the creeping, mysterious, fearsome Oriental shadow. But once more doubts arise when he writes about scholars.

These doubts are of two kinds. First, Mr. Said adopts a certain style or tone which may make the reader uneasy; his awareness of the style of other writers makes us the more conscious of his own. At the beginning of the book he has told us in a frank and moving way of the personal motive which partly led to the writing of it: as a Palestinian Arab living in the West, he finds his life "disheartening . . . the web of racism, cultural stereotypes, political imperialism, dehumanizing ideology holding in the Arab or the Muslim is very strong indeed." In this last section, the tone is that of one struggling to break out of the web; his forceful criticisms go, in some places, as far as accusations of bad faith against other scholars. If these charges had been systematic and sustained, they would have been an obstacle to rational discourse; even coming as they do in two or three places, they may cause grave offence and lead to the book being taken less seriously than it should be.

Apart from this, someone working in the field of Middle Eastern studies may find this part of the book a little old-fashioned. Mr. Said is considering not so much the work being done today, and expressed in articles, monographs, and the words of teachers, but rather those works of synthesis which, by their nature, embody yesterday's work. Both in Europe and America, the best of today's work does seem to have broken out of the "Orientalist" frame, to have turned critically on itself, and to be fertilized by the ideas of the human sciences of the age. To some extent Mr. Said is aware of this: he mentions the work of Jacques Berque and Maxime Rodinson in France, Clifford Geertz in America, and Roger Owen in England. But he might have gone further, and written of the continued or revived tradition of religious history in Germany, and the new French historical work molded by Marxism and the *Annales* school; the greatest Middle Eastern historian of our day, Claude Cahen, is not once mentioned. This field of study, like almost all others, is now being rejuvenated by younger American scholars: historians, anthropologists, and now— despite what he says about the neglect of literature—students of poetry.

The last word however must be his. Today's work still expresses, to a great extent, a European and American conception of the Muslim East: "the Arab and Islamic world remains a second-order power in terms of the production of culture, knowledge and scholarship." There are some exceptions: no Ottoman historian would neglect the work of Halil Inalcik and other great Turkish historians, and no student of North Africa in future will be able to ignore the profound and original ideas of Abdullah Laroui. But in general it is true that the Western student of the Arabs and Persians still works within a structure of ideas created by other Western students. Arabs and Persians, "as a genuinely felt and experienced force," are still not present in Western culture; but it would need another book to explain why this is so.

Leon Wieseltier (review date 7 April 1979)

SOURCE: A review of *Orientalism*, in *The New Republic*, Vol. 180, No. 14, April 7, 1979, pp. 27-33.

[*In the harsh review below, Wieseltier demonstrates how politics inform many of Said's arguments in* Orientalism, *suggesting that "the methodological gadgetry and 'iconoclastic' analysis of his book issue in little more than the abject canards of Arab propaganda."*]

Edward Said's angry book [***Orientalism***] is about a collusion of knowledge with power. The knowledge is Orientalism and the power is imperialism. Said contends that images of the Orient in the West's traditions of learning and literature are of a piece with the institutions of conquest and administration that it loosed upon the East. Fictions about Islam and the Arabs were manufactured to justify, and even exalt, Europe's rapacious political and cultural designs. In Said's account the self-serving misperceptions appear already in Aeschylus (Peter Brown once called this sort of thing "the Plato-to-NATO" school of intellectual history); Said lingers, too, over hostile caricatures of Muslims in Dante's *Inferno,* as if Christians in 13th-century Arab works fared any better. But it is with Napoleon that his arraignment of the Orientalist abuse gets fully underway. Napoleon's campaign in Egypt was, according to Said, the first of many colonial enterprises underwritten by the expertise of scholars and writers on the Orient:

> For Napoleon Egypt was a project that acquired reality in his mind, and later in his preparations for its conquest, through experiences that belong to the realm of ideas and myths culled from texts, not empirical reality. His plans for Egypt therefore became the first in a long series of European encounters with the Orient in which the Orientalist's special expertise was put directly to functional colonial use.

The philological and historiographical achievements of Silvestre de Sacy and Ernest Renan, of Louis Massignon and H. A. R. Gibb, were all mortgaged to the global interest of capitalist France and Great Britain. The scholars furnished an Orient that was immobile, aberrant, supine, exotic—an Orient, in short, ripe for possession, and which possession would only improve. And the scholars' version became canonical, so that Europe knew only the Arabs in the texts, and nothing of what Arabs really were. "They cannot represent themselves; they must be represented"—Said cites this verse from Marx to describe exactly the powerlessness of the Arabs before the authority of Orientalism.

Said's indictment of the professors for their part in the cultural preparation of imperialism is, however, not a little skewed. The correlation of learning with policy was neither as tight nor as foul as he purports. Not as tight, because Orientalism's greatest strides of scholarship were made in countries that had no hand in the occupation of Arabia. They took place in the Netherlands, in Austria, and, of course, in Germany; by scholars such as de Groeje, Hurgronje, Noeldeke, Muller, Goldziher, Wellhausen, Becker, Weil, Dozy. These figures Said treats scoutishly or not at all. And not as foul, because Said's assumptions about the conduct of humanistic scholarship are decidedly contestable.

Said begins his book with an attack on objectivity. "No production of knowledge in the human sciences can ever ignore or disclaim its author's involvement as a human subject in his own circumstances." There are cultural values and political premises buried even in the tomes of the philologists. In fact that is most of what is buried there:

> I believe it needs to be made clear about cultural discourse and exchange within a culture that what is commonly circulated by it is not "truth" but representations. . . . The value, efficacy, strength, apparent veracity of a written statement about the Orient therefore relies very little, and cannot instrumentally depend, on the Orient as such. . . . The things to look at are style, figures of speech, setting, narrative devices, historical and social circumstances, not the correctness of the representation nor its fidelity to some great original.

The human sciences tell primarily of themselves, of the real and perceived conditions to which they are in thrall.

Such strictures are not merely in order, they are commonplace. Of course objectivity is confounded by the impurities of the scholar's life in the world. Yet we continue to distinguish the study that is more precise, the judgment that is more just, from that which is less. And that is not because the scholar has transcended the presuppositions with which his work is overrun, or because "truth" has been miraculously discovered, but because it is possible for practicing historians—if not for voyeur theorists—to recognize a point at which the evidence stops and the interpretation begins, and to measure one against the other. This they do at least often and effectively enough to make their activity meaningful. Partisan scholars may turn up truths, and they may not. What will decide is their intellectual responsibility and professional competence; and, for these requirements not even the noblest intention may stand in.

Conor Cruise O'Brien has warned against the impairment of scholarly integrity by political inhibitions. Such vigilance is surely preferable to the well-heeled complacence of many political scientists and foundation boards. For objectivity may often be abused: much error and much evil have been the work of experts. Renan's racism, for example, is plain. But Renan's views must be rejected not only because they are villainous, but because they were wrong, and that is not the same. It is one thing to fear a betrayal by the intellectuals, and quite another to believe in the impossibility of knowledge.

How, then, evaluate the production of the human sciences? Having banished "correctness" and "fidelity," Said collapses egregiously into politics. "No person academically involved with the Near East—no Orientalist, that is—has ever . . . culturally and politically identified himself wholeheartedly with the Arabs." This, then, is what is wanting. Critical detachment is a chimera, malice breeds untruth: all that remains are sympathy, participation ("The Orientalist is outside the Orient," Said laments), and service. Said is entirely dead to the gains in understanding promised by an adversary attitude—gains of the sort illustrated, for instance, by the writings of Solzhenitsyn, the Medvedevs, Aleksandr Nekrich. Much of what we know about the political system and recent history of the Soviet Union we have learned from scholars and writers who oppose it. And those in the West most sympathetic have proved in many ways to be the most mistaken. Enlightenment is frequently the fruit of dissent, and certainly of skepticism.

But not for Said. Criticism, in his view, is only an expression of treachery. As in this passage:

> Ignaz Goldziher's appreciation of Islam's tolerance toward other religions was undercut by his dislike of Mohammed's anthropomorphisms and Islam's too-exterior theology and jurisprudence; Duncan Black Macdonald's interest in Islamic piety and orthodoxy was vitiated by his perception of what he considered Islam's heretical Christianity; Carl Becker's understanding of Islamic civilization made him see it as a sadly undeveloped one; C. Snouck Hurgronje's highly refined studies of Islamic mysticism (which he considered the essential part of Islam) led him to a harsh judgement of its crippling limitations; and Louis Massignon's extraordinary identification with Islamic theology, mystical passion, and poetic art kept him curiously unforgiving to Islam for what he regarded as its unregenerate revolt against the idea of incarnation. The manifest differences in their methods emerge as less important than their Orientalist consensus on Islam: latent inferiority.

Inferiority? No, it is only imperfection of which Islam stands here accused, and for Said Islam must be perfect. Perhaps Mohammed's anthropomorphisms were not all that objectionable, and the limitations of Islamic mysticism not all that crippling. But monopoly capitalism seems strangely served by the belief to the contrary.

Scholarship for Said, we may conclude, must political muster. Only scholars who champion the Arabs comprehend them. These are not many, but they include Jacques Berque, Maxime Rodinson and Roger Owen. It suffices for Noam Chomsky to have written tirelessly on the Arabs' behalf to be also counted among the exemplary *érudit*. The mantle of the Orientalists, on the other hand, has fallen most firmly on Bernard Lewis. Said concludes his book with an hysterical attack on Lewis. At issue is the etymology of *thawra*, the Arabic word for revolution. Lewis proposed that "the root *th-w-r* in classical Arabic meant to rise up (e.g., as a camel), to be stirred, excited, and . . . hence to rebel." Said smells an enemy: "Why introduce the idea of a camel rising as an etymological root for modern Arab revolution except as a clever way of discrediting the modern?" And more: "Lewis's association of *thawra* with a camel rising and generally with excitement (and not with a struggle on behalf of values) hints . . . that the Arab is scarcely more than a neurotic sexual being." And still more: "But . . . it is a 'bad' sexuality he ascribes to the Arab. In the end, since [he is] not really equipped for serious action, the sexual excitement is no more noble than a camel's rising up." And, finally, because Lewis notes that *thawra* was "often used in the context of establishing a petty, independent sovereignty," and not to denote a full political and social revolution, his real meaning is "that instead of copulation the Arab can achieve foreplay, masturbation, coitus interruptus."

All that is patently fatuous, but it is precisely what Said is up to. I know of no word for revolution in any language whose root refers to "a struggle on behalf of values"; the English certainly does not. Said does not prove, moreover, that Lewis's etymology is wrong, only that it is politically unacceptable. It happens that none other than Jacques Berque has put forward an alternative. Berque maintains that *thawra* means "effervescence," and likens it to a usage in medieval physics which referred to the rising of a hair on a head. Now an upright hair flatters Ben Bella and Habash no more than an upright camel; and, if sex is at stake, camels rise more naturally and for longer than hairs. But of Berque's suggestion we hear nothing. Berque is with the revolution, and so may pass. (The revolution still eats its own: a few years ago there appeared in *Les Temps Modernes* a vigorous denunciation of Jacques Berque for just those Orientalist sins against which Said rails.)

As Said construes the human sciences, then, it would be impossible to regard skeptically any aspect of the Arab world without being a tool of imperialism. Scholarly integrity, intellectual responsibility, professional competence—these aspirations he would no doubt dismiss as sentimental and ingenuous. And they are, in a sense, ingenuous; or, rather, they are a matter of philosophical conviction. One believes in free inquiry or one does not. Said does not:

"learned and imaginative writing are never free." There is no room in his scheme for an exercise of intelligence that is not exhaustively determined by its social, political and cultural environment. When the Orientalism is not "manifest" it is "latent." Or, as he bluntly puts it, "every European, in what he could say about the Orient, was . . . a racist, an imperialist and almost totally ethnocentric."

"Every European": there were malefactors outside the academy as well. The authority of Orientalism is, in fact, most apparent in its grip upon the imagination—upon writers such as Chateaubriand, Nerval and Flaubert, upon painters such as Gérôme and Delacroix. (Gérôme's languorous and very beautiful *Snake Charmers* may be consulted on the dust jacket of Said's book. *Orientalism,* it says, above the fetching little ass of an Arab boy displaying himself and a snake to a group of rapt Arab warriors. A shrewd advertisement, this: sort of like selling feminism with a Vargas girl.) Said does not discuss the painters—many of Delacroix's florid Orientals were Jews anyway—but he takes pains to describe the deployment of the Orient in the literary geography of the last century. This he does instructively. He is particularly good on those writers—Edward William Lane, most poignantly—who were caught between Orientalist expectations and their experience of the Orient. None entirely overcame this division. It was no mere prejudice, however, with which they wrestled. Orientalism is more than the sum of scholars' myths and poets' fancies. It is, we are finally admonished, an epistemology.

Presiding over Said's philippic is the mighty methodological vision of Michel Foucault. Foucault's subject is the incarceration of man in concepts; surely no historian of ideas has ever drawn so tenebrous a portrait of human life's enslavement to its own intellectual creations. Foucault's extraordinary books are chapters in a terrible history of utter domination by discourse: by the discourse of medicine, natural science, political economy, penology, sex. These are not so much departments of learning, Foucault counsels, but instruments of control; they are "discursive systems" which ordain their own "enunciative possibilities and impossibilities," what may and may not be said in their field, and so govern absolutely. Orientalism is nothing less than such a system, as insurmountable and as injurious. And yet, pleads Said, it must be unlearned.

Dissolve to the West Bank.

II

Our Zionist faith and aspirations were composed of two things, and two things only: the people of Israel and the land of Israel. This faith was not created or sustained by the Turks, or Kaiser Wilhelm, or Balfour.

—Ben Gurion, 1937

Edward Said's essay is not, as Albert Hourani has timidly suggested, about "the way in which intellectual traditions are created and transmitted." It is about the way in which intellectual traditions bedevil contemporary politics. More specifically, it is about how Orientalism is responsible for the failure of Palestinian nationalism.

Hard as it is to detect amid the allusions and abstractions with which the book is swollen, the real argument of *Orientalism* is that Palestinians continue to elude their political destiny because the epistemological habits of the French and the British have been inherited by the Israelis and the Americans. The argument is in three parts: Zionism is colonialism, American policy in the Middle East is imperialism (thus are the Palestinians awarded the cachet of third world cant), the Palestinians remain unheeded. *Orientalism* establishes Edward Said as among the more formidable of Zionism's cultured despisers. For the methodological gadgetry and "iconoclastic" analysis of his book issue in little more than the abject canards of Arab propaganda.

"The Semitic myth bifurcated in the Zionist movement: one Semite went the way of Orientalism, the other, the Arab, was forced to go the way of the Oriental." Or, elsewhere: "The difference between Renan and Weizman is that the latter had already gathered behind his rhetoric the solidity of institutions whereas the former had not." The ignorance in such passages is staggering. Said knows virtually nothing about the modern history of the Jews, about the origins and nature of the Zionist impulse. Someone as incensed as he by hasty and politically duplicitous scholarship might have taken the trouble to examine more closely the ideological and political development of the movement he impugns. Said prefers his rage. He adduces Balfour, and Weizman to Balfour, and crudely concludes that Zionism was another monstrous colonial adventure.

Zionism was a movement of national liberation. With a difference, to be sure: it required for its fulfillment the resettlement of an oppressed (according to Albert Memmi, a colonized) Jewish population. This resettlement, which was a return from exile, and in the event disappointed all Zionist hopes, was the optical illusion which made many cry colonialism; it was, too, the movement's tragic feature, for it insured that Zionism would have victims. Yet Zionism was, in the words of the astute Hayim Greenberg, "in recent history . . . the first instance of colonization free from imperialist ambition or the desire to rule any part of the population." The leaders of the *yishuv*—not merely the lofty likes of Judah Magnes, but figures of real political consequence within Labor Zionism—were ardently committed to cooperation with the Arabs, with whom many wished to collaborate in the social and democratic reconstruction of Palestine. (Not so Jabotinsky, whose writings are sadly marred by slurs and stereotypes, and by a proclivity to empire.) They were, no doubt, too sanguine. The inhabitants of Palestine could hardly have blessed the Jewish pioneers, though it is interesting to note that neither the first nor the second *aliyah* was perceived by them as imperialistic. The opposition of the fellahin who had—and still have—their rights, however, has nothing to do with the legitimacy of Jewish nationalism. And as the decades passed the crisis in Europe grew dire, and Zionism became a program for return in an hour of emergency, and Europe became a charnel house for the Jews.

The doctrine that Zionism is colonialism is not new—even Orwell delivered himself of the opinion that "the Palestine issue is partly a colour issue, and an Indian nationalist . . . would probably side with the Arabs"—but it has in recent years enjoyed renewed currency, and so it is important to understand precisely in what the slander consists. It is not merely political. Would that it were: political differences allow for solutions, as Anwar Sadat has demonstrated. What is denied is rather that Jewish politics has a national motive—that is, that the Jews are a nation, that they possess the legitimate rights and privileges of a nation, that they have a history out of which certain practical conclusions must be drawn. Zionism is just such a conclusion. It is the genuine expression of a moral, psychological and political evolution within the Jewish world; it cannot be understood otherwise. Said and his ilk, therefore, have not understood it. They look to the history of the Europeans when they should be looking to the history of the Jews. The immolation of the Jews in Nazi Europe moves them not at all. (In a recent essay on **"The Idea of Palestine in the West"** Said observes sardonically that support for the idea of a Jewish state surged "with the advent of Fascism in Europe." He may be assured that the Zionists would have done without that particular stroke of fortune.) Said sees Zionists in Palestine representing not themselves, but others; he sees Jews in the service only of the British.

British interests were for a time identified with the growth of the Jewish community in Palestine, and that growth certainly owed something to the British endorsement of Zionist claims. But that endorsement, even Balfour's, was not why Zionism won, and anyway it did not always come. The instruments of policy emitted by the Foreign Office in the 1920s and 1930s were in the main designed to diminish the benefits accruing to the *yishuv* from Balfour's largesse. Zionism's struggle, furthermore, was as often with the mandatory as it was with the citrus crop and the fedayeen. "In every hour of our lives as Jews and as workers," Berl Katznelson remarked in 1931, "as citizens and in our colonization activity, we feel the [British] administration to be colonial and absolutistic. We are hurt by its degradations and its insults." The notion of Zionist fealty to the British in Palestine is, in short, preposterous. Nor was the attitude of the Palestinian community toward the British any less ambiguous. It courted the Crown as well, and turned against it whenever it appeared that Jews were all the burden the white man wanted to bear. Significant elements in the Palestinian leadership decided expediently to become clients of the Nazis. How Hitler's Orientalism must have grated!

Zionism has once in its parlous career allied itself proudly with the affairs of a great power. That power is the United States, for which Israel dependably speaks. And this makes Israel, in Said's view, an agent of imperialism. "From the beginning of the nineteenth century France and Britain dominated the Orient and Orientals; since World War II America has dominated the Orient, and approaches it as France and Britain once did." The prize this time around is oil. But this time may be the first that the profits have redounded to the natives. It is a curious kind of imperialism that distorts its own economy, imposes the hardship on its own people, and alters its own foreign policy, all to meet the gross political and commercial demands of the peoples it was supposed to plunder. The oil cartel is untouched, the oil fields uninvaded—which any imperialist worth his salt would have seen to long ago. And hundreds of millions of imperialist dollars annually feed and arm the vanguard of the revolution. (What does Said think is filling the PLO's coffers? Chomsky's royalties?) With enemies like these, who needs friends?

The desire to rid the region of major powers and their Mephistophelian bargains is very estimable. It is not, however, Said's. He is aware that lesser states and movements cannot prosecute their interests without the patronage of such a power. Their own weaknesses, and global rivalries, forbid it. And so his orations against Western imperialism and its wickedness translate into a concrete political choice: the Soviet Union. The preference appears coyly at various places in the book; but it is glaring in the absence of any even desultory consideration of Soviet Orientalism and the fitful development of Soviet policy toward the Arabs. Before Bandung the Arabs were treated by Russian academicians with ignorance or indifference. But by the 1950s it was clear to the Russians that the Arabs could be used; and new journals of Oriental studies began to appear, and the shibboleths of the restive third world came to be intoned by the supple Mikoyan and his successors. There is no reason to believe that Soviet scholars understand their subject any better than their Western peers. Their government, however, stands behind radical forces in the Arab countries, and that will do. The Marxist-Leninist minions training in the hills of Lebanon, Syria and Iraq seem not to care that they are fighting imperialism with imperialism, and neither does Said.

The gravest threat posed by the West, Said continues, may lie in the export of its civilization. The Arab world, he writes, is "an intellectual . . . and cultural satellite" of the United States. "The Arab and Islamic world as a whole is hooked into the Western market system"—as, indeed, is Israel, where the quality of culture is in some ways also imperilled by "transistors, blue jeans, and Coca Cola." Said is alarmed by the proliferation in the Middle East of American consumerism and its corruptions. But the influence of the West upon the Arab nations has surely been more complex. It might best be described as a mixed curse. And not merely because of the blandishments of modernization—which, as the glorious women of Iran have shown, will not be so swiftly renounced. From the West there has also been introduced into Arab society the ideological equipment for its own awakening, the very concepts of rationality and progress, nation and revolution, in the name of which Arabs criticize and revolt. The Arab left was not created out of the Koran. And here is Said, excoriating the West in the dialectical sonorities of Gramsci and Foucault.

III

Which brings us, at last, to the myth of the invisible Palestinian. "There exists [in America] an almost unanimous consensus that politically he does not exist." Or, as Said wrote last spring, "we seem scarcely capable of making actual and legitimate the bare facts of our presence." The West simply does not see the Palestinian, we are told, because its *episteme* will not permit.

But this is dramatically untrue. The Palestinians are the political heroes of the season, and of many before and many to come. They have almost completely usurped the moral prestige which once attached to Zionism; and the obloquy into which Zionism has fallen is as good a sign as any of how twisted are the times. *Bien-pensants* everywhere are beside themselves in the Palestinians' support. The United Nations cannot pay them sufficient tribute. And they are the centerpiece of the solution of the Arab-Israeli conflict for which American policymakers most ache. Carter's pronouncement in Clinton in 1977 constitutes nothing less than a Balfour Declaration for the Palestinians: the president of the United States announced that his government views with favor the establishment of a homeland for them in Palestine. The Mideast expert in residence at the National Security Council is a scholar whose reputation was made in the study of Algerian and Palestinian nationalism. He and the other professor are plainly doing their very best to evict the Israelis from the West Bank. In high places the Palestinians are sitting rather pretty.

But perhaps not in lower places. "Since World War II, and more noticeably after each Arab-Israeli war, the Arab Muslim has become a figure in American popular culture." But an unsavory figure, complains Said: the American media depict the Arab always beside a gas pump or with a gun in his hands. How unfair. Perhaps this has something to do with the fact that the Palestinians and their supporters have relied most upon oil and murder. No anti-Arab bias, after all, robbed Sadat of America's admiration. But, we must recall, "the things to look at are style, figures of speech, setting, narrative devices, historical and social circumstances, *not* the correctness of the representation or its fidelity to some great original." Study the Americans, not the Arabs.

In his account of Orientalist scholarship Said's method suffers for his politics. Here his politics suffers for his method. And yet it is not their reading of Renan that prods security guards at Western airports to have another poke at Libyan and Iraqi pouches. The application of a Foucault-like holism to the realities of the political world has the consequence only of absolving the actors of their accountability. There are politicians in Israel who, without such sophistication, arrive at a similar and equally explosive despair; Said resembles no one so much as those on the other side who attribute all that befalls them to anti-Semitism, for whom all there will ever be is war. But the Jews did not build their state with such self-pity or paranoia, and neither will the Palestinians.

Nor did Jews build it with terror; right-wing militants whose appetite for confrontation threatened the rewards of decades of hard work and slow growth were harshly brought into line, and may be again. On Palestinian strategy Said is silent. His *jusq'auboutisme,* however, is unmistakable. How, indeed, do battle with an epistemology? Strong measures are called for. To overthrow the triumphalist dogmas of Western consciousness it may be necessary to smuggle a few bombs into Israeli pickle barrels. Discursive systems die hard.

Said's foray into cultural history is, then, just another apology for rejectionism. And there is something morally pusillanimous about its appearance in the current political climate. In the wake of Sadat's initiative and the accords at Camp David—which Said attacked last September—the Israelis are in the throes of a strenuous reassessment of their designs upon the territories. Peace Now proved that it has finally become respectable in Israeli society to wish to exchange territories for peace. And as a growing number of Israelis come at last to question their claim to Nablus Said sets out to show that they have no claim even to Tel Aviv.

But where is Peace Now's counterpart among the Palestinians? Who among them has the courage to condemn their own crimes and engage the Israelis? Where is their Eliav, their Yariv, their Weizman? Where, indeed, is their Begin? Nowhere in the history of Palestinian nationalism since the 1920s is there to be found anything but boycott and violence. The Palestinians have their own feral and fruitless tactics to blame for their failure to achieve a state: the maximalists fulfilled their own fears. As they surely will again. The leadership of the PLO today is good only for assassinations and interviews. It still has no eye for the main chance. It dreams instead of social revolution, and lately of Islam. No wonder, then, that the architects of the region's first blueprint for peace have to speak for the Palestinians. They cannot represent themselves; they must be represented.

It is a vital interest of Israel that the national and political needs of the people with whom it must live be met. The autonomy plan, for all its shortcomings, is at least the beginning of the end of Palestinian tutelage, and so should be honored. Reports in the Israeli press of proposals before the Israeli cabinet to restrict even further the scope of Palestinian self-rule are disturbing; bad faith now will only make matters worse. The Israeli government must stand up to fear, and greed, and the madness of petty messianists who disfigure Judaism even as they endanger Israel. ("The Jews did not come to Israel to be safe," Geula Cohen recently explained.) But it has made a fine opening move. It is finally Arafat and his pack, and not Gush Emunim, who make the Israelis go slowly. As the Israelis must, the imprecations of diplomats and intellectuals notwithstanding, until the Palestinians abandon their holy anger for credible objectives, and terrorism becomes statesmanship. The Palestinians have the right to determine their own future. They do not have the right to determine Israel's. For both it is the moment of truth.

Edward Said with Salman Rushdie (interview date 1986)

SOURCE: "On Palestinian Identity: A Conversation with Edward Said," in *Imaginary Homelands: Essays and Criticism 1981-1991,* Granta Books, 1991, pp. 166-84.

[In the following interview which took place at the PEN Congress in New York in 1986, Said discusses the identity of the Palestinian conscious based on historical and literary themes in his writings.]

For those of us who see the struggle between Eastern and Western descriptions of the world as both an internal and an external struggle, Edward Said has for many years been an especially important voice. Professor of English and Comparative Literature at Columbia and author of literary criticism on, among others, Joseph Conrad, Edward has always had the distinguishing feature that he reads the world as closely as he reads books. We need only think of the major trilogy which precedes his new book, *After the Last Sky.* In the first volume, *Orientalism,* he analysed 'the affiliation of knowledge with power', discussing how the scholars of the period of Empire helped to create an image of the East which provided the justification for the supremacist ideology of imperialism. This was followed by *The Question of Palestine,* which described the struggle between a world primarily shaped by Western ideas—that of Zionism and later of Israel—and the largely 'oriental' realities of Arab Palestine. Then came *Covering Islam,* subtitled 'How the Media and the Experts Determine How We See the Rest of the World', in which the West's invention of the East is, so to speak, brought up to date through a discussion of responses to the Islamic revival.

After the Last Sky is a collaborative venture with Jean Mohr—a photographer who may be known to you from John Berger's study of immigrant labour in Europe, *A Seventh Man.* Its title is taken from a poem, 'The Earth is Closing on Us', by the national poet of Palestine, Mahmoud Darwish:

> The earth is closing on us, pushing us through the last
> passage, and we tear off our limbs to pass through.
> The earth is squeezing us. I wish we were its wheat
> so we could die and live again. I wish the earth was
> our mother
> So she'd be kind to us. I wish we were pictures on
> the rocks for our dreams to carry
> As mirrors. We saw the faces of those to be killed by
> the last of us in the last defence of the soul.
> We cried over their children's feast. We saw the faces
> of those who will throw our children
> Out of the window of this last space. Our star will
> hang up mirrors.
> Where should we go after the last frontiers? Where
> should the birds fly after the last sky?
> Where should the plants sleep after the last breath of
> air?
> We will write our names with scarlet steam,
> We will cut off the hand of the song to be finished by
> our flesh.
> We will die here, here in the last passage. Here and
> here our blood will plant its olive tree.

After the last sky there is no sky. After the last border there is no land. The first part of Said's book is called 'States'. It is a passionate and moving meditation on displacement, on landlessness, on exile and identity. He asks, for example, in what sense Palestinians can be said to exist. He says: 'Do we exist? What proof do we have? The further we get from the Palestine of our past, the more precarious our status, the more disrupted our being, the more intermittent our presence. When did we become a people? When did we stop being one? Or are we in the process of becoming one? What do those big questions have to do with our intimate relationships with each other and with others? We frequently end our letters with the motto "Palestinian love" or "Palestinian kisses". Are there really such things as Palestinian intimacy and embraces, or are they simply intimacy and embraces—experiences common to everyone, neither politically significant nor particular to a nation or a people?'

Said comes, as he puts it, from a 'minority inside a minority'—a position with which I feel some sympathy, having also come from a minority group within a minority group. It is a kind of Chinese box that he describes: 'My family and I were members of a tiny Protestant group within a much larger Greek Orthodox Christian minority, within the larger Sunni Muslim majority.' He then goes on to discuss the condition of Palestinians through the mediation of a number of recent literary works. One of these, incorrectly called an Arab *Tristram Shandy* in the blurb, is a wonderful comic novel about the secret life of somebody called Said, *The Ill-Fated Pessoptimist.* A pessoptimist, as you can see, is a person with a problem about how he sees the world. Said claims all manner of things, including, in chapter one, to have met creatures from outer space: 'In the so-called age of ignorance before Islam, our ancestors used to form their gods from dates and eat them when in need. Who is more ignorant then, dear sir, I or those who ate their gods? You might say it is better for people to eat their gods than for the gods to eat them. I would respond, yes, but their gods were made of dates.'

A crucial idea in *After the Last Sky* concerns the meaning of the Palestinian experience for the form of works of art made by Palestinians. In Edward's view, the broken or discontinuous nature of Palestinian experience entails that classic rules about form or structure cannot be true to that experience; rather, it is necessary to work through a kind of chaos or unstable form that will accurately express its essential instability. Edward then proceeds to introduce the theme—which is developed later in the book—that the history of Palestine has turned the insider (the Palestinian Arab) into the outsider. This point is illustrated by a photograph of Nazareth taken from a position in what is called Upper Nazareth—an area which did not exist in the time of Arab Palestine. Thus Arab Palestine is seen from the point of view of a new, invented Palestine, and the inside experience of the old Palestine has become the external experience in the photograph. And yet the Palestinians have remained.

> It would be easier
> to catch fried fish in the milky way
> to plough the sea
> or to teach the alligator speech
> than to make us leave.

In part two, 'Interiors', which greatly develops the theme of the insider and the outsider, Edward refers to a change in the status of the Palestinians who are inside Palestine. Until recently, among the Palestinian community in general, there was a slight discounting of those who remained inside, as if they were somehow contaminated by the proximity of the Jews. Now, however, the situation has been inverted: those who go on living there, maintaining a Palestinian culture and obliging the world to recognize their existence, have acquired a greater status in the eyes of other Palestinians.

This experience of being inside Palestinianness is presented as a series of codes which, though incomprehensible to outsiders, are instantly communicated by Palestinians when they meet one another. The only way in which to show your insiderness is precisely through the expression of those codes. There is a very funny incident in which Professor Said receives a letter, via a complete stranger, from a man who has built his *Palestinian* identity as a karate expert. 'What was the message to me?' Said asks. 'First of all he was inside, and using the good offices of a sympathetic outsider to contact me, an insider who was now outside Jerusalem, the place of our common origin. That he wrote my name in English was as much a sign that he too could deal with the world I lived in as it was that he followed what I did. The time had come to demonstrate that the Edward Saids had better remember that we were being watched by karate experts. Karate does not stand for self-development but only for the repeated act of being a Palestinian expert. A Palestinian—it is as if the activity of repeating prevents us and others from skipping us or overlooking us entirely.'

He then gives a number of other examples of repeating behaviour in order to make it Palestinian behaviour, and thus existing through that repetition. There also seems to be a compulsion to excess, illustrated in various ways, both tragic and comic, within the book. One of the problems of being Palestinian is that the idea of interior is regularly invaded by other people's descriptions, by other people's attempts to control what it is to occupy that space—whether it be Jordanian Arabs who say there is no difference between a Jordanian and a Palestinian, or Israelis who claim that the land is not Palestine but Israel.

The third part, 'Emergence', and the fourth part, 'Past and Future', turn to a discussion of what it actually is or might be to be a Palestinian. There is also an account of the power to which Palestinians are subject, of the way in which even their names have been altered through the superimposition of Hebrew transliteration. As a mark of resistance, Palestinians are now seeking to reassert their identity by going back to the old Arabic forms: Abu Ammar, for example, instead of Yasser Arafat. On various occasions the very meaning of names has been changed. Thus the largest refugee camp in Lebanon, Ein el Hilwé, which is written with an

'h' in the Arabic transliteration, has become Ein el Khilwé in the Hebrew transliteration: a name which means 'sweet spring' has been turned into something like 'spring in the empty place'. Said sees in this an allusion to mass graves and the regularly razed and not always rebuilt camps. 'I also register the thought,' he writes, 'that Israel has indeed emptied the camp with its Palestinian wellspring.'

The text goes on to talk about Zionism, which he addressed in his earlier book *The Question of Palestine.* We should note the difficulty in making any kind of critique of Zionism without being instantly charged with anti-Semitism. Clearly it is important to understand Zionism as a historical process, as existing in a context and having certain historical functions. A further idea in these later sections of the book is that, in the West, everyone has come to think of exile as a primarily literary and bourgeois state. Exiles appear to have chosen a middle-class situation in which great thoughts can be thought. In the case of the Palestinians, however, exile is a mass phenomenon: it is the mass that is exiled and not just the bourgeoisie.

Finally Said poses a series of questions which come down to the original one of Palestinian existence: 'What happens to landless people? However you exist in the world, what do you preserve of yourselves? What do you abandon?' I find one passage particularly valuable, as it connects with many things I have been thinking about. 'Our truest reality,' he writes, 'is expressed in the way we cross over from one place to another. We are migrants and perhaps hybrids, in but not of any situation in which we find ourselves. This is the deepest continuity of our lives as a nation in exile and constantly on the move.' He also criticizes the great concentration of the Palestinian cause on its military expression, referring to the dangers of cultural loss or absence.

Professor Said periodically receives threats to his safety from the Jewish Defense League in America, and I think it is important for us to appreciate that to be a Palestinian in New York—in many ways *the* Palestinian—is not the easiest of fates.

[*Salman Rushdie:*] *One of my sisters was repeatedly asked in California where she came from. When she said 'Pakistan' most people seemed to have no idea what this meant. One American said: 'Oh, yes, Pakestine!' and immediately started talking about his Jewish friends. It is impossible to overestimate the consequences of American ignorance on world affairs. When I was at the PEN Congress in New York in 1986, the American writer Cynthia Ozick took it upon herself to circulate a petition which described Chancellor Kreisky of Austria as an anti-Semite. Why was he an anti-Semite—this man who is himself a Jew and has given refuge to tens, perhaps hundreds, of thousands of Jews leaving the Soviet Union? Because he had had a conversation with Yasser Arafat. The alarming thing is that this petition, on the face of it quite absurd, should have been taken so seriously by participants at the congress. There was even a moment when I felt nervously that since no one else seemed to be speaking for Palestine, I might have to myself. But the defence came from Pierre Trudeau of all people, who spoke very movingly about the Palestinian cause. These are some of the extraordinary things that happen in New York. Edward, you are the man on the spot. Is it getting worse or better? How does it feel?*

[Edward Said:] Well, I think it is getting worse. First of all, most people in New York who feel strongly about Palestine and Palestinians have had no direct experience at all. They think of them essentially in terms of what they have seen on television: bomb scares, murders and what the Secretary of State and others call terrorism. This produces a kind of groundless passion, so that when I am introduced to someone who may have heard of me, they react in a very strange way that suggests 'maybe you're not as bad as you seem.' The fact that I speak English, and do it reasonably well, adds to the complications, and most people eventually concentrate on my work as an English professor for the rest of the conversation. But you do feel a new kind of violence around you which is a result of 1982. An important break with the past occurred then, both for people who have supported Israel in the United States, and for people like us, for whom the destruction of Beirut, our Beirut, was the end of an era. Most of the time you can feel that you are leading a normal life, but every so often you are brought up against a threat or an allusion to something which is deeply unpleasant. You always feel outside in some way.

Has there been any change in your ability to publish or talk about the Palestinian issue?

To some extent. This is one issue on which, as you know, there is a left-right break in America, and there are still a few groups, a few people—like Chomsky or Alexander Cockburn—who are willing to raise it publicly. But most people tend to think that it is better left to the crazies. There are fewer hospitable places, and you end up publishing for a smaller audience. Ironically, you also become tokenized, so that whenever there is a hijacking or some such incident, I get phone-calls from the media asking me to come along and comment. It's a very strange feeling to be seen as a kind of representative of terrorism. You're treated like a diplomat of terrorism, with a place at the table. I remember one occasion, though, when I was invited to a television debate with the Israeli ambassador—I think it was about the *Achille Lauro* incident. Not only would he not sit in the same room with me; he wanted to be in a different building, so as not to be contaminated by my presence.

The interviewer said to the national audience: 'You know, Professor Said and Ambassador Netanyahu refuse to speak to each other, the Israeli ambassador won't speak to him and he won't. . . .' But then I interrupted and said: 'No, no, I am perfectly willing to speak to him, but he won't. . . .' The moderator replied: 'Well, I stand corrected. Mr. Ambassador, why won't you speak to Professor Said?' 'Because he wants to kill me.' The moderator, without batting an eyelid, urged: 'Oh really, tell us about it.' And the ambassador went on about how Palestinians want to kill the Israelis, and so on. It was really a totally absurd situation.

You say you don't like calling it a Palestinian diaspora. Why is that?

I suppose there is a sense in which, as one man wrote in a note to me from Jerusalem, we are 'the Jews of the Arab world'. But I think our experience is really quite different and beyond such attempts to draw parallels. Perhaps its dimension is much more modest. In any case the idea that there is a kind of redemptive homeland doesn't answer to my view of things.

So let me put to you your own question. Do you exist? And if so, what proof do you have? In what sense is there a Palestinian nation?

First of all, in the sense that a lot of people have memories or show great interest in looking into the past for a sign of coherent community. Many, too—especially younger-generation scholars—are trying to discover things about the Palestinian political and cultural experience that mark it off from the rest of the Arab world. Secondly, there is the tradition of setting up replicas of Palestinian organizations in places as far afield as Australia or South America. It is quite remarkable that people will come to live in, say, Youngstown, Ohio—a town I don't know, but you can imagine what it's like—and remain on top of the latest events in Beirut or the current disagreements between the Popular Front and Al Fatah, and yet not even know the name of the mayor of Youngstown or how he is elected. Maybe they will just assume that he is put there by somebody rather than being elected. Finally, you can see from Jean Mohr's pictures that the Palestinians are a people who move a lot, who are always carrying bags from one place to another. This gives us a further sense of identity as a people. And we say it loudly enough, repetitiously enough and stridently enough, strong in the knowledge that they haven't been able to get rid of us. It is a great feeling—call it positive or pessoptimistic—to wake up in the morning and say: 'Well they didn't bump me off.'

To illustrate this point that things could be worse, you tell the story of a mother whose son died very soon after his wedding. While the bride is still mourning she

says: 'Thank God it has happened in this way and not
in another way!' The bride then gets very angry and
says: 'How dare you say that! What could possibly be a
worse way?' But the mother-in-law replies: 'Well, you
know, if he grew old and you left him for another man
and then he died, that could be worse. So it's better that
he dies now.'

Exactly. You are always inventing worse scenarios.

*It's very difficult to work out whether this is optimism
or pessimism. That's why it is called pessoptimism.
Would you like to say something now about the codes
by which Palestinians exist and recognize each other
and about the idea of repetition and excess as a way
of existing?*

Let me tell you another story that will show you what I
mean. A close friend of mine once came to my house and
stayed overnight. In the morning we had breakfast, which
included yogurt cheese with a special herb, *za'atar*. This
combination probably exists all over the Arab world, and
certainly in Palestine, Syria and Lebanon. But my friend
said: 'There, you see. It's a sign of a Palestinian home that
it has *za'atar* in it.' Being a poet, he then expatiated at great
and tedious length on Palestinian cuisine, which is generally very much like Lebanese and Syrian cuisine, and by the
end of the morning we were both convinced that we had a
totally distinct national cuisine.

*So, because a Palestinian chooses to do something it be-
comes the Palestinian thing to do?*

That's absolutely right. But even among Palestinians there
are certain code words that define which camp or group the
speaker comes from; whether from the Popular Front,
which believes in the complete liberation of Palestine, or
from the Fatah, which believes in a negotiated settlement.
They will choose a different set of words when they talk
about national liberation. Then there are the regional accents. It is very strange indeed to meet a Palestinian kid in
Lebanon who was born in some refugee camp and has never
been to Palestine but who carries the inflections of Haifa,
or Jaffa, in his Lebanese Arabic.

*Let us turn to the idea of excess. You talk about how you
find yourself obliged to carry too much luggage wherever you go. But more seriously, I remember that dialogue
between a captured Palestinian guerrilla and an Israeli
broadcaster in which the guerrilla appears to be implicating himself in the most heinous crimes but is in fact
sending up the entire event by a colossal excess of apolo-
gies. The broadcaster is too tuned into his own set of attitudes to realize what is going on.*

Yes. It was in 1982 in southern Lebanon, when Israeli radio would often put captured guerrillas on the air as a form
of psychological warfare. But in the case you are talking
about, no one was deceived. In fact, the Palestinians in
Beirut made a cassette recording of the whole show and
played it back in the evening as a way of entertaining
people. Let me translate a sample:

Israeli broadcaster: Your name?

Captured Palestinian: Ahmed Abdul Hamid Abu Site.

Israeli: What is your movement name?

Palestinian: My movement name is Abu Lell [which in
English means Father of Night, with a rather threatening, horrible sound to it].

Israeli: Tell me, Mr. Abu Lell, to which terrorist organization do you belong?

Palestinian: I belong to the Popular Front for the Liberation. . . . I mean terrorization of Palestine.

Israeli: And when did you get involved in the terrorist
organization?

Palestinian: When I first became aware of terrorism.

Israeli: What was your mission in South Lebanon?

Palestinian: My mission was terrorism. In other words,
we would enter villages and just terrorize the occu-
pants. And whenever there were women and children
in particular, we would terrorize everything, and all we
did was terrorism.

Israeli: And did you practise terrorism out of belief in
a cause or just for money?

Palestinian: No, just for money. What kind of cause is this
anyway? Is there still a cause? We sold out a long time
ago.

Israeli: Tell me . . . where do the terrorist organizations
get their money?

Palestinian: From anyone who has spare money for terrorism.

Israeli: What is your opinion of the terrorist Arafat?

Palestinian: I swear that he is the greatest terrorist of
all. He is the one who sold us and the cause out. His
whole life is terrorism. [Of course, to a Palestinian this

could mean that he is the most committed of all, but it sounds as if he is just a total sellout.]

Israeli: What is your opinion of the way in which the Israeli defence forces have conducted themselves?

Palestinian: On my honour, we thank the Israeli defence forces for their good treatment of each terrorist.

Israeli: Do you have any advice for other terrorists, who are still terrorizing the IDF?

Palestinian: My advice to them is to surrender their arms to the IDF. What they will find there is the best possible treatment.

Israeli: Lastly, Mr. Terrorist, would you like to send a message to your family?

Palestinian: I would like to assure my family and friends that I am in good health. I would also like to thank the enemy broadcasting facility for letting me speak out like this.

Israeli: You mean the Voice of Israel?

Palestinian: Yes, yes, sir. Thank you, sir. Yes of course, sir.

And this went out over the air?

Absolutely. It was put out on a daily basis, and recorded in Beirut and played back to the guerrillas.

It's a very funny and wonderful story.

You also talk about a photo article in a fashion magazine, under the headline 'Terrorist Culture', which claims that the Palestinians are not really Palestinians because they have simply hijacked Arab dress and renamed it Palestinian.

We do it all the time!

The article also claims that this supposedly distinctive dress is not that of the people but of the upper middle class. Referring to the American author of the article, Sharon Churcher, you write: 'In the larger scheme of things . . . she is somebody doing a hack job on a hack fashion magazine.' And yet, you say you feel the need to go right back to the beginning, to explain the whole history of Palestine in order to unmake Sharon Churcher's lie and show that this is in fact genuinely popular Palestinian dress. Doesn't this need to go back again and again over the same story become tiring?

It does, but you do it anyway. It is like trying to find the magical moment when everything starts, as in *Midnight's Children*. You know midnight, and so you go back. But it is very hard to do that because you have to work out everything and get past a lot of questions in the daily press about why Palestinians don't just stay where they are and stop causing trouble. That immediately launches you into a tremendous harangue, as you explain to people: 'My mother was born in Nazareth, my father was born in Jerusalem . . . .' The interesting thing is that there seems to be nothing in the world which sustains the story: unless you go on telling it, it will just drop and disappear.

The need to be perpetually told.

Exactly. The other narratives have a kind of permanence of institutional existence and you just have to try to work away at them.

This is one of the things that you criticize from within Palestinianness: the lack of any serious effort to institutionalize the story, to give it an objective existence.

That's right. It is interesting that right up to 1948, most of the writing by Palestinians expressed a fear that they were about to lose their country. Their descriptions of cities and other places in Palestine appeared as a kind of pleading before a tribunal. After the dispersion of the Palestinians, however, there was a curious period of silence until a new Palestinian literature began to develop in the fifties and, above all, the sixties. Given the size of this achievement, it is strange that no narrative of Palestinian history has ever been institutionalized in a definitive masterwork. There never seems to be enough time, and one always has the impression that one's enemy—in this case the Israelis—are trying to take the archive away. The gravest image for me in 1982 was of the Israelis shipping out the archives of the Palestine Research Centre in Beirut to Tel Aviv.

In the context of literature rather than history, you argue that the inadequacy of the narrative is due to the discontinuity of Palestinian existence. Is this connected with the problem of writing a history?

Yes. There are many different kinds of Palestinian experience, which cannot all be assembled into one. One would therefore have to write parallel histories of the communities in Lebanon, the occupied territories, and so on. That is the central problem. It is almost impossible to imagine a single narrative: it would have to be the kind of crazy history that comes out in *Midnight's Children*, with all those little strands coming and going in and out.

You have talked of The Pessoptimist *as a first manifestation of the attempt to write in a form which appears to be formlessness, and which in fact mirrors the instability of the situation. Could you say some more about this?*

It's a rather eccentric view, perhaps. I myself am not a scholar of Palestinian and certainly not Arabic literature in general. But I am fascinated by the impression made on everyone by, for instance, Kanafani's novel *Men in the Sun*, whose texture exemplifies the uncertainty whether one is talking about the past or the present. One story of his, called, I think, 'The Return to Haifa', follows a family who left in 1948 and resettled in Ramallah. Much later they return to visit their house in Haifa, and to meet again the son they had left behind in a panic and who was adopted by an Israeli family. Throughout the novel there is a powerful sense of endless temporal motion, in which past, present and future intertwine without any fixed centre.

Perhaps we could now turn to the lengthy discussion in **After the Last Sky** *about the unheard voices of Palestinian women. You write: 'And yet, I recognize in all this a fundamental problem—the crucial absence of women. With few exceptions, women seem to have played little more than the role of hyphen, connective, transition, mere incident. Unless we are able to perceive at the interior of our life the statements women make: concrete, watchful, compassionate, immensely poignant, strangely invulnerable—we will never fully understand our experience of dispossession.' The main illustration you then give is a film,* The Fertile Memory, *by the young Palestinian director Michel Khleifi, which deals with the experience of two Palestinian women.*

Yes. This film made a very strong impression on me. One of the most striking scenes revolves around the older woman, who is actually Khleifi's aunt. She has a piece of property in Nazareth which a Jewish family has been living on for many years, but one day her daughter and son-in-law come with the news that this family now wants to buy up the title deeds. She makes it clear that she is not interested. 'But what do you mean?' they insist. 'They are living on it; it's their land. They just want to make things easier for you by giving you money in return for the deeds.' 'No, I won't do that,' she replies. It is a totally irrational position, and Khleifi registers the expression of stubbornness, almost transcendent foolishness, on her face. 'I don't have the land now,' she explains. 'But who knows what will happen? We were here first. Then the Jews came and others will come after them. I own the land and I'll die, but it will stay there despite the comings and goings of people.' She is then taken to see her land for the first time—it had been left to her by her husband, who went to Lebanon in 1948 and died there. Khleifi records her extraordinary experience of walking on the land that she owns but does not own, treading gently and turning round and round. Then suddenly her expression changes as she realizes the absurdity

of it all and walks away. This scene typified for me the persistent presence of the woman in Palestinian life—and, at the same time, the lack of acknowledgement which that presence has elicited. There is a strong misogynist streak in Arab society: a kind of fear and dislike existing alongside respect and admiration. I remember another occasion when I was with a friend looking at a picture of a rather large and formidable yet happy Palestinian woman, her arms folded across her chest. This friend summed up the whole ambivalence with his remark: 'There is the Palestinian woman, in all her strength . . . and her ugliness.' The picture of this woman, by Jean Mohr, seems to say something that we have not really been able to touch upon. That experience is one that I, as a man, in this Palestinian sort of mess, am beginning to try to articulate.

In **After the Last Sky** *you say that, having lived inside Western culture for a long time, you understand as well as any non-Jew can hope to do what is the power of Zionism for the Jewish people. You also describe it as a programme of slow and steady acquisition that has been more efficient and competent than anything the Palestinians have been able to put up against it. The problem is that any attempt to provide a critique of Zionism is faced, particularly nowadays, with the charge that it is anti-Semitism in disguise. The retort that you are not anti-Semitic but anti-Zionist is always, or often, greeted with: 'Oh yes, we know that code.' What you have done in this book and in* **The Question of Palestine** *is to offer a very useful, emotionally neutral critique of Zionism as an historical phenomenon. Perhaps you could say a few words about this.*

In my opinion, the question of Zionism is the touchstone of contemporary political judgement. A lot of people who are happy to attack apartheid or US intervention in Central America are not prepared to talk about Zionism and what it has done to the Palestinians. To be a victim of a victim does present quite unusual difficulties. For if you are trying to deal with the classic victim of all time—the Jew and his or her movement—then to portray yourself as the victim of the Jew is a comedy worthy of one of your own novels. But now there is a new dimension, as we can see from the spate of books and articles in which any kind of criticism of Israel is treated as an umbrella for anti-Semitism. Particularly in the United States, if you say anything at all, as an Arab from a Muslim culture, you are seen to be joining classical European or Western anti-Semitism. It has become absolutely necessary, therefore, to concentrate on the particular history and context of Zionism in discussing what it represents for the Palestinian.

The problem, then, is to make people see Zionism as being like anything else in history, as arising from sources and going somewhere. Do you think that Zionism has changed its nature in recent years, apart from the fact that it has become subject to criticism?

One of my main concerns is the extent to which people are not frozen in attitudes of difference and mutual hostility. I have met many Jews over the last ten years who are very interested in some kind of exchange, and events in the sixties have created a significant community of Jews who are not comfortable with the absolutes of Zionism. The whole notion of crossing over, of moving from one identity to another, is extremely important to me, being as I am—as we all are—a sort of hybrid.

I would like to ask you a couple of more personal questions. You say that to be a Palestinian is basically to come from a Muslim culture, and yet you are not a Muslim. Do you find that a problem? Have there been any historical frictions in this respect?

All I can say is that I have had no experience of such frictions. My own sense is that our situation as Palestinians is very different from Lebanon, where conflicts between Sunnis, Shiites, Maronites, Orthodox and so forth have been sharply felt historically. One of the virtues of being a Palestinian is that it teaches you to feel your particularity in a new way, not only as a problem but as a kind of gift. Whether in the Arab world or elsewhere, twentieth-century mass society has destroyed identity in so powerful a way that it is worth a great deal to keep this specificity alive.

You write: 'The vast majority of our people are now thoroughly sick of the misfortunes that have befallen us, partly through our own fault, partly because of who the dispossessors are, and partly because our cause has a singular ineffectuality to it, capable neither of sufficiently mobilizing our friends nor of overcoming our enemies. On the other hand, I have never met a Palestinian who is tired enough of being a Palestinian to give up entirely.'

That's rather well put!

This brings me to my final point that, unlike your previous three books, which centred on the dispute between Eastern and Western cultures, **After the Last Sky** *focuses much more on an inner dispute or dialectic at the heart of Palestinianness. After a period of extroversion, you suggest, many Palestinians are themselves experiencing a certain turning inwards. Why is this so? What has been your own experience?*

Well, obviously much of it has to do with disillusion. Most people in my own generation—and I can't really speak for others—grew up in an atmosphere of despondency. But then in the late sixties and early seventies, a tremendous enthusiasm and romantic glamour attached to the rise of a

new movement out of the ashes. In a material sense it accomplished very little: no land was liberated during that period. Moreover, the excitement of the Palestinian resistance, as it was called in those days, was a rather heady atmosphere, forming part of Arab nationalism and even—in an ironic and extraordinary way—part of the Arab oil boom. Now all that is beginning to crumble before our eyes, giving way to a sense of disillusionment and questioning about whether it was ever worthwhile and where we are to go from here. It was as an expression of this mood that I wrote *After the Last Sky.* The photographs were important in order to show that we are not talking just of our own personal, hermetic disillusion. For the Palestinians have become a kind of commodity or public possession, useful, for example, to explain the phenomenon of terrorism. I found myself writing from the point of view of someone who had at last managed to connect the part that was a professor of English and the part that lived, in a small way, the life of Palestine. Luckily Jean Mohr had built up quite a large archive of pictures since he worked for the Red Cross in 1949. We came together under strange circumstances: he was putting up some pictures and I was working as a consultant for the United Nations. Since they would not let us write what we wanted, we said: 'Let's have a book and do it in our own way.' It represented a very personal commitment on both our parts.

The picture on the cover is really quite extraordinary— a man with a kind of starburst on the right lens of his glasses. As you say, he has been blinded by a bullet in one eye, but has learned to live with it. He is still wearing the spectacles . . . still smiling.

Jean told me that he took the photo as the man was en route to visit his son, who had been sentenced to life imprisonment.

Dinitia Smith (essay date 23 January 1989)

SOURCE: "Arafat's Man in New York," in *New York*, Vol. 22, No. 4, January 23, 1989, pp. 40-6.

[*In the essay below, Smith provides an overview of Said's life and career.*]

On the afternoon of December 14, a Columbia University professor returning home from London, where he'd delivered a lecture on Yeats, pushed open the door of his Morningside Heights apartment and found his wife and two children gathered around the television set. History was being made.

It was history that Edward Said, a Palestinian-born professor of English and comparative literature, had helped create. Said joined his family around the TV and listened as Secretary of State George P. Shultz announced that the United States—after years of refusing to recognize the Palestine Liberation Organization—would begin talks with the group's representatives in Tunis. Said sank into a chair. "The taboo has been lifted," he said.

For years, the Palestinians, Israel, and the United States had been caught in a deadlock over the future of Israel. Now some of the old assumptions had begun to change—though how much is not yet clear. With prodding from the Americans, PLO chairman Yasser Arafat had finally made statements at a press conference, declaring Israel's right to exist and renouncing terrorism. The Palestinian National Covenant—the PLO charter—still pledges to "liquidate the Zionist presence in Palestine." But Arafat's statements—the last of a series of comments he made over several weeks—were seen as a significant move forward. All through these weeks, Said had been on the phone to colleagues in the PLO hierarchy, urging that Arafat make his position unambiguous.

As soon as Shultz's press conference broke off, the phone began ringing in Said's dark-paneled apartment. The news shows were calling to ask for more interviews.

In recent months, Said has become a familiar figure on American television, a distinguished-looking man of 53 dressed in well-cut suits, speaking in a perfect American accent, with a perfectly American demeanor—espousing the Palestinian cause. He is nothing if not a man of paradoxes. An American citizen, he has been a member of the Palestine National Council—the Palestinian parliament-in-exile-since 1977, and in November, at the P.N.C. meeting in Algiers, he helped draft the Palestinian declaration of independence. He serves as an independent, unaffiliated member of the council, not officially connected to the PLO (or any of its constituent groups, such as Fatah or the Popular Front for the Liberation of Palestine), though he is a PLO supporter.

Baptized as an Episcopalian, Said is a member of a minority within a minority—most Christian Arabs are Greek Orthodox. He has spent almost all his adult life in the United States, yet he is fighting for a land he's barely seen since childhood. He is an intellectual—one of America's leading literary critics—thrust into the role of political activist.

Said is a Palestinian living in a city of almost 2 million Jews—"My friends are *only* Jews," he says with perhaps only a little exaggeration. Yet he is an admirer of Yasser Arafat, a symbol of terrorism for most Jews. To Said, Arafat is a hero—"the old man," in the words that Arafat's follow-

ers often use to describe him. In the December [1988] *Interview* magazine, Said gave an affectionate account of sitting down with Arafat in Tunis for breakfast (a large salad bowl filled with cornflakes, over which the PLO leader poured hot tea. "I invented this during the siege of Beirut," he said). Said wrote that Arafat's "international stature has come to him as leader of a genuinely national and popular movement, with a clearly legitimate goal of self-determination for his people."

Opinions like that have put Said in a curious and sometimes dangerous position. There are phone threats, hate letters. In 1985, Said's office at Columbia was torn apart. (Victor Vancier, a member of the Jewish Defense League convicted of a series of J.D.L. bombings, later told writer Robert I. Friedman that the vandalism was the work of "Jewish patriots," but he would not say whether the J.D.L. had been involved.) Said worries about the security in his home and almost never gives out his phone number. But he says he tries not to become obsessed by the threats. "I'd get paralyzed," he says. When threats do come, "the city police and the FBI have been cooperative."

Perhaps the greatest paradox of all is that Edward Said is an academic, living and working in the world of ideas, while serving as a spokesman for a militant cause sometimes associated with terrorism. "I totally repudiate terrorism in all forms," he says. "Not just Palestinian terrorism—I'm also against Israeli terrorism, the bombing of refugee camps. I'm against collective punishment, like the detention of 850,000 Gazans by Israeli forces in their homes for a week during the meeting of the P.N.C. in Algiers."

Even Said's enemies acknowledge that he has never been involved personally in terrorist acts. Yet, in Algiers last November, Said sat in the same conference hall as Mohammed Abul Abbas, a member of the PLO executive committee who was convicted in absentia by an Italian court for the murder of the American Leon Klinghoffer, an old man in a wheelchair, during the 1985 hijacking of the cruise ship *Achille Lauro*.

Abbas is "a s—, a degenerate," says Said. Yet, "in the conditions of exile politics, very strange things occur." What's more, Said says, Shultz and President Reagan have met with Israeli prime ministers Menachem Begin and Yitzhak Shamir. "Shamir was involved with terrorist activities in the Stern Gang," Said says, "and Begin at Deir Yassin," the Arab village attacked in 1948 by the Irgun, Zionist commandos led by Begin. Several hundred Arab men, women, and children were killed.

Questions about terrorism stalk Said wherever he goes, often overwhelming his analysis of the Middle East situation. Last year, while being interviewed for a BBC documentary,

Said was again asked to explain his position on terrorism. "I'm totally against it," he said. But "I've always been much more impressed by the extent of Palestinian suffering."

"That seems very clear," the interviewer commented, "but very cold and unfeeling."

Said looked taken aback. "I'm not sure what you mean—unfeeling."

The interviewer said he was referring to Said's response.

Again Said expressed disapproval of terrorism. "It doesn't advance a political goal," he said—and then pointed out that "terrorism was first introduced into the Middle East by Zionists in the twenties."

For Said, all questions of Palestinian terrorism are overshadowed by what he sees as Israeli terrorism against Palestinian civilians. "The situation of the Palestinian is that of a victim," he says. "There is a moral difference. They're the dispossessed, and what they do by way of violence and terrorism is understandable. But what the Israelis do, in killing Palestinians on a much larger scale, is a continuation of the horrific and unjust dispossession of the Palestinian people. Far more Palestinians—by a ratio of 100 to 1—have been killed by Israelis than Israelis have been killed by Palestinians."

Many prominent Jews are troubled by Said's statements. Rabbi Arthur Hertzberg, former vice-president of the World Jewish Congress, is a research scholar at Columbia's Middle East Institute. He has debated Said publicly. "I called Sabra and Shatilla a pogrom in 1982," says Hertzberg, referring to the massacres of Palestinian refugees outside Beirut by right-wing Christians while Israeli troops stood by. "When he has spoken out against Arab terrorism, his voice has been very muted and politically circumspect," Hertzberg says.

"He puts on a very nice face for an American audience," says Yossi Gal, a spokesman for the Israeli embassy in Washington. "With his American accent, he tries to put on a positive picture in an attempt to manipulate the media—that this is what the PLO is all about. Americans know the PLO equals terrorism, not the PLO equals Edward Said equals Columbia University."

Morris B. Abram, former chairman of the Conference of Presidents of Major American Jewish Organizations, calls Said "a skillful propagandist. If Professor Said is the man he would have Americans believe he is, let him urge that the Palestine National Council repeal the Palestinian Covenant, which calls for the destruction of Israel."

Said has heard these criticisms before. "I'm not an apologist or paid propagandist," he says. "I do what I do out of commitment. I want people like Abram to point to things I've said that are not true. People don't refute my arguments—they just attack me personally. This attempt to defame my character and to slander me is because they cannot answer the factual truth of what I say."

As for the Palestinian National Covenant, "it nowhere calls for the destruction of Israel," says Said. He argues that when the framers of the document in 1964 wrote about the need to "liquidate the Zionist presence in Palestine," they "didn't say 'Jews.' The word 'Zionist' meant the movement that threw us out of our own country. That had to be defied and reversed." He goes on to add that, in any case, he thinks Arafat's statements and the resolutions of the P.N.C. "directly supersede" the covenant.

Increasingly, Said is being asked to explain the Palestinian cause to American audiences. Last March, George Shultz invited Said and his friend and colleague on the P.N.C., Ibrahim Abu-Lughod, professor of political science at Northwestern University, to Washington to talk about the Palestinian situation. Before they got down to business, Said and Shultz discussed their alma mater, Princeton. "Shultz said we needed credible and representative Palestinians," says Said—adding, with irony in his voice, "like myself, who have Ph.D.'s, not terrorists."

Also in March, Said was invited to attend Sabbath services and deliver a talk at Congregation B'nai Yisrael in Armonk, New York. It was Said's first time in a synagogue. "I was moved," he says. "I appreciated the gesture very much." Rabbi Douglas E. Krantz says the reactions to Said's talk "were more or less positive," but "what was most important about the visit was that the conflict was humanized in our sanctuary."

Last December, Said was invited to speak at a lunch at Columbia's School of International and Public Affairs. Guests included Zbigniew Brzezinski, a Columbia professor who was Jimmy Carter's national-security adviser, and Robert Jervis, professor of political science and a specialist in national security. The atmosphere was cordial, yet Said was nervous, the sweat running down his face, his voice dry as he delivered a summary of the Palestinian uprising and of events in Algiers.

Brzezinski, for once, seemed to be on Said's side. "I admit the Palestinian position has evolved, whereas the Israeli position has not," he said.

There were questions from around the table. Jervis asked if one of the problems in the Middle East wasn't "the floridness" and the "exaggeration" of the Arabic language itself, "making for the difficulty of a political understanding."

Later, Said observed that Jervis's remark "typifies the clichés that come from ignorance and fear. Arabic is no more florid than any other great language. It can be used floridly, to conceal intention, but that's true of *every* language!"

The gathering was in many ways typical of Said's daily life. Always a gentleman, yet always a stranger, he in some ways never quite seems to belong.

He was born into an old Jerusalem family in 1935, delivered, he says, by a Jewish midwife. His father, Wadie, was already an American citizen, having fled to the United States to avoid the Ottoman draft. In 1917, Wadie joined the American Army and served in France. After attending college in Cleveland, he returned to Palestine and became a wealthy businessman, the head of a company that made office equipment and published books. Said's mother is half Palestinian and half Lebanese. She grew up in Nazareth, where her father was the first Baptist minister in Palestine.

The family home was in a comfortable neighborhood of West Jerusalem, near the King David Hotel. Said was the oldest and the only boy. Mother and son were very close. Wadie Said was more severe. "He taught me to judge myself and others by unmeetable standards," says his son.

Said's memories of Jerusalem are filled with "images of the sun, pastel colors, people wearing dark-colored clothes, peasants and sheepherders. . . ." He remembers "idyllic" family gatherings on the slopes of Mount Carmel, at picnic lunches along the Sea of Galilee. A family picture of Said from his early childhood shows a little Arab boy with dark skin and curly hair, wearing a kaffiyeh. In Palestine, he says, he had "a sense of belonging that I never had after that again." But his father "hated Jerusalem," Said remembers. "He said it reminded him of death."

Said went to St. George's, an Anglican school attended by Jerusalem's aristocracy, where his father had been a student and star athlete. A plaque with his father's name among the first elevens (the equivalent of the varsity cricket team) still hangs there, and Said says he dreams of one day taking his own son, Wadie, to see it.

As Said approached his twelfth birthday, the British Mandate in Palestine was in its final days, and Jerusalem had been divided into zones. Soon Said would need a pass to get from his home to his school. "The situation was dangerous and inconvenient," Said remembers. Said's family left in December 1947 for Cairo. "I certainly didn't think I was never going to return," Said says.

In the spring of 1948, with the British gone, war broke out between the Arabs and the Jews after the Arabs rejected a U.N.-sponsored partition of the country. Within months, the rest of the Said family were refugees. "I have uncles in Athens, Washington, in Amman, in Pittsburgh, England, Switzerland," says Said.

While many Palestinians landed in refugee camps, Said and his parents, like other upper-class families, resumed their privileged existence. (Some of the children of these families later formed the nexus of the modern PLO leadership.) Compared with other Palestinians, "I suffered very little," Said admits.

But for all Palestinians, no matter what their class, says Said, the loss of Palestine has been known forever after as the *nakbah,* the disaster. "Since ancient times," he says, "the worst punishment given a man was exile and separation from his natal place. It is the most horrible fate, a permanent fall from paradise."

In Cairo, Said attended the American School along with the children of U.S. diplomats. Later, he entered Victoria College in Cairo, known as the Eton of the Middle East. Among the students at the school (which had a branch in Alexandria) were the future King Hussein of Jordan and Adnan Khashoggi. The head boy in Said's house at the school was the future actor Omar Sharif, then known as Michel Chalhoub. Said says Sharif—who was four years older—was a bully and Said "hated" him. Said felt like a stranger. "Most of the people at the school had been there all their lives," he says.

Victoria College was supposed to turn its students into little English gentlemen. Some of the teachers were shell-shocked veterans of World War II. One, Said recalls, "sometimes started to shake" in class. Said remembers writing "essays on the enclosure system in England. I knew more about the enclosure bill than any other subject. Arab language and literature were comic subjects."

Said's mother arranged for him to be tutored in Arabic and given lessons in riding, boxing, gymnastics, and piano. On Sundays, "I went to Sunday school at the Anglican church in the morning and in the evening went to the Presbyterian church. I know the King James Version and the Book of Common Prayer very well." The result of these lessons was to turn Said into something of a modern polymath, an expert on the literature of many lands, an excellent athlete, a pianist of nearly concert-level skill.

In 1951, Said defied one of his teachers at Victoria College, and his parents and the faculty agreed that "my career in the British system was not going to prosper." So he was sent to Mount Hermon, an "austere evangelist school," as he recalls it, in Massachusetts. Said was miserable. He had never been away from home before, he had "no place to go at Christmas," and he saw his parents only in the summer. "I did brilliantly, but I was always penalized somehow," he remembers. "There was always a moral disapproval." He was happy, though, at Princeton. "For the first time in my life, I was able intellectually to flourish," he says.

During the summers, Said continued to return to Cairo, but Nasser's revolution in Egypt in 1952 changed forever the nature of Arab politics, marking the rise of Arab nationalism. By 1963, with a "wave of socialism" passing over Egypt, "there was no place for a man like my father," says Said. The family moved to Lebanon. "My life has marked a period of cataclysmic changes," he says. "Whole countries disappearing, whole nations realigning." The exodus from Cairo was traumatic for the Saids, and ever since then, the phrase "after Cairo" has been a family refrain. Said's father died in Lebanon in 1971. His mother and two of his sisters lived through the siege of Beirut by Israeli forces in 1982, and—though his mother is currently in Washington—she and the sisters maintain homes in West Beirut.

In 1962, as a graduate student in comparative literature at Harvard, Said met his first wife, an Estonian-American who was a friend of his sister's at Vassar. The marriage was troubled. Said says his wife had "little interest in Arab culture."

For his Harvard Ph.D. dissertation, Said chose the Polish-born writer Joseph Conrad, like Said an exile. Conrad became a crucial figure in his life. In an essay, **"The Mind of Winter: Reflections on a Life in Exile,"** published in *Harper's* in 1984, Said quotes Conrad: "It is indeed hard upon a man to find himself a lost stranger, helpless, incomprehensible, and of mysterious origin, in some obscure corner of the earth." The dissertation was later turned into his first book, *Joseph Conrad and the Fiction of Autobiography.*

In his early years in America, Said says, he had "little political consciousness of myself as an Arab." But the 1967 defeat of the Arabs in the war with Israel changed him forever. He saw "the tremendous support for the Israeli victory and the total lack of support for the Arab position. I began to radically question my presence in this society."

He separated from his first wife in 1968 and began to "rediscover" his identity as an Arab. On a trip to Lebanon in 1970, Said met Mariam Cortas, a Lebanese Quaker who, like Said, came from a wealthy family. "I fell in love with her," says Said, and they were married at the end of the year. They have two children: Wadie, now seventeen, and Najla, fourteen, both students at the Trinity School.

At the time of his second marriage, Said was teaching at Columbia and making his reputation as a scholar. He was among the first literary critics to introduce the writing of French structuralists like Claude Lévi-Strauss, and the post-structuralist Michel Foucault, to American audiences. The French structuralists wrote that the human mind has an innate structuring capacity, which it imposes on the outside world. Human thought, consciousness itself, human myths and kinship patterns, all have "deep structures," and it is the scholar's task to uncover them. In 1975, Said published *Beginnings: Intention and Method,* about the way intellectual endeavors—works of history, novels, and poems—begin and the significance of the author's choice of a beginning. Like much of Said's early scholarly writing, it is influenced by the structuralists and nearly impossible for an ordinary person to read. The book was awarded Columbia's Lionel Trilling prize.

During the seventies, Said became increasingly involved in the Palestinian cause. His cousin by marriage, Kamal Nasser, a poet and spokesman for the PLO in Amman, was killed in Lebanon in 1973 by Israeli commandos coming in from the sea, Said says. In 1977, he became a member of the Palestine National Council. "I've never really wanted to have even a semi-official affiliation," Said says. "I did it out of solidarity and commitment."

In 1978, he published the book for which he's best known, *Orientalism,* an examination of the way the West perceives the Islamic world. The book has a striking cover: a nineteenth-century painting, *The Snake Charmer,* by the French artist Jean-Léon Gérôme. The painting shows a naked Arab boy, with a snake wound round his body, being regarded lasciviously by a group of Arab men. To Said, the painting epitomizes the West's "malicious" misconceptions about Arabs.

In the book, Said purports to show the way the Orient is portrayed as "mysterious" and "sensual" and Arabs and Muslims as "evil, totalitarian and terroristic." To Said, the West's vision of the Islamic world is "a web of racism, cultural stereotypes [and] dehumanizing ideology." He argues that Orientalism is like a form of anti-Semitism, as if "the Jew of pre-Nazi Germany has bifurcated. What we have now is a Jewish hero . . . and his creeping, mysteriously fearsome shadow, the Arab Oriental."

The book caused an uproar. Bernard Lewis, professor of Near Eastern studies at Princeton, called it "false" and "absurd." He argued that it "reveals a disquieting lack of knowledge of what scholars do and what scholarship is about."

Still, *Orientalism* was nominated for the National Book Critics Circle Award and has changed the face of scholarship on the Arab world and the Third World in general. Professional groups have devoted symposia to the book, and it has been translated into fifteen languages.

Since *Orientalism,* Said has turned away from pure literary scholarship. In *The World, the Text, and the Critic* (1983), which won the René Wellek Prize of the American Comparative Literature Association, Said argued that scholars are social beings interpreting works that have been created in the midst of political events. His books *The Question of Palestine* (1979), *Covering Islam* (1981), *After the Last Sky* (1986), and *Blaming the Victims* (1988) have taken on an increasingly political tone. A new book, *Culture and Imperialism,* is scheduled to be published next year.

Today, Said continues to live uneasily poised between two cultures, Arab and American.

"Whether I'm with Americans or with Arabs, I always feel incomplete," says Said. "Part of myself can't be expressed. I always have a sense of being slightly at a disadvantage. There is always the sense that being Arab carries a special charge of being delinquent, guilty by association."

At home, he speaks Arabic—"a language I have loved more than any other," he has written. (Said also speaks French and reads Italian, German, Spanish, and Latin.) His apartment is filled with the mixed symbols of the cultures he inhabits—a poinsettia for Christmas, pillows covered with Palestinian weavings, jeweled boxes of beaten silver from Egypt.

In the outside world, Said seems thoroughly American, playing squash at the Columbia gym with friends, many of them Jews. To his close friend Jonathan R. Cole, recently named the provost of Columbia, Said is "a brilliant scholar, in his own way equal to Lionel Trilling.

"We haven't had a great many political discussions," says Cole, who is Jewish. "I definitely agree with him that we have to have an accommodation to the Palestinian question. The question is whether or not his friends reconstruct his positions to what they want to hear. If he supports the stereotypical PLO position calling for the annihilation of Israel, then I don't agree with him."

To some of Said's friends, his quality of separateness, of being apart from the dominant culture, has the effect of making him seem like a Jew. David Stern, assistant professor of medieval-Hebrew literature at the University of Pennsylvania, was an undergraduate student at Columbia when he first met Said. Stern is an observant Jew and a Zionist. "I felt a kind of sympathy with him as an outsider, in the same way as I felt an outsider," says Stern.

To Cole, Said "is a marginal man, as many Jews are. It's difficult for Edward to feel of a place. Of course, that's a situation that Jews have been in for many centuries. Edward and many of his Jewish friends are more similar to each other than to people who came from Western Europe."

Yet the similarity between Said and Jews ends when Said is asked about the Holocaust. Three years ago, he and his wife went to see *Shoah,* Claude Lanzmann's movie about memories of the Holocaust. "I'm sure we were the only Arabs there," Said remarked in the BBC documentary. Today, he says he was disappointed in the movie. "I knew Lanzmann had gotten money from the Israeli government for it," he says. "It was a disturbing film because of what it revealed about European anti-Semitism, [yet] ideologically, it provided an argument for Zionism that impinged on me as a Palestinian. It seemed to me much more about present-day politics than it did about the past. It's all part of a justification for the Palestinian situation, an argument for dispossessing Palestinians.

"I don't say there is an equation between the suffering of the Jews and the Palestinians," Said adds, "but the suffering of Jews doesn't thereby entitle them to dispossess us!"

Despite Said's commitment to the Palestinian cause, he has never gone back to Jerusalem and has visited the West Bank only twice, briefly, for family weddings (both times before 1967). Now that he's become a prominent spokesman for the Palestinian cause, Said is no longer welcome in Israel. Last year, when he was invited to Bir Zeit University on the West Bank to lecture, Israeli prime minister Yitzhak Shamir said he would refuse Said a visa if he tried to return.

But even if there were a Palestinian state, Said would probably never live there. "It's too late for me. I'm past the point of uprooting myself again," he says. Besides, "New York is the exilic city. You can be anything you want here, because you are always playacting; you never really belong."

If he will never live in Palestine, why fight so hard for a Palestinian homeland? "I'm not fighting for the nationalistic element," Said says. "I'm fighting because I have a tremendous anger at an unacknowledged injustice to an entire people. Not a day goes by when I don't think in the minutest detail of how a relatively innocent people have been made to suffer this kind of tragedy, while the Western World celebrated their oppressors."

Now that the United States is talking to the PLO, Said says, his goal is an international peace conference. "We want to break down the taboos and naturalize the Palestinians, so they are not seen as monsters, as Nazis, etc. It's very important that American Jews and Israeli Jews understand how the Palestinians require from them acknowledgement of the immense historical injustice inflicted on us as a nation."

Said's hope is for "an independent Palestinian state alongside Israel, in some kind of confederation with Jordan. There is an Israeli law of return; there should be an equivalent Palestinian law of return—that is an extremely important and sensitive issue. All Palestinians feel they have a right of return. But we are talking about numbers, both Jewish and Palestinian, that will simply overwhelm the capacity of both states to absorb—there have to be limitations on both states. They can't do everything they want. They have to negotiate some formula together."

Even as Said envisions a future Palestinian state, the thought of it makes the scholar-intellectual in him uneasy. "I feel deeply uncomfortable with nationalism," he says. "My commitment to the cause is because of the injustice to and sufferings of people of whom I'm a part. Nationalism itself doesn't interest me. I can see it as a necessity, but I myself am not interested in successful nationalism."

There is no sign that Said's advocacy of the Palestinian cause has affected him professionally. At Columbia, where he makes a distinctive figure striding about campus in a loden-green coat and a red-paisley scarf, Said is something of a cult figure. His lectures, which touch on fashionable trends in structuralism and deconstruction, are well attended. In 1983, he was invited to deliver the University Lecture at Columbia, considered a great honor. He is constantly invited to speak at other universities and has won most of the major awards of his profession. It takes twelve pages on his résumé to list all his books and essays. (In his spare time, he is also music critic for the *Nation*.) Three years ago, when he turned down an important offer from Harvard, Columbia gave him a bigger apartment with a new kitchen. "I get promotions, salary increases, all the perks," he says.

Last December, after the P.N.C. conference in Algiers, New York *Times* publisher Arthur Ochs Sulzberger invited Said to have lunch with editors at the paper. Two days before the lunch was held, Arafat issued his statement recognizing Israel. Usually, discussions about the Palestinian situation have been dominated by questions about the Palestinians' refusal to recognize Israel. Now, at the luncheon, "it was as if an obstacle to discourse had been removed," Said says. The editors asked about the events that had led up to Arafat's statements and about the future. The conversation was so lively that Said hardly had time to eat the seafood salad that had been set before him.

Still, even as he and the newspaper editors sat together in an eleventh-floor dining room, in Israel, on the West Bank, the violence was increasing. By the end of the day, eight

Palestinians in a funeral procession had been shot dead by Israeli soldiers, and the Palestinians were continuing to riot.

Edward Said with Bonnie Marranca, Marc Robinson, and Una Chaudhuri (interview date March 1989)

SOURCE: "Criticism, Culture, and Performance," in *Performing Arts Journal*, Vol. 1, No. 37, January, 1991, pp. 21-42.

[*In the following interview, which originally took place in March, 1989, Said speaks out about his music criticism, the role of the public intellectual, the significance of performance of drama and music, and the influence of "interculturalism" on the construction of artistic canons.*]

I

[*Bonnie Marranca:*] *Since you write on music performance, tell us how you feel about this activity in your life, and how it is perceived by others in the literary world.*

[Edward Said:] I think the isolation of musical culture from what is called literary culture is almost total. What used to be assumed to be a kind of passing knowledge or literacy on the part of literary people with regard to music is now non-existent. I think there are a few desultory efforts to be interested in the rock culture and pop music, that whole mass culture phenomenon, on the part of literary intellectuals. But the world that I'm interested in, the music of classical performance and opera and the so-called high-culture dramas that have persisted largely from the nineteenth century, is almost totally mysterious to literary people. I think they regard what I do as a kind of lark. I've demonstrated my seriousness by giving a series of lectures last spring, the Wellek Lectures at the University of California at Irvine, which are normally very heavy-duty literary theory lectures. I gave them on what I call musical elaborations, of which the first lecture of three was on performance. It was called **"Performance as an extreme occasion."** I was interested in the role of music in the creation of social space. In the third lecture I talked about music and solitude and melody, which are subjects that interest me a great deal. But I don't think one can really worry about music seriously without some active participation in musical life. My own background is that of a pianist. I studied piano quite seriously when I was an undergraduate at Princeton and with teachers at Juilliard. So I think what interests me in the whole phenomenon is not so much the reviewing aspect. I prefer trying to deal with the problem of the composer and the problem of performance as separate but interrelated issues.

[*Marranca:*] *Your music criticism seems to be different from your literary criticism. Not only is the subject matter different, but it doesn't seem to be as—let me see if I can choose the right word, because I don't want to mean it in any kind of pejorative sense—it's lighter, it's not as dense and politically engaged. Of course, it doesn't always lend itself to that, depending on the subject matter. On the other hand, the piece that you did on Verdi's* Aida *is a model for a new kind of theatre history. But it seems to me that there is something you allow yourself to do in music criticism that is not there in your literary criticism.*

What I'm moved by in music criticism are things that I'm interested in and like. I am really first motivated by pleasure. And it has to be sustained over a long period of time. I don't write reviews; I think that's a debased form, to write a kind of scorecard, morning-after kind of thing about performance. So what I like to do is to go to many more performances than I would ever write about and then over a period of time, certain things crystallize out of my mind as I reflect on them and think about them, and the music I'll play over. In the end, what I really find abides are the things that I care about. I don't know what those are until after a period of time has elapsed. It's a different type of occasional writing from the kind that I do in literary criticism, where I'm involved in much longer terms of debates. Whereas in this I don't really engage with too much in music criticism, because most of it is to me totally uninteresting. There are a couple of interesting music critics around. Not the journalistic ones. Andrew Porter in the *New Yorker* I think is challenging and quite brilliant at times. And then there are people who write from the extreme right wing, like Samuel Lipman, who writes for *The New Criterion,* and Edward Wasserstein, who writes for the *New Republic,* who are very intelligent music critics. And that's about it. The rest is really a desert—people who write about music in a non-musicological way.

On the other hand, I have had lots of response from young musicologists, who write me about some of the issues that come up. For example, I wrote a piece about feminism in music and the problem of that. And I've written about the problems of political power and representation over years in some of the things I've done for *The Nation.* But my overriding concern is a record of a certain kind of enjoyment, which I think can be given literary form, without drawing attention to itself as a kind of tour de force. "Lighter" is the word you used, I would call it glib and superficial.

[*Una Chaudhuri:*] *Do you think that performance, as a category, has something to do with the difference?*

Tremendously. That's what I'm really interested in. I think the thing that got me started was Glenn Gould. It was really the first extended piece that I wrote which appeared the year he died, or the year after he died—'82 or '83—in *Vanity Fair.* I'd long been fascinated with him. And I also was very interested in the phenomenon of Toscanini. Just because it seemed to me that both of them seemed to be musicians whose work, in a certain sense, was *about* performance. There was no attempt to pretend they were doing something else, but they had sort of fixated on the notion of performance and carried it to such an extreme degree that it compelled attention on its own, and it attracted attention to the artificiality of performance. And to the conventions of it, and to the strange—in the case of Toscanini—well, Bonnie, you write about it, too, in your essay on performance versus singing—the difference between performers who heighten the occasion and those who turn it into a kind of extension of the drawing room or social occasion. So performance is very interesting because then there's the other problem, that you don't have either in theatre, the visual and/or literary arts, in that the performance of music is so momentary—it's over!—I mean, you can't go back to it, anyway, really. And so there's a kind of sporting element that I'm trying to capture. I talked about it once with Arthur Danto who said, for example, if you read his pieces, they're all about going back over to an exhibition, leaving aside what he says and what his attitudes and his ideas are about art. I can't do that. So I have to go back, really, to my recollection. And my attempts, in my own mind, to restate it or experience it in another context.

[*Marc Robinson:*] *On the whole idea of performance, let me draw you out a bit on opera performance, especially the staging of it. For so many people in the theatre, the whole world of opera is a foggy, dead zone that most of us don't go to because the theatricality of it is so conservative. But now many of the experimental directors are going back to opera—Robert Wilson, Peter Sellars, Andre Serban—and trying to revive it from a theatre background. Where do you see opera performance going?*

Well, it's a tremendously interesting subject that excites me in many different ways. I think for the most part there is a deadness at the heart of opera performance, largely because of institutions like the Met, which for one reason or another—some of the reasons are perfectly obvious—has been dominated by what I call Italian *verismo* opera—and strengthened in this ridiculous kind of thing by the revival, that began in the '60s, of the *bel canto* tradition. The result of this is that a kind of hegemony has formed between the blue chip opera companies like the Met, and this repertory, and has frozen out a large amount of really extraordinary music. It has hardened performance style into a ridiculous conventionalism which has now become the norm. It infects everybody, even the greatest singers. It is certainly true of Pavarotti, sort of on the right; and on the left, Jessye Norman. You see what I'm trying to say? It's narcotized audiences. The thing I cannot understand is how people can sit through operas at the Met.

[*Robinson:*] *I remember when you reviewed the Strauss opera* Erwartung *and were so disappointed. Didn't you say something about how it would be much more rewarding just to stay at home and stage it in your mind?*

Exactly. Or watch it as a concert performance with Jessye Norman. It's the story of a woman who's going mad. And she's looking for her betrothed. The text is written—texts in operas are very interesting—by a Viennese medical student. The text is not of great literary value, but it's about hysteria and it bears an interesting relation, Adorno says, to Freud's case studies. So it is a minute, seismographic dissolution of a consciousness. Now here is this wonderful singer who hasn't got a clue what it's about, much too large in size to represent neurasthenia and hysteria and all this kind of stuff. As the opera progresses she goes deeper and deeper into the forest losing her mind and looking for her fiancé. And then it's discovered she really might be a patient in a mental institution who's run away. And right in the middle of the set—right in the middle of the stage—is this enormous grand piano. What is a grand piano doing in the middle of a forest? So I opined that the reason she was going mad was that she couldn't figure out what to do with the grand piano. Which produces a kind of—I mean, you could say—it's a kind of perverse version of the opera. It's a glorious misinterpretation of the opera. That's not what's intended; it was supposed to be a deeply serious kind of thing, and it just didn't work. That's what the Met does, and I don't understand how it continues to do that.

[*Robinson:*] *Maybe the consequence of that is there are certain works of music-theatre that simply shouldn't be staged. You always hear that with dramatic literature, there are certain "unstageable" texts—an awful lot of Shakespeare . . .*

Yes, that's certainly true, but a lot of those derive from performances where the unstageability of the piece can be made evident, you know, like a late Ibsen play, *When We Dead Awaken.* It has a lot to do with musical performance as well as opera, . . . That is to say, how do these—this is a sort of Gramscian phrase—how do these hegemonic canons get formed? I mean, for example, the exclusion of French opera is really quite extraordinary. There is a wonderful tradition of French music and French drama—music-drama—that just doesn't find its way onto the American stages. Think of Rameau; think of Berlioz; think of most of Rossini, aside from *The Barber of Seville.* I mean, Rossini was a French opera writer. Berlioz; you never see him. Bizet is the author of ten operas, of which *Carmen*

gets fitful performances—*Carmen* is one of the great masterpieces—but precisely because it's kind of an anti-French and anti-German opera, in a way. Then there's Massenet and Fauré. Why all this *verismo* and then a little smattering of Wagner—Wagner sort of turned into Italian. . . .

[*Marranca:*] *I think the last time we spoke we talked a little bit about the Philip Glass operas, about whether you had seen* Einstein on the Beach, Akhnaten, *or* Satyagraha. *Are you interested in the contemporary repertoire?*

I am. I've heard those and I've seen videos of them—one or two of Glass's things. It's not a musical aesthetic that moves me tremendously. It doesn't seem to me to exploit to the maximum what is available there.

[*Marranca:*] *What about as critical material, in the sense of writing about or looking at the* Akhnaten *opera. . . . Even in terms of political themes I would have thought they'd attract your attention.*

That's true. It's just . . . I don't know, I can't explain it. As I say, I work with fairly strong likes and dislikes, pleasures and so on . . . I don't derive the kind of interest from Glass that I would have found, say, in other contemporary composers, like Henze. I think Henze is a more interesting writer of opera.

[*Marranca:*] *I was interested to read in a recent interview—one of the things you mentioned in talking about your writing—how the concepts of polyphonic voice and chorus interest you. Could you elaborate on that in terms of your own critical writing?*

These are things it takes a while to fetch out of one's own interests and predilections. I seem to have always been interested in the phenomenon of polyphony of one sort or another. Musically, I'm very interested in contrapuntal writing, and contrapuntal forms. The kind of complexity that is available, aesthetically, to the whole range from consonant to dissonant, the tying together of multiple voices in a kind of disciplined whole, is something that I find tremendously appealing.

[*Marranca:*] *How do you extend it to your own essays?*

I extend it, for example, in an essay I did on exile, basing it on personal experience. If you're an exile—which I feel myself, in many ways, to have been—you always bear within yourself a recollection of what you've left behind and what you can remember, and you play it against the current experience. So there's necessarily that sense of counterpoint. And by counterpoint I mean things that can't be reduced to homophony. That can't be reduced to a kind of simple reconciliation. My interest in comparative literature is based on the same notion. I think the one thing that I find, I guess, the most—I wouldn't say repellent, but I would say antagonistic—for me is identity. The notion of a *single* identity. And so multiple identity, the polyphony of many voices playing off against each other, without, as I say, the need to reconcile them, just to hold them together, is what my work is all about. More than one culture, more than one awareness, both in its negative and its positive modes. It's basic instinct.

[*Chaudhuri:*] *Do you think there are certain cultures and cultural practices that are more encouraging of polyphony?*

Absolutely. For example, in music, one of the things I've been very interested in—and it occupies the last part of the three sections of my book on music [**Musical Elaborations**], which will appear next year, is a kind of opposition between forms that are based upon development and domination. Like sonata. Sonata form is based on statement, rigorous development, recapitulation. And a lot of things go with that: the symphony, for example, I'm staying within the Western, classical world; certain kinds of opera are based upon this, versus forms that are based upon what I would call developing variations, in which conflict and domination and the overcoming of tension through forced reconciliation is not the issue. There the issue is to prolong, like in a theme and variation, in fugal forms. In polyphony like, in my own tradition, the work of Um Kulthum. She was the most famous classical Arab singer of the twentieth century. Her forms are based upon an inhabiting of time, not trying to dominate it. It's a special relationship with temporality. Or the music of Messiaen, for example, the great French avant-garde composer who I think is divine. You see the dichotomy of that. On the one hand, domination/development; on the other, a kind of proliferation through variation and polyphonic relationship. Those are the culture practices that I think one could use as a typology of *other* culture practices: they're based on the whole idea of community, overlapping vs. coercive domination and enlightenment—the narratives of enlightenment and achievement that are to be found in novels.

[*Chaudhuri:*] *I'm very interested in what you say about this idea of inhabiting the time of performance, instead of dominating it.*

Trying to ride it. It's a phrase that comes out of Gerard Manley Hopkins who has a very strange relationship with time in his poetry, especially the last part of his first great poem, *The Wreck of the Deutschland.* There's this whole thing where the question of whether you try to resist the time and erect the structure, or you try to ride time and live inside the time.

[*Chaudhuri:*] *I think of theatre performance as such, as somehow demanding that the time be inhabited. That is, it makes its own demands, even in the masterful performer, who may try to dominate it, but may not succeed.*

Yes. There really is a difference in musical performance between people who are involved in remaking the music and inhabiting it in that way, as opposed to just dispatching it with efficiency and tremendous technical skill.

[*Robinson:*] *It is also very much in the nature of the exile. I mean, there's a sense that you're either living in the past or living in an ideal future, and the present is such a dangerous equivocal realm where you can't place yourself, and yet you're forced to.*

What's interesting about it is, of course, that you get a sense of its provisionality. That's what I like about it. There's no attempt made to pretend that it's the natural way to do it. It's giving up in a temporal sort of way to that moment.

[*Robinson:*] *Such a balancing act too. Both in terms of time, but also in terms of the exile's relationship to the world. On the one hand, you have the wonderful worldliness or the ability to partake of so many regions. And on the other hand, the enforced isolation. How does one balance between those two?*

I don't know. I don't think there's a formula for it. I think one can call it a kind of traffic between those situations.

II

[*Robinson:*] *The whole idea of private space connects to that and might be a topic to pursue. I'm often very moved by your idea of the secular intellectual, the secular artist, partaking of the public world in a real, strong way. And yet all the changes that are going on now in Eastern Europe started me thinking about alternatives to that point of view. There was an anecdote of the East German playwright Heiner Müller—he had always been in opposition to the government—who was asked by somebody from Western Europe, "Aren't you excited now that the chains are off, you're able to write your plays that really do take on the political situation, take on the government, what have you . . ." And he said, "No, actually, freedom now means freedom to read Proust, to stay at home in my library." That seems to signal a rediscovery of private space, a retreat from what used to be an enforced secularity.*

Privacy for me is very jealously guarded, because so out of my control is the public dimension of the world I live in, which has to do with a peculiar sensitivity and intransigence of the Palestinian situation. And thinking about it for the last fifteen or twenty years has been very difficult for me to guard. Partly the music has been very much that way, because it's a non-verbal idiom. I've been involved in the thick of these battles over what one says, what one can say, and all that kind of stuff. The public has been so much with me it's been impossible for me to retreat into the private. Although, obviously, we all do have a kind of intimate private life. But it's not recoverable for me in any easy way. In the last couple of years—partly because I'm getting older—I've been deeply resentful of how much, quite against my will and intention and any plan that I might have had, public life has usurped so much of my time and effort. By that, I don't mean only politics. I mean teaching, writing, the whole sense of having an audience—sometimes completely unpredictable and against my will. So that inwardness is a very, very rare commodity. I'm not sure that my case is a special case. I think it may be true of more people than we suspect.

[*Chaudhuri:*] *Do you think that somehow a certain kind of engaged intellectual is being made to carry more cultural burden than ever before?*

Well, I feel it. I can't speak for others. I find it very hard to speak for others, because I'm in a strange position. I mean, I don't have as much time for reflection. And that's why, for me, the musical experience has been so important. Because it's something that isn't charged and inflected in quite the ways that some of the other things I've been doing have been. I just feel that for the public intellectual it can be extremely debilitating. It's almost paranoid: something you say can be twisted into a thousand different forms or only one different form that can have untold consequences. And in my case, also, I have many quite different and totally impermeable audiences. I write a monthly column in Arabic for one of the largest weeklies in the Arab world. And then the constituencies you have, necessarily, in the world of European languages is also very different. So it's extremely draining, just to try to keep up with it, much less to contribute.

[*Robinson:*] *I wonder if we're going to see some of the models of the intellectual artist change, as is the case already in Eastern Europe, with many who are now retreating from that public role—seeing it as a burden, and now evolving into a secluded hermeticism. A lot of the artists there want to rediscover beauty.*

I understand that perfectly. What we live in, in a way, is what Eliot called a wilderness of mirrors: endless multiplication, without tremendous significance, but just a spinning on. And you just want to say: enough. I don't want too much to do with that. And therefore, one of the things that I find myself thinking about, not only privacy that as we talked

about earlier is virtually impossible, but also looking at performance exactly like Gould, who understood this problem, and because of that, therefore, was able to focus and specialize and control what he did to the extent that it wasn't a limitless spinning out. There was this kind of—now this hasn't been written enough about or noted about Gould enough—massive effort on his part from the moment he thought about a work to practicing, preparing, and then performing it, and then recording it. He is one of the unique examples of somebody who was a public performer, whose attempt was to enrich the art of performance by, at the same time, controlling it. There is something, of course, quite cold and deadening about it, at the same time. But on the other hand, it's an interesting model to think about. Not many people do that. Most people tend to be profligate and they want more multiplication. There is a sense in which he wanted that, but he wanted to control it as much as possible. Perhaps because he feared that being on the stage had already showed him what was likely to happen: that he would just become a creature of this public space.

[*Robinson:*] *Genet might be another example, a man who was always preserving the private realm.*

Exactly.

[*Robinson:*] *He was able to understand what went on in the Mid-East because of his experience of outsiderhood.*

[*Chaudhuri:*] *And also in the plays as well.*

[*Marranca:*] *Beckett, too.*

But what you feel in Genet and Gould you don't feel in Beckett, that is, that there's a flirting with danger. I've never felt that about Beckett. Who can't admire him—but on the other hand there is a kind of safety in Beckett's work that you don't find in Genet. In Genet you feel the incredible risk involved in all of his drama.

[*Chaudhuri:*] *It's also a provocation, isn't it?*

[*Marranca:*] *One of the things that strikes me about Beckett is that he's so great a writer and so overpowers theatricality that it's not necessary ever to see him performed. But Genet gains by being in the theatre. . . . We've been talking about the private moment and the Eastern European situation, the sense of aloneness and solitude that somehow seems to be demanded after so strong a public life.*

The death of Beckett set many people wondering about just what will come after Beckett, of course. And in some ways it seems it's the end of the universal playwright and the international dramatic repertoire. Also, because cul-

ture has become so public and so much a part of spectacle, and where there's so little emphasis on the private
moment, it seems to me that drama, which is such a private, reflective, intimate form anyway, is falling further
and further down in the hierarchy of forms experienced
by serious people who would ordinarily have gone to theatre, those who read serious novels and go to the opera.
People like Havel and Fugard became known not necessarily because they are great playwrights. They got into
the international repertoire because of their politics and
their symbolic value. It seems more and more that drama
will be a kind of local knowledge. And in the theatre we
see the ascendancy of spectacle, of performance, rather
than drama. International performers like, say, Laurie
Anderson or Wilson, make things that can travel in culture.

Or Peter Brook. . . . But even Laurie Anderson, and Brook
in particular—what underlies them, also, paradoxically is
a kind of modesty of means. It's not like a traveling opera.
It has, in fact, a kind of easily-packed baggage, which you
can transport from country to country and do with a small
repertory, the same pieces. But I think one thing that you
didn't mention about drama—that in the Palestinian situation, for example, which is the only one I can speak about
with any assurance—is that the drama has a testimonial
value, which is different from symbolic, when you talk
about symbolic. That is to say—take Joseph Papp cancel-
ling that Palestinian play, *The Story of Kufur Shamma* last
summer. It wasn't because of the content of the play, it was
Palestinians talking about *their* experience. *That* was what
was threatening. And that's why he had to cancel it. So on
that level it is local knowledge, but a local knowledge that
is frequently engaged in translocal issues. Things that are
of interest to other places. I suppose the burden placed
upon the playwright and the performer is somehow to translate this local situation into an idiom that is contiguous to
and touches other situations.

[*Marranca:*] *In that way, I suppose, drama can travel. But
so much of it now, when you compare the theatre of the
last four, five, or six decades—what used to be considered international and of interest to an international audience—no longer appears on Broadway. For example,
when was the last, say, German or Hungarian or French
play on Broadway? In this sense the international repertoire is shrinking.*

Although, I'll tell you, Bonnie, I was in Delphi last summer giving a talk at an International Conference on Greek
tragedy. I talked about Wagner, I believe. Every night there
was a performance of a play in the theatre at Delphi. And I
was there for two performances, the second of which was
extraordinary, the performance by Wajda's troupe of a Pol-
ish-language *Antigone* . . .

[*Robinson:*] *I saw it in Poland.*

You saw it in Poland. Well, I saw it in Delphi. And the audience was entirely Greek . . . modern Greeks, obviously.
It was overwhelming. It seemed to me to have there a peculiar mix of things. It was the "OK cultural festival," it was
the antique representation of self that was acceptable to the
powers-that-be, because it's sponsored by the Greek government which is in a great crisis at the moment. It was an
occasion for the local folk. OK, all that. But in addition, it
was for me a very powerful theatrical experience. I don't
know which performance you saw, because there were several versions. Where did you see it?

[*Robinson:*] *In Krakow in '85. It was a very bad time, politically, for Poland.*

Were there transformations of the chorus?

[*Robinson:*] *Yes. The chorus changed throughout the
play—moving from bureaucrats—maybe Parliament
members—to protesting students to, finally, shipyard
workers, like those from Gdansk who started Solidarity.
In a Polish theatre, it becomes extremely powerful. Actually, it's an event that makes me question or at least
want to take issue with your idea, Bonnie, about the universality of a play, and mourning the loss of Beckett.*

No, I think what she's talking about—which I'm interested
in—the great master theatrical talent that produces, I have
to keep using the word over and over again, a masterwork
of the sort that created the nineteenth century repertory
theatre, that continues into the late symbolic tragedies of
Ibsen and Strindberg, and then moves into Brecht and then
Beckett. There's a pedigree here that you're alluding to:
people who dominate the stage. The model is one of domination. I don't regret its end, to be perfectly honest with
you, because of a lot of what goes with it. In the same way
that you could say, well what about the great—think of
this—what about the great Austro-Germanic symphonic tradition that begins with Haydn, goes through Mozart,
Beethoven, Schumann, Brahms, I suppose Wagner's in there
a little bit, Mahler, Bruckner, Schöenberg . . . and then what?
Nothing. It ends. And you get these local nationalists, you
know, Bartok. I mean, it took place, but we can live without it. It can be respected and memorialized in various
ways, but I'm not so sure of that, given the damage to other
surrounding clumps it overshadows and dominates. It produces a certain canon or canonicity.

[*Robinson:*] *Yeah, and aren't we all trashing the canon!*

Not trashing. It isn't the be-all-and-end-all, is what I'm
saying.

[*Marranca:*] *I understand your point of view about attacking universality, of course, but the issue is that in drama there's almost nothing else. There are plenty of musical traditions to follow. There are plenty of great novels that are breaking out of the mode and being enjoyed by wide groups and nationalities.*

Yes, that's true.

[*Marranca:*] *But with drama, the whole thing collapses, because if there's no international repertoire, then it's a gradual decreasing of the form itself. And what's left are just the bestsellers, the topical plays that somehow travel, and then the classics. But maybe two of Ibsen, or a few of Brecht. What I'm saying is the other traditions are so much richer, and the repertories are so wide, but if you begin to have a form which worldwide audiences lose interest in—in terms of the new—then I think it's a problem for the form, and that that's different than, say, the situation in music.*

[*Robinson:*] *But isn't that a Romantic idea, that of an international work of art?*

[*Marranca:*] *But they still exist in art, if you look at paintings from many, many countries, a lot of it even looks largely the same, and there are good and bad works. I see nothing wrong with large groups of people in different cultures around the world appreciating the same work. That always happens in terms of fiction, for example.*

The way you describe it, it certainly sounds special and peculiar to the drama. But why is it?

[*Marranca:*] *One of the things I hinted at before is that what we are seeing now are international spectacles found in several cultural festivals, works by Brook or Laurie Anderson, whose recent piece can be just as accessible in Japan or Western Europe or Brazil, or someplace else. Often we're seeing a kind of internationalization of performance. When I use the word "performance," I mean something different from the theatre. It's not textbound, it doesn't deal with a play. Performance work is often highly technological, it reflects a certain transfer of pop imagery and music.*

Recognizable and commodified styles.

[*Marranca:*] *Exactly. And they are understood by people all over the world now, because of the international youth culture. And that has unseated drama somewhat . . .*

And also because of film and television and all the apparatus of the culture industry.

[*Marranca:*] *So that the great theatres now tend to remain in their own countries and build their repertoires on the classics, redo them, and are rejuvenated by new people. But we don't see this travel in theatre that we're seeing in video or visual arts, or fiction, or "performance" as a genre in itself.*

And, of course, in music you find it in the cult of the traveling maestro or the celebrated pianist or the important diva and tenor, and so on and so forth.

[*Robinson:*] *Maybe theatre is less suited to this kind of travel because of the holdover of the idea that a play should somehow address the issues of the people in front of it, the audiences. It's the most socially-connected of the arts, of course. And I would think people would be reluctant to give up that possibility of engagement that the theatre provides, in a much more immediate way than art, music, or TV.*

[*Chaudhuri:*] *There's another way of looking at this. There has always been this dimension of locality in the theatre, this connection to a specific time and place. And it's always been special to the drama. Now, for all its power technology is not going to promote a better means of a direct collaboration with people than the theatre event. So that this "local knowledge" characteristic may be what will save the theatre, and give it its future.*

But she mourns it. I think you really do have a nostalgia for the great figures. Or the great forms. It's a kind of Lukacian, early Lukacs—you know, *The Soul and Its Forms* . . . a kind of Lukacian forlornness and melancholy, which is there. I think you're right. I'm not saying you're wrong.

[*Marranca:*] *To tell you the truth, I'm more interested in the idea of performance than I am in drama, with a very few exceptions. Of course, as a publisher, knowing what it's like to sell books world-wide, on a very practical basis I find a loss of interest in drama.*

What does that mean? You've lost interest in the drama and you watch the performance. In other words, it would matter more to you that Vanessa Redgrave was acting in a play, rather than the play was, say, *Macbeth*, or something like that. Is that what you mean by performance?

[*Marranca:*] *No. I mean something else. I've lost interest in conventionalized stagings of drama. In that case, I would rather sit home with a play and not see it. Though I take a larger interest in performances such as Wilson's work, and some avant-garde performance.*

[*Chaudhuri:*] *That's really a question of quality, isn't it?*

[*Marranca:*] *Yes.*

See, the other part of it is, and I think it's very important for people like us, who are interested in these issues and questions, not simply to celebrate the avant-garde—that is to say, the novel, or the exciting and unusual that come along in the cases of Peter Sellars or Wilson—but also, to stimulate greater dissatisfaction and anger on the part of audiences who now sit sheepishly through unacceptably boring reproductions of masterpieces. That's the part that I find the most puzzling of all. Why is it that the level of critical sensibility has sunk so low? The threshhold for pain is so high, that people can sit through abysmal "conventional" reproductions of classical masterpieces in the theatre or in opera or in music rather than experience something quite new in a contemporary work or a dangerous or innovative re-staging of a classical work. I don't understand that. Do you understand it?

[*Marranca:*] *Well, certainly part of it, but not all of it, is that the commentary is so bad on the papers of note—that's one major issue.*

Well, there it becomes an important thing to talk about. This is where some of Gramsci's analysis of culture is very important, where you can look at the papers of note and the people who write commentary as sort of organic intellectuals for theatre interests. In other words, they are advance guard, in the military sense—advance guard organizers of opinion and manufacturers of consent for important interests in the theatre, whose role is to colonize and narcotize and lobotomize audiences into accepting certain kinds of conventions as the norm. I think that's an important part of one's work: to raise dissatisfaction at this time.

[*Marranca:*] *You know, the other thing is that, unlike the art audience, for example, which always wants to see something new, the theatre audience and music audience basically want to see the greatest hits in familiar settings. And so the audiences are fundamentally different, even though they might be the same people.*

[*Robinson:*] *But sometimes that struggling with those greatest hits can be very fruitful, and writers are doing it all the time. Hofmannsthal will deal with the* Electra *story as handed down and absorb it into a creation of his own. Heiner Müller will write* Hamletmachine *in order to kill* Hamlet.

Or, in some cases, to keep adapting to the changing conditions of performance imposed on him by the patrons.

[*Robinson:*] *It seems like there are two ways for contemporary artists to deal with this burden or oppressiveness of the classic tradition, and the canon. One is just to keep pushing it aside and write or compose new work. And then the other one—Hofmannsthal, Heiner Müller—is to try to absorb it and then remake it somehow, to kind of neutralize it, recharge it in a subversive way.*

I'm of the second opinion. In all of the discussions that have been going on in literary studies about the canon, and the whole question of the Western tradition, it seems to me that one of the great fallacies, in my view, has been the one that suggests that you, first of all, show how the canon is the result of a conspiracy—a sort of white male cabal—of people who, for example, turned Hawthorne into one of the great cult figures of American literature and prevented a whole host of, for example, more popular women writers of the time, or regional writers, and so on. . . . Therefore what is enjoined upon holders of this view is you push aside Hawthorne and you start reading these other people. But that is to supplant one canon by another, which, it seems to me, really reinforces in whole idea of canon and, of course, all of the authority that goes with it. That's number one. Number two—half of this is my education and half of this is my age and predilection—I'm interested in the canon. I'm very conservative in the sense that I think that there is something to be said, at least on the level of preference and pleasure, for aspects of work that has persisted and endured and has acquired and accreted to it a huge mass of differing interpretations, ranging from hatred to reverence. It's something that I find enriching as a part of knowledge. So I'm not as willing as a lot of people to scuttle it. My view is to assimilate to canons these other contrapuntal lines.

You could take the extreme view of Benjamin: every document of civilization is also a document of barbarity. You can show—and I've tried to show it in this book that I've been writing on cultural imperialism for ten years—that the great monuments (well, I did it in the *Aida* case) of culture are not any less monuments for their, in the extreme version, complicity with rather sordid aspects of the world. Or, in the less extreme case, for their participation, their engagement in social, historical processes. I find that interesting. I'm less willing to toss them overboard and say, "Let's focus on the new." I mean, I find the idea of novelty in and of itself doesn't supply me with quite enough nourishment.

[*Robinson:*] *The whole canon becomes an incredibly sharp weapon for a non-Western writer, too. Somebody like Soyinka can take* The Balcony, *or* The Bacchae, *or* Threepenny Opera *and rewrite them as parables of colonialism.*

And not only that, but in the best instances—I think more interesting than Soyinka is the work of the Sudanese novelist Tayeb Salih. He's written several novels, but his masterpiece is a novel called *The Season of Migration to the North*—it came out in the late '60s—that is quite consciously a work that is reacting to, writing back to, Conrad's *Heart of Darkness*. This is a story, not of a white man who comes to Africa, but a black man who goes to Europe. And the result is, on one level, of course, a reaction to Conrad. In other words, this is a post-colonial fable of what happens when a black man goes to London and wreaks havoc upon a whole series of English women. There's a kind of sexual fable. But if you look at it more deeply, it not only contains within it the history of decolonization and reaction to Western imperialism, but it also, in my opinion, deepens the tragedy by showing this man's reactive revenge, which to many readers in the Third World, in the Arab and African world, is a just revenge. But Salih does it fresh because it's futile, pathetic and ultimately tragic. Because it reinforces the cycle of isolation as insufficiency of the politics of identity. It is not enough to just be a black wreaking havoc on a white, there's another world that you have to live in. And in that sense, it's a much richer and more interesting work than Conrad, because it dramatizes the limitations of Conrad. And I'm second to none in my admiration for Conrad, but this is a quite amazing type of thing which is in the novel, which is quite powerful in its own sense—it's in Arabic not in English—depends on the Conrad novel, but is independent of it at the same time. It's quite fascinating.

[*Robinson:*] *And that may be a solution, as it were, to the whole problem of locality of a work of art. Because what you are describing can be both a very potent work in a local context, but it's also an intercultural work.*

Absolutely. And that's where I finally disagree with Bonnie's idea. In the implied contrast between the local and the universal, I think the local is more interesting than the universal. It depends where you look at it from. If you look at it from the point of view of the colonized world, as Fanon says, the universal is always achieved at the expense of the native. I'll give you a perfect example—look at the case of Camus. Camus is the writer who, practically more than anyone in modern French culture, represents universality. A more careful reading of the work shows that in every instance of his major fiction, and even the collections of stories, most of them are set in Algeria. Yet, they're not of Algeria. They're always parables of the German occupation of France. You look even more carefully at that and you look for the point of view of Algerian independence, which was achieved after Camus's death in 1962—and of course, Genet answers to this, because Genet was involved in the same issue in *The Screens*. If you look at that and you see what Camus was doing throughout his work was using the cultural discourse of the French Lycée—which gives rise to universalism and the human condition and the resistance to Nazism and Fascism and all the rest of it—as a way of

blocking the emergence of an independent Algeria. . . . It seems to me, *there* is the importance of local knowledge which you bring to bear upon this text. And put it back in its situation and locale. And there it doesn't become any less interesting, it becomes more interesting, precisely because of this discrepancy between its universal reach and scope on the one hand, and reputation; and on the other, its rather more complicit local circumstances. But maybe we're making too much of it . . .

[*Marranca:*] *I think in some sense we're talking about dissimilar things. Literature and the general secular intellectual life lead a more ongoing life in terms of debate and internal politics than drama does. I simply wanted to point out, if drama was no longer going to add in some sense to an international repertoire, and we were only going to have a local drama, which I value also, then that means something entirely different. For example, in drama we don't really have secular theatre intellectuals in the sense that literature does. Almost all discourse and dialogue and debate on theatre issues is either in the reviewing mechanisms of the popular papers, which don't have any kind of interesting debate going on internally, or in marginalized journals like our own, or in the academic world. So that theatre issues are not brought to bear on general cultural-political issues in the same way that other subjects are treated now, in science or in literature. So I think that this kind of loss is more serious for theatre than it would be in the novel.*

I think you're absolutely right, and I think—yes, I see your point. That's a much larger way of putting it.

III

[*Chaudhuri:*] *About the canon—this idea of not just throwing over one canon and putting another one in its place—it really seems that what's missing in that approach is that many people are not looking at how these things are taught and how they're presented. They're really only looking at what is taught.*

Yes, exactly, although "what" is important, also. The exclusion of certain "whats" is very interesting.

[*Chaudhuri:*] *But it's almost as if one doesn't want to give up something deeper, which is certain models of evaluating texts. . . .*

I call them models of veneration, and that's what they are.

[*Chaudhuri:*] *That veneration is transferred to something else, and it leaves you in the same abject position vis-à-vis the text or the art work or whatever.*

Well, it is one of the constitutive problems of academic debate in general, but it's basically unanchored in real engagement with the real world. It's largely theoretical. So the "what," on the one level, is equally important. It's a claim to certain kinds of authority and turf and so on. But the "how," you know, the "how" becomes relatively weightless, in a certain sense; it becomes one method among others. I'll give you an example of what I'm trying to say. Look at the result of all the massive infusion that American literary, and I suppose, cultural studies in general, have received through "theory" in the last thirty years: structuralism, poststructuralism, deconstruction, semiotics, Marxism, feminism, all of it. Effectively they're all weightless, I mean they all represent academic choices and a lot of them are not related to the circumstances that originally gave rise to them. For example, Third World studies in the university are a very different thing from Soyinka or Salih in their own immediately post-colonial situation trying to write a narrative of the experience. You know how sometimes a critic like Ngugi talking about decolonizing the mind is one thing for somebody who's been in prisons, lived through the whole problems of neo-imperialism, the problems of the native language vs. English, etc. They're very different things than somebody deciding, well, I'm going to specialize in decolonization or the discourse of colonialism. So that's a very great problem.

[Chaudhuri:] The academy is actively rendering them weightless . . .

In a certain sense you can't completely do away with that, because the university is a kind of utopian place. To a certain extent, these things should happen. Perhaps the disparity between the really powerful and urgent originary circumstances of a cultural method, and its later transmutation as a theoretical choice in the university, is too great.

[Chaudhuri:] Do you think it should remain utopian? Maybe that's part of the problem, that this is a model that has outgrown its usefulness.

I think that's where we are right now. We're watching a very interesting transformation. Most students, I think, the good students here, my students—and I know this from direct contact with them—are really no longer interested in theory. They're really interested in these historical, cultural contests that have characterized the history of the late twentieth century. Between racism and imperialism, colonialism, various forms of authority, various types of liberation and independence as they are reflected in culture, in aesthetic forms, in discourses and so on. So that's where I go. The problem is how you relate that to social change at a time when it seems everything is now moving away from the contests that determined the history of the twentieth century hitherto—the contests between socialism and capi-

talism, and so on. So it's a very troubling moment. I think the important thing is to be exploratory.

[Marranca:] You know, in fact, in the little piece in The Guardian *that you wrote, you mention that you felt somehow the history of philosophy and politics, and general drift of intellectual life, was really almost inadequate to deal with the new situations.*

I think it is. I think it certainly is.

[Marranca:] What directions might this view of the arts and sciences coming together somehow in some new understanding take? Where would you like to take it in your world?

Without getting too specific and detailed, I think that if you take a general thing that you've been interested in, interculturalism, I think that's obviously where it's going. That is to say, various types of integration between formerly disparate or different realms, like politics, history, and aesthetics. But rather than just leaving it at that, it seems to me that new kinds of formations seem to be particularly interesting and important. One would be relationships of interdependence and overlapping. We've had a tendency, you see, to think of experiences in national terms. We say there's the Polish experience, there's the French experience, there's the Haitian experience, there's the Brazilian experience. It seems to me that that's pretty much over, where one could give a certain amount of fidelity and attention to basic national identities. What's interesting is the way the national identities have historically, in fact—and the present moment facilitates that—interacted and depended upon each other. I mean the relationship between Brazil and North America is very, very dramatic now in the situation of the rain forests. The relationship between North Africa and the European metropolis is very dramatic now because of the presence of a large number of Muslim immigrants in France.

What you begin to realize is the universality, therefore, not of stabilities, which have been the prevailing norm in cultural studies, but of migrations: these massive transversals of one realm into another. That seems to me an entirely new subject matter. Refugee studies versus the studies of stable cultural institutions which have characterized the paradigms of the social sciences and the humanities of the past. That would be one major thing. Another would be the study of what I call integrations and interdependence versus the studies dominated by nationalities and national traditions. The conflict between emergent transnational forces like Islam which is a subcontinental presence, it's an Arab presence, it's now a European presence. There's a total reconfiguration of the cultural scene that can only be understood, in my opinion, historically. You could see elements of it already in the conflict between Europe and the Orient, for example, which I talked about twelve or thirteen years ago.

[Marranca:] Do you have any thoughts on interculturalism as it relates to performance or any of the other kinds of things you might want to take to your work, besides the Aida model of doing theatre history?

Not at this stage, no, because I'm so mired in *contested* regions between cultures. I'm very much, I'm afraid, marked by that. In other words, I'm really a creature whose current interest is very much controlled by the conflict between the culture in which I was born and the culture in which I live at present. Which is really quite a strange phenomenon. It's not just that they're different, you know, but there's a war going on and I'm involved on both sides of that. So it's very difficult for me to talk about interculturalism, which would suggest a kind of sanity and calm reflectiveness.

[Marranca:] Do you think of interculturalism as a kind of orientalism?

Well, it can be. Yes, absolutely. Because I think there's a whole range of what is acceptable and what is not acceptable. We haven't gotten to that stage yet, I don't think, of being able to talk about it in an uninflected way, in a way that doesn't bear the scars of contests between the North and the South, or the East and the West. I mean, the geographical configuration of the world is still very strongly inscribed, at least in my vision of things.

*[Robinson:] Drawing out of what's just been said, it seems that there's good interculturalism and bad interculturalism. But after I read **Orientalism**, a great paralysis set in.*

Sorry about that.

[Robinson:] Every time I consider or reflect on another culture, I feel my "power" position coming into relief. But is the alternative to that power just a greater distance or isolationism? I don't want that.

No, no, no. I don't think it's possible. You know, I think one of the great flaws of *Orientalism* is the sense that it may have communicated that there is no alternative to that, which is a sort of hands-off sort of thing. That's not what I would imply. And I think, at the very end I say something like that. That there is a kind of "already given," you know, a sort of messiness and involvement of everyone of everyone else. It's just that I would like to think that the inequalities, as between, say, a native informant and a white ethnographic eye, weren't so great. I don't know how to talk

about this without seeming to congratulate myself, but it was interesting, to me at any rate, that *Orientalism*—partly because I think that it was already in the air—seemed to have released a lot of quite interesting work that went way beyond it. It instigated a certain kind of self-consciousness about cultural artifacts that had been considered to be impervious to this kind of analysis. And the irony is it didn't make them less interesting, it made them more interesting. So I think the history of orientalism—I don't mean the book, I mean the problem—is really the history of human—how shall I put it?—human meddling, without which we can't live.

Look, any time you globalize, let's say East vs. West, you can come up with convincing formulas that always suggest the triumph of the West. That's why Naipaul is successful. I mean, that's the basis for the Naipaul appeal. He says the world is made up of people who invent telephones and those who use them. Where are the people who use telephones? We don't know that. See, you can always fall into that trap; the trap that C. L. James never fell into, because he said if you're a white man you can say you have Beethoven, and the black man's not supposed to listen to Beethoven, he supposed to listen to Calypso. That's a trap you can't fall into. You've got to be able to make the distinctions and use what you want and think of it as part of the possession of all mankind or humankind. I don't know how to get to that point without waging the struggle on some very local and clearly circumscribed level.

So on one level it seems to me that there's a need for historical understanding of various contests. That's why I don't believe in "literary studies." I don't believe in the study of English literature by itself. It should be looked at with West Indian literature, with American literature, with French literature, with African literature, with Indian—you understand what I'm saying? The deep historicization of the circumstances of production of culture and along with that, an acute understanding of the extent to which every cultural document contains within it a history of a contest of rulers and ruled, of leaders and led. And third, that what we require is a deep understanding of where we would like to go.

Frank Kermode (review date 7 November 1991)

SOURCE: "Off the Edge," in *London Review of Books*, Vol. 13, No. 21, November 7, 1991, pp. 3-4.

[In the following review, Kermode discusses the musical and political themes of Musical Elaborations.*]*

The Wellek Library Lectures at the University of California, Irvine, are meant to be about Critical Theory, and up to now they have, for good or ill, been faithful (in their fashion) to that intention: but it was an enlivening idea to ask Edward Said to talk about music as well, or instead. Said is a good enough pianist to understand what the professionals are up to. He knows a great deal more about music than most amateurs, and argues persuasively that it should not be left entirely to the rigorous mercies of the musicologists. The result is this very interesting, excited, crammed little book [**Musical Elaborations**], in which admirable and questionable propositions jostle one another so bewilderingly that it isn't always easy to know exactly where one is, or what might come next, rather as in a late Beethoven quartet.

There are really two principal subjects, and they remain somewhat at odds with one another. The first is a dutiful act of loyalty to the fashionable notion that works of art must be removed from the sphere of aesthetics for subjection to cultural-historical analysis. The most illuminating sort of writing about music, Said says, is 'humanistic' rather than merely aesthetic or technical—it must have its various roles in society and in history, its relation to the discourses of political power, strenuously investigated, just as literature is nowadays primarily a matter for 'cultural studies' and routinely submits 'to ideological or psychoanalytic analysis'. Many pages of the book politely argue with Adorno, who did that sort of thing, though before it became the vogue, with magisterial strength and gloomy inclusiveness. Said, deferential but still his own man, characteristically points out that to treat modern music as a reflection or portent of the world's present or impending ruin is actually a Eurocentric view, taken, with unconscious colonialist arrogance, to apply universally.

He knows far too much about music to believe that the musical canon is, like the literary one, a white male bourgeois fraud, and the second subject of his transgressive sonata is, roughly, the experience of music in solitude, of private performance and properly creative listening. This is far more interesting, and it establishes the right of Said's book to be taken more seriously than if it had offered nothing but a Foucauldian exercise in musical 'archaeology' or a New Historicist negotiation between musical and other discourses.

His views on world politics, and on literary and cultural history, are seriously held and already well-known, and he was of course under no obligation to put them aside when writing these lectures, even if they seem to have no very intimate connection with his personal experience of music. His most political moment occurs in a slightly apologetic digression on the life and work of Paul de Man. As everybody knows, de Man's most notorious war-time article argued that to tidy the Jews away somewhere—say, into 'a

Jewish colony isolated from Europe'—would not be much of a loss to European culture; and commentators have rightly been shocked at this perhaps juvenile but callous anti-semitism. Said's point, however, is that at the time when de Man was writing there already was such a homeland, in which the indigenous population was already being expropriated. The youthful Nazi sympathiser was casually recommending Zionism; and Said, whatever he's supposed to be discussing, will not lose his opportunity to point out the connection that existed between right-wing Zionism (now represented by Yitzhak Shamir) and 'officials of the Third Reich'.

These are serious matters but they have very little to do with music. It is as if he wanted to remind himself, and us, that there are things that are important beyond all this fiddle. It cannot have been easy for one who can lose himself, as Said can, in the apparently autonomous structures and private pleasures of music to take this line, but a sense of civic or intellectual duty drags him away from contemplation and compels him to write about these 'worldly' matters.

More germane to his musical interests, though still classifiable as cultural criticism, is his study of the conditions of modern performance—for instance, the alienating social arrangements of the concert hall. 'Performances of Classical music', he rightly observes, are 'highly concentrated, rarefied and extreme occasions'. Performance is a feat quite distinct from composing, which it has in large measure displaced from public interest.

Nowadays sharply differentiated from composers, performers are also clearly marked as separate from their audiences. They are even dressed differently. Most members of the audience play no instrument, can't get to know music by playing piano transcriptions as they once did, and in any case couldn't hope to play the way the pianist does: so they observe him or her in alienated but reverential ignorance, much as they might a pole vaulter.

True; and more might be said on this head. The most effective deterrent to concert-going is the nonsense in which all, performers and audience alike, feel obliged to participate, perhaps to establish that elusive rapport—the absurd, ritually prolonged applause, the ceremonial entrances of leader and conductor, the marching off and on-stage, the standing up and sitting down, all reaching its farcical nadir in the yelling, stamping foolery of the Proms. Nor can these antics be altogether avoided by staying away, for they are invariably described with affectionate condescension by Radio 3 announcers, who, day in and day out, do so much to represent every kind of music as a cosy indulgence for retired persons.

Said laments, along with Adorno and many others, that social and technological developments have gone far towards ruining Classical music by making it available in this way, or in recorded performance, invariant and therefore falsifying. He also deplores the musical pollution of our aural environment ('the demotion of music to commodity status'). On the other hand, he dislikes the way musicologists barricade themselves behind abstruse textual analysis, not risking the more 'humanistic' approach which places music in social and psychological settings. It sometimes appears that he wants music to suffer all the pains literature is currently undergoing (often at the hands of critics who remain unfamiliar with the private experiences that literature can provide).

This is conscientious, but it seems strikingly at odds with the preferred inwardness of his own experience of music; and it makes for a certain apparent confusedness of exposition. It is not easy to grasp the structure of these three lectures right away; listening to them must have been strenuous, despite the relief of musical illustrations. Said talks about a great many things, digresses, honours his critical commitments, and returns, with some relief but too rarely, to music as such. So there is a continual struggle between an intense private love of music and a conviction that the modern way of treating the discourses of art as unprivileged in relation to other discourses ought to be applied to music as to everything else.

Hence the stress on professional performance. The pages devoted to Toscanini and Glenn Gould are extraordinary. Said has to weigh against their admired interpretative skills the fact that they in different ways conspire to the maintenance of a social order: Toscanini giving performance appropriate to the sponsorship of a giant industrial concern, Gould abjuring the concert hall but making that very gesture an index of apartness and a permanent part of his performance. He most approves works which transgress social norms, or musical norms socially imposed—for example, *Cosi fan tutte* and Bach's 'Canonic Variations' on *Von Himmel hoch,* the latter because it is so enormously and gratuitously in excess of the 'pious technical sententiousness' of the chorale: 'pure musicality in a social space off the edge'.

He nevertheless complains about Bach fawning on the Elector of Saxony (and, presumably, Frederick the flautist), insisting that we ought to 'read' the B minor Mass not only for its 'astonishing demonstration of piety and invention' but as an instance of this crawling servility: 'the awe we feel in the Credo . . . reinforces the separation between ruler and ruled, and this in turn is made to feel "right" in great outbursts of joy (*et resurrexit* and *hosanna*).'

I don't find this acceptable. Is there not a surprisingly elementary confusion between music and how it was paid for?

Not that it is wrong to be interested in the original situation of such a work, or for that matter to relate *Aida* to the 'European domination of the Near East', or, for that matter, to acknowledge Mozart's endless willingness to comply with the demands of the people he wrote for and the customs of the countries he wrote in. But some discrimination is surely needed. The tone of dedications and letters soliciting patronage from potentates may strike us as embarrassing, but their language was surely well understood as conventional. You wouldn't write so when sending a manuscript to a publisher or even applying to the Arts Council for a grant, but in either case you would do appropriately what Bach was doing appropriately. Dr. Johnson wanted a patron for the *Dictionary* and the fact that we remember the case chiefly because he didn't get one doesn't mean he didn't quite properly try to. And surely the equation between specific sections of the Mass and the reinforcement of the political hierarchy is rather crude? Who would be bold enough to say that Said's own achievements are attributable to his willingness to benefit by pleasing the American academy? That the arguments of his splendid **Orientalism** are the counterpart of his desire to establish himself as an original, an émigré with distinctive gifts, and that we should 'read' him in this mode as well as the other? For he is surely affected by consciousness of his position in the top rank of American critics—at times he even writes like them, affecting that slightly condescending clumsiness that now passes for a grace in those circles. Yet I, and I daresay he too, would call it an impertinence to judge his work in that manner.

What makes his book valuable is simply his profound understanding of music and its performance. There is, in the final lecture, a fascinating account of what it was like to listen to Alfred Brendel playing the Brahms Piano Variations, Op. 18, a work he had not known, though he at once realised its connection with the String Sextet in B flat. He subtly distinguishes between that experience, and the experience of listening, in the same recital, to the Diabelli Variations, a work he knew well, so that during its performance he was attending to Brendel's interpretation rather than to the music itself, as he had done with the Brahms.

What is admirable in such anecdotes—including a few pages on the Arabic singer Umm Kalthoum, heard in his youth in Cairo, and a reminiscence of his own teacher Ignace Tiegerman—is an unmistakable and eloquent musicianship. The final lecture takes off from Proust's many meditations on music, and again Said's deepest pleasure seems to lie not in exhibitions of cultural criticism but in the recognition of music that occupies 'a social space off the edge', music that he experiences as indifferent to, as 'transgressing', cultural norms and conventions.

He applauds (but cannot spell) Messiaen and admires the

Metamorphosen of Richard Strauss, 'an essay in almost pure repetition and contemplation'—'pure' because independent of contemporary preoccupations and pressures not strictly musical, 'radically, beautifully elaborative, music whose pleasures and discoveries are premised upon letting go, upon not asserting a central authorising identity'.

This passage, stressing the privacy of his experience of this late Strauss work, comes almost at the end of his book. It seems decisive, until he adds a last sentence that hardly seems relevant to what he has just been saying: 'in the perspective afforded by such a work as *Metamorphosen*, music . . . becomes an art not primarily or exclusively about authorial power and social authority, but a mode for thinking through or thinking with the integral variety of human cultural practices, generously, noncoercively, and, yes, in a utopian cast, if by utopian we mean worldly, possible, attainable, knowable.' Here the exaltation he feels when he listens to the Strauss, sensing its solitude within his own, has got itself illicitly transferred, out of a sort of academic loyalty, to a professional critical programme for which he probably cares much less.

In short, the switch from private ecstasy to 'cultural practices' reflects a conscientious unwillingness to let go himself, and, in writing about music, to refrain transgressively from obeisance to professional formations and deformations. And yet, in the end, his awareness of the conflict between pleasure and duty adds to the interest of a remarkably rich and interesting book. Some obscurity, and some wavering of the expository line, may at least tempt one to read it again in search of the full sense of the argument, thus to be rewarded by the proof Said offers, out of his own experience, that when great music is heard by good listeners all talk of cultural criticism, and of aural pollution and European decadence, ceases for the moment to matter very much. Here if anywhere, in the solitude of the intent listener, is that small utopia, worldly, possible, attainable, knowable.

Malcolm Bowie (review date 29 November 1991)

SOURCE: "A Whole New Approach," in *Times Literary Supplement,* November 29, 1991, p. 8.

[*In the review below, Bowie praises Said's diverse insights and ideas about music in* Musical Elaborations, *concluding that the book enriches yet further problematizes music criticism.*]

Let it not be said that writers on music cannot write, for some of them certainly can. Here is Gerald Abraham, for example, discussing Chopin as melodist in *A Hundred Years of Music:*

> He had an instinct amounting to genius for inventing melodies that would be actually ineffective if sung or played on an instrument capable of sustaining tone but which, picked out in percussive points of sound each beginning to die as soon as born, are enchanting and give an illusion of singing that is often lovelier than singing itself.

The contrast between the continuous cantilena of, say, Bellini's melodies and the broken continuity of Chopin's has found its way into Abraham's syntax and given his sentence its own tune. He works hard to combine the technical description of sound-production with a lively account of musical pleasure being sought and found. But writing about music often goes awry when this sort of equilibrium is lost. Music criticism as a humanistic discipline is threatened on the one hand by technical analysis far in excess of its occasion and, on the other, by an empty striving for expressive effect.

Edward Said, in [*Musical Elaborations,* a] lecture series originally delivered at the Irvine campus of the University of California, is extraordinarily good at getting the balance right and at enlisting new rhetorical tools for the description of musical composition and performance. The lectures offer a set of trenchant notes towards a new kind of interpretative criticism. What writers on music most need, according to Professor Said, is an active awareness of what has been going on recently in neighbouring fields of interpretation, including feminism, cultural sociology and deconstruction, and a greater willingness to reconnect the quasi-autonomous musical work to the social and political force-fields in which it is produced, heard and studied. The new critical discourse that Said envisages is not, however, designed simply to create a public envelope for private artistic experiences. Said has much grander ambitions for it: to find ways of building bridges between the intimate, note-by-note unfolding of structured musical argument and the ambient structures of society, and, in due course, to do this systematically, without resorting to a trivial play of analogy between the two realms.

In producing his provisional sketch of this new, wide-ranging yet integrated approach, and in beginning to map an acoustic space that is also a social space, he is greatly assisted by the semi-technical term announced in his title: elaboration. This, it soon emerges, is a matter of working out and working through, of bringing complex structures to birth from simple-seeming initial motifs, and of allowing the labour and the laboriousness of musical craft to be commemorated by the critic even as he relives the easeful rapture that listening to music can bring. For music to be elaborate in Said's sense—which is derived in part from Gramsci—it has to be multiform, occupy the realm of transformational process and produce its effects of complexity, plenitude and completeness by an arduous espousal of the temporal dimension. And there is no real point in trying to cheat your way out of your time-boundedness, for music that refuses to be elaborate and temporal rapidly becomes shallow.

Said writes brilliantly about the musical works that for him best exemplify the self-delighting "elaborative" imagination at work. Bach's canonic variations on "Von Himmel hoch" are the supreme emblem of this creative *furor*. This work is

> an exercise in pure combinatorial virtuosity. The melody is set first in the bass, then in the soprano, then in middle voices, all the time that the figural elaborations imitate each other in strict canon writing at different chordal intervals. Yet the overall impression communicated by the work is of something plastic and benign: the fearsomely problematic contrapuntal difficulties negotiated by Bach are, as it were, completely disguised. Moreover, the chorale melody itself is displaced so often from one register to the other that we sense Bach's ability to dislodge even the chorale's pious technical sententiousness with polyphonic manipulations that testify to a demonic power.

By skilful use of notions drawn from modern literary study, writing of this kind speaks with appropriate energy and nuance about qualities of Bach's counterpoint that could easily have been allowed to ebb away in a well-behaved technical analysis. Even the unexplained side-step from "benign" to "demonic", in describing the general potency of a single piece, has its own contribution to make: Bach's inventiveness can indeed strike the hearer as obliging at one moment and disruptive the next—or by turns supremely sane and almost mad. Glenn Gould caught something of the same terrifying uncertainty when he spoke of the great fugues as belonging both to the civilized intercourse of human beings and to the unpeopled Northern wastes.

Baroque fugal and variation forms suit Said's argument well when he needs to characterize the ordered multifariousness of musical thought, for these forms allow many things to happen at once and do not drive over-zealously towards a pre-ordained harmonic goal. Over and against this vision of creative freedom, he sets the actual or potential rigidities of sonata form. For Said, the trouble with this celebrated organizing device, especially in its long-lived Viennese incarnation, is that it encourages a cult of wilfulness and control among composers. If they fail to take precautions, their chosen structure can make them: dominative, coercive, authoritative, combative, overtly administrative and executive. . . .

These and other adjectives, as they rain upon the sonata principle during the final pages of the book, seem to be gate-crashers from another kind of polemic altogether. They are charges that a gentle university humanist might be goaded into making against a particularly offensive Dean, but they have little aesthetic or political force when directed at Haydn, Mozart and Beethoven, or even at their imitators. Said caricatures the role of the sonata development section—it is "the space opened up between two strongly marked poles, the inaugural declarations, which is where the theme first gets stated, and at the end, which is where a final cadential formula winds things up"—and has nothing to say about the extremes of tonal uncertainty and waywardness that the great Viennese composers discovered there. The very longevity of sonata form can be explained in terms very different from those that Said deploys with such relish. Could it not be that the centrally placed zone of uncertainty in sonata movements remained fascinating for so long precisely because it introduced an asymmetry between the "strongly marked poles" of exposition and recapitulation, made it impossible for the one simply to repeat the other and provided an ironic counter-weight to the rhetoric of authority and control?

This is a wonderfully alert and audacious book, and one that, inhabiting border territory, has a proper readiness to be speculative and to take risks. Said is one of those major scholars who can bring a new comparative discipline into view before our eyes without appointing himself as its founding mandarin or its proprietor. He never loses sight of the fact that there is still much shared work for literary and musical scholars to do if the project sketched here is to bear fruit. And the book has an informing tension that other border-dwellers will immediately recognize. The pleasure principle draws Said back to an enraptured intimacy with the work of art, and an astute anthropological intelligence draws him away again to the highly organized social world that composers, patrons, performers, entrepreneurs and concert goers inhabit. The book is full of insights into matters that fall in the transitional region between "pure" musicality and music as social act: from the pianist or composer as superstar, to the rise of audio culture and to the role of personal reminiscence in the listener's experience of musical time. Said proceeds with zest and demythologizing acerbity.

At the end of the final lecture, the elegiac self-referentiality of Richard Strauss's last works brings Said to his own profession of faith. What the humane study of music now most requires is "a mode for thinking through or thinking with the integral variety of human cultural practices, generously, non-coercively, and, yes, in a utopian cast, if by utopian we mean worldly, possible, attainable, knowable". It is perhaps rather strange that the inward and backward-looking intensities of Strauss's *Metamorphosen* should bring us so abruptly to a progressive, public-spirited and outward-looking research programme such as this, and stranger still, when we remember the author's earlier exhortations, that nothing should be said about the ruined fabric of German society at the time. The pursuit of musical pleasure has won the day, in the present book at least. But as a whole, Professor Said's pioneering work makes possible a richer and more problematic view of *Metamorphosen,* and of much else.

J. B. Kelly (review date 26 April 1993)

SOURCE: "Imperial Masquerade," in *National Review,* Vol. XLV, No. 8, April 26, 1993, pp. 48-50.

[*In the review below, Kelly blasts Said's representations of the British empire in* Culture and Imperialism.]

In the beginning was the word. *Impérialisme* was coined 150 years ago, during the period of the July Monarchy in France, as a label for the attempts being made within the country to reclaim Napoleonic ideas and to reimpose the former imperial system. Passing into English as "imperialism," it was employed by British political writers in the 1850s and 1860s to describe the principles, imperial rather than republican, upon which Louis Napoléon sought to organize the government of France after he assumed the title of Emperor in 1852. The word had no connection at the time with what was later to be known as "the British Empire." Indeed, even so scathing a critic of Britain's acquisition of overseas territories as Richard Cobden never employed the word in his diatribes against imperial rule.

Only in the last quarter of the century did "imperialism" come into use to denote, usually with a degree of disapprobation, the process of imperial expansion. It was used by the Liberal leader William Gladstone in the aftermath of the Eastern Crisis of 1877-78 to condemn the conduct of the Tory prime minister, Benjamin Disraeli, in moving the British fleet to the Dardanelles, dispatching Indian troops to Malta, and annexing Cyprus. Gladstone was not opposed to the existence of the British Empire but rather, as he explained at the time, to its extension by armed conquest and its maintenance by military force, a system he termed "imperialism." Four years later, of course, he occupied Egypt. The word was also used in British political circles by critics of the Second Afghan War (1878-79) and of the Zulu War, which took place at the same time. Once introduced into the sphere of African affairs, the word

spread and flourished over the next twenty years during what came to be known as "the Scramble for Africa."

Since that day it has undergone countless changes of meaning in everyday usage, largely under the influence of Marxist-Leninist dogma. Not only has "imperialist" supplanted "imperial" as the adjective normally derived from "empire" but it has proceeded through a series of mutations, each more outlandish than its predecessor, until now it is no more than a husk of a word into which anyone may cram whatever tortured meaning he cares to. So it is with Edward W. Said, who in his new book subsumes under the heading "imperialism" virtually every contact Europe has had with the outside world since the eighteenth century. Not being an historian, he obviously feels himself absolved from any obligation to respect the imperatives of historical scholarship, and free to prosecute the Western world at will for the crimes he says it has committed against the peoples of Asia, Africa, and Latin America.

Culture and Imperialism continues and broadens the attack Said launched a dozen or so years ago in *Orientalism,* which argued that the very study of the Middle East by Western scholars was an imperialist act, for it furthered the aims of imperial powers and contributed to Western perceptions of the Arabs as inferior and of Islamic culture as second-rate. Now he argues, more ambitiously, that not only did the West lay Africa and most of Asia under the imperialist yoke, but it also forced its culture, especially its literary culture, upon the African and Asian peoples, at the same time deriding or denigrating their indigenous cultures. However, as opposition to imperial rule grew, eventually finding expression in nationalist struggles for independence, a literature of resistance and liberation developed among the native intelligentsia and their sympathizers in the West, which ultimately neutralized the pernicious influence of imperialist literature and paved the way for the downfall of European dominion in Asia and Africa.

At least this is what I understand Said's thesis to be. His writing is so diffuse, obscure, and overwrought that it is difficult to make out what it is he is trying to say—even though he repeats himself *ad infinitum* throughout the book. Take, for instance, this passage, on British histories of India.

> Whereas these official versions of history try to do this for identitarian authority (to use Adornian terms)—the caliphate, the state, the orthodox clergy, the Establishment—the disenchantments, the disputatious and systematically skeptical investigations in the innovative work I have cited submit these composite, hybrid identities to a negative dialectic which dissolves them into variously constructed components. What matters a great deal more than the stable identity kept current in

official discourse is the contestatory force of an interpretative method whose material is the disparate, but intertwined and interdependent, and above all overlapping streams of historical experience.

There are interminable acres of prose like this—muddled, inflated, impenetrable—which testify to nothing more than the author's awesome capacity for self-indulgence.

According to Said, the English novel was "immensely important" in the formation of imperial attitudes. "The novel, as a cultural artifact of bourgeois society, and imperialism are unthinkable without each other." A dubious proposition at best; but let it go. He chooses four novelists whose work for him embodies and promotes the ideas current in their day about the British Empire—Conrad, Kipling, Jane Austen, and Dickens. Conrad and Kipling one can understand, especially as they knew the East at first hand. But Austen and Dickens? It seems that by casually referring to Antigua in *Mansfield Park* Austen revealed that she had the empire in the back of her mind most of the time, that she was nevertheless indifferent to the condition of the subject peoples ("in *Mansfield Park* [she] sublimates the agonies of Caribbean existence to a mere half dozen passing references to Antigua"), and that she dodged facing up to her true responsibility to denounce imperialism and all its works.

Dickens in *Great Expectations* sent the convict Magwitch off to Australia, apparently a dreadful place unfit for decent Englishmen, which showed that Dickens knew a thing or two about what it felt like to be a despised colonial lad. Conrad, of course, as evidenced by the sentiments he expressed in *Nostromo, Lord Jim,* and *Heart of Darkness,* was a hopeless case, handicapped by "crucial limitations in vision," imbued with the "paternalistic arrogance of imperialism," and willfully blind to the existence of Africa's native culture. Kipling, surprisingly, is let off fairly lightly: although irredeemably tainted with the sin of imperialism, at least he knew India intimately and wrote about its people with sympathy.

To Said the *mission civilisatrice* of Britain and France in Asia and Africa was little more than a fraud. It conferred no benefits upon the native peoples but resulted only in "the murder, subversion and endless instability of 'primitive' societies." The eminent social anthropologist Ernest Gellner, of Cambridge University, has already exposed at length in the *Times Literary Supplement* the errors, omissions, and fallacies of Said's arguments about the French Empire in North Africa. I shall confine myself, therefore, to Said's animadversions on the British Empire, which take up a good third of his book.

It need hardly be said that he hasn't a good word to say for the empire. Its sole purpose, it seems, was to oppress and exploit the peoples of Asia and Africa who were unfortunate enough to fall under Britain's malevolent sway. The only legacy it conferred was to make its former subjects, whether white, black, or brown, feel rejected and despised. How Said could come up with such a grotesque caricature, so much at odds with the historical evidence, defies understanding. The answer, in part at least, may lie in the sources he cites in his notes. These consist in the main of *parti-pris* works of Marxist or neo-Marxist provenance, among which revisionist studies of the New Left school predominate—the "innovative work" to which he refers in the passage quoted earlier. His exemplars include such authors as V. G. Kiernan, Noam Chomsky, and Ali Mazrui. His sacred texts are vituperative tracts such as Frantz Fanon's *The Wretched of the Earth.* The standard authorities, such as the six-volume *Cambridge History of the British Empire* or the equally massive *Cambridge History of India,* are nowhere to be seen. Nor are any of the works of the great scholars of British imperial history. Very peculiar.

Said's big thought, which he proudly italicizes, is that "the enterprise of empire depends upon the *idea of having an empire.*" Not for him the old notion that much of the empire was acquired haphazardly, in a fit of absentmindedness, as it were. No, it was all part of a grand design, the intellectual foundations of empire being laid before the edifice was created. This, of course, is all nonsense. What Said is obviously unaware of is that the very word "empire," as applied to the overseas possessions of the Crown, did not come into use in Britain before the middle of the nineteenth century, by which time all these possessions, with the exception of the tropical African dependencies, the Boer republics, and a handful of Pacific islands, had already been acquired.

His lack of acquaintance with elementary facts about the empire shows up prominently in his section on British India, which he examines through the medium of Kipling's *Kim.* After beginning with the solecism of the "British East India Company" he goes on to speak of "British colonial officials" (India was never a colony administered by the Colonial Office but. eventually, an empire administered by the India Office), and to categorize India as "a territory dominated by Britain for three hundred years." In reality, it was not until the Battle of Plassey in 1757, which consolidated the hold of the English East India Company on Bengal, that one can properly speak of the beginnings of British rule in India. It was not until nearly a century later, with the conquest of Sind and the Punjab in the 1840s, that one could talk of British "domination" in India. From there to independence in 1947 was a hundred years.

Said seems to believe that the abolition of suttee and female slavery only came in the wake of the Indian nationalist movement. So much for the labors of Dalhousie as governor-general in the 1830s. Incidentally, Said is strangely silent about the centuries-old Arab slave trade from Africa, which was suppressed not by Arab nationalists but by intransigent "imperialists" like Palmerston.

The "Great Game" is defined by Said as "a sort of political economy of control over India," which would have raised a laugh beyond the Hindu Kush. Does he know when and how the term originated, or anything at all about the contest between Britain and Czarist Russia in Central Asia? Has he at least read Curzon? One doubts it. The great viceroy never appears in his book—although Christopher Hitchens, Alexander Cockburn, and Anthony Lewis all get favorable mention. Said further informs us that "after 1857 the East India Company was replaced by the much more formal Government of India." It was not. The Government of India had existed, in name and in fact, since 1834. It was the Crown, on the revocation of the Company's charter in 1858, that assumed through the India Office (the renamed Board of Control) direct responsibility for the governing of India, and sovereignty over those territories where the Company had been sovereign. Details, perhaps, but one tends to weary of an author whose pages are studded with historical inaccuracies of every kind, who has never read an imperial dispatch in the original, yet considers himself fully entitled to pontificate at will about the deplorable nature of British rule in India.

He is equally at sea with the rest of the empire. Until the eve of the Second World War, he tells us, Canada, Australia, New Zealand, and South Africa, like the tropical colonies, protectorates, and other dependencies, were governed directly from London. Evidently he knows nothing of the Balfour Declaration (of 1926 on Dominion status, not that of 1917 on Palestine) or of the Statute of Westminster of 1931 which accorded constitutional recognition to the independence of the Dominions. That's what comes of failing to read the right books on the subject. Another instance of this failure, one among many, occurs in the section of his book devoted to the literature of resistance to imperialism. He writes, basing himself on a book by an Arab nationalist, George Antonius, that "the Arabs, after liberating themselves from the Ottomans in 1917 and 1918, took British promises for Arab independence as the literal truth." If the Arabs "liberated themselves" from Ottoman rule, one wonders what the armies of the British Empire were doing in 1914-18 in places like Gallipoli, Egypt, Palestine, and Iraq. As for the accusation of British bad faith toward the Arabs, Said is on shaky ground in relying upon Antonius's book, *The Arab Awakening,* which is a work of pure advocacy, written for the purpose of influencing British thinking on Palestine on the eve of the Second World War. Moreover, its shortcomings have been devastatingly exposed by a far greater scholar than Antonius, the late Elie Kedourie, in his classic study *In the Anglo-Arab Labyrinth.* Said does not so much as mention this book, the existence of which he surely must, as a committed Palestinian nationalist, have been aware of.

The final fifty pages of his book are so embarrassing to read that it would be a kindness to draw a veil over them. He is outraged by the American air raid on Libya but not by the destruction of the Pan American airliner over Lockerbie or the French UTA airliner over Niger, the handiwork of Libyan terrorists. He deplores the war against Iraq, although he admits that Saddam Hussein was naughty to attack Kuwait. He concedes that the Middle East is in an appalling mess, the causes of which he quickly ascribes to the period of British and French domination, although he then goes on to lament that in those days, as compared with now, one could travel freely and in safety from Syria to Egypt. He holds the United States responsible for the Indonesian massacres in East Timor. He blames many of the troubles in the world on a demonic trio of "fundamentalists"—Ayatollah Khomeini, Pope John Paul II, and Margaret Thatcher. And so on.

What emerges from these semi-coherent ramblings is Said's abiding hatred of everything the British Empire stood for and everything the United States stands for in the world today. A strange emotion for someone who was educated at Victoria College in Egypt, an institution founded by the British for the education of the scions of the Arab upper classes, and who has found a rewarding academic career in the United States, crowned by appointment to a chair at Columbia University. But that is his affair.

Robert Hughes (essay date 21 June 1993)

SOURCE: "Envoy to Two Cultures," in *Time,* Vol. 141, No. 25, June 21, 1993, pp. 60-2.

[*In the following essay, Hughes summarizes the controversies and achievements of Said's life.*]

Huge as American academe is, it has few public intellectuals—men or women whose views carry weight with general readers off-campus. Near the top of any list of such people is a tall, elegantly tailored, 57-year-old American of Palestinian descent who for the past 30 years has taught English and comparative literature at Columbia University in New York City: Edward Said.

Said (pronounced Sigh-*eed*) owes his fame partly to his cultural criticism, notably his 1978 book *Orientalism,* a study of how ideas and images about the Arab world were contrived by Western writers and why. Now comes *Culture and Imperialism.* A plum pudding of a book, with excursions on such matters as Irish-nationalist poetry and the building of an opera house in Cairo for the launch of Verdi's *Aida,* it is the product of a culturally hypersaturated mind, moving between art and politics, showing how they do or might intermesh—but never with the coarse ideological reductiveness of argument so common in America nowadays. Said's theme is how the three big realities of empire—imperialism, "native" resistance, decolonization—helped shape, in particular, the English and French novel. *Culture and Imperialism* includes brilliant readings of Conrad, Kipling, Camus, Yeats and other writers. It has been extolled by such critics as Camille Paglia and Henry Louis Gates Jr., and roundly damned by others, especially English ones, who fixated on Said's suggestion that an awareness of Caribbean slavery ran under the ironic tranquillity of Jane Austen's *Mansfield Park.* In England you can dump on God, Churchill or Prince Charles, but touch Jane Austen and you're toast.

So is Jane Austen why Said's office at Columbia has been vandalized, and why he has received death threats from Jews, Iraqis, Palestinian extremists and Syrians? Is his dislike of poststructuralism the reason why thousands of American Jews think of him as an enemy, the P.L.O.'s man in New York? Guess again.

The fact is that Said, though by no means the only public Arab intellectual in America, is the most visible one: the voice of Palestine in exile. For more than 20 years he has been writing in defense of Palestinian rights and against the usurpation of Palestine territory by Jordan and Israel. His books on the subject, like *The Question of Palestine* (1979), are written, he says, "to bear witness to the historical experience of Palestinians."

Hence the attacks. A few years ago, an article on Said ran in *Commentary* magazine under the defamatory headline "The Professor of Terror." In 1985 his name turned up on a "confidential" blacklist circulated by the Anti-Defamation League of B'nai B'rith, implying that he was one of a group of "pro-Arab propagandists" in American academe who "use their anti-Zionism merely as a guise for their deeply felt anti-Semitism." When an academic association exposed this document, B'nai B'rith hastily retracted it and disowned its author. But trying to defend Palestinians against Israel's massive propaganda resources in America is, by any standard, an uphill slog, and Said has no illusions about it. "My endless beef with the Palestinian leadership is that they've never grasped the importance of America as clearly and as early as the Jews," he says. "Most Palestinian leaders, like Arafat, grew up in tyrannical countries like Syria or Jordan, where there's no democracy at all. They don't understand the institutions of civil society, and that's the most important thing!"

Said is not, in fact, a Muslim, but an Anglican. He was born in Jerusalem in 1935, the son of Arab Christians; his father, a wealthy merchant, fled to Cairo in 1947. English church, English education. In Cairo he went to Victoria College, "the Eton of the Middle East"—an anomaly, as Said remembers it, in an Egypt seething with anti-British feeling. Willy-nilly, this training ground for the colonial élite made him a child of Empire, giving him "a wonderful, very tough, English public-school education—ceaseless work." Its teachers were all English, extras from Lawrence Durrell's *Alexandria Quartet,* "nostalgic for home and free to cane the little wogs under their tutelage. There was general denigration of Arab society and the Arab world. The place to be was England. What mattered was English culture and English ideas."

At 15, fractious young Edward was expelled for "rowdyness," whereupon his father, who held dual Palestinian-U.S. citizenship, sent him to a boarding school in Massachusetts—"a tremendous dislocation for me, but academically very easy, after what I'd come from." At 18 Said became an American citizen. He went to Princeton for a year, studying literature, music and moral philosophy. Then he transferred to Harvard, where, after five years, he got a doctorate in English literature. Looking back, Said thinks, the odd thing about his student years was that "I never attached myself to a mentor, never at all. It's my perverse streak—I'm a natural autodidact."

This liking for the self-taught is at the heart of Said's attitude toward work. He thinks the narrowness of students' reference is "one of the great generational dividers," and dislikes the current academic obsession with "professionalism," which basically means finding and keeping your knowledge slot in an overpopulated field. This, he complains, is apt to turn lively undergraduates into timid graduate students "afraid of stepping outside the consensus." Professionalism, as understood in American academe today, "means you learn all the current rules of how to say things. I think that's one of the reasons why intellectual life in America is so stunted. It's a colossal bore. I'm much happier being a shameless amateur, in the original sense of loving things and doing them because you're curious about them, not because you have to."

Said's amateur passion, his *violon d'Ingres,* is music. He is an accomplished pianist; in April he gave duet recitals in New York and Washington with the Lebanese pianist Diana Takieddine. For some years he wrote music criticism for *The Nation,* and in 1991 he published a collection of his essays, *Musical Elaborations.* Today, afflicted by leukemia and acutely aware of the shortness of life, he is thinking of writing "a memoir of my pre-political life, which ended in 1967. What a strange world I grew up in!—a vanished world now. It's very hard even to find traces of it. I can let memory play all the tricks it wants. I want that, actually. Then maybe I'll write some fiction."

His writing and teaching have always ranged widely. Their base—laid long ago at Harvard—is the tradition of German philology, exemplified in America by the émigré scholar Erich Auerbach (1892-1957), that explores the modes and levels of representation in Western writing. "Representation"—how we see other cultures, how we depict them in our own through imagination and stereotype—is the core of Said's work, especially of *Orientalism* and *Culture and Imperialism.* But Said despises what he calls "the minority mentality" on American campuses. "My books are one long protest against it. The status of victim is not a passive blanket that you pull over yourself. You can always do something. Anyway, there's no such thing as a pure unmediated culture, any more than there's a pure unmediated self. All people, all cultures, are hybrid. I'm against essentialism. I'm against provincial nationalism. Yet people still insist on getting it wrong; they make the most absurd constructions on my work. It's not about saying imperialism was bad—you don't need a book to tell you that." Not the least absurd is the idea that Said's criticism aims to downgrade the classics by unmasking some of their authors' social or political assumptions. "How can you not believe in quality? I can't stand that line, it's so stupid."

Politics—and the haunting, obsessive questions of Arab identity—entered Said's life long after music and literature. His effort to put them together started after the 1967 war with the seizure of the West Bank. "Many of my friends who had studied in America began to be drawn back, and I began to be involved in the re-emergence of Palestinian nationalism." He set out to relearn classical Arabic. He got extra encouragement from his wife Mariam Cortas, the daughter of a Lebanese educator. "Mariam also grew up in the Middle East, but in an entirely Arab system."

The canard that Said supports Arab terrorism goes back to the '70s, and it is supported, his critics say, by the fact that from 1977 until 1991 he was a member of the Palestine National Council, a Palestinian parliament-in-exile consisting of some 400 members worldwide, which serves as an umbrella for the P.L.O. as well as for nonmilitary and nonterrorist organizations. Never mind that Said has always urged the P.L.O. to seek the conference table, not the car bomb, or that, to the U.S. government, the P.N.C. and the P.L.O. were wholly distinct. For the Israeli right and its American supporters they were one and the same thing. Thus in 1988, at the height of the Israeli crackdown in occupied Palestine, when Secretary of State George Shultz proposed talking to Said and another Palestinian-American professor, Ibrahim Abu-Lughod, to discuss his Middle East peace effort, Israel's Prime Minister Yitzhak Shamir vehemently objected. The meeting took place anyway.

None of Said's political foes have been able to cite a single utterance by him that could be construed as anti-Semitic or as condoning either tyranny or terrorism. Hence they fall back on innuendo, smear tactics or—in the case of Kanan Makiya, an Iraqi whose recent book *Cruelty and Silence,* directed against Arab acquiescence in the horrors of Saddam's regime, also fiercely attacks Said—on distortions of his views. The feud between Makiya and Said has been seized on, to the pleasure of neither, by American anti-Arabists. Said, declaimed A. M. Rosenthal in the New York *Times* last April, is the kind of Arab intellectual who preaches to other Arabs that "the enemy is, guess—the West, not the despotisms among whom they chose not to seek tenure." Such folk, he added, are the "silent servants" of terrorism and tyranny.

And such punditry is wide of the mark. Far from lending support to Middle Eastern despotisms, Said has harshly criticized them. He spoke out (while academe remained largely silent) for Salman Rushdie against the Iranian mullahs and their *fatwa:* "Those of us from the Moslem part of this world cannot accept the notion that democratic freedoms should be abrogated to protect Islam." He has inveighed against Saddam Hussein in Iraq and Hafez Assad in Syria. The "traditional discourse" of Arab nationalism, he wrote on the eve of the Gulf War, is "unresponsive, anomalous, even comic." The Arab media are "a disgrace," incapable of dealing with "life in the Arab world today with its terrible inequities, its self-inflicted wounds, its crushing mediocrity in science and many cultural fields." In sum, if Said is the Arab world's propagandist, it should hire a new one fast. He has always rejected the "tyranny and atavism" of Islamic fundamentalism, in the name of the secular, liberal and humane strand in Arab culture whose voices are silenced by Middle Eastern regimes and ignored in America. "People try to characterize me as a spokesman for the Arab states," says Said, "but I'm not. I've always tried to retain my independence. I've always spoken out against the leaders."

He isn't optimistic about the future, on either side. He sees Americans clinging to their Arab stereotypes—the fat grasping sheik, the crazy fundamentalist bomber. Meanwhile, "most Arabs today, including cultivated ones, have no hope of any kind of cultural exchange between them and the West. The mood is so desperate. The fundamentalist movement is in a sense an act of desperation: "The West won't listen to us, so we turn away from them.' That's the most discouraging thing, to me—the wholesale condemnation of America and the West, without trying to discover that America is a very contradictory, various place." Were ever two cultures so far apart, so blinded by their own distorted images of each other? But what better subject could there be, in this insanely fractured time, for an authentic humanist like Said?

Michael Wood (review date 3 March 1994)

SOURCE: "Lost Paradises," in *New York Review of Books*, Vol. 41, March 3, 1994, pp. 44-7.

[*In the following review, Wood appraises the strengths and weaknesses of* Culture and Imperialism, *linking its ideas to Said's earlier writings.*]

What redeems certain empires, or perhaps only the British, according to Conrad's Marlow, what saves them from mere rapacity, from being "just robbery with violence, aggravated murder on a great scale," is "the idea only. An idea at the back of it; not a sentimental pretence but an idea; and an unselfish belief in the idea—something you can set up, and bow down before, and offer a sacrifice to." At this point in *Heart of Darkness* Marlow is said to break off. It is "only after a long silence" and "in a hesitating voice" that he speaks again, and starts to tell the story of his journey to Africa and his meeting with the mysterious and dying Kurtz.

Marlow stops speaking, presumably, because he is troubled by the metaphor he has stumbled into. Bowing down and offering a sacrifice don't sound like the activities of an organized and enlightened Western mind. They sound like idolatry, even if the recipient is an idea rather than a barbarous deity. The very thing that (perhaps genuinely) distinguishes the British from the ancient Roman and the modern Belgian empires identifies it with the supposed savages it is unselfishly dispossessing of their land, and worse still, with Kurtz himself, the European who has gone native, whose house is surrounded by human skulls, and who has himself become someone to bow down before and offer a sacrifice to. African chiefs are said to "crawl" to him. As so often in Conrad, an argument begins to collapse into its opposite. There is a slippage at the heart of empire, a crack in its definition of itself.

Other features of empire are intact and unthreatened in *Heart of Darkness,* though, and even Conrad seems quite untroubled by them. The epigraph to Edward Said's powerful recent book picks up the passage on Marlow's idea a little earlier, and continues into the quotation as given above:

> The conquest of the earth, which mostly means the taking it away from those who have a different complexion or slightly flatter noses than ourselves, is not a pretty thing when you look into it too much. What redeems it is the idea only. An idea at the back of it . . .

As the carefully understated irony makes clear, Conrad was not a racist in the most obvious and virulent sense; he did not believe in the superiority of one race over another, and repeatedly mocks the very notion. But he did believe in race itself, as almost everyone did until more recently than we care to remember. Conrad welcomed the stereotype of the African savage, even if he thought (or because he thought) we were all savages at heart. He could see that Europeans might be as wild and morally benighted as Africans, or even more so, because of the veneer of their hypocrisy and refinement; he could not see that Africans might have their own enlightenment and civilization.

This is an effect of culture, or rather of power experienced as a cultural inflection, and such matters are the theme of Said's book [*Culture and Imperialism*]. But culture doesn't simply respond to power; it shapes the moral world in which power is exercised and encountered. In one sense *Culture and Imperialism* is a sequel to Said's *Orientalism* (1978); in another it is, as he says, "an attempt to do something else." Like *Orientalism* the newer work describes a culture of dominance, the way realities of power are both registered and masked in language and behavior; but it also explores cultures of resistance, the ways in which an ancient or emerging culture can speak within and against domination.

Thus *Culture and Imperialism* has a brilliant, affectionate chapter on Kipling's *Kim* ("we can watch a great artist . . . blinded by his own insights about India"), a scrupulous and painful chapter on Camus's fiction and its relation to Algerian independence ("Camus's narratives have a negative vitality, in which the tragic human seriousness of the colonial effort achieves its last great clarification before ruin overtakes it"); a complex, many-angled account of Verdi's *Aida* and its first performance in Egypt. But the book also has an intricate response to Yeats's situation as an entangled postcolonial poet ("His greatest decolonizing works concern the birth of violence, or the violent birth of change"), and a passionate account of what Said calls the voyage in, the moment in writing when the children of empire take up their own argument in the alien language they have been taught. Said's chief examples of this voyage, discussed in sympathetic detail, are C. L. R. James's *The Black Jacobins* and George Antonius's *The Arab Awakening:* he also makes acute comments on Ranajit Guha's *A Rule of Property for Bengal* and S. H. Alatas's *The Myth of the Lazy Native*.

> No longer does the logos dwell exclusively, as it were, in London and Paris. No longer does history run unilaterally, as Hegel believed, from east to west, or from south to north, becoming more sophisticated and developed, less primitive and backward as it goes.

The new perspective requires not a denial of what comparative literature used to be in the grand days of Spitzer, Auerbach, and Curtius but an extension of its interest to works of historical and sociological learning, and a reexamination of its old hierarchies, its (sometimes) implicit but (always) unmistakable Eurocentrism.

The real hero of Said's book is anonymous and collective; everyone who has been silenced or misrepresented by an empire, but who has said enough, or left marks enough, to encourage the chance of liberation. Frantz Fanon comes close to being the named hero, the bearer of a "cultural energy" which could move us beyond nationalism, seen as the continuing grip of empire's hand, into an authentic humanism, a term to be stripped of its conservative and self-congratulating intonation. "It is a misreading of Fanon," Said suggests, "not to see in him something considerably beyond a celebration of violent conflict." I'm sure this is right, although Said's dismissal of Fanon's support of armed struggle as "at most tactical" is a little swift—it was more than that—and doesn't even evoke "the justified violence of the oppressed," a phrase Said uses elsewhere.

However, Said's topic at this point is not violence but nationalism, and he already has enough difficulties on his hands. He doesn't want to refuse nationalism its legitimacy as a form of resistance to its imperial domination; he wants us to see that there are many forms of nationalism, courageous as well as crazy and tyrannical ones. But he also wants nationalism to be critical of itself. Only in this way can it modulate into liberation, and put an end even to the ghosts of empire. At this point, words like "universal" might make a comeback, because they would represent not the projection into time and space of whatever our civilization happens to be, but the discovery of authentically shared human grounds, old and new.

It will be more difficult to rehabilitate "objective," a word often found in the same lexicon, not because there are no common truths or because subjectivity is all we have left, but because "objectivity" has served too many forms of Realpolitik, has too often meant merely an insufficient curiosity about the status quo, as when the facts (our facts) are assumed to take care of all argument. Said quotes Fanon as saying that "for the native, objectivity is always directed against him." There are other objectivities, of course, which may be helpful to the native or which may be the native's own, as when an investigation reveals the lies and distortions of a crooked or unscrupulous oppressor. But even there, even when a relative objectivity can be substantiated and agreed on, there are also passion and polemic, not the mere, aloof disinterestedness the word "objectivity" mostly seems to proclaim.

This is a delicate matter, which haunts all of Said's work—indeed haunts much modern scholarship in all kinds of fields. He acknowledges the force of various Nietzschean skepticisms about the possibility of truth and knowledge, but clings to the idea that "there is such a thing as knowledge that is less, rather than more partial than the individual . . . who produces it" and that what he calls "the seductive degradation of knowledge" can be resisted. All knowledge is potentially political, we might say; it doesn't have to be, shouldn't be politicized.

Taking a cue from Raymond Williams, Said describes the elaborate involvement of culture in empire as "a structure of attitude and reference." This capacious phrase, almost obsessively repeated, begins to wear a little thin, or to look more like a talisman than a concept. Of course Said must have some such ample container if he is to recognize the ways in which texts are and are not determined by historical circumstance, but I still worry about the bagginess of the term. Is there anything that won't go into it? Like Williams, and like Lukács, his other *maître à penser*, Said deals frequently in the very broadest of propositions. The difficulty with them is not that we can't assent to them but that we can scarcely see what it would mean not to.

Said himself is certainly aware of this problem, and in his earlier book *The World, the Text, and the Critic* (1983) speaks of the risk of "soupy" designations and "sloppy" notions. Here he writes of the "unacceptable vagueness" which may attend words like imperialism, and offers two responses to this concern: we need to look at the details and differences concealed by the general term; we must not use them to avoid the hard realities lurking in the vagueness itself. This is persuasive, and in the case of empire the vagueness is a product of the sheer size of the phenomenon, of the fact, say, cited by Said, that by 1914 "Europe held a grand total of roughly 85 percent of the earth as colonies, protectorates, dependencies, dominions, and commonwealths." As a result, empire lingers almost everywhere, in minds and economies, even when it is supposed to have gone, and Said can plausibly speak of our political "context" as still "primarily imperial." We need to remember that the culture of empire often includes a magisterial denial of the possession of anything like an empire, or an interest in any such thing, as when the interventions of the United States in Asia and Latin America and the Middle East are pictured not as imperial gestures but as humble, even altruistic acts of peace-keeping. Or when the British and the Belgians indulged in the metaphors of bringing light to darkness which so caught Conrad's attention.

There are overstatements in *Culture and Imperialism*, uncertainties, contradictions. "The novel . . . and imperialism are unthinkable without each other." This is either untrue (people have been thinking of them separately for ages, that is what Said wishes to change) or a truism (all historical connections, however tenuous, look inevitable to hindsight). Said eloquently identifies and rejects the rhetoric of blame which riddles so many discussions of empire, but what he himself says very often sounds like blame, and he's the one who tells us that Conor Cruise O'Brien lets Camus "off the hook" by converting the historical fact of Western dominance in Algeria into the more metaphysical notion of "Western consciousness and conscience in relation to the non-Western world." There is an interesting analogy between Verdi's "imperial notion" of the total art work and the imperial gesture (Verdi's and others') which premieres in Egypt an opera about the same country's ancient splendors and miseries, a form of homage that looks a little like a takeover. But "imperial" is still a metaphor here, it elides Verdi's own opposition to Austrian imperialism, and to say that the notion and the gesture "dovetailed conveniently" makes the suggestive network of connections, what Said calls the "ghostly notations" of musical and political history, look like a pretty blunt operation after all. I'm still puzzling over what I think is wrong with the suggestion that Austen "sublimates the agonies of Caribbean existence to a mere half dozen passing references to Antigua." Is it that they are not agonies to her, even if we feel they should be; and that the word sublimates blurs the issue?

To note all this is not to demand of the critic some impossible delicacy or poise, but to remind ourselves that Said, like the rest of us, has more than one passion. A Palestinian who lives and works in New York, and a Christian Arab who was educated in Egypt and the United States, he inhabits a complicated, multiple world; and his book itself is speaking to several different audiences. If some readers are distressed by his insistence on the worldly embroilments of literature, others are upset by his kindness to his enemies. It is surprising, and affecting, to read that Said finds the famous images of empire—Gordon at Khartoum, Kurtz in Africa, T. E. Lawrence conspiring in the desert, Rhodes "establishing countries, estates, funds as easily as other men might have children," Bugeaud frenchifying Algeria, "the concubines, dancing girls, odalisques of Gérôme, Delacroix's *Sardanapalus*, Matisse's North Africa, Saint-Saëns's *Samson and Delilah*"—"haunting, strangely attractive, compelling." Some of those images seem a good deal more haunting and attractive than others, and certainly Said goes further than I would when he thinks Yeats's espousal of fascism "arrogant if charming."

What is important about Said's "contrapuntal reading" of works of literature—a reading in which ordinarily separate histories are allowed to play against each other, to produce not harmony but a complicated polyphony—is not its occasional bluntness or its sometimes overstated claims, but the range of insight and argument it makes possible. It is not only a matter, as he too modestly says, of provoking "a newly engaged interest" in canonical texts, or of making them "more valuable as works of art." It is a matter of learning how to find, in literature and elsewhere, what Said calls "a heightened form of historical experience": which I take to mean finding history in places where it ought not to have been lost, amid our favorite formalisms and decorums, for example.

This is what Said's demanding discussions of Camus, Flaubert, Forster, Gide, Yeats, Césaire, Neruda, and many others do for us. The point, to parody Marx, is not to appreciate the world but to understand it. We see the "strengths" and "limitations" of works we care about, Conrad's *Nostromo,* for example; we catch the references they themselves make to things we have forgotten, as I shall suggest in a moment in relation to Jane Austen; we gain or regain a "sense of the human community and the actual contests" that go into the formation of national and other histories, those of the British in India, for instance, and the Indians under the British; and we recognize in empire and its legacy "a compellingly important and interesting configuration in the world of power and nations." There is no exaggeration in such a claim, and by analogy we recognize other missed or displaced configurations too.

Culture and Imperialism is a hospitable book—surprisingly hospitable perhaps for a volume with such a turbulent topic, and for an author with such a (well-earned) reputation as a polemicist. It is a work of prodigious learning, littered with warm acknowledgments of authors and titles. Its very pages look like an active community of scholarship, and Said speaks eloquently of the university as a "utopian space" where politics are (must be) an issue but where such issues are not "imposed or resolved." We may think of the space as wider than the university, as appearing wherever thought and argument are active, wherever criticism in Said's sense occurs. The "social goal" of criticism, he says in ***The World, the Text, and the Critic,*** is "noncoercive knowledge produced in the interests of human freedom": and he asks, in a rather Jamesian turn, "What is critical consciousness at bottom if not an unstoppable predilection for alternatives?"

Literature itself would be a utopia in this sense, an idea we find in Kundera, for instance ("the novel is incompatible with the totalitarian universe"). But then this same utopian, critical space, if much wider than the university, is still pretty slender overall, threatened even within the university, vulnerable to all sorts of conformities, and always at risk when the predilection for alternatives, whichever way they run, is treated as treason.

There is an excellent example of regainable historical experience in Austen's *Mansfield Park,* which Said controversially discusses in ***Culture and Imperialism.*** Said's case seems at first sight very much overworked; a few mentions of Sir Thomas Bertram's possessions in Antigua support a whole structure of argument about empire and sla-very. Said shows analogies between running an estate and writing a novel, and between restoring order at home, where the young folks have been putting on a play, and keeping order abroad, where the natives are no doubt restless. When he writes that "there is nothing in *Mansfield Park* that would contradict us" if we were to pursue such connec-tions, a proper skepticism arises in us. This is how lawyers talk when their evidence or their witnesses are shaky.

But Said's evidence is not shaky, and he is if anything too discreet about it. He says, correctly but without quoting, that Austen continues to link colonial expansion with do-mestic morality "right up to the last sentence." If we turn to that last sentence with questions about slavery in our mind, we are likely to find it disconcerting. Should we have questions about slavery in our mind? Well, Austen had; it's her later readers who haven't.

In the last words of the novel we learn that the parsonage at Mansfield

> which. . . Fanny had never been able to approach but with some painful sensation of restraint or alarm, soon grew as dear to her heart, and as thoroughly perfect in her eyes, as every thing else, within the view and patronage of Mansfield Park, had long been.

The restraint and alarm have to do with the former inhabit-ants of the parsonage, who include Fanny's meddling and snobbish aunt, her glittering rival for the love of her cousin Edmund, and a man who made her an offer it seemed she couldn't refuse; but "patronage" reaches out into a world beyond Fanny's immediate experiences, and picks up dis-cussions earlier in the novel.

There is surely a smile at Fanny's enthusiasm in the words "thoroughly perfect," and a restriction implied by "in her eyes." The place is not perfect, because nowhere is. Austen has just said, in one of her milder relativizing touches, that "the happiness of the married cousins . . . must appear as secure as earthly happiness can be." How secure is that? How secure did Austen think it was? She goes on to specify by implication that this happiness involves "affection and comfort," and—a nice touch—the death of the incumbent at the parsonage, so the happy couple can move in. I don't think we should read Austen as sneering here, or doubting the happiness of the married cousins. But it is a worldly happiness, and the projected perfection, as Fanny herself knows, involves a plantation in Antigua, part of the patron-age if not of the view of Mansfield Park. Said's point is that it is precisely not part of the view because it is taken for granted: "Austen reveals herself to be *assuming* . . . the importance of an empire to the situation at home." This is true enough, although of course there is no reason why

Austen should not make such an assumption. More trou-bling is the implied attitude to the management of empire, and here Austen begins to look rather more like Conrad than you would expect.

Austen, like Conrad (and most other English novelists writ-ing before this century), accepts the idea of overseas pos-session; she fails to express any considerable interest in the human objects of British colonial attention, undoubt-edly caught up in the "recent losses" Sir Thomas Bertram has sustained "on his West India Estate," part of the "expe-rience and anxiety" he met there—although indeed his losses and anxiety may well have to do with the approach-ing abolition of the British slave trade rather than its heart-less flourishing.

But Austen does express unease, or allow space for unease, about the morality of overseas possession. Sir Thomas, hav-ing taken his mousy niece into his house as an act of kind-ness, is surprised, on his return from Antigua, to find she has grown into an attractive young woman. "Your uncle thinks you very pretty, dear Fanny," her cousin Edmund says. "You must really begin to harden yourself to the idea of be-ing worth looking at. . . . You must try not to mind growing up into a pretty woman." Edmund means to be kind, and has tried to frame his father's compliments with an appropri-ate moral reservation: "Though they may be chiefly on your person, you must put up with it, and trust to his seeing as much beauty of mind in time." Even so, "being worth look-ing at" is pretty brutal, and "beauty of mind" here sounds like the stuff you get at question time in the Miss World contest.

But the real problem here, which makes Fanny "distressed by more feelings than he was aware of," is that she is in love with Edmund, and we are to imagine the strange tor-ture of hearing these things from his mouth but not from his mind and heart. Edmund, blind to all this and not yet in love with Fanny, says she needs to talk to her uncle more, she is "one of those who are too silent in the evening circle." At this point Austen makes an astonishing connec-tion, which I should certainly not have seen without Said's instigation, between the commodification of women and a more notorious commerce in human flesh. Fanny says:

> "But I do talk to him more than I used. I'm sure I do, Did not you hear me ask him about the slave trade last night?"

> "I did—and was in hopes the question would be fol-lowed up by others. It would have pleased your uncle to be inquired of farther."

> "And I longed to do it—but there was such a dead silence!"

Fanny goes on to explain her diffidence: she didn't want to seem more interested in her uncle's doings in the West Indies, or specifically, "his information," than the man's own daughters were.

There is a lot of work for the reader to do here, and different readers will do different work. It's possible to see this moment as not *about* the slave trade at all; mention of it merely signals Fanny's seriousness and the empty-headedness of the Bertram girls. The dead silence is one of boredom. This certainly is how Edmund sees the matter, but his mind is not fully on it: he is thinking, as his next speech shows, about how wonderful Mary Crawford, the woman he is currently attracted to, is. And can it be true that Sir Thomas would have been pleased by further questions about the slave trade? What was his answer to the first? Perhaps the dead silence was his, and Fanny describes her diffidence because she doesn't want to seem to complain. Or she is embarrassed at the memory: she didn't mean to cause trouble or seem like some sort of radical, she only wanted a wise and authoritative answer to her no doubt foolish qualms.

For Said the dead silence suggests that the cruelty of the West Indies could not be connected with the civility of places like Mansfield Park, "since there simply is no common language for both." This is certainly the effect of the silence, and it is certainly the way many readers of Jane Austen see the matter. Several English reviews of Said's book thought the idea that Austen might (or might not) have anything to say about slavery was his chief and most ridiculous idea, and were illustrated with rather demure-looking prints of the novelist, as if she were a cultural icon to be saved from political desecration. But the silence in the novel must be local, rather than a reflection of the culture at large. The British slave trade was abolished in 1807, and most commentators assume the novel (written in 1811) to be set in the years just before that. The subject would have been much discussed, and might have been discussed even at places like Mansfield Park. Fanny was trying and failing to talk about the *news*. If the silence is Sir Thomas's, rather than simply that of boredom, we still have to guess at its source. Is he an embarrassed anti-abolitionist, or does he just think women shouldn't talk about these things? Is he fed up with all the talk about the slave trade, or just too distressed to talk any more?

Of course, we can't take these questions very far without writing our own novel; but that is not a reason for dropping them entirely. Slavery is not questioned in such a scene; but it is remembered, and there is no comfortable place for a critic or reader to be. The writing is so understated, so delicately unforthcoming, that at first we can only note the presence in it of a question that, in older, less contrapuntal readings, Fanny might be thought too frightened to ask and Austen might be thought too genteel to entertain.

Austen offers several stories here, or several possibilities of story, and such a move invites us to think about Said's suggestion that "narrative itself is the representation of power," a point he also made some time ago in a *London Review of Books* article called **"Permission to Narrate."** It's not that the powerless don't have stories, and it's not only that they don't get to tell the stories they do have. It's that they are scarcely perceived as capable of having stories, their stories are not so much refused as ruled out, unimaginable as pieces of recognized history. "With no acceptable narrative to rely on, with no sustained permission to narrate, you feel crowded out and silenced."

It's true that the acceptance of official stories often leaves little room for anything else, and that a person who doesn't share the assumptions of those stories will often seem to be mute. But there are narratives of resistance as well as of dominance, and Said's own work—his literary and cultural criticism, his writing on music, his polemical writing, his moving essay-memoir *After the Last Sky* (1986)—is itself full of stories, even if they are often brief and submerged, and sometimes only implied.

Or they are counternarratives, reversals, recoveries, refusals of a familiar or prevalent tale, the one that takes up most of our space and time. They are like the story of Said's mother's Palestinian passport, told in *After the Last Sky*: it is torn up by a British official during the Mandate in Palestine, since as a married woman she can no longer need it and since, the official told her, her administrative absence would create a legal space for a Jewish immigrant from Europe. Or the story, told in *Culture and Imperialism*, of the Arab Protestant minister who learns that the European and American authorities in his community now want Arab Christians to join the Orthodox Church, to return to the East, so to speak, as if a whole hundred years' missionary venture was just a Western caprice which could simply be called off.

Said sometimes writes of alternatives to narrative, of "lateral, non-narrative connections," or "anti-narrative energy" or "anti-narrativist waywardness"; but these are actually narratives themselves, other ways of telling, to adapt the title of one of John Berger's books. They are "broken narratives," in Said's own phrase, scraps of story, dissolutions, or diversions of the tyrannical single narrative. *After the Last Sky* transcribes a grimly comic interview in which a captured Palestinian is interviewed on Israeli radio:

"And what was your mission in South Lebanon?"

"My mission was terrorism . . . in other words, we

would enter villages and just terrorize. And wherever there were women and children, we would terrorize. Everything and all we did was terrorism. . . ."

"What's your opinion of the terrorist Arafat?"

"I swear he's the greatest terrorist of all. . . . His whole life is terrorism."

At one point, Said indicates, the man being interviewed makes a terrible linguistic joke or slip. He belongs to the "Popular Front for the Liberation [*tahrir*]—I mean Terrorization [*takhrib*]—of Palestine."

What is happening here relates only indirectly or ironically to the actual horrors of terrorism and violence, on either side of the fearful situation in Israel and Palestine. Even if this man were a terrorist, his performance would be a parody, a caricature of a nightmare. Of course, he might be frightened into this talk and just groveling. Or he may be brutally, blatantly cynical.

But the reading Said offers is the most persuasive one. The man lives inside a powerful story, and can defend himself against it only by mockingly accepting everything it says. We are looking at a dominant myth in action, one which says that there is only one kind of terrorism ("theirs") and that all captured Palestinians are terrorists. You can't answer such a myth, you can't even tell a clear counterstory that anyone will believe. You can only travesty it, repeat it as if it were a buried fable. Said says,

> This story and several others like it circulate among Palestinians like epics; there are even cassettes of it available for an evening's entertainment.

That story is scary too, of course. What if the parody turns back into a simplified, murderous version of the real thing? Well, we have to believe in the dark and lively sense of humor of those who are being entertained, which is a way of saying we have to believe they are as human as we are; no more, no less.

Two of Said's broken narratives in particular bring his work into focus for me, hang in my mind like elusive emblems of what that work is about. One concerns artists of great gifts, composers, novelists, or critics, whose historical situation or relation to language becomes a cage or an impasse: their very achievements lead them to frustration, they demand more of the world and themselves than either can give, their immense successes are caught up in what feels to them like failure. Swift, Hopkins, Conrad, in Said's accounts of them, all enact versions of this grand but hard story. There is also Yeats, struggling to "announce the contours of an imagined or ideal community" in the violent re-verse of an ideal world. Put together, these glimpses of brilliant and baffled artistic careers begin to resemble Adorno's account of modern music, which finds an austere integrity in the dead end into which it drives itself. And also lurking somewhere here perhaps is the example of Said's Princeton teacher R. P. Blackmur, who spoke of failure as "the expense of greatness," and said (of Henry Adams) "a genuine failure comes hard and slow, and, as in a tragedy, is only full realized at the end."

Said is drawn to these tales, and Adorno is an important figure in the argument of *Musical Elaborations* (1991), and in the relaxed and elegiac Lord Northcliffe Lectures which Said recently gave at University College, London. But the story I hear in his work is finally less stately and more dynamic than the one Adorno tells, more direct and less mournful than the one we meet in Blackmur. The artist is a hero, not because he wins or loses but because he acts, because he is faithful against the odds to a difficult idea of the self and the world.

The other broken narrative is a version, or an anticipation, of the story of the obliging terrorist. It echoes through Said's writing in quite different contexts, early and late, and it is the implied story, the narrative behind the narrative, of *Orientalism.* This book is very emphatically about the "system of ideas" by which the West has mapped the East, and says it acknowledges only "tacitly" the "lives, histories, and customs" of those who actually live in so-called Eastern lands. Said insists that he doesn't believe in any "real or true Orient," "some Oriental essence" to be opposed to a set of essentially wrong Western views. It's the very invention of the Orient that is the problem; it allows learning and sympathy and literature and adventure but it always risks tumbling into myth. Said quotes the scholar Duncan Macdonald on the Oriental's "*liability* to be stampeded by a single idea," and comments on the liability of Macdonald and his colleagues to be stampeded by a single idea about the Orient. In one of the quietest and most telling moments in the book, Said suggests that the "difference is slight" between the history the West has given the Arab since 1940 and the history it has taken from him. Much is to be learned from the thought that a theft and a gift might, in certain contexts or perspectives, be almost the same.

But then there are real people in the imaginary East, and Said's tacit acknowledgment of actualities is louder than he perhaps thought it was at the time, since it embodies a genuine passion for the unrepresented, for those who can't speak, but who flicker in the pages of *Orientalism* whenever Said invokes a neglected human history. He writes for example of "the disparity between texts and reality," of "the Islamic people as humans," of "individual Arabs with narratable life histories." What else but this reality, the untold story of this reality, would make Orientalism such a

problem-filled enterprise? Just how narratable those neglected life histories are, and by whom, is of course the
question we are looking at. Said doesn't want to speak for
the silenced or the ignored—the Orientalists are already
doing that—he wants their silence to be heard.

Not all Orientals are silent, of course, and not only Orientals are silenced; Said's broken narrative comes into play
wherever representation overwhelms the represented, and
we can all think of parallel examples. This is to say that the
story, as a story, concerns a group or groups of people who
are unable to represent themselves not because they cannot speak or have no stories, and not even because they
have been repressed, although that is often also the case.
It is not even chiefly a question of their access to the
means of distribution of narrative, although that too is of
course important. They cannot represent themselves, Said
is saying, because they are already represented, like the interviewed terrorist. A monstrous imitation stands in their
place, and is worked like the chess-playing puppet Walter
Benjamin evokes at the start of his "Theses on the Philosophy of History." They are different from us and their difference, usually but not always construed as inferiority, is
who they are. They have no other life.

At the same time the silence of these peoples has a charm
of its own and is a criticism of our noisy speech. This is
not to justify their silencing but to say they are not only
victims, and I find I want to associate the habits of secrecy
Said attributes to the Palestinians in *After the Last Sky*
("We are a people of messages and signals, of allusions and
indirect expression," there is "something withheld from an
immediate deciphering") with what he calls the "reticence,
mystery, or allusive silence" of music, the modesty of its
wordlessness. These reticences are worlds apart, of course,
but they share the sense of a realm that language can point
to but cannot name, that only community or the art of listening can inherit. In *Musical Elaborations* Said quotes
Proust on the subject of books being the work of solitude
and the children of silence, and thinks of the phrase in relation to Brahms: "I found myself coming to a sort of
unstatable, or inexpressible, aspect of his music, the music of his music, which I think anyone who listens to, plays,
or thinks about music carries within oneself." This is not a
retreat from the world, or a denial of worldliness. It is one
of the ways, and among the most valuable, in which we live
in the world. Solitude is part of who we are, and it can, in
communities of trust, open out onto shared silences, the
imagined music of our music.

Such communities are fragile and intermittent. They are
places where allusions are enough, and silences count as
much as words; where words too still count but have been
relieved of the burden of assertion and will. They are often more a memory than a fact, and sometimes not even a

memory. They are like home as Said describes it at the end
of *Culture and Imperialism,* evoking the exile of Erich
Auerbach, who fell into the East at Istanbul and found in
his mind the Europe he had lost. Said quotes Hugo of Saint
Victor, who thought that love of home should give way to
a love of "every soil," which in turn, for the person who
had become "perfect," should yield to a sense that "the entire world is a foreign place." Said's comments on this passage are wonderfully delicate and subtle, and can be seen
as offering an original reading of Proust's suggestion that
true paradises are lost paradises:

> Exile is predicated on the existence of, love for, and a
> real bond with one's native place; the universal truth
> of exile is not that one has lost that love or home, but
> that inherent in each is an unexpected, unwelcome loss.
> Regard experiences then as if they were about to dis-
> appear.

This is a truth for those who have lost their love and home,
and for those who have not; and for those who have returned
to them. Exile, as Said suggests earlier in this book, can
be a happy and an unhappy condition, a chance of belonging "to more than one history." It can be suffered or sought,
or imaginatively borrowed. It is a way of understanding
loss, and a way of knowing what there is to lose, the paradise that can't exist until it's gone.

David K. Shipler (review date 26 June 1994)

SOURCE: "From a Wellspring of Bitterness," in *The New
York Times Book Review,* Vol. 99, June 26, 1994, pp. 9-
10.

[*In the following review, Shipler expresses mixed emotions for the themes of* The Politics of Dispossession.]

Quite some time ago, in what I believe was my only encounter with Edward W. Said, we compared notes on where
we lived in Jerusalem—he as a Palestinian boy until 1947,
I as a correspondent for *The New York Times* more than
30 years later. It turned out that both our homes were in
the lovely, quiet neighborhood of Talbiya, an elegant quarter where well-to-do Arab families earlier in this century
built houses with thick stone walls, now covered with flowering vines of bougainvillea. The places where Mr. Said and
I lived were separated by a few blocks, a few decades, a few
wars and the great divide of dispossession.

Talbiya's Arab residents began fleeing in 1947, just ahead
of the warfare that engulfed Arabs and Jews as Israel
struggled to be born. Jews quickly occupied the abandoned
houses, making Talbiya a mixed, and tense, neighborhood

until February 1948, when Jewish troops used a sound truck to threaten the remaining Arabs into leaving. Since then, Talbiya has been populated almost entirely by Israeli Jews, which has made Mr. Said's truncated childhood in Jerusalem a wellspring of bitterness.

This may be important in understanding why a man of such intellect does not know how to speak to people who do not already agree with him. Buried in his newest collection of vitriolic writings, *The Politics of Dispossession: The Struggle for Palestinian Self-Determination, 1989-1994*, are serious ideas about Islam, the Arab world, Palestinian strategy and United States policy. These are coupled with provocative and justifiable assaults on American caricatures of Islam and Arabs and on the unwillingness of American society to give the Palestinian people "permission to narrate" their own story. The Arab world is condemned for failing to understand the West and for squandering its oil wealth on new hotels instead of great libraries.

> . . . reading Mr. Said is like being yelled at for hours on end, and it takes a good and willing ear to appreciate his calmer passages of insight, to hear the essential melodies that run beneath the discordant onslaughts.
> —David K. Shipler

But reading Mr. Said is like being yelled at for hours on end, and it takes a good and willing ear to appreciate his calmer passages of insight, to hear the essential melodies that run beneath the discordant onslaughts. Consider the 1991 gulf war, on which he spends several chapters. He assaults "the unmistakably racist prescriptions of William Safire and A. M. Rosenthal of *The New York Times,* as well as Fouad Ajami of CBS." And what is the author's basis for this grave charge of racism? That they "urged the most unrestrained military attacks against Iraq." That hardly proves racism, an epithet he uses to try to silence the opposing side in a broader debate over how the Middle East should be interpreted—the side that gives weight to the region's historical tribal instincts as elements of contemporary conflict. Mr. Said calls that view "Orientalism," condemns it as racist and thereby muddies his legitimate complaint about the American demonization of Saddam Hussein and the underlying perception of Arabs and of Palestinians as primitive, corrupt, sub-human, worthy only of being bombed and humiliated.

Mr. Said is a master of overstatement whose numbing invective often vitiates his arguments. But he does put his finger on a crucial truth about the way we see Arabs, pointing to a remarkably ignorant sentence about Saddam Hussein

in a 1990 *Foreign Affairs* article: "He came from a brittle land, a frontier country between Persia and Arabia, with little claim to culture and books and grand ideas." Mr. Said counters that Baghdad was "the seat of Abbasid civilization, the highest flowering of Arab culture between the ninth and 12th centuries, which produced works of literature still read today as Shakespeare, Dante and Dickens are still read. . . . Baghdad produced at least five of the greatest 20th century Arab poets, and without any question all of the top artists and sculptors."

He might help us see more clearly the Arab world's multi-layered cultures and histories if he wrote less about American misperceptions and more about Arab reality; an example is his final chapter, "The Other Arab Muslims," which expertly distinguishes between what is Islamic and what is Arab, between orthodox Islamic observance and militant politics. Since Mr. Said is a professor of English and comparative literature at Columbia University and not a scholar of the Middle East, he is most readable when he is slightly journalistic, etching sharp portraits of thinkers he meets on a visit to Egypt, for instance, or recounting his first trip to Israel, in 1992.

Aside from an introduction and an epilogue, *The Politics of Dispossession* is a collection of essays, Op-Ed pieces and dialogues (most notably one between Mr. Said and Salman Rushdie) published from 1969 to 1993 in *The Nation, The New York Times, The New Statesman, Arab Studies Quarterly, The New Left Review, Mother Jones,* and elsewhere. Structurally, they produce an unfortunate result: Because each is immersed in the issue of the moment, together they create a drumbeat of repetitiveness and no sense of evolution in the author's thinking. They repeat factual errors of the time, such as the exaggerated figure of 20,000 killed in Israel's 1982 invasion of Lebanon. They contain only superficial accounts of policy developments in the Palestine Liberation Organization, despite Mr. Said's membership on the Palestine National Council, the Palestinians' nominal parliament, from 1977 to 1991. Consequently, *The Politics of Dispossession* is susceptible to the same criticism that Mr. Said levels against Bernard Lewis's *Semites and Anti-Semites* in a review reprinted here. "He has now patched together a disorganized and tendentious book out of articles that have appeared elsewhere."

Two shifts of viewpoint are evident but unexplained. After years of excoriating Israel as racist and imperialist, he writes abruptly in 1991: "Israelis are not white Afrikaners; nor are they like French settlers in Algeria. They have a history of suffering and of persecution."

The second concerns Yasir Arafat. In 1983, when he was organizing terrorism and preaching the defeat of Israel, Mr. Said saw him as "a major leader" who had shaped Palestinians into "a national community" and "made the P.L.O. a genuinely representative body." Eleven years and 300 pages later, after signing the "ill-considered and stupid" P.L.O. agreement of mutual recognition with Israel, Mr. Arafat is suddenly autocratic, remote, not freely elected and, with his colleagues, "should step aside." Edward Said thus becomes the Norman Podhoretz of the Palestinians.

I confess to an unfair advantage: I know most of the people Mr. Said assails, including moderate Israelis who have long worked for coexistence with the Palestinians; he attacks them not only for their ideas but also personally, with a contemptuous tone that sounds false notes in every case. His line about Thomas L. Friedman of *The New York Times,* for example, could easily apply to Mr. Said himself: "He offers advice to everyone about how much better they could be doing if they paid attention to him." Still, this book makes you think—if you can think while gritting your teeth.

Ian Gilmour (review date 10 July 1994)

SOURCE: "The Broken Promised Land," in *The Observer,* No. 10578, July 10, 1994, p. 16.

[*Below, Gilmour sympathizes with Said's attitude about the Palestinian issues discussed in* The Politics of Dispossession.]

The most remarkable feature of the Arab-Israeli conflict has been not the great military and political success of the state of Israel or the hardship and misery imposed on the Palestinian people, but the West's heaping of praise and reward on the oppressors, and blame and penalty on the victims—a stark contrast to South Africa. Europe has for some time been more even-handed; not so the United States.

The struggle for Palestine is often thought to be one between two rights: both Arabs and Jews have a right to the land, But, initially at least, that was far from true. As late as 1917, Palestine was 90 per cent Arab. There had long been a small Jewish presence there, but by no stretch of imagination did the Jews have a secular right to Palestine. Hence, God had to be invoked.

The difficulty was that religious Jews did not believe in political Zionism—which means the turning of Arab land into Jewish, and the substitution of Jews for Arabs—and political Zionists did not believe in God. Virtually all leading Zionists had been non-believers. The founder of political Zionism, Theodor Herzl, was so little guided by the Old Testament that he would have been happy to settle for Uganda as the Jewish State.

As George Steiner put it: 'Zionism was created by Jewish nationalists who drew their inspiration from Bismarck and followed a Prussian model.' Yet somehow the idea got home that God had given Palestine to the Jews who, therefore, had a natural right to the land. So, as Edward Said writes in this impressive collection of finely textured essays, *The Politics of Dispossession,* 'a national movement whose provenance and ideas were European took a land away from a non-European people settled there for centuries'.

Unfortunately, that process was begun by the British. By the Balfour Declaration of 1917, wrote Arthur Koestler, 'one country solemnly promised to another the country of a third'. That promise was not only freakish, as Koestler said, it was politically frivolous. Having been Chief Secretary of Ireland, Balfour well knew the results of sectarian bitterness and land disputes, yet he recklessly foisted them on to Palestine with the disastrous consequences that we know. In 1948, by a strikingly thorough policy of ethnic and geographical cleansing, the Israelis drove out five sixths of the Palestinian population and so comprehensively destroyed 400 out of 500 Palestinian villages that no trace of them now remains.

Edward Said is chiefly concerned, however, with the last 25 years when the Palestinians have had to contend not with British frivolity but with American malevolence. He himself was born in Jerusalem, and when his family was 'dispossessed and displaced in 1948' he finished his education in the United States, where he is now Professor of English and Comparative Literature at Columbia. In 1967 he became actively involved in Palestinian affairs; since then in addition to writing a number of notable books he has been the most cogent and eloquent defender of the Palestinians and their right to self-determination.

That has been no easy task. There is no decent argument against Palestinian self-determination, as the American public evidently recognises. But the Palestinians are 'the victims of a victim' who in America is unusually powerful, and the views of the public count for little against the pro-Israeli lobby, to which the Senate is unfailingly obedient. Hence the Palestinian case has been customarily vilified or ignored, and American aid showered upon Israel. (That relatively well-off country gets nearly half the total American foreign aid budget. Per capita, Israel gets 700 times as much as sub-Sahara Africa.) With few exceptions American governing circles have been humiliatingly subservient to the Israelis.

The US media are little better. The owner of the once-liberal *Atlantic Monthly* and *US News and World Report* was only uncommonly candid in directing: 'I will not have a word of criticism of Israel in any of my publications.' Columnists such as A. M. Rosenthal and William Safire are mere Zionist propagandists. Others such as Anthony Lewis, William Pfaff and Stephen Rosenfeld are brave and fair, but they are a small minority.

Israel, therefore, can do much as it likes, and the unconsulted American tax-payer foots the bill. The internationally recognised frontiers of Israel leave the Palestinians just 23 per cent of Palestine—hardly an excessive proportion for the indigenous inhabitants. Yet, by building a mass of illegal settlements, Israel has stolen some 40 per cent of that remnant. In the Gaza strip 5,000 Israeli settlers and the Israeli army still occupy more than half as much land as 800,000 Palestinians.

The United States has underwritten such activities as well as the accompanying Israeli violence. It has effectively paid for the bullets which have enforced a brutal occupation—live ammunition has routinely been fired at children throwing stones, hundreds of whom had been killed and wounded. Torture has been prevalent, yet American hypocrisy is easily equal to treating the Palestinians as the offenders instead of as victims who deserve reparations.

As the settlements still grow apace, Said is gloomy about the future. He has no time for the Arab governments, little for Yasser Arafat. And he believes the incompetently negotiated Oslo Peace Accord to be 'an instrument of Palestinian surrender'. This fine book shows him to be an angry man; it also shows that he has much to be angry about.

Tom Narin (review date 8 September 1994)

SOURCE: "What Nations Are for," in *London Review of Books*, Vol. 16, No. 17, September 8, 1994, pp. 7-8.

[*In the following review, Narin relates the dual themes of dispossession and nationalism of* The Politics of Dispossession *and* Representations of the Intellectual *to Said's politics and personal philosophy.*]

The politics of dispossession is nationalism—an overgeneralisation which at once calls for precise qualification. It is quite true that not all nationalists are dispossessed: possessors have their own (often strident) variations on the theme. It is also true that nationality politics did not originate among the crushed and uprooted: indeed its primary source was the *nouveaux riches* or upwardly mobile of Early Modern times, in Holland, England and France.

However, their national-state politics only became nationalism later on, when these entrepreneurial societies inflicted their success on the rest of the world in the 19th century.

This infliction was Progress, which caused the un-progressed to feel for the first time dispossessed in the general and inescapable sense which amounts to an '-ism'. And it was out of that sense that the storm of modernisation emerged. The rest of humanity's patchwork-quilt could neither evade industrialisation nor put up with it on the imperial terms initially offered. The result was a counter-blast aiming at modernity 'on our own terms'—the terms (inevitably) of what existed before the newly-rich (and armed) nations emerged to rewrite the entire script.

That script—the 'history' which some imagined terminating around the year 1990—was mined by the very reality which it sought to recompose. In the dominant storm-centre itself a certain calmness could prevail: a false calm, as Edward Said repeatedly says in these books [*The Politics of Dispossession* and *Representations of the Intellectual*], founded on arrogance, ignorance and superior military force. The metropolitan view was that Progress was greater than its bearers and destined to triumph, regardless of the particular language it spoke. The Russo-Soviet or Anglo-British empires were simply vehicles for its dissemination. But outside the centre, wherever the contemporary frontiers of 'development' happened to be, metropolitanism was perceived as the exploitation of Progress in order to eternalise a particular national hegemony. *Their civilisation* will end by dispossessing us.

For collectivities, dispossession brings decease. The same is not of course true for individuals. All individual Palestinians could theoretically have opted to become, or at least have tried to become, Israeli, Jordanian, Syrian or (one of Said's own identity-dilemmas) American. This option has always been warmly viewed in imperial or sub-imperial capitals like Tel Aviv. But in practice it applies only to the educated. The unvoiced logic beneath it goes like this: if only the 'intellectuals' (trouble-makers) would mind their own (individual) businesses and honestly assimilate, then the non-intellectual majority would, after a certain lapse of time, well . . . disappear. Before nationalism arrived to change things, most ethno-linguistic communities we know about did disappear—or more accurately, were 'disappeared' in the Argentinian sense, like the Picts of North-Eastern Scotland. There was a time not long ago when the Palestinians looked like ideal candidates for disappearance. They could see the last sky coming, and after it nothing. Right up until the peace agreement last year there was no certainty of reprieve.

Another way of reading nationalism is just that: no more disappearance. For the majority of the collectivity, the collectivity itself remains the sole redemptive possibility. Hence its 'death', though metaphorical, is all too easily translatable into individual or familial terms. On the West Bank and Gaza, even though many Palestinians became successful exiles and émigrés like Said, there could never have been two million individual escape routes of that kind. If 'Palestine' doesn't make it, few Palestinians will. The point is not quite that nationalism is a matter of life or death—like the rawer nature which once prevailed—but that 'nationalism' has altered the nature of the species to make it such a matter.

The Politics of Dispossession and *Representations of the Intellectual* can be read as a single meditation on this theme. An intellectual ear marked for escape and successful metropolitan assimilation has turned back, and tried to assume the burden of those left behind. The burden is a crushing one. In a sense frankly admitted in these pages, it is too much for him or for any other individual. He has become the best-known intellectual spokesman of the Palestinian cause, yet was always far too honest and too honourable to be merely its loudspeaker. As the gross contradictions and failings of the cause have accumulated over thirty years, he has been unable to avoid registering and criticising them. So more is collected in *Politics of Dispossession* than scattered essays and reviews. It reads like a memoir of the Stations of the Cross, one continuous journey through the agonies and humiliations which have broken him apart—above all when inflicted, as so often, by those 'on his own side'. The critique of Arab nationalism and Palestinian parochialism in these pages is more devastating than anything put out by Zionists or the US Israeli lobby.

Said suffers from acute identity problems. So do all nationalist intellectuals. But since he is a famously fashion-conscious individual critics have rarely resisted the temptation to mock his identity-pangs. Paul Johnson wrote of him recently in the *Sunday Times* as 'a fashionable figure' with 'modish problems of identity . . . It is not clear to me,' Johnson continued, 'who, or what, the real Edward Said is.' The implication is that 'identity' in the political or nationalist sense is something like posturing in front of a mirror, but Johnson is the poseur here, not Said.

> My father as a boy sold crowns of thorns to tourists near the Sepulchre . . . Yet a few yards away, underneath a declivity in the city wall, we stumbled on Zalatimo, the renowned pastry shop whose speciality *mtaqaba* was a great family favourite. A wizened old baker was in there stoking the oven, but his ancient form suggested something only barely surviving.

Astonishingly, Said Sr., the Jerusalem relic-vendor, turned into an ace moderniser: he was the man who, via his Egyptian business, introduced filing and the typewriter into Arabic culture. He saw identity principally as a question of backbone, and was chronically upset by his son's inability to stand up straight, in the ramrod style approved by the Boy

Scouts and Victoria College, Cairo. The family were Greek-Orthodox Christians, converted to Anglicanism in the late 19th century. When young Edward's vertebral slackness got too pronounced for them he was packed off to America, aged 15. He had never seen snow, and was compelled to invent a new personality at a puritanical New England boarding school. A few years later he escaped to Princeton, and then in 1963 to New York's Columbia University as a teacher, where he has remained for thirty years.

This background provides an unusual identity-humus. What he likes most about New York is its anonymity. Self-consciously nationalist intellectuals are often susceptible to cosmopolitanism: secretly (or in Said's case openly) they feel most at home on the neutral terrain of exile and alienation. The very mechanism of identification—'standing up for' a people and a cause—requires a certain distance, an implicit separation of the self from background and community. A nation can only realise itself—register its patent rights, so to speak—in a voice that is recognisable to another, broader community, and which can give those rights an objective, inter-national resonance. The intellectuals, who articulate the message, can seem to occupy an ambiguous position; both sides can accuse them of betrayal. Said has had more than his fill of this.

Conservative metropolitans such as Johnson like to portray nationalism as an invention of intellectuals. There is some trite truth in this: all ideologies, including fogeyism, must initially be synthesised by the educated, a process which may then be misrepresented as wilful 'forging', 'dreaming up' etc. However, an ideology which has convulsed the world must be more than wilful. At this deeper level it is nationalism which has invented modern intellectuals. Their pre-history lay in the European Renaissance and Enlightenment; but these only prepared the ground for the increasingly extra-European modernity of which nationalism is an inescapable part.

The development of industrial modernity could not avoid gross unevenness; the antagonisms that arose from such disparity were bound to be registered; those observing and reacting to them sought another language for the new facts; that language had to be at once vernacular (accessible to the less educated) and universal (translatable into rights and principles). It had to transcend, rather than 'disappear', the parochial and ethnic. It had to establish a new connection with the universal and only the paradox of 'nation-ism' (as it might also have been called) could do this. Its machinery for doing so took the form of distinct nationalist intelligentsias: egg-heads of ethnos, who placed (as Said does) increasing emphasis on the choice of what once lay far beneath any conscious choice: 'identity'.

'Nationalism' is in one sense no more than a general title

for this language—the evolving tongue of modernity. Said began to speak it in earnest in 1967, after the Six-Day War; 'That awful week in June', he calls it, when he grasped more fully that 'I was an Arab, and we—"you" to most of my embarrassed friends—were being whipped.' From this cat-o'-nine-tails initiation was born *Orientalism,* his most celebrated work. Imperialism had fostered a self-interested mythology of the Arab Orient, he argued, in which academics and poets had colluded with missionaries, statesmen and entrepreneurial desperadoes. The result was a romantic conception frequently exalted by love. But (alas) this was love for the noble natives as they were, or rather as they were imagined to have been—infants of an Edenic Islam untarnished by Atlantic pollution (including filing cabinets and typewriters). The converse of such affection was of course contempt, mutating into hatred whenever the natives went 'beyond themselves'. Orientalism demanded they stick to their true, veiled selves. Failure to do so merely revealed (as in the 1967 war) their congenital inability to adapt to modern ways: as useless with tanks as with democracy and women.

Arabism and anti-Arabism have something in common: the belief in a Pan-Arab *Geist* capable of effective, nationalist-style unity. Although he started off wanting to subscribe to this, an irreverent observer like Said could not long put up with it. He soon realised that it was no better than Pan-Hellenism and Pan-Slavism: conservative ideological trances induced by a rhetoric of racial solidarity to stifle popular and national trouble-makers—notably trouble-makers like him. In the introduction to *The Politics of Dispossession* (one of the best parts) he recounts how an earlier study of Palestine failed to find an Arab publisher.

> It's an interesting footnote to all this that when *The Question of Palestine* came out . . . a Beirut publishing house approached me about an Arabic translation. When I agreed, I was stunned to learn a moment later that I would be expected to remove from the text any criticism I had made of Syria, Saudi Arabia, and the rest. I refused, and to this day none of my books on Palestine has been translated into Arabic.

His new one stands even less chance, unless West Bank self-rule makes unexpectedly quick progress.

To get anywhere, Palestinian nationalism had to distinguish itself from this miasma. The author's quaint way of putting it is as 'a reductive process', or 'an attempt to decompose Arab nationalism into discreter units finely sensitive to the true cost of real independence'. It took the Palestinians twenty-five years, through a series of fearful defeats—the worst of them at Arab hands, in Jordan, Lebanon and Kuwait. 'The countries that make the loudest noise in support of Palestine treat Palestinians the worst,' he remarks an-

grily. On the other hand, when the *intifadah* mobilised the population of the Occupied Territories against Israeli control from 1987 onwards, it met with at least limited success quite rapidly. 'Recognition' is not a gratuitous extra benefit for a nationalist movement: in a sense it is the whole point (even if elaborate negotiations are needed subsequently to establish a polity). By March 1988, Said recalls, this was in effect won and symbolised in the meeting between himself, another Palestinian professor and Secretary of State George Shultz: the world now had to confront the reality of a limited but indefeasible national demand, one which would not be disappeared. Even so the effects of the confrontation were further postponed by the Gulf War, and the PLO's reckless support for Saddam Hussein.

Said sometimes wobbles badly on the latter topic. 'Both wrong and embarrassingly silly,' he concedes; but at the same time he denounces Israeli peaceniks for using such support as an excuse to break off relations—'as if the Palestinian situation under Israeli military occupation had been just wonderful before the Gulf War.' This is feeble rhetoric. I shouldn't imagine the Israelis thought that for a second; but the Iraqi Government had just been raining missiles down on them (as well as preparing a new big-gun variant of the Final Solution).

Orientalism was a scathing analysis of metropolitan-racialist nonsense. But nationalist counterblast always carries its own danger: an obsessive over-attunement to its object of denunciation. Reading these pages, one feels that the-cat-o'-nine-tails will never cease its work, the skin never grow back over the tortured nerve-endings. In part this has been a consequence of Said's particular circumstances. In New York he has had to endure daily combat with another kind of exile intelligentsia, the formidably organised Israeli-American lobby. European readers who are not aware of how aggressive and unscrupulous that mode of nationalism can be will find *The Politics of Dispossession* enlightening. It must have been like fighting the Six-Day War over and over again.

The obsessive undertow of *Orientalism* brought Said into conflict with Ernest Gellner. Reviewing a successor-volume, *Culture and Imperialism,* in the *Times Literary Supplement,* Gellner accused him of 'inventing a bogy called Orientalism' and attributing to it a far too pervasive cultural influence. The attack was twofold. First, Gellner was accusing Said of not locating his chosen cultural polemic accurately enough within a grander, epochal framework—the 'transition from agrarian to industrial society', which has long been Gellner's own preferred theme. He argued, secondly, that because it lacked this degree of theoretical articulation, the anti-Orientalist crusade had too often sunk into a banal vindication of its victims. If most Western scholarship and writing about the East is

Orientalist conspiracy, then hope must lie exclusively on the other side: in the camp of those put down, crassly categorised, or adored for the wrong reasons. But the trouble with this anti-imperialist 'camp' is the hopelessness of so much of it: vile dictators, censorship, clerical mania, and traditionalism incompatible with any sort of modernisation (Western-led or not).

On the first count I feel Gellner is quite right. Said is no theorist, and rarely situates his cultural forays within a wider historical perspective. It is quite true that Progress was bound to take off in one region of the world rather than another. Unevenness could only have been avoided with guidance from outer space by something like the miracle-stones in Arthur C. Clarke's *2001*. Progress might have erupted out of China, in which case some Atlantic equivalent of Edward Said might by now be denouncing Occidentalism and the near-universal contempt displayed by the academic lackeys of Peking for the bulbous-nosed and straight-eyed. Or it might (like *homo sapiens* itself) have come out of Africa. In that case both Said and Gellner would today be fulminating jointly over Septentrionalist delusions about colourlessness: the vacant brain-pans supposed natural to the pigmentally-challenged, with their slime-grey eyes, ratty hair and squeaky-voiced irrationality. In fact, for reasons still imperfectly understood, it originated in Atlantic seaboard societies and gave the initial leverage to a congeries of pinkoid clans.

On the second count, I am not so sure. Out of unevenness came nationalism, including the sort Edward Said defends, and I would have thought that *in the long run* the victims would be likely to tell a better and more accurate story about what happened to them, and about their own social and cultural histories before the big developmental change.

The trouble is, we live in the short run. And within this they will go on finding it extremely difficult to tell their story without rhetorical aspiration (which is what Gellner was denouncing). The reasons for this are not (as the victim-ideology tends to assume) subjective and moral ones—betrayal, bad faith and so on. They are institutional. Colonised and less-developed societies lack the means to evolve an adequate cultural riposte to the 'advanced' offensive. By contrast, the imperialists are over-endowed with professorships, research institutes, well-heeled anthropologists and literary periodicals (as well as with missiles and aircraft-carriers). Most serious inquiry can only be done from their point of view, even if the risks of Orientalist astigmatism remain inherent in it. All the same, to get a sense of the opposite and what it means, *The Politics of Dispossession* will serve better than Gellner. 'There isn't a single decent library in the Arab world,' Said complains:

To do research on our own past, our culture, our lit-

erature, we still have to come to the West, to study at the feet of Orientalists, many of whom have openly declared themselves enemies to Islam and the Arabs . . . [But neither has there been] any effort to pour money into Western universities to promote the study of Arab and Islamic civilisation, to promote that study in *our* interests. On all sides it is evident that as Arabs we are the world's intellectual and moral *lumpen-proletariat*.

So what 'the long run' entails is long indeed; a more integral process of modernisation, within which 'lumpenproletarian' status can be left behind, and both state and civil institutions built up. That is what nations are for. Or at least, no better way of doing it has yet been lastingly demonstrated. 'The Arab world,' Said continues, 'is undergoing a premature technocratisation' on the lines laid down by his own father: typewriters before democracy, as it were, leading to the ascendancy of the right-wing brutalism typified by Saddam Hussein and President Assad.

However, 'the Arab world' is a large part of this problem, not a solution. It denotes not a nation but something more like a 'people', in that purplish after-dinner sense so dear to Winston Churchill: 'the English-speaking Peoples' who have spread themselves round a bit, acquired a sense of destiny, retained certain elements of common culture—and never quite got over it. Under Thatcher some of us thought that curse would never go away. One of the few alleviating features of Majorism has been that it too has faded amid the general grime. Feeling that 'a world' is on one's side is a serious malfunction. Yet victim-status makes it more tempting to indulge such feelings, since 'worlds' may always be imagined as possessing a redemptive secret denied to mere nationalities. If the secular version lets down the dispossessed, then an even headier possibility can step in: the 'other world' of a common faith, in this case Islam.

Not that Said can be accused of wobbling in that direction. He remains aggressively secular: 'We must see the issues concretely, not in terms of the happy and airy abstractions that tend to dominate our discussions. What distinguishes the truly struggling intellectual is, first, his or her effort to grasp things as they are in the proper methodological and political perspective, and, second, the conception of his or her work as activity, not as passive contemplation.' This is the recipe for struggle which is also outlined in ***Representations of the Intellectual.*** Said has nobly lived up to its criteria during his long activity as champion of the Palestinian national cause. Among nationalist intellectuals I know or have read about, I cannot think of anyone less like the 'Professor of Terrorism' so often invoked by the US-Israeli lobby.

The accusation has been revived none the less, in connection with his denunciation of last year's agreement between Arafat and Rabin. The story here is mainly in the Introduction and the Epilogue to **The Politics of Dispossession.** The former recounts his mounting disillusionment with the PLO leadership long before the historic accord. The most surprising aspect of this to many readers will be the mulish parochialism of that leadership. In Said's account it had no idea at all of how American politics and public opinion functioned. All through the Eighties

> Arafat was neither fighting to expand solidarity for Palestinians in the West nor nurturing the logical Palestinian constituency . . . of liberals; dissenters, the women's movement, and so on. Instead he and his associates seemed to be looking for patrons in the West who would get them a solution of some sort. This quixotic fantasy originated in the notion that the United States worked like, say, Syria or Iraq: get close to someone close to the Maximum leader and all doors will open.

When the door did inch open at last, Arafat rushed to get his foot in. In 1985 he had told Said that he had no intention of ending up 'with nothing to show for his decades of effort against the Zionist movement'. Said now accuses the PLO of accepting something uncomfortably close to nothing: the tiny roof of Gaza and Jericho against the last sky, the most cramped space for manoeuvre one can imagine qualifying for 'self-government'.

But Said's denunciation of this climb-down is at once accompanied by modest, practical proposals for making the most of it—for enlarging the space and turning his country into a genuine nation. He contrasts the old nation-building slogan of Zionism—'another acre, another goat'—to the apocalyptic assertiveness which has dogged both Arab and PLO rhetoric. In the new situation, he suggests, a version of the former must now be worked out for Palestinians.

This 'counter-strategy' is a nation-building prospectus founded upon maximisation of the very few assets the Palestinians possess. This almost uniquely dispossessed people, he argues, has one hugely under-exploited advantage: perhaps the largest, most able and most dispersed intelligentsia any national movement has ever been able to claim. Zionism is the obvious historical precedent; but it should also be remembered how divided Jewish intellectuals were, and how strong anti-Zionism remained among them until World War Two. By contrast, Said observes:

> Throughout the Arab world, Europe, and the United States there are extraordinarily large numbers of gifted and successful Palestinians who have made a mark in medicine, law, banking, planning, architecture, journalism, industry, education, contracting. Most of these

people have contributed only a tiny fraction of what they could to the Palestinian national effort.

What is now required is an international effort at nation-state building—qualitatively different from the earlier efforts of the PLO and the *intifadah*—an invention of 'ways of countering the facts with our own facts and institutions, and finally of asserting our national presence, democratically and with mass participation'. Small-country, secular, democratic, institutional, acre-and-goat nationalism, in other words, assisted by a diaspora middle class. It resembles Jewish nationalism minus the Zionist component. Also, it is virtually the opposite of what Saddam Hussein, King Hussein, President Assad and (intermittently) the PLO have stood for: the 'Arab world' of dictatorial cliques, violent paranoia, mass oppression and (potentially) theocratic convulsions. No wonder they hate the Palestinians so much: paradoxically, the most hopeless of causes offers the only real hope on the Middle Eastern scene.

George M. Wilson (review date October 1994)

SOURCE: "Edward Said on Contrapuntal Reading," in *Philosophy and Literature*, Vol. 18, No. 2, October, 1994, pp. 265-73.

[*In the following review, Wilson examines Said's notion of "contrapuntal reading" exemplified by Said's close reading of Jane Austen's novel* Mansfield Park *in* Culture and Imperialism.]

Edward Said's rich and powerful new book, **Culture and Imperialism,** offers, as one strand of its multifaceted discussion, methodological reflections on the reading and interpretation of works of narrative fiction. More specifically, Said delineates and defends what he calls a "contrapuntal" reading (or analysis) of the texts in question. I am sympathetic to much of what Said aims to accomplish in this endeavor, but I am also puzzled about some key aspects of his proposal. I will begin by presenting a brief sketch of my understanding of what a contrapuntal reading involves, and I will then explain some of the doubts and puzzlement I feel. Unfortunately, there is much that Said says about even this limited topic that I will have to by-pass, but I hope to say enough to initiate some helpful discussion of the issues. I should note that although the topic of "contrapuntal reading" recurs with significant emphasis throughout his book, Said's direct explication of the enterprise is scattered across several chapters, and the relevant remarks tend to be, in each instance, fairly brief. Given this state of affairs, I have tried to extract a reasonably unified account from a wide range of passages, and I hope to have done so as sympathetically and accurately as possible. Nevertheless, the fact remains that what follows is my reconstruction of the view that Said adumbrates.

Contrapuntal readings are meant to interweave, mutually qualify, and above all, superimpose the legitimate claims of internal or intrinsic readings of a work, on the one hand, and the claims of various forms of external critique, on the other. Such readings rest upon the fact that any literary fiction refers to or depicts a complex of materials that have been drawn from the actual world, e.g., actual people, places, institutions, and practices. These items are taken up and variously deployed within the wider imaginative project of the work. It is crucial to this deployment that the intended audience can be expected to bring to the text a set of background "attitudes" concerning the relevant real world materials, and that these beliefs, concerns, ideological presuppositions, etc., are elaborated within the work's embedded patterns. Thus, the text is anchored in what Said calls "a structure of reference and attitude," and this structure constitutes the base from which a contrapuntal reading chiefly proceeds. Reading contrapuntally, interpreters move back and forth between an internal and external standpoint on the work's imaginative project, with special attention to the structure of reference and attitudes it contains. From an internal standpoint, interpretation aims at explanation that respects the strategies and the density of the textual elements they implicate. It is important that the internal standpoint articulate the work's vision as compellingly as possible, not only because this has an obvious interest of its own, but because the persuasiveness of commentary from an external standpoint depends upon giving full credit to the sophistication of the text. (We will return to this point shortly.)

An external standpoint examines the problematic seductiveness of the work's capacity to guide its audience's responses and seeks to define the limited degrees of freedom within whatever complexity it establishes. By reminding us of information about the structure of reference that the work ignores, distorts, or minimizes *and* by reminding us that the structure of invoked attitudes has plausible alternatives that the work has effectively excluded, the external standpoint situates the text critically within a wider field of imaginative possibilities. As Said formulates the point, we read from an external perspective " . . . with an effort to draw out, extend, give emphasis and voice to what is silent or marginally present or ideologically represented" in the work.

In elaborating the account above, I have spoken of "intrinsic readings" of narrative fictions, and it will help to fill in my sketch if I specify the fairly standard conception I have in mind. Said does not address this as a separate topic, but I believe that the following remarks are fully compatible with what he seems to presuppose. In reading a story, it is fictional for the reader that he or she is learning of a sequence of narrative events, and the reader is generally licensed to ask after *explanations* of why and how the fictional history transpires as it does, where these explanations are to be framed in terms of the "implied" workings of the fictional world. The agents, events, and situations of that world are configured into various significant connections, and it is this network of fictional explanatory connections that readers try to infer. In searching for a global meaning of the work, audiences hope to arrive at a surveyable pattern of narrative-based explanation and thus to survey the narrative events in a manner that opens them up to plausible perspectives of moral, psychological, or political evaluation. When they read from an internal standpoint, readers employ a framework of explanatory background assumptions and normative principles that they take to be *authorized* for the work in question—authorized, perhaps, in the light of the author's intentions concerning such matters. However, when these same readers move contrapuntally outside their internal standpoint, they will knowingly adopt explanatory and evaluative frameworks that depart more or less radically from anything that the author or the intended audience could be expected to endorse. And they will do so on the grounds that the alternatives chosen are relevant to the questions raised by the work and are justified by what is independently known or seriously contended about its real world references. Within the internal dimension of a contrapuntal reading, one constructs the articulated upshot of participation in an authorized game of make-believe. Within the external dimension, one's reading rides piggy-back upon this participation and is responsive to whatever grounds one has for rejecting or, at least, resisting full involvement in the imaginative enterprise encouraged by the text.

As I mentioned earlier, Said does not attempt to work out in detail an explicit account of contrapuntal analysis. It is clear, in fact, that readers are intended to be instructed by the various extended examples of the practice that he provides. The first such extended instance is given in his commentary on Jane Austen's *Mansfield Park,* and it is the special role of this analysis to initiate readers into the methods and rewards that contrapuntal reading purports to offer. This sample interpretation does seem to me to be highly instructive, but I think we are taught equally about the prospects *and* the problems that a contrapuntal strategy engenders. Since Said discusses the novel at some length, I will consider only some of the arguments he puts forward, but, for reasons I will subsequently explain, the issues that emerge are, in my judgement, symptomatic of deficiencies or lacunae in his overall account.

Said reminds us that Thomas Bertram, Sr., the owner of Mansfield Park, is also the owner of extensive plantations in Antigua. In fact, through most of the first half of the book, he is absent from his home and from England because he has had to attend to his troubled business affairs on that island. This absence is crucial to the early development of the plot. Because he is away and his rather stern domestic management has lapsed, the normal ordering of life at Mansfield Park is falling into serious disarray. The situation is dire: heavy and improper flirting has been dangerously intermixed with indecorous preparations for an amateur theatrical. Fortunately, Mr. Bertram returns from his journey just in time to rout the imminent production and to quash the immediate causes of this decline into impropriety.

As Said notes, references to Mr. Bertram's Antigua holdings are relatively few in number, and they are made almost in passing. For example, it is never explained just what business it is that calls him to his plantation, and we learn nothing about how this business is resolved. From Austen's point of view—or so it seems—the visit to Antigua is little more than a plot device designed to motivate Mr. Bertram's lengthy absence, and that absence is made to last just long enough to build to a significant mid-point crisis. On a standard reading of the novel, the fact that *it is at his Antigua plantation* that Mr. Bertram is occupied appears to be incidental to the main narrative and thematic concerns.

However, Said's contrapuntal analysis of *Mansfield Park* insists that we are not to accept the targeted fictional fact as being merely incidental in this way. If the book invites us to unthinkingly and unblinkingly pass over the point that the economy and well-being of Mansfield Park substantially depends upon a distant Caribbean plantation, we are required to resist this heavily freighted invitation. And this is so, Said contends, because we need to reimagine the novel in full cognizance of the imperialistic presuppositions that lie only thinly buried beneath the apparently casual references to Mr. Bertram's overseas ventures. Whatever Austen did or didn't know about British colonialism in the Caribbean and elsewhere, *we* know that Mr. Bertram's fortune is sustained by the exploitation of foreign territory, the oppression of native peoples, and, more specifically, upon slavery among the workers on his land. Out of all these matters and more, in the novel only the question of slavery flutters equivocally into sight for just an instant and then immediately disappears.

Now, it is important that we be tolerably clear about what is supposed to be at stake in connection with a contrapuntal reading here. We can surely grant that Jane Austen and her readers accept, apparently without hesitation or demurral, most of the ideological underpinnings of British imperialism in the early 1800s. Moreover, as Said repeatedly points out, this situation remains largely unchanged as we pass through the ranks of major and minor British writers during the century. Said is also absolutely right to claim that

it is disturbing to observe how thoroughly even the crudest presuppositions of empire are left unquestioned within English literature despite the wealth of liberal and humanistic values that much of this literature supports and even celebrates. Still, as deplorable as this massive historical circumstance may be, it is by now a familiar fact that the English public, from economic top to bottom, were deeply and unreflectively imbued with the precepts, perceptions, and assumptions that underwrote for them the legitimacy of colonialism. It is really not surprising to discover that a stringently imperialist ideology recurs in work after work during the period in question. It may shock for a moment that even Jane Austen is implicated in the framework of imperialist thought, but, having registered the shock, we should conclude that it would be more amazing if she were not. Suppose, therefore, that all of this is granted. Nevertheless, none of these reflections do much to clarify the more particular promise that contrapuntal readings of *Mansfield Park* and other canonical novels will alter, in substantial detail, our comprehension of fine-grained narrative development. How, according to Said, is this elaborate counterpoint of interpretative vision supposed to be achieved?

In his analysis of *Mansfield Park,* Said advances several lines of commentary that might seem to help us with this question. For example, he suggests that we should view the heroine, Fanny Price, as a value-laden import into the Bertram household. That is, much as imports from the Antigua plantation are needed to support the domestic arrangements at Mansfield Park, so also, but in a complementary fashion, Fanny should be seen as the bearer of resources from outside which serve to reconsolidate and strengthen the Bertram family's power and standing. Working from this analogy, Said is able to read much of Fanny's story as a kind of allegory of the Bertram's unacknowledged dependence upon the wealth and other goods that they must regularly appropriate and employ. He says, "It is no exaggeration to interpret the concluding sections of *Mansfield Park* as the coronation of an arguably unnatural (or at very least, illogical) principle at the heart of a desired English order."

However, the comparison of Fanny to exports from Antigua strikes me as thin and arbitrary. It is simply too easy to propose linkages of this ilk and to spin alternative "allegories" from them. First, the sense in which Fanny has been imported into the Bertram circle is equivocal. It is true that they have brought her from her home in Portsmouth to live at Mansfield Park, but it is also true that the Bertrams are her kin—she is their niece and cousin. Second, and more important to present concerns, it is arguable that Fanny embodies the natural piety and virtue that give moral sense to Mr. Bertram's principles and a spiritual foundation to the proper way of life at Mansfield Park. Of course, the influence of this piety and virtue has been, like Fanny herself, neglected and misunderstood by the Bertrams. It takes the sundry disasters occurring toward the end of the novel to recall them to the true nature and importance of these underlying values. If one chooses to adopt this analogy instead, one will not be inclined to view Fanny as an import from outside, but rather as the unlikely receptacle of the values that have always supplied the Bertrams with their solidity and strength as a family. When the hearts and heads of others have been temporarily distracted, it is Fanny who holds fast to the family's ethical heritage. At any rate, this suggestion, quite different in force from Said's, seems at least its equal in plausibility.

Said also elaborates a different proposal that is considerably more promising. Our basic conception of Mr. Bertram and all that he stands for in the novel can seem to be transformed if we attempt to grasp and assess the character of the man while bearing sharply in mind the implications of his undepicted role as owner of a plantation in Antigua. On the whole, the book treats him as a worthy and honorable person. In particular, it endorses the strictness of his management of Mansfield Park. The estate will not run properly without his constant surveillance of its daily affairs, without his rigorous regimentation of his family's behavior, and without the overall discipline he enforces. The novel plainly demonstrates the vigilance that is demanded if plausible but pernicious threats like the Crawford siblings are to be rebuffed. And yet, when we imaginatively consider what Mr. Bertram's surveillance, regimentation, and discipline might amount to in the Antiguan context, we can easily form a vivid idea of how his stern, uncompromising 'virtues' could have a darker, more disturbing cast. Said suggests that we should view Mr. Bertram's rule over his plantation as a natural extension of the regime he has established at Mansfield Park. But, the former, we may be sure, will not have been tempered by familial affection nor by the laws and civilities that govern genteel life in the English countryside. Thus, according to Said, we are licensed to use our presumptive knowledge of Mr. Bertram's activities in Antigua to fill out our sense of his values, attitudes, and temperament. When we do refashion our moral portrait of him in this manner, the novel's largely benign conception of the man will be significantly disturbed.

In some ways, it seems to me that this proposal has considerable force, but, at the same time, it is also difficult to place it coherently within a broader reading of the novel. Let me offer just one illustration of what I have in mind. Said nowhere mentions the fact that Jane Austen renders some stern judgments of her own about Mr. Bertram, and one can wonder where these judgments fit within a contrapuntal reading in Said's mode. For instance, it is made very clear that Mr. Bertram has enthusiastically pushed his oldest daughter into a disastrous marriage with a rich and fatu-

ous neighbor, and his enthusiasm for her nuptials derives significantly from the prospect of the vast, adjoining properties that the united families will control. Similarly, Mr. Bertram turns rather ferociously upon poor Fanny when she perspicaciously rejects Henry Crawford's proposal of marriage. In his view, Fanny has been offered a startling promotion in wealth and social standing, a promotion to which she has no natural claim, and her perversity in refusing the offer moves him to considerable harshness towards his niece. There is no question but that Austen shows Mr. Bertram to be seriously wrong in his actions and judgments in these two cases. He is convicted, at a minimum, of greed, pride of place, cold insensitivity, and a considerable degree of outright cruelty. Mr.. Bertram is supposed to be a "good man," but, in these matters and some others, he is unambiguously condemned. Now, if we are reading *Mansfield Park* contrapuntally, it seems as if we should be allowed to employ these indictments to condition and modify our sense of the novel's relations to its Antiguan references. If Mr. Bertram is found to be at fault within his own family in the ways just described, why shouldn't we extend the verdicts and read him as even more strenuously faulted for his conduct as a colonial exploiter? Certainly, these very same "faults" would yield much graver consequences when exercised at his West Indian plantation. On Said's approach, as we have seen, we are entitled to bring our knowledge of British imperialism to bear upon our assessments of Mr. Bertram when he is portrayed at home. This is held to be a reasonable extension of our background knowledge into our imaginative involvement with the story. But then, why isn't it equally legitimate to bring the novel's negative moral judgments to bear upon the character when we imagine him in his business in Antigua? Isn't this an equally reasonable extension from the contents of the novel to our broader impressions of the implicit background? And, if this kind of extension is sanctioned, do we have in *Mansfield Park* a very early exemplar of an anticolonial novel, albeit one that is framed within the trappings of a domestic moral tale?

Naturally, I regard these last interpretative suggestions to be as absurd as Said himself would take them to be. Nevertheless, I don't see that there is anything in Said's discussion of and methodology for contrapuntal reading that would rule them out. We cannot object, as we might naturally wish to, that the whole subject of Antigua in Mansfield Park is too incidental to bear this sort of interpretative weight. As I indicated earlier, Said insists that the topic is not to be dismissed upon these grounds. What troubles me, in this and other of Said's examples, is the following. For all the merit of Said's objectives in developing the concept of contrapuntal reading, the constraints he appears to recognize upon acceptable analyses are far too weak. Given the goal of opening up a work to a range of alternative external perspectives, readers are permitted to employ any background assumptions and evaluative principles that have *some* relevance to *some* facet or dimension of the work. After all, even perspectives that are severely marginalized within the work are to be admitted. What is more, readers are not to rely upon their normal perceptions concerning the relative weight and importance of various elements in the text. And, finally, there can be no overall requirement that contrapuntal interpretative views must be consistent with the work taken in its entirety. The contrapuntal reader will often take special interest in the contradictions that a text can be forced to reveal. But then it is no wonder that, when these and similar constraints have been dropped, readers find themselves floundering among a confusing motley of radically diverse possibilities. (I have only hinted at the ease with which a host of possibilities can, with a little ingenuity, be constructed.)

The chief difficulty, in my opinion, is not that there are somehow too many possibilities, as if we knew the number of satisfactory readings that a work can generate. Rather, we should be troubled by the following consideration. Whenever we have a particular, powerful contrapuntal reading, such as the ones that Said produces in his book, it is usually a minor exercise to conceive of alternatives which apparently have equal force and epistemic status but which also contradict or stand in significant conceptual tension with the original. And then, viewing the overall situation from this perspective of interpretative conflict, it is likely to strike a reasonable critic that the choice of any one of the competing readings will be arbitrary and tendentious. It is liable to seem that each of the alternatives generated is less the result of sensitive but responsible attention to the text and more the product of an adamantly insisted upon outside agenda. Since Said, in his impressive investigations, plainly wants to avoid this insidious appearance, he needs to tell us more about the nature and evidential requirements of interpretation in the style he favors. He needs to fill out, as he has not yet done in *Culture and Imperialism,* the conditions that a convincing contrapuntal reading must satisfy.

Fawzia Afzal-Khan (review date Winter 1994)

SOURCE: A review of *Culture and Imperialism,* in *World Literature Today,* Vol. 68, No. 1, Winter, 1994, pp. 229-30.

[*Below, Afzal-Khan favorably reviews* Culture and Imperialism, *noting the lucidity of Said's prose style.*]

Edward Said's latest book, *Culture and Imperialism,* is, as the title more or less announces, a study of the ways in which the culture of imperialism preceded and undergirded the colonial enterprises of the big European powers of yes-

teryear, England and France, and, in today's world, how the same process continues with America playing the role of imperial giant. In many ways, the book is a continuation of the kind of "worldly" scholarly criticism Said inaugurated in his groundbreaking study, *Orientalism,* and in both books he is at pains to show how "great" works of Western literature have not been produced in a sociopolitical vacuum dubbed "objective art" but rather have been cultural expressions of the age's zeitgeist. Such a thesis allows Said to proffer what he himself calls "situated" or "contrapuntal" readings of texts as varied as Conrad's *Heart of Darkness,* Jane Austen's *Mansfield Park,* and Kipling's *Kim.* Thus, he is able to show how the so-called domestic novel of manners—of which *Mansfield Park* is such a typical example—derives from and is dependent for much of its value-coding on Britain's imperial activities abroad, a connection or "collusion" which has not been much commented upon by critics until very recently (or much noted in contemporary cultural work of the West): "More clearly than anywhere else in her fiction, Austen here synchronizes domestic and international authority, making it plain that to hold and rule Mansfield Park is to hold and rule an imperial estate in close, not to say inevitable association with it. What assures the domestic tranquillity and attractive harmony of one is the productivity and regulated discipline of the other."

> **Reading Said's prose is a most gratifyingly lucid experience for the critic and student of literature overburdened with the theoretical jargon that gained so much ascendancy in the past decade or two in the American academy....**
> **—*Fawzia Afzal-Khan***

Reading Said's prose is a most gratifyingly lucid experience for the critic and student of literature overburdened with the theoretical jargon that gained so much ascendancy in the past decade or two in the American academy, following its infatuation with French poststructuralism. It is heartening also to read someone whose scholarship is as wide-ranging and learned as his. It is therefore puzzling and somewhat disappointing that he should show so little awareness or acknowledgment of the work done by many postcolonial feminist critics on the topic of gender and imperialism, most especially that of Gayatri Spivak ("Three Women's Texts and a Critique of Imperialism") and, more recently, Jenny Sharpe in *The Allegories of Empire.* Aijaz Ahmad's critique (in *In Theory*) of Said's "difficulties with gender" certainly ring true here, but then Ahmad doesn't do much better himself; after all, the triad he concentrates on is all-male: Said, Rushdie, and Marx!

What propels *Culture and Imperialism* forward from

Orientalism is its acknowledgment and explication of the "Culture[s] of resistance" which sprang up and continue to do so everywhere in the world as a response to colonialism and imperialism and which have, in the realm of culture, led to a proliferation of counternarratives that have subverted the dominant discourse. The chapter "Resistance and Opposition" is well worth reading for its insightful references to and analyses of the works and lives of such great anticolonialist figures as Aimé Césaire, Amil Cabral, Frantz Fanon, and C. L. R. James; a very interesting portion of the chapter concerns Yeats and his legacy in the Irish resistance to Britain's hegemony.

By far the most moving section, however, is the concluding one, "Collaboration, Independence and Liberation," which may be said to reveal Said's idealistic core, what Ahmad deridingly refers to as his commitment to "High Humanism" but which I prefer to think of as his hope and belief in the highest principles of humanity. What is ironic (vis-à-vis Ahmad) is that Said links this vision for a future of humanity with Marx's vision as well—a vision, based in the words of Césaire and linked by James to the words of T. S. Eliot, that would embrace all of humankind and not just an elite class of the West. The lines that Said quotes many times in his book come from Césaire's famous poem "Return to My Native Land": "And no race possesses the monopoly of beauty, / of intelligence, of force, and there / is a place for all at the rendezvous / of victory." He also cites James's "contrapuntal" use of these lines, with other similar ones from Eliot's poem "Incarnation" ("Here the impossible union / of spheres of existence is actual"). This is how Said interprets James's contrapuntal usage:

> By moving so unexpectedly from Césaire to Eliot's "Dry Salvages," verses by a poet who, one might think, belongs to a totally different sphere, James rides the poetic force of Césaire's "truth unto itself" as a vehicle for crossing over from the provincialism of one strand of history into an apprehension of other histories, all of them animated by and actualized in an "impossible union." This is a literal instance of Marx's stipulated beginning of human history, and it gives to his prose the dimension of a social community as actual as the history of a people, as general as the vision of a poet.

Now granted that this is a very "liberal" interpretation of Marx's vision, and indeed Said himself goes on to acknowledge a few sentences later that he doubts there is any kind of "repeatable doctrine, reusable theory . . . much less the bureaucracy of a future state" to be gleaned from such an anti-imperialist liberatory rhetoric. Nevertheless, such an acknowledgment of the rhetorical power as well as the limits of discursivity (projecting an ideal unity of West and non-West) also gives the lie at least to Ahmad's charge of

poststructural "irrationalism" against Said, which appears rather irrationally founded (not to say contradictory) itself.

Far from "pander[ing] to the most sentimental, the most extreme forms of Third-Worldist nationalism" (Ahmad), *Culture and Imperialism,* which is a culmination of Said's evolutionary thought to date, embodies transnational and transcultural hopes and aspirations—fitting for an intellectual who has carved an admirable space for himself in the metropolitan culture of American academe, exiled from his native Palestine. It is not that, as an exile, he has forgotten or rejected what he calls a very "real bond with one's native place." A sense of homeland is indeed very sweet, but intellectual integrity born of exile demands that one not "derive satisfaction from substitutes furnished by illusion or dogma, whether deriving from pride in one's heritage or from certainty about who 'we' are." For, as Said astutely notes, no one today is "purely one thing." Labels like "Indian, or woman, or Muslim, or American" are just that: labels. Although Said recognizes the weight and reality of cultural differences, traditions, languages, et cetera, he is convinced that "survival . . . is about the connections between things." To be able to think sympathetically and "contrapuntally" about others means, in the Saidian scenario, "not trying to rule others, not trying to classify them or put them into hierarchies."

Barbara Smith (review date 28 January 1996)

SOURCE: "After Oslo," in *The New York Times Book Review,* Vol. 101, January 28, 1996, p. 19.

[*In the review below, Smith generally praises the themes and tone of* Peace and Its Discontents *but notes that "the articles are dated."*]

An intellectual, says Edward W. Said, a professor of English and comparative literature at Columbia University, must be a rebel against prevailing ideas. In *Peace and Its Discontents* he follows his own precept well: few can match the pungency with which he challenges conventional wisdom on the Middle East peace process—the belief that it is an ineluctably good thing, threatened by self-evidently bad extremists.

Mr. Said mounts his challenge from high moral ground, having long favored a political solution to the Arab-Israeli conflict. But the Oslo compromise he finds contemptible. His people, the Arab-American argues fiercely, have been gulled into giving away their trump—Israeli desire for Arab recognition—for little more than a pat on the back from the United States. The interim argument leaves residents of the West Bank and Gaza subservient to Israel, and also subject to the petty dictatorship of Yasir Arafat, a leader he finds beyond redemption.

A fatal weakness of the peace agreement, he argues, is that it squanders the gains and sacrifices of the intifada without getting in return any commitment from Israel on Palestinian self-determination, the status of East Jerusalem or repatriation or compensation for the Palestinian refugees. It splits the Palestinian nation in half, writes Mr. Said (who was displaced from his birthplace in Jerusalem in 1948), offering no future at all to the 55 percent, many of them stateless, who live outside the occupied territories.

Peace and Its Discontents brings together articles written after the September 1993 Rabin-Arafat handshake and is addressed primarily to an Arab audience. Though some of the articles have also been published in American and European magazines, they were originally written for Al Hayat, a leading Saudi-owned Arabic newspaper published in London, or for Al Ahram, a weekly newspaper published in Cairo.

Their sorrow and their anger are good, scolding stuff, an articulate tirade against perceived folly and uncritical applause. But, inevitably, the articles are dated. And since they were written before Yitzhak Rabin's assassination, some are off-key. Mr. Said's argument is based on the premise that the Oslo agreement enabled Israel to attain all its strategic and tactical objectives without its having to cede anything of value in return. Tell that to the Likud opposition, let alone to Rabin's confessed murderer. His assumption, moreover, that the terms of the agreement give Israel no cause for complaint or fear sits oddly with the current state of that country, now torn by religious and political dissension.

Mr. Said writes that Palestine must be restored "to its place not simply as a small piece of territory between the Mediterranean Sea and the Jordan River, but as *an idea* that for years galvanized the Arab world into thinking about and fighting for social justice, democracy and a different kind of future." This sounds high-minded, but the Palestinians' fight, so far as it existed, got nobody anywhere: the Arab world obtained neither social justice nor democracy, and Palestinians in the West Bank and Gaza continued to suffer from a repressive occupation. Now, at least, Israel has moved its troops out of most of the main towns in the West Bank and Gaza, and Palestinians have held free elections. What happens next is unknown.

The Oslo agreement is a gamble. The issues that matter most were left to the talks on a permanent solution, due to start in May. The Palestinians have no guarantee of getting what they want, or anything like it. Mr. Said expects the worst and could well turn out to be right: he certainly has reason to mourn the gap now yawning between the Palestinians in the West Bank and Gaza and those in the diaspora. But he tosses aside the inevitable question: what should the Palestinians do instead? Surely, he says impatiently, among six million Palestinians any number of alternatives could be found. Yes, but what were they then and what are they now?

FURTHER READING

Criticism

Alexander, Edward. "Professor of Terror." *Commentary* 88, No. 2 (August 1989): 49-50.
> Alleges Said's role in PLO activities, vilifying Said as "a literary scholar and ideologue of terrorism."

Bové, Paul. "Mendacious Innocents, or, The Modern Genealogist as Conscientious Intellectual: Nietzsche, Foucault, Said." In *Why Nietzsche Now?*, edited by Daniel O'Hara, pp. 359-88. Bloomington: Indiana University Press, 1985.
> Discusses the function of the intellectual figure in Nietzsche's *Genealogy of Morals*, Foucault's *Discipline and Punish*, and Said's *Orientalism.*

Brombert, Victor. "Orientalism and the Scandals of Scholarship." *The American Scholar* 48 (Autumn 1979): 532-42.
> Finds *Orientalism* "provocative," but suggests Said's fervent polemicism "colours" the book's arguments.

Brooks, Peter. "The Modern Element." *Partisan Review* XXXV, No. 4 (Fall 1968): 630-38.
> Brief analysis of *Joseph Conrad and the Fiction of Autobiography,* concluding that the book seems "dangerously to encourage psychological platitude."

Davis, Robert Con. "Theorizing Opposition: Aristotle, Greimas, Jameson, Said." *L'Esprit Créateur* XXVII, No. 2 (Summer 1987): 5-18.
> Discusses the theoretical implications of oppositional criticism, defining conflict and showing its limitations.

Gallagher, Catherine. "Politics, the Profession, and the Critic." *diacritics* (Summer 1985): 37-43.
> Examines Said's writings as a convergence of literary criticism and political activism.

Robbins, Bruce. "Edward Said's *Culture and Imperialism,* A Symposium." *Social Text* 12, No. 4 (Fall 1994): 1-24.
> Proceedings of a symposium at the Modern Language Association in Toronto, Ontario, in December 1993, including a response by Said.

Walzer, Michael. "The Solipsist as Hero." *The New Republic,* No. 4164 (7 November 1994): 38-40.

    Faults *Representation of the Intellectual* for its romanticism, solipsism, and autobiographical content.

Wander, Philip. "Marxism, Post-Colonialism, and Rhetorical Contextualization." *Quarterly Journal of Speech* 82 (1996): 402-35.

    Compares and contrasts the political aspects of James Arnt Aune's *Rhetoric and Marxism* to *Culture and Imperialism.*

Interviews

"Interview with Edward W. Said." *diacritics* 6, No. 3 (Fall 1976): 3-47.

    Addresses Said's position in the "critical avant-garde," the state of academic criticism, and the development of his thesis about Western orientalism.

Salusinszky, Imre. "Edward Said." In *Criticism in Society,* pp. 123-48. New York: Methuen, 1987.

    Speaks to Said's background, Palestinian activism, influences, and literary work.

Additional coverage of Said's life and career is contained in the following sources published by Gale: *Contemporary Authors,* **Vols. 21-24R;** *Contemporary Authors New Revision Series,* **Vol. 45; and** *Dictionary of Literary Biography,* **Vol. 67.**

Anne Sexton
1928-1974

[Born Anne Gray Harvey] American poet, playwright, children's writer, short story writer, and essayist.

The following entry presents an overview of Sexton's career. For further information on her life and works, see *CLC,* Volumes 2, 4, 6, 8, 10, 15, and 53.

INTRODUCTION

Anne Sexton is among the most celebrated and tragic poets of the confessional school. Her highly emotional, self-reflexive verse, characterized by preoccupations with childhood guilt, mental illness, motherhood, and female sexuality, is distinguished for its stunning imagery, artistry, and remarkable cadences. An unlikely latecomer to poetry, Sexton underwent a rapid metamorphosis from suburban housewife to major literary figure during the early 1960s. Her first three volumes of poetry, *To Bedlam and Part Way Back* (1960), *All My Pretty Ones* (1962), and *Live or Die* (1967), garnered critical acclaim and established her reputation as an important poet. Subsequent volumes, especially *Love Poems* (1969) and *Transformations* (1971), won her a large public audience, as did her popular appearances at poetry readings. A gifted, glamorous, and deeply troubled woman, Sexton's art and life—punctuated by her suicide—converged with the convictions of the contemporary feminist movement, drawing attention to the oppressive, circumscribed existence of women in American society.

Biographical Information

Born Anne Gray Harvey in Newton, Massachusetts, Sexton was the youngest of three daughters raised by her parents, a housewife and the owner of a prosperous wool company, in an upper middle-class home near Boston. Sexton graduated from Rogers Hall preparatory school for girls in 1947, where her first poetry appeared in the school yearbook. After a year at Garland Junior College, a finishing school in Boston, she eloped with Alfred Muller "Kayo" Sexton II in 1948, an impulsive marriage that endured separations and infidelities until their divorce in 1973. From 1949 to 1952 Sexton worked as a model, lingerie salesperson, and bookstore clerk while Kayo served in the Navy Reserve during the Korean War. She gave birth to their first daughter, Linda Gray, in 1953, followed by a second, Joyce "Joy" Ladd, in 1955. After the arrival of Joyce, Sexton received psychiatric treatment for severe depression, followed by a period of hospitalization and a suicide attempt in 1956. Sexton suffered bouts of suicidal depression throughout the

rest of her life, necessitating continual psychotherapy and subsequent hospitalizations. Upon the suggestion of her psychiatrist, Sexton began writing poetry during her recovery in 1956. The next year she joined a poetry workshop headed by John Holmes at the Boston Center for Adult Education, where she befriended Maxine Kumin. Sexton's first published poem, "Eden Revisited," appeared in *The Fiddlehead Review* in 1958. During the same year, Sexton received a scholarship to attend the Antioch Writers' Conference to study under W. D. Snodgrass. Later that year, she enrolled in Robert Lowell's writing seminar at Boston University, where she was introduced to Sylvia Plath, and in 1959 participated in the Bread Loaf Writers Conference on a Robert Frost fellowship. Her first volume of poetry, *To Bedlam and Part Way Back,* received a National Book Award nomination in 1960, as did her second volume, *All My Pretty Ones,* winner of the Levison Prize from *Poetry* magazine in 1962. *Selected Poems* (1964), published in England, consists of poetry from both *To Bedlam and Part Way Back* and *All My Pretty Ones.* After an appointment at the Radcliffe Institute from 1961 to 1963, Sexton travelled to Europe on an American Academy of Arts and Letters fellowship in 1963. She received a Ford Foundation grant for residence with the Charles Playhouse in Boston in 1964. During this time, Sexton also collaborated with Kumin on *Eggs of Things* (1963) and *More Eggs of Things* (1964), the first of several children's books followed by *Joey and the Birthday Present* (1971) and *The Wizard's Tears* (1975). Her next major volume of poetry, *Live or Die,* received a Pulitzer Prize and Shelley Award from the Poetry Society of America in 1967. Shortly after the publication of *Love Poems* in 1969, she was awarded a Guggenheim fellowship to work on her only dramatic work, *Mercy Street,* produced Off-Broadway by the American Place Theatre in 1969. In the next years she published additional volumes of poetry, including *Transformations, The Book of Folly* (1972), *The Death Notebooks* (1974), and *The Awful Rowing Toward God* (1975), which she completed only months before her death. The recipient of honorary degrees from Harvard and Radcliffe, Sexton gave frequent poetry readings and taught creative writing at Boston University from 1970 until her death. During the 1970s, Sexton's mental and physical health deteriorated, exacerbated by addictions to alcohol and sleeping pills. She committed suicide by carbon monoxide poisoning in 1974.

Major Works

Regarded as a confessional poet, Sexton's writing is in many ways a candid autobiographic record of her struggle to overcome the feelings of guilt, loss, inadequacy, and suicidal despair that tormented her. Inspired by years of intensive psychotherapy, Sexton's carefully crafted poetry often addresses her uncertain self-identity as a daughter, wife, lover, mother, and psychiatric patient. Her first volume, *To Bedlam and Part Way Back,* consists of poems written shortly after her confinement in a mental hospital, during which she lost custody of her children. "The Double Image," among the most accomplished works of the volume, is a sequence of seven poems describing Sexton's schism with her mother in the imagery of two portraits facing each other from opposite walls. Other poems, notably "You, Doctor Martin," "Music Swims Back To Me," and "Ringing the Bells" relate Sexton's experiences and emotional state while hospitalized. "Unknown Girl in the Maternity Ward," which involves an unwed mother who prepares to abandon her illegitimate child, alludes to Sexton's guilt at having lost her own children. Another significant poem from the volume, "For John, Who Begs Me Not to Enquire Further," is Sexton's response to poet John Holmes's criticism of her transgressive subject matter, representing Sexton's defense of the confessional mode and her own poetic voice. The poems of *All My Pretty Ones* further illustrate Sexton's aptitude for invoking musical rhythms and arresting imagery. Entitled after a line from Shakespeare's *Macbeth,* this volume contains the oft-anthologized poems "The Truth the Dead Know," written upon

the death of her father, "All My Pretty Ones," "The Abortion," and "Letter Written on a Ferry While Crossing Long Island Sound," all of which probe emotions surrounding loss. "With Mercy For the Greedy," also from this volume, anticipates Sexton's proclivity for Christian motifs in much of her subsequent work. The poems of *Live or Die* explore Sexton's ongoing vacillation between life and maternal responsibility and her attraction to suicide. Her obsession with death, a prominent recurring theme in all of her work, is explicit in the poems "Sylvia's Death," about Sylvia Plath's suicide, and "Wanting to Die," countered by the life-affirming poem "Live" at the end of the volume. Also included are the well known poems "Flee on Your Donkey," "Menstruation at Forty," "The Addict," "Little Girl, My Stringbean, My Lovely Woman," a tender paean to her daughter, and "Somewhere in Africa," a eulogy on the death of Holmes. Less concerned with psychic trauma, *Love Poems* contains verse ranging from elegant depiction of erotic desire in "The Breast," "Song for a Lady," and "Eighteen Days Without You," praise for womanhood in "In Celebration of My Uterus," the pain of love's end in "For My Lover, Returning to His Wife," "You All Know the Story of the Other Woman," and "The Ballad of the Lonely Masturbator," and her relationship with her husband in "Loving the Killer." In *Transformations,* a collection of loosely reinterpreted Grimm fairy tales, Sexton relies upon biting satire and dark humor to shatter the notion of happy or conventional endings. For example, "Snow White and the Seven Dwarfs" portrays the heroine as vindictive and vain, "Rapunzel" involves a lesbian relationship between Rapunzel and Mother Gothel, and "Briar Rose," based on the Sleeping Beauty story, features a young girl haunted by the incestuous advances of her father. Sexton's late volumes reveal the poet's mounting anguish, coloring her work with an increasing morbidity and overriding religiosity. The themes of alienation, death, and deliverance are evident in "The Death of Fathers" and "The Jesus Papers" in *The Book of Folly,* "The Death Baby" and "O Ye Tongues," a sequence of psalms, in *The Death Notebooks,* and "The Rowing Endeth," the final poem of *The Awful Rowing Toward God* in which the speaker arrives at "the island called God" to play a hand of cards with the deity himself. The balance of Sexton's poetry is collected in the posthumous volumes *45 Mercy Street* (1976) and *Words for Dr. Y* (1978).

Critical Reception

Sexton is recognized as one of the most significant American poets of the postwar era. Widely praised for the forceful imagery, compelling associations, affective elegiac tone, and meticulously arranged tonal patterns of her best verse, she is considered among the most talented representatives of the first generation confessional poets, along with Lowell and Plath. Critics frequently comment on the dual nature of Sexton's poetry as a cathartic process and destructive urge. While many find courage in Sexton's willingness to transmute painful personal experience and taboo sexual topics into art, others condemn such themes as exhibitionistic and inappropriate. As poet James Dickey wrote of Sexton's poems in his now famous review of *To Bedlam and Part Way Back,* "One feels tempted to drop them furtively into the nearest ashcan, rather than be caught with them in the presence of such naked suffering." Despite the limitations of Sexton's unabashed self-scrutiny, many critics discern profound archetypal motifs in her work, particularly allusions to the Oedipus myth in themes of incest and the relentless search for forbidden truth. Though *Love Poems* and *Transformations* were Sexton's best-selling and most popular volumes during her life, her critical reputation rests largely upon the poems of *To Bedlam and Part Way Back, All My Pretty Ones,* and *Live or Die.* Renowned for her heavily revised verse in earlier volumes, most critics note Sexton's declining artistic discipline in hastily composed later volumes such as *The Book of Folly, The Death Notebooks,* and *The Awful Rowing Toward God.* A celebrity and trenchant poetess whose frank discussion of sex and mental illness offered liberating honesty for many, Sexton remains among the most important female poets of her generation.

PRINCIPAL WORKS

To Bedlam and Part Way Back (poetry) 1960

All My Pretty Ones (poetry) 1962

Eggs of Things [with Maxine Kumin] (juvenilia) 1963

More Eggs of Things [with Maxine Kumin] (juvenilia) 1964

Selected Poems (poetry) 1964

Live or Die (poetry) 1966

Love Poems (poetry) 1969

Mercy Street (drama) 1969

Joey and the Birthday Present [with Maxine Kumin] (juvenilia) 1971

Transformations (poetry) 1971

The Book of Folly (poetry) 1972

O Ye Tongues (poetry) 1973

The Death Notebooks (poetry) 1974

The Awful Rowing Toward God (poetry) 1975

The Wizard's Tears [with Maxine Kumin] (juvenilia) 1975

45 Mercy Street (poetry) 1976

Anne Sexton: A Self Portrait in Letters (correspondence) 1977

Words for Dr. Y: Uncollected Poems with Three Stories (poetry and short stories) 1978

The Complete Poems (poetry) 1981

No Evil Star: Selected Essays, Interviews, and Prose (essays, interviews, and prose) 1985

Selected Poems of Anne Sexton (poetry) 1988

CRITICISM

Suzanne Juhasz (essay date 1979)

SOURCE: "Seeking the Exit or the Home: Poetry and Salvation in the Career of Anne Sexton," in *Shakespeare's Sisters: Feminist Essays on Women Poets,* edited by Sandra M. Gilbert and Susan Gubar, Indiana University Press, 1979, pp. 261-8.

[*In the following essay, Juhasz explores Sexton's creative urge as both a curse and cathartic force in her life. Juhasz maintains that Sexton's dual identity as housewife and poet proved a source of inspiration and despair.*]

If you are brought up to be a proper little girl in Boston, a little wild and boycrazy, a little less of a student and more of a flirt, and you run away from home to elope and become a proper Boston bride, a little given to extravagance and a little less to casseroles, but a proper bride nonetheless who turns into a proper housewife and mother, and if all along you know that there lives inside you a rat, a "gnawing pestilential rat," what will happen to you when you grow up? If you are Anne Sexton, you will keep on paying too much attention to the rat, will try to kill it, and yourself, become hospitalized, be called crazy. You will keep struggling to forget the rat and be the proper Boston housewife and mother you were raised to be. And into this struggle will come, as an act of grace, poetry, to save your life by giving you a role, a mission, a craft: an act, poetry, that is you but is not you, outside yourself. Words, that you can work and shape and that will stay there, black and true, while you do this, turn them into a poem, that you can send away to the world, a testimony of yourself. Words that will change the lives of those who read them and your own life, too. So that you can know that you are not only the wife and mother, not only the rat, but that you are the poet, a person who matters, who has money and fame and prizes and students and admirers and a name, Anne Sexton.

But what about the mother and wife, and what about the rat, when Anne Sexton becomes a poet? This essay is about the end of Sexton's career and poetry, and it looks at the role that her poems played in her life and in ours. It is a tale for our times, because it is also about what poetry can do for women and what it cannot do for women. Something we need to know.

Since the recent publication of Sexton's letters, there is now no doubt how conscious she was of the craft of poetry, of the work that it is, and how devoted she was to doing that work. "You will make it if you learn to revise," she wrote to an aspiring poet in 1965:

if you take your time, if you work your guts out on one poem for four months instead of just letting the miracle (as you must feel it) flow from the pen and then just leave it with the excuse that you are undisciplined.

Hell! I'm undisciplined too, in everything but my work . . . and the discipline the reworking the forging into being is the stuff of poetry. . . .

In fact, for Sexton the poem existed as a measure of control, of discipline, for one whom she defined as "given to excess." "I have found that I can control it best in a poem," she says. "If the poem is good then it will have the excess under control . . . it is the core of the poem . . . there like stunted fruit, unseen but actual."

Yet the poem had another function in her life, the one which gives rise to that label "confessional," which has always dogged her work and is not usually complimentary. Her poetry is highly personal. She is either the overt or the implicit subject of her poem, and the she as subject is the person who anguishes, who struggles, who seems mired in the primary soil of living: the love/hate conflict with mother and father, the trauma of sex, the guilt of motherhood. The person in the poem is not the proper lady and mother and wife who is always trying her best to tidy up messes and cover them with a coating of polish and wax. Rather, it is the rat, a creature of nature rather than culture, who is crude and rude, "with its bellyful of dirt / and its hair seven inches long"; with its "two eyes full of poison / and routine pointed teeth." The rat person, with her "evil mouth" and "worried eyes," knows that living is something about which to worry: she sees and tells. In form her poem often follows a psychoanalytic model, as I have pointed out in an earlier essay, beginning in a present of immediate experience and probing into a past of personal relationships in order to understand the growth (and the damaging) of personality. As such, the poem for Sexton is an important agent in her quest for salvation: for a way out of the madness that the rat's vision engenders, a way that is not suicide.

Very early in her career, in **"For John, Who Begs Me Not to Enquire Further,"** she presents an aesthetics of personal poetry which is conscious that the poem, because it is an object that communicates and mediates between person and person, can offer "something special" for others as well as oneself.

> I tapped my own head;
> it was glass, an inverted bowl.
> It is a small thing
> to rage in your own bowl.
> At first it was private.
> Then it was more than myself;

> it was you, or your house
> or your kitchen.
> And if you turn away
> because there is no lesson here
> I will hold my awkward bowl,
> with all its cracked stars shining
> like a complicated lie,
> and fasten a new skin around it
> as if I were dressing an orange
> or a strange sun.
> Not that it was beautiful,
> but that I found some order there.
> There ought to be something special
> for someone
> in this kind of hope.

In such poetry, she warns, there is no "lesson," no universal truth. What there is is the poem of herself, which, as she has made it, has achieved an order; that very order a kind of hope (a belief in salvation) that might be shared. The poem of herself is, however, not herself but a poem. The imagery of this poem attests to that fact, as it turns self into object, a bowl, an orange, a sun, while it turns the poem about self into a coating or covering that surrounds the self. The bowl is like a planet in a heaven of "cracked stars shining / like a complicated lie"; if he should turn from this poem, she promises to "fasten a new skin around" or "dress" her orange, that strange sun.

Of course Sexton was right when she said that there ought to be something special in that gesture her poems made toward others. People responded to her poetry because she had the courage to speak publicly of the most intimate of personal experiences, the ones so many share. She became a spokesperson for the secret domestic world and its pain. And her audience responded as strongly as it did, not only because of what she said but because of how she said it. She was often, although not always, a good poet, a skilled poet, whose words worked insight upon her subject matter and irradiated it with vision.

But what about herself, in the process? What did her poems do for her?

In a letter she speaks of the necessity for the writer to engage in a vulnerable way with experience.

> I think that writers . . . must try *not* to avoid knowing what is happening. Everyone has somewhere the ability to mask the events of pain and sorrow, call it shock . . . when someone dies for instance you have this shock that carries you over it, makes it bearable. But the creative person must not use this mechanism anymore than they have to in order to keep breathing. Other people may. But not you, not us. Writing is "life"

in capsule and the writer must feel every bump edge scratch ouch in order to know the real furniture of his capsule . . . I, myself, alternate between hiding behind my own hands protecting myself anyway possible, and this other, this seeing ouching other. I guess I mean that creative people must not avoid the pain that they get dealt. I say to myself, sometimes repeatedly "I've got to get the hell out of this hurt" . . . But no. Hurt must be examined like a plague.

The result of this program, as she says in a letter to W. D. Snodgrass, is writing "real." "Because that is the one thing that will save (and I do mean save) other people."

And yet the program is not only altruistic in intent. Personal salvation remains for her an equally urgent goal. As she writes in **"The Children,"** from one of her last books, *The Awful Rowing Toward God* (1975):

> The place I live in
> is a kind of maze
> and I keep seeking
> the exit or the home.

In describing this position of vulnerability necessary for poetry, she tells Snodgrass that a poet must remain "the alien." In her vocabulary for herself, that alien is of course the rat. But there is a serious problem here, because Anne Sexton the woman (who is nonetheless the poet, too) does not like the rat. The existence of the rat obstructs salvation. In **"Rowing,"** the opening poem of *The Awful Rowing Toward God,* salvation is described as an island toward which she journeys. This island, her goal, is "not perfect," having "the flaws of life, / the absurdities of the dinner table, / but there will be a door":

> and I will open it
> and I will get rid of the rat inside me.
> the gnawing pestilential rat.

In the **"Ninth Psalm"** of her long poem, *O Ye Tongues,* an extended description of the state of salvation includes this vision: "For the rat was blessed on that mountain. He was given a white bath."

In other words, Sexton, recognizing at the age of twenty-eight her possession of a talent, turned her mad self to good work (and works): into a writer, an active rather than a passive agent. For she had defined madness as fundamentally passive and destructive in nature. "Madness is a waste of time. It creates nothing . . . nothing grows from it and you, meanwhile, only grow into it like a snail. Yet the rat who is the mad lady is also the poet. To have become a poet was surely an act toward salvation for Sexton. It gave her something to do with the knowledge that the rat possessed. Left

to her silence, the rat kept seeing too much and therefore kept seeking "the exit." Words brought with them power, power to reach others. They gave her as well a social role, "the poet," that was liberating. Being the poet, who could make money with her poetry, who could be somebody of consequence in the public world, was an act that helped to alleviate some of the frustration, the impotence, the self-hatred that Sexton the woman experienced so powerfully in her life. The poet was good: how good she was Sexton, as teacher and reader and mentor, made a point of demonstrating.

But the rat was not good; in yet another image of self-identification, Sexton called that hated, evil, inner self a demon.

> My demon,
> too often undressed,
> too often a crucifix I bring forth,
> too often a dead daisy I give water to
> too often the child I give birth to
> and then abort, nameless, nameless . . .
> earthless.
>
> Oh demon within,
> I am afraid and seldom put my hand up
> to my mouth and stitch it up
> covering you, smothering you
> from the public voyeury eyes
> of my typewriter keys.

These lines are from **"Demon,"** which appears in her posthumous volume, *45 Mercy Street.* The poem begins with an epigraph from D. H. Lawrence: "A young man is afraid of his demon and puts his hand over the demon's mouth sometimes." It goes on to show why the demon, though frightening, cannot be covered, smothered, or denied speech: because the demon, exposed, is at the center of her poetry. At the same time the poem, with its bitter repetition of "too often," reveals a hatred, not only of the demon, but of the act of uncovering and parading it. Of the act that is nonetheless essential to making the poem.

Finally, the poem's imagery points to a further aspect of the demon that is for Sexton perhaps the most terrible of all. The demon is crucifix, icon of salvation through death; is dead daisy for which the poem alone provides water; is child which, through the act of the poem, is both birthed and aborted. The demon may begin as something that lives within and is a part (albeit frightening and nasty) of herself; but the poem, in being written, turns the demon into an object separate and alien from herself. This disassociation, this conversion of self into other, is as distressing to Sexton as the self-hatred that she must experience each time she acknowledges the existence of the demon or the rat. Because, as **"Demon"** makes clear, the self as object, the self in the poem, is dead. To use the self in making poems is to lose the self, for the poem is never the experience that produces it. The poem is always an artifice, as she herself observes in another poem from *45 Mercy Street,* **"Talking to Sheep":**

> Now,
> in my middle age,
> I'm well aware
> I keep making statues
> of my acts, carving them with my sleep—

The poems can never offer personal salvation for their poet, and she has come to understand why. First, because she defines salvation as a life freed at last from the rat and her pain ("I would sell my life to avoid / the pain that begins in the crib / with its bars or perhaps / with your first breath"), and yet she cannot kill the rat without killing the vision that is the source of her poetry. Second, because the poems themselves are a kind of suicide. She knows that poetry must be craft as well as vision; that the very act of crafting objectifies the poem's content. What has lived within her, externalized and formalized by art, becomes something other than herself; is form but not flesh.

That the woman and the poet were different "selves," and in conflict with each other, she was well aware.
—*Suzanne Juhasz*

She expresses this new knowledge in the only way she knows, by making poetry of it. In poems like those quoted, or in the following lines from **"Cigarettes and Whiskey and Wild, Wild Women,"** the other side of **"For John, Who Begs Me Not to Enquire Further"** is revealed: the implications of this aesthetic of personal poetry for the poet herself.

> Now that I have written many words,
> and let out so many loves, for so many,
> and been altogether what I always was—
> a woman of excess, of zeal and greed,
> I find the effort useless.
> Do I not look in the mirror,
> these days,
> and see a drunken rat avert her eyes?
> Do I not feel the hunger so acutely
> that I would rather die than look
> into its face?
> I kneel once more,
> in case mercy should come
> in the nick of time.

In an earlier essay on Sexton I maintained that poetry had

saved her from suicide. It did, for the years in which she wrote and was the poet. But it is equally true that poetry could not prevent her death, "the exit," because it could not bring her to salvation, "the home."

For Sexton, salvation would have meant sanity: peace rather than perpetual conflict, integration rather than perpetual fragmentation. Sanity would have meant vanquishing at last her crazy bad evil gnawing self, the rat, the demon. Yet the rat was, at the same time, the source of her art. Its anxious visions needed to be nurtured so that she might be a poet. Sanity might bring peace to the woman, but it would destroy the poet. And it was not the woman, who made the peanut butter sandwiches and the marriage bed, whom Sexton liked. It was the poet. The discipline of her craft and the admiration, respect, and power that it brought allowed her to feel good about herself. That the woman and the poet were different "selves," and in conflict with each other, she was well aware. "I do not live a poet's life. I look and act like a housewife," she wrote. "I live the wrong life for the person I am." Although this fragmentation of roles wrought conflict and confusion, it nonetheless made possible the kind of poetry that Sexton wrote. But more and more in her final years she seemed to have come to despise the balancing act itself, demanding all or, finally, nothing.

Perhaps the kind of salvation that Sexton sought was unattainable, because its very terms had become so contradictory. Certainly, her poetry could not offer it. In poetry she could make verbal and public what she knew about her private self; she could shape this knowledge, control it, give it a form that made it accessible to others. But she could not write what she did not know, so that while her poems document all the rat has seen, they never offer an alternative vision. They are always too "close" to herself for that. And they are at the same time too far from her. By creating through externalization and formalization yet another self with which to deal, her poetry increased her sense of self-fragmentation in the midst of her struggle toward wholeness.

Yet Sexton's poetry has offered salvation to others. Personal poetry of this kind, a genre that many women, in their search for self-understanding and that same elusive wholeness, have recently adopted, must be understood to have a different function for its readers and for its writers. Art as therapy appears less profitable for the artist, who gives the gift of herself, than for its recipients. I think that I can learn from Sexton's poems as she never could. They project a life that is like my own in important ways; I associate my feelings with hers, and the sense of a shared privacy is illuminating. At the same time, they are not my life; their distance from me permits a degree of objectivity, the ability to analyze as well as empathize. Possibly I can use the insights produced by such a process to further change in my own life. For the artist, however, because the distance between herself and the poem is at once much closer and much greater, it is more difficult, perhaps impossible, to use the poem in this way. Salvation for the artist must come, ultimately, from developing a life that operates out of tensions which are creative rather than destructive. Sexton's life, art, and death exemplify some of the difficulties faced by women artists in achieving this goal and also dramatically underline the necessity of overcoming them.

William H. Shurr (essay date 1980)

SOURCE: "Anne Sexton's *Love Poems:* The Genre and the Differences," in *Modern Poetry Studies,* Vol. 10, 1980, pp. 58-68.

[*In the following essay, Shurr discusses the composition and central motifs of* Love Poems. *According to Shurr, in* Love Poems *Sexton "merges the possibility of the ancient genre of erotic love poetry with the immediacy of modern experience."*]

At least half of Anne Sexton's published volumes of poetry show a tight unity of construction. Though virtually all of the poems were published separately in various periodicals, and thus each can stand by itself as a complete poem, in the collections they are brought into programmatic relation to one another. This is most obvious in *Transformations,* where the subjects are all known fairy tales and the speaker and the format of presentation is in every case the same. But study of *Love Poems, The Death Notebooks,* and *The Awful Rowing Toward God*—and, to a lesser extent, *Live or Die*—can uncover a similar continuity of experience. In the remaining volumes the reader finds suites of poems in which each can be taken separately but which yield a still "higher" synthesis when taken together.

Love Poems (1969) is more than simply a collection of love poems; it is the record of a love affair which, as it is presented in the volume, lasted about four years. As shaped in the volume the experience was characterized by intense moments which the lovers had together as well as frequent separations, and it finally ended definitively. One senses in *Love Poems* a conscious attempt to isolate the experience from all others, to shape it into a unity and present the stages of its evolution as typical. A clue to Sexton's intention in shaping the collection is the forcefully suggestive passage from Yeats with which she introduced it:

> One should say before sleeping, "I have
> lived many lives. I have been a slave and a
> prince. Many a beloved has sat upon my knees
> and I have sat upon the knees of many a beloved.

> Everything that has been shall be again."

What we are to make of this is perhaps that Sexton is searching for essential contours, for a pattern of events that is repeatable and has been repeated a billion times in human history. Any collection of love poetry, or any suite of love poems, celebrates essentially the same sequence: the fascination, the awakening, the consummation, the celebration, the love-sickness in absence, the parting and the end of the affair: "everything that has been shall be again." But so intensely lived is the experience that it seems to the lovers that it must be their unique experience alone; John Donne would persuade us that no other lovers had ever existed, that he exists as priest to unfold the wonders of this experience to the laity, gradually, according to their ability to understand. As Sexton introduces her poems, through the quotation from Yeats, she would interpret the genre to us as one in which we may appreciate again the universal moments in the experience and look as well for her own personal heightenings and insights.

By far the most highly dramatized moment of the collection, and the most intensely erotic, is the poem which celebrates **"That Day."** The poem has some elements of the medieval *alba:* reliving the experience and celebrating its stages in lavish detail, praising the lover's beauty (here, the details of the erection which she herself has manipulated), the union, and watching over the lover's sleep afterward. In the Troubadours, the sexual reward is the Lady's "gift," and Sexton rewrites and modernizes the tradition, "I bore gifts for your gift." Also in medieval love poetry, one finds the convention of the lovers' prayer to avoid the excesses of the unfortunate lovers of old. Medea is mentioned, and more frequently Dido, the Queen of Carthage who wanted to marry Aeneas even though she knew the Fates had decreed another wife for him, who begged at least to have a child by him as a permanent reminder of their love, and who finally committed suicide. Sexton's prayer, against this background, is chilling:

> Then I knew you in your dream and prayed of our time
> that I would be pierced and you would take root in me
> and that I might bring forth your born, might bear
> the you or the ghost of you in my little household.

The lovely eroticism of **"That Day"** is further heightened, interpreted, by its own framework. The typical dawn setting of the *alba* has been displaced. The experience of **"That Day"** is recounted the *next* day; the beloved is absent. In his place, quite literally where he had been, the mechanical typewriter is now in her hands. The end is foreseen and her aloneness frames the poem. The last lines read: "but this is the typewriter that sits before me and love is where yesterday is at."

"That Day" is the fifth poem of the collection and is preceded by three poems of preparation: the awakening of "The Hand," which will touch the beloved for the first time; the awakening of "The Kiss," which suddenly becomes adult, erotic; the awakening of "The Breast," which finds its best function in giving and receiving pleasure, in mothering the lover. What is perceived and repeated in each of these poems is the transition to a higher plane of being, the unfolding of a different function and a different kind of experience. The consummation of these preparations in "That Day" is then orchestrated with a powerful unleashing of new emotional forces. Some of Sexton's most striking lines appear in these three poems. In a vivid image she describes the hand, before its awakening, as "sealed off / in a tin box." An image of transformation at the end of "The Kiss" arrests the attention: "Darling, the composer has stepped / into fire." In each case the suspension caused by the enjambement adds to the effect. Where the musical suggestion is here Wagnerian, it becomes playful in the next poem, "The Breast," where she describes her previously childish body as "A xylophone maybe with skin stretched over it awkwardly."

The natural flow, however, seems arrested by the difficult fourth poem in this initial group of five. It is called "The Interrogation Of The Man Of Many Hearts." It interrupts the continuity of the three preparatory poems with the following fulfillment poem. While the attention it requires seems to break the erotic line of development, it nevertheless clearly defines the situation of the affair and states themes which develop later as the painful dimension of the experience. It is as if Sexton were deliberately interrupting the pleasant expectations of the reader, to insist on the full reality of the matter.

"The Interrogation Of The Man Of Many Hearts" probes the psychology of the male, who obviously enjoys the sexual experience with the interrogating woman, but who will inevitably rest in a more permanent married relationship with another woman. His instinct to marry another is not entirely reasonable. He acknowledges that

> She's my real witch, my fork, my mare,
> my mother of tears, my skirtful of hell,
> the stamp of my sorrows, the stamp of my bruises . . .

But still, he says, "I'm caught deep in the dye of her." The poem is a sequence of questions from the woman, with answers from the man. Once again the tradition of medieval love poetry comes to mind. Andreas Capellanus states that, among the rules for Courtly Love marriage is actually an impediment to romantic love; the experience is heightened to its fullest only by the excitement of being extramarital, adulterous. Still another poetic technique of the Troubadours, the conversation between the lovers, the alternating *debat* between the man and the woman, is embodied in these lines.

The woman is sympathetically aware of the compulsive drives of the male. He admits that his polygamous instincts conflict with her essentially monogamous needs; what is a temporary need for him is permanent need for her:

> I have not only bedded her down.
> I have tied her down with a knot.

Sexton leads the reader through the nuances of reality, deeply felt and rendered with clear verbal intelligence. The wisdom she retrieves from this painful interrogation is the fact of the mutability of all experience, an ancient piece of wisdom traceable through Spenser and Boethius back to Ecclesiastes. Whether sanctioned by society and traditions or not, the final lesson of human experience is the same:

> and every bed has been condemned
> not by morality or law,
> but by time

Insertion of "The Interrogation Of The Man Of Many Hearts" at this point in the collection—between the awakening poems and the consummation poem—immediately elevates the meditations to a plane of high seriousness, from erotic romance to profound realism.

The rest of the poems in *Love Poems* are in fact rays from this initial cluster. A second sequence can be discerned in which the subject is the sexual awakening of the woman. "Song For A Red Nightgown" is the lightly humorous attempt at a precise description of a woman's night dress, the costume that signals the change from caterpillar to butterfly: "the butterfly owns her now." In another poem, "It Is A Spring Afternoon," the girl senses the change of seasons as parallel to her own profound and silent maturing. She falls in love with her new body, "her animal loveliness," in a series of healing and healthy images:

> Because of this
> the ground, that winter nightmare,
> has cured its sores and burst
> with green birds and vitamins.
> Because of this
> the trees turn in their trenches
> and hold up little rain cups
> by their slender fingers.
> Because of this
> a woman stands by her stove
> singing and cooking flowers.
> Everything here is yellow and green.

The swiftness and completeness of the transition is expressed in diction borrowed from Robert Frost's poem, "For Once, Then, Something":

> The face of the child wrinkles
> in the water and is gone forever.

The most striking of these "awakening" poems appears at the beginning of the sequence and bears the flagrant title **"In Celebration Of My Uterus."** The poem fits into the collection only because of the context there. It derives, actually, as the opening lines make clear, from the medical problem Sexton had in 1959, when she feared that she had cancer, the disease from which her mother had recently died. The diagnosis and operation, however, disclosed only a benign tumor which was removed. The event itself was described in clinical detail in the poem called **"The Operation"** from *All My Pretty Ones* (1962). But, while the event itself happened several years before the affair began (as dated in *Love Poems*), still we may judge that this celebration of her womanly sexuality, where "each cell has a life," has been successfully inserted into its present place in the volume. The poem has been noticed by others, and while it may not be her strongest one there are elements in it that suggest a further respect for Anne Sexton's poetry as a whole. From this point of view, the Whitmanesque diction of the poem assumes primary importance. She invents a twelve-item catalogue, for example, of typical women; toward the end of the poem, the same phrase "Let me . . . " introduces eight separate lines of rhythmically parallel syntax; further, the Whitmanesque word "sing" and its variations occur prominently some half-dozen times, as does Whitman's divine "I am" phrase. Where Whitman celebrates the phallus, Sexton assumes the role of female counterpart, celebrating the uterus. There are reasons for seeing Sexton in the tradition of Whitman; she creates a female singer of the Self to match his male persona.

A third sequence of poems can be discerned later in the volume, celebrating the affair at its height. Leaving open the possibility that other poems and parts of poems touch the same subject, we can list the following as poems which follow without interruption in this sequence: **"Now,"** **"Us,"** **"Mr. Mine,"** **"Song For A Lady,"** and **"Knee Song."** The poems are characterized by innocence and spontaneity, by the security that the moment of love is eternal. In such a situation, play is the characteristic activity: "We are here on a raft, exiled from dust." The motifs rise to a high point in the final poem, where Molly Bloom's soliloquy is mined for dramatic effect: "Yes oh yes yes yes . . . yes yes yes." The poems are lovely as erotic celebration. The sensual details are fresh and moving. **"Song For A Lady"** is a small gem of a song intricately rhymed. But even within this sequence can be heard time's winged chariot, which chills all lovers. Crystalized in a unique trope, this startling image is her version of the *carpe diem* theme:

> The shoemaker will come and he will rebuild
> this room. He will lie on your bed
> and urinate and nothing will exist.
> Now is the time. Now!

This suggests the theme of a fourth discernible sequence in *Love Poems,* a series of poems on the bitter aftermath of the affair. Once again, Sexton's placement of the poems is telling. Actually, this series comes third among the four sequences I have been suggesting, after the awakening poems and immediately before the fulfillment poems just described. It is as if Sexton would mold our responses to a harsh reality, as she had in the opening sequence of five poems: the most intense sensual pleasures are the most compelling reminders of our temporariness. It is as if Sexton were holding herself to the fire to find all the wisdom she could in a moment that was as transitory as it was beautiful. The poems that follow without interruption in this sequence are **"Just Once,"** **"Again And Again And Again,"** **"You All Know The Story Of The Other Woman,"** and **"Moon Song, Woman Song,"** The sequence is ended by the powerful **"Ballad Of The Lonely Masturbator."**

The first poem, which was actually written and published several years earlier, describes the affair as definitely over and ends with the irony that "these constants" are now "gone." The following poems are filled with bitterness: a frog "sits on my lips and defecates"; "the blackness is murderous"; she senses herself as having been used and abandoned; all lovers are "full of lies. / They are eating each other." On first reading, it is perhaps **"The Ballad Of The Lonely Masturbator"** which strikes the reader as most original, but the poem that precedes it may have profounder rewards. **"Moon Song, Woman Song"** is a meditation into the ancient archetype of the moon as woman, virgin, goddess, the betrayed lover. The poem sets the speech in the mouth of the moon:

> I have been oranging and fat,
> carrot colored, gaped at,
> allowing my cracked o's to drop on the sea . . .

The male is present in the poem as violator, "tall in your battle dress." The opposition of figures is ancient and worth considering again, but for this most recent version of the story Sexton suggests a modern context that strikingly authenticates the perennial applicability of the archetypal story. The male is lightly suggested as astronaut by the phrases "coverall man" and "blast off," and the moon passively awaits still another rough assault from him. The poem ends with a further insight; the ends of the male and the female are eternally unreconcilable: for him she is only "headquarters of an area," whereas she sees herself as "house of a dream."

> *Love Poems*, then, merges the possibilities of the ancient genre of erotic love poetry with the immediacy of modern experience.
> —*William H. Shurr*

Tight as the generic unity is, two poems seem to resist inclusion in *Love Poems*. The first is called **"The Break,"** and since it follows **"For My Lover, Returning To His Wife,"** the title suggests a smooth sequence of events. But the poem is an account of the broken hip she actually suffered from an accidental fall downstairs, on November 9, 1966. The fall and the subsequent operation were to leave her a virtual invalid for nearly a year. The muses of poetry were handing her difficult materials to transmute into a series of love poems. But poetry has rules that are different from those of biography and another careful reading is required for signs of Sexton's intention in placing the poem here. A key phrase appears: "I'm Ethan Frome's wife," and the reader recalls the end of Edith Wharton's story, where the two intense lovers are crippled and embittered finally, with the betrayed wife left to move them around at whim. The poem then suggests guilt and the fear of retribution, of poetic justice: a broken hip is the "right" punishment for an adulterous relationship. An earlier allusion, to Icarus, in line 13 confirms this suggestion of poetic justice. Congruent with this point of entry is the contrast, developed throughout the poem, between the broken hip and the broken heart. The poem begins, "It was also my violent heart that broke"; it ends with the acceptance of reality of her situation, the broken hip and "the violent heart." Her final comment draws on the phrase from the New Testament (John 2:17) to summarize her situation: "The zeal / of my house doth eat me up"—the driving energies of the violent heart have somehow resulted in the crack-up of the body. The seven other references to "heart" in this poem confirm the connection. The heart, "old hunger motor," "thought it could call all the shots." "The heart burst with love and lost its breath." With some problems, then, the poem inserts itself within the thematic patterns of *Love Poems,* suggesting that the love is a guilty one, that such overreaching cannot long escape the notice of the gods. If this is the intent of the poem, as it finds its place in *Love Poems,* then two lines in the third stanza arrest the attention:

> Yes, I was like a box of dog bones.
> But now they've wrapped me in like a nun.

In the last collection of poems she was to see through the press, *The Awful Rowing Toward God,* her love becomes a mystical love for the divine; her use of "Ms. Dog" indicates some marital relation to its reverse, "God." The lines above suggest some earlier beginning of this perception; the failure of human love isolates her for the divine.

The second poem which resists inclusion into the unity of *Love Poems* is **"The Papa And Mama Dance."** The poem is the recollection of a fictional brother and herself, as children, dressing in their parents' old clothes, and engaging in some intensely incestuous behavior. Sexton had no brother and the fantasy is the same as those found in other volumes of her poetry, in **"To Johnny Pole On The Forgotten Beach"** in *To Bedlam And Part Way Back* (1960), and in the Christopher poems in *The Death Notebooks* (1974). These poems, including the present one, are like the other moments when Sexton manufactures "autobiography" for the more intense personalization of her experiences. While **"The Papa And Mama Dance,"** then, seems to come from another corner of the poet's mind, it is worth recalling that the convention of lovers pretending to be brother and sister, to heighten the erotic intimacy of the relationship, is at least as old as the Song of Solomon. There is, in addition, another detail which ties this poem to the present collection. It begins with the sister criticizing the brother for not burning his draft card, for going off to war instead. In the concluding sequence of the book, the poem **"December 9th,"** she complains to her lover:

> Two years ago, Reservist,
> you would have burned
> your draft card . . .

This poem as well, then, has multiple ties to the collection in which it appears.

An early reviewer of *Love Poems* complained that the volume seemed to him to suffer from hasty construction, and that "most of the poems seem to have been written far too quickly, as if she were rather nervous of overcooking emotional raw material." It can be argued, however, that just the opposite is true, that the materials of the collection are quite cooled, quite thoroughly manipulated and artistically arranged, that the *impression* of raw emotion was precisely the one the poet was eager to convey. For example, the reader of Linda Gray Sexton's book, *Anne Sexton: A Self-Portrait in Letters,* comes to realize that two poems, **"The Nude Swim"** and **"Loving the Killer,"** derive their setting and quite likely their personae from Anne's European trips with her husband. Still another poem, **"Just Once,"** fits the composite picture of *Love Poems* perfectly, but it was first published in 1958, several years before the affair began according to the internal datings of the volume. The raw experience has been cooked here quite thoroughly. Sexton had a talent for "pseudobiography," for the presentation of her poems as if they were raw emotional experiences.

What embarrassed some early critics even as unsanctionable invasion of her own privacy turned out, at least at times, to be an intense fictional realism, the inventive talent of the poet-storyteller.

Love Poems, then, merges the possibilities of the ancient genre of erotic love poetry with the immediacy of modern experience. The contours of the genre which Sexton has emphasized are the awakening, the experience, the enjoyment and celebration of love, with the bitter aftermath of the definitive break as the controlling context for the whole. Individual poems are alive with a pulse of their own; the cool, ironic *encadrement* is the timeless theme of Mutability.

Diane Wood Middlebrook (essay date December 1983)

SOURCE: "Housewife into Poet: The Apprenticeship of Anne Sexton," in *New England Quarterly,* Vol. 56, No. 4, December, 1983, pp. 483-503.

[*In the following essay, Middlebrook examines Sexton's artistic development from suburban mother to celebrated poet, focusing on the significance of her literary mentors, particularly her relationship with John Holmes.*]

In April 1960, Anne Sexton for the first time wrote "poet" rather than "housewife" in the "occupation" block of her income tax return. Married since 1948, mother of two daughters, Sexton had been publishing poetry for three years. The change in her status as citizen was significant for Sexton and for American literature. No poet before her had written so frankly of the female realm of family life, nor of its pathologies. And few poets, women or men, achieved success so expeditiously: nine years from drafting her first poem to being awarded the Pulitzer Prize.

Sexton's unprecedented metamorphosis from suburban housewife into major poet appears, at first glance, a fairy tale. The real interest of its improbability, though, lies in Sexton's exemplary struggle against two seemingly unrelated handicaps: that of being a suburban wife and mother without a college education and that of being, at recurring intervals, certifiably mad. At age twenty-eight, Anne Sexton quite unexpectedly began turning herself into an artist. During the years of her apprenticeship, in which she produced two highly regarded books, Sexton's good fortune included working with several established younger poets—W. D. Snodgrass, Robert Lowell, James Wright—who immediately recognized her originality and with the Boston poet-teacher John Holmes, who censured it. Friend and adversary, Holmes measured Sexton's work by the literary standards and conventions of an older generation. The

chronicle of their relationship provides numerous insights into the development of Sexton's self-awareness as an artist.

I. 1956—57: Discovering "Language"

Sexton began writing poetry at home. Following her hospitalization for suicidal depressiveness in 1956, Sexton's two young children had been removed to the care of grandmothers; Sexton found herself with no occupation but psychotherapy and convalescence. Her doctor suggested that she use her free time to improve her education. "One night I saw I. A. Richards on educational television reading a sonnet and explaining its form," she told an interviewer. "I thought to myself, 'I could do that, maybe; I could try.' So I sat down and wrote a sonnet. The next day I wrote another one, and so forth." She measured progress by changes in the furniture supporting her work. At first she used a card table "because I didn't think I was a poet. When I put in a desk, it was in our dining room. [. . .] Then I put up some book shelves—everything was tentative."

This "tentative" rearrangement of the household was symbolic of Sexton's changed relation to domestic life in 1957. Postpartum depression following the birth of Sexton's first daughter, Linda, led in 1954 to her first psychiatric hospitalization. On her own birthday in 1956 she had made the first of many suicide attempts. And though family members were initially reluctant to acknowledge how serious Sexton's psychological problems had become, they were generous with support once she entered regular treatment. Husband Kayo's father, George Sexton, paid for Sexton's psychotherapy; after Sexton's second major breakdown, in 1955, Kayo's mother took infant Joy into her home for three years, while Anne's sister Blanche periodically cared for Linda. Anne's mother, Mary Gray, paid for regular housekeeping, and Kayo took over the shopping and cooking when Anne could not manage.

Working alone at home, free from other responsibilities, Sexton found writing an effective therapy. "My doctor encouraged me to write more. 'Don't kill yourself,' he said. 'Your poems might mean something to someone else someday.' That gave me a feeling of purpose, a little cause, something to *do* with my life." "I was quite naive. I thought he knew everything. Of course, he wouldn't know a good poem from a bad poem, but luckily I didn't think of that."

Sexton marked her development as a poet, rather than convalescing mental patient, from the evening she enrolled in a poetry workshop offered by the Boston Center for Adult Education. The teacher was John Holmes, a member of the senior faculty at Tufts University, who supplemented his income by offering instruction in writing to the "nontraditional" types who enroll in adult education courses. Holmes was warm and unintimidating as a teacher. What Sexton derived from the class, however, was not simply how to tell a good poem from a bad poem. Attempting to characterize this period of her life for an interviewer, Sexton drew an analogy between Holmes's poetry class and the mental hospital.

> I started in the middle of the term, very shy, writing very bad poems, solemnly handing them in for the eighteen others in the class to hear. The most important aspect of that class was that I felt I belonged somewhere. When I first got sick and became a displaced person, I thought I was quite alone, but when I went into the mental hospital, I found I wasn't, that there were other people like me. It made me feel better—more real, sane. I felt, "These are my people." Well, at the John Holmes class that I attended for two years, I found I belonged to the poets, that I was *real* there, and I had another, "These are my people."

Working out the implications of this association between the hospital and class provides a way of understanding some of the social significance of Sexton's art.

Until diagnosed as mentally ill, Sexton had been regarded by her exasperated family as childish, selfish, incompetent. Her mother-in-law remembered the shock with which she first watched Sexton throw herself, pounding and screaming, on the floor because she was enraged at being asked to do an errand. Later, Sexton's anger sometimes threatened the safety of her young children; Linda Sexton indicates that the poem **"Red Roses"** (in the posthumously published **45 Mercy Street**) recreates such an incident. But in the hospital, removed from the dynamics of family life, Sexton assumed another identity. As a madwoman she was a member of a distinct social class. Even the forms of her suffering, symptomatic of the disease she embodied, were not unique but generic. Most important for her later development, in the hospital she was given a hearing by therapists trained to decode her symptoms and clarify their function in her life. And she found herself in a social group that used language in a special way, to communicate indirectly.

Years after this first hospitalization, Sexton described the discovery—"I thought I was quite alone, but [. . .] I found I wasn't"—to a psychiatrist friend:

> It is hard to define. When I was first sick I was thrilled [. . .] to get into the Nut House. At first, of course, I was just scared and crying and very quiet (who me!) but then I found this girl (very crazy of course) (like me I guess) who talked language. What a relief! I mean, well . . . someone! And then later, a while later, and quite a while, I found out that [Dr.] Martin talked language. [. . .] By the way, [husband] Kayo has never once understood one word of language.

By "language," Sexton seems to mean forms of speech in which meaning is condensed and indirect and where breaks and gaps demand as much interpretation as what is voiced. Schizophrenics use language this way, and so do poets: "figurative language" is the term Sexton might have used here, except she meant to indicate that the crucible of formation was urgent need. Being permitted to communicate in "language" made her feel "real"—unlike the speech transactions of family life, which made her feel doll-like:

> Someone pretends with me—
> I am walled in solid by their noise—
> or puts me upon their straight bed.
> They think I am me!
> Their warmth is not a friend!
> They pry my mouth for their cups of gin
> and their stale bread.

Psychotherapy following hospitalization, further developing the sense of liberation achieved in the hospital, provided Sexton with a form of education. Intensive scrutiny of her illness introduced her, haphazardly but usefully, to the theory of psychoanalysis, techniques of association, and an arena in which to display her verbal cunning. Equally important, it freed her from confinement in the family. Demonstrably unfit for the occupation of housewife and mother, Sexton turned to other work. And because she had the good fortune to live in Greater Boston, she found her way, merely by enrolling, into another social group that spoke "language": "I found I belonged to the poets, that I was *real* there."

Boston in the late 1950s was full of poets. "Being a 'poet' in Boston is not so difficult," Anne Sexton wrote Carolyn Kizer in February 1959, "except there are hoards of us living here. The place is jammed with good writers." Such abundance offered numerous advantages to the apprentice. Many well-known writers taught workshops that carried no academic prerequisites. In few places outside Boston might a professor of poetry like I. A. Richards have found an audience for lectures on the sonnet, or a TV station to air them. Both the teacher and Sexton's fellow students at the Boston Center for Adult Education reflected the exceptional literacy of Greater Boston. In John Holmes's class Sexton met Maxine Kumin, a Radcliffe graduate who had decided after some years of motherhood to return to serious writing. Kumin's career was to flourish in tandem with Sexton's, each eventually receiving the Pulitzer Prize in poetry.

It was part of Sexton's transformative good luck, I think, that she found both the instruction and, later, the academic credentials she needed without passing through the advantaged but in important ways—for poets—repressive educational systems that shaped the early work of her Boston cohorts, Adrienne Rich and Sylvia Plath. Rigorous academic training of the period led young poets to imitate the masters of the British tradition, particularly the metaphysical poets and the intensely intellectual modernists. The early writings of both Plath and Rich indicate that they were excellent students, striving for correctness in these modes. As strong poets, and like men who became strong poets under the same academic influences, Plath and Rich survived this academic phase by growing out of it; in their characteristic mature work, the mannerisms of their early models have disappeared. In the realm of the university, however, not only were their literary models intellectual men, but their teachers and lovers were too, and the best women students tended to marry them and then vanish into the underclass of academic life.

Sexton avoided this common predicament of her contemporaries, paradoxically, by marrying young. Having no further academic ambitions after finishing high school, she went on to the Garland School in Boston, where girls were taught home management. She eloped within a few months. Her struggles to mature during the early years of marriage and motherhood took place almost completely within an extended family; her husband was frequently absent on business, and both parents and in-laws were important, frequently intrusive, presences. The illnesses from which she suffered throughout her adult life burgeoned in this context of censorious parental scrutiny. Problematic as her family relations were, however, they formed a different universe of concern from the one she entered as an apprentice to poetry and did not impede her development once she found her way out of the house. She turned from sufferer into poet, a social role different altogether.

II. 1958-59: Becoming Visible

Transforming the insights won in therapy into the poetry she wrote between 1958 and 1960, Sexton was like the miller's daughter, in her own poem "Rumpelstiltskin," who acquires the gift of spinning straw into gold. Developing this gift took about three years. From the time she enrolled in John Holmes's course at the Adult Education Center, Sexton worked hard at learning the craft. The day following the first class meeting, Maxine Kumin ran into Sexton at the Newton public library, where Sexton was trying to locate the contemporary poetry shelves. Here began a collaboration that was to last until Sexton's suicide. Kumin knew her way around a library but, like Sexton, initially felt intimidated by the literary world. Two housewives, they pooled cars and other resources, converted house and garden into workspace, and conducted an ongoing informal seminar in the craft of poetry over the telephone.

Sexton and Kumin were apprentices together, but Kumin possessed credentials Sexton had to acquire another way.

Following the Boston Center course, Sexton spent several weeks during the summer of 1958 at the Antioch College Writer's Conference. Attracted by the poem "Heart's Needle," she went expressly to work with W. D. Snodgrass. This peculiarly American institution—the writer's workshop, the writer's conference—suited Sexton because it assumed no common denominator but a gift (or the delusion of a gift) and provided the valuable attention of professionals. Working with Snodgrass at Antioch was decisive. Sexton was already quite a capable writer; under Snodgrass she began to abandon certain of the conventions she had picked up in the poetry workshop—such as attaching the poem to an elevating literary allusion or founding the poem on an abstraction. "Heart's Needle," a poem about Snodgrass's separation from his daughter through divorce, came at a moment when American poetry had grown dull and academic. The poem had a large impact on Robert Lowell, for one, who said "Heart's Needle" had encouraged the production of his *Life Studies*. Snodgrass's influence on Sexton is visible in two of the finest poems of *To Bedlam*, **"Unknown Girl in a Maternity Ward"** and **"The Double Image"**—poems that raise troubled questions about the relation of mother to child. Whereas Lowell had taken from Snodgrass courage to write about the general anguish of family life, Sexton grasped in his model license to explore her sickness as it pertained to her roles as daughter and mother. Working with Snodgrass, Sexton acquired the distinctive voice of her early poetry.

Back in the Boston suburbs with a cache of new manuscripts and encouragement from Snodgrass, Sexton was accepted by Robert Lowell in September 1958 to audit his graduate writing seminar at Boston University. George Starbuck and Sylvia Plath joined this class in the winter. The three—Sexton, Starbuck, Plath—formed an intense triangle whose emotional dynamics are encoded in Sylvia Plath's journal from the period and in Sexton's hilarious and tender memorial essay to Plath, **"The Barfly Ought to Sing."**

Within a year from her first session in a poetry workshop, then, Sexton had acquired enviable visibility and respect in the poetry world. She did so by working demonically. "She would willingly push a poem through twenty or more drafts," Maxine Kumin remembers. "She had an unparalleled tenacity in those early days." Despite an acute personal shyness, she also became an active self-promoter: cultivating contacts shamelessly; submitting poems anywhere she could expect editorial advice, if not publication; accepting profuse invitations to give public readings. During 1958-59, Sexton lost both her parents, within months of each other, to severe illnesses, and was hospitalized for psychiatric treatment several times herself. Nonetheless, she continued the discipline of long days at the typewriter and regular meetings with groups of poets in which she tested her developing skills.

At least as important as the Lowell class was Sexton's participation in the meetings John Holmes convened in the fall of 1958 to continue working with his star poets from the Boston Center, Sexton, Kumin, and Sam Albert. George Starbuck also joined the group. After Starbuck's departure for Italy in September 1961, the workshop had a shifting population of visitors, but until then it was a remarkably stable collective. Altogether, what came to be known as "the John Holmes workshop" met for three and one-half years, twice monthly until Holmes died of cancer in 1962. During this time Sexton, Kumin, and Starbuck produced widely noticed first books, and Holmes brought out *The Fortune Teller,* nominated for a National Book Award in 1962. Most of the poems in these four books had been "workshopped" into shape during long evening sessions at one or another of the participants' homes.

The structure of the workshop was informal: each poet in turn became first among equals as a poem was dissected and interrogated. Holmes, however, assigned himself the presiding role. He was senior in age; he also held a respectable position in the literary establishment peculiar to Boston. President of the New England Poetry Club, for a time poetry critic at the *Boston Evening Transcript,* anthologist and teacher of poetry, Holmes eventually received appointment to the American Academy of Arts and Sciences; but his writing had an old-fashioned quality, an Arnoldian judiciousness that made him an odd contemporary for the younger writers.

With Maxine Kumin and George Starbuck, Holmes was confiding and affectionate; he squired them around to meet other literary people and proposed them for teaching positions. Sexton, however, set his teeth on edge. In life as in art, Sexton possessed a commanding physical presence. Photographs from one of the workshop evenings show her sitting on the floor, a glamour girl with long legs extended, her bright red lipstick and sweater in startling contrast to the subdued coloration of her companions. When the workshop met in the Holmes's living room, Holmes's widow Doris Eyges remembers, Sexton's raucous cries penetrated to the upstairs study: "YOU'VE GOT TO HEAR THIS! IT WORKS! IT WORKS!—FANTASTIC!" The loud voice demanded and got a large share of the group's attention. Too much, Holmes grumbled to Maxine Kumin: Anne "is on my mind unpleasantly too much of the time between our workshops. [. . .] I'm impatient with her endless demands."

III. 1959—61: Sexton and the Censor

During her years of apprenticeship, Sexton was to have two deeply significant confrontations with John Holmes, whose role in her life was, I believe, to disclose to her, in opposing him, her definitive strengths as a poet. The first conflict occurred in February 1959. Writing several poems a week and opening them for discussion both in the workshop and in Lowell's class, Sexton had amassed enough material to consider compiling a book. When she submitted a preliminary version for Holmes's criticism, his response revealed that his differences with her went far deeper than the mild offense his personal standoffishness had communicated.

> **The courage of acknowledgment in the poetry of *To Bedlam* comes from Sexton's lucidity about how general is the suffering that must be experienced as personal but can be grasped and expressed in metaphor.**
> **—*Diane Wood Middlebrook***

Like a good teacher, Holmes began his critique on a positive note: "It's a book, all right, well put together." Next he suggested a change in the proposed title, for marketing reasons: "I really think booksellers and publishers would be wary." Then he went on to give the full substance of his advice, a view he had been holding silently since their earliest days of working together.

> I distrust the very source and subject of a great many of your poems, namely, all those that describe and dwell on your time in the hospital. [. . .] I am uneasy [. . .] that what looks like a brilliant beginning might turn out to be so self-centered and so narrowed a diary that it would be clinical only.

> Something about asserting the hospital and psychiatric experience seems to me very selfish—all a forcing others to listen to you, and nothing given the listeners, nothing that teaches them or helps them. [. . .] It bothers me that you use poetry this way. It's all a release for you, but what is it for anyone else except a spectacle of someone experiencing release? [. . .]

> Don't publish it in a book. You'll certainly outgrow it, and become another person, then this record will haunt and hurt you. It will even haunt and hurt your children, years from now. [8 February 1959]

Sexton's first response was a rattled letter she drafted but did not send. ("Of course I love you. [. . .] From true poets I want truth. Anything else would prove us unreal, after all. Thank you, John, for being real.") The reply she did send encloses a poem, "the condensation of it all," titled **"For John, Who Begs Me Not to Enquire Further."** Sexton had concluded that Holmes's motive in advising her about the manuscript was not to critique but to censor her. Useful criticism empowers creative revision, and Sexton knew how to profit from the attention of another poet. But

Holmes was not saying "Revise"; he was saying "Don't publish it." Sexton's reply is a defense not only of her manuscript but of a whole genre of poetry that would come to be called "confessional."

> I tapped my own head;
> it was glass, an inverted bowl.
> [. . . . .]
> And if you turn away
> because there is no lesson here
> I will hold my awkward bowl
> with all its cracked stars shining
> [. . . . .]
> This is something I would never find
> in a lovelier place, my dear,
> although your fear is anyone's fear
> like an invisible veil between us all . . .
> and sometimes in private,
> my kitchen, your kitchen,
> my face, your face.

Shrewd as neurotic people often are about the concealed anxieties of others, Sexton insists to Holmes that his rejection of her poetry is in part a defense against the power of her art, which tells not a private but a collective truth and, to his horror, includes and reveals him. Sexton may or may not have heard in literary circles gossip about the gruesome suicide of Holmes's first wife or about Holmes's successful recovery from alcoholism. His life had been "ragged with horrors," as his widow put it but by the late 1950s was outwardly peaceful and secure. His advice to Sexton was possibly advice he had followed himself: "Don't publish it . . . you will certainly outgrow it and become another person." But Sexton based her work on a different understanding of suffering. In her imagery, "tapping" the head produces "stars," signs radiant with significance, uniting sufferer and beholder despite the "glass bowl" that shuts them off from other forms of contact. "Anyone's fear" of the sick inhibits this identification; the courage of acknowledgment in the poetry of *To Bedlam* comes from Sexton's lucidity about how general is the suffering that must be experienced as personal but can be grasped and expressed in metaphor.

Far from discouraging publication of the *Bedlam* poems, Holmes's reaction gave Sexton insight into what the book was really about. The poem she wrote in reply contains an allusion in its title to a letter from Schopenhauer to Goethe: "most of us carry in our heart the Jocasta who begs Oedipus for God's sake not to inquire further." The longer quotation of this letter became the epigraph of *To Bedlam and Part Way Back,* and **"For John . . ."** became the introductory poem to Part II, in which Sexton collected her most ambitious and self-revealing poems. Holmes had been "real"—truth-telling—in his response to her, and thus she

dared be the same; moreover, his reaction provided a foil Sexton, anticipating the distaste these poems were bound to arouse, could use in her book.

Houghton Mifflin accepted the manuscript in May 1959, just as Lowell's class was ending; it appeared in March 1960 with a jacket blurb by Lowell, which insured that the book would be widely reviewed. The reviews did not change John Holmes's opinion of the work. As Sexton workshopped poems that would shortly appear in her second collection (*All My Pretty Ones,* October 1962), Holmes's hostility deepened. "I suppose I don't want her to know how I feel," he wrote Maxine Kumin. "But I think more often than you'd ever realize that I can't stand another meeting with her there. [. . .] She is utterly selfish" (6 August 1961). The objectionable characteristics of the person were equally objectionable in the poems.

> I said way back, that she was going to have a hard time to change subject matter, after the book, and it's true. I think her search for subject matter is desperate, and that we could talk to her about it, get her to try different things [. . .] she writes so absolutely selfishly, of herself, to bare and shock and confess. Her motives are wrong, artistically, and finally the self-preoccupation comes to be simply damn boring. [. . .] [W]asn't it once understood that the whole intent of writing the bedlam poems was to get rid of them, and to cure herself, to grow up, to become through writing poetry a mature and rich person? [. . .] As it is, she merely re-infects herself, and doesn't seem to know any better than to enjoy it. [16 August 1961]

Holmes took a proprietary interest in the workshop. In February 1960 he had circulated a two-page memo listing four ways to improve its efficacy; many times he would follow up a meeting with letters to one or another of the poets that expanded on his first-sight critiques. Thus in the name of straightening out a problem, he engaged Sexton in a second open confrontation in January 1961. Galled by what he referred to as Anne's "greedy and selfish demands" at one of the workshop sessions, Holmes wrote letters to each of the participants venting his spleen. To Anne he was most tactful, but he made his points:

> I was sort of upset about the workshop, as a matter of fact. [. . .] [Y]ou gave Sam an awfully rough time, I felt, too much of it, and hard for a man to take, and he took it like a good sport. But it went on and on. Also I thought you took too much time, more than anyone else got, and also, for the first time I've ever minded, I thought you and Max had too much to drink, and that it took the meaning and responsible thinking away from the poems. [25 January 1961]

Holmes wanted the workshop to work; Sexton thought it was working. Certainly it was working for her: she could audition drafts of poems within a circle of intimates she trusted to know what effects she was after. "What kind of workshop is this?" she fumed to Holmes in her reply to his letter. "Are we mere craftsmen or are we artists! [. . .] I resent the idea that an almost good poem isn't worth any amount of time if we can make it better and first the actual writer has got to be able to HEAR." As Sexton realized, however, the conflict was not merely over workshop manners: it involved behavior indistinguishable from poetics. For Sexton, the unbridled excitements of the group process frequently led to inspired revision. "This is a great strength and a great, but mutual, creative act each time it happens," she argued; to repress the process would be to kill the work. Moreover, she knew the issue was not merely a disproportion in amounts of attention meted out in the workshop. She was not privy to Holmes's judgment in his letter to Sam Albert that she was "like a child and three times as selfish" (24 January 1961), but Sexton's reply indicates that she had felt symbolic family roles being acted out in the group.

> In the long pull, John, where you might be proud of me, you are ashamed of me. I keep pretending not to notice . . . But then, you remind me of my father (and I KNOW that's not your fault.) But there is something else here . . . who do I remind you of?

The group went on meeting, its format unchanged, until Holmes developed cancer a year later. Holmes's disgust with Sexton increased. He seems to have diffused the problem by inviting others to confide their mistrust and dislike of Sexton and to confirm his judgment that she was a bad influence with reference to both art and manners. "I have heard lately two lengthy judgments of her, exactly like my bitterest feelings, and the impression is shared by others that she does you harm," he warned Maxine Kumin on 6 August.

For Sexton, however, the exchange of letters in February had a clarifying significance, elaborated in a dream she reported to her therapist a few days after writing the letter.

> AS: This perfect voice was enunciating very carefully as if to tell me exactly how it was—and yet he was kind and patient about it—very irritated but patient all at once—and this was terrible because whatever he was telling me I was seeing the reverse. [. . .] [H]e'd talk reasonably, reasonably, and he wouldn't stop telling me, you know, just nicely [. . .] it would become so frightening that I would pound on the floor [. . .] maybe screaming stop it, stop it, [. . .] that would be the feeling: LISTEN! and then I'd try something else. PLEASE. Like HE COULDN'T HEAR ME.

> Dr: There is one thing I have trouble understanding; that is, what you wanted when you had to pound on the floor.

> AS: Well, associate. If you're pounding on the floor then you must be down on the floor. You don't stand up. Crouched [. . .] more like a child or an animal or someone very afraid. It's kind of crazy to be on the floor—and yet it's kind of afraid, really. [. . .] He keeps telling me what's so and probably he's right but it isn't so for me so I've got to try again to make the same thing so for both of us so we can make sense to each other. Otherwise, I'm crazy. I'm lost.

> Dr: If you can talk to one person, you're not crazy?

> AS: Right. [. . .] One sane person, that is.

Like the poem **"For John . . ."** with which Sexton had replied to his letter the year before, this dream is also a "condensation of it all." The unnamed masculine speaker, a composite censor, blends several identities—teacher, critic, father, mother, doctor, senior poet: those in charge of telling "exactly how it is" and unable to "HEAR," Present only as "this perfect voice," his identity may include some of the prestigious reviewers of Sexton's first book: possibly James Dickey ("one feels tempted to drop them furtively into the nearest ashcan, rather than be caught with them in the presence of so much naked suffering"); possibly Geoffrey Hartman ("With such a theme, [. . .] did the poet have to exploit the more sensational aspect of her experience?"). "Kind of patient, telling me about it just nicely," he devastates her.

The doctor asks—reasonably, reasonably—what she wants pounding on the floor, a question Sexton answers rather indirectly. Is the only way to stop the senior poet's voice an act of violence performed in fear, "like a child or an animal"? No: Sexton wants in the dream what she wanted from the workshop, what she had described in her letter to Holmes, the "mutual intuitive creative act" by which the individual poets merged their strengths through disciplined listening. "Probably he's right," but this only makes him distant and self-absorbed. Disengaging from the craziness and fear inspired by being ignored ("you remind me of my father"), Sexton acknowledges—almost in spite of herself—the powers she can marshal against the censor: "I've got to try again [. . .] so we can make sense to each other."

The dream images, like the "awkward bowl / with all its cracked stars shining," radiate outward into other significant relationships formed around words. Among those unable to HEAR, by this date, are Sexton's father and mother, both dead in the spring of 1959, the same spring Houghton Mifflin accepted *To Bedlam and Part Way Back.* They did not live to read Anne Harvey Sexton's words in a book nor to see the world confirm her as a poet. As in her dream, their impenetrability inspired stubborn efforts to "make the same thing so for both of us"; from *All My Pretty Ones* through *The Awful Rowing Toward God,* Mother and Father remain in Sexton's poems the powerful withholders of confirming attention, now cleverly dead and beyond appeal.

Out in the real world, however, Sexton's bond with Maxine Kumin involved much reciprocal listening. Kumin has described how each had a special phone installed in her study: "we sometimes connected with a phone call and kept that line linked for hours at a stretch [. . .]; we whistled into the receiver for each other when we were ready to resume." The relationship, fruitful for both, helped Sexton engage her critical faculties once she had completed the process she referred to as "milking the unconscious." Describing it to an interviewer, Sexton said "all poets have a little critic in their heads. [. . .] [Y]ou have to turn off the little critic while you are beginning a poem so that it doesn't inhibit you. Then you have to turn it on again when you are revising and refining." Whistling into the receiver for Maxine was a way of calling up the inner critic by paging an external one. Sexton made use of such a model throughout her life: as playwright; as member of the chamber rock group "Her Kind" that performed her poems to music; as a teacher herself; and, of course, in the workshop.

If John Holmes is one of the identities of the censor in Sexton's dream, then her struggle was not with Holmes the man but with Holmes the Man of Letters: paragon of correctness, arbiter of taste, warden of the literary tradition. The rather playful, even daughterly, tone of Sexton's reply to Holmes's attack suggests that she had already detected the sense that might be made of their mutual hostility. Holmes's distaste for Sexton's work was not based on a judgment that she was a second-rate poet. "What you have is a genius," he had written her in the letter rejecting the *Bedlam* manuscript, "an unaccountable, unconscious, startling gift with words, and emotions, and patterns for them." His quarrel was with her subject, "your time in the hospital and the complications that took you there" (8 February 1959).

What took Sexton to the hospital was a preference for suicide over the role of mother as she had construed it from her own glamorous, intelligent, repressive, and punitive mother—in the world's eyes, a competent, well-bred woman. The disturbing subject of the *Bedlam* poems is Sexton's experience of the female roles of mother and daughter as in themselves a sickness, and not merely her sickness. Thus in poems like ' The Double Image," she writes of her horror at passing on femaleness itself.

> [. . .] this was the cave of the mirror,
> that double woman who stares

> at herself, as if she were petrified
> [. . . . .]
> I, who was never quite sure
> about being a girl, needed another
> life, another image to remind me.
> And this was my worst guilt; you could not cure
> nor soothe it. I made you to find me.

Sexton resisted Holmes's judgment that *To Bedlam* contained "so self-centered and narrow a diary that it would be clinical only," just as she later resisted the label "confessional" for her poetry. Speaking in the name of art ("Her motives are wrong, artistically") and asking another woman writer to agree that Sexton's subject matter was an extension of her intrusive social behavior ("she writes to bare and shock and confess"), Holmes insisted that the sick woman was discontinuous with the poet. But Sexton knew the poetry was a revelation and a critique, faithful to the female unconscious; it reflected the high cost of socializing women into feminine roles. Hers were truths that had not been put into poetry before, or with quite the same emphases, by a woman writer. "There's something else here . . . who do I remind you of?" Sexton was asking the question of an entire tradition largely devoid of the voice of female consciousness—though it was a voice the auditor might be expected to recognize, having heard it at home, or in his own bad dreams.

IV. Coda: Assimilating "Female" to "Poet"

All of Sexton's poems about the hospital and the complications that took her there were published and proceeded to make her reputations: first as a "confessional" poet and then as a woman poet—a category that was developing in literature at the time of her death. The large audiences for her work included mental patients, psychotherapists, and great numbers of women, most of whom did not share Holmes's point of view concerning Sexton's subject matter. The exchange of letters in 1961 was, apparently, the last open confrontation between them; however, it remained for Sexton, who outlived John Holmes after all, to write the interpretive coda to their relationship, in an elegy written shortly after Holmes's death in 1962. Titled **"Somewhere in Africa,"** the poem takes up the themes of reasonableness and wildness expressed in her dream and in her letter to Holmes and synthesizes them in a new way.

> Must you leave, John Holmes, with the prayers and
>   psalms
> you never said, said over you? Death with no rage
> to weigh you down? Praised by the mild God, his arm
> over the pulpit, leaving you timid, with no real age,
>
> whitewashed by belief, as dull as the windy preacher!
> Dead of a dark thing, John Holmes, you've been lost

in the college chapel, mourned as father and teacher,
mourned with piety and grace under the University
    Cross.
Your last book unsung, your last hard words
    unknown,
abandoned by science, cancer blossomed in your
    throat,
rooted like bougainvillea into your gray backbone,
ruptured your pores until you wore it like a coat.

The thick petals, the exotic reds, the purples and
    whites
covered up your nakedness and bore you up with all
their blind power. I think of your last June nights
in Boston, your body swollen but light, your eyes
    small

as you let the nurses carry you into a strange land.
. . . If this is death and God is necessary let him be
    hidden
from the missionary, the well-wisher and the glad
    hand.
Let God be some tribal female who is known but
    forbidden.

Let there be this God who is a woman who will place
    you
upon her shallow boat, who is a woman naked to the
    waist,
moist with palm oil and sweat, a woman of some
    virtue
and wild breasts, her limbs excellent, unbruised and
    chaste.

Let her take you. She will put twelve strong men at
    the oars
for you are stronger than mahogany and your bones
    fill
the boat high with fruit and bark from the interior.
She will have you now, whom the funeral cannot kill.

John Holmes, cut from a single tree, lie heavy in her
    hold
and go down that river with the ivory, the copra and
    the gold.

In Sexton's elegy reasonableness and wildness became two gods: one male, identified with institutions; one female, identified with poetry. The formal art of the piece reinforces the ceremonial tone, yet its argument insists that poetry belongs to the territory of wildness: libido, darkness, fertility, beauty, strangeness. The poem seems to tap all Sexton's ambivalent love for Holmes. It praises his integrity ("cut from a single tree") and claims him for the paradise reserved for the tribe of poets, but it also distinguishes the censor from the artist in him. Separating the

dead poet from the authority figures in the poem—"mild God," "windy preacher"—Sexton conveys her understanding that the conflict between her and Holmes was not merely a conflict between two temperaments. It was a successful struggle, on her side, against the conventions and "standards" John Holmes affirmed, which Sexton experienced as powers, powers that could repress, even extinguish, the growth of her art. Criticizing her work, Holmes invariably used the words "childish" and "selfish"; he saw the poems only as referring to the person, whom he deplored, not as radiant signs. It was fortunate for Sexton that neither she nor Holmes was willing to abandon the struggle until it had forced her to clarify this difference for herself. Holmes never failed to assert his standards—which were highly acceptable ones in literary Boston and elsewhere—as part of a process of taking her seriously. Under his gentlemanly disapproval she acquired knowledge of herself as a poet of damage and resistance.

By the time she wrote **"Somewhere in Africa,"** Sexton had achieved genuine separation from all her early mentors—Snodgrass, Lowell, James Wright—who were also, of course, censors; she had acquired a public persona and voice that was distinctively female. And if the female subjects of her poems were dismembered, bruised, unchaste, and self-vilifying, the female god of art in her elegy is none of these. In Sexton's apprenticeship, femaleness itself was an aspect of identity that had, with great difficulty, been assimilated to the sense of authority necessary to mastery. **"Somewhere in Africa"** identifies femaleness as one of the poet's powers; with all the strength of the known but forbidden, the poet carries her censor and teacher to his final resting place in her hold, on her terms.

Diana Hume George (essay date Fall 1985)

SOURCE: "Is It True? Feeding, Feces, and Creativity in Anne Sexton's Poetry," in *Soundings: An Interdisciplinary Journal*, Vol. 68, No. 3, Fall, 1985, pp. 357-71.

[*In the following essay, George explores the psychoanalytic significance of infant feeding, nurturance, and excretion in Sexton's poetry, especially as evident in* O Ye Tongues. *According to George, "In her version of the emergence of poetic consciousness, the infant's ambivalent attachment to feces becomes a metaphor for fertilization of the imagination and for the creation of a sustaining self."*]

This is an essay on beginnings and endings, feces and fruit, in the poetry of Anne Sexton. I will end it in the place of specifically female grace made accessible by Stephanie Demetrakopoulos' mediation, "The Nursing Mother and

Feminine Metaphysics." But I begin earlier in the feeding cycle, at a moment that is by its nature far less graceful. The extremities in Anne Sexton's poetry might be aberrant, but her dilemma belongs to a lesser degree to all women, and certainly to all women poets. The dilemma and its poetic resolution have to do with the development of creativity in infancy, with the relationship between feces and language. Sexton explores the uses of oral ingestion and anal defiance as primary sources of power in poetry. In her version of the emergence of poetic consciousness, the infant's ambivalent attachment to feces becomes a metaphor for fertilization of the imagination and for the creation of a sustaining self. Her poetic journey from psychoanalysis to myth ends with power and goodness, but begins with impotence and evil.

Anne Sexton believed that evil crawled into her, "something I ate" (**"Is It True?"**). The ingestion of evil begins with birth, with lactation and feeding, whereby "all my need took you down like a meal." She needs the white love of mother's milk, but because this feeding depletes the mother, she ingests evil, becomes the body of evil in the act of feeding.

> When I tell the priest I am full
> of bowel movement, right into the fingers,
> he shrugs. To him shit is good.
> To me, to my mother, it was poison
> and the poison was all of me
> in the nose, in the ears, in the lungs.
> That's why language fails.
> Because to one, shit is a feeder of plants,
> to another the evil that permeates them
> and although they try,
> day after day of childhood,
> they can't push the poison out.
> So much for language.
> So much for psychology.
> God lives in shit—I have been told.

"Is it true?" she asks. In **"The Hoarder,"** "there is something there / I've got to get and I dig / down." She finds the objects and sins of her past as she digs—the aunt's clock she broke, the five dollars belonging to her sister that she ripped up—until she reaches "my first doll that water went / into and water came out of"; yet what she must find is deeper still:

> earlier it was the diaper I wore
> and the dirt thereof and my
> mother hating me for it and me
> loving me for it but the hate
> won didn't it yes the distaste
> won the disgust won and because
> of this I am a hoarder of words

> I hold them in though they are
> dung oh God I am a digger
> I am not an idler
> am I?

If the problem begins at birth and deepens with the enculturation embodied in toilet training, it can become endlessly cyclical, for we must all eat and defecate. Sexton identified with and loved that creature—"body, you are good goods"—yet was so ambivalent toward it that the struggle between creatureliness and creativity ripped her apart. "Is it true?" became a central question of her quest as spiritual seeker, as poet, as woman. Is it true that God blesses feces, lives in it, that the smell of it is the smell of life rather than of death? Is it true that God can love the rat? (Is it true that God is the rat? That the rat accomplishes and keeps the miracle, as in **"The Deep Museum?"**) If only she could be sure. But she is not. There is no certainty, and Sexton craved absolutes as she craved the sun that shone on her like a "dozen glistening haloes."

The parable of maturation from infancy centers on the feeding/digesting/excreting cycle that makes us creatures so entirely. In this story, as in the scenario envisioned by psychoanalytic theory, the infant loves her own feces, is proud of its production, naps in the ooze of its warmth; in Sexton's version, unlike that of psychoanalysis, it is at this moment that the infant is most able to move toward imaginative invention. When the infant discovers that this dear production in the aura of which it ruminates for lonely hours is suddenly distasteful to the parents, its emerging sense of clean and creaturely identity is forever betrayed. And where does waste come from? From feeding, by which the infant gains its life sustenance at the mother's breast. Although it will be years before the maturing human knows about this relationship—before, in other words, it is fully introduced into the symbolic order—its body may well "know" it from the start; surely the mother knows, and can in nursing communicate her acceptance and/or disgust. Henceforth, the connection between nourishment and waste will be ambivalent. Ironically, almost embarrassingly, this is Sexton's version of the ideal moment before experience teaches its brutal lesson: this moment of the unity of waste and creativity. The God that is said to be all soul—and also, heretically, all immanence—embodies the same ambivalence. The trinity's division of spiritual from bodily and human aspects of godhead becomes emblematic of that division in the civilized human creature. Even Christian culture's God, it seems, is not able to endure the body. At death, we project the reunion of soul and body into the last moments of time, relegating it to an eternity that begins, tellingly, with the Day of Judgment.

Thus the question, "Is it true?" is central to Sexton's spiritual quest. It is also central to her dilemma as both poet and woman. Juhasz, Ostriker, Lauter, and Middlebrook have detailed the ways in which Sexton's femaleness became her central preoccupation as poet-person. According to Ostriker, "she gives us full helpings of her breasts, her uterus, her menstruation, her abortion, her 'tiny jail' of a vagina, her mother's and daughters' breasts, everyone's operations, the act of eating . . . , even the trauma of her childhood enemas." In her review of **The Complete Poems** Middlebrook says that Sexton's lasting importance as a modern poet "lies in her bold exploration of female sexuality and female spirituality." Beginning with **Live or Die,** Middlebrook finds, Sexton "begins to explore the suspicion that what she suffers from is femaleness itself, and is probably incurable." Is it true? Can God love her less, or not at all, or just as much, because she is a woman? Can she love herself? Is it true that "we must all eat beautiful women," that self-sacrifice is the condition and the mandate of femininity? Is it true that she is defective because female, or is it true, more hopefully, that although woman is more rat than man is, God will take that rat in his arms and embrace her? Or might it be true that woman's nurturance, her creativity in the body, makes her more beloved of God? Does the Father-God love his own image best—that of man—or does he crave that "other" not only human and bodied, but also female? Or does "his own image" include both genders as suggested by "male and female created he them"?

These are questions Sexton answered continuously and contradictorily throughout her personal and poetic lives. If the relationship between nurturance and creativity is of the reciprocal and imaginative sort emblemized by the serpent of eternity with its tail in its mouth, then she will be blessed. But Sexton's persona suspects that the waste with which she is sullied soon after birth, once dear and now evil, is specifically female; that mother and father, and therefore God, find female waste the really messy stuff, the manure of the universe. If "shit is the evil that permeates them" to some, and the feeder of plants to others, it will be, ironically, the nurturant and recreative female who is most likely to experience it as permeation. If the body's unruly creatureliness is the antithesis of what is valued by civilization—well-known for its discontent with anything messy—then what body is indeed the messiest, the most creaturely? That body is of course woman's, "fastened to the earth, listening for its small animal noises," according to Sexton, pulled by the tide of sea and moon, bringing forth humanity between urine and feces, in blood and ooze. Neither God nor man, it seems, will ever forgive woman his ignominious source between her thighs—nor may she forgive herself in Anne Sexton's world, no matter how hard she tries, "day after day of childhood," to "push the poison out."

That, says Sexton, is "why language fails." The direct connection between feces and language made so explicit in **"The Hoarder"** and **"Is It True?"** is implicit throughout

Sexton's poetry and is peculiar to her dilemma as female *poet,* that double bind. To "hoard" words, as the human infant sometimes is said to hoard bowel movements, unable to push them out, filled with them to the lungs and fingertips, is to curse oneself; in Blake's metaphor, it is to "murder an infant in its cradle." If your mother and your father—your culture—hate you for smelling up the hearth, then you will try to keep your waste inside. By analogy, the effort to push it out, to speak, will meet with equal contempt, because the woman's waste, her special evil, is the bodily reminder of mortality and creatureliness.

When I say that this was Sexton's dilemma as poet, I mean that literally. The contempt reserved for Sexton and "her kind" is special indeed, quite different and more vitriolic than that first dispensed in careful and restrained doses to Robert Lowell and W. D. Snodgrass. If the sneer derives from fear, as Alicia Ostriker says—and certainly she is right—that is warmer comfort for critics than it must have been for the poet. Ostriker points out with wry irritation that "Anne Sexton is the easiest poet in the world to condescend to. Critics get in line for the pleasure of filing her under N for Narcissist and announcing that she lacks reticence."

For the living poet, the process began immediately, with the special and almost haunted contempt of her teacher, John Holmes, quoted at previously unavailable length by Sexton's biographer, Diane Middlebrook. Bear in mind the scatological foundation of this discussion while I cite a few of the positions taken by Sexton's critics, both friends and enemies. Holmes "distrusts the very source and subject of a great many of your poems." He is deeply bothered "that you use poetry this way. It's all a release for you, but what is it for anyone else except a spectacle of someone experiencing release?" James Dickey's now famous review of the poems in **To Bedlam and Part Way Back** is perhaps the most appropriate: "One feels tempted to drop them furtively into the nearest ashcan, rather than be caught with them in the presence of such naked suffering." More recently, Rosemary Johnson, who approaches Sexton with some sympathy and respect, still feels obliged (only partly ironically) to wonder whether "such messy preoccupations will remain to stain the linen of the culture for long or whether good taste bleaches out the most stubborn stain eventually."

To underscore the obvious: a woman of "her kind" is more than invited, is indeed required, to feel that "infantile" connection between feces and words. If she hoards her words, then she is full with waste to the fingertips. If she shares them, the critics declare that she has messed her pants in public, that such "confessions" are indeed nothing but waste matter, smelly soil that belongs—where else?—in the ashcan, furtively dropped there by the reader lest he be "caught with them." The male critic wants to drop it in the can, while the female critic, in wry, womanly fashion, wonders rather how we will get out the stain left on the linen of culture. Holmes even advised other workshop members to stay away from Sexton, believing her influence to be dangerous and pernicious. He speaks for many of us in his "distrust of the source and subject" of her poetry: her own very bodily, excruciatingly female, madness.

If psychoanalytic theory sometimes seems silly because of the attention it pays to toilet training and to its symbolic meaning and lasting influence on our lives, the reaction of critics to Anne Sexton's poetry seems to prove its case. Perhaps, after all, a great deal of our enduring conflicts, joys, suffering, confidence or lack of it, emerges from this first encounter with enculturation. Perhaps, indeed, it all has something fundamental to do with language, imagination, creativity. And why should these concerns not be within the domain of our poetry?

Swallowing Magic, Delivering Anne

I am directed back by Diane Middlebrook and Stephanie Demetrakopoulos to *O Ye Tongues.* They find this psalm sequence among Sexton's most accomplished poems, formally and thematically. I did not share this opinion until recently, probably because I have been among those disposed to see early Sexton as best Sexton, and late Sexton as sloppy and self-parodic, I locate the central poem for the relationship between infancy and creativity, and between waste and language, in the **"Third Psalm."** In *O Ye Tongues,* Sexton employs what Middlebrook calls "that most nurturant rhetoric: praise." I want here to employ that same rhetoric to suggest some of Sexton's finest poetic accomplishments. I consider this poem significant for its mythic and prophetic qualities, and its place in Sexton's radical retelling of the story of humanity's creation, fall and renewal in the poetry that begins with *Transformations* and includes **"The Jesus Papers," "The Death of the Fathers,"** and the **"Furies"** and **"Angels"** sequences.

O Ye Tongues begins with a tone reminiscent of the Psalms; its subject is Genesis:

> Let the waters divide so that God may wash his face
> in first light.
> Let there be pin holes in the sky in which God puts
> his little
>   finger.
>   . . .
> Let there be seasons so the sky dogs will jump across
> the sun in
>   December.
>   . . .
> Let there be a heaven so that man may outlive his
> grasses.

A tonally non-violent flood—"Let Noah build an ark out of the old lady's shoe and fill it with the creatures of the Lord,"—is conducted by a largely benevolent God who is presented only once in a slightly ironic light when the ark of salvation serves to "notch his belt repeatedly." The joyous bulk of humanity imagined at its daily tasks and delights is finally particularized in the **"Third Psalm"** with an "I" not quite or only Anne Sexton; she is the human infant in civilization. That this infant is American and urban is specified by her coming "from the grave of my mama's belly into the commerce of Boston."

Here Anne Sexton achieves the perfect and delicate balance between telling her own story and telling the story of us all; this is, as Middlebrook points out, "an eerily, beautifully sustained account of the emergence of the symbol-making consciousness in infancy," and a "parable of liberation from confinement by means of invention." I am especially interested here in the part played in that drama by eating and defecating. Sexton envisions for us an infant, alone with herself in the new universe for many more hours each day than she is accompanied by adults (the "big balloons" that "bend us over"), a baby full of human intelligence and not yet able to occupy her mind with the mental activity that precedes articulated identity.

> For I could not read or speak and on the long nights
>   I could not turn the moon off or count the lights
>   of cars across the ceiling.

What does such a one do, alone and newly birthed from one kind of grave? In Sexton's story, she begins to engage in mental creativity, a "reproduction" that is at the same time a splitting. Such a process had long been surmised and theoretically posited by psychoanalysis to take place only with and through the infant's contact with the mother:

> For Anne and Christopher were born in my head as I
>   howled at the grave of the roses, the ninety-four
>   rose creches of my bedroom.

The imaginary brother, or other self, functions in Sexton's parable as an animus figure, who prior to the formation of a fully recognizable "I" is united (and split) into a "we," a "kind of company when the big balloons did not bend over us." Here Sexton implicitly locates the source both of wholeness and fragmentation in the emerging psyche, dependent crucially not only upon the *presence* of the big balloons (alienating, even if needed for nurture and as a reference point for the emergence of identity) but upon their sustained and frequent *absence*. With no one to talk to, to gaze upon and therefrom gain a sense of reality and identity, the infant creates its own companion within the psyche. We have long recognized that the "imaginary companion" of very young childhood emerges from such a need to fill up lonely hours, but popular mythology and formal theory alike place its emergence later. Sexton, sometimes more psychoanalytic than the theory itself, sometimes seems capable of being, presses back the boundaries toward birth, supposing that the infant will engage in the process it has just been through: a birth which sunders it from connection, yet ironically brings it from death into life. Both imitative and inventive by nature, Sexton's infant makes an analogy of the birth trauma, compensating for its loss, celebrating its life. In an analogy to the psychoanalytic concept of penis envy, Sexton conflates developmental stages into this creative act of the brother's mental birth: Christopher is her twin, "holding his baby cock like a minnow."

When the balloons appear, then the infant lapses into passivity, even if that passivity is sometimes angry:

> For I lay pale as flour and drank moon juice from a
> rubber tip.

And what else does the infant do? It wets its pants and it shits, and when it does, "Christopher smiled and said let the air be sweet with your soil." Here Christopher becomes that self-affirming voice of confidence, assuring Anne that she is altogether good. She can listen to Christopher, "unless the balloon came and changed my bandage." The *body* that experiences the cleansing and feeding rituals is the female body, in this case, so it is "she" who first experiences humiliation and distaste from the balloons. Christopher, entirely mental, escapes censure and confusion. As I read him here, Christopher is not only the aspect of self that infuses one with self-confidence, but also the infant and imaginative forerunner of Sexton's later Christ as "ragged brother" and fellow-traveler, the human figure of godhead with whom she can identify, and whom she eventually lost; for Christopher in enlarged form will later change from self/brother to Father/God. Oscillation between identification with and alienation from this later-exiled aspect of the self is foreshadowed even here:

> For I lay as single as death. Christopher lay beside
>   me.
>   He was living.

Christopher takes care of her when the balloons disappear, and they talk together. In answer to her question, "where are we?" (she is experiencing the "boundaries of the closed room"), Christopher says, "Jail." When Christopher sleeps, and is not there to answer the questions or to reassure her, the infant "Anne" learns to rely on herself, surmounting the frustration of the fingers that "would not stay," and that "broke out of my mouth." Although I suspect that other plausible readings might call forth less happy inferences about Christopher's otherness and "Anne's" separation from him, he still remains her infant's own creation, a symbol for self-

insemination when they ruminate together, and for the necessity of lonely self-reliance when he is unavailable to her.

> For I was prodding myself out of my sleep, out the
> green room.
> The sleep of the desperate who travel backwards into
> darkness.

Momentarily alone, she knows she must be her own awakener, must bring herself out of sleep even while Christopher sleeps, "making sea sounds."

What "Anne" figures out alone, and then with Christopher when he reawakens, is the final lesson of the parable, and a fair account of the ambiguous polarities of Anne Sexton's subsequent life; perhaps, read another way, it speaks of all of our lives:

> For birth was a disease and Christopher and I
> invented the cure.
> For we swallow magic and we deliver Anne.

Considering Anne Sexton's life and death, and the context of such imagery in the rest of her poetry, we can only read these lines as radically ambiguous. Sexton apparently did consider even her very birth and existence a disease; the invention of "cure" in "swallowing magic" has ironically defeating references to her dependence upon drugs and her repeated efforts to kill herself with pills. In **"Wanting to Die,"** she writes:

> Twice I have so simply declared myself,
> have possessed the enemy, eaten the enemy,
> have taken on his craft, his magic.

"The enemy" can be either life or death; in either case, to take on the craft and the magic refers to killing oneself through a parody of normal nurturance, through ingestion that cures once and for all the disease of life sustained from the beginning by that other ingestion of food which results in the waste one cannot get out of one's fingers or one's soul.

Sexton always placed herself in the middle and mediating positions of mother-daughter constellations.
—*Diana Hume George*

But whatever the echoed allusion here to previous and future sources of disease and cure, the function of "magic" in *O Ye Tongues* is the creation of a sustaining self; not only of a sustaining self, but of a creative impulse. The

"Anne" delivered in the rest of the sequence is the heroine of her own story, coming of age into womanhood, motherhood, and poetry. From her beginnings, lying in quiet and in soiled diapers, talking to herself, inventing Christopher, surrounded by her own sweet soil and its smell, she rises into yet another birth, this one meant to correct the flaws of the first. In the **"Fourth Psalm,"** Anne and Christopher "come forth" from "soil" and make "poison sweet." The mole who comes from the ground—that "artificial anus"—into the light is capable of "swallowing the sun." Every image in the **"Fourth Psalm"** is natural, earthly, and regenerative: daisy, orange, snail, squid, cauliflower, rose, daffodil, dog, carp, leopard, even cockroach, all are blessed. Given little praise for her creatureliness or her femaleness either by culture or by its designated enforcers in the persons of parents, "Anne" celebrates that feminine creature from soil and sea, as she does in so many poems. In the **"Seventh Psalm,"** she takes on the female function of reproduction as an embodiment of "a magnitude," a "many," each of us "patting ourselves dry with a towel." At the same time she is a solitary figure, "in the dark room putting bones into place." Seeing the large design, she births her baby into "many worlds of milk."

The progress from her infancy to her own motherhood marks a transformation of the meaning of the feeding cycle; that transformation is from psychoanalysis to myth. Sexton always placed herself in the middle and mediating positions of mother-daughter constellations. Her poems about the mother-daughter relationship in which she is daughter are always painfully ambivalent, while her poems to her own daughters are joyfully ambivalent. Understanding what went awry between herself and her mother, she endeavors to ensure that she will not do to her daughters what was done to her. She will try to experience nursing not as psychic depletion, but as spiritual abundance. The terms of this transformation are theoretically outlined in antithetical essays by Freud ("On the Transformation of Instincts") and Stephanie Demetrakopoulos ("The Nursing Mother and Feminine Metaphysics").

"To begin with," says Freud, "it would appear that in the products of the unconscious—spontaneous ideas, phantasies, symptoms—the conceptions *faeces* (money, gift), *child,* and *penis* are seldom distinguished and are easily interchangeable." While I agree with the feminist contention that what women "envy" is "power," I support the psychoanalytic contention that the metaphor is grounded in an always bodily reality—i.e., "penis envy" is a valid term. Sexton's infant conjures up a penis of her own in Christopher, "holding his baby cock like a minnow." It is through the mediation of fecal matter that the infant first experiences the desire for "power," experienced in Sexton's poem as invention and creativity. The infant engages in that other "birthing" in which she does indeed deliver a child. In

Freud's scenario, this will take place over a period of years and will normally end with the female's relinquishment of the desire for the penis in the substitute "child." In Sexton the process in the early psalms of *O Ye Tongues* is entirely imaginative; she has already begun to transform the terms of psychoanalysis into mythic structures. Freud is concerned in his essay to trace adult character traits that have their sources in the anal stage, and among these traits is obstinacy, stubbornness, or defiance. Defecation affords the infant and young child its first occasion to decide between a "narcissistic and an object-loving attitude." He or she can offer up feces as a gift, or else retain them as a means of "asserting his own will." Because he is concerned to trace the etiology of neurosis, Freud's language is censorious; failure to relinquish the gift results in defiant, obstinate attitudes that spring from a "narcissistic clinging to the pleasure of anal eroticism."

Anne Sexton has been called "narcissistic," and in other poems she does speak of withholding feces, but I want to transform the meanings of the Freudian terminology. The story of Sexton's infant may indeed be that of a developing neurosis; yet it is also a description of another and creative kind of "defiance," a primary source of energy and power in Sexton's poetry. The early formation of an individualized, courageous stance in art may be connected to this infant drama of giving and withholding. Sexton's infant wants to keep that penis, that power, that child. It belongs to her, more especially since it is rejected rather than welcomed by the mother because of its female character. The nursing experienced by the mother as depletion results in this product she will also despise, and Sexton's infant makes of this situation the best that could be hoped for. In the contest of wills between resentful mother and defiant infant, the infant cuts her losses in the real world by compensating in her imaginative life. What Freud mourns as symptom, Sexton celebrates as power.

When Sexton's infant grows into maternity herself, she tries to perceive nursing differently, aware that her perception of it will have vast consequences for the child:

> For the baby suckles and there is a people made
> of milk for her to use. There are milk trees to
> hiss her on. There are milk beds in which to
> lie and dream of a warm room. There are milk
> fingers to fold and unfold. There are milk
> bottoms that are wet and caressed and put into
> their cotton. For there are many worlds of milk
> to walk through under the moon.

Stephanie Demetrakopoulos uses Sexton's psalms to forward a thesis about nursing. If Levi Strauss's metaphor "The Raw and the Cooked" is a central image for raw nature turning into culture, then "woman cooking, woman gestating, woman nursing" are all images of that process:

> Woman's alchemy changes blood to milk; her body
> is a transmutation system that has the power to
> change her very body to food which becomes in turn
> the physical and psychic energy of her
> child. She is creating an incarnate soul,
> assisting its growth.

Demetrakopoulos sees Sexton's imagery of nursing in the **"Seventh Psalm"** as a sign of specifically female grace. She experiences it as the "connective tissue, the flow, the indisputable plenitude of a loving ground of being, a goddess who seems to amalgamate Demeter with Sophia."

This movement from compensatory struggle to assisting the growth of an incarnate soul was clearly conceived by Sexton as midwifed by the mother who governs the tone of the feeding cycle.

> For the baby grows and the mother places her giggle-
> jog
>   on her knee and sings a song of Christopher and
>   Anne.
> For the mother sings songs of the baby that knew.

"Anne" herself, now become a mother, is the "baby that knew" what we all know in some private reach of unconsciousness inaccessible to many of us, accessible to Anne Sexton throughout her life; the loneliness *and* the companionable creativity of infancy are the double source of all we are, all we might become. "For the mother remembers the baby she was and never locks and twists or puts lonely into a foreign place." This is, after all, a hopeful fiction, a myth, for motherhood precipitated Anne Sexton's first mental breakdown, and her illness later did compel her to "put lonely into a foreign place." She acknowledged in many poems that despite her efforts to make it so, love has no simple, "uncomplicated hymn."

Thus the mother of the ninth and final psalm sees that motherhood cannot be her only creation. She must "climb her own mountain." For this woman, the mountain is poetry:

> For I am placing fist over fist on rock and plunging
>   into the altitude of words. The silence of words.

Even as the mother does so, the daughter "starts up her own mountain" to "build her own city and fill it with her own oranges, her own words." The image of the orange functions in *O Ye Tongues* as an embryo of the human form: the expectant mother "has swallowed a bagful of oranges and she is well pleased." Now the same orange is equated with language, especially the language of poetry that oper-

ates by the creation of metaphor and images—another gestation, another birthing. Sexton has come full circle from feces to fruit, from language to babies, in the regenerative cycle. Sometimes her false pregnancies have filled her with waste. But she bears ripe fruit in moments of genuine conception, of greater grace. The child is mother to the woman. The poem arises from the imaginative impregnation of the self.

William H. Shurr (essay date Fall 1985)

SOURCE: "Mysticism and Suicide: Anne Sexton's Last Poetry," in *Soundings: An Interdisciplinary Journal,* Vol. 68, No. 3, Fall, 1985, pp. 335-56.

[*In the following essay, Shurr discusses the significance of Sexton's increasing religiosity and impending suicide revealed in* The Awful Rowing Toward God.]

> Schweigen. Wer inniger schwieg rührt an die Wurzeln
> der Rede.
> —Rilke

> And Rilke, think of Rilke with his terrible pain.
> —Anne Sexton

When Anne Sexton died in 1974, she had just produced what she intended to be her final book of poems, *The Awful Rowing Toward God.* Before that volume the direction of her work was unclear. There had been seven earlier books of poetry, beginning with the forceful and unsettling poems of *To Bedlam and Part Way Back* (1960). Her signature was the clear line of personal narrative; but it was frequently not clear whether the narratives were true biography or a kind of artistically manipulated pseudo-biography. She became famous, with the Pulitzer Prize in 1966, and the reader became familiar with such frequently anthologized poems as **"Unknown Girl in the Maternity Ward," "The Truth the Dead Know," "The Farmer's Wife,"** and **"The Abortion."** We knew her voice, but each poem seemed an unrelated victory. Her early classification among the "confessional poets" never seemed to confer the insights it had promised. One fellow poet dismissed her work as garbage; at the other pole, Sandra Gilbert canonized her divine madness in an essay entitled "Jubilate Anne."

The reader's reward was finally *The Awful Rowing Toward God,* the book of a mature poet whose dedication to art was single-minded and supreme, who could finally declare with utter simplicity "I am in love with words." Sexton had prepared and intended *The Awful Rowing Toward God* as a posthumous publication. A year before she died she told an interviewer that she had written the first drafts of these poems in two and a half weeks, that she would continue to polish them, but that she would allow publication only after her death. Her published letters add the chilling information that she had then sent the manuscript to her publisher and was actually reading the galley proofs on the day she took her own life.

The volume gains authority as Anne Sexton's intended final work. The shape and direction of her poetic career finally becomes clear. Clear also is the grim fact that the suicide is a consciously intended part of the book. We miss her meaning, the total program she provided for her reader to experience, without this stark fact.

As the "Rowing" of the title suggests, the image of the Sea pervades this collection; and it soon becomes obvious that this metaphorical Sea is the carrier for one of the most profound and pervasive ideas of western culture.

One of Sexton's earliest reviewers noticed the prominence of the Sea in her work, and when a later interviewer asked her about it she affirmed its personal importance to her. She was a New Englander: the sea was in her history and in her daily experience. The imagery aligns her, also, with some of the most prominent American writers. Emily Dickinson was another virtually land-locked lady in whose poetry the Sea is pervasive. The New England tradition was remembered as having begun with a dangerous adventure across the unknown ocean; the culture was supported throughout its history by commerce on the sea. For Sexton personally, the sea was escape and renewal, where the family had vacationed since her childhood. It is both a danger and life-support system. In most of her poetry it is also the setting for the journey of the soul. The phrase most often quoted by the reviewers from her early books was the one she retrieved from Kafka and used as epigraph for *All My Pretty Ones:* ". . . a book should serve as the axe for the frozen sea within us."

In her final volume this Sea becomes warm with swarming life. The two poems which begin and end the collection, **"Rowing"** and **"The Rowing Endeth,"** set up a framework of sea-exploration, and there are overt references to the Sea in two-thirds of the poems. The Sea is quite literally the fluid medium in which the mental life of this poetry takes place. The first poem begins with the emergence of the Self from non-being; the child is gradually able to do more human things but feels itself still "undersea all the time." We are only seven pages into the collection when the perception becomes clear that the Sea is the source of all life:

> From the sea came up a hand,
> ignorant as a penny,
> troubled with the salt of its mother,

> mute with the silence of the fishes,
> quick with the altars of the tides,
> and God reached out of His mouth
> and called it man.
> Up came the other hand
> and God called it woman.
> The hands applauded.
> And this was no sin.
> It was as it was meant to be.

There is a calm rightness carrying this statement along, a sense of order, and—new for Sexton—an untroubled account of the invention of sexuality. The poem achieves dignity and authority by its imitation of Biblical diction.

But the Sea is not only origin; it is also metaphor for the continuing flow of life within the human being. Sexton, for example, perceives the pulse that beats in her arteries as "the sea that bangs in my throat." The figure is extended a few pages later, where "the heart / . . . swallows the tides / and spits them out cleansed." The Sea is simultaneously within and without. Even the ears are "conch shells," fashioned to bring in the sound of the Sea constantly to human consciousness. This seems to intimate that human beings live in a Sea of Life, but if one knows that the conch shell really amplifies the rush of the blood within the hearer, then this line also indicates that the Sea of Life is within.

There are negative elements in this massive symbolic Sea-world. On the margin between sea and land, between spirit and matter, are the crab who causes painful cancer, the sand flea who might enter the ear and cause madness in the brain, the turtle who furnishes an image of human sloth and insensitivity. There is also the land itself which supports human iniquity and furnishes images for spiritual dryness and desolation. But in this world the margin between sea and land is also creative; it is the area where "the sea places its many fingers on the shore" and opposites can interact. The sea is necessary "mother," as the earth is necessary "father," and without interaction between the two there is no life.

Still another perception unfolds as Sexton explores her sea-subject: "Perhaps the earth is floating" on the Sea. The world of matter floats on the Sea of spirit and life; and so that Sea is never far off from any of us. Even the earthbound can dig wells in the middle of the desert, and tap into that Sea, as the Sphinx advises the poet to do in another poem:

> I found the well [of God]
> . . . and there was water,
> and I drank,
> . . . Then the well spoke to me.
> It said: Abundance is scooped from abundance,
> Yet abundance remains.

The appreciative reader has now arrived, at this point in the book, at the ancient literary perception of a metaphoric Sea that surrounds and animates all life with a creative vitality, the fluid medium in which things live and move and have their being, a creative "Abundance" prodigal of its forms. This is the same perception that is behind much literature that can be described as "Romantic," "Enthusiastic," or in any way "Mystical."

These figures and tropes carry us to one of Sexton's most moving poems, the only poem in the collection in which the obvious and awaited word "Logos" appears:

> When man
> enters woman,
> like the surf biting the shore,
> again and again,
> and the woman opens her mouth in pleasure
> and her teeth gleam
> like the alphabet,
> Logos appears milking a star,
> and the man
> inside of woman
> ties a knot
> so that they will
> never again be separate
> and the woman
> climbs into a flower
> and swallows its stem
> and Logos appears
> and unleashes their rivers.

Sexton recapitulates twenty-five centuries of western erotic mysticism here, where the imagery of the *Song of Solomon* merged early with the worship of the *Torah,* and then developed through the writings of St. John the Divine into the Logos Christology of the Greek Fathers, who were themselves influenced by Plato's lovely idea, in the *Timaeus,* of the world as divine creative Body. Divine creative energy, which unleashes itself in permanent joyous activity, has—according to the poem—its momentary analogue in human ecstasy: the human being can, at least briefly during intercourse, "reach through / the curtain of God" to participate by immediate contact in the creative flow of life.

Image carries idea. The most important function of the Sea images in *The Awful Rowing Toward God* is to carry the items that produce this Logos mysticism as Sexton's final achievement, the final life-conferring idea her work came to embody.

One of the most important poems in this personal synthesis then becomes the strange one called **"The Fish that Walked."** The title introduces the scenario: a fish enters the human element for a period, finds the place "awkward" and "without grace": "There is no rhythm / in this country of dirt" he says. But the experience stimulates deep memories in the poet-observer, of her own vague pre-existence in the Sea, floating in "the salt of God's belly," with deep longings "for your country, fish." In view of the Logos poem which immediately precedes it, this poem is not so strange. With its allusions to grace and to the traditional symbol of fish as Christ, this is Anne Sexton's highly personal version of the Logos made flesh and dwelling among men. Sexton asserts that she herself has enjoyed the mystical experience of living in the flowing life of the Divine: the poem ends with conversation between the lady-poet and the fish-Logos.

Sexton's Logos-intuition is itself creative, generating further imaginative work. More developments follow, and more connections are made. God is incomplete without a body, for example: according to a poem called **"The Earth,"**

> God owns heaven,
> but He craves the earth
> . . . but most of all He envies the bodies,
> He who has no body.

And in a later poem in the collection, the Logos would like to be incarnated more than once:

> I have been born many times, a false Messiah,
> but let me be born again
> into something true.

Such a world, in which the Logos is the Sea where the poet lives, is charged with Personality or Personhood. Near the end of the collection a poem begins

> I cannot walk an inch
> without trying to walk to God.
> I cannot move a finger
> without trying to touch God.

The grounds here are those of mystics and theologians who have perceived the Logos as eternally existing, responsible for the creation of the physical world, and responsible also for preventing its lapse back into non-being.

The image of the Sea, as it merges into the idea of the Logos, is thus the underlying metaphor that gives *The Awful Rowing Toward God* its largest meaning and its undeniable power: the Sea-Logos gives life initially, sustains and supports it, and finally receives it back. The Sea-Logos is the personalized arena for the struggle of the human mind; it is as well the goal of the human mind and affections. And the poet's consciousness is at the center of this world. Her genius comes alive in this vital connection with its source. With this collection Anne Sexton's work creates a highly personal synthesis of the mystical potential in Western civilization.

It is startling to find such traditional piety in the sophisticated lady whose conversation was sprinkled with conventional obscenities, whose trademark was the ever-present pack of Salems. In the photographs that accompany her works she is immaculately groomed, expensively dressed, posing against a glassed-in sunporch amid wicker furniture and potted plants. If this is the setting of anguish, it seems mockingly ironic. On the evidence of the photographs one might almost accuse Anne Sexton of self-indulgence; we might almost agree with one of her early critics that she is "a poet without mystical inclinations." But her voice is deeply formed from layers of authentic experience. Style in this last volume has grown lean and precise, the presentation of a personal idiom.

It is surprising also to find the lady so learned in the tradition. She despised her formal education: "I'm not an intellectual of any sort I know of. . . . I had never gone to college, I absolutely was a flunk-out in any schooling I had, I laughed my way through exams. . . . And until I started at twenty-seven, hadn't done much reading." Her comments led one sympathetic friend to write (mistakenly, I think): "Nor was Sexton a particularly reflective or intellectual person. She came to poetry late, to learning even later, and though she worked hard to educate herself, she never acquired a vocabulary to discuss her ideas on a level of enduring interest or value." But the reader emerges from *The Awful Rowing Toward God* with the sense of having been put deeply in touch with the tradition of letters and religious sensibility; she embodies both the length and the richness of that tradition.

For example, the title, *The Awful Rowing Toward God* seems to arrest with its overtones from Emily Dickinson, some of whose love poems feature images of rowing to safe harbor. And, indeed, one of the first impressions that the book makes is that it recapitulates the American experience in literature. The myth from Poe's *Eureka* is reflected in these lines: "I will take a crowbar / and pry out the broken / pieces of God in me." She repeats Whitman in calling her poems "a song of myself." The later voice of T. S. Eliot can surely be heard in these lines:

> Listen.
> We must all stop dying in the little ways,
> in the craters of hate,
> in the potholes of indifference—
> a murder in the temple.
> The place I live in
> is a kind of maze

> and I keep seeking
> the exit or the home.
> Yet if I could listen
> to the bulldog courage of those children
> and turn inward into the plague of my soul
> with more eyes than the stars
> I could melt the darkness. . . .

There must be a nod to Thoreau's personified pond as she notices "the pond wearing its mustache of frost." There is direct engagement with one of Emily Dickinson's poems when she says, "Perhaps I am no one." The American Indian legacy is briefly regarded as she imagines a reservation with "their plastic feathers, / the dead dream" and tries herself to revitalize those Indian dreams of fire, vulture, coyote, and wren. The great American writers are also apparent in the sea imagery on almost every page of *The Awful Rowing Toward God.* She extends as well an American writer's interest in evolution: the two themes emerge in one poem, where "the sea . . . is the kitchen of God."

But she can be found even more intensely among the Modernist concerns of the century. She sounds like Yeats early in her collection: "[the children] are writing down their life / on a century fallen to ruin." She has learned the modern temper from Kierkegaard and in one poem gives her own personal version of "The Sickness Unto Death." She has learned from Beckett to construct scenarios of the Absurd with her own life as the text. She has learned the metaphysical seriousness of *The Seventh Seal* of Ingmar Bergman: the last poem of this collection imagines Sexton playing her royal flush against the lyrically wild cards of God. She has learned from Lowell, Berryman, and Snodgrass so to liberate her writing as to match the tones and concerns of modern inner speech. The language taboos are broken through: the banal reductions of ordinary speech are as telling, in context, as were the flights of fancy in former times. Formal structures of versification in her final work are valid only for the individual poem—each poem has its own form.

The Awful Rowing Toward God embodies a stratum of even deeper and longer historical traditions. What will make the poetry of Anne Sexton permanently valid is her modernization of the perennial meditative wisdom of the West. C. S. Lewis said many years ago that "Humanity does not pass through phases as a train passes through stations: being alive, it has the privilege of always moving yet never leaving anything behind." Heaven and hell remain useful for the mind to locate itself, even for a population without the "faith" to regard them as actual places. Anne Sexton's last volume presents a very personalized compendium of the permanent wisdom of the West, of those questions that frame our enquiry, those values that are constantly meditated on in our solitude. She has written her own psalm sequences, her own proverbs of wisdom. She can look at traces of evil within and strike a playful explanation from the first text of Western Literature: "Not meaning to be [evil], you understand, / just something I ate." The fabric is densely woven by a woman of "little education."

The Awful Rowing Toward God describes not only perception of the Logos, but also the traditional journey of the ascetic soul towards encounter. A voice present from the earliest volumes reiterates the neurotic intensity of her perceptions, the hyper-sensitivity produced by inner disorder. But in this final book the voice that had earliest spoken her madness now seems cultivated for insight. The room where she writes has become sacred and magical: the electric wall sockets are perhaps "a cave of bees," the phone takes root and flowers, "birds explode" outside the window; her typewriter is at the center, with forty-eight eyeballs that never shut; it holds carols for the dance of Joy, songs that come from God. This room of the writer becomes the geographical center of her poems, as her writing becomes the one passion that has mercilessly excluded all others—the lover who had been celebrated in *Love Poems,* the recently divorced husband, the growing daughters, the friends who have been alienated or abandoned, have all dropped beneath the mental horizon of this collection. Perhaps there is the ruthless egotism that Perry Miller believed he saw in Thoreau, the violent simplification to gain her writer's solitude. But perhaps it is the last instinct of the ascetic, ruthlessly to exclude everything from one's life that suggests this world, that does not furnish essential baggage for the next.

The journey within this room begins with savage emptying. Sexton imagines herself as the Witch, a figure from earlier poems now assumed as a personal identity. She goes to her window only to shout "Get out of my life." She imagines herself as old and ridiculous to look at.

> I am shovelling the children out,
> scoop after scoop. . . .
> Maybe I am becoming a hermit,
> opening the door for only
> a few special animals. . . .
> Maybe I have plugged up my sockets
> to keep the gods in . . .

But it is all required, she says in a magnificent phrase, for "climbing the primordial climb."

In the earliest stages of the climb, the power of evil intrudes and impedes. She senses "the bomb of an alien God":

> The children are all crying in their pens. . . .
> They are old men who have seen too much,
> their mouths full of dirty clothes,

> The tongues poverty, tears like pus.

She takes this evil upon herself and sings the lament of the ancient psalmist:

> God went out of me
> as if the sea had dried up like sandpaper,
> as if the sun had become a latrine.
> God went out of my fingers.
> They became stone.
> My body became a side of mutton
> and despair roamed the slaughterhouse.

As a sufferer herself her compassion expands to all of humanity caught in the hell of a bad dream:

> They are mute.
> They do not cry help
> except inside
> where their hearts are covered with grubs.

And insight arrives with compassion. She senses that her heart is dead, but only because she called it Evil. And further light appears when she sees that physical isolation is an aspect of human misery; in a poem called **"Locked Doors"** she looks into the human hell: "The people inside have no water / and are never allowed to touch." In the earliest poem in this collection she had already started this theme of isolation:

> Then there was life
> with its cruel house
> and people who seldom touched—
> though touch is all.

Three poems which appear near the center of the collection recapitulate aspects of the journey towards perception of the Logos. The most historically based poem of the collection is called **"The Sickness unto Death,"** and it is a Kierkegaardian meditation on the human sense of loss and isolation, of estrangement from the Sea of Life. What is left is evil, excremental; it must be eaten slowly and bitterly. The poem stands as a pivot at the center of the book and it ends with a turn upwards, with a catharsis:

> tears washed me
> wave after cowardly wave. . . .
> and Jesus stood over me looking down
> and He laughed to find me gone
> and put His mouth to mine
> and gave me His air.

The next poem in this series follows a few pages later and continues this upward development. **"The Wall"** begins with the paradox that over the millions of years of evolution the only thing that has not changed in nature is the phenomenon of change; mutability is the only constant. It is a part of wisdom to participate consciously in this reality. At the end the poet's voice assumes great authority and formality. She is now the seer who has lived close enough to her experience to emerge with wisdom worth imparting:

> For all you who are going,
> and there are many who are climbing their pain,
> many who will be painted out with a black ink
> suddenly and before it is time,
> for these many I say,
> awkwardly, clumsily,
> take off your life like trousers,
> your shoes, your underwear,
> then take off your flesh,
> unpick the lock of your bones.
> In other words take off the wall
> that separates you from God.

**It is quite obvious in the later collections
that she becomes progressively more
interested in exploring aspects of the
western religious tradition.**
—*William H. Shurr*

The road upwards, the journey of affirmation, contains moments of joy and vision. The grounding insight, which regulates the rest of the ascent, comes in a third poem called **"Is It True?"** the longest poem in the collection and also located near the book's center. It is a poem of occupations and blessings for ordinary things, which become transparent and holy. But in the midst of these the poet still senses herself "in this country of black mud" and can see herself as animal, filled with excrement, living in a country which still prosecuted the Vietnam War. The poem begins with the natural instinct of the human to stop his work and look up at the sun occasionally; it ends with looking up to find Christ in the figure of the wounded seagull:

> For I look up,
> and in a blaze of butter is
> Christ,
> soiled with my sour tears,
> Christ,
> a lamb that has been slain,
> his guts drooping like a sea worm,
> but who lives on, lives on
> like the wings of an Atlantic seagull.
> Though he has stopped flying,
> the wings go on flapping
> despite it all,
> despite it all.

The next poem records moments of pure ecstasy, where daily chores and ordinary occupations are permeated with the presence of the divine: "There is joy / in all." She is transported by the impulse "to faint down by the kitchen table / in a prayer of rejoicing." She expands in a poem called **"The Big Heart"** a few pages later, accepting a new repose at a higher level of reconciliation:

> And God is filling me,
> though there are times of doubt
> as hollow as the Grand Canyon,
> still God is filling me.
> He is giving me the thoughts of dogs,
> the spider in its intricate web,
> the sun
> in all its amazement,
> and the slain ram
> that is the glory,
> the mystery of great cost,
> and my heart,
> which is very big,
> I promise it is very large,
> a monster of sorts,
> takes it all in—
> and in comes the fury of love.

This leads, in the poems that follow, to multiple reconciliations. Friends are gathered around her, valued for their "abundance." Words sometimes fail the poet, but they are "miraculous" nevertheless,

> I am in love with words.
> They are the doves falling out of the ceiling.
> They are six holy oranges sitting in my lap.
> They are the trees, the legs of summer,
> and the sun, its passionate face.

She becomes reconciled with the Mother who had been a harsh presence in earlier volumes; she relives life at the breast, life at the knee, and now feels the strength necessary to face what she calls "the big people's world." The whole of the mystical tradition now becomes her personal domain, and she can speak of the Jesus of Christianity as "the Christ who walked for me."

We must, then, come down to Anne Sexton as a *religious* poet; critics have found this aspect of her poetry more difficult than her shocking language or her revelation of family secrets. It is quite obvious in the later collections that she becomes progressively more interested in exploring aspects of the western religious tradition. Barbara Kevles was the interviewer who as able to probe most deeply into this aspect of Sexton's experience. In the *Paris Review* interview of 1971 her gently persistent questions led Sexton to reveal a great deal about her religious experiences.

She protested initially that she was not "a lapsed Catholic" as some had conjectured; she was religious on her own Protestant terms. The most starling revelation of this interview was her experience with visions: "I have visions— sometimes ritualized visions—that come of me of God, or of Christ, or of the Saints, and I feel that I can touch them almost . . . that they are a part of me. . . . If you want to know the truth, the leaves talk to me every June. . . . I feel very much in touch with things after I've had a vision. It's somewhat like the beginning of writing a poem; the whole world is very sharp and well defined, and I'm intensely alive. . . ." One recalls the story that Hilda Doolittle told on herself— it was only after she mentioned to Sigmund Freud that she had religious visions that Freud felt she was sufficiently interesting, and sufficiently sick, for him to take her on as a patient. But in this interview Sexton was able to keep religion and mental illness separated at least to her own satisfaction: "When you're mad, [the visions are] silly and out of place, whereas if it's so-called mystical experience, you've put everything in its proper place." She protested that speaking of these things to the interviewer caused her some discomfort and she would prefer to move on to other subjects. But the line of questioning produced this final insight: "I think in time to come people will be more shocked by my mystical poetry than by my so-called confessional poetry."

The mystical poetry has not been universally appreciated. For one hostile critic, the religious poems read like "verbal comicstrips . . . the pathetic figure of 'Mrs. Sexton' reminds one less of St. Theresa than of Charlie Brown." Another critic, though, could recognize in her the "sacerdotal . . . a priestess celebrating mysteries," and could use such words as "hieratic . . . sibyl . . . vatic."

It may be that Sexton herself was somewhat surprised or even embarrassed by this turn of her interests, this direction of her own growth. At least this seems a possible explanation for her decision to leave the poems for posthumous publication—though the careful reader can already discern seeds of this book, hints of this evolution, in her earlier collections.

We come then finally to deal with Saint Anne, who found the western tradition of spirituality anything but bankrupt. Towards the end of this collection we find that she has been reading the lives of the saints, and that she even has meditations on the three theological virtues of faith, hope, and charity. Faith is initially described as a great weight of information hung on a small wire. The small wire then becomes a thin vein with love pulsing back and forth through it, sustaining the believer with a higher life. The relation is life-giving and life-sustaining, as the twig feeds life to the grape, from another figure in the poem. The ending is dramatically modern, with one of Sexton's reductive banalizing

similes: the pulsing vein of faith is man's contract with God, who "will enter your hands / as easily as ten cents used to / bring forth a Coke." The poem is remarkable for its intelligence and its compactness, as well as for its historical sweep.

Two rowing poems bracket this collection and give its title. The two poems are the only ones to use the rowing metaphor. The first is a poem of beginnings: recollections of the crib, dolls, early schoolyears, the gradual recognition of inner pain and loneliness. Consciousness emerges from all of these experiences as if rising from under a sea, gradually discerning God as an island goal. The rower as in a dream fights absurd obstacles, but has the hope of possible calm and resolution at journey's end.

The last poem is full of joy. The rowing has ended, the struggle is over. The surprise in the poem is the game of poker which God requires of the newcomer. He deals her a royal flush, the complete family of cards. But he has tricked her—with a wild card he holds five aces. The game and the trickery serve to release the final tensions of the volume. Laughter spills out and the hoop of his laughter rolls into her mouth, joining God and the Rower in intimate union.

> Then I laugh, the fishy dock laughs,
> the sea laughs. The Island laughs.
> The Absurd laughs.

The poem and the volume end with love for the wild card, the "Dearest dealer," the "eternal . . . and lucky love."

The Awful Rowing Toward God seems a complex harmonium, a radical simplification achieved at great personal expense. Anais Nin once described her own work as a writer in the following way: "Why one writes is a question I can answer easily, having so often asked it of myself. I believe one writes because one has to create a world in which one can live. I could not live in any of the worlds offered to me—the world of my parents, the world of war, the world of politics. I had to create a world of my own, like a climate, a country, an atmosphere in which I could breathe, reign, and recreate myself when destroyed by living. That, I believe, is the reason for every work of art."

The Awful Rowing Toward God is a polished and completed "alternative world," inevitable like every great work of art. It is the personal embodiment of one of the oldest and most invigorating ideas in the Western tradition, the idea of the Logos. She does not die as does Henry James's character Dencombe, in *The Middle Years,* feeling that he had never completed the artistic work for which his whole life had been a preparation. But her achievement in this book of poems is penultimate; the final action, the suicide, remains to be pondered.

There is a body of scientific theory on the nature of suicide. One socio-psychological theorist begins with questions such as: "Why does man induce so fearful a thing as death when nothing so terrifying as death is imminent?" His assumption is that death is always and in every case "fearful" and "terrifying." Sexton's final work is contrary evidence. "Exhilaration" would be a more appropriate word.

It may be that we are closer to the reality with A. Alvarez. In his extraordinary study of literature and suicide Alvarez writes that "each suicide is a closed world with its own irresistible logic." Each suicide is special, wrapped in its own individual mystery. We must then build a theory for each case, and for a start we may cull a brief anthology of Sexton's comments on death, from her letters to friends:

> "Killing yourself is merely a way to avoid pain."
> "Suicide is the opposite of a poem."
> "Once I thought God didn't want me up there in the sky. Now I'm convinced he does."
> "In my opinion Hemingway did the right thing."
> "One writes to forestall being blotted out."
> "I'm so God damned sure I'm going to die soon."

The list is chronological, and though the statements are in ragged prose, unsupported by the framework of a poem, they show progression, from a conventional and guilt-ridden attitude toward suicide to a more open understanding of it. Sexton's ideas on suicide obviously changed as she came closer to her own death.

Much of Sexton's artistic speculation on suicide she herself gathered in her third book of poems, *Live or Die* (1966), and a full account of the genesis of her thought would have to deal extensively with these explorations. A brief tour through that book produces several direct statements about "the almost unnameable lust" for self-destruction:

> But suicides have a special language.
> Like carpenters they want to know *which tools*.
> They never ask *why build*.

Her voyage has already set in that direction. But so in a more general sense has everyone's:

> But surely you know that everyone has a death,
> his own death,
> waiting for him.
> So I will go now without old age or disease. . . .

The last poem of *Live or Die* was actually called a "hokey"

ending to the collection by an unsympathetic reader. But it can be seen as strongly defining the collection. The decision not to take one's life is "a sort of human statement," a celebration

> of the sun
> the dream, the excitable gift.

It was about this time that Sexton recorded her psychiatrist's plea, "Don't kill yourself. Your poems might mean something to someone else some day." It was as if she sensed a mission still to be completed.

But what may be the most powerful poem in the 1966 volume comes in the center, **"To Lose the Earth."** The reader is arrested by the epigraph, from Thomas Wolfe:

> To lose the earth you know, for greater knowing;
> to lose the life you have, for greater life;
> to leave the friends you loved for greater loving;
> to find a land more kind than home, more large
> than earth. . . .

The poem itself goes on to conduct the reader's entry into a work of art, and it is a remarkably moving experience. It is an entry into the world of timeless beauty which is elevating and utterly mind-altering. But introduced as it is by the quotation from Wolfe, the poem is ambivalent: it is, equally, the experience of death into which she conducts us. The poem is Sexton's "Ode on a Grecian Urn" and "Ode to a Nightingale" stated simultaneously: the lure of death merges with the idea of timeless beauty. It is escape of the Ego, with its Imagination, into the eternal stasis of beauty and truth. Joyce Carol Oates wrote, much more sympathetically, that "Sexton yearned for that larger experience, that rush of near divine certainty that the self *is* immortal." Freud had already generalized on this phenomenon: "Our unconscious . . . does not believe in its own death; it behaves as if it were immortal." We need, then, a broader set of categories for suicide.

As a young man Ralph Waldo Emerson speculated quite generously on the variety of motivations leading to suicide, and provided this listing:

> It is wrong to say generally that the suicide is a hero or that he is a coward. . . . The merit of the action must obviously depend in all cases upon the particular condition of the individual. It may be in one the effect of despair, in one of madness, in one of fear, in one of magnanimity, in one of ardent curiosity to know the wonders of the other world.

Emerson's last two categories, startling for a young clergyman, carry us farther towards meanings latent in *The Awful Rowing Toward God.*

One accomplishment of the collection is an enormous expansion of awareness, of consciousness. As Sexton grows from inner disorder to inner harmony, from madness to poetry, the themes and images of the mystical tradition provide rungs for that "primordial climb." A vast inwardness develops: silence and introspection sculpt the inner world until it matches the larger lineaments of the common tradition of western mysticism. The journey is the dangerous work of solitude:

> One must listen hard to the animal within,
> one must walk like a sleepwalker
> on the edge of the roof,
> one must throw some part of her body
> into the devil's mouth.

The flight from multiplicity, in the search for "the pure, the everlasting, the immortal and unchanging," which Plato described in *The Phaedo,* results in a sense of accomplishment, of self control and rest, of "being in communion with the unchanging." Sexton comes to embody one form of the long tradition of liberal inquiry and inward search for concepts and values which, as Socrates observed, make human life worth living. There results a sense, as in Poe's *Eureka,* of the return from fragmentation to unity, to the primordial Paradise, the home of Life, Beauty, Intelligence. The preliminary report of this world can now be tendered by one "in love with words," but the reality itself is fully experienced only when one takes the final step into the Great Silence which climaxes Thoreau's journey in *A Week on the Concord and Merrimack Rivers.* To borrow a phrase from Rilke, Sexton "steps, festively clothed, out of the great darkness" of her solitude. She has achieved, in her climactic work, exactly what Emerson called "magnanimity."

The major actions of her final months seem deliberate attempts at *denouement:* the final book was shaped to its final order; the final task was to act the *finis.*
—William H. Shurr

It is not enough to say that literature is an imitation of life. It is rather an abstract of life and a forced patterning of life. Time, in art, is stopped, repeatable, arranged, enriched, reversible—as it is not in life. The events that befall a person in a drama or a narrative may be the experiences of a real person in real life. But there is an important difference. In real life the experience is part of a flow; significant experiences are merged with experiences of entirely different meaning or of no apparent meaning at all. The pattern of significance is clouded over by other events. Even

the profoundest introspection may not uncover the exact beginning or the final end of the reverberations of an experience. In art, on the other hand, even the most abstract art, there is selectivity and conscious pattern. Art and the life-experience are rarely identical. There are cases where life becomes significant when it tries to imitate art, as closely as possible, as when one might try to live up to a code or an ideal.

Sexton became totally an artist, to the exclusion of any other role, an artist whose medium, in the final event, was her own life. The major actions of her final months seem deliberate attempts at *denouement:* the final book was shaped to its final order; the final task was to act the *finis.* How else guarantee the permanence of the accomplishment; how else act authentically on the present state of insight?

The most famous twentieth-century comment on suicide was Albert Camus's, in *The Myth of Sisyphus:* "There is only one philosophical problem which is truly serious; it is suicide. To judge whether life itself is or is not worth the trouble of being lived—that is the basic question of philosophy." It is generally assumed, in the context of Camus's thought, that suicide would be a negative judgment of the "worth" of life. In Sexton's case the contrary is true.

In Sexton's case, one can see suicide as grounded in "magnanimity," as the result of "ardent curiosity," the self-chosen final capstone to a structure of life and art now satisfactorily completed. Suicide becomes a version of Kierkegaard's leap of faith, a step into what the imagination had seemed, by its harmonizings, to authenticate. Should there be no light beyond, at least the adventurer has left behind a vision of sublime light. Sexton's way is not everyone's, but it has its own rationale and, as artistic vision, its own extraordinary beauty.

Diana Hume George (essay date 1987)

SOURCE: "The Poetic Heroism of Anne Sexton," in *Literature and Psychology,* Vol. 33, Nos. 3-4, 1987, pp. 76-88.

[*In the following essay, George examines the significance of forbidden knowledge, incest, and psychic guilt in Sexton's poetry. George contends that Sexton's truth-seeking resembles that of the mythical Oedipus of Greek tragedy and psychoanalytic theory.*]

> Not that it was beautiful,
> but that I found some order there.
> There ought to be something special
> for someone
> in this kind of hope.
> This is something I would never find
> in a lovelier place, my dear,
> although your fear is anyone's fear

like an invisible veil between us all . . .
and sometimes in private,
my kitchen, your kitchen,
my face, your face.

—Anne Sexton, **"For John, Who Begs Me**
Not to Enquire Further"
To Bedlam and Part Way Back

What the story of the Sphinx seems to emphasize is that the answer to the riddle of life is not just man, but each person himself. . . . In contemplating Sophocles' *Oedipus* as Freud did, one realizes that the entire play is essentially Oedipus' struggle to get at the hidden truth. It is a battle for knowledge in which Oedipus has to overcome tremendous inner resistance against recognizing the truth about himself, because he fears so much what he might discover. . . . What forms the essence of our humanity—and of the play—is not our being victims of fate, but our struggle to discover the truth about ourselves.

—Bruno Bettelheim, *Freud and Man's Soul*

BETTELHEIM'S OEDIPUS

Oedipus, Sophocles, Freud: this is preeminently a man's story, told by men to and for men, about a tragically fated hero who unknowingly slays his father and marries his mother. Despite Freud's attribution of the Oedipus complex to women as well as to men, the story of Oedipus has also remained essentially masculine in the popular imagination. That imagination, sensing perhaps the culturally masculine tenor not only of the myth but of its symbolic meanings, has even tried (with a brief assist from psychoanalysis) to provide a womanly equivalent: The Elektra complex. But Freud stuck stubbornly to his assertion that the story of Oedipus was that of all humankind, and a number of revisionist theorists and practitioners have attempted to explain why. Among the most convincing retellings is Juliet Mitchell's in *Psychoanalysis and Feminism,* in which she urges us to construe the Oedipus complex as more than a term for normal childhood sexual conflicts revolving around intense attachments to the parents, by which measure the significance attributed to it by psychoanalysis may indeed seem inflated. According to Mitchell, the Oedipus complex designates a set of internal and external acts through which every person is initiated into the cultural order; it is not only "a metaphor for the psychic structure of the bourgeois nuclear family under Viennese capitalism," but "a law that describes the way in which all [Western] culture is acquired by each individual."

Critics have been endlessly irritated by the recurring themes of infancy and the relationship to the mother and father in Anne Sexton's poetry. Beginning with her first teacher, John Holmes, Sexton has been accused of childishness and of infantile preoccupations. She insisted that these themes were at the heart of the matter—and not only her matter, but by implication, everyone's. "Grow up," said the decorous world of poetry to her throughout her career; "Stop playing in the crib and the sandbox—and especially stop sniveling about your childhood." Her poetic reply frightened the critics who disliked her work—most of them transparently opposed to psychoanalytic theory—for that reply asserted again and again that grown woman though she might be, successful professional though she might be, the process of working out her relationship to her parents and her childhood was a life's work. Nor did she permit the poetic community to suppose it was only *her* life's work. If we acknowledged it as hers, and as the legitimate domain of poetry, then we would have to come to terms with the possibility that it might be our own lifelong process as well. Blind as Teiresias, she revealed to all of us the truth about Laius' murder. As Bruno Bettelheim writes in *Freud and Man's Soul,* "we encounter in Teiresias the idea that having one's sight turned away from the external world and directed inward—toward the inner nature of things—gives true knowledge and permits understanding of what is hidden and needs to be known."

But it is not Teiresias, finally, with whom I identify Anne Sexton. Rather, it is Oedipus, and specifically the Oedipus of *Freud and Man's Soul.* Bettelheim attempts yet another re-reading of Freud's Oedipus, and I find it the most moving and accessible that contemporary psychoanalysis has offered to an audience larger than its own members. Freud's Oedipus, through Bettelheim, takes on the luminosity of the prophet, and becomes not merely a tragic victim, but an embattled seer. According to Bettelheim, the suggestiveness and referential richness of the Oedipal story only *includes* the implication that little boys want to kill the man they *know* is their father and marry the woman they *know* is their mother. This "common and extreme simplification" ignores the fact that Oedipus did not know what he was doing when he killed Laius and married Jocasta, and that "his greatest desire was to make it *impossible* for himself to harm those he thought were his parents." This crucial detail expands the story's mythic power to include "the child's anxiety and guilt for having patricidal and incestuous wishes," and the consequences of acting on such wishes.

As Bettelheim reads both the Sophocles play and Freud's adaptation of it, the central issues are Oedipus' guilt and his discovery of the truth. Oedipus' lack of initial awareness about what he has done is reflected in psychoanalysis' version of the story by the repression in adulthood of both the murderous feelings toward the parent of the same sex, and the incestuous feelings toward the parent of the opposite sex. Oedipus behaved as he did as a consequence of his real parents having rejected him in the most brutal and literal way possible; he loved the parents he thought were his. "It is only our love for our parents and our conscious wish to protect them that leads us to repress our negative and sexual feelings for them."

Bettelheim also emphasizes another portion of the story often glossed over by theory and by practice: when he fled Corinth, Oedipus did not fully heed the temple inscription, "Know thyself," which implicitly warned against misunderstandings of the oracle's prophecies. He was not sufficiently self-aware in his flight, and later acted out his metaphorical blindness by literally blinding himself. So Oedipus, truth-seeker, sought the complex truths too late; or, translated into psychic parlance, self-knowledge requires an understanding of the "normally unconscious aspects of ourselves." It's Bettelheim's conviction and that of psychoanalysis—and here I part company with him and it regretfully—that knowledge really is power, that to know the unconscious is to be able to control it, and more or less completely. "This is a crucial part of the myth," writes Bettelheim: "as soon as the unknown is made known . . . the pernicious consequences of the Oedipal deeds disappear." That is indeed the most hopeful reading of the cease of pestilence in Thebes, but not the only one. No one, after all, can restore Oedipus' sight to him, and his wanderings toward ultimate peace in Colonus are still torturous and tragic. Not until he awaits death does he find his peace. Bettelheim sees the Oedipus in us all as able to be "free" from our own "destructive powers" and their ability to "harm us." This is, of course, the expression of psychoanalysis' own profound wish that it might provide "cure," a wish that Freud himself became suspicious of near the end of his life. I prefer a more realistic phrasing of what the search for self-knowledge might hope to accomplish: a lessening of the destructive hold of unconscious material over people's lives, and a diminished likelihood that one might single-handedly cause a pestilence in the city.

This important reservation aside, I find Bettelheim's reading of Oedipus convincing and important, if not entirely new: Oedipus is a hero who is fated to feel guilty for something he has done but did not know he was doing and did not mean to do; and, more importantly, he is a quester after truth against tremendous inner and external odds, determined to recognize that truth when he finds it, no matter how painful it may be for him and for other people he loves. That truth is peculiarly his own—Bettelheim points out, through DeQuincey, that the Sphinx posed different problems for different people, so that the answer to the riddle is not merely man in general, but Oedipus in particular. But it is also universal. "The answer to the riddle of life is not just man, but each person himself."

In the Oedipus story, it is the woman/mother/wife, Jocasta,

who says that she does not want to know the truth and who cannot cope with it when it is revealed. She kills herself because she possesses unwanted knowledge—not, as Bettleheim points out, the knowledge that she has committed incest, but repressed knowledge that she helped to abandon her son to death years earlier. Perhaps it is ironic that I should see Anne Sexton as Oedipus and not as Jocasta. Anne Sexton killed herself. Yet despite that final irony, the essential characteristics of Anne Sexton's poetry identify her not with the overwhelmed and helpless victim/victimizer, Jocasta, but with the hero Oedipus, whose struggle for the truth was determined and tragic. As Alicia Ostriker says in a comparison of Plath and Sexton, Sexton "fought hard with love, greed, and laughter to save herself, and failed." Her "failure" was heroic rather than pathetic, courageous rather than cowardly, Unlike Jocasta, who is immediately defeated by the revelation of the truth, Sexton grappled with her truth again and again, in a deadly hand to hand combat she might be said, on some terms, to have won.

ANNE'S OEDIPUS

That Anne Sexton identified herself with Oedipus is evident in only one modest place in her poetry, in the first collection, *To Bedlam and Part Way Back.* The epigraph for the collection is from a letter of Schopenhauer to Goethe in 1815:

> It is the courage to make a clean breast of it in face of every question that makes the philosopher. He must be like Sophocles' Oedipus, who, seeking enlightenment concerning his terrible fate, pursues his indefatigable enquiry, even when he divines that appalling horror awaits him in the answer, But most of us carry in our heart the Jocasta who begs Oedipus for God's sake not to inquire further . . .

Sexton's biographer, Diane Middlebrook, reveals the previously unavailable details of the story that led to Sexton's use of this epigraph, and to the poem that opens Part II of *Bedlam,* which contains the most intensely confessional material in the collection. **"For John, Who Begs Me Not to Enquire Further,"** was Sexton's ultimate poetic reply to John Holmes' fierce objections to Sexton's "sources and subject matter." She should not, he warned, write about her experiences in mental institutions or her private neuroses; these were not legitimate subjects for poetry, and were more dangerous than useful. Although Sexton could not have known it at the time, Holmes was to be only the first of a series of Jocastas whom Sexton would have to confront in the many years of productivity remaining to her. Her argument in this poem is that of the truth-seeking Oedipus:

> Not that it was beautiful,

but that, in the end, there was
a certain sense of order there;
something worth learning
in that narrow diary of my mind,
in the commonplaces of the asylum . . .

Like that other star-crossed poet, Plath, Sexton is trapped in her bell jar, "an inverted bowl."
—Diana Hume George

Like Oedipus, Sexton does not pretend to be a seeker after beauty here, though she will seek beauty as well later in her poetic life; she seeks, rather, "a certain sense of order," if knowing the truth about oneself, however awful, can yield a pattern, a structure, that will teach one "something worth learning" about how one's mystery can be unwoven. The "narrow diary of my mind" elicits images of the private person confiding confidences to a small and secret book, and she is aware that in employing this image, she addresses the implicit reservations anyone might have about the divulgence of confidences. Yet it seems to me that straight as this image is, Sexton must have intended some slight irony, angry as she had been during the process that led up to this finally loving, forgiving, giving poem addressed to a father figure, teacher, and friend who was, as she later said, "in the long run, ashamed of me where you might be proud of me." The "commonplaces of the asylum" include the "cracked mirror," in which the beholder must acknowledge the fragmented pieces of the self, held up to the scrutiny of whatever wholeness that perceiver can manage. It also prefigures the next and central image of the poem, which Diane Middlebrook finds central not only to this poem, but to Sexton's entire poetics:

I tapped my own head;
it was glass, an inverted bowl,
It is a small thing
to rage in your own bowl.
At first it was private.
Then it was more than myself;
it was you, or your house
or your kitchen.

Like that other star-crossed poet, Plath, Sexton is trapped in her bell jar, "an inverted bowl." But by the act of tapping it, she tentatively releases powers that reveal to her that her pain is more than private, that she shares with other isolated beings this "small thing" enlarged by sympathy and empathy.

The scene of this coming into connection with others trapped in their inverted bowls is, significantly, the "house," and more particularly the kitchen, locale of so many of Sexton's scenes of recognition, as it was of Plath's. It is not only, I think, that the kitchen is such a female place, but that here the ritual of preparing and eating food takes place; here all modern people are most literally nourished. This is the room in which her world, suburban America, finds itself most at home. The domesticity suggested by the kitchen implies that here, in this most ordinary and yet formally ritualized room, the most extraordinary human truths will emerge, in the midst of simple converse about the everyday matters of commonplace lives. In this respect, the kitchen and the asylum are perhaps closely related. Neither is Thebes or Corinth, but either may be the crossroads at which one kills one's father, or the ceremonial place in which one marries one's mother.

And if you turn away
because there is no lesson here
I will hold my awkward bowl,
with all its cracked stars shining
like a complicated lie,
and fasten a new skin around it
as if I were dressing an orange
or a strange sun.

It is on this passage that Middlebrook bases her contention that tapping the head "produces 'stars,' signs radiant with significance, uniting sufferer and beholder despite the 'glass bowl' that shuts them off from other forms of contact." To that insight, I would add that the cracked stars resulting from tapping the bowl are yet another reflection of the cracked mirror in the asylum, that we all, in kitchens or madhouses, aim toward the same general human truths that shine differently in different lives. The speaker, under the critical scrutiny of the one who has "turned away," must hold her bowl awkwardly, partially disarmed by the withdrawal of an invited commonality. The cracked stars shine "like a complicated lie," Sexton's acknowledgement that we each create our own story, are trapped within our own private perspectives in which we style and shape a truth that has as much of the necessary lie as of authenticity; the lie is "complicated" by our complicity in the egotistical desire to make ourselves, perhaps, the heroes of our stories. There is also a suggestion here, muted from reprimand into plea, that the stars will more likely constitute that "complicated lie," that partial denial of the sought truth, if the invited other rejects the partnership by which a complicated *truth* might emerge: "And if you turn away . . ." When the fellow sufferer changes to the detached or disdainful observer, the speaker has no choice but to "fasten a new skin" around the bowl, an action which defensively separates her from him, and blocks any progress that they might together make toward an understanding; yet the stars still shine underneath, a luminous invitation toward truth.

This is something I would never find

in a lovelier place, my dear,
although your fear is anyone's fear,
like an invisible veil between us all . . .
and sometimes in private
my kitchen, your kitchen,
my face, your face.

Whatever truth the speaker seeks, it will not be available in "lovelier places" than the private mind speaking its halting language to another private mind, trying to make contact. What separates them, she knows, is the hearer's fear, "anyone's fear," not only of the sick or mad or sordid; "your fear" is also the subject of the inquiry itself. Although the grammatical construction of the last lines is ambiguous, I read them to mean secondarily that the fear pulls down the veil between them in their kitchens and on their faces, and primarily that this "something," this "special sort of hope," takes place in the kitchen and is revealed, through the mutually cracked glass bowls, on their distorted, human, striving faces.

The two lengthy poems that follow this preface to Part II of *Bedlam* reveal the "source and subject" of the cracked stars that John/Jocasta does not want to hear. **"The Double Image"** and **"The Division of Parts"** show us this other "cracked mirror" of the mother, image of fragmentation and wholeness for the speaker.

> . . . my mocking mirror, my overthrown
> love, my first image. She eyes me from that face,
> that stony head of death
> I had outgrown.

Addressed to her daughter, **"The Double Image"** tells the story of a thirty-year-old mother who goes to live with her own mother after the speaker's suicide attempt. An "outgrown child," she inhabits her mother's house as an unwelcome guest who must submit to her mother's resentment for her suicide attempt, and who must sit for a portrait of herself to be hung on a wall opposite her mother's portrait, freezing in time her dependence on her mother, herself as reflection of that "mocking mirror," and her stubborn refusal to become that bitter woman. The mother contracts cancer (blaming her daughter), the daughter is institutionalized again, and the mother begins her slow dying. The speaker estranged from her own daughter by her inability to mother her tells herself one of those complicated lies, and then unravels it:

> . . . And you came each
> weekend. But I lie,
> You seldom came. I just pretended
> you . . .

The lesson she learns that she must pass on to her daughter—this complicated truth made up of so many self-serving lies that must be exploded—is "why I would rather / die than love." And this has much to do, she knows, with her relationship to that "overthrown love," and the speaker's need to turn away from her:

> The artist caught us at the turning;
> we smiled in our canvas home
> before we chose our foreknown separate ways.
> And this was the cave of the mirror,
> that double woman who stares
> at herself, as if she were petrified
> in time . . .

If she is to survive, she will have to acknowledge that she is unwillfully guilty of her own mother's sin, passed now to another generation:

> And this was my worst guilt; you could not cure
> nor soothe it, I made you to find me.

In telling her young daughter this truth, she is giving that child a chance to escape the prison of poisonous identifications handed from mother to daughter to mother to daughter. Mary Gray, Sexton's mother, could not admit or acknowledge this human truth inherent in the reproductive urge; it is Sexton's hope that in admitting her own complicity in this complicated lie, she will provide her child with a way to escape its implications; or if not to escape them entirely, then to know that the trap lies baited for her.

But I have called Anne Sexton Oedipus, and Oedipus wanted to marry his mother, not to harm her. Sexton's Oedipus/Anne knows that the mother is the "first overthrown love" for both sexes, and that the differentiation of desire in males and females occurs later. It is my contention that Oedipus/Anne does "slay" her mother and "marry" her father, just as Oedipus slew his father and married his mother. That Sexton thought herself guilty of her mother's death, and of marrying her father, is explicit throughout her canon. (In **"All My Pretty Ones,"** she also acknowledges the possibility of an unconscious guilt connected with her father's death). Here I will concentrate on her self-perception of this deadly configuration in three poems ranging throughout her career: **"The Double Image,"** (*Bedlam*); **"Those Times . . ."** (*Live or Die*); and **"Divorce, Thy Name is Woman"** (*45 Mercy Street*). In **"Double Image,"** she is accused of her mother's death; in **"Those Times"** she acknowledges this unintentional sin; and in **"Divorce, Thy Name is Woman,"** she speaks of her "marriage" throughout life to her father. This is what Oedipus must discover himself guilty of: the murder of the parent of the same sex, and forbidden incest with the parent of the opposite sex.

"The Double Image" includes one of the most startling

and frightening of Sexton's stanzas, made more so by the clever facility and unexpectedness of the rhyme:

> They hung my portrait in the chill
> north light, matching
> me to keep me well,
> Only my mother grew ill.
> She turned from me, as if death were catching,
> as if death transferred,
> as if my dying had eaten inside of her.
> That August you were two, but I timed my days with
> doubt.
> On the first of September she looked at me
> and said I gave her cancer.
> They carved her sweet hills out
> and still I couldn't answer.

The speaker of this poem is the same woman who remembers putting "bees in my mouth" to keep from devouring her mother in the nursing process as an infant; who knows that "all my need took you down like a meal"; who, though she does not know it as a child, will utterly defeat her mother in **"Those Times . . ."**

> I did not know that my life, in the end,
> would run over my mother's like a truck
> and all that would remain
> from the year I was six
> was a small hole in my heart, a deaf spot,
> so that I might hear
> the unsaid more clearly.

The "hole in the heart," that "deaf spot," becomes the poet's source of the knowledge of absence; blocked by childhood indignities from hearing the ordinary music of daily life, she takes on the special sensual acuity of the handicapped: what she will hear is the unsaid, just as blind Oedipus will "see" with the sight of the blind visionary.

And like Oedipus, Sexton did not want to run over her mother's life like a truck, or to give her cancer, or to defeat her, or to slay her; she intended, rather, like Oedipus, the opposite; to protect that beloved if rejecting parent. Oedipus is utterly rejected by his biological parents, who wish to murder him that he might not murder his father; his other parents, unknowingly adoptive, are those he loves and flees Corinth to protect when he hears the Oracle. In so fleeing, he fulfills the prophecy. In the Oedipus myth, then, the parental figures are split; the actual and rejecting parents, and the adoptive and loving ones, who might after all be called the "real" parents. In the normative infant and childhood psyche, these roles of rejecting and loving parents are united, so that reality and imago emerge from the same identities and bodies; it is the real parents we love and wish to protect, their imagos we wish to murder and

marry. Seeking this complex truth, Sexton knows that she must make reparation for the split inside her that duplicates the split in the psyches of her parents, who both rejected *and* loved her, just as she rejects *and* loves them.

Having "murdered" her mother in the psychic sense, she processed such guilt as if fated to do so. It matters little, I would say, whether or not Mary Gray actually told Anne Sexton that Sexton "gave her cancer," matters equally little whether the mother's trauma over her daughter's suicide attempt actually contributed to the development of her disease. Like Oedipus, she has sought and found her psychic truth: she slew her mother, who had literary aspirations that Sexton would fulfill, who was jealous of this beautiful daughter; *and* she dearly loved the mother that she slew. That is a hard truth. It is peculiarly Anne Sexton's; it is also mine, may be any woman's. Daughters both "love" and "slay" their mothers.

Oedipus/Anne acknowledges the other half of her sin in the countless father poems distributed throughout the canon. Having detailed this intense and lifelong romance elsewhere, I will here rely on the late poem, probably composed almost fifteen years after **"The Double Image,"** in which she most explicitly acknowledges her marriage to the father. Part of the sequence in **45 Mercy Street** called **"Eating the Leftovers," "Divorce, Thy Name is Woman"** begins in the aftermath of that lifelong marriage:

> I am divorcing daddy—Dybbuk! Dybbuk /
> I have been doing it daily all my life . . .

In this poem, Sexton constructs a kind of allegory for woman in western culture. The marriage of daughter to father is represented as literal.

> Later,
> When blood and eggs and breasts
> dropped onto me,
> Daddy and his whiskey breath
> made a long midnight visit
> in a dream that is not a dream
> and then called his lawyer quickly.
> Daddy divorcing me.

The "dream that is not a dream" is a psychic fact, a fact of mental life, something that "actually happens" in the netherland of unconscious primary process. The father seduces the daughter, then rejects her, disowning his own passion and hers. "I have been divorcing him ever since" in the interior world of psychic realities, where the Mother is her witness in the courtroom. The daughter keeps on divorcing him, "adding up the crimes / Of how he came to me, / how he left me." Sexton's speaker takes on the voice of any woman working out her childhood love for her father, any woman still

> waiting, waiting for Daddy to come home
> and stuff me so full of our infected child
> that I turn invisible, but married,
> at last.

To be born a woman in a patriarchy is often to be compelled to live out precisely this ritual. The maternal urge becomes a parody of its first manifestation in the desire to present the father with a child. This, in the tortured psychic world of the poem, is the only true marriage; all others are only pale and inadequate reflections of this primal union. To marry one's father is, indeed, to "turn invisible," for it means that the daughter becomes not herself, not her mother, but an inverted parody of herself *and* her mother, of wife *and* daughter. Acknowledging the incestuous foundations of romantic love on which not only the family, but all western culture is based, Sexton exposes the underbelly of the myth—that we are all "the infected child" of incest, that we all become "invisible," effaced, in the need to "marry, at last." Marriage is the sanctification of incest, the sacred profanity whose nature we expend our sublimated energies denying. We are all possessed by the dybbuks of our personal and cultural pasts. What Sexton speaks of here is as narrow as the room of each womb we come from, and as broad as our dedication to Classical culture. We are all implicated, fathers and daughters alike, all dwelling in a shadow world in which the realities we perceive are shadows of original forms—and of original desires. We stay in the cave willingly, perceiving reflected forms, because we cannot look upon those forms directly without becoming "invisible." Yet we seek that original form, that original desire, never quite content with its substitute.

While Sexton breaks this ultimate taboo, thereby acknowledging her self-effacement, her speaker also wants to affirm the divorce. The "solution" of the poem is a continual process of divorce, an unending courtroom scene, but one which always returns from courtroom to bedroom, where the woman is "opening and shutting the windows. Making the bed and tearing it apart." Before and after the divorce of man and wife is this continuous marriage to and divorce from the father, a permanent oscillation between two conflicting desires: to divorce and be done with; and to "marry, at last."

Far from being done with the horrors he discovers in his pursuit of truth when he does indeed uncover it and blind himself, Oedipus does not find peace until he awaits death at Colonus, in the wake of years of blind wandering. The Jocastas in Anne Sexton's life begged her not to inquire further; when she did, psychoanalysis held out to her the hope of which Bettelheim speaks on behalf of psychoanalysis: that knowledge of the truth will set one free. Her truth, tougher by far than either the willed ignorance of Jocasta which cannot endure revelation, or the mandated "liberty" of analytic cure, is more like that of the original Oedipus: complex, tragic, visionary. Sexton did not, like Jocasta, find the sought truth and simply die of it; in the many years between her first exploration of truth in *Bedlam* and her death in 1974, she triumphed over her guilt and her ghosts again and again. The "strange goddess face" of the slain mother whom the infant ate—"all my need took / you down like a meal"—is redeemed in a dream of reparation and mutual forgiveness in **"Dreaming the Breasts:"**

> The breasts I knew at midnight
> beat like the sea in me now.
> Mother, I put bees in my mouth
> to keep from eating
> yet it did you no good.
> In the end they cut off your breasts
> and milk poured from them
> into the surgeon's hand
> and he embraced them.
> I took them from him
> and planted them.

The planting of the mother's severed breasts enables "those dear white ponies" to "go galloping, galloping, / wherever you are;" and the daughter, for the moment of this poem, is renewed into her own life, free of guilt and pain. In **"All My Pretty Ones,"** the daughter discovering her father's flaws after his death in her mother's diary is able, by coming to terms with them and with their small duplications in her own life, to reach some kind of catharsis of pity and fear:

> Only in this hoarded span will love persevere.
> Whether you are pretty or not, I outlive you,
> bend down my strange face to yours and forgive you.

If this act of mutual forgiveness with mother and father must be repeated more than once, this is not a sign of weakness of resolve and will and heart, but of their strengths and determination. No resolution is ever quite so permanent as humans might wish. Anne Sexton could not be utterly and finally freed of her ghosts and her guilt in this life, and her poetry thus reveals these other "complicated lies:" of poetry as celebration only, of knowledge as ultimate freedom. "What forms the essence of our humanity—and of [*Oedipus Rex*]—is not our being victims of fate, but our struggle to discover the truth about ourselves." What forms the essence of Anne Sexton's poetic achievement is not her status as victim, but her struggle to discover the truth about herself, to turn her blindness into insight. And unless we "turn away," like Jocasta, like John Holmes, there ought indeed to be "something special" in "this kind of hope," perhaps in private.

my kitchen, your kitchen,
my face, your face.

Liz Porter Hankins (essay date Summer 1987)

SOURCE: "Summoning the Body: Anne Sexton's Body Poems," in *Midwest Quarterly,* Vol. 28, No. 4, Summer, 1987, pp. 511-24.

[*In the following essay, Hankins explores Sexton's response to patriarchal oppression and search for feminine identity in her portrayal of the female body. According to Hankins, "Her body poetry represents her journey to herself, for in accepting and learning to love her body, she is accepting and learning herself."*]

Robert Boyers so aptly said of Anne Sexton, "There is something awesome, even sublime in a woman who is not afraid to sound crude or shrill so long as she is honest, who in her best work sounds neither crude nor shrill precisely because she is honest." Mrs. Sexton reliably and openly confesses in her work; she seldom, if ever, yields to distortion or illusion. Her poems reflect the intimacy and complexity of her life and her struggle; she dares to set it in verse with the same force with which she lived it. Although many critics have been drawn to Mrs. Sexton's attraction to madness, they have repeatedly failed to deal with her femininity—her intimate search into herself for redemption. She found her answer in her work, not in suicide, through search and affirmation. Her solution lies in the long journey into herself when she transcends in verse the limitations of the physical and when the temple of her body becomes her ideological universe. She summons usage and experience, the world, through her body poetry.

Weston and Wellesley, Massachusetts, like Salem, or even Atlanta or Meridian, are proper settings in terms of absorbed religiosity, leftovers of the fitful, raging sermons of Jonathan Edwards, of the whispered accusations of Salem. Mrs. Sexton, and Sylvia Plath as well, reached maturity surrounded by and rooted deeply in the Puritan tradition of New England. It is from this tradition of expectations (especially those for women), that this tension, this order and balance that much of the content of modern American poetry derives. The Puritan ethos provided the lens through which the poet viewed his/her poetic world—its subjects, messages, choice of language, technique, and style. Its transparency reveals a man basically corrupt, living his life in a world which is equally corrupt and which offers little or no hope for salvation. Puritan poetry, whether Robert Lowell's or others', focuses on man's limitations and corruption, and usually uses complex and metaphysical compositions. Humans are basically evil living with the Adamic

legacy whose only salvation must come through suffering. There is no holy self, as there exists only personal corruption from within and without. There is no vision of a New Jerusalem, unlike John Donne's assurance of the cleansing of the soul in God's abode. Man drowns in a sea of sin which offers only doom. Mrs. Sexton, as others, is victimized by her own madness which seems to have resulted from an effort to cope with her feelings of sin and guilt in this hopeless world devoid of hope of salvation. When she summons herself through her body, she approaches metaphysics as her body becomes ideas leaving the isolated self behind on the physical plane. She transcends history, rationality, society, and assumes her own unique identity—she *becomes* through her body and its parts.

The militancy of seventeenth-century England, when militancy was no longer useful or necessary, seemed to turn itself inward and within the Church—churchmen converted their militant drives into doctrine and dogma. Women became convenient, silent recipients of that former militant enthusiasm. They were assigned roles of submission and reproduction to perpetuate and enhance the patriarchal institution. Sinful woman was to make her retribution by quietly accepting domination. Her role was prescribed by biblical complainers like Martha, who dared to question, who was shamed into submission.

> **Anne Sexton's works . . . clearly contain her efforts at defining herself as a woman— the daughter, mother, wife, lover.**
> **—*Liz Porter Hankins***

Mrs. Sexton's search for herself in her poetry and her life led her in many directions. Her efforts to comply with the expectations of others were admirable, one supposes, as she said in a 1968 interview:

> All I wanted was a little piece of life, to be married, to have children. . . . I was trying my damnedest to lead a conventional life, for that was how I was brought up, and it was what my husband wanted of me. But one can't build little white picket fences to keep the nightmares out.

Although Mrs. Sexton's poetry does not cry out with the same timbre of rage as does that of Adrienne Rich, a large portion of her work deals with the role of women in a patriarchal society. Only a female can possibly know what it is like to be female in a society which says just such femininity is inferior and must be dominated. Admittedly males suffer and feel and cry also, but they do so on male terms.

Anne Sexton's works, especially the poetry contained in *To*

Bedlam and Part Way Back and **Love Poems,** clearly contain her efforts at defining herself as a woman—the daughter, mother, wife, lover. As a daughter she alludes to her drunken father and her masochistic memory:

> You have worn my underwear.
> You have read my newspaper.
> You have seen my father whip me,
> You have seen me stroke my father's whip.

(**Death Notebooks**)

Looking at her own baby picture she wonders "Anne, / who were you?" Often vulnerable, often guilty, often a victim of circumstance, she becomes a mother herself and looks upon that role as being a daughter once again:

> I, who was never quite sure
> about being a girl, needed another
> life, another image to remind me.
> And this was my worst guilt; you could
> not cure nor soothe it. I made you to
> find me.

(**To Bedlam and Part Way Back**)

Her **Love Poems** underscore her Puritan up[...] a wife. She constantly strives to be the good [...] of submission, the dominated lover, carryi[...] structions just as she was taught:

> Swift boomerang, come get!
> I am delicate. You've been gone.
> The losing has hurt me some, yet
> I must bend for you. See me arch.
> I'm turned on....
>
> Draw me good, draw me warm.
> Bring me your raw-boned wrist and your [...]
> strange, Mr. Bind, strange stubborn horn [...]

(**Love Poems**)

She is a lover in the lesbian affair of "S[...] and outlines a tenderness for her own body as it is reflected by an identical one:

> On the day of breasts and small hips
> the window pocked with bad rain,
> rain coming on like a minister,
> we coupled, so sane and insane.
> We lay like spoons while the sinister
> rain dropped like flies on our lips
> and our glad eyes and our small hips.

> 'The room is so cold with rain,' you said
> and you, feminine you, with your flower
> said novenas to my ankles and elbows.
> You are a national product and power.
> Oh my swan, my drudge, my dear wooly rose,
> even a notary would notarize our bed
> as you knead me and I rise like bread.

Again as a lover, alluding to the objectification of her body in "**You All Know the Story of the Other Woman**," she is used by a man:

> He puts his bones back on,
> turning the clock back an hour.
> She knows flesh, that skin balloon,
> the unbound limbs, the boards,
> the roof, the removable roof.
> She is his selection, part time.
> You know the story too! Look,
> when it is over he places her,
> [...] phone, back on the hook.

[...]urning To His Wife," she is a tem- [...]ntial lover in comparison to the le-

> [...]d singular.
> [...]yourself and your dream.
> [...]onument, step after step.

> [...]a watercolor.

[...]defining herself, Mrs. Sexton comes to [...]body as an object which, she feels, is [...]men. She, however uneasily, comes to [...]her sexual relationships with men and by [...]h her body is offered and used as a sac-[...]ure about her body in regard to her pre-[...]role—she shows it, uses it, permits it to [...]it. She searches with her body for answers [...]age, and in tradition. She contrasts almost [...]maleness with maleness in these lines from [...]ocks":

> Whereas last night
> the cock knew its way home,
> as stiff as a hammer,
> battering in with all
> its awful power.
> That theater.
> Today it is tender,
> a small bird,
> as soft as a baby's hand.

She is the house.
He is the steeple.
When they fuck they are God.
When they break away they are God.
When they snore they are God.

(*Death Notebooks*)

She is an object again in **"Barefoot"**:

. . . Barefoot,
I drum up and down your back.
In the morning I run from door to door
of the cabin playing chase me.
Now you grab me by the ankles.
Now you work your way up the legs
and come to pierce me at my hunger mark.

(*Love Poems*)

In **"Man and Wife"** she sees the entrapment of being a wife; marriage provides no answers either:

Now they are together
like strangers in a two-seater outhouse,
eating and squatting together.

(*Live or Die*)

Mrs. Sexton, the constant female persona in these poems, strikes back in her own poetic/creative way against the oppression of men, against the Puritan tradition that continues to make demands of her womanhood. She often sees her body as grotesque, repulsive, and ridden with the sin and guilt possessed by all women. These lines are from **"Those Times"**:

At six
I lived in a graveyard full of dolls,
avoiding myself,
my body, the suspect
in its grotesque house.

She is repelled by the notion of her own nudity in **"The Nude Swim"**:

The walls of that grotto
were every color blue and
you said, 'Look! Your eyes
are seacolor. Look! Your eyes
are skycolor.' And my eyes
shut down as if they were
suddenly ashamed.

(*Love Poems*)

The woman sees herself, her body, in the eyes of her lover and is ashamed. Paul's message to the Corinthians concerning the body as a temple reminds Mrs. Sexton of her guilt and her sense of sin. Sometimes, as in **"The Nude Swim,"** the body corrects the mind's mistakes.

She tries over and over again "to lead a conventional life," but the burden of sin seems to be ever present in a haunting, ghost-like shadow from which she can find no escape. She strokes the whip of her father because little girls are so carefully taught the uniquely female traits of obedience and submission, and that women's identity is complete only with men.

The hope for Mrs. Sexton (and other women as well) lies in accepting and loving herself—as a woman, as a vessel into which she chooses to pour others' love. It is in this hope that she may become herself, not because of someone else, but because she *is;* she has achieved an identity apart from that dependence on someone else. Her body poetry represents her journey to herself, for in accepting and learning to love her body, she is accepting and learning herself. There is no one there to help her—it is a process of being feminine, of being alone, and of searching. Her Puritan ideals, her men, her womanhood, all prove useless until she faces the judges in the courtroom of her body and all of its parts.

In a 1965 interview with Patricia Marx, Mrs. Sexton refers to Franz Kafka's letter from which she quotes in *All My Pretty Ones:*

The books we read are the kind that act upon us like
a misfortune, that make us suffer like the death of someone we love more than ourselves. A book should serve
as the ax for the frozen sea within us.

She says in reply, "I feel my poetry should do that. I think it should be a shock to the senses." Her body poems, true to their confessional nature, do just that—shock us with their honesty, yet take us along into herself, into her search for womanhood.

The harvesting within her body, the letting of blood, the cessation of the menses, marks her realization of completing one phase, yet continuing on a journey of a different kind. She puts away fertility from within in order to perceive it somewhere else in **"Menstruation at Forty"**:

The womb is not a clock
nor a bell tolling,
but in the eleventh month of its life
I feel the November
of the body as well as the calendar.
In two days it will be my birthday

and as always the earth is done with its harvest. . . .

Woman,
weaving a web over your own,
a thin and tangled poison.

(***Live or Die***)

When reproduction ceases, does her body as a woman cease to exist? Only until she is willing to seek further within herself for an answer. In **"Little Girl, My String Bean, My Lovely Woman,"** she gives to her oldest daughter advice on womanhood that she herself has not followed:

I hear
as in a dream
the conversation of the old wives
speaking of *womanhood.*
I remember that I heard nothing myself.
I was alone.
I waited like a target.

Oh, darling, let your body in,
let in tie you in,
in comfort.
What I want to say, Linda,
is that women are born twice. . . .
there is nothing in your body that lies.
All that is new is telling the truth.
I'm here, that somebody else,
an old tree in the background.

She begins to admit to herself things that she has been refusing to admit. In **"The Breast"** she gives in:

This is the key to it.
This is the key to everything.
Preciously.

(***Love Poems***)

In **"In Celebration of My Uterus"** she simply "sings" for that female part:

Sweet weight,
in celebration of the woman I am.
and of the soul of the woman I am
and of the central creature and its delight
I sing for you. I dare to live.

She is approaching unity with her ideological self. She begins to glorify her body instead of feeling guilty because of it.

In **"Hurry Up Please It's Time"** she is back to the begin-

ning of the search and role-playing Eve, except the fruit is an orange this time, and, once again, the body is somewhat threatening. Thinking as an Eve, she swallows an orange, yet records it more as a Lillith might:

I dream I'm a boy with a zipper.
It's so practical, la de dah.
The trouble with being a woman, Skeezix,
is being a little girl in the first place.
Not all the books of the world will change that.
I have swallowed an orange, being woman.
You have swallowed a ruler, being man.

(***Death Notebooks***)

Through the miles and miles of journeying, Mrs. Sexton comes full circle from the exploration of herself in her many different roles to the realization that she must, indeed, allow herself to love herself and her body. These lines are from **"The Double Image"**:

. . . And I had to learn
why I would rather
die than love. . . .

(***To Bedlam and Part Way Back***)

In order to love oneself, one must, in particular, women must, as she says, be "fastened to the earth, listening for its small animal noises." The ax for the frozen sea is beginning to hone itself when Mrs. Sexton finally realizes that she has a need for herself, her body and all its parts—she must reserve some of herself for herself. She says to her young daughter Joyce in **"The Double Image"**:

. . . love your self's self where it lives.

. . . The time I did not love
myself, I visited your shoveled walks; you held my glove.

There was new snow after this.

(***To Bedlam and Part Way Back***)

"The Farmer's Wife" portrays Mrs. Sexton's new awareness that sometimes a woman can find strength in being alone, in being a woman. The old humdrum routine does offer hope to the farmer's wife:

. . . she has been his habit;
as again tonight he'll say
honey bunch let's go
and she will not say how there
must be more to living
than this brief bright bridge

of the raucous bed or even
the slow braille touch of him
like a heavy god grown light,
that old pantomime of love
that she wants although
it leaves her still alone,
built back again at last,
mind's apart from him, living
her own self in her own words
and hating the sweat of the house. . . .

The old woman, although still obliged to perform sexual and wifely duties to her husband, finds herself "Built back again at last." Afterwards she is herself and Anne Sexton begins looking to herself again, this time in utter honesty in **"The Hoarder"**: "There is something there / I've got to get and I dig down / into the depths to find it" (**Book of Folly**). It is the acceptance she is after, and in **"The Ballad of the Lonely Masturbator"** she is alone, touching her body, and admitting it. She has transformed all her fears, her confusion, her Puritan upbringing, and in this moment has come to realize that all of her body—her uterus, her brown legs, her hands, her feet, her breasts, her fingers, are hers and hers alone. She is beyond her attitude of before when in **"The Touch"** she says: "For months my hand had been sealed off / in a tin box" (**Love Poems**). She transcends biology and approaches the metaphysical at the instant of realization that her body has become ideological. Everything else in her life has seemed somewhat trivial and undependable until this moment. Her femaleness, her body, offer her stability in the wake of madness and the middle-class obsession for suburban life. They come to represent everything—her ideals of femininity, her craft as a poet, her link to the physical reality of life. In **"The Ballad of the Lonely Masturbator"** Mrs. Sexton deals with the body as an idea when she "breaks out of my body this way." Once again the body corrects the mistakes of the mind:

> The end of the affair is always death.
> She's my workshop. Slippery eye,
> out of the tribe of myself my breath
> finds you gone. I horrify
> those who stand by. I am fed.
> At night, alone, I marry the bed.
>
> Finger to finger, now she's mine.
> She's not too far. She's my encounter.
> I beat her like a bell. I recline
> in the bower where you used to mount her.
> You borrowed me on the flowered spread.
> At night, alone, I marry the bed.
> I break out of my body this way,
> an annoying miracle. . . .

(**Love Poems**)

So, to Mrs. Sexton, the poetess, the searching madwoman, came the realization that one must first love oneself, that it is the first step in learning and loving others. One must journey far down into the depths of one's soul, past history, community, society, and the guilt imposed by these and more. Mrs. Sexton, in glorious but fleeting moments, got in touch with herself through her body—her female body. In those moments her body acquired ideological power enabling the poet to rise above all the limitations of the earthly life for women—sin and guilt, suppression and domination. That transcendence truly and surely became her "ax for the frozen sea within" her.

One wonders, going one step further, if perhaps Mrs. Sexton was not contemplating or even suggesting the Phoenix-like rebirth of an androgynous being, for she makes numerous references to such. In **"Begat"** she writes: "Red. Red. Father, you are blood red. / Father, / we are two birds on fire" (**Book of Folly**), and in **"Angel of Fire and Genitals"**: "Fire-woman, you of the ancient flame, / . . . Mother of fire, let me stand at your devouring gate / as the sun dies in your arms and you loosen its terrible weight." Phoenix-like, through her metaphysical union between the body and the mind, this woman will shuck the bonds of gender, and will rise from the ash as in **"Consorting With Angels"** she dreams:

> I was tired of being a woman,
> tired of the spoons and the pots. . . .
> But I was tired of the gender of things.
> . . . I was not a woman anymore,
> not one thing or the other. . . .
> I'm no more a woman
> than Christ was a man.

(**Live or Die**)

One is reminded of *sui genesis*, the rebirth, or self-birth alluded to in **"The Breast"**:

> Ignorant of men I lay next to my sisters
> and rising out of the ashes I cried
> *my sex will be transfixed!*

(**Love Poems**)

Mrs. Sexton has run the gamut in the search for herself, her female identity. She finally summons herself through her body, and in so doing, transcends physical limitations—her body becomes mental, metaphysical, in that it places her in absolute touch with herself. It almost possesses super powers, thus enabling her to entertain thoughts of self-birthing, regenerating as a mental or spiritual force forging the "ax for the frozen sea within."

Diane Wood Middlebrook (essay date 1992)

SOURCE: "Anne Sexton: The Making of 'The Awful Rowing Toward God,'" in *Rossetti to Sexton: Six Women Poets at Texas,* edited by Dave Oliphant, University of Texas at Austin, 1992, pp. 223-35.

[*In the following essay, Middlebrook discusses Sexton's friendship with James Wright and the composition* The Awful Rowing Toward God.]

Between 10 and 30 January 1973, Anne Sexton wrote—"with two days out for despair and three days out in a mental hospital"—an entire volume of poems. Eventually titled **The Awful Rowing Toward God,** this proved to be the last book Sexton saw into print. A few hours after correcting the galleys on 4 October 1974, she committed suicide. Important in its own right as Anne Sexton's "last" book, this volume gains great interest from being viewed in the context of collections of worksheets, correspondence, and other items in the Sexton archive at the Harry Ransom Humanities Research Center at The University of Texas at Austin.

The HRHRC acquired the Sexton archive in 1980, sixteen years after the poet's death. Sexton's elder daughter Linda, executor of the estate, decided that all manuscripts and correspondence and miscellany—including Anne Sexton's library—should be sold together. She rightly assumed that Sexton's voluminous papers would interest scholars, since Sexton, virtually an autodidact, kept careful track of her own progress as an artist and businesswoman—and as a patient in psychotherapy.

The Sexton archive offers an unusually full range of materials pertaining to the poet's life and work. Born Anne Gray Harvey in 1928 in Wellesley, Massachusetts, Sexton acquired a love of books from her mother, Mary Gray Staples Harvey, who collected fine editions. Sexton's maternal grandfather Arthur Gray Staples was a writer, and for many years editor of a newspaper in Lewiston, Maine. During her teenage years, Anne began keeping letters, pictures, and memorabilia in scrapbooks, many of which made their way into vertical files in the HRHRC's Sexton archive. At age 19, Anne Harvey married Alfred Muller Sexton II (nicknamed "Kayo"); they had two daughters: Linda Gray Sexton, born 1953, and Joyce Ladd Sexton, born 1955. Anne Sexton's career as a poet began with treatment for a "nervous breakdown" in 1956, when her first psychiatrist, Martin Orne, suggested writing as a form of therapy.

A resident of suburban Boston, Sexton sought formal training in local workshops, and rapidly developed a very professional attitude toward writing. From the outset, she kept letters she received from other writers, and made carbons of her own letters; thus, both sides of Sexton's correspondence are available to readers at the HRHRC. Moreover, she was a careful steward of her own manuscripts. Abundant worksheets for each published volume of Sexton's work make possible a full view of the development of many individual poems and all of her books. In addition, the HRHRC contains worksheets and completed versions of stories and plays by Anne Sexton, most of which remain unpublished, as well as voluminous unpublished business correspondence which provides a detailed view of the economics of her career. Finally, the Sexton archive contains numerous audiotapes and films that convey the poet's skills as a performer of her own work.

At the time Anne Sexton wrote **The Awful Rowing Toward God,** she was preparing to leave her marriage of twenty-five years. Her husband Kayo, a wool salesman whose hobbies were hunting and fishing, had never taken much interest in poetry or poets. Both daughters—Joy now age 18, Linda 20—had left the family home for boarding school and college. Like many couples of their era, Anne and Kayo found that the departure of their children opened a void across which they measured how little else they had in common. Moreover, career success had given Anne Sexton the confidence and financial security to make divorce a viable option. By 1973 she held a position as Professor of Creative Writing at Boston University, and had made herself one of the best-paid performers on the poetry circuit that burgeoned on American campuses during the 1960s. Correspondence with universities shows Sexton setting fees at the level James Dickey had established when he moved into the poetry business out of advertising. In 1973, Sexton regularly demanded $1200-$1500 for any reading that required airplane travel or an overnight stay out of town. Letters to her department head at Boston University regarding raises and job security show Sexton calling attention to the three honorary degrees she received in 1970-1971 and threatening—just a joke, of course—to post a feminist fist on his office door if her salary did not rise to meet that of her male colleagues. The daughter of one salesman and the wife of another, Sexton knew how to deal in the literary marketplace. That, indeed, was the theme of many poems in the new book she had in press in January 1973, **The Death Notebooks,** which bore an epigraph from Ernest Hemingway's *A Movable Feast:* "Look, you con man, make a living out of your death."

In contrast, **The Awful Rowing Toward God** is a book exclusively about religious belief. Though in 1973 Sexton belonged to no established church, spiritual questions engaged her deeply. She exulted to a friend that the thirty-nine poems of **Awful Rowing** emerged from "two and a half weeks of frantic, devout inspiration." Religious themes had appeared in Sexton's work from the beginning, and had recurred with increasing significance in each succeeding vol-

ume, attracting the interest of priests, nuns, and other religious people with whom Sexton enjoyed corresponding;
particularly rich are letters Sexton exchanged with Brother
Dennis O'Brien, F.S.C., between 1961-1963, on deposit at
the HRHRC. But nowhere are Sexton's questions about religious faith pursued with the urgency expressed in *Awful
Rowing.* In these poems Sexton aggressively probes the
possibility of God's immanence in the secular world of her
daily life. If God is everywhere, the devout must be able
to find him even in their kitchens, even in themselves at
their worst.

> I will take a crowbar
> and pry out the broken
> pieces of God in me.
> Just like a jigsaw puzzle,
> I will put Him together again
> with the patience of a chess player.
>
> How many pieces?
> It feels like thousands,
> God dressed up like a whore
> in a slime of green algae.
> God dressed up like an old man
> staggering out of His shoes.
> God dressed up like a child,
> all naked,
> even without skin,
> soft as an avocado when you peel it.

Characteristically scatological, transgressive, exhibitionistic, the poems of *Awful Rowing* struggle to bring God
down to a level with Sexton's sense of the evil that inhabited her body in the forms of obsessional neuroses, depression, addiction. The principle that united Sexton with God,
in her personal system of belief, was the gift of language
that could connect *anything* to *anything else,* via the syntax of metaphor. She states the principle simply in a poem
from *Awful Rowing:* "the typewriter [. . .] is my church /
with an altar of keys always waiting."

Language and imagery were rampant in Sexton during those
weeks of composition, and the craft of association she had
developed permitted the poems to lengthen down the page
without false starts or revision. Rapidity resulted in thematic focus: the poems of *Awful Rowing* are organized
around congregated images of the body in pain: references
to veins, blood, skin, tongue, hands, eyeballs, nakedness recur in the poems (as in **"The Big Heart":** "The artery of
my soul has been severed / and soul is spurting out . . .").
A worksheet Sexton filed carefully with the first draft of
the book shows her calculating her output: on several days
in January 1973 she wrote as many as three different poems. The abundance was unusual even for her; in earlier
work, Sexton would typically put every poem through many

drafts. (For example, the HRHRC files contain 38
worksheets spanning four years for Sexton's **"Flee on Your
Donkey,"** before its acceptance at *The New Yorker* and its
appearance as a major poem in the Pulitzer-prizewinning
volume *Live or Die,* 1966.)

Sexton considered another title for the book: *Washing the
Feet of God,* suggestive of a relationship between the
speaker of her poems and Mary Magdalene, the "fallen"
woman who wiped the feet of Jesus with her hair. She also
considered titling it *The Life Notebooks,* to point the contrast between this devotional volume and its immediate predecessor *The Death Notebooks.* But in several of the
poems themselves, metaphors of rowing and swimming are
used to express intense, laborious struggle toward a longed-
for ground of faith. Worksheets reveal Sexton shuffling and
reshuffling the order of the poems; eventually she decided
to open and close the volume with **"Rowing"** and **"The
Rowing Endeth."**

By early February the manuscript was ready to send to her
agent Cindy Degener at Sterling Lord Agency. It was
Degener who would negotiate the contract with Sexton's
publisher, Houghton Mifflin Company, and who would try
to market any unsold poems to high-paying magazines such
as *Cosmopolitan* and *Vogue.* Sexton herself began doling
out several pages at a time to Howard Moss for consideration at *The New Yorker,* where she had held a "first reading" contract since 1961. Sexton always dealt personally
with editors she knew well, such as Moss.

Following her usual practice, Sexton also sent the manuscript to poets whose advice she trusted, hoping for detailed
criticism. Her first editor, George Starbuck—now her
"boss," as head of Creative Writing at Boston University—
received a copy, as did John Malcolm Brinnin, a senior colleague at B.U. who had the office next door to her own.
Perhaps on impulse, Sexton also decided to request criticism from her old friend James Wright. Wright's very interesting response is well-detailed in the manuscript
collection at the HRHRC; to grasp its importance requires
a bit of background.

Anne Sexton's friendship with James Wright had begun in
February 1960, when she impulsively sent a note praising
his new book of poems, *Saint Judas:*

> Dear Mr. Wright, I doubt you remember meeting me
> at Robert Lowell's class and later at a party at John
> Holmes' house, but at any rate . . . I am writing to say
> in all sincerity, having re-read your book for the six[th]
> time thou wast born altogether a great poet.

This fan letter inaugurated what quickly turned into a passionate correspondence; in the next eleven months Sexton

wrote and received from Wright what she described as "several hundred 'faintly scarlet' letters." Most of these letters disappeared mysteriously after her death. However, enough remain in the Sexton archives at the HRHRC to reveal that, for a time in 1960, Wright filled an enormous void at the center of Sexton's life. Offering her what quickly developed, on paper, into a blend of mentorship and courtship, Wright answered her hunger for affectionate recognition with a hunger of his own.

In his surviving letters, as in person, Wright was garrulous, gossipy, warmheartedly pedantic. His advice about music and reading came complete with serial numbers of recordings by favorite conductors, his reading notes convey a quirky, avid intelligence. Introducing Sexton to a pair of translations of Neruda's "Walking Around," Wright thought it useful to inform her,

> [Neruda] is a South American Communist, which is a historically complicated kind of creature. In any case, he is, like, say, Mayakovsky in that his directly *political* poems are so bad as to be, not funny, but distressing, as if you were seeing Sir John Gielgud forget several lines at the very dramatic crisis of *Hamlet.*

Wright was translating Neruda at this time, as part of an effort to transform his formal style into a poetry more spare and imagistic. His own early work had been snubbed for its "plodding sincerity" by James Dickey in a review that roused a controversy in the *Sewanee Review* for a few issues, before Wright, endearingly, decided he agreed with Dickey's judgment and gave up the argument. Wright then turned to translating poets such as Georg Trakl, an Austrian writer whose imagery had an immediacy he admired. In this undertaking he found an ally in Robert Bly. At the time Sexton and Wright were becoming ardent correspondents, Wright and Bly were collaborating on several volumes of translations from Trakl, César Vallejo, and Neruda.

Wright held a place of magical significance in Anne Sexton's development as a poet, for the first book of poems she ever bought for herself . . . was James Wright's *The Green Wall. . . .*
—*Diane Wood Middlebrook*

The formation of Wright's friendship with both Sexton and Bly occurred at an important phase of transition in his life, when he was leaving his marriage and attempting to reach some authentic mode of expressing his own inwardness in compelling imagery. He was, briefly, disposed to find in Sexton a muse who reconnected him to inspiration. Wright's name for Anne Sexton—"Blessing," sometimes "Bee," or "B,"—was also the title of a much-admired poem he wrote during the period of their intimacy. "My beautiful kind Blessing, my discovered love," he called her. "In the midst of everything you do you can know you are utterly loved. [. . .] I survive by sitting and thinking of you." Sometimes they wrote each other two or three letters in a single day. "It was wonderful for her: an enchantment," Maxine Kumin remembered. Wright's feelings in these documents are not so much for Sexton herself—whom he knew only through letters and phone calls, not from any day-to-day contact—as for the sense of himself that writing to her gave him. This is manifest in the remarks that accompanied his gift to her in July of a book he treasured, the collected poems of Edward Thomas, now at the HRHRC:

> Ten years ago I secretly bought and hid this book and another copy which is identical to it [. . .] I also had an old, very personal copy of Whitman. But once about a year ago, in despair, I tore the Whitman to pieces and thrust it down into the rankest mucky bottom sludge of an old garbage can near a dirty railroad track in Minneapolis; then I burned my manuscripts. Years of them. A symbolic suicide, if there ever was one. [. . .] But whatever in me has been worthy of life, for ten years, clings to each page of this book. I always (even in the worst times) hoped to be worthy of giving this book to somebody. Oh, I knew you would come. But it was a long time. Thank you for being alive and for letting me give you this book. Because, in letting me give the gift, you give me at the same time a gift in return: myself.

For many months this feeling was completely mutual. Wright held a place of magical significance in Anne Sexton's development as a poet, for the first book of poems she ever bought for herself—long before sending him that first fan letter—was James Wright's *The Green Wall,* prizewinner in the Yale Younger Poets series in 1957, her copy of which is at the HRHRC. In one of her long letters to Wright, Sexton recalled that one day she had made $2.75 selling Beauty Counselor Cosmetics door to door: "I wasn't poor, but I had to work awfully hard selling face cream to strangers who wouldn't open the door and besides I'd just come out of the booby hatch and I was nervous with strangers, I was even nervous with face cream." She'd taken the job in order to pay her psychiatrist's fees. On the way home that particular day she went into a bookstore to look at poetry.

> I had never heard of you . . . but I had never heard of Yeats either. I read SHE HID IN THE TREES FROM THE NURSES (I think that is right) and a few others. I took out my face cream money and bought the book. At first I didn't read it, that day I didn't. I was saving it. The next day I went to visit my mother who lived

on top of a large rock that overlooked the ocean. I went to spend a weekend with her. It is funny how I have forgotten all this. But the clear memory was when I left my mother's very nicely cruelly perfect living room (don't think I didn't love her—it was just that now I had something of my own to do. I had a book of poems and they were mine . . . unlike her perfect room.) I went out on the rocks, high over the sea and found a little nitch [sic] there, hidden from the land in a way. I [sic] little place, such as children find to hide in and to keep themselves in. A MY place. I took a pack of cigarettes and this green book that I had bought with my face cream money. The sea was there, and the sun and wind. It was a nice day. It was my place, my book, words written for me, to me. I held it in my hand and it moved, not like the sea below me, but like a small mechanical heart might. I say that, extravagant or not, because the book told me who I was, who I could be. The book was more alive than all the ruined sea.

On her own side of the correspondence that they were conducting in 1960, Sexton fed her deep hunger for growth as a poet on Wright's unflagging attention. Just beginning her second book in 1960, she was anxious for new sources of encouragement, new models, a wider intellectual horizon. Under Wright's tutelage Sexton read eclectically in world poetry: many worksheets for poems written in 1961 and 1962 have carbon typescript translations from other poets on the back, which Wright probably either sent her or recommended to her.

Just as Wright welcomed Sexton's letters, he welcomed manuscripts of her poems in progress, and was liberal, even prodigal, with advice. He would write all over her drafts of poems with a blunt soft lead pencil in tiny script. Wright had direct influence on several of the poems Sexton wrote in 1960 and 1961. Worksheets of manuscripts of Sexton's **"The Truth the Dead Know"** and **"A Curse Against Elegies"** suggest that they may have started out as the same poem, titled "Refusal"; in August 1960 a letter from Wright notes their similarity to his own poem, "The Refusal," observing that Sexton's two versions have different themes, and that in following him, she chooses the "narrower and less powerful" theme. He tried to dissuade her from imitation of him. "B. must trust her own imagination: call her own stubbornness to aid!" he advises.

But it was not so much Wright's practical advice as his acceptance of her as a peer that mattered to Sexton, helping her internalize the identity she was rapidly acquiring in the professional world of poetry. Shortly after their correspondence began, Wright sent her a copy of Rainer Maria Rilke's *Letters to a Young Poet,* with a sibylline inscription:

To Anne Sexton, for whom this book was written—

"Let those who may complain that it was only upon paper remember that only upon paper have humanity yet achieved glory, beauty, truth, knowledge, virtue and abiding love" (G. B. Shaw, on his letters to Ellen Terry)—Jim Wright, Spring 1960.

Wright may have been thinking of Rilke's miserable record as a husband, father, and lover of other human beings, much in contrast with the commitment to love and work that Rilke idealizes in *Letters to a Young Poet.* Both Wright and Sexton were married to loyal, hardworking spouses, and Wright, a guilty soul, apparently did not acknowledge to others his attachment to Sexton. In any case, his literary advice was excellent. Sexton adopted *Letters to a Young Poet* as a personal manifesto, and re-read it whenever she wanted to make emotional contact with Wright.

This old connection, then, lay in the background of Sexton's decision to send Wright the manuscript of *The Awful Rowing Toward God,* in January 1973. She wrote him an affectionate letter and signed it with his old name of endearment, "Bee." Wright's reply was most ambivalent. He returned the manuscript with numerous penciled annotations on various poems; he also returned Sexton's letter, with a terse reply written in pencil below her signature:

> Dear Bee, I'm returning your manuscript in faith for you and your poetic genius. I have no intention of excusing your bad verse and your bad prose. There are some poems here that I think are fine. There are some that I think are junk. The choice between them is yours.
>
> —C[omfort].

Pedantic, impassioned, Wright argued both with Sexton's craft and her theology. "Leave God his own poems, and cut these lines out. God damn it Bee, stop trying to be a saint. Be a poet, and get rid of the junk.—Cf 'The Sea,' by Cecilia Moraes (of Brazil)." Regarding **"The Earth Falls Down"** he commanded, "Delete this poem. For Christ's sake, Bee, read Jung's analysis of *Job.*" He urged her to abandon all but three lines of **"After Auschwitz,"** adding, "Bee, what I ask is a terrible sacrifice. But *listen, listen;* trust your own strange voice."

Wright's commentary generated a second and third layer of marginal glosses as Sexton reacted with irritation and chagrin to his exhortations, then passed along the manuscript to Maxine Kumin. Around the margins of this draft, a small but heated war goes on, with aggressive reactions to Wright in the neat handwriting of Kumin and in Sexton's big scrawl. **"The Fallen Angels"** had elicited from Wright a whole column of irritable dispute over the nature of heaven, culminating in the advice, "Bee, stop making stupid cute remarks about angels. We don't even know enough about each other." Sexton had penned a big black X through the poem; but Maxine came to its defense in the left margin: "I like this poem—it isn't intended as a deep theological investigation but a way of hoarding up the good signs, or omens to keep going." The poem stayed, as did other poems and stanzas and images that Wright rejected.

Undoubtedly, Sexton should have given Wright's advice more weight; reviewers would echo Wright's privately-voiced criticism of the poems. But Sexton was in a hurry to finish this book. Her divorce from Kayo proved psychologically damaging in ways she might have foreseen, and did not. Both inspiration and health deserted her in the months following their separation; and worries about money distracted her constantly. Most of the Sexton correspondence dating from 1973-1974 is concerned with the business of poetry, not the process of creation.

Nonetheless, the final version of *The Awful Rowing Toward God* reflected Wright's intervention. Imploring her to "listen, listen" and to "strip the language and shackle accidents," Wright had guided Sexton's attention to arbitrary similes and rhythmically wooden passages which she sometimes decided to revise. Readying the final manuscript for publication, Sexton completed it with a dedication: "For Brother Dennis, wherever he is, and for James Wright, who would know." With Maxine Kumin's help, Sexton corrected the galleys of the book the day she died. Her touching acknowledgment shows that the spirit and not the letter was of use to her as she brought this final manuscript to press, in what were to be the last months, days, and hours of her life.

Mikhail Ann Long (essay date Spring-Summer 1993)

SOURCE: "As If Day Had Rearranged Into Night: Suicidal Tendencies in the Poetry of Anne Sexton," in *Literature and Psychology,* Vol. 39, Nos. 1-2, Spring-Summer, 1993, pp. 26-41.

[*In the following essay, Long examines Sexton's preoccupation with death and suicide as an integral feature of her writing. According to Long, "Her poems clearly reflect her understanding of, and attempt to come to terms with, her mental illness and suicidal behavior."*]

> as if day had rearranged
> into night and bats flew in the sun.

Was Anne Sexton's poetry primarily about the nature of the closed world of suicide? Most critics agree on the fact that Sexton definitely wrote about wanting to die, and the nature of suicide, from a very personal point of view. Many

critics believe that at least some of Sexton's poetry reflects this suicidal "lust." According to Diane Hume George, there are "at least twenty poems primarily dedicated to explaining what it feels like to want, or need, to die." Kathleen Spivack, in her article "Poet and Friend" notes that "Anne was obsessed with death—one has only to read *Live or Die* to see to what extent." Spivack goes on to tell us that:

> Ultimately, death took precedence in her imagination. Anne had . . . almost a what-the-hell attitude toward death: Her wish to destroy herself was a deep compulsion.

So Sexton's deep-seated desire to die is apparent to most, if not all, of her critics, and readers. But is it omnipresent, woven into the fabric of all, or nearly all, of her poetry, or is it only in a few pieces?

Sexton resumed writing poetry (she had written as a child and young woman), according to Maxine Kumin's introductory essay in Sexton's *Complete Poems,* after her first breakdown and suicide attempt. Her psychiatrist Dr. Martin Orne encouraged her writing as a kind of therapy, an emotional outlet, to enable her to return to, or develop, a stable inner life. Therefore all of her published poetry was written after she had entered Allen Alvarez's "closed world of the suicide." This explains the unremitting background of despair and pain that is clearly visible in even the most pleasant of her poems. But the obvious connection between Sexton's urgency towards death and suicide and her poetic expression is blurred in most critics' minds. They fail to analyze Sexton's work based on the fact that since she was suicidal during her entire writing career, her poetry could well be judged by assuming this suicidal nature as foundational to any real understanding.

Was Sexton consciously aware of her desire to die? According to Ari Kiev in his 1971 article about "Suicide Prevention,"

> The suicidal act in most of our patients was characterized by impulsivity and the absence of premeditation. . . . patients were often so emotionally disturbed at the time of the attempt that they not only did not consider but could not use the telephone to call for help. . . . Another factor which cuts across age, sex and diagnostic groups, was non-recognition of an underlying psychiatric illness or emotional disturbance which the patient was experiencing prior to the attempt.

Although this impulsive behavior may have characterized several of Sexton's suicide attempts, the overall thrust of her writing indicates premeditated action on her part. Her poems clearly reflect her understanding of, and attempt to come to terms with, her mental illness and suicidal behavior. She tried to work these conflicts out on paper as well as with numerous therapists and psychiatrists. Another suicidologist, Joseph Richman, discusses the fact that

> Suicide itself is a communication. It is a cry for help, an appeal to others, a method of retaliation or revenge, an expression of atonement and a confession . . . What has been largely overlooked . . . is the reciprocal, two-way nature of communication. . . . There also seems to be an imperviousness or non-reception to verbal messages from the suicidal person by the relatives.

This "reciprocal nature" of suicide as communication comes into play not only with the family and friends of Sexton but with her readers since she expressed her despair and her darker nature in her poetry. This communication was used by Sexton to attempt to reach other souls that were as tormented as she herself was.

Sexton, writing as a "confessional poet," undoubtedly used her own persona in much of her poetry. Kumin refers to "Sexton's deeply rooted conviction that poems not only could, but had to be, made out of the detritus of her life." Therefore her poetry can be assumed to be a reflection of her underlying view of life and her deepest feelings about suicide. I will provide an alternative reading for several of Sexton's apparently non-suicidal poems, by isolating Sexton's suicidal tendencies as a major thematic element that runs through not only the "suicide/death" poems, but many of the others, and by analyzing her poetry using data from a study of *Suicidal Women: Their Thinking and Feeling Patterns* done by Charles Neuringer and Dan J. Lettieri in 1982.

In their study Neuringer and Lettieri postulated that "the key to suicide does not lie in the area of personality and motivational forces but is the product of the cognitive and intellectual organization of the suicidal individual. . . . there is a particular style of thinking. . . . that leads some people to organize their experience in such a way that suicide is the only possible choice for them." Originally Neuringer had also hoped to compare this potential using gender but was unable to as no comparable study had yet been conducted using male potential suicides.

The Neuringer study consisted of forty women, thirty of whom had evidenced definite suicidal tendencies, and a control group of ten who were in crisis but not suicidal. All thirty of the suicidal women had contacted a suicide "hotline" in Los Angeles, and had been analyzed concerning their suitability for this particular study. The potential suicides were divided into groups of ten and ranked from low to high suicide potential. The subjects were then followed for three weeks, on a daily basis, using a combination of questionnaires and personal interviews to monitor their mental and emotional status. The findings isolated data on four "ingredients" and attempted to find the pattern for identifying potential suicides. I will be dealing with the findings for the highly suicidal woman since Sexton clearly fell in this category throughout her writing career.

The first "ingredient" is the subject's attitude toward life, death, and suicide. According to Neuringer the highly suicidal woman does not find life attractive. Her evaluations of life are in the negative zone. Death seems to be perceived as non-frightening, neutral, or even attractive. A desire to escape from her life seems to predominate.

The second "ingredient" in the suicidal personality is the particular manner the subject chooses to organize her way of viewing the world. Neuringer maintains that this consists of dichotomous thinking carried to one or more extremes. Stark alternatives and extreme polarities of life and death characterize the highly suicidal woman's thinking patterns. "No-Win" situations and severely limited problem-solving mechanisms seem to be part of the pattern. "The massive dichotomous thinking [of the highly suicidal woman] curtails the use of conceptual and intellectual tools that could provide a wide variety of alternative solutions to their difficulties. . . . For these women life and death are perceived as clear and opposing alternatives; intermediate ways of living are not possible." Howard M. Bogard also describes this dichotomous thinking in his article, the "Collected Thoughts of a Suicidologist" when he describes how differently a situation can appear to a suicidal person. He states that

> The loss of jobs, love objects and status must be viewed within the eye and the psychology of the individual involved. The loss of a job will mean something far more devastating to a man who has rigorously over-invested his work . . . Should a man's career be part of a compensatory struggle to deny feelings of minimal self worth, loss of his position will set off feelings of failure, humiliation, impotence, uselessness, depression and perhaps of suicide. Thus, if I lose my job, I am nothing . . . if I am nothing I am [or should be] dead.

This is a clear illustration of the fact that alternate ways of living do not appear possible to the suicidal person.

The third "ingredient" of the suicidal personality seems to be the suicidal urge that is more or less present at all times. The desire or urgency fluctuates from day to day but only within a narrow range: "The person never feels free enough from suicidal feelings to develop adequate problem-solving behavior. . . . The horror continues and will continue, reinforced by the very presence of negative life attitudes and dichotomous thinking. These lethal ingredients to not permit the adoption of life-saving orientations." Allen Alvarez explains this urge very clearly in his book *The Savage God:*

> For them [the suicidal ones], the act is neither rash nor operatic nor, in any obvious way, unbalanced. Instead it is, insidiously, a vocation. . . . there never seems to have been a time when one was not suicidal . . . so the suicide feels he has always been preparing in secret for this last act.

So death is always in the back of their minds, a viable choice if nothing else works out.

The final "ingredient" is the affective state, the level of feelings and emotions. The highly suicidal woman reports greater suffering, and "seems to be living in a world devoid of interest and [apparently] joyless. They cannot be aroused by stimuli; they are angry and dissatisfied by what they are and what they do; they feel inadequate, they dislike themselves and are profoundly depressed." Otto Rank isolated this tendency in his 1945 book *Will Therapy and Truth and Reality* when he states that the suicide

> perceives himself as unreal and reality as unbearable, because with him the mechanisms of illusion are known and destroyed by self-consciousness. He can no longer deceive himself about himself and disillusions [sic] even his own ideal of personality. He perceives himself as bad, guilt laden, inferior, as a small, weak, helpless creature, which is the truth about mankind, as Oedipus also discovered in the crash of his heroic fate. All other is illusion, deception, but necessary deception in order to be able to bear one's self and thereby life.

Neuringer attempts to find a relationship between these ingredients for the seriously suicidal woman and finds that, in addition to this already "lethal brew" there is one final factor not found in the other women in the study. The "seriously suicidal woman is not oriented toward others . . . [therefore] possible social restraints in the environment have no inhibiting power for her . . . [this] allows her to act in socially non-sanctioned ways and . . . makes the decision to escape from life easy." These findings concur on a scientific level with Allen Alvarez's more colloquial description of the "closed world" of the suicide in his book.

A close examination of Sexton's poems, one about death and suicide, and several others that do not appear to be about death, will reveal Neuringer's five "ingredients."

"Sylvia's Death," written in 1963 is probably the best of Sexton's explorations of wanting to die. Diane Hume George dislikes this poem intensely, making her reasons clear in her discussion of Sexton's so-called "suicide se-

ries" in her book *Oedipus Anne.* George sees the poem as "self-serving, self-pity[ing] and self-aggrandizing" and she feels that she is "overhearing a pathetic competition between suicides, one accomplished and one potential, full of petty jealousy and envy masquerading as eulogy." This view of the poem is echoed by Kathleen Spivack when she discusses Sexton's "jealousy that Sylvia had actually managed to kill herself," but if this poem is viewed as an expression of Sexton's actual feelings about Plath's death, and about her own suicide attempts, then perhaps the apparent pettiness and jealousy could be construed as simply symptoms of the suicidal mind set rather than self-pity.

Neuringer's first "ingredient" can be seen in this poem with Sexton's expressed view of life as "a dead box of stones and spoons," and death as "an old belonging," and finally her view of suicide as "the ride home with our boy." These attitudes reflect a necessary view of death, one which makes suicide a plausible alternative to Sexton rather than simply expressing pettiness and envy.

The second "ingredient" is the dichotomous or polarized view of life and death. This must be assumed in this poem because death is the only subject. Death is not only affirmed as precious, "the death we drank to," but is seen as the only thing of value throughout the poem. Sexton does not remind Plath of the beauties of life, indeed she never refers to any values of life at all. She merely reiterates their previous obsession with death as "the one we talked of so often."

The third "ingredient" is the suicidal urge which appears near the end of the poem: "And I see now that we store him up / year after year, old suicides / and I know at the news of your death, / a terrible taste for it, like salt," Alvarez refers to this endless desire when he quotes an English novelist as saying "For me suicide's a constant temptation. It never slackens . . . it's been a pattern ever since I can remember."

The fourth "ingredient" is the emotional or affective state of mind of Sexton and she is clearly feeling abandoned by Plath, left behind in this terrifying life where "the moon's bad / and the king's gone, / and the queen's at her wit's end." Death is obviously preferable, and Sexton seems to feel only that Plath has gone ahead, without warning Sexton of her departure for the promised land. Sexton herself had a pact with Maxine Kumin that seems similar. She was to ask Kumin for the "Death Baby" if she ever decided to kill herself again. Possibly Sexton felt that Plath had owed her a similar warning in their suicidal "closed world."

The final factor, according to Neuringer, was the feeling of isolation from the surrounding culture's social mores. This lack of interest in what is important to "other people" seems obvious when Sexton does not remind Sylvia of her obligation to stay alive for her children's sakes. It is also apparent from the fact that Sexton herself, a potential suicide, was completely unaware that Plath was on the verge again. Allen Alvarez (also a member of the "closed society" of which he wrote) refers to his own lack of perception when he admits that he as a fairly good friend of Plath, completely missed the message, and finally he rationalizes this oversight by trying to prove that Plath really didn't mean to kill herself. So Sexton's loss of contact with the world outside could also be assumed by her feeling that she did not have a responsibility to stay closely enough in touch with her friend's pain or terrors to attempt to alleviate or deflect them. So all five ingredients can be found in this "suicide" poem. But can they be found in Sexton's other, less stridently death-oriented, poetry?

Unlike **"Sylvia's Death," "The Nude Swim"** is a poem that has probably never been classified as a suicide/death poem. It appeared in *Love Poems* in 1969. William H. Shurr sees the poem as part of a record of a love affair, and although he feels that the poem "derives its setting and quite likely [its] personae from Anne's European trips with her husband," still he perceives the poem on a very superficial "travel documentary" level. The poem does appear to be a momentary break in Sexton's ongoing depressive state, and yet when analyzed according to Neuringer's criteria, it has all of the "ingredients" for a suicidal interpretation. A brief plot summary isolates some of its key elements. Two people swim into an "unknown grotto," where they can "lose all their loneliness," and the "real fish" ignore them. The water is clear and buoyant, and the speaker poses on its surface mimicking a painting of a seductive woman. Her companion tells the speaker that her eyes are "seacolor / skycolor" which then seems to destroy her mood.

Sexton's view of life, death and suicide in this poem appears to be that life is only pleasant when one escapes to an exotic place like Capri, and even there reality looms so large that a further escape to an "unknown grotto" is required to allow the speaker to "release [her] loneliness." Entering the "unknown grotto" can be seen as mysterious or even ominous. Water is a symbol of the subconscious, of oblivion, and can be death-dealing as well as life-giving. Therefore the "clear [and] buoyant" water becomes significant as a symbol when the speaker floats on top of it, plays with it, and finally views it as "a couch as deep as a tomb." Sexton's dichotomous thinking is apparent in the juxtaposition of "real" with unreal fish. The real fish are able to survive in the water, and they ignore these unreal fish as they "trail" over the surface. The speaker and her companion seem only to be pretending to be alive and will never be "real."

The suicidal urge can be traced in the speaker's perceptions

of the swim as a momentary release from her loneliness, and yet she knows that she is only posing, only pretending to be a vivid and sensuous woman, while she is floating on the unreal and tomb-like water. Her affective state appears dreamy as she describes this fantasy scene. But her companion destroys the mood by telling her that she is "sky" and "sea colored," a positive view of the speaker basically, and this is a reminder of the living world of which she is a part. This compliment forces her to close her eyes, in an attempt to remain hidden, and then to revert to an ashamed and self-hating state. This is a reenactment of her usual feelings of inadequacy, and worthlessness which are typical of a suicidal person.

The isolation of the cave and the swimmers from the "real world" of Capri indicates that the speaker is oriented away from the world. She has lost touch with others and feels suffocated and constrained by the real world. This freedom of the cave, in reality, is freedom for the speaker to toy with oblivion and death.

In another poem from *Love Poems* (1969), **"For my Lover, Returning to his Wife,"** Sexton again exhibits the "particular style of thinking" that Neuringer contends leads to suicide. Paul Lacey describes the entire volume of poems as "affirm[ing] the body in a way not to be found in her earlier poetry . . . the whole body and its separate parts are celebrated and delighted in." Karl Malkoff describes the *Love Poems* as "further[ing] the reintegration of the self." But within the actual poem itself Sexton's view of life, death, and suicide is again clearly weighted against the speaker's own right to existence. She compares herself to the "Wife" and finds that the wife is "solid" while the speaker is "a watercolor. / I wash off." This also provides a concise view of the dichotomy between the real world of "the wife," and the unreal world of "the mistress" and as usual the speaker loses. She "wash[es] off." She is "momentary," and an "experiment." Therefore, she perceives the wife as the ideal that she, the speaker, cannot attain, and realizes that her only alternative is to disappear. This disappearance is part of the on-going urge toward total oblivion. To die is to lose her awareness that she is not "solid" like the wife, and will enable her to forget that she has been "wash[ed] off" and dissolved.

And in the speaker's muffled anger and rage at being abandoned, there are curious echoes of what she feels she is not. Sexton's own affective state shows in her description of the wife. If the wife is "exquisite," "fireworks," "real," "harmony," and his "have to have," in addition to the "bitch in her," then what is the speaker? The opposite descriptive adjectives are ugly, boring, unreal, and inharmonious, and his unnecessary object. That the wife has a "bitch in her" does not mitigate the speaker's sense of being second-best. And the speaker clearly agrees with the lover that she is less valuable than his wife when she "give[s him] permission . . . [to] answer the call . . . [to] climb her like a monument . . . [because] she is so solid."

Sexton does not consider herself a part of the real world within the context of the poem because she describes herself as "momentary," "a luxury," with her hair "rising like smoke," and her very existence is "out of season." And while she does not discuss suicidal feelings in direct terms, the absence of any rationale that would enable her to live, coupled with her complete invisibility, and lack of worth in her relationship to the lover and his wife, would lead most seriously disturbed people to feel like death was a serious alternative to such despair. Instead of rationalizing her situation, or rejecting and devaluing her lover, she has turned the knife of worthlessness against her own life. Or in the words of Neuringer, the speaker has organized her thinking patterns "in such a way that suicide is the only possible choice" for her.

In **"The Double Image"** the suicidal undertones are even more markedly present. Published in her first book, *To Bedlam and Part Way Back* in 1960, it is ostensibly a long explanation, addressed to her three-year-old daughter, of Sexton's suicide attempts, and therefore her past inability to be a good mother for the child. Written as though Sexton now felt "together" and stable, the poem's speaker is in reality precariously balanced on the verge of oblivion. Greg Johnson describes the poem as "tender [with a] carefully modulated voice . . . firmly aligned on the side of health." And although Johnson describes Sexton as aware of her "continued vulnerability" he focuses on her "desire for an affectionate, healthy relationship with the child." In truth Sexton is already isolated from life and unable to relate to her child at all.

> **Sexton's desire to die, and also her separation from the immediacies of the world, are seen in her use of language and imagery that distances, not only the audience, but the speaker, from the story being unfolded.**
> —*Mikhail Ann Long*

Beginning with the first section, and running throughout the poem, her view of life can be seen as strongly negative: nature "goes queer," and autumn leaves do not believe in themselves or else they fall. Life "was an old debt," that is filled with "blame" and "doom," and can be understood only by "witches" and "ugly angels" who tell Sexton what her life means, and what she must do. Sexton warns her daughter that if she doesn't believe in herself she will fall as the leaves are falling. By the second section of the poem life

is filled with lies and hypocrisy where one is locked up in the cupboards of a church. Death, on the other hand, is "simpler than [she'd] thought," and will, with the witches' help, "take away [her] guilty soul."

The suicidal view of life as having only one solution or alternative to death is seen in her repeated failures to find a place to be, not only for her daughter, but for herself. Sexton tries to die, she ends up in a mental hospital, she then tries to go home again to her mother's house, again she tries to die, she tries to go back to her husband in Boston, and so on and so on. She seems to be searching for the perfect place in the world for her weary spirit to rest, and exist, and never seems to succeed. The end of the poem remains inconclusive since, although she has her daughter back with her full time, she does not tell the reader where they finally are, or even give the feeling that they really are settled at all.

Sexton's desire to die, and also her separation from the immediacies of the world, are seen in her use of language and imagery that distances, not only the audience, but the speaker, from the story being unfolded. A formal, unemotional retelling of all of these desperate failures of the spirit of Sexton's part creates a sense of disinterest in, or at best, clinical curiosity about, the details of her life. She is not committed to this life, or even to this child. She calls her daughter an "image," a "small piglet," a "butterfly girl," a "splendid stranger," and "a small milky mouse." All terms of endearment to be sure, but also basically non-human terms, and such terms could also serve to remove the child from the immediate world where her mother would feel responsibility for her. So the child could conceivably end up being part of the world that Neuringer feels the suicidal person can ignore. However adorable, who needs to feel responsible for an image or a mouse?

Sexton's affective state is the most easily isolated. It consists of total despair, a complete and over-riding sense of guilt and failure, and a self-image that is disastrous. Sexton sees herself through her mother's eyes, or at least as she imagines her mother sees her, and what she finds is the "stony head of death," "the double woman who stares / at herself, as if she were petrified / in time," and most dreadfully, she sees herself as "rot[ting] on the wall, [her] own / Dorian Gray." Sexton has no hope for her own future or for the future of the relationship with her child. She begins the poem in futility, "all the medical hypothesis / that explained my brain will never be as true as these / struck leaves letting go," and ends it in guilt and confusion: "I, who was never quite sure / about being a girl, needed another / life, another image to remind me. / And this was my worst guilt; you could not cure / nor soothe it. I made you to find me." The final terrifying fact that the reader notices is that the entire poem, with the exception of the opening line, is written in the past tense. The poem ends in the past, not in the present or the future.

Sexton's *Live or Die* (1966) ends with the poem **"Live."** Paul Lacey finds that this poem "express[es] a new equilibrium," and Robert Boyers calls it "a triumph of determination and insight, a final resolution of irreconcilabilities that had threatened to remain perpetually suspended and apart . . . a rebirth of astounding proportions." Most other critics also agree that the poem affirms life and announces Sexton's determination to live. But in this poem Neuringer's five "ingredients" appear clearly, and they do so with even more violence simply because the tone is so strong and positive. This poem does not offer a counter to Sexton's suicidal nature but rather represents her state of mind when she is feeling stronger and more capable of dealing with her problems. Clearly however, her on-going obsession with death, her inability to achieve equilibrium in her life, her vision of the world as joyless and cruel, and her lack of connection with the people around her remain as marked and symptomatic as in her other works.

Beginning with Sexton's view of life, death, and suicide, we see immediately that she remains obsessed with death although she describes it in less seductive terms. Death, relegated to the background like "mud, day after day," is still far from being safely removed from her. The assumption that Sexton is merely setting the stage for her reader in the first two stanzas by explaining her emotional state does not ameliorate her terrifying view of life. She calls herself mutilated, dismembered, "somebody's doll" and says that she has a "dwarf's heart." The only human is the "death-baby," which has been cooked and sewn with "little maggots" by "somebody's mother." And in the subsequent supposedly affirmative stanzas, life remains "a dream," and even less positive, a magic ritual as she "turn[s her] shadow [and not her substance] three times round." Sexton maintains that life has given her "the answer" and she sees it as "moving feverishly." Her tone becomes increasingly angry and even sarcastic as she progresses through the poem and describes her "new" outlook. Sexton's depiction of the sun or life as an egg with a tumbling center is as deadly as her other more obviously negative life images. She ends "Live, Live because of the sun, / the dream, the excitable gift." Such images are not necessarily positive since none of the three is susceptible to man's control, and the effects of these images are equally uncontrollable and unknown. The sun can kill and so can a dream. And what exactly is an "excitable gift?" It is something offered by another person, at their convenience, and for their own reasons. To "excite" means to set in motion, awaken, call forth, or stir-up, according to the Oxford English Dictionary, and all these terms are capable of being extremely positive or extremely negative. That Sexton chooses such strong words capable

of divergent and polarized meanings is indicative of her true inner mood.

Sexton's view of herself becomes increasingly impenetrable; she decides that she needs a "purifier," and sleeps in a "corruptible bed." While she feels that she is not a "killer," she remains hidden behind an "apron" and carries her kisses inside her "hood." Her role appears to be to "love more if they come," to nurture, to feed, and to provide roses (beauty) from "the hackles" (her inner anger) of her throat. She is not creative in herself she says; her typewriter is the one that writes and does not break. In fact, she herself has frequently broken and been yelled at and told to shut-up by the people in her world. Ironically, the hammer or the power to kill herself has not been discarded because she has come to love life, but because she now understands that "people don't like to be told / that you're sick."

Sexton's mood remains strongly dichotomous as she portrays her world as a heartless place where her pain is used sadistically, or trivialized, by those around her. When she burns, they roast marshmallows over her flames, and when she freezes emotionally, they skate on her in cute little costumes. When she becomes a witch, they paint her pink, disguising her real nature for a moment. Even more indicative of their insensitivity is her comment that rather than help her change or get well, those around her simply oversimplify her complexity, and say that she is as "nice as a chocolate bar" when she is crazy.

But the primary key to Sexton's mood is that the people around her remain inhuman, or at best non-human, throughout the poem. Her lovers are "celery stalks," her husband is a "redwood," and her two daughters are "sea urchins." Even the puppies are not compared to living creatures but are called "cordwood [and] birch trees." So Sexton remains oriented away from those around her, and while she is not going to wear her hospital shift or quote her Black Masses at this time, she does not unequivocally state that they are no longer in her repertoire of life. Suicide and death remain in the recesses of her mind because life continues to be something that she "all the time want[s] to get rid of."

So Neuringer's five "lethal ingredients" can be found in many other Sexton poems, certainly many more than the twenty or so ostensibly "suicidal" poems that the critics cite. And these ingredients may well be present in them all, either wholly or in part. Sexton's view of the world seems always a little askew, and her sense of futility is always very strong. The awareness of all her incapacities, failures, and secret sins, seems to underlie many, if not all, of her poems. And Sexton constantly reiterates her view that death is easy, plausible, welcoming, and so attractive that "I am in love with it" (in the poem **"Leaves That Talk"**). Perhaps Diane Hume George's theory of the existence of a special language of the suicide is true, and this special language has muffled Sexton's deathly view of life in the minds of critics. Perhaps only someone who has also heard the "green girls" can understand Sexton's language, and agree with her that "They call, they call their green death call. They want me. They need me. / I belong lying down under them, / letting the green coffin fold and unfold / above me as I go out."

Other elements, of course, go into the making of Sexton's, or any poet's work. Gary Blankenburg, among other critics, notes that Sexton's poetry is written primarily from the stance of "mental, physical, and spiritual illness." Sexton suffered severe bouts with mental illness during her entire writing career, and indeed much of her poetry can be viewed from the therapeutic angle. There are numerous critical articles written about Sexton's therapy sessions, her hospitalizations, and her frequent descent into mental distress. But she was also a consummate poet. Anyone capable of writing such lines as "Johnny, your dream moves summers / inside my mind," or ". . . what / I remember best is that / the door to your room was / the door to mine," was a gifted craftsman of the language. That she also had a strong sense of humor about life and death can be seen by lines such as "the dead turn over casually, / thinking . . . / Good! No visitors today." These and hundreds of other perfectly crafted lines prove that Sexton's poetry is readable on any number of levels.

But her suicidal tendencies drove her, and ultimately claimed her, and stopped her mouth with death. Ernest Becker seems to be describing Sexton, and all creative geniuses, when he discusses the root of the suicidal wish:

> What we call the well-adjusted man has just this capacity to partialize the world for comfortable action . . . men aren't built to be gods, to take in the whole world; they are built like other creatures, to take in the piece of ground in front of their noses . . . as soon as a man lifts his nose from the ground and starts sniffing at eternal problems like life and death, the meaning of a rose or a star cluster—then he is in trouble.

And Sexton definitely began sniffing at eternal problems, eternal paradoxes and so lost her way forever. But her poetry remains to tell us about ourselves, the darker parts, the parts of ourselves that we try to ignore. And she tells us, whether we understand her or not, how it feels to live in the endless night of a suicidal nature.

FURTHER READING

Criticism

Gallagher, Brian. "The Expanded Use of Simile in Anne Sexton's *Transformations*." *NMAL: Notes on Modern American Literature* 3 (1979): Item 20.

> Examines the narrative and allusive function of similes in *Transformations*.

George, Diana Hume. "Anne Sexton's Suicide Poems." *Journal of Popular Culture* 18, No. 2 (Fall 1984): 17-31.

> Explores the articulation of suicidal longing in Sexton's poetry and public disdain for self-inflicted death.

George, Diana Hume. "How We Danced: Anne Sexton on Fathers and Daughters." *Women's Studies* 12, No. 2 (1986): 179-202.

> Offers a psychoanalytic reading of family dynamics and father-daughter relationships in Sexton's poetry.

Locke, Maryel F. "Anne Sexton Remembered." In *Rossetti to Sexton: Six Women Poets at Texas*, edited by Dave Oliphant, pp. 155-63. Austin: University of Texas at Austin, 1992.

> Offers personal reflection upon the life, work, and death of Sexton.

Nichols, Kathleen L. "The Hungry Beast Rowing Toward God: Anne Sexton's Later Religious Poetry." *NMAL: Notes on Modern American Literature* 3 (1979): Item 21.

> Discusses the significance of Christian themes and the journey motif in *The Awful Rowing Toward God*.

Skorczewski, Dawn. "What Prison Is This? Literary Critics Cover Incest in Anne Sexton's `Briar Rose.'" *Signs: Journal of Women in Culture and Society* 21, No. 2 (Winter 1996): 309-42.

> Examines critical response to father-daughter incest portrayed in "Briar Rose."

Interviews

Fitzgerald, Gregory. "The Choir from the Soul: A Conversation with Anne Sexton." *Massachusetts Review* 19 (1978): 69-88.

> Sexton discusses her poetry, literary influences, and artistic development.

Additional coverage of Sexton's life and career is contained in the following sources published by Gale: *Concise Dictionary of American Literary Biography, 1941-1968; Contemporary Authors,* Vols. 1-4R, 53-56; *Contemporary Authors Bibliographical Series,* Vol. 2; *Contemporary Authors New Revision Series,* Vols. 3, 36; *Dictionary of Literary Biography,* Vols. 5, 169; *DISCovering Authors; DISCovering Authors: British; DISCovering Authors: Canadian; DISCovering Authors Modules: Most-Studied and Poets; Major Twentieth Century Writers; Poetry Criticism,* Vol. 2; *Something about the Author,* Vol. 10; and *World Literature Criticism.*

☐ Contemporary Literary Criticism

Indexes

Literary Criticism Series
Cumulative Author Index
Cumulative Topic Index
Cumulative Nationality Index
Title Index, Volume 123

How to Use This Index

The main references

Camus, Albert
1913-1960 . . . . . . .CLC 1, 2, 4, 9, 11,
14, 32, 69; DA; DAB; DAC; DAM
DRAM, MST, NOV; DC2; SSC 9;
WLC

list all author entries in the following Gale Literary Criticism series:

BLC = *Black Literature Criticism*
BLCS = *Black Literature Criticism Supplement*
CLC = *Contemporary Literary Criticism*
CLR = *Children's Literature Review*
CMLC = *Classical and Medieval Literature Criticism*
DA = *DISCovering Authors*
DAB = *DISCovering Authors: British*
DAC = *DISCovering Authors: Canadian*
DAM = *DISCovering Authors Modules*
  DRAM = *dramatists;* *MST* = *most-studied*
  authors; *MULT* = *multicultural authors;* *NOV* =
  novelists; *POET* = *poets;* *POP* = *popular/genre*
  writers; *DC* = *Drama Criticism*
HLC = *Hispanic Literature Criticism*
LC = *Literature Criticism from 1400 to 1800*
NCLC = *Nineteenth-Century Literature Criticism*
PC = *Poetry Criticism*
SSC = *Short Story Criticism*
TCLC = *Twentieth-Century Literary Criticism*
WLC = *World Literature Criticism, 1500 to the Present*
WLCS = *World Literature Criticism Supplement*

The cross-references

See also CA 89-92; DLB 72; MTCW

list all author entries in the following Gale biographical and literary sources:

AAYA = *Authors & Artists for Young Adults*
AITN = *Authors in the News*
BEST = *Bestsellers*
BW = *Black Writers*
CA = *Contemporary Authors*
CAAS = *Contemporary Authors Autobiography Series*
CABS = *Contemporary Authors Bibliographical Series*
CANR = *Contemporary Authors New Revision Series*
CAP = *Contemporary Authors Permanent Series*
CDALB = *Concise Dictionary of American Literary Biography*
CDBLB = *Concise Dictionary of British Literary Biography*

DLB = *Dictionary of Literary Biography*
DLBD = *Dictionary of Literary Biography Documentary Series*
DLBY = *Dictionary of Literary Biography Yearbook*
HW = *Hispanic Writers*
JRDA = *Junior DISCovering Authors*
MAICYA = *Major Authors and Illustrators for Children and Young Adults*
MTCW = *Major 20th-Century Writers*
NNAL = *Native North American Literature*
SAAS = *Something about the Author Autobiography Series*
SATA = *Something about the Author*
YABC = *Yesterday's Authors of Books for Children*

Literary Criticism Series
Cumulative Author Index

See Giraudoux, (Hippolyte) Jean

Andrade, Carlos Drummond de .... **CLC 18**
See also Drummond de Andrade, Carlos

Andrade, Mario de 1893-1945 ...... **TCLC 43**

Andreae, Johann V(alentin) 1586-1654 **LC 32**
See also DLB 164

Andreas-Salome, Lou 1861-1937 ... **TCLC 56**
See also CA 178; DLB 66

Andress, Lesley
See Sanders, Lawrence

Andrewes, Lancelot 1555-1626 .... **LC 5**
See also DLB 151, 172

Andrews, Cicily Fairfield
See West, Rebecca

Andrews, Elton V.
See Pohl, Frederik

Andreyev, Leonid (Nikolaevich) 1871-1919
TCLC 3
See also CA 104

Andric, Ivo 1892-1975 .... **CLC 8; SSC 36**
See also CA 81-84; 57-60; CANR 43, 60; DLB
147; MTCW 1

Androvar
See Prado (Calvo), Pedro

Angelique, Pierre
See Bataille, Georges

Angell, Roger 1920- .... **CLC 26**
See also CA 57-60; CANR 13, 44, 70; DLB 171,
185

Angelou, Maya 1928- **CLC 12, 35, 64, 77; BLC
1; DA; DAB; DAC; DAM MST, MULT,
POET, POP; WLCS**
See also AAYA 7, 20; BW 2, 3; CA 65-68;
CANR 19, 42, 65; CDALBS; CLR 53; DLB
38; MTCW 1, 2; SATA 49

Anna Comnena 1083-1153 .... **CMLC 25**

Annensky, Innokenty (Fyodorovich) 1856-1909
TCLC 14
See also CA 110; 155

Annunzio, Gabriele d'
See D'Annunzio, Gabriele

Anodos
See Coleridge, Mary E(lizabeth)

Anon, Charles Robert
See Pessoa, Fernando (Antonio Nogueira)

Anouilh, Jean (Marie Lucien Pierre) 1910-1987
**CLC 1, 3, 8, 13, 40, 50; DAM DRAM; DC
8**
See also CA 17-20R; 123; CANR 32; MTCW
1, 2

Anthony, Florence
See Ai

Anthony, John
See Ciardi, John (Anthony)

Anthony, Peter
See Shaffer, Anthony (Joshua); Shaffer, Peter
(Levin)

Anthony, Piers 1934- .... **CLC 35; DAM POP**
See also AAYA 11; CA 21-24R; CANR 28, 56,
73; DLB 8; MTCW 1, 2; SAAS 22; SATA 84

Anthony, Susan B(rownell) 1916-1991 **TCLC
84**
See also CA 89-92; 134

Antoine, Marc
See Proust, (Valentin-Louis-George-Eugene-)
Marcel

Antoninus, Brother
See Everson, William (Oliver)

Antonioni, Michelangelo 1912- .... **CLC 20**
See also CA 73-76; CANR 45, 77

Antschel, Paul 1920-1970
See Celan, Paul
See also CA 85-88; CANR 33, 61; MTCW 1

Anwar, Chairil 1922-1949 .... **TCLC 22**
See also CA 121

Anzaldua, Gloria 1942-
See also CA 175; DLB 122; HLCS 1

Apess, William 1798-1839(?) **NCLC 73; DAM
MULT**
See also DLB 175; NNAL

Apollinaire, Guillaume 1880-1918 **TCLC 3, 8,
51; DAM POET; PC 7**
See also Kostrowitzki, Wilhelm Apollinaris de
See also CA 152; MTCW 1

Appelfeld, Aharon 1932- .... **CLC 23, 47**
See also CA 112; 133

Apple, Max (Isaac) 1941- .... **CLC 9, 33**
See also CA 81-84; CANR 19, 54; DLB 130

Appleman, Philip (Dean) 1926- .... **CLC 51**
See also CA 13-16R; CAAS 18; CANR 6, 29,
56

Appleton, Lawrence
See Lovecraft, H(oward) P(hillips)

Apteryx
See Eliot, T(homas) S(tearns)

Apuleius, (Lucius Madaurensis) 125(?)-175(?)
CMLC 1
See also DLB 211

Aquin, Hubert 1929-1977 .... **CLC 15**
See also CA 105; DLB 53

Aquinas, Thomas 1224(?)-1274 ..... **CMLC 33**
See also DLB 115

Aragon, Louis 1897-1982 .. **CLC 3, 22; DAM
NOV, POET**
See also CA 69-72; 108; CANR 28, 71; DLB
72; MTCW 1, 2

Arany, Janos 1817-1882 .... **NCLC 34**

Aranyos, Kakay
See Mikszath, Kalman

Arbuthnot, John 1667-1735 .... **LC 1**
See also DLB 101

Archer, Herbert Winslow
See Mencken, H(enry) L(ouis)

Archer, Jeffrey (Howard) 1940- ..... **CLC 28;
DAM POP**
See also AAYA 16; BEST 89:3; CA 77-80;
CANR 22, 52; INT CANR-22

Archer, Jules 1915- .... **CLC 12**
See also CA 9-12R; CANR 6, 69; SAAS 5;
SATA 4, 85

Archer, Lee
See Ellison, Harlan (Jay)

Arden, John 1930- **CLC 6, 13, 15; DAM DRAM**
See also CA 13-16R; CAAS 4; CANR 31, 65,
67; DLB 13; MTCW 1

Arenas, Reinaldo 1943-1990 . **CLC 41; DAM
MULT; HLC 1**
See also CA 124; 128; 133; CANR 73; DLB
145; HW 1; MTCW 1

Arendt, Hannah 1906-1975 .... **CLC 66, 98**
See also CA 17-20R; 61-64; CANR 26, 60;
MTCW 1, 2

Aretino, Pietro 1492-1556 .... **LC 12**

Arghezi, Tudor 1880-1967 .... **CLC 80**
See also Theodorescu, Ion N.
See also CA 167

Arguedas, Jose Maria 1911-1969 **CLC 10, 18;
HLCS 1**
See also CA 89-92; CANR 73; DLB 113; HW 1

Argueta, Manlio 1936- .... **CLC 31**
See also CA 131; CANR 73; DLB 145; HW 1

Arias, Ron(ald Francis) 1941-
See also CA 131; CANR 81; DAM MULT; DLB
82; HLC 1; HW 1, 2; MTCW 2

Ariosto, Ludovico 1474-1533 .... **LC 6**

Aristides

See Epstein, Joseph

Aristophanes 450B.C.-385B.C. **CMLC 4; DA;
DAB; DAC; DAM DRAM, MST; DC 2;
WLCS**
See also DLB 176

Aristotle 384B.C.-322B.C. ... **CMLC 31; DA;
DAB; DAC; DAM MST; WLCS**
See also DLB 176

Arlt, Roberto (Godofredo Christophersen)
1900-1942 **TCLC 29; DAM MULT; HLC 1**
See also CA 123; 131; CANR 67; HW 1, 2

Armah, Ayi Kwei 1939- **CLC 5, 33; BLC 1;
DAM MULT, POET**
See also BW 1; CA 61-64; CANR 21, 64; DLB
117; MTCW 1

Armatrading, Joan 1950- .... **CLC 17**
See also CA 114

Arnette, Robert
See Silverberg, Robert

**Arnim, Achim von (Ludwig Joachim von
Arnim)** 1781-1831 ...... **NCLC 5; SSC 29**
See also DLB 90

Arnim, Bettina von 1785-1859 .... **NCLC 38**
See also DLB 90

Arnold, Matthew 1822-1888 **NCLC 6, 29; DA;
DAB; DAC; DAM MST, POET; PC 5;
WLC**
See also CDBLB 1832-1890; DLB 32, 57

Arnold, Thomas 1795-1842 .... **NCLC 18**
See also DLB 55

Arnow, Harriette (Louisa) Simpson 1908-1986
CLC 2, 7, 18
See also CA 9-12R; 118; CANR 14; DLB 6;
MTCW 1, 2; SATA 42; SATA-Obit 47

Arouet, Francois-Marie
See Voltaire

Arp, Hans
See Arp, Jean

Arp, Jean 1887-1966 .... **CLC 5**
See also CA 81-84; 25-28R; CANR 42, 77

Arrabal
See Arrabal, Fernando

Arrabal, Fernando 1932- .... **CLC 2, 9, 18, 58**
See also CA 9-12R; CANR 15

Arreola, Juan Jose 1918-
See also CA 113; 131; CANR 81; DAM MULT;
DLB 113; HLC 1; HW 1, 2

Arrick, Fran .... **CLC 30**
See also Gaberman, Judie Angell

Artaud, Antonin (Marie Joseph) 1896-1948
TCLC 3, 36; DAM DRAM
See also CA 104; 149; MTCW 1

Arthur, Ruth M(abel) 1905-1979 ...... **CLC 12**
See also CA 9-12R; 85-88; CANR 4; SATA 7,
26

Artsybashev, Mikhail (Petrovich) 1878-1927
TCLC 31
See also CA 170

Arundel, Honor (Morfydd) 1919-1973 **CLC 17**
See also CA 21-22; 41-44R; CAP 2; CLR 35;
SATA 4; SATA-Obit 24

Arzner, Dorothy 1897-1979 .... **CLC 98**

Asch, Sholem 1880-1957 .... **TCLC 3**
See also CA 105

Ash, Shalom
See Asch, Sholem

Ashbery, John (Lawrence) 1927- **CLC 2, 3, 4,
6, 9, 13, 15, 25, 41, 77; DAM POET; PC 26**
See also CA 5-8R; CANR 9, 37, 66; DLB 5,
165; DLBY 81; INT CANR-9; MTCW 1, 2

Ashdown, Clifford
See Freeman, R(ichard) Austin

Ashe, Gordon

See Mikszath, Kalman

Balzac, Honore de 1799-1850 **NCLC 5, 35, 53; DA; DAB; DAC; DAM MST, NOV; SSC 5; WLC**
See also DLB 119

Bambara, Toni Cade 1939-1995 **CLC 19, 88; BLC 1; DA; DAC; DAM MST, MULT; SSC 35; WLCS**
See also AAYA 5; BW 2, 3; CA 29-32R; 150; CANR 24, 49, 81; CDALBS; DLB 38; MTCW 1, 2

Bamdad, A.
See Shamlu, Ahmad

Banat, D. R.
See Bradbury, Ray (Douglas)

Bancroft, Laura
See Baum, L(yman) Frank

Banim, John 1798-1842 .... **NCLC 13**
See also DLB 116, 158, 159

Banim, Michael 1796-1874 .... **NCLC 13**
See also DLB 158, 159

Banjo, The
See Paterson, A(ndrew) B(arton)

Banks, Iain
See Banks, Iain M(enzies)

Banks, Iain M(enzies) 1954- .... **CLC 34**
See also CA 123; 128; CANR 61; DLB 194; INT 128

Banks, Lynne Reid .... **CLC 23**
See also Reid Banks, Lynne
See also AAYA 6

Banks, Russell 1940- .... **CLC 37, 72**
See also CA 65-68; CAAS 15; CANR 19, 52, 73; DLB 130

Banville, John 1945- .... **CLC 46, 118**
See also CA 117; 128; DLB 14; INT 128

Banville, Theodore (Faullain) de 1832-1891 **NCLC 9**

Baraka, Amiri 1934- **CLC 1, 2, 3, 5, 10, 14, 33, 115; BLC 1; DA; DAC; DAM MST, MULT, POET, POP; DC 6; PC 4; WLCS**
See also Jones, LeRoi
See also BW 2, 3; CA 21-24R; CABS 3; CANR 27, 38, 61; CDALB 1941-1968; DLB 5, 7, 16, 38; DLBD 8; MTCW 1, 2

Barbauld, Anna Laetitia 1743-1825 **NCLC 50**
See also DLB 107, 109, 142, 158

Barbellion, W. N. P. .... **TCLC 24**
See also Cummings, Bruce F(rederick)

Barbera, Jack (Vincent) 1945- .... **CLC 44**
See also CA 110; CANR 45

Barbey d'Aurevilly, Jules Amedee 1808-1889 **NCLC 1; SSC 17**
See also DLB 119

Barbour, John c. 1316-1395 .... **CMLC 33**
See also DLB 146

Barbusse, Henri 1873-1935 .... **TCLC 5**
See also CA 105; 154; DLB 65

Barclay, Bill
See Moorcock, Michael (John)

Barclay, William Ewert
See Moorcock, Michael (John)

Barea, Arturo 1897-1957 .... **TCLC 14**
See also CA 111

Barfoot, Joan 1946- .... **CLC 18**
See also CA 105

Barham, Richard Harris 1788-1845 **NCLC 77**
See also DLB 159

Baring, Maurice 1874-1945 .... **TCLC 8**
See also CA 105; 168; DLB 34

Baring-Gould, Sabine 1834-1924 .. **TCLC 88**
See also DLB 156, 190

Barker, Clive 1952- .... **CLC 52; DAM POP**

See also AAYA 10; BEST 90:3; CA 121; 129; CANR 71; INT 129; MTCW 1, 2

Barker, George Granville 1913-1991 **CLC 8, 48; DAM POET**
See also CA 9-12R; 135; CANR 7, 38; DLB 20; MTCW 1

Barker, Harley Granville
See Granville-Barker, Harley
See also DLB 10

Barker, Howard 1946- .... **CLC 37**
See also CA 102; DLB 13

Barker, Jane 1652-1732 .... **LC 42**

Barker, Pat(ricia) 1943- .... **CLC 32, 94**
See also CA 117; 122; CANR 50; INT 122

Barlach, Ernst 1870-1938 .... **TCLC 84**
See also CA 178; DLB 56, 118

Barlow, Joel 1754-1812 .... **NCLC 23**
See also DLB 37

Barnard, Mary (Ethel) 1909- .... **CLC 48**
See also CA 21-22; CAP 2

Barnes, Djuna 1892-1982 **CLC 3, 4, 8, 11, 29; SSC 3**
See also CA 9-12R; 107; CANR 16, 55; DLB 4, 9, 45; MTCW 1, 2

Barnes, Julian (Patrick) 1946- **CLC 42; DAB**
See also CA 102; CANR 19, 54; DLB 194; DLBY 93; MTCW 1

Barnes, Peter 1931- ....**CLC 5, 56**
See also CA 65-68; CAAS 12; CANR 33, 34, 64; DLB 13; MTCW 1

Barnes, William 1801-1886 .... **NCLC 75**
See also DLB 32

Baroja (y Nessi), Pio 1872-1956 **TCLC 8; HLC 1**
See also CA 104

Baron, David
See Pinter, Harold

Baron Corvo
See Rolfe, Frederick (William Serafino Austin Lewis Mary)

Barondess, Sue K(aufman) 1926-1977 **CLC 8**
See also Kaufman, Sue
See also CA 1-4R; 69-72; CANR 1

Baron de Teive
See Pessoa, Fernando (Antonio Nogueira)

Baroness Von S.
See Zangwill, Israel

Barres, (Auguste-) Maurice 1862-1923 **TCLC 47**
See also CA 164; DLB 123

Barreto, Afonso Henrique de Lima
See Lima Barreto, Afonso Henrique de

Barrett, (Roger) Syd 1946- .... **CLC 35**

Barrett, William (Christopher) 1913-1992 **CLC 27**
See also CA 13-16R; 139; CANR 11, 67; INT CANR-11

Barrie, J(ames) M(atthew) 1860-1937 **TCLC 2; DAB; DAM DRAM**
See also CA 104; 136; CANR 77; CDBLB 1890-1914; CLR 16; DLB 10, 141, 156; MAICYA; MTCW 1; SATA 100; YABC 1

Barrington, Michael
See Moorcock, Michael (John)

Barrol, Grady
See Bograd, Larry

Barry, Mike
See Malzberg, Barry N(athaniel)

Barry, Philip 1896-1949 .... **TCLC 11**
See also CA 109; DLB 7

Bart, Andre Schwarz
See Schwarz-Bart, Andre

Barth, John (Simmons) 1930- **CLC 1, 2, 3, 5, 7,**

9, 10, 14, 27, 51, 89; **DAM NOV; SSC 10**
See also AITN 1, 2; CA 1-4R; CABS 1; CANR 5, 23, 49, 64; DLB 2; MTCW 1

Barthelme, Donald 1931-1989 **CLC 1, 2, 3, 5, 6, 8, 13, 23, 46, 59, 115; DAM NOV; SSC 2**
See also CA 21-24R; 129; CANR 20, 58; DLB 2; DLBY 80, 89; MTCW 1, 2; SATA 7; SATA-Obit 62

Barthelme, Frederick 1943- ...... **CLC 36, 117**
See also CA 114; 122; CANR 77; DLBY 85; INT 122

Barthes, Roland (Gerard) 1915-1980 **CLC 24, 83**
See also CA 130; 97-100; CANR 66; MTCW 1, 2

Barzun, Jacques (Martin) 1907- .... **CLC 51**
See also CA 61-64; CANR 22

Bashevis, Isaac
See Singer, Isaac Bashevis

Bashkirtseff, Marie 1859-1884 ...... **NCLC 27**

Basho
See Matsuo Basho

Basil of Caesaria c. 330-379 .... **CMLC 35**

Bass, Kingsley B., Jr.
See Bullins, Ed

Bass, Rick 1958- .... **CLC 79**
See also CA 126; CANR 53; DLB 212

Bassani, Giorgio 1916- .... **CLC 9**
See also CA 65-68; CANR 33; DLB 128, 177; MTCW 1

Bastos, Augusto (Antonio) Roa
See Roa Bastos, Augusto (Antonio)

Bataille, Georges 1897-1962 .... **CLC 29**
See also CA 101; 89-92

Bates, H(erbert) E(rnest) 1905-1974 **CLC 46; DAB; DAM POP; SSC 10**
See also CA 93-96; 45-48; CANR 34; DLB 162, 191; MTCW 1, 2

Bauchart
See Camus, Albert

Baudelaire, Charles 1821-1867 **NCLC 6, 29, 55; DA; DAB; DAC; DAM MST, POET; PC 1; SSC 18; WLC**

Baudrillard, Jean 1929- .... **CLC 60**

Baum, L(yman) Frank 1856-1919 ... **TCLC 7**
See also CA 108; 133; CLR 15; DLB 22; JRDA; MAICYA; MTCW 1, 2; SATA 18, 100

Baum, Louis F.
See Baum, L(yman) Frank

Baumbach, Jonathan 1933- ....**CLC 6, 23**
See also CA 13-16R; CAAS 5; CANR 12, 66; DLBY 80; INT CANR-12; MTCW 1

Bausch, Richard (Carl) 1945- .... **CLC 51**
See also CA 101; CAAS 14; CANR 43, 61; DLB 130

Baxter, Charles (Morley) 1947- **CLC 45, 78; DAM POP**
See also CA 57-60; CANR 40, 64; DLB 130; MTCW 2

Baxter, George Owen
See Faust, Frederick (Schiller)

Baxter, James K(eir) 1926-1972 .... **CLC 14**
See also CA 77-80

Baxter, John
See Hunt, E(verette) Howard, (Jr.)

Bayer, Sylvia
See Glassco, John

Baynton, Barbara 1857-1929 .... **TCLC 57**

Beagle, Peter S(oyer) 1939- .... **CLC 7, 104**
See also CA 9-12R; CANR 4, 51, 73; DLBY 80; INT CANR-4; MTCW 1; SATA 60

Bean, Normal
See Burroughs, Edgar Rice

See Wodehouse, P(elham) G(renville)

Brooke-Rose, Christine 1926(?)- .... **CLC 40**
See also CA 13-16R; CANR 58; DLB 14

Brookner, Anita 1928- **CLC 32, 34, 51; DAB; DAM POP**
See also CA 114; 120; CANR 37, 56; DLB 194; DLBY 87; MTCW 1, 2

Brooks, Cleanth 1906-1994 **CLC 24, 86, 110**
See also CA 17-20R; 145; CANR 33, 35; DLB 63; DLBY 94; INT CANR-35; MTCW 1, 2

Brooks, George
See Baum, L(yman) Frank

Brooks, Gwendolyn 1917- **CLC 1, 2, 4, 5, 15, 49; BLC 1; DA; DAC; DAM MST, MULT, POET; PC 7; WLC**
See also AAYA 20; AITN 1; BW 2, 3; CA 1-4R; CANR 1, 27, 52, 75; CDALB 1941-1968; CLR 27; DLB 5, 76, 165; MTCW 1, 2; SATA 6

Brooks, Mel .... **CLC 12**
See also Kaminsky, Melvin
See also AAYA 13; DLB 26

Brooks, Peter 1938- .... **CLC 34**
See also CA 45-48; CANR 1

Brooks, Van Wyck 1886-1963 .... **CLC 29**
See also CA 1-4R; CANR 6; DLB 45, 63, 103

Brophy, Brigid (Antonia) 1929-1995 **CLC 6, 11, 29, 105**
See also CA 5-8R; 149; CAAS 4; CANR 25, 53; DLB 14; MTCW 1, 2

Brosman, Catharine Savage 1934- ..... **CLC 9**
See also CA 61-64; CANR 21, 46

Brossard, Nicole 1943- .... **CLC 115**
See also CA 122; CAAS 16; DLB 53

Brother Antoninus
See Everson, William (Oliver)

The Brothers Quay
See Quay, Stephen; Quay, Timothy

Broughton, T(homas) Alan 1936- ..... **CLC 19**
See also CA 45-48; CANR 2, 23, 48

Broumas, Olga 1949- .... **CLC 10, 73**
See also CA 85-88; CANR 20, 69

Brown, Alan 1950- .... **CLC 99**
See also CA 156

Brown, Charles Brockden 1771-1810 **N C L C 22, 74**
See also CDALB 1640-1865; DLB 37, 59, 73

Brown, Christy 1932-1981 .... **CLC 63**
See also CA 105; 104; CANR 72; DLB 14

Brown, Claude 1937- **CLC 30; BLC 1; DAM MULT**
See also AAYA 7; BW 1, 3; CA 73-76; CANR 81

Brown, Dee (Alexander) 1908- .. **CLC 18, 47; DAM POP**
See also AAYA 30; CA 13-16R; CAAS 6; CANR 11, 45, 60; DLBY 80; MTCW 1, 2; SATA 5

Brown, George
See Wertmueller, Lina

Brown, George Douglas 1869-1902 **TCLC 28**
See also CA 162

Brown, George Mackay 1921-1996 **CLC 5, 48, 100**
See also CA 21-24R; 151; CAAS 6; CANR 12, 37, 67; DLB 14, 27, 139; MTCW 1; SATA 35

Brown, (William) Larry 1951- .... **CLC 73**
See also CA 130; 134; INT 133

Brown, Moses
See Barrett, William (Christopher)

Brown, Rita Mae 1944- **CLC 18, 43, 79; DAM NOV, POP**

See also CA 45-48; CANR 2, 11, 35, 62; INT CANR-11; MTCW 1, 2

Brown, Roderick (Langmere) Haig-
See Haig-Brown, Roderick (Langmere)

Brown, Rosellen 1939- .... **CLC 32**
See also CA 77-80; CAAS 10; CANR 14, 44

Brown, Sterling Allen 1901-1989 **CLC 1, 23, 59; BLC 1; DAM MULT, POET**
See also BW 1, 3; CA 85-88; 127; CANR 26; DLB 48, 51, 63; MTCW 1, 2

Brown, Will
See Ainsworth, William Harrison

Brown, William Wells 1813-1884 ...**NCLC 2; BLC 1; DAM MULT; DC 1**
See also DLB 3, 50

Browne, (Clyde) Jackson 1948(?)- .... **CLC 21**
See also CA 120

Browning, Elizabeth Barrett 1806-1861 **NCLC 1, 16, 61, 66; DA; DAB; DAC; DAM MST, POET; PC 6; WLC**
See also CDBLB 1832-1890; DLB 32, 199

Browning, Robert 1812-1889 . **NCLC 19, 79; DA; DAB; DAC; DAM MST, POET; PC 2; WLCS**
See also CDBLB 1832-1890; DLB 32, 163; YABC 1

Browning, Tod 1882-1962 .... **CLC 16**
See also CA 141; 117

Brownson, Orestes Augustus 1803-1876 **NCLC 50**
See also DLB 1, 59, 73

Bruccoli, Matthew J(oseph) 1931- ... **CLC 34**
See also CA 9-12R; CANR 7; DLB 103

Bruce, Lenny .... **CLC 21**
See also Schneider, Leonard Alfred

Bruin, John
See Brutus, Dennis

Brulard, Henri
See Stendhal

Brulls, Christian
See Simenon, Georges (Jacques Christian)

Brunner, John (Kilian Houston) 1934-1995 **CLC 8, 10; DAM POP**
See also CA 1-4R; 149; CAAS 8; CANR 2, 37; MTCW 1, 2

Bruno, Giordano 1548-1600 .... **LC 27**

Brutus, Dennis 1924- **CLC 43; BLC 1; DAM MULT, POET; PC 24**
See also BW 2, 3; CA 49-52; CAAS 14; CANR 2, 27, 42, 81; DLB 117

Bryan, C(ourtlandt) D(ixon) B(arnes) 1936- **CLC 29**
See also CA 73-76; CANR 13, 68; DLB 185; INT CANR-13

Bryan, Michael
See Moore, Brian

Bryant, William Cullen 1794-1878 . **NCLC 6, 46; DA; DAB; DAC; DAM MST, POET; PC 20**
See also CDALB 1640-1865; DLB 3, 43, 59, 189

Bryusov, Valery Yakovlevich 1873-1924 **TCLC 10**
See also CA 107; 155

Buchan, John 1875-1940 ..... **TCLC 41; DAB; DAM POP**
See also CA 108; 145; DLB 34, 70, 156; MTCW 1; YABC 2

Buchanan, George 1506-1582 .... **LC 4**
See also DLB 152

Buchheim, Lothar-Guenther 1918- .... **CLC 6**
See also CA 85-88

Buchner, (Karl) Georg 1813-1837 . **NCLC 26**

Buchwald, Art(hur) 1925- ....**CLC 33**
See also AITN 1; CA 5-8R; CANR 21, 67; MTCW 1, 2; SATA 10

Buck, Pearl S(ydenstricker) 1892-1973 **CLC 7, 11, 18; DA; DAB; DAC; DAM MST, NOV**
See also AITN 1; CA 1-4R; 41-44R; CANR 1, 34; CDALBS; DLB 9, 102; MTCW 1, 2; SATA 1, 25

Buckler, Ernest 1908-1984 .... **CLC 13; DAC; DAM MST**
See also CA 11-12; 114; CAP 1; DLB 68; SATA 47

Buckley, Vincent (Thomas) 1925-1988 **CLC 57**
See also CA 101

Buckley, William F(rank), Jr. 1925- **CLC 7, 18, 37; DAM POP**
See also AITN 1; CA 1-4R; CANR 1, 24, 53; DLB 137; DLBY 80; INT CANR-24; MTCW 1, 2

Buechner, (Carl) Frederick 1926- **CLC 2, 4, 6, 9; DAM NOV**
See also CA 13-16R; CANR 11, 39, 64; DLBY 80; INT CANR-11; MTCW 1, 2

Buell, John (Edward) 1927- ....**CLC 10**
See also CA 1-4R; CANR 71; DLB 53

Buero Vallejo, Antonio 1916- ..... **CLC 15, 46**
See also CA 106; CANR 24, 49, 75; HW 1; MTCW 1, 2

Bufalino, Gesualdo 1920(?)- ....**CLC 74**
See also DLB 196

Bugayev, Boris Nikolayevich 1880-1934 **TCLC 7; PC 11**
See also Bely, Andrey
See also CA 104; 165; MTCW 1

Bukowski, Charles 1920-1994 **CLC 2, 5, 9, 41, 82, 108; DAM NOV, POET; PC 18**
See also CA 17-20R; 144; CANR 40, 62; DLB 5, 130, 169; MTCW 1, 2

Bulgakov, Mikhail (Afanas'evich) 1891-1940 **TCLC 2, 16; DAM DRAM, NOV; SSC 18**
See also CA 105; 152

Bulgya, Alexander Alexandrovich 1901-1956 **TCLC 53**
See also Fadeyev, Alexander
See also CA 117

Bullins, Ed 1935- **CLC 1, 5, 7; BLC 1; DAM DRAM, MULT; DC 6**
See also BW 2, 3; CA 49-52; CAAS 16; CANR 24, 46, 73; DLB 7, 38; MTCW 1, 2

Bulwer-Lytton, Edward (George Earle Lytton) 1803-1873 ....**NCLC 1, 45**
See also DLB 21

Bunin, Ivan Alexeyevich 1870-1953 **TCLC 6; SSC 5**
See also CA 104

Bunting, Basil 1900-1985 ..... **CLC 10, 39, 47; DAM POET**
See also CA 53-56; 115; CANR 7; DLB 20

Bunuel, Luis 1900-1983 .. **CLC 16, 80; DAM MULT; HLC 1**
See also CA 101; 110; CANR 32, 77; HW 1

Bunyan, John 1628-1688 ... **LC 4; DA; DAB; DAC; DAM MST; WLC**
See also CDBLB 1660-1789; DLB 39

Burckhardt, Jacob (Christoph) 1818-1897 **NCLC 49**

Burford, Eleanor
See Hibbert, Eleanor Alice Burford

Burgess, Anthony **CLC 1, 2, 4, 5, 8, 10, 13, 15, 22, 40, 62, 81, 94; DAB**
See also Wilson, John (Anthony) Burgess
See also AAYA 25; AITN 1; CDBLB 1960 to Present; DLB 14, 194; DLBY 98; MTCW 1

Burke, Edmund 1729(?)-1797 **LC 7, 36; DA; DAB; DAC; DAM MST; WLC**
See also DLB 104

Burke, Kenneth (Duva) 1897-1993**CLC 2, 24**
See also CA 5-8R; 143; CANR 39, 74; DLB 45, 63; MTCW 1, 2

Burke, Leda
See Garnett, David

Burke, Ralph
See Silverberg, Robert

Burke, Thomas 1886-1945 .... **TCLC 63**
See also CA 113; 155; DLB 197

Burney, Fanny 1752-1840 .... **NCLC 12, 54**
See also DLB 39

Burns, Robert 1759-1796 . **LC 3, 29, 40; DA; DAB; DAC; DAM MST, POET; PC 6; WLC**
See also CDBLB 1789-1832; DLB 109

Burns, Tex
See L'Amour, Louis (Dearborn)

Burnshaw, Stanley 1906- .... **CLC 3, 13, 44**
See also CA 9-12R; DLB 48; DLBY 97

Burr, Anne 1937- .... **CLC 6**
See also CA 25-28R

Burroughs, Edgar Rice 1875-1950 . **TCLC 2, 32; DAM NOV**
See also AAYA 11; CA 104; 132; DLB 8; MTCW 1, 2; SATA 41

Burroughs, William S(eward) 1914-1997**CLC 1, 2, 5, 15, 22, 42, 75, 109; DA; DAB; DAC; DAM MST, NOV, POP; WLC**
See also AITN 2; CA 9-12R; 160; CANR 20, 52; DLB 2, 8, 16, 152; DLBY 81, 97; MTCW 1, 2

Burton, Sir Richard F(rancis) 1821-1890 **NCLC 42**
See also DLB 55, 166, 184

Busch, Frederick 1941- ..... **CLC 7, 10, 18, 47**
See also CA 33-36R; CAAS 1; CANR 45, 73; DLB 6

Bush, Ronald 1946- .... **CLC 34**
See also CA 136

Bustos, F(rancisco)
See Borges, Jorge Luis

Bustos Domecq, H(onorio)
See Bioy Casares, Adolfo; Borges, Jorge Luis

Butler, Octavia E(stelle) 1947- **CLC 38, 121; BLCS; DAM MULT, POP**
See also AAYA 18; BW 2, 3; CA 73-76; CANR 12, 24, 38, 73; DLB 33; MTCW 1, 2; SATA 84

Butler, Robert Olen (Jr.) 1945-**CLC 81; DAM POP**
See also CA 112; CANR 66; DLB 173; INT 112; MTCW 1

Butler, Samuel 1612-1680 .... **LC 16, 43**
See also DLB 101, 126

Butler, Samuel 1835-1902 . **TCLC 1, 33; DA; DAB; DAC; DAM MST, NOV; WLC**
See also CA 143; CDBLB 1890-1914; DLB 18, 57, 174

Butler, Walter C.
See Faust, Frederick (Schiller)

Butor, Michel (Marie Francois) 1926-**CLC 1, 3, 8, 11, 15**
See also CA 9-12R; CANR 33, 66; DLB 83; MTCW 1, 2

Butts, Mary 1892(?)-1937 .... **TCLC 77**
See also CA 148

Buzo, Alexander (John) 1944- .... **CLC 61**
See also CA 97-100; CANR 17, 39, 69

Buzzati, Dino 1906-1972 .... **CLC 36**
See also CA 160; 33-36R; DLB 177

Byars, Betsy (Cromer) 1928-............. **CLC 35**
See also AAYA 19; CA 33-36R; CANR 18, 36, 57; CLR 1, 16; DLB 52; INT CANR-18; JRDA; MAICYA; MTCW 1; SAAS 1; SATA 4, 46, 80; SATA-Essay 108

Byatt, A(ntonia) S(usan Drabble) 1936-**C L C 19, 65; DAM NOV, POP**
See also CA 13-16R; CANR 13, 33, 50, 75; DLB 14, 194; MTCW 1, 2

Byrne, David 1952-............................ **CLC 26**
See also CA 127

Byrne, John Keyes 1926-
See Leonard, Hugh
See also CA 102; CANR 78; INT 102

Byron, George Gordon (Noel) 1788-1824 **NCLC 2, 12; DA; DAB; DAC; DAM MST, POET; PC 16; WLC**
See also CDBLB 1789-1832; DLB 96, 110

Byron, Robert 1905-1941 .... **TCLC 67**
See also CA 160; DLB 195

C. 3. 3.
See Wilde, Oscar

Caballero, Fernan 1796-1877 .... **NCLC 10**

Cabell, Branch
See Cabell, James Branch

Cabell, James Branch 1879-1958 .... **TCLC 6**
See also CA 105; 152; DLB 9, 78; MTCW 1

Cable, George Washington 1844-1925**T C L C 4; SSC 4**
See also CA 104; 155; DLB 12, 74; DLBD 13

Cabral de Melo Neto, Joao 1920- ... **CLC 76; DAM MULT**
See also CA 151

Cabrera Infante, G(uillermo) 1929-**CLC 5, 25, 45, 120; DAM MULT; HLC 1**
See also CA 85-88; CANR 29, 65; DLB 113; HW 1, 2; MTCW 1, 2

Cade, Toni
See Bambara, Toni Cade

Cadmus and Harmonia
See Buchan, John

Caedmon fl. 658-680 .... **CMLC 7**
See also DLB 146

Caeiro, Alberto
See Pessoa, Fernando (Antonio Nogueira)

Cage, John (Milton, Jr.) 1912-1992 .. **CLC 41**
See also CA 13-16R; 169; CANR 9, 78; DLB 193; INT CANR-9

Cahan, Abraham 1860-1951 .... **TCLC 71**
See also CA 108; 154; DLB 9, 25, 28

Cain, G.
See Cabrera Infante, G(uillermo)

Cain, Guillermo
See Cabrera Infante, G(uillermo)

Cain, James M(allahan) 1892-1977**CLC 3, 11, 28**
See also AITN 1; CA 17-20R; 73-76; CANR 8, 34, 61; MTCW 1

Caine, Mark
See Raphael, Frederic (Michael)

Calasso, Roberto 1941- .... **CLC 81**
See also CA 143

Calderon de la Barca, Pedro 1600-1681 .. **L C 23; DC 3; HLCS 1**

Caldwell, Erskine (Preston) 1903-1987**CLC 1, 8, 14, 50, 60; DAM NOV; SSC 19**
See also AITN 1; CA 1-4R; 121; CAAS 1; CANR 2, 33; DLB 9, 86; MTCW 1, 2

Caldwell, (Janet Miriam) Taylor (Holland) 1900-1985**CLC 2, 28, 39; DAM NOV, POP**
See also CA 5-8R; 116; CANR 5; DLBD 17

Calhoun, John Caldwell 1782-1850**NCLC 15**
See also DLB 3

Calisher, Hortense 1911-**CLC 2, 4, 8, 38; DAM NOV; SSC 15**
See also CA 1-4R; CANR 1, 22, 67; DLB 2; INT CANR-22; MTCW 1, 2

Callaghan, Morley Edward 1903-1990**CLC 3, 14, 41, 65; DAC; DAM MST**
See also CA 9-12R; 132; CANR 33, 73; DLB 68; MTCW 1, 2

Callimachus c. 305B.C.-c. 240B.C. **CMLC 18**
See also DLB 176

Calvin, John 1509-1564 .... **LC 37**

Calvino, Italo 1923-1985**CLC 5, 8, 11, 22, 33, 39, 73; DAM NOV; SSC 3**
See also CA 85-88; 116; CANR 23, 61; DLB 196; MTCW 1, 2

Cameron, Carey 1952- .... **CLC 59**
See also CA 135

Cameron, Peter 1959- .... **CLC 44**
See also CA 125; CANR 50

Camoens, Luis Vaz de 1524(?)-1580
See also HLCS 1

Camoes, Luis de 1524(?)-1580
See also HLCS 1

Campana, Dino 1885-1932 .... **TCLC 20**
See also CA 117; DLB 114

Campanella, Tommaso 1568-1639 .... **LC 32**

Campbell, John W(ood, Jr.) 1910-1971 **C L C 32**
See also CA 21-22; 29-32R; CANR 34; CAP 2; DLB 8; MTCW 1

Campbell, Joseph 1904-1987 .... **CLC 69**
See also AAYA 3; BEST 89:2; CA 1-4R; 124; CANR 3, 28, 61; MTCW 1, 2

Campbell, Maria 1940- .... **CLC 85; DAC**
See also CA 102; CANR 54; NNAL

Campbell, (John) Ramsey 1946-**CLC 42; SSC 19**
See also CA 57-60; CANR 7; INT CANR-7

Campbell, (Ignatius) Roy (Dunnachie) 1901-1957 .... **TCLC 5**
See also CA 104; 155; DLB 20; MTCW 2

Campbell, Thomas 1777-1844 .... **NCLC 19**
See also DLB 93; 144

Campbell, Wilfred .... **TCLC 9**
See also Campbell, William

Campbell, William 1858(?)-1918
See Campbell, Wilfred
See also CA 106; DLB 92

Campion, Jane .... **CLC 95**
See also CA 138

Campos, Alvaro de
See Pessoa, Fernando (Antonio Nogueira)

Camus, Albert 1913-1960**CLC 1, 2, 4, 9, 11, 14, 32, 63, 69; DA; DAB; DAC; DAM DRAM, MST, NOV; DC 2; SSC 9; WLC**
See also CA 89-92; DLB 72; MTCW 1, 2

Canby, Vincent 1924- .... **CLC 13**
See also CA 81-84

Cancale
See Desnos, Robert

Canetti, Elias 1905-1994**CLC 3, 14, 25, 75, 86**
See also CA 21-24R; 146; CANR 23, 61, 79; DLB 85, 124; MTCW 1, 2

Canfield, Dorothea F.
See Fisher, Dorothy (Frances) Canfield

Canfield, Dorothea Frances
See Fisher, Dorothy (Frances) Canfield

Canfield, Dorothy
See Fisher, Dorothy (Frances) Canfield

Canin, Ethan 1960- .... **CLC 55**
See also CA 131; 135

Cannon, Curt
See Hunter, Evan

See also BEST 90:2; CA 21-24R; CAAS 10;
CANR 21, 32, 76; DLBY 89; HW 1; MTCW
1, 2

Celan, Paul .... **CLC 10, 19, 53, 82; PC 10**
See also Antschel, Paul
See also DLB 69

Celine, Louis-Ferdinand **CLC 1, 3, 4, 7, 9, 15,
47**
See also Destouches, Louis-Ferdinand
See also DLB 72

Cellini, Benvenuto 1500-1571 .... **LC 7**

Cendrars, Blaise 1887-1961 ..... **CLC 18, 106**
See also Sauser-Hall, Frederic

Cernuda (y Bidon), Luis 1902-1963 **CLC 54;
DAM POET**
See also CA 131; 89-92; DLB 134; HW 1

Cervantes, Lorna Dee 1954-
See also CA 131; CANR 80; DLB 82; HLCS 1;
HW 1

Cervantes (Saavedra), Miguel de 1547-1616
**LC 6, 23; DA; DAB; DAC; DAM MST,
NOV; SSC 12; WLC**

Cesaire, Aime (Fernand) 1913- . **CLC 19, 32,
112; BLC 1; DAM MULT, POET; PC 25**
See also BW 2, 3; CA 65-68; CANR 24, 43,
81; MTCW 1, 2

Chabon, Michael 1963- .... **CLC 55**
See also CA 139; CANR 57

Chabrol, Claude 1930- .... **CLC 16**
See also CA 110

Challans, Mary 1905-1983
See Renault, Mary
See also CA 81-84; 111; CANR 74; MTCW 2;
SATA 23; SATA-Obit 36

Challis, George
See Faust, Frederick (Schiller)

Chambers, Aidan 1934- .... **CLC 35**
See also AAYA 27; CA 25-28R; CANR 12, 31,
58; JRDA; MAICYA; SAAS 12; SATA 1, 69,
108

Chambers, James 1948-
See Cliff, Jimmy
See also CA 124

Chambers, Jessie
See Lawrence, D(avid) H(erbert Richards)

Chambers, Robert W(illiam) 1865-1933
TCLC 41
See also CA 165; DLB 202; SATA 107

Chandler, Raymond (Thornton) 1888-1959
TCLC 1, 7; SSC 23
See also AAYA 25; CA 104; 129; CANR 60;
CDALB 1929-1941; DLBD 6; MTCW 1, 2

Chang, Eileen 1920-1995 .... **SSC 28**
See also CA 166

Chang, Jung 1952- .... **CLC 71**
See also CA 142

Chang Ai-Ling
See Chang, Eileen

Channing, William Ellery 1780-1842 **NCLC
17**
See also DLB 1, 59

Chao, Patricia 1955- .... **CLC 119**
See also CA 163

Chaplin, Charles Spencer 1889-1977 **CLC 16**
See Chaplin, Charlie
See also CA 81-84; 73-76

Chaplin, Charlie
See Chaplin, Charles Spencer
See also DLB 44

Chapman, George 1559(?)-1634 **LC 22; DAM
DRAM**
See also DLB 62, 121

Chapman, Graham 1941-1989 .... **CLC 21**

See also Monty Python
See also CA 116; 129; CANR 35

Chapman, John Jay 1862-1933 .... **TCLC 7**
See also CA 104

Chapman, Lee
See Bradley, Marion Zimmer

Chapman, Walker
See Silverberg, Robert

Chappell, Fred (Davis) 1936- ..... **CLC 40, 78**
See also CA 5-8R; CAAS 4; CANR 8, 33, 67;
DLB 6, 105

Char, Rene(-Emile) 1907-1988 **CLC 9, 11, 14,
55; DAM POET**
See also CA 13-16R; 124; CANR 32; MTCW
1, 2

Charby, Jay
See Ellison, Harlan (Jay)

Chardin, Pierre Teilhard de
See Teilhard de Chardin, (Marie Joseph) Pierre

Charles I 1600-1649 .... **LC 13**

Charriere, Isabelle de 1740-1805 ..**NCLC 66**

Charyn, Jerome 1937- .... **CLC 5, 8, 18**
See also CA 5-8R; CAAS 1; CANR 7, 61;
DLBY 83; MTCW 1

Chase, Mary (Coyle) 1907-1981 .... **DC 1**
See also CA 77-80; 105; SATA 17; SATA-Obit
29

Chase, Mary Ellen 1887-1973 .... **CLC 2**
See also CA 13-16; 41-44R; CAP 1; SATA 10

Chase, Nicholas
See Hyde, Anthony

Chateaubriand, Francois Rene de 1768-1848
NCLC 3
See also DLB 119

Chatterje, Sarat Chandra 1876-1936(?)
See Chatterji, Saratchandra
See also CA 109

Chatterji, Bankim Chandra 1838-1894**NCLC
19**

Chatterji, Saratchandra .... **TCLC 13**
See also Chatterje, Sarat Chandra

Chatterton, Thomas 1752-1770 .**LC 3; DAM
POET**
See also DLB 109

Chatwin, (Charles) Bruce 1940-1989**CLC 28,
57, 59; DAM POP**
See also AAYA 4; BEST 90:1; CA 85-88; 127;
DLB 194, 204

Chaucer, Daniel
See Ford, Ford Madox

Chaucer, Geoffrey 1340(?)-1400 **LC 17; DA;
DAB; DAC; DAM MST, POET; PC 19;
WLCS**
See also CDBLB Before 1660; DLB 146

Chavez, Denise (Elia) 1948-
See also CA 131; CANR 56, 81; DAM MULT;
DLB 122; HLC 1; HW 1, 2; MTCW 2

Chaviaras, Strates 1935-
See Haviaras, Stratis
See also CA 105

Chayefsky, Paddy .... **CLC 23**
See also Chayefsky, Sidney
See also DLB 7, 44; DLBY 81

Chayefsky, Sidney 1923-1981
See Chayefsky, Paddy
See also CA 9-12R; 104; CANR 18; DAM
DRAM

Chedid, Andree 1920- .... **CLC 47**
See also CA 145

Cheever, John 1912-1982 **CLC 3, 7, 8, 11, 15,
25, 64; DA; DAB; DAC; DAM MST, NOV,
POP; SSC 1; WLC**
See also CA 5-8R; 106; CABS 1; CANR 5, 27,

76; CDALB 1941-1968; DLB 2, 102; DLBY
80, 82; INT CANR-5; MTCW 1, 2

Cheever, Susan 1943- .... **CLC 18, 48**
See also CA 103; CANR 27, 51; DLBY 82; INT
CANR-27

Chekhonte, Antosha
See Chekhov, Anton (Pavlovich)

Chekhov, Anton (Pavlovich) 1860-1904**TCLC
3, 10, 31, 55, 96; DA; DAB; DAC; DAM
DRAM, MST; DC 9; SSC 2, 28; WLC**
See also CA 104; 124; SATA 90

Chernyshevsky, Nikolay Gavrilovich 1828-1889
NCLC 1

Cherry, Carolyn Janice 1942-
See Cherryh, C. J.
See also CA 65-68; CANR 10

Cherryh, C. J. .... **CLC 35**
See also Cherry, Carolyn Janice
See also AAYA 24; DLBY 80; SATA 93

Chesnutt, Charles W(addell) 1858-1932
TCLC 5, 39; BLC 1; DAM MULT; SSC 7
See also BW 1, 3; CA 106; 125; CANR 76; DLB
12, 50, 78; MTCW 1, 2

Chester, Alfred 1929(?)-1971 .... **CLC 49**
See also CA 33-36R; DLB 130

Chesterton, G(ilbert) K(eith) 1874-1936
**TCLC 1, 6, 64; DAM NOV,POET; PC 28;
SSC 1**
See also CA 104; 132; CANR 73; CDBLB
1914-1945; DLB 10, 19, 34, 70, 98, 149,
178; MTCW 1, 2; SATA 27

Chiang, Pin-chin 1904-1986
See Ding Ling
See also CA 118

Ch'ien Chung-shu 1910- .... **CLC 22**
See also CA 130; CANR 73; MTCW 1, 2

Child, L. Maria
See Child, Lydia Maria

Child, Lydia Maria 1802-1880 ...**NCLC 6, 73**
See also DLB 1, 74; SATA 67

Child, Mrs.
See Child, Lydia Maria

Child, Philip 1898-1978 .... **CLC 19, 68**
See also CA 13-14; CAP 1; SATA 47

Childers, (Robert) Erskine 1870-1922 **T C L C
65**
See also CA 113; 153; DLB 70

Childress, Alice 1920-1994**CLC 12, 15, 86, 96;
BLC 1; DAM DRAM, MULT, NOV; DC 4**
See also AAYA 8; BW 2, 3; CA 45-48; 146;
CANR 3, 27, 50, 74; CLR 14; DLB 7, 38;
JRDA; MAICYA; MTCW 1, 2; SATA 7, 48,
81

Chin, Frank (Chew, Jr.) 1940- .... **DC 7**
See also CA 33-36R; CANR 71; DAM MULT;
DLB 206

Chislett, (Margaret) Anne 1943- ...... **CLC 34**
See also CA 151

Chitty, Thomas Willes 1926- .... **CLC 11**
See also Hinde, Thomas
See also CA 5-8R

Chivers, Thomas Holley 1809-1858**NCLC 49**
See also DLB 3

Choi, Susan .... **CLC 119**

Chomette, Rene Lucien 1898-1981
See Clair, Rene
See also CA 103

Chopin, Kate **TCLC 5, 14; DA; DAB; SSC 8;
WLCS**
See also Chopin, Katherine
See also CDALB 1865-1917; DLB 12, 78

Chopin, Katherine 1851-1904
See Chopin, Kate

30
See also CA 5-8R; 25-28R; DLB 9

Costantini, Humberto 1924(?)-1987 . **CLC 49**
See also CA 131; 122; HW 1

Costello, Elvis 1955- .... **CLC 21**

Costenoble, Philostene
See Ghelderode, Michel de

Cotes, Cecil V.
See Duncan, Sara Jeannette

Cotter, Joseph Seamon Sr. 1861-1949 **T C L C 28; BLC 1; DAM MULT**
See also BW 1; CA 124; DLB 50

Couch, Arthur Thomas Quiller
See Quiller-Couch, SirArthur (Thomas)

Coulton, James
See Hansen, Joseph

Couperus, Louis (Marie Anne) 1863-1923 **TCLC 15**
See also CA 115

Coupland, Douglas 1961-**CLC 85; DAC; DAM POP**
See also CA 142; CANR 57

Court, Wesli
See Turco, Lewis (Putnam)

Courtenay, Bryce 1933- .... **CLC 59**
See also CA 138

Courtney, Robert
See Ellison, Harlan (Jay)

Cousteau, Jacques-Yves 1910-1997 .. **CLC 30**
See also CA 65-68; 159; CANR 15, 67; MTCW 1; SATA 38, 98

Coventry, Francis 1725-1754 .... **LC 46**

Cowan, Peter (Walkinshaw) 1914- .... **SSC 28**
See also CA 21-24R; CANR 9, 25, 50

Coward, Noel (Peirce) 1899-1973**CLC 1, 9, 29, 51; DAM DRAM**
See also AITN 1; CA 17-18; 41-44R; CANR 35; CAP 2; CDBLB 1914-1945; DLB 10; MTCW 1, 2

Cowley, Abraham 1618-1667 .... **LC 43**
See also DLB 131, 151

Cowley, Malcolm 1898-1989 .... **CLC 39**
See also CA 5-8R; 128; CANR 3, 55; DLB 4, 48; DLBY 81, 89; MTCW 1, 2

Cowper, William 1731-1800 . **NCLC 8; DAM POET**
See also DLB 104, 109

Cox, William Trevor 1928- .... **CLC 9, 14, 71; DAM NOV**
See Trevor, William
See also CA 9-12R; CANR 4, 37, 55, 76; DLB 14; INT CANR-37; MTCW 1, 2

Coyne, P. J.
See Masters, Hilary

Cozzens, James Gould 1903-1978**CLC 1, 4, 11, 92**
See also CA 9-12R; 81-84; CANR 19; CDALB 1941-1968; DLB 9; DLBD 2; DLBY 84, 97; MTCW 1, 2

Crabbe, George 1754-1832 .... **NCLC 26**
See also DLB 93

Craddock, Charles Egbert
See Murfree, Mary Noailles

Craig, A. A.
See Anderson, Poul (William)

Craik, Dinah Maria (Mulock) 1826-1887 **NCLC 38**
See also DLB 35, 163; MAICYA; SATA 34

Cram, Ralph Adams 1863-1942 ..... **TCLC 45**
See also CA 160

Crane, (Harold) Hart 1899-1932 **TCLC 2, 5, 80; DA; DAB; DAC; DAM MST, POET; PC 3; WLC**

See also CA 104; 127; CDALB 1917-1929; DLB 4, 48; MTCW 1, 2

Crane, R(onald) S(almon) 1886-1967**CLC 27**
See also CA 85-88; DLB 63

Crane, Stephen (Townley) 1871-1900 **T C L C 11, 17, 32; DA; DAB; DAC; DAM MST, NOV, POET; SSC 7; WLC**
See also AAYA 21; CA 109; 140; CDALB 1865-1917; DLB 12, 54, 78; YABC 2

Cranshaw, Stanley
See Fisher, Dorothy (Frances) Canfield

Crase, Douglas 1944- .... **CLC 58**
See also CA 106

Crashaw, Richard 1612(?)-1649 .... **LC 24**
See also DLB 126

Craven, Margaret 1901-1980 . **CLC 17; DAC**
See also CA 103

Crawford, F(rancis) Marion 1854-1909**TCLC 10**
See also CA 107; 168; DLB 71

Crawford, Isabella Valancy 1850-1887**N C L C 12**
See also DLB 92

Crayon, Geoffrey
See Irving, Washington

Creasey, John 1908-1973 .... **CLC 11**
See also CA 5-8R; 41-44R; CANR 8, 59; DLB 77; MTCW 1

Crebillon, Claude Prosper Jolyot de (fils) 1707-1777 .... **LC 1, 28**

Credo
See Creasey, John

Credo, Alvaro J. de
See Prado (Calvo), Pedro

Creeley, Robert (White) 1926-**CLC 1, 2, 4, 8, 11, 15, 36, 78; DAM POET**
See also CA 1-4R; CAAS 10; CANR 23, 43; DLB 5, 16, 169; DLBD 17; MTCW 1, 2

Crews, Harry (Eugene) 1935- **CLC 6, 23, 49**
See also AITN 1; CA 25-28R; CANR 20, 57; DLB 6, 143, 185; MTCW 1, 2

Crichton, (John) Michael 1942-**CLC 2, 6, 54, 90; DAM NOV, POP**
See also AAYA 10; AITN 2; CA 25-28R; CANR 13, 40, 54, 76; DLBY 81; INT CANR-13; JRDA; MTCW 1, 2; SATA 9, 88

Crispin, Edmund .... **CLC 22**
See Montgomery, (Robert) Bruce; Montgomery, (Robert) Bruce
See also CA 179; DLB 87

Cristofer, Michael 1945(?)- .... **CLC 28; DAM DRAM**
See also CA 110; 152; DLB 7

Croce, Benedetto 1866-1952 .... **TCLC 37**
See also CA 120; 155

Crockett, David 1786-1836 .... **NCLC 8**
See also DLB 3, 11

Crockett, Davy
See Crockett, David

Crofts, Freeman Wills 1879-1957 .. **TCLC 55**
See also CA 115; DLB 77

Croker, John Wilson 1780-1857 .... **NCLC 10**
See also DLB 110

Crommelynck, Fernand 1885-1970 .. **CLC 75**
See also CA 89-92

Cromwell, Oliver 1599-1658 .... **LC 43**

Cronin, A(rchibald) J(oseph) 1896-1981**C L C 32**
See also CA 1-4R; 102; CANR 5; DLB 191; SATA 47; SATA-Obit 25

Cross, Amanda
See Heilbrun, Carolyn G(old)

Crothers, Rachel 1878(?)-1958 ...... **TCLC 19**

See also CA 113; DLB 7

Croves, Hal
See Traven, B.

Crow Dog, Mary (Ellen) (?)- .... **CLC 93**
See also Brave Bird, Mary
See also CA 154

Crowfield, Christopher
See Stowe, Harriet (Elizabeth) Beecher

Crowley, Aleister .... **TCLC 7**
See also Crowley, Edward Alexander

Crowley, Edward Alexander 1875-1947
See Crowley, Aleister
See also CA 104

Crowley, John 1942- .... **CLC 57**
See also CA 61-64; CANR 43; DLBY 82; SATA 65

Crud
See Crumb, R(obert)

Crumarums
See Crumb, R(obert)

Crumb, R(obert) 1943- .... **CLC 17**
See also CA 106

Crumbum
See Crumb, R(obert)

Crumski
See Crumb, R(obert)

Crum the Bum
See Crumb, R(obert)

Crunk
See Crumb, R(obert)

Crustt
See Crumb, R(obert)

Cruz, Victor Hernandez 1949-
See also BW 2; CA 65-68; CAAS 17; CANR 14, 32, 74; DAM MULT, POET; DLB 41; HLC 1; HW 1, 2; MTCW 1

Cryer, Gretchen (Kiger) 1935- .... **CLC 21**
See also CA 114; 123

Csath, Geza 1887-1919 .... **TCLC 13**
See also CA 111

Cudlip, David R(ockwell) 1933- ...... **CLC 34**
See also CA 177

Cullen, Countee 1903-1946**TCLC 4, 37; BLC 1; DA; DAC; DAM MST, MULT, POET; PC 20; WLCS**
See also BW 1; CA 108; 124; CDALB 1917-1929; DLB 4, 48, 51; MTCW 1, 2; SATA 18

Cum, R.
See Crumb, R(obert)

Cummings, Bruce F(rederick) 1889-1919
See Barbellion, W. N. P.
See also CA 123

Cummings, E(dward) E(stlin) 1894-1962**CLC 1, 3, 8, 12, 15, 68; DA; DAB; DAC; DAM MST, POET; PC 5; WLC**
See also CA 73-76; CANR 31; CDALB 1929-1941; DLB 4, 48; MTCW 1, 2

Cunha, Euclides (Rodrigues Pimenta) da 1866-1909 .... **TCLC 24**
See also CA 123

Cunningham, E. V.
See Fast, Howard (Melvin)

Cunningham, J(ames) V(incent) 1911-1985 **CLC 3, 31**
See also CA 1-4R; 115; CANR 1, 72; DLB 5

Cunningham, Julia (Woolfolk) 1916-**CLC 12**
See also CA 9-12R; CANR 4, 19, 36; JRDA; MAICYA; SAAS 2; SATA 1, 26

Cunningham, Michael 1952- .... **CLC 34**
See also CA 136

Cunninghame Graham, R(obert) B(ontine) 1852-1936 .... **TCLC 19**
See also Graham, R(obert) B(ontine)

Cunninghame
See also CA 119; DLB 98

Currie, Ellen 19(?)- .... **CLC 44**

Curtin, Philip
See Lowndes, Marie Adelaide (Belloc)

Curtis, Price
See Ellison, Harlan (Jay)

Cutrate, Joe
See Spiegelman, Art

Cynewulf c. 770-c. 840 .... **CMLC 23**

Czaczkes, Shmuel Yosef
See Agnon, S(hmuel) Y(osef Halevi)

Dabrowska, Maria (Szumska) 1889-1965**CLC 15**
See also CA 106

Dabydeen, David 1955- .... **CLC 34**
See also BW 1; CA 125; CANR 56

Dacey, Philip 1939- .... **CLC 51**
See also CA 37-40R; CAAS 17; CANR 14, 32, 64; DLB 105

Dagerman, Stig (Halvard) 1923-1954 **TCLC 17**
See also CA 117; 155

Dahl, Roald 1916-1990**CLC 1, 6, 18, 79; DAB; DAC; DAM MST, NOV, POP**
See also AAYA 15; CA 1-4R; 133; CANR 6, 32, 37, 62; CLR 1, 7, 41; DLB 139; JRDA; MAICYA; MTCW 1, 2; SATA 1, 26, 73; SATA-Obit 65

Dahlberg, Edward 1900-1977 .. **CLC 1, 7, 14**
See also CA 9-12R; 69-72; CANR 31, 62; DLB 48; MTCW 1

Daitch, Susan 1954- .... **CLC 103**
See also CA 161

Dale, Colin .... **TCLC 18**
See also Lawrence, T(homas) E(dward)

Dale, George E.
See Asimov, Isaac

Dalton, Roque 1935-1975
See also HLCS 1; HW 2

Daly, Elizabeth 1878-1967 .... **CLC 52**
See also CA 23-24; 25-28R; CANR 60; CAP 2

Daly, Maureen 1921- .... **CLC 17**
See also AAYA 5; CANR 37; JRDA; MAICYA; SAAS 1; SATA 2

Damas, Leon-Gontran 1912-1978 .... **CLC 84**
See also BW 1; CA 125; 73-76

Dana, Richard Henry Sr. 1787-1879**NCLC 53**

Daniel, Samuel 1562(?)-1619 .... **LC 24**
See also DLB 62

Daniels, Brett
See Adler, Renata

Dannay, Frederic 1905-1982 . **CLC 11; DAM POP**
See also Queen, Ellery
See also CA 1-4R; 107; CANR 1, 39; DLB 137; MTCW 1

D'Annunzio, Gabriele 1863-1938**TCLC 6, 40**
See also CA 104; 155

Danois, N. le
See Gourmont, Remy (-Marie-Charles) de

Dante 1265-1321 .... **CMLC 3, 18; DA; DAB; DAC; DAM MST, POET; PC 21; WLCS**

d'Antibes, Germain
See Simenon, Georges (Jacques Christian)

Danticat, Edwidge 1969-..................... **CLC 94**
See also AAYA 29; CA 152; CANR 73; MTCW 1

Danvers, Dennis 1947- .... **CLC 70**

Danziger, Paula 1944- .... **CLC 21**
See also AAYA 4; CA 112; 115; CANR 37; CLR 20; JRDA; MAICYA; SATA 36, 63, 102; SATA-Brief 30

Da Ponte, Lorenzo 1749-1838 .... **NCLC 50**

Dario, Ruben 1867-1916 .... **TCLC 4; DAM MULT; HLC 1; PC 15**
See also CA 131; CANR 81; HW 1, 2; MTCW 1, 2

Darley, George 1795-1846 .... **NCLC 2**
See also DLB 96

Darrow, Clarence (Seward) 1857-1938**TCLC 81**
See also CA 164

Darwin, Charles 1809-1882 .... **NCLC 57**
See also DLB 57, 166

Daryush, Elizabeth 1887-1977 ...... **CLC 6, 19**
See also CA 49-52; CANR 3, 81; DLB 20

Dasgupta, Surendranath 1887-1952**TCLC 81**
See also CA 157

Dashwood, Edmee Elizabeth Monica de la Pasture 1890-1943
See Delafield, E. M.
See also CA 119; 154

Daudet, (Louis Marie) Alphonse 1840-1897 **NCLC 1**
See also DLB 123

Daumal, Rene 1908-1944 .... **TCLC 14**
See also CA 114

Davenant, William 1606-1668 .... **LC 13**
See also DLB 58, 126

Davenport, Guy (Mattison, Jr.) 1927-**CLC 6, 14, 38; SSC 16**
See also CA 33-36R; CANR 23, 73; DLB 130

Davidson, Avram (James) 1923-1993
See Queen, Ellery
See also CA 101; 171; CANR 26; DLB 8

Davidson, Donald (Grady) 1893-1968**CLC 2, 13, 19**
See also CA 5-8R; 25-28R; CANR 4; DLB 45

Davidson, Hugh
See Hamilton, Edmond

Davidson, John 1857-1909 .... **TCLC 24**
See also CA 118; DLB 19

Davidson, Sara 1943- .... **CLC 9**
See also CA 81-84; CANR 44, 68; DLB 185

Davie, Donald (Alfred) 1922-1995 . **CLC 5, 8, 10, 31**
See also CA 1-4R; 149; CAAS 3; CANR 1, 44; DLB 27; MTCW 1

Davies, Ray(mond Douglas) 1944- ... **CLC 21**
See also CA 116; 146

Davies, Rhys 1901-1978 .... **CLC 23**
See also CA 9-12R; 81-84; CANR 4; DLB 139, 191

Davies, (William) Robertson 1913-1995 **CLC 2, 7, 13, 25, 42, 75, 91; DA; DAB; DAC; DAM MST, NOV, POP; WLC**
See also BEST 89:2; CA 33-36R; 150; CANR 17, 42; DLB 68; INT CANR-17; MTCW 1, 2

Davies, William Henry 1871-1940 ... **TCLC 5**
See also CA 104; 179; DLB 19, 174

Davies, Walter C.
See Kornbluth, C(yril) M.

Davis, Angela (Yvonne) 1944-**CLC 77; DAM MULT**
See also BW 2, 3; CA 57-60; CANR 10, 81

Davis, B. Lynch
See Bioy Casares, Adolfo; Borges, Jorge Luis

Davis, B. Lynch
See Bioy Casares, Adolfo

Davis, Harold Lenoir 1894-1960 ...... **CLC 49**
See also CA 178; 89-92; DLB 9, 206

Davis, Rebecca (Blaine) Harding 1831-1910 **TCLC 6**
See also CA 104; 179; DLB 74

Davis, Richard Harding 1864-1916**TCLC 24**
See also CA 114; 179; DLB 12, 23, 78, 79, 189; DLBD 13

Davison, Frank Dalby 1893-1970 ...... **CLC 15**
See also CA 116

Davison, Lawrence H.
See Lawrence, D(avid) H(erbert Richards)

Davison, Peter (Hubert) 1928- .... **CLC 28**
See also CA 9-12R; CAAS 4; CANR 3, 43; DLB 5

Davys, Mary 1674-1732 .... **LC 1, 46**
See also DLB 39

Dawson, Fielding 1930-....................... **CLC 6**
See also CA 85-88; DLB 130

Dawson, Peter
See Faust, Frederick (Schiller)

Day, Clarence (Shepard, Jr.) 1874-1935 **TCLC 25**
See also CA 108; DLB 11

Day, Thomas 1748-1789 .... **LC 1**
See also DLB 39; YABC 1

Day Lewis, C(ecil) 1904-1972 . **CLC 1, 6, 10; DAM POET; PC 11**
See also Blake, Nicholas
See also CA 13-16; 33-36R; CANR 34; CAP 1; DLB 15, 20; MTCW 1, 2

Dazai Osamu 1909-1948 .... **TCLC 11**
See also Tsushima, Shuji
See also CA 164; DLB 182

de Andrade, Carlos Drummond 1892-1945
See Drummond de Andrade, Carlos

Deane, Norman
See Creasey, John

Deane, Seamus (Francis) 1940- .... **CLC 122**
See also CA 118; CANR 42

de Beauvoir, Simone (Lucie Ernestine Marie Bertrand)
See Beauvoir, Simone (Lucie Ernestine Marie Bertrand) de

de Beer, P.
See Bosman, Herman Charles

de Brissac, Malcolm
See Dickinson, Peter (Malcolm)

de Chardin, Pierre Teilhard
See Teilhard de Chardin, (Marie Joseph) Pierre

Dee, John 1527-1608 ....**LC 20**

Deer, Sandra 1940- .... **CLC 45**

De Ferrari, Gabriella 1941- .... **CLC 65**
See also CA 146

Defoe, Daniel 1660(?)-1731 ..... **LC 1, 42; DA; DAB; DAC; DAM MST, NOV; WLC**
See also AAYA 27; CDBLB 1660-1789; DLB 39, 95, 101; JRDA; MAICYA; SATA 22

de Gourmont, Remy(-Marie-Charles)
See Gourmont, Remy (-Marie-Charles) de

de Hartog, Jan 1914- .... **CLC 19**
See also CA 1-4R; CANR 1

de Hostos, E. M.
See Hostos (y Bonilla), Eugenio Maria de

de Hostos, Eugenio M.
See Hostos (y Bonilla), Eugenio Maria de

Deighton, Len .... **CLC 4, 7, 22, 46**
See also Deighton, Leonard Cyril
See also AAYA 6; BEST 89:2; CDBLB 1960 to Present; DLB 87

Deighton, Leonard Cyril 1929-
See Deighton, Len
See also CA 9-12R; CANR 19, 33, 68; DAM NOV, POP; MTCW 1, 2

Dekker, Thomas 1572(?)-1632 ..**LC 22; DAM DRAM**
See also CDBLB Before 1660; DLB 62, 172

Delafield, E. M. 1890-1943 .... **TCLC 61**

See also Dashwood, Edmee Elizabeth Monica
de la Pasture
See also DLB 34
de la Mare, Walter (John) 1873-1956TCLC 4,
53; DAB; DAC; DAM MST, POET; SSC
14; WLC
See also CA 163; CDBLB 1914-1945; CLR 23;
DLB 162; MTCW 1; SATA 16
Delaney, Franey
See O'Hara, John (Henry)
Delaney, Shelagh 1939-CLC 29; DAM DRAM
See also CA 17-20R; CANR 30, 67; CDBLB
1960 to Present; DLB 13; MTCW 1
Delany, Mary (Granville Pendarves) 1700-1788
LC 12
Delany, Samuel R(ay, Jr.) 1942-CLC 8, 14, 38;
BLC 1; DAM MULT
See also AAYA 24; BW 2, 3; CA 81-84; CANR
27, 43; DLB 8, 33; MTCW 1, 2
De La Ramee, (Marie) Louise 1839-1908
See Ouida
See also SATA 20
de la Roche, Mazo 1879-1961 .... CLC 14
See also CA 85-88; CANR 30; DLB 68; SATA
64
De La Salle, Innocent
See Hartmann, Sadakichi
Delbanco, Nicholas (Franklin) 1942- CLC 6,
13
See also CA 17-20R; CAAS 2; CANR 29, 55;
DLB 6
del Castillo, Michel 1933- .... CLC 38
See also CA 109; CANR 77
Deledda, Grazia (Cosima) 1875(?)-1936
TCLC 23
See also CA 123
Delgado, Abelardo B(arrientos) 1931-
See also CA 131; CAAS 15; DAM MST, MULT;
DLB 82; HLC 1; HW 1, 2
Delibes, Miguel .... CLC 8, 18
See also Delibes Setien, Miguel
Delibes Setien, Miguel 1920-
See Delibes, Miguel
See also CA 45-48; CANR 1, 32; HW 1; MTCW
1
DeLillo, Don 1936- CLC 8, 10, 13, 27, 39, 54,
76; DAM NOV, POP
See also BEST 89:1; CA 81-84; CANR 21, 76;
DLB 6, 173; MTCW 1, 2
de Lisser, H. G.
See De Lisser, H(erbert) G(eorge)
See also DLB 117
De Lisser, H(erbert) G(eorge) 1878-1944
TCLC 12
See also de Lisser, H. G.
See also BW 2; CA 109; 152
Deloney, Thomas 1560(?)-1600 .... LC 41
See also DLB 167
Deloria, Vine (Victor), Jr. 1933-CLC 21, 122;
DAM MULT
See also CA 53-56; CANR 5, 20, 48; DLB 175;
MTCW 1; NNAL; SATA 21
Del Vecchio, John M(ichael) 1947- ... CLC 29
See also CA 110; DLBD 9
de Man, Paul (Adolph Michel) 1919-1983
CLC 55
See also CA 128; 111; CANR 61; DLB 67;
MTCW 1, 2
De Marinis, Rick 1934- .... CLC 54
See also CA 57-60; CAAS 24; CANR 9, 25, 50
Dembry, R. Emmet
See Murfree, Mary Noailles
Demby, William 1922-CLC 53; BLC 1; DAM

MULT
See also BW 1, 3; CA 81-84; CANR 81; DLB
33
de Menton, Francisco
See Chin, Frank (Chew, Jr.)
Demetrius of Phalerum c. 307B.C.-CMLC 34
Demijohn, Thom
See Disch, Thomas M(ichael)
de Molina, Tirso 1580-1648
See also HLCS 2
de Montherlant, Henry (Milon)
See Montherlant, Henry (Milon) de
Demosthenes 384B.C.-322B.C. ...... CMLC 13
See also DLB 176
de Natale, Francine
See Malzberg, Barry N(athaniel)
Denby, Edwin (Orr) 1903-1983 .... CLC 48
See also CA 138; 110
Denis, Julio
See Cortazar, Julio
Denmark, Harrison
See Zelazny, Roger (Joseph)
Dennis, John 1658-1734 .... LC 11
See also DLB 101
Dennis, Nigel (Forbes) 1912-1989 ...... CLC 8
See also CA 25-28R; 129; DLB 13, 15; MTCW
1
Dent, Lester 1904(?)-1959 .... TCLC 72
See also CA 112; 161
De Palma, Brian (Russell) 1940-....... CLC 20
See also CA 109
De Quincey, Thomas 1785-1859 ...... NCLC 4
See also CDBLB 1789-1832; DLB 110; 144
Deren, Eleanora 1908(?)-1961
See Deren, Maya
See also CA 111
Deren, Maya 1917-1961 .... CLC 16, 102
See also Deren, Eleanora
Derleth, August (William) 1909-1971CLC 31
See also CA 1-4R; 29-32R; CANR 4; DLB 9;
DLBD 17; SATA 5
Der Nister 1884-1950 .... TCLC 56
de Routisie, Albert
See Aragon, Louis
Derrida, Jacques 1930- .... CLC 24, 87
See also CA 124; 127; CANR 76; MTCW 1
Derry Down Derry
See Lear, Edward
Dersonnes, Jacques
See Simenon, Georges (Jacques Christian)
Desai, Anita 1937-CLC 19, 37, 97; DAB; DAM
NOV
See also CA 81-84; CANR 33, 53; MTCW 1,
2; SATA 63
Desai, Kiran 1971- .... CLC 119
See also CA 171
de Saint-Luc, Jean
See Glassco, John
de Saint Roman, Arnaud
See Aragon, Louis
Descartes, Rene 1596-1650 .... LC 20, 35
De Sica, Vittorio 1901(?)-1974 .... CLC 20
See also CA 117
Desnos, Robert 1900-1945 .... TCLC 22
See also CA 121; 151
Destouches, Louis-Ferdinand 1894-1961C L C
9, 15
See also Celine, Louis-Ferdinand
See also CA 85-88; CANR 28; MTCW 1
de Tolignac, Gaston
See Griffith, D(avid Lewelyn) W(ark)
Deutsch, Babette 1895-1982 .... CLC 18
See also CA 1-4R; 108; CANR 4, 79; DLB 45;

SATA 1; SATA-Obit 33
Devenant, William 1606-1649 .... LC 13
Devkota, Laxmiprasad 1909-1959 . TCLC 23
See also CA 123
De Voto, Bernard (Augustine) 1897-1955
TCLC 29
See also CA 113; 160; DLB 9
De Vries, Peter 1910-1993 CLC 1, 2, 3, 7, 10,
28, 46; DAM NOV
See also CA 17-20R; 142; CANR 41; DLB 6;
DLBY 82; MTCW 1, 2
Dewey, John 1859-1952 .... TCLC 95
See also CA 114; 170
Dexter, John
See Bradley, Marion Zimmer
Dexter, Martin
See Faust, Frederick (Schiller)
Dexter, Pete 1943- ... CLC 34, 55; DAM POP
See also BEST 89:2; CA 127; 131; INT 131;
MTCW 1
Diamano, Silmang
See Senghor, Leopold Sedar
Diamond, Neil 1941- .... CLC 30
See also CA 108
Diaz del Castillo, Bernal 1496-1584 .. LC 31;
HLCS 1
di Bassetto, Corno
See Shaw, George Bernard
Dick, Philip K(indred) 1928-1982CLC 10, 30,
72; DAM NOV, POP
See also AAYA 24; CA 49-52; 106; CANR 2,
16; DLB 8; MTCW 1, 2
Dickens, Charles (John Huffam) 1812-1870
NCLC 3, 8, 18, 26, 37, 50; DA; DAB; DAC;
DAM MST, NOV; SSC 17; WLC
See also AAYA 23; CDBLB 1832-1890; DLB
21, 55, 70, 159, 166; JRDA; MAICYA; SATA
15
Dickey, James (Lafayette) 1923-1997 CLC 1,
2, 4, 7, 10, 15, 47, 109; DAM NOV, POET,
POP
See also AITN 1, 2; CA 9-12R; 156; CABS 2;
CANR 10, 48, 61; CDALB 1968-1988; DLB
5, 193; DLBD 7; DLBY 82, 93, 96, 97, 98;
INT CANR-10; MTCW 1, 2
Dickey, William 1928-1994 ....CLC 3, 28
See also CA 9-12R; 145; CANR 24, 79; DLB 5
Dickinson, Charles 1951- .... CLC 49
See also CA 128
Dickinson, Emily (Elizabeth) 1830-1886
NCLC 21, 77; DA; DAB; DAC; DAM
MST, POET; PC 1; WLC
See also AAYA 22; CDALB 1865-1917; DLB
1; SATA 29
Dickinson, Peter (Malcolm) 1927-CLC 12, 35
See also AAYA 9; CA 41-44R; CANR 31, 58;
CLR 29; DLB 87, 161; JRDA; MAICYA;
SATA 5, 62, 95
Dickson, Carr
See Carr, John Dickson
Dickson, Carter
See Carr, John Dickson
Diderot, Denis 1713-1784 .... LC 26
Didion, Joan 1934-CLC 1, 3, 8, 14, 32; DAM
NOV
See also AITN 1; CA 5-8R; CANR 14, 52, 76;
CDALB 1968-1988; DLB 2, 173, 185;
DLBY 81, 86; MTCW 1, 2
Dietrich, Robert
See Hunt, E(verette) Howard, (Jr.)
Difusa, Pati
See Almodovar, Pedro
Dillard, Annie 1945- .. CLC 9, 60, 115; DAM

NOV
See also AAYA 6; CA 49-52; CANR 3, 43, 62;
DLBY 80; MTCW 1, 2; SATA 10
Dillard, R(ichard) H(enry) W(ilde) 1937-
CLC 5
See also CA 21-24R; CAAS 7; CANR 10; DLB
5
Dillon, Eilis 1920-1994 .... **CLC 17**
See also CA 9-12R; 147; CAAS 3; CANR 4,
38, 78; CLR 26; MAICYA; SATA 2, 74;
SATA-Essay 105; SATA-Obit 83
Dimont, Penelope
See Mortimer, Penelope (Ruth)
Dinesen, Isak .... **CLC 10, 29, 95; SSC 7**
See also Blixen, Karen (Christentze Dinesen)
See also MTCW 1
Ding Ling .... **CLC 68**
See also Chiang, Pin-chin
Diphusa, Patty
See Almodovar, Pedro
Disch, Thomas M(ichael) 1940- .... **CLC 7, 36**
See also AAYA 17; CA 21-24R; CAAS 4;
CANR 17, 36, 54; CLR 18; DLB 8;
MAICYA; MTCW 1, 2; SAAS 15; SATA 92
Disch, Tom
See Disch, Thomas M(ichael)
d'Isly, Georges
See Simenon, Georges (Jacques Christian)
Disraeli, Benjamin 1804-1881NCLC 2, 39, 79
See also DLB 21, 55
Ditcum, Steve
See Crumb, R(obert)
Dixon, Paige
See Corcoran, Barbara
Dixon, Stephen 1936- .... **CLC 52; SSC 16**
See also CA 89-92; CANR 17, 40, 54; DLB 130
Doak, Annie
See Dillard, Annie
Dobell, Sydney Thompson 1824-1874 **N C L C
43**
See also DLB 32
Doblin, Alfred .... **TCLC 13**
See also Doeblin, Alfred
Dobrolyubov, Nikolai Alexandrovich 1836-1861
NCLC 5
Dobson, Austin 1840-1921 .... **TCLC 79**
See also DLB 35; 144
Dobyns, Stephen 1941-...................... **CLC 37**
See also CA 45-48; CANR 2, 18
Doctorow, E(dgar) L(aurence) 1931- **CLC 6,
11, 15, 18, 37, 44, 65, 113; DAM NOV, POP**
See also AAYA 22; AITN 2; BEST 89:3; CA
45-48; CANR 2, 33, 51, 76; CDALB 1968-
1988; DLB 2, 28, 173; DLBY 80; MTCW 1,
2
Dodgson, Charles Lutwidge 1832-1898
See Carroll, Lewis
See also CLR 2; DA; DAB; DAC; DAM MST,
NOV, POET; MAICYA; SATA 100; YABC 2
Dodson, Owen (Vincent) 1914-1983 **CLC 79;
BLC 1; DAM MULT**
See also BW 1; CA 65-68; 110; CANR 24; DLB
76
Doeblin, Alfred 1878-1957............. **TCLC 13**
See also Doblin, Alfred
See also CA 110; 141; DLB 66
Doerr, Harriet 1910-........................... **CLC 34**
See also CA 117; 122; CANR 47; INT 122
Domecq, H(onorio Bustos)
See Bioy Casares, Adolfo
Domecq, H(onorio) Bustos
See Bioy Casares, Adolfo; Borges, Jorge Luis
Domini, Rey

See Lorde, Audre (Geraldine)
Dominique
See Proust, (Valentin-Louis-George-Eugene-)
Marcel
Don, A
See Stephen, SirLeslie
Donaldson, Stephen R. 1947- **CLC 46; DAM
POP**
See also CA 89-92; CANR 13, 55; INT CANR-
13
Donleavy, J(ames) P(atrick) 1926-**CLC 1, 4, 6,
10, 45**
See also AITN 2; CA 9-12R; CANR 24, 49, 62,
80; DLB 6, 173; INT CANR-24; MTCW 1,
2
Donne, John 1572-1631**LC 10, 24; DA; DAB;
DAC; DAM MST, POET; PC 1; WLC**
See also CDBLB Before 1660; DLB 121, 151
Donnell, David 1939(?)- .... **CLC 34**
Donoghue, P. S.
See Hunt, E(verette) Howard, (Jr.)
Donoso (Yanez), Jose 1924-1996**CLC 4, 8, 11,
32, 99; DAM MULT; HLC 1; SSC 34**
See also CA 81-84; 155; CANR 32, 73; DLB
113; HW 1, 2; MTCW 1, 2
Donovan, John 1928-1992 .... **CLC 35**
See also AAYA 20; CA 97-100; 137; CLR 3;
MAICYA; SATA 72; SATA-Brief 29
Don Roberto
See Cunninghame Graham, R(obert) B(ontine)
Doolittle, Hilda 1886-1961**CLC 3, 8, 14, 31, 34,
73; DA; DAC; DAM MST, POET; PC 5;
WLC**
See also H. D.
See also CA 97-100; CANR 35; DLB 4, 45;
MTCW 1, 2
Dorfman, Ariel 1942- ...... **CLC 48, 77; DAM
MULT; HLC 1**
See also CA 124; 130; CANR 67, 70; HW 1, 2;
INT 130
Dorn, Edward (Merton) 1929- ... **CLC 10, 18**
See also CA 93-96; CANR 42, 79; DLB 5; INT
93-96
Dorris, Michael (Anthony) 1945-1997 .. **C L C
109; DAM MULT, NOV**
See also AAYA 20; BEST 90:1; CA 102; 157;
CANR 19, 46, 75; CLR 58; DLB 175;
MTCW 2; NNAL; SATA 75; SATA-Obit 94
Dorris, Michael A.
See Dorris, Michael (Anthony)
Dorsan, Luc
See Simenon, Georges (Jacques Christian)
Dorsange, Jean
See Simenon, Georges (Jacques Christian)
Dos Passos, John (Roderigo) 1896-1970**C L C
1, 4, 8, 11, 15, 25, 34, 82; DA; DAB; DAC;
DAM MST, NOV; WLC**
See also CA 1-4R; 29-32R; CANR 3; CDALB
1929-1941; DLB 4, 9; DLBD 1, 15; DLBY
96; MTCW 1, 2
Dossage, Jean
See Simenon, Georges (Jacques Christian)
Dostoevsky, Fedor Mikhailovich 1821-1881
**NCLC 2, 7, 21, 33, 43; DA; DAB; DAC;
DAM MST, NOV; SSC 2, 33; WLC**
Doughty, Charles M(ontagu) 1843-1926
TCLC 27
See also CA 115; 178; DLB 19, 57, 174
Douglas, Ellen .... **CLC 73**
See also Haxton, Josephine Ayres; Williamson,
Ellen Douglas
Douglas, Gavin 1475(?)-1522 .... **LC 20**
See also DLB 132

Douglas, George
See Brown, George Douglas
Douglas, Keith (Castellain) 1920-1944**T C L C
40**
See also CA 160; DLB 27
Douglas, Leonard
See Bradbury, Ray (Douglas)
Douglas, Michael
See Crichton, (John) Michael
Douglas, (George) Norman 1868-1952**T C L C
68**
See also CA 119; 157; DLB 34, 195
Douglas, William
See Brown, George Douglas
Douglass, Frederick 1817(?)-1895**NCLC 7, 55;
BLC 1; DA; DAC; DAM MST, MULT;
WLC**
See also CDALB 1640-1865; DLB 1, 43, 50,
79; SATA 29
Dourado, (Waldomiro Freitas) Autran 1926-
CLC 23, 60
See also Autran Dourado, Waldomiro Freitas
See also CA 25-28R; 179; CANR 34, 81; DLB
145; HW 2
Dourado, Waldomiro Autran 1926-
See Dourado, (Waldomiro Freitas) Autran
See also CA 179
Dove, Rita (Frances) 1952-**CLC 50, 81; BLCS;
DAM MULT, POET; PC 6**
See also BW 2; CA 109; CAAS 19; CANR 27,
42, 68, 76; CDALBS; DLB 120; MTCW 1
Doveglion
See Villa, Jose Garcia
Dowell, Coleman 1925-1985 .... **CLC 60**
See also CA 25-28R; 117; CANR 10; DLB 130
Dowson, Ernest (Christopher) 1867-1900
TCLC 4
See also CA 105; 150; DLB 19, 135
Doyle, A. Conan
See Doyle, Arthur Conan
Doyle, Arthur Conan 1859-1930**TCLC 7; DA;
DAB; DAC; DAM MST, NOV; SSC 12;
WLC**
See also AAYA 14; CA 104; 122; CDBLB 1890-
1914; DLB 18, 70, 156, 178; MTCW 1, 2;
SATA 24
Doyle, Conan
See Doyle, Arthur Conan
Doyle, John
See Graves, Robert (von Ranke)
Doyle, Roddy 1958(?)- .... **CLC 81**
See also AAYA 14; CA 143; CANR 73; DLB
194
Doyle, Sir A. Conan
See Doyle, Arthur Conan
Doyle, Sir Arthur Conan
See Doyle, Arthur Conan
Dr. A
See Asimov, Isaac; Silverstein, Alvin
Drabble, Margaret 1939-**CLC 2, 3, 5, 8, 10, 22,
53; DAB; DAC; DAM MST, NOV, POP**
See also CA 13-16R; CANR 18, 35, 63; CDBLB
1960 to Present; DLB 14, 155; MTCW 1, 2;
SATA 48
Drapier, M. B.
See Swift, Jonathan
Drayham, James
See Mencken, H(enry) L(ouis)
Drayton, Michael 1563-1631 ...... **LC 8; DAM
POET**
See also DLB 121
Dreadstone, Carl
See Campbell, (John) Ramsey

See also DLB 176
Epsilon
See Betjeman, John
Epstein, Daniel Mark 1948- .... **CLC 7**
See also CA 49-52; CANR 2, 53
Epstein, Jacob 1956- .... **CLC 19**
See also CA 114
Epstein, Jean 1897-1953 .... **TCLC 92**
Epstein, Joseph 1937- .... **CLC 39**
See also CA 112; 119; CANR 50, 65
Epstein, Leslie 1938- .... **CLC 27**
See also CA 73-76; CAAS 12; CANR 23, 69
Equiano, Olaudah 1745(?)-1797 **LC 16; BLC
2; DAM MULT**
See also DLB 37, 50
ER .... **TCLC 33**
See also CA 160; DLB 85
Erasmus, Desiderius 1469(?)-1536 ...... **LC 16**
Erdman, Paul E(mil) 1932- .... **CLC 25**
See also AITN 1; CA 61-64; CANR 13, 43
Erdrich, Louise 1954-**CLC 39, 54, 120; DAM
MULT, NOV, POP**
See also AAYA 10; BEST 89:1; CA 114; CANR
41, 62; CDALBS; DLB 152, 175, 206;
MTCW 1; NNAL; SATA 94
Erenburg, Ilya (Grigoryevich)
See Ehrenburg, Ilya (Grigoryevich)
Erickson, Stephen Michael 1950-
See Erickson, Steve
See also CA 129
Erickson, Steve 1950- .... **CLC 64**
See also Erickson, Stephen Michael
See also CANR 60, 68
Ericson, Walter
See Fast, Howard (Melvin)
Eriksson, Buntel
See Bergman, (Ernst) Ingmar
Ernaux, Annie 1940- .... **CLC 88**
See also CA 147
Erskine, John 1879-1951 .... **TCLC 84**
See also CA 112; 159; DLB 9, 102
Eschenbach, Wolfram von
See Wolfram von Eschenbach
Eseki, Bruno
See Mphahlele, Ezekiel
Esenin, Sergei (Alexandrovich) 1895-1925
TCLC 4
See also CA 104
Eshleman, Clayton 1935- .... **CLC 7**
See also CA 33-36R; CAAS 6; DLB 5
Espriella, Don Manuel Alvarez
See Southey, Robert
Espriu, Salvador 1913-1985 .... **CLC 9**
See also CA 154; 115; DLB 134
Espronceda, Jose de 1808-1842 ..... **NCLC 39**
Esquivel, Laura 1951(?)-
See also AAYA 29; CA 143; CANR 68; HLCS
1; MTCW 1
Esse, James
See Stephens, James
Esterbrook, Tom
See Hubbard, L(afayette) Ron(ald)
Estleman, Loren D. 1952-**CLC 48; DAM NOV,
POP**
See also AAYA 27; CA 85-88; CANR 27, 74;
INT CANR-27; MTCW 1, 2
Euclid 306B.C.-283B.C. .... **CMLC 25**
Eugenides, Jeffrey 1960(?)- .... **CLC 81**
See also CA 144
Euripides c. 485B.C.-406B.C.**CMLC 23; DA;
DAB; DAC; DAM DRAM, MST; DC 4;
WLCS**
See also DLB 176

Evan, Evin
See Faust, Frederick (Schiller)
Evans, Caradoc 1878-1945 .... **TCLC 85**
Evans, Evan
See Faust, Frederick (Schiller)
Evans, Marian
See Eliot, George
Evans, Mary Ann
See Eliot, George
Evarts, Esther
See Benson, Sally
Everett, Percival L. 1956- .... **CLC 57**
See also BW 2; CA 129
Everson, R(onald) G(ilmour) 1903- . **CLC 27**
See also CA 17-20R; DLB 88
Everson, William (Oliver) 1912-1994 **CLC 1,
5, 14**
See also CA 9-12R; 145; CANR 20; DLB 212;
MTCW 1
Evtushenko, Evgenii Aleksandrovich
See Yevtushenko, Yevgeny (Alexandrovich)
Ewart, Gavin (Buchanan) 1916-1995**CLC 13,
46**
See also CA 89-92; 150; CANR 17, 46; DLB
40; MTCW 1
Ewers, Hanns Heinz 1871-1943 ..... **TCLC 12**
See also CA 109; 149
Ewing, Frederick R.
See Sturgeon, Theodore (Hamilton)
Exley, Frederick (Earl) 1929-1992 **CLC 6, 11**
See also AITN 2; CA 81-84; 138; DLB 143;
DLBY 81
Eynhardt, Guillermo
See Quiroga, Horacio (Sylvestre)
Ezekiel, Nissim 1924- .... **CLC 61**
See also CA 61-64
Ezekiel, Tish O'Dowd 1943- .... **CLC 34**
See also CA 129
Fadeyev, A.
See Bulgya, Alexander Alexandrovich
Fadeyev, Alexander .... **TCLC 53**
See also Bulgya, Alexander Alexandrovich
Fagen, Donald 1948- .... **CLC 26**
Fainzilberg, Ilya Arnoldovich 1897-1937
See Ilf, Ilya
See also CA 120; 165
Fair, Ronald L. 1932- .... **CLC 18**
See also BW 1; CA 69-72; CANR 25; DLB 33
Fairbairn, Roger
See Carr, John Dickson
Fairbairns, Zoe (Ann) 1948- .... **CLC 32**
See also CA 103; CANR 21
Falco, Gian
See Papini, Giovanni
Falconer, James
See Kirkup, James
Falconer, Kenneth
See Kornbluth, C(yril) M.
Falkland, Samuel
See Heijermans, Herman
Fallaci, Oriana 1930- .... **CLC 11, 110**
See also CA 77-80; CANR 15, 58; MTCW 1
Faludy, George 1913- .... **CLC 42**
See also CA 21-24R
Faludy, Gyoergy
See Faludy, George
Fanon, Frantz 1925-1961 ... **CLC 74; BLC 2;
DAM MULT**
See also BW 1; CA 116; 89-92
Fanshawe, Ann 1625-1680 .... **LC 11**
Fante, John (Thomas) 1911-1983 ..... **CLC 60**
See also CA 69-72; 109; CANR 23; DLB 130;
DLBY 83

Farah, Nuruddin 1945-**CLC 53; BLC 2; DAM
MULT**
See also BW 2, 3; CA 106; CANR 81; DLB
125
Fargue, Leon-Paul 1876(?)-1947 ... **TCLC 11**
See also CA 109
Farigoule, Louis
See Romains, Jules
Farina, Richard 1936(?)-1966 .... **CLC 9**
See also CA 81-84; 25-28R
Farley, Walter (Lorimer) 1915-1989 **CLC 17**
See also CA 17-20R; CANR 8, 29; DLB 22;
JRDA; MAICYA; SATA 2, 43
Farmer, Philip Jose 1918- .... **CLC 1, 19**
See also AAYA 28; CA 1-4R; CANR 4, 35; DLB
8; MTCW 1; SATA 93
Farquhar, George 1677-1707 ... **LC 21; DAM
DRAM**
See also DLB 84
Farrell, J(ames) G(ordon) 1935-1979 **CLC 6**
See also CA 73-76; 89-92; CANR 36; DLB 14;
MTCW 1
Farrell, James T(homas) 1904-1979**CLC 1, 4,
8, 11, 66; SSC 28**
See also CA 5-8R; 89-92; CANR 9, 61; DLB 4,
9, 86; DLBD 2; MTCW 1, 2
Farren, Richard J.
See Betjeman, John
Farren, Richard M.
See Betjeman, John
Fassbinder, Rainer Werner 1946-1982**CLC 20**
See also CA 93-96; 106; CANR 31
Fast, Howard (Melvin) 1914- **CLC 23; DAM
NOV**
See also AAYA 16; CA 1-4R; CAAS 18; CANR
1, 33, 54, 75; DLB 9; INT CANR-33; MTCW
1; SATA 7; SATA-Essay 107
Faulcon, Robert
See Holdstock, Robert P.
Faulkner, William (Cuthbert) 1897-1962**CLC
1, 3, 6, 8, 9, 11, 14, 18, 28, 52, 68; DA; DAB;
DAC; DAM MST, NOV; SSC 1, 35; WLC**
See also AAYA 7; CA 81-84; CANR 33;
CDALB 1929-1941; DLB 9, 11, 44, 102;
DLBD 2; DLBY 86, 97; MTCW 1, 2
Fauset, Jessie Redmon 1884(?)-1961**CLC 19,
54; BLC 2; DAM MULT**
See also BW 1; CA 109; DLB 51
Faust, Frederick (Schiller) 1892-1944(?)
TCLC 49; DAM POP
See also CA 108; 152
Faust, Irvin 1924- .... **CLC 8**
See also CA 33-36R; CANR 28, 67; DLB 2,
28; DLBY 80
Fawkes, Guy
See Benchley, Robert (Charles)
Fearing, Kenneth (Flexner) 1902-1961 . **C L C
51**
See also CA 93-96; CANR 59; DLB 9
Fecamps, Elise
See Creasey, John
Federman, Raymond 1928- .... **CLC 6, 47**
See also CA 17-20R; CAAS 8; CANR 10, 43;
DLBY 80
Federspiel, J(uerg) F. 1931- .... **CLC 42**
See also CA 146
Feiffer, Jules (Ralph) 1929- ..... **CLC 2, 8, 64;
DAM DRAM**
See also AAYA 3; CA 17-20R; CANR 30, 59;
DLB 7, 44; INT CANR-30; MTCW 1; SATA
8, 61
Feige, Hermann Albert Otto Maximilian
See Traven, B.

60
See also CA 77-80; 164; CANR 44; DLBY 82, 98

Genet, Jean 1910-1986CLC 1, 2, 5, 10, 14, 44, 46; DAM DRAM
See also CA 13-16R; CANR 18; DLB 72; DLBY 86; MTCW 1, 2

Gent, Peter 1942- .... CLC 29
See also AITN 1; CA 89-92; DLBY 82

Gentile, Giovanni 1875-1944 .... TCLC 96
See also CA 119

Gentlewoman in New England, A
See Bradstreet, Anne

Gentlewoman in Those Parts, A
See Bradstreet, Anne

George, Jean Craighead 1919- .... CLC 35
See also AAYA 8; CA 5-8R; CANR 25; CLR 1; DLB 52; JRDA; MAICYA; SATA 2, 68

George, Stefan (Anton) 1868-1933TCLC 2, 14
See also CA 104

Georges, Georges Martin
See Simenon, Georges (Jacques Christian)

Gerhardi, William Alexander
See Gerhardie, William Alexander

Gerhardie, William Alexander 1895-1977 CLC 5
See also CA 25-28R; 73-76; CANR 18; DLB 36

Gerstler, Amy 1956- .... CLC 70
See also CA 146

Gertler, T. .... CLC 34
See also CA 116; 121; INT 121

Ghalib ....NCLC 39, 78
See also Ghalib, Hsadullah Khan

Ghalib, Hsadullah Khan 1797-1869
See Ghalib
See also DAM POET

Ghelderode, Michel de 1898-1962CLC 6, 11; DAM DRAM
See also CA 85-88; CANR 40, 77

Ghiselin, Brewster 1903- .... CLC 23
See also CA 13-16R; CAAS 10; CANR 13

Ghose, Aurabinda 1872-1950 .... TCLC 63
See also CA 163

Ghose, Zulfikar 1935- .... CLC 42
See also CA 65-68; CANR 67

Ghosh, Amitav 1956- .... CLC 44
See also CA 147; CANR 80

Giacosa, Giuseppe 1847-1906 .... TCLC 7
See also CA 104

Gibb, Lee
See Waterhouse, Keith (Spencer)

Gibbon, Lewis Grassic .... TCLC 4
See also Mitchell, James Leslie

Gibbons, Kaye 1960-CLC 50, 88; DAM POP
See also CA 151; CANR 75; MTCW 1

Gibran, Kahlil 1883-1931 . TCLC 1, 9; DAM POET, POP; PC 9
See also CA 104; 150; MTCW 2

Gibran, Khalil
See Gibran, Kahlil

Gibson, William 1914- .. CLC 23; DA; DAB; DAC; DAM DRAM, MST
See also CA 9-12R; CANR 9, 42, 75; DLB 7; MTCW 1; SATA 66

Gibson, William (Ford) 1948- ... CLC 39, 63; DAM POP
See also AAYA 12; CA 126; 133; CANR 52; MTCW 1

Gide, Andre (Paul Guillaume) 1869-1951 TCLC 5, 12, 36; DA; DAB; DAC; DAM MST, NOV; SSC 13; WLC
See also CA 104; 124; DLB 65; MTCW 1, 2

Gifford, Barry (Colby) 1946- .... CLC 34
See also CA 65-68; CANR 9, 30, 40

Gilbert, Frank
See De Voto, Bernard (Augustine)

Gilbert, W(illiam) S(chwenck) 1836-1911 TCLC 3; DAM DRAM, POET
See also CA 104; 173; SATA 36

Gilbreth, Frank B., Jr. 1911- .... CLC 17
See also CA 9-12R; SATA 2

Gilchrist, Ellen 1935-CLC 34, 48; DAM POP; SSC 14
See also CA 113; 116; CANR 41, 61; DLB 130; MTCW 1, 2

Giles, Molly 1942- .... CLC 39
See also CA 126

Gill, Eric 1882-1940 .... TCLC 85

Gill, Patrick
See Creasey, John

Gilliam, Terry (Vance) 1940- .... CLC 21
See also Monty Python
See also AAYA 19; CA 108; 113; CANR 35; INT 113

Gillian, Jerry
See Gilliam, Terry (Vance)

Gilliatt, Penelope (Ann Douglass) 1932-1993 CLC 2, 10, 13, 53
See also AITN 2; CA 13-16R; 141; CANR 49; DLB 14

Gilman, Charlotte (Anna) Perkins (Stetson) 1860-1935 .... TCLC 9, 37; SSC 13
See also CA 106; 150; MTCW 1

Gilmour, David 1949- .... CLC 35
See also CA 138, 147

Gilpin, William 1724-1804 .... NCLC 30

Gilray, J. D.
See Mencken, H(enry) L(ouis)

Gilroy, Frank D(aniel) 1925- .... CLC 2
See also CA 81-84; CANR 32, 64; DLB 7

Gilstrap, John 1957(?)- .... CLC 99
See also CA 160

Ginsberg, Allen 1926-1997CLC 1, 2, 3, 4, 6, 13, 36, 69, 109; DA; DAB; DAC; DAM MST, POET; PC 4; WLC
See also AITN 1; CA 1-4R; 157; CANR 2, 41, 63; CDALB 1941-1968; DLB 5, 16, 169; MTCW 1, 2

Ginzburg, Natalia 1916-1991CLC 5, 11, 54, 70
See also CA 85-88; 135; CANR 33; DLB 177; MTCW 1, 2

Giono, Jean 1895-1970 .... CLC 4, 11
See also CA 45-48; 29-32R; CANR 2, 35; DLB 72; MTCW 1

Giovanni, Nikki 1943- CLC 2, 4, 19, 64, 117; BLC 2; DA; DAB; DAC; DAM MST, MULT, POET; PC 19; WLCS
See also AAYA 22; AITN 1; BW 2, 3; CA 29-32R; CAAS 6; CANR 18, 41, 60; CDALBS; CLR 6; DLB 5, 41; INT CANR-18; MAICYA; MTCW 1, 2; SATA 24, 107

Giovene, Andrea 1904- .... CLC 7
See also CA 85-88

Gippius, Zinaida (Nikolayevna) 1869-1945
See Hippius, Zinaida
See also CA 106

Giraudoux, (Hippolyte) Jean 1882-1944 TCLC 2, 7; DAM DRAM
See also CA 104; DLB 65

Gironella, Jose Maria 1917- .... CLC 11
See also CA 101

Gissing, George (Robert) 1857-1903TCLC 3, 24, 47
See also CA 105; 167; DLB 18, 135, 184

Giurlani, Aldo

See Palazzeschi, Aldo

Gladkov, Fyodor (Vasilyevich) 1883-1958 TCLC 27
See also CA 170

Glanville, Brian (Lester) 1931- .... CLC 6
See also CA 5-8R; CAAS 9; CANR 3, 70; DLB 15, 139; SATA 42

Glasgow, Ellen (Anderson Gholson) 1873-1945 TCLC 2, 7; SSC 34
See also CA 104; 164; DLB 9, 12; MTCW 2

Glaspell, Susan 1882(?)-1948TCLC 55; DC 10
See also CA 110; 154; DLB 7, 9, 78; YABC 2

Glassco, John 1909-1981 .... CLC 9
See also CA 13-16R; 102; CANR 15; DLB 68

Glasscock, Amnesia
See Steinbeck, John (Ernst)

Glasser, Ronald J. 1940(?)- .... CLC 37

Glassman, Joyce
See Johnson, Joyce

Glendinning, Victoria 1937- .... CLC 50
See also CA 120; 127; CANR 59; DLB 155

Glissant, Edouard 1928- . CLC 10, 68; DAM MULT
See also CA 153

Gloag, Julian 1930- .... CLC 40
See also AITN 1; CA 65-68; CANR 10, 70

Glowacki, Aleksander
See Prus, Boleslaw

Gluck, Louise (Elisabeth) 1943-CLC 7, 22, 44, 81; DAM POET; PC 16
See also CA 33-36R; CANR 40, 69; DLB 5; MTCW 2

Glyn, Elinor 1864-1943 .... TCLC 72
See also DLB 153

Gobineau, Joseph Arthur (Comte) de 1816-1882 .... NCLC 17
See also DLB 123

Godard, Jean-Luc 1930- .... CLC 20
See also CA 93-96

Godden, (Margaret) Rumer 1907-1998 C L C 53
See also AAYA 6; CA 5-8R; 172; CANR 4, 27, 36, 55, 80; CLR 20; DLB 161; MAICYA; SAAS 12; SATA 3, 36; SATA-Obit 109

Godoy Alcayaga, Lucila 1889-1957
See Mistral, Gabriela
See also BW 2; CA 104; 131; CANR 81; DAM MULT; HW 1, 2; MTCW 1, 2

Godwin, Gail (Kathleen) 1937- CLC 5, 8, 22, 31, 69; DAM POP
See also CA 29-32R; CANR 15, 43, 69; DLB 6; INT CANR-15; MTCW 1, 2

Godwin, William 1756-1836 .... NCLC 14
See also CDBLB 1789-1832; DLB 39, 104, 142, 158, 163

Goebbels, Josef
See Goebbels, (Paul) Joseph

Goebbels, (Paul) Joseph 1897-1945 TCLC 68
See also CA 115; 148

Goebbels, Joseph Paul
See Goebbels, (Paul) Joseph

Goethe, Johann Wolfgang von 1749-1832 NCLC 4, 22, 34; DA; DAB; DAC; DAM DRAM, MST, POET; PC 5; WLC
See also DLB 94

Gogarty, Oliver St. John 1878-1957TCLC 15
See also CA 109; 150; DLB 15, 19

Gogol, Nikolai (Vasilyevich) 1809-1852NCLC 5, 15, 31; DA; DAB; DAC; DAM DRAM, MST; DC 1; SSC 4, 29; WLC
See also DLB 198

Goines, Donald 1937(?)-1974CLC 80; BLC 2; DAM MULT, POP

See also BW 1; CA 33-36R; CANR 24; DLB 41

Harper, Mrs. F. E. W.
See Harper, Frances Ellen Watkins

Harris, Christie (Lucy) Irwin 1907- **CLC 12**
See also CA 5-8R; CANR 6; CLR 47; DLB 88; JRDA; MAICYA; SAAS 10; SATA 6, 74

Harris, Frank 1856-1931 .... **TCLC 24**
See also CA 109; 150; CANR 80; DLB 156, 197

Harris, George Washington 1814-1869 **NCLC 23**
See also DLB 3, 11

Harris, Joel Chandler 1848-1908 ... **TCLC 2; SSC 19**
See also CA 104; 137; CANR 80; CLR 49; DLB 11, 23, 42, 78, 91; MAICYA; SATA 100; YABC 1

Harris, John (Wyndham Parkes Lucas) Beynon 1903-1969
See Wyndham, John
See also CA 102; 89-92

Harris, MacDonald .... **CLC 9**
See also Heiney, Donald (William)

Harris, Mark 1922- .... **CLC 19**
See also CA 5-8R; CAAS 3; CANR 2, 55; DLB 2; DLBY 80

Harris, (Theodore) Wilson 1921- ..... **CLC 25**
See also BW 2, 3; CA 65-68; CAAS 16; CANR 11, 27, 69; DLB 117; MTCW 1

Harrison, Elizabeth Cavanna 1909-
See Cavanna, Betty
See also CA 9-12R; CANR 6, 27

Harrison, Harry (Max) 1925- .... **CLC 42**
See also CA 1-4R; CANR 5, 21; DLB 8; SATA 4

Harrison, James (Thomas) 1937- **CLC 6, 14, 33, 66; SSC 19**
See also CA 13-16R; CANR 8, 51, 79; DLBY 82; INT CANR-8

Harrison, Jim
See Harrison, James (Thomas)

Harrison, Kathryn 1961- .... **CLC 70**
See also CA 144; CANR 68

Harrison, Tony 1937- .... **CLC 43**
See also CA 65-68; CANR 44; DLB 40; MTCW 1

Harriss, Will(ard Irvin) 1922- .... **CLC 34**
See also CA 111

Harson, Sley
See Ellison, Harlan (Jay)

Hart, Ellis
See Ellison, Harlan (Jay)

Hart, Josephine 1942(?)- **CLC 70; DAM POP**
See also CA 138; CANR 70

Hart, Moss 1904-1961 **CLC 66; DAM DRAM**
See also CA 109; 89-92; DLB 7

Harte, (Francis) Bret(t) 1836(?)-1902 **TCLC 1, 25; DA; DAC; DAM MST; SSC 8; WLC**
See also CA 104; 140; CANR 80; CDALB 1865-1917; DLB 12, 64, 74, 79, 186; SATA 26

Hartley, L(eslie) P(oles) 1895-1972 **CLC 2, 22**
See also CA 45-48; 37-40R; CANR 33; DLB 15, 139; MTCW 1, 2

Hartman, Geoffrey H. 1929- .... **CLC 27**
See also CA 117; 125; CANR 79; DLB 67

Hartmann, Sadakichi 1867-1944 ... **TCLC 73**
See also CA 157; DLB 54

Hartmann von Aue c. 1160-c. 1205 **CMLC 15**
See also DLB 138

Hartmann von Aue 1170-1210 ...... **CMLC 15**

Haruf, Kent 1943- .... **CLC 34**

See also CA 149

Harwood, Ronald 1934- .... **CLC 32; DAM DRAM, MST**
See also CA 1-4R; CANR 4, 55; DLB 13

Hasegawa Tatsunosuke
See Futabatei, Shimei

Hasek, Jaroslav (Matej Frantisek) 1883-1923 **TCLC 4**
See also CA 104; 129; MTCW 1, 2

Hass, Robert 1941- ... **CLC 18, 39, 99; PC 16**
See also CA 111; CANR 30, 50, 71; DLB 105, 206; SATA 94

Hastings, Hudson
See Kuttner, Henry

Hastings, Selina .... **CLC 44**

Hathorne, John 1641-1717 .... **LC 38**

Hatteras, Amelia
See Mencken, H(enry) L(ouis)

Hatteras, Owen .... **TCLC 18**
See also Mencken, H(enry) L(ouis); Nathan, George Jean

Hauptmann, Gerhart (Johann Robert) 1862-1946 .... **TCLC 4; DAM DRAM**
See also CA 104; 153; DLB 66, 118

Havel, Vaclav 1936- **CLC 25, 58, 65, 123; DAM DRAM; DC 6**
See also CA 104; CANR 36, 63; MTCW 1, 2

Haviaras, Stratis .... **CLC 33**
See also Chaviaras, Strates

Hawes, Stephen 1475(?)-1523(?) .... **LC 17**
See also DLB 132

Hawkes, John (Clendennin Burne, Jr.) 1925-1998 .. **CLC 1, 2, 3, 4, 7, 9, 14, 15, 27, 49**
See also CA 1-4R; 167; CANR 2, 47, 64; DLB 2, 7; DLBY 80, 98; MTCW 1, 2

Hawking, S. W.
See Hawking, Stephen W(illiam)

Hawking, Stephen W(illiam) 1942- **CLC 63, 105**
See also AAYA 13; BEST 89:1; CA 126; 129; CANR 48; MTCW 2

Hawkins, Anthony Hope
See Hope, Anthony

Hawthorne, Julian 1846-1934 .... **TCLC 25**
See also CA 165

Hawthorne, Nathaniel 1804-1864 **NCLC 39; DA; DAB; DAC; DAM MST, NOV; SSC 3, 29; WLC**
See also AAYA 18; CDALB 1640-1865; DLB 1, 74; YABC 2

Haxton, Josephine Ayres 1921-
See Douglas, Ellen
See also CA 115; CANR 41

Hayaseca y Eizaguirre, Jorge
See Echegaray (y Eizaguirre), Jose (Maria Waldo)

Hayashi, Fumiko 1904-1951 .... **TCLC 27**
See also CA 161; DLB 180

Haycraft, Anna
See Ellis, Alice Thomas
See also CA 122; MTCW 2

Hayden, Robert E(arl) 1913-1980 **CLC 5, 9, 14, 37; BLC 2; DA; DAC; DAM MST, MULT, POET; PC 6**
See also BW 1, 3; CA 69-72; 97-100; CABS 2; CANR 24, 75, 82; CDALB 1941-1968; DLB 5, 76; MTCW 1, 2; SATA 19; SATA-Obit 26

Hayford, J(oseph) E(phraim) Casely
See Casely-Hayford, J(oseph) E(phraim)

Hayman, Ronald 1932- .... **CLC 44**
See also CA 25-28R; CANR 18, 50; DLB 155

Haywood, Eliza (Fowler) 1693(?)-1756 **LC 1, 44**

See also DLB 39

Hazlitt, William 1778-1830 .... **NCLC 29**
See also DLB 110, 158

Hazzard, Shirley 1931- .... **CLC 18**
See also CA 9-12R; CANR 4, 70; DLBY 82; MTCW 1

Head, Bessie 1937-1986 **CLC 25, 67; BLC 2; DAM MULT**
See also BW 2, 3; CA 29-32R; 119; CANR 25, 82; DLB 117; MTCW 1, 2

Headon, (Nicky) Topper 1956(?)- ..... **CLC 30**

Heaney, Seamus (Justin) 1939- **CLC 5, 7, 14, 25, 37, 74, 91; DAB; DAM POET; PC 18; WLCS**
See also CA 85-88; CANR 25, 48, 75; CDBLB 1960 to Present; DLB 40; DLBY 95; MTCW 1, 2

Hearn, (Patricio) Lafcadio (Tessima Carlos) 1850-1904 .... **TCLC 9**
See also CA 105; 166; DLB 12, 78, 189

Hearne, Vicki 1946- .... **CLC 56**
See also CA 139

Hearon, Shelby 1931- .... **CLC 63**
See also AITN 2; CA 25-28R; CANR 18, 48

Heat-Moon, William Least .... **CLC 29**
See also Trogdon, William (Lewis)
See also AAYA 9

Hebbel, Friedrich 1813-1863 **NCLC 43; DAM DRAM**
See also DLB 129

Hebert, Anne 1916- **CLC 4, 13, 29; DAC; DAM MST, POET**
See also CA 85-88; CANR 69; DLB 68; MTCW 1, 2

Hecht, Anthony (Evan) 1923- **CLC 8, 13, 19; DAM POET**
See also CA 9-12R; CANR 6; DLB 5, 169

Hecht, Ben 1894-1964 .... **CLC 8**
See also CA 85-88; DLB 7, 9, 25, 26, 28, 86

Hedayat, Sadeq 1903-1951 .... **TCLC 21**
See also CA 120

Hegel, Georg Wilhelm Friedrich 1770-1831 **NCLC 46**
See also DLB 90

Heidegger, Martin 1889-1976 .... **CLC 24**
See also CA 81-84; 65-68; CANR 34; MTCW 1, 2

Heidenstam, (Carl Gustaf) Verner von 1859-1940 .... **TCLC 5**
See also CA 104

Heifner, Jack 1946- .... **CLC 11**
See also CA 105; CANR 47

Heijermans, Herman 1864-1924 .... **TCLC 24**
See also CA 123

Heilbrun, Carolyn G(old) 1926- .... **CLC 25**
See also CA 45-48; CANR 1, 28, 58

Heine, Heinrich 1797-1856 **NCLC 4, 54; PC 25**
See also DLB 90

Heinemann, Larry (Curtiss) 1944- ... **CLC 50**
See also CA 110; CAAS 21; CANR 31, 81; DLBD 9; INT CANR-31

Heiney, Donald (William) 1921-1993
See Harris, MacDonald
See also CA 1-4R; 142; CANR 3, 58

Heinlein, Robert A(nson) 1907-1988 **CLC 1, 3, 8, 14, 26, 55; DAM POP**
See also AAYA 17; CA 1-4R; 125; CANR 1, 20, 53; DLB 8; JRDA; MAICYA; MTCW 1, 2; SATA 9, 69; SATA-Obit 56

Helforth, John
See Doolittle, Hilda

Hellenhofferu, Vojtech Kapristian z
See Hasek, Jaroslav (Matej Frantisek)

Ilf, Ilya .... **TCLC 21**
See also Fainzilberg, Ilya Arnoldovich

Illyes, Gyula 1902-1983 .... **PC 16**
See also CA 114; 109

Immermann, Karl (Lebrecht) 1796-1840
NCLC 4, 49
See also DLB 133

Ince, Thomas H. 1882-1924 .... **TCLC 89**

Inchbald, Elizabeth 1753-1821 ...... **NCLC 62**
See also DLB 39, 89

Inclan, Ramon (Maria) del Valle
See Valle-Inclan, Ramon (Maria) del

Infante, G(uillermo) Cabrera
See Cabrera Infante, G(uillermo)

Ingalls, Rachel (Holmes) 1940- .... **CLC 42**
See also CA 123; 127

Ingamells, Reginald Charles
See Ingamells, Rex

Ingamells, Rex 1913-1955 .... **TCLC 35**
See also CA 167

Inge, William (Motter) 1913-1973 . **CLC 1, 8, 19; DAM DRAM**
See also CA 9-12R; CDALB 1941-1968; DLB 7; MTCW 1, 2

Ingelow, Jean 1820-1897 .... **NCLC 39**
See also DLB 35, 163; SATA 33

Ingram, Willis J.
See Harris, Mark

Innaurato, Albert (F.) 1948(?)- .. **CLC 21, 60**
See also CA 115; 122; CANR 78; INT 122

Innes, Michael
See Stewart, J(ohn) I(nnes) M(ackintosh)

Innis, Harold Adams 1894-1952 .... **TCLC 77**
See also DLB 88

Ionesco, Eugene 1909-1994CLC 1, 4, 6, 9, 11, 15, 41, 86; DA; DAB; DAC; DAM DRAM, MST; WLC
See also CA 9-12R; 144; CANR 55; MTCW 1, 2; SATA 7; SATA-Obit 79

Iqbal, Muhammad 1873-1938 .... **TCLC 28**

Ireland, Patrick
See O'Doherty, Brian

Iron, Ralph
See Schreiner, Olive (Emilie Albertina)

Irving, John (Winslow) 1942-CLC 13, 23, 38, 112; DAM NOV, POP
See also AAYA 8; BEST 89:3; CA 25-28R; CANR 28, 73; DLB 6; DLBY 82; MTCW 1, 2

Irving, Washington 1783-1859 . **NCLC 2, 19; DA; DAB; DAC; DAM MST; SSC 2; WLC**
See also CDALB 1640-1865; DLB 3, 11, 30, 59, 73, 74, 186; YABC 2

Irwin, P. K.
See Page, P(atricia) K(athleen)

Isaacs, Jorge Ricardo 1837-1895 ... **NCLC 70**

Isaacs, Susan 1943- .... **CLC 32; DAM POP**
See also BEST 89:1; CA 89-92; CANR 20, 41, 65; INT CANR-20; MTCW 1, 2

Isherwood, Christopher (William Bradshaw) 1904-1986 .... **CLC 1, 9, 11, 14, 44; DAM DRAM, NOV**
See also CA 13-16R; 117; CANR 35; DLB 15, 195; DLBY 86; MTCW 1, 2

Ishiguro, Kazuo 1954- ..CLC 27, 56, 59, 110; DAM NOV
See also BEST 90:2; CA 120; CANR 49; DLB 194; MTCW 1, 2

Ishikawa, Hakuhin
See Ishikawa, Takuboku

Ishikawa, Takuboku 1886(?)-1912 **TCLC 15; DAM POET; PC 10**
See also CA 113; 153

Iskander, Fazil 1929- .... **CLC 47**
See also CA 102

Isler, Alan (David) 1934- .... **CLC 91**
See also CA 156

Ivan IV 1530-1584 .... **LC 17**

Ivanov, Vyacheslav Ivanovich 1866-1949
TCLC 33
See also CA 122

Ivask, Ivar Vidrik 1927-1992 .... **CLC 14**
See also CA 37-40R; 139; CANR 24

Ives, Morgan
See Bradley, Marion Zimmer

Izumi Shikibu c. 973-c. 1034 .... **CMLC 33**

J. R. S.
See Gogarty, Oliver St. John

Jabran, Kahlil
See Gibran, Kahlil

Jabran, Khalil
See Gibran, Kahlil

Jackson, Daniel
See Wingrove, David (John)

Jackson, Jesse 1908-1983 .... **CLC 12**
See also BW 1; CA 25-28R; 109; CANR 27; CLR 28; MAICYA; SATA 2, 29; SATA-Obit 48

Jackson, Laura (Riding) 1901-1991
See Riding, Laura
See also CA 65-68; 135; CANR 28; DLB 48

Jackson, Sam
See Trumbo, Dalton

Jackson, Sara
See Wingrove, David (John)

Jackson, Shirley 1919-1965 . **CLC 11, 60, 87; DA; DAC; DAM MST; SSC 9; WLC**
See also AAYA 9; CA 1-4R; 25-28R; CANR 4, 52; CDALB 1941-1968; DLB 6; MTCW 2; SATA 2

Jacob, (Cyprien-)Max 1876-1944 .... **TCLC 6**
See also CA 104

Jacobs, Harriet A(nn) 1813(?)-1897NCLC 67

Jacobs, Jim 1942- .... **CLC 12**
See also CA 97-100; INT 97-100

Jacobs, W(illiam) W(ymark) 1863-1943
TCLC 22
See also CA 121; 167; DLB 135

Jacobsen, Jens Peter 1847-1885 .... **NCLC 34**

Jacobsen, Josephine 1908- .... **CLC 48, 102**
See also CA 33-36R; CAAS 18; CANR 23, 48

Jacobson, Dan 1929- .... **CLC 4, 14**
See also CA 1-4R; CANR 2, 25, 66; DLB 14, 207; MTCW 1

Jacqueline
See Carpentier (y Valmont), Alejo

Jagger, Mick 1944- .... **CLC 17**

Jahiz, al- c. 780-c. 869 .... **CMLC 25**

Jakes, John (William) 1932- ..CLC 29; DAM NOV, POP
See also BEST 89:4; CA 57-60; CANR 10, 43, 66; DLBY 83; INT CANR-10;MTCW 1, 2; SATA 62

James, Andrew
See Kirkup, James

James, C(yril) L(ionel) R(obert) 1901-1989
CLC 33; BLCS
See also BW 2; CA 117; 125; 128; CANR 62; DLB 125; MTCW 1

James, Daniel (Lewis) 1911-1988
See Santiago, Danny
See also CA 174; 125

James, Dynely
See Mayne, William (James Carter)

James, Henry Sr. 1811-1882 .... **NCLC 53**

James, Henry 1843-1916 **TCLC 2, 11, 24, 40, 47, 64; DA; DAB; DAC; DAM MST, NOV; SSC 8, 32; WLC**
See also CA 104; 132; CDALB 1865-1917; DLB 12, 71, 74, 189; DLBD 13; MTCW 1, 2

James, M. R.
See James, Montague (Rhodes)
See also DLB 156

James, Montague (Rhodes) 1862-1936T C L C 6; SSC 16
See also CA 104; DLB 201

James, P. D. 1920- .... **CLC 18, 46, 122**
See also White, Phyllis Dorothy James
See also BEST 90:2; CDBLB 1960 to Present; DLB 87; DLBD 17

James, Philip
See Moorcock, Michael (John)

James, William 1842-1910 .... **TCLC 15, 32**
See also CA 109

James I 1394-1437 .... **LC 20**

Jameson, Anna 1794-1860 .... **NCLC 43**
See also DLB 99, 166

Jami, Nur al-Din 'Abd al-Rahman 1414-1492
LC 9

Jammes, Francis 1868-1938 .... **TCLC 75**

Jandl, Ernst 1925- .... **CLC 34**

Janowitz, Tama 1957- .. **CLC 43; DAM POP**
See also CA 106; CANR 52

Japrisot, Sebastien 1931- .... **CLC 90**

Jarrell, Randall 1914-1965CLC 1, 2, 6, 9, 13, 49; DAM POET
See also CA 5-8R; 25-28R; CABS 2; CANR 6, 34; CDALB 1941-1968; CLR 6; DLB 48, 52; MAICYA; MTCW 1, 2; SATA 7

Jarry, Alfred 1873-1907 .. **TCLC 2, 14; DAM DRAM; SSC 20**
See also CA 104; 153; DLB 192

Jarvis, E. K.
See Bloch, Robert (Albert)

Jeake, Samuel, Jr.
See Aiken, Conrad (Potter)

Jean Paul 1763-1825 .... **NCLC 7**

Jefferies, (John) Richard 1848-1887NCLC 47
See also DLB 98, 141; SATA 16

Jeffers, (John) Robinson 1887-1962CLC 2, 3, 11, 15, 54; DA; DAC; DAM MST, POET; PC 17; WLC
See also CA 85-88; CANR 35; CDALB 1917-1929; DLB 45, 212; MTCW 1, 2

Jefferson, Janet
See Mencken, H(enry) L(ouis)

Jefferson, Thomas 1743-1826 .... **NCLC 11**
See also CDALB 1640-1865; DLB 31

Jeffrey, Francis 1773-1850 .... **NCLC 33**
See also DLB 107

Jelakowitch, Ivan
See Heijermans, Herman

Jellicoe, (Patricia) Ann 1927- .... **CLC 27**
See also CA 85-88; DLB 13

Jen, Gish .... **CLC 70**
See also Jen, Lillian

Jen, Lillian 1956(?)-
See Jen, Gish
See also CA 135

Jenkins, (John) Robin 1912- .... **CLC 52**
See also CA 1-4R; CANR 1; DLB 14

Jennings, Elizabeth (Joan) 1926- .CLC 5, 14
See also CA 61-64; CAAS 5; CANR 8, 39, 66; DLB 27; MTCW 1; SATA 66

Jennings, Waylon 1937- .... **CLC 21**

Jensen, Johannes V. 1873-1950 ...... **TCLC 41**
See also CA 170

Lampman, Archibald 1861-1899 ... **NCLC 25**
See also DLB 92

Lancaster, Bruce 1896-1963 .... **CLC 36**
See also CA 9-10; CANR 70; CAP 1; SATA 9

Lanchester, John .... **CLC 99**

Landau, Mark Alexandrovich
See Aldanov, Mark (Alexandrovich)

Landau-Aldanov, Mark Alexandrovich
See Aldanov, Mark (Alexandrovich)

Landis, Jerry
See Simon, Paul (Frederick)

Landis, John 1950- .... **CLC 26**
See also CA 112; 122

Landolfi, Tommaso 1908-1979 .... **CLC 11, 49**
See also CA 127; 117; DLB 177

Landon, Letitia Elizabeth 1802-1838 **NCLC 15**
See also DLB 96

Landor, Walter Savage 1775-1864 **NCLC 14**
See also DLB 93, 107

Landwirth, Heinz 1927-
See Lind, Jakov
See also CA 9-12R; CANR 7

Lane, Patrick 1939- ... **CLC 25; DAM POET**
See also CA 97-100; CANR 54; DLB 53; INT 97-100

Lang, Andrew 1844-1912 .... **TCLC 16**
See also CA 114; 137; DLB 98, 141, 184; MAICYA; SATA 16

Lang, Fritz 1890-1976 .... **CLC 20, 103**
See also CA 77-80; 69-72; CANR 30

Lange, John
See Crichton, (John) Michael

Langer, Elinor 1939- .... **CLC 34**
See also CA 121

Langland, William 1330(?)-1400(?) ... **LC 19; DA; DAB; DAC; DAM MST, POET**
See also DLB 146

Langstaff, Launcelot
See Irving, Washington

Lanier, Sidney 1842-1881 ..... **NCLC 6; DAM POET**
See also DLB 64; DLBD 13; MAICYA; SATA 18

Lanyer, Aemilia 1569-1645 .... **LC 10, 30**
See also DLB 121

Lao-Tzu
See Lao Tzu

Lao Tzu fl. 6th cent. B.C.- .... **CMLC 7**

Lapine, James (Elliot) 1949- .... **CLC 39**
See also CA 123; 130; CANR 54; INT 130

Larbaud, Valery (Nicolas) 1881-1957 **TCLC 9**
See also CA 106; 152

Lardner, Ring
See Lardner, Ring(gold) W(ilmer)

Lardner, Ring W., Jr.
See Lardner, Ring(gold) W(ilmer)

Lardner, Ring(gold) W(ilmer) 1885-1933 **TCLC 2, 14; SSC 32**
See also CA 104; 131; CDALB 1917-1929; DLB 11, 25, 86; DLBD 16; MTCW 1, 2

Laredo, Betty
See Codrescu, Andrei

Larkin, Maia
See Wojciechowska, Maia (Teresa)

Larkin, Philip (Arthur) 1922-1985 **CLC 3, 5, 8, 9, 13, 18, 33, 39, 64; DAB; DAM MST, POET; PC 21**
See also CA 5-8R; 117; CANR 24, 62; CDBLB 1960 to Present; DLB 27; MTCW 1, 2

Larra (y Sanchez de Castro), Mariano Jose de 1809-1837 .... **NCLC 17**

Larsen, Eric 1941- .... **CLC 55**

See also CA 132

Larsen, Nella 1891-1964 .... **CLC 37; BLC 2; DAM MULT**
See also BW 1; CA 125; DLB 51

Larson, Charles R(aymond) 1938- ... **CLC 31**
See also CA 53-56; CANR 4

Larson, Jonathan 1961-1996 .... **CLC 99**
See also AAYA 28; CA 156

Las Casas, Bartolome de 1474-1566 ... **LC 31**

Lasch, Christopher 1932-1994 .... **CLC 102**
See also CA 73-76; 144; CANR 25; MTCW 1, 2

Lasker-Schueler, Else 1869-1945 ... **TCLC 57**
See also DLB 66, 124

Laski, Harold 1893-1950 .... **TCLC 79**

Latham, Jean Lee 1902-1995 .... **CLC 12**
See also AITN 1; CA 5-8R; CANR 7; CLR 50; MAICYA; SATA 2, 68

Latham, Mavis
See Clark, Mavis Thorpe

Lathen, Emma .... **CLC 2**
See also Hennissart, Martha; Latsis, Mary J(ane)

Lathrop, Francis
See Leiber, Fritz (Reuter, Jr.)

Latsis, Mary J(ane) 1927(?)-1997
See Lathen, Emma
See also CA 85-88; 162

Lattimore, Richmond (Alexander) 1906-1984 **CLC 3**
See also CA 1-4R; 112; CANR 1

Laughlin, James 1914-1997 .... **CLC 49**
See also CA 21-24R; 162; CAAS 22; CANR 9, 47; DLB 48; DLBY 96, 97

Laurence, (Jean) Margaret (Wemyss) 1926-1987 .. **CLC 3, 6, 13, 50, 62; DAC; DAM MST; SSC 7**
See also CA 5-8R; 121; CANR 33; DLB 53; MTCW 1, 2; SATA-Obit 50

Laurent, Antoine 1952- .... **CLC 50**

Lauscher, Hermann
See Hesse, Hermann

Lautreamont, Comte de 1846-1870 **NCLC 12; SSC 14**

Laverty, Donald
See Blish, James (Benjamin)

Lavin, Mary 1912-1996 **CLC 4, 18, 99; SSC 4**
See also CA 9-12R; 151; CANR 33; DLB 15; MTCW 1

Lavond, Paul Dennis
See Kornbluth, C(yril) M.; Pohl, Frederik

Lawler, Raymond Evenor 1922- .... **CLC 58**
See also CA 103

Lawrence, D(avid) H(erbert Richards) 1885-1930 . **TCLC 2, 9, 16, 33, 48, 61, 93; DA; DAB; DAC; DAM MST, NOV, POET; SSC 4, 19; WLC**
See also CA 104; 121; CDBLB 1914-1945; DLB 10, 19, 36, 98, 162, 195; MTCW 1, 2

Lawrence, T(homas) E(dward) 1888-1935 **TCLC 18**
See also Dale, Colin
See also CA 115; 167; DLB 195

Lawrence of Arabia
See Lawrence, T(homas) E(dward)

Lawson, Henry (Archibald Hertzberg) 1867-1922 .... **TCLC 27; SSC 18**
See also CA 120

Lawton, Dennis
See Faust, Frederick (Schiller)

Laxness, Halldor .... **CLC 25**
See also Gudjonsson, Halldor Kiljan

Layamon fl. c. 1200- .... **CMLC 10**
See also DLB 146

Laye, Camara 1928-1980 **CLC 4, 38; BLC 2; DAM MULT**
See also BW 1; CA 85-88; 97-100; CANR 25; MTCW 1, 2

Layton, Irving (Peter) 1912- **CLC 2, 15; DAC; DAM MST, POET**
See also CA 1-4R; CANR 2, 33, 43, 66; DLB 88; MTCW 1, 2

Lazarus, Emma 1849-1887 .... **NCLC 8**

Lazarus, Felix
See Cable, George Washington

Lazarus, Henry
See Slavitt, David R(ytman)

Lea, Joan
See Neufeld, John (Arthur)

Leacock, Stephen (Butler) 1869-1944 **TCLC 2; DAC; DAM MST**
See also CA 104; 141; CANR 80; DLB 92; MTCW 2

Lear, Edward 1812-1888 .... **NCLC 3**
See also CLR 1; DLB 32, 163, 166; MAICYA; SATA 18, 100

Lear, Norman (Milton) 1922- .... **CLC 12**
See also CA 73-76

Leautaud, Paul 1872-1956 .... **TCLC 83**
See also DLB 65

Leavis, F(rank) R(aymond) 1895-1978 **CLC 24**
See also CA 21-24R; 77-80; CANR 44; MTCW 1, 2

Leavitt, David 1961- ..... **CLC 34; DAM POP**
See also CA 116; 122; CANR 50, 62; DLB 130; INT 122; MTCW 2

Leblanc, Maurice (Marie Emile) 1864-1941 **TCLC 49**
See also CA 110

Lebowitz, Fran(ces Ann) 1951(?)- **CLC 11, 36**
See also CA 81-84; CANR 14, 60, 70; INT CANR-14; MTCW 1

Lebrecht, Peter
See Tieck, (Johann) Ludwig

le Carre, John .... **CLC 3, 5, 9, 15, 28**
See also Cornwell, David (John Moore)
See also BEST 89:4; CDBLB 1960 to Present; DLB 87; MTCW 2

Le Clezio, J(ean) M(arie) G(ustave) 1940- **CLC 31**
See also CA 116; 128; DLB 83

Leconte de Lisle, Charles-Marie-Rene 1818-1894 .... **NCLC 29**

Le Coq, Monsieur
See Simenon, Georges (Jacques Christian)

Leduc, Violette 1907-1972 .... **CLC 22**
See also CA 13-14; 33-36R; CANR 69; CAP 1

Ledwidge, Francis 1887(?)-1917 .... **TCLC 23**
See also CA 123; DLB 20

Lee, Andrea 1953- .... **CLC 36; BLC 2; DAM MULT**
See also BW 1, 3; CA 125; CANR 82

Lee, Andrew
See Auchincloss, Louis (Stanton)

Lee, Chang-rae 1965- .... **CLC 91**
See also CA 148

Lee, Don L. .... **CLC 2**
See also Madhubuti, Haki R.

Lee, George W(ashington) 1894-1976 **CLC 52; BLC 2; DAM MULT**
See also BW 1; CA 125; DLB 51

Lee, (Nelle) Harper 1926- .. **CLC 12, 60; DA; DAB; DAC; DAM MST, NOV; WLC**
See also AAYA 13; CA 13-16R; CANR 51; CDALB 1941-1968; DLB 6; MTCW 1, 2; SATA 11

Lee, Helen Elaine 1959(?)- .... **CLC 86**

See also CA 148

Lee, Julian
See Latham, Jean Lee

Lee, Larry
See Lee, Lawrence

Lee, Laurie 1914-1997 **CLC 90; DAB; DAM POP**
See also CA 77-80; 158; CANR 33, 73; DLB 27; MTCW 1

Lee, Lawrence 1941-1990 .... **CLC 34**
See also CA 131; CANR 43

Lee, Li-Young 1957- .... **PC 24**
See also CA 153; DLB 165

Lee, Manfred B(ennington) 1905-1971**CLC 11**
See also Queen, Ellery
See also CA 1-4R; 29-32R; CANR 2; DLB 137

Lee, Shelton Jackson 1957(?)- .... **CLC 105; BLCS; DAM MULT**
See also Lee, Spike
See also BW 2, 3; CA 125; CANR 42

Lee, Spike
See Lee, Shelton Jackson
See also AAYA 4, 29

Lee, Stan 1922- .... **CLC 17**
See also AAYA 5; CA 108; 111; INT 111

Lee, Tanith 1947- .... **CLC 46**
See also AAYA 15; CA 37-40R; CANR 53; SATA 8, 88

Lee, Vernon .... **TCLC 5; SSC 33**
See Paget, Violet
See also DLB 57, 153, 156, 174, 178

Lee, William
See Burroughs, William S(eward)

Lee, Willy
See Burroughs, William S(eward)

Lee-Hamilton, Eugene (Jacob) 1845-1907 **TCLC 22**
See also CA 117

Leet, Judith 1935- .... **CLC 11**

Le Fanu, Joseph Sheridan 1814-1873**NCLC 9, 58; DAM POP; SSC 14**
See also DLB 21, 70, 159, 178

Leffland, Ella 1931- .... **CLC 19**
See also CA 29-32R; CANR 35, 78, 82; DLBY 84; INT CANR-35; SATA 65

Leger, Alexis
See Leger, (Marie-Rene Auguste) Alexis Saint-Leger

Leger, (Marie-Rene Auguste) Alexis Saint-Leger 1887-1975 . **CLC 4, 11, 46; DAM POET; PC 23**
See also CA 13-16R; 61-64; CANR 43; MTCW 1

Leger, Saintleger
See Leger, (Marie-Rene Auguste) Alexis Saint-Leger

Le Guin, Ursula K(roeber) 1929- **CLC 8, 13, 22, 45, 71; DAB; DAC; DAM MST, POP; SSC 12**
See also AAYA 9, 27; AITN 1; CA 21-24R; CANR 9, 32, 52, 74; CDALB 1968-1988; CLR 3, 28; DLB 8, 52; INT CANR-32; JRDA; MAICYA; MTCW 1, 2; SATA 4, 52, 99

Lehmann, Rosamond (Nina) 1901-1990**CLC 5**
See also CA 77-80; 131; CANR 8, 73; DLB 15; MTCW 2

Leiber, Fritz (Reuter, Jr.) 1910-1992 **CLC 25**
See also CA 45-48; 139; CANR 2, 40; DLB 8; MTCW 1, 2; SATA 45; SATA-Obit 73

Leibniz, Gottfried Wilhelm von 1646-1716**LC 35**
See also DLB 168

Leimbach, Martha 1963-
See Leimbach, Marti
See also CA 130

Leimbach, Marti .... **CLC 65**
See also Leimbach, Martha

Leino, Eino .... **TCLC 24**
See also Loennbohm, Armas Eino Leopold

Leiris, Michel (Julien) 1901-1990..... **CLC 61**
See also CA 119; 128; 132

Leithauser, Brad 1953- .... **CLC 27**
See also CA 107; CANR 27, 81; DLB 120

Lelchuk, Alan 1938- .... **CLC 5**
See also CA 45-48; CAAS 20; CANR 1, 70

Lem, Stanislaw 1921- .... **CLC 8, 15, 40**
See also CA 105; CAAS 1; CANR 32; MTCW 1

Lemann, Nancy 1956- .... **CLC 39**
See also CA 118; 136

Lemonnier, (Antoine Louis) Camille 1844-1913 **TCLC 22**
See also CA 121

Lenau, Nikolaus 1802-1850 .... **NCLC 16**

L'Engle, Madeleine (Camp Franklin) 1918- **CLC 12; DAM POP**
See also AAYA 28; AITN 2; CA 1-4R; CANR 3, 21, 39, 66; CLR 1, 14, 57; DLB 52; JRDA; MAICYA; MTCW 1, 2; SAAS 15; SATA 1, 27, 75

Lengyel, Jozsef 1896-1975 .... **CLC 7**
See also CA 85-88; 57-60; CANR 71

Lenin 1870-1924
See Lenin, V. I.
See also CA 121; 168

Lenin, V. I. .... **TCLC 67**
See also Lenin

Lennon, John (Ono) 1940-1980 . **CLC 12, 35**
See also CA 102

Lennox, Charlotte Ramsay 1729(?)-1804 **NCLC 23**
See also DLB 39

Lentricchia, Frank (Jr.) 1940- .... **CLC 34**
See also CA 25-28R; CANR 19

Lenz, Siegfried 1926- .... **CLC 27; SSC 33**
See also CA 89-92; CANR 80; DLB 75

Leonard, Elmore (John, Jr.) 1925-**CLC 28, 34, 71, 120; DAM POP**
See also AAYA 22; AITN 1; BEST 89:1, 90:4; CA 81-84; CANR 12, 28, 53, 76; DLB 173; INT CANR-28; MTCW 1, 2

Leonard, Hugh .... **CLC 19**
See also Byrne, John Keyes
See also DLB 13

Leonov, Leonid (Maximovich) 1899-1994 **CLC 92; DAM NOV**
See also CA 129; CANR 74, 76; MTCW 1, 2

Leopardi, (Conte) Giacomo 1798-1837**NCLC 22**

Le Reveler
See Artaud, Antonin (Marie Joseph)

Lerman, Eleanor 1952- .... **CLC 9**
See also CA 85-88; CANR 69

Lerman, Rhoda 1936- .... **CLC 56**
See also CA 49-52; CANR 70

Lermontov, Mikhail Yuryevich 1814-1841 **NCLC 47; PC 18**
See also DLB 205

Leroux, Gaston 1868-1927 .... **TCLC 25**
See also CA 108; 136; CANR 69; SATA 65

Lesage, Alain-Rene 1668-1747 .... **LC 2, 28**

Leskov, Nikolai (Semyonovich) 1831-1895 **NCLC 25; SSC 34**

Lessing, Doris (May) 1919-**CLC 1, 2, 3, 6, 10, 15, 22, 40, 94; DA; DAB; DAC; DAM MST, NOV; SSC 6; WLCS**
See also CA 9-12R; CANR 33, 54, 76; CDBLB 1960 to Present; DLB 15, 139; DLBY 85; MTCW 1, 2

Lessing, Gotthold Ephraim 1729-1781 . **LC 8**
See also DLB 97

Lester, Richard 1932- .... **CLC 20**

Lever, Charles (James) 1806-1872 **NCLC 23**
See also DLB 21

Leverson, Ada 1865(?)-1936(?) ...... **TCLC 18**
See also Elaine
See also CA 117; DLB 153

Levertov, Denise 1923-1997**CLC 1, 2, 3, 5, 8, 15, 28, 66; DAM POET; PC 11**
See also CA 1-4R, 178; 163; CAAE 178; CAAS 19; CANR 3, 29, 50; CDALBS; DLB 5, 165; INT CANR-29; MTCW 1, 2

Levi, Jonathan .... **CLC 76**

Levi, Peter (Chad Tigar) 1931-......... **CLC 41**
See also CA 5-8R; CANR 34, 80; DLB 40

Levi, Primo 1919-1987 . **CLC 37, 50; SSC 12**
See also CA 13-16R; 122; CANR 12, 33, 61, 70; DLB 177; MTCW 1

Levin, Ira 1929- .... **CLC 3, 6; DAM POP**
See also CA 21-24R; CANR 17, 44, 74; MTCW 1, 2; SATA 66

Levin, Meyer 1905-1981 . **CLC 7; DAM POP**
See also AITN 1; CA 9-12R; 104; CANR 15; DLB 9, 28; DLBY 81; SATA 21; SATA-Obit 27

Levine, Norman 1924-...................... **CLC 54**
See also CA 73-76; CAAS 23; CANR 14, 70; DLB 88

Levine, Philip 1928-**CLC 2, 4, 5, 9, 14, 33, 118; DAM POET; PC 22**
See also CA 9-12R; CANR 9, 37, 52; DLB 5

Levinson, Deirdre 1931-...................**CLC 49**
See also CA 73-76; CANR 70

Levi-Strauss, Claude 1908-.............. **CLC 38**
See also CA 1-4R; CANR 6, 32, 57; MTCW 1, 2

Levitin, Sonia (Wolff) 1934-............. **CLC 17**
See also AAYA 13; CA 29-32R; CANR 14, 32, 79; CLR 53; JRDA; MAICYA; SAAS 2; SATA 4, 68

Levon, O. U.
See Kesey, Ken (Elton)

Levy, Amy 1861-1889 .... **NCLC 59**
See also DLB 156

Lewes, George Henry 1817-1878 ... **NCLC 25**
See also DLB 55, 144

Lewis, Alun 1915-1944 .... **TCLC 3**
See also CA 104; DLB 20, 162

Lewis, C. Day
See Day Lewis, C(ecil)

Lewis, C(live) S(taples) 1898-1963**CLC 1, 3, 6, 14, 27; DA; DAB; DAC; DAM MST, NOV, POP; WLC**
See also AAYA 3; CA 81-84; CANR 33, 71; CDBLB 1945-1960; CLR 3, 27; DLB 15, 100, 160; JRDA; MAICYA; MTCW 1, 2; SATA 13, 100

Lewis, Janet 1899-1998 ....**CLC 41**
See also Winters, Janet Lewis
See also CA 9-12R; 172; CANR 29, 63; CAP 1; DLBY 87

Lewis, Matthew Gregory 1775-1818**NCLC 11, 62**
See also DLB 39, 158, 178

Lewis, (Harry) Sinclair 1885-1951 . **TCLC 4, 13, 23, 39; DA; DAB; DAC; DAM MST, NOV; WLC**
See also CA 104; 133; CDALB 1917-1929;

68; DAM POET

See also CA 9-12R; 106; CANR 33, 63; CDALBS; DLB 4, 7, 45; DLBY 82; MTCW 1, 2

MacLennan, (John) Hugh 1907-1990 **CLC 2, 14, 92; DAC; DAM MST**

See also CA 5-8R; 142; CANR 33; DLB 68; MTCW 1, 2

MacLeod, Alistair 1936- **CLC 56; DAC; DAM MST**

See also CA 123; DLB 60; MTCW 2

Macleod, Fiona

See Sharp, William

MacNeice, (Frederick) Louis 1907-1963 **C L C 1, 4, 10, 53; DAB; DAM POET**

See also CA 85-88; CANR 61; DLB 10, 20; MTCW 1, 2

MacNeill, Dand

See Fraser, George MacDonald

Macpherson, James 1736-1796 .... **LC 29**

See also Ossian

See also DLB 109

Macpherson, (Jean) Jay 1931- .... **CLC 14**

See also CA 5-8R; DLB 53

MacShane, Frank 1927- .... **CLC 39**

See also CA 9-12R; CANR 3, 33; DLB 111

Macumber, Mari

See Sandoz, Mari(e Susette)

Madach, Imre 1823-1864 .... **NCLC 19**

Madden, (Jerry) David 1933- .... **CLC 5, 15**

See also CA 1-4R; CAAS 3; CANR 4, 45; DLB 6; MTCW 1

Maddern, Al(an)

See Ellison, Harlan (Jay)

Madhubuti, Haki R. 1942- **CLC 6, 73; BLC 2; DAM MULT, POET; PC 5**

See also Lee, Don L.

See also BW 2, 3; CA 73-76; CANR 24, 51, 73; DLB 5, 41; DLBD 8; MTCW 2

Maepenn, Hugh

See Kuttner, Henry

Maepenn, K. H.

See Kuttner, Henry

Maeterlinck, Maurice 1862-1949 ... **TCLC 3; DAM DRAM**

See also CA 104; 136; CANR 80; DLB 192; SATA 66

Maginn, William 1794-1842 .... **NCLC 8**

See also DLB 110, 159

Mahapatra, Jayanta 1928- .... **CLC 33; DAM MULT**

See also CA 73-76; CAAS 9; CANR 15, 33, 66

Mahfouz, Naguib (Abdel Aziz Al-Sabilgi) 1911(?)-

See Mahfuz, Najib

See also BEST 89:2; CA 128; CANR 55; DAM NOV; MTCW 1, 2

Mahfuz, Najib .... **CLC 52, 55**

See also Mahfouz, Naguib (Abdel Aziz Al-Sabilgi)

See also DLBY 88

Mahon, Derek 1941- .... **CLC 27**

See also CA 113; 128; DLB 40

Mailer, Norman 1923- **CLC 1, 2, 3, 4, 5, 8, 11, 14, 28, 39, 74, 111; DA; DAB; DAC; DAM MST, NOV, POP**

See also AITN 2; CA 9-12R; CABS 1; CANR 28, 74, 77; CDALB 1968-1988; DLB 2, 16, 28, 185; DLBD 3; DLBY 80, 83; MTCW 1, 2

Maillet, Antonine 1929- . **CLC 54, 118; DAC**

See also CA 115; 120; CANR 46, 74, 77; DLB 60; INT 120; MTCW 2

Mais, Roger 1905-1955 .... **TCLC 8**

See also BW 1, 3; CA 105; 124; CANR 82; DLB 125; MTCW 1

Maistre, Joseph de 1753-1821 .... **NCLC 37**

Maitland, Frederic 1850-1906 .... **TCLC 65**

Maitland, Sara (Louise) 1950- .... **CLC 49**

See also CA 69-72; CANR 13, 59

Major, Clarence 1936- **CLC 3, 19, 48; BLC 2; DAM MULT**

See also BW 2, 3; CA 21-24R; CAAS 6; CANR 13, 25, 53, 82; DLB 33

Major, Kevin (Gerald) 1949- ..**CLC 26; DAC**

See also AAYA 16; CA 97-100; CANR 21, 38; CLR 11; DLB 60; INT CANR-21; JRDA; MAICYA; SATA 32, 82

Maki, James

See Ozu, Yasujiro

Malabaila, Damiano

See Levi, Primo

Malamud, Bernard 1914-1986 **CLC 1, 2, 3, 5, 8, 9, 11, 18, 27, 44, 78, 85; DA; DAB; DAC; DAM MST, NOV, POP; SSC 15; WLC**

See also AAYA 16; CA 5-8R; 118; CABS 1; CANR 28, 62; CDALB 1941-1968; DLB 2, 28, 152; DLBY 80, 86; MTCW 1, 2

Malan, Herman

See Bosman, Herman Charles; Bosman, Herman Charles

Malaparte, Curzio 1898-1957 .... **TCLC 52**

Malcolm, Dan

See Silverberg, Robert

Malcolm X .... **CLC 82, 117; BLC 2; WLCS**

See also Little, Malcolm

Malherbe, Francois de 1555-1628 .... **LC 5**

Mallarme, Stephane 1842-1898 **NCLC 4, 41; DAM POET; PC 4**

Mallet-Joris, Francoise 1930- .... **CLC 11**

See also CA 65-68; CANR 17; DLB 83

Malley, Ern

See McAuley, James Phillip

Mallowan, Agatha Christie

See Christie, Agatha (Mary Clarissa)

Maloff, Saul 1922- .... **CLC 5**

See also CA 33-36R

Malone, Louis

See MacNeice, (Frederick) Louis

Malone, Michael (Christopher) 1942- **CLC 43**

See also CA 77-80; CANR 14, 32, 57

Malory, (Sir) Thomas 1410(?)-1471(?)**LC 11; DA; DAB; DAC; DAM MST; WLCS**

See also CDBLB Before 1660; DLB 146; SATA 59; SATA-Brief 33

Malouf, (George Joseph) David 1934-**CLC 28, 86**

See also CA 124; CANR 50, 76; MTCW 2

Malraux, (Georges-)Andre 1901-1976**CLC 1, 4, 9, 13, 15, 57; DAM NOV**

See also CA 21-22; 69-72; CANR 34, 58; CAP 2; DLB 72; MTCW 1, 2

Malzberg, Barry N(athaniel) 1939- ... **CLC 7**

See also CA 61-64; CAAS 4; CANR 16; DLB 8

Mamet, David (Alan) 1947-**CLC 9, 15, 34, 46, 91; DAM DRAM; DC 4**

See also AAYA 3; CA 81-84; CABS 3; CANR 15, 41, 67, 72; DLB 7; MTCW 1, 2

Mamoulian, Rouben (Zachary) 1897-1987 **CLC 16**

See also CA 25-28R; 124

Mandelstam, Osip (Emilievich) 1891(?)-1938(?) **TCLC 2, 6; PC 14**

See also CA 104; 150; MTCW 2

Mander, (Mary) Jane 1877-1949 ... **TCLC 31**

See also CA 162

Mandeville, John fl. 1350- .... **CMLC 19**

See also DLB 146

Mandiargues, Andre Pieyre de .... **CLC 41**

See also Pieyre de Mandiargues, Andre

See also DLB 83

Mandrake, Ethel Belle

See Thurman, Wallace (Henry)

Mangan, James Clarence 1803-1849**NCLC 27**

Maniere, J.-E.

See Giraudoux, (Hippolyte) Jean

Mankiewicz, Herman (Jacob) 1897-1953 **TCLC 85**

See also CA 120; 169; DLB 26

Manley, (Mary) Delariviere 1672(?)-1724**L C 1, 42**

See also DLB 39, 80

Mann, Abel

See Creasey, John

Mann, Emily 1952- .... **DC 7**

See also CA 130; CANR 55

Mann, (Luiz) Heinrich 1871-1950 ... **TCLC 9**

See also CA 106; 164; DLB 66, 118

Mann, (Paul) Thomas 1875-1955 **TCLC 2, 8, 14, 21, 35, 44, 60; DA; DAB; DAC; DAM MST, NOV; SSC 5; WLC**

See also CA 104; 128; DLB 66; MTCW 1, 2

Mannheim, Karl 1893-1947 .... **TCLC 65**

Manning, David

See Faust, Frederick (Schiller)

Manning, Frederic 1887(?)-1935 ... **TCLC 25**

See also CA 124

Manning, Olivia 1915-1980 ....**CLC 5, 19**

See also CA 5-8R; 101; CANR 29; MTCW 1

Mano, D. Keith 1942- ....**CLC 2, 10**

See also CA 25-28R; CAAS 6; CANR 26, 57; DLB 6

Mansfield, Katherine **TCLC 2, 8, 39; DAB; SSC 9, 23; WLC**

See also Beauchamp, Kathleen Mansfield

See also DLB 162

Manso, Peter 1940- .... **CLC 39**

See also CA 29-32R; CANR 44

Mantecon, Juan Jimenez

See Jimenez (Mantecon), Juan Ramon

Manton, Peter

See Creasey, John

Man Without a Spleen, A

See Chekhov, Anton (Pavlovich)

Manzoni, Alessandro 1785-1873 .... **NCLC 29**

Map, Walter 1140-1209 .... **CMLC 32**

Mapu, Abraham (ben Jekutiel) 1808-1867 **NCLC 18**

Mara, Sally

See Queneau, Raymond

Marat, Jean Paul 1743-1793 .... **LC 10**

Marcel, Gabriel Honore 1889-1973 . **CLC 15**

See also CA 102; 45-48; MTCW 1, 2

March, William 1893-1954 .... **TCLC 96**

Marchbanks, Samuel

See Davies, (William) Robertson

Marchi, Giacomo

See Bassani, Giorgio

Margulies, Donald .... **CLC 76**

Marie de France c. 12th cent. - **CMLC 8; PC 22**

See also DLB 208

Marie de l'Incarnation 1599-1672 ...... **LC 10**

Marier, Captain Victor

See Griffith, D(avid Lewelyn) W(ark)

Mariner, Scott

See Pohl, Frederik

Marinetti, Filippo Tommaso 1876-1944**TCLC 10**

See also CA 107; DLB 114

Marivaux, Pierre Carlet de Chamblain de 1688-
1763 .... **LC 4; DC 7**

Markandaya, Kamala .... **CLC 8, 38**
See also Taylor, Kamala (Purnaiya)

Markfield, Wallace 1926- .... **CLC 8**
See also CA 69-72; CAAS 3; DLB 2, 28

Markham, Edwin 1852-1940 .... **TCLC 47**
See also CA 160; DLB 54, 186

Markham, Robert
See Amis, Kingsley (William)

Marks, J
See Highwater, Jamake (Mamake)

Marks-Highwater, J
See Highwater, Jamake (Mamake)

Markson, David M(errill) 1927- .... **CLC 67**
See also CA 49-52; CANR 1

Marley, Bob .... **CLC 17**
See also Marley, Robert Nesta

Marley, Robert Nesta 1945-1981
See Marley, Bob
See also CA 107; 103

Marlowe, Christopher 1564-1593 **LC 22, 47;**
DA; DAB; DAC; DAM DRAM, MST; DC
1; WLC
See also CDBLB Before 1660; DLB 62

Marlowe, Stephen 1928-
See Queen, Ellery
See also CA 13-16R; CANR 6, 55

Marmontel, Jean-Francois 1723-1799 .. **LC 2**

Marquand, John P(hillips) 1893-1960**CLC 2,**
10
See also CA 85-88; CANR 73; DLB 9, 102;
MTCW 2

Marques, Rene 1919-1979 ..... **CLC 96; DAM**
MULT; HLC 2
See also CA 97-100; 85-88; CANR 78; DLB
113; HW 1, 2

Marquez, Gabriel (Jose) Garcia
See Garcia Marquez, Gabriel (Jose)

Marquis, Don(ald Robert Perry) 1878-1937
TCLC 7
See also CA 104; 166; DLB 11, 25

Marric, J. J.
See Creasey, John

Marryat, Frederick 1792-1848 .... **NCLC 3**
See also DLB 21, 163

Marsden, James
See Creasey, John

Marsh, (Edith) Ngaio 1899-1982 **CLC 7, 53;**
DAM POP
See also CA 9-12R; CANR 6, 58; DLB 77;
MTCW 1, 2

Marshall, Garry 1934- .... **CLC 17**
See also AAYA 3; CA 111; SATA 60

Marshall, Paule 1929- .. **CLC 27, 72; BLC 3;**
DAM MULT; SSC 3
See also BW 2, 3; CA 77-80; CANR 25, 73;
DLB 157; MTCW 1, 2

Marshallik
See Zangwill, Israel

Marsten, Richard
See Hunter, Evan

Marston, John 1576-1634**LC 33; DAM DRAM**
See also DLB 58, 172

Martha, Henry
See Harris, Mark

Marti (y Perez), Jose (Julian) 1853-1895
NCLC 63; DAM MULT; HLC 2
See also HW 2

Martial c. 40-c. 104 .... **CMLC 35; PC 10**
See also DLB 211

Martin, Ken

See Hubbard, L(afayette) Ron(ald)

Martin, Richard
See Creasey, John

Martin, Steve 1945- .... **CLC 30**
See also CA 97-100; CANR 30; MTCW 1

Martin, Valerie 1948- .... **CLC 89**
See also BEST 90:2; CA 85-88; CANR 49

Martin, Violet Florence 1862-1915 **TCLC 51**

Martin, Webber
See Silverberg, Robert

Martindale, Patrick Victor
See White, Patrick (Victor Martindale)

Martin du Gard, Roger 1881-1958 **TCLC 24**
See also CA 118; DLB 65

Martineau, Harriet 1802-1876 .... **NCLC 26**
See also DLB 21, 55, 159, 163, 166, 190; YABC
2

Martines, Julia
See O'Faolain, Julia

Martinez, Enrique Gonzalez
See Gonzalez Martinez, Enrique

Martinez, Jacinto Benavente y
See Benavente (y Martinez), Jacinto

Martinez Ruiz, Jose 1873-1967
See Azorin; Ruiz, Jose Martinez
See also CA 93-96; HW 1

Martinez Sierra, Gregorio 1881-1947**TCLC 6**
See also CA 115

Martinez Sierra, Maria (de la O'LeJarraga)
1874-1974 .... **TCLC 6**
See also CA 115

Martinsen, Martin
See Follett, Ken(neth Martin)

Martinson, Harry (Edmund) 1904-1978**C L C**
14
See also CA 77-80; CANR 34

Marut, Ret
See Traven, B.

Marut, Robert
See Traven, B.

Marvell, Andrew 1621-1678 ... **LC 4, 43; DA;**
DAB; DAC; DAM MST, POET; PC 10;
WLC
See also CDBLB 1660-1789; DLB 131

Marx, Karl (Heinrich) 1818-1883 . **NCLC 17**
See also DLB 129

Masaoka Shiki .... **TCLC 18**
See also Masaoka Tsunenori

Masaoka Tsunenori 1867-1902
See Masaoka Shiki
See also CA 117

Masefield, John (Edward) 1878-1967**CLC 11,**
47; DAM POET
See also CA 19-20; 25-28R; CANR 33; CAP 2;
CDBLB 1890-1914; DLB 10, 19, 153, 160;
MTCW 1, 2; SATA 19

Maso, Carole 19(?)- .... **CLC 44**
See also CA 170

Mason, Bobbie Ann 1940-**CLC 28, 43, 82; SSC**
4
See also AAYA 5; CA 53-56; CANR 11, 31,
58; CDALBS; DLB 173; DLBY 87; INT
CANR-31; MTCW 1, 2

Mason, Ernst
See Pohl, Frederik

Mason, Lee W.
See Malzberg, Barry N(athaniel)

Mason, Nick 1945- .... **CLC 35**

Mason, Tally
See Derleth, August (William)

Mass, William
See Gibson, William

Master Lao

See Lao Tzu

Masters, Edgar Lee 1868-1950 **TCLC 2, 25;**
DA; DAC; DAM MST, POET; PC 1;
WLCS
See also CA 104; 133; CDALB 1865-1917;
DLB 54; MTCW 1, 2

Masters, Hilary 1928- .... **CLC 48**
See also CA 25-28R; CANR 13, 47

Mastrosimone, William 19(?)- .... **CLC 36**

Mathe, Albert
See Camus, Albert

Mather, Cotton 1663-1728 .... **LC 38**
See also CDALB 1640-1865; DLB 24, 30, 140

Mather, Increase 1639-1723 .... **LC 38**
See also DLB 24

Matheson, Richard Burton 1926- ..... **CLC 37**
See also CA 97-100; DLB 8, 44; INT 97-100

Mathews, Harry 1930- .... **CLC 6, 52**
See also CA 21-24R; CAAS 6; CANR 18, 40

Mathews, John Joseph 1894-1979 .. **CLC 84;**
DAM MULT
See also CA 19-20; 142; CANR 45; CAP 2;
DLB 175; NNAL

Mathias, Roland (Glyn) 1915- .... **CLC 45**
See also CA 97-100; CANR 19, 41; DLB 27

Matsuo Basho 1644-1694 .... **PC 3**
See also DAM POET

Mattheson, Rodney
See Creasey, John

Matthews, Brander 1852-1929 ...... **TCLC 95**
See also DLB 71, 78; DLBD 13

Matthews, Greg 1949- .... **CLC 45**
See also CA 135

Matthews, William (Procter, III) 1942-1997
CLC 40
See also CA 29-32R; 162; CAAS 18; CANR
12, 57; DLB 5

Matthias, John (Edward) 1941- .... **CLC 9**
See also CA 33-36R; CANR 56

Matthiessen, Peter 1927-**CLC 5, 7, 11, 32, 64;**
DAM NOV
See also AAYA 6; BEST 90:4; CA 9-12R;
CANR 21, 50, 73; DLB 6, 173; MTCW 1, 2;
SATA 27

Maturin, Charles Robert 1780(?)-1824**NCLC**
6
See also DLB 178

Matute (Ausejo), Ana Maria 1925- .. **CLC 11**
See also CA 89-92; MTCW 1

Maugham, W. S.
See Maugham, W(illiam) Somerset

Maugham, W(illiam) Somerset 1874-1965
CLC 1, 11, 15, 67, 93; DA; DAB; DAC;
DAM DRAM, MST, NOV; SSC 8; WLC
See also CA 5-8R; 25-28R; CANR 40; CDBLB
1914-1945; DLB 10, 36, 77, 100, 162, 195;
MTCW 1, 2; SATA 54

Maugham, William Somerset
See Maugham, W(illiam) Somerset

Maupassant, (Henri Rene Albert) Guy de 1850-
1893**NCLC 1, 42; DA; DAB; DAC; DAM**
MST; SSC 1; WLC
See also DLB 123

Maupin, Armistead 1944-**CLC 95; DAM POP**
See also CA 125; 130; CANR 58; INT 130;
MTCW 2

Maurhut, Richard
See Traven, B.

Mauriac, Claude 1914-1996 .... **CLC 9**
See also CA 89-92; 152; DLB 83

Mauriac, Francois (Charles) 1885-1970 **C L C**
4, 9, 56; SSC 24
See also CA 25-28; CAP 2; DLB 65; MTCW 1,

2

Mavor, Osborne Henry 1888-1951
See Bridie, James
See also CA 104

Maxwell, William (Keepers, Jr.) 1908-**CLC 19**
See also CA 93-96; CANR 54; DLBY 80; INT 93-96

May, Elaine 1932- .... **CLC 16**
See also CA 124; 142; DLB 44

Mayakovski, Vladimir (Vladimirovich) 1893-1930 .... **TCLC 4, 18**
See also CA 104; 158; MTCW 2

Mayhew, Henry 1812-1887 .... **NCLC 31**
See also DLB 18, 55, 190

Mayle, Peter 1939(?)- .... **CLC 89**
See also CA 139; CANR 64

Maynard, Joyce 1953- .... **CLC 23**
See also CA 111; 129; CANR 64

Mayne, William (James Carter) 1928-**CLC 12**
See also AAYA 20; CA 9-12R; CANR 37, 80; CLR 25; JRDA; MAICYA; SAAS 11; SATA 6, 68

Mayo, Jim
See L'Amour, Louis (Dearborn)

Maysles, Albert 1926- .... **CLC 16**
See also CA 29-32R

Maysles, David 1932- .... **CLC 16**

Mazer, Norma Fox 1931- .... **CLC 26**
See also AAYA 5; CA 69-72; CANR 12, 32, 66; CLR 23; JRDA; MAICYA; SAAS 1; SATA 24, 67, 105

Mazzini, Guiseppe 1805-1872 .... **NCLC 34**

McAuley, James Phillip 1917-1976 .. **CLC 45**
See also CA 97-100

McBain, Ed
See Hunter, Evan

McBrien, William Augustine 1930-.. **CLC 44**
See also CA 107

McCaffrey, Anne (Inez) 1926-**CLC 17; DAM NOV, POP**
See also AAYA 6; AITN 2; BEST 89:2; CA 25-28R; CANR 15, 35, 55; CLR 49; DLB 8; JRDA; MAICYA; MTCW 1, 2; SAAS 11; SATA 8, 70

McCall, Nathan 1955(?)- .... **CLC 86**
See also BW 3; CA 146

McCann, Arthur
See Campbell, John W(ood, Jr.)

McCann, Edson
See Pohl, Frederik

McCarthy, Charles, Jr. 1933-
See McCarthy, Cormac
See also CANR 42, 69; DAM POP; MTCW 2

McCarthy, Cormac 1933- **CLC 4, 57, 59, 101**
See also McCarthy, Charles, Jr.
See also DLB 6, 143; MTCW 2

McCarthy, Mary (Therese) 1912-1989**CLC 1, 3, 5, 14, 24, 39, 59; SSC 24**
See also CA 5-8R; 129; CANR 16, 50, 64; DLB 2; DLBY 81; INT CANR-16; MTCW 1, 2

McCartney, (James) Paul 1942- **CLC 12, 35**
See also CA 146

McCauley, Stephen (D.) 1955- .... **CLC 50**
See also CA 141

McClure, Michael (Thomas) 1932-**CLC 6, 10**
See also CA 21-24R; CANR 17, 46, 77; DLB 16

McCorkle, Jill (Collins) 1958- .... **CLC 51**
See also CA 121; DLBY 87

McCourt, Frank 1930- .... **CLC 109**
See also CA 157

McCourt, James 1941- .... **CLC 5**
See also CA 57-60

McCourt, Malachy 1932-................. **CLC 119**

McCoy, Horace (Stanley) 1897-1955**TCLC 28**
See also CA 108; 155; DLB 9

McCrae, John 1872-1918 .... **TCLC 12**
See also CA 109; DLB 92

McCreigh, James
See Pohl, Frederik

McCullers, (Lula) Carson (Smith) 1917-1967 **CLC 1, 4, 10, 12, 48, 100; DA; DAB; DAC; DAM MST, NOV; SSC 9, 24; WLC**
See also AAYA 21; CA 5-8R; 25-28R; CABS 1, 3; CANR 18; CDALB 1941-1968; DLB 2, 7, 173; MTCW 1, 2; SATA 27

McCulloch, John Tyler
See Burroughs, Edgar Rice

McCullough, Colleen 1938(?)- **CLC 27, 107; DAM NOV, POP**
See also CA 81-84; CANR 17, 46, 67; MTCW 1, 2

McDermott, Alice 1953- .... **CLC 90**
See also CA 109; CANR 40

McElroy, Joseph 1930- .... **CLC 5, 47**
See also CA 17-20R

McEwan, Ian (Russell) 1948- .... **CLC 13, 66; DAM NOV**
See also BEST 90:4; CA 61-64; CANR 14, 41, 69; DLB 14, 194; MTCW 1, 2

McFadden, David 1940- .... **CLC 48**
See also CA 104; DLB 60; INT 104

McFarland, Dennis 1950- .... **CLC 65**
See also CA 165

McGahern, John 1934-**CLC 5, 9, 48; SSC 17**
See also CA 17-20R; CANR 29, 68; DLB 14; MTCW 1

McGinley, Patrick (Anthony) 1937- . **CLC 41**
See also CA 120; 127; CANR 56; INT 127

McGinley, Phyllis 1905-1978 .... **CLC 14**
See also CA 9-12R; 77-80; CANR 19; DLB 11, 48; SATA 2, 44; SATA-Obit 24

McGinniss, Joe 1942- .... **CLC 32**
See also AITN 2; BEST 89:2; CA 25-28R; CANR 26, 70; DLB 185; INT CANR-26

McGivern, Maureen Daly
See Daly, Maureen

McGrath, Patrick 1950- .... **CLC 55**
See also CA 136; CANR 65

McGrath, Thomas (Matthew) 1916-1990**CLC 28, 59; DAM POET**
See also CA 9-12R; 132; CANR 6, 33; MTCW 1; SATA 41; SATA-Obit 66

McGuane, Thomas (Francis III) 1939-**CLC 3, 7, 18, 45**
See also AITN 2; CA 49-52; CANR 5, 24, 49; DLB 2, 212; DLBY 80; INT CANR-24; MTCW 1

McGuckian, Medbh 1950- ..... **CLC 48; DAM POET; PC 27**
See also CA 143; DLB 40

McHale, Tom 1942(?)-1982 .... **CLC 3, 5**
See also AITN 1; CA 77-80; 106

McIlvanney, William 1936- .... **CLC 42**
See also CA 25-28R; CANR 61; DLB 14, 207

McIlwraith, Maureen Mollie Hunter
See Hunter, Mollie
See also SATA 2

McInerney, Jay 1955-**CLC 34, 112; DAM POP**
See also AAYA 18; CA 116; 123; CANR 45, 68; INT 123; MTCW 2

McIntyre, Vonda N(eel) 1948- .... **CLC 18**
See also CA 81-84; CANR 17, 34, 69; MTCW 1

McKay, Claude   **TCLC 7, 41; BLC 3; DAB; PC 2**
See also McKay, Festus Claudius
See also DLB 4, 45, 51, 117

McKay, Festus Claudius 1889-1948
See McKay, Claude
See also BW 1, 3; CA 104; 124; CANR 73; DA; DAC; DAM MST, MULT, NOV, POET; MTCW 1, 2; WLC

McKuen, Rod 1933- .... **CLC 1, 3**
See also AITN 1; CA 41-44R; CANR 40

McLoughlin, R. B.
See Mencken, H(enry) L(ouis)

McLuhan, (Herbert) Marshall 1911-1980 **CLC 37, 83**
See also CA 9-12R; 102; CANR 12, 34, 61; DLB 88; INT CANR-12; MTCW 1, 2

McMillan, Terry (L.) 1951- **CLC 50, 61, 112; BLCS; DAM MULT, NOV, POP**
See also AAYA 21; BW 2, 3; CA 140; CANR 60; MTCW 2

McMurtry, Larry (Jeff) 1936-**CLC 2, 3, 7, 11, 27, 44; DAM NOV, POP**
See also AAYA 15; AITN 2; BEST 89:2; CA 5-8R; CANR 19, 43, 64; CDALB 1968-1988; DLB 2, 143; DLBY 80, 87; MTCW 1, 2

McNally, T. M. 1961- .... **CLC 82**

McNally, Terrence 1939- .... **CLC 4, 7, 41, 91; DAM DRAM**
See also CA 45-48; CANR 2, 56; DLB 7; MTCW 2

McNamer, Deirdre 1950- .... **CLC 70**

McNeal, Tom .... **CLC 119**

McNeile, Herman Cyril 1888-1937
See Sapper
See also DLB 77

McNickle, (William) D'Arcy 1904-1977 **C L C 89; DAM MULT**
See also CA 9-12R; 85-88; CANR 5, 45; DLB 175, 212; NNAL; SATA-Obit 22

McPhee, John (Angus) 1931- .... **CLC 36**
See also BEST 90:1; CA 65-68; CANR 20, 46, 64, 69; DLB 185; MTCW 1, 2

McPherson, James Alan 1943-.. **CLC 19, 77; BLCS**
See also BW 1, 3; CA 25-28R; CAAS 17; CANR 24, 74; DLB 38; MTCW 1, 2

McPherson, William (Alexander) 1933- **C L C 34**
See also CA 69-72; CANR 28; INT CANR-28

Mead, George Herbert 1873-1958 . **TCLC 89**

Mead, Margaret 1901-1978 .... **CLC 37**
See also AITN 1; CA 1-4R; 81-84; CANR 4; MTCW 1, 2; SATA-Obit 20

Meaker, Marijane (Agnes) 1927-
See Kerr, M. E.
See also CA 107; CANR 37, 63; INT 107; JRDA; MAICYA; MTCW 1; SATA 20, 61, 99

Medoff, Mark (Howard) 1940- ... **CLC 6, 23; DAM DRAM**
See also AITN 1; CA 53-56; CANR 5; DLB 7; INT CANR-5

Medvedev, P. N.
See Bakhtin, Mikhail Mikhailovich

Meged, Aharon
See Megged, Aharon

Meged, Aron
See Megged, Aharon

Megged, Aharon 1920- .... **CLC 9**
See also CA 49-52; CAAS 13; CANR 1

Mehta, Ved (Parkash) 1934- .... **CLC 37**
See also CA 1-4R; CANR 2, 23, 69; MTCW 1

Melanter
See Blackmore, R(ichard) D(oddridge)

Melies, Georges 1861-1938 .... **TCLC 81**
Melikow, Loris
See Hofmannsthal, Hugo von
Melmoth, Sebastian
See Wilde, Oscar
Meltzer, Milton 1915- .... **CLC 26**
See also AAYA 8; CA 13-16R; CANR 38; CLR 13; DLB 61; JRDA; MAICYA; SAAS 1; SATA 1, 50, 80
Melville, Herman 1819-1891 NCLC 3, 12, 29, 45, 49; DA; DAB; DAC; DAM MST, NOV; SSC 1, 17; WLC
See also AAYA 25; CDALB 1640-1865; DLB 3, 74; SATA 59
Menander c. 342B.C.-c. 292B.C. ..... **CMLC 9; DAM DRAM; DC 3**
See also DLB 176
Menchu, Rigoberta 1959-
See also HLCS 2
Menchu, Rigoberta 1959-
See also CA 175; HLCS 2
Mencken, H(enry) L(ouis) 1880-1956 **T C L C 13**
See also CA 105; 125; CDALB 1917-1929; DLB 11, 29, 63, 137; MTCW 1, 2
Mendelsohn, Jane 1965(?)- .... **CLC 99**
See also CA 154
Mercer, David 1928-1980 CLC 5; DAM DRAM
See also CA 9-12R; 102; CANR 23; DLB 13; MTCW 1
Merchant, Paul
See Ellison, Harlan (Jay)
Meredith, George 1828-1909 . **TCLC 17, 43; DAM POET**
See also CA 117; 153; CANR 80; CDBLB 1832-1890; DLB 18, 35, 57, 159
Meredith, William (Morris) 1919- CLC 4, 13, 22, 55; DAM POET; PC 28
See also CA 9-12R; CAAS 14; CANR 6, 40; DLB 5
Merezhkovsky, Dmitry Sergeyevich 1865-1941 **TCLC 29**
See also CA 169
Merimee, Prosper 1803-1870 NCLC 6, 65; SSC 7
See also DLB 119, 192
Merkin, Daphne 1954- .... **CLC 44**
See also CA 123
Merlin, Arthur
See Blish, James (Benjamin)
Merrill, James (Ingram) 1926-1995 CLC 2, 3, 6, 8, 13, 18, 34, 91; DAM POET; PC 28
See also CA 13-16R; 147; CANR 10, 49, 63; DLB 5, 165; DLBY 85; INT CANR-10; MTCW 1, 2
Merriman, Alex
See Silverberg, Robert
Merriman, Brian 1747-1805 .... **NCLC 70**
Merritt, E. B.
See Waddington, Miriam
Merton, Thomas 1915-1968 CLC 1, 3, 11, 34, 83; PC 10
See also CA 5-8R; 25-28R; CANR 22, 53; DLB 48; DLBY 81; MTCW 1, 2
Merwin, W(illiam) S(tanley) 1927- CLC 1, 2, 3, 5, 8, 13, 18, 45, 88; DAM POET
See also CA 13-16R; CANR 15, 51; DLB 5, 169; INT CANR-15; MTCW 1, 2
Metcalf, John 1938- .... **CLC 37**
See also CA 113; DLB 60
Metcalf, Suzanne
See Baum, L(yman) Frank
Mew, Charlotte (Mary) 1870-1928 .. **TCLC 8**

See also CA 105; DLB 19, 135
Mewshaw, Michael 1943- .... **CLC 9**
See also CA 53-56; CANR 7, 47; DLBY 80
Meyer, June
See Jordan, June
Meyer, Lynn
See Slavitt, David R(ytman)
Meyer-Meyrink, Gustav 1868-1932
See Meyrink, Gustav
See also CA 117
Meyers, Jeffrey 1939- .... **CLC 39**
See also CA 73-76; CANR 54; DLB 111
Meynell, Alice (Christina Gertrude Thompson) 1847-1922 .... **TCLC 6**
See also CA 104; 177; DLB 19, 98
Meyrink, Gustav .... **TCLC 21**
See also Meyer-Meyrink, Gustav
See also DLB 81
Michaels, Leonard 1933- CLC 6, 25; SSC 16
See also CA 61-64; CANR 21, 62; DLB 130; MTCW 1
Michaux, Henri 1899-1984 .... **CLC 8, 19**
See also CA 85-88; 114
Micheaux, Oscar (Devereaux) 1884-1951 **TCLC 76**
See also BW 3; CA 174; DLB 50
Michelangelo 1475-1564 .... **LC 12**
Michelet, Jules 1798-1874 .... **NCLC 31**
Michels, Robert 1876-1936 .... **TCLC 88**
Michener, James A(lbert) 1907(?)-1997 **C L C 1, 5, 11, 29, 60, 109; DAM NOV, POP**
See also AAYA 27; AITN 1; BEST 90:1; CA 5-8R; 161; CANR 21, 45, 68; DLB 6; MTCW 1, 2
Mickiewicz, Adam 1798-1855 .... **NCLC 3**
Middleton, Christopher 1926- .... **CLC 13**
See also CA 13-16R; CANR 29, 54; DLB 40
Middleton, Richard (Barham) 1882-1911 **TCLC 56**
See also DLB 156
Middleton, Stanley 1919- .... **CLC 7, 38**
See also CA 25-28R; CAAS 23; CANR 21, 46, 81; DLB 14
Middleton, Thomas 1580-1627 LC 33; DAM DRAM, MST; DC 5
See also DLB 58
Migueis, Jose Rodrigues 1901- .... **CLC 10**
Mikszath, Kalman 1847-1910 .... **TCLC 31**
See also CA 170
Miles, Jack .... **CLC 100**
Miles, Josephine (Louise) 1911-1985 CLC 1, 2, 14, 34, 39; DAM POET
See also CA 1-4R; 116; CANR 2, 55; DLB 48
Militant
See Sandburg, Carl (August)
Mill, John Stuart 1806-1873 .... **NCLC 11, 58**
See also CDBLB 1832-1890; DLB 55, 190
Millar, Kenneth 1915-1983 .... **CLC 14; DAM POP**
See Macdonald, Ross
See also CA 9-12R; 110; CANR 16, 63; DLB 2; DLBD 6; DLBY 83; MTCW 1, 2
Millay, E. Vincent
See Millay, Edna St. Vincent
Millay, Edna St. Vincent 1892-1950 **TCLC 4, 49; DA; DAB; DAC; DAM MST, POET; PC 6; WLCS**
See also CA 104; 130; CDALB 1917-1929; DLB 45; MTCW 1, 2
Miller, Arthur 1915- CLC 1, 2, 6, 10, 15, 26, 47, 78; DA; DAB; DAC; DAM DRAM, MST; DC 1; WLC
See also AAYA 15; AITN 1; CA 1-4R; CABS

3; CANR 2, 30, 54, 76; CDALB 1941-1968; DLB 7; MTCW 1, 2
Miller, Henry (Valentine) 1891-1980 CLC 1, 2, 4, 9, 14, 43, 84; DA; DAB; DAC; DAM MST, NOV; WLC
See also CA 9-12R; 97-100; CANR 33, 64; CDALB 1929-1941; DLB 4, 9; DLBY 80; MTCW 1, 2
Miller, Jason 1939(?)- .... **CLC 2**
See also AITN 1; CA 73-76; DLB 7
Miller, Sue 1943- .... **CLC 44; DAM POP**
See also BEST 90:3; CA 139; CANR 59; DLB 143
Miller, Walter M(ichael, Jr.) 1923- CLC 4, 30
See also CA 85-88; DLB 8
Millett, Kate 1934- .... **CLC 67**
See also AITN 1; CA 73-76; CANR 32, 53, 76; MTCW 1, 2
Millhauser, Steven (Lewis) 1943- CLC 21, 54, 109
See also CA 110; 111; CANR 63; DLB 2; INT 111; MTCW 2
Millin, Sarah Gertrude 1889-1968 ... **CLC 49**
See also CA 102; 93-96
Milne, A(lan) A(lexander) 1882-1956 TCLC 6, 88; DAB; DAC; DAM MST
See also CA 104; 133; CLR 1, 26; DLB 10, 77, 100, 160; MAICYA; MTCW 1, 2; SATA 100; YABC 1
Milner, Ron(ald) 1938- CLC 56; BLC 3; DAM MULT
See also AITN 1; BW 1; CA 73-76; CANR 24, 81; DLB 38; MTCW 1
Milnes, Richard Monckton 1809-1885 N C L C 61
See also DLB 32, 184
Milosz, Czeslaw 1911- CLC 5, 11, 22, 31, 56, 82; DAM MST, POET; PC 8; WLCS
See also CA 81-84; CANR 23, 51; MTCW 1, 2
Milton, John 1608-1674 LC 9, 43; DA; DAB; DAC; DAM MST, POET; PC 19; WLC
See also CDBLB 1660-1789; DLB 131, 151
Min, Anchee 1957- .... **CLC 86**
See also CA 146
Minehaha, Cornelius
See Wedekind, (Benjamin) Frank(lin)
Miner, Valerie 1947- .... **CLC 40**
See also CA 97-100; CANR 59
Minimo, Duca
See D'Annunzio, Gabriele
Minot, Susan 1956- .... **CLC 44**
See also CA 134
Minus, Ed 1938- .... **CLC 39**
Miranda, Javier
See Bioy Casares, Adolfo
Miranda, Javier
See Bioy Casares, Adolfo
Mirbeau, Octave 1848-1917 .... **TCLC 55**
See also DLB 123, 192
Miro (Ferrer), Gabriel (Francisco Victor) 1879-1930 .... **TCLC 5**
See also CA 104
Mishima, Yukio 1925-1970 CLC 2, 4, 6, 9, 27; DC 1; SSC 4
See also Hiraoka, Kimitake
See also DLB 182; MTCW 2
Mistral, Frederic 1830-1914 .... **TCLC 51**
See also CA 122
Mistral, Gabriela .... **TCLC 2; HLC 2**
See also Godoy Alcayaga, Lucila
See also MTCW 2
Mistry, Rohinton 1952- .... **CLC 71; DAC**
See also CA 141

Mitchell, Clyde
See Ellison, Harlan (Jay); Silverberg, Robert

Mitchell, James Leslie 1901-1935
See Gibbon, Lewis Grassic
See also CA 104; DLB 15

Mitchell, Joni 1943- .... **CLC 12**
See also CA 112

Mitchell, Joseph (Quincy) 1908-1996**CLC 98**
See also CA 77-80; 152; CANR 69; DLB 185;
DLBY 96

Mitchell, Margaret (Munnerlyn) 1900-1949
TCLC 11; DAM NOV, POP
See also AAYA 23; CA 109; 125; CANR 55;
CDALBS; DLB 9; MTCW 1, 2

Mitchell, Peggy
See Mitchell, Margaret (Munnerlyn)

Mitchell, S(ilas) Weir 1829-1914 ... **TCLC 36**
See also CA 165; DLB 202

Mitchell, W(illiam) O(rmond) 1914-1998**CLC
25; DAC; DAM MST**
See also CA 77-80; 165; CANR 15, 43; DLB
88

Mitchell, William 1879-1936 .... **TCLC 81**

Mitford, Mary Russell 1787-1855 ... **NCLC 4**
See also DLB 110, 116

Mitford, Nancy 1904-1973................. **CLC 44**
See also CA 9-12R; DLB 191

Miyamoto, (Chujo) Yuriko 1899-1951 **T C L C
37**
See also CA 170, 174; DLB 180

Miyazawa, Kenji 1896-1933 .... **TCLC 76**
See also CA 157

Mizoguchi, Kenji 1898-1956 .... **TCLC 72**
See also CA 167

Mo, Timothy (Peter) 1950(?)-............ **CLC 46**
See also CA 117; DLB 194; MTCW 1

Modarressi, Taghi (M.) 1931- .... **CLC 44**
See also CA 121; 134; INT 134

Modiano, Patrick (Jean) 1945- .... **CLC 18**
See also CA 85-88; CANR 17, 40; DLB 83

Moerck, Paal
See Roelvaag, O(le) E(dvart)

Mofolo, Thomas (Mokopu) 1875(?)-1948
TCLC 22; BLC 3; DAM MULT
See also CA 121; 153; MTCW 2

Mohr, Nicholasa 1938-**CLC 12; DAM MULT;
HLC 2**
See also AAYA 8; CA 49-52; CANR 1, 32, 64;
CLR 22; DLB 145; HW 1, 2; JRDA; SAAS
8; SATA 8, 97

Mojtabai, A(nn) G(race) 1938- **CLC 5, 9, 15,
29**
See also CA 85-88

Moliere 1622-1673**LC 10, 28; DA; DAB; DAC;
DAM DRAM, MST; WLC**

Molin, Charles
See Mayne, William (James Carter)

Molnar, Ferenc 1878-1952 .. **TCLC 20; DAM
DRAM**
See also CA 109; 153

Momaday, N(avarre) Scott 1934- **CLC 2, 19,
85, 95; DA; DAB; DAC; DAM MST,
MULT, NOV, POP; PC 25; WLCS**
See also AAYA 11; CA 25-28R; CANR 14, 34,
68; CDALBS; DLB 143, 175; INT CANR-
14; MTCW 1, 2; NNAL; SATA 48; SATA-
Brief 30

Monette, Paul 1945-1995 .... **CLC 82**
See also CA 139; 147

Monroe, Harriet 1860-1936 .... **TCLC 12**
See also CA 109; DLB 54, 91

Monroe, Lyle
See Heinlein, Robert A(nson)

Montagu, Elizabeth 1720-1800 .... **NCLC 7**

Montagu, Mary (Pierrepont) Wortley 1689-
1762 .... **LC 9; PC 16**
See also DLB 95, 101

Montagu, W. H.
See Coleridge, Samuel Taylor

Montague, John (Patrick) 1929- **CLC 13, 46**
See also CA 9-12R; CANR 9, 69; DLB 40;
MTCW 1

Montaigne, Michel (Eyquem) de 1533-1592
LC 8; DA; DAB; DAC; DAM MST; WLC

Montale, Eugenio 1896-1981**CLC 7, 9, 18; PC
13**
See also CA 17-20R; 104; CANR 30; DLB 114;
MTCW 1

Montesquieu, Charles-Louis de Secondat 1689-
1755 .... **LC 7**

Montgomery, (Robert) Bruce 1921-1978
See Crispin, Edmund
See also CA 179; 104

Montgomery, L(ucy) M(aud) 1874-1942
TCLC 51; DAC; DAM MST
See also AAYA 12; CA 108; 137; CLR 8; DLB
92; DLBD 14; JRDA; MAICYA; MTCW 2;
SATA 100; YABC 1

Montgomery, Marion H., Jr. 1925- .... **CLC 7**
See also AITN 1; CA 1-4R; CANR 3, 48; DLB
6

Montgomery, Max
See Davenport, Guy (Mattison, Jr.)

Montherlant, Henry (Milon) de 1896-1972
CLC 8, 19; DAM DRAM
See also CA 85-88; 37-40R; DLB 72; MTCW
1

Monty Python
See Chapman, Graham; Cleese, John
(Marwood); Gilliam, Terry (Vance); Idle,
Eric; Jones, Terence Graham Parry; Palin,
Michael (Edward)
See also AAYA 7

Moodie, Susanna (Strickland) 1803-1885
NCLC 14
See also DLB 99

Mooney, Edward 1951-
See Mooney, Ted
See also CA 130

Mooney, Ted .... **CLC 25**
See also Mooney, Edward

Moorcock, Michael (John) 1939-**CLC 5, 27, 58**
See also Bradbury, Edward P.
See also AAYA 26; CA 45-48; CAAS 5; CANR
2, 17, 38, 64; DLB 14; MTCW 1, 2; SATA
93

Moore, Brian 1921-1999**CLC 1, 3, 5, 7, 8, 19,
32, 90; DAB; DAC; DAM MST**
See also CA 1-4R; 174; CANR 1, 25, 42, 63;
MTCW 1, 2

Moore, Edward
See Muir, Edwin

Moore, G. E. 1873-1958 .... **TCLC 89**

Moore, George Augustus 1852-1933**TCLC 7;
SSC 19**
See also CA 104; 177; DLB 10, 18, 57, 135

Moore, Lorrie .... **CLC 39, 45, 68**
See also Moore, Marie Lorena

Moore, Marianne (Craig) 1887-1972**CLC 1, 2,
4, 8, 10, 13, 19, 47; DA; DAB; DAC; DAM
MST, POET; PC 4; WLCS**
See also CA 1-4R; 33-36R; CANR 3, 61;
CDALB 1929-1941; DLB 45; DLBD 7;
MTCW 1, 2; SATA 20

Moore, Marie Lorena 1957-
See Moore, Lorrie

See also CA 116; CANR 39

Moore, Thomas 1779-1852 .... **NCLC 6**
See also DLB 96, 144

Mora, Pat(ricia) 1942-
See also CA 129; CANR 57, 81; CLR 58; DAM
MULT; DLB 209; HLC 2; HW 1, 2; SATA
92

Morand, Paul 1888-1976 .... **CLC 41; SSC 22**
See also CA 69-72; DLB 65

Morante, Elsa 1918-1985 .... **CLC 8, 47**
See also CA 85-88; 117; CANR 35; DLB 177;
MTCW 1, 2

Moravia, Alberto 1907-1990**CLC 2, 7, 11, 27,
46; SSC 26**
See also Pincherle, Alberto
See also DLB 177; MTCW 2

More, Hannah 1745-1833 .... **NCLC 27**
See also DLB 107, 109, 116, 158

More, Henry 1614-1687 .... **LC 9**
See also DLB 126

More, Sir Thomas 1478-1535 .... **LC 10, 32**

Moreas, Jean .... **TCLC 18**
See also Papadiamantopoulos, Johannes

Morgan, Berry 1919- .... **CLC 6**
See also CA 49-52; DLB 6

Morgan, Claire
See Highsmith, (Mary) Patricia

Morgan, Edwin (George) 1920- .... **CLC 31**
See also CA 5-8R; CANR 3, 43; DLB 27

Morgan, (George) Frederick 1922- .. **CLC 23**
See also CA 17-20R; CANR 21

Morgan, Harriet
See Mencken, H(enry) L(ouis)

Morgan, Jane
See Cooper, James Fenimore

Morgan, Janet 1945- .... **CLC 39**
See also CA 65-68

Morgan, Lady 1776(?)-1859 .... **NCLC 29**
See also DLB 116, 158

Morgan, Robin (Evonne) 1941- .... **CLC 2**
See also CA 69-72; CANR 29, 68; MTCW 1;
SATA 80

Morgan, Scott
See Kuttner, Henry

Morgan, Seth 1949(?)-1990 .... **CLC 65**
See also CA 132

Morgenstern, Christian 1871-1914 . **TCLC 8**
See also CA 105

Morgenstern, S.
See Goldman, William (W.)

Moricz, Zsigmond 1879-1942 .... **TCLC 33**
See also CA 165

Morike, Eduard (Friedrich) 1804-1875**NCLC
10**
See also DLB 133

Moritz, Karl Philipp 1756-1793 .... **LC 2**
See also DLB 94

Morland, Peter Henry
See Faust, Frederick (Schiller)

Morley, Christopher (Darlington) 1890-1957
TCLC 87
See also CA 112; DLB 9

Morren, Theophil
See Hofmannsthal, Hugo von

Morris, Bill 1952- .... **CLC 76**

Morris, Julian
See West, Morris L(anglo)

Morris, Steveland Judkins 1950(?)-
See Wonder, Stevie
See also CA 111

Morris, William 1834-1896 .... **NCLC 4**
See also CDBLB 1832-1890; DLB 18, 35, 57,
156, 178, 184

Morris, Wright 1910-1998 CLC **1, 3, 7, 18, 37**
See also CA 9-12R; 167; CANR 21, 81; DLB 2, 206; DLBY 81; MTCW 1, 2

Morrison, Arthur 1863-1945 .... TCLC **72**
See also CA 120; 157; DLB 70, 135, 197

Morrison, Chloe Anthony Wofford
See Morrison, Toni

Morrison, James Douglas 1943-1971
See Morrison, Jim
See also CA 73-76; CANR 40

Morrison, Jim .... CLC **17**
See also Morrison, James Douglas

Morrison, Toni 1931- CLC **4, 10, 22, 55, 81, 87;**
BLC **3;** DA; DAB; DAC; DAM MST, MULT, NOV, POP
See also AAYA 1, 22; BW 2, 3; CA 29-32R; CANR 27, 42, 67; CDALB 1968-1988; DLB 6, 33, 143; DLBY 81; MTCW 1, 2; SATA 57

Morrison, Van 1945- .... CLC **21**
See also CA 116; 168

Morrissy, Mary 1958- .... CLC **99**

Mortimer, John (Clifford) 1923- CLC **28, 43;**
DAM DRAM, POP
See also CA 13-16R; CANR 21, 69; CDBLB 1960 to Present; DLB 13; INT CANR-21; MTCW 1, 2

Mortimer, Penelope (Ruth) 1918- .... CLC **5**
See also CA 57-60; CANR 45

Morton, Anthony
See Creasey, John

Mosca, Gaetano 1858-1941 .... TCLC **75**

Mosher, Howard Frank 1943- .... CLC **62**
See also CA 139; CANR 65

Mosley, Nicholas 1923- .... CLC **43, 70**
See also CA 69-72; CANR 41, 60; DLB 14, 207

Mosley, Walter 1952- . CLC **97; BLCS; DAM MULT, POP**
See also AAYA 17; BW 2; CA 142; CANR 57; MTCW 2

Moss, Howard 1922-1987 CLC **7, 14, 45, 50;**
DAM POET
See also CA 1-4R; 123; CANR 1, 44; DLB 5

Mossgiel, Rab
See Burns, Robert

Motion, Andrew (Peter) 1952- .... CLC **47**
See also CA 146; DLB 40

Motley, Willard (Francis) 1909-1965 CLC **18**
See also BW 1; CA 117; 106; DLB 76, 143

Motoori, Norinaga 1730-1801 .... NCLC **45**

Mott, Michael (Charles Alston) 1930- CLC **15, 34**
See also CA 5-8R; CAAS 7; CANR 7, 29

Mountain Wolf Woman 1884-1960 .. CLC **92**
See also CA 144; NNAL

Moure, Erin 1955- .... CLC **88**
See also CA 113; DLB 60

Mowat, Farley (McGill) 1921- CLC **26; DAC; DAM MST**
See also AAYA 1; CA 1-4R; CANR 4, 24, 42, 68; CLR 20; DLB 68; INT CANR-24; JRDA; MAICYA; MTCW 1, 2; SATA 3, 55

Mowatt, Anna Cora 1819-1870 ..... NCLC **74**

Moyers, Bill 1934- .... CLC **74**
See also AITN 2; CA 61-64; CANR 31, 52

Mphahlele, Es'kia
See Mphahlele, Ezekiel
See also DLB 125

Mphahlele, Ezekiel 1919- .. CLC **25; BLC 3; DAM MULT**
See also Mphahlele, Es'kia
See also BW 2, 3; CA 81-84; CANR 26, 76; MTCW 2

Mqhayi, S(amuel) E(dward) K(rune Loliwe)

1875-1945 TCLC **25; BLC 3; DAM MULT**
See also CA 153

Mrozek, Slawomir 1930- .... CLC **3, 13**
See also CA 13-16R; CAAS 10; CANR 29; MTCW 1

Mrs. Belloc-Lowndes
See Lowndes, Marie Adelaide (Belloc)

Mtwa, Percy (?)- .... CLC **47**

Mueller, Lisel 1924- .... CLC **13, 51**
See also CA 93-96; DLB 105

Muir, Edwin 1887-1959 .... TCLC **2, 87**
See also CA 104; DLB 20, 100, 191

Muir, John 1838-1914 .... TCLC **28**
See also CA 165; DLB 186

Mujica Lainez, Manuel 1910-1984 ... CLC **31**
See also Lainez, Manuel Mujica
See also CA 81-84; 112; CANR 32; HW 1

Mukherjee, Bharati 1940- CLC **53, 115; DAM NOV**
See also BEST 89:2; CA 107; CANR 45, 72; DLB 60; MTCW 1, 2

Muldoon, Paul 1951- CLC **32, 72; DAM POET**
See also CA 113; 129; CANR 52; DLB 40; INT 129

Mulisch, Harry 1927- .... CLC **42**
See also CA 9-12R; CANR 6, 26, 56

Mull, Martin 1943- .... CLC **17**
See also CA 105

Muller, Wilhelm .... NCLC **73**

Mulock, Dinah Maria
See Craik, Dinah Maria (Mulock)

Munford, Robert 1737(?)-1783 .... LC **5**
See also DLB 31

Mungo, Raymond 1946- .... CLC **72**
See also CA 49-52; CANR 2

Munro, Alice 1931- .... CLC **6, 10, 19, 50, 95;**
DAC; DAM MST, NOV; SSC **3; WLCS**
See also AITN 2; CA 33-36R; CANR 33, 53, 75; DLB 53; MTCW 1, 2; SATA 29

Munro, H(ector) H(ugh) 1870-1916
See Saki
See also CA 104; 130; CDBLB 1890-1914; DA; DAB; DAC; DAM MST, NOV; DLB 34, 162; MTCW 1, 2; WLC

Murdoch, (Jean) Iris 1919-1999 CLC **1, 2, 3, 4, 6, 8, 11, 15, 22, 31, 51; DAB; DAC; DAM MST, NOV**
See also CA 13-16R; 179; CANR 8, 43, 68; CDBLB 1960 to Present; DLB 14, 194; INT CANR-8; MTCW 1, 2

Murfree, Mary Noailles 1850-1922 ... SSC **22**
See also CA 122; 176; DLB 12, 74

Murnau, Friedrich Wilhelm
See Plumpe, Friedrich Wilhelm

Murphy, Richard 1927- .... CLC **41**
See also CA 29-32R; DLB 40

Murphy, Sylvia 1937- .... CLC **34**
See also CA 121

Murphy, Thomas (Bernard) 1935- ... CLC **51**
See also CA 101

Murray, Albert L. 1916- .... CLC **73**
See also BW 2; CA 49-52; CANR 26, 52, 78; DLB 38

Murray, Judith Sargent 1751-1820 NCLC **63**
See also DLB 37, 200

Murray, Les(lie) A(llan) 1938- CLC **40; DAM POET**
See also CA 21-24R; CANR 11, 27, 56

Murry, J. Middleton
See Murry, John Middleton

Murry, John Middleton 1889-1957 TCLC **16**
See also CA 118; DLB 149

Musgrave, Susan 1951- .... CLC **13, 54**

See also CA 69-72; CANR 45

Musil, Robert (Edler von) 1880-1942 T C L C **12, 68;** SSC **18**
See also CA 109; CANR 55; DLB 81, 124; MTCW 2

Muske, Carol 1945- .... CLC **90**
See also Muske-Dukes, Carol (Anne)

Muske-Dukes, Carol (Anne) 1945-
See Muske, Carol
See also CA 65-68; CANR 32, 70

Musset, (Louis Charles) Alfred de 1810-1857 NCLC **7**
See also DLB 192

Mussolini, Benito (Amilcare Andrea) 1883-1945 TCLC **96**
See also CA 116

My Brother's Brother
See Chekhov, Anton (Pavlovich)

Myers, L(eopold) H(amilton) 1881-1944 TCLC **59**
See also CA 157; DLB 15

Myers, Walter Dean 1937- . CLC **35; BLC 3; DAM MULT, NOV**
See also AAYA 4, 23; BW 2; CA 33-36R; CANR 20, 42, 67; CLR 4, 16, 35; DLB 33; INT CANR-20; JRDA; MAICYA; MTCW 2; SAAS 2; SATA 41, 71, 109; SATA-Brief 27

Myers, Walter M.
See Myers, Walter Dean

Myles, Symon
See Follett, Ken(neth Martin)

Nabokov, Vladimir (Vladimirovich) 1899-1977 CLC **1, 2, 3, 6, 8, 11, 15, 23, 44, 46, 64; DA; DAB; DAC; DAM MST, NOV; SSC 11; WLC**
See also CA 5-8R; 69-72; CANR 20; CDALB 1941-1968; DLB 2; DLBD 3; DLBY 80, 91; MTCW 1, 2

Nagai Kafu 1879-1959 .... TCLC **51**
See also Nagai Sokichi
See also DLB 180

Nagai Sokichi 1879-1959
See Nagai Kafu
See also CA 117

Nagy, Laszlo 1925-1978 .... CLC **7**
See also CA 129; 112

Naidu, Sarojini 1879-1943 .... TCLC **80**

Naipaul, Shiva(dhar Srinivasa) 1945-1985 CLC **32, 39; DAM NOV**
See also CA 110; 112; 116; CANR 33; DLB 157; DLBY 85; MTCW 1, 2

Naipaul, V(idiadhar) S(urajprasad) 1932- CLC **4, 7, 9, 13, 18, 37, 105; DAB; DAC; DAM MST, NOV**
See also CA 1-4R; CANR 1, 33, 51; CDBLB 1960 to Present; DLB 125, 204, 206; DLBY 85; MTCW 1, 2

Nakos, Lilika 1899(?)- .... CLC **29**

Narayan, R(asipuram) K(rishnaswami) 1906- CLC **7, 28, 47, 121; DAM NOV; SSC 25**
See also CA 81-84; CANR 33, 61; MTCW 1, 2; SATA 62

Nash, (Frediric) Ogden 1902-1971 . CLC **23; DAM POET; PC 21**
See also CA 13-14; 29-32R; CANR 34, 61; CAP 1; DLB 11; MAICYA; MTCW 1, 2; SATA 2, 46

Nashe, Thomas 1567-1601(?) .... LC **41**
See also DLB 167

Nashe, Thomas 1567-1601 .... LC **41**

Nathan, Daniel
See Dannay, Frederic

Nathan, George Jean 1882-1958 ... TCLC **18**

See also Hatteras, Owen
See also CA 114; 169; DLB 137
Natsume, Kinnosuke 1867-1916
See Natsume, Soseki
See also CA 104
Natsume, Soseki 1867-1916 .... **TCLC 2, 10**
See also Natsume, Kinnosuke
See also DLB 180
Natti, (Mary) Lee 1919-
See Kingman, Lee
See also CA 5-8R; CANR 2
Naylor, Gloria 1950-**CLC 28, 52; BLC 3; DA; DAC; DAM MST, MULT, NOV, POP; WLCS**
See also AAYA 6; BW 2, 3; CA 107; CANR 27, 51, 74; DLB 173; MTCW 1, 2
Neihardt, John Gneisenau 1881-1973**CLC 32**
See also CA 13-14; CANR 65; CAP 1; DLB 9, 54
Nekrasov, Nikolai Alekseevich 1821-1878
NCLC 11
Nelligan, Emile 1879-1941 .... **TCLC 14**
See also CA 114; DLB 92
Nelson, Willie 1933- .... **CLC 17**
See also CA 107
Nemerov, Howard (Stanley) 1920-1991**CLC 2, 6, 9, 36; DAM POET; PC 24**
See also CA 1-4R; 134; CABS 2; CANR 1, 27, 53; DLB 5, 6; DLBY 83; INT CANR-27; MTCW 1, 2
Neruda, Pablo 1904-1973**CLC 1, 2, 5, 7, 9, 28, 62; DA; DAB; DAC; DAM MST, MULT, POET; HLC 2; PC 4; WLC**
See also CA 19-20; 45-48; CAP 2; HW 1; MTCW 1, 2
Nerval, Gerard de 1808-1855**NCLC 1, 67; PC 13; SSC 18**
Nervo, (Jose) Amado (Ruiz de) 1870-1919
TCLC 11; HLCS 2
See also CA 109; 131; HW 1
Nessi, Pio Baroja y
See Baroja (y Nessi), Pio
Nestroy, Johann 1801-1862 .... **NCLC 42**
See also DLB 133
Netterville, Luke
See O'Grady, Standish (James)
Neufeld, John (Arthur) 1938- .... **CLC 17**
See also AAYA 11; CA 25-28R; CANR 11, 37, 56; CLR 52; MAICYA; SAAS 3; SATA 6, 81
Neville, Emily Cheney 1919- .... **CLC 12**
See also CA 5-8R; CANR 3, 37; JRDA; MAICYA; SAAS 2; SATA 1
Newbound, Bernard Slade 1930-
See Slade, Bernard
See also CA 81-84; CANR 49; DAM DRAM
Newby, P(ercy) H(oward) 1918-1997 **CLC 2, 13; DAM NOV**
See also CA 5-8R; 161; CANR 32, 67; DLB 15; MTCW 1
Newlove, Donald 1928- .... **CLC 6**
See also CA 29-32R; CANR 25
Newlove, John (Herbert) 1938- .... **CLC 14**
See also CA 21-24R; CANR 9, 25
Newman, Charles 1938- .... **CLC 2, 8**
See also CA 21-24R
Newman, Edwin (Harold) 1919- .... **CLC 14**
See also AITN 1; CA 69-72; CANR 5
Newman, John Henry 1801-1890 .. **NCLC 38**
See also DLB 18, 32, 55
Newton, (Sir)Isaac 1642-1727 .... **LC 35, 52**
Newton, Suzanne 1936- .... **CLC 35**
See also CA 41-44R; CANR 14; JRDA; SATA

5, 77
Nexo, Martin Andersen 1869-1954 **TCLC 43**
Nezval, Vitezslav 1900-1958 .... **TCLC 44**
See also CA 123
Ng, Fae Myenne 1957(?)- .... **CLC 81**
See also CA 146
Ngema, Mbongeni 1955- .... **CLC 57**
See also BW 2; CA 143
Ngugi, James T(hiong'o) .... **CLC 3, 7, 13**
See also Ngugi wa Thiong'o
Ngugi wa Thiong'o 1938- .. **CLC 36; BLC 3; DAM MULT, NOV**
See also Ngugi, James T(hiong'o)
See also BW 2; CA 81-84; CANR 27, 58; DLB 125; MTCW 1, 2
Nichol, B(arrie) P(hillip) 1944-1988 **CLC 18**
See also CA 53-56; DLB 53; SATA 66
Nichols, John (Treadwell) 1940- .... **CLC 38**
See also CA 9-12R; CAAS 2; CANR 6, 70; DLBY 82
Nichols, Leigh
See Koontz, Dean R(ay)
Nichols, Peter (Richard) 1927- **CLC 5, 36, 65**
See also CA 104; CANR 33; DLB 13; MTCW 1
Nicolas, F. R. E.
See Freeling, Nicolas
Niedecker, Lorine 1903-1970 .... **CLC 10, 42; DAM POET**
See also CA 25-28; CAP 2; DLB 48
Nietzsche, Friedrich (Wilhelm) 1844-1900
TCLC 10, 18, 55
See also CA 107; 121; DLB 129
Nievo, Ippolito 1831-1861 .... **NCLC 22**
Nightingale, Anne Redmon 1943-
See Redmon, Anne
See also CA 103
Nightingale, Florence 1820-1910 ... **TCLC 85**
See also DLB 166
Nik. T. O.
See Annensky, Innokenty (Fyodorovich)
Nin, Anais 1903-1977**CLC 1, 4, 8, 11, 14, 60; DAM NOV, POP; SSC 10**
See also AITN 2; CA 13-16R; 69-72; CANR 22, 53; DLB 2, 4, 152; MTCW 1, 2
Nishida, Kitaro 1870-1945 .... **TCLC 83**
Nishiwaki, Junzaburo 1894-1982 .... **PC 15**
See also CA 107
Nissenson, Hugh 1933- .... **CLC 4, 9**
See also CA 17-20R; CANR 27; DLB 28
Niven, Larry .... **CLC 8**
See also Niven, Laurence Van Cott
See also AAYA 27; DLB 8
Niven, Laurence Van Cott 1938-
See Niven, Larry
See also CA 21-24R; CAAS 12; CANR 14, 44, 66; DAM POP; MTCW 1, 2; SATA 95
Nixon, Agnes Eckhardt 1927- .... **CLC 21**
See also CA 110
Nizan, Paul 1905-1940 .... **TCLC 40**
See also CA 161; DLB 72
Nkosi, Lewis 1936- .... **CLC 45; BLC 3; DAM MULT**
See also BW 1, 3; CA 65-68; CANR 27, 81; DLB 157
Nodier, (Jean) Charles (Emmanuel) 1780-1844
NCLC 19
See also DLB 119
Noguchi, Yone 1875-1947 .... **TCLC 80**
Nolan, Christopher 1965- .... **CLC 58**
See also CA 111
Noon, Jeff 1957- .... **CLC 91**
See also CA 148

Norden, Charles
See Durrell, Lawrence (George)
Nordhoff, Charles (Bernard) 1887-1947
TCLC 23
See also CA 108; DLB 9; SATA 23
Norfolk, Lawrence 1963- .... **CLC 76**
See also CA 144
Norman, Marsha 1947-**CLC 28; DAM DRAM; DC 8**
See also CA 105; CABS 3; CANR 41; DLBY 84
Normyx
See Douglas, (George) Norman
Norris, Frank 1870-1902 .... **SSC 28**
See also Norris, (Benjamin) Frank(lin, Jr.)
See also CDALB 1865-1917; DLB 12, 71, 186
Norris, (Benjamin) Frank(lin, Jr.) 1870-1902
TCLC 24
See also Norris, Frank
See also CA 110; 160
Norris, Leslie 1921- .... **CLC 14**
See also CA 11-12; CANR 14; CAP 1; DLB 27
North, Andrew
See Norton, Andre
North, Anthony
See Koontz, Dean R(ay)
North, Captain George
See Stevenson, Robert Louis (Balfour)
North, Milou
See Erdrich, Louise
Northrup, B. A.
See Hubbard, L(afayette) Ron(ald)
North Staffs
See Hulme, T(homas) E(rnest)
Norton, Alice Mary
See Norton, Andre
See also MAICYA; SATA 1, 43
Norton, Andre 1912- .... **CLC 12**
See also Norton, Alice Mary
See also AAYA 14; CA 1-4R; CANR 68; CLR 50; DLB 8, 52; JRDA; MTCW 1; SATA 91
Norton, Caroline 1808-1877 .... **NCLC 47**
See also DLB 21, 159, 199
Norway, Nevil Shute 1899-1960
See Shute, Nevil
See also CA 102; 93-96; MTCW 2
Norwid, Cyprian Kamil 1821-1883**NCLC 17**
Nosille, Nabrah
See Ellison, Harlan (Jay)
Nossack, Hans Erich 1901-1978 .... **CLC 6**
See also CA 93-96; 85-88; DLB 69
Nostradamus 1503-1566 .... **LC 27**
Nosu, Chuji
See Ozu, Yasujiro
Notenburg, Eleanora (Genrikhovna) von
See Guro, Elena
Nova, Craig 1945- .... **CLC 7, 31**
See also CA 45-48; CANR 2, 53
Novak, Joseph
See Kosinski, Jerzy (Nikodem)
Novalis 1772-1801 .... **NCLC 13**
See also DLB 90
Novis, Emile
See Weil, Simone (Adolphine)
Nowlan, Alden (Albert) 1933-1983 **CLC 15; DAC; DAM MST**
See also CA 9-12R; CANR 5; DLB 53
Noyes, Alfred 1880-1958 ...... **TCLC 7; PC 27**
See also CA 104; DLB 20
Nunn, Kem .... **CLC 34**
See also CA 159
Nye, Robert 1939- .. **CLC 13, 42; DAM NOV**
See also CA 33-36R; CANR 29, 67; DLB 14;

1810-1850
See Fuller, Margaret
See also SATA 25
Ostrovsky, Alexander 1823-1886 **NCLC 30, 57**
Otero, Blas de 1916-1979 .... **CLC 11**
See also CA 89-92; DLB 134
Otto, Rudolf 1869-1937 .... **TCLC 85**
Otto, Whitney 1955- .... **CLC 70**
See also CA 140
Ouida .... **TCLC 43**
See also De La Ramee, (Marie) Louise
See also DLB 18, 156
Ousmane, Sembene 1923- .... **CLC 66; BLC 3**
See also BW 1, 3; CA 117; 125; CANR 81;
MTCW 1
Ovid 43B.C.-17 **CMLC 7; DAM POET; PC 2**
See also DLB 211
Owen, Hugh
See Faust, Frederick (Schiller)
Owen, Wilfred (Edward Salter) 1893-1918
**TCLC 5, 27; DA; DAB; DAC; DAM MST,
POET; PC 19; WLC**
See also CA 104; 141; CDBLB 1914-1945;
DLB 20; MTCW 2
Owens, Rochelle 1936- .... **CLC 8**
See also CA 17-20R; CAAS 2; CANR 39
Oz, Amos 1939- **CLC 5, 8, 11, 27, 33, 54; DAM
NOV**
See also CA 53-56; CANR 27, 47, 65; MTCW
1, 2
Ozick, Cynthia 1928- **CLC 3, 7, 28, 62; DAM
NOV, POP; SSC 15**
See also BEST 90:1; CA 17-20R; CANR 23,
58; DLB 28, 152; DLBY 82; INT CANR-
23; MTCW 1, 2
Ozu, Yasujiro 1903-1963 .... **CLC 16**
See also CA 112
Pacheco, C.
See Pessoa, Fernando (Antonio Nogueira)
Pacheco, Jose Emilio 1939-
See also CA 111; 131; CANR 65; DAM MULT;
HLC 2; HW 1, 2
Pa Chin .... **CLC 18**
See also Li Fei-kan
Pack, Robert 1929- .... **CLC 13**
See also CA 1-4R; CANR 3, 44, 82; DLB 5
Padgett, Lewis
See Kuttner, Henry
Padilla (Lorenzo), Heberto 1932- ..... **CLC 38**
See also AITN 1; CA 123; 131; HW 1
Page, Jimmy 1944- .... **CLC 12**
Page, Louise 1955- .... **CLC 40**
See also CA 140; CANR 76
Page, P(atricia) K(athleen) 1916- **CLC 7, 18;
DAC; DAM MST; PC 12**
See also CA 53-56; CANR 4, 22, 65; DLB 68;
MTCW 1
Page, Thomas Nelson 1853-1922 .... **SSC 23**
See also CA 118; 177; DLB 12, 78; DLBD 13
Pagels, Elaine Hiesey 1943- .... **CLC 104**
See also CA 45-48; CANR 2, 24, 51
Paget, Violet 1856-1935
See Lee, Vernon
See also CA 104; 166
Paget-Lowe, Henry
See Lovecraft, H(oward) P(hillips)
Paglia, Camille (Anna) 1947- .... **CLC 68**
See also CA 140; CANR 72; MTCW 2
Paige, Richard
See Koontz, Dean R(ay)
Paine, Thomas 1737-1809 .... **NCLC 62**
See also CDALB 1640-1865; DLB 31, 43, 73,
158

Pakenham, Antonia
See Fraser, (Lady) Antonia (Pakenham)
Palamas, Kostes 1859-1943 .... **TCLC 5**
See also CA 105
Palazzeschi, Aldo 1885-1974 .... **CLC 11**
See also CA 89-92; 53-56; DLB 114
Pales Matos, Luis 1898-1959
See also HLCS 2; HW 1
Paley, Grace 1922- **CLC 4, 6, 37; DAM POP;
SSC 8**
See also CA 25-28R; CANR 13, 46, 74; DLB
28; INT CANR-13; MTCW 1, 2
Palin, Michael (Edward) 1943- .... **CLC 21**
See also Monty Python
See also CA 107; CANR 35; SATA 67
Palliser, Charles 1947- .... **CLC 65**
See also CA 136; CANR 76
Palma, Ricardo 1833-1919 .... **TCLC 29**
See also CA 168
Pancake, Breece Dexter 1952-1979
See Pancake, Breece D'J
See also CA 123; 109
Pancake, Breece D'J .... **CLC 29**
See also Pancake, Breece Dexter
See also DLB 130
Panko, Rudy
See Gogol, Nikolai (Vasilyevich)
Papadiamantis, Alexandros 1851-1911 **TCLC 29**
See also CA 168
Papadiamantopoulos, Johannes 1856-1910
See Moreas, Jean
See also CA 117
Papini, Giovanni 1881-1956 .... **TCLC 22**
See also CA 121
Paracelsus 1493-1541 .... **LC 14**
See also DLB 179
Parasol, Peter
See Stevens, Wallace
Pardo Bazan, Emilia 1851-1921 .... **SSC 30**
Pareto, Vilfredo 1848-1923 .... **TCLC 69**
See also CA 175
Parfenie, Maria
See Codrescu, Andrei
Parini, Jay (Lee) 1948- .... **CLC 54**
See also CA 97-100; CAAS 16; CANR 32
Park, Jordan
See Kornbluth, C(yril) M.; Pohl, Frederik
Park, Robert E(zra) 1864-1944 ...... **TCLC 73**
See also CA 122; 165
Parker, Bert
See Ellison, Harlan (Jay)
Parker, Dorothy (Rothschild) 1893-1967 **CLC
15, 68; DAM POET; PC 28; SSC 2**
See also CA 19-20; 25-28R; CAP 2; DLB 11,
45, 86; MTCW 1, 2
Parker, Robert B(rown) 1932- **CLC 27; DAM
NOV, POP**
See also AAYA 28; BEST 89:4; CA 49-52;
CANR 1, 26, 52; INT CANR-26; MTCW 1
Parkin, Frank 1940- .... **CLC 43**
See also CA 147
Parkman, Francis, Jr. 1823-1893 .. **NCLC 12**
See also DLB 1, 30, 186
Parks, Gordon (Alexander Buchanan) 1912-
CLC 1, 16; BLC 3; DAM MULT
See also AITN 2; BW 2, 3; CA 41-44R; CANR
26, 66; DLB 33; MTCW 2; SATA 8, 108
Parmenides c. 515B.C.-c. 450B.C. **CMLC 22**
See also DLB 176
Parnell, Thomas 1679-1718 .... **LC 3**
See also DLB 94
Parra, Nicanor 1914- ...... **CLC 2, 102; DAM**

MULT; HLC 2
See also CA 85-88; CANR 32; HW 1; MTCW
1
Parra Sanojo, Ana Teresa de la 1890-1936
See also HLCS 2
Parrish, Mary Frances
See Fisher, M(ary) F(rances) K(ennedy)
Parson
See Coleridge, Samuel Taylor
Parson Lot
See Kingsley, Charles
Partridge, Anthony
See Oppenheim, E(dward) Phillips
Pascal, Blaise 1623-1662 .... **LC 35**
Pascoli, Giovanni 1855-1912 .... **TCLC 45**
See also CA 170
Pasolini, Pier Paolo 1922-1975 . **CLC 20, 37,
106; PC 17**
See also CA 93-96; 61-64; CANR 63; DLB 128,
177; MTCW 1
Pasquini
See Silone, Ignazio
Pastan, Linda (Olenik) 1932- **CLC 27; DAM
POET**
See also CA 61-64; CANR 18, 40, 61; DLB 5
Pasternak, Boris (Leonidovich) 1890-1960
**CLC 7, 10, 18, 63; DA; DAB; DAC; DAM
MST, NOV, POET; PC 6; SSC 31; WLC**
See also CA 127; 116; MTCW 1, 2
Patchen, Kenneth 1911-1972 ... **CLC 1, 2, 18;
DAM POET**
See also CA 1-4R; 33-36R; CANR 3, 35; DLB
16, 48; MTCW 1
Pater, Walter (Horatio) 1839-1894 .. **NCLC 7**
See also CDBLB 1832-1890; DLB 57, 156
Paterson, A(ndrew) B(arton) 1864-1941
TCLC 32
See also CA 155; SATA 97
Paterson, Katherine (Womeldorf) 1932- **CLC
12, 30**
See also AAYA 1; CA 21-24R; CANR 28, 59;
CLR 7, 50; DLB 52; JRDA; MAICYA;
MTCW 1; SATA 13, 53, 92
Patmore, Coventry Kersey Dighton 1823-1896
NCLC 9
See also DLB 35, 98
Paton, Alan (Stewart) 1903-1988 **CLC 4, 10,
25, 55, 106; DA; DAB; DAC; DAM MST,
NOV; WLC**
See also AAYA 26; CA 13-16; 125; CANR 22;
CAP 1; DLBD 17; MTCW 1, 2; SATA 11;
SATA-Obit 56
Paton Walsh, Gillian 1937-
See Walsh, Jill Paton
See also CANR 38; JRDA; MAICYA; SAAS 3;
SATA 4, 72, 109
Patton, George S. 1885-1945 .... **TCLC 79**
Paulding, James Kirke 1778-1860 ... **NCLC 2**
See also DLB 3, 59, 74
Paulin, Thomas Neilson 1949-
See Paulin, Tom
See also CA 123; 128
Paulin, Tom .... **CLC 37**
See also Paulin, Thomas Neilson
See also DLB 40
Paustovsky, Konstantin (Georgievich) 1892-
1968 .... **CLC 40**
See also CA 93-96; 25-28R
Pavese, Cesare 1908-1950 ... **TCLC 3; PC 13;
SSC 19**
See also CA 104; 169; DLB 128, 177
Pavic, Milorad 1929- .... **CLC 60**
See also CA 136; DLB 181

See also CA 29-32R; CAAS 4; CANR 58;
DLBY 82, 98; MTCW 2
Pinta, Harold
See Pinter, Harold
Pinter, Harold 1930-**CLC 1, 3, 6, 9, 11, 15, 27,
58, 73; DA; DAB; DAC; DAM DRAM,
MST; WLC**
See also CA 5-8R; CANR 33, 65; CDBLB 1960
to Present; DLB 13; MTCW 1, 2
Piozzi, Hester Lynch (Thrale) 1741-1821
NCLC 57
See also DLB 104, 142
Pirandello, Luigi 1867-1936**TCLC 4, 29; DA;
DAB; DAC; DAM DRAM, MST; DC 5;
SSC 22; WLC**
See also CA 104; 153; MTCW 2
Pirsig, Robert M(aynard) 1928-**CLC 4, 6, 73;
DAM POP**
See also CA 53-56; CANR 42, 74; MTCW 1,
2; SATA 39
Pisarev, Dmitry Ivanovich 1840-1868 **NCLC
25**
Pix, Mary (Griffith) 1666-1709 .... **LC 8**
See also DLB 80
Pixerecourt, (Rene Charles) Guilbert de 1773-
1844 .... **NCLC 39**
See also DLB 192
Plaatje, Sol(omon) T(shekisho) 1876-1932
TCLC 73; BLCS
See also BW 2, 3; CA 141; CANR 79
Plaidy, Jean
See Hibbert, Eleanor Alice Burford
Planche, James Robinson 1796-1880**NCLC 42**
Plant, Robert 1948- .... **CLC 12**
Plante, David (Robert) 1940- **CLC 7, 23, 38;
DAM NOV**
See also CA 37-40R; CANR 12, 36, 58, 82;
DLBY 83; INT CANR-12; MTCW 1
Plath, Sylvia 1932-1963 **CLC 1, 2, 3, 5, 9, 11,
14, 17, 50, 51, 62, 111; DA; DAB; DAC;
DAM MST, POET; PC 1; WLC**
See also AAYA 13; CA 19-20; CANR 34; CAP
2; CDALB 1941-1968; DLB 5, 6, 152;
MTCW 1, 2; SATA 96
Plato 428(?)B.C.-348(?)B.C. .... **CMLC 8; DA;
DAB; DAC; DAM MST; WLCS**
See also DLB 176
Platonov, Andrei .... **TCLC 14**
See also Klimentov, Andrei Platonovich
Platt, Kin 1911- .... **CLC 26**
See also AAYA 11; CA 17-20R; CANR 11;
JRDA; SAAS 17; SATA 21, 86
Plautus c. 251B.C.-184B.C..**CMLC 24; DC 6**
See also DLB 211
Plick et Plock
See Simenon, Georges (Jacques Christian)
Plimpton, George (Ames) 1927-........ **CLC 36**
See also AITN 1; CA 21-24R; CANR 32, 70;
DLB 185; MTCW 1, 2; SATA 10
Pliny the Elder c. 23-79 .... **CMLC 23**
See also DLB 211
Plomer, William Charles Franklin 1903-1973
CLC 4, 8
See also CA 21-22; CANR 34; CAP 2; DLB
20, 162, 191; MTCW 1; SATA 24
Plowman, Piers
See Kavanagh, Patrick (Joseph)
Plum, J.
See Wodehouse, P(elham) G(renville)
Plumly, Stanley (Ross) 1939- .... **CLC 33**
See also CA 108; 110; DLB 5, 193; INT 110
Plumpe, Friedrich Wilhelm 1888-1931**TCLC
53**

See also CA 112
Po Chu-i 772-846 .... **CMLC 24**
Poe, Edgar Allan 1809-1849 **NCLC 1, 16, 55,
78; DA; DAB; DAC; DAM MST, POET;
PC 1; SSC 34; WLC**
See also AAYA 14; CDALB 1640-1865; DLB
3, 59, 73, 74; SATA 23
Poet of Titchfield Street, The
See Pound, Ezra (Weston Loomis)
Pohl, Frederik 1919- .... **CLC 18; SSC 25**
See also AAYA 24; CA 61-64; CAAS 1; CANR
11, 37, 81; DLB 8; INT CANR-11; MTCW
1, 2; SATA 24
Poirier, Louis 1910-
See Gracq, Julien
See also CA 122; 126
Poitier, Sidney 1927- .... **CLC 26**
See also BW 1; CA 117
Polanski, Roman 1933- .... **CLC 16**
See also CA 77-80
Poliakoff, Stephen 1952- .... **CLC 38**
See also CA 106; DLB 13
Police, The
See Copeland, Stewart (Armstrong); Summers,
Andrew James; Sumner, Gordon Matthew
Polidori, John William 1795-1821 . **NCLC 51**
See also DLB 116
Pollitt, Katha 1949- .... **CLC 28, 122**
See also CA 120; 122; CANR 66; MTCW 1, 2
Pollock, (Mary) Sharon 1936-**CLC 50; DAC;
DAM DRAM, MST**
See also CA 141; DLB 60
Polo, Marco 1254-1324 .... **CMLC 15**
Polonsky, Abraham (Lincoln) 1910- **CLC 92**
See also CA 104; DLB 26; INT 104
Polybius c. 200B.C.-c. 118B.C. ...... **CMLC 17**
See also DLB 176
Pomerance, Bernard 1940-.... **CLC 13; DAM
DRAM**
See also CA 101; CANR 49
Ponge, Francis (Jean Gaston Alfred) 1899-1988
CLC 6, 18; DAM POET
See also CA 85-88; 126; CANR 40
Poniatowska, Elena 1933-
See also CA 101; CANR 32, 66; DAM MULT;
DLB 113; HLC 2; HW 1, 2
Pontoppidan, Henrik 1857-1943 .... **TCLC 29**
See also CA 170
Poole, Josephine .... **CLC 17**
See also Helyar, Jane Penelope Josephine
See also SAAS 2; SATA 5
Popa, Vasko 1922-1991 .... **CLC 19**
See also CA 112; 148; DLB 181
Pope, Alexander 1688-1744 **LC 3; DA; DAB;
DAC; DAM MST, POET; PC 26; WLC**
See also CDBLB 1660-1789; DLB 95, 101
Porter, Connie (Rose) 1959(?)- .... **CLC 70**
See also BW 2, 3; CA 142; SATA 81
Porter, Gene(va Grace) Stratton 1863(?)-1924
TCLC 21
See also CA 112
Porter, Katherine Anne 1890-1980**CLC 1, 3, 7,
10, 13, 15, 27, 101; DA; DAB; DAC; DAM
MST, NOV; SSC 4, 31**
See also AITN 2; CA 1-4R; 101; CANR 1, 65;
CDALBS; DLB 4, 9, 102; DLBD 12; DLBY
80; MTCW 1, 2; SATA 39; SATA-Obit 23
Porter, Peter (Neville Frederick) 1929-**CLC 5,
13, 33**
See also CA 85-88; DLB 40
Porter, William Sydney 1862-1910
See Henry, O.
See also CA 104; 131; CDALB 1865-1917; DA;

DAB; DAC; DAM MST; DLB 12, 78, 79;
MTCW 1, 2; YABC 2
Portillo (y Pacheco), Jose Lopez
See Lopez Portillo (y Pacheco), Jose
Portillo Trambley, Estela 1927-1998
See also CANR 32; DAM MULT; DLB 209;
HLC 2; HW 1
Post, Melville Davisson 1869-1930 **TCLC 39**
See also CA 110
Potok, Chaim 1929- ... **CLC 2, 7, 14, 26, 112;
DAM NOV**
See also AAYA 15; AITN 1, 2; CA 17-20R;
CANR 19, 35, 64; DLB 28, 152; INT CANR-
19; MTCW 1, 2; SATA 33, 106
Potter, (Helen) Beatrix 1866-1943
See Webb, (Martha) Beatrice (Potter)
See also MAICYA; MTCW 2
Potter, Dennis (Christopher George) 1935-1994
CLC 58, 86, 123
See also CA 107; 145; CANR 33, 61; MTCW 1
Pound, Ezra (Weston Loomis) 1885-1972
**CLC 1, 2, 3, 4, 5, 7, 10, 13, 18, 34, 48, 50,
112; DA; DAB; DAC; DAM MST, POET;
PC 4; WLC**
See also CA 5-8R; 37-40R; CANR 40; CDALB
1917-1929; DLB 4, 45, 63; DLBD 15;
MTCW 1, 2
Povod, Reinaldo 1959-1994 .... **CLC 44**
See also CA 136; 146
Powell, Adam Clayton, Jr. 1908-1972**CLC 89;
BLC 3; DAM MULT**
See also BW 1, 3; CA 102; 33-36R
Powell, Anthony (Dymoke) 1905-**CLC 1, 3, 7,
9, 10, 31**
See also CA 1-4R; CANR 1, 32, 62; CDBLB
1945-1960; DLB 15; MTCW 1, 2
Powell, Dawn 1897-1965 .... **CLC 66**
See also CA 5-8R; DLBY 97
Powell, Padgett 1952- .... **CLC 34**
See also CA 126; CANR 63
Power, Susan 1961- .... **CLC 91**
Powers, J(ames) F(arl) 1917-**CLC 1, 4, 8, 57;
SSC 4**
See also CA 1-4R; CANR 2, 61; DLB 130;
MTCW 1
Powers, John J(ames) 1945-
See Powers, John R.
See also CA 69-72
Powers, John R. .... **CLC 66**
See also Powers, John J(ames)
Powers, Richard (S.) 1957- .... **CLC 93**
See also CA 148; CANR 80
Pownall, David 1938- .... **CLC 10**
See also CA 89-92; CAAS 18; CANR 49; DLB
14
Powys, John Cowper 1872-1963**CLC 7, 9, 15,
46**
See also CA 85-88; DLB 15; MTCW 1, 2
Powys, T(heodore) F(rancis) 1875-1953
TCLC 9
See also CA 106; DLB 36, 162
Prado (Calvo), Pedro 1886-1952 ... **TCLC 75**
See also CA 131; HW 1
Prager, Emily 1952- .... **CLC 56**
Pratt, E(dwin) J(ohn) 1883(?)-1964 **CLC 19;
DAC; DAM POET**
See also CA 141; 93-96; CANR 77; DLB 92
Premchand .... **TCLC 21**
See also Srivastava, Dhanpat Rai
Preussler, Otfried 1923- .... **CLC 17**
See also CA 77-80; SATA 24
Prevert, Jacques (Henri Marie) 1900-1977
CLC 15

See also CA 77-80; 69-72; CANR 29, 61; MTCW 1; SATA-Obit 30

Prevost, Abbe (Antoine Francois) 1697-1763 **LC 1**

Price, (Edward) Reynolds 1933-**CLC 3, 6, 13, 43, 50, 63; DAM NOV; SSC 22**
See also CA 1-4R; CANR 1, 37, 57; DLB 2; INT CANR-37

Price, Richard 1949- .... **CLC 6, 12**
See also CA 49-52; CANR 3; DLBY 81

Prichard, Katharine Susannah 1883-1969 **CLC 46**
See also CA 11-12; CANR 33; CAP 1; MTCW 1; SATA 66

Priestley, J(ohn) B(oynton) 1894-1984**CLC 2, 5, 9, 34; DAM DRAM, NOV**
See also CA 9-12R; 113; CANR 33; CDBLB 1914-1945; DLB 10, 34, 77, 100, 139; DLBY 84; MTCW 1, 2

Prince 1958(?)- .... **CLC 35**

Prince, F(rank) T(empleton) 1912- .. **CLC 22**
See also CA 101; CANR 43, 79; DLB 20

Prince Kropotkin
See Kropotkin, Peter (Aleksieevich)

Prior, Matthew 1664-1721 .... **LC 4**
See also DLB 95

Prishvin, Mikhail 1873-1954 .... **TCLC 75**

Pritchard, William H(arrison) 1932- **CLC 34**
See also CA 65-68; CANR 23; DLB 111

Pritchett, V(ictor) S(awdon) 1900-1997 **C L C 5, 13, 15, 41; DAM NOV; SSC 14**
See also CA 61-64; 157; CANR 31, 63; DLB 15, 139; MTCW 1, 2

Private 19022
See Manning, Frederic

Probst, Mark 1925-............................. **CLC 59**
See also CA 130

Prokosch, Frederic 1908-1989 ...... **CLC 4, 48**
See also CA 73-76; 128; CANR 82; DLB 48; MTCW 2

Propertius, Sextus c. 50B.C.-c. 16B.C.**C M L C 32**
See also DLB 211

Prophet, The
See Dreiser, Theodore (Herman Albert)

Prose, Francine 1947- ....**CLC 45**
See also CA 109; 112; CANR 46; SATA 101

Proudhon
See Cunha, Euclides (Rodrigues Pimenta) da

Proulx, Annie
See Proulx, E(dna) Annie

Proulx, E(dna) Annie 1935-... **CLC 81; DAM POP**
See also CA 145; CANR 65; MTCW 2

Proust, (Valentin-Louis-George-Eugene-) Marcel 1871-1922 **TCLC 7, 13, 33; DA; DAB; DAC; DAM MST, NOV; WLC**
See also CA 104; 120; DLB 65; MTCW 1, 2

Prowler, Harley
See Masters, Edgar Lee

Prus, Boleslaw 1845-1912 .... **TCLC 48**

Pryor, Richard (Franklin Lenox Thomas) 1940- **CLC 26**
See also CA 122; 152

Przybyszewski, Stanislaw 1868-1927**TCLC 36**
See also CA 160; DLB 66

Pteleon
See Grieve, C(hristopher) M(urray)
See also DAM POET

Puckett, Lute
See Masters, Edgar Lee

Puig, Manuel 1932-1990**CLC 3, 5, 10, 28, 65; DAM MULT; HLC 2**

See also CA 45-48; CANR 2, 32, 63; DLB 113; HW 1, 2; MTCW 1, 2

Pulitzer, Joseph 1847-1911 .... **TCLC 76**
See also CA 114; DLB 23

Purdy, A(lfred) W(ellington) 1918-**CLC 3, 6, 14, 50; DAC; DAM MST, POET**
See also CA 81-84; CAAS 17; CANR 42, 66; DLB 88

Purdy, James (Amos) 1923-**CLC 2, 4, 10, 28, 52**
See also CA 33-36R; CAAS 1; CANR 19, 51; DLB 2; INT CANR-19; MTCW 1

Pure, Simon
See Swinnerton, Frank Arthur

Pushkin, Alexander (Sergeyevich) 1799-1837 **NCLC 3, 27; DA; DAB; DAC; DAM DRAM, MST, POET; PC 10; SSC 27; WLC**
See also DLB 205; SATA 61

P'u Sung-ling 1640-1715........**LC 49; SSC 31**

Putnam, Arthur Lee
See Alger, Horatio, Jr.

Puzo, Mario 1920-1999 **CLC 1, 2, 6, 36, 107; DAM NOV, POP**
See also CA 65-68; CANR 4, 42, 65; DLB 6; MTCW 1, 2

Pygge, Edward
See Barnes, Julian (Patrick)

Pyle, Ernest Taylor 1900-1945
See Pyle, Ernie
See also CA 115; 160

Pyle, Ernie 1900-1945 .... **TCLC 75**
See also Pyle, Ernest Taylor
See also DLB 29; MTCW 2

Pyle, Howard 1853-1911 .... **TCLC 81**
See also CA 109; 137; CLR 22; DLB 42, 188; DLBD 13; MAICYA; SATA 16, 100

Pym, Barbara (Mary Crampton) 1913-1980 **CLC 13, 19, 37, 111**
See also CA 13-14; 97-100; CANR 13, 34; CAP 1; DLB 14, 207; DLBY 87; MTCW 1, 2

Pynchon, Thomas (Ruggles, Jr.) 1937-**CLC 2, 3, 6, 9, 11, 18, 33, 62, 72, 123; DA; DAB; DAC; DAM MST, NOV, POP; SSC 14; WLC**
See also BEST 90:2; CA 17-20R; CANR 22, 46, 73; DLB 2, 173; MTCW 1, 2

Pythagoras c. 570B.C.-c. 500B.C. .. **CMLC 22**
See also DLB 176

Q
See Quiller-Couch, SirArthur (Thomas)

Qian Zhongshu
See Ch'ien Chung-shu

Qroll
See Dagerman, Stig (Halvard)

Quarrington, Paul (Lewis) 1953- ..... **CLC 65**
See also CA 129; CANR 62

Quasimodo, Salvatore 1901-1968 ..... **CLC 10**
See also CA 13-16; 25-28R; CAP 1; DLB 114; MTCW 1

Quay, Stephen 1947-......................... **CLC 95**

Quay, Timothy 1947-......................... **CLC 95**

Queen, Ellery .... **CLC 3, 11**
See also Dannay, Frederic; Davidson, Avram (James); Lee, Manfred B(ennington); Marlowe, Stephen; Sturgeon, Theodore (Hamilton); Vance, John Holbrook

Queen, Ellery, Jr.
See Dannay, Frederic; Lee, Manfred B(ennington)

Queneau, Raymond 1903-1976 **CLC 2, 5, 10, 42**
See also CA 77-80; 69-72; CANR 32; DLB 72;

MTCW 1, 2

Quevedo, Francisco de 1580-1645 .... **LC 23**

Quiller-Couch, SirArthur (Thomas) 1863-1944 **TCLC 53**
See also CA 118; 166; DLB 135, 153, 190

Quin, Ann (Marie) 1936-1973 .... **CLC 6**
See also CA 9-12R; 45-48; DLB 14

Quinn, Martin
See Smith, Martin Cruz

Quinn, Peter 1947-............................. **CLC 91**

Quinn, Simon
See Smith, Martin Cruz

Quintana, Leroy V. 1944-
See also CA 131; CANR 65; DAM MULT; DLB 82; HLC 2; HW 2

Quiroga, Horacio (Sylvestre) 1878-1937 **TCLC 20; DAM MULT; HLC 2**
See also CA 117; 131; HW 1; MTCW 1

Quoirez, Francoise 1935-..................... **CLC 9**
See also Sagan, Francoise
See also CA 49-52; CANR 6, 39, 73; MTCW 1, 2

Raabe, Wilhelm (Karl) 1831-1910. **TCLC 45**
See also CA 167; DLB 129

Rabe, David (William) 1940-... **CLC 4, 8, 33; DAM DRAM**
See also CA 85-88; CABS 3; CANR 59; DLB 7

Rabelais, Francois 1483-1553**LC 5; DA; DAB; DAC; DAM MST; WLC**

Rabinovitch, Sholem 1859-1916
See Aleichem, Sholom
See also CA 104

Rabinyan, Dorit 1972- .... **CLC 119**
See also CA 170

Rachilde 1860-1953 .... **TCLC 67**
See also DLB 123, 192

Racine, Jean 1639-1699 . **LC 28; DAB; DAM MST**

Radcliffe, Ann (Ward) 1764-1823**NCLC 6, 55**
See also DLB 39, 178

Radiguet, Raymond 1903-1923 ...... **TCLC 29**
See also CA 162; DLB 65

Radnoti, Miklos 1909-1944 .... **TCLC 16**
See also CA 118

Rado, James 1939-............................. **CLC 17**
See also CA 105

Radvanyi, Netty 1900-1983
See Seghers, Anna
See also CA 85-88; 110; CANR 82

Rae, Ben
See Griffiths, Trevor

Raeburn, John (Hay) 1941- .... **CLC 34**
See also CA 57-60

Ragni, Gerome 1942-1991 .... **CLC 17**
See also CA 105; 134

Rahv, Philip 1908-1973 .... **CLC 24**
See also Greenberg, Ivan
See also DLB 137

Raimund, Ferdinand Jakob 1790-1836**N C L C 69**
See also DLB 90

Raine, Craig 1944-..................... **CLC 32, 103**
See also CA 108; CANR 29, 51; DLB 40

Raine, Kathleen (Jessie) 1908- ...... **CLC 7, 45**
See also CA 85-88; CANR 46; DLB 20; MTCW 1

Rainis, Janis 1865-1929 .... **TCLC 29**
See also CA 170

Rakosi, Carl 1903-............................. **CLC 47**
See also Rawley, Callman
See also CAAS 5; DLB 193

Raleigh, Richard
See Lovecraft, H(oward) P(hillips)

Raleigh, Sir Walter 1554(?)-1618 . **LC 31, 39**
See also CDBLB Before 1660; DLB 172

Rallentando, H. P.
See Sayers, Dorothy L(eigh)

Ramal, Walter
See de la Mare, Walter (John)

Ramana Maharshi 1879-1950 .... **TCLC 84**

Ramoacn y Cajal, Santiago 1852-1934**T C L C 93**

Ramon, Juan
See Jimenez (Mantecon), Juan Ramon

Ramos, Graciliano 1892-1953 .... **TCLC 32**
See also CA 167; HW 2

Rampersad, Arnold 1941- .... **CLC 44**
See also BW 2, 3; CA 127; 133; CANR 81; DLB 111; INT 133

Rampling, Anne
See Rice, Anne

Ramsay, Allan 1684(?)-1758 .... **LC 29**
See also DLB 95

Ramuz, Charles-Ferdinand 1878-1947**T C L C 33**
See also CA 165

Rand, Ayn 1905-1982 **CLC 3, 30, 44, 79; DA; DAC; DAM MST, NOV, POP; WLC**
See also AAYA 10; CA 13-16R; 105; CANR 27, 73; CDALBS; MTCW 1, 2

Randall, Dudley (Felker) 1914-**CLC 1; BLC 3; DAM MULT**
See also BW 1, 3; CA 25-28R; CANR 23, 82; DLB 41

Randall, Robert
See Silverberg, Robert

Ranger, Ken
See Creasey, John

Ransom, John Crowe 1888-1974**CLC 2, 4, 5, 11, 24; DAM POET**
See also CA 5-8R; 49-52; CANR 6, 34; CDALBS; DLB 45, 63; MTCW 1, 2

Rao, Raja 1909- ..... **CLC 25, 56; DAM NOV**
See also CA 73-76; CANR 51; MTCW 1, 2

Raphael, Frederic (Michael) 1931-**CLC 2, 14**
See also CA 1-4R; CANR 1; DLB 14

Ratcliffe, James P.
See Mencken, H(enry) L(ouis)

Rathbone, Julian 1935- .... **CLC 41**
See also CA 101; CANR 34, 73

Rattigan, Terence (Mervyn) 1911-1977**CLC 7; DAM DRAM**
See also CA 85-88; 73-76; CDBLB 1945-1960; DLB 13; MTCW 1, 2

Ratushinskaya, Irina 1954- .... **CLC 54**
See also CA 129; CANR 68

Raven, Simon (Arthur Noel) 1927- .. **CLC 14**
See also CA 81-84

Ravenna, Michael
See Welty, Eudora

Rawley, Callman 1903-
See Rakosi, Carl
See also CA 21-24R; CANR 12, 32

Rawlings, Marjorie Kinnan 1896-1953**T C L C 4**
See also AAYA 20; CA 104; 137; CANR 74; DLB 9, 22, 102; DLBD 17; JRDA; MAICYA; MTCW 2; SATA 100; YABC 1

Ray, Satyajit 1921-1992 .. **CLC 16, 76; DAM MULT**
See also CA 114; 137

Read, Herbert Edward 1893-1968 ..... **CLC 4**
See also CA 85-88; 25-28R; DLB 20, 149

Read, Piers Paul 1941- .... **CLC 4, 10, 25**
See also CA 21-24R; CANR 38; DLB 14; SATA 21

Reade, Charles 1814-1884 .... **NCLC 2, 74**
See also DLB 21

Reade, Hamish
See Gray, Simon (James Holliday)

Reading, Peter 1946- .... **CLC 47**
See also CA 103; CANR 46; DLB 40

Reaney, James 1926- .. **CLC 13; DAC; DAM MST**
See also CA 41-44R; CAAS 15; CANR 42; DLB 68; SATA 43

Rebreanu, Liviu 1885-1944 .... **TCLC 28**
See also CA 165

Rechy, John (Francisco) 1934- **CLC 1, 7, 14, 18, 107; DAM MULT; HLC 2**
See also CA 5-8R; CAAS 4; CANR 6, 32, 64; DLB 122; DLBY 82; HW 1, 2; INT CANR-6

Redcam, Tom 1870-1933 .... **TCLC 25**

Reddin, Keith .... **CLC 67**

Redgrove, Peter (William) 1932- ..**CLC 6, 41**
See also CA 1-4R; CANR 3, 39, 77; DLB 40

Redmon, Anne .... **CLC 22**
See also Nightingale, Anne Redmon
See also DLBY 86

Reed, Eliot
See Ambler, Eric

Reed, Ishmael 1938-**CLC 2, 3, 5, 6, 13, 32, 60; BLC 3; DAM MULT**
See also BW 2, 3; CA 21-24R; CANR 25, 48, 74; DLB 2, 5, 33, 169; DLBD 8; MTCW 1, 2

Reed, John (Silas) 1887-1920 .... **TCLC 9**
See also CA 106

Reed, Lou .... **CLC 21**
See also Firbank, Louis

Reeve, Clara 1729-1807 .... **NCLC 19**
See also DLB 39

Reich, Wilhelm 1897-1957 .... **TCLC 57**

Reid, Christopher (John) 1949- .... **CLC 33**
See also CA 140; DLB 40

Reid, Desmond
See Moorcock, Michael (John)

Reid Banks, Lynne 1929-
See Banks, Lynne Reid
See also CA 1-4R; CANR 6, 22, 38; CLR 24; JRDA; MAICYA; SATA 22, 75

Reilly, William K.
See Creasey, John

Reiner, Max
See Caldwell, (Janet Miriam) Taylor (Holland)

Reis, Ricardo
See Pessoa, Fernando (Antonio Nogueira)

Remarque, Erich Maria 1898-1970 **CLC 21; DA; DAB; DAC; DAM MST, NOV**
See also AAYA 27; CA 77-80; 29-32R; DLB 56; MTCW 1, 2

Remington, Frederic 1861-1909 .... **TCLC 89**
See also CA 108; 169; DLB 12, 186, 188; SATA 41

Remizov, A.
See Remizov, Aleksei (Mikhailovich)

Remizov, A. M.
See Remizov, Aleksei (Mikhailovich)

Remizov, Aleksei (Mikhailovich) 1877-1957 **TCLC 27**
See also CA 125; 133

Renan, Joseph Ernest 1823-1892 ..**NCLC 26**

Renard, Jules 1864-1910 .... **TCLC 17**
See also CA 117

Renault, Mary .... **CLC 3, 11, 17**
See also Challans, Mary
See also DLBY 83; MTCW 2

Rendell, Ruth (Barbara) 1930- . **CLC 28, 48; DAM POP**
See also Vine, Barbara
See also CA 109; CANR 32, 52, 74; DLB 87; INT CANR-32; MTCW 1, 2

Renoir, Jean 1894-1979 .... **CLC 20**
See also CA 129; 85-88

Resnais, Alain 1922- .... **CLC 16**

Reverdy, Pierre 1889-1960 .... **CLC 53**
See also CA 97-100; 89-92

Rexroth, Kenneth 1905-1982**CLC 1, 2, 6, 11, 22, 49, 112; DAM POET; PC 20**
See also CA 5-8R; 107; CANR 14, 34, 63; CDALB 1941-1968; DLB 16, 48, 165,212; DLBY 82; INT CANR-14; MTCW 1, 2

Reyes, Alfonso 1889-1959**TCLC 33; HLCS 2**
See also CA 131; HW 1

Reyes y Basoalto, Ricardo Eliecer Neftali
See Neruda, Pablo

Reymont, Wladyslaw (Stanislaw) 1868(?)-1925 **TCLC 5**
See also CA 104

Reynolds, Jonathan 1942- .... **CLC 6, 38**
See also CA 65-68; CANR 28

Reynolds, Joshua 1723-1792 .... **LC 15**
See also DLB 104

Reynolds, Michael Shane 1937- .... **CLC 44**
See also CA 65-68; CANR 9

Reznikoff, Charles 1894-1976 .... **CLC 9**
See also CA 33-36; 61-64; CAP 2; DLB 28, 45

Rezzori (d'Arezzo), Gregor von 1914-1998 **CLC 25**
See also CA 122; 136; 167

Rhine, Richard
See Silverstein, Alvin

Rhodes, Eugene Manlove 1869-1934**TCLC 53**

Rhodius, Apollonius c. 3rd cent. B.C.- **C M L C 28**
See also DLB 176

R'hoone
See Balzac, Honore de

Rhys, Jean 1890(?)-1979 **CLC 2, 4, 6, 14, 19, 51; DAM NOV; SSC 21**
See also CA 25-28R; 85-88; CANR 35, 62; CDBLB 1945-1960; DLB 36, 117, 162; MTCW 1, 2

Ribeiro, Darcy 1922-1997 .... **CLC 34**
See also CA 33-36R; 156

Ribeiro, Joao Ubaldo (Osorio Pimentel) 1941- **CLC 10, 67**
See also CA 81-84

Ribman, Ronald (Burt) 1932- .... **CLC 7**
See also CA 21-24R; CANR 46, 80

Ricci, Nino 1959- .... **CLC 70**
See also CA 137

Rice, Anne 1941- .... **CLC 41; DAM POP**
See also AAYA 9; BEST 89:2; CA 65-68; CANR 12, 36, 53, 74; MTCW 2

Rice, Elmer (Leopold) 1892-1967 **CLC 7, 49; DAM DRAM**
See also CA 21-22; 25-28R; CAP 2; DLB 4, 7; MTCW 1, 2

Rice, Tim(othy Miles Bindon) 1944- **CLC 21**
See also CA 103; CANR 46

Rich, Adrienne (Cecile) 1929-**CLC 3, 6, 7, 11, 18, 36, 73, 76; DAM POET; PC 5**
See also CA 9-12R; CANR 20, 53, 74; CDALBS; DLB 5, 67; MTCW 1, 2

Rich, Barbara
See Graves, Robert (von Ranke)

Rich, Robert
See Trumbo, Dalton

Richard, Keith .... **CLC 17**
See also Richards, Keith

Richards, David Adams 1950- **CLC 59; DAC**
See also CA 93-96; CANR 60; DLB 53
Richards, I(vor) A(rmstrong) 1893-1979**C L C 14, 24**
See also CA 41-44R; 89-92; CANR 34, 74; DLB 27; MTCW 2
Richards, Keith 1943-
See Richard, Keith
See also CA 107; CANR 77
Richardson, Anne
See Roiphe, Anne (Richardson)
Richardson, Dorothy Miller 1873-1957**TCLC 3**
See also CA 104; DLB 36
Richardson, Ethel Florence (Lindesay) 1870-1946
See Richardson, Henry Handel
See also CA 105
Richardson, Henry Handel .... **TCLC 4**
See also Richardson, Ethel Florence (Lindesay)
See also DLB 197
Richardson, John 1796-1852**NCLC 55; DAC**
See also DLB 99
Richardson, Samuel 1689-1761**LC 1, 44; DA; DAB; DAC; DAM MST, NOV; WLC**
See also CDBLB 1660-1789; DLB 39
Richler, Mordecai 1931-**CLC 3, 5, 9, 13, 18, 46, 70; DAC; DAM MST, NOV**
See also AITN 1; CA 65-68; CANR 31, 62; CLR 17; DLB 53; MAICYA; MTCW 1, 2; SATA 44, 98; SATA-Brief 27
Richter, Conrad (Michael) 1890-1968**CLC 30**
See also AAYA 21; CA 5-8R; 25-28R; CANR 23; DLB 9, 212; MTCW 1, 2; SATA 3
Ricostranza, Tom
See Ellis, Trey
Riddell, Charlotte 1832-1906 .... **TCLC 40**
See also CA 165; DLB 156
Ridgway, Keith 1965- .... **CLC 119**
See also CA 172
Riding, Laura .... **CLC 3, 7**
See also Jackson, Laura (Riding)
Riefenstahl, Berta Helene Amalia 1902-
See Riefenstahl, Leni
See also CA 108
Riefenstahl, Leni .... **CLC 16**
See also Riefenstahl, Berta Helene Amalia
Riffe, Ernest
See Bergman, (Ernst) Ingmar
Riggs, (Rolla) Lynn 1899-1954 ..... **TCLC 56; DAM MULT**
See also CA 144; DLB 175; NNAL
Riis, Jacob A(ugust) 1849-1914 ..... **TCLC 80**
See also CA 113; 168; DLB 23
Riley, James Whitcomb 1849-1916**TCLC 51; DAM POET**
See also CA 118; 137; MAICYA; SATA 17
Riley, Tex
See Creasey, John
Rilke, Rainer Maria 1875-1926**TCLC 1, 6, 19; DAM POET; PC 2**
See also CA 104; 132; CANR 62; DLB 81; MTCW 1, 2
Rimbaud, (Jean Nicolas) Arthur 1854-1891 **NCLC 4, 35; DA; DAB; DAC; DAM MST, POET; PC 3; WLC**
Rinehart, Mary Roberts 1876-1958**TCLC 52**
See also CA 108; 166
Ringmaster, The
See Mencken, H(enry) L(ouis)
Ringwood, Gwen(dolyn Margaret) Pharis 1910-1984 .... **CLC 48**
See also CA 148; 112; DLB 88

Rio, Michel 19(?)- .... **CLC 43**
Ritsos, Giannes
See Ritsos, Yannis
Ritsos, Yannis 1909-1990 .... **CLC 6, 13, 31**
See also CA 77-80; 133; CANR 39, 61; MTCW 1
Ritter, Erika 1948(?)- .... **CLC 52**
Rivera, Jose Eustasio 1889-1928 ... **TCLC 35**
See also CA 162; HW 1, 2
Rivera, Tomas 1935-1984
See also CA 49-52; CANR 32; DLB 82; HLCS 2; HW 1
Rivers, Conrad Kent 1933-1968 .... **CLC 1**
See also BW 1; CA 85-88; DLB 41
Rivers, Elfrida
See Bradley, Marion Zimmer
Riverside, John
See Heinlein, Robert A(nson)
Rizal, Jose 1861-1896 .... **NCLC 27**
Roa Bastos, Augusto (Antonio) 1917-**CLC 45; DAM MULT; HLC 2**
See also CA 131; DLB 113; HW 1
Robbe-Grillet, Alain 1922-**CLC 1, 2, 4, 6, 8, 10, 14, 43**
See also CA 9-12R; CANR 33, 65; DLB 83; MTCW 1, 2
Robbins, Harold 1916-1997 ..... **CLC 5; DAM NOV**
See also CA 73-76; 162; CANR 26, 54; MTCW 1, 2
Robbins, Thomas Eugene 1936-
See Robbins, Tom
See also CA 81-84; CANR 29, 59; DAM NOV, POP; MTCW 1, 2
Robbins, Tom .... **CLC 9, 32, 64**
See also Robbins, Thomas Eugene
See also BEST 90:3; DLBY 80; MTCW 2
Robbins, Trina 1938- .... **CLC 21**
See also CA 128
Roberts, Charles G(eorge) D(ouglas) 1860-1943 **TCLC 8**
See also CA 105; CLR 33; DLB 92; SATA 88; SATA-Brief 29
Roberts, Elizabeth Madox 1886-1941 **T C L C 68**
See also CA 111; 166; DLB 9, 54, 102; SATA 33; SATA-Brief 27
Roberts, Kate 1891-1985 .... **CLC 15**
See also CA 107; 116
Roberts, Keith (John Kingston) 1935-**CLC 14**
See also CA 25-28R; CANR 46
Roberts, Kenneth (Lewis) 1885-1957**TCLC 23**
See also CA 109; DLB 9
Roberts, Michele (B.) 1949- .... **CLC 48**
See also CA 115; CANR 58
Robertson, Ellis
See Ellison, Harlan (Jay); Silverberg, Robert
Robertson, Thomas William 1829-1871**NCLC 35; DAM DRAM**
Robeson, Kenneth
See Dent, Lester
Robinson, Edwin Arlington 1869-1935**TCLC 5; DA; DAC; DAM MST, POET; PC 1**
See also CA 104; 133; CDALB 1865-1917; DLB 54; MTCW 1, 2
Robinson, Henry Crabb 1775-1867**NCLC 15**
See also DLB 107
Robinson, Jill 1936- .... **CLC 10**
See also CA 102; INT 102
Robinson, Kim Stanley 1952-........... **CLC 34**
See also AAYA 26; CA 126; SATA 109
Robinson, Lloyd
See Silverberg, Robert

Robinson, Marilynne 1944- .... **CLC 25**
See also CA 116; CANR 80; DLB 206
Robinson, Smokey .... **CLC 21**
See also Robinson, William, Jr.
Robinson, William, Jr. 1940-
See Robinson, Smokey
See also CA 116
Robison, Mary 1949- .... **CLC 42, 98**
See also CA 113; 116; DLB 130; INT 116
Rod, Edouard 1857-1910 .... **TCLC 52**
Roddenberry, Eugene Wesley 1921-1991
See Roddenberry, Gene
See also CA 110; 135; CANR 37; SATA 45; SATA-Obit 69
Roddenberry, Gene .... **CLC 17**
See also Roddenberry, Eugene Wesley
See also AAYA 5; SATA-Obit 69
Rodgers, Mary 1931-......................... **CLC 12**
See also CA 49-52; CANR 8, 55; CLR 20; INT CANR-8; JRDA; MAICYA; SATA 8
Rodgers, W(illiam) R(obert) 1909-1969**CLC 7**
See also CA 85-88; DLB 20
Rodman, Eric
See Silverberg, Robert
Rodman, Howard 1920(?)-1985 .... **CLC 65**
See also CA 118
Rodman, Maia
See Wojciechowska, Maia (Teresa)
Rodo, Jose Enrique 1872(?)-1917
See also CA 178; HLCS 2; HW 2
Rodriguez, Claudio 1934-.................. **CLC 10**
See also DLB 134
Rodriguez, Richard 1944-
See also CA 110; CANR 66; DAM MULT; DLB 82; HLC 2; HW 1, 2
Roelvaag, O(le) E(dvart) 1876-1931**TCLC 17**
See also CA 117; 171; DLB 9
Roethke, Theodore (Huebner) 1908-1963**CLC 1, 3, 8, 11, 19, 46, 101; DAM POET; PC 15**
See also CA 81-84; CABS 2; CDALB 1941-1968; DLB 5, 206; MTCW 1, 2
Rogers, Samuel 1763-1855 .... **NCLC 69**
See also DLB 93
Rogers, Thomas Hunton 1927- .... **CLC 57**
See also CA 89-92; INT 89-92
Rogers, Will(iam Penn Adair) 1879-1935 **TCLC 8, 71; DAM MULT**
See also CA 105; 144; DLB 11; MTCW 2; NNAL
Rogin, Gilbert 1929-......................... **CLC 18**
See also CA 65-68; CANR 15
Rohan, Koda .... **TCLC 22**
See also Koda Shigeyuki
Rohlfs, Anna Katharine Green
See Green, Anna Katharine
Rohmer, Eric .... **CLC 16**
See also Scherer, Jean-Marie Maurice
Rohmer, Sax .... **TCLC 28**
See also Ward, Arthur Henry Sarsfield
See also DLB 70
Roiphe, Anne (Richardson) 1935- ..**CLC 3, 9**
See also CA 89-92; CANR 45, 73; DLBY 80; INT 89-92
Rojas, Fernando de 1465-1541**LC 23; HLCS 1**
Rojas, Gonzalo 1917-
See also HLCS 2; HW 2
Rojas, Gonzalo 1917-
See also CA 178; HLCS 2
Rolfe, Frederick (William Serafino Austin Lewis Mary) 1860-1913 .... **TCLC 12**
See also CA 107; DLB 34, 156
Rolland, Romain 1866-1944 .... **TCLC 23**
See also CA 118; DLB 65

Rolle, Richard c. 1300-c. 1349 ...... **CMLC 21**
 See also DLB 146
Rolvaag, O(le) E(dvart)
 See Roelvaag, O(le) E(dvart)
Romain Arnaud, Saint
 See Aragon, Louis
Romains, Jules 1885-1972 .... **CLC 7**
 See also CA 85-88; CANR 34; DLB 65; MTCW
 1
Romero, Jose Ruben 1890-1952 .... **TCLC 14**
 See also CA 114; 131; HW 1
Ronsard, Pierre de 1524-1585 .. **LC 6; PC 11**
Rooke, Leon 1934- .. **CLC 25, 34; DAM POP**
 See also CA 25-28R; CANR 23, 53
Roosevelt, Franklin Delano 1882-1945**T C L C
 93**
 See also CA 116; 173
Roosevelt, Theodore 1858-1919 ..... **TCLC 69**
 See also CA 115; 170; DLB 47, 186
Roper, William 1498-1578 .... **LC 10**
Roquelaure, A. N.
 See Rice, Anne
Rosa, Joao Guimaraes 1908-1967 .. **CLC 23;
 HLCS 1**
 See also CA 89-92; DLB 113
Rose, Wendy 1948-**CLC 85; DAM MULT; PC
 13**
 See also CA 53-56; CANR 5, 51; DLB 175;
 NNAL; SATA 12
Rosen, R. D.
 See Rosen, Richard (Dean)
Rosen, Richard (Dean) 1949- .... **CLC 39**
 See also CA 77-80; CANR 62; INT CANR-30
Rosenberg, Isaac 1890-1918 .... **TCLC 12**
 See also CA 107; DLB 20
Rosenblatt, Joe .... **CLC 15**
 See also Rosenblatt, Joseph
Rosenblatt, Joseph 1933-
 See Rosenblatt, Joe
 See also CA 89-92; INT 89-92
Rosenfeld, Samuel
 See Tzara, Tristan
Rosenstock, Sami
 See Tzara, Tristan
Rosenstock, Samuel
 See Tzara, Tristan
Rosenthal, M(acha) L(ouis) 1917-1996 . **C L C
 28**
 See also CA 1-4R; 152; CAAS 6; CANR 4, 51;
 DLB 5; SATA 59
Ross, Barnaby
 See Dannay, Frederic
Ross, Bernard L.
 See Follett, Ken(neth Martin)
Ross, J. H.
 See Lawrence, T(homas) E(dward)
Ross, John Hume
 See Lawrence, T(homas) E(dward)
Ross, Martin
 See Martin, Violet Florence
 See also DLB 135
Ross, (James) Sinclair 1908-1996 ... **CLC 13;
 DAC; DAM MST; SSC 24**
 See also CA 73-76; CANR 81; DLB 88
Rossetti, Christina (Georgina) 1830-1894
 **NCLC 2, 50, 66; DA; DAB; DAC; DAM
 MST, POET; PC 7; WLC**
 See also DLB 35, 163; MAICYA; SATA 20
Rossetti, Dante Gabriel 1828-1882 . **NCLC 4,
 77; DA; DAB; DAC; DAM MST, POET;
 WLC**
 See also CDBLB 1832-1890; DLB 35
Rossner, Judith (Perelman) 1935-**CLC 6, 9, 29**

 See also AITN 2; BEST 90:3; CA 17-20R;
 CANR 18, 51, 73; DLB 6; INT CANR-18;
 MTCW 1, 2
Rostand, Edmond (Eugene Alexis) 1868-1918
 **TCLC 6, 37; DA; DAB; DAC; DAM
 DRAM, MST; DC 10**
 See also CA 104; 126; DLB 192; MTCW 1
Roth, Henry 1906-1995 ..... **CLC 2, 6, 11, 104**
 See also CA 11-12; 149; CANR 38, 63; CAP 1;
 DLB 28; MTCW 1, 2
Roth, Philip (Milton) 1933-**CLC 1, 2, 3, 4, 6, 9,
 15, 22, 31, 47, 66, 86, 119; DA; DAB; DAC;
 DAM MST, NOV, POP; SSC 26; WLC**
 See also BEST 90:3; CA 1-4R; CANR 1, 22,
 36, 55; CDALB 1968-1988; DLB 2, 28, 173;
 DLBY 82; MTCW 1, 2
Rothenberg, Jerome 1931- .... **CLC 6, 57**
 See also CA 45-48; CANR 1; DLB 5, 193
Roumain, Jacques (Jean Baptiste) 1907-1944
 TCLC 19; BLC 3; DAMMULT
 See also BW 1; CA 117; 125
Rourke, Constance (Mayfield) 1885-1941
 TCLC 12
 See also CA 107; YABC 1
Rousseau, Jean-Baptiste 1671-1741 ...... **LC 9**
Rousseau, Jean-Jacques 1712-1778**LC 14, 36;
 DA; DAB; DAC; DAM MST; WLC**
Roussel, Raymond 1877-1933 .... **TCLC 20**
 See also CA 117
Rovit, Earl (Herbert) 1927- .... **CLC 7**
 See also CA 5-8R; CANR 12
Rowe, Elizabeth Singer 1674-1737 ...... **LC 44**
 See also DLB 39, 95
Rowe, Nicholas 1674-1718 .... **LC 8**
 See also DLB 84
Rowley, Ames Dorrance
 See Lovecraft, H(oward) P(hillips)
Rowson, Susanna Haswell 1762(?)-1824
 NCLC 5, 69
 See also DLB 37, 200
Roy, Arundhati 1960(?)- .... **CLC 109**
 See also CA 163; DLBY 97
Roy, Gabrielle 1909-1983 **CLC 10, 14; DAB;
 DAC; DAM MST**
 See also CA 53-56; 110; CANR 5, 61; DLB 68;
 MTCW 1; SATA 104
Royko, Mike 1932-1997 .... **CLC 109**
 See also CA 89-92; 157; CANR 26
Rozewicz, Tadeusz 1921- .. **CLC 9, 23; DAM
 POET**
 See also CA 108; CANR 36, 66; MTCW 1, 2
Ruark, Gibbons 1941- .... **CLC 3**
 See also CA 33-36R; CAAS 23; CANR 14, 31,
 57; DLB 120
Rubens, Bernice (Ruth) 1923- .... **CLC 19, 31**
 See also CA 25-28R; CANR 33, 65; DLB 14,
 207; MTCW 1
Rubin, Harold
 See Robbins, Harold
Rudkin, (James) David 1936- .... **CLC 14**
 See also CA 89-92; DLB 13
Rudnik, Raphael 1933- .... **CLC 7**
 See also CA 29-32R
Ruffian, M.
 See Hasek, Jaroslav (Matej Frantisek)
Ruiz, Jose Martinez .... **CLC 11**
 See also Martinez Ruiz, Jose
Rukeyser, Muriel 1913-1980**CLC 6, 10, 15, 27;
 DAM POET; PC 12**
 See also CA 5-8R; 93-96; CANR 26, 60; DLB
 48; MTCW 1, 2; SATA-Obit 22
Rule, Jane (Vance) 1931- .... **CLC 27**
 See also CA 25-28R; CAAS 18; CANR 12; DLB

 60
Rulfo, Juan 1918-1986 ...... **CLC 8, 80; DAM
 MULT; HLC 2; SSC 25**
 See also CA 85-88; 118; CANR 26; DLB 113;
 HW 1, 2; MTCW 1, 2
Rumi, Jalal al-Din 1297-1373 .... **CMLC 20**
Runeberg, Johan 1804-1877 .... **NCLC 41**
Runyon, (Alfred) Damon 1884(?)-1946**T C L C
 10**
 See also CA 107; 165; DLB 11, 86, 171; MTCW
 2
Rush, Norman 1933- .... **CLC 44**
 See also CA 121; 126; INT 126
Rushdie, (Ahmed) Salman 1947-**CLC 23, 31,
 55, 100; DAB; DAC; DAM MST, NOV,
 POP; WLCS**
 See also BEST 89:3; CA 108; 111; CANR 33,
 56; DLB 194; INT 111; MTCW 1, 2
Rushforth, Peter (Scott) 1945- .... **CLC 19**
 See also CA 101
Ruskin, John 1819-1900 .... **TCLC 63**
 See also CA 114; 129; CDBLB 1832-1890;
 DLB 55, 163, 190; SATA 24
Russ, Joanna 1937- .... **CLC 15**
 See also CANR 11, 31, 65; DLB 8; MTCW 1
Russell, George William 1867-1935
 See Baker, Jean H.
 See also CA 104; 153; CDBLB 1890-1914;
 DAM POET
Russell, (Henry) Ken(neth Alfred) 1927-**C L C
 16**
 See also CA 105
Russell, William Martin 1947- .... **CLC 60**
 See also CA 164
Rutherford, Mark .... **TCLC 25**
 See also White, William Hale
 See also DLB 18
Ruyslinck, Ward 1929- .... **CLC 14**
 See also Belser, Reimond Karel Maria de
Ryan, Cornelius (John) 1920-1974 ..... **CLC 7**
 See also CA 69-72; 53-56; CANR 38
Ryan, Michael 1946- .... **CLC 65**
 See also CA 49-52; DLBY 82
Ryan, Tim
 See Dent, Lester
Rybakov, Anatoli (Naumovich) 1911-1998
 CLC 23, 53
 See also CA 126; 135; 172; SATA 79; SATA-
 Obit 108
Ryder, Jonathan
 See Ludlum, Robert
Ryga, George 1932-1987**CLC 14; DAC; DAM
 MST**
 See also CA 101; 124; CANR 43; DLB 60
S. H.
 See Hartmann, Sadakichi
S. S.
 See Sassoon, Siegfried (Lorraine)
Saba, Umberto 1883-1957 .... **TCLC 33**
 See also CA 144; CANR 79; DLB 114
Sabatini, Rafael 1875-1950 .... **TCLC 47**
 See also CA 162
Sabato, Ernesto (R.) 1911-**CLC 10, 23; DAM
 MULT; HLC 2**
 See also CA 97-100; CANR 32, 65; DLB 145;
 HW 1, 2; MTCW 1, 2
Sa-Carneiro, Mario de 1890-1916 . **TCLC 83**
Sacastru, Martin
 See Bioy Casares, Adolfo
Sacastru, Martin
 See Bioy Casares, Adolfo
Sacher-Masoch, Leopold von 1836(?)-1895
 NCLC 31

Sachs, Marilyn (Stickle) 1927- .... **CLC 35**
See also AAYA 2; CA 17-20R; CANR 13, 47;
CLR 2; JRDA; MAICYA; SAAS 2; SATA 3,
68

Sachs, Nelly 1891-1970 .... **CLC 14, 98**
See also CA 17-18; 25-28R; CAP 2; MTCW 2

Sackler, Howard (Oliver) 1929-1982 **CLC 14**
See also CA 61-64; 108; CANR 30; DLB 7

Sacks, Oliver (Wolf) 1933- .... **CLC 67**
See also CA 53-56; CANR 28, 50, 76; INT
CANR-28; MTCW 1, 2

Sadakichi
See Hartmann, Sadakichi

Sade, Donatien Alphonse Francois, Comte de
1740-1814 .... **NCLC 47**

Sadoff, Ira 1945- .... **CLC 9**
See also CA 53-56; CANR 5, 21; DLB 120

Saetone
See Camus, Albert

Safire, William 1929- .... **CLC 10**
See also CA 17-20R; CANR 31, 54

Sagan, Carl (Edward) 1934-1996 **CLC 30, 112**
See also AAYA 2; CA 25-28R; 155; CANR 11,
36, 74; MTCW 1, 2; SATA 58; SATA-Obit
94

Sagan, Françoise .... **CLC 3, 6, 9, 17, 36**
See also Quoirez, Françoise
See also DLB 83; MTCW 2

Sahgal, Nayantara (Pandit) 1927-.... **CLC 41**
See also CA 9-12R; CANR 11

Said, Edward W. 1935- .... **CLC 123**

Saint, H(arry) F. 1941- .... **CLC 50**
See also CA 127

St. Aubin de Teran, Lisa 1953-
See Teran, Lisa St. Aubin de
See also CA 118; 126; INT 126

Saint Birgitta of Sweden c. 1303-1373 **CMLC
24**

Sainte-Beuve, Charles Augustin 1804-1869
NCLC 5

Saint-Exupery, Antoine (Jean Baptiste Marie
Roger) de 1900-1944 **TCLC 2, 56; DAM
NOV; WLC**
See also CA 108; 132; CLR 10; DLB 72;
MAICYA; MTCW 1, 2; SATA 20

St. John, David
See Hunt, E(verette) Howard, (Jr.)

Saint-John Perse
See Leger, (Marie-Rene Auguste) Alexis Saint-
Leger

Saintsbury, George (Edward Bateman) 1845-
1933 .... **TCLC 31**
See also CA 160; DLB 57, 149

Sait Faik .... **TCLC 23**
See also Abasiyanik, Sait Faik

Saki .... **TCLC 3; SSC 12**
See also Munro, H(ector) H(ugh)
See also MTCW 2

Sala, George Augustus .... **NCLC 46**

Salama, Hannu 1936- .... **CLC 18**

Salamanca, J(ack) R(ichard) 1922- **CLC 4, 15**
See also CA 25-28R

Salas, Floyd Francis 1931-
See also CA 119; CAAS 27; CANR 44, 75;
DAM MULT; DLB 82; HLC 2; HW 1, 2;
MTCW 2

Sale, J. Kirkpatrick
See Sale, Kirkpatrick

Sale, Kirkpatrick 1937- .... **CLC 68**
See also CA 13-16R; CANR 10

Salinas, Luis Omar 1937- ...... **CLC 90; DAM
MULT; HLC 2**
See also CA 131; CANR 81; DLB 82; HW 1, 2

Salinas (y Serrano), Pedro 1891(?)-1951
TCLC 17
See also CA 117; DLB 134

Salinger, J(erome) D(avid) 1919- **CLC 1, 3, 8,
12, 55, 56; DA; DAB; DAC; DAM MST,
NOV, POP; SSC 2, 28; WLC**
See also AAYA 2; CA 5-8R; CANR 39; CDALB
1941-1968; CLR 18; DLB 2, 102, 173;
MAICYA; MTCW 1, 2; SATA 67

Salisbury, John
See Caute, (John) David

Salter, James 1925- .... **CLC 7, 52, 59**
See also CA 73-76; DLB 130

Saltus, Edgar (Everton) 1855-1921 . **TCLC 8**
See also CA 105; DLB 202

Saltykov, Mikhail Evgrafovich 1826-1889
NCLC 16

Samarakis, Antonis 1919- .... **CLC 5**
See also CA 25-28R; CAAS 16; CANR 36

Sanchez, Florencio 1875-1910 .... **TCLC 37**
See also CA 153; HW 1

Sanchez, Luis Rafael 1936- .... **CLC 23**
See also CA 128; DLB 145; HW 1

Sanchez, Sonia 1934- .... **CLC 5, 116; BLC 3;
DAM MULT; PC 9**
See also BW 2, 3; CA 33-36R; CANR 24, 49,
74; CLR 18; DLB 41; DLBD 8; MAICYA;
MTCW 1, 2; SATA 22

Sand, George 1804-1876 **NCLC 2, 42, 57; DA;
DAB; DAC; DAM MST, NOV; WLC**
See also DLB 119, 192

Sandburg, Carl (August) 1878-1967 **CLC 1, 4,
10, 15, 35; DA; DAB; DAC; DAM MST,
POET; PC 2; WLC**
See also AAYA 24; CA 5-8R; 25-28R; CANR
35; CDALB 1865-1917; DLB 17, 54;
MAICYA; MTCW 1, 2; SATA 8

Sandburg, Charles
See Sandburg, Carl (August)

Sandburg, Charles A.
See Sandburg, Carl (August)

Sanders, (James) Ed(ward) 1939- .. **CLC 53;
DAM POET**
See also CA 13-16R; CAAS 21; CANR 13, 44,
78; DLB 16

Sanders, Lawrence 1920-1998 **CLC 41; DAM
POP**
See also BEST 89:4; CA 81-84; 165; CANR
33, 62; MTCW 1

Sanders, Noah
See Blount, Roy (Alton), Jr.

Sanders, Winston P.
See Anderson, Poul (William)

Sandoz, Mari(e Susette) 1896-1966 .. **CLC 28**
See also CA 1-4R; 25-28R; CANR 17, 64; DLB
9, 212; MTCW 1, 2; SATA 5

Saner, Reg(inald Anthony) 1931- .... **CLC 9**
See also CA 65-68

Sankara 788-820 .... **CMLC 32**

Sannazaro, Jacopo 1456(?)-1530 .... **LC 8**

Sansom, William 1912-1976 **CLC 2, 6; DAM
NOV; SSC 21**
See also CA 5-8R; 65-68; CANR 42; DLB 139;
MTCW 1

Santayana, George 1863-1952 .... **TCLC 40**
See also CA 115; DLB 54, 71; DLBD 13

Santiago, Danny .... **CLC 33**
See also James, Daniel (Lewis)
See also DLB 122

Santmyer, Helen Hoover 1895-1986 . **CLC 33**
See also CA 1-4R; 118; CANR 15, 33; DLBY
84; MTCW 1

Santoka, Taneda 1882-1940 .... **TCLC 72**

Santos, Bienvenido N(uqui) 1911-1996 . **C L C
22; DAM MULT**
See also CA 101; 151; CANR 19, 46

Sapper .... **TCLC 44**
See also McNeile, Herman Cyril

Sapphire
See Sapphire, Brenda

Sapphire, Brenda 1950- .... **CLC 99**

Sappho fl. 6th cent. B.C.- ...... **CMLC 3; DAM
POET; PC 5**
See also DLB 176

Saramago, Jose 1922- ...... **CLC 119; HLCS 1**
See also CA 153

Sarduy, Severo 1937-1993 **CLC 6, 97; HLCS 1**
See also CA 89-92; 142; CANR 58, 81; DLB
113; HW 1, 2

Sargeson, Frank 1903-1982 .... **CLC 31**
See also CA 25-28R; 106; CANR 38, 79

Sarmiento, Domingo Faustino 1811-1888
See also HLCS 2

Sarmiento, Felix Ruben Garcia
See Dario, Ruben

Saro-Wiwa, Ken(ule Beeson) 1941-1995 **C L C
114**
See also BW 2; CA 142; 150; CANR 60; DLB
157

Saroyan, William 1908-1981 **CLC 1, 8, 10, 29,
34, 56; DA; DAB; DAC; DAM DRAM,
MST, NOV; SSC 21; WLC**
See also CA 5-8R; 103; CANR 30; CDALBS;
DLB 7, 9, 86; DLBY 81; MTCW 1, 2; SATA
23; SATA-Obit 24

Sarraute, Nathalie 1900- **CLC 1, 2, 4, 8, 10, 31,
80**
See also CA 9-12R; CANR 23, 66; DLB 83;
MTCW 1, 2

Sarton, (Eleanor) May 1912-1995 **CLC 4, 14,
49, 91; DAM POET**
See also CA 1-4R; 149; CANR 1, 34, 55; DLB
48; DLBY 81; INT CANR-34; MTCW 1, 2;
SATA 36; SATA-Obit 86

Sartre, Jean-Paul 1905-1980 **CLC 1, 4, 7, 9, 13,
18, 24, 44, 50, 52; DA; DAB; DAC; DAM
DRAM, MST, NOV; DC 3; SSC 32; WLC**
See also CA 9-12R; 97-100; CANR 21; DLB
72; MTCW 1, 2

Sassoon, Siegfried (Lorraine) 1886-1967 **C L C
36; DAB; DAM MST, NOV, POET; PC 12**
See also CA 104; 25-28R; CANR 36; DLB 20,
191; DLBD 18; MTCW 1, 2

Satterfield, Charles
See Pohl, Frederik

Saul, John (W. III) 1942- **CLC 46; DAM NOV,
POP**
See also AAYA 10; BEST 90:4; CA 81-84;
CANR 16, 40, 81; SATA 98

Saunders, Caleb
See Heinlein, Robert A(nson)

Saura (Atares), Carlos 1932- .... **CLC 20**
See also CA 114; 131; CANR 79; HW 1

Sauser-Hall, Frederic 1887-1961 ...... **CLC 18**
See also Cendrars, Blaise
See also CA 102; 93-96; CANR 36, 62; MTCW
1

Saussure, Ferdinand de 1857-1913 **TCLC 49**

Savage, Catharine
See Brosman, Catharine Savage

Savage, Thomas 1915- .... **CLC 40**
See also CA 126; 132; CAAS 15; INT 132

Savan, Glenn 19(?)- .... **CLC 50**

Sayers, Dorothy L(eigh) 1893-1957 **TCLC 2,
15; DAM POP**
See also CA 104; 119; CANR 60; CDBLB 1914-

1945; DLB 10, 36, 77, 100; MTCW 1, 2

Sayers, Valerie 1952- .... **CLC 50, 122**
See also CA 134; CANR 61

Sayles, John (Thomas) 1950- . **CLC 7, 10, 14**
See also CA 57-60; CANR 41; DLB 44

Scammell, Michael 1935- .... **CLC 34**
See also CA 156

Scannell, Vernon 1922- .... **CLC 49**
See also CA 5-8R; CANR 8, 24, 57; DLB 27;
SATA 59

Scarlett, Susan
See Streatfeild, (Mary) Noel

Scarron
See Mikszath, Kalman

Schaeffer, Susan Fromberg 1941- **CLC 6, 11, 22**
See also CA 49-52; CANR 18, 65; DLB 28;
MTCW 1, 2; SATA 22

Schary, Jill
See Robinson, Jill

Schell, Jonathan 1943- .... **CLC 35**
See also CA 73-76; CANR 12

Schelling, Friedrich Wilhelm Joseph von 1775-1854 .... **NCLC 30**
See also DLB 90

Schendel, Arthur van 1874-1946 ... **TCLC 56**

Scherer, Jean-Marie Maurice 1920-
See Rohmer, Eric
See also CA 110

Schevill, James (Erwin) 1920- .... **CLC 7**
See also CA 5-8R; CAAS 12

Schiller, Friedrich 1759-1805 . **NCLC 39, 69;
DAM DRAM**
See also DLB 94

Schisgal, Murray (Joseph) 1926- .... **CLC 6**
See also CA 21-24R; CANR 48

Schlee, Ann 1934- .... **CLC 35**
See also CA 101; CANR 29; SATA 44; SATA-Brief 36

Schlegel, August Wilhelm von 1767-1845 **NCLC 15**
See also DLB 94

Schlegel, Friedrich 1772-1829 .... **NCLC 45**
See also DLB 90

Schlegel, Johann Elias (von) 1719(?)-1749 **LC 5**

Schlesinger, Arthur M(eier), Jr. 1917- **CLC 84**
See also AITN 1; CA 1-4R; CANR 1, 28, 58;
DLB 17; INT CANR-28; MTCW 1, 2; SATA 61

Schmidt, Arno (Otto) 1914-1979 ...... **CLC 56**
See also CA 128; 109; DLB 69

Schmitz, Aron Hector 1861-1928
See Svevo, Italo
See also CA 104; 122; MTCW 1

Schnackenberg, Gjertrud 1953- .... **CLC 40**
See also CA 116; DLB 120

Schneider, Leonard Alfred 1925-1966
See Bruce, Lenny
See also CA 89-92

Schnitzler, Arthur 1862-1931 **TCLC 4; SSC 15**
See also CA 104; DLB 81, 118

Schoenberg, Arnold 1874-1951 ...... **TCLC 75**
See also CA 109

Schonberg, Arnold
See Schoenberg, Arnold

Schopenhauer, Arthur 1788-1860 . **NCLC 51**
See also DLB 90

Schor, Sandra (M.) 1932(?)-1990 ...... **CLC 65**
See also CA 132

Schorer, Mark 1908-1977 .... **CLC 9**
See also CA 5-8R; 73-76; CANR 7; DLB 103

Schrader, Paul (Joseph) 1946- .... **CLC 26**

See also CA 37-40R; CANR 41; DLB 44

Schreiner, Olive (Emilie Albertina) 1855-1920 **TCLC 9**
See also CA 105; 154; DLB 18, 156, 190

Schulberg, Budd (Wilson) 1914-... **CLC 7, 48**
See also CA 25-28R; CANR 19; DLB 6, 26, 28; DLBY 81

Schulz, Bruno 1892-1942 **TCLC 5, 51; SSC 13**
See also CA 115; 123; MTCW 2

Schulz, Charles M(onroe) 1922- .... **CLC 12**
See also CA 9-12R; CANR 6; INT CANR-6; SATA 10

Schumacher, E(rnst) F(riedrich) 1911-1977 **CLC 80**
See also CA 81-84; 73-76; CANR 34

Schuyler, James Marcus 1923-1991 **CLC 5, 23;
DAM POET**
See also CA 101; 134; DLB 5, 169; INT 101

Schwartz, Delmore (David) 1913-1966 **CLC 2, 4, 10, 45, 87; PC 8**
See also CA 17-18; 25-28R; CANR 35; CAP 2;
DLB 28, 48; MTCW 1, 2

Schwartz, Ernst
See Ozu, Yasujiro

Schwartz, John Burnham 1965- .... **CLC 59**
See also CA 132

Schwartz, Lynne Sharon 1939- .... **CLC 31**
See also CA 103; CANR 44; MTCW 2

Schwartz, Muriel A.
See Eliot, T(homas) S(tearns)

Schwarz-Bart, Andre 1928- .... **CLC 2, 4**
See also CA 89-92

Schwarz-Bart, Simone 1938- .. **CLC 7; BLCS**
See also BW 2; CA 97-100

Schwitters, Kurt (Hermann Edward Karl Julius) 1887-1948 .... **TCLC 95**
See also CA 158

Schwob, Marcel (Mayer Andre) 1867-1905 **TCLC 20**
See also CA 117; 168; DLB 123

Sciascia, Leonardo 1921-1989 . **CLC 8, 9, 41**
See also CA 85-88; 130; CANR 35; DLB 177;
MTCW 1

Scoppettone, Sandra 1936- .... **CLC 26**
See also AAYA 11; CA 5-8R; CANR 41, 73;
SATA 9, 92

Scorsese, Martin 1942- .... **CLC 20, 89**
See also CA 110; 114; CANR 46

Scotland, Jay
See Jakes, John (William)

Scott, Duncan Campbell 1862-1947 **TCLC 6;
DAC**
See also CA 104; 153; DLB 92

Scott, Evelyn 1893-1963 .... **CLC 43**
See also CA 104; 112; CANR 64; DLB 9, 48

Scott, F(rancis) R(eginald) 1899-1985 **CLC 22**
See also CA 101; 114; DLB 88; INT 101

Scott, Frank
See Scott, F(rancis) R(eginald)

Scott, Joanna 1960- .... **CLC 50**
See also CA 126; CANR 53

Scott, Paul (Mark) 1920-1978 .... **CLC 9, 60**
See also CA 81-84; 77-80; CANR 33; DLB 14, 207; MTCW 1

Scott, Sarah 1723-1795 .... **LC 44**
See also DLB 39

Scott, Walter 1771-1832 .. **NCLC 15, 69; DA;
DAB; DAC; DAM MST, NOV, POET; PC 13; SSC 32; WLC**
See also AAYA 22; CDBLB 1789-1832; DLB 93, 107, 116, 144, 159; YABC 2

Scribe, (Augustin) Eugene 1791-1861 **NCLC 16; DAM DRAM; DC 5**

See also DLB 192

Scrum, R.
See Crumb, R(obert)

Scudery, Madeleine de 1607-1701 .... **LC 2**

Scum
See Crumb, R(obert)

Scumbag, Little Bobby
See Crumb, R(obert)

Seabrook, John
See Hubbard, L(afayette) Ron(ald)

Sealy, I. Allan 1951- .... **CLC 55**

Search, Alexander
See Pessoa, Fernando (Antonio Nogueira)

Sebastian, Lee
See Silverberg, Robert

Sebastian Owl
See Thompson, Hunter S(tockton)

Sebestyen, Ouida 1924- .... **CLC 30**
See also AAYA 8; CA 107; CANR 40; CLR 17;
JRDA; MAICYA; SAAS 10; SATA 39

Secundus, H. Scriblerus
See Fielding, Henry

Sedges, John
See Buck, Pearl S(ydenstricker)

Sedgwick, Catharine Maria 1789-1867 **NCLC 19**
See also DLB 1, 74

Seelye, John (Douglas) 1931- .... **CLC 7**
See also CA 97-100; CANR 70; INT 97-100

Seferiades, Giorgos Stylianou 1900-1971
See Seferis, George
See also CA 5-8R; 33-36R; CANR 5, 36;
MTCW 1

Seferis, George .... **CLC 5, 11**
See also Seferiades, Giorgos Stylianou

Segal, Erich (Wolf) 1937- . **CLC 3, 10; DAM POP**
See also BEST 89:1; CA 25-28R; CANR 20, 36, 65; DLBY 86; INT CANR-20; MTCW 1

Seger, Bob 1945- .... **CLC 35**

Seghers, Anna .... **CLC 7**
See also Radvanyi, Netty
See also DLB 69

Seidel, Frederick (Lewis) 1936- .... **CLC 18**
See also CA 13-16R; CANR 8; DLBY 84

Seifert, Jaroslav 1901-1986 .. **CLC 34, 44, 93**
See also CA 127; MTCW 1, 2

Sei Shonagon c. 966-1017(?) .... **CMLC 6**

Sejour, Victor 1817-1874 .... **DC 10**
See also DLB 50

Sejour Marcou et Ferrand, Juan Victor
See Sejour, Victor

Selby, Hubert, Jr. 1928- **CLC 1, 2, 4, 8; SSC 20**
See also CA 13-16R; CANR 33; DLB 2

Selzer, Richard 1928- .... **CLC 74**
See also CA 65-68; CANR 14

Sembene, Ousmane
See Ousmane, Sembene

Senancour, Etienne Pivert de 1770-1846 **NCLC 16**
See also DLB 119

Sender, Ramon (Jose) 1902-1982 **CLC 8; DAM MULT; HLC 2**
See also CA 5-8R; 105; CANR 8; HW 1;
MTCW 1

Seneca, Lucius Annaeus c. 1-c. 65 . **CMLC 6;
DAM DRAM; DC 5**
See also DLB 211

Senghor, Leopold Sedar 1906- **CLC 54; BLC 3; DAM MULT, POET; PC 25**
See also BW 2; CA 116; 125; CANR 47, 74;
MTCW 1, 2

Senna, Danzy 1970- .... **CLC 119**

1846-1916 .... **TCLC 3**
See also CA 104; 134
Sierra, Gregorio Martinez
See Martinez Sierra, Gregorio
Sierra, Maria (de la O'LeJarraga) Martinez
See Martinez Sierra, Maria (de la O'LeJarraga)
Sigal, Clancy 1926- .... **CLC 7**
See also CA 1-4R
Sigourney, Lydia Howard (Huntley) 1791-1865
NCLC 21
See also DLB 1, 42, 73
Siguenza y Gongora, Carlos de 1645-1700 **L C
8; HLCS 2**
Sigurjonsson, Johann 1880-1919 ... **TCLC 27**
See also CA 170
Sikelianos, Angelos 1884-1951 .... **TCLC 39**
Silkin, Jon 1930- .... **CLC 2, 6, 43**
See also CA 5-8R; CAAS 5; DLB 27
Silko, Leslie (Marmon) 1948-**CLC 23, 74, 114;
DA; DAC; DAM MST, MULT, POP;
WLCS**
See also AAYA 14; CA 115; 122; CANR 45,
65; DLB 143, 175; MTCW 2; NNAL
Sillanpaa, Frans Eemil 1888-1964 ... **CLC 19**
See also CA 129; 93-96; MTCW 1
Sillitoe, Alan 1928- ... **CLC 1, 3, 6, 10, 19, 57**
See also AITN 1; CA 9-12R; CAAS 2; CANR
8, 26, 55; CDBLB 1960 to Present; DLB 14,
139; MTCW 1, 2; SATA 61
Silone, Ignazio 1900-1978 .... **CLC 4**
See also CA 25-28; 81-84; CANR 34; CAP 2;
MTCW 1
Silver, Joan Micklin 1935- .... **CLC 20**
See also CA 114; 121; INT 121
Silver, Nicholas
See Faust, Frederick (Schiller)
Silverberg, Robert 1935- **CLC 7; DAM POP**
See also Jarvis, E. K.
See also AAYA 24; CA 1-4R; CAAS 3; CANR
1, 20, 36; CLR 59; DLB 8; INTCANR-20;
MAICYA; MTCW 1, 2; SATA 13, 91; SATA-
Essay 104
Silverstein, Alvin 1933- .... **CLC 17**
See also CA 49-52; CANR 2; CLR 25; JRDA;
MAICYA; SATA 8, 69
Silverstein, Virginia B(arbara Opshelor) 1937-
CLC 17
See also CA 49-52; CANR 2; CLR 25; JRDA;
MAICYA; SATA 8, 69
Sim, Georges
See Simenon, Georges (Jacques Christian)
Simak, Clifford D(onald) 1904-1988**CLC 1, 55**
See also CA 1-4R; 125; CANR 1, 35; DLB 8;
MTCW 1; SATA-Obit 56
Simenon, Georges (Jacques Christian) 1903-
1989 .. **CLC 1, 2, 3, 8, 18, 47; DAM POP**
See also CA 85-88; 129; CANR 35; DLB 72;
DLBY 89; MTCW 1, 2
Simic, Charles 1938- .... **CLC 6, 9, 22, 49, 68;
DAM POET**
See also CA 29-32R; CAAS 4; CANR 12, 33,
52, 61; DLB 105; MTCW 2
Simmel, Georg 1858-1918 .... **TCLC 64**
See also CA 157
Simmons, Charles (Paul) 1924- .... **CLC 57**
See also CA 89-92; INT 89-92
Simmons, Dan 1948- ..... **CLC 44; DAM POP**
See also AAYA 16; CA 138; CANR 53, 81
Simmons, James (Stewart Alexander) 1933-
CLC 43
See also CA 105; CAAS 21; DLB 40
Simms, William Gilmore 1806-1870 **NCLC 3**
See also DLB 3, 30, 59, 73

Simon, Carly 1945- .... **CLC 26**
See also CA 105
Simon, Claude 1913-1984 .. **CLC 4, 9, 15, 39;
DAM NOV**
See also CA 89-92; CANR 33; DLB 83; MTCW
1
Simon, (Marvin) Neil 1927-**CLC 6, 11, 31, 39,
70; DAM DRAM**
See also AITN 1; CA 21-24R; CANR 26, 54;
DLB 7; MTCW 1, 2
Simon, Paul (Frederick) 1941(?)- ..... **CLC 17**
See also CA 116; 153
Simonon, Paul 1956(?)- .... **CLC 30**
Simpson, Harriette
See Arnow, Harriette (Louisa) Simpson
Simpson, Louis (Aston Marantz) 1923-**CLC 4,
7, 9, 32; DAM POET**
See also CA 1-4R; CAAS 4; CANR 1, 61; DLB
5; MTCW 1, 2
Simpson, Mona (Elizabeth) 1957- .... **CLC 44**
See also CA 122; 135; CANR 68
Simpson, N(orman) F(rederick) 1919-**CLC 29**
See also CA 13-16R; DLB 13
Sinclair, Andrew (Annandale) 1935-. **CLC 2,
14**
See also CA 9-12R; CAAS 5; CANR 14, 38;
DLB 14; MTCW 1
Sinclair, Emil
See Hesse, Hermann
Sinclair, Iain 1943- .... **CLC 76**
See also CA 132; CANR 81
Sinclair, Iain MacGregor
See Sinclair, Iain
Sinclair, Irene
See Griffith, D(avid Lewelyn) W(ark)
Sinclair, Mary Amelia St. Clair 1865(?)-1946
See Sinclair, May
See also CA 104
Sinclair, May 1863-1946 .... **TCLC 3, 11**
See also Sinclair, Mary Amelia St. Clair
See also CA 166; DLB 36, 135
Sinclair, Roy
See Griffith, D(avid Lewelyn) W(ark)
Sinclair, Upton (Beall) 1878-1968 **CLC 1, 11,
15, 63; DA; DAB; DAC; DAM MST, NOV;
WLC**
See also CA 5-8R; 25-28R; CANR 7; CDALB
1929-1941; DLB 9; INT CANR-7; MTCW
1, 2; SATA 9
Singer, Isaac
See Singer, Isaac Bashevis
Singer, Isaac Bashevis 1904-1991**CLC 1, 3, 6,
9, 11, 15, 23, 38, 69, 111; DA; DAB; DAC;
DAM MST, NOV; SSC 3; WLC**
See also AITN 1, 2; CA 1-4R; 134; CANR 1,
39; CDALB 1941-1968; CLR 1; DLB 6, 28,
52; DLBY 91; JRDA; MAICYA; MTCW 1,
2; SATA 3, 27; SATA-Obit 68
Singer, Israel Joshua 1893-1944 .... **TCLC 33**
See also CA 169
Singh, Khushwant 1915- .... **CLC 11**
See also CA 9-12R; CAAS 9; CANR 6
Singleton, Ann
See Benedict, Ruth (Fulton)
Sinjohn, John
See Galsworthy, John
Sinyavsky, Andrei (Donatevich) 1925-1997
CLC 8
See also CA 85-88; 159
Sirin, V.
See Nabokov, Vladimir (Vladimirovich)
Sissman, L(ouis) E(dward) 1928-1976**CLC 9,
18**

See also CA 21-24R; 65-68; CANR 13; DLB 5
Sisson, C(harles) H(ubert) 1914- .... **CLC 8**
See also CA 1-4R; CAAS 3; CANR 3, 48; DLB
27
Sitwell, Dame Edith 1887-1964 **CLC 2, 9, 67;
DAM POET; PC 3**
See also CA 9-12R; CANR 35; CDBLB 1945-
1960; DLB 20; MTCW 1, 2
Siwaarmill, H. P.
See Sharp, William
Sjoewall, Maj 1935- .... **CLC 7**
See also CA 65-68; CANR 73
Sjowall, Maj
See Sjoewall, Maj
Skelton, John 1463-1529 .... **PC 25**
Skelton, Robin 1925-1997 .... **CLC 13**
See also AITN 2; CA 5-8R; 160; CAAS 5;
CANR 28; DLB 27, 53
Skolimowski, Jerzy 1938- .... **CLC 20**
See also CA 128
Skram, Amalie (Bertha) 1847-1905 **TCLC 25**
See also CA 165
Skvorecky, Josef (Vaclav) 1924- **CLC 15, 39,
69; DAC; DAM NOV**
See also CA 61-64; CAAS 1; CANR 10, 34,
63; MTCW 1, 2
Slade, Bernard .... **CLC 11, 46**
See also Newbound, Bernard Slade
See also CAAS 9; DLB 53
Slaughter, Carolyn 1946- .... **CLC 56**
See also CA 85-88
Slaughter, Frank G(ill) 1908- .... **CLC 29**
See also AITN 2; CA 5-8R; CANR 5; INT
CANR-5
Slavitt, David R(ytman) 1935- ...... **CLC 5, 14**
See also CA 21-24R; CAAS 3; CANR 41; DLB
5, 6
Slesinger, Tess 1905-1945 .... **TCLC 10**
See also CA 107; DLB 102
Slessor, Kenneth 1901-1971 .... **CLC 14**
See also CA 102; 89-92
Slowacki, Juliusz 1809-1849 .... **NCLC 15**
Smart, Christopher 1722-1771 .. **LC 3; DAM
POET; PC 13**
See also DLB 109
Smart, Elizabeth 1913-1986 .... **CLC 54**
See also CA 81-84; 118; DLB 88
Smiley, Jane (Graves) 1949-**CLC 53, 76; DAM
POP**
See also CA 104; CANR 30, 50, 74; INT CANR-
30
Smith, A(rthur) J(ames) M(arshall) 1902-1980
CLC 15; DAC
See also CA 1-4R; 102; CANR 4; DLB 88
Smith, Adam 1723-1790 .... **LC 36**
See also DLB 104
Smith, Alexander 1829-1867 .... **NCLC 59**
See also DLB 32, 55
Smith, Anna Deavere 1950- .... **CLC 86**
See also CA 133
Smith, Betty (Wehner) 1896-1972 .... **CLC 19**
See also CA 5-8R; 33-36R; DLBY 82; SATA 6
Smith, Charlotte (Turner) 1749-1806 **N C L C
23**
See also DLB 39, 109
Smith, Clark Ashton 1893-1961 .... **CLC 43**
See also CA 143; CANR 81; MTCW 2
Smith, Dave .... **CLC 22, 42**
See also Smith, David (Jeddie)
See also CAAS 7; DLB 5
Smith, David (Jeddie) 1942-
See Smith, Dave
See also CA 49-52; CANR 1, 59; DAM POET

Smith, Florence Margaret 1902-1971
  See Smith, Stevie
  See also CA 17-18; 29-32R; CANR 35; CAP 2;
  DAM POET; MTCW 1, 2
Smith, Iain Crichton 1928-1998 .... **CLC 64**
  See also CA 21-24R; 171; DLB 40, 139
Smith, John 1580(?)-1631 .... **LC 9**
  See also DLB 24, 30
Smith, Johnston
  See Crane, Stephen (Townley)
Smith, Joseph, Jr. 1805-1844 .... **NCLC 53**
Smith, Lee 1944- .... **CLC 25, 73**
  See also CA 114; 119; CANR 46; DLB 143;
  DLBY 83; INT 119
Smith, Martin
  See Smith, Martin Cruz
Smith, Martin Cruz 1942- ..... **CLC 25; DAM
MULT, POP**
  See also BEST 89:4; CA 85-88; CANR 6, 23,
  43, 65; INT CANR-23; MTCW 2; NNAL
Smith, Mary-Ann Tirone 1944- .... **CLC 39**
  See also CA 118; 136
Smith, Patti 1946- .... **CLC 12**
  See also CA 93-96; CANR 63
Smith, Pauline (Urmson) 1882-1959 **TCLC 25**
Smith, Rosamond
  See Oates, Joyce Carol
Smith, Sheila Kaye
  See Kaye-Smith, Sheila
Smith, Stevie .... **CLC 3, 8, 25, 44; PC 12**
  See also Smith, Florence Margaret
  See also DLB 20; MTCW 2
Smith, Wilbur (Addison) 1933- .... **CLC 33**
  See also CA 13-16R; CANR 7, 46, 66; MTCW
  1, 2
Smith, William Jay 1918- .... **CLC 6**
  See also CA 5-8R; CANR 44; DLB 5; MAICYA;
  SAAS 22; SATA 2, 68
Smith, Woodrow Wilson
  See Kuttner, Henry
Smolenskin, Peretz 1842-1885 .... **NCLC 30**
Smollett, Tobias (George) 1721-1771 **LC 2, 46**
  See also CDBLB 1660-1789; DLB 39, 104
Snodgrass, W(illiam) D(e Witt) 1926- **CLC 2,
6, 10, 18, 68; DAM POET**
  See also CA 1-4R; CANR 6, 36, 65; DLB 5;
  MTCW 1, 2
Snow, C(harles) P(ercy) 1905-1980 **CLC 1, 4,
6, 9, 13, 19; DAM NOV**
  See also CA 5-8R; 101; CANR 28; CDBLB
  1945-1960; DLB 15, 77; DLBD 17; MTCW
  1, 2
Snow, Frances Compton
  See Adams, Henry (Brooks)
Snyder, Gary (Sherman) 1930- **CLC 1, 2, 5, 9,
32, 120; DAM POET; PC 21**
  See also CA 17-20R; CANR 30, 60; DLB 5,
  16, 165, 212; MTCW 2
Snyder, Zilpha Keatley 1927- .... **CLC 17**
  See also AAYA 15; CA 9-12R; CANR 38; CLR
  31; JRDA; MAICYA; SAAS 2; SATA 1, 28,
  75
Soares, Bernardo
  See Pessoa, Fernando (Antonio Nogueira)
Sobh, A.
  See Shamlu, Ahmad
Sobol, Joshua .... **CLC 60**
Socrates 469B.C.-399B.C. .... **CMLC 27**
Soderberg, Hjalmar 1869-1941 ..... **TCLC 39**
Sodergran, Edith (Irene)
  See Soedergran, Edith (Irene)
Soedergran, Edith (Irene) 1892-1923 **T C L C
31**

Softly, Edgar
  See Lovecraft, H(oward) P(hillips)
Softly, Edward
  See Lovecraft, H(oward) P(hillips)
Sokolov, Raymond 1941- .... **CLC 7**
  See also CA 85-88
Solo, Jay
  See Ellison, Harlan (Jay)
Sologub, Fyodor .... **TCLC 9**
  See also Teternikov, Fyodor Kuzmich
Solomons, Ikey Esquir
  See Thackeray, William Makepeace
Solomos, Dionysios 1798-1857 .... **NCLC 15**
Solwoska, Mara
  See French, Marilyn
Solzhenitsyn, Aleksandr I(sayevich) 1918-
  **CLC 1, 2, 4, 7, 9, 10, 18, 26, 34, 78; DA;
DAB; DAC; DAM MST, NOV; SSC 32;
WLC**
  See also AITN 1; CA 69-72; CANR 40, 65;
  MTCW 1, 2
Somers, Jane
  See Lessing, Doris (May)
Somerville, Edith 1858-1949 .... **TCLC 51**
  See also DLB 135
Somerville & Ross
  See Martin, Violet Florence; Somerville, Edith
Sommer, Scott 1951- .... **CLC 25**
  See also CA 106
Sondheim, Stephen (Joshua) 1930- . **CLC 30,
39; DAM DRAM**
  See also AAYA 11; CA 103; CANR 47, 68
Song, Cathy 1955- .... **PC 21**
  See also CA 154; DLB 169
Sontag, Susan 1933- **CLC 1, 2, 10, 13, 31, 105;
DAM POP**
  See also CA 17-20R; CANR 25, 51, 74; DLB
  2, 67; MTCW 1, 2
Sophocles 496(?)B.C.-406(?)B.C. ...**CMLC 2;
DA; DAB; DAC; DAM DRAM, MST; DC
1; WLCS**
  See also DLB 176
Sordello 1189-1269 .... **CMLC 15**
Sorel, Georges 1847-1922 .... **TCLC 91**
  See also CA 118
Sorel, Julia
  See Drexler, Rosalyn
Sorrentino, Gilbert 1929- **CLC 3, 7, 14, 22, 40**
  See also CA 77-80; CANR 14, 33; DLB 5, 173;
  DLBY 80; INT CANR-14
Soto, Gary 1952- **CLC 32, 80; DAM MULT;
HLC 2; PC 28**
  See also AAYA 10; CA 119; 125; CANR 50,
  74; CLR 38; DLB 82; HW 1, 2; INT 125;
  JRDA; MTCW 2; SATA 80
Soupault, Philippe 1897-1990 .... **CLC 68**
  See also CA 116; 147; 131
Souster, (Holmes) Raymond 1921- **CLC 5, 14;
DAC; DAM POET**
  See also CA 13-16R; CAAS 14; CANR 13, 29,
  53; DLB 88; SATA 63
Southern, Terry 1924(?)-1995 .... **CLC 7**
  See also CA 1-4R; 150; CANR 1, 55; DLB 2
Southey, Robert 1774-1843 .... **NCLC 8**
  See also DLB 93, 107, 142; SATA 54
Southworth, Emma Dorothy Eliza Nevitte
  1819-1899 .... **NCLC 26**
Souza, Ernest
  See Scott, Evelyn
Soyinka, Wole 1934- **CLC 3, 5, 14, 36, 44; BLC
3; DA; DAB; DAC; DAM DRAM, MST,
MULT; DC 2; WLC**
  See also BW 2, 3; CA 13-16R; CANR 27, 39,

82; DLB 125; MTCW 1, 2
Spackman, W(illiam) M(ode) 1905-1990 **C L C
46**
  See also CA 81-84; 132
Spacks, Barry (Bernard) 1931- .... **CLC 14**
  See also CA 154; CANR 33; DLB 105
Spanidou, Irini 1946- .... **CLC 44**
Spark, Muriel (Sarah) 1918- **CLC 2, 3, 5, 8, 13,
18, 40, 94; DAB; DAC; DAM MST, NOV;
SSC 10**
  See also CA 5-8R; CANR 12, 36, 76; CDBLB
  1945-1960; DLB 15, 139; INTCANR-12;
  MTCW 1, 2
Spaulding, Douglas
  See Bradbury, Ray (Douglas)
Spaulding, Leonard
  See Bradbury, Ray (Douglas)
Spence, J. A. D.
  See Eliot, T(homas) S(tearns)
Spencer, Elizabeth 1921- .... **CLC 22**
  See also CA 13-16R; CANR 32, 65; DLB 6;
  MTCW 1; SATA 14
Spencer, Leonard G.
  See Silverberg, Robert
Spencer, Scott 1945- .... **CLC 30**
  See also CA 113; CANR 51; DLBY 86
Spender, Stephen (Harold) 1909-1995 **CLC 1,
2, 5, 10, 41, 91; DAM POET**
  See also CA 9-12R; 149; CANR 31, 54; CDBLB
  1945-1960; DLB 20; MTCW 1, 2
Spengler, Oswald (Arnold Gottfried) 1880-1936
  TCLC 25
  See also CA 118
Spenser, Edmund 1552(?)-1599 **LC 5, 39; DA;
DAB; DAC; DAM MST, POET; PC 8;
WLC**
  See also CDBLB Before 1660; DLB 167
Spicer, Jack 1925-1965 **CLC 8, 18, 72; DAM
POET**
  See also CA 85-88; DLB 5, 16, 193
Spiegelman, Art 1948- .... **CLC 76**
  See also AAYA 10; CA 125; CANR 41, 55, 74;
  MTCW 2; SATA 109
Spielberg, Peter 1929- .... **CLC 6**
  See also CA 5-8R; CANR 4, 48; DLBY 81
Spielberg, Steven 1947- .... **CLC 20**
  See also AAYA 8, 24; CA 77-80; CANR 32;
  SATA 32
Spillane, Frank Morrison 1918-
  See Spillane, Mickey
  See also CA 25-28R; CANR 28, 63; MTCW 1,
  2; SATA 66
Spillane, Mickey .... **CLC 3, 13**
  See also Spillane, Frank Morrison
  See also MTCW 2
Spinoza, Benedictus de 1632-1677 .... **LC 9**
Spinrad, Norman (Richard) 1940- ... **CLC 46**
  See also CA 37-40R; CAAS 19; CANR 20; DLB
  8; INT CANR-20
Spitteler, Carl (Friedrich Georg) 1845-1924
  TCLC 12
  See also CA 109; DLB 129
Spivack, Kathleen (Romola Drucker) 1938-
  CLC 6
  See also CA 49-52
Spoto, Donald 1941- .... **CLC 39**
  See also CA 65-68; CANR 11, 57
Springsteen, Bruce (F.) 1949- .... **CLC 17**
  See also CA 111
Spurling, Hilary 1940- .... **CLC 34**
  See also CA 104; CANR 25, 52
Spyker, John Howland
  See Elman, Richard (Martin)

Stout, Rex (Todhunter) 1886-1975 ..... **CLC 3**
See also AITN 2; CA 61-64; CANR 71
Stow, (Julian) Randolph 1935- .. **CLC 23, 48**
See also CA 13-16R; CANR 33; MTCW 1
Stowe, Harriet (Elizabeth) Beecher 1811-1896
**NCLC 3, 50; DA; DAB; DAC; DAM MST,
NOV; WLC**
See also CDALB 1865-1917; DLB 1, 12, 42,
74, 189; JRDA; MAICYA; YABC 1
Strachey, (Giles) Lytton 1880-1932 **TCLC 12**
See also CA 110; 178; DLB 149; DLBD 10;
MTCW 2
Strand, Mark 1934- **CLC 6, 18, 41, 71; DAM
POET**
See also CA 21-24R; CANR 40, 65; DLB 5;
SATA 41
Straub, Peter (Francis) 1943- . **CLC 28, 107;
DAM POP**
See also BEST 89:1; CA 85-88; CANR 28, 65;
DLBY 84; MTCW 1, 2
Strauss, Botho 1944- .... **CLC 22**
See also CA 157; DLB 124
Streatfeild, (Mary) Noel 1895(?)-1986**CLC 21**
See also CA 81-84; 120; CANR 31; CLR 17;
DLB 160; MAICYA; SATA 20; SATA-Obit
48
Stribling, T(homas) S(igismund) 1881-1965
CLC 23
See also CA 107; DLB 9
Strindberg, (Johan) August 1849-1912**T C L C
1, 8, 21, 47; DA; DAB; DAC; DAM DRAM,
MST; WLC**
See also CA 104; 135; MTCW 2
Stringer, Arthur 1874-1950 .... **TCLC 37**
See also CA 161; DLB 92
Stringer, David
See Roberts, Keith (John Kingston)
Stroheim, Erich von 1885-1957 ..... **TCLC 71**
Strugatskii, Arkadii (Natanovich) 1925-1991
CLC 27
See also CA 106; 135
Strugatskii, Boris (Natanovich) 1933-**CLC 27**
See also CA 106
Strummer, Joe 1953(?)- .... **CLC 30**
Strunk, William, Jr. 1869-1946 ...... **TCLC 92**
See also CA 118; 164
Stryk, Lucien 1924- .... **PC 27**
See also CA 13-16R; CANR 10, 28, 55
Stuart, Don A.
See Campbell, John W(ood, Jr.)
Stuart, Ian
See MacLean, Alistair (Stuart)
Stuart, Jesse (Hilton) 1906-1984**CLC 1, 8, 11,
14, 34; SSC 31**
See also CA 5-8R; 112; CANR 31; DLB 9, 48,
102; DLBY 84; SATA 2; SATA-Obit 36
Sturgeon, Theodore (Hamilton) 1918-1985
CLC 22, 39
See also Queen, Ellery
See also CA 81-84; 116; CANR 32; DLB 8;
DLBY 85; MTCW 1, 2
Sturges, Preston 1898-1959 .... **TCLC 48**
See also CA 114; 149; DLB 26
Styron, William 1925-**CLC 1, 3, 5, 11, 15, 60;
DAM NOV, POP; SSC 25**
See also BEST 90:4; CA 5-8R; CANR 6, 33,
74; CDALB 1968-1988; DLB 2, 143; DLBY
80; INT CANR-6; MTCW 1, 2
Su, Chien 1884-1918
See Su Man-shu
See also CA 123
Suarez Lynch, B.
See Bioy Casares, Adolfo; Borges, Jorge Luis

Suassuna, Ariano Vilar 1927-
See also CA 178; HLCS 1; HW 2
Suckow, Ruth 1892-1960 .... **SSC 18**
See also CA 113; DLB 9, 102
Sudermann, Hermann 1857-1928 .. **TCLC 15**
See also CA 107; DLB 118
Sue, Eugene 1804-1857 .... **NCLC 1**
See also DLB 119
Sueskind, Patrick 1949- .... **CLC 44**
See also Suskind, Patrick
Sukenick, Ronald 1932- .... **CLC 3, 4, 6, 48**
See also CA 25-28R; CAAS 8; CANR 32; DLB
173; DLBY 81
Suknaski, Andrew 1942- .... **CLC 19**
See also CA 101; DLB 53
Sullivan, Vernon
See Vian, Boris
Sully Prudhomme 1839-1907 .... **TCLC 31**
Su Man-shu .... **TCLC 24**
See also Su, Chien
Summerforest, Ivy B.
See Kirkup, James
Summers, Andrew James 1942- .... **CLC 26**
Summers, Andy
See Summers, Andrew James
Summers, Hollis (Spurgeon, Jr.) 1916-**CLC 10**
See also CA 5-8R; CANR 3; DLB 6
Summers, (Alphonsus Joseph-Mary Augustus)
Montague 1880-1948 .... **TCLC 16**
See also CA 118; 163
Sumner, Gordon Matthew .... **CLC 26**
See also Sting
Surtees, Robert Smith 1803-1864 .. **NCLC 14**
See also DLB 21
Susann, Jacqueline 1921-1974 .... **CLC 3**
See also AITN 1; CA 65-68; 53-56; MTCW 1,
2
Su Shih 1036-1101 .... **CMLC 15**
Suskind, Patrick
See Sueskind, Patrick
See also CA 145
Sutcliff, Rosemary 1920-1992**CLC 26; DAB;
DAC; DAM MST, POP**
See also AAYA 10; CA 5-8R; 139; CANR 37;
CLR 1, 37; JRDA; MAICYA; SATA 6, 44,
78; SATA-Obit 73
Sutro, Alfred 1863-1933 .... **TCLC 6**
See also CA 105; DLB 10
Sutton, Henry
See Slavitt, David R(ytman)
Svevo, Italo 1861-1928 . **TCLC 2, 35; SSC 25**
See also Schmitz, Aron Hector
Swados, Elizabeth (A.) 1951- .... **CLC 12**
See also CA 97-100; CANR 49; INT 97-100
Swados, Harvey 1920-1972 .... **CLC 5**
See also CA 5-8R; 37-40R; CANR 6; DLB 2
Swan, Gladys 1934- .... **CLC 69**
See also CA 101; CANR 17, 39
Swarthout, Glendon (Fred) 1918-1992**CLC 35**
See also CA 1-4R; 139; CANR 1, 47; SATA 26
Sweet, Sarah C.
See Jewett, (Theodora) Sarah Orne
Swenson, May 1919-1989**CLC 4, 14, 61, 106;
DA; DAB; DAC; DAM MST, POET; PC
14**
See also CA 5-8R; 130; CANR 36, 61; DLB 5;
MTCW 1, 2; SATA 15
Swift, Augustus
See Lovecraft, H(oward) P(hillips)
Swift, Graham (Colin) 1949- ...... **CLC 41, 88**
See also CA 117; 122; CANR 46, 71; DLB 194;
MTCW 2
Swift, Jonathan 1667-1745 ..... **LC 1, 42; DA;**

**DAB; DAC; DAM MST, NOV, POET; PC
9; WLC**
See also CDBLB 1660-1789; CLR 53; DLB 39,
95, 101; SATA 19
Swinburne, Algernon Charles 1837-1909
**TCLC 8, 36; DA; DAB; DAC; DAM MST,
POET; PC 24; WLC**
See also CA 105; 140; CDBLB 1832-1890;
DLB 35, 57
Swinfen, Ann .... **CLC 34**
Swinnerton, Frank Arthur 1884-1982**CLC 31**
See also CA 108; DLB 34
Swithen, John
See King, Stephen (Edwin)
Sylvia
See Ashton-Warner, Sylvia (Constance)
Symmes, Robert Edward
See Duncan, Robert (Edward)
Symonds, John Addington 1840-1893 **N C L C
34**
See also DLB 57, 144
Symons, Arthur 1865-1945 .... **TCLC 11**
See also CA 107; DLB 19, 57, 149
Symons, Julian (Gustave) 1912-1994 **CLC 2,
14, 32**
See also CA 49-52; 147; CAAS 3; CANR 3,
33, 59; DLB 87, 155; DLBY 92; MTCW 1
Synge, (Edmund) J(ohn) M(illington) 1871-
1909 ... **TCLC 6, 37; DAM DRAM; DC 2**
See also CA 104; 141; CDBLB 1890-1914;
DLB 10, 19
Syruc, J.
See Milosz, Czeslaw
Szirtes, George 1948- .... **CLC 46**
See also CA 109; CANR 27, 61
Szymborska, Wislawa 1923- .... **CLC 99**
See also CA 154; DLBY 96; MTCW 2
T. O., Nik
See Annensky, Innokenty (Fyodorovich)
Tabori, George 1914- .... **CLC 19**
See also CA 49-52; CANR 4, 69
Tagore, Rabindranath 1861-1941**TCLC 3, 53;
DAM DRAM, POET; PC 8**
See also CA 104; 120; MTCW 1, 2
Taine, Hippolyte Adolphe 1828-1893 . **N C L C
15**
Talese, Gay 1932- .... **CLC 37**
See also AITN 1; CA 1-4R; CANR 9, 58; DLB
185; INT CANR-9; MTCW 1, 2
Tallent, Elizabeth (Ann) 1954- .... **CLC 45**
See also CA 117; CANR 72; DLB 130
Tally, Ted 1952- .... **CLC 42**
See also CA 120; 124; INT 124
Talvik, Heiti 1904-1947 .... **TCLC 87**
Tamayo y Baus, Manuel 1829-1898 **NCLC 1**
Tammsaare, A(nton) H(ansen) 1878-1940
TCLC 27
See also CA 164
Tam'si, Tchicaya U
See Tchicaya, Gerald Felix
Tan, Amy (Ruth) 1952- . **CLC 59, 120; DAM
MULT, NOV, POP**
See also AAYA 9; BEST 89:3; CA 136; CANR
54; CDALBS; DLB 173; MTCW 2; SATA
75
Tandem, Felix
See Spitteler, Carl (Friedrich Georg)
Tanizaki, Jun'ichiro 1886-1965**CLC 8, 14, 28;
SSC 21**
See also CA 93-96; 25-28R; DLB 180; MTCW
2
Tanner, William
See Amis, Kingsley (William)

See Ainsworth, William Harrison

Tieck, (Johann) Ludwig 1773-1853 **NCLC 5, 46; SSC 31**
See also DLB 90

Tiger, Derry
See Ellison, Harlan (Jay)

Tilghman, Christopher 1948(?)- .... **CLC 65**
See also CA 159

Tillinghast, Richard (Williford) 1940-**CLC 29**
See also CA 29-32R; CAAS 23; CANR 26, 51

Timrod, Henry 1828-1867 .... **NCLC 25**
See also DLB 3

Tindall, Gillian (Elizabeth) 1938- ...... **CLC 7**
See also CA 21-24R; CANR 11, 65

Tiptree, James, Jr. .... **CLC 48, 50**
See also Sheldon, Alice Hastings Bradley
See also DLB 8

Titmarsh, Michael Angelo
See Thackeray, William Makepeace

Tocqueville, Alexis (Charles Henri Maurice Clerel, Comte) de 1805-1859
.... **NCLC 7, 63**

Tolkien, J(ohn) R(onald) R(euel) 1892-1973 **CLC 1, 2, 3, 8, 12, 38; DA; DAB; DAC; DAM MST, NOV, POP; WLC**
See also AAYA 10; AITN 1; CA 17-18; 45-48; CANR 36; CAP 2; CDBLB 1914-1945; CLR 56; DLB 15, 160; JRDA; MAICYA; MTCW 1, 2; SATA 2, 32, 100; SATA-Obit 24

Toller, Ernst 1893-1939 .... **TCLC 10**
See also CA 107; DLB 124

Tolson, M. B.
See Tolson, Melvin B(eaunorus)

Tolson, Melvin B(eaunorus) 1898(?)-1966 **CLC 36, 105; BLC 3; DAM MULT, POET**
See also BW 1, 3; CA 124; 89-92; CANR 80; DLB 48, 76

Tolstoi, Aleksei Nikolaevich
See Tolstoy, Alexey Nikolaevich

Tolstoy, Alexey Nikolaevich 1882-1945**T C L C 18**
See also CA 107; 158

Tolstoy, Count Leo
See Tolstoy, Leo (Nikolaevich)

Tolstoy, Leo (Nikolaevich) 1828-1910**TCLC 4, 11, 17, 28, 44, 79; DA; DAB; DAC; DAM MST, NOV; SSC 9, 30; WLC**
See also CA 104; 123; SATA 26

Tomasi di Lampedusa, Giuseppe 1896-1957
See Lampedusa, Giuseppe (Tomasi) di
See also CA 111

Tomlin, Lily .... **CLC 17**
See also Tomlin, Mary Jean

Tomlin, Mary Jean 1939(?)-
See Tomlin, Lily
See also CA 117

Tomlinson, (Alfred) Charles 1927-**CLC 2, 4, 6, 13, 45; DAM POET; PC 17**
See also CA 5-8R; CANR 33; DLB 40

Tomlinson, H(enry) M(ajor) 1873-1958**TCLC 71**
See also CA 118; 161; DLB 36, 100, 195

Tonson, Jacob
See Bennett, (Enoch) Arnold

Toole, John Kennedy 1937-1969 **CLC 19, 64**
See also CA 104; DLBY 81; MTCW 2

Toomer, Jean 1894-1967**CLC 1, 4, 13, 22; BLC 3; DAM MULT; PC 7; SSC 1; WLCS**
See also BW 1; CA 85-88; CDALB 1917-1929; DLB 45, 51; MTCW 1, 2

Torley, Luke
See Blish, James (Benjamin)

Tornimparte, Alessandra

See Ginzburg, Natalia

Torre, Raoul della
See Mencken, H(enry) L(ouis)

Torrey, E(dwin) Fuller 1937- .... **CLC 34**
See also CA 119; CANR 71

Torsvan, Ben Traven
See Traven, B.

Torsvan, Benno Traven
See Traven, B.

Torsvan, Berick Traven
See Traven, B.

Torsvan, Berwick Traven
See Traven, B.

Torsvan, Bruno Traven
See Traven, B.

Torsvan, Traven
See Traven, B.

Tournier, Michel (Edouard) 1924-**CLC 6, 23, 36, 95**
See also CA 49-52; CANR 3, 36, 74; DLB 83; MTCW 1, 2; SATA 23

Tournimparte, Alessandra
See Ginzburg, Natalia

Towers, Ivar
See Kornbluth, C(yril) M.

Towne, Robert (Burton) 1936(?)- ..... **CLC 87**
See also CA 108; DLB 44

Townsend, Sue .... **CLC 61**
See also Townsend, Susan Elaine
See also AAYA 28; SATA 55, 93; SATA-Brief 48

Townsend, Susan Elaine 1946-
See Townsend, Sue
See also CA 119; 127; CANR 65; DAB; DAC; DAM MST

Townshend, Peter (Dennis Blandford) 1945- **CLC 17, 42**
See also CA 107

Tozzi, Federigo 1883-1920 .... **TCLC 31**
See also CA 160

Traill, Catharine Parr 1802-1899 .. **NCLC 31**
See also DLB 99

Trakl, Georg 1887-1914 .... **TCLC 5; PC 20**
See also CA 104; 165; MTCW 2

Transtroemer, Tomas (Goesta) 1931-**CLC 52, 65; DAM POET**
See also CA 117; 129; CAAS 17

Transtromer, Tomas Gosta
See Transtroemer, Tomas (Goesta)

Traven, B. (?)-1969 .... **CLC 8, 11**
See also CA 19-20; 25-28R; CAP 2; DLB 9, 56; MTCW 1

Treitel, Jonathan 1959- .... **CLC 70**

Tremain, Rose 1943- .... **CLC 42**
See also CA 97-100; CANR 44; DLB 14

Tremblay, Michel 1942- **CLC 29, 102; DAC; DAM MST**
See also CA 116; 128; DLB 60; MTCW 1, 2

Trevanian .... **CLC 29**
See also Whitaker, Rod(ney)

Trevor, Glen
See Hilton, James

Trevor, William 1928-**CLC 7, 9, 14, 25, 71, 116; SSC 21**
See also Cox, William Trevor
See also DLB 14, 139; MTCW 2

Trifonov, Yuri (Valentinovich) 1925-1981 **CLC 45**
See also CA 126; 103; MTCW 1

Trilling, Lionel 1905-1975 ...... **CLC 9, 11, 24**
See also CA 9-12R; 61-64; CANR 10; DLB 28, 63; INT CANR-10; MTCW 1, 2

Trimball, W. H.

See Mencken, H(enry) L(ouis)

Tristan
See Gomez de la Serna, Ramon

Tristram
See Housman, A(lfred) E(dward)

Trogdon, William (Lewis) 1939-
See Heat-Moon, William Least
See also CA 115; 119; CANR 47; INT 119

Trollope, Anthony 1815-1882**NCLC 6, 33; DA; DAB; DAC; DAM MST, NOV; SSC 28; WLC**
See also CDBLB 1832-1890; DLB 21, 57, 159; SATA 22

Trollope, Frances 1779-1863 .... **NCLC 30**
See also DLB 21, 166

Trotsky, Leon 1879-1940 .... **TCLC 22**
See also CA 118; 167

Trotter (Cockburn), Catharine 1679-1749**L C 8**
See also DLB 84

Trout, Kilgore
See Farmer, Philip Jose

Trow, George W. S. 1943- .... **CLC 52**
See also CA 126

Troyat, Henri 1911- .... **CLC 23**
See also CA 45-48; CANR 2, 33, 67; MTCW 1

Trudeau, G(arretson) B(eekman) 1948-
See Trudeau, Garry B.
See also CA 81-84; CANR 31; SATA 35

Trudeau, Garry B. .... **CLC 12**
See also Trudeau, G(arretson) B(eekman)
See also AAYA 10; AITN 2

Truffaut, Francois 1932-1984 .. **CLC 20, 101**
See also CA 81-84; 113; CANR 34

Trumbo, Dalton 1905-1976 .... **CLC 19**
See also CA 21-24R; 69-72; CANR 10; DLB 26

Trumbull, John 1750-1831 .... **NCLC 30**
See also DLB 31

Trundlett, Helen B.
See Eliot, T(homas) S(tearns)

Tryon, Thomas 1926-1991 . **CLC 3, 11; DAM POP**
See also AITN 1; CA 29-32R; 135; CANR 32, 77; MTCW 1

Tryon, Tom
See Tryon, Thomas

Ts'ao Hsueh-ch'in 1715(?)-1763 .... **LC 1**

Tsushima, Shuji 1909-1948
See Dazai Osamu
See also CA 107

Tsvetaeva (Efron), Marina (Ivanovna) 1892-1941 .... **TCLC 7, 35; PC 14**
See also CA 104; 128; CANR 73; MTCW 1, 2

Tuck, Lily 1938- .... **CLC 70**
See also CA 139

Tu Fu 712-770 .... **PC 9**
See also DAM MULT

Tunis, John R(oberts) 1889-1975 ...... **CLC 12**
See also CA 61-64; CANR 62; DLB 22, 171; JRDA; MAICYA; SATA 37; SATA-Brief 30

Tuohy, Frank .... **CLC 37**
See also Tuohy, John Francis
See also DLB 14, 139

Tuohy, John Francis 1925-1999
See Tuohy, Frank
See also CA 5-8R; 178; CANR 3, 47

Turco, Lewis (Putnam) 1934- ...... **CLC 11, 63**
See also CA 13-16R; CAAS 22; CANR 24, 51; DLBY 84

Turgenev, Ivan 1818-1883 .... **NCLC 21; DA; DAB; DAC; DAM MST, NOV; DC 7; SSC 7; WLC**

Turgot, Anne-Robert-Jacques 1727-1781 **L C 26**

Turner, Frederick 1943- .... **CLC 48**
See also CA 73-76; CAAS 10; CANR 12, 30, 56; DLB 40

Tutu, Desmond M(pilo) 1931-**CLC 80; BLC 3; DAM MULT**
See also BW 1, 3; CA 125; CANR 67, 81

Tutuola, Amos 1920-1997**CLC 5, 14, 29; BLC 3; DAM MULT**
See also BW 2, 3; CA 9-12R; 159; CANR 27, 66; DLB 125; MTCW 1, 2

Twain, Mark **TCLC 6, 12, 19, 36, 48, 59; SSC 34; WLC**
See also Clemens, Samuel Langhorne
See also AAYA 20; CLR 58; DLB 11, 12, 23, 64, 74

Tyler, Anne 1941-. **CLC 7, 11, 18, 28, 44, 59, 103; DAM NOV, POP**
See also AAYA 18; BEST 89:1; CA 9-12R; CANR 11, 33, 53; CDALBS; DLB 6, 143; DLBY 82; MTCW 1, 2; SATA 7, 90

Tyler, Royall 1757-1826 .... **NCLC 3**
See also DLB 37

Tynan, Katharine 1861-1931 .... **TCLC 3**
See also CA 104; 167; DLB 153

Tyutchev, Fyodor 1803-1873 .... **NCLC 34**

Tzara, Tristan 1896-1963 ...... **CLC 47; DAM POET; PC 27**
See also CA 153; 89-92; MTCW 2

Uhry, Alfred 1936-... **CLC 55; DAM DRAM, POP**
See also CA 127; 133; INT 133

Ulf, Haerved
See Strindberg, (Johan) August

Ulf, Harved
See Strindberg, (Johan) August

Ulibarri, Sabine R(eyes) 1919-**CLC 83; DAM MULT; HLCS 2**
See also CA 131; CANR 81; DLB 82; HW 1, 2

Unamuno (y Jugo), Miguel de 1864-1936 **TCLC 2, 9; DAM MULT, NOV; HLC 2; SSC 11**
See also CA 104; 131; CANR 81; DLB 108; HW 1, 2; MTCW 1, 2

Undercliffe, Errol
See Campbell, (John) Ramsey

Underwood, Miles
See Glassco, John

Undset, Sigrid 1882-1949**TCLC 3; DA; DAB; DAC; DAM MST, NOV;WLC**
See also CA 104; 129; MTCW 1, 2

Ungaretti, Giuseppe 1888-1970**CLC 7, 11, 15**
See also CA 19-20; 25-28R; CAP 2; DLB 114

Unger, Douglas 1952- .... **CLC 34**
See also CA 130

Unsworth, Barry (Forster) 1930- ..... **CLC 76**
See also CA 25-28R; CANR 30, 54; DLB 194

Updike, John (Hoyer) 1932-**CLC 1, 2, 3, 5, 7, 9, 13, 15, 23, 34, 43, 70; DA; DAB; DAC; DAM MST, NOV, POET, POP; SSC 13, 27; WLC**
See also CA 1-4R; CABS 1; CANR 4, 33, 51; CDALB 1968-1988; DLB 2, 5, 143; DLBD 3; DLBY 80, 82, 97; MTCW 1, 2

Upshaw, Margaret Mitchell
See Mitchell, Margaret (Munnerlyn)

Upton, Mark
See Sanders, Lawrence

Upward, Allen 1863-1926 .... **TCLC 85**
See also CA 117; DLB 36

Urdang, Constance (Henriette) 1922-**CLC 47**
See also CA 21-24R; CANR 9, 24

Uriel, Henry
See Faust, Frederick (Schiller)

Uris, Leon (Marcus) 1924- **CLC 7, 32; DAM NOV, POP**
See also AITN 1, 2; BEST 89:2; CA 1-4R; CANR 1, 40, 65; MTCW 1, 2; SATA 49

Urista, Alberto H. 1947-
See Alurista
See also CA 45-48; CANR 2, 32; HLCS 1; HW 1

Urmuz
See Codrescu, Andrei

Urquhart, Jane 1949- .... **CLC 90; DAC**
See also CA 113; CANR 32, 68

Usigli, Rodolfo 1905-1979
See also CA 131; HLCS 1; HW 1

Ustinov, Peter (Alexander) 1921- .... **CLC 1**
See also AITN 1; CA 13-16R; CANR 25, 51; DLB 13; MTCW 2

U Tam'si, Gerald Felix Tchicaya
See Tchicaya, Gerald Felix

U Tam'si, Tchicaya
See Tchicaya, Gerald Felix

Vachss, Andrew (Henry) 1942- .... **CLC 106**
See also CA 118; CANR 44

Vachss, Andrew H.
See Vachss, Andrew (Henry)

Vaculik, Ludvik 1926- .... **CLC 7**
See also CA 53-56; CANR 72

Vaihinger, Hans 1852-1933 .... **TCLC 71**
See also CA 116; 166

Valdez, Luis (Miguel) 1940- ..**CLC 84; DAM MULT; DC 10; HLC 2**
See also CA 101; CANR 32, 81; DLB 122; HW 1

Valenzuela, Luisa 1938- **CLC 31, 104; DAM MULT; HLCS 2; SSC 14**
See also CA 101; CANR 32, 65; DLB 113; HW 1, 2

Valera y Alcala-Galiano, Juan 1824-1905 **TCLC 10**
See also CA 106

Valery, (Ambroise) Paul (Toussaint Jules) 1871-1945 ..... **TCLC 4, 15; DAM POET; PC 9**
See also CA 104; 122; MTCW 1, 2

Valle-Inclan, Ramon (Maria) del 1866-1936 **TCLC 5; DAM MULT; HLC 2**
See also CA 106; 153; CANR 80; DLB 134; HW 2

Vallejo, Antonio Buero
See Buero Vallejo, Antonio

Vallejo, Cesar (Abraham) 1892-1938**TCLC 3, 56; DAM MULT; HLC 2**
See also CA 105; 153; HW 1

Valles, Jules 1832-1885 .... **NCLC 71**
See also DLB 123

Vallette, Marguerite Eymery
See Rachilde

Valle Y Pena, Ramon del
See Valle-Inclan, Ramon (Maria) del

Van Ash, Cay 1918- .... **CLC 34**

Vanbrugh, Sir John 1664-1726 **LC 21; DAM DRAM**
See also DLB 80

Van Campen, Karl
See Campbell, John W(ood, Jr.)

Vance, Gerald
See Silverberg, Robert

Vance, Jack .... **CLC 35**
See also Kuttner, Henry; Vance, John Holbrook
See also DLB 8

Vance, John Holbrook 1916-
See Queen, Ellery; Vance, Jack

See also CA 29-32R; CANR 17, 65; MTCW 1

Van Den Bogarde, Derek Jules Gaspard Ulric Niven 1921-1999
See Bogarde, Dirk
See also CA 77-80; 179

Vandenburgh, Jane .... **CLC 59**
See also CA 168

Vanderhaeghe, Guy 1951- .... **CLC 41**
See also CA 113; CANR 72

van der Post, Laurens (Jan) 1906-1996**CLC 5**
See also CA 5-8R; 155; CANR 35; DLB 204

van de Wetering, Janwillem 1931- ... **CLC 47**
See also CA 49-52; CANR 4, 62

Van Dine, S. S. .... **TCLC 23**
See also Wright, Willard Huntington

Van Doren, Carl (Clinton) 1885-1950 **T C L C 18**
See also CA 111; 168

Van Doren, Mark 1894-1972 .... **CLC 6, 10**
See also CA 1-4R; 37-40R; CANR 3; DLB 45; MTCW 1, 2

Van Druten, John (William) 1901-1957**TCLC 2**
See also CA 104; 161; DLB 10

Van Duyn, Mona (Jane) 1921- **CLC 3, 7, 63, 116; DAM POET**
See also CA 9-12R; CANR 7, 38, 60; DLB 5

Van Dyne, Edith
See Baum, L(yman) Frank

van Itallie, Jean-Claude 1936- .... **CLC 3**
See also CA 45-48; CAAS 2; CANR 1, 48; DLB 7

van Ostaijen, Paul 1896-1928 .... **TCLC 33**
See also CA 163

Van Peebles, Melvin 1932- **CLC 2, 20; DAM MULT**
See also BW 2, 3; CA 85-88; CANR 27, 67, 82

Vansittart, Peter 1920- .... **CLC 42**
See also CA 1-4R; CANR 3, 49

Van Vechten, Carl 1880-1964 .... **CLC 33**
See also CA 89-92; DLB 4, 9, 51

Van Vogt, A(lfred) E(lton) 1912- .... **CLC 1**
See also CA 21-24R; CANR 28; DLB 8; SATA 14

Varda, Agnes 1928- .... **CLC 16**
See also CA 116; 122

Vargas Llosa, (Jorge) Mario (Pedro) 1936- **CLC 3, 6, 9, 10, 15, 31, 42, 85; DA; DAB; DAC; DAM MST, MULT, NOV; HLC 2**
See also CA 73-76; CANR 18, 32, 42, 67; DLB 145; HW 1, 2; MTCW 1, 2

Vasiliu, Gheorghe 1881-1957
See Bacovia, George
See also CA 123

Vassa, Gustavus
See Equiano, Olaudah

Vassilikos, Vassilis 1933- .... **CLC 4, 8**
See also CA 81-84; CANR 75

Vaughan, Henry 1621-1695 .... **LC 27**
See also DLB 131

Vaughn, Stephanie .... **CLC 62**

Vazov, Ivan (Minchov) 1850-1921 . **TCLC 25**
See also CA 121; 167; DLB 147

Veblen, Thorstein B(unde) 1857-1929 **T C L C 31**
See also CA 115; 165

Vega, Lope de 1562-1635 ..... **LC 23; HLCS 2**

Venison, Alfred
See Pound, Ezra (Weston Loomis)

Verdi, Marie de
See Mencken, H(enry) L(ouis)

Verdu, Matilde
See Cela, Camilo Jose

Verga, Giovanni (Carmelo) 1840-1922 T C L C
3; SSC 21
See also CA 104; 123
Vergil 70B.C.-19B.C. ... CMLC 9; DA; DAB;
DAC; DAM MST, POET; PC 12; WLCS
See also Virgil
Verhaeren, Emile (Adolphe Gustave) 1855-1916
TCLC 12
See also CA 109
Verlaine, Paul (Marie) 1844-1896NCLC 2, 51;
DAM POET; PC 2
Verne, Jules (Gabriel) 1828-1905TCLC 6, 52
See also AAYA 16; CA 110; 131; DLB 123;
JRDA; MAICYA; SATA 21
Very, Jones 1813-1880 .... NCLC 9
See also DLB 1
Vesaas, Tarjei 1897-1970 .... CLC 48
See also CA 29-32R
Vialis, Gaston
See Simenon, Georges (Jacques Christian)
Vian, Boris 1920-1959 .... TCLC 9
See also CA 106; 164; DLB 72; MTCW 2
Viaud, (Louis Marie) Julien 1850-1923
See Loti, Pierre
See also CA 107
Vicar, Henry
See Felsen, Henry Gregor
Vicker, Angus
See Felsen, Henry Gregor
Vidal, Gore 1925-CLC 2, 4, 6, 8, 10, 22, 33, 72;
DAM NOV, POP
See also AITN 1; BEST 90:2; CA 5-8R; CANR
13, 45, 65; CDALBS; DLB 6, 152; INT
CANR-13; MTCW 1, 2
Viereck, Peter (Robert Edwin) 1916- CLC 4;
PC 27
See also CA 1-4R; CANR 1, 47; DLB 5
Vigny, Alfred (Victor) de 1797-1863NCLC 7;
DAM POET; PC 26
See also DLB 119, 192
Vilakazi, Benedict Wallet 1906-1947TCLC 37
See also CA 168
Villa, Jose Garcia 1904-1997 .... PC 22
See also CA 25-28R; CANR 12
Villarreal, Jose Antonio 1924-
See also CA 133; DAM MULT; DLB 82; HLC
2; HW 1
Villaurrutia, Xavier 1903-1950 ...... TCLC 80
See also HW 1
Villiers de l'Isle Adam, Jean Marie Mathias
Philippe Auguste, Comte de 1838-1889
NCLC 3; SSC 14
See also DLB 123
Villon, Francois 1431-1463(?) .... PC 13
See also DLB 208
Vinci, Leonardo da 1452-1519 .... LC 12
Vine, Barbara .... CLC 50
See Rendell, Ruth (Barbara)
See also BEST 90:4
Vinge, Joan (Carol) D(ennison) 1948-CLC 30;
SSC 24
See also CA 93-96; CANR 72; SATA 36
Violis, G.
See Simenon, Georges (Jacques Christian)
Viramontes, Helena Maria 1954-
See also CA 159; DLB 122; HLCS 2; HW 2
Virgil 70B.C.-19B.C.
See Vergil
See also DLB 211
Visconti, Luchino 1906-1976 .... CLC 16
See also CA 81-84; 65-68; CANR 39
Vittorini, Elio 1908-1966 .... CLC 6, 9, 14
See also CA 133; 25-28R

Vivekananda, Swami 1863-1902 .... TCLC 88
Vizenor, Gerald Robert 1934-CLC 103; DAM
MULT
See also CA 13-16R; CAAS 22; CANR 5, 21,
44, 67; DLB 175; MTCW 2; NNAL
Vizinczey, Stephen 1933- .... CLC 40
See also CA 128; INT 128
Vliet, R(ussell) G(ordon) 1929-1984 CLC 22
See also CA 37-40R; 112; CANR 18
Vogau, Boris Andreyevich 1894-1937(?)
See Pilnyak, Boris
See also CA 123
Vogel, Paula A(nne) 1951- .... CLC 76
See also CA 108
Voigt, Cynthia 1942- .... CLC 30
See also AAYA 3, 30; CA 106; CANR 18, 37,
40; CLR 13, 48; INT CANR-18; JRDA;
MAICYA; SATA 48, 79; SATA-Brief 33
Voigt, Ellen Bryant 1943- .... CLC 54
See also CA 69-72; CANR 11, 29, 55; DLB 120
Voinovich, Vladimir (Nikolaevich) 1932-CLC
10, 49
See also CA 81-84; CAAS 12; CANR 33, 67;
MTCW 1
Vollmann, William T. 1959- ..CLC 89; DAM
NOV, POP
See also CA 134; CANR 67; MTCW 2
Voloshinov, V. N.
See Bakhtin, Mikhail Mikhailovich
Voltaire 1694-1778 . LC 14; DA; DAB; DAC;
DAM DRAM, MST; SSC 12; WLC
von Aschendrof, BaronIgnatz
See Ford, Ford Madox
von Daeniken, Erich 1935- .... CLC 30
See also AITN 1; CA 37-40R; CANR 17, 44
von Daniken, Erich
See von Daeniken, Erich
von Heidenstam, (Carl Gustaf) Verner
See Heidenstam, (Carl Gustaf) Verner von
von Heyse, Paul (Johann Ludwig)
See Heyse, Paul (Johann Ludwig von)
von Hofmannsthal, Hugo
See Hofmannsthal, Hugo von
von Horvath, Odon
See Horvath, Oedoen von
von Horvath, Oedoen
See Horvath, Oedoen von
von Liliencron, (Friedrich Adolf Axel) Detlev
See Liliencron, (Friedrich Adolf Axel) Detlev
von
Vonnegut, Kurt, Jr. 1922-CLC 1, 2, 3, 4, 5, 8,
12, 22, 40, 60, 111; DA; DAB; DAC; DAM
MST, NOV, POP; SSC 8; WLC
See also AAYA 6; AITN 1; BEST 90:4; CA 1-
4R; CANR 1, 25, 49, 75; CDALB 1968-
1988; DLB 2, 8, 152; DLBD 3; DLBY 80;
MTCW 1, 2
Von Rachen, Kurt
See Hubbard, L(afayette) Ron(ald)
von Rezzori (d'Arezzo), Gregor
See Rezzori (d'Arezzo), Gregor von
von Sternberg, Josef
See Sternberg, Josef von
Vorster, Gordon 1924- .... CLC 34
See also CA 133
Vosce, Trudie
See Ozick, Cynthia
Voznesensky, Andrei (Andreievich) 1933-
CLC 1, 15, 57; DAM POET
See also CA 89-92; CANR 37; MTCW 1
Waddington, Miriam 1917- .... CLC 28
See also CA 21-24R; CANR 12, 30; DLB 68
Wagman, Fredrica 1937- .... CLC 7

See also CA 97-100; INT 97-100
Wagner, Linda W.
See Wagner-Martin, Linda (C.)
Wagner, Linda Welshimer
See Wagner-Martin, Linda (C.)
Wagner, Richard 1813-1883 .... NCLC 9
See also DLB 129
Wagner-Martin, Linda (C.) 1936- .... CLC 50
See also CA 159
Wagoner, David (Russell) 1926-CLC 3, 5, 15
See also CA 1-4R; CAAS 3; CANR 2, 71; DLB
5; SATA 14
Wah, Fred(erick James) 1939- .... CLC 44
See also CA 107; 141; DLB 60
Wahloo, Per 1926-1975 .... CLC 7
See also CA 61-64; CANR 73
Wahloo, Peter
See Wahloo, Per
Wain, John (Barrington) 1925-1994 . CLC 2,
11, 15, 46
See also CA 5-8R; 145; CAAS 4; CANR 23,
54; CDBLB 1960 to Present; DLB 15, 27,
139, 155; MTCW 1, 2
Wajda, Andrzej 1926- .... CLC 16
See also CA 102
Wakefield, Dan 1932- .... CLC 7
See also CA 21-24R; CAAS 7
Wakoski, Diane 1937- CLC 2, 4, 7, 9, 11, 40;
DAM POET; PC 15
See also CA 13-16R; CAAS 1; CANR 9, 60;
DLB 5; INT CANR-9; MTCW 2
Wakoski-Sherbell, Diane
See Wakoski, Diane
Walcott, Derek (Alton) 1930-CLC 2, 4, 9, 14,
25, 42, 67, 76; BLC 3; DAB; DAC; DAM
MST, MULT, POET; DC 7
See also BW 2; CA 89-92; CANR 26, 47, 75,
80; DLB 117; DLBY 81; MTCW 1, 2
Waldman, Anne (Lesley) 1945- .... CLC 7
See also CA 37-40R; CAAS 17; CANR 34, 69;
DLB 16
Waldo, E. Hunter
See Sturgeon, Theodore (Hamilton)
Waldo, Edward Hamilton
See Sturgeon, Theodore (Hamilton)
Walker, Alice (Malsenior) 1944- CLC 5, 6, 9,
19, 27, 46, 58, 103; BLC 3; DA; DAB;
DAC; DAM MST, MULT, NOV, POET,
POP; SSC 5; WLCS
See also AAYA 3; BEST 89:4; BW 2, 3; CA
37-40R; CANR 9, 27, 49, 66, 82; CDALB
1968-1988; DLB 6, 33, 143; INT CANR-27;
MTCW 1, 2; SATA 31
Walker, David Harry 1911-1992 .... CLC 14
See also CA 1-4R; 137; CANR 1; SATA 8;
SATA-Obit 71
Walker, Edward Joseph 1934-
See Walker, Ted
See also CA 21-24R; CANR 12, 28, 53
Walker, George F. 1947- . CLC 44, 61; DAB;
DAC; DAM MST
See also CA 103; CANR 21, 43, 59; DLB 60
Walker, Joseph A. 1935- .... CLC 19; DAM
DRAM, MST
See also BW 1, 3; CA 89-92; CANR 26; DLB
38
Walker, Margaret (Abigail) 1915-1998CLC 1,
6; BLC; DAM MULT; PC 20
See also BW 2, 3; CA 73-76; 172; CANR 26,
54, 76; DLB 76, 152; MTCW 1, 2
Walker, Ted .... CLC 13
See also Walker, Edward Joseph
See also DLB 40

Wallace, David Foster 1962- ..... **CLC 50, 114**
  See also CA 132; CANR 59; MTCW 2
Wallace, Dexter
  See Masters, Edgar Lee
Wallace, (Richard Horatio) Edgar 1875-1932
    TCLC 57
  See also CA 115; DLB 70
Wallace, Irving 1916-1990 **CLC 7, 13; DAM
    NOV, POP**
  See also AITN 1; CA 1-4R; 132; CAAS 1;
    CANR 1, 27; INT CANR-27; MTCW 1, 2
Wallant, Edward Lewis 1926-1962 **CLC 5, 10**
  See also CA 1-4R; CANR 22; DLB 2, 28, 143;
    MTCW 1, 2
Wallas, Graham 1858-1932 .... **TCLC 91**
Walley, Byron
  See Card, Orson Scott
Walpole, Horace 1717-1797 .... **LC 49**
  See also DLB 39, 104
Walpole, Hugh (Seymour) 1884-1941 **TCLC 5**
  See also CA 104; 165; DLB 34; MTCW 2
Walser, Martin 1927- .... **CLC 27**
  See also CA 57-60; CANR 8, 46; DLB 75, 124
Walser, Robert 1878-1956 **TCLC 18; SSC 20**
  See also CA 118; 165; DLB 66
Walsh, Jill Paton .... **CLC 35**
  See also Paton Walsh, Gillian
  See also AAYA 11; CLR 2; DLB 161; SAAS 3
Walter, Villiam Christian
  See Andersen, Hans Christian
Wambaugh, Joseph (Aloysius, Jr.) 1937- **CLC
    3, 18; DAM NOV, POP**
  See also AITN 1; BEST 89:3; CA 33-36R;
    CANR 42, 65; DLB 6; DLBY 83; MTCW 1,
    2
Wang Wei 699(?)-761(?) .... **PC 18**
Ward, Arthur Henry Sarsfield 1883-1959
  See Rohmer, Sax
  See also CA 108; 173
Ward, Douglas Turner 1930- .... **CLC 19**
  See also BW 1; CA 81-84; CANR 27; DLB 7,
    38
Ward, E. D.
  See Lucas, E(dward) V(errall)
Ward, Mary Augusta
  See Ward, Mrs. Humphry
Ward, Mrs. Humphry 1851-1920 .. **TCLC 55**
  See also DLB 18
Ward, Peter
  See Faust, Frederick (Schiller)
Warhol, Andy 1928(?)-1987 .... **CLC 20**
  See also AAYA 12; BEST 89:4; CA 89-92; 121;
    CANR 34
Warner, Francis (Robert le Plastrier) 1937-
    CLC 14
  See also CA 53-56; CANR 11
Warner, Marina 1946- .... **CLC 59**
  See also CA 65-68; CANR 21, 55; DLB 194
Warner, Rex (Ernest) 1905-1986 ...... **CLC 45**
  See also CA 89-92; 119; DLB 15
Warner, Susan (Bogert) 1819-1885 **NCLC 31**
  See also DLB 3, 42
Warner, Sylvia (Constance) Ashton
  See Ashton-Warner, Sylvia (Constance)
Warner, Sylvia Townsend 1893-1978 **CLC 7,
    19; SSC 23**
  See also CA 61-64; 77-80; CANR 16, 60; DLB
    34, 139; MTCW 1, 2
Warren, Mercy Otis 1728-1814 ..... **NCLC 13**
  See also DLB 31, 200
Warren, Robert Penn 1905-1989 **CLC 1, 4, 6,
    8, 10, 13, 18, 39, 53, 59; DA; DAB; DAC;
    DAM MST, NOV, POET; SSC 4; WLC**

  See also AITN 1; CA 13-16R; 129; CANR 10,
    47; CDALB 1968-1988; DLB 2, 48, 152;
    DLBY 80, 89; INT CANR-10; MTCW 1, 2;
    SATA 46; SATA-Obit 63
Warshofsky, Isaac
  See Singer, Isaac Bashevis
Warton, Thomas 1728-1790 ..... **LC 15; DAM
    POET**
  See also DLB 104, 109
Waruk, Kona
  See Harris, (Theodore) Wilson
Warung, Price 1855-1911 .... **TCLC 45**
Warwick, Jarvis
  See Garner, Hugh
Washington, Alex
  See Harris, Mark
Washington, Booker T(aliaferro) 1856-1915
    TCLC 10; BLC 3; DAM MULT
  See also BW 1; CA 114; 125; SATA 28
Washington, George 1732-1799 .... **LC 25**
  See also DLB 31
Wassermann, (Karl) Jakob 1873-1934 **T C L C
    6**
  See also CA 104; 163; DLB 66
Wasserstein, Wendy 1950- ... **CLC 32, 59, 90;
    DAM DRAM; DC 4**
  See also CA 121; 129; CABS 3; CANR 53, 75;
    INT 129; MTCW 2; SATA 94
Waterhouse, Keith (Spencer) 1929- . **CLC 47**
  See also CA 5-8R; CANR 38, 67; DLB 13, 15;
    MTCW 1, 2
Waters, Frank (Joseph) 1902-1995 .. **CLC 88**
  See also CA 5-8R; 149; CAAS 13; CANR 3,
    18, 63; DLB 212; DLBY 86
Waters, Roger 1944- .... **CLC 35**
Watkins, Frances Ellen
  See Harper, Frances Ellen Watkins
Watkins, Gerrold
  See Malzberg, Barry N(athaniel)
Watkins, Gloria 1955(?)-
  See hooks, bell
  See also BW 2; CA 143; MTCW 2
Watkins, Paul 1964- .... **CLC 55**
  See also CA 132; CANR 62
Watkins, Vernon Phillips 1906-1967 **CLC 43**
  See also CA 9-10; 25-28R; CAP 1; DLB 20
Watson, Irving S.
  See Mencken, H(enry) L(ouis)
Watson, John H.
  See Farmer, Philip Jose
Watson, Richard F.
  See Silverberg, Robert
Waugh, Auberon (Alexander) 1939- .. **CLC 7**
  See also CA 45-48; CANR 6, 22; DLB 14, 194
Waugh, Evelyn (Arthur St. John) 1903-1966
    **CLC 1, 3, 8, 13, 19, 27, 44, 107; DA; DAB;
    DAC; DAM MST, NOV, POP; WLC**
  See also CA 85-88; 25-28R; CANR 22; CDBLB
    1914-1945; DLB 15, 162, 195; MTCW 1, 2
Waugh, Harriet 1944- .... **CLC 6**
  See also CA 85-88; CANR 22
Ways, C. R.
  See Blount, Roy (Alton), Jr.
Waystaff, Simon
  See Swift, Jonathan
Webb, (Martha) Beatrice (Potter) 1858-1943
    TCLC 22
  See also Potter, (Helen) Beatrix
  See also CA 117; DLB 190
Webb, Charles (Richard) 1939- .... **CLC 7**
  See also CA 25-28R
Webb, James H(enry), Jr. 1946- .... **CLC 22**
  See also CA 81-84

Webb, Mary (Gladys Meredith) 1881-1927
    TCLC 24
  See also CA 123; DLB 34
Webb, Mrs. Sidney
  See Webb, (Martha) Beatrice (Potter)
Webb, Phyllis 1927- .... **CLC 18**
  See also CA 104; CANR 23; DLB 53
Webb, Sidney (James) 1859-1947 .. **TCLC 22**
  See also CA 117; 163; DLB 190
Webber, Andrew Lloyd .... **CLC 21**
  See also Lloyd Webber, Andrew
Weber, Lenora Mattingly 1895-1971 **CLC 12**
  See also CA 19-20; 29-32R; CAP 1; SATA 2;
    SATA-Obit 26
Weber, Max 1864-1920 .... **TCLC 69**
  See also CA 109
Webster, John 1579(?)-1634(?) ... **LC 33; DA;
    DAB; DAC; DAM DRAM, MST; DC 2;
    WLC**
  See also CDBLB Before 1660; DLB 58
Webster, Noah 1758-1843 .... **NCLC 30**
  See also DLB 1, 37, 42, 43, 73
Wedekind, (Benjamin) Frank(lin) 1864-1918
    TCLC 7; DAM DRAM
  See also CA 104; 153; DLB 118
Weidman, Jerome 1913-1998 .... **CLC 7**
  See also AITN 2; CA 1-4R; 171; CANR 1; DLB
    28
Weil, Simone (Adolphine) 1909-1943 **TCLC 23**
  See also CA 117; 159; MTCW 2
Weininger, Otto 1880-1903 .... **TCLC 84**
Weinstein, Nathan
  See West, Nathanael
Weinstein, Nathan von Wallenstein
  See West, Nathanael
Weir, Peter (Lindsay) 1944- .... **CLC 20**
  See also CA 113; 123
Weiss, Peter (Ulrich) 1916-1982 **CLC 3, 15, 51;
    DAM DRAM**
  See also CA 45-48; 106; CANR 3; DLB 69, 124
Weiss, Theodore (Russell) 1916- **CLC 3, 8, 14**
  See also CA 9-12R; CAAS 2; CANR 46; DLB
    5
Welch, (Maurice) Denton 1915-1948 **TCLC 22**
  See also CA 121; 148
Welch, James 1940- ..... **CLC 6, 14, 52; DAM
    MULT, POP**
  See also CA 85-88; CANR 42, 66; DLB 175;
    NNAL
Weldon, Fay 1931- **CLC 6, 9, 11, 19, 36, 59, 122;
    DAM POP**
  See also CA 21-24R; CANR 16, 46, 63; CDBLB
    1960 to Present; DLB 14, 194; INT CANR-
    16; MTCW 1, 2
Wellek, Rene 1903-1995 .... **CLC 28**
  See also CA 5-8R; 150; CAAS 7; CANR 8; DLB
    63; INT CANR-8
Weller, Michael 1942- .... **CLC 10, 53**
  See also CA 85-88
Weller, Paul 1958- .... **CLC 26**
Wellershoff, Dieter 1925- .... **CLC 46**
  See also CA 89-92; CANR 16, 37
Welles, (George) Orson 1915-1985 **CLC 20, 80**
  See also CA 93-96; 117
Wellman, John McDowell 1945-
  See Wellman, Mac
  See also CA 166
Wellman, Mac 1945- .... **CLC 65**
  See also Wellman, John McDowell; Wellman,
    John McDowell
Wellman, Manly Wade 1903-1986 .... **CLC 49**
  See also CA 1-4R; 118; CANR 6, 16, 44; SATA
    6; SATA-Obit 47

See also AAYA 20; CAAS 5; DLB 8; INT
CANR-17
Wilhelm, Katie Gertrude 1928-
See Wilhelm, Kate
See also CA 37-40R; CANR 17, 36, 60; MTCW
1
Wilkins, Mary
See Freeman, Mary Eleanor Wilkins
Willard, Nancy 1936- .... CLC 7, 37
See also CA 89-92; CANR 10, 39, 68; CLR 5;
DLB 5, 52; MAICYA; MTCW 1; SATA 37,
71; SATA-Brief 30
William of Ockham 1285-1347 ..... CMLC 32
Williams, Ben Ames 1889-1953 ..... TCLC 89
See also DLB 102
Williams, C(harles) K(enneth) 1936-CLC 33,
56; DAM POET
See also CA 37-40R; CAAS 26; CANR 57; DLB
5
Williams, Charles
See Collier, James L(incoln)
Williams, Charles (Walter Stansby) 1886-1945
TCLC 1, 11
See also CA 104; 163; DLB 100, 153
Williams, (George) Emlyn 1905-1987CLC 15;
DAM DRAM
See also CA 104; 123; CANR 36; DLB 10, 77;
MTCW 1
Williams, Hank 1923-1953 .... TCLC 81
Williams, Hugo 1942- .... CLC 42
See also CA 17-20R; CANR 45; DLB 40
Williams, J. Walker
See Wodehouse, P(elham) G(renville)
Williams, John A(lfred) 1925-CLC 5, 13; BLC
3; DAM MULT
See also BW 2, 3; CA 53-56; CAAS 3; CANR
6, 26, 51; DLB 2, 33; INT CANR-6
Williams, Jonathan (Chamberlain) 1929-
CLC 13
See also CA 9-12R; CAAS 12; CANR 8; DLB
5
Williams, Joy 1944- .... CLC 31
See also CA 41-44R; CANR 22, 48
Williams, Norman 1952- .... CLC 39
See also CA 118
Williams, Sherley Anne 1944-CLC 89; BLC 3;
DAM MULT, POET
See also BW 2, 3; CA 73-76; CANR 25, 82;
DLB 41; INT CANR-25; SATA 78
Williams, Shirley
See Williams, Sherley Anne
Williams, Tennessee 1911-1983CLC 1, 2, 5, 7,
**8, 11, 15, 19, 30, 39, 45, 71,111; DA; DAB;
DAC; DAM DRAM, MST; DC 4; WLC**
See also AITN 1, 2; CA 5-8R; 108; CABS 3;
CANR 31; CDALB 1941-1968; DLB 7;
DLBD 4; DLBY 83; MTCW 1, 2
Williams, Thomas (Alonzo) 1926-1990CLC 14
See also CA 1-4R; 132; CANR 2
Williams, William C.
See Williams, William Carlos
Williams, William Carlos 1883-1963CLC 1, 2,
**5, 9, 13, 22, 42, 67; DA; DAB; DAC; DAM
MST, POET; PC 7; SSC 31**
See also CA 89-92; CANR 34; CDALB 1917-
1929; DLB 4, 16, 54, 86; MTCW 1, 2
Williamson, David (Keith) 1942- ...... CLC 56
See also CA 103; CANR 41
Williamson, Ellen Douglas 1905-1984
See Douglas, Ellen
See also CA 17-20R; 114; CANR 39
Williamson, Jack .... CLC 29
See also Williamson, John Stewart

See also CAAS 8; DLB 8
Williamson, John Stewart 1908-
See Williamson, Jack
See also CA 17-20R; CANR 23, 70
Willie, Frederick
See Lovecraft, H(oward) P(hillips)
Willingham, Calder (Baynard, Jr.) 1922-1995
CLC 5, 51
See also CA 5-8R; 147; CANR 3; DLB 2, 44;
MTCW 1
Willis, Charles
See Clarke, Arthur C(harles)
Willis, Fingal O'Flahertie
See Wilde, Oscar
Willy
See Colette, (Sidonie-Gabrielle)
Willy, Colette
See Colette, (Sidonie-Gabrielle)
Wilson, A(ndrew) N(orman) 1950- ... CLC 33
See also CA 112; 122; DLB 14, 155, 194;
MTCW 2
Wilson, Angus (Frank Johnstone) 1913-1991
CLC 2, 3, 5, 25, 34; SSC 21
See also CA 5-8R; 134; CANR 21; DLB 15,
139, 155; MTCW 1, 2
Wilson, August 1945- ... CLC 39, 50, 63, 118;
**BLC 3; DA; DAB; DAC; DAM DRAM,
MST, MULT; DC 2; WLCS**
See also AAYA 16; BW 2, 3; CA 115; 122;
CANR 42, 54, 76; MTCW 1, 2
Wilson, Brian 1942- .... CLC 12
Wilson, Colin 1931- .... CLC 3, 14
See also CA 1-4R; CAAS 5; CANR 1, 22, 33,
77; DLB 14, 194; MTCW 1
Wilson, Dirk
See Pohl, Frederik
Wilson, Edmund 1895-1972CLC 1, 2, 3, 8, 24
See also CA 1-4R; 37-40R; CANR 1, 46; DLB
63; MTCW 1, 2
Wilson, Ethel Davis (Bryant) 1888(?)-1980
CLC 13; DAC; DAM POET
See also CA 102; DLB 68; MTCW 1
Wilson, John 1785-1854 .... NCLC 5
Wilson, John (Anthony) Burgess 1917-1993
See Burgess, Anthony
See also CA 1-4R; 143; CANR 2, 46; DAC;
DAM NOV; MTCW 1, 2
Wilson, Lanford 1937- CLC 7, 14, 36; DAM
DRAM
See also CA 17-20R; CABS 3; CANR 45; DLB
7
Wilson, Robert M. 1944- .... CLC 7, 9
See also CA 49-52; CANR 2, 41; MTCW 1
Wilson, Robert McLiam 1964- .... CLC 59
See also CA 132
Wilson, Sloan 1920- .... CLC 32
See also CA 1-4R; CANR 1, 44
Wilson, Snoo 1948- .... CLC 33
See also CA 69-72
Wilson, William S(mith) 1932- .... CLC 49
See also CA 81-84
Wilson, (Thomas) Woodrow 1856-1924TCLC
79
See also CA 166; DLB 47
Winchilsea, Anne (Kingsmill) Finch Counte
1661-1720
See Finch, Anne
Windham, Basil
See Wodehouse, P(elham) G(renville)
Wingrove, David (John) 1954- .... CLC 68
See also CA 133
Winnemucca, Sarah 1844-1891 ..... NCLC 79
Winstanley, Gerrard 1609-1676 .... LC 52

Wintergreen, Jane
See Duncan, Sara Jeannette
Winters, Janet Lewis .... CLC 41
See also Lewis, Janet
See also DLBY 87
Winters, (Arthur) Yvor 1900-1968 CLC 4, 8,
32
See also CA 11-12; 25-28R; CAP 1; DLB 48;
MTCW 1
Winterson, Jeanette 1959-CLC 64; DAM POP
See also CA 136; CANR 58; DLB 207; MTCW
2
Winthrop, John 1588-1649 .... LC 31
See also DLB 24, 30
Wirth, Louis 1897-1952 .... TCLC 92
Wiseman, Frederick 1930- .... CLC 20
See also CA 159
Wister, Owen 1860-1938 .... TCLC 21
See also CA 108; 162; DLB 9, 78, 186; SATA
62
Witkacy
See Witkiewicz, Stanislaw Ignacy
Witkiewicz, Stanislaw Ignacy 1885-1939
TCLC 8
See also CA 105; 162
Wittgenstein, Ludwig (Josef Johann) 1889-1951
TCLC 59
See also CA 113; 164; MTCW 2
Wittig, Monique 1935(?)- .... CLC 22
See also CA 116; 135; DLB 83
Wittlin, Jozef 1896-1976 .... CLC 25
See also CA 49-52; 65-68; CANR 3
Wodehouse, P(elham) G(renville) 1881-1975
**CLC 1, 2, 5, 10, 22; DAB; DAC; DAM
NOV; SSC 2**
See also AITN 2; CA 45-48; 57-60; CANR 3,
33; CDBLB 1914-1945; DLB 34, 162;
MTCW 1, 2; SATA 22
Woiwode, L.
See Woiwode, Larry (Alfred)
Woiwode, Larry (Alfred) 1941- .... CLC 6, 10
See also CA 73-76; CANR 16; DLB 6; INT
CANR-16
Wojciechowska, Maia (Teresa) 1927-CLC 26
See also AAYA 8; CA 9-12R; CANR 4, 41; CLR
1; JRDA; MAICYA; SAAS 1; SATA 1, 28,
83; SATA-Essay 104
Wolf, Christa 1929- .... CLC 14, 29, 58
See also CA 85-88; CANR 45; DLB 75; MTCW
1
Wolfe, Gene (Rodman) 1931- CLC 25; DAM
POP
See also CA 57-60; CAAS 9; CANR 6, 32, 60;
DLB 8; MTCW 2
Wolfe, George C. 1954- .... CLC 49; BLCS
See also CA 149
Wolfe, Thomas (Clayton) 1900-1938TCLC 4,
**13, 29, 61; DA; DAB; DAC; DAM MST,
NOV; SSC 33; WLC**
See also CA 104; 132; CDALB 1929-1941;
DLB 9, 102; DLBD 2, 16; DLBY 85, 97;
MTCW 1, 2
Wolfe, Thomas Kennerly, Jr. 1930-
See Wolfe, Tom
See also CA 13-16R; CANR 9, 33, 70; DAM
POP; DLB 185; INT CANR-9; MTCW 1, 2
Wolfe, Tom .... CLC 1, 2, 9, 15, 35, 51
See also Wolfe, Thomas Kennerly, Jr.
See also AAYA 8; AITN 2; BEST 89:1; DLB
152
Wolff, Geoffrey (Ansell) 1937- .... CLC 41
See also CA 29-32R; CANR 29, 43, 78
Wolff, Sonia

See Levitin, Sonia (Wolff)

Wolff, Tobias (Jonathan Ansell) 1945- . C L C **39, 64**
See also AAYA 16; BEST 90:2; CA 114; 117; CAAS 22; CANR 54, 76; DLB 130;INT 117; MTCW 2

Wolfram von Eschenbach c. 1170-c. 1220 **CMLC 5**
See also DLB 138

Wolitzer, Hilma 1930- .... **CLC 17**
See also CA 65-68; CANR 18, 40; INT CANR-18; SATA 31

Wollstonecraft, Mary 1759-1797 .... **LC 5, 50**
See also CDBLB 1789-1832; DLB 39, 104, 158

Wonder, Stevie .... **CLC 12**
See also Morris, Steveland Judkins

Wong, Jade Snow 1922- .... **CLC 17**
See also CA 109

Woodberry, George Edward 1855-1930 **TCLC 73**
See also CA 165; DLB 71, 103

Woodcott, Keith
See Brunner, John (Kilian Houston)

Woodruff, Robert W.
See Mencken, H(enry) L(ouis)

Woolf, (Adeline) Virginia 1882-1941**TCLC 1, 5, 20, 43, 56; DA; DAB; DAC; DAM MST, NOV; SSC 7; WLC**
See also Woolf, Virginia Adeline
See also CA 104; 130; CANR 64; CDBLB 1914-1945; DLB 36, 100, 162; DLBD 10; MTCW 1

Woolf, Virginia Adeline
See Woolf, (Adeline) Virginia
See also MTCW 2

Woollcott, Alexander (Humphreys) 1887-1943 **TCLC 5**
See also CA 105; 161; DLB 29

Woolrich, Cornell 1903-1968 .... **CLC 77**
See also Hopley-Woolrich, Cornell George

Wordsworth, Dorothy 1771-1855 ..**NCLC 25**
See also DLB 107

Wordsworth, William 1770-1850..**NCLC 12, 38; DA; DAB; DAC; DAM MST, POET; PC 4; WLC**
See also CDBLB 1789-1832; DLB 93, 107

Wouk, Herman 1915-**CLC 1, 9, 38; DAM NOV, POP**
See also CA 5-8R; CANR 6, 33, 67; CDALBS; DLBY 82; INT CANR-6; MTCW 1, 2

Wright, Charles (Penzel, Jr.) 1935-**CLC 6, 13, 28, 119**
See also CA 29-32R; CAAS 7; CANR 23, 36, 62; DLB 165; DLBY 82; MTCW 1, 2

Wright, Charles Stevenson 1932- ... **CLC 49; BLC 3; DAM MULT, POET**
See also BW 1; CA 9-12R; CANR 26; DLB 33

Wright, Frances 1795-1852 .... **NCLC 74**
See also DLB 73

Wright, Frank Lloyd 1867-1959 .... **TCLC 95**
See also CA 174

Wright, Jack R.
See Harris, Mark

Wright, James (Arlington) 1927-1980**CLC 3, 5, 10, 28; DAM POET**
See also AITN 2; CA 49-52; 97-100; CANR 4, 34, 64; CDALBS; DLB 5, 169; MTCW 1, 2

Wright, Judith (Arandell) 1915- **CLC 11, 53; PC 14**
See also CA 13-16R; CANR 31, 76; MTCW 1, 2; SATA 14

Wright, L(aurali) R. 1939- .... **CLC 44**
See also CA 138

Wright, Richard (Nathaniel) 1908-1960 **C L C 1, 3, 4, 9, 14, 21, 48, 74; BLC 3; DA; DAB; DAC; DAM MST, MULT, NOV; SSC 2; WLC**
See also AAYA 5; BW 1; CA 108; CANR 64; CDALB 1929-1941; DLB 76, 102; DLBD 2; MTCW 1, 2

Wright, Richard B(ruce) 1937- .... **CLC 6**
See also CA 85-88; DLB 53

Wright, Rick 1945- .... **CLC 35**

Wright, Rowland
See Wells, Carolyn

Wright, Stephen 1946- .... **CLC 33**

Wright, Willard Huntington 1888-1939
See Van Dine, S. S.
See also CA 115; DLBD 16

Wright, William 1930- .... **CLC 44**
See also CA 53-56; CANR 7, 23

Wroth, LadyMary 1587-1653(?) .... **LC 30**
See also DLB 121

Wu Ch'eng-en 1500(?)-1582(?) .... **LC 7**

Wu Ching-tzu 1701-1754 .... **LC 2**

Wurlitzer, Rudolph 1938(?)- .... **CLC 2, 4, 15**
See also CA 85-88; DLB 173

Wyatt, Thomas c. 1503-1542 .... **PC 27**
See also DLB 132

Wycherley, William 1641-1715**LC 8, 21; DAM DRAM**
See also CDBLB 1660-1789; DLB 80

Wylie, Elinor (Morton Hoyt) 1885-1928 **TCLC 8; PC 23**
See also CA 105; 162; DLB 9, 45

Wylie, Philip (Gordon) 1902-1971 ... **CLC 43**
See also CA 21-22; 33-36R; CAP 2; DLB 9

Wyndham, John .... **CLC 19**
See also Harris, John (Wyndham Parkes Lucas) Beynon

Wyss, Johann David Von 1743-1818**NCLC 10**
See also JRDA; MAICYA; SATA 29; SATA-Brief 27

Xenophon c. 430B.C.-c. 354B.C. .... **CMLC 17**
See also DLB 176

Yakumo Koizumi
See Hearn, (Patricio) Lafcadio (Tessima Carlos)

Yamamoto, Hisaye 1921-**SSC 34; DAM MULT**

Yanez, Jose Donoso
See Donoso (Yanez), Jose

Yanovsky, Basile S.
See Yanovsky, V(assily) S(emenovich)

Yanovsky, V(assily) S(emenovich) 1906-1989 **CLC 2, 18**
See also CA 97-100; 129

Yates, Richard 1926-1992 .... **CLC 7, 8, 23**
See also CA 5-8R; 139; CANR 10, 43; DLB 2; DLBY 81, 92; INT CANR-10

Yeats, W. B.
See Yeats, William Butler

Yeats, William Butler 1865-1939**TCLC 1, 11, 18, 31, 93; DA; DAB; DAC; DAM DRAM, MST, POET; PC 20; WLC**
See also CA 104; 127; CANR 45; CDBLB 1890-1914; DLB 10, 19, 98, 156; MTCW 1, 2

Yehoshua, A(braham) B. 1936-.. **CLC 13, 31**
See also CA 33-36R; CANR 43

Yep, Laurence Michael 1948-............ **CLC 35**
See also AAYA 5; CA 49-52; CANR 1, 46; CLR 3, 17, 54; DLB 52; JRDA; MAICYA; SATA 7, 69

Yerby, Frank G(arvin) 1916-1991 .**CLC 1, 7, 22; BLC 3; DAM MULT**
See also BW 1, 3; CA 9-12R; 136; CANR 16, 52; DLB 76; INT CANR-16; MTCW 1

Yesenin, Sergei Alexandrovich
See Esenin, Sergei (Alexandrovich)

Yevtushenko, Yevgeny (Alexandrovich) 1933- **CLC 1, 3, 13, 26, 51; DAM POET**
See also CA 81-84; CANR 33, 54; MTCW 1

Yezierska, Anzia 1885(?)-1970 .... **CLC 46**
See also CA 126; 89-92; DLB 28; MTCW 1

Yglesias, Helen 1915- .... **CLC 7, 22**
See also CA 37-40R; CAAS 20; CANR 15, 65; INT CANR-15; MTCW 1

Yokomitsu Riichi 1898-1947 .... **TCLC 47**
See also CA 170

Yonge, Charlotte (Mary) 1823-1901**TCLC 48**
See also CA 109; 163; DLB 18, 163; SATA 17

York, Jeremy
See Creasey, John

York, Simon
See Heinlein, Robert A(nson)

Yorke, Henry Vincent 1905-1974 ...... **CLC 13**
See also Green, Henry
See also CA 85-88; 49-52

Yosano Akiko 1878-1942 .... **TCLC 59; PC 11**
See also CA 161

Yoshimoto, Banana .... **CLC 84**
See also Yoshimoto, Mahoko

Yoshimoto, Mahoko 1964-
See Yoshimoto, Banana
See also CA 144

Young, Al(bert James) 1939-**CLC 19; BLC 3; DAM MULT**
See also BW 2, 3; CA 29-32R; CANR 26, 65; DLB 33

Young, Andrew (John) 1885-1971 ...... **CLC 5**
See also CA 5-8R; CANR 7, 29

Young, Collier 1917-1994
See Bloch, Robert (Albert)
See also CA 179; CAAE 179

Young, Edward 1683-1765 .... **LC 3, 40**
See also DLB 95

Young, Marguerite (Vivian) 1909-1995 **C L C 82**
See also CA 13-16; 150; CAP 1

Young, Neil 1945- .... **CLC 17**
See also CA 110

Young Bear, Ray A. 1950-...... **CLC 94; DAM MULT**
See also CA 146; DLB 175; NNAL

Yourcenar, Marguerite 1903-1987**CLC 19, 38, 50, 87; DAM NOV**
See also CA 69-72; CANR 23, 60; DLB 72; DLBY 88; MTCW 1, 2

Yurick, Sol 1925- .... **CLC 6**
See also CA 13-16R; CANR 25

Zabolotsky, Nikolai Alekseevich 1903-1958 **TCLC 52**
See also CA 116; 164

Zagajewski, Adam .... **PC 27**

Zamiatin, Yevgenii
See Zamyatin, Evgeny Ivanovich

Zamora, Bernice (B. Ortiz) 1938- .. **CLC 89; DAM MULT; HLC 2**
See also CA 151; CANR 80; DLB 82; HW 1, 2

Zamyatin, Evgeny Ivanovich 1884-1937 **TCLC 8, 37**
See also CA 105; 166

Zangwill, Israel 1864-1926 .... **TCLC 16**
See also CA 109; 167; DLB 10, 135, 197

Zappa, Francis Vincent, Jr. 1940-1993
See Zappa, Frank
See also CA 108; 143; CANR 57

Zappa, Frank .... **CLC 17**
See also Zappa, Francis Vincent, Jr.

Zaturenska, Marya 1902-1982 ...... **CLC 6, 11**

Literary Criticism Series
Cumulative Topic Index

This index lists all topic entries in Gale's *Classical and Medieval Literature Criticism, Contemporary Literary Criticism, Literature Criticism from 1400 to 1800, Nineteenth-Century Literature Criticism,* and *Twentieth-Century Literary Criticism.*

Contemporary Literary Criticism
Cumulative Nationality Index

Nationality Index

Nationality Index

Nationality Index

Nationality Index

Nationality Index

Nationality Index

CLC-123 Title Index

557

Title Index

ISBN 0-7876-3198-1

9 780787 631987

90000